International
Business Transactions

International Business Transactions

Problems, Cases, and Materials

Daniel C.K. Chow

Robert J. Nordstrom/Porter Wright Morris & Arthur Designated Professor of Law, The Ohio State University Michael E. Moritz College of Law

Thomas J. Schoenbaum

George Washington University School of Law, Washington, DC, and International Christian University, Tokyo

ASPEN

PUBLISHERS

111 Eighth Avenue, New York, NY 10011
www.aspenpublishers.com

© 2005 Aspen Publishers, Inc.
A Wolters Kluwer Company
www.aspenpublishers.com

      Permissions
      Aspen Publishers
      111 Eighth Avenue
      New York, NY 10011

Printed in the United States of America.

1 2 3 4 5 6 7 8 9 0

ISBN 0-7355-3985-5

To my wife Qing and our son Alan

DC

To my children — Geoffrey, Liz, Lucius, Cecilia, and Kelsey — from a proud and admiring father

TJS

Summary of Contents

Contents

2   *International Sale of Goods*   **59**

4   *Letters of Credit*   251

5 *Nonestablishment Forms of International Business: Agency and Distributorships, Technology Transfer, Contract Manufacturing, and Franchising*   **321**

6 *Foreign Direct Investment* 393

Preface

We are pleased to offer to our law school colleagues, professors in business schools, students, and international lawyers a casebook that takes a new approach to the field of international business transactions. This approach reflects many hours of thinking and discussion as well as our own experimentation with ways of teaching this vast field. As we explain further below and in Chapter 1, we envision international business transactions as the field of private business transactions that are international in character and that are governed by a blend of international private law and the private law aspects of public international law.

International business transactions is a subject that, despite its practical usefulness and theoretical attractiveness, often falls betwixt and between. International business programs tend to regard it as a course for legal specialists; many law schools leave it to schools of business or position it as an advanced course in international law. As a result, few law and business students have been exposed to the course.

We believe that, in this era of globalization, a course in international business transactions is an essential part of the training of all business lawyers and of people in the corporate world as well. There is no longer a clear distinction between businesses that operate in the United States and those with foreign operations. Sooner or later, every successful business will have an international aspect. This was brought home vividly when one of the authors received a phone call from a lawyer in a small town in Georgia. This lawyer was drafting a contract for an export sale to France on behalf of a client and called the state law school to inquire whether there was any special law that he should know about. He was saved from possible malpractice by learning that the contract would be subject to the United Nations Convention on Contracts for the International Sale of Goods. This episode suggests that a course in international business transactions, then, hardly should be considered esoteric.

We also believe that in the modern era, when trade and commerce have become truly global, international business transactions can no longer be viewed as being dominated by developed nations in North America and Europe. The increasing importance of developing nations, as well as the emergence of China and Asia as economic powers, requires in-depth coverage of non-Western countries, regions, and cultures that were not traditionally covered in casebooks on international law and business, which were strongly oriented toward Western developed countries.

In the past, one reason for sweeping international business transactions off into a corner was the disagreement about what kind of a course it is or should be. Is it international law? Commercial law? Trade law?

To be sure, international business transactions is a cross-disciplinary course and must be taught that way. To be manageable, however, the range of subjects must be integrated into a coherent whole. Using our compact book in a three-hour curriculum package, the course can be covered in appropriate depth and scope. Our integrative approach is based on certain pedagogical assumptions.

First, it is not appropriate — or even possible — to teach transactional law together with international trade law in the same basic course. In the past, we have used casebooks that have covered both international trade law and private transactions. Combining the two subjects resulted in books of such length, density, and complexity that our attempts to cover the bulk of such material in a single-semester, three-hour course tested the tolerance of our students and exceeded our own powers of will and endurance. The rules of the multilateral trading system and their domestic law transformations are now simply too extensive and complex to be combined with the law of private transactions. These rules of international trade are also qualitatively different: they are public international law and domestic public and administrative law. While some coverage is necessary, we have limited our coverage of international trade law, with the idea that students should cover these in a separate course devoted entirely to that important field.

Second, we have found that the problem method is the most appropriate approach for this kind of course and that short, focused problems, rather than long, complex, and abstract ones, are the most effective pedagogically. Most of the problems in this book can be answered by reading one or two cases or statutes that immediately follow the case. Targeted problems help students to get the point and move on. We have used all the problems in our classrooms, so they are "combat tested."

Third, international business transactions is a course that, despite its name, combines domestic laws and foreign laws as well as what is traditionally called international law. The field of international business transactions involves a new kind of international law that is a mix of international private law, international public law, and a *sui generis* law known as the new *lex mercatoria*.

We have included statutory and legal texts in the casebook so that it is not necessary to consult outside statutory materials, with the exceptions of Chapter 3 on the sales contract, which requires use of the Convention on Contracts for the International Sale of Goods; Chapter 4 on the letter of credit, which requires use of the Uniform Credits and Documentary Practices; and Chapter 6, which requires use of the Foreign Corrupt Practices Act. We have prepared a short documents supplement for use with these chapters, which adopters of this book can obtain as a Word document by contacting Professor Chow at the address below.

We hope that you find these materials as stimulating and as challenging as we do. We welcome your comments and can be contacted at chow.1@osu.edu and (614) 292-0948 and at tschoen@icu.ac.jp.

Daniel C.K. Chow
Columbus, Ohio

Thomas J. Schoenbaum
Tokyo, Japan

Acknowledgments

Behar, Richard, *Bejing's Phony War Against Fakes*, Fortune Magazine, p. 188 (October 30, 2000). Reprinted with the permission of Fortune Magazine and the author.

Bent, Maureen A., *Export Hazardous Industries: Should American Standards Apply?* 20 Int'l L. & Pol., 777, 778-781 (1988). Reprinted with the permission of NYU Journal of International Law and Politics.

Bowman, M.J., *The Convention on Civil Liability for Damages Resulting from Activities Dangerous to the Environment*, Centre for Environmental Law, University of Nottingham. Reprinted with the permission of Lawtext Publishing Ltd., www.lawtext.com.

Bradlow, D.D., & A. Escher, *Current Developments, Legal Challenges and Definition of FDI*, in *Legal Aspects of Foreign Direct Investment* (1999). Reprinted with the permission of Kluwer Law International and the authors.

Charney, Jonathan, *Transnational Corporations and Developing Public International Law*, 1983 Duke L.J. 748, 762-769. Reprinted with the permission of Duke University School of Law.

Chow, Daniel C.K., *Counterfeiting in the People's Republic of China*, 78 Wash. U.L.Q. 1 (2000). Reprinted with the permission of Washington University School of Law and the author.

Chow, Daniel C.K., *The Legal System of the People's Republic of China in a Nutshell*, pp. 20-34 — excerpt (words only), and p. 33 — Chart: GDP of Top Ten Countries. Reprinted with the permission of Thomson West and the author.

Chow, Daniel C.K., *The Role of Organized Crime, Local Protectionism and the Trade in Counterfeit Goods in China*, 14 China Econ. Rev., 473-481, 482. Reprinted with the permission of Elsevier Science and the author.

Davidson, John, *International Business Negotiations in the United Kingdom*, in *The ABA Guide to International Business Negotiations* (James R. Silkenat & Jeffrey M. Aresty, eds., ABA 2000), pp. 667, 669-675. Reprinted with the permission of the American Bar Association and the author.

Denton, Charles M., *Scope of ISO 14001*, International Environment Reporter (BNA) (August 7, 1996), p. 715. Reprinted with the permission of the Bureau of National Affairs, Inc.

Divan, Shyam, & Armin Rosencranz, *The Bhopal Settlement*, 19 Envtl. Pol'y & L. 166-169 (1989). Reprinted with the permission of IOS Press B.V. and the authors.

Gouvea, Raul, *Brazil: A Strategic Approach*, Thunderbird Int'l Bus. Rev. Reprinted with the permission of John Wiley & Sons, World Bank Publications, Melhores e Maiores/Exame/Editora Abril, Target Semonsen Associados/Brasil em Exame/Editora, and the author.

Halvorssen, Anita Margrethe, *Book Review: Changing Course: A Global Business Perspective on Development and the Environment*, 4 Colorado J. Int'l Envtl. L. & Pol'y 241, 243-248 (1993). Reprinted with the permission of University of Colorado School of Law.

Hanlon, James, *European Community Law* (Thomson Sweet & Maxwell, 2003), pp. 1-17 and 260-265. Reprinted with the permission of the author.

Hixson, Kathleen, *Extraterritorial Jurisdiction Under the Third Restatement of the Foreign Relations Law of the United States*, 12 Fordham Int'l L.J. 127, 129-137 (1988). Reprinted with the permission of the author.

Israel, Brian D., *Environmental and Safety Management in Large Companies: Avoiding Pitfalls*, ABA Trends (Jan./Feb. 2004), pp. 4-5. Reprinted with the permission of the American Bar Association, Environment, Energy and Resources Section.

Karamanian, Susan, *The Road to the Tribunal and Beyond: International Arbitration and the United States*, 34 Geo. Wash. Int'l L. Rev. 17, 19-21. Reprinted with the permission of George Washington University.

Leonard, H. Jeffrey, *Confronting Industrial Pollution in Rapidly Industrializing Countries: Myths, Pitfalls and Opportunities*, 12 Ecology L.Q. (1985). Reprinted with the permission of the Regents of the University of California and the author.

Low, Lucinda A., & William M. McGlone, *Avoiding Problems Under the Foreign Corrupt Practices Act, U.S. Antiboycott Laws. OFAC Sanctions, Export Controls, and the Economic Espionage Act*, in *Negotiating and Structuring International Commercial Transactions* (M. Sandstrom & D. Goldweig, eds., 2d ed., 2003). Reprinted with the permission of the American Bar Association, International Law and Practices Section.

Lowenfeld, Andreas F., *Lex Mercatoria: An Arbitrator's View*, 6 Arb. Int'l 133, 137-140 (1990). Reprinted with the permission of Graham & Trotman (a member of the Kluwer Academic Publishers Group).

Lowenfeld, Andreas F., *International Economic Law*, 432-438 (Oxford UP, 2002). Reprinted with the permission of Oxford University Press.

Lowenfeld, Andreas F., *International Economic Law*, 456-461, 473-492 (Oxford UP, 2002). Reprinted with the permission of Oxford University Press.

Lyons, Francis X., *Sarbanes-Oxley and the Changing Face of Environmental Liability Disclosure Obligations*, ABA Trends (Nov./Dec. 2003), pp. 10-11. Reprinted with the permission of the American Bar Association, Environment, Energy and Resources Section.

Matsushita, M., T.J. Schoenbaum, & P.C. Mavroidis, *The World Trade Organization* (2003), pp. 228-239 and 522-525. Reprinted with the permission of Oxford University Press and the authors.

McCaffrey, Stephen C., *Accidents Do Happen: Hazardous Technology and International Tort Litigation*, 1 Transnat'l Law. 41, 48-51 (1988). Reprinted with the permission of the University of the Pacific McGeorge Law Review and the author.

Neumeyer, Eric, *Greening International Trade and Investment* (2001), pp. 164-166. Reprinted with the permission of James & James (Science Publishers) Ltd.

Organization for Economic Cooperation and Development, *Council Recommendation on the Application of the Polluter-Pays Principle to Accidental Pollution*, 28 I.L.M.

1320 (1989). Reprinted with the permission of the American Society of International Law.

Organization for Economic Cooperation and Development, *The OECD Guidelines for Multinational Enterprises*, 40 I.L.M. 237 (2000). Reprinted with the permission of the American Society of International Law.

Paust, Jordan J., *Human Rights Responsibilities of Private Corporations*, 35 Vanderbilt J. Transnat'l L., 801, 802-812 (2002). Reprinted with the permission of Vanderbilt University Law School.

Sandstrom, Mark R., Julia McCalmon, & Teresa M. Goody, *The Impact of Trade and Customs Laws upon International Commercial Transactions*, in *Negotiating and Structuring International Commercial Transactions* (M. Sandstrom & D. Goldweig, eds., 2d ed., 2003). Reprinted with the permission of the Copyright Clearance Center.

Sarrailhé, Philippe, *International Business Negotiations in France*, in *The ABA Guide to International Business Negotiations* (James R. Silkenat & Jeffrey M. Aresty, eds., ABA 2000), pp. 425-428, 430-431. Reprinted with the permission of the American Bar Association and the author.

Sobin, Sturgis M., *U.S. Courts Can Obtain Jurisdiction over a Foreign Parent Company*, in the International Business Law Update (Winter 1999/2000). Reprinted with the permission of the author.

The Japan Times, *U.S. Oil Firm Leaves Toxic Legacy in Ecuador* (Jan. 30, 2004), p. 14. Reprinted with the permission of the Japan Times and the author.

The New York Times, *Japanese Capital and Jobs Flow into China* (Feb. 17, 2004), p. C1. Reprinted with the permission of the New York Times Co.

Verhoeven, Thomas O., *International Business Negotiations in Germany*, in *The ABA Guide to International Business Negotiations* (James R. Silkenat & Jeffrey M. Aresty, eds., ABA 2000), pp. 447-455. Reprinted with the permission of the American Bar Association and the author.

Vogelson, Jay M., *Dispute Resolution*, in *Negotiating and Structuring International Commercial Transactions* (1991), pp. 116-118 and 184-185. Reprinted with the permission of the American Bar Association.

Walls, Michael P., *Disclosure Responsibilities for Exporters*, 4 Nat. Resources & Env't 3, 10 (1990). Reprinted with the permission of the American Bar Association and the author.

Wena Hotels Ltd. v. Arab Republic of Egypt, 41 I.L.M. 881 (2002). Reprinted with the permission of the American Society of International Law.

International
Business Transactions

1 *Introduction*

In this chapter, we will first discuss the scope of this book and the major themes of the developing field of international business transactions that we will be exploring in subsequent chapters.

I. Some Background Considerations

A. Scope and Approach of This Book

This book concerns international business transactions (IBTs), by which we mean private business transactions that are international in character. The international element exists when the parties have their places of business in different nation-states; when these transactions involve the movement of goods, services, capital, or technology across the boundaries of different nations; or when transactions between parties of one state have a direct effect in a different state.

IBTs may be categorized, at least in general terms, according to the extent of penetration in international markets. The very first level of penetration is a simple export-import transaction, for example, a contract for the sale of goods involving a seller from the United States and a buyer from Germany. If this is successful, and the company finds a sufficient and continuing demand for its products, the seller may decide to become more involved in dealing with the German and European markets by establishing a sales agent in Germany or a distributor of its products who will attempt to increase the seller's penetration of the targeted markets. After this step, the seller may decide to undertake a third level of penetration of the European market by licensing a German entity to manufacture its products in Germany for sale and distribution in Germany and other European countries. A significant issue in such a licensing transaction is technology transfer, as the seller will need to allow the German manufacturer some access to the seller's intellectual property rights, know-how, and other forms of proprietary information. Alternatively or after the term of the licensing agreement, the company may decide to establish its own operations in Germany by establishing a business entity of which it is the sole or part owner. Technology transfer issues are also important in this transaction as the levels of technology involved in foreign investment can often be more advanced than those involved in licensing. The U.S. company would have the choice of establishing its own operations from scratch or of buying an existing German business entity. In either case, this would be what is termed foreign direct investment (FDI). This would also involve incorporating a German or European subsidiary company or, rarely, a branch office.

If there is sufficient demand for the company's products, not only in Germany and Europe, but around the world, our imaginary U.S. company may employ similar strategies in many nations and many foreign markets. If it is successful, our company will become a world-class business known as a transnational corporation (TNC) or multinational enterprise (MNE). A similar scenario would exist if the seller in the example above were selling services, such as financial services or insurance, instead of products.

This book will examine all of these transactions and trace this progression from the simple contract of sale to the establishment of foreign direct investment and the many collateral issues involved. Of course, each international transaction has its own particular character, and real IBTs are variations on the themes just described. Nevertheless, we believe this progression is a useful way of studying the subject in an academic setting. After this introductory chapter provides some background considerations, the next five chapters of this book will trace this progression. Chapters 2, 3, and 4 concern the international sales transaction and Chapters 5 and 6 examine agency/distributorships, contract manufacturing, and foreign direct investment. Although we weave intellectual property issues into most of the earlier chapters, we devote all of Chapter 7 to the protection of in-tellectual property rights, an issue of fundamental importance in international business today. Chapter 8 then turns to dispute resolution in an international business context. Finally, Chapter 9 concerns corporate social responsibility and examines the obligations of multinational enterprises concerning issues of human rights, labor conditions, and the environment.

Note that the transactions that are the focus of this book are private transac-tions by which we mean transactions that affect the commercial, economic, and business interests of private or nongovernmental parties. The parties to most of the transactions examined in this book are business entities, companies, or MNEs. In some cases, however, one or more of the parties to the transaction may be a government entity or a business entity under the control of a government. These transactions are also included within the scope of this book when the government entity is acting in a commercial or entrepreneurial capacity. We want to distinguish the transactions that are the subject of this book from international transactions that affect public rights such as where government entities engage in commercial activity that may affect the rights of its citizens as a whole and the rights of other nations such as when one nation engages in the sale of military equipment to another or when one nation assists another in rebuilding its economy and industry after some calamity, such as war.

The IBTs that we examine in this book not only involve private parties or entities acting in a commercial or private capacity but they also involve areas of commerce traditionally deemed as areas of private law such as contracts, property, and torts. Public laws that affect IBTs such as antitrust, securities, customs, exchange controls, and general economic regulation will be discussed by way of background but will not be the focus of this book. Note that one of the hallmarks of private law is that the parties have the freedom and authority to contractually alter private law rights and obligations. One of the major themes that will be explored throughout this book is the way in which parties can structure IBTs to protect and further their interests against a background of private laws that permit bargains to be formed by contract. By contrast, public laws are generally mandatory in nature and do not permit parties to alter their impact or effect. The distinction between private and public law brings us to another important point about the focus and orientation of this book.

We want to distinguish the scope and subject matter of this book from another field, the regulation of international trade and economic relations among nations.

While this field is related to the field that is the subject matter of this book, we believe that it is fruitful to view international business transactions and the regulation of international trade and economic relations as separate, although related fields that should be the subject of separate courses in the law school curriculum. The regulation of international trade concerns the attempts by nations, acting in their sovereign capacities, to regulate economic and commercial activity between themselves and the conduct of such activity by their nationals through mandatory public laws. For example, export and import controls such as customs classifications, quotas, tariffs, and other customs controls belong to the field of international trade and economic regulation. Laws governing unfair trade practices that allow import nations to impose sanctions on unfairly priced imports also belong to the field of international trade law. Transnational antitrust and anticompetition laws are another example. The principal intergovernmental international organization that is involved in the regulation of world trade and economic relations is the World Trade Organization (WTO). Another important body in the regulation of world trade is the European Union (EU), consisting of 25 states (as of May 1, 2004), including virtually all the nations of western and central Europe. On trade and economic issues, the EU is charged with the complete economic integration of its member economies by eliminating all trade barriers and by adopting a common economic policy, including customs duties, with respect to nonmember states. While we consider the WTO, the EU, and other international and regional economic institutions in this book and how they impact the private transactions that are the subject of this book, the WTO, regional economic institutions, and domestic implementation of WTO obligations will not be our focus as in a course on the regulation of international trade and economic regulations.

One other area in which this book differs from some other approaches is that we include the topic of foreign investment within our treatment of private international transactions. Foreign investment is commonly treated under other approaches as part of the field of international economic regulatory law and "international trade and investment" is commonly referred to as a specialty or field of study. While the public law aspects of foreign investment are treated in regulatory courses, the transactional aspects of foreign investment are often not treated at all in private law courses. While there are, of course, many important regulatory issues concerning foreign investment, in this book we take a close and detailed look at the transactional aspects of foreign direct investment, including how to establish and operate a foreign investment enterprise in a developing country. We believe that FDI is best understood as the final step in a progression from the most simple type of IBT, the simple export sales transaction, to the most complex. We do not, however, treat the regulatory aspects of foreign investment in complete fashion and include such treatment only by way of background and introduction.

To be sure, we wish to emphasize that we cover topics relating to the regulation of international trade in this book and that some of this coverage will be in depth because all international business transactions operate against the background of international economic regulation. You will find that in many chapters we blend and interweave topics of international trade law into our materials on private transactions. Our approach is to select those topics of international trade law that are most pertinent as the necessary background for understanding the progression of topics that we cover: The sales contract, distribution, licensing, and foreign direct investment. Moreover, although you will find that some parts of this book will cover certain international trade topics in detail, our coverage of international trade is selective as it is for the primary purpose of understanding the private transaction. We do not attempt to provide systematic coverage of international trade and international economic law as we would be in a casebook devoted to that important field.

To give you a sense of how we use and select international trade law topics in this book, consider that in our materials covering the sales transaction we will cover the importer's compliance with U.S. customs laws, a trade law topic, in detail. We believe that this is the trade law topic that is most closely connected to the transactional issues related to the sale of goods and that affects the IBT practitioner on a micro level on a day-to-day basis. Our assumption is that when our students go on to represent one of the parties in an international sale they are most likely to represent a U.S. party. The trade law issues of most importance to the U.S. party will generally occur when the U.S. party is the buyer-importer. The buyer must satisfy U.S. Customs laws governing all imports as this compliance will usually determine the amount of tax or customs duty that must be paid by the buyer-importer. As the amount of duty that must be paid is a significant issue for most buyers, we cover this topic in depth. On the other hand, we believe that the trade law issues are generally less complex when the U.S. party is the seller. In this case, the U.S. seller must comply with U.S. export controls and related laws, but these issues are generally less complex in most cases so we cover this topic in less detail, reflecting its lower level of complexity. Of course, there are other trade law issues and some of them are quite important macro law issues that implicate important issues concerning economic relations between states. If this were a casebook in international trade and economic relations, we would cover the export trade compliance issues in depth. As for our coverage of imports, after import customs compliance issues we would then go on to consider unfair competition issues such as dumping, that is, when imported goods are sold at a lower price than in the exporter's home market, which can result in the imposition of an antidumping duty to offset the margin of dumping. We would also cover subsidies, that is, payments by the country of export to the exporter that provides a price advantage, which can be offset by the imposition of a countervailing duty. We would then go on to cover "safeguards," that is, measures available to a state to limit fairly traded imports that are causing harm to domestic industries. However, we do not go on to cover all of the trade law topics in our consideration of an international sales contract. Rather, our approach to the trade law topics is selective and reflects our best judgment on what international trade topics are most vital for understanding the private transaction that is taught within the confines of a three- or four-credit course on international business transactions. Note that our approach to treating the trade law issues in a sales contract discussed above reflects how we treat the trade law issues in all of the areas covered in this book: We cover selected trade law materials that are most important to the private transaction. In some cases, you will find that we introduce the selected trade law materials at the end of a chapter (Chapter 2 on the sales contract and Chapter 7 on the protection of intellectual property), at the beginning (Chapter 6 on foreign direct investment), and in some cases we interweave the trade law material throughout the materials on the private transaction (Chapter 5 on technology transfer).

We believe that a book focusing on the private business transaction against a carefully selected set of materials relating to international economic regulation offers enough materials and challenges for a separate course. We also believe that a fruitful course of study for the student interested in international business law would be a course on international business transactions followed by a separate, advanced course on the regulation of international trade and economic relations between nations.

NOTES AND QUESTIONS

1. As the fields of international business transactions and international trade law are different, will a lawyer practicing in both fields need different skills? If so, how do the skills necessary for IBTs differ from those necessary for international trade law issues? In the area of IBT, the focus is on *negotiating* and *structuring* transactions against a background of private laws that allow flexibility for bargains altering rights and obligations by contract. In IBTs, the party sitting across the table is usually another private party. In international trade law, the focus is on *compliance* with mandatory public laws, and the party that one normally deals with is a governmental authority with regulatory and enforcement powers. In some cases, the distinction that we draw here is blurred as in the case of doing business in some developing countries where the issue of compliance is often a process of negotiation with local governments. However, we believe that this distinction is useful in an academic setting to demonstrate that the skills needed by a lawyer in each area are different. Both types of skills are necessary to help clients take full advantage of business opportunities. Many IBTs also concern international trade law issues so a lawyer will need to exercise both sets of skills.

2. We introduce a number of basic technical concepts throughout this chapter that you may be unfamiliar with but that you will need to master. Do not confuse *public law* discussed above with *public international law*, which we introduce shortly, or *private law* with *private international law*, also introduced later in this chapter.

B. Counsel in International Business

Another topic that we wish to introduce in this first chapter is the role of the lawyer in international business transactions. It should not be surprising that the growth of international business and trade of all kinds in the latter part of the twentieth century has also transformed the legal profession. As MNEs expand abroad, many will require their company lawyers to spend extended assignments overseas and advise their overseas businesses. As many of the world's most successful law firms have multinational enterprises as their clients and as their clients have expanded their reach around the world, law firms have also expanded their capabilities and offices in order to meet their clients' changing needs. We are now in the era of the multinational law firm as many firms believe that it is essential to have international capability in order to survive in today's competitive marketplace. Some of the world's largest law firms have branch offices around the world and follow a business model that is similar to that of MNEs.

NOTES AND QUESTIONS

1. Large law firms are routinely engaged in international transactions and some of them are global firms with branch offices in many countries around the

world. While a typical large firm may have separate departments for corporate, tax, intellectual property, and litigation, these firms generally do not have an international business department. Why? Which department handles international transactions?

2. Given the realities of law firm practice, would you counsel law students to present themselves to law firms as aspiring IBT lawyers?

1. Issues Faced by Lawyers

The issues confronting a lawyer in an international business transaction can be divided into two categories: Issues of competence and issues of ethics. As to issues of competence, no lawyer can be expected to be an authority on all of the legal issues that can arise in the context of a private international transaction that presents unique challenges and issues. A lawyer will often be faced with foreign laws and foreign languages. How should the lawyer best advise his or her clients in this situation? Where the lawyer is a partner in a law firm, the client is often an MNE; where the lawyer is in-house counsel, the client is usually top management such as the chief executive officer (CEO) or a vice president of international development. The role of the lawyer in these situations may be to manage a group of local foreign lawyers and experts.

Issues of ethics can be very complex in an international setting. Most nations, including the United States, have codes of professional ethics for the licensed attorney. In an international setting, one issue that arises is whether the lawyer is subject to the ethical standards and rules of the foreign nation in which the client is doing business. How should the lawyer advise a client when dealing with a culture in which corruption is rampant and where bribery of government officials and private parties is commonplace? Does a lawyer have any duty to take into consideration larger economic and political issues in representing MNE clients that are doing business in a developing nation? These are also issues that we will be exploring in this book.

2. Role of Counsel for an MNE

As the most important actors in IBTs today are MNEs (as we further discuss in §IV.B. later), we now provide an overview of the legal department of an MNE and the work and challenges of an "in-house" international lawyer. Our hypothetical MNE is Acme, Ltd., a Fortune 500 company based in the United States and engaged in the consumer products industry with operations around the world. Acme has a large worldwide legal department headed by a general counsel with many in-house lawyers. Large companies have in-house lawyers because these lawyers, as employees of the company, are viewed as being more loyal and as having a greater familiarity with the business of the company. In-house lawyers are always available to work with the company's business managers. Many companies like to know that a business manager can simply walk down the hall and chat with a company lawyer or pick up the phone and ask a lawyer to attend a meeting or to answer a quick question. Most companies realize that business managers are less likely to enjoy this level of service or have such ready access to legal services if they depend only on outside counsel.

Today, the general counsel may be called the "global general counsel" to reflect the realities of the modern global corporation. Most general counsels are members of the elite top-management group of the MNE and are at the level of a vice president or senior vice president of the corporation, which is usually one level below that of the most senior executives (often called presidents who head up entire important regions or business units of the company, such as "President of Acme, North America" where geographical divisions are used or "President, Acme Hair Care" where business divisions are used). Presidents are usually one level below and general counsel is usually two levels below the CEO. Note that in most companies the legal department is viewed as "support" because the main business of the MNE is the product or service that it sells. The main business of Nike is producing athletic shoes and sports apparel and the main business of Coca-Cola is producing soft drinks; the role of their legal departments is to provide support for the main business of the company. This is one major distinction between an in-house lawyer and a lawyer at a law firm where the main business of the company is providing legal services. The reporting structure for in-house lawyers is generally divided along two lines. On legal work, in-house lawyers in general report to business managers. The general counsel would report to presidents of business regions or business departments and to the CEO. Each lawyer would also report functionally to his or her department head or superior in the legal hierarchy with the general counsel at the top.

Our hypothetical MNE will have a U.S. headquarters where the global general counsel will be located. In addition, the MNE will have regional general counsels, such as a "General Counsel, Asia-Pacific" or a "General Counsel, Europe." These lawyers report to the global general counsel and are one level below the general counsel (but who aspire to attain that position eventually) and are either vice presidents or directors. A country with major business operations will also have a country general counsel, who is generally one level below the regional general counsel in the hierarchy, that is, "General Counsel, Greater China," and is either a director or an associate director within the company. The country general counsel will have a legal staff of lawyers who are senior counsels or below.

To give you a sense of the legal work of an in-house lawyer, let's take a look at the work of the legal department of Acme (China), Ltd., our hypothetical foreign investment enterprise in China that is further examined in Chapter 6 on foreign direct investment. Acme is a world-class company that manufactures famous brands of shampoo, soap, skin lotion, cosmetics, and other household products for the booming China market whose growing middle class seems to have an insatiable appetite for premium international brands and international glamour. The role of Acme's lawyers is to provide legal support for its China business managers and to protect the company by making sure that it complies with all laws and regulations. What are the types of tasks that these lawyers are expected to undertake?

Acme's lawyers in the China legal department had helped to set up the initial joint ventures engaged in the various consumer products industries by drafting the legal documents when Acme first entered the Chinese market. For the very first joint venture established by Acme in 1988, Acme hired an international law firm to draft the joint venture documents and to work with Acme in securing all of the approvals required by China's government authorities. After the first joint venture, Acme's in-house lawyers in China had acquired a set of joint venture documents and familiarity with the approval process so Acme's management then internalized all of this work to save on costs. Although Acme's joint ventures and other foreign invested business enterprises are now well established in China, Acme must still have contacts with China's many government authorities on a regular basis and the contacts are usually done through the legal department, which is designated as the single point of contact within the company (although sometimes the government affairs department is also involved). Acme's joint ventures, although given managerial autonomy by law, are still formally under the supervision of a government authority with regulatory power over its industry. Acme must file reports with supervisory authorities once a quarter on its business activities and will regularly consult with tax authorities on the amount of the company's tax liabilities and submit tax invoices to the government. All of these contacts between Acme and Chinese authorities will be conducted through the legal department. As Acme is planning to establish new joint ventures in other product lines, to reorganize and combine some of its joint ventures as wholly foreign-owned subsidiaries of Acme, and to increase the capital of some of its existing joint ventures, Acme's lawyers are very busy meeting with Acme China's general manager and finance managers to review and plan all of these changes. Acme's lawyers must also meet with Chinese government authorities on a regular and ongoing basis to keep them apprised of the planned changes as their approval is needed for all of these organizational changes. Chinese authorities will also provide Acme with their input on whether such changes are feasible and how to structure the transactions. All of this work, of course, requires that Acme's lawyers be intimately familiar with China's laws and legal and political system. While Acme's lawyers can now handle most issues, they occasionally seek help from outside law firms on issues that require special expertise, such as tax and reorganization and merger issues.

As Acme is an aggressive and ambitious company, it is always offering new products for the China market and aggressively promoting existing products. Acme's legal department needs to file new trademark applications with China's national trademark authorities for each new brand that is introduced in China and for each new variation on an existing trademark, which the marketing department is constantly proposing as it changes the style and appearance of the products to keep them fresh and appealing to changing consumer tastes. Where products involve new patents, Acme's lawyers must also file patent applications with China's national patent authority. Acme's legal department also works closely with the marketing department, which is organized with brand managers in charge of each brand such as Seagull Shampoo. Acme's brand managers work extensively with international advertising agencies to promote new commercials, and Acme's in-house lawyers must review all advertising to see that it complies with China's stringent advertising laws. The legal department also works with the marketing department to secure approvals from China's Ministry of Telecommunications in Beijing for all new television advertisements. Acme's lawyers also review sales and purchasing contracts from Acme's purchasing department, which must buy a large amount of raw materials from local suppliers in order to manufacture its products. In addition, Acme's lawyers are busy offering advice to Acme China's human resources department on the many personnel and labor issues that arise on a daily basis.

Acme also currently has a serious commercial piracy problem in China as many counterfeit Acme products have appeared on the market that capitalize on Acme's success. Acme's in-house lawyers protect their intellectual property rights by hiring private investigation companies and outside law firms specializing in intellectual property to pursue counterfeiters and enforcement actions.

Counterfeiting in China is a major problem, and we will examine this in detail in Chapter 7.

3. Challenges for the International Lawyer

The picture presented above shows Acme's lawyers and its business managers busily working harmoniously and as a team in promoting Acme's business and earning profits, but there are opportunities for conflicts and challenges in the workplace. One of the important tasks of Acme's lawyers is to ensure that Acme is in compliance with all of China's laws and regulations and this may involve reining in some of the more aggressive tactics of Acme's business managers. This role sometimes casts the company in-house lawyer in the role of a "naysayer" who is always perceived as saying "no" and as bringing negative news to the business department. In some companies, lawyers may even be disliked by the business departments if they are viewed as too conservative and risk averse and constantly creating obstacles to business plans or frustrating the "can't miss" strategies of an up-and-coming star manager.

Of course, in-house lawyers occasionally experience these types of conflicts with business departments on a domestic level as well, but these conflicts can be especially acute in an international setting for several reasons. Business managers who are assigned abroad are usually given three- to five-year assignments with the understanding that a promotion awaits them after a successful performance abroad and a return to the MNE's headquarters in the United States. Managers are judged on what they have accomplished, that is, how many new joint ventures they have established, how many new products were introduced in the market, and how much they have increased sales revenue during their assignments. These business managers feel pressure to perform and produce within a short period of time during their overseas assignment, which is now often considered to be critical for significant long-term advancement within many corporations. Some business managers have been tempted to pursue risks and very aggressive strategies, knowing that they will be rewarded when their assignment is over and that problems with their risky strategies may not arise until years later — long after they have departed the foreign branch and have been promoted. In this situation, there can often be conflict between ambitious business managers who seek business results (and professional advancement within the company) and the in-house lawyer whose job is to protect the company from unnecessary risks.

Another reason for greater potential conflict in the international workplace is that often the laws of developing countries are incomplete or unclear and the legal system less than predictable. For example, like that of many other developing countries, China's legal system contains many gaps and ambiguities and is subject to rapid change. There are many gray areas in China's legal system where the legality of certain actions is subject to legitimately differing opinions and where, as a result, risk is more difficult to assess. But China is not alone in having an undeveloped legal system. The lack of a mature, predictable legal system and the general absence of the rule of law are common problems in developing countries all over the world. Conducting business in an environment that lacks a mature legal system can give rise to greater uncertainty and more frequent and serious disagreements on the degree of risk involved than in a developed legal system, such as that of the United States.

A developing country's lack of a mature legal system also creates challenges in dealing with local foreign lawyers. For example, in China the ranks of the legal profession have increased dramatically with the opening up of China to foreign direct investment in 1978. The prospect of undreamed-of riches for the elite of the legal profession, intense competition for a handful of multinational clients necessary for any lucrative practice, and a nascent awareness of legal ethics all contribute to a professional environment in which sharp practices and improper conduct are all too common. For many Chinese lawyers, the goal is to achieve the result desired by the client by whatever means necessary so as to retain the client's business rather than to use independent judgment to offer candid and objective legal advice that may not always be what the client wants to hear. Using illegal tactics such as bribing a judge, a prosecutor, or other government officials without the client's knowledge is made easier in a legal environment that is often inaccessible to foreign clients. Lacking Chinese language skills and contacts within the Chinese legal system, many foreign clients have no means to independently verify or to check on the work done by their local lawyers and the methods that are used. The client is pleased with the result and does not ask too many questions. We stress, however, these issues are not unique to China by any means. Issues of legal ethics arising from the lack of a professional bar that is either self-regulating or subject to supervision by a legal system with a strong code of legal ethics and disciplinary measures are common problems among developing countries.

PROBLEM 1-1

Foreign investment laws in China currently provide that applications to establish joint ventures with a capital investment of over $30 million must be submitted to central authorities in Beijing for approval and that investments that do not exceed $30 million can be approved at the local level. In the 1990s, some local approval authorities began the practice of allowing joint venture applicants to split a single application to establish a joint venture of over $30 million into two or more applications on the theory that local approval is legal so long as each application is under $30 million. The local authorities allowed the splitting of applications even though all of the applications really concerned a single joint venture and even though the total capital invested in the joint venture that was finally established was over $30 million. Some lawyers viewed this tactic as an artifice to circumvent central-level requirements, but many parties viewed this approach as an attractive option as it would avoid an application to Beijing with all of the delays and more intense scrutiny of the deal that this would entail.

A senior finance manager in Acme (China), Ltd., comes to you, Acme's in-house counsel, and says, "Can we just split our application to establish our new $50 million joint venture to make detergent into two $25 million applications and submit them to the local authorities who have promised to approve the deal in 30 days so that we avoid the hassle and the two-year wait for approval in Beijing? You know that I need to get this done because I am going back to the United States next year when I'm up for VP. I'll also put in a good word with your boss in the United States who says that he is looking for a new General Counsel, North America. Look, I know that you have some reservations but you admit that the law is unclear. Anyway, the local authorities have already told us that they will approve the application so we are covered because if Beijing raises any issues we can always say that we were advised by the local authorities that this procedure is lawful and that they also approved the application. So please draw up the two applications and get them to me by the end of the week. Let's get a beer after work at the White Swan Hotel and talk about this further. My treat." As you leave work that evening for the White Swan, you remember from your professional ethics class in law school that you are to represent your client zealously and within the boundaries of the law but then realize that this axiom isn't very helpful in this situation. You also think about how nice it would be to move back to the United States. What do you tell the finance manager?

PROBLEM 1-2

You are in-house counsel at Acme's subsidiary in Russia and have a disagreement with a business manager over the legality of certain payments that are being made to the local government authorities in connection with some needed approvals. You are concerned that these payments might be considered to be illegal bribes under local law and may also raise problems under the U.S. Foreign Corrupt Practices Act (see Chapter 6, pp. 448-473), but your business manager argues that these are lawful administrative fees and that at best this is a "gray area" as all of Acme's competitors are paying them. You have a meeting with the business manager and lay out the five reasons you think that the payments are illegal, but the manager says, "Okay, you've done your job by laying out all the risks for me. I'm willing to take the risks so let's make the payments." As you are quite opposed to the payments, you then suggest that the company get an opinion letter from an outside local counsel on the legality of the payments. You can see that the business manager is irritated with you (and you worry momentarily about your annual review from the manager), but the manager finally agrees to abide by the opinion letter of the local lawyers. You hire one of a number of newly established local Russian law firms specializing in foreign investment and you explain to them your position and the position of the business manager on the payments. One week later, you get an opinion letter signed by the local firm which states that, under local law, it is absolutely clear that the payments are illegal and lists the five reasons that you stated. You also get a bill for $10,000 and a letter with a long list of other areas in which the law firm is eager to help you. Do you give the opinion letter to the business manager? How would you suggest getting an opinion letter from outside counsel in this situation? What cautions about dealing with outside law firms does this episode suggest?

C. Cultural Concerns

In an age where people, goods, services, capital, and technology now routinely cross national boundaries, issues of differences and clashes in culture that affect IBTs have also become more common. By culture, we refer to the values and norms shared by a group and the group's economic, social, political, and religious institutions. Although consideration of cultural issues may not have been traditionally considered part of the work of an international transactions lawyer, a lawyer who ignores cultural issues in a business transaction does so at his or her own peril in this rapid age of globalization.

We will examine some of the cultural and political issues that divide developing and developed nations as groups and that have an impact in international policy-making arenas such as the World Trade Organization, the United Nations, and other international organizations. In addition to having an impact in the policy-making arena, cultural differences between countries also have a direct impact on particular IBTs in two ways. First, cultural issues should be part of the background "business case" for a private transaction, but unlike economic, legal, and marketing issues, all part of traditional business and legal analysis, cultural issues may be ignored to the detriment of the transaction. For example, when the Walt Disney Company bought a tract of land near Paris to construct EuroDisney, Disney's U.S. management assumed that the promise of jobs and economic development would mean widespread local support for the new theme park. Instead, the local populace valued its traditional agricultural lifestyle over economic development and offered spirited resistance to the Disney project, much to the surprise of Disney's management. In addition, a Disney theme park had been a spectacular success in Japan, but the Japanese were far more receptive to U.S. culture than many of the French who, if anything, were lukewarm toward American culture. Although these were important considerations, the experienced business and legal officials at Disney never considered the cultural factors. *See* Jeanne M. Brett, *Negotiating Globally* 8 (2002). One possible explanation for the failure of the Disney officials to fully consider the cultural factors is that these factors are not present in the company's transactions in the United States, the business environment to which Disney officials were accustomed, and so were ignored in the company's initial forays into the international market.

A second way that differences in culture can affect international business transactions is in negotiating styles. Lawyers are often called on by their clients to negotiate across cultures: The same lawyer may negotiate a sales contract with a German buyer and a joint venture with a Brazilian partner for the same client. Understanding differences in negotiating styles can be advantageous to the lawyer or business executive. On the other hand, failure to understand cultural differences might result in "value being left on the table," that is, in a deal where both parties are not as well off as they could be if barriers in culture and negotiating styles could be overcome. Cross-cultural negotiation skills have become highly sought after skills in the modern age as we have acquired a better understanding of cultural differences. According to one view, there are certain prevalent cultural categories that are reflected in negotiation strategies and styles: Individualism versus collectivism, egalitarianism versus hierarchy, and low-context versus high-context communications. *See* Brett, *supra*, 15-21. Most countries fall into these categories. Individualist cultures place the interests of the individual above those of the collective; hierarchical cultures, unlike egalitarian cultures, emphasize differentiated social status and deference to social superiors and associate social power with social status; negotiators from low-context-communications cultures emphasize direct, explicit communications, whereas those from high-context-communications cultures emphasize indirect communications that must be understood against a complex and often unstated background of social values. *See id.* Negotiators from individualist, egalitarian, and low-context-communications cultures such as the United States use direct, confrontational styles, whereas negotiators from collectivist, hierarchical, and high-context-communications cultures such as China prefer to use indirect negotiation styles that avoid confrontation. Where there is a negotiation between persons with clashing negotiation styles, such as from the United States and China, the difference in styles could lead to poor communication and misunderstanding that results in a less than optimal result for both parties. Another, perhaps even greater concern to lawyers and their clients is that they may be disadvantaged and exploited by the other party's skillful negotiators who are used to working in cross-cultural contexts. From the viewpoint of the lawyer negotiating on behalf of a client, the goal is to avoid both results that can arise from the pitfalls of culture.

NOTES AND QUESTIONS

1. A large literature on cultural issues in international business transactions has emerged. In particular, experts urge caution in dealing with Asian and other non-Western cultures that may have deeply embedded cultural traditions that differ in significant respects from Western values. Take the following example of how to deal with the Chinese:

> A U.S. company had a contract from a German buyer to sell bicycles produced in China. When the first shipment was ready, there was a problem. The bikes rattled. The U.S. buyer did not want to accept the shipment, knowing that they would not be acceptable to the German customer, whose high-end market niche was dominated by bikes that were whisper quiet. What to do? In U.S. culture, the normal approach would be to tell the manufacturer that the rattling bikes were unacceptable and that the problem had to be fixed. In China, such a direct confrontation would be extremely rude and cause much loss of face. Knowing this, the U.S. manager went to the Chinese plant, inspected the bicycles, rode a few, and asked about the rattle. "Is this rattle normal? Do all the bikes rattle? Do you think the German buyer will think there is something wrong with the bike if it rattles?" Then he left. The next shipment of bikes had no rattles.[1]

Under the suggested approach, when does the U.S. manager find out whether the problem has been resolved? Do you see any other issues with this approach? How would you suggest handling this problem without causing "loss of face"?

2. How should managers handle cross-cultural negotiations? Here is one suggestion:

> Be prepared for interests and priorities to have a cultural basis. If you are proposing to bring economic development to a region, find out how people in the region feel about economic development before you get to the negotiation table. Prepare for the negotiation by understanding the culture. See how the culture is classified according to the cultural values of individualism versus collectivism and egalitarianism versus hierarchy. Do some background research so you have a good understanding of the other negotiator's political, economic, and social environment. Make sure you have your own interpreter. Use your interpreter to help you understand the cultural factors influencing the other party's interests and priorities.[2]

Suppose that you are advising a senior vice president in charge of international business development who is scheduled to fly to Japan for a three-day meeting with

---

1. Brett, *supra*, at 8.
2. Brett, at 204-205.

Japanese officials on establishing a joint venture and then will need to travel to Chile to negotiate a foreign direct investment deal the following week. Would you advise the business executive to follow this prescription? What would you suggest?

PROBLEM 1-3

In light of the success of fast-food franchises such as McDonald's and Pizza Hut in China, Joe's Economy Burgers (JEB), an Ohio company with locations around the Midwest, is considering expansion into China. JEB has been able to successfully compete against famous fast-food chains in the Midwest based on its no-frills, "blue-collar" working-class image, offering burgers at half the price of more pricey fast-food chains. JEB's decor also reflects its image and approach. JEB's founders grew up during the Great Depression and have consistently stressed frugality in the company's corporate philosophy. Food is served in clean but plain and somewhat dull surroundings. JEB has signs in various places in its restaurants stressing frugality in daily life, a return to the simple nonmaterialistic values of rural America, and the rejection of a wasteful, luxury lifestyle. JEB has developed quite a following among its niche in the U.S. market and has been earning modest but steady profits for many years. JEB's management sees no reason why using the same strategy to compete against fast-food competitors in China will not be just as successful as in the United States. Do you see any issues relating to culture with JEB's approach to China?

PROBLEM 1-4

Texas Barbecue Ribs (TBR), a successful Houston-based restaurant chain, is considering an expansion into Europe. TBR serves supersize portions of smoked ribs, southern-style cole slaw, and crunchy fries with its slogan "Everything Comes Bigger in Texas" in an interior setting with bold colors, a southwestern motif, and loud Texas country music. The restaurant has been quite successful in the Southwest and the South. What cultural issues might TBR face in European markets?

II. *The Growth of International Business Since the Second World War*

This section explores some of the important developments in the international arena that form the modern historical background for international commercial and business transactions. The second half of the twentieth century, particularly the past two decades, has been marked by a surge in transnational commercial transactions of all kinds and the integration of the economies of the world to a greater extent than ever before. Today, the immense flow of commercial activity across national boundaries on a daily basis is a distinguishing feature of the modern world. The international sale of goods, the transfer of services, the movement of capital across national boundaries, the transfer of knowledge and technology, and foreign investment in the form of joint ventures and wholly foreign-owned subsidiaries are commonplace.

FIGURE 1-1
Exports of Goods and Services as a
Percentage of Gross Domestic Product
(Measured at Current Prices)

Country	1960	2001
Canada	17.2	43.8
France	14.5	27.9
Germany	19.0	35.1
Japan	10.7	10.4
Netherlands	47.7	65.3
Sweden	22.8	45.2
Switzerland	29.3	45.1
United Kingdom	20.9	27.1
United States	5.2	10.3

Source: OECD National Accounts Volume 2003.

This surge in international commercial activity can be traced to several major historical events. First, at the end of the Second World War, the United States and some of its allies met at the Bretton Woods Conference in New Hampshire, which led to the creation of the legal institutions that would create the postwar legal framework for world trade: The International Monetary Fund (IMF), the World Bank, and the General Agreement on Tariffs and Trade (GATT). The world economy had just endured a decade and a half of immense turmoil and disruption. Protectionist trade measures in the form of excessive tariffs and protective currency regulations had triggered hostilities among nations, a worldwide depression, and an immensely destructive world war, the consequences of which are still being felt today. The United States and its allies wanted to put into place the type of international institutions that would help to prevent the types of economic policies that led to world tensions and hostilities. One of the lessons affirmed by the Second World War is that when economic conflict exists among nations, military conflict may not be too far behind. The IMF was established to create restrictions on national regulation of currency and foreign exchange controls. The IMF also became a lender of last resort for those developing nations that were unable to repay their foreign loans. The World Bank was created in 1944, first to aid in the reconstruction of Europe and then to provide loans to support the economic development of the developing world and the world's poorest nations. A third organization, the International Trade Organization (ITO) was proposed to encourage free trade by reducing tariffs, the high customs duties that were imposed on goods imported into a nation in order to protect the nation's own domestic industries. However, the ITO's ambitious charter extended beyond free trade to include rules on employment, commodity agreements, restrictive business practices, and international investment and services. Even before the ITO charter was finally approved, a group of nations decided to negotiate tariff reductions to give an early boost to trade liberalization after the Second World War and to remove the protectionist measures that had remained in place since the 1930s. The result of these negotiations was the General Agreement on Tariffs and Trade, the GATT, which was a combined package of tariff concessions and some of the trade rules contained in the ITO charter. Because the parties wanted to protect the value of the package they had negotiated, they allowed the GATT to enter into force on a provisional basis in January 1948 while the ITO was still being negotiated. Once established, the ITO was envisioned as the administering body for the GATT. Due mainly to opposition from the U.S. Congress, however, the ITO never came into existence. Note that the GATT was created as a treaty, not an international organization. With the demise of the ITO, a small staff was created in Geneva to handle basic administrative tasks. This blossomed into the GATT, which was an international organization without a charter. This difficulty was corrected in 1995 by the creation of the World Trade Organization, which assumed the role originally intended for the ITO.

Although these international institutions helped to increase international commerce, there were limitations on the expansion of free trade and free markets in the first decades following the Second World War. First, the existence of the Soviet Union and its satellite countries and the People's Republic of China and its Asian sphere of influence meant that the expansion of commerce excluded a significant portion of the world as the Cold War froze in place the barriers to trade, commerce, and business that existed between the West and the East at the end of the Second World War. For the first several decades after the Second World War, China purposefully isolated itself by shutting its doors to the world (with the exception of trade with the Soviet Union until China split with the Soviet Union in the 1960s) in a fervent, if misguided, attempt at self-sufficiency. In addition, there was a period, however brief, in the latter half of the twentieth century when a viable argument could be made that communism was a legitimate competitor to free-market capitalism as an economic system and that a competition existed between these systems championed by rival nations for the alliance of other nations around the world. Second, because GATT was viewed as a rich nation's club, many developing nations did not participate in GATT for the first several decades of its existence. Many developing nations believed that they had more to lose from complying with the GATT's requirements than they would gain from the benefits of trade. In addition, until the 1980s, many developing nations, some freed from colonization only at the end of the Second World War, viewed developed nations with a certain amount of suspicion and mistrust and, as a result, erected their own restrictive laws against international business and trade. For example, many developing nations had highly restrictive laws regulating foreign investment that had the effect, perhaps intended, of discouraging investment altogether.

In the past two decades, several significant developments have vastly accelerated the pace of international business and commerce. The disintegration of the Soviet Union and its satellites in Eastern Europe has removed the barriers to trade and exchanges that have existed since the end of the Second World War. The watershed decision by the Third Plenum of the Chinese Communist Party in 1978 to adopt economic reforms that would institute some free markets in China and to engage the rest of the world in trade has created one of the world's most vibrant and important markets for foreign trade and investment. These changes also signaled the emergence of free-market capitalism as the dominant economic model in the world today. There is no longer a viable argument that that there is a serious competitor to capitalism as the world's most successful economic model. Even in China, where the official position is that the nation has a mixed system of "socialism with unique Chinese characteristics," the system can be characterized as socialist in name only. In conjunction with this vast sea change in the political arena, the information technology revolution, started in the United States in the 1990s, created vast new opportunities for trade and world integration that seemed impossible only a decade before. The disintegration of the communist bloc of nations and the technology revolution also coincided with a more receptive attitude of developing nations toward commerce and trade with developed nations. Developing nations now actively and aggressively compete for investment dollars from developed nations, and many nations have enacted new laws that encourage foreign investment. During the last round of GATT negotiations that led to the establishment of the World Trade Organization, a large number of developing nations played an important role in the negotiations. Today, about three-quarters of WTO members are developing countries and countries in transition to market economies. One of the major developments of the Fourth Ministerial Conference of the WTO held in Doha, Qatar, in November 2001 was the explicit recognition of the importance of the needs of developing and least developed countries in the future work program of the WTO.

III. Modern Forms and Patterns of International Business and Commerce

There are four principal channels of economic exchange and integration between nations in the modern era: Trade in goods, trade in services, foreign direct investment, and transfer of knowledge and technology. At the risk of repeating ourselves, we want to emphasize that our focus in this book is on the private transactions in each of these four channels and not the public regulatory aspects that we will examine only by way of background. Each of these topics will be the focus of one or more chapters or sections of this book, and we now introduce these topics and the themes that we will be exploring in depth.

A. Trade in Goods

Traditionally, states engaged in transnational economic exchanges principally through trade in goods and services. Since the end of the Second World War, international trade has been driving the process of globalization and integration of the world's economies. Merchandise exports have almost tripled from approximately $1.9 trillion in 1980 to $6 trillion in 2001.

FIGURE 1-2
Growth of World Merchandise Exports in the Past Two Decades (in $ Billions) and Percentage Share

Year	World	Developed Countries	EU	USA	Developing Countries
1980	1,932	65.5	36.4	11.7	34.5
1985	1,875	68.4	35.6	11.7	31.6
1990	3,423	71.7	40.5	11.5	28.3
1995	5,104	68.0	40.4	11.5	32.0
1999	5,577	66.9	39.1	12.6	33.1
2001	5,984	75.1	37.7	13.6	20.3

Source: IMF and UNCTAD (2000).

The traditional measure of trade competitiveness has been determined by share of world exports. Under this criterion, 20 economies, consisting primarily of developed countries led by the United States, Germany, and Japan, maintained about a two-thirds share of world trade for the past two decades. However, if one focuses on percentage gains in share of world exports for the period from 1985 to 2000, then a different list emerges that is led by China and other developing countries and economies in transition. In other words, the face of world trade is changing rapidly and a number of developing countries are the most significant beneficiaries. This foretells a greater role for developing nations in world trade and business in the future and suggests that the concerns of developing nations will assume a more significant role in world trade and business.

FIGURE 1-3

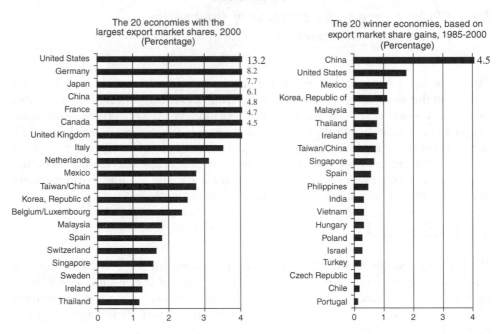

Source: *UNCTAD World Investment Report* 143 (2002).

Another significant trend is that the growth in exports is tied directly to the level of technology involved. Exports grow faster the higher the level of technology involved in the product and the less the reliance on natural resources as a source for the product. In the area of technology-intensive exports, developing countries are growing faster than their developed counterparts. High-technology products are now the largest source of foreign exchange for developing countries. In 2000, exports of technology-intensive products by developing countries reached $450 billion—$64 billion more than exports of primary products, $45 billion more than low-technology exports, $140 billion more than medium-technology exports, and $215 billion more than exports of products derived from natural resources. *See UNCTAD World Investment Report* at 145. The role of high technology and intellectual property as the engine of world trade and economic development for developing nations is another emerging world trend.

B. Trade in Services

Unlike the trade in goods, the international trade in services involves no package crossing a national boundary and a customs frontier. The intangible nature of the trade in services makes it inherently more difficult to measure in concrete terms. Some trade in services can be defined by a physical activity such as transport, hotel, or insurance services, but other types of services such as consultancy or education are more intangible and may be more difficult to define and measure. While the measurement of the trade in services is subject to greater difficulties than the measurement of the trade in goods, there is consensus that this trade has been growing on a rapid basis paralleling the growth in the trade in goods.[3]

In 2001, services accounted for more than two-thirds of the gross domestic product (GDP) of developed countries, the world's principal export markets for services. By 1999, services had surpassed 50 percent of GDP in developing countries and 57 percent of GDP in economies in transition. *See* UNCTAD, 2001, at 300-315. While services have become an important part of domestic economies, trade in services has so far lagged trade in goods. Of the almost $7.5 trillion in total trade in merchandise and commercial services in 2000, trade in goods accounted for $6.2 trillion while trade in services accounted for $1.4 trillion. However, among developed countries, the world's principal export markets, the export of commercial services has grown at a slightly faster rate (8.6%) than the growth in the export of goods (8.3%) for the period from 1985 to 2000. Examples of major services exports are sea and air transportation, travel, communications, insurance, financial, computer and information, legal, and other business services.

As the tradeability of services increases as a result of modern information and communication technologies, it can be expected that the production of a growing number of services will shift to developing countries as was the case with manufacturing. Another indicator of the potential for growth in the trade in services is that the international expansion of foreign direct investment fueled primarily by multinational enterprises discussed in greater detail in a later section may foreshadow an expansion in the export of services. As companies expand their operations on a global basis, they will also move research and development, marketing, sales, accounting, human resources, and other services abroad as well. A number of MNEs are relocating these services to lower-cost sites or places that make more logistical sense and are exporting them back to the United States from there. In the developing world, Asia appears to be more advanced than other regions in attracting the relocation of services that are then exported to other locations around the world. Industries that perform support services, such as law firms and accounting firms, are following their clients abroad by establishing branch offices around the world.

An indication of the recognition of the growing importance of trade in services is the inclusion of trade in services in the GATT negotiations that resulted in the General Agreement on Trade in Services (GATS) during the Uruguay Round of negotiations that culminated in the establishment of the WTO.

---

3. Methods of data collection for the trade in services are from six main sources: International transactions reporting systems (mainly from central banks), surveys of enterprises, surveys of households, administrative data, government data, and information obtained from partner countries and international organizations. Some of these data may be supplemented by modeling and estimation techniques.

C. Foreign Direct Investment

Foreign direct investment (FDI) refers to the acquisition by a business entity resident in one nation of a lasting ownership interest in a business entity resident in another nation, usually obtained through the investment of capital, technology, and other resources. Up to the mid-1980s, foreign trade in goods was the most significant channel of transnational commercial activity and economic exchanges between states. Exports grew much faster than FDI in the 1950s, 1960s, and 1970s. In the 1980s, however, this pattern began to change and the growth rates in FDI began to exceed the growth rates in trade. Coinciding with the disintegration of the Soviet Union, Eastern Europe, and the bulk of the socialist world, FDI began to rise dramatically in the 1980s and has now become the principal impetus behind the deepening of world economic integration. As the following diagram indicates, world real industrial production has risen by 60 percent over this 24-year period or by an annual growth rate of 2 percent. International trade as represented by export figures has increased by 210 percent over this whole period or by 4.8 percent annually, more than twice as rapidly as industrial production. An even more dramatic increase occurred in the area of FDI. From 1973 to 1997, FDI increased by 780 percent or by an annual growth rate of 9.5 percent, twice as large as the export growth rate.

FIGURE 1-4

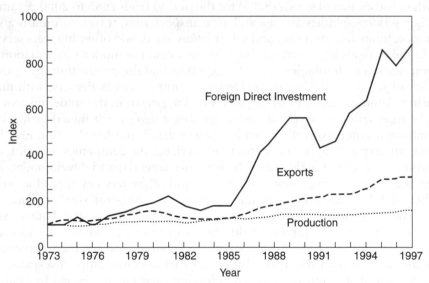

Source: IMF and other statistics.

The bulk of FDI inflows is concentrated in developed countries, with 68 percent of the world total in 2001. Some developing countries, however, have made gains in attracting FDI inflows reflecting the same pattern that we saw in the area of exports. In 2001, FDI inflows in developing countries reached 28 percent compared to an average of 18 percent during the previous two years.

According to UNCTAD, the following forces are the main drivers behind the surge in foreign investment:

The first is policy liberalization: opening up national markets and allowing all kinds of FDI and non-equity arrangements. In 2001, 208 changes in FDI laws were made by 71 countries. More than 90 percent aimed at making the investment climate more favourable to inward FDI. In addition, last year, as many as 97 countries were involved in the conclusion of 158 bilateral investment treaties, bringing the total of such treaties to 2,099 by the end of 2001. Similarly, 67 new double taxation treaties were concluded. Moreover, the investment issue figured prominently in the Fourth WTO Ministerial Conference in Doha, Qatar, in November 2001. Part of the follow-up work involves a substantial effort to help developing countries evaluate better the implications of closer multilateral cooperation in the investment area for their development process.

The second force is rapid technological change, with its rising costs and risks, which makes it imperative for firms to tap world markets and to share these costs and risks. On the other hand, falling transport and communication costs—the "death" of distance—have made it economical to integrate distant operations and ship products and components across the globe in the search for efficiency. This is contributing, in particular, to efficiency seeking FDI, with important implications for the export competitiveness of countries.

The third force, a result of the previous two, is increasing competition. Heightened competition compels firms to explore new ways of increasing their efficiency, including by extending their international reach to new markets at an early stage and by shifting certain production activities to reduce costs. It also results in international trade taking new forms, with new ownership and contractual arrangements, and new activities being located in new sites abroad.

UNCTAD World Investment Report at xv-xvi.

D. Knowledge and Technology Transfer

In the modern era, intellectual property serves a vital role in promoting economic development of all kinds. The legal issues that arise from the transfer of intellectual property will be one of the key themes that we will explore in this book. How is technology transfer related to the issues discussed so far in this book? Improving export competitiveness and attracting FDI are important goals for all states in the world today but these goals are not ends in themselves. Rather, they serve as the means to a more overarching end: Economic development. For developed nations, this means continuing advancement in living standards and improvement in economic conditions; for developing nations, this means modernization and industrialization of their economies. For all nations, knowledge and technology are critical to achieving these goals as they are the engines that drive both trade and FDI.

Because of their importance in promoting economic development, intellectual property rights are the source of some of the sharpest disagreements between developed and developing nations. Developed countries dominate in the creation of knowledge and advanced technology; developing nations tend to be importers and consumers of knowledge and technology created in developed countries. Most developing nations are urgently seeking advanced technology and knowledge transfer as they believe that these are the key ingredients for modernization and industrialization. Many developing nations believe that intellectual property rights are unduly restricting their access to technology by denying access altogether or only through the payment of burdensome royalty and licensing fees. Developed nations argue that intellectual property rights protect their substantial investments in research and development and offer a fair return for their efforts.

As we have seen in the discussion of exports, the higher the level of technology the faster the growth in exports. In the area of FDI, in many instances the most important contribution of the FDI is not the capital investment but the technology, know-how, and skills of the foreign investor. The element that is critical to the success of the foreign investment is often the knowledge-based component in the form of intellectual property such as patents, trademarks, copyrights, trade secrets, know-how, and other forms of intellectual property.

As an indication of the growing importance of intellectual property, the international transfer of knowledge and technology, as measured by payments for royalties and licensing fees, increased dramatically at about the same rate as FDI in the past two decades. Technology payments rose from $12 billion in 1983 to $80 billion in 1999; the annual growth rate for technology payments in the decade of the 1990s was 11.1 percent, even exceeding the growth rate for FDI at 9.9 percent. *See* Jorn Kleinert, *The Role of Multinational Enterprises in Globalization: An Empirical Overview* 9 (2001). It should not be surprising that developed countries dominate in the area of technology transfer. In the 1990s, almost 90 percent of all of the royalties and licensing fees on a worldwide basis were received by five countries: The United States (58%), Japan (10%), the United Kingdom (9%), Germany (6%), and France (4%) *See id.* at 10.

IV. Some Important New Developments

A. The Rise of China and East and South Asia

One of the world trends that has emerged within the past two decades is the rise of Asian economies. Of the top ten countries that had the largest percentage gains in exports for the 1985-2000 period, six countries (China, South Korea, Malaysia, Thailand, Taiwan, and Singapore) were from Asia — and this list does not include Japan, which, as an established economic power, had the third largest market share of exports in the world in 2000. Of the Asian economies, China stands apart. China's share of foreign trade has risen from twenty-seventh in the world in 1978 with $20.6 billion to sixth in the world in 2001 with $510 billion, an increase of almost 25 fold. The emergence of China has changed the way that many multinational enterprises do business in the world. Many of the world's largest corporations have targeted China as a key strategic market and have poured in billions of dollars of foreign investment. Within the span of just two decades, China has grown from an insignificant target of FDI to surpass the United States to become the world's largest recipient of FDI with capital inflows of about $50 billion in 2002.

According to current forecasts, China may have the world's largest economy measured by GDP during the early part of the twenty-first century. If this were to occur, then two of the three largest economies in the world would be from Asia (China and Japan in third place) along with the United States. This could signal a shift of economic dominance away from the West for the first time in modern history. The United States dominates world trade and business in the modern era and was preceded by Britain in the nineteenth century. The rise of Asia can have many repercussions for world business and trade as many Asia countries harbor views on significant issues, such as intellectual property and the sharing of high technology, that differ from views held by the United States and other developed countries. There are also many other significant cultural differences between the West and East that were often ignored in the past as Western nations dominated world trade, but cultural issues can and often are relevant in IBTs today. We will be also exploring some of these themes in this volume.

B. The Role of Multinational Enterprises

We have so far discussed four main channels of world economic integration: Trade in goods, trade in services, foreign direct investment, and knowledge and technology transfer. The transnational corporation or multinational enterprise[4] stands at the center of all of these developments and is the major vehicle for promoting all these channels in the international arena. First, MNEs play a major role in increasing the export competitiveness in the area of goods and services of host countries, especially developing countries, by providing additional capital and know-how as well as access to global, regional, and home markets. It is also estimated that over one-third of all worldwide trade takes place within MNEs and that about 80 percent of all world trade involves at least one MNE on one side of the trade. *See* Kleinert, *supra*, at 24-25. Second, FDI is tied directly to MNEs as they serve as the foreign investor and provide the capital and resources in the vast bulk of FDI transactions in the world today. Third, MNEs are now also the owners of the world's most valuable patents, trademarks, copyrights, and other forms of intellectual property and dominate the transfer of knowledge and technology on a worldwide basis.

A sense of the importance of MNEs in world trade and business is provided by the following UNCTAD summary:

> Recent estimates suggest that there are about 65,000 TNCs today, with about 850 foreign affiliates across the globe. Their economic impact can be measured in different ways. In 2001, foreign affiliates accounted for about 54 million employees, compared to 24 million in 1990; their sales of almost $19 trillion were more than twice as high as world exports in 2001, compared to 1990 when both were roughly equal; and the stock of outward foreign direct investment increased from $1.7 trillion to $6.6 trillion over the same period. Foreign affiliates now account for one-tenth of world GDP and one-third of world exports. Moreover, if the value of worldwide TNC activities associated with non-equity relationships (e.g. international subcontracting, licensing, contract manufacturers) is considered, TNCs would account for even larger shares in these global aggregates.

---

4. A classic definition of the MNE has described it as

a number of affiliated businesses which function simultaneously in different countries, are joined together by ties of common ownership or control, and are responsible to a common mangement strategy. From the headquarters company (and country) flow direction and control, and from the affiliates (branches, subsidiaries and joint enterprises) products, revenues, and information. Management may be organized in either monocentric or polycentric fashion. In the former case, top management is centered in one headquarters company; in the latter, management has been divided into geographic zones and a separate headquarters company has been established for each zone.

W. Feld, *Nongovernmental Forces and World Politics: A Study of Business, Labor, and Political Groups* 23 (1972).

UNCTAD World Investment Report at xv. As an indicator of the influence of some MNEs in the world economy, according to some economic measures the largest MNEs are larger than many countries. In a comparison of the sales volume of firms with the GDP of countries, the sales of the top 200 firms accounted for 26 percent of world GDP in 1997; of the world's 100 largest economies, 51 were MNEs and 49 were countries. *See* Sarah D. Anderson & John Cavanagh, *The Field Guide to the Global Economy* 67-68 (2000).

As MNEs have assumed a major role in globalization and in the economic development of nations, a host of new issues have arisen. Should MNEs be subject to international ethical obligations because of their importance in the world economy? MNEs are subject to laws against corruption in the United States and a growing number of countries. But these are laws that restrain specific behavior. Do MNEs have affirmative obligations to assist in development as well? We shall be exploring these issues in this book but for now consider the role of MNEs in the context of the following debate concerning globalization.

C. Globalization

The term "globalization" has become a watchword of our time, a word that provokes debate and controversy. For some, globalization is a benign and inevitable development. For others, it represents the summation and cause of all social and economic ills. For most of us, however, globalization is something in between these two extremes: It brings us benefits but also creates problems that have to be dealt with and managed. What is globalization? There are many definitions, but we prefer a short and simple one. Globalization, at least in the economic sphere, is the relatively free movement of goods, services, money, people, technology, information, and communication over the entire planet. Globalization has happened in the lifetimes of many who witnessed a world of nations that were separated by rigid physical, political, and technological boundaries; the pace of change has been stunning. The achievement of globalization in our time is a "first" in human history.

Most observers assume that the growth and expansion of trade and the elimination of market and trade barriers is beneficial for all the nations involved and particularly for developing nations. MNEs, which stand to reap significant benefits from the elimination of trade barriers, are some of the most ardent proponents of further trade expansion. MNEs based in the United States have pressed the U.S. government to promote further trade and investment liberalization around the world. Recall the earlier discussion that in the post–Cold War world free-market capitalism now has no viable challengers as the world's dominant economic model. The U.S. government not only wishes to support the important constituency of U.S.-based MNEs, but also believes that promoting free trade and eliminating market barriers will serve an important political purpose by promoting democracy, which appears to go hand in hand with free-market capitalism. These are propositions that do not find universal acceptance either by experts or by ordinary people. It is beyond the scope of this book to consider the full impact of globalization on civil society, but consider the implications of the points in the following essay:

> During the 1980s and 1990s, Anglo-American efforts to establish a single global market were further strengthened through comprehensive trade-liberalization agreements that increased the flow of economic resources across national borders. The rising neoliberal paradigm received further legitimation with the 1969-1991 collapse

of command-type economies in Eastern Europe. Shattering the postwar economic consensus on Keynesian principles, free-market theories pioneered by Friedrich Hayek and Milton Friedman established themselves as the new economic orthodoxy, advocating the reduction of the welfare state, the downsizing of government, and the deregulation of the economy. A strong emphasis on "monetarist" measures to combat inflation led to the abandonment of the Keynesian goal of full employment in favor of establishing "flexible" labor markets. In addition, the dramatic shift from a state-dominated to a market-dominated world was accompanied by technological innovations that lowered the costs of transportation and communication. The value of world trade increased from $57 billion in 1947 to $56 trillion in the 1990s.

Perhaps the two most important aspects of economic globalization relate to the changing nature of the production process and the internationalization of financial transactions. Indeed, many analysts consider the emergence of a transnational financial system the most fundamental feature of our time. As sociologist Manuel Castells points out, the process of financial globalization accelerated dramatically in the late 1980s as capital and securities markets in Europe and the United States were deregulated. The liberalization of financial tracing allowed for the increased mobility among different segments of the financial industry with fewer restrictions and a global market of investment opportunities. In addition, advances in data processing and information technology contributed to the explosive growth of tradeable financial value. However, a large part of the money involved in expanding markets had little to do with supplying capital for productive investment—putting together machines, raw materials, and employees to produce saleable commodities and the like. Most of the growth occurred in the purely money-dealing currency and securities markets that trade claims to draw profits from future production. Aided by new communication technologies, global speculators earned spectacular incomes by taking advantage of weak financial and banking regulations in the emerging markets of developing countries. By the late 1990s, the equivalent of nearly two trillion dollars was being exchanged daily in global currency markets alone.

While the creation of international financial markets represents a crucial aspect of economic globalization, another important economic development of the past three decades also involves the changing nature of global production. Transnational corporations (TNCs) consolidated their global operations in an increasingly deregulated global-labor market. The availability of cheap labor, resources, and favorable production conditions in the Third World enhanced both the mobility and the profitability of TNCs. Accounting for over 70 percent of world trade, these gigantic enterprises expanded their global reach as their direct foreign investments arose approximately 15 percent annually during the 1990s. Their ability to disperse manufacturing processes into many discrete phases carried out in many different locations around the world is often cited as one of the hallmarks of economic globalization. Indeed, the formation of such "global commodity chains" allows huge corporations such as Nike and General Motors to produce, distribute, and market their products on a global scale. Nike, for example, subcontracts 100 percent of its goods production to 75,000 workers in China, South Korea, Malaysia, Taiwan, and Thailand.

Transnational production systems augment the power of global capitalism by enhancing the ability of TNCs to bypass the nationally-based political influence of trade unions and other workers' organizations in collective wage-bargaining processes. While rejecting extreme accounts of economic globalization, the political economist Robert Gilpin nonetheless concedes that the growing power of TNCs has profoundly altered the structure and functioning of the global economy:

> These giant firms and their global strategies have become major determinants of trade flows and the location of industries and other economic activities around the world. Most investment is in capital-intensive and technology-intensive sectors. These firms have become central in the expansion of technology

flows to both industrialized and industrializing economies. As a consequence, multinational firms have become extremely important in determining the economic, political, and social welfare of many nations. Controlling much of the world's investment capital, technology, and access to global markets, such firms have become major players not only in international economic, but political affairs as well.

Manfred B. Steger, *Globalism* 26-28 (2002).

NOTES AND QUESTIONS

1. While globalization has powerful and ardent proponents, it also has vocal and passionate opposition. One group of objectors to globalization can be categorized as "nationalist-protectionist." This group tends to blame globalization for certain social, economic, and political ills affecting their home countries. Political figures such as Pat Buchanan in the United States condemn neoliberal internationalism, free trade, and MNEs for loss of jobs at home and moral decline. A second group of antiglobalists such as Ralph Nader argue that economic globalization has undermined the democratic accountability of MNEs and that they are free to exploit workers and damage the environment around the world. Intergovernmental organizations such as the IMF, the World Bank, and the World Trade Organization are antidemocratic institutions dominated by the MNEs. A third group, which includes academics like Amy Chua, denounces globalization for its exploitation of developing countries, for causing instability and social turmoil among developing countries, and for its exacerbation of the economic disparities between the developed and the developing worlds. Most opponents of globalization concede, however, that reversal of the process is impossible and that, to the contrary, the further deepening of this process is probably inexorable. The real battleground, then, is how to control the damaging effects of globalization and who should bear these costs. We further explore these important issues in depth in the last chapter of this book, but for now consider these issues in light of the following questions that are currently being debated.

2. What kind of corporate social responsibility or obligations do MNEs have to meet these objections? Because MNEs are propelling the process of globalization forward and some MNEs have economic power equivalent to that of nations, do MNEs acquire certain obligations to cure some of globalization's ill effects? For example, do MNEs have a social responsibility to channel the wealth-creating effects of their activities to poor nations and to poor socioeconomic groups in nations where MNEs invest? Do MNEs acquire humanitarian obligations? For example, should MNEs donate drugs that combat deadly diseases such as AIDS (acquired immunodeficiency syndrome) to countries that cannot afford to pay for them?

3. What responsibility do states and intergovernmental organizations have to manage the process of globalization so as to reduce its deleterious impact on civil society?

PROBLEM 1-5

Assume that you are the foreign trade minister of Z, a developing country that has a host of serious economic and social problems. You are the leader of a group of developing countries that will attend a world economic summit with a group of advanced industrialized countries. At the summit, you will give a speech arguing that historical events have created a moral duty on the part of developed nations and their MNEs to provide financial assistance and reparations to developing countries to assist them in economic development. The second part of your argument is that developing nations should be exempt from stringent international environmental controls on industrial development and Western intellectual property laws. As trade minister, can you make these arguments on behalf of the developing nations? Now assume you are the leader of a developed nation that is home to many powerful MNEs. How do you respond to these arguments?

V.   The Legal Framework for International Business Transactions

A.   Introductory Considerations

As we now turn to the legal framework for international business transactions, we start with a basic question: Is this an international law course? The answer to this question is "yes and no." International business transactions is not a traditional field of law like torts, contracts, or even competition law and securities law or public international law. Rather, the international business lawyer must be familiar with many specialized fields of law. International business transactions cut across and concern many legal fields and categories. Frequently, an IBT will concern both international law and domestic law, sometimes of the lawyer's home country, but perhaps also the domestic laws of several countries.

IBTs also cut across and concern both private law, which governs legal relations between private individuals and firms, and public law, which deals with regulation by governments. Moreover, IBTs cut across many legal subjects, including but not limited to commercial law, torts, administrative law, and a great number of regulatory law fields.

Although the international business lawyer deals in both international and domestic law, in this course we will, of course, emphasize the international aspects of international business practice since the domestic laws frequently encountered are covered in other law school courses. We emphasize, however, that there is no bright-line distinction between the international and domestic aspects of the practice. With this caveat in mind, we now turn to an overview of the legal framework in which most private international transactions occur. This framework consists of the choice of law principles and substantive rules of law that apply to a particular transaction and the primary legal institutions and forums that create and interpret the law.

B.   International Conflicts of Law and Choice of Law

One of the most basic tasks for any lawyer engaged in international business transactions is to determine what substantive law or laws apply to an international business transaction in order to advise clients and to structure transactions. This can be a complicated task in an international business transaction as there can be a number of different applicable laws from both national and international sources. Moreover, in many situations, the various aspects of a single transaction may be governed by more than one set of laws. How is the choice of law determination made in an international context and what principles govern this choice?

International law is traditionally divided into two fields: *Public international law*, which is the system of laws governing the relations of nation-states, intergovernmental organizations, and, to a limited extent, the private conduct of individuals; and *private international law*, which refers to the use of domestic choice of law rules by domestic courts to resolve issues of conflicts of laws in an international context. We return to a more detailed discussion of public international law later in this chapter, but for now we wish to focus on private international law as international business transactions have traditionally been associated with this field.

A transaction that involves the movement of goods, services, or capital across the national boundaries of country A and country B creates a choice of law issue of what substantive law governs the transaction because the legal systems of both country A and country B may be involved. In a situation where the parties themselves had not made an effective choice of law, or where the transaction was not governed by a superseding law such as an international treaty, the choice of law among the domestic law of country A, country B, or perhaps a combination of the two to govern the transaction was called private international law. The underlying assumption of this traditional approach was that all private international transactions were governed by national, not international law, and the rules of private international law helped to resolve which national law applied to the transaction.

Thus, the term *private international law* was really a misnomer. Private international law is really a field of domestic law because it refers to use of domestic choice of law rules by a domestic legal system to resolve conflicts of law issues in an international context involving the choice between the laws of two or more nations. The end of the process is domestic law as well because the application of the choice of law rules leads either to the use of local domestic law or to the use of foreign domestic law in national courts.

In applying its own domestic choice of law rules in an international conflicts of law context—which becomes an application of private international law—a domestic court typically weighs a number of factors, including

(a) the needs of the interstate and international systems,
(b) the relevant policies of the forum,
(c) the relevant policies of other interested states and the relative interests of those states in the determination of the particular issue,
(d) the protection of justified expectations,
(e) the basic policies underlying the particular field of law,
(f) certainty, predictability and uniformity of result, and
(g) ease in the determination and application of the law to be applied.

Restatement, Conflicts of Law (Second) §188 (1971).[5] As you can see, the factors are broad in scope, and courts will inevitably use their discretion in according

---

5. Note in the case of the United States, international choice of law issues can involve either (i) the choice of the law of one of the 50 states and the law of a foreign nation or (ii) the choice of federal law and the law of a foreign nation. The Restatement provision quoted in

weight to these factors. This approach leads to an inherent lack of predictability in results. Moreover, the Restatement factors set forth above is a restatement of the choice of law approach of U.S. courts, and the domestic courts of each nation will apply their own version of international choice of law principles. While many choice of law approaches across nations are similar, the many differing regimes added an additional level of unpredictability to the system. To deal with the lack of predictability and uniformity in the area of private international law rules, the Hague Conference on Private International Law was established in 1893 in order to promote uniform conflicts or private international law rules as a major part of its work program. The Hague Conference is a self-standing intergovernmental organization created under a statute adopted by a treaty in 1955 and currently has 45 members, including the United States, which did not join the conference until 1964. The conference has prepared conventions prescribing rules for ascertaining the substantive law applicable to testamentary dispositions, products liability, matrimonial property, and contracts for the international sale of goods. The United States is not a party to these conventions, but has signed, although not yet ratified, the Convention on the Law Applicable to Trusts and Their Recognition. The United States is also a party to two well-known procedural conventions promulgated by the Hague Conference, the Convention on the Service Abroad of Judicial and Extra-judicial Documents in Civil or Commercial Matters, 20 U.S.T. 361, 658 U.N.T.S. 163, entered into force on February 23, 1969, and the Convention on the Taking of Evidence Abroad in Civil or Commercial Matters, 23 U.S.T. 2555, 847 U.N.T.S. 231, entered into force on October 7, 1972.

C. The New Lex Mercatoria (Law Merchant)

In medieval times before the rise of the nation-state, business transactions were carried on across the existing frontiers of Europe. However, transborder conflicts of law did not arise in the modern sense because merchants in different European kingdoms employed common forms and legal principles to resolve disputes. This body of law was known as the *lex mercatoria* or medieval law merchant and was a

---

the text sets out the factors to be weighed when there is a choice between the law of a state and the law of a foreign nation. In many situations involving private transactions, such as in the case of a contract for the sale of goods, the choice is between the law of one of the 50 states, often the state's version of the Uniform Commercial Code, and the law of a foreign country. Under long-standing practice, state courts do not hesitate to use their usual choice of approaches, as exemplified by the Restatement provision quoted above, to international cases even where the foreign relations of the United States may be implicated. *See* Daniel C.K. Chow, *Limiting Erie in a New Age of International Law: Toward a Federal Common Law of International Choice of Law*, 74 Iowa L. Rev. 165 (1988). Federal courts exercising diversity jurisdiction are to apply the substantive law of the state in which they are located under *Erie R.R. Co. v. Tompkins*, 304 U.S. 64 (1938), including the state's choice of law rules. *See Klaxon v. Stentor Elec. Mfg.*, 3132 U.S. 487 (1941).

   In some cases, however, there is a conflict between a federal law of the United States and the law of a foreign nation. For example, in the area of antitrust or securities regulation, U.S. laws may apply to govern a transaction abroad that may also be at the same time subject to a foreign law. Many of the situations involving a conflict between a federal law and a foreign law occur in the context of laws regulating international trade and economic relations. In these cases involving the choice between U.S. federal law and the law of a foreign nation, a different set of choice of law considerations apply. *See* Restatement, Foreign Relations Law (Third) §403.

special type of supranational common law applicable to commercial transactions among European merchants. Special international commercial courts were created to deal with international business problems. This situation had a long history in Europe; the medieval *lex mercatoria* was the heir to the *jus gentium* of Roman law. Thus, the traditional conflicts of law approach to international business problems is exceptional; it dates back only to the rise of nation-states since the seventeenth century and the creation of national bodies of law. *See* Filip De Ly, *International Business Law and Lex Mercatoria* (1992).

During the last 50 years and continuing today at an accelerating pace, a new *lex mercatoria* has developed that functions in a similar fashion to the *lex mercatoria* of old. We have now and are continuing to create a truly international body of rules and forms to govern international business transactions. As a result, the domestic body of law known as private international law is diminishing in relevance and importance. We no longer need conflicts of law principles if we develop and use a body of law and legal tools that ensure that legal conflicts no longer arise. Of course, it is too strong to say that conflicts of law are now rare. They still arise and private international law is still needed. What we have in truth is a hybrid system of the *lex mercatoria* and private international law.

There are basically three reasons for the new lex mercatoria and the diminution of private international law. First, for many years sustained efforts have been made by both nations and private entities to harmonize international economic and commercial law through the promulgation of international treaties and uniform codes. These and other law creation methods have given us a vast body of doctrine that is truly international in character. Second, courts now freely allow parties to choose the applicable law that will govern their relations. As we will see, parties may even choose to apply general equitable principles and avoid choosing any domestic system of law. Third, the availability and popularity of arbitration as a dispute resolution technique means that many disputes are now resolved by international bodies, not by national courts. These international arbitration bodies are comfortable operating outside the parameters of national laws and forums. Traditional private international law analysis does continue to be applicable, however, where no superseding international law is applicable or where the parties have not chosen a source of law to govern the transaction. In these cases, a private international law analysis would result in the application of the domestic law of one of the nations involved in the transaction.

D.   Sources of Law for International Business Transactions

The Hague Conference discussed in the previous section is an example of an attempt to harmonize international commercial law through the adoption of uniform rules of international choice of law that would lead to predictability and uniformity in the procedures by which a substantive law was chosen by a domestic court to govern cases with connections to more than one nation's laws. During the latter half of the twentieth century, however, many additional approaches to harmonization have gained extensive support from the international community.

Professor Roy Goode of St. John's College, Oxford, has written on the currently accepted sources of international business law as follows:

The Instruments of Harmonization

The Range of Available Instruments

There are at least nine methods by which harmonization may be either effected or in some measure inducted, namely:

(1)   a multilateral Convention without a Uniform Law as such;
(2)   a multilateral Convention embodying a Uniform Law;
(3)   a set of bilateral Treaties;
(4)   [European] Community legislation — typically a Directive;[6]
(5)   a Model Law;
(6)   a codification of custom and usage promulgated by an international non-governmental body;
(7)   international trade terms promulgated by such an organization;
(8)   model contracts and general contractual conditions;
(9)   restatements by scholars and other experts.

The characteristic of the first four is that they have the force of law, subject to such constitutional acts as may be necessary to give them force in the territory of a particular Contracting State.[7] The Model is, as its name implies, a model which can be adopted in its entirety, adapted, or simply used as the basis for ideas; it has no legal force as such. The next four instruments depend on their efficacy upon incorporation into contracts, though a codification of custom and usage could perhaps be relied on as the best evidence of custom and usage and as such be imported by implication into a contract, whilst the adoption of general contractual conditions is not the exclusive prerogative of private parties but can also be achieved by embodiment in bilateral or multilateral Conventions implemented by dispositive legislation in the various participating States.

Roy Goode, *Reflections on the Harmonization of Commercial Law* reprinted in Ross Cranston & Roy Goode, *Commercial and Consumer Law* 6-7 (Oxford 1993). In the discussion below, we will categorize the sources of international law applicable to international business transactions. Professor Goode's nine instruments of harmonization fall into two of the three categories of the sources of law for international business transactions that we further discuss below.

We should note that there is a historical precedent for a uniform supranational law applying to commercial transactions, the lex mercatoria discussed in the previous section. As we have noted, the *lex mercatoria* was a set of international legal rules created by custom and usage that supplemented what was at that time the often-incomplete commercial law of states. By the nineteenth century as most nations had absorbed the medieval *lex mercatoria* into their national laws or had replaced it by their own national commercial law, and international transactions became largely governed by national law, some legal theorists rejected the very notion of a supranational merchant law altogether, stating instead that all

---

6. See pp. 58 and 477-517 *infra* for a further discussion of the European Union.

7. Note that a nation that is a signatory to a treaty is referred to as a contracting state, which underscores that the treaty is a legal text, whereas a nation that belongs to an international organization is a member. Thus, the original GATT had contracting parties, whereas the WTO has members. — EDS.

international business transactions were necessarily governed by national law. Note, however, that some vestiges of *lex mercatoria* as a set of customary legal rules still remains, and it is possible that courts may still refer to long-standing rules of international commerce that may differ somewhat from national laws. Note further that the concept of a *lex mercatoria* has been given new life by the many harmonizing codes, model laws, and systems of terms, further discussed below, that have been created in the latter part of the twentieth century.

E. International Forums and Institutions

We now turn to some of the principal institutions and forums that are the sources of the harmonization of the law applicable to international business and commercial transactions. Perhaps the most important are the following:

1. UNCITRAL

The United Nations Commission on International Trade Law (UNCITRAL or the commission) is the core legal body of the United Nations[8] in the field of international commerce and trade. Today, UNCITRAL is the most prolific source of proposals for the unification of commercial law. The body was established by the United Nations (UN) General Assembly, the plenary body of the UN, in 1966. The commission continues to report to the General Assembly. The commission is dedicated to formulating modern rules on commercial transactions and to furthering the harmonization and unification of the law of international commerce. The commission is presently composed of 36 member states elected by the General Assembly, although membership in the commission has been recently expanded to 60 states. The states are elected for a term of six years with the terms of half of the members expiring every three years. Membership is structured so as to be representative of the world's various geographic regions as well as its principal legal and economic systems. Some of the current members of the commission include France, Germany, Cameroon, Rwanda, Russia, Lithuania, and Mexico. The United States has been represented on the commission since its inception. The commission's secretariat, its main administrative body, is located in Vienna, with working sessions held in alternative years at the UN headquarters in New York and in Vienna.

One of UNCITRAL's most important and influential roles is to create multilateral conventions or treaties on international commerce that have the force of

---

8. Established on October 24, 1945 when its charter, a multilateral treaty, came into force, the United Nations is a universal organization that is charged with peacekeeping responsibilities; with the development of friendly relations among nations; with the achievement of international cooperation in solving international problems of an economic, social, cultural, and humanitarian character; and with the promotion of human rights and fundamental freedoms for all human beings without discrimination. *See* UN Charter, art. 1. At the time of its founding, the United Nations consisted of 51 states. Today, its membership has grown to over 190 states, consisting of virtually all of the independent states of the world. The United Nations replaced a predecessor organization, the League of Nations, founded in 1920, by the Treaty of Versailles, which ended World War I. The League of Nations met its demise after it failed to prevent World War II and at the end of that conflict, a new international organization, the UN was formed.

law, binding all of the nations that ratify the treaty. Conventions drafted by UNCITRAL are formally approved as official UN instruments at a diplomatic conference convened by the General Assembly. The convention then is open for signature for those nations that wish to adopt the treaty. In some cases, the conventions provide by their own terms that they do not enter into force unless a minimum number of nations adopt and ratify the treaty. Among the major results of the commission is the Convention on Contracts for the International Sale of Goods (1980) (CISG), which has established a comprehensive code of legal rules governing the formation of contracts for the international sale of goods, obligations of the buyer and seller, and remedies for breach and other aspects of the contract. Some other notable conventions are the Convention on the Limitation Period in the International Sale of Goods (concluded 1974, entry into force 1988), setting forth uniform limitation periods for bringing actions arising from international sales contracts, and the Convention on the Carriage of Goods by Sea (concluded 1978, entry into force 1992) — the "Hamburg Rules" — which establishes a uniform legal regime governing the rights and obligations of shippers, carriers, and consignees under a contract of carriage of goods by sea. The United States has yet to ratify this treaty although it has already come into force for some 20 countries. The widely adopted New York Convention on the Recognition and Enforcement of Foreign Arbitral Awards (1958) was prepared by the UN prior to the establishment of UNCITRAL, but the commission has been instrumental in promoting the convention and its acceptance by nations.

In addition to creating and promulgating conventions, UNCITRAL also drafts model laws for incorporation by governments worldwide such as the UNCITRAL Model Law on Procurement of Goods, Construction and Services (1994), designed to assist developing countries in reforming and modernizing their laws on government procurement. UNCITRAL also creates legal rules that parties can directly incorporate by contract to govern their transaction. Examples are the UNCITRAL Arbitration Rules (1976), which parties may agree on for the conduct of arbitral proceedings arising out of their commercial relationships, and the UNCITRAL Conciliation Rules (1980). UNCITRAL also provides other services such as technical assistance for states on law reform projects and legal and legislative guides.

2. *UNIDROIT*

The International Institute for the Unification of Private Law (UNIDROIT or the institute) is an independent intergovernmental organization with its headquarters in Rome. The goals of UNIDROIT are somewhat similar to those of UNCITRAL: To study the needs and methods for modernizing and harmonizing private law and, in particular, commercial law between states. The reason for these overlapping roles can be traced to history. UNIDROIT was established in 1926 as an organ of the League of Nations, the predecessor organization to the United Nations. Following the demise of the League of Nations, the institute was re-established in 1940 on the basis of a multilateral treaty, the UNIDROIT Statute. The institute remained an independent body when the United Nations was established in 1945. When the UN decided that it needed a body to focus on issues of commercial law, the UN established UNCITRAL. For these reasons, both UNIDROIT and UNCITRAL have overlapping goals, although as we shall see the work of the two bodies differs in methods and in emphasis.

Membership in UNIDROIT currently consists of 59 members with some overlap with the membership of UNCITRAL. The United States joined UNIDROIT in 1964. The membership of the institute is designed to include a variety of legal, economic, and political systems as well as different cultural backgrounds. The institute is funded by annual contributions by its member states and consists of a secretariat, the main administrative body; a governing council, a policy body; and a general assembly, the ultimate decision-making organ made up of representatives from each of the member states.

As UNIDROIT is an independent organization devoted to private and commercial law, its work is less influenced by political issues and tends to focus on more technical issues. This emphasis distinguishes the work of the institute from UNCITRAL, which, as a body of the United Nations, continues to report to the General Assembly, the plenary body of the UN, and is subject to the influence of political issues and is particularly sensitive to the issues of developing nations. A second distinction is that while UNIDROIT has sought to promulgate its work through international treaties that represent all views, the principal drafters of UNIDROIT treaties in the past have mainly been Western European nations. Many governments have been reluctant to adopt UNIDROIT treaties as they tend to reflect the legal traditions of Western Europe but not traditions elsewhere. For example, after 30 years of work, two uniform laws on international sales were adopted under the auspices of UNIDROIT in 1964: The Uniform Law on International Sale of Goods and the Uniform Law on the Formation of Contracts for the International Sale of Goods. Only a handful of states, mostly Western European, adopted the two 1964 conventions. Most countries such as the United States and a large number of the developing nations refused to adopt the conventions. This failure led the United Nations to search for a more universally acceptable contracts convention that culminated in the CISG. To date, the only UNIDROIT convention that the United States has signed and ratified is the Convention Providing for a Uniform Law on the Form of an International Will, although Congress has yet to pass implementing legislation. The United States is also a signatory to two other UNIDROIT conventions, the Convention on International Factoring and the Convention on International Financial Leasing, but neither has been submitted to Congress for ratification.

In recent years, UNIDROIT has shifted its work to nonbinding instruments such as model laws that may influence the development of domestic legislation and general principles that are addressed directly to judges, arbitrators, and private parties who are left to decide whether to use them or not. UNIDROIT does continue to draft treaties for ratification and to do preliminary work on treaties that are later promulgated by other international organizations, but its role as a source of international commercial law conventions has diminished with the rise of UNCITRAL. Perhaps UNIDROIT's most influential recent work has been the development of the Principles of International Commercial Contracts (1994), which are applicable to all commercial contracts and are not limited to contracts for the sale of goods like the CISG. Unlike the CISG, the principles were not drafted as an international treaty. In addition, the principles are not intended as a model law that states can adopt or enact and thus confer the force of law. Rather, the principles are intended as a type of restatement of the law that draws upon sources from around the world and serve as a source of ideas for drafting domestic legislation, international conventions, or international commercial contracts. Note also that the principles are offered as an interpretive tool that can supplement gaps in existing international or domestic law or in existing commercial agreements. On a more controversial level, the principles are also intended to be a distillation or even a source for the *lex mercatoria*, the supranational law of commerce that has ancient roots and that continues to lurk as a possible source of international commercial law.

3. The International Chamber of Commerce

Founded in 1919, the International Chamber of Commerce (ICC) is a private not-for-profit organization whose members consist of national chambers of commerce, trade and business associations, and companies from about 130 countries. Note that unlike UNCITRAL and UNIDROIT the ICC is a nongovernmental agency whose goal is to represent the interests of private business and industry before national governments and international organizations. A second goal of the ICC is to create uniform rules and standards for international business. As the ICC is a private body, it operates mainly through the promulgation of nonbinding rules that private parties can adopt by contract. Among the ICC's most influential contributions are Incoterms and the Uniform Customs and Practice for Documentary Credits (UCP), both discussed further in the next section on sources of substantive law. Both of these sets of rules are widely adopted by private parties to govern their transactions in the sale, transport, and financing of goods. In later chapters, we will examine Incoterms and the UCP in some detail.

The ICC also provides specialized services to facilitate international commerce. One of the ICC's services is its court of arbitration, which, since its establishment in 1922, has handled more than 10,000 commercial arbitrations and since 1999 has received new cases at the rate of 500 per year, more than any other organization. We will be examining the process of commercial arbitration in later sections of this book.

Besides UNCITRAL, UNIDROIT, and the ICC, the Hague Conference and the International Maritime Committee (known under its French title, Comité Maritime International) have also played an important role in unifying or codifying international commercial law. On a regional level, the Council of the European Union and the European Parliament, institutions within the European Union, are the most important regional law-making institutions. Note that these EU institutions differ from UNCITRAL and UNIDROIT in that they have direct law-making powers and can create supranational laws that, upon enactment, are immediately effective as a superseding international law within its membership. UNCITRAL and UNIDROIT draft treaties that are then open for adoption on a voluntary basis by participating nations. Another regional organization engaged in harmonization is the Organization of American States (OAS), which is based in Washington, D.C., and currently consists of 35 states. The OAS is the oldest regional organization in the world; although it was established in its present form in 1948 when its charter came into existence, the OAS traces its origins to a number of predecessor entities dating to the first decade of the twentieth century. Today, OAS membership is open to all independent American states. Although much of the work of the OAS has focused on political issues and matters of public international law, it has recently held a series of conferences on private law. The OAS has produced a number of conventions that attempt to harmonize private commercial law, but the United States is a contracting party only to the Convention on International Commercial Arbitration and the Convention on Letters Rogatory.

F.   Major Categories of International Business Law

A distinguishing feature of the modern era since the end of the Second World War is that private international transactions are often governed in whole or in part by a source of law that is other than the law of one of the countries involved in the transnational movement of goods, services, capital, or technology. Note that this is quite a departure from the approach in the nineteenth century when legal theorists posited that all international commercial transactions were necessarily governed by national, not international, rules (with the possible exception of the ancient *lex mercatoria*).

The modern law that applies to IBTs is a blend of domestic private law and the business law aspects of public international law. We can classify the law of international business transactions into four categories.

1.   Public International Law

As we have previously noted, the traditional field of public international law concerned the law that governed relations between states. Under the traditional view, only states were subjects of international law and only states had rights and obligations. Any rights or obligations in individuals or other entities were deemed to be derivative from their relationship to the state. Public international law also traditionally concerned political issues, diplomatic activity, and public rights such as the determination of statehood, the right of peoples to self-determination, the use of force, and the recognition of governments. Most law school courses on international law continue to focus on these and related topics of the traditional public international law field. The primary sources of public international law are treaties, which are essentially explicit contracts between states, and customary international law, which we further discuss below.

Today, public international law is no longer confined to relations between states but also applies to intergovernmental international organizations and even to individuals, although to a more limited extent. *See* Restatement of the Law of Foreign Relations (Third) §101 (1987). Moreover, the field of public international law not only encompasses public rights but also is a significant source of law governing commercial activity that occurs between private parties. The applicability of international treaties to private business transactions and private rights signals a shift in modern public international law. In the twentieth century, however, particularly after the end of the Second World War, the dramatic rise of international commerce and transactions of all kinds crossing national boundaries have led nations to focus their attention on international commercial activity. Today, public international law in the form of treaties between states is an important source of law for international business transactions. Treaties can be bilateral or multilateral in nature. One example of a multilateral treaty that is an important source of law for international business transactions is the CISG, which sets forth a uniform law governing certain international contracts for the sale of goods. As of October 2004, 63 countries, including the United States, China, Russia, and Germany, were signatories to the treaty. We will shortly discuss the application of the CISG and other treaties to private transactions and their relationship to the domestic laws of the United States and other countries. For now, it is important to understand that the CISG and other law treaties can apply directly to a sales contract and other business transactions between private parties.

Aside from treaties, customary international law is the other major source of traditional public international law. The basic idea behind customary international law is that states in and by their international practice may consent to the creation and application of international legal rules among themselves. Whereas treaties are evidence of an explicit consent between nations to be bound by contract, customary international law can be understood as a form of implied consent to be bound. The practice of states refers to official government conduct in the form of official statements at international conferences, national legislative measures, national court decisions, and diplomatic statements and practices or other actions taken by governments to deal with issues in the international area. The practice of states alone was not sufficient to become law; the practice had to be accompanied by a sense of legal obligation in order to become customary international law. As we have previously discussed, the ancient *lex mercatoria* was one type of international law that was applied in national courts up until the nineteenth century, and some vestiges of the traditional *lex mercatoria* may continue to have some application today. Aside from the law merchant, however, in the area of international business transactions, customary international law does not play a significant role as it applies mostly in the traditional areas of political issues, such as the determination of boundaries, and diplomatic issues, such as the granting of asylum. Customary international law, as traditionally applied, is not a significant source of law for private international business transactions although, as we shall see in the next section, custom of a different sort in the form of custom or industry practice can play a significant role through the intermediary of private and intergovernmental institutions.

2. *Regional Supranational Law*

Within a regional economic organization such as the European Union, there are instances in which a supranational law in the form of a treaty or regulation will apply directly to its member countries and will supersede national law in the case of conflict. Thus, a business transaction with a connection to Germany may be subject in part or in whole to an EC *law or regulation* that overrides German law. In other cases in the EU, a *directive* will require a member country to ensure that its laws conform to EU law and policy.[9]

3. *Uniform Codes and Other Harmonizing Measures*

An important and perhaps unique source of law applicable to international business transactions are the codes or rules created by intergovernmental and by private and nongovernmental bodies for the purposes of promoting harmonization. These rules codify international commercial custom and usage and define trade terms. Unlike treaties, which are legally binding instruments creating legal duties and obligations, the codes themselves have no inherent legal force but become legally effective when they are incorporated by contract by the parties. A prominent example of a widely adopted code are Incoterms (from International Commercial Terms) promulgated by the International Chamber of Commerce, an international nongovernmental body consisting of national chambers of commerce as its members. Incoterms provide a lexicon as well as define rights and duties for exporters and forwarders involved in the international shipment of

---

9. See p. 341 *infra*.

goods. Concepts such as CIF (cost, insurance, and freight) and FOB (free on board) are given a uniform definition by Incoterms that the parties can adopt. This avoids the problem that these terms could have different meanings to a seller from the United States and a buyer from England. Another striking example is provided by the Uniform Customs and Practice for Documentary Credits (UCP) of the International Chamber of Commerce, which governs letters of credit and has been adopted by banks throughout the world. The UCP applies to the account party's application to its bank to open the credit, the credit itself, the relationship between the beneficiary and the advising and confirming banks, and the relationships of the banks among themselves. Each of the relevant contracts incorporates the provisions of the UCP by reference, creating a network of contracts subject to a uniform set of rules and definitions.

The role that these codifications play in providing a source of law for international business transactions appears to have no direct analogy in domestic law. The harmonizing measures promulgated by the ICC and other nongovernmental organizations are not intended to be model laws that may be adopted by legislatures or restatements of the law that are an attempt to influence the development of the law by courts or legislatures. Rather, they are intended for incorporation by contract by private parties to directly govern their transactions. Note that these codifications appear to be unique in international law — although they are related to the ancient *lex mercatoria* as they attempt to codify and set out in precise terms some of the customs and usages of international commerce. Unlike the *lex mercatoria*, however, these codifications do not purport to be a type of customary international law that is binding on domestic courts; rather, these codifications are binding because of incorporation by contract by the parties. Together with other sources of international commercial law, these codifications may constitute a new *lex mercatoria* for the modern age.

4. *Domestic Law*

Domestic law, including private international law, continues to be an important source of law for many international business transactions. In a business transaction between parties in different states, the domestic law of one of the states will apply to the transaction in the absence of a superseding treaty or the explicit adoption of a uniform code by the parties. Conflicts and choice of law as well as recognition and enforcement of judgments in an international context continue to be governed by the principles of private international law. Domestic law may be the substantive law applicable to a business transaction because it is chosen under domestic conflicts of law rules, that is, private international law, or because the parties have agreed to have the transaction governed by domestic law. In a sales contract between a U.S. seller and a Germany buyer, the parties may agree to have U.S. law govern the contract. Certain international treaties, including the CISG, allow the parties to opt out and to choose domestic law. In the example just given, the sales contract would, in the absence of an election to opt out by the parties, be subject to the CISG. A party may decide to have U.S. law govern a letter of credit transaction and choose not to adopt the UCP. Note that even where a transaction is governed by one of the nondomestic sources of law for international business transactions discussed in this section, some aspects of the transaction may nevertheless be governed by domestic law. For example, the CISG explicitly excludes some contract issues, such as validity, from the scope of its coverage, and these issues will be governed by domestic law. Domestic law continues to play an important role in every IBT even where a nondomestic source of law appears to be the governing law. Whenever there is an issue that falls into a "gap" in the application of law to an IBT that is otherwise governed by a nondomestic source of law, the gap needs to be filled and domestic law becomes a prime candidate to serve as this gap filler.

NOTES AND QUESTIONS

1. *Public international law*, which we discuss above, should not be confused with the concept of *public law* (i.e., antitrust, securities, and other mandatory laws dealing with public rights that may apply in an international context) that we introduced on p. 2 *supra*. Also be careful to distinguish between *private international law*, which we introduced on p. 28 and which refers to the application of domestic choice of law rules to an international choice of law situation, with *private law* (i.e., substantive laws dealing with contract, property, torts, and other fields dealing with private rights that may apply in an international context) that we also introduced on p. 2. You will need to keep these distinctions clear in order to have a solid grasp of the complex law applicable to IBTs and international economic relations.

PROBLEM 1-6

To test your understanding of these concepts and to emphasize that a single IBT can be subject to many different sources and types of law, can you explain how a single IBT, an international transaction for the sale of goods involving a sales contract, export compliance, and import clearance issues (see p. 4 *supra*), can involve:

(1a)   a private international law analysis?
(1b)   a public international law that deals with private law issues?
(2a)   a domestic law that deals with private law issues?
(2b)   a domestic law that deals with public law issues?

G.   Relationship of Sources of International Law to Domestic Law

The previous discussion indicated that the law governing international business transactions is drawn from a number of sources. Among the most important sources now is public international law. What is the relationship between public international law and domestic U.S. law governing IBTs?

As a historical matter, international law was part of the law of England and, as such, it was also part of the law of the U.S. colonies. With independence, international law became part of the law of the United States. From the beginning, international law was incorporated into the law of the United States without the need for any action by the President or Congress, and U.S. courts, both state and federal, have applied it and given it effect as did the courts of England. With respect to treaties, the Supremacy Clause of the U.S. Constitution states that treaties of the United States, as well as the Constitution and laws of the United States, are to be "the supreme Law of the Land." *See* U.S. CONST. art. VI. With respect to customary international law, the U.S. Supreme Court has stated that it is "a part of our law." *See The Paquete Habana*, 175 U.S. 677, 700 (1900). This equates customary international law to the law of treaties and other international agreements as part of the law of the United States.[10]

Both treaties and customary international law are regarded as a type of federal law, equivalent in rank to the laws of the United States and supreme over the laws of the states. It was long ago established in U.S. jurisprudence that where there is a conflict between international law and state law, the former prevails. *See Ware v. Hylton*, 3 U.S. (3 Dall.) 199, 326 (1796). Where there is conflict between a treaty and a federal statute, the one that is later in time controls. *See Whitney v. Robertson*, 124 U.S. 190, 194 (1888). Note that the treaties that have the benefit of the Supremacy Clause and Article VI need not necessarily be treaties made pursuant to Article II of the Constitution, which are those made by the President with the advice and consent of two-thirds of the Senate. There are two other common types of international agreements that are also given the same effect as treaties entered into pursuant to Article II of the Constitution: Statutory agreements or congressional-executive agreements where the President entered into international agreements pursuant to ordinary congressional legislation authorizing such activity and executive agreements or agreements concluded by the President alone without any congressional participation.

While international law is a type of federal law, there is an important distinction between treaties and other types of federal law. With respect to treaties, in *Foster v. Neilson*, 27 U.S. 253 (1829), Chief Justice Marshall drew a distinction between self-executing and non-self-executing treaties that is now followed by many other countries. A self-executing treaty has a direct effect within the United States as soon as the treaty enters into force without the need for implementing domestic legislation. A non-self-executing treaty requires implementing legislation passed by Congress before the treaty is given effect. Note that in the case of a non-self executing treaty, it is the domestic implementing legislation that has legal effect within the United States, not the treaty itself. Examples of non-self-executing treaties are the many WTO agreements that contemplate implementing domestic legislation. Customary international law, where applicable, is given direct effect in U.S. courts.

How does one determine whether a treaty is self-executing? One common approach by courts in the United States is to examine the intent of the states that are party to the treaty. The court examines the provisions of the treaty to determine whether they are aimed directly at the courts and not at the Congress requiring legislation. *See Foster v. Neilson, supra*, 27 U.S. at 314; *see also Cheung v. United States*, 213 F.2d 82, 95 (2d Cir. 2000) (explicit statement by executive that treaty will not require implementing legislation). A few years later, Justice Marshall, who held that the treaty at issue in *Foster* was non-self-executing, held that the very same article at issue in a Spanish language version of the treaty was self-executing, indicating the broad interpretive discretion of the courts. *See United States v. Percheman*, 32 U.S. 51 (1833). For other approaches on how to determine

---

10. Some scholars, however, dispute the current relevance of customary international law unless it has been explicitly incorporated into U.S. law. *See, e.g.*, J. Patrick Kelly, *The Twilight of Customary International Law*, 40 Va. J. of Int'l L. 449 (2000).

whether a treaty is self-executing, *see* Jordan Paust, *Self-Executing Treaties*, Am. J. Int'l L. 760 (1988).

In the area of international business transactions, self-executing treaties and domestic legislation enacted for the purpose of implementing non-self-executing treaties may be sources of law applicable to a particular transaction. In some cases, the different aspects of the same transaction may be subject to different sources of law. For example, a sales contract may be subject to the CISG but the letter of credit procured by the parties to finance the sale may be subject to the Uniform Customs and Practice for Documentary Credits of the ICC, which by agreement of the parties displaces or supersedes domestic law that would otherwise govern the letter of credit. The carriage of the goods by sea may be subject to a different international treaty or to a different federal statute such as the Carriage of Goods by Sea Act. Even where certain aspects of a transaction appear to fall under one set of legal rules such as letters of credit under the UCP, where questions arise that are not treated in the UCP, gaps in the UCP may be filled by resort to domestic law, such as the Uniform Commercial Code. For now, it is important to understand that the emerging law of international business transactions is often an amalgamation or hybrid of many different sources of law. We have identified the primary ones in this section, but the process of determining which law governs a particular aspect of a transaction can be complex and any transaction may be subject to different sources of law.

PROBLEM 1-7

A successful Ohio law firm uses a standard form for its domestic sales contracts. The standard form has a choice of law clause choosing Ohio law. The law firm has been retained by a long-time client that wishes to sell sophisticated equipment to be adapted for use in Argentina. The law firm has represented the client in the past in its domestic transactions quite successfully through the use of its standard contracts. The law firm is considering adopting the standard sales contract to the international sale and retaining the choice of law clause stipulating Ohio law. The senior partner of the firm reasoned that the firm has been quite successful in resolving any disputes under Ohio law and rather than subjecting the transaction to the various sources of law governing international business transactions, the law firm would simply retain its choice of law clause and avoid the complexities of applying unfamiliar sources of law. The lawyers in the firm are familiar with Ohio law, learned it in law school, and would save the client the expense involved in having the firm's lawyers research Argentine law or learn about various sources of international law applicable to the contract. Do you see any problems with this approach? Consider this problem in light of the following:

(1) Assume that Argentine law does not have the same types of implied warranties that are contained under the Ohio version of the Uniform Commercial Code such as an implied warranty of fitness. How does this affect your answer?

(2) Both the United States and Argentina are parties to the Convention on Contracts for the International Sale of Goods mentioned in the discussion above. The CISG allows parties to opt out of the convention in favor of another law, including domestic law. Assume that the choice of law clause in the law firm's standard contract is sufficient to opt out of the CISG. How would you advise

the Ohio law firm in light of the following discussion of whether a lawyer involved in an international contract needs to be aware of the CISG:

> This question is not a difficult one. The duty of competence set forth in Model Rule 1.1 clearly requires of a lawyer "the legal knowledge, skill, thoroughness and preparation reasonably necessary for the representation." Any lawyer involved in the negotiation or litigation of a contract for which the parties have their places of business in different countries has a duty to determine [whether the Convention applies.] If . . . the lawyer determines that the Sales Convention applies to the transaction, he or she then has a duty to understand fully the rules of the Convention and the application of those rules to the transaction. If the representation is in the context of negotiations, the lawyer is also responsible for determining and advising the client whether exercising the Article 6 possibility of "opting out" of the Convention rules would be to the benefit of the client. If the representation is in the context of litigation, the lawyer clearly has an obligation to know (1) whether the Convention applies to the transaction in question, and (2) if it does, the impact on his or her client of application of the Convention rules. The failure to understand and properly apply the Convention in regard to any of these obligations clearly constitutes a violation of Rule 1.1.

Ronald A. Brand, *Professional Responsibility in a Transnational Transactions Practice*, 17 J. L. & Comm. 301, 335-336 (1998).

PROBLEM 1-8

A, an Illinois company, has entered into a contract to sell goods to B, a German company. Both the United States and Germany are contracting parties to the CISG. Article 1 of the CISG provides that "this Convention applies to contracts of sale of goods between parties whose places are in different States . . . when the States are Contracting States." Article 6 of the CISG further provides, "The parties may exclude the application of this Convention or . . . derogate from or vary the effect of any of its provisions." Suppose that the contract has a choice of law clause that provides, "This contract is to be governed exclusively by the laws of Illinois." Suppose that A brings a lawsuit in an Illinois state court on the contract.

(1) Should the Illinois court apply Illinois state law, German law, the CISG, or some other law? *See Asante Technologies, Inc. v. PMC-Sierra, Inc.*, 164 F. Supp. 2d 1142, 1150 (N.D. Cal. 2001) (a choice of law provision selecting British Columbia law did not, without more, "evince a clear intent to opt out of the CISG. . . . Defendant's choice of applicable law adopts the law of British Columbia, and it is undisputed that the CISG *is* the law of British Columbia."). *See also Ajax Tool Works, Inc. v. Can Eng Manufacturing Ltd.*, 2003 WL 223187 at 3 (N.D. Ill. 2003) ("The parties' contract states that the 'agreement shall be governed by the laws of the Province of Ontario, Canada.' Obviously, this clause does not exclude the CISG."); *St. Paul Guardian Ins. Co. v. Neuromed Medical Systems & Support, GmbH*, 2002 WL 465312 at 3 (S.D.N.Y. 2002) (the CISG applies "[w]here parties, as here, designate a choice of law clause in their contract — selecting the law of a Contracting State without expressly excluding application of the CISG. . . . To hold otherwise would undermine the objectives of the Convention which Germany has agreed to uphold.").

(2) How would you draft the choice of law clause to exclude the CISG?

(3) With respect to the CISG, is it a self-executing treaty that has direct effect within U.S. courts or must the Illinois court look to domestic implementing legislation?

VI.   *International Economic Law: The Public Law Institutions and Rules That Facilitate and Regulate International Business*

Governments, of course, play a large role in both facilitating and regulating international business. Governments levy taxes (called tariffs) on imports, and they have the ability to influence trade, encouraging some and cutting off other transactions. Governments also have the ability to regulate international transactions just as they do domestic business through competition laws, securities laws, environmental laws, labor laws, taxation, and social legislation.

Theoretically, the doctrines of sovereignty and the existence of the nation-state system of world order would allow any state to impose whatever tax or regulation on international business it deemed necessary. This, of course, would be chaotic and damaging to world business. Fortunately, in the last 60 years an imposing structure of international rules and intergovernmental organizations has been created to impose some order on the way governments regulate international business. Without this framework, international business as we know it today would be literally impossible.

The legal mechanism used to create this framework of international institutions and rules is the international agreement or treaty, which was previously considered in our discussion of public international law. This legal method is a primary way of creating public international law, and this body of law is a specialized branch of public international law known as *international economic law* and also known as *international trade law*.

International economic law (IEL) consists, therefore, of the framework of intergovernmental organizations and international rules that govern international economic relations. IEL is created through bilateral, regional, and multilateral treaties. Such treaties cover all four of the areas of international business, trade in goods, trade in services, foreign investment, and technology transfer. Once the rules have been formulated internationally through the treaty-making process, the responsibility of participating governments is to transform these international obligations into domestic legislation and to apply them faithfully. Thus, the international business lawyer will deal with these rules more on the level of domestic law than as international law. Nevertheless, their international law source must be understood.

International economic law is such a vast and difficult subject that it is or should be the subject of separate courses in the law school curriculum. Most of this subject is beyond the scope of this book, which concerns the law of international business transactions.

However, in each of the chapters of this book, IEL concepts will be introduced since they are an integral part of the legal practice relating to international business transactions. In this introductory chapter, we introduce the principal institutions and sources of IEL that the international business lawyer must learn to deal with.

PROBLEM 1-9

Medtech, Inc., manufactures medical devices in its factory in Columbus, Georgia. It is a small, but very successful closely held corporation (no public stock outstanding) that has developed a market for its products in the south, east, and midwestern United States. John Bell, the dynamic and ambitious CEO and founder, now is thinking of expanding the business internationally. He has the following questions:

(1)   Europe, he feels, is a natural extension of the market for his products. However, there are many different countries all with different languages and cultures. Bell is concerned that these many cultural differences will be reflected in many different legal systems, including differing customs rates, export requirements, and the use of many different currencies. These differences could make doing business in Europe complex and costly. How difficult would it be to develop a European market for Medtech products?

(2)   What about starting closer to home? Should Medtech expand to Canada? Mexico? Other countries in Latin America?

(3)   How easy would it be to expand to Japan, China, Vietnam, Indonesia, and other Asian markets? How would developing a common strategy for Asia compare with developing a common approach for Europe?

(4)   What about developing countries such as those in Africa?

(5)   Where can he get some help about what export markets would be best for Medtech's products? What if Medtech ran into difficulty in the form of an unfair or arbitrary action by a foreign government that prevented foreign sales, like an unruly customs agency that held up the distribution of Medtech products?

(6)   Suppose that he goes to the trouble of developing a foreign market and Medtech products are successful. Can the foreign government raise taxes or otherwise shut down his operations?

(7)   What about foreign competition for his products in the United States? Can anything be done if foreign competitors are "dumping" their products in the United States, that is, selling their products at prices below what are charged in the home markets in order to obtain a market access at the expense of Medtech?

In considering this problem, review the following materials in §§A-H below.

A.   The World Trade Organization

The World Trade Organization (WTO) was founded in Geneva on January 1, 1995, as the successor to the General Agreement on Tariffs and Trade (GATT).[11] The WTO carries on the work of the GATT, but on a much larger scale with major new responsibilities. The WTO at this writing has 146 members,

---

11. Agreement Establishing the World Trade Organization, 1994, available at *www.wto.org*.

including all major commercial states except Russia, which is expected to become a member shortly. The functions and structure of the WTO are analyzed in the following excerpt from Mitsuo Matsushita, Thomas J. Schoenbaum, & Petros Mavroidis, *The World Trade Organization: Law, Practice and Policy* 3-14 (Oxford 2003):

1. The WTO: Functions and Structure

The WTO exists to "facilitate the implementation, administration, and operation as well as to further the objectives" of the WTO agreements. Beyond this general purpose, the WTO has four specific tasks: (1) to provide a forum for negotiations among Members both as to current matters and any future agreements; (2) to administer the system of dispute settlement; (3) to administer the Trade Policy Review Mechanism; and (4) to cooperate as needed with the IMF and the World Bank, the two other Bretton Woods institutions.

The WTO is formally endowed with existence, legal personality and legal capacity as an international organization. It must be accorded privileges and immunities that are in accordance with its functions.

The WTO has two governing bodies: the Ministerial Conference and the General Council. The Ministerial Conference is the supreme authority. It is composed of representatives of all WTO Members and meets at least once every two years. The General Council is the chief decision-making and policy body between meetings of the Ministerial Conference. The General Council also discharges the responsibilities of two important subsidiary bodies, namely, the Dispute Settlement Body and the Trade Policy Review Body. The General Council is composed of all WTO Members and meets "as appropriate."

Specialized Councils and Committees that report to the General Council do much of the day-to-day work of the WTO. The WTO Agreement establishes these Councils: a Council for Trade in Goods; a Council for Trade in Services; and Council for Trade-Related Aspects of Intellectual Property Rights (TRIPS). These Councils have the power to establish committees (or subsidiary bodies) as required. The Ministerial Conference has also established committees: a Committee on Trade and Development; a Committee on Balance of Payments; a Committee on Budget, Finance and Administration; and, by special action on 14 April 1994, a Committee on Trade and Environment. Additional councils and committees oversee the Plurilateral Trade Agreements. These also report to the WTO General Council.

The WTO has a Secretariat located in Geneva and presided over by a Director-General, who is appointed by the Ministerial Conference. The Ministerial Conference sets the powers and term of office of the Director-General, and the Director-General has the power to appoint the staff and direct the duties of the WTO Secretariat. Neither the Director-General nor the Members of the Secretariat may seek or accept instructions from any national government, and both must act as international officials.

2. Decision-Making

There are two primary modes of decision-making: decision by consensus and voting. For general decision-making, WTO bodies continue to follow the practice of the GATT 1947 of deciding by consensus. The WTO provides that "[t]he body concerned shall be deemed to have decided by consensus if no Member, present at the meeting when the decision is taken, formally objects to the proposed decision." Thus, consensus differs from unanimity. In consensus decision-making, the minority will normally go along with the majority unless it has a serious objection. The majority will, in turn, not ramrod decision through by vote but will deal with the objections of the minority. The consensus decision-making process takes a great deal of time.

Voting occurs in the WTO only when a decision cannot be taken by consensus. In the Ministerial Conference and the General Council, decisions are taken by "a majority of the votes cast" unless otherwise specified in the relevant WTO agreement. Each Member has one vote. Thus, the decision-making process of the WTO is quite different from the IMF and the World Bank, where weighted voting favours the larger, more important states.

3. A Summary of GATT Obligations

[While GATT no longer exists as an international organization, the GATT continues to live on as one of the three principal agreements of the WTO along with the General Agreement on Trade in Services (GATS) and the Agreement on Trade-Related Intellectual Property Rights (TRIPS). The original text is now called "GATT 1947" and the updated version is called "GATT 1994," the subject of the following discussion.] The GATT lowers tariffs by limiting tariff charges to those agreed in the Schedules of Concessions (Article II) and giving the benefit of these concessions to all GATT contracting parties (Article I). The tariff schedules are annexed to the GATT. The GATT is a code of general rules regulating the conduct of the parties. Most of these rules are designed to assure that the tariff concessions work as intended and are not undermined. The GATT contains the following additional provisions:

(1) A requirement of national treatment of imports with respect to taxes and regulations (Article III);
(2) A prohibition on quotas, import or export licenses and other measures, with some exceptions (Article XI), and a special provision relating to quotas on cinematograph files (Article IV);
(3) Guarantees of freedom of transit (Article V);
(4) Rules relating to subsidies and antidumping and countervailing duties (Articles VI and XVI);
(5) Rules on valuation for customs purposes (Article VII);
(6) Rules on fees and formalities connected with importation and exportation (Article VIII);
(7) Rules on marks of origin (Article IX);
(8) Rules on transparency and publication of national trade regulations (Article X);
(9) Rules on currency exchange regulation (Article XV);
(10) Rules on state-trading enterprises (Article XVII); and
(11) Rules on government assistance to economic development (Article XVIII).

In addition, the GATT contains provisions that allow some exceptions to the basic GATT rules:

(1) Exceptions for quotas for balance-of-payments purposes (Articles XII, XIII, XIV, XV and XVII, Section B);
(2) Exceptions for developing countries (Article XVIII and Part IV);
(3) An exception for emergency action where serious injury is caused or threatened to a domestic industry (Article XIX) (the so-called escape clause);
(4) An exception for health, safety, the protection of natural resources and other matters (Article XX);
(5) An exception for national security (Article XXI);
(6) An exception for customs unions and free trade areas (Article XXIV);
(7) An exception for waivers by the contracting parties (Article XXV); and
(8) An exception allowing a GATT contracting party to "opt out" of a GATT relationship on a one-time basis only, when a new contracting party joins the GATT (Article XXXV).

Two GATT provisions relate to the settlement of disputes: Article XXII, which provides for consultation, and Article XXIII, which allows a GATT contracting party to make a complaint and permits the GATT Contracting Parties to investigate and make recommendations for resolving the dispute. These provisions were the basis on which the GATT system of dispute resolution was developed and are the foundation for WTO dispute settlement procedures.

Finally, the GATT contains a number of provisions relating to procedure:

(1) Procedures for modifying the Schedules of Concessions (Article XXVIII) and conducting tariff negotiations (Article XXVIII *bis*);

(2) Procedures for withholding or withdrawing concessions if a state withdraws or fails to become a contracting party (Article XXVII);

(3) Procedures defining which countries may be the contracting parties and for accession to the GATT (Articles XXXII and XXXIII);

(4) Procedures for amending the GATT (Article XXX);

(5) Procedures for withdrawing from the GATT on six months' notice (Article XXXI); and

(6) Procedures for acceptance, entry into force and registration of the GATT (Article XXVI).

The GATT also contains an Annex with notes and supplementary interpretations of various Articles. The GATT was modified and superseded in part by the GATT 1994, one of the WTO agreements. The "original" GATT, as amended, is now known as the GATT 1947.

4. The GATT Tariff Negotiating Rounds

Despite its birth defects, the GATT served as the basis for eight "rounds" of multilateral trade negotiations. These rounds were held periodically to reduce tariffs and other barriers to international trade and were increasingly complex and ambitious. All were successful.

The principal accomplishment of the GATT was its success in reducing tariffs and other trade barriers on a worldwide basis.

The various negotiating rounds were named after the place in which the negotiations began or the person associated with initiating the round. The names and dates of the rounds are as follows:

- Geneva   1947
- Annecy   1949
- Torquay   1950
- Geneva   1956
- Dillon   1960-61
- Kennedy   1962-67
- Tokyo   1973-79
- Uruguay   1986-94

The objectives of the early GATT negotiating rounds were primarily to reduce tariffs. Non-tariff barriers later emerged as a vital concern as well. The objectives of the Tokyo and Uruguay Rounds were primarily to reduce non-tariff barriers. The Uruguay Round culminated in the creation of an immense new body of international law relating to trade: the basic texts of the WTO agreements exceeded 400 pages, and the Final Act signed in Marrakesh, Morocco on 15 April 1994 was over 26,000 pages.

The Final Act of the Uruguay Round transformed the GATT into a new, fully fledged international organization called the World Trade Organization (WTO).

5. The Creation of the WTO

The idea of creating a World Trade Organization emerged slowly from various needs and suggestions. Even at the beginning of the Uruguay Round, negotiators and observers realized that significant new agreements would require better institutional mechanisms and a better system for resolving disputes. One of the 15 negotiations undertaken at the beginning of the Round was on the "functioning of the GATT system", dubbed with the acronym "FOGS". Negotiators were particularly concerned with how new agreements would come into force and whether they would be binding on all GATT contracting parties. Many countries wanted to avoid the problems of the Tokyo Round, which had resulted in significant new "side agreements" that were binding only on those GATT contracting parties that accepted them (GATT à la carte).

Thus, Uruguay Round negotiators were receptive to the suggestion, first made by Professor Jackson, to use the Uruguay Round as an occasion to found a new "World Trade Organization". Jackson argued that it was time to cure the "birth defects" of the GATT by creating an organization that would be a United Nations specialized agency with an organizational structure and a dispute settlement mechanism. The creation of such an organization could solve the problems of "GATT à la carte". It would be necessary to accept all the Uruguay Round agreements to be a Member of the new World Trade Organization.

The idea of a new world trade organization was taken up in the FOGS negotiation. When the Draft Final Act of the Uruguay Round was issued in 1991, it contained a proposal for a new "Multilateral Trade Organization." Working groups and negotiators did further work, and the name was changed to the World Trade Organization. The Draft Final Act included agreements on transitional arrangements and the termination of the GATT 1947 and the Tokyo Round agreements on subjects covered by new WTO agreements. Finally, the negotiators decided that the WTO would come into being on 1 January 1995. The package of agreements that brought the WTO into being was opened for signature at Marrakesh on 15 April 1994. The package consisted of multilateral trade agreements annexed to a single document, namely, the Marrakesh Agreement Establishing the World Trade Organization (WTO Agreement). Through this ingenious device, all agreements annexed to the WTO Agreement become binding on all Members as a single body of law.

Annex 1 of the WTO Agreement is divided into three parts. Annex 1A consists of the GATT 1994 and the following agreements:

- Agreement on Agriculture
- Agreement on the Application of Sanitary and Phytosanitary Measures
- Agreement on Textiles and Clothing
- Agreement on Technical Barriers to Trade
- Agreement on Trade Related Investment Measures
- Agreement on Implementation of Article VI of the General Agreement on Tariffs and Trade 1994 (Antidumping Agreement)
- Agreement on Implementation of Article VII of the General Agreement on Tariffs and Trade 1994 (Customs Valuation Agreement)
- Agreement on Preshipment Inspection
- Agreement on Rules of Origin
- Agreement on Import Licensing Procedures
- Agreement on Subsidies and Countervailing Measures
- Agreement on Safeguards

Annex 1A includes a General Interpretive Note that provides that, if there is a "conflict" between provisions of the GATT 1994 and another Annex 1A Agreement, the provision of the latter controls.

Annex 1B consists of the General Agreement on Trade in Services (GATS) and its annexes. Annex 1C consists of the Agreement on Trade-Related Aspects of Intellectual Property Rights (TRIPS Agreement).

Annex 2 consists of the Understanding on Rules and Procedures Governing Settlement of Disputes (Dispute Settlement Understanding or DSU), which establishes the procedures for resolving trade disputes among WTO Members.

Annex 3 consists of the Trade Policy Review Mechanism, which establishes a periodic review of each WTO Member's compliance with WTO agreements and commitments.

Annex 4 consists of the Plurilateral Trade Agreements:

- Agreement on Trade in Civil Aircraft
- Agreement on Government Procurement
- International Dairy Agreement
- International Bovine Meat Agreement

The plurilateral agreements are binding only on the parties that have accepted them.

B. The North American Free Trade Agreement

The North American Free Trade Agreement (NAFTA) is the most important example of its kind. There are scores of such free-trade agreements (FTAs) functioning in the world today. FTAs exist in every region of the world and every member of the WTO is a party to at least one. They are both bilateral and multilateral. The United States has free-trade agreements with Israel, Jordan, Singapore, and Chile in addition to NAFTA, and more are on the way. FTAs are political as well as economic instruments. Politically, they tie states together. In economic terms, FTAs both create and divert trade. They create trade between members, but part of this trade is diverted away from third-party states. Thus, in pure economic terms, FTAs are mixed blessings.

NAFTA is a prototypical example of an FTA that is extremely important to North American business entities, but almost as important to non-NAFTA countries that do business with Mexico, the United States, and Canada.

NAFTA encompasses all trade between Mexico, the United States, and Canada. As of 2003, virtually all customs duties (tariffs) have been eliminated on products moving between the three countries considered to have "North American content" (more on the definition of this in Chapter 2). All three members retain, however, complete control over their commercial policies toward non-NAFTA states. This is the essence of an FTA: The parties do not give up their economic independence. They can also apply their unfair trade practice laws (antidumping and countervailing duty) against their NAFTA partners.

1. NAFTA Objectives

NAFTA became effective on January 1, 1994. NAFTA creates free movement of goods and to a large extent fosters cross-border trade in services and investment flows. NAFTA also covers to some extent other economic issues such as labor, protection of the environment (through side agreements), intellectual property, and competition law. The excerpt below provides a good general overview of NAFTA's objectives:

United States Department of Commerce,
A Guide to Customs Procedures (2004)
Description of the NAFTA

Objectives

The objectives of this Agreement, as elaborated more specifically through its principles and rules, including national treatment, most-favored-nation treatment and transparency, are to:

- Eliminate barriers to trade in, and facilitate the cross-border movement of, goods and services between the territories of the Parties;
- Promote conditions of fair competition in the free trade area;
- Increase substantially investment opportunities in the territories of the Parties;
- Provide adequate and effective protection and enforcement of intellectual property rights in each Party's territory;
- Create effective procedures for the implementation and application of this Agreement, for its joint administration and for the resolution of disputes;
- Establish a framework for further trilateral, regional and multilateral cooperation to expand and enhance the benefits of this Agreement.

Tariff Phaseout

The NAFTA eliminates tariffs on most goods originating in Canada, Mexico and the United States over a maximum transition period of fifteen years. The schedule to eliminate tariffs already established in the Canada–United States Free Trade Agreement will continue as planned so that all Canada–United States trade is duty-free in 1998. For most Mexico–United States and Canada-Mexico trade, the NAFTA will either eliminate existing customs duties immediately or phase them out in five to ten years. On a few sensitive items, the Agreement will phase out tariffs over fifteen years. NAFTA-member countries may agree to a faster phaseout of tariffs on any goods.

Generally, tariffs will only be eliminated on goods that "originate" as defined in Article 401 of the NAFTA. That is, transshipping goods made in, say Guatemala, through Mexico will not entitle them to preferential NAFTA duty rates. The NAFTA does provide for reduced duties on some goods of Canada, Mexico and the United States that do not originate but that meet specified conditions. For example, limited quantities of goods that are non-originating may be eligible for preferential NAFTA treatment under special tariff-rate quotas.

2.   *Dispute Resolution Under NAFTA*

We will go into the technicalities of NAFTA in subsequent chapters of this book, but we now introduce the operation of the NAFTA Free Trade Commission, one of the few institutions created by NAFTA, and the agreed process of NAFTA dispute resolution:

Chapter 20 of the NAFTA contains the general provision for the resolution of disputes.***

Recourse to dispute settlement procedures under Chapter 20 can be had for "all disputes between the Parties regarding the interpretation or application" of NAFTA and where "a Party considers that an actual or proposed measure of another Party is or would be inconsistent with the obligations of [the] Agreement or cause nullification or impairment" of the Agreement. (NAFTA, Ch. 20, Art. 2004)

Recourse to dispute resolution procedures is only available to a government "Party." (Art. 2004) The US has stated, however, that it will "automatically trigger panel review in response to a timely request from any person who otherwise could have challenged the determination in court." (59 Fed. Reg., Monday, Jan. 3, 1994, p. 228) Also, the NAFTA calls upon all the Parties to facilitate the judicial enforcement in their own territory of arbitration awards obtained in another Party's country. (Art. 2022) Thus, it will be prudent for private parties to have detailed international arbitration clauses in their contracts.

Article 2001 creates a Free Trade Commission composed of Cabinet-level officials or their designees. The Commission oversees the implementation and operation of the NAFTA and supervises all committees and working groups created under the Agreement including resolution of disputes. Article 2002 establishes a permanent, trilateral Secretariat to assist the Commission.

Under NAFTA, if the dispute arises within the jurisdiction of both GATT and NAFTA, the complaining party chooses the forum for settlement. (Art. 2005) Private practitioners should be familiar both with GATT's new rules and NAFTA's to assess which forum suits their client's situation. If one Party objects to GATT, then the dispute must be heard pursuant to NAFTA. If one of the Parties to a dispute involving the environment, or health, sanitary or phytosanitary issues, so requests, the dispute must be resolved pursuant to NAFTA. The forum that is chosen or required will be the exclusive forum for the resolution of that dispute.

Chapter 20 strongly encourages cooperation among the parties to resolve disputes before resulting to arbitration. (Art. 2003) The first step in dispute resolution requires the Parties to proceed through a period of consultation and negotiation. (Art. 2006) Thereafter, the Parties may request a meeting of the Free Trade Commission to utilize good offices, conciliation, mediation and expert advice. (Art. 2007) The assistance of Scientific Review Boards may be especially helpful for environmental disputes. (Arts. 2014 & 2015)

If the parties cannot resolve their differences through consultations, or through the Commission, a Party may request that the matter be referred to an arbitration panel. (Art. 2008) Chapter 20 permits third Parties "with a significant interest" to participate as a complaining Party in the process. (Art. 2008.3)

Arbitrators are chosen from a roster of legal, trade and other experts, including nationals from non-Parties. (Arts. 2009 & 2010) The panels are composed of five members. (Art. 2011) The Parties must agree on a chair within 15 days or else a Party is chosen by lot to select the chair. Thereafter, each Party chooses two more panelists. Any party may exercise a preemptory challenge against an individual not on the roster. (Id.) Separate panel selection rules exist for when there are more than two parties.

Ninety days after the panel has been selected, or such other time period established by the Model Rules-of-Procedure, or by agreement of the Parties, the panel issues a confidential initial report to the Parties. (Art. 2016) The Parties then have 14 days in which to submit comments to the panel. A final report follows that may not state which panelists decided with the majority and which with the minority. (Art. 2017) The report is forwarded to the Free Trade Commission for publication 15 days later, unless it decides otherwise.

Upon issuance of the Final Report, the Parties are again to negotiate the dispute without resorting to compensation. (Art. 2018) If the final resolution of the dispute involves a finding that a measure is inconsistent with the obligations of the NAFTA, or causes a nullification or impairment of a NAFTA benefit, the emphasis is placed on taking action in the form of amending or removing the offending domestic law. Compensation is only to be used as a last resort, and then only pursuant to narrow parameters. (Art. 2019) The injured Party may suspend benefits to the offend-ing Party in the same sector(s) affected by the measure.

Leslie Alan Glick, *Understanding the North American Free Trade Agreement*, 20-23 (2d ed. 1994).

C.   The European Union

The European Union (EU) is a political and economic union of 25 nations of Europe. After 2005, when a new "European Constitution" is expected to enter into force, the EU will function very much like a sovereign state, although through veto power EU members will retain some autonomy in certain areas such as foreign policy and defense.

What is now the EU began as an economic customs union in the 1950s. A customs union, in contrast to a free-trade area, is a union of sovereign states whose members not only agree to abolish tariffs and obstacles to trade within the union but also agree to maintain a common commercial and economic policy toward nonmember states. As a result, companies trading with member states of the EU face a single set of common tariffs and customs requirements.

A customs union and common market were formed in Europe as the European Economic Community in 1957 and the Single European Act of 1987. In 1993, the Maastricht Treaty on European Union created the EU, which rests on three pillars: (1) an economic union, (2) a common foreign and security policy, and (3) a common justice and home affairs policy. A common currency, the euro, was created among a majority of EU members. From the original membership of six states in the 1950s, the EU now has 25 members and more states will join in the future.

The EU rather than the members now controls virtually all aspects of eco-nomic and trade policy toward nonmembers. Customs duties within the EU have been eliminated. The EU formulates legislation through a complex process involv-ing three institutions: The EU Commission, the Parliament, and the Council of Ministers. The European Court of Justice has ultimate power to interpret EU laws and review legislation. There is also a political body, the European Council, which, under the new EU Constitution expected to be adopted by 2005, will have a president and a foreign minister. For all practical purposes, the EU functions as a federal state as far as non-EU multinational business is concerned.

D.   Free Trade in Asia

Asia is a vast area that varies greatly in terms of nations, cultures, and peoples. In south Asia the principal nation is India, a developing country but with pockets of very advanced technology and industry. In east and northeast Asia, Japan and China dominate; however, each is at a very different stage of political and eco-nomic development. In southeast Asia, the largest state is Indonesia, which has severe political and economic problems. Singapore is an island of stability and relative prosperity — it has recently concluded free-trade agreements with Japan, South Korea, and the United States.

In addition to having great disparity in levels of economic development, Asia is also marked by areas of political instability and long-term unresolved political problems such as the North and South Korea predicament and China's claim to sovereignty over Taiwan. These economic and political issues have retarded the formation of any significant economic, political, and security architecture and multilateral institutions. This may change, but for now only two significant organizational groupings are relevant: The Association of Southeast Asian Nations (ASEAN) and the Asia Pacific Economic Cooperation forum (APEC), which also includes the United States and countries from outside of Asia that border on the Pacific Ocean.

1. ASEAN

ASEAN was established on August 8, 1967, in Bangkok and now consists of ten countries: Brunei, Cambodia, Indonesia, Laos, Malaysia, Myanmar, Philippines, Singapore, Thailand, and Vietnam. The ASEAN region has a population of about 500 million, a total of 4.5 million square kilometers, a combined gross domestic product of U.S.$737 billion, and a total trade of U.S.$720 billion. The objectives of ASEAN are to promote economic growth and regional peace and stability.

One of ASEAN's first initiatives was the Preferential Trading Arrangement of 1977, which created tariff preferences among member nations in order to improve what were insignificant levels of intra-ASEAN trade that were between 12 and 15 percent in the late 1960s and early 1970s. In 1992, the Fourth ASEAN Summit in Singapore adopted plans for an ASEAN Free Trade Area or AFTA, which would eventually eliminate tariff and nontariff barriers among member countries. Other ASEAN initiatives include plans to create trans-ASEAN networks for air, land, and sea transportation; telecommunications; and energy. ASEAN cooperation has led to some significant increases in trade. Within three years of the launching of AFTA, exports among ASEAN countries grew from U.S.$43.26 billion in 1993 to almost U.S.$80 billion in 1996, an average yearly growth rate of 28.3 percent. Intraregional ASEAN trade grew during the same period to almost 25 percent of total trade.

2. APEC

APEC is an informal cooperation forum of nations that border the Pacific Ocean rim. APEC was established in 1989 and currently has 21 members: Australia; Brunei Darussalam; Canada; Chile; People's Republic of China; Hong Kong, China; Indonesia; Japan; Republic of Korea; Malaysia; Mexico; New Zealand; Papua New Guinea; Peru; Republic of the Philippines; Russia; Singapore; Chinese Taipei (Taiwan); Thailand; United States; and Vietnam. As a trading group, APEC now accounts for about half of the world's exports and imports. APEC meetings allow leaders from member countries to discuss major issues in the APEC region in an informal setting. APEC meetings, such as that hosted by the United States in 1989 on Blake Island, Washington, provide a forum for leaders to meet on a regular basis as a group to discuss APEC's goals of free trade and investment and to discuss current issues and resolve disputes. Although these meetings are informal, they have resulted in significant market liberalization of APEC markets. APEC has also played a significant role in promoting the adoption of economic policies to stimulate growth and attract investment and has also addressed social issues such as environmental and labor standards, education, and disease prevention and control.

E.   The Proposed Free Trade Area of the Americas

The United States is leading an effort to create a Free Trade Area of the Americas (FTAA), which would encompass all of the economies of the Western Hemisphere. Formal work on creating the FTAA began at the Summit of the Americas, which was held in December 1994 in Miami when the leaders of the 34 democracies in the region agreed to complete negotiations for the FTAA agreement by 2005, which will result in the gradual elimination of barriers to trade and investment. A draft FTAA agreement was made available to the public in all four official languages on July 3, 2001.

The goal of the FTAA is to create a free-trade zone in the Western Hemisphere that will be consistent with or exceed the requirements of WTO rules and disciplines. The FTAA will be designed to coexist with bilateral and subregional agreements, such as NAFTA, and countries may negotiate and accept the obligations of the FTAA individually or as members of a subregional integration group. Special attention will be given to the needs of the smaller economies. Among the topics that are the current subject of negotiations are market access, investment, services, government procurement, dispute settlement, agriculture, intellectual property rights, subsidies, antidumping and countervailing duties, and competition policy. The original plan of the FTAA negotiators was to conclude a comprehensive agreement by January 2005 that would enter into force in December 2005. However, reality and international politics appear to have made that goal impossible. Instead, the United States has entered into separate free trade agreements with Chile (2003) and with five Central American nations — Costa Rica, Guatemala, Nicaragua, El Salvador, and Honduras (2004) as well as with a Caribbean nation, the Dominican Republic. It now appears that the Free Trade Area of the Americas will be accomplished, if at all, in a step-by-step fashion.

F.   Developing Countries

Importing from or to and investing in so-called developing countries involves special considerations. However, a threshold question is: What is the definition of a developing country?

There is no universally accepted definition of this important term, but the classification scheme developed by the World Bank is widely used. The World Bank classifies countries in terms of per capita income. A low-income developing country is one with a per capita income of $755 or less. Nations with per capita income of $756 to $2,995 are classified as lower-middle developing countries. Nations having per capita income from $2,995 to $9,265 are upper-middle developing countries. Nations with per capita income greater than $9,265 are high-income countries eligible for membership in organizations of the industrialized countries such as the Paris-based Organization of Economic Cooperation and Development.

It is apparent that the term *developing country* encompasses most of the countries of the world and most of the membership of the WTO. However, the term includes widely different countries located in many different areas of the world. An umbrella organization that deals with the economic interests of developing countries is the Geneva-based United Nations Conference on Trade and Development (UNCTAD). As an arm of the United Nations Economic and Social Council, UNCTAD undertakes a wide variety of activities to further the interests of developing countries.

In trade, developing countries benefit from what is known as the Generalized System of Preferences (GSP). This was intended to implement Part IV of the GATT, which called for preferential tariff rates for products manufactured in developing countries:

> Part IV of the GATT was a disappointment for many developing countries that had hoped to get new provisions allowing preferences. The demand for preferences was finally granted in 1971 when the GATT contracting parties adopted waivers authorizing the Generalized System of Preferences (GSP) and tariff preferences among developing countries. These two waivers became permanent policy through the adoption of the Enabling Clause in 1979. Between 1971 and 1976, most OECD countries, including the United States and the EU/EC, implemented the GSP by adopting national legislation authorizing tariff preferences for developing countries. These GSP programmes generally provide duty-free treatment for industrial products and reduced tariffs for agricultural products. The United States has implemented GSP through Title V of the Trade Act of 1974 as well as programmes to benefit certain geographical areas. The EU/EC supplements its GSP programmes with an international convention, the Cotonou Agreement, conferring broad benefits on 77 (including 55 WTO Members) associated nations from Africa, the Caribbean, and the Pacific (so-called ACP countries).
>
> These GSP programmes have had limited impact on the economic development of beneficiary countries. The range of products allowed duty-free treatment is limited by political considerations, and the list of beneficiary countries is often arbitrary. Rule-of-origin criteria are strictly applied to exclude even bona fide products: US courts have held that a double substantial transformation is required before goods made from imported parts qualify. In addition to at least 35 percent value added, the constituent materials of the eligible article must be "wholly the growth, product or manufacture of the beneficiary developing country". Rules such as these render GSP treatment very technical and uncertain for developing country exporters.
>
> As Constantine Michalopoulos, a senior official at the World Bank, has stated, "the GSP turned out to be less than it has been touted to be at its inception. It was important for some products, for some countries, for some of the time. But it [has not] served to strengthen the integration of developing countries into the world trading system."

Mitsuo Matsushita, Thomas J. Schoenbaum, & Petros Mavroidis, *The World Trade Organization: Law, Practice and Policy* 383-384 (2003) (citations omitted).

An industry that has capitalized on the GSP and the U.S. African Growth and Opportunity Act (AGOA) is South Africa's auto industry. As a result of the AGOA, the auto industry has become South Africa's largest export sector; in 2001, the first year of the program, the industry's exports rose by 387 percent to $359 million. In 2002, exports grew again to $572.9 million.

G. The Organization for Economic Cooperation and Development

The Organization for Economic Cooperation and Development (OECD) is a grouping of 30 industrialized countries based in Paris. The OECD produces internationally agreed-on instruments, decisions, and recommendations to promote international rules where multilateral agreement is necessary. These are produced by dialogue, peer review, pressure, and consensus.

The member states are Australia, Austria, Belgium, Canada, Czech Republic, Denmark, Finland, France, Germany, Greece, Hungary, Iceland, Ireland, Italy,

Japan, Korea, Luxembourg, Mexico, Netherlands, New Zealand, Norway, Poland, Portugal, Slovak Republic, Spain, Sweden, Switzerland, Turkey, the United Kingdom, and the United States.

H.   Trade Institutions and Policy in the United States

In the United States, international economic and trade policy is controlled by the Congress, which has the constitutional power over foreign commerce (U.S. CONST. art. I, §8). However, the President and the executive branch of the U.S. government exercise practical control through congressional delegation of power and because the President has the constitutional authority to negotiate with foreign nations (U.S. CONST. art. II). The U.S. Court of International Trade (CIT) has exclusive jurisdiction to hear civil actions arising out of import transactions, and the CIT exercises judicial review of final agency decisions concerning U.S. trade laws. Decisions of the CIT can be appealed to the U.S. Court of Appeals for the Federal Circuit.

Authority over international trade and investment is divided among several agencies of the U.S. government.

(1)   The U.S. Customs Service, a part of the Department of Homeland Security, has primary authority over imports into the United States.

(2)   The U.S. Department of Commerce is the primary agency for both export promotion and the regulation of exports under U.S. law. One of its departments, the International Trade Administration (ITA), provides help to individual businesses that desire to develop export markets anywhere in the world. The Commercial Law Development Program fosters the opening of new export markets in developing countries. The Office of Export Licensing administers export licensing requirements.

(3)   U.S. trade laws involving import competition are administered by both the ITA and an independent agency, the International Trade Commission (ITC), which consists of six persons appointed by the President for nine-year terms. The U.S. import competition trade laws are conceptually divided into the regulation of fair and unfair trade. Fair-trade imports that cause or threaten to cause serious injury to U.S. industries may be regulated by decision of the ITC, which issues escape clause (§201) and market disruption (§406) import relief determinations to the President. Private interests may petition the ITC for import relief.

The ITC also has major responsibility for administration of U.S. trade laws involving unfair trade practices and shares responsibility with the Department of Commerce. The ITC administers §337 proceedings involving imports that infringe U.S. laws concerning intellectual property. The ITC also decides whether U.S. industry is materially injured by foreign dumping or subsidies. The ITA, part of the Commerce Department, decides questions of the existence of dumping or subsidies in these antidumping or countervailing duty cases. If dumping exists and if there is a material injury to U.S. industry, the ITC can order the imposition of an antidumping duty on the imported product, that is, a duty to offset the margin of dumping and equalize the prices for the product imported into the United States with the price in its home market. A private business can petition for import relief under these unfair trade practice laws.

(4)   The Office of the United States Trade Representative (USTR) is in the Office of the President of the United States, and the USTR is appointed by the President with the advice and consent of the U.S. Senate. The USTR offers policy advice and handles trade negotiations with foreign nations. The USTR receives complaints from U.S. businesses concerning breaches of international trade agreements or unjustifiable, unreasonable, or discriminating foreign practices. Under §301 of the Trade Act of 1974, the USTR can trigger a dispute settlement proceeding against a foreign entity on behalf of U.S. businesses at the WTO or in NAFTA and can authorize retaliatory trade actions.

NOTES AND QUESTIONS

1. This great body of international economic law (IEL) is the result of states following their perceived interests and negotiating trade arrangements and mutual trade concessions over the last half century. This law provides the framework in which international business must operate. IEL usually does not directly affect private contracts, but the international business lawyer ignores it at his or her peril.

2. IEL rules can have a negative impact on international business, particularly if the rules are ignored. For example, an export transaction may be affected by export controls or an antidumping or countervailing duty complaint in the importing nation. Franchising and distributorship agreements with geographical restrictions may also be subject to antitrust and anticompetition laws, which are part of IEL. In most cases, however, IEL will facilitate international business transactions, by removing or lowering tariffs and other import barriers and by providing a procedure to obtain redress for possible foreign practices that impede trade. How can a U.S. company obtain help from the USTR? If a U.S. company enlists the help of the USTR in a dispute with a foreign company, what types of actions can the USTR undertake? Are there any negative consequences for a U.S. company that enlists the help of the USTR? Companies from other countries can also call on their governments for help.

3. A knowledge of IEL, in addition to knowledge about the law of international business transactions, is indispensable for the lawyer who wants to help his or her client take full advantage of international business opportunities.

2 *International Sale of Goods*

This chapter and the next two (Chapters 3 and 4) should be considered as one unit as all three concern the international sale of goods. The following two chapters (Chapters 5 and 6) can also be considered as one unit as they are two closely inter-related chapters that focus on the next steps in IBTs beyond the sales transaction. Chapters 5 and 6 focus on the progressive involvement and integration of a U.S. corporation in its overseas business expansion through agency/distributorships, contract manufacturing, and foreign direct investment.

We begin this chapter with an overview of the entire international sale of goods transaction, the most basic and most common form of international business transactions. The next two chapters will focus on two topics introduced here, that is, the contract of sale itself and financing options through letters of credit. These topics are of such importance in IBTs that we devote entire chapters to their coverage.

In this chapter, we focus most of our attention on providing an overview of the documentary sales transaction, which continues to be the preferred method used by most parties today. Note that the documentary sales transaction actually involves at least three different contracts: (1) the sales contract, (2) the letter of credit for payment, and (3) the bill of lading and contract of affreightment for the transport of the goods. For our purposes, the most important of these are the sales contract and letter of credit, which are treated in detail in Chapters 3 and 4, respectively. In this chapter, after the overview materials, we provide a brief treatment of the bill of lading, contract of affreightment, and insurance issues.

In the final part of this chapter, we examine international trade law matters relating to the export and import issues in an international sales transaction. These are the trade issues that we believe most directly affect the legal practitioner on a micro level.

I. Overview of the International Sales Transaction

To understand the international sale of goods, we want to first turn to the basic expectations and risks of the seller and the buyer in any sales transaction. We want to focus on the transaction where the buyer and seller are strangers without a prior course of dealing that has established a level of trust and familiarity between the parties. This type of transaction is becoming increasingly common in the modern age: Parties that wish to do business together but that are not familiar with each other and do not necessarily trust each other.

A. Expectations of the Parties

We start with the expectations of the typical buyer and seller. Both parties want the bargain to be completed: The buyer wishes to receive the bargained-for goods and the seller wishes to receive payment as expeditiously as possible. This can occur with minimal risks and costs to both parties in a face-to-face transaction where the seller delivers the goods to the buyer; the buyer inspects the goods immediately to determine whether they conform to the contract, and the buyer makes payment to the seller. But such face-to-face transactions are rare in today's modern age where sellers and buyers are separated by great distances and many never meet face to face even after many years of doing business together.

Once we introduce the separation of time and distance that is common in the modern age into the sales transaction, we can better understand the risks to the parties. The buyer's concern is in receiving the goods as bargained for in the sales contract. In many instances, the buyer will wish to first inspect the goods and make payment only after the buyer is satisfied that the goods conform to the contract. The buyer does not wish to first pay for the goods and only later discover that the goods are unsuitable for the buyer's purposes. At this point, the buyer has already parted with its payment and is now in possession of goods that are not suitable. On the other hand, the seller wishes to receive payment as expeditiously as possible and does not wish to be endure an extended waiting period while the buyer inspects the goods. In addition, if the buyer has the right to inspect the goods, the seller is also subject to the risk that the buyer will reject the goods as non-conforming and refuse payment. At this point, the seller has already parted with the goods that are now in the possession of the buyer. The seller now has to deal with the recovery or disposition of goods that may be a great distance away and with a buyer who refuses to make payment.

In the context of a domestic sale within the United States, these risks are often manageable. For both parties, a great deal of information is easily accessible from public sources about many businesses in the United States. The buyer can also inquire into the seller's reputation for honesty and dependability. If the buyer is involved in an industry network, such an inquiry should not be difficult. In some instances, the buyer and the seller may have other already established business relationships with each other or their affiliates. Even where there is a disagreement, the parties may believe that they can work out their differences if they are both easily accessible for meetings, by telephone, or by other communications.

In a domestic sale, the legal issues should also be manageable. If the transaction crosses state lines, there will be a choice of law issue but the laws governing contracts are not likely to differ significantly from state to state. Many states have adopted the Uniform Commercial Code (UCC) to govern contracts and one state's version is likely to be almost identical to another state's version. The court systems of the 50 states vary to some degree but these differences are minor. In many instances, after having established a level of trust and familiarity through a series of transactions, the parties may decide to operate on an open-account basis. Under this arrangement, the seller ships the goods to buyer, the buyer accepts and inspects the goods, and the seller's credit department will send an invoice to the buyer usually with credit terms (e.g., payment in 30 or 60 days).

B. The International Context

When we move from a domestic to an international context, the expectations of the parties generally remain the same but the risks can increase significantly. When the sale involves a seller in the United States and a buyer in Germany, China, or Brazil, the distances are far greater, making communications more difficult even in this modern age of information technology. There can be differences in time zones that delay communications and differences in language that may create additional hurdles. While English is the dominant business language in the world today, the level of English proficiency of a foreign party can vary from case to case and even in the best of circumstances, there can continue to be misunderstandings where one of the parties must operate in a foreign language.

In an international sale, the buyer will have greater difficulty in ascertaining the reputation and trustworthiness of the seller. Representatives from the buyer may have first encountered the seller's goods only briefly at an international trade show or even through the Internet where the seller had a Web page introducing its goods. Whereas a buyer in a domestic transaction could check on the reputation of the seller by making some inquiries with associates and affiliates that have had past dealings with the seller, the buyer in an international transaction may have no contacts with those who have previously dealt with the seller. Whereas a buyer from Ohio could visit a seller's factory in California, the time and expense of a visit may preclude a buyer from China or Germany from visiting the same factory. The seller will also have greater difficulty in checking the creditworthiness of the buyer. If the buyer is a large corporation from an industrialized country such as Germany, the seller may be able to obtain reliable financial information about the buyer with some ease. But if the buyer is from a developing country such as China, Vietnam, or a newly industrialized nation such as South Korea or Taiwan, reliable information may be difficult to obtain. Detailed financial information about business enterprises in China, for example, are not available publicly and there is no reliable government sources of information about creditworthiness or business reputation.

Note also that while the expectations of the parties may not change in an international transaction, the risks of nonperformance are far greater for both the seller and the buyer. As in the domestic context, the buyer will wish to inspect the goods before payment and the seller will want payment as expeditiously as possible. In the international context, all of these risks are magnified. If the buyer has the right to inspect the goods before payment, the risk to the seller of rejection of the goods by the buyer is compounded by what may be the thousands of miles that the goods have traveled only to be left at a foreign port and unclaimed by the buyer. For the buyer, the risk of making a payment before inspection of the goods is compounded by difficulties of time and distance in communicating with the seller that the goods are unsuitable and by the obstacles created by national boundaries and different legal systems in seeking the return of the funds or other remedial measures. What were relatively minor legal issues in the domestic context also become far more significant in the international context. Choice of law issues in the domestic U.S. context are often not major issues because the differences between the laws of the 50 states are minor in many instances and there are no significant differences in the legal systems of the states. In an international context, however, differences in law and legal systems can be quite significant. In a sales transaction to China, whether U.S. law or Chinese law governs the transaction can be quite a significant and contentious issue between the parties. In addition, whether disputes are decided in a U.S. forum or a Chinese forum can be a critical or even dispositive issue as the two legal systems are divided by fundamental differences, including a significant language difference, that can add costs in time and expense far greater than what the parties might anticipate. There is also the time and expense for the party that must appear in the foreign forum. In addition, in an international sale of goods transaction, unlike a domestic transaction, the sale may involve the application of a third substantive law, the UN Convention on Contracts for the International Sale of Goods, in addition to or in place of the domestic law of each of the parties. All of these considerations indicate that the parties must carefully consider how to manage all of the risks involved in the sale. At the same time, the management of risk cannot result in the creation of costs and obligations that are so burdensome that they become a detriment to completion of the transaction altogether.

The response of the international trading community to the expectations and risks of the parties involved in the international sale described above has taken the following forms. First, with respect to the expectations of the parties, the international trading community has created a special lexicon of commercial terms that assigns duties and obligations in the sale. Terms such as FOB, CIF, negotiable bill of lading, nonnegotiable bill of lading, letter of credit, and confirmed letter of credit have specialized meanings that define, for example, whether the buyer has the right to inspect the goods before payment, when payment is to be made, and how payment is to be made. These terms are contained in the International Chamber of Commerce's Incoterms and the Uniform Customs and Practice for Documentary Credits, both of which can be adopted by the parties by contract, and in other sources. These terms, many of which long predate the ICC's codification efforts, help to clearly define rights and duties in the sales transaction so that there is less risk of misunderstanding about the expectations of the parties. We set out some of the most frequently used terms in the materials that follow.

The second type of response deals with the risks of nonperformance. As we noted earlier, the situation that best minimizes the risks for the parties occurs in a face-to-face transaction when the seller delivers the goods and the buyer inspects the goods immediately and then makes payment. Where the parties are separated by large distances and international boundaries, this arrangement does not appear to be possible. But what if the parties were able to substitute a surrogate for the goods in the form of documents that are the equivalent of the goods themselves because the documents represent title to and control of the goods? While the transport of goods for delivery over long distances can involve weeks or months, the delivery of a set of documents can be done in a matter of a day or two except perhaps to the most remote locations. Under this arrangement, called the documentary sale, delivery of the documents constitutes a symbolic delivery of the goods and payment is then to occur upon delivery of the documents. The seller delivers a set of predetermined documents to the buyer and the buyer inspects the documents and then makes payment to the seller. Having obtained the documents, the buyer now has legal control of the goods and can obtain physical possession of the goods at the port of importation from the carrier by presenting the documents to the carrier. But what if the seller does not trust the buyer to make payment after delivery of the documents anymore than after the buyer receives delivery of the goods in a nondocumentary sale? In this case, the seller will insist that the buyer engage a bank in the buyer's home jurisdiction that will pay the seller upon delivery of the documents from the seller; the bank then either seeks reimbursement from the buyer in exchange for the documents or debits the buyer's account with the bank and forwards the documents to the buyer. Now with the documents in hand, the buyer goes to the port to obtain possession of the goods.

The documentary sale that we have described above actually consists of at least three contracts: (1) the sales contract between the seller and buyer for the goods, which can consist of one writing or a series of writings; (2) the letter of credit between the buyer's bank and the seller for payment; and (3) the bill of lading between the seller and the carrier for shipment of the goods. Note that in a documentary sale the parties need not use a letter of credit because the seller can submit the documents directly to the buyer for payment. As we mentioned earlier, however, the seller often does not wish to bear the risk that the buyer will not pay against the documents. As a result, the seller will require the buyer to have a bank issue a letter of credit to address this risk. We will proceed through the documentary sale that uses a letter of credit as the payment device, but remember that it is possible to have a documentary sale without the use of letters of credit.

Note that while these three contracts are interrelated, they are considered to be separate and independent of each other. We will further explore these concepts in the materials below but for now let us now turn to a brief overview of each of these three contracts.

1. The Sales Contract

The international sales contract, like any other contract, is usually formed through negotiations leading to an offer by the buyer and an acceptance by the seller. In many cases, the first contact between the parties is initiated by the buyer who sends a letter requesting information on the price of goods that the buyer seeks to purchase. The letter often seeks a pro forma invoice from the seller that includes several pricing options that will include the price of the goods and will vary depending on the shipping arrangements that the seller is asked to make on behalf of the buyer and on whether the shipper is to obtain insurance on the goods. Note that the buyer and seller use commercial terms such as FOB (free on board) and CIF (cost, insurance, and freight) that through long usage have acquired an established meaning for dividing the responsibilities of the parties and that have been given standard definitions by the International Chamber of Commerce. After considering the terms of the pro forma invoice, the buyer decides to make a purchase and sends a purchase order. The purchase order repeats some of the terms of the pro forma invoice. It is the policy of most sellers that all purchase orders are such to an order acknowledgment.

FORM 2-1
Letter of Inquiry

Mr. Paulo Netto, General Manager
GLOBO Products, S.A.
76 Rua Rui Barbosa
Rio de Janeiro, Brazil

<u>By Fax</u>   June 1, 2005

Dear Mr. Netto:

We enjoyed visiting your display at the Rio de Janeiro Trade Fair on April 20th of this year. Thank you for taking the time to come to our reception at the Hotel Central. We, too, are excited about possible business development opportunities for Value Industries in Brazil. Our Vice President for Business Development, Ms. Samantha Williams, will be in Rio de Janeiro in September and will be in contact with you to arrange for a factory visit to discuss business possibilities.

We now wish to order Christmas ornaments. Please sends us a <u>pro forma</u> <u>invoice in triplicate</u> covering:

Item #15	50,000 Christmas Lights in Red, Green, and Yellow
Item #21	5,000 White Angel Ornaments
Item #13	5,000 Candy Cane Ornaments
Item #4	5,000 Sparkling Red Bells
Item #8	10,000 Super Deluxe 18″ Christmas Wreaths

Please include your <u>best price</u>, <u>including packaging</u>, <u>FOB Rio de Janeiro</u>, C&F <u>Newark</u>, New Jersey, and <u>CIF Newark</u>. Thank you and we look forward to your response.

FOB - Free on bd.
C&F - cost & freight
CIF - cost, insurance, freight

Sincerely,

Henry Williams
Sales Director, North America
Value Industries, Inc.
Worthington, Ohio

FORM 2-2
Pro Forma Invoice

GLOBO Products, S.A.
76 Rua Rui Barbosa
Rio de Janeiro, Brazil

To: Mr. Henry Williams
    Sales Director
    Value Industries, Inc.   June 15, 2005

Pro Forma Invoice No. 522

Description	Price per Unit (USD)	Total Price
50,000 Christmas Lights in Red, Green, and Yellow	$.25	$12,500
5,000 White Angel Ornaments	.75	3,750
5,000 Candy Cane Ornaments	.95	4,750
5,000 Sparkling Red Bells	.95	4,750
10,000 Super Deluxe 18″ Christmas Wreaths	3.50	35,000
Total Price FOB Rio de Janeiro		$60,750
Ocean Freight to Newark, New Jersey		2,500
Total Price C&F Newark		$63,250
Insurance at 110%		515
Total Price CIF Newark		$63,765

The prices quoted above are <u>firm for 60 days</u>. Payment terms are payment under a confirmed irrevocable <u>letter of credit issued</u> by a U.S. Bank and confirmed by the <u>Banco do Brasil, Rio de Janeiro Branch</u>. Shipment will occur in approximately <u>15 days from receipt of your order</u> and advice of credit. All purchase orders subject to written acknowledgment from us.

[handwritten margin note: irrevocable letter of credit]

Yours Truly,

Paulo Netto
General Manager

FORM 2-3
Purchase Order

GLOBO Products, S.A.
76 Rua Rui Barbosa
Rio de Janeiro, Brazil

<u>By Fax</u>   July 1, 2005

Dear Mr. Netto:

Please supply us in accordance with your Pro Forma Invoice No. 522 dated June 15, 2005 with the following items:

Item #15	50,000 Christmas Lights in Red, Green, and Yellow @ $.25 USD per unit
Item #21	5,000 White Angel Ornaments @ .75
Item #13	5,000 Candy Cane Ornaments @ .95
Item #4	5,000 Sparkling Red Bells @ .95
Item #8	10,000 Super Deluxe 18″ Christmas Wreaths @ 3.50

Total Price CIF Newark, New Jersey $63,765.00

Delivery Date: Prior to September 1, 2005

payment

We have instructed Mid-America Bank to open a confirmed irrevocable letter of credit per your pro forma invoice and to ask the Banco do Brasil, Rio de Janeiro Branch, for its confirmation. We look forward to your early acknowledgment by mail.

Sincerely,

Henry Williams
Sales Director, North America
Value Industries, Inc.
Worthington, Ohio

Note in a routine sales transaction such as this one that the person handling the sale for the buyer is often a purchasing department or an agent and that a sales manager handles the sale for the seller. <u>No lawyers are involved in this transaction although the parties may use form documents that have been drafted or reviewed by lawyers, but even this may not be the case.</u> Many corporations routinely enter into sales transactions without legal counsel and <u>in the vast majority of these transactions, legal counsel are never involved as no problems arise</u>. Some corporations even have policy guidelines on when sales contracts need to be reviewed by the in-house legal department of the corporation. Usually, these guidelines provide that only contracts exceeding certain sums or long-term contracts need review by legal counsel.

need for legal counsel is little unless
K is big or long

QUESTIONS

1. Why would the buyer ask for various alternatives on shipping costs from the seller? Do you think that the seller would be able to make these arrangements at any cost savings to the buyer? *yes — varying prices*

2. Why is it usually the policy of the seller to require an order acknowledgment in any sales transaction? *a clear acceptance*

3. When is a contract formed between the parties through an offer and an acceptance? Of the documents discussed above, which represents the offer and which the acceptance? *pro forma invoice — offer / purchase order — acceptance*

2. Letter of Credit *(m.o.p.)*

The method of payment for this sale of goods is the letter of credit, mentioned in both the pro forma invoice and the purchase order. We give a quick overview of the letter of credit in this chapter so that you can see its role in the overall sales transaction. We return to a more detailed examination of the letter of credit in Chapter 4.

The letter of credit allows the seller to obtain payment from the buyer's bank upon the presentation of certain documents, usually including a bill of lading, which provides evidence that the goods have been shipped. To obtain a letter of credit, the buyer usually goes to its bank in the foreign nation and asks the bank to issue a credit in favor of the seller. To obtain the credit, the buyer may give the bank a copy of the pro forma invoice that the bank can use as a basis for detailing the contents of the credit. The buyer can either deposit funds for the amount of the credit with the bank or the buyer may have other accounts with the bank containing funds that can be debited once payment on the credit is made. In some cases, the buyer may neither deposit funds nor have current accounts with the bank, but the bank may be willing to provide the funds for the credit and then seek reimbursement from the buyer after the bank makes payment. The ability of the buyer to obtain a letter of credit is an indication of the creditworthiness of the buyer as the bank will assess whether the buyer is a good credit risk in deciding to issue the credit. By requiring a letter of credit from the buyer, the seller is able to obtain an assessment of the buyer's creditworthiness by a financial institution in the buyer's home location. *[margin: → determine if buyer is a good credit risk]*

To obtain payment under the letter of credit, the seller must submit to the buyer's bank a set of required documents detailed in the credit, which usually include a bill of lading, a commercial invoice, and an insurance certificate. The seller must usually comply exactly with the requirements of the terms of the credit as failure to submit a required document or the submission of a defective document will result in a refusal to pay by the bank. The seller obtains a bill of lading from the carrier after the seller delivers the goods to the carrier and the carrier loads the goods. At this point, the carrier will issue a bill of lading to the seller. The commercial invoice details the quantity and nature of the goods that have been delivered to the carrier. The insurance certificate is evidence that the goods have been insured during transit. Once the buyer's bank receives the documents as required by the terms of the credit, the bank must pay the seller. *[margin: To get payment] [margin: Bill of lading / commercial invoice / insurance cert.]*

We have so far examined the unconfirmed letter of credit, which requires the seller to submit the documents directly to the buyer's bank. In the case of a confirmed letter of credit, another bank, usually a bank located in the seller's nation

confirmed vs. unconfirmed

that the seller is familiar with or that has an already established relationship with the seller, will add its confirmation that it will pay the seller under the letter of credit when presented with the proper documents by the seller. This bank is the confirming bank, sometimes also called the seller's bank. The reason the seller might insist on a confirmed letter of credit is that the seller might not trust the buyer's bank any more than it trusts the buyer. In an unconfirmed credit, the seller must submit the documents to the buyer's bank usually situated in the same foreign location as the buyer. If the buyer's bank refuses to pay, then the seller, which has already parted with the goods, can sue the buyer's bank but this may not be a practicable option given the distance, time, and expense involved in a foreign litigation. To address these concerns, the seller may insist on the additional obligation of a local bank in the seller's location to pay the seller on presentation of the documents. Once the confirming bank pays the seller, the confirming bank will then forward the documents to the buyer's bank for reimbursement. The seller is usually in a better position to assess the reputation of the confirming bank and the seller has more effective means of recourse should the confirming bank refuse to pay.

Note that the confirming bank has added its own obligation to pay the seller on presentation of documents, but this does not alter the original obligation of the issuing bank to pay on the letter of credit. If the seller decides to forward the documents directly to the issuing bank, it must pay the seller. In the case of an unconfirmed credit, the buyer's bank may notify the seller directly of the letter of credit or it may have a local bank in the seller's location notify the seller. In the latter case, the bank is a notifying bank, but it does not have any obligation to pay under the letter of credit.

QUESTIONS

1. The distinction between the sales contract and the letter of credit is sometimes summed up by saying that the former is a contract for the sale of goods while the latter is a contract for the sale of documents. Can you explain what this means?

2. Why do you suppose that the international trading community has established the independence rule requiring payment on the letter of credit regardless of nonperformance of the underlying sales contract? In answering this question, think about the following: Suppose that instead of this rule, we had a rule that banks paid at their peril on the letter of credit (i.e., the banks will be unable to get reimbursement from the buyer) if there was some defect in the performance of the underlying sales contract. What would be the effect of such a rule on the international banking community and how would it affect the international sales transaction?

FORM 2-4
Commercial Letter of Credit

Banco do Brasil
18 Setor Bancario Sul
Rio de Janeiro, Brazil
Mr. Paulo Netto

GLOBO Products, S.A.
76 Rua Rui Barbosa
Rio de Janeiro, Brazil   July 5, 2005

Dear Mr. Netto:

We have been instructed by the Mid-America Bank of Worthington, Ohio, USA that they have opened an irrevocable credit in your favor in the amount of USD $63,750.00 available by your sight drafts on the Mid-America Bank accompanied by:

1. Full Original Set On Board Negotiable Bills of Lading in triplicate properly endorsed to the Banco do Brasil, Rio de Janeiro Branch. *3 doc's required*
2. Insurance Policy covering marine and war risk at 110% of value.
3. Commercial invoice in triplicate issued by Globo Products covering:

    50,000 Christmas Lights in Red, Green, and Yellow
    5,000 White Angel Ornaments
    5,000 Candy Cane Ornaments
    5,000 Sparkling Red Bells
    10,000 Super Deluxe 18″ Christmas Wreaths

All documents must indicate Letter of Credit No. 7151-C. All drafts must be marked "drawn under Letter of Credit No. 7151-C confirmed by the Banco do Brasil, Rio de Janeiro Branch." Drafts must be presented to us by no later than July 31, 2005.

This credit is subject to the Uniform Customs and Practice for Documentary Credits (UCP 500) 1993 version, International Chamber of Commerce Publication No. 500. *UCP*

We confirm the credit and hereby undertake to purchase all drafts drawn as specified above and accompanied by the documents so specified. *purchase drafts*

Sincerely,

                Cesar Calmon
                General Manager, International Credit Dept.

3.   The Bill of Lading and the Contract of Affreightment

The third contract usually involved in the documentary sale is the contract of affreightment or carriage for the shipment of the goods from the seller to the buyer. Once the sales contract has been executed and the seller has received notification that the letter of credit has been established, the seller must now manufacture and ship the goods. To make the shipping arrangements, most shippers will engage a freight forwarder, which is a specialist in this field. The freight forwarder will make the appropriate arrangements for transporting the goods from the factory to the port of shipment. When the goods are loaded on board the carrier, the carrier will then issue a bill of lading to cover the goods. The bill of lading usually serves two functions: It is a contract of carriage under which the carrier promises to transport the goods to a certain destination and the seller promises to pay the carrier's fee. The bill of lading also determines to whom the carrier should deliver the goods. If the bill of lading is *nonnegotiable* (also known as a straight or white bill of lading for the color of paper on which it is printed), the carrier is to deliver the goods to the person named as the consignee in the bill or to an agent or person designated by the consignee. The consignee need not submit the original of the nonnegotiable bill to the carrier to obtain possession of the goods. If the bill is *negotiable* (also known as a yellow bill of lading), then the carrier is to deliver the goods only to the person in possession of the original negotiable bill properly endorsed. (Several sets of originals are usually issued.) The carrier must first obtain surrender of the negotiable bill before delivering the goods. Note that a negotiable bill thus represents control of the goods themselves because whoever has possession of a properly endorsed bill has the right to obtain possession of the goods. Most shippers use standard form contracts for bills of lading and fill in the information required. You can determine whether a bill is negotiable or nonnegotiable by examining the space reserved for naming the consignee. If the bill names a specific person, then the bill is nonnegotiable. If the bill is filled out "To Order of Shipper," then the bill is a negotiable bill and anyone to whom the bill has been properly endorsed by the shipper and by subsequent persons can obtain possession of the goods. In a documentary sales transaction, a negotiable bill must be used. The carrier issues the bill to the seller after the goods have been loaded on board. The seller, in turn, endorses the bill to the issuing bank and submits the other required documents for payment. Once the bank pays the seller, the bank then forwards the documents to the buyer for reimbursement. The bank endorses the bill of lading to the buyer who then submits the bill to the carrier and receives custody of the goods.

The bill of lading will contain a description of the goods but the description refers in general to what is loaded in containers (e.g., "Christmas ornaments and decorations") and is too general to provide any indication whether the goods will meet the buyer's expectations. The commercial invoice, however, should provide detailed information about the goods as it should repeat the bulk of the buyer's purchase order. Read in combination, the bill of lading and the commercial invoice provide a reliable indication of whether the goods loaded on board the carrier are what the buyer expects to receive under the sales contract. Note also that the bill of lading may be stamped "Clean on Board." This notation means that the goods have not been damaged in the process of being loaded on board the vessel. Carriers also provide a "Received for Shipment" notation but this notation

FORM 2-5

BILL OF LADING For Multimodal Transport or Port to Port Shipment

Hapag-Lloyd

SHIPPER: GLOBO Products, S.A.		HAPAG-LLOYD REFERENCE HL-B-07915	
Consignee		(5) BOOKING NO. B-1592	(5A) BILL OF LADING NO. B-256
To order of Shipper		(6) EXPORT REFERENCE3	
Notify Address (Carrier not responsible for failure to notify; see clause 20 (1) hereof:		(7) FORWARDING AGENT, F.M.C. NO. F.L. Monteiro & Co. 50 Rua General Jadim Rio de Janeiro Phone: (55) (21) 291-1224	
		(8) POINT AND COUNTRY OF ORIGIN Rio de Janeiro, Brazil	
(4) NOTIFY PARTY (COMPLETE NAME AND ADDRESS) Value Industries, Inc. Worthington, OH		(9) ALSO NOTIFY – ROUTING & INSTRUCTIONS Notify on arrival in Rio de Janeiro Port Mrs. J. Monteiro for further instructions	
(12) PRE-CARRIAGE BY* Container Trucks	(13) PLACE OF RECEIPT BY PRE-CARRIER* Rio de Janeiro	Phone: 136-735-0311 Trucks to deliver to Pier 15 Docks receipts required	
(14) VESSEL VOY FLAG M/V Reefer Sun II	(15) PORT OF LOADING Rio de Janeiro	(10) LOADING PIER/TERMINAL Pier 15	(10A) ORIGINALS(S) TO BE RELEASED AT
(18) PORT OF DISCHARGE Newark, N.J.	(17) PLACE OF DELIVERY BY ON-CARRIER*	(11) TYPE OF MOVE (IF MIXED, USED BLOCK 20 AS APPROPRIATE)	

PARTICULARS FURNISHED BY SHIPPER					
MKS. & NOS. / CONTAINER NOS. (18)	NO. OF PKGS. (19)	HM	DESCRIPTION OF PACKAGES AND GOODS (20)	GROSS WEIGHT (21)	MEASUREMENT (22)
Value Industries, Inc. Order No. 52 Made in Brazil			Container 56A–TRU 1,424 Cartons Christmas Decorations Import License No. 14776 Letter of Credit No. 7151-C **CLEAN ON BOARD** **NO TRANSSHIPMENT ALLOWED**	5,252 lbs.	1,950 C.F.

(23) Declared Value $ _____ If shipper enters a value, carriers "package" limitation of liability does not apply and the ad valorem rate will be charged.

(23A) RATE OF EXCHANGE

(24) **FREIGHT**
PAYABLE
AT/BY

IP	RATED AS	PER	RATE	PREPAID	COLLECT	LOCAL CURRENCY
TOTAL CHARGES						

If this box is checked, goods have been loaded, stowed and counted by Shipper. Carrier has NOT done so and is not responsible for accuracy of count, condition or nature of goods described in PARTICULARS FURNISHED BY SHIPPER

THE RECEIPT, CUSTODY, CARRIAGE, AND DELIVERY OF THE GOODS ARE SUBJECT TO THE TERMS APPEARING ON THE FACE AND BACK HEREOF AND TO CARRIER'S APPLICABLE TARIFF

In witness whereof three (3) original bills of lading all of the same tenor and date one of which being accomplished the others to stand void, have been issued by the originating carrier for and on behalf of itself other participating carriers, the vessel and new master and owners or charterers

Dated ....

At ....

.... (Originating Carrier)

By ....

BILL OF LADING NO.   DATE   *APPLICABLE ONLY WHEN USED FOR MULTIMODAL TRANSPORTATION does not evidence that the goods have been loaded on board the vessel without suffering damage. Sales contracts and letters of credit usually require clean bills of lading.

As we have stated earlier, the bill of lading is also a contract of carriage between the shipper (here the seller) and the carrier. On the reverse side of the bill of lading are standard terms that govern the rights and obligations of the parties. The carrier undertakes the responsibility from the moment it takes receipt of the goods to deliver the goods to the port of discharge or a named place of delivery. The liability of the carrier for any damage to the goods if the carriage is to or from the United States is governed to the federal Carriage of Goods by Sea Act (COGSA), 46 U.S.C. §§1300 *et seq.*, which limits the liability of the carrier to $500 per package unless the shipper declares otherwise in the bill of lading. *See id.* at §1304(5). Other carriages may be subject to an international convention such as the International Convention for Unification of Certain Rules Relating to Bills of Lading (1924), also known as the Hague Rules. In most cases, the parties will also have insurance covering the goods during the carriage for the benefit of the buyer.

NOTES AND QUESTIONS

1. In a documentary sale, involving payment against documents, a negotiable bill of lading must be used. Why?

2. If the buyer is a wholesaler or a distributor, the documentary sale can be very useful because it allows the buyer to sell the goods while they are still in transit. Can you explain how? For this to happen, a negotiable bill of lading is essential.

3. The per package limitation of $500 on the carrier's liability was established by COGSA in 1936 and has never been changed. Today, such a limitation would appear to be less than adequate to cover damage to the goods in many cases. Take a look at the bill of lading and find where the shipper is allowed to make a declaration of the value of the goods that would negate the application of the $500 per package limitation of liability under COGSA. Why wouldn't a shipper simply declare a higher value in all cases where the value of the goods per package exceeds $500?

4. If the per package limitation of $500 applies, what would prevent an unscrupulous carrier from theft of a precious cargo and claiming that it was lost at sea?

4.   Overview of the Entire Documentary Sale Transaction

Now that we have reviewed all of the basic contracts of the documentary sale, see if you can follow all of the steps in the transaction involving a confirmed letter of credit in the figure below.

FIGURE 2-1

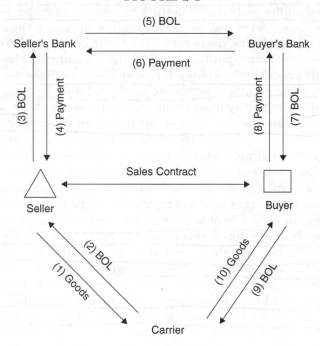

Let's review each of the steps:

(1) Seller manufactures the goods and delivers them to Carrier;
(2) Carrier loads the goods and issues a bill of lading to Seller;
(3) Seller presents the bill of lading and other documents such as a commercial invoice and certificate of insurance to Seller's Bank, which acts as a confirming bank;
(4) Seller's Bank examines the bill of lading and other documents to determine whether they conform to the letter of credit; Seller's bank decides that the documents are conforming and makes payment to Seller;
(5) Seller's Bank forwards the documents to Buyer's Bank, which is the issuing bank;
(6) Buyer's Bank examines the documents to determine whether they conform to the terms of the letter of credit; Buyer's Bank decides that the documents are conforming and reimburses Seller's Bank for payment under the letter of credit;
(7) Buyer's Bank forwards the documents to Buyer;
(8) Buyer's Bank debits Buyer's account or Buyer makes payment to Buyer's Bank;
(9) Buyer presents bill of lading to Carrier; and
(10) Carrier delivers goods to Buyer.

Note the use of the documentary sale has allowed the parties to address some of the risks involved in the international sales transaction where the parties are strangers to each other and there is not an established level of trust and familiarity. What were a set of risks and unknowns for the seller and buyer have now been broken down into a smaller set of discrete risks, and the task of assessing the risk has been placed on the party that is in the best position to make the assessment. For example, while the seller may not be in a position to make an assessment of the creditworthiness of the buyer, the buyer's bank or the issuing bank for the letter of credit should be in a better position to make this assessment. The buyer's bank may have an already established business relationship with the buyer or else is in a position to determine whether issuing the credit in favor of the buyer is a good commercial risk. By requiring payment under a letter of credit, the seller now has also the creditworthiness of the buyer's bank to rely on in addition to that of the buyer. If the seller is uncertain of the creditworthiness of the buyer's bank, the seller can ask for a confirmed letter of credit, which requires the seller's bank to make an additional assessment of the creditworthiness of the buyer's bank. As the seller's bank is a member of the international banking community, it is in a good position to make an assessment of the reputation of the buyer's bank.

In addition, the seller is able to obtain expeditious payment because the seller will have all of the documents usually required by a letter of credit after it has delivered the goods to the carrier at the port of shipment and can submit them to the confirming bank for immediate payment. The seller can then receive payment while the goods are still en route to the buyer. As for the buyer, its interests are protected by the documents submitted by the seller for payment, which usually include the bill of lading, a commercial invoice, and a certificate of insurance. With these documents, the buyer has evidence that the goods have been safely loaded aboard a carrier bound for the buyer; that the goods loaded fit the description in the commercial invoice, which is identical to the description in the sales contract; and that the goods are protected from damage or destruction by insurance during the carriage. Note, however, that under the documentary sale, payment is made before the buyer inspects the goods. Some buyers address this concern by requiring a certificate of inspection as one of the documents that must be submitted for payment under the letter of credit. The buyer will engage some third party who will inspect the goods and provide a certification that they conform to the terms of the contract.

Although the documentary credit has been designed to manage risks in an international sale, there are still many ways in which things can go wrong. Here are some of the more common ways:

(1) The seller ships conforming goods but obtains documents from the carrier that do not conform to the requirements of the letter of credit;

(2) The seller ships nonconforming or defective goods and then submits forged documents to the confirming bank for payment;

(3) The carrier damages the goods during loading or transport or the goods are stolen;

(4) War, fire, or other supervening events prevent the seller from producing the goods or the carrier from completing the transport of the goods altogether or in a timely fashion;

(5) The buyer receives conforming documents but when the buyer receives and inspects the goods, the buyer discovers that the goods do not conform to the sales contract.

We will be exploring these situations in the materials that follow.

NOTES AND QUESTIONS

1. In the transaction above, the buyer must pay against shipping documents provided by the seller. Suppose that the documents all conform to the requirements of the sales contract and the letter of credit and the confirming bank makes payment, the issuing banking reimburses the confirming bank, and the buyer's account with the issuing bank is debited. The buyer goes to the port of destination and presents the bill of lading to the carrier. Upon inspecting the goods, however, the buyer finds that the goods are nonconforming. What remedies are available to the buyer? What disadvantages does the buyer confront in this situation? Can you think of a method for the buyer to protect itself from receiving nonconforming goods? Think in terms of the documentary credit. What type of document might the buyer require from the seller for payment that might reduce this risk?

warranty?

2. In a documentary sale involving letters of credit as the method of payment, banks will insist on a negotiable bill of lading, which serves as security to protect the bank's interest in the goods. Can you explain how? Can you explain why a nonnegotiable bill fails to protect the bank's interests in the goods?

- To order or shipper, rather than specific person

to bearer

C. Commercial Terms Under the ICC Incoterms

As our previous discussion has indicated, there are numerous steps in the sales transaction. Many of these steps may be mechanical and routine such as arranging for the shipment of the goods from the seller's factory to the carrier, clearing the goods for export and import, and packaging the goods, but it is still important that the parties have a clear understanding of who is to perform each of the many tasks necessary to complete the transaction. Avoiding confusion and misunderstandings in the allocation of responsibilities for these mechanical tasks is essential in order for the sales transaction to be accomplished efficiently, but the parties may not always be able to achieve this result. Frequently, parties to an international contract are unaware of the trading practices in their different states. These differences can give rise to disputes and litigation, resulting in the needless and wasteful expenditure of time and money. To deal with these problems, the International Chamber of Commerce first published in 1936 a set of rules and definitions to guide the interpretation of commonly used commercial terms, called Incoterms (1936) ("Incoterms" comes from international commercial terms), which parties can adopt by contract that then determine the allocation of responsibilities between the parties for the various necessary tasks in the international sales transaction. Where these terms are adopted, they acquire legal force by contract and displace any inconsistent terms in domestic law that are part of the common law or are contained in a private law, which, as we noted earlier, most nations allow parties to alter by contract. Amendments and additions were later added to Incoterms in 1953, 1967, 1976, 1990, and 2000 to make these terms consistent with international practice and usage.

The scope of application of Incoterms is very specific and limited. Incoterms apply only to matters concerning the duties and obligations of sellers and buyers to a contract of sale relating to the delivery of tangible goods sold. As we have noted earlier in a documentary sale involving letters of credit, there are at least three contracts: The contract of sale, the carriage contract, and the letter of credit. Incoterms are directly relevant only to the first of these contracts and only in certain respects. In particular, avoid the common misunderstanding that Incoterms apply also to the carriage contract between the shipper and the carrier for the transport of the goods. In addition, Incoterms do not apply to all of the other rights and obligations under a sales contract that are not directly related to the delivery of the goods. Matters such as formation of the contract, warranties, breach of contract, damages, and other remedies are all outside the scope of Incoterms. Many of these other matters are covered by a substantive contract law. In the international context, the sales contract may be governed by the Convention on Contracts for the International Sale of Goods. In all instances, where Incoterms have been adopted by the parties, they will apply hand in hand with a substantive contract law such as the CISG, another international convention, or a domestic contract law of one of the parties.

One important area in which commercial terms have traditionally applied is to the issue of risk of loss for the goods. In the documentary credit that we described in the previous section, an important issue between the buyer and the seller is who bears the risk of loss should the goods become damaged or destroyed before the buyer can take possession and title. How is this risk allocated? The basic approach is that the risk of loss remains with the seller until it has satisfied its delivery obligations to the buyer. But when is the delivery obligation satisfied? Let us begin with a contract for the sale of goods under which the seller is to deliver the goods to the buyer at the buyer's place of business. In these circumstances, the risk of loss (and title) does not pass from the seller to the buyer until the seller delivers physical possession of the goods into the custody of the buyer. For example, if the goods are lost or damaged while being shipped by sea by the seller, the seller must bear the risk of loss and must still meet its obligations under the contract.

In most cases in international sales today, however, the parties generally do not provide that the seller is required to provide physical possession to the buyer at the buyer's place of business. Rather, a common arrangement is for the buyer to ask the seller to make shipping arrangements at the seller's port on behalf of the buyer. The seller would then arrange for a carrier on behalf of the buyer and load the goods on board the ship. Whether the seller who makes these arrangements will also pay for them is subject to agreement by the parties, which we discuss further below. However, whether the seller pays on behalf of the buyer or not, risk of loss was determined to pass from the seller to the buyer at the same point in time. Under this arrangement, when does the seller satisfy its delivery obligations transferring risk of loss (and title) to the buyer? In the absence of an explicit agreement between the parties, it was understood as a matter of commercial practice and then codified under Incoterms that the risk of loss under an FOB or CIF transaction passed from the seller to the buyer when the goods were delivered by the seller into the custody of the carrier. This occurred when the goods "passed the ship's rail." If you can picture the goods being hoisted from the dock by a lift, the risk passed from the seller to the buyer at the moment that the goods came under the custody of the carrier, that is, when they passed the ship's rail. Prior to this point, the seller assumed the risk of loss and thus the seller would be not be relieved from the sales contract if, for example, the goods were damaged in transit from its factory to the carrier. After the goods passed the ship's rail, however, the buyer assumed the risk of loss—which is why most buyers will procure insurance for the goods from this point forward.

While the procedure of passing the ship's rail might have described traditional delivery procedures, in modern maritime practice, goods are often delivered by the seller to a point on land where they are stored in a container in a warehouse for subsequent transport by sea or by a combined means of transport (sea, air, or land) in a multimodal transport. As a result, Incoterms have been revised to reflect modern international practice. The 1980 revision added the term free carrier (FCA) to deal with the frequent case where the reception point in maritime commerce was no longer the traditional passing of the ship's rail in an FOB transaction but a point on land prior to the loading of the goods on the vessel. The 1990 revision also added clauses to permit the seller's obligation to provide proof of delivery through electronic data interchange (EDI) messages in place of the traditional paper documentation, provided that the parties agreed to communicate electronically. Note, however, in a documentary sale the bill of lading allows the buyer to obtain possession of the goods while in transit and the buyer surrenders the bill of lading in exchange for the goods from the carrier. Actual delivery of the paper document to the carrier makes the bill of lading difficult to replace by electronic communications. No doubt Incoterms will continue to be periodically revised to reflect changes in international maritime trade.

We wish to emphasize that Incoterms are not intended as a type of law of contracts. Incoterms are intended only to clarify which party has to perform the various tasks necessary for the delivery of goods under the contract of sale. However, as Incoterms do create obligations on the part of the parties to perform certain tasks, these obligations can result in certain legal rights and obligations that arise under a background substantive contract law such as the CISG. Moreover, while Incoterms apply only to the sales contract, the adoption of certain terms in Incoterms may necessarily limit the parties with respect to the other contracts. For example, a seller having agreed to a sale CFR (cost and freight) or CIF cannot use a mode of transportation other than carriage by sea as the seller must present a bill of lading or other maritime document to the buyer, which is simply not possible if other modes of transportation are used. In addition, the documents required for payment under a letter of credit will depend on the mode of transportation used.

Before we set forth some of the more commonly used provisions of Incoterms, we start with a general overview of the structure and organization of Incoterms. Note that, with all of the terms, the parties have certain uniform obligations. The seller must provide conforming goods and a commercial invoice and assist the buyer in procuring documents and other arrangements for the shipment of the goods. The buyer must make payment and, in some cases, notify the seller of the details of the shipping arrangement, such as the name of the carrier or port of destination. The 1990 version of Incoterms sorted all of the terms into four groups, starting with the group where the seller has only the obligation to make the goods available to the buyer at the seller's premises (the "E" term: EXW). In the second group, the "F" terms (FCA, FAS, and FOB), the seller must deliver the goods to a carrier named by the buyer. Under the "C" terms (CFR, CIF, CPT, and CIP), the seller has to contract for carriage but without assuming the risk of loss to the goods or additional costs past the point of shipment. Under the last group, the

"D" terms (DAF, DES, DEQ, DDU, and DDP), the seller has to bear all costs and risks needed to bring the goods to the place of destination.

Under all of these terms, the risk of loss for the goods as well as the obligation for bearing the costs relating to the goods passes from the seller to the buyer once the seller has completed its delivery obligation.

The following chart summarizes all of these terms:

INCOTERMS 2000

Group E	**Departure**
	EXW: Ex Works (. . . named place)
Group F	**Main carriage unpaid by seller**
	FCA: Free Carrier (. . . named place)
	FAS: Free Alongside Ship (. . . named port of shipment)
	FOB: Free on Board (. . . named port of shipment)
Group C	**Main carriage paid by seller**
	CFR: Cost and Freight (. . . named port of destination)
	CIF: Cost, Insurance, and Freight (. . . named port of destination)
	CPT: Carriage Paid To (. . . named place of destination)
	CIP: Carriage and Insurance Paid To (. . . named place of destination)
Group D	**Arrival**
	DAF: Delivered at Frontier (. . . named place)
	DES: Delivered Ex Ship (. . . named port of destination)
	DEQ: Delivered Ex Quay (. . . named port of destination)
	DDU: Delivered Duty Unpaid (. . . named place of destination)
	DDP: Delivered Duty Paid (. . . named place of destination).

PROBLEM 2-1

A U.S. seller and an English buyer enter into a contract for the sale of books "FOB seller's factory, Rose Hill, New York. This contract incorporates Incoterms 2000." In accordance with its usual practice, the seller arranges for transport of the goods inland to New York City where the goods are to be loaded aboard the carrier nominated by the buyer and bound for England. However, the carrier nominated by the buyer does not arrive at New York before the goods. The seller arranges for storage of the books in a transit warehouse at New York port and immediately notifies the buyer that the goods have been stored pending notification of a substitute carrier by the buyer. One week later, the buyer's instructions naming the substitute carrier are received by the seller, but in the meantime, the books are destroyed by a fire in the storage facility. The seller seeks payment for the cost of transporting the goods from the factory to the port in New York, the cost of storage, and payment of the purchase price. The buyer responds that it has no obligation to pay for the inland transport and that, under an FOB sale, the seller assumed the risk of loss until the books were delivered "across the ship's rail." Moreover, the buyer argues that as the seller cannot now deliver the books, there is a total failure of consideration for the contract and the buyer does not have to pay the purchase price. In addition, the buyer argues that the seller should have insured the books against risk of loss or damage. Does the buyer have to pay for the books, inland passage, and storage? See Incoterms on the FOB term below, especially at introductory paragraph, A3, B3, A4, B4, A5, B5, A6, B6, A7, and B7.

INCOTERMS 2000 ICC OFFICIAL RULES FOR THE INTERPRETATION OF TRADE TERMS

FOB   FREE ON BOARD (. . . named port of shipment)

"Free on board" means that the seller delivers when the goods pass the ship's rail at the named port of shipment. This means that the buyer has to bear all costs and risks of loss or damage to the goods from that point. The FOB term requires the seller to clear the goods for export. This term can be used only for sea or inland waterway transport. If the parties do not intend to deliver the goods across the ship's rail, the FCA term should be used.

A THE SELLER'S OBLIGATIONS	B THE BUYER'S OBLIGATIONS
A1 Provision of Goods in Conformity with the Contract	**B1 Payment of the Price**
The seller must provide the goods and the commercial invoice, or its equivalent electronic message, in conformity with the contract of sale and any other evidence of conformity which may be required by the contract.	The buyer must pay the price as provided in the contract of sale.
A2 Licences, Authorizations and Formalities	**B2 Licences, Authorizations and Formalities**
The seller must obtain at his own risk and expense any export licence or other official authorization and carry out, where applicable, all customs formalities necessary for the export of the goods.	The buyer must obtain at his own risk and expense any import licence or other official authorization and carry out, where applicable, all customs formalities for the import of the goods and, where necessary, for their transit through any country.
A3 Contracts of Carriage and Insurance	**B3 Contracts of Carriage and Insurance**

a) Contract of carriage
    No obligation.
	a) Contract of carriage
	    The buyer must contract at his own expense for the carriage of the goods from the named port of shipment.

b) Contract of insurance
    No obligation.
	b) Contract of insurance
	    No obligation.

A4   Delivery

The seller must deliver the goods on the date or within the agreed period at the named port of shipment and in the manner customary at the port on board the vessel nominated by the buyer.

A5   Transfer of Risks

The seller must, subject to the provisions of B5, bear all risks of loss of or damage to the goods until such time as they have passed the ship's rail at the named port of shipment.

A6   Division of Costs

The seller must, subject to the provisions of B6, pay

- all costs relating to the goods until such time as they have passed the ship's rail at the named port of shipment; and
- where applicable, the costs of customs formalities necessary for export as well as all duties, taxes and other charges payable upon export.

A7   Notice to the Buyer

The seller must give the buyer sufficient notice that the goods have been delivered in accordance with A4.

B4   Taking Delivery

The buyer must take delivery of the goods when they have been delivered in accordance with A4.

B5   Transfer of Risks

The buyer must bear all risks of loss of or damage to the goods

- from the time they have passed the ship's rail at the named port of shipment; and
- from the agreed date or the expiry date of the agreed period for delivery which arise because he fails to give notice in accordance with B7, or because the vessel nominated by him fails to arrive on time, or is unable to take the goods, or closes for cargo earlier than the time notified in accordance with B7, provided, however, that the goods have been duly appropriated to the contract, that is to say, clearly set aside or otherwise identified as the contract goods.

B6   Division of Costs

The buyer must pay

- all costs relating to the goods from the time they have passed the ship's rail at the named port of shipment; and
- any additional costs incurred, either because the vessel nominated by him fails to arrive on time, or is unable to take the goods, or closes for cargo earlier than the time notified in accordance with B7, or because the buyer has failed to give appropriate notice in accordance with B7, provided, however, that the goods have been duly appropriated to the contract, that is to say, clearly set aside or otherwise identified as the contract goods; and
- where applicable, all duties, taxes and other charges as well as the costs of carrying out customs formalities payable upon import of the goods and for their transit through any country.

B7   Notice to the Seller

The buyer must give the seller sufficient notice of the vessel name, loading point and required delivery time.

A8 Proof of Delivery, Transport Document or Equivalent Electronic Message

The seller must provide the buyer at the seller's expense with the usual proof of delivery in accordance with A4.

Unless the document referred to in the preceding paragraph is the transport document, the seller must render the buyer, at the latter's request, risk and expense, every assistance in obtaining a transport document for the contract of carriage (for example, a negotiable bill of lading, a non-negotiable sea waybill, an inland waterway document, or a multimodal transport document).

Where the seller and buyer have agreed to communicate electronically, the document referred to in the preceding paragraph may be replaced by an equivalent electronic data interchange (EDI) message.

A9 Checking — Packaging — Marking

The seller must pay the costs of those checking operations (such as checking quality, measuring, weighing, counting) which are necessary for the purpose of delivering the goods in accordance with A4.

The seller must provide at his own expense packaging (unless it is usual for the particular trade to ship the goods of the contract description unpacked) which is required for the transport of the goods, to the extent that the circumstances relating to the transport (for example modalities, destination) are made known to the seller before the contract of sale is concluded. Packaging is to be marked appropriately.

A10 Other Obligations

The seller must render the buyer at the latter's request, risk and expense, every assistance in obtaining any documents or equivalent electronic messages (other than those mentioned in A8) issued or transmitted in the country of shipment and/or of origin which the buyer may require for the import of the goods and, where necessary, for their transit through any country.

The seller must provide the buyer, upon request, with the necessary information for procuring insurance.

B8 Proof of Delivery, Transport Document or Equivalent Electronic Message

The buyer must accept the proof of delivery in accordance with A8.

B9 Inspection of Goods

The buyer must pay the costs of any pre-shipment when such inspection is mandated by the authorities of the country of export.

B10 Other Obligations

The buyer must pay all costs and charges incurred in obtaining the documents or equivalent electronic messages mentioned in A10 and reimburse those incurred by the seller in rendering his assistance in accordance therewith.

PROBLEM 2-2

A French seller and a U.S. buyer agree on the sale of a quantity of handbags "CIF Los Angeles with payment against documents. This contract is subject to Incoterms 2000." The seller loads the goods on board the carrier at Marseilles. To save on costs, the seller asks the carrier for a straight or nonnegotiable bill of lading made out in the name of the U.S. buyer. The seller forwards the bill of lading to the buyer, a commercial invoice, and other documents and asks for payment against documents. The buyer argues that the seller must submit a negotiable bill of lading under a CIF transaction.

(1) Must the seller submit a negotiable bill of lading to the buyer? *yes*
(2) Who must arrange and pay for the contract of carriage? *yes a-3-a*
(3) Who must arrange and pay for insurance for the goods?
(4) Suppose that no one pays for insurance and that the goods are damaged or lost during the ocean carriage. Did the risk of loss for the goods pass from the seller to the buyer?

To answer these questions, see Incoterms on the CIF term below, especially at introductory paragraph, A3, B3, A5, B5, A8, and B8.

CIF   COST INSURANCE AND FREIGHT (. . . named port of destination)

"Cost, insurance and freight" means that the seller delivers when the goods pass the ship's rail in the port of shipment.

The seller must pay the costs and freight necessary to bring the goods to the named port of destination *but* the risk of loss of or damage to the goods, as well as any additional costs due to events occurring after the time of delivery, are transferred from the seller to the buyer. However, in CIF the seller also has to procure marine insurance against the buyer's risk of loss of or damage to the goods during the carriage.

Consequently, the seller contracts for insurance and pays the insurance premium. The buyer should note that, under the CIF term, the seller is required to obtain insurance only on minimum cover. Should the buyer wish to have the protection of greater cover, he would either need to agree as much expressly with the seller or to make his own extra insurance arrangements.

The CIF term requires the seller to clear the goods for export.

This term can be used only for sea and inland waterway transport. If the parties do not intend to deliver the goods across the ship's rail, the CIP term should be used.

A THE SELLER'S OBLIGATIONS	B THE BUYER'S OBLIGATIONS
A1 Provision of Goods in Conformity with the Contract	**B1 Payment of the Price**
The seller must provide the goods and the commercial invoice, or its equivalent electronic message, in conformity with the contract of sale and any other evidence of conformity which may be required by the contract.	The buyer must pay the price as provided in the contract of sale.

A2 Licences, Authorizations and Formalities

The seller must obtain at his own risk and expense any export licence or other official authorization and carry out, where applicable, all customs formalities necessary for the export of the goods.

A3 Contracts of Carriage and Insurance

a) Contract of carriage

The seller must contract on usual terms at his own expense for the carriage of the goods to the named port of destination by the usual route in a seagoing vessel (or inland waterway vessel as the case may be) of the type normally used for the transport of goods of the contract description.

b) Contract of insurance

The seller must obtain at his own expense cargo insurance as agreed in the contract, such that the buyer, or any other person having an insurable interest in the goods, shall be entitled to claim directly from the insurer and provide the buyer with the insurance policy or other evidence of insurance cover.

The insurance shall be contracted with underwriters or an insurance company of good repute and, failing express agreement to the contrary, be in accordance with minimum cover of the Institute Cargo Clauses (Institute of London Underwriters) or any similar set of clauses. The duration of insurance cover shall be in accordance with B5 and B4. When required by the buyer, the seller shall provide at the buyer's expense war, strikes, riots and civil commotion risk insurances if procurable. The minimum insurance shall cover the price provided in the contract plus ten per cent (i.e. 110%) and shall be provided in the currency of the contract.

A4 Delivery

The seller must deliver the goods on board the vessel at the port of shipment on the date or within the agreed period.

A5 Transfer of Risks

The seller must, subject to the provisions of B5, bear all risks of loss of or

B2 Licences, Authorizations and Formalities

The buyer must obtain at his own risk and expense any import licence or other official authorization and carry out, where applicable, all customs formalities for the import of the goods and for their transit through any country.

B3 Contracts of Carriage and Insurance

a) Contract of carriage
   No obligation.

b) Contract of insurance
   No obligation.

B4 Taking Delivery

The buyer must accept delivery of the goods when they have been delivered in accordance with A4 and receive them from the carrier at the named port of destination.

B5 Transfer of Risks

The buyer must bear all risks of loss of or damage to the goods from the time damage to the goods until such time as they have passed the ship's rail at the port of shipment.

they have passed the ship's rail at the named port of shipment.

The buyer must, should he fail to give notice in accordance with B7, bear all risks of loss of or damage to the goods from the agreed date or the expiry date of the period fixed for shipment provided, however, that the goods have been duly appropriated to the contract, that is to say, clearly set aside or otherwise identified as the contract goods.

A6   Division of Costs
The seller must, subject to the provisions of B6, pay
- all costs relating to the goods until such time as they have been delivered in accordance with A4; and
- the freight and all other costs resulting from A3 a), including the costs of loading the goods on board; and
- the costs of insurance resulting from A3 b); and
- any charges for unloading at the agreed port of discharge which were for the seller's account under the contract of carriage; and
- where applicable, the costs of customs formalities necessary for export as well as all duties, taxes and other charges payable upon export, and for their transit through any country if they were for the seller's account under the contract of carriage.

B6   Division of Costs
The buyer must, subject to the provisions of A3, pay
- all costs relating to the goods from the time they have been delivered in accordance with A4; and
- all costs and charges relating to the goods whilst in transit until their arrival at the port of destination, unless such costs and charges were for the seller's account under the contract of carriage; and
- unloading costs including lighterage and wharfage charges, unless such costs and charges were for the seller's account under the contract of carriage; and
- all additional costs incurred if he fails to give notice in accordance with B7, for the goods from the agreed date or the expiry date of the period fixed for shipment, provided, however, that the goods have been duly appropriated to the contract, that is to say, clearly set aside or otherwise identified as the contract goods; and
- where applicable, all duties, taxes and other charges as well as the costs of carrying out customs formalities payable upon import of the goods and, where necessary, for their transit through any country unless included within the cost of the contract of carriage.

A7   Notice to the Buyer
The seller must give the buyer sufficient notice that the goods have been delivered in accordance with A4 as well as any other notice required in order to allow the buyer to take measures which are normally necessary to enable him to take the goods.

B7   Notice to the Seller
The buyer must, whenever he is entitled to determine the time for shipping the goods and/or the port of destination, give the seller sufficient notice thereof.

A8 Proof of Delivery, Transport Document or Equivalent Electronic Message

The seller must, at his own expense, provide the buyer without delay with the usual transport document for the agreed port of destination.

This document (for example, a negotiable bill of lading, a non-negotiable sea waybill or an inland waterway document) must cover the contract goods, be dated within the period agreed for shipment, enable the buyer to claim the goods from the carrier at the port of destination and, unless otherwise agreed, enable the buyer to sell the goods in transit by the transfer of the document to a subsequent buyer (the negotiable bill of lading) or by notification to the carrier.

When such a transport document is issued in several originals, a full set of originals must be presented to the buyer.

Where the seller and the buyer have agreed to communicate electronically, the document referred to in the preceding paragraphs may be replaced by an equivalent electronic data interchange (EDI) message.

A9 Checking — Packaging — Marking

The seller must pay the costs of those checking operations (such as checking quality, measuring, weighing, counting) which are necessary for the purpose of delivering the goods in accordance with A4.

The seller must provide at his own expense packaging (unless it is usual for the particular trade to ship the goods of the contract description unpacked) which is required for the transport of the goods arranged by him. Packaging is to be marked appropriately.

A10 Other Obligations

The seller must render the buyer at the latter's request, risk and expense, every assistance in obtaining any documents or equivalent electronic messages (other than those mentioned in A8) issued or transmitted in the country of shipment and/or of origin which the

B8 Proof of Delivery, Transport Document or Equivalent Electronic Message

The buyer must accept the transport document in accordance with A8 if it is in conformity with the contract.

B9 Inspection of Goods

The buyer must pay the costs of any pre-shipment inspection except when such inspection is mandated by the authorities of the country of export.

B10 Other Obligations

The buyer must pay all costs and charges incurred in obtaining the documents or equivalent electronic messages mentioned in A10 and reimburse those incurred by the seller in rendering his assistance in accordance therewith.

buyer may require for the import of the
goods and, where necessary, for their
transit through any country.

The seller must provide the buyer, upon
request, with the necessary information
for procuring any additional insurance.

The buyer must provide the seller,
upon request, with the necessary information for procuring insurance.

D.   Interpretation of Commercial Terms

While Incoterms and other attempts at harmonization have alleviated many of the
difficulties involved in the interpretation of international commercial terms and
international commercial law, none of the modern instruments of harmonization
can be expected to answer all questions that may arise in the course of an international contract or other form of international business transaction. There will
inevitably be issues that fall into the gaps of any text and other questions that are
not squarely addressed by any instrument. Moreover, the drafters of modern
instruments of harmonization never intended for the instruments to be completely
comprehensive but have always viewed these instruments as needing supplementation from time to time from the traditional sources of international commercial
law. To deal with gaps and unanswered issues, lawyers must continue to look to
other sources of international practice, and among them are cases from domestic
legal systems. One of the most famous cases involving the interpretation of commercial terms is *Biddell Brothers* below in which the English courts established the
foundations for the modern understanding of the CIF term.

    Biddell Brothers involved a CIF contract where the parties did not explicitly
provide for payment against documents. In such a situation, must the buyer pay
against the bill of lading or can the buyer wait until actual delivery and after the
buyer inspects the goods?

PROBLEM 2-3

    A U.S. seller and an Egyptian buyer meet at an agricultural trade fair. The
seller deals in Grade A extra-fine grain and the buyer is a wholesale distributor of
grain for the African continent. The buyer mentions to the seller that the buyer
must be able to sell the grain while it is in transit from the United States. After
several days of negotiations, the parties agree to a sales contract, which provides in
part:

> Seller is to arrange and prepay inland transportation to port of shipment and freight
> from port of shipment to the port of destination in Cairo. Purchase price includes
> freight. Payment in net cash upon delivery.

The seller arranges for the carriage and loads the goods aboard the carrier, which
issues a bill of lading to the seller. The seller forwards the bill of lading to the buyer
and asks for payment. While the carrier is en route, however, heavy storms cause
damage to the carrier's deck and cargo. The buyer now has the bill of lading but
takes the position that as the contract did not explicitly call for payment against

documents, it has the option of either paying against the bill of lading or paying against delivery of the goods and after inspection. The buyer argues that the term "[p]ayment in net cash against delivery" refers to delivery of the goods. The buyer wishes to inspect the grain to make sure that it is suitable for its customers and to also ensure that the goods did not suffer damage during transit, especially as no one procured insurance. The seller argues that the buyer must pay against documents and that the reference to "[p]ayment against delivery" refers to delivery of the documents. Must the buyer pay? Did anyone have an obligation to procure insurance? Read *Biddell Brothers* below.

Biddell Brothers v. E. Clemens Horst Company
In the Court of Appeals
[1911] 1 King's Bench 934

Appeal from the judgment of HAMILTON J. in an action tried by him without a jury.

The action was brought to recover damages for alleged breaches of two contracts, dated respectively October 13, 1904, and December 21, 1904.

The first contract, which was made at Sunderland between the defendants, of San Francisco and London, parties of the first part, and Vaux & Sons, Limited, of the city of Sunderland, parties of the second part, provided that "the parties of the first part agree to sell to the parties of the second part one hundred (100) bales, equal to or better than choice brewing Pacific Coast hops of each of the crops of the years 1905 to 1912 inclusive.

"The said hops to be shipped to Sunderland.

"The parties of the second part shall pay for the said hops at the rate of ninety (90) shillings sterling per 112 lbs., c.i.f. to London, Liverpool, or Hull (tare 5 lbs. Per bale).

"Terms net cash.

"It is agreed that this contract is severable as to each bale.

"The sellers may consider entire unfulfilled portion of this contract violated by the buyers in case of refusal by them to pay for any hops delivered and accepted hereunder or if this contract or any part of it is otherwise violated by the buyers.

"Time of shipment to place of delivery, or delivery at place of delivery, during the months (inclusive) of October to March following the harvest of each year's crop.

"If for any reason the parties of the second part shall be dissatisfied with or object to all or any part of any lot of hops delivered hereunder, the parties of the first part may, within thirty days after receipt of written notice thereof, ship or deliver other choice hops in place of those objected to."

The second contract was between the same parties, and in the same terms, except that it provided for the sale by the defendants to Vaux & Sons, Limited, of fifty bales of British Columbian hops equal to or better than choice Pacific Coast hops of each of the crops of the years 1906 to 1912 inclusive; c.i.f. to London.

Upon August 11, 1908, Vaux & Sons, Limited, assigned for value to the plaintiffs all their rights and benefits under the two contracts, and express notice thereof in writing was given by the plaintiffs to the defendants.

Correspondence passed between the parties as to the shipment of the 150 bales of the 1909 crop, and on January 29, 1910, the defendants wrote to the plaintiffs stating that they were ready to make shipment of the 150 bales of the 1909 crop of the contracted quality, and that "for the invoice price less freight we will value on your good selves at sight with negotiable bills of lading and insurance certificates attached to draft, and if you wish we will also attach certificates of quality of the Merchants' Exchange, San Francisco, or other competent authority to cover the shipment." On February 1 the plaintiffs replied that they were prepared to take delivery on the terms of the contracts, and that it was "in accordance with the universal practice of the trade and the custom adopted by you in your dealings with other purchasers of your hops, and it has also been your custom with our assignors to submit samples, and the samples having been accepted to give delivery in bulk in accordance with the samples; but if you decline to adopt the usual and undoubtedly most convenient course, we can only pay for the hops against delivery and examination of each bale. We cannot fall in with your suggestion of accepting the certificate of quality of the Merchants' Exchange, San Francisco." On February 5 the defendants' solicitors wrote to the plaintiffs' solicitors that the refusal of the plaintiffs to pay for the hops except upon terms which were not in accordance with the contracts was a clear breach of the contracts by the plaintiffs, and, that being so, the defendants would not now ship to the plaintiffs the 150 bales of the 1909 crop, and they reserved all their rights in respect of the breach of contract by the plaintiffs.

Upon March 11, 1910, the plaintiffs issued the writ in this action claiming damages for breach of contract in refusing to ship or deliver the 150 bales of hops. The defence, after stating that the defendants raised no defence with reference to the assignment of the agreements, alleged that, by reason of the plaintiffs' violation of the entire unfulfilled portion of the agreements in refusing to pay for the hops in accordance with the terms of the agreements, the defendants were entitled to refuse to further perform the agreements, and they counterclaimed against the plaintiffs for damages for breach of contract in refusing to take and pay for the 150 bales of hops.

Hamilton J. gave judgment for the defendants.

Vaughan Williams L.J.: It was argued before Hamilton J. on behalf of the defendants that the terms "net cash" in a c.i.f. contract necessarily mean "cash against documents." Hamilton J. affirmed the proposition just set forth as to performance of a c.i.f. contract by the seller, but in no way based his conclusion on the assumption that "terms net cash" means "cash against documents," and expressed his opinion that the words "terms net cash" in themselves mean only, in the absence of proof of trade custom or trade meaning, no credit and no deduction by way of discount or rebate or otherwise, which the law would have implied.

The judgment of the learned judge is based primarily [not] upon any authorities upon the meaning of the terms "cost freight and insurance," but is based upon the proposition that the terms c.i.f. "are now settled and, I hope I may add, well understood." Those are the words of the learned judge, and he goes on to say that it is not and cannot be contended but "that the seller under a c.i.f. contract has first of all to arrange to put on board a ship at the port of shipment goods of the description contained in the contract; secondly to arrange for a contract of affreightment under which they will be delivered at the destination contemplated in the contract; thirdly to arrange for an insurance upon the usual terms current in the trade, available for the benefit of the buyer; to make out an invoice; and, finally, he has to tender to the buyer those documents so that the buyer may know what freight he has to pay in order to obtain delivery of the goods, if they are intact, or so that he may recover for the loss of them if they have gone to the bottom."

There is no evidence in the present case of any law merchant or custom which reads such words as "payment to be made against shipping documents," or words to that effect, into the contract. As to the construction of the contract, I certainly think it very difficult to construe this c.i.f. contract as containing an implied condition for payment of "cash against documents."

The appeal, therefore, must be allowed, and judgment entered for the plaintiffs.

FARWELL L.J.: I will assume that as a matter of usage the seller is bound to tender the bill of lading to the buyer when it arrives, and, if the buyer accepts it, he must, of course, pay for the goods on such acceptance, because the delivery of the bill of lading is a symbolical delivery of the goods, and, if the goods are accepted, the right of antecedent (though not of subsequent) inspection before payment is thereby waived, just as it would be in the case of acceptance of the goods themselves without inspection. But I fail to follow the consequence said by the learned judge to ensue. The duty on A to tender to B a document before he can require payment does not impose on B a duty to accept such document as equivalent to goods, if he has a right to inspect such goods before accepting and paying for them. B has the option of choosing between two alternative rights: he may accept symbolical delivery or actual delivery, but in the absence of express contract it is at his option, not at the seller's. In the great majority of cases, it suits both buyer and seller better to give and accept symbolical delivery by the bill of lading, and the existence and exercise of this option explain why in cases where the c.i.f. contract does not contain the words "cash against documents," or the like, the contract is in fact often so carried out. But this is no evidence of usage for the buyer to accept in all cases, or, in other words, to waive the option. If the goods were lost at sea, the option would at once cease because inspection would have been rendered impossible, and the buyer would be bound to pay against documents.

The basis of my judgment is that the buyer has a common law right (now embodied in the Sale of Goods Act) to have inspected goods against payment, and this cannot be taken away from him without some contract expressed or implied, and here I can find neither.

In my opinion the appeal should be allowed and judgment entered for the plaintiffs.

KENNEDY L.J.: [T]he plaintiffs' assertion of the right under a cost freight and insurance contract to withhold payment until delivery of the goods themselves, and until after an opportunity of examining them, cannot possibly be effectuated except in one of two ways. Landing and delivery can rightfully be given by the shipowner only to the holder of the bill of lading. Therefore, if the plaintiffs' contention is right, one of two things must happen. Either the seller must surrender to the purchaser the bill of lading, whereunder the delivery can be obtained, without receiving payment, which, as the bill of lading carries with it an absolute power of disposition, is, in the absence of a special agreement in the contract of sale, so unreasonable as to be absurd; or, alternatively, the vendor must himself retain the bill of lading, himself land and take delivery of the goods, and himself store the goods on quay (if the rules of the port permit), or warehouse the goods, for such time as may elapse before the purchaser has an opportunity of examining them. But this involves a manifest violation of the express terms of the contract "90s. per 112 lbs. Cost freight and insurance." The parties have in terms agreed that for the buyer's benefit the price shall include freight and insurance, and for his benefit nothing beyond freight and insurance. But, if the plaintiffs' contention were to prevail, the vendor must be saddled with the further payment of those charges at the port of discharge which would be added to the freight and insurance premium which alone he has by the terms of the contract undertaken to defray.

Finally, let me test the soundness of the plaintiffs' contention that according to the true meaning of this contract their obligation to pay arises only when delivery of the goods has been tendered to them after they have had an opportunity of examination, in this way. Suppose the goods to have been shipped, the bill of lading taken, and the insurance for the benefit of the buyer duly effected by the seller, as expressly stipulated in the contract. Suppose the goods then during the ocean transit to have been lost by the perils of the sea. The vendor tenders the bill of lading, with the insurance policy and the other shipping documents (if any) to the purchaser, to whom from the moment of shipment the property has passed, and at whose risk, covered by the insurance, the goods were at the time of loss. Is it, I ask myself, arguable that the purchaser could be heard to say,

"I will not pay because I cannot have delivery of and an examination of the goods"? But it is just this which is necessarily involved in the contention of these plaintiffs. The seller's answer, and I think conclusive answer, is, "You have the bill of lading and the policy of insurance."

In my judgment, the judgment of Hamilton J. was right, and this appeal, so far as relates to the plaintiffs' claim, should be dismissed.

Disposition: Appeal allowed.

NOTES AND QUESTIONS

1. Lord Justice Vaughn Williams and Lord Justice Farwell argue that in the absence of an express provision calling for payment against documents in a CIF transaction, payment is to be made against delivery of the goods, which is the default position. The court, according to these judges, should not insert a provision that the parties themselves have not. Lord Justice Kennedy argues that the nature of a CIF transaction involving a negotiable bill of lading requires payment against documents.

2. In an omitted part of his opinion, Kennedy also reviewed *Parker v. Schuller*, 17 T.L.R. 299 (1901). In *Parker*, the plaintiff buyers entered into contracts for the sale of certain chemicals that were to be shipped from Germany for delivery in Liverpool. The goods were never shipped by the sellers, and the buyers brought a lawsuit, alleging breach of the CIF contract. In the trial court, plaintiffs argued that the nondelivery of the *goods* to Liverpool constituted a breach of the CIF contract instead of arguing, as they should have, that the nondelivery of the *documents* constituted a breach of the CIF contract. As the goods were never shipped, the defendant sellers could not have obtained a bill of lading and certificate of insurance for the goods. So the sellers could not deliver these documents to the buyers in Liverpool. This argument, if properly raised, would have succeeded for the plaintiffs. Plaintiffs, however, did not raise these arguments at the trial court

but the trial judge, Judge Lawrance, ruled that the nondelivery of the goods was a breach of the CIF contract. On appeal, plaintiff's lawyer, one Horridge, attempted to raise the arguments about the nondelivery of the documents for the first time but the court of appeals refused to consider the arguments by Horridge because these arguments were never raised in the papers and the court felt that it could not consider them and would consider only the argument that nondelivery of the goods breached the CIF contract. This claim was rejected by the court of appeals and the judgment of the trial court holding that a nondelivery of the goods breached the CIF contract was reversed. *Parker v. Schuller* stands for the proposition that in a CIF contract the delivery obligation is satisfied by a delivery of the documents or is breached by a failure to deliver the documents, not the goods.

3. The judgment of the court of appeals in *Biddell Brothers* was appealed by the defendants E. Clemens Horst Company with the following result below.

E. Clemens Horst Company v. Biddell Brothers
House of Lords
[1912] A.C. 18

EARL LOREBURN L.C.: My Lords, in this case there has been a remarkable divergence of judicial opinion. For my part I think it is reasonably clear that this appeal ought to be allowed; and the remarkable judgment of Kennedy L.J., illuminating, as it does, the whole field of controversy, relieves me from the necessity of saying much upon the subject.

Now s. 28 of the Sale of goods Act says in effect that payment is to be against delivery. Accordingly we have supplied by the general law an answer to the question when this cash is to be paid. But when is there delivery of goods which are on board ship? That may be quite a different thing from delivery of goods on shore. The answer is that delivery of the bill of lading when the goods are at sea can be treated as delivery of the goods themselves, this law being so old that I think it is quite unnecessary to refer to authority for it.

Now in this contract there is no time fixed at which the seller is entitled to tender the bill of lading. He therefore may do so at any reasonable time; and it is wrong to say that he must defer the tender of the bill of lading. He therefore may do so at any reasonable time; and it is wrong to say that he must defer the tender of the bill of lading until the ship has arrived; and it is still more wrong to say that he must defer the tender of the bill of lading until after the goods have been landed, inspected, and accepted.

Accordingly, Hamilton J.'s order ought to be restored so far as the claim is concerned. Order of the Court of Appeal reversed.

NOTES AND QUESTIONS

1. In reversing the court of appeals, Lord Chancellor Earl Loreburn states "[D]elivery of the bill of lading when the goods are at sea can be treated as delivery of the goods themselves, this law being so old that I think it is quite unnecessary to refer to authority for it." As the early decisions indicated, there did not appear to be any clear English authority on this issue. If so, what "law" is he referring to?

2. Compare the opinions of Farwell and Kennedy. Farwell argues that in a CIF transaction where the parties have not explicitly agreed on payment against documents, when the seller tenders a negotiable bill of lading to the buyer, the buyer has the option of making payment either against symbolical delivery, that is, delivery of the bill of lading which represents the goods, or against actual delivery of the goods themselves. If the buyer accepts the bill, then the seller endorses the bill to the buyer and the buyer then must pay. Alternatively, the buyer can refuse to accept the bill and exercise its right to inspect the goods before payment. The buyer's duty to pay arises under this alternative only after the buyer determines that the seller has proffered conforming goods. The choice is up to the buyer. The buyer's right of inspection is based on the common law and embodied in the English Sale of Goods Act. Under Farwell's position, what choice do you think a rational buyer would make in most cases?

Kennedy argues that as the seller is under a duty to present the bill of lading as expeditiously as possible to the buyer, the buyer has a corresponding duty to pay the seller against the documents. He further argues that not only is this the correct legal analysis but it is the only practicable position. He argues that otherwise, either the seller will have to surrender the bill of lading to the buyer, which is the equivalent of delivery of the goods to the buyer but without receiving payment, or the seller must retain the bill of lading and arrange to land, take delivery of the goods as the carrier will surrender possession of the goods only to the person with the bill of lading, and also store the goods in a warehouse where the buyer can inspect them. After the buyer approves the goods, the seller then presents the bill of lading to the buyer, which the buyer will then forward to the carrier or warehouse custodian to obtain possession of the goods. He rejects both alternatives.

Note that both Farwell and Kennedy are allocating the risk of nonperformance in a case where the parties have not explicitly agreed on an allocation of risk. Under Farwell's position, the seller bears the risk that the buyer will insist on inspection of the goods before payment and then refuse to pay on the grounds that the goods are nonconforming. Under Kennedy's position, the buyer bears the risk that the buyer will pay against the documents and then discover that the goods are nonconforming when they arrive at the buyer's location and the buyer retrieves the goods from the carrier in exchange for the bill of lading. Under Farwell's position, the seller becomes the plaintiff in an international dispute, whereas the buyer becomes the plaintiff under Kennedy's view. One way of understanding the work of the courts is that they attempt to identify the commercial risks in international business transactions, determine which risks are more reasonable to bear, and allocate those risks to the parties that are in the best position to manage and bear the risks. Under this view, Farwell is stating that the seller is in a better position to bear the risk of nonperformance, whereas Kennedy believes that the buyer is in the better position. Of the seller and the buyer in a CIF transaction, which party do you think is in the better position to manage and bear the risk of nonperformance?

3. To test your understanding of the principles set forth in *Biddell Brothers*, suppose that the parties had agreed on the use of a nonnegotiable or straight bill of lading but were otherwise silent on payment. Under this arrangement, when is payment to be made? Does the buyer have the right of inspection?

4. The position set forth by Kennedy and upheld by the House of Lords that a CIF transaction implies payment against documents is now the standard position.

Section 320(4) of the Uniform Commercial Code (2003) provides:

> Under the term C.I.F. or C.&F., unless otherwise agreed the buyer must make payment against tender of the required documents and the seller may not tender nor the buyer demand delivery of the goods in substitution for the documents.

Review Incoterms CIF B(1) and B(8). Can you explain how the Incoterms definition of CIF also requires payment against documents?

E. Documents of Title

The negotiable bill of lading is crucial to a CIF or payment against documents transaction. Delivery of the bill of lading passes title to the goods and is equivalent to delivery of the goods. Are there other documents that can also serve as a document of title, such as a delivery order, that is, an order from the seller directed at the carrier to deliver the goods to the buyer? This raises the more basic question: What is the essential legal requirement that makes a document a document of title? These issues are explored in the cases and materials that follow.

PROBLEM 2-4

An English seller and a Pakistani buyer enter into a contract for the sale of wheat. The contract provides for "Sale of wheat CIF Pakistan at a port to be designated by buyer; payment against documents; seller can submit either a bill of lading or a delivery order." The seller loads the shipment aboard the carrier in exchange for a negotiable bill of lading. The seller gives the buyer a delivery order made out to the ship's master with instructions to the master to deliver the wheat to the buyer. The seller also gives the buyer an insurance policy insuring the goods against marine risk at 110 percent of value. While the ship is on its way to Pakistan, there is a brief military skirmish involving Pakistani and Indian ships and the carrier is damaged and the wheat is lost as a result. The seller demands payment from the buyer, but the buyer refuses to pay on the grounds that the contract was one for payment against the delivery of goods, despite the use of the CIF term, and as the goods were lost, there was a total failure of consideration. Must the buyer pay? Does it make a difference whether the freight was prepaid or collect? See *The Julia* below. On the insurance issue, see Incoterms CIF, A3.

Comptoir d'Achat et de Vente Du Boerenbond Belge S/A v. Luis de Ridder Limitada
(The Julia)
House of Lords
[1949] A.C. 293

[On April 24, 1940, Luis de Ridder, an Argentinian grain exporting firm (seller), contracted to sell 500 tons of rye for about $5,000 to Comptoir d'Achat et de Vente du Boerenbond Belge (buyer), CIF Antwerp with payment against documents. The 500 tons of rye were part of a 1,120-ton shipment of rye that the seller had already loaded on board the *Julia* on April 18 prior to contracting with the buyer. The master of the *Julia* had given the seller a negotiable bill of lading covering the entire load of rye made out to the order of the seller's agent in Belgium, Belgian Grain and Produce Company (Belgian Grain).

Under the contract with the buyer, the seller was entitled to present either a delivery order or a bill of lading to the buyer. After the *Julia* set sail, the seller instructed Belgian Grain to present the buyer with a provisional invoice and a delivery order. The provisional invoice was for the amount of $5,000 covering the cost of the goods and insurance. The delivery order was addressed to the seller's cargo superintendent in Belgium, F. Van Bree, S.A. (Van Bree), with instructions to release the goods to the buyer upon presentation of the delivery order. The delivery order also stated that the buyer had a share in the insurance policy purchased by the seller covering the entire shipment of rye on board the *Julia*. The share given to the buyer was 2 percent over the invoice value of the rye purchased by the buyer. Before the delivery order was transmitted to the buyer, it was signed and endorsed by Van Bree promising to honor the delivery order in favor of the bearer. The buyer accepted both the provisional invoice and the delivery order and paid $5,000 to Belgian Grain. The same day, the seller presented two insurance certificates referenced in the delivery order to Van Bree (one certificate was for marine risks and the other was for war risks). The certificates provided that they represented the original policy of insurance with its coverage of the full shipment and conveyed all of the rights of the original policy holder (the seller) and could be exchanged for a duly stamped policy if and when required. The certificates also provided that they were invalid unless countersigned by Belgian Grain. The record does not indicate whether they were ever signed. From the record, it appears that these certificates were never delivered to the buyer.

To obtain delivery of the goods, the buyer followed a rather complicated procedure that the parties had been using for 8 to 11 years and would have used in this case if the *Julia* had actually arrived in Antwerp. After the ship arrived, the buyer would give the delivery order with a check for the freight charges to its own agent, Carga S.A. (Carga), who served as the buyer's cargo superintendent at Antwerp. Carga would then hand the check to Belgian Grain for the freight charges and present the delivery order at the same time. Belgian Grain would then make an inscription at the bottom of the delivery order acknowledging receipt of the freight charges and would return the order so annotated to Carga. Next, Carga would hand the delivery order to Van Bree, seller's cargo superintendent, which retained the delivery order and issued a *laissez suivre* or release addressed to themselves authorizing the delivery to Carga. Before Van Bree could obtain possession of the goods from the ship, however, the ship's master had to issue a captain's release. The master would issue the release only upon proof that the freight had been paid to the agents of the ship. Once the ship's captain was satisfied that the freight charges had been paid, he would issue a release instructing his staff or superintendents aboard the ship to release them to Van Bree. In turn, Van Bree would release them to Carga who would deliver the goods to the buyer.

Before the *Julia* could arrive at Antwerp, however, the Germans invaded Belgium and occupied Antwerp. The ship was diverted to Lisbon where the rye was sold at a considerably lower price than the price paid by the buyer. The seller offered to give the buyer the amount realized on this sale, but the buyer sought a refund of the entire purchase price. After the war, the buyer sought arbitration before an umpire and claimed that the nondelivery of the rye at Antwerp constituted a total failure of consideration under the contract and that the buyer was entitled to recover the purchase price. The umpire found that the contract was a genuine CIF contract and that the seller had delivered the documents to the buyer as required under the contract and was entitled to payment. The umpire's award was upheld by the court of first instance and by the court of appeals from which the sellers have appealed.]

LORD PORTER: In the present case it is true, no doubt, to say that some steps had been taken towards the performance of this contract, e.g., the goods had been shipped, an invoice sent, the customary so-called delivery order had been transmitted and that delivery order amongst its provisions contained a declaration by the sellers' agents, Belgian Grain and Produce Co. Ld., that they gave a share of the present delivery order to $4,973 in a certificate of insurance. But the taking of steps towards performance is not necessarily a part performance of a contract. The question is whether the purchaser has got what he is entitled to in return for the price. That practice seems to me rather to show that the payment was not made for the documents but as an advance payment for a contract afterwards to be performed.

No doubt the contract could have been so performed as to make it subject to the ordinary principles which apply to a c.i.f. contract. The tender of a bill of lading or even of a delivery order upon the ship, at any rate if attorned to by the master, and a policy or a certificate of insurance delivered to or even held for them might well put it in that category. But the type of delivery order tendered in the present case was a preliminary step only. A complicated procedure had to be followed before the goods would be released. The buyers had to hand the sum due for freight to their agents; those agents would then pay the freight and present the delivery order to the Belgian Grain and Produce Co. Ld., who would sign a note on it acknowledging receipt of the freight; the agents thereupon would hand the delivery order to Van Bree who would retain it and issue a "laissez suivre" or release to themselves authorizing delivery to the agents. But before physical delivery of the goods could take place Van Bree must have received a "Captain's laissez suivre" authorizing delivery to them. "It was thus," as the umpire says, "the effective document upon which Van Bree obtained physical possession of the goods; it was issued to Van Bree and was never physically in the buyers' hands." Similarly, "the insurance certificates," as the umpire also finds, "were received by Van Bree from the Belgian Grain and Produce Co. Ld., and would not have passed through the hands of, or even have been seen by, the buyers." He further finds that Van Bree "were at no time and in no respect agents of the buyers and that the sellers did not, by delivering the certificates to Van Bree, constructively deliver them to the buyers nor did Van Bree at any time hold the certificates (whether countersigned by the Belgian Grain and Produce Co. Ld. or not) at the disposal of the buyers." In these circumstances the fact that the sellers twice collected the insurance money for a total loss and handed it to the buyers does not lead very far. It was a convenient method of settling accounts between the parties and, despite the extra two per cent., is in substance no more than a repayment of the money given for the goods.

The vital question in the present case, as I see it, is whether the buyers paid for the documents as representing the goods or for the delivery of the goods themselves. But the whole circumstances have to be looked at and where, as, in my opinion, is the case here, no further security beyond that contained in the original contract passed to the buyers as a result of payment, where the property and possession both remained in the sellers until delivery in Antwerp, where the sellers were to pay for deficiency in bill of lading weight, guaranteed condition on arrival and made themselves responsible for all averages, the true view, I think, is that it is not a c.i.f. contract even in a modified form but a contract to deliver at Antwerp. If this be the true view there was plainly a frustration of the adventure — indeed the sellers admit so much in their pleadings — and no part performance and the consideration had wholly failed. The buyers are accordingly entitled to recover the money which they have paid. I would allow the appeal and pronounce for the alternative award with costs in your Lordships' House and in the courts below.

LORD SIMONDS: My Lords, there is, in my opinion, no finding of fact by the umpire which would justify your Lordships in holding that the delivery order which was handed to the buyers had any commercial value in the ordinary sense. That it was not a document of title by itself entitling the buyers to delivery of the goods was expressly found. It is a matter of conjecture whether in these circumstances it had any commercial value, and your Lordships cannot found on conjecture. The case is, however, put not only on the general commercial value of such a document but upon the special value which is said to have accrued to the buyers from its terms. This is the view which was taken by the learned Master of the Rolls, whose words I have already cited. At this stage I would remind your Lordships that "when one is considering the law of failure of consideration and of the quasi-contractual right to recover money on that ground, it is, generally speaking, not the promise which is referred to as the consideration, but the performance of the promise." To this I would add that the receipt by the promisee of something which the promisor did not promise will not prevent a total failure of consideration. The value consideration which the Master of the Rolls thought the buyers received was a personal undertaking and guarantee by Van Bree, the local agents at Antwerp of the sellers, which was to be found in their indorsement of the delivery note. I cannot accept this view. It is, I think, reasonably clear that the words I have cited give rise to no independent contractual rights against Van Bree. There is nothing in the umpire's award to suggest that Van Bree were acting in any other capacity than as agents for the sellers. If they were in fact acting or purporting to act as principals in respect of their indorsement of the delivery note, then, if, as I assume to be the case in the absence of evidence to the contrary, Belgian law is the same as English law, the buyers acquired against them no enforceable rights; for, so far as they at least were concerned, there was no consideration for their engagement. But, as I have said, in my view Van Bree were acting throughout as agents, and, seen in its true perspective, their undertaking indorsed on the delivery order was not "a part of what they [the buyers] contracted to pay for," but a part of the machinery by which the sellers were to carry out their bargain. What the buyers bought was 500 tons of rye, not an indorsement on a piece of paper which brought them not a step nearer their rye until the ship arrived at Antwerp. I come, then, to the conclusion that the sellers performed neither all nor, in any material sense, a part of what they were required to do under the contract and the buyers obtained no part of that which they had contracted to buy. There was therefore failure of consideration.

LORD NORMAND: It is agreed that the delivery order was not the equivalent of the goods in the sense that its possession conferred on the holder the right of property in the goods valid against all the world. But the consideration for the price is nothing less than that right, unless there are special terms in the contract. If the delivery order had some value otherwise than as the equivalent of the goods the fact has not been proved, and if proved it would be without relevance. If, as is I think plain on the facts found, the delivery order is merely a cogwheel in the machinery for enabling the sellers to transfer the property, it cannot be treated as to any extent consideration for the price, for the consideration for the price is not what the seller does in order to effect the transfer but the actual transfer of the property itself. It is not therefore necessary to consider whether Van Bree intended to bind themselves personally by their signature to any of the undertakings contained in the delivery order. But I can find no evidence of such an intention and I can find no consideration moving from the buyers to Van Bree.

These subsidiary arguments by themselves therefore avail nothing, and the sellers must rely on their contention that the contract by its special terms provides that between the sellers and the buyers the delivery order shall be treated as equivalent to the goods. The sellers laid weight on the description of the price as a c.i.f. price and on the description of the business as c.i.f. business. They also founded on the clause dealing with payment which, they said, treated the delivery order as the equivalent of the bill of lading and the price as paid for it. I think, however, that the explanation of the description c.i.f. in relation to the price and the business carried on by these two parties is that the contract stipulates for a price the components of which were cost, insurance and freight, and that the printed form of the contract used was one which was suitable for an orthodox c.i.f. transaction though also for other transactions not conforming to the c.i.f. model. The use of the label c.i.f. was therefore not significant and I agree with Asquith L.J., that the question is not whether the label was appropriate but what was the effect of the terms of the contract when it was not intended or possible to perform it as an orthodox c.i.f. contract is performed. The stipulation that the price or part of it was to be paid in exchange for a bill of lading and policy or in exchange for a delivery order and certificate does not carry with it the implication that in relation to the rights of the parties inter se the delivery order is to have the effect of a bill of lading, and I can see no reason for reading into the words "in exchange for" anything more than their literal meaning or to read "payment . . . in exchange for . . . delivery order" as meaning "payment for the delivery order." But I think that if the words "delivery order" had had to be construed without the aid of the previous course of dealing, it would have been held to mean a document addressed to and accepted by one in physical possession of the goods. The sellers would then have been bound to tender a document which was in fact the legal equivalent of the goods. The effect of the course of dealing was to release the sellers from that obligation and to entitle them to payment on tender of a document which contains no more than a personal obligation. I do not find evidence in the contract that the parties have undertaken to treat this document as a document of title as between themselves. I would therefore allow the appeal, with costs, both here and in the courts below.

Appeal allowed.

NOTES AND QUESTIONS

1. Did the House of Lords find that this was a contract for payment against documents or a contract for payment against delivery of the goods?

2. If the lordships had found that this was a true CIF contract, would the buyer have recovered the purchase price?

3. In *The Julia*, what was the legally effective document that gave possession to the goods? Was this document ever delivered to the buyer?

4. Why was it the practice of the London and Belgium grain merchants to require the seller to hire a sales agent (Belgian Grain) as well as a cargo superintendent (Van Bree)?

5. For a number of years, the parties had engaged in a rather complex arrangement for the sale of rye under the rules of the London Corn Trade Association. This arrangement helped to create flexibility in the sales transaction for both the London merchants and the Belgium buyers and the industry had developed a sophisticated system of agents and superintendents to support this practice. The seller is able to load a large bulk shipment of rye on board the carrier destined for Antwerp without first having obtained any purchase orders. After the goods are loaded, the carrier issues a negotiable bill of lading that is made out to the seller's agent, Belgian Grain, in Antwerp. The seller also takes out two insurance policies for the entire shipment of rye to protect itself against damage or loss of the rye due to marine or war risks while en route to Antwerp. The seller can then sell all or a portion of the rye while the vessel is en route to Belgium. Once the seller and a buyer agree on a sale, the seller will issue a delivery order to its agent in Antwerp. Note that as the bill of lading covers the entire shipment of rye, the seller cannot instruct its Antwerp agent to endorse the bill of lading to the buyer unless the buyer purchases the entire shipment. As the seller ships a very large shipment in order to economize on costs, it is unlikely that any single buyer will purchase the entire shipment but rather each shipment may be subject to several orders from several different buyers each purchasing a portion of the shipment. As a result, the seller will issue delivery orders addressed to its cargo superintendent to distribute a portion of the rye to each buyer. If all of the rye is not purchased by buyers while en route to Antwerp, the seller's Antwerp agent would pay the carrier for the freight charges and the seller's cargo superintendent would take possession of the rye by presenting the bill of lading to the carrier. The cargo superintendent would then deliver the rye to the agent who would then attempt to sell the rye on behalf of the seller.

As with the bill of lading, the insurance policies purchased by the seller also covered the entire shipment against loss during the carriage. Thus, the seller could not endorse the policies and deliver the policies to the buyer unless the buyer purchased the entire shipment, which, as we noted, was not likely given the large size of the shipments that the seller used to save on shipment costs. Instead, the practice used by the London Corn Trade Association was to have the seller note on the delivery order that the buyer was the beneficiary of a "share" of the two insurance policies covering marine and war risk covering the portion purchased by the buyer; then the seller gave two "certificates of insurance," signed by the seller's insurance brokers, to the seller's cargo superintendent in Antwerp. The certificates purported to represent all of the rights in the original insurance policies with full coverage of the entire shipment and purported to convey all of these rights to the transferee. The combination of the notation on the delivery order specifying the buyer's share in the insurance policies and the delivery of the certificates representing the policies was thought to be sufficient to transfer a valid interest in the policies to the buyer to cover the portion of the rye purchased by the buyer against marine and war risk. Note in *The Julia* that Lord Porter doubted whether any valid interests in the insurance policies had been actually transferred to the buyer. Why?

Once the seller and buyer conclude a sale, the seller will instruct its Antwerp agent to issue a provisional invoice and a delivery order with the insurance annotation to the buyer. Against delivery of these documents, the buyer makes payment to the seller's agent. When the goods arrive, the buyer then instructs its local cargo superintendent to present an additional check for the freight charges and the delivery order to the seller's agent for its endorsement. The cargo was shipped freight collect with payment for the freight charges due before discharge of the goods. This arrangement saved the seller the expense of advancing the freight charges and placed the burden of paying these charges on the buyer as the ship would not discharge the goods until the freight was paid. From the buyer's viewpoint, however, the buyer did not wish to pay the freight while the ship was still en route. The insurance certificates endorsed to the buyer covered only the loss of the cargo, not the freight charges. If the buyer paid the freight charges while the carrier was en route and the carrier was lost due to no negligence of the ship's master, the buyer would suffer the loss of the freight charges. To deal with this risk, the buyer paid the freight charges after the arrival of the ship. Once the seller's agent received the freight charges, it then signed a note at the bottom of the delivery order acknowledging receipt of the freight and handed the delivery order back to the buyer's cargo superintendent who, in turn, handed it to the seller's superintendent. As the seller's Antwerp agent was a sales agent and distributor for the seller and not qualified to handle cargo, the seller had to engage another entity — F. Van Bree, S.A. in *The Julia* — specifically for the purpose of receiving and moving cargo from the carrier. The delivery order, however, did not entitle the seller's cargo superintendent to possession of the goods because the ship's master would only release the goods when he was satisfied that the freight had been paid. When the master was satisfied that the freight charges were paid, he would issue the captain's release (*laissez suivre*), which was addressed to the ship's crew and authorized the delivery of the cargo. Without the captain's release, the crew would not unload any cargo. Only this document, issued after the ship's master was satisfied that the costs of affreightment had been paid, would authorize the delivery of the goods to the seller's cargo superintendent who was under instructions to hand the goods to the buyer's cargo agent who would then hand over the goods to the buyer.

6. In *The Julia*, the buyer argued that in exchange for payment it received neither possession nor property from the seller. Thus, there was a total failure of consideration and the buyer was entitled to recoup the purchase price. The seller argued that the contract was a modified CIF transaction but still retained the essential CIF characteristic of payment against documents. In this case, the parties had agreed to acceptance of a delivery order instead of documents. Lord Porter rejected the argument that the transaction was a modified CIF transaction. He argued that, under a CIF transaction, the buyer must be given a document containing the right to the goods. Porter argued that the buyer was never given this right and so it was impossible to characterize this as a CIF transaction. Review Porter's opinion at p. 94 *supra*. Can you explain his argument that the buyer never had

the right to the goods? Also review the opinion of Lord Normand, who argued that calling a transaction CIF does not make it so unless documents of title are used.

The seller also argued that handing over the delivery order, even if it was not a document of title, was part performance of the contract and, that the delivery order had some commercial value. As a result, there could not have been the total failure of consideration as alleged by the buyer. Lord Simonds rejected both of these arguments. Simonds viewed the contract as one for the delivery of goods either by way of actual delivery of the goods themselves or by way of symbolic delivery, which involved handing over a document representing the goods, such as a negotiable bill of lading. There clearly was no actual delivery. Nor was there symbolic delivery because the order was not a document of title giving the buyer the right to the goods. As to the argument that the seller must have performed some part of the contract because it handed over the delivery order, Simonds noted "when one is considering the law of failure of consideration and of the quasi-contractual right to recover money on that ground, it is, generally speaking, not the promise which is referred to as the consideration, but the performance of the promise. To this I would add that the receipt by the promisee of something which the promisor did not promise will not prevent a total failure of consideration." See p. 95 *infra*. As to the commercial value of the delivery order, Simonds rejected the notion that the commercial value of the order was founded on obligations of Van Bree to deliver the goods. Under Simonds' view, the buyer acquired no enforceable rights against Van Bree as a result of the delivery order. Van Bree was merely the agent of the seller and the arrangement was merely a mechanism by which the seller was to perform its obligations under the contract. The delivery order to Van Bree did not create any additional rights in the buyer.

7. Are the lordships establishing a rule restricting the freedom of the parties to agree under the sales contract that payment is to be made upon presentation of a delivery order even though it is not a document of title and has no commercial value? If the delivery order is not a document of title, then the buyer is, in essence, making an advance payment of the purchase price against the delivery of the goods to occur later and assuming the risk if the goods are lost at sea. Granted this is a risky transaction for the buyer, but why shouldn't the parties be able to make such a bargain if they wish? Note that the effect of payment against delivery orders that are not documents of title is that the risk of loss for the goods shifts to the buyer even though no property or title passes. In an orthodox CIF transaction, the risk of loss shifts to the buyer once the goods are safely loaded aboard the ship, but the buyer is protected because it has a document of title such as a negotiable bill of lading and also a policy of insurance. The argument that the parties have artificially agreed that the buyer would pay upon the presentation of a document that gave no title or enforceable right to delivery of the goods would shift the risk of loss to the buyer who must pay for the goods if they are lost at sea even though the buyer has no property or title until the goods are landed and delivered to the buyer. But why should courts prevent sophisticated commercial parties from entering into such an arrangement if this is what they wish to do? Perhaps the seller is willing to give the buyer a lower price because the buyer is willing to bear additional risks and the buyer has made a calculated decision that such risks are worth bearing. Wouldn't rejecting such a bargain made by the parties be an unjustifiable restriction on the freedom of contract? Lord Normand responded to this argument in his opinion. Carefully review his opinion. Is Normand saying that the

parties can never freely contract for the buyer to make advance payment against later delivery of the goods and to shift the risk of loss to the buyer even though no property passes?

8. As noted earlier, the merchants in London and Antwerp had been using the complex arrangement described in note 5 above for a number of years for the sale of rye. Presumably, both the buyers and the sellers were sophisticated merchants and businesspeople. Why would the Belgian buyers pay against delivery orders that did not pass title or possession?

9. One commentator has summarized the effect of the decision as follows:

1. A pure c.i.f. contract is one in which the seller performs his obligations by tendering a clean bill of lading, an invoice and a marine insurance policy covering only the goods sold and in which the buyer is bound to accept them and pay irrespective of what happens to the goods themselves.

2. The parties may expressly agree to substitute other documents (e.g. a delivery order and insurance certificate) for the bill of lading and insurance policy.

3. Where they do so it is a question of construction in each case whether the other normal obligations of a c.i.f. contract remain unaffected so that the documents take the place of the goods. The use of the express c.i.f. is far from decisive, it may merely indicate that the seller is to arrange shipment and insurance and be paid accordingly.

4. The courts will be very reluctant to construe these hybrid c.i.f. contracts as providing that the documents take the place of the goods unless the substituted documents are such as to give the buyers an immediate and enforceable right to obtain the goods (e.g. a delivery order attorned to by the master) and rights which can be made effective against the insurer in the event of loss. In other cases they will strive to construe the contract as one in which the seller is obliged to deliver the goods themselves at the named port of destination and in which the risk remains with him until he does so.

L.G.B. Bower, *CIF Contracts*, 12 Mod. L. Rev. 241, 245 (1949).

PROBLEM 2-5

An international dealer in bulk agricultural goods comes to your law office and asks for advice light of *The Julia* on how to set up a payment against documents transaction so the dealer can load the goods in bulk on board a carrier freight collect and sell the goods while in transit to several buyers and receive payment against documents. Please advise.

F.   The Contract of Affreightment, Bills of Lading, and Insurance

1.   The Contract of Affreightment

In an international sales transaction, one of the parties will arrange the transportation of the goods. Typically, this duty falls to the seller; it is easier for the seller to arrange everything and charge the buyer. Thus, most export transactions are CIF in form. The seller will arrange this transport through an intermediary, a broker, or a freight forwarder.

There are four possible modes of transport: Air, rail, road, and water. Often, more than one mode must be used, especially if door-to-door delivery is sought. This is known as multimodal transport. The most frequent device used in shipping goods is the container, a metal box that can be loaded onto a ship as well as carried by rail or truck.

In international trade, transport by ship is frequently employed. In general, there are two types of ship transport: Common carriage and private carriage. A common carrier is one that holds itself out to the general public as engaged in the business of marine transport for compensation. In private carriage, a ship will be leased in whole or in part by special arrangement. The contract of private carriage is known as a charter party.

At common law, distinctly different legal consequences attached to common carriage and private carriage. The common carrier was chargeable as an insurer of the goods, accountable for any damage or loss happening in the course of the conveyance. There are only narrow exceptions to this liability: Acts of God, acts of the public enemy, and inherent vices or faults of the shipper. *See, e.g., New Jersey Steam Navigation Co. v. Merchant's Bank of Boston*, 47 U.S. (6 How.) 344, 381, 12 L. Ed. 465 (1848); *The Niagra v. Cordes*, 62 U.S. (21 How.) 7, 16 L. Ed. 41 (1858). By contrast, the shipowner engaged in private carriage was not subject to insurer's liability, but was only liable for loss or damage to the extent this was proximately caused by a breach of an obligation contained in a contract of carriage. *See, e.g., Commercial Molasses Corp. v. New York Tank Barge Corp.*, 314 U.S. 104, 62 S. Ct. 156, 86 L. Ed. 89 (1941); *Pure Oil Co. v. M/V Caribbean*, 235 F. Supp. 299 (W.D. La. 1964), *aff'd sub nom, Pure Oil v. Boyne*, 370 F.2d 121 (5th Cir. 1966).[1] A ship hired for a specific voyage to carry a particular cargo for charterers was not a common carrier, but a bailee for hire required to exercise only ordinary skill and care. *See The Wildenfels*, 161 F. 864 (2d Cir. 1908).

The following case concerns some of the problems that may arise concerning the contract of affreightment.

F.D. Import & Export Corp. v. M/V Reefer Sun
United States District Court, Southern District of New York, 2002
248 F. Supp. 2d 240

SCHEINDLIN, District Judge.

BACKGROUND

A. THE PARTIES

F.D. Import is a New York corporation that engages in international trade. Defendants Arctic Reefers Corp. ("Arctic Reefers"), Bright Sapphire Maritime,

---

1. At common law, the private carrier would be held liable only for negligence as a bailee, but since the private carrier was not "subject to the exceptional and extraordinary duties and liabilities of common carriers, . . . they may carry for whom they choose, and for such compensation and upon such conditions as may be agreed upon." *The Fri*, 154 F. 333, 338 (2d Cir. 1907). The law of private carriage is now essentially charter party law.

Inc. ("Sapphire"), Oesterreichischer Lloyd Ship Management GES MBH ("OLSM"), South Pacific Shipping Co., Ltd. ("South Pacific"), and the vessel, M/V Reefer Sun ("Reefer Sun") are all foreign entities with places of business in Bermuda, Austria, Panama, Denmark, or New York. Each entity engages in the common carriage of cargo between international ports.

Exportadora Bananera Noboa ("EBN"), Frutera Jambeli Frujasa C.A. ("Frutera"), and Grupo Noboa are all foreign entities with offices in New York. *Id.* Pacific Fruit Co., Italy SpA ("Pacific Fruit"), is a foreign entity with offices located in Italy and Ecuador. *Id.* These entities supply fruit for international trade.

B. FACTUAL BACKGROUND

This case involves a shipment of bananas from Guayaquil, Ecuador to Nikolaev, Ukraine. In 2001, F.D. Import arranged the shipment of bananas to its affiliate and customer located in Ukraine — Avrora, Inc. F.D. Import had an oral agreement for the purchase of bananas from Pacific Fruit, a banana supplier.

On March 19, 2001, a Charter Party was executed for the shipment of the bananas on the vessel Reefer Sun, a ship owned and operated by Arctic Reefers. The only signatories to the Charter Party were Arctic Reefers and the charterer — South Pacific. Pursuant to Clause 27 of the Charter Party, "[a]ll disputes arising under this Charter Party [are] to be referred to arbitration in London (English Law to apply)."

Six clean Bills of Lading for the shipment of the bananas were executed on March 28, 2001. According to the Bills of Lading, fresh green Ecuadorian bananas were loaded onto the Reefer Sun in Ecuador and were to be discharged in Ukraine. On the Bills of Lading, the shipper is named as Frutera, "on behalf of: F.D. Import." Avrora is named as the consignee. Paragraph 1 of the Conditions of Carriage located on the reverse side of the Bills of Lading provides that "[a]ll terms and conditions, liberties and exceptions of the Charter Party . . . including the Law and Arbitration Clause are herewith incorporated."

On March 28, 2001, the Reefer Sun received 200,354 boxes of bananas in Ecuador, allegedly in good condition per the Bills of Lading, and the bananas were shipped to Ukraine. Although F.D. Import had an oral understanding with Frutera regarding the purchase of bananas, a written Purchase Agreement was not signed until April 5, 2001. Per the agreement, F.D. Import purchased approximately 120,000 boxes of bananas from Pacific Fruit. On April 13, the parties amended the Purchase Agreement to include an additional 80,354 boxes of bananas.

On April 18, 2001, the shipment arrived in Ukraine and unloading began. On April 24, F.D. Import made the final payment on the purchase price of $1.9 million. Upon unloading the ship, Avrora discovered that the bananas were fraudulently and intentionally packed in Bonita boxes to conceal their true brand names. Avrora also discovered that 3,672 boxes were spoiled and unsalable. Finally, on May 4, Avrora realized that 20% of all the boxes showed signs of disease. As a result, 80,000 boxes of bananas were destroyed.

F.D. Import brought this action on April 16, 2002, seeking over $980,000 in damages. F.D. Import names nine defendants who fall into one of two categories. First, there are the companies involved in supplying the bananas — EBN, Pacific

Fruit, Frutera, and Grupo Noboa (collectively "suppliers"). Second, there is the vessel, the vessel's owners/operators, and the charterer — Reefer Sun, Bright Sapphire Maritime, Inc., OLSM, Arctic Reefers, South Pacific Shipping Co. (collectively "carriers"). With respect to the carriers, F.D. Import claims that they breached the Bills of Lading and Charter Party by failing to operate the vessel in the proper condition which resulted in the damaged fruit. With respect to the suppliers, plaintiff claims that they breached the Purchase Agreement because they did not properly grow and maintain the fruit. Plaintiff seeks to hold each defendant jointly and severally liable for the damage. Arctic Reefer brings cross-claims against its co-defendants EBN, Pacific Fruit, and Frutera, seeking indemnification and/or contribution. All Defendants contend that provisions in the Charter Party and Bills of Lading require arbitration and move to dismiss these proceedings, or in the alternative, stay the proceedings pending arbitration.

LEGAL STANDARD

Pursuant to the Federal Arbitration Act ("FAA"), "a district court must stay proceedings if satisfied that the parties have agreed in writing to arbitrate an issue or issues underlying the district court proceeding." *McMahan Sec. Co. v. Forum Capital Mkts. L.P.*, 35 F.3d 82, 85 (2d Cir. 1994). *See* 9 U.S.C. §3 (2001). The statute applies to certain arbitration agreements concerning interstate commerce or maritime transactions (*e.g.*, provisions in charter parties and bills of lading of water carriers). *See* 9 U.S.C. §§1, 2.

To stay proceedings pending arbitration, a court must consider four factors: (1) whether the parties agreed to arbitrate, (2) the scope of the agreement, (3) if federal statutory claims are asserted, whether Congress intended those claims to be non-arbitrable, and (4) if only some of the claims are arbitrable, whether to stay the balance of the proceedings pending arbitration.

AGREEMENT TO ARBITRATE

To establish a valid arbitration agreement under the FAA, there must be evidence of a written provision in a maritime transaction or commercial contract providing that controversies arising from the contract or transaction are subject to arbitration. Although there is a strong federal presumption in favor of arbitrability, "arbitration is a matter of contract and a party cannot be required to submit to arbitration any dispute which [the party] has not agreed so to submit." *AT & Techs., Inc. v. Communications Workers of Am.*, 475 U.S. 643, 648, 106 S. Ct. 1415, 89 L. Ed. 2d 648 (1986).

Here, F.D. Import claims that it did not agree to arbitration because it was not a signatory to the Charter Party or Bills of Lading, and had no notice of the provisions of these instruments. For the purpose of this motion, the parties concede that F.D. Import had no actual notice of the arbitration clause. The issue, then, is whether an arbitration clause in a bill of lading and a charter party are enforceable if the plaintiff had no notice of these clauses. The final question is whether the claims asserted here fall within the scope of this arbitration agreement.

A. NOTICE

1. Binding Parties Without Actual Notice

A party does not need actual notice to be bound by an arbitration agreement. Constructive notice is sufficient to create a binding arbitration agreement. Consequently, an arbitration agreement can govern a party that did not sign the agreement or is not mentioned in the agreement. In a related context, but not involving an arbitration clause, the Second Circuit has held that the terms of a charter party or bill of lading are usually binding on non-signatories because to do otherwise would "impose 'far too heavy a burden on the carriers.'" *Stolt Tank Containers, Inc. v. Evergreen Marine Corp.*, 962 F.2d 276, 280 (2d Cir. 1992). In that case, the court found that a plaintiff who was not a party to the bill of lading was nevertheless bound by its terms because plaintiff had constructive notice that its shipper had an agreement with the carrier.

"[C]ourts have 'consistently drawn a distinction between arbitration clauses specifically identifying the parties to which it applies, and a broader form of arbitration clause which does not restrict the parties.'" *See id.* If an arbitration clause is broad, it may govern disputes of non-signatories and parties not listed in the contract. A broad clause is one that states that it covers "all disputes" arising under the charter. In contrast, a narrow arbitration clause only applies to certain parties. A limited clause typically states that it governs "disputes between owners and charterers" or other specified groups. Therefore, a broad arbitration clause in a charter party is binding on those parties with constructive notice of its terms.

"Constructive notice can be defined, crudely, as a rule in which 'if you should have known something, you'll be held responsible for what you should have known.'" *Steel Warehouse*, 141 F.3d at 237 (citation omitted). A plaintiff has constructive notice of the terms of a charter party if the terms were properly incorporated into the bill of lading. *See id.* An arbitration clause is properly incorporated where the bill of lading explicitly refers to the charter party's arbitration clause. *See Son Shipping v. De Fosse & Tanghe*, 199 F.2d 687, 688 (2d Cir. 1952) ("Where terms of the charter party are, as here, expressly incorporated into the bills of lading, they are a part of the contract of carriage and are binding upon those making claim for damages for the breach of the contract just as they would be if the dispute were between the charterer and the shipowner.").

2. F.D. Import's Lack of Actual Notice

The Charter Party does not list F.D. Import as a party to the agreement. Instead, it is signed by the charterer (South Pacific) and the ship owner (Arctic Reefers). However, the language of Clause 27 is broad, providing that "all disputes" arising under the Charter Party will be referred to arbitration in London. Because the arbitration agreement is broad, F.D. Import is bound by its terms if it had constructive notice of the terms.

The Bills of Lading provided F.D. Import with constructive knowledge of the Charter Party's arbitration clause because the Bills of Lading properly incorporated the clause. Paragraph 1 of the conditions of carriage on the reverse side of the Bills of Lading states that "all terms and conditions" of the Charter Party "including the Law and Arbitration Clause" are herewith incorporated. This is a clear incorporation of the clause and thereby gave F.D. Import constructive notice.

F.D. Import was listed as a party on the Bills of Lading and its affiliate, Avrora, was a holder of the Bills of Lading.

IV. SCOPE OF ARBITRATION AGREEMENT

The final question is whether the claims at issue are within the scope of this agreement.

After reviewing the factual allegations in the Complaint, it is apparent that F.D. Import's claims relating to the Bills of Lading and Charter Party fall within the scope of the arbitration clause. As [previously] explained, the language of the arbitration agreement is broad and applies to "all" issues arising under the Charter Party. F.D. Import's claim that the shipment of the bananas did not comply with the Bills of Lading and Charter Party arises out of these agreements, which provide for the shipment of bananas in satisfactory condition. The cross-claim brought by Arctic Reefers against EBN, South Pacific, Frutera, and Grupo Noboa are also within the scope of the arbitration agreement. If Arctic Reefers is found liable for Plaintiff's losses, it seeks indemnification or contribution from the co-defendants. This cross-claim is within the scope of the arbitration clause because the claim arises from the Charter Party. Arctic Reefers is only liable to Plaintiff if it breached its obligations under the Charter Party and this breach is the only way the cross-claim would be triggered.

In contrast, Plaintiff's claims related to the planting and maintenance of the fruit are not within the scope of the arbitration clause because they do not touch matters covered under the Charter Party or Bills of Lading. These allegations concern the condition of the fruit before shipment, and the Charter Party and Bills of Lading only cover the condition of the fruit once in the carrier's possession. As a result, these claims are governed under the provisions of the Purchase Agreement and are not subject to the arbitration clause.

V. BALANCE OF PROCEEDINGS

The only remaining question is whether the Court should stay the proceedings related to the non-arbitrable issues. Under 9 U.S.C. §3, if the claims fall within the scope of an arbitration agreement, a court *must* stay proceedings, as it has no discretion to deny the stay. When there is a combination of arbitrable and non-arbitrable issues, a court has discretion to stay the non-arbitrable issues pending arbitration. The non-arbitrable issues here are completely separate from F.D. Import's suit against the carriers. *First*, the claims against the suppliers are brought under the Purchase Agreement as opposed to the Bills of Lading and Charter Party. *Second*, the role of the fruit growers and suppliers is unrelated and distinct from that of the carriers who were responsible for the actual shipment of the fruit. *Finally*, court proceedings concerning the suit against the suppliers will not affect the outcome of the arbitration, or vice versa. Therefore, to reach an efficient resolution of these disputes, the non-arbitrable proceedings will continue in this Court. The first issue to be resolved in these proceedings is whether the forum selection clause of the Purchase Agreement binds the parties and requires the Court to dismiss the claims.

VI. CONCLUSION

For the reasons stated above, I find that F.D. Import entered into a binding arbitration agreement with the following defendants: Reefer Sun, Arctic Reefers, Sapphire, OLSM, and South Pacific. Claims against these defendants are dismissed. The arbitration agreement does not govern claims brought against the following defendants: EBN, Pacific Fruit, Frutera, and Grupo Noboa. Defendants' motion to stay proceedings pending arbitration is denied and this action shall continue.

NOTES AND QUESTIONS

1. What was the contract of carriage in the *M/V Reefer Sun, supra*? How was it formed?
2. Arbitration clauses are favored by both courts and parties as a method of dispute settlement. An arbitration clause will be enforced even in a bill of lading alone. *See Vimar Seguros y Reaseguros v. M/V Sky Reefer*, 515 U.S. 528, 115 S. Ct. 2322, 132 L. Ed. 462 (1995).
3. Why was the plaintiff in the *M/V Reefer Sun* anxious to avoid arbitration?
4. What lessons are contained in this case for the future?

G.   The Bill of Lading

The bill of lading is an ancient commercial document dating from medieval times and in general use since the sixteenth century. The traditional bill of lading is a document that is signed by the carrier of goods or his agent acknowledging that goods have been received for shipment. At a minimum, the bill of lading describes the goods and contains the names of the parties, the date, and the places of shipment and destination. Each carrier has its own form of bill of lading.

The bill of lading serves three functions. First, it may be the contract or evidence of the contract of carriage. Second, it serves as a receipt for the goods. Third, it may serve as a document of title to the goods if treated this way by the parties. The issuance of a bill of lading is common in both private and common carriage. What was the function of the bills of lading in the *M/V Reefer Sun*?

In the United States, bills of lading issued in interstate commerce and in export (but not import) transactions are subject to the Federal Bill of Lading Act (also known as the Pomerene Act), 49 U.S.C. §§80101–80116. This act categorizes all bills as either negotiable or nonnegotiable (sometimes called "straight") bills of lading. As we noted earlier, a negotiable bill of lading is one that allows transfer by indorsement. This feature allows the right to claim the goods to be transferred from person to person quite easily by signing the bill. A bill may even be signed in blank and not to the order of a named person. It is these features that allow the bill of lading to serve as a document of title. A straight bill, on the other hand, is made out to a named consignee and cannot be transferred by indorsement. When issuing a bill, the carrier is required to specify on its face which category of bill is involved. The Federal Bill of Lading Act protects the good-faith purchaser of a bill. The person negotiating or transferring a bill also warrants that the bill is genuine and that the goods covered by the bill are merchantable and fit for a particular purpose. The issuer of a bill — a carrier — is liable for misleading statements about the goods and has a duty to deliver the goods to the consignee or the holder of the bill. In this way, the law reinforces the integrity of commercial transactions.

Traditionally, bills of lading are issued in paper form, and this is still true today for security reasons. However, electronic bills of lading are gradually replacing paper bills. *See* Emmanuel T. Laryea, *Payment for Paperless Trade: Are There Viable Alternatives to the Documentary Credit?* 33 Law & Pol'y Int'l Bus. 3 (2001).

The bill of lading is used in all four modes of transport — air, water, rail, and road — but in international trade bills of lading issued by sea carriers tend to dominate. These are sometimes ocean bills of lading covering transport by sea, but more often through bills of lading are issued covering the whole trip between the exporters' and importers' places of business.

What law is applicable to bills of lading? The Federal Bill of Lading Act does not deal with the details of transport and the very important question of liability for lost or damaged cargo. These matters were traditionally left open, and it was up to the common law or to the parties themselves to handle these matters by agreement. By the late nineteenth century, however, two categories of problems arose. First, since carriers had more bargaining power than shippers, bills of lading often included clauses absolving carriers from liability. Second, tremendous disparity in bills of lading became apparent, especially since different jurisdictions differed on the question of how far carriers could go in limiting or excluding their own liability. National differences on these matters tended to disrupt international trade.

The solution was to introduce uniformity and standardization by international agreement. In the early and middle twentieth century, the four different modes of transport were functionally separate; thus, international regimes that differed from each other were introduced for each of the four modes. We will concentrate on only one of the modes — carriage by water — since this is dominant today in international trade.

Certain organizations, such as the International Law Association and the Comité Maritime International (CMI), took the lead in urging uniform international regulation of the rights and duties of carriers of ocean cargo. After several years of preparatory work, the International Law Association, at its Hague meeting in 1921, adopted a body of principles known as the "Hague Rules, 1921." This was followed by a tentative draft international convention incorporating the rules, which was submitted by the Belgian government to the Fifth Diplomatic Conference on Maritime Law held in Brussels in October 1922. The negotiations at this conference culminated in a final act, known as the International Convention for the Unification of Certain Rules of Law relating to Bills of Lading,[2] signed in Brussels on August 25, 1924.

This convention was not conceived as a comprehensive and self-sufficient code regulating the carriage of goods by sea; it was intended merely to unify certain rules relating to bills of lading damage to hull cargo (live animals excepted) between the time of loading and discharge. All bills of lading covered by the convention were made subject to minimum standards that define both the risks assumed by the carrier that cannot be altered by contrary agreement and the immunities the carrier may enjoy unless otherwise agreed by the parties.

---

2. 51 Stat. 233; T.S. No. 931; 120 U.N.T.S. 155, entered into force for the United States, Dec. 29, 1937.

In general, clauses relieving the carrier from liability for negligence in the loading, handling, stowing, keeping, carrying, and the discharge of the goods or diminishing its obligation to furnish a seaworthy vessel were declared null and void. The carrier, in turn, was relieved from liability for negligence in "navigation or in the management" of the vessel and from the absolute warranty of seaworthiness. The convention applies to "all bills of lading issued in any of the contracting States."

It was hoped that by balancing the conflicting policies of maritime nations and the interests of shippers and carriers, the Brussels Convention would standardize the liabilities of carriers on the international level. Moreover, it was expected that, as to matters regulated by the convention, the outcome of litigation would be the same in the courts of any of the contracting states. The optimism that prevailed at the time the convention was signed has been only partially vindicated. Most maritime nations did ratify or adhere to the Brussels Convention; other countries, without formally adhering to the convention, enacted special legislation incorporating its rules. Despite the substantial uniformity of domestic legislation, however, conflicts in the determination of the carriers' liability and the validity of negligence clauses in bills of lading remained. States adopted the rules with modifications and textual variations; thus, differing rules and interpretations developed and persist.

In 1968, the so-called Visby Rules[3] (the Brussels Protocol of Amendments to the Hague Rules) were signed at a diplomatic conference called by the Belgian government in response to a request by the CMI. The occasion for the call of this conference was the widespread belief that the per unit limitation of liability (100 pounds sterling per package) as well as other provisions of the Hague Rules had become inadequate. The Visby Amendments adjusted the limits to 30 francs Poincaré per kilogram (U.S.$.09 per pound) and 10,000 francs Poincaré per package (U.S.$662). (The franc Poincaré is a unit of account consisting of 65.6 milligrams of gold at a standard fineness of .00009.)

Many shipping nations have adopted the Visby Amendments, which came into force in 1977. By their terms (Art. X), they apply to (1) bills of lading issued in a contracting state, (2) carriage from a port in a contracting state, and (3) bills of lading incorporating the rules, "whatever may be the nationality of the ship, the carrier, the shipper, the consignee, or any interested person." The Visby Amendments have not been ratified by the United States.

The adoption and application of the Visby Rules were complicated by the fact that in 1971, by international agreement and domestic legislation in the United States, gold lost its monetary functions and no longer has an official price. In 1979, however, a protocol to the Visby Rules was adopted substituting the special drawing right (SDR) for the franc Poincaré as a unit of account.[4] An SDR is the unit of account used by the International Monetary Fund (IMF). Its value fluctuates and is published daily based on the weighted average of the values of a "basket" of key currencies. Since the value of an SDR is subject to daily fluctuations, many

---

3. Protocol to Amend the International Convention for the Unification of Certain Rules Relating to Bills of Lading, Brussels, 1968, 2 (U.N.) Register of Texts, Ch. 2. The Protocol came into force on June 27, 1977, in 11 countries.

4. 6 Benedict on Admiralty Doc. No. 1-2A. References to gold francs are converted into SDRs, either 666.7 SDRs per package or unit or 2 SDRs per kilogram, whichever is greater. This protocol entered into force in 1984.

countries that have ratified Hague/Visby (as well as only Hague) have adopted a "gold clause agreement" or other mechanisms to fix the package limitation formula to a specific amount of their own currency. Thus, even among states that have ratified Visby, different limitations may apply.

The most recent initiative to revise the Brussels Convention was undertaken under the auspices of the United Nations Conference for Trade and Development and the related United Nations Commission on International Trade Law. These forums were sympathetic to developing countries who believed that organizations like the CMI did not suit their needs. The developing countries argued that the rules of international private maritime law had been written by traditional maritime states and were unfairly biased in favor of shipowners and carriers. UNCTAD has established a Permanent Committee on Shipping that has adopted as its mission a thorough ongoing review of virtually all the international conventions relating to shipping. This has created tension and disagreement with the more traditional organizations, the CMI and the International Maritime Organization (IMO), which consider themselves the guardians of the Brussels Conventions.

In 1978, a new convention, the Hamburg Rules,[5] was promulgated under the sponsorship of UNCTAD and UNCITRAL to replace the Hague/Visby Rules on carrier liability. The Hamburg Rules substitute a unitary rebuttable presumption of carrier liability for the complex risk allocation system of Hague/Visby. They are intended to increase carrier liability for lost and damaged cargo. As a result, the Hamburg Rules are quite controversial and have not been accepted by any important maritime state.

As this story makes clear, uniformity in the law concerning bills of lading and transport of goods by sea is still elusive. The U.S. law dates from 1936 — the Carriage of Goods by Sea Act (COGSA), 46 U.S.C. §§1301 *et seq*. Virtually all other shipping nations have modernized their law in recent years so that the U.S. COGSA is quite conservative and protective of the carrier. One of the main features of COGSA is its limitation on the liability of the carrier to $500 per package. *See* 46 U.S.C. §1304(5).

There is a new effort by the CMI to draft a convention suitable for the twenty-first century, *see http://www.comitemaritime.org*, but progress is very slow.

PROBLEM 2-6

A U.S. seller entered into a charter party for the M/V Reefer Sun II to ship a large quantity of high-definition plasma flat-screen televisions packed into five shipping containers from the port of New Orleans to its final destination in a Mediterranean country. The shipment called for the M/V Reefer Sun II to arrive in Italy where the standard containers would be unloaded on to trucks and transported inland to a second port on the other side of the peninsula where they would be reloaded on board a second carrier, the M/V Appollonia, for its final destination. As this was a form of "multimodal transport" involving more than one type of transportation, the carrier issued a single through bill of lading covering all phases

---

5. United Nations Convention on the Carriage of Goods by Sea, 1978, U.N. Doc. A/CONF. 89/14 (1978), reprinted in 17 ILM 608 (1978).

of the voyage until the goods were loaded on board the second carrier when it would issue a second bill of lading to cover the voyage to the final port of destination. A clause in the through bill of lading stated: "Himalaya Clause: All exceptions, defenses, immunities, limitations of liability, privileges and conditions applicable by COGSA to the carrier shall be extended to the benefit of all persons performing services on behalf of the carrier."

After the M/V Reefer Sun II arrives in Italy at the first port, the following events occur:

(1) The Italian stevedores hired by the carrier to unload the cargo damaged the first container containing 20 package units, causing $1 million in damage. *liable but limited $500 per package ➝ $10,000*

(2) When the M/V Reefer Sun II arrives, not all of the trucks are at the port of call due to an oversight by the U.S. seller. The second container is loaded on to a truck for transshipment while the third, fourth, and fifth containers are placed in a dock warehouse where they await the arrival of *no liability)* additional trucks. While in the warehouse, a fire destroys the third container, resulting in a total loss of the cargo worth $4 million. *— himalaya clause*

(3) The fourth and fifth containers are transshipped by truck to the second port where they arrive in the late afternoon. The containers are loaded on board the second vessel, the M/V Appollonia, which issues a bill of *fruit* lading with a Clause Paramount, providing that the bill of lading is subject to COGSA. The Appollonia is scheduled for departure the next *depends* morning but overnight, the fourth container is broken into aboard the vessel and all of the goods are stolen, resulting in a loss of $4 million.

What is the liability, if any, of the stevedores, the warehouse company, the trucking company, and the M/V Appollonia? See *Fruit of the Loom* and *Steel Coils* below and the accompanying notes.

Fruit of the Loom v. Arawak Caribbean Line Ltd.
United States District Court, Southern District of Florida, 1998
126 F. Supp. 2d 1337

LYNCH, United States Magistrate Judge.

ARAWAK is an ocean carrier and at the times relevant to this matter operated a ocean liner service between the Ports of Kingston, Jamaica and Port Everglades, Florida. SEASIDE is a domestic motor carrier.

FRUIT's Amended Complaint alleges that FRUIT tendered delivery of its cargoes to ARAWAK in Kingston, Jamaica, and that ARAWAK agreed to deliver FRUIT's cargoes to Jamestown, Kentucky. FRUIT's Amended Complaint further alleges that after the cargoes were carried by ARAWAK as far as Port Everglades, ARAWAK then sub-contracted the services of SEASIDE to complete the inland domestic portion of the motor carriage from Port Everglades, Florida on to Jamestown, Kentucky. FRUIT alleges that the carriers failed to deliver the cargoes to FRUIT.

FRUIT's Amended Complaint alleges three causes of action: Negligence (Count III); Breach of Bailment (Count V) and Breach of Contract (Count I) against ARAWAK. On January 9, 1997, ARAWAK filed its Motion to Dismiss the counts for Negligence and Bailment. On December 5, 1997, this Court granted ARAWAK's Motion to Dismiss as to the count for Negligence (as being violative of the Economic Loss Rule) and denied the Motion, without prejudice, as to the count for Bailment based upon the Court's finding that the factual record was not yet sufficiently developed as to FRUIT's knowledge and consent to the use of SEASIDE as a sub-contractor/sub-bailee.

The Plaintiff's cargoes were comprised of cotton tee-shirts and baseball jackets. FRUIT had completed the process of manufacturing the cargoes in the nation of Jamaica. They were loaded into a total of four (4) standard forty-foot (40′) ocean shipping containers belonging to ARAWAK in Kingston, Jamaica. These four ocean containers were loaded onto vessels under charter to ARAWAK and were conveyed to Port Everglades, Florida on various dates in August or September, 1995. These cargo movements were part of many hundreds of other similar shipping movements which ARAWAK had performed for FRUIT during the course of the 1995 calendar year. At the time of the loss, numerous other FRUIT cargoes were in various stages of transit with ARAWAK.

Upon arrival at Port Everglades, the cargo was removed from the ocean containers and "trans-loaded" into two standard fifty-three foot (53′) highway tractor-trailers operated by the trucking company, SEASIDE. As these two trucks passed through Martin County, Florida during their transit from South Florida to FRUIT's distribution center in Jamestown, Kentucky, they were hijacked. Both of the tractor-trailers were subsequently found empty and abandoned near Interstate 95. The Federal Bureau of Investigation (FBI) conducted a criminal investigation and later recovered a portion of the cargoes from persons in South Florida who purchased some of the cargo from unknown persons.

Both Bills of Lading issued by ARAWAK showed the final destination as Jamestown, Kentucky, consigned to FRUIT. Further, ARAWAK contracted directly with SEASIDE to transport the subject shipments from Port Everglades, Florida to Jamestown, Kentucky. SEASIDE was to be paid by ARAWAK for its services.

The reverse side of ARAWAK's Ocean Bills of Lading contain the following provisions:

> 1. APPLICABILITY OF BILL OF LADING. The following terms and conditions govern the contractual relationship between Carrier and Shipper with respect to the goods. . . .

When a Bill of Lading is issued to destination, it is a through bill and all connecting carriage is subject to its terms. *Mexican Light & Power Co. v. Texas Mexican Railway*, 331 U.S. 731, 67 S. Ct. 1440, 91 L. Ed. 1779 (1947). As there is only one Bill of Lading which governed each of the shipments at issue and SEASIDE was a connecting carrier under each of the respective Bills of Lading, these Bills of Lading governed during the entire transit period.

The Carriage of Goods by Sea Act ("COGSA"), 46 U.S.C.App. §1300, *et seq.*, governs this shipment. ARAWAK's Bills of Lading indicate that, as permitted by 46 U.S.C.App. §1312, the parties have agreed that the Carriage of Goods by Sea Act is applicable. In Paragraph 4, Clause Paramount, the following language appears:

> 4. GOVERNING LAWS (CLAUSE PARAMOUNT). This bill of lading is subject to the provisions in the Carriage of Goods by Sea Act of the United States. . . . The defenses and limitations of said Act shall apply to the

> goods . . . before the goods are loaded on and/or after goods are discharged
> from the Vessel, and throughout the entire time the goods are in the custody
> or are the responsibility of the Carrier, whether acting as carrier, bailee,
> stevedore, or terminal operator.

Therefore, COGSA applied rather than the Interstate Commerce Act and COGSA governed during the entire transit period, including the land carriage portion of the trip after the goods were transferred from the vessel. See also, 46 U.S.C.App. §1307 which provides:

> Nothing contained in this chapter shall prevent a carrier or a shipper from entering into any agreement, stipulation, condition, reservation, or exemption as to the responsibility and liability of the carrier or the ship for the loss or damage to or in connection with the custody and care and handling of goods prior to the loading on and subsequent to the discharge from the ship on which the goods are carried by sea.

Each of ARAWAK's Bills of Lading provides:

5. INTERMODAL OR SUBSTITUTED SERVICE. . . . At all times when goods are in the care, custody or control of a connecting air, land or water carrier, such connecting carrier shall be entitled to all rights, privileges, liens, limitations of and exonerations from liability, and to optional or discretionary rights of indemnity granted to Carrier hereunder to the full extent permitted to carriers under any rules and regulations and laws relating to carriers.

6. PERSONS COVERED (HIMALAYA CLAUSE). All exceptions, exemptions, defenses, immunities, limitations of liability, privileges and conditions granted or provided by this Bill of Lading, applicable tariff, or by COGSA or by any applicable statute for the benefit of the Vessels or Carrier shall also apply to and for the benefit of . . . all parties performing services for or on behalf of the Vessel or Carrier as employees, servants, agents or contractors of Carrier. . . .

The parties to a bill of lading may extend a contractual benefit to a third party by clearly expressing their intent to do so. *Robert C. Herd and Co. v. Krawill Machinery Corp.*, 359 U.S. 297, 79 S. Ct. 766, 3 L. Ed. 2d 820. As SEASIDE is included within the scope of parties covered by ARAWAK's Bills of Lading, SEASIDE's liability is controlled by and limited as set forth in these Bills of Lading. This contractual extension of liability terms to SEASIDE comports with the Harter Act's applicability to a shipment after discharge, until "proper delivery is made to the consignee." 46 U.S.C.App. §190.

SEASIDE is included within the scope of parties covered by ARAWAK's Bills of Lading. Therefore, it is entitled to all of the same benefits, exonerations, and limitations available to ARAWAK, including the Exceptions Clause found at paragraph 18 of the ocean Bill of Lading. This clause provides:

18. EXCEPTIONS CLAUSE. Carrier shall not be liable for any loss, damage, delay or failure in performance hereunder occurring at any time, including before loading on or after discharge from the Vessel or during any voyage, arising or resulting from the happening and/or threat and/or after effects of one or more of the following: . . . acts of public enemies, thieves, pirates, [or] assailing thieves . . . .

The losses of the two containers in September, 1995 due to the criminal acts of hijackers is within the specific language of the Exceptions Clause of the ARAWAK Bills of Lading. Since Paragraphs 4, 5 and 6 of the ARAWAK Bills of Lading do exactly that, SEASIDE is afforded the same protection against the actions of hijackers as ARAWAK. Paragraph 5 of the ARAWAK Bills of Lading states that SEASIDE is entitled to "all rights, privileges, liens, limitations of and exonerations from liability, and to optional or discretionary rights of indemnity granted to Carrier hereunder to the full extent permitted to carriers under any rules and regulations and laws relating to carriers."

SEASIDE is a "connecting carrier," and the Exceptions Clause is meant to apply not only to the vessel, but to all participating land carriers in the absence of alternative terms. The Eleventh Circuit held in *Certain Underwriters v. Barber Blue Sea Line*, 675 F.2d 266 (11th Cir. 1982), that a Himalaya Clause's use of "agent" and "independent contractor" was sufficient to apply the benefits of the bill of lading to a terminal operator, particularly since it was a through bill of lading (Yokohama to Miami), and it was clear that the ocean carrier could not deliver to the port of Miami without using an agent or contractor to make the actual delivery.

The plain language which the parties used to allocate the risk of loss for various events in this case loss due to " . . . thieves, pirates, assailing thieves . . . " does not include any qualifications as to whether the hijackers were employees of either of the parties. It is difficult to imagine an unsolved cargo theft in which endless conjecture could not be made as to the potential identities of the criminals.

One of the very reasons the parties assigned to one another, by contractual agreement, the various risks of loss was to bring a measure of predictability and certainty to their relationship. Both parties to this transportation agreement employed numerous persons who would have had knowledge of the movement of the various cargoes. Both parties were at risk that criminals could be employed by one party or the other. The unqualified language used by the parties to categorically define the risk: cargo loss due to " . . . thieves, pirates, assailing thieves . . . ," makes no distinction as to where such a criminal might hijack the cargo. Had these two parties allocated the risk of criminal hijacking to that of the carrier instead of the shipper, conjecture about the involvement of one of FRUIT's employees would have been equally unavailing to ARAWAK. The Court finds that FRUIT bargained for a transportation contract with ARAWAK wherein FRUIT assumed the risk of cargo loss resulting from criminal hijackings.

PROBLEM 2-7

Suppose that in Problem 2-6 above the additional following events occur. When the M/V *Appollonia* arrives at the port of final destination and the fifth (and final) container is unpacked there is evidence of damage to the container, resulting in $2 million in damages to the goods. The U.S. seller has a clean bill of lading issued by the first carrier, the M/V Reefer Sun II. The cargo inspector hired by the seller to inspect the cargo as it was unloaded from the M/V Reefer Sun II in Italy issued a report indicating "clean unblemished exteriors" on all of the containers. The containers were then transported by the truckers to the Appollonia, which also issued a clean bill of lading that is in the custody of the seller. Who is liable for the damage and what, if any, limitations on liability exist?

Suppose instead that the M/V Appollonia issued an "unclean" bill describing several dents in the container when it received them for shipment. Is anyone liable and for how much? See *Steel Coils* below and the accompanying notes.

Steel Coils, Inc. v. M/V Lake Marion
United States Court of Appeals, Fifth Circuit, 2003
331 F.3d 422, *cert. denied*, 124 S. Ct. 400 (2003)

HIGGINBOTHAM, Circuit Judge.

I.

The plaintiff, Steel Coils, Inc., is an importer of steel products with its principal office in Deerfield, Illinois. It ordered flat-rolled steel from a steel mill in Russia. Itochu, which then owned ninety percent of the stock of Steel Coils, purchased the steel and entered into a voyage charter with Western Bulk for the M/V LAKE MARION to import the steel to the United States.[6] Western Bulk had time chartered the vessel from Lake Marion, Inc.[7] As Lake Marion, Inc.'s manager, Bay Ocean employed the master and crew of the vessel.

The LAKE MARION took on the steel coils at the Latvian port of Riga between February 26 and March 2, 1997. The steel had traveled to port by rail from the Severstal steel mill 400 miles north of Moscow. At Riga, the hot rolled coils were stored outside, while the cold rolled and galvanized coils were encased in protective steel wrappers and stored in a warehouse at the port.[8]

After departing Riga, the vessel stopped at another Latvian port, Ventspils, where it took on more steel coils.[9] The ship departed Ventspils on March 7, 1997 and arrived at Camden, New Jersey, on March 28, 1997. After Camden, the ship stopped at New Orleans and Houston. Steel Coils alleged that the coils unloaded at New Orleans and Houston were damaged by saltwater, which required Steel Coils to have the cargo cleaned and recoated.

II.

Steel Coils filed suit under COGSA against the M/V LAKE MARION *in rem* and against Lake Marion, Inc., Bay Ocean Management, and Western Bulk Carriers *in personam*, requesting $550,000 in damages, with a separate claim of negligence against Bay Ocean. The vessel interests and Western Bulk filed

---

6. "A voyage charter is a contract for the hire of a vessel for one or a series of voyages. . . . " *Citrus Mktg. Bd. of Israel* v. *J. Lauritzen A/S*, 943 F.2d 220, 221 n. 3 (2d Cir. 1991) (internal quotation marks omitted).

7. "A time charter is a contract to use a vessel for a particular period of time, although the vessel owner retains possession and control." *Id.* at 221 n. 2 (internal quotation marks omitted).

8. Evidence at trial showed that cold rolled and galvanized coils are susceptible to corrosion if exposed to any type of moisture, while hot rolled coils corrode only if exposed to saltwater.

9. These coils are not the subject of the present suit.

cross-claims against each other for indemnification, and Western Bulk filed a third party complaint for indemnification against Itochu.

After a bench trial, the district court held the defendants jointly and severally liable to Steel Coils for $262,000, and Bay Ocean liable for an additional $243,358.94. The court further found that Western Bulk was entitled to indemnity from Lake Marion, Inc. for any amount it pays to Steel Coils.

III.

Defendants M/V LAKE MARION, Lake Marion, Inc., and Bay Ocean contend that the district court improperly shifted the burden to them to prove that the steel cargo was not in good condition prior to loading or was in undamaged condition at discharge, that it erred in finding that they failed to exercise due diligence to ensure that the vessel was seaworthy at the commencement of the voyage, and that it was wrong in disregarding their defenses to COGSA liability of peril of the sea and latent defect.

IV.

COGSA provides a complex burden-shifting procedure. Initially, the plaintiff must establish a prima facie case by demonstrating that the cargo was loaded in an undamaged condition and discharged in a damaged condition. For the purpose of determining the condition of the goods at the time of receipt by the carrier, the bill of lading serves as prima facie evidence that the goods were loaded in the condition therein described. If the plaintiff presents a prima facie case, the burden shifts to the defendants to prove that they exercised due diligence to prevent the damage or that the damage was caused by one of the exceptions set forth in section 1304(2) of COGSA, including "[p]erils, dangers, and accidents of the sea or other navigable waters" and "[l]atent defects not discoverable by due diligence." If the defendants show that the loss was caused by one of these exceptions, the burden returns to the shipper to establish that the defendants' negligence contributed to the damage. Finally, if the shipper is able to establish that the defendants' negligence was a contributory cause of the damage, the burden switches back to the defendants to segregate the portion of the damage due to the excepted cause from that portion resulting from the carrier's own negligence.

A.

The vessel interests first assert that the district court reversed the burden of proof, requiring them to demonstrate that the goods were loaded in a damaged condition or were unloaded in an undamaged condition instead of requiring Steel Coils to prove that the coils were loaded undamaged and discharged damaged. These defendants mischaracterize the district court's decision. The district court properly explained that under COGSA a plaintiff must establish a prima facie case by "proving that the cargo for which the bills of lading were issued was loaded in an undamaged condition, and discharged in a damaged condition." Applying this law the trial court determined that Steel Coils demonstrated its prima facie case by proving that "the cargo was delivered to the LAKE MARION in good order and condition" and "was unloaded at the ports of New Orleans and Houston in a damaged condition."

The district court cited specific evidence proffered by Steel Coils to support these conclusions. In determining that the coils were loaded in good condition, it examined "mates receipts, bills of lading containing comments on the condition of the cargo, and a cargo survey taken at the load port in Riga that contained commentary about and photographs of the cargo." It explained that although some of these documents contained notations regarding "atmospheric rust on the hot rolled coils and damage to the wrapping of the cold rolled and galvanized coils," the evidence showed that "these conditions did not damage the coils" and were not the result of exposure to seawater prior to embarkation.

We conclude that the district court in this case did not clearly err in finding that the hot rolled coils were in good condition prior to loading. That the rust noted on the coils was atmospheric and nondamaging in nature, and that the moisture on the coils also did not affect their good condition is supported by the evidence.

As for the cold rolled and galvanized coils, the vessel interests argue that the bill of lading notation that the condition of these coils was unknown fatally undermined Steel Coils's attempt to prove a prima facie case of good condition. For this argument they rely on *Caemint Food, Inc. v. Lloyd Brasileiro Companhia de Navegacao*, in which the Second Circuit reasoned:

> Although a clean bill of lading normally constitutes prima facie evidence that cargo was in good condition at the time of shipment . . . it does not have this probative force where . . . the shipper seeks to recover for damage to goods shipped in packages that would have prevented the carrier from observing the damaged condition had it existed when the goods were loaded.[10]

Caemint held that a plaintiff could not recover for corned beef it claimed was ruined during the voyage because it could not present evidence as to the condition of the corned beef, which was inside metal containers, before shipment.

We have similarly stated that "[w]here because of the perishable or intrinsic nature of the commodity, the internal condition is not adequately revealed by external appearances, cargo may have a considerable burden of going further to prove actual condition."[11] That is not the case here. Captain Sparks testified that although the wrappers of the cold rolled and galvanized coils loaded at Riga were wet due to condensation, there was no evidence of "drip-down" or "run-down" of moisture to the coils and no mention in the bills of lading of "white rust or white oxidation marks," which are normal preshipment clauses indicating possible rust damage to the coils. He concluded that "[t]he amount of moisture on those coils must have been negligible" and "[t]here was no damage to those coils."

The evidence at trial showed that, had the cold rolled or galvanized coils been damaged by rust, their outer wrappers would have revealed it. Because the wrappers had no indication of rust, and the moisture on the outside of the wrappers was

---

10. 647 F.2d 347, 352 (2d Cir. 1981).
11. *United States v. Lykes Bros. S.S. Co.*, 511 F.2d 218, 223 (5th Cir. 1975) (internal quotation marks omitted).

not dripping down into the coils, it was not clearly erroneous for the district court to conclude that the cold rolled and galvanized coils were in an undamaged state prior to loading.

The vessel interests further assert clear error in the finding that the steel coils were damaged upon unloading. The contention is that seawater could not have entered through the hatches because the top-stowed cargo unloaded at Camden had no seawater damage, and that perhaps the steel coils rusted on the way from the ship to their ultimate inland destinations.

The vessel interests' arguments are belied by a wealth of evidence relied upon by the district court that at unloading the cargo was damaged by seawater rust. For instance, the McLarens Toplis survey conducted in New Orleans noted "rust stains to coils to varying extents," and "[r]andom tests on the rust stained areas with a solution of silver nitrate proved positive" with respect to chlorides, "indicating water ingress." The McLarens Toplis survey in Houston similarly stated that "[t]he cargo was examined and found to be extremely rusty," and that "[e]xtensive silver nitrate tests were conducted with strong positive results. It is our opinion [that] the . . . cargo came into contact with sea water, most likely through the poorly maintained hatch covers. . . . "

The vessel interests have not cited any evidence in the record that disputes these conclusions. Their argument that the district court "simply accepted plaintiff's survey reports and testimony *en masse* as setting forth the proper measure of damages, and that the damage was proven at discharge" implicitly acknowledges that substantial evidence in the record supports the district court's conclusions as to the damage evident at unloading.

B.

Facing a prima facie case, a defendant may escape liability if it shows that it exercised "due diligence . . . to make the ship seaworthy, and to secure that the ship is properly manned, equipped, and supplied, and to make the holds . . . and all other parts of the ship in which goods are carried fit and safe for their reception, carriage, and preservation."[12] The vessel interests urge that even if Steel Coils carried its initial burden, they exercised due diligence in making the vessel seaworthy and thus should have escaped liability.

In making its determination that the defendants did not exercise due diligence, the district court correctly noted that seaworthiness is defined as "reasonable fitness to perform or do the work at hand,"[13] and explained that, under COGSA, the carrier's duty to exercise due diligence in making the vessel seaworthy is nondelegable. It concluded that the ship was not reasonably fit to perform the work at hand — shipping steel coils — because the hatches were not maintained in good condition and had not been tested for watertightness before embarkation, which had resulted in an ingress of seawater during the voyage, and because the holds, which had previously carried a cargo of rock salt, had not been washed out with fresh water before the steel was loaded.

---

12. 46 U.S.C. §1304.

13. *See Farrell Lines, Inc. v. Jones*, 530 F.2d 10 n. 2 (5th Cir. 1976) (internal quotations marks omitted).

That the hatches were insufficiently maintained is further supported by the observations of the Seaspan Marine Consultants surveyor who inspected the hatches after the vessel docked in Camden. He noted that the rubber gaskets of the hatch panels had deep grooves in them, were worn out in several places, were heavily rusted and bent or waved in certain areas, and that parts of the gaskets were missing or cut in some places.

The vessel interests also argue that they were not responsible for conducting a watertightness test on the hatch covers prior to embarkation because pursuant to the voyage charter Itochu was supposed to "make an inspection of holds and test watertightness of hatches." This argument ignores the COGSA carrier's nondelegable duty to ensure that the vessel is reasonably fit to carry steel cargo.

In *Jamaica Nutrition Holdings, Ltd. v. United Shipping Co., Ltd.*, we rejected a similar argument.[14] There the trial court had found the defendant carrier liable for failing to adequately clean out the pipes of the vessel before loading its cargo of soybean oil. The ship's previous cargo had been molasses. Prior to loading the oil, a surveyor had visually inspected the ship's pipes and tanks and determined that they were suitable for carrying the oil. After the ship reached its destination, another surveyor examined the oil and found it contaminated with molasses. Based on this evidence, the district court concluded that the defendant's failure to clean adequately the vessel's tanks, pipes, and pumps rendered the vessel unseaworthy.

On appeal, the defendant argued it should escape liability because the voyage charter party provided: "Vessel to clean tanks, lines and pumps *to Charterer's surveyor's satisfaction.*" It contended that because the charterer's surveyor had inspected the vessel's tanks and found them suitable, the carrier's obligation to the shipper was fulfilled. However, we concluded otherwise, reasoning:

> COGSA, whether applicable by its own force or by virtue of the clause paramount, imposed a nondelegable duty on [the carrier] to exercise due diligence to make the vessel fit for carriage of the cargo shipment. This duty was not abrogated by its covenant also to clean the vessel to the charterer's satisfaction. By permitting molasses residue to remain in the system, [the carrier] violated its duty.[15]

Because the duty to exercise due diligence to ensure the seaworthiness of a vessel is nondelegable, the district court here did not reversibly err in concluding that the vessel interests failed to exercise due diligence in part because they did not test the watertightness of the hatches.

C.

The vessel interests contend that even if the district court's finding on due diligence can be sustained, the coils became damaged due to causes for which COGSA liability is excepted.

1.

Under section 1304(2) of COGSA, "[n]either the carrier nor the ship shall be responsible for loss or damage arising or resulting from . . . [p]erils, dangers,

---

14. 643 F.2d 376 (5th Cir. 1981).
15. *Id.* at 379.

and accidents of the sea or other navigable waters." At trial the defendants argued that a storm encountered by the M/V LAKE MARION on its transatlantic voyage constituted a "peril of the sea" and caused the saltwater to enter the holds. The ship's captain testified that he encountered very rough weather during the journey, with strong winds that occasionally reached Beaufort Scale Force 10 and, at their peak, reached force 11 to 12 for approximately two hours on March 26.

The trial judge rejected the peril of the sea defense for two reasons. First, such weather conditions were foreseeable in the North Atlantic during the late winter months. Second, no damage to the vessel resulted from the voyage, and the only conditions noted in the surveys at the discharge ports indicated preexisting damage as a result of prolonged neglect.

We sustain the district court's refusal to find the rough weather encountered by the M/V LAKE MARION to have been a peril of the sea given the ship's lack of injury. We cannot conclude on this record that the noted storm, even with its force 12 winds, constituted a peril "of an extraordinary nature or aris[ing] from irresistible force or overwhelming power" which could not "be guarded against by the ordinary exertions of human skill and prudence."[16]

2.

The vessel interests also urge another exception to COGSA liability. COGSA exempts any damage caused by "[l]atent defects not discoverable by due diligence."[17] Defendants argued at trial that a crack found in Hold No. 1 while the vessel was docked in New Orleans, which ruined 123 coils in that hold, was a latent defect that could not have been discovered through due diligence. The trial judge rejected the contention that the fracture was a latent defect.

"A true latent defect is a flaw in the metal and is not caused by the use of the metallic object" or by "gradual deterioration."[18] Such a defect "is one that could not be discovered by any known and customary test."[19] The ship owner has the burden to demonstrate that the defect was not discoverable.

The vessel interests posit that since a latent defect is one not discoverable in the ordinary course of surveys or inspections, and the M/V LAKE MARION's holds were inspected during the loading process, the crack was by definition a latent defect. However, Marine surveyor Captain Rasaretnam inspected the crack and determined that it was old, and had existed in some form since crews installed a doubling plate at the fracture site. The district court concluded that the crack was an extension of an old crack, and at least part of it had been present since the doubling plate had been put in place. Moreover, Captain Sparks hypothesized that the crack was caused by gradual deterioration, not by a defect in the metal. We cannot conclude that the district court clearly erred in finding that the fracture was old and in rejecting the latent defect defense.

V.

In addition to its COGSA claims, Steel Coils asserted a general maritime negligence claim against Lake Marion, Inc.'s managing agent, Bay Ocean. The

---

16. *J. Gerber & Co.*, 437 F.2d at 588 (internal quotations omitted).
17. 46 U.S.C. App. §1302(2)(p).
18. *Waterman S.S. v. U.S. Smelting Ref. & Mining Co.*, 155 F.2d 687 (5th Cir. 1946).
19. *Id.*

claim is that Bay Ocean, as vessel manager, hired the crew and was responsible for maintaining the vessel's condition, and that it was negligent in maintaining and testing the hatch covers, failing to repair the crack in Hold No. 1, and in washing the holds with seawater. Bay Ocean contended at trial that Steel Coils could not assert a negligence claim against it outside of COGSA.

The district court disagreed, holding Bay Ocean liable in tort for its negligence separate from the COGSA claim, and finding Bay Ocean liable for the entire amount requested by Steel Coils because Bay Ocean was not entitled to claim the $500-per-package limitation on liability found in COGSA. These are conclusions of law and we conduct a *de novo* review.

"One of COGSA's most important provisions limits a [vessel or] carrier's liability to five hundred dollars . . . per package unless a higher value is declared by the shipper."[20] The term "carrier" includes "the owner or the charterer who enters into a contract of carriage with a shipper."[21] We have held that as long as an entity is a party to the contract of carriage, it is a carrier. In *Sabah Shipyard Sdn. Bhd. v. M/V HARBEL TAPPER*,[22] we stated, "[t]o determine whether a party is a COGSA carrier, we have followed COGSA's plain language, focusing on whether the party entered into a contract of carriage with a shipper. . . . [A] party is considered a carrier under COGSA if that party 'executed a contract of carriage.' "[23]

It is undisputed that Bay Ocean is not explicitly named in the applicable contract of carriage, the voyage charter between Western Bulk and Itochu.[24]

Bay Ocean argues that even if it is nothing more than an agent of the carrier it may avoid liability altogether on Steel Coils's separate negligence claim because COGSA is the exclusive remedy for suits for damage to cargo. However, in a similar case, *Citrus Marketing Board of Israel v. J. Lauritzen A/S*,[25] the Second Circuit held that a plaintiff may sue a ship's manager in tort for damage to cargo and that COGSA does not govern such an action. The *Citrus Marketing* court rejected the manager's argument and the district court's holding that COGSA controlled the claim, explaining that COGSA only applied to disputes between shippers and carriers.[26] It explained, however, that a Himalaya Clause, which extends a carrier's rights under COGSA to agents of the carrier, might apply to save the manager from liability and remanded that issue for the district court to consider at trial.

---

20. *Mannesman Demag Corp. v. M/V Concert Express*, 225 F.3d 587, 589 (5th Cir. 2000); *see* 46 U.S.C. App. §1304(5).

21. §1301(a).

22. 178 F.3d 400 (5th Cir. 1999).

23. *Id.* at 405 (internal quotations omitted).

24. The district court concluded that the voyage charter party, rather than the bill of lading, was the applicable contract of carriage because if a bill of lading is held by the same shipper that executed the voyage charter party, the charter party governs the transaction. *See In re Marine Sulphur Queen*, 460 F.2d 89, 103 (2d Cir. 1972). The trial court found that Itochu, in entering into the voyage charter, acted as Steel Coils's agent. Since Steel Coils was the shipper that held the bills of lading and was a party to the voyage charter by virtue of its agency relationship with Itochu, the voyage charter party was the contract of carriage. Steel Coils did not argue in its original brief that Itochu was not its agent, and thus waived the argument. See *Peavy v. WFAA-TV, Inc.*, 221 F.3d 158, 179 (5th Cir. 2000).

25. 943 F.2d 2200 (2d Cir. 1991).

26. *Id.* at 220.

Bay Ocean charges that the district court's ruling that Bay Ocean cannot take advantage of the $500-per-package limitation "ignores the reality of maritime commerce," because it is common for one-vessel corporations such as Lake Marion, Inc., who have no employees, to act solely through their managing agents. It also argues that this result will "allow shippers to circumvent not only the package limitation, but all of COGSA, when contracting with a vessel with a separate managing agent." However, Bay Ocean chose to separate itself from Lake Marion by binding only Lake Marion to the time charter. In doing so Bay Ocean chose that only Lake Marion would become a carrier for purposes of COGSA.[27]

We agree with the Second Circuit that a noncarrier can be held liable in tort outside of COGSA. Steel Coils's negligence action against Bay Ocean was not subject to the COGSA package limitation.

VI.

For these reasons, we affirm the district court's judgment.

NOTES AND QUESTIONS

1. COGSA is applicable to all contracts for the carriage of goods by sea to or from ports of the United States in foreign trade. See 46 U.S.C. §1312. Private carriage under a charter party is not subject to COGSA under §1305, but COGSA is usually incorporated through a Clause Paramount as discussed in *Fruit of the Loom.* Even in private carriage to or from ports of the United States, however, where there is a bill of lading that forms the contract of carriage, COGSA will apply. What was the governing law in *F.D. Import & Export, supra?*

2. As COGSA applies to all carriage of goods by sea from "tackle to tackle," COGSA normally does not apply to inland carriage that is typical of today's multi-modal transport contracts and does not apply to any party that is not considered to be a carrier. However, COGSA can also be extended to (1) cover third parties and (2) inland carriage on a through bill of lading. How is this done?

3. If COGSA is found not to apply to inland transport, the applicable law will be state law as well as any applicable federal statutory regime of liability, such as the Carmack Amendment, 49 U.S.C. §11707. See, e.g., *Project Hope v. M/V IBN SINA,* 250 F.3d 67 (2d Cir. 2001). Where the loss of cargo occurs during land transport in a foreign country, foreign law or an international conventional regime will apply. See *Hartford Fire Ins. Co. v. Orient Overseas Containers Lines (UK) Ltd.,* 230 F.3d 549 (2d Cir. 2000).

4. State the allocation of burdens of proof under COGSA. A feature of this law is that there is a list of causes of loss for which the carrier is not liable. The two most important exceptions to carrier liability are losses caused by perils of the seas and losses caused by negligent navigation of the ship. What is the purpose of these exclusions?

5. There is also a provision limiting liability to $500 per package or "customary freight unit." See 46 U.S.C. §1304(5). How are these limitations applied? See

---

27. Bay Ocean also ignores the availability of a Himalaya Clause.

Groupe Chegaray/V de Chalus v. P & O Containers, 251 F.3d 1359 (11th Cir. 2001). Note that in the principal case, there were four defendants. How many of these defendants were entitled to claim the $500 per package limitation and why? The plaintiff Steel Coils recovered a total judgment of $505,358.64 in the district court. What is the effect of the $500 per package or customary freight unit limitation on the plaintiff's ability to collect the full amount of this judgment? Which of the defendants is Steel Coils likely to pursue to satisfy the judgment?

6. The ability of the carrier to avoid liability as well as other risks makes it necessary for the buyer or seller to purchase a policy of insurance in connection with shipping goods in international trade. The following case shows some aspects of such a transaction.

H. Marine Insurance

American National Fire Insurance Co. v. Mirasco, Inc.
United States District Court, Southern District of New York, 2003
249 F. Supp. 2d 303

SWEET, District Judge.

[American National Fire Insurance Co. (American National) and Great American Insurance Co. (Great American) (collectively the Insurers) and Mirasco, Inc. (Mirasco), have cross-moved for summary judgment on issues regarding a coverage issue under an ocean marine transportation policy.]

DECREE 465

On November 22, 1997, the Egyptian Government issued Decree 465, which, according to a translation provided by the Insurers, provided in part:

B) packets in which products must be firmly closed and healthy authorized. Moreover, the following information must be written, in a fixed unerasable material, on a card put inside the packet and also written outside it in [A]rabic (it might be written in two languages if [A]rabic is one):

  its Certificate of Origin

  product name and trade mark if exist[ing]

  Importers' name and address

  the authority which supervised the slay to [I]slamic sharia should be accredited by the trade office in the Certificate of Origin

  slaughter house name

  slay date.

As a result of Decree 465's labeling requirements, Mirasco marked all shipments with "Mirasco Misr" ("Misr"), one of Mirasco's largest customers, as the importer, even though a portion of the shipments was set aside for other customers. Misr would receive the product, clear it and turn over to Mirasco's other customers their portion of the shipment. Misr is a proprietorship organized under the laws of the nation of Egypt and maintains its principal place of business in Alexandria, Egypt. The Insurers claim, and Mirasco disputes, that Misr is controlled by Mirasco and used to facilitate clearing the cargo through Egyptian customs in light of Decree 465.

DECREE #6

In October 1998, the Egyptian authorities rejected a shipment of beef livers imported by Hady Enterprises and produced by one of Mirasco's suppliers, Iowa Beef Products ("IBP"), due to purported labeling irregularities in violation of Decree 465.

On January 3, 1999, the Egyptian government issued Decree #6 (the "Decree"). The Decree became effective on January 14, 1999, when it was officially published. According to a translation provided by the Insurers, the Decree stated that "[a]n embargo is placed on trade with the American company I.B.P. Corp in the United States of America as well as with any company with which it is associated." The Decree did not apply to cargo shipped by Mirasco's other suppliers, Excel Corporation ("Excel") or Monfort, Inc. ("Monfort").

Mirasco asserts, and the Insurers contest, that the Decree did not apply under Egyptian law to any IBP cargo that was shipped prior to January 14, 1999.

In an e-mail dated May 19, 1999, one of the Insurer's agents, Pam Kobin, the Divisional Assistant Vice-President for Specialty Claims of Great American's Cincinnati, Ohio office, stated that the decree "was not an embargo [of a ship] but it certainly was a prohibition." Although Mirasco asserts otherwise, Kobin has attested that she was not the one responsible for denying Mirasco's claim but that the decision was made by personnel of the New York Ocean Marine Business Unit.

THE BEEF LIVER SHIPMENT ON THE M/V SPERO

On December 31, 1998, stevedores hired and paid for by Mirasco completed the loading of the M/V Spero in Houston, Texas. The cargo consisted of 219,072 cartons of beef liver, including 132,535 cartons of IBP products (60.5 percent of the shipment), for which Mirasco had paid $1,081,500; 60,502 cartons of Excel products (27.6 percent of the shipment), for which Mirasco had paid $562,570.21; and 26,035 cartons of Monfort products (11.9 percent of the shipment), for which Mirasco had paid $285,450. The brands were not strictly segregated into different holds or hatches; instead, while Mirasco attempted not to break up lots of the same product, lots from different brands were stored together. The cartons of frozen beef liver were hard frozen and in apparently sound condition at the time of loading aboard the M/V Spero. In addition, the shipment was packed and labeled solely for Misr, but was to be sold to five customers, including Misr, upon the shipment's importation into Egypt.

After loading the cargo aboard M/V Spero in Houston, Mirasco obtained fifteen (15) bills of lading for carriage of the cargo to Alexandria, Egypt. Eight (8) bills of lading covered the IBP cargo, and seven (7) bills of lading covered the Monfort and Excel cargo.

The M/V Spero arrived in Alexandria on January 23, 1999. Yossif El Menoufy ("El Menoufy"), a representative of Sea Horse International ("Sea Horse"), which had been hired by the Insurers to investigate and report on the shipment, was present when the M/V Spero arrived and observed the later inspection of the Spero.

As discussed above, Decree #6 had gone into effect after the M/V Spero's departure but prior to the M/V Spero's arrival. Thus Mirasco then unsuccessfully attempted to convince the Egyptian authorities that the IBP cargo of the M/V Spero should be exempted from the Decree because the shipment sailed prior to the issuance thereof.

THE RETURN OF THE SHIPMENT

The M/V Spero sailed from Alexandria on March 26, 1999, with all cargo still aboard. The cargo was otherwise found in sound condition except for 387 cartons that thawed during the return trip due to stowage too close to heated fuel tanks. These cartons were destroyed, and the Insurers paid for them in the amount of $6,164 after the commencement of this lawsuit.

Mirasco marketed the rest of the rejected cargo to traders and buyers. The cargo was sold in the United States in May, June and July of 1999. Because the market had been steadily falling since August of 1998, the prices received by Mirasco for the M/V Spero cargo ranged as low as $0.115 per pound although the cargo had been purchased back in the fall of 1998 for as much as $0.34 per pound.

THERE IS NO DISPUTE OF MATERIAL FACT THAT THE EGYPTIAN AUTHORITIES REJECTED THE CARGO

The Insurers argue that the cargo was not rejected by the Egyptian authorities pursuant to the terms of the Policy. This question requires an analysis of the term "rejection" as used in the Policy.

As an initial matter, the Insurers do not appear to contest that the 60.5 percent of the shipment that was IBP brand was rejected and/or condemned as those words are defined under the policy because of Decree #6 and based on the fact that the inspectors never even sampled the IBP products. Indeed, the Insurers provided return freight as provided for by Clause D of the Rejection Coverage even though Mirasco did not present any Notices of Rejection or any other formal papers attesting to the fact that the cargo was rejected due to Decree #6.

This fact therefore contradicts the Insurers' contentions that "rejection" under the Policy is defined by custom and usage by the Egyptian government as requiring a Final Rejection Certificate after sampling and testing and adverse lab results, and an unsuccessful appeal. The Insurers did not require any such documents and appeal before sending return freight on the goods it claimed were embargoed. Indeed, this restrictive definition would mean that coverage would not exist if a governmental authority arbitrarily (1) refused to sample and/or test the cargo; (2) declined to permit and/or decide an appeal; or (3) did not issue "final rejection certificates." As Mirasco points out, such restrictive definition would undermine the purpose of rejection insurance, which is a type of political risks insurance that insures against the arbitrary acts of a government, including arbitrary rejection or detention or miscarriage of administrative determination.

The Insurers' unsupported allegations that the customs documents and [Misr's] testimony cannot be trusted or should not be construed to support a finding of rejection are insufficient to raise a material issue of fact. Similarly, the fact that Mirasco was originally given the opportunity to discharge 10 percent of the cargo per day to segregate the mislabeled cargo does not mean the cargo was not rejected, as discharge does not mean that the goods were accepted for import.

As a result, there is no genuine dispute of material fact that the M/V Spero cargo was rejected by the Egyptian authorities as that term is defined in the Policy.

SUMMARY JUDGMENT MAY BE GRANTED TO THE INSURERS IN PART BASED ON THE EXCLUSIONS

The Insurers contend that even if the cargo was rejected as that term is defined in the Policy, Mirasco is not entitled to coverage because of exclusions to the Rejection Coverage, including an exclusion (1) for loss of market as to all goods, (2) for recovery for anything but return freight due to an embargo announced after a shipment has set sail, as against the IBP cargo, and (3) of mislabeling as against the Excel and Monfort cargoes. Each will be addressed in turn.

A. THE LOSS OF MARKET EXCLUSION DOES NOT APPLY

The Insurers point out that Mirasco was able to sell its cargo once it returned to the United States, albeit for drastically lower prices than they would have received in Egypt due to the collapse of the market for beef livers. As a result, they claim that the Policy's loss of market exclusion applies. Mirasco replies that what occurred in this case was loss of market value, rather than loss of market.

Both parties rely on the same case arising in the Tenth Circuit Court of Appeals, *Boyd Motors, Inc. v. Employers Ins. of Wausau*, 880 F.2d 270 (10th Cir. 1989). *Boyd* involved an action to recover under a commercial inland marine policy, which included a "loss of market" exclusion, due to diminished value of automobiles damaged by hail. *Id.* at 271. The plaintiff had already received reimbursement for the cost of repairing the automobiles, and sought in this action an additional $40,609.48 based on its claim that the vehicles were worth less after the damage. *Id.* The district court had held that "the diminution [in] value which occurs after an accident, despite repairs, clearly is defined as loss in market." *Id.* at 273. The Tenth Circuit disagreed, stating that the above situation involved loss of market value, rather than loss of market, and that recovery was not precluded by the exclusion. In reaching this conclusion, the court discussed the two concepts of loss of market and loss of market value:

> "[M]arket" refers collectively to matters external to any particular product item, namely those conditions that determine the degree to which supply of that commodity exceeds or falls short of demand, whereas "market value" is a function of the qualities (*e.g.*, age, state of repair) inherent in the individual item itself, and refers to that price

that that specific article with those qualities would command in a given market. Thus, . . . a market is lost when, for example, due to delay in distribution, changes in consumer habits, etc., a certain type of product is no longer in demand with its intended purchasers, while what is involved in the present case, in which particular merchandise in Boyd's inventory has allegedly suffered depreciation due to physical alteration (damage and restoration), is a loss of market value.

Id. at 273.

The discussion of "loss of market" above suggests that the loss must occur in the original market for which the goods are intended.

There is no evidence that Mirasco lost its customers in Egypt who had already agreed to purchase a good portion of the beef livers on the M/V Spero. As a result, and in the absence of any legal showing to the contrary from the Insurers, the loss of market exclusion does not apply and the Insurers' motion for summary judgment on this ground is denied.

B. THE IBP CARGO WAS REJECTED AS A RESULT OF AN "EMBARGO," AND THUS MIRASCO IS ENTITLED ONLY TO RETURN FREIGHT

The Policy explicitly provides that no claim may attach under Rejection Coverage "[i]n the event of any embargo or prohibition being declared or in being by importing country," except that return freight is provided where the embargo is announced or enforced after shipments have sailed. Rejection Coverage, Clause D. Decree #6 was announced after the beef liver shipment had sailed. Therefore, if Decree #6 is an "embargo or prohibition" under the Policy, the Insurers are only responsible for paying the return freight of $400,000, which they have already paid.

There is nothing in Clause D to suggest that the term "embargo" is ambiguous. Therefore, the Court will look to the ordinary meaning of the term. According to the United States Supreme Court, "the ordinary meaning of 'embargo' . . . is a governmentally imposed quantitative restriction — of zero — on the importation of merchandise." *K mart Corp. v. Cartier*, 485 U.S. 176, 185, 108 S. Ct. 950, 957, 99 L. Ed. 2d 151 (1988).

K mart provided examples of other embargoes imposed by the United States, and referred not only to the embargo on Cuba, 22 U.S.C. §2370(a), but also to a number of "embargoes" imposed against general types of products. *Id.* at 184, 108 S. Ct. at 957 (*citing* 21 U.S.C. §381 (embargo against adulterated, misbranded or unapproved foods, drugs and cosmetics); 15 U.S.C. §1397 (embargo against motor vehicles that do not conform to federal safety standards); 19 U.S.C. §1305 (embargo against obscene pictures, lottery tickets and articles for causing unlawful abortion); 15 U.S.C. §§1241-44 (embargo on switchblade knives); and 19 C.F.R. §12.60 (1987) (embargo on fur-seal or sea-otter skins)).

It is true that the above examples involve embargoes against specific products or groups of products, rather than against products of a particular manufacturer. The definition of "embargo" should nonetheless cover this situation, as Egypt has imposed in Decree #6 "a quantitative restriction of zero" on the importation of IBP products.

As a result, the ban on all IBP products in Decree #6 constitutes an embargo or prohibition pursuant to Clause D, and the embargo or prohibition was the cause of the rejection of the goods. As a result, Mirasco is only entitled to the return freight for the IBP products, which constitute 60.5 percent of the claim. Because the Insurers have already provided such return freight, they are entitled to judgment on their claims with regard to the IBP products, and Mirasco's cross-motion for summary judgment is denied inasmuch as it relates to the IBP products.

C. THE EXCEL AND MONFORT CARGO

As an initial matter, there is no dispute that some percentage of the Excel and Monfort Cargo was rejected solely for mislabeling and thus falls under the exclusion in Clause C, Part 5. What is disputed, however, is exactly how much of the cargo falls under this exclusion. Mirasco contends that the correct percentage is represented by the settlements it reached with Excel and Monfort. The Insurers, relying on Mirasco's initial claims for complete remuneration from Excel and Monfort, assert that all of the Excel and Monfort cargo was mislabeled. Given this dispute, it can only be concluded at this time that at least as much of the cargo was mislabeled as was represented in the Excel and Monfort settlements — and potentially more.

What remains is the portion of the cargo that was purportedly rejected for either health and sanitary discrepancies alone or for mislabeling and health and sanitary violations. In seeking summary judgment against these claims, the Insurers assert that Mirasco chose to ship back the cargo after discovering it was rejected on the ground of noncovered events — Decree #6 and mislabeling — and therefore that any rejection on the basis of health was not the proximate cause of Mirasco's losses.

The Insurers have failed to establish that there is a dispute of material fact with regard to whether Mirasco's losses were proximately caused, at least in part, by events covered by the Policy. As a result, the Insurers' motion for summary judgment is denied. Mirasco's motion for summary judgment is denied because an issue of fact remains as to what portion of the Excel and Monfort cargo, if any, was rejected on grounds covered by the Policy.

SUE AND LABOR CLAUSE

For the first time in their reply papers, the Insurers have raised the defense that Mirasco failed to comply with Clause 34 of the Policy, the "sue and labor" clause, which states:

> In case of any imminent or actual loss or misfortune, it shall be lawful and necessary to and for The Insured, his or their factors, servants and assigns, to sue, labor and travel for, in and about the defense; safeguard and recovery of the said goods and merchandise, or any part thereof, without prejudice to this insurance. . . .

"When a policy contains a sue and labor clause, an insurer may be able to argue that the insured has forfeited its coverage if it does not sue and labor to minimize the covered loss." *International Commodities Export Corp. v. American Home Assurance Co.*, 701 F. Supp. 448, 452 (S.D.N.Y. 1988).

The Insurers claim that Mirasco should have unloaded the cargo at the permitted 10 percent-per-day rate and segregated the mislabeled Excel and

Monfort goods from the correctly labeled goods. Thus, they argue, the correctly labeled goods could have been sold. There is no factual basis for the claim, however, that the goods could have been sold if they were, in fact, discharged and segregated.

Indeed, Mirasco contends that it did not begin unloading because it was awaiting the lab results from the inspectors and because of the general attitude of the Egyptian authorities, leading Mirasco to believe that even if it did segregate the correctly labeled cargo, the Egyptian authorities would find another reason to reject it. In addition, Mirasco contends (and the Insurers dispute) that the Insurers, through Sea Horse, ordered Mirasco to ship the cargo back to the United States and thus was obligated to follow that directive.

Because the Insurers have not established a genuine dispute with regard to whether Mirasco could have even imported the correctly labeled Excel and Monfort products even if they had discharged and segregated them at a rate of 10 percent per day, their motion for summary judgment is denied.

NOTES AND QUESTIONS

1. There are a variety of insurance products that can be purchased to safeguard an international sale of goods. The most comprehensive is "all risks" insurance for which, of course, a higher premium must be paid. In the event of loss or damage, the owner of the goods, usually the buyer, is paid the insured value, and the insurer is subrogated to any claim against the carrier. The insurer can proceed against the carrier, standing in the shoes of the insured.

2. The law of marine insurance is remarkably uniform over much of the world. This is because of the influence of London underwriters that still dominate the market and the remarkable codification of English law, the Marine Insurance Act of 1906, Edw. 7, Ch. 41. Versions of this law have been enacted in most countries. Because of the high risks of the insurance industry and the possibility of fraud, English law long ago established the basic principle of the duty of absolute good faith on the part of the parties to the insurance contract.

3. Standard forms of cargo insurance are provided by the Institute Cargo Clauses of the Institute of London Underwriters. These Institute Clauses provide three alternative sets of forms — A, B, and C — which define the risks covered and the losses for which cover is excluded. Clause A provides the most extensive, "all risks" cover. Clause B is intermediate, and Clause C provides the least cover — only loss or damage reasonably attributable to fire, explosion, collision, jettison or general average, that is, intentional loss of cargo when necessary to save the ship. It must be emphasized that there are many exclusions even for "all risks" cover. The importer may want to insist on additional cover, for example, the Institute War Clauses or the Strikes, Riots, and Civil Commotions Clause. What was the cover in the principal case? When is such cover a good idea? Who decides on the extent of cover?

4. The law of marine insurance has never been codified in the United States. However, the basic substantive law of marine insurance is federal maritime law, and the Supreme Court has stated that U.S. courts should look to English law for the applicable rules because of the "special reasons for keeping in harmony with the marine insurance laws of England, the great field of this business." *Queens Ins. Co. of America v. Globe & Rutgers Fire Ins. Co.*, 263 U.S. 487, 493 (1924). However, in

Wilburn Boat Co. v. Fireman's Fund Ins. Co., 348 U.S. 310, *reh'g denied*, 349 U.S. 907 (1955), the Supreme Court ruled that in the absence of a controlling federal admiralty law principle to guide the resolution of a particular issue, the courts must apply the applicable state law rule. The *Wilburn Boat* decision both surprised and puzzled the admiralty bar.

Wilburn Boat was the typical "hard case" that makes bad law; it involved an insurance policy on a small houseboat used for commercial carriage of passengers on Lake Texoma, an inland lake between Oklahoma and Texas. The original owners of the boat, the insured parties under the policy, had conveyed the boat and policy to a corporation in which they were the sole stockholders, and the boat was subsequently mortgaged. The insurance policy issued by the defendant insurance company provided that without the consent of the underwriter, the boat could not be sold, transferred, assigned, or pledged or used for anything other than private pleasure purposes.

After the boat was destroyed by fire, the corporate owner brought suit on the policy to recover for the loss. The insurance company denied liability, alleging breach of the warranty involving the transfer, pledge, and use of the boat. In response, the boat owner contended that under Texas law the policy provision against pledging was invalid, and the claimed policy breaches were immaterial unless they contributed to the loss. The district court and court of appeals denied recovery, holding that federal admiralty law—not state law—applied, and the established rule required literal fulfillment of every policy warranty. The Supreme Court reversed on the grounds that no federal admiralty rule existed to deal with the consequences of warranty breaches in marine insurance policies, and that the void should be filled by applying state law.

PROBLEM 2-8

Medtech, Inc. is exporting medical equipment to its Russian subsidiary company. Medtech procures an "all risks" cargo insurance policy. At the time the premium is paid, ABC is aware of unrest in the port of destination (St. Petersburg), but this knowledge was not disclosed to the insurer, American Northern Insurance Co. (ANI). When the cargo arrived, it was confiscated by the port authorities on a pretext and sold. ANI has since discovered Medtech's non-disclosure. Should ANI refuse to cover the loss and, if so, on what grounds? What law applies to this controversy? Even if Medtech was in good faith, does an "all risks" policy cover this type of loss?

II.   The International Sales Contract and International Trade Law Considerations

In addition to the private law aspects that must be dealt with in an international sales transaction, there are public law questions. Although these complex issues merit detailed treatment in a separate course, we briefly cover the salient points here. For detailed explanations, *see* Mitsuo Matsushita, Thomas J. Schoenbaum, &

Petros C. Mavroidis, *The World Trade Organization: Law, Practice and Policy* (Oxford 2003).

An international sale of goods is both an export from the country of the seller and an import into the country of the buyer. Thus, in the country of the seller applicable laws concerning exports are relevant and must be observed. Most countries encourage exports since they improve their international balance of payments, create jobs, and cause an inflow of foreign exchange. Accordingly, in most cases, export regulations are not a concern. However, if politically sensitive products, such as goods that can be used for military purposes or advanced technology, are the subject of the transaction, export controls can come into play. Moreover, some countries, most notably the United States, have additional laws that concern exports. Political and foreign policy sanctions may preclude exports to certain countries. The United States also enforces antiboycott laws and regulations against foreign corrupt practices and economic espionage.

For the importer in an international sales transaction, there are very different considerations. The importer must deal with the customs laws and regulations of the importing country and normally a tax — a tariff — must be paid. In the case of a few countries, there may be currency controls that govern the extent to which local currency can be used as payment. These will not be treated here since, fortunately, they are of minimal importance today.

A tariff is a border tax levied on imported goods. Typically, it is paid by the importer, normally the buyer in an international sale of goods transaction. There are three basic kinds of tariffs: (1) ad valorem, (2) specific, and (3) mixed. An ad valorem tariff is a tax that is expressed as a percentage of the value of an imported item. A specific tariff is a flat tax per imported item. A mixed tariff combines aspects of both of these. A common mixed tariff is a tariff-quota, a tax that sets one, usually lower, charge on the first x number of units imported and a much higher charge on units imported above x. A tariff inhibits imports by making them more expensive for the importer who must typically pass on some of the cost to its consumers in addition to raising money for the importing country's government.

Another kind of import regulation that may be important in certain cases is a quota or quantitative restriction. A quota is a numerical limit on the number of units of a category of product that can be imported. A quota is more effective than a tariff because it completely eliminates the products in excess of the number specified. The use of a tariff, however, results in revenue for the importing nation whereas a quota does not.

There are other customs problems that the importer must deal with in certain cases. There may be onerous customs procedures, charges, and formalities. There may be testing and certification procedures to assure that products comply with national standards and quality controls. There may be regulations concerning the safety and health of products and their effect on the environment.

Fortunately, most of these issues are addressed and harmonized by international legal norms. Tariffs and customs formalities are regulated by the agreements administered by the World Trade Organization, and these must be observed by all 146 WTO members. In most cases, the applicable tariff will be "bound" — a ceiling amount will be fixed under Article II of the General Agreement on Tariffs and Trade (GATT). Arbitrary customs procedures and formalities are prohibited by GATT Articles II and XI. Most quotas are illegal under GATT Article XI.

There are three variables in the calculation of a tariff: (1) the category or "classification" of the imported product, (2) the product's value, and (3) the place of origin of the product. All of these matters are regulated by WTO international criteria.

Product standards and health and safety measures that affect imports are also controlled by two WTO agreements — the Technical Barriers to Trade Agreement and the Sanitary and Phytosanitary Measures Agreement.

All of these matters are also addressed by regional free-trade and customs union agreements.

A. Export Trade Matters

PROBLEM 2-9

Apex Co. is a company located in northern Virginia and incorporated in Delaware. Apex has developed an extensive line of software products with business applications ranging from automated systems recovery to computer models to predict severe weather occurrences, which have been adapted to use by the U.S. Coast Guard. Apex Co. is investigating opportunities to sell its products internationally through foreign distributors located in various countries.

A distributor located in a Middle Eastern country says that to market in that country Apex will have to provide assurances that it does not presently do business with the government of the state of Israel. Apex, in fact, has never sold its products in Israel and is considering writing a letter to the distributor to explain this.

Certain distributors located in the European Union tell Apex that sales will be easy to make if no restrictions are placed on the possible resale of the software so that the purchasers are not necessarily the ultimate customers for the products.

Advise Apex as to the legal problems that may arise with regard to its export plans.

PROBLEM 2-10

Universal Electronics (UE) is a large diversified U.S. multinational enterprise with interests in financial services and heavy industry. UE has just been approached by the Cuban government and has been offered a multi-billion-dollar contract to sell oil refinery services to Cuba. Concerned about the consequences of accepting such a contract, UE has suggested to the Cuban government that it hire Universal Electronics (Indonesia), Ltd., to perform the contract. UE has no ownership interest in UE (Indonesia) but several of the directors of the board of UE (Indonesia) are also directors of UE. What legal issues are involved?

PROBLEM 2-11

Microtel, a leading U.S. computer manufacturer and software developer, has just hired a senior vice president from its arch rival, Zurich Systems, based in Switzerland. The senior executive has been intimately involved in Zurich's product development and marketing strategies for its bold new operating system for the

European Union. Microtel is elated because it wishes to sell its products in the EU. Should Microtel have any concerns?

For Problems 2-9 through 2-11, consult the following reading.

Lucinda A. Low and William M. McGlone,
Avoiding Problems Under . . . U.S. Antiboycott Laws,
OFAC Sanctions, Export Controls, and the Economic
Espionage Act, **in Negotiating and Structuring**
International Commercial Transactions, p. 193
(Mark R. Sandstrom and David N. Goldsweig, eds. 2d ed. 2003)

U.S. TRADE AND TRANSACTIONAL CONTROLS

Beyond antibribery laws, the United States imposes other aggressive and far-reaching controls on international trade, transactions, and investment. Known popularly as sanctions and export controls, these controls are imposed under a variety of different regulatory regimes, are administered by different government agencies, are based on different policy objectives, target different kinds of activities, and differ in jurisdictional coverage. These rules often overlap with one another, both in terms of persons covered and proscribed activities. Certain transactions may be prohibited by two or more sets of rules; sometimes an activity is permitted by one law, but prohibited under another. In many instances, the lawfulness of a transaction turns on differences in jurisdictional coverage. Some controls apply directly to the activities of foreign persons and companies; others are more limited in their extraterritorial reach. In all cases, however, these rules apply to companies based in the United States and to individuals who are citizens or residents of the United States, wherever they are located. In addition, all of these rules apply to conduct — by any person — that occurs in the United States.

1. PERSON-BASED CONTROLS

Substantive Prohibitions

The bulk of the person-based controls discussed in this section are trade and transactional sanctions that are contained in country-specific regulations administered by the U.S. Treasury Department's Office of Foreign Assets Control (OFAC). The legal authorities for the majority of these controls are the Trading with the Enemy Act (TWEA) and the International Emergency Economic Powers Act (IEEPA). There is a separate set of OFAC regulations for each targeted country or sanctions regime, and each set of regulations contains its own definitions of prohibited activities and persons or property subject to control. OFAC currently administers trade and/or investment embargoes against Cuba, Iran, Libya, Sudan, North Korea, and Burma — and scores of entities and individuals designated for terrorism or narcotics trafficking reasons.

Most of the OFAC regulations restrict U.S. persons and companies from engaging in or participating in transactions involving "property" in which the targeted country, group, or individual has any "interest." These concepts are defined broadly in the regulations to prohibit covered persons from engaging or participating in — directly or indirectly — any transaction involving a targeted country or person, even if the subject matter of the transaction is not of U.S. origin.

Although the substantive prohibitions of the sanctions regimes differ in their details, the following similarities are worth noting:

- The range of prohibited business transactions typically includes import and export, trade, investment, financing, technology transfers, and others, including assisting, participating in, approving, or facilitating any transactions that would be prohibited as to U.S. persons.

- Most sanctions regimes also block the property and any interests in property of the sanctioned country. These blocking orders, or asset freezes, apply to any blocked property that comes within the jurisdiction of the United States or the possession or control of a U.S. person. In this sense, they are a hybrid of person- and property-based controls and can create issues for foreign entities and persons that are not otherwise covered by the person-based controls. For example, payments through an overseas branch of a U.S. bank by a noncovered foreign entity for Libyan goods can become subject to a blocking order, even though the underlying transaction is not otherwise subject to U.S. control.

- All sanctions regimes prohibit "evasion" by persons subject to the controls. The concept of evasion is a broad one. It prohibits indirect as well as direct efforts to engage in prohibited transactions, as well as approval, support, or facilitation of transactions by noncovered persons. In its classic sense, the prohibition against evasion would prevent a covered person from restructuring the terms of a proposed transaction with a targeted country to avoid U.S. jurisdiction, by assigning contract performance to a noncovered foreign affiliate or individual, for example.

- Each regime targets a particular government, and entities that are deemed to be instrumentalities of that government are called "Specially Designated Nationals" (SDNs). SDNs may or may not be based in the targeted country; often they are found in third countries. Generally speaking, covered persons are barred from dealing with SDNs to the same extent that they are prohibited from dealing with the targeted country government. OFAC maintains a list of hundreds of SDNs.

- In addition to the country-based controls, OFAC regulations similarly prohibit U.S. persons from engaging in nearly all transactions involving numerous specially-designated individuals and entities. These include the following categories of designated persons: foreign terrorists and terrorist organizations, foreign narcotics traffickers and "drug kingpins," proliferators of weapons of mass destruction, certain Yugoslavian war criminals, and persons deemed to threaten international stabilization efforts in the western Balkans.

Apart from the OFAC rules, certain other person-based controls are imposed on the activities of U.S. persons and companies under the Commerce Department's Export Administration Regulations (EAR). These more limited, person-based controls bar U.S. companies and individuals from providing assistance or support to certain foreign entities or projects that are engaged in the development, production, or stockpiling of weapons of mass destruction, including nuclear items, chemical and biological weapons, and their missile delivery systems. The EAR also prohibits U.S. persons from providing technical assistance in support of the overseas development of sensitive encryption products. These restrictions apply to covered persons, wherever they are located, who knowingly participate in or support proscribed activities. Like the OFAC controls mentioned above, these controls apply based on the identity of the person engaging in the transaction, regardless of whether the transaction involves any activity within the United States or any U.S.-origin goods or technology.

JURISDICTIONAL REACH

Notwithstanding the substantive differences of these person-based controls, the following are generally true under each regulatory regime:

- All person-based controls apply to companies organized under U.S. law, including their foreign branches, and U.S. companies that are subsidiaries of foreign companies.
- All person-based controls also apply to U.S. citizens and residents, even if they are living abroad and working for a foreign entity (with minor exceptions for U.S. citizens residing abroad in the case of the Iran sanctions). For example, a U.S. director (i.e., a citizen or resident of the United States) of a foreign entity not subject to the person-based controls would be individually barred from voting to approve any transaction between the entity and a targeted country.
- Two of the OFAC sanctions programs — those based on TWEA (North Korea and Cuba) — include person-based controls that apply to foreign entities that are "owned or controlled" by a U.S. company or individual (e.g., foreign subsidiaries). Although the regulations do not define the factors that determine ownership or control, OFAC takes the position that any entity that is wholly or majority-owned by a U.S. person is covered. In addition, foreign entities that are effectively controlled by U.S. companies also are caught; although not defined, "control" can arise where a U.S. company has the authority to control the management or board of a foreign company or if it has exclusive managerial control over the foreign entity.
- Even where a foreign subsidiary is not directly covered, its parent company can be held liable under the person-based controls for actions taken by the subsidiary, for example if it authorized the subsidiary to enter into a contract or restructured its activities to evade the sanctions. All of the person-based controls include explicit prohibitions against evasion, and all are construed to bar U.S. persons from *approving or facilitating* any transaction that would be prohibited as to U.S. persons. The parent company, to be liable for such facilitation, would either have to be a U.S. company or a foreign company acting within U.S. territory in relation to the prohibited activity. These broad approval and facilitation prohibitions effectively expand the jurisdictional reach of the person-based controls by barring any person in the United States (even foreign citizens and companies) from taking any action in support of an otherwise noncovered, third-country transaction with a targeted country.

- Where a country is subject to a multilateral sanctions regime, foreign subsidiaries that may not be subject to U.S. law may be subject to a parallel
  foreign law.

Any U.S. company would, of course, be subject to these person-based restrictions under the EAR. In addition, any U.S. citizen or resident is covered, even if he
or she is living abroad and working for a foreign company. While a foreign entity
(and its foreign branches and subsidiaries) would not be covered, all of its
U.S. personnel would be. Moreover, consistent with the person-based controls
discussed above, U.S. persons are barred from facilitating, approving, or supporting activities by foreign entities that are prohibited as to U.S. persons, and foreign
persons are subject to these restrictions if they are acting within the United States.

Foreign entities and individuals also may be subject to other foreign export
control laws or blocking orders that can impose additional or conflicting obligations on their business activities. These other rules are described briefly below.

2. PROPERTY-BASED CONTROLS

Apart from the person-based controls discussed above, several U.S. laws
regulate trade transactions that involve U.S.-origin goods or technology without
regard to the nationality of the person engaging in the transaction. Although some
of these restrictions appear in OFAC sanctions programs, they are housed principally in U.S. export and reexport controls laws. The more comprehensive of these
export control laws is the Commerce Department's Export Administration
Regulations (EAR), which apply to shipments of nonmilitary and so-called
"dual-use" goods and technology. Separately, the Arms Export Control Act, as
implemented by the State Department's International Traffic in Arms
Regulations (ITAR), controls the export (and import) of U.S.-origin defense articles, information, and services. And finally, OFAC's sanctions programs often
include property-based export and reexport controls, as well as blocking orders,
that apply to property subject to U.S. jurisdiction.

Substantive Prohibitions

Consumer products are generally subject to the EAR. At the other end of the
spectrum, military aircraft, satellites, and items specifically designed for military
use — as well as related parts, components, and technology — are subject to ITAR
control. This assumes, of course, that the items being shipped are subject to U.S.
jurisdiction.

3. EXPORT ADMINISTRATION REGULATIONS

The Export Administration Act authorizes the President to control exports "*of
any item subject to the jurisdiction of the United States* or exported by any person subject
to the jurisdiction of the United States." With the exception of certain person-
based nonproliferation and encryption controls the Commerce Department generally relies on the first leg of this statutory authority by controlling items (goods
and technology) that are subject to U.S. jurisdiction. An item is deemed to be
subject to EAR jurisdiction if it has been produced in the United States or has

entered the customs territory of the United States. In addition, as explained below, certain foreign-produced commodities that incorporate U.S. origin parts or components or are the "direct products" of U.S. origin technology may be subject to EAR control. Because the EAR generally exercises control based on the origin of the item rather than the identity or nationality of the exporter, these property-based controls apply to exports and reexports by any person or entity, domestic or foreign, of items subject to U.S. jurisdiction.

Whether or not a particular export or reexport transaction is subject to a prohibition or licensing requirement depends on the country of destination, the sophistication of the items to be shipped, the identity of the end-user, and the intended end-use of the items. Currently, the EAR imposes a total export and reexport embargo on shipments of U.S. goods and technology to Cuba, Libya, and North Korea (except for EAR99 items). In addition, OFAC maintains export and reexport embargoes with respect to Iran and Sudan. The EAR also imposes documentation and record-keeping requirements.

For EAR-controlled items, the Commerce Control List (CCL) describes the technical parameters of each controlled item, the reason for the control, the countries to which the export is controlled, and the circumstances under which the item may be exported. Items that fall under EAR99 of the CCL typically may be exported to most destinations without an export license. Exceptions to this general rule, however, arise for more sophisticated items (including state-of-the-art manufacturing equipment and technology) and shipments to restricted countries (the six embargoed countries listed above, and others depending on the item in question), entities, organizations, or individuals of concern, or proscribed proliferation activities.

The EAR also prohibits shipments — by any person — of U.S. origin items if there is knowledge or reason to know that a violation has occurred or will occur. This means that no person or entity (even foreign companies and their foreign personnel) may ship U.S. origin products to any country if it has knowledge that the products are ultimately bound for an embargoed destination in violation of U.S. export or reexport controls. A shipment of products to a distributor in Egypt, for example, with the requisite level of knowledge that they will be resold to Libya could give rise to a violation of the EAR. Under the EAR, the knowledge or reason-to-know threshold can be met if there are "red flags" or suspicious circumstances that would put a reasonably prudent person on notice that a violation is likely to occur.

Apart from the controls described above, the EAR prohibits all exports and reexports to individuals and entities listed on the Denied Persons List. In addition, the EAR imposes restrictions on shipments to projects of proliferation concern, i.e., entities that are known to be developing weapons of mass destruction such as nuclear, chemical, and biological weapons, and their missile delivery systems. These so-called "nonproliferation" controls prohibit shipments of *any* items to entities or projects that have been listed in the EAR, or are otherwise "known" to the exporter, as being engaged in prohibited proliferation activities.

Jurisdictional Reach. In general terms, these export and reexport control laws consist primarily of property-based controls. This means that the principal test for determining whether or not they apply depends on whether the shipment in question involves goods or technology that originated in the United States. The property-based controls apply to exports of goods or technology from the United

States to any country (with certain exceptions for Canada) and to reexports of U.S. origin items from one foreign country to another. The term "export" is defined broadly to include domestic transfers of technology to foreign nationals, as well as physical exports from the United States. As noted above, whether or not a given export or reexport is prohibited depends on a variety of factors, including the nature of the item, the country of destination, the identity of the end-user, and the proposed end-use.

Many of these export controls, particularly those housed in the EAR, overlap with the sanctions programs described above. For example, the EAR also prohibits exports and reexports of U.S. goods and technology to most of the countries subject to OFAC sanctions. In this sense, the EAR adds a property-based overlay to the person-based OFAC sanctions. As a result, a transaction involving U.S. origin items may be subject to EAR control, even if the same transaction escapes OFAC jurisdiction. For example, an export by an independent foreign company of U.S.-manufactured product to Cuba will be prohibited under the EAR, even though the company making the shipment is not subject to the U.S. person controls (by virtue of the fact that it is not owned or controlled by a U.S. person).

As noted above, export jurisdiction and reexport jurisdiction are based principally on the origin of the product or technology involved, and not on the nationality of — or territorial links to — the persons engaging in the transaction.

Exports of Goods or Technology from the United States.   The property-based controls apply to any shipment or transfer from the United States to any other country. Goods or technology are deemed to be of "U.S. origin" if they were either produced in the United States or have entered any territories, dependencies, or possessions of the United States. This means that foreign-produced goods or technology that enter or transit the customs territory of the United States are, for export control purposes, treated the same as goods or technology that were produced in the United States. For example, foreign-manufactured products that have been imported into the United States become subject to U.S. jurisdiction and, therefore, may be shipped from the United States only in accordance with the applicable U.S. export and reexport control laws.

Reexports of U.S.-Origin Goods or Technology.   In addition to restricting direct exports from the United States, U.S. law imposes aggressive and far-reaching controls on reexports of goods and technology that originated in the United States. Under these rules, no person may reexport goods or technology received from the United States to any third country unless specifically authorized to do so by the relevant U.S. regulatory authority. Similarly, a U.S. exporter may not transfer goods or technology from the United States if it knows that the items will be reexported directly or indirectly, in whole or in part, to an unauthorized destination under U.S. law.

All companies and individuals around the world, U.S. or foreign, are subject to these reexport rules to the extent they deal in goods or technology subject to the rules. This means that no person in any country may ship U.S.-origin goods or technology to any other country unless the U.S. government authorizes such shipment, either under the terms of the regulations or specific licensing approval. Thus, to the extent a foreign entity is dealing in U.S.-origin items, any shipment of those items from any other country is treated the same as a direct export from the United States. In their simplest form, these reexport rules would bar a shipment from France to Libya, for example, of products that have been manufactured in and originally exported from the United States. As explained in the following paragraphs, aggressive definitions of "U.S. origin" extend these reexport controls to a far more complex and far-reaching set of circumstances as well.

ANTIBOYCOTT LAWS

The United States maintains two "antiboycott laws" designed to prevent U.S. companies from supporting or participating in boycotts of countries friendly to the United States. While both laws are drafted without reference to any particular boycott, their principal target is the Arab League's long-standing economic boycott of Israel. Both laws impose far-reaching restrictions on boycott-related actions, agreements, and even the furnishing of information, and often apply directly to the activities of foreign affiliates of U.S. companies. Penalties for violations can include civil and criminal fines, imprisonment, and the loss of tax credits or export privileges.

1. COMMERCE DEPARTMENT'S ANTIBOYCOTT LAW

The more sweeping of the two U.S. antiboycott laws is maintained by the U.S. Department of Commerce in its Export Administration Regulations. The substantive prohibitions and the reporting requirements of the Commerce Department's antiboycott law apply if the person taking the action in question is a "U.S. person" *and* the activity is an activity in the "interstate or foreign commerce of the United States."

Jurisdictional Coverage

The terms "U.S. person" and "interstate or foreign commerce of the United States" are defined broadly and reflect the extraterritorial reach of other U.S. laws discussed above. The term "U.S. person" includes "controlled-in-fact" foreign affiliates of U.S. corporations. The regulations define "control in fact" as "the authority or ability of a domestic concern to establish the general policies or to control day-to-day operations of its foreign subsidiary, partnership affiliate, branch, office or other permanent foreign establishment." A foreign affiliate of a U.S. company is presumed to be controlled in fact when it meets one or more of the following conditions:

- The domestic concern owns or controls (either indirectly or directly) over 50 percent of the outstanding voting securities of the foreign subsidiary or affiliate.
- The domestic concern owns or controls (whether directly or indirectly) 25 percent or more of the voting securities of the foreign subsidiary or affiliate, if no other person owns or controls (whether directly or indirectly) an equal or larger percentage.
- The domestic concern operates the foreign subsidiary or affiliate under an exclusive management contract.
- A majority of the members of the board of directors of the foreign subsidiary or affiliate also are members of the comparable governing body of the domestic concern.

- The domestic concern has authority to appoint the majority of the members of the board of directors of the foreign subsidiary or affiliate.
- The domestic concern has authority to appoint the chief operating officer of the foreign subsidiary or affiliate.

Under the Commerce Department's regulations, the presence of one or more of these factors creates a rebuttable presumption that the foreign entity is controlled in fact.

The term "interstate or foreign commerce of the United States" includes activities by or with persons physically present in the United States, including imports and exports, the provision of services, and even the provision of information. Any transaction between a controlled-in fact foreign entity and a person located in the United States is an activity in U.S. commerce. Similarly, transactions between controlled-in-fact foreign entities and persons not physically located in the United States may also constitute activities in U.S. commerce. When such a transaction involves goods or services that were originally obtained from the United States, the transaction may be considered an activity in U.S. commerce.

Prohibitions

The Commerce antiboycott law prohibits all of the following actions:

- refusing to do business with Israel, Israeli companies, or Israelis; in Israel, or with "blacklisted" companies;
- furnishing boycott-related information — including information about one's business relationships with Israel, Israeli companies, Israelis, or "blacklisted" companies;
- discriminating against any U.S. person on the basis of race, religion, sex, or national origin; and
- evasion.

Reporting Requirements

U.S. companies and their controlled-in-fact foreign affiliates must report the receipt of requests to take any action that has the effect of furthering or supporting the boycott. Boycott-related requests — whether oral or written — are generally reportable regardless of whether the requested action is prohibited or permitted and regardless of whether the recipient complies with the request.

Enforcement and Penalties

The Commerce Department's Office of Antiboycott Compliance (OAC) is very aggressive in its enforcement actions and investigations, most of which surface in the U.S. press. Violations are subject to the full range of civil and criminal penalties available under the Export Administration Regulations, including fines, imprisonment, and the denial of export privileges. The maximum civil fine is US$10,000 *per violation*. If a single letter were to contain 10 pieces of prohibited information, the U.S. person could be charged with 10 violations, amounting to US$100,000 in fines.

2. TREASURY DEPARTMENT'S ANTIBOYCOTT LAW

Section 999 of the Internal Revenue Code requires U.S. taxpayers to report their operations in boycotting countries and penalizes taxpayers who "participate in or cooperate with" an unsanctioned foreign boycott by denying them certain tax benefits.

IMPERMISSIBLE AGREEMENTS

The following types of agreements are impermissible and subject to penalties under section 999:

- agreements to refuse to do business directly or indirectly within a country or with a country's government, companies, or nationals;
- agreements to refuse to do business with U.S. persons who do business in a country or with its government, companies, or nationals;
- agreements to refuse to do business with companies owned or managed by individuals of a particular race, religion, or nationality;
- agreements to refrain from employing persons of a particular race, religion, or nationality; and
- agreements to refuse to ship or insure products on carriers owned or operated by persons who do not participate in or cooperate with the boycott.

ECONOMIC ESPIONAGE ACT

The Economic Espionage Act of 1996 (EEA) was enacted in response to the growing thefts of trade secrets from U.S. companies by foreign governments and competitors, as well as by U.S. companies and individuals. Industrial espionage, and the need for stronger federal criminal prohibitions to address it, were highlighted in 1993 by the well-publicized case of Jose Ignacio Lopez, a General Motors executive who defected to Volkswagen with boxes of confidential GM documents.

The EEA addresses the problem of industrial espionage by making it a federal crime to copy or otherwise steal trade secrets with the intent or knowledge that the misappropriation will (1) benefit a foreign government, foreign instrumentality, or foreign agent; or (2) injure the owner of the trade secret and provide an economic benefit to another person. The Act imposes significant penalties in the form of fines, imprisonment, and criminal forfeiture of property or proceeds derived from or used in the violation.

The jurisdictional reach of the Act is broad. It applies to U.S. and foreign persons, and to conduct within and in some instances outside the United States. Thus, although the Act provides some protection to U.S. companies and its subsidiaries from theft of trade secrets by U.S. and foreign competitors and governments, by its terms it could also be used against that company by any other company that suspects that it has improperly obtained "trade secrets."

NOTES

1. One of the most important export trade law regimes governing IBTs that we do not cover in this section is the Foreign Corrupt Practices Act (FCPA), 15

U.S.C. §78 *et seq.* Among its other requirements, the FCPA prohibits U.S. companies from paying bribes to foreign government officials to obtain or retain business or to secure an improper advantage. The FCPA should be a major concern to any U.S. company or person who does international business and applies in a wide variety of contexts, including to the simplest of IBTs, the international sale of goods. For example, suppose that a U.S. seller pays a bribe to a foreign government official and is then rewarded with a contract under which the foreign government purchases goods from the seller. This type of transaction, even though both the demand and the payment may occur entirely outside the United States, is subject to regulation under the FCPA and the U.S. seller and its officers might be subject to criminal and civil liability. Because of its importance, the FCPA merits extended coverage, which we have postponed to a later chapter. While FCPA issues can arise in an international sale, these issues usually arise in the foreign direct investment context. We return to an extended treatment of the FCPA in Chapter 6 on foreign investment.

2. One of the most important tasks for the seller-exporter in the United States is to determine whether the transaction is subject to the EAR and whether the items being exported are subject to the Commerce Control List (CCL) or the Export Control Classification Number (ECCN). If the items are classified under the CCL or the ECCN, the exporter may be required to submit a license application and obtain an export license for the products before they can be lawfully exported. The burden is upon the exporter to see that it fully complies with the EAR. A detailed list of instructions is contained in 15 C.F.R. Part 730.

3. After the 9/11 attacks on the United States, broad antiterrorist legislation was enacted by the U.S. Congress, including the USA Patriot Act, Pub. L. No. 107-56, 115 Stat. 272 (2001). Title III of this act, which deals with money laundering, requires the reporting of certain types of international payments.

B.   Import Trade Matters

PROBLEM 2-12

Acme Tool Co. is a Chicago-based company incorporated in Illinois in the business of manufacturing and selling a complete line of hand tools for home use. Acme markets its products through various hardware stores in the midwestern United States. Because of high demand, Acme finds it necessary from time to time to purchase hand tools from other suppliers to fill its orders. At present, Acme needs to purchase 1,000 screwdrivers and 1,000 electric power drills to fill pending orders from its U.S. customers.

Acme has the option of purchasing from suppliers in Peru, Israel, Belgium Mexico, and the United States. The prices quoted are as follows (all FOB):

For screwdrivers:

Peru	$110
Israel	$115
Belgium	$120
Mexico	$118
United States	$120

For power drills:

Peru	$450
Israel	$550
Belgium	$400
Mexico	$500
United States	$560

Acme must handle all aspects of the importation of the tools if it chooses to purchase them outside the United States. Where is the best source of the tools in question? What other information might you need?

PROBLEM 2-13

Everlast Tools, Inc., an Indiana company, is the importer of record of a large shipment of hand tools made in China. The tools arrive in large crates with the notation "Made in China," but the tools themselves are unmarked. After clearing the goods with Customs, Everlast unpacks the crates and sends one shipment of tools to several specialty tool manufacturers, which break down, reshape, and rebuild the tools as specialty tools for sale to selected industrial consumers. When Everlast ships the tools to the manufacturers, the tools are shipped in containers marked "hand tools" and Everlast then separately sends an invoice marked "product of China" to each of the manufacturers. The manufacturers sell the reconfigured tools in packages marked "Proudly Made in the United States."

Everlast also incorporates some of the imported tools into a toolbox kit that contains other commonly used hand tools for everyday use. The toolbox is sold as a single unit and marked "Everlast Home Toolbox. The Everlast Tool Co., Indiana, USA." The Chinese tools meet all industry standards and are the equal, if not superior, of Everlast tools made in its Indiana plant. Have any laws been violated?

PROBLEM 2-14

Nihon Kaisha (NK) is a Japanese company whose business is the manufacture of automobiles. NK has decided to set up a manufacturing facility in Mexico that will turn out substantial numbers of its best-selling line of autos. NK intends to import auto parts from Japan into Mexico (which has a low tariff rate for auto parts), assemble the automobiles in Mexico, and then take advantage of NAFTA by exporting the finished cars from Mexico into the United States and Canada duty free. Is this possible? If so, how?

NK also plans to establish a factory in France, import parts, and assemble the cars in France in order to sell its cars in the 25 countries that are members of the EU. Is this a good plan? What is the difference between the plan for NAFTA and the plan for the EU?

PROBLEM 2-15

National Semiconductor of Taiwan (NST) is considering Mexico or Peru as a location for its new factory, which will build laptop computers for export to the

United States. NST will supply the plasma display ($200), the microprocessor ($250), and the motherboard ($150) to the factory, but the keyboard ($25), other electronic components ($200), and the costs of labor, production, and assembly ($175) will be supplied by its factory abroad. Assume that NST's products will be subject to rules of origin, including tests for regional value content. Should NST locate the factory in Mexico or Peru? Assume that the duty on laptop computers is 12 percent ad valorem.

For Problems 2-12 through 2-15, consult the reading below and the accompanying notes.

Mark R. Sandstrom, Julia M. McCalmon, and Teresa M. Goody, *The Impact of Trade and Customs Laws upon International Commercial Transactions*, in Negotiating and Structuring International Commercial Transactions, p. 135
(Mark R. Sandstrom and David N. Goldsweig, eds. 2003)

TARIFFS

Tariffs are clearly significant to international commercial transactions given that they represent direct costs imposed upon imports of raw materials, components, or finished products as they enter the destined foreign market. Specifically, where the parties to a transaction have a choice of options regarding the sourcing of components and/or the place of manufacture of finished products, duty implications of the various alternatives should be considered to efficiently structure production processes by minimizing the cost of duties. As more fully discussed below, in order to assess a tariff, three determinations must be made: the classification of the article under the Harmonized Tariff Schedule, the value of the article, and the country of origin of the article.

CLASSIFICATIONS

All major trading countries maintain tariff schedules that establish duty rates for imported products according to specifically defined tariff classifications. These tariff schedules conform to the International Convention on the Harmonized Commodity Description and Coding System of 1988 ("Convention"). The Convention was drafted under the auspices of the World Customs Organization ("WCO"), formerly known as the Customs Cooperation Council, based in Brussels, Belgium. The Convention is essentially a system of tariff schedules broken down into 97 Chapters covering all goods and products traded among member countries. Within the Convention, and in the corresponding tariff schedules of the WCO member countries, Chapters are designated on a two-digit basis. Within each Chapter, product classifications are subdivided into four-digit "subheadings". The convention, as well as each WCO member country's tariff schedules, are identical down to the subheadings at the six-digit level.

The tariff schedules in effect in the United States are the Harmonized Tariff Schedules of the United States ("HTSUS"). A copy of representative excerpt from the HTSUS is included on pages [146-147]. This excerpt, which covers certain hand tools, is representative of the organization of the HTSUS, and its general characteristics are mirrored in the tariff schedules of other trading countries. Hand tools are classified under heading 8205 of the HTSUS, which is included in Chapter 82 of the tariff schedules. The classification descriptions in the specific six-digit subheadings (e.g. 8205.40) — screwdrivers; 8205.51 — household tools descriptions found in the tariff schedules of all other WCO countries. Duties are assessed at the eight-digit level (e.g., 8205.20.30 Hammers with heads over 1.5 kg. — General duty rate — 6.2%; 8205.51.45 — household tools of copper — General duty rate — Free). Classifications at the eight-digit levels and corresponding duty levels vary from country to country. In certain cases, the HTSUS contains 10-digit classifications (e.g., 8205.51.3030 — iron or steel kitchen and table implements). These subheadings are subcategories that have been broken out for statistical purposes. Import statistics are generated and published on the basis of 10-digit subheadings, but the subheadings at this level have no impact on the determination of duty rates.

Duty rates are generally imposed on an ad valorem basis, i.e., a percentage of the appraised value of the imported article. The duty rates in the first, "General" column are known as Normal Trade Relations ("NTR") rates, which are the normal rate of duty applied to goods from most developed countries. As previously mentioned, NTR rates were formerly known as Most-Favored-Nation ("MFN") rates. The duty rates in the second, "Special" column are preferential duty rates established pursuant to various preferential duty programs and free trade agreements for eligible articles imported from eligible countries. The duty rates in the third column, "Column 2," are the old Smoot-Hawley tariffs established by Congress in 1932. The NTR rates represent reductions in the Smoot-Hawley tariffs which have been negotiated under the many aforementioned rounds of multilateral trade negotiations in GATT/WTO. The column 2 rates apply only to articles imported from Cuba, Laos, and North Korea. Similarly, most developed countries maintain both standard NTR as well as preferential duty rates under tariff schedules, which are akin to the United States' schedule.

Valuation

Specific duty rates are assigned to each tariff schedule classification. In most cases, if the classification is not duty free, the duty rate will be based upon an ad valorem, percentage figure. Thus, in order to determine the amount of the duty, the appraised value of the imported product must be determined. Most WTO and WCO members have adopted the Agreement on Implementation of Article VII of the General Agreement on Tariffs and Trade 1994 negotiated as part of the Uruguay Round of Multilateral Trade Negotiations, the so-called WTO Valuation Code. The Code balances the needs of importing countries and exporters by simplifying valuation procedures, requiring customs services to observe minimum fairness and transparency standards, and eliminating many of the protectionist features of foreign customs valuation systems.

The Code, upon which the valuation regulations of the United States and other WTO member countries is based, contains a hierarchy of five valuation methodologies: transaction value, transaction value of identical merchandise, transaction value of similar merchandise, deductive value, and computed value. Of these, transaction value is the preferred and most utilized basis for appraising the value of imported merchandise. It is defined as the price actually paid or

Harmonized Tariff Schedule of the United States (2002)*

Heading/ Subheading	Stat. Suffix	Article Description	Unit of Quantity	Rates of Duty		2
				1		
				General	Special	
8205		Handtools (including glass cutters) not elsewhere specified or included; blow torches and similar self-contained torches; vises, clamps and the like, other than accessories for and parts of machine tools; anvils; portable forges; hand- or pedal-operated grinding wheels with frameworks; base parts thereof:				
8205.10.00	00	Drilling, threading or tapping tools, and parts thereof	X	6.2%	Free (A, CA, E, IL, J, MX) 3.1% (JO)	45%
8205.20		Hammers and sledge hammers, and parts thereof:				
8205.20.30	00	With heads not over 1.5 kg each	doz	6.2%	Free (A, CA, E, IL, J, MX) 3.1% (JO)	45%
8205.20.60	00	With heads over 1.5 kg each	doz	Free		20%
8205.30		Planes, chisels, gouges and similar cutting tools for working wood, and parts thereof:				
8205.30.30	00	With cutting part containing by weight over 0.2 percent of chromium, molybdenum, or tungsten or over 0.1 percent of vanadium	X	5.7%	Free (A, CA, E, IL, J, MX) 2.8% (JO)	60%
8205.30.60	00	Other (including parts)	X	5%	Free (A, CA, E, IL, J, MX)	45%
8205.40.00	00	Screwdrivers, and parts thereof	X	6.2%	Free (A, CA, E, IL, J, MX) 3.1% (J)	45%

(continued)

Heading/ Subheading	Stat. Suffix	Article Description	Unit of Quantity	Rates of Duty		
				1		2
				General	Special	
8205.51		Other handtools (including glass cutters) and parts thereof: Household tools, and parts thereof: Of iron or steel:				
8205.51.15	00	Carving and butcher steels, with or without handles	No	Free		8¢ each +45%
8205.51.30		Other (including parts)	No	3.7%	Free (A, CA, E, IL, J, MX)	40%
	30	Kitchen and table implements	X			
	60	Other (including parts)	X			
8205.51.45	00	Of copper	X	Free		40%
8205.51.60	00	Of aluminum	Kg	2.2¢/kg +5%	Free (A, CA, E, IL, J, MX) 1.1¢/kg + 2.5% (JO)	19¢/kg +40%
8205.51.75	00	Other	X	3.7%	Free (A, CA, E, IL, J, MX)	40%
8205.59		Other:				
8205.59.10	00	Pipe tools, and parts thereof	X	7.2%	Free (A, CA, E, IL, J, MX) 3.6% (JO)	45%
8205.59.20	00	Power-actuated handtools, and parts thereof:	X	27.5%	Free (A, CA, E, IL, J, MX)	45%
8205.59.30	00	Crowbars, track tools and wedges, and Parts thereof	kg	Free		3¢/kg

* In the Special column there are the following preferences: A = GSP beneficiaries; A = Censala; E = Caribbean Basin Economic Recovery Act beneficiaries; IL = Israel; J = Andean Trade Preferences Act beneficiaries; MX = Mexico; JO = Jordan. New preference programs will add African Growth and Opportunity Act beneficiaries; Singapore; and Chile. More will certainly follow.

payable for the merchandise when sold for export to the country of importation. Transaction value is usually equivalent to the invoice price of the goods at the time of exportation from the country in which the goods are produced. Cargo, insurance, and freight ("CIF") costs are not included in the appraised value. Additions are made for certain costs if not included in the invoice price, including the cost of packing, selling commissions, assists (materials, parts, tools, design work, etc. provided to the foreign seller by the buyer free of charge or at reduced cost), certain royalties and proceeds to the seller from subsequent sales in the country of importation.

In certain cases transaction value cannot be used, including where the exporter and importer are related parties and the relationship influences the price of the goods, or where there is no sale at the time of export, such as in a consignment transaction. Where transaction value cannot be used as a method of appraisement, valuation is made on the basis, in order of preference, of deductive value or computed value. Deductive value is determined by starting with the resale price of the goods to unrelated customers by the importer in the country of importation, and backing out commissions or profits, general expenses, all CIF costs, and the value of any further processing incurred in the country of importation to approximate the price of the goods at the port of exportation. Computed value is determined by adding the costs of materials, fabrication, general expenses, and profits incurred in producing the product in the country of exportation.

COUNTRY OF ORIGIN FOR MARKING

There are other requirements relating to the importation of goods which are common in many countries, one of which being the ability to identify the country of origin of products. For example, in the United States, each imported article must be marked in a conspicuous place, as legibly, indelibly, and permanently as the nature of the article permits, to indicate to the "ultimate purchaser" the name of the foreign country in which the article was manufactured or produced. The "ultimate purchaser" is defined as the last person in the United States who will receive the article in the form in which it is imported. If the imported good is not altered after importation, the foreign country of origin marking must remain on the good until it reaches the ultimate purchaser. However, if an imported good, such as a component or part, is substantially transformed by a manufacturer into a new product with a new name, character, or use different from the imported good, then the manufacturer is deemed to be the ultimate purchaser. In such a case, the manufactured product need no longer be marked with the foreign country of origin of the imported component or part when shipped from the manufacturer's facility.

In the case of goods traded among the United States, Canada, and Mexico, the member countries of the NAFTA, special rules apply to determine the country of origin for marking purposes. In most cases the NAFTA marking rules are based upon an objective test, the so-called tariff shift test. If the manufacturing process changes the tariff classification of the imported good to a different classification specified in the NAFTA marking rule, the country of origin of the manufactured product is deemed to change to that of the country in which the finished good is manufactured. However, it should be stressed that the NAFTA country of origin marking rules are separate and distinct from the NAFTA rules of origin which are used to determine eligibility for NAFTA preferential duty rates.

IMPORT RESTRICTIONS ON SPECIFIC PRODUCTS

Enforcement of customs and duty laws is generally performed by the country's customs authorities. In the United States, that role is played by the United States Customs Service. Depending on the products involved, imports may be subject to additional requirements and restrictions. The regulation of specific products by United States Federal Agencies provides a representative example of some of the restrictions which can apply. Under U.S. laws, imports of food and agricultural products are subject to requirements administered by the Food and Drug Administration, Department of Agriculture, and the Department of Health and Human Services. The Food and Drug Administration and the Department of Health and Human Services also regulate imported drugs, cosmetics and medical devices. Imports of household appliances must comply with energy standards and labeling requirements administered by the Department of Energy and the Federal Trade Commission. Importation of electronic products are subject to radiation performance standards administered by the Food and Drug Administration and to radio emission standards of the Federal Communications Commission. Toxic substance imports are regulated by the Customs Service and the Environmental Protection Agency. Hazardous substances are regulated by the Food and Drug Administration, the Consumer Products Safety Commission, and the Department of Transportation. Textile, wool, and fur products are subject to strict labeling requirements.

RULES OF ORIGIN IN GENERAL

The growing number of bilateral and multilateral preferential trade agreements being negotiated by developed and developing countries alike are becoming an increasingly important factor influencing international trade and investment determinations of companies manufacturing goods for sale in international markets. Whether or not particular imported products will benefit from these preferential trade agreements will depend primarily upon the application of rules of origin to such products and the processes by which they are manufactured. Rules of origin are also key determinants of the application of non-preferential trading measures, such as antidumping and countervailing duties, quantitative restrictions (quotas), buy-national government procurement requirements, and country of origin marking requirements, all of which significantly impact the international trade of goods.

In the desire to optimize and rationalize the production of finished goods, manufacturers are increasingly required to take into consideration preferential duty agreements and programs as they increase the use of multi-country sources of raw materials and components in the production of finished products. Likewise, manufacturing operations are being split up into various processing stages, which are often performed in more than one country. In order to deal with the segmentation and disbursement of these manufacturing processes, rules of origin have become more complex in their language and implementation.

The application of rules of origin can serve as an impediment to trade in many circumstances. On the other hand, such rules of origin are for the most part transparent, well-defined, and predictable in their application. Thus, a proper understanding of the applicable rules of origin, can enable companies to plan their investment, production, and distribution strategies so as to minimize the cost of multi-market production and sales operations and, therefore, maximize the profits generated from their international commercial transactions.

Where a product is produced in one country from raw materials and components originating in that country, the designation of the country of origin of that good is easily accomplished. However, where a good is produced from raw materials or intermediate components sourced from more than one country and/ or where the manufacturing processes necessary to complete the finished good are performed in more than one country, the question as to country of origin of the finished good becomes more difficult to answer. To establish the country of origin in such cases, rules of origin apply certain tests which must be satisfied in order to determine the country of origin of the good. The tests applied under rules of origin may be divided into two categories, those which are subjective in nature and those which apply objective criteria subject to little room for interpretation.

SUBJECTIVE TESTS

In the U.S., the primary test used to determine the country of origin of a good involving materials or processing from more than one country is the substantial transformation test. In order for a product to be considered a product of a certain country, it must be substantially transformed in that country. Since there can be only one country of origin for rules of origin purposes, the test refers to the country in which the "last" substantial transformation takes place. Under U.S. law, a product is substantially transformed when it is transformed into a new and different article having a distinctive name, character, or use.

In applying the "name, character, or use" test, the Customs Service and the courts have analyzed each case on the basis of the specific facts presented using a variety of criteria. In addition to the criteria of whether the transformation creates a new name, character, or use, other tests have been applied, such as: the "article of commerce" test, the "essence" test, and the "value added" test. As observed by the court in [*Koru North America v. United States*, 701 F. Supp. 229, 234 n. 9 (CIT 1988)]:

> The plethora of tests results from the cases on substantial transformation being "very product specific and . . . often distinguishable on that basis, rather than by their statutory underpinnings." Courts have not adhered rigidly to a single test because of the "importance of focusing on the facts of each case." . . . Courts find it "difficult to take concepts applicable to products such as textiles and apply them to combinations of liquids or fabrication of steel articles."

Thus, this subjective test of rule of origin is often of little help in providing guidance as to whether the fabrication of an imported article will be considered a substantial transformation of that article.

Other countries apply subjective rules of origin tests which are similar to that applied in the United States. In the European Union, the rules of origin are based primarily upon a determination of the country in which the last substantial

transformation occurred in the case of rules of country of origin marking requirements, government procurement, and the collection of import statistics. However,
in recent years, there has been a general movement toward the use of objective
tests to determine the country of origin of an imported product.

OBJECTIVE TESTS

By objective, it is meant that the country of origin of a particular product can
be determined on the basis of specifically defined or quantitative criteria which can
be applied to a particular fact situation to yield an unambiguous and consistently
repeatable result. Goods traded within free trade areas and customs unions must
be given consistent and predictable tariff treatment by all members of such trading
agreements. Otherwise, significant distortions can occur in trade to and within
such geographic areas to the economic detriment of producers and industries in
one or more participating member countries.

For the U.S., this issue arose in connection with the United States–Canada
Free Trade Agreement ("CFTA"), which entered into effect January 1, 1989. The
CFTA was the first major, all-sector, free trade agreement entered into by the
U.S. The primary rule of origin test adopted under the CFTA was based upon
a change in tariff classification, the so-called tariff-shift test. This tariff-shift rule
of origin test was also utilized, in a much more detailed and complex form
under the NAFTA, which succeeded the CFTA when Mexico was included as a
member of the free trade agreement. The NAFTA entered into effect on January 1,
1994.

Another widely used objective rule of origin test is the so-called local or
regional value (or value-added) test. As discussed in more detail below, a local
value test generally stipulates a minimum percentage of the total value of a product which must be accounted for by the value of materials, labor and other
processing costs originating or performed in one of more of the member countries
in order for that product to qualify as "originating" in a member country of the
free trade agreement.

A final objective test, which is applied more rarely in rules of origin, is a test
that requires certain processing operations to be performed on a raw material or
component to produce the finished good. For instance, a process-based rule of
origin could require that a finished textile article be cut and sewn in a particular
country in order for that country to be deemed the country of origin of the
finished textile article.

FREE TRADE AGREEMENTS AND CUSTOMS UNIONS

The GATT provision permitting the formation of Free Trade Areas ("FTA"s)
and Customs Unions ("CU"s), is an important exception to the Most-Favored
Nation obligation of non-discrimination. Free Trade Areas involve agreements
among member countries to reduce and eliminate duties on goods traded across
national borders within the free trade area, while permitting each member country
to maintain its own, separate system of tariffs on imports from non-member countries. Alternatively, Customs Union agreements involve the elimination of duties
on trade within the customs union as well as the establishment of a common

external tariff on imports from third countries. Consequently, there necessarily has to be more political and economic coordination between countries in a CU, as contrasted to the coordination needed between countries in a FTA. Rules of origin play an important role in commercial transactions with countries which are part of a free trade area or customs union. Rules of origin establish the standard for determining when a good, which is processed in a FTA or CU member country, but is processed from articles imported from a third, non-member country, can enjoy the benefits of preferential duty treatments accorded under the FTA or CU when exported to other member countries. In the case of free trade areas, the rules of origin become more complex, because the external import duty on imports from third countries will vary from one member country to another. Exporters will have an incentive to "shop" for the country with the lowest external duty when attempting to penetrate the FTA market.

The customs laws specific to free trade areas are very complex. Rules of origin play an important role in commercial transactions involving regional trading blocs since they determine the origin of the product and consequently, its treatment. For the purposes of this chapter, the NAFTA rules will be used to elucidate the manner in which rules of origin are applied in such regional trade agreements.

The Free Trade Agreement, NAFTA, has significantly altered and enhanced trade among the U.S., Canada, and Mexico. Moreover, it has also significantly affected trade in goods produced by companies located in third-countries, both outside and within North America. In order to obtain the benefit of NAFTA preferential rates on goods imported into one NAFTA country from another, the good must "originate" in one or more NAFTA member countries. If a good is wholly obtained or produced in Canada, Mexico, or the United States, then it is clearly deemed to originate in that country and is eligible for preferential NAFTA duty treatment when imported into another NAFTA country. However, if a good is produced in a NAFTA country from raw materials or components sourced in non-NAFTA countries, then the eligibility of the finished good will be determined by application of the NAFTA rules or origin. Trade in "originating goods" between the U.S. and Canada is duty free for most products. Tariffs on dutiable items traded between Mexico on the one hand, and the U.S. and Canada on the other, have been considerably reduced since NAFTA was implemented, and will continue to be reduced, in annual stages, to zero for most products by 2003.

The NAFTA rules of origin are classification-specific, in that individual classifications or groups of classifications in the U.S. Harmonized Tariff Schedule ("HTSUS") are assigned separate and distinct rules of origin. Thus, it is not possible to determine the rule of origin applicable to a good to be imported into the customs territory of a NAFTA member country until the tariff classification of the good is established. For purposes of the NAFTA rules of origin, the term "good" refers to the product subject to the rule of origin determination in the country into which it has been imported. The term "material" refers to an intermediate article that is used in the production of the good in question, and includes a part, component, raw material or an ingredient used to produce the good.

The NAFTA rules of origin are based primarily on the two objective tests: the tariff-shift test and the regional value content tests. In rarer cases, primarily with respect to textile products, the NAFTA rules of origin also incorporate tests based upon required manufacturing or processing operations.

TARIFF SHIFT

A tariff shift test generally requires that the processing of a material imported from a non-NAFTA country into a finished good "shift" the tariff classification of the material from a permissible tariff classification to the tariff classification of the finished good corresponding to the pertinent rule of origin. A representative example of the tariff-shift test is the rule of origin applicable to carbon steel seamless standard pipe classified under HTSUS subheading *7304.39.00* This HTSUS subheading covers certain circular tubes, pipes, seamless, of iron or non-alloy steel. The NAFTA rule of origin applicable to this subheading requires: *"A change to subheadings 7304.10 through 7304.39 from any other chapter."* HTSUS subheadings *7304.10* through *7304.39* cover all types of carbon steel seamless pipe. In order to be eligible for NAFTA duty rates, i.e., in order to be deemed an "originating product," the raw material used to produce the seamless pipe must be classified outside of Chapter 73. Chapter 73 covers fabricated articles of iron and steel. Carbon steel seamless pipe is generally produced by the extrusion of a heated billet over a mandrel, or by the rotary piercing of heated round steel bar. Steel billets and steel bars are classified under Chapter 72 of the HTSUS, which covers basic iron and steel mill products. Thus, the process of producing carbon steel welded pipe from a steel billet or bar satisfies the applicable NAFTA rule of origin. It "shifts" the classification of the raw material from Chapter 72, a Chapter outside HTSUS Chapter 73, to the specified subheadings for seamless pipe, consistent with the requirement of the rule of origin corresponding to that subheading. Accordingly, any carbon steel seamless pipe produced from a billet or bar in any NAFTA member country would, by the nature of the manufacturing process, be eligible for NAFTA duty rates upon importation into any of the other NAFTA countries. The seamless pipe would be eligible for NAFTA preferential duty rates even if the steel billet or bar were sourced from a non-NAFTA member country.

For a finished good to be considered eligible for NAFTA, the NAFTA rules of origin require that all non-originating materials satisfy the tariff-shift requirement. Thus, if any non-originating material does not satisfy the tariff shift requirement, the finished good would not meet the test and the good would not qualify for NAFTA duty treatment. However, an exception is made in the case of non-originating materials with insignificant value. The de minimis provision of the NAFTA rules of origin permits a good to qualify as originating if the value of any non-originating material which does not meet the tariff shift requirement is not more than seven percent of the value of the finished good.

Accessories, spare parts, and tools that are delivered with originating goods and that form part of the goods' standard accessories, parts, or tools are considered originating and are also disregarded in determining whether all the non-originating materials undergo the requisite tariff shift. However, as discussed more fully below, accessories, parts, and tools are not disregarded for purposes of calculating regional value content.

Even if a good satisfies a tariff shift, rule of origin requirement, it will not be considered an originating good if the shift in tariff classification results from either, (1) mere dilution with water or another substance that does not materially alter the characteristics of the good, or (2) any production or pricing practice with respect to which it may be demonstrated, on the basis of a preponderance of evidence, that the object was to circumvent the NAFTA rules of origin.

Regional Value Content

The negotiators of NAFTA were concerned that a tariff-shift requirement would be inadequate in ensuring that sufficient local materials and value-adding processing would be required to qualify for NAFTA eligibility. These reservations were especially prevalent with regard to import-sensitive products such as automobiles and textiles. Specifically, the U.S. and Canada had concern that third-country companies could use minor processing operations in Mexico, which has relatively lower labor costs, as a platform for duty-free shipments to the other NAFTA countries. Accordingly many of the NAFTA rules of origin incorporate a regional value content ("RVC") test in lieu of, or in conjunction with, a tariff-shift test.

In the case of most goods, two alternative methods are available for the calculation of RVC, the transaction value method and the net cost method. Under the transaction value method, the value of the goods and processing, originating or conducted in one or more NAFTA countries, must equal 60 percent or more of the transaction value of the good. The transaction value of a good is defined as the transaction value of the good for purposes of customs appraisal under generally accepted customs valuation principles set forth in the WTO Agreement on Implementation of Article VII of the General Agreement on Tariffs and Trade 1994. As defined, the transaction value generally approximates the ex-factory price of a good sold to an independent buyer on an arms-length basis. The formula used to calculate RVC on the basis of Transaction Value is as follows:

$$RVC = \frac{TV - VNM}{TV} \times 100$$

> *where RVC is the Regional Value Content*
> *TV is Transaction Value*
> *VNM is the value of non-originating materials used by the producer in the production of*
>> *the good.*

The second basis for calculating RVC is the net cost method. Under the net cost method, fifty percent of the net cost to produce the good must be based upon costs incurred in one or more NAFTA countries. Net cost is defined as all costs of producing the good, including materials, labor, overhead (but not profit), less expenses for sales promotion (including marketing and after sales service), royalties, shipping and packing costs, and non-allowable interest costs. The percentage content requirement for the net cost method is lower than that of the transaction value method, since profits and sales expenses are excluded in the calculation of the former method. The formula used to calculate RVC on the basis of the net cost method is as follows:

$$RVC = \frac{NC - VNM}{NC} \times 100$$

> *where RVC is the Regional Value Content*
> *NC is the Net Cost*
> *VNM is the value of non-originating materials used by the producer in the production of*
>> *the good.*

An example of the application of the RVC test is provided by the NAFTA rule of origin applicable to portable steel hibachis, used to grill meat outdoors, which are classified under HTSUS subheading 7321.13.0020. For purposes of this example, it is assumed that a hibachi is fabricated in Mexico using parts from various countries. The steel shell of the hibachi is imported from Japan and is valued at $4.00. The legs of the hibachi are imported from Canada and have a value of $2.00. The grill used on the hibachi is produced in the U.S. with a value of $3.00. The legs of the hibachi and the grill are "originating" materials since they are sourced from *NAFTA* countries. The steel shell of the hibachi is a non-originating material since it is sourced from Japan. The transaction value (fob invoice price) of the finished hibachi is $12.00

The NAFTA rule of origin applicable to HTSUS subheading 7321.13.0020 requires:

A change to subheadings 7321.12 *through* 7321.83 *from any other heading; or*
A change to subheadings 7321.12 *through* 7321.83 *from subheading* 7321.90 *[parts of hibachis], whether or not there is also a change from any other heading, provided there is a regional value content of not less than:*

> (1)   *Sixty percent where the transaction value method is used, or*
> (2)   *Fifty percent where the net cost method is used.*

The shell, legs and grill of the Hibachi are classified as parts of cooking appliances other than stoves or ranges under HTSUS subheading 7321.90.6030. The process of producing the hibachi transforms the tariff classification of the non-originating material, the steel shell, from HTSUS subheading 7321.90.6030 (parts) to subheading 7321.13.0020 (hibachi). However, the rule of origin requires a transfer from a heading outside 7321. Thus, any non-originating material classified under heading 7321, including parts, cannot be transformed in a way which would satisfy the tariff-shift rule of origin.

However, the rule of origin also contains an alternative test which permits a hibachi manufactured from non-originating hibachi parts to qualify for NAFTA eligibility, provided that finished good contains sufficient NAFTA regional value. Applying the Transaction Value, the RVC of the hibachi is 66.7%:

$$RVC = \frac{TV - VNM}{TV} \times 100\% = \frac{\$12 - \$4}{\$12} \times 100 = \frac{\$8}{\$12} \times 100\% = 66.7\%$$

Thus the RVC of the finished hibachi is greater than the minimum sixty percent required by the Transaction Value method and the hibachi can be imported into the U.S. at the NAFTA rate of duty.

The RVC test for automobiles and certain significant automotive parts is more stringent than that applied generally to other products. For instance, major automotive components and subassemblies are subject to the "tracing" principle whereby the value of any non-originating material remains non-originating, regardless of the amount of processing and the number of transformations which the material may undergo in one or more NAFTA countries before incorporation into the finished automobile. In addition, the RVC for automotive products subject to regional value tests must be conducted on the basis of the Net Cost method. Furthermore, the minimum RVC percentages for such products increased from 50 percent to 55–56 percent in 1998, and to 60–62.5 percent in 2002.

Processing Operations

As indicated earlier, certain import sensitive products are accorded very strict rules of origin which ensure that NAFTA eligibility will be granted only if a substantial amount of material and processing is sourced or conducted in one or more NAFTA countries. The tariff shift rules applicable to textile articles are an example of such strict requirement. Most textile articles will qualify for NAFTA treatment only if they are produced from fabric produced from yarn or fiber produced in a NAFTA country. These textile rules of origin are known as "yarn-forward" or, in the case of man-made-fiber articles, the "fiber-forward" rules.

In a limited number of cases, the NAFTA rules of origin require that certain specified processing operations be conducted upon a good before it will be deemed originating and eligible for NAFTA duty treatment. Such processing requirements are found primarily in the rules of origin applicable to textile articles. A representative example of such a requirement is found in the rule of origin applicable to men's and boy's wool overcoats and similar articles classified under HTSUS subheading 6101.10.0000. The NAFTA rule of origin corresponding to this subheading requires:

> *A change to subheadings 6101.10 through 6101.30 from any other chapter, except from headings . . . [reference to excluded yarn, fiber and fabric headings], provided that:*
>
> (A)   *the good is both cut (or knit to shape) and sewn or otherwise assembled in the territory of one or more of the NAFTA parties,*
> (B)   *the visible lining fabric listed in chapter rule 1 for chapter 61 satisfies the tariff change requirements provided therein.*

As is apparent, the NAFTA rules of origin are often complex. In fact, other more complex NAFTA concepts have not been covered in this chapter, such as cost averaging methods used in Rye calculations and inventory management methodologies used to determine the origin of fungible, originating and non-originating, materials used to produce a finished good. On the other hand, as indicated earlier, the NAFTA rules of origin, as drafted and implemented by the customs authorities of the three NAFTA countries, do enable companies to plan investment in manufacturing and distribution operations; companies know in advance what is required to obtain eligibility for *NAFTA* and what the duty consequences of any particular combination of manufacturing and distribution operations will be.

PREFERENTIAL DUTY PROGRAMS

The U.S., as well as Japan and the most other developed countries, has adopted programs under which imports of specifically designated products from specifically designated beneficiary developing countries are eligible for duty free treatment. The [principal] U.S. preferential duty program is known as the Generalized System of Preferences ("GSP"). In general terms, the U.S.

GSP program is similar to the preferential duty programs maintained by other developed countries.

Under GSP, a wide range of products imported from more than 100 countries and territories may be imported duty free into the U.S., provided that certain requirements are satisfied. Among these is the GSP rule of origin, which provides in relevant part:

The duty free treatment provided under this subchapter shall apply to any eligible article which is the growth, product, or manufacture of a beneficiary developing country if

 (1) *that article is imported directly from a beneficiary developing country into the customs territory of the United States; and*

 (2) *the sum of*

  (a) *the cost or value of the materials produced in the beneficiary developing country or any two or more such countries that are members of the same association of countries and are treated as one country under section 2467(2) of this title, plus*

  (b) *the direct costs of processing operations performed in such beneficiary developing country or such member countries, is not less than 35 percent of the appraised value of such article at the time it is entered.*

In order to be eligible for GSP duty treatment, an article must originate in an eligible country. Thus, the article must be substantially transformed in a beneficiary developing country ("BDC") in order to be deemed as originating in that country. The article must be imported directly to the U.S. from that country. Finally, the local value requirement of the GSP is similar to the Net Cost method of calculating regional value content under NAFTA, except that only thirty-five percent of the value must be local. Furthermore, only materials and direct costs of processing may be included, which excludes overhead and other nonallocable general and administrative costs. As under NAFTA, no article is deemed eligible for GSP benefits merely by undergoing simple combining or packing operations, or mere dilution with water or another substance which does not materially alter the characteristics of the article.

Another duty preference program in effect in the U.S. is the so-called Caribbean Basin Initiative ("CBI"), established under the Caribbean Basin Economic Recovery Act. The CBI program is similar to GSP, except that it is limited to countries in the Caribbean basin including countries in the Caribbean Sea and in Central America.

In 1991, the U.S. Congress enacted the Andean Trade Preference Act ("ATPA"). The ATPA created a preferential duty program for the four members of the Andean Pact: Bolivia, Ecuador, Colombia, and Peru. The ATPA rules of origin are, for the most part, the same as those that apply to CBI.

In 1985, the U.S. implemented a free trade agreement with Israel, under which preferential duty treatment is accorded to designated imports from that country. The rules of origin established under the Israel Free Trade Agreement are essentially the same as those established under CBI and ATPA.

The African Growth and Opportunity Act ("AGOA"), enacted in 2000, provides preferential duty treatment relating to articles not subject to GSP preferences to forty-eight sub-Saharan countries in Africa. The products covered are primarily textile and apparel products, which are permitted to enter the United States free of duty and free from quantitative restriction [subject to certain conditions].

Companies which have available manufacturing operations in more than one country should review the rules of origin applied under the various preferential duty agreements and programs in force in the country or countries in which the finished goods are eventually to be sold. By doing so, such companies will be able to structure their manufacturing operations so as to minimize the impact of duties upon the sales of the goods. [W]here it may not be possible to meet a regional value content test of sixty percent under NAFTA, [it may be possible to meet] the thirty-five percent test applied under GSP, CBI, or ATPA. From the viewpoint of a company based outside North America which desires to produce offshore for sale in the U.S., it may make little difference whether a plant is located in Mexico (NAFTA) or Costa Rica (GSP, CBI).

NOTES AND QUESTIONS

1. As a matter of international law, all states that are members of the World Trade Organization or that are parties to bilateral or regional economic arrangements have an obligation not to charge a tariff or to take any import measure that is different from their agreed ("bound") import schedules. The remedy for any violation of these international norms is a dispute settlement proceeding conducted by the WTO. *See, e.g., Argentina-Measures Affecting Imports of Footwear, Textiles, Apparel and Other Items*, complaint by the United States, WTO Appellate Body, WT/DS 56/AB/R (1998) (Argentina held to have violated its obligations by charging more than the agreed bound tariff).

2. *Free-Trade Agreements and Customs Unions*: Free-trade areas (FTAs) and customs unions (CUs) share a common feature in that all goods from member states pass within the territory duty free. However, FTAs and CUs have some significant differences in how their members deal with goods from nonmembers. NAFTA is an example of a free-trade area. While members of NAFTA have eliminated duties on goods traveling across national boundaries of each of its members, each member is free to maintain its own separate tariff system on imports from nonmember countries; that is, the United States, Mexico, and Canada each has its own tariff system and levies its own set of duties on goods from nonmembers. By contrast the EU is a customs union that maintains a common external tariff on goods from all nonmember countries. Once the goods lawfully enter any country in the EU, they are allowed to freely circulate within the EU without the payment of any additional duties. This means that goods entering the EU are subject to one uniform tariff no matter where they enter and then they are free to circulate within the EU duty free. By contrast, as each country in an FTA enjoys its own authority to set its tariffs, it becomes possible for a nonmember to select the member of the FTA with the lowest tariffs as a point of entry into the FTA market and then to export the goods duty free to other members of the FTA. Suppose that Mexico has lower tariffs for certain goods than the United States. The nonmember could ship to Mexico, pay a lower tariff, conduct some simple processing operations, and then ship the goods to the United States duty free, saving the difference between the United States duty and the Mexican duty. To prevent or limit this type of strategic behavior, an FTA will normally have rules of origin that will determine whether the processed product will be treated as a product originating in the FTA and thus receive duty-free treatment or whether the product will be treated as a

nonoriginating product and subject to the individual external tariffs of each member country of the FTA. In our previous example, the United States may determine that although the goods are traveling from Mexico they are really of non-FTA origin as they originally came from a nonmember state and will subject those goods to the regular U.S. tariff. (This would mean that the nonoriginating goods were subject to two tariffs, one when they entered Mexico and a second tariff when they entered the United States, not what the exporter intended!) In some circumstances, however, the FTA rules of origin may provide that the goods from the nonmember state should be deemed to originate in Mexico and enjoy duty-free status within the FTA. These rules of origin can be complex and may also include a regional content value requirement for certain goods as in the case of NAFTA. The concept of regional content value (RCV) is a simple one even if the calculations in a specific case may be complex. The basic concept is that the product will be treated as originating in NAFTA and thus allowed free movement within NAFTA only if a certain percentage of the total value of the product is attributable to NAFTA.

3. *Bonded Facilities and Foreign Trade Zones:* A bonded facility is a duty-free customs area used for storage, repacking, clearing, or sorting of imported merchandise. Duty must be paid only when the goods are withdrawn and put into the stream of commerce. A foreign trade zone is a specifically designated area where goods can be landed without the payment of duty. It may be possible to perform assembly or processing operations in this zone.

4. *Temporary Importation Under Bond:* Placing goods in an approved warehouse and posting bond equal to twice the estimated duty allows a delay in paying a duty for up to one year. This is particularly useful for goods that will be re-exported because it avoids the delay of the duty drawback process.

5. What happens if goods are imported and then exported as a whole or after processing? In this case, the importer/exporter can apply for and receive a duty drawback which is usually 99 percent of the duty originally paid. *See, e.g., Texport Oil Co. v. United States*, 1 F. Supp. 2d 1393 (CIT 1998) (company entitled to drawback on exports of petroleum products).

6. In this book, we concentrate on U.S. Customs rules. Note that every country or economic area has its own distinctive rules. For example, the 25-member European Union enforces EU-wide customs and allows free circulation of goods within the EU itself. *See* Edwin A. Vermulst, *EC Customs Classification Rules: Should Ice Cream Melt?* 15 Mich. J. of Int'l L. 1241 (1994).

7. How realistic are the NAFTA origin rules? Former Secretary of Labor Robert Reich, writing in 1991, pointed out the following:

> When an American buys a Pontiac Le Mans from General Motors, for example, he engages unwittingly in an international transaction. Of the $10,000 paid to GM, about $3,000 goes to South Korea for routine labor and assembly operations, $1,850 to Japan for advanced components (engines, transaxles, and electronics), $700 to the former West Germany for styling and design engineering, $400 to Taiwan, Singapore, and Japan for small components, $250 to Britain for advertising and marketing services, and about $50 to Ireland and Barbados for data processing. The rest— less than $4,000—goes to strategists in Detroit, lawyers and bankers in New York, lobbyists in Washington, insurance and health care workers all over the country, and to General Motors shareholders all over the world.

The Wall Street Journal, July 5, 1991, p. A6.

1. Import Cases

The importer, typically the buyer in an international sale of goods, is normally responsible for handling all aspects of compliance with the customs laws of the importing country. Of primary concern to importers is determining the amount of customs duties that are due on imported goods. In the United States, contested issues arise more often in import cases than in export cases. Litigation and controversy centers around the following issues: (1) classification, (2) valuation, (3) rules of origin, and (4) marking. As these are among the principal trade law issues that you may encounter in any international sales transaction, we explore each of these issues in the sections below.

Customs duties are determined by the U.S. Customs Service. An importer can contest a customs determination through resort to two specialized federal courts, the Court of International Trade, which is a trial court, and the U.S. Court of Appeals for the Federal Circuit. The following cases discuss the main questions that arise.

A. **CLASSIFICATION ISSUES**

North American Processing Co. v. United States
United States Court of Appeals, Federal Circuit, 2001
236 F.3d 695

LOURIE, Circuit Judge.

The imported goods at issue in this case are bovine fat trimmings containing thirty-five percent chemical lean[28] and sixty-five percent fat, which were imported by North American on October 14, 1992. Customs originally classified the entry under subheading 1502.00.00 as "[f]ats of bovine animals . . . ," dutiable at a rate of 0.95¢/kg. Subheading 1502.00.00 reads as follows:

> 1502.00.00 Fats of bovine animals, sheep or goats, raw or rendered, whether or not pressed or solvent-extracted

HTSUS, subheading 1502.00.00. Customs later reliquidated the merchandise on February 23, 1993, and classified it under subheading 0202.30.60 as "[m]eat of bovine animals . . . ," dutiable at a rate of 4.4¢/kg. Subheading 0202.30.60 reads as follows:

> 0202 Meat of bovine animals, frozen: . . .
> 0202.30 Boneless:
> 0202.30.60 Other
> HTSUS, heading 0202.

[North American filed a protest with Customs, which was denied. North American challenged the denial with the Court of International Trade, which agreed with Customs. North American then appealed to the court of appeals.]

---

28. "Chemical lean" indicates the results of an analysis where the fat content of a sample of the imported merchandise is determined by chemical assay under standard laboratory conditions.

DISCUSSION

Determining whether imported merchandise has been properly classified under an appropriate tariff provision is ultimately an issue of statutory interpretation and thus a question of law. Resolution of that issue entails a two-step process: (1) ascertaining the proper meaning of specific terms in the tariff provision; and (2) determining whether the merchandise at issue comes within the description of such terms as properly construed. The first step is a question of law over which this court exercises complete and independent review. The second step is a question of fact that this court reviews for clear error. Furthermore, Customs' classification determinations are presumed to be correct. 28 U.S.C. §2639(a)(1) (1994).

Applied in numerical order, the GRIs of the HTSUS and the Additional United States Rules of Interpretation govern the proper classification of merchandise entering the United States. *Carl Zeiss, Inc. v. United States*, 195 F.3d 1375, 1379 (Fed. Cir. 1999). According to GRI 1, "classification shall be determined according to the terms of the headings and any relevant section or chapter notes." Thus, "a court first construes the language of the heading, and any section or chapter notes in question, to determine whether the product at issue is classifiable under the heading." *Baxter*, 182 F.3d at 1337. Absent contrary legislative intent, HTSUS terms are to be construed according to their common and commercial meaning. *Carl Zeiss*, 195 F.3d at 1379. A court may rely upon its own understanding of the terms used, lexicographic and scientific authorities, dictionaries, and other reliable information. *Id.*

We agree with the government that the merchandise is properly classified under subheading 0202.30.60. The Explanatory Notes to chapter 2 expressly state that "[a]nimal fat presented separately is excluded . . . , but fat presented in the carcass *or adhering to meat* is treated as forming part of the meat." HTSUS, ch. 2 Explanatory Notes (emphasis added). Although the Explanatory Notes are not legally binding or dispositive, they may be consulted for guidance and are generally indicative of the proper interpretation of the various HTSUS provisions. *E.g., Carl Zeiss*, 195 F.3d at 1378 n. 1 (citing H.R. Conf. Rep. No. 100-576, at 549 (1988), *reprinted in* 1998 U.S.C.C.A.N. 1547, 1582). Therefore, it is clear that Congress intended that the presence of fat in a mixture containing lean and fat components does not preclude its classification as "meat." In the present case, the subject merchandise is comprised of fat which adheres to a lean component, and is not separately presented. It thus fits within that classification. Moreover, USDA regulations define "meat" as "[t]he part of the muscle of any cattle, sheep, swine, or goats . . . *with or without the accompanying and overlying fat*. . . ." 9 C.F.R. §301.2 (2000) (emphasis added). While USDA regulations are not dispositive of whether a Customs classification ruling is correct, we find them to be persuasive regarding this issue. *See Carl Zeiss*, 195 F.3d at 1379 (permitting courts to consult any reliable information source to determine the proper classification of merchandise). Accordingly, we find that the imported merchandise at issue is properly classified as "meat" under subheading 0202.30.60.

We also agree with the government that the imported merchandise may not be classified as "fats" under subheading 1502.00.00. The government presented undisputed testimony at trial that the USDA considers trimmings that contain less than twelve percent lean to be properly classified as fat. Therefore, because the subject merchandise contains a lean component that comprises far more than twelve percent of the total mixture, it may not be classified as "fats." The dictionary definition of the term "fat" further supports this conclusion. "Fat" is defined as

> [the] part of the tissues of an animal that consists chiefly of cells distended with greasy or oily matter . . . [;] the oily or greasy substance that makes up the bulk of the cell contents of adipose tissue and occurs in smaller quantities in many other parts of animals and in plants. . . .

Webster's Third New International Dictionary 827 (1981). Accordingly, we conclude that subheading 1502.00.00 is inapplicable to the merchandise at issue.

JVC Co. of America v. United States
United States Court of Appeals, Federal Circuit, 2000
234 F.3d 1348

LOURIE, Circuit Judge.

The imported goods at issue in this case are video camera recorders, otherwise known as camcorders, which were imported by JVC in 1992. *JVC*, 62 F. Supp. 2d at 1133. The parties agree that JVC's camcorders are "electrical machine[s] or apparatus possessing two independent functions generally used in conjunction with one another; a television camera and a video tape recorder." *Id.* Customs classified the camcorders under subheading 8525.30.00, under the broader heading of 8525 of the HTSUS, as "television cameras," dutiable at a rate of 4.2 *ad valorem*. *Id.* at 1134. Heading 8525 and subheading 8525.30.00 read as follows:

> 8525 Transmission apparatus for radiotelephony, radiotelegraphy, radio-broadcasting or television, whether or not incorporating reception apparatus or sound recording or reproducing apparatus; television cameras: . . .
> 8525.30.00 Television cameras

JVC timely protested Customs' classification and paid all of the liquidated duties that were due. *JVC*, 62 F. Supp. 2d at 1134. JVC then challenged Customs' classification in the Court of International Trade, arguing that its camcorders should have been classified under subheading 8543.80.90. Heading 8543 and subheadings 8543.80 and 8543.80.90 read as follows:

> 8543 Electrical machines and apparatus, having individual functions, not specified or included elsewhere in this chapter; parts thereof: . . .
> 8543.80 Other machines and apparatus: . . .
> 8543.80.90 Other

HTSUS, heading 8543. JVC alternatively argued that its camcorders should have been classified under subheading 8479.89.90. *JVC*, 62 F. Supp. 2d at 1134. Heading 8479 and subheadings 8479.89 and 8479.89.90 read as follows:

> 8479 Machines and mechanical appliances having individual functions, not specified or included elsewhere in this chapter; parts thereof: . . .
> Other machines and mechanical appliances: . . .
>
> 8479.89 Other
> 8479.89.80 Other

Merchandise classified under subheadings 8543.80.90 and 8479.89.90 are dutiable at the respective rates of 3.9% and 3.7% *ad valorem*.

[Customs classified JVC's camcorders under subheading 8525.30.00 as "television cameras." The ruling was challenged in the Court of International Trade where both parties cross-moved for summary judgment. The Court of International Trade upheld the ruling by Customs and JVC timely appealed.]

DISCUSSION

Determining the meaning of a tariff term in the HTSUS is an issue of statutory interpretation and thus a question of law. In this case, because the structure and use of the imported camcorders are not in dispute, and Customs has not promulgated any regulations interpreting the tariff terms at issue, our analysis of whether the imported merchandise has been properly classified turns on the determination of the proper meaning and scope of the relevant tariff classifications.

Applied in numerical order, the GRIs of the HTSUS and the Additional United States Rules of Interpretation govern the proper classification of merchandise entering the United States. Under GRI 3(a), when goods are *prima facie* classifiable under two or more headings, the court should determine which heading is the most specific, comparing only the language of the headings and not the language of the subheadings. Only after determining that a product is classifiable under a particular heading should the court look to the subheadings to find the proper classification.

As an initial matter, we agree with the government that the merchandise is *prima facie* classifiable under heading 8525. As an *eo nominee* provision, heading 8525 includes all forms of the named article, *i.e.*, "television cameras." *Carl Zeiss*, 195 F.3d at 1379. The Explanatory Notes to heading 8525 expressly state that "[t]his heading covers television cameras. . . . Cameras for underwater work and portable cameras with or without a built-in video recorder are also classified here." Explanatory Notes, §XVI, 85.25(c), at 1375 (1986). Although the Explanatory Notes are not legally binding or dispositive, they may be consulted for guidance and are generally indicative of the proper interpretation of the various HTSUS provisions. In addition, according to the McGraw-Hill Encyclopedia of Science & Technology, "[a] television camera may fall within one of several categories: studio, *portable*, or telecine." 18 McGraw-Hill Encyclopedia of Sci. & Tech. 212 (8th ed. 1997) (emphasis added). This reference further states that:

> Television cameras intended for . . . portable use are usually one piece, with all elements of the camera system contained in one assembly. *Such cameras may be combined with a detachable or built-in videocassette recorder to form a camcorder* (Fig. 2). . . . Portable cameras . . . usually combine all of the basic elements into one package and may be used for a multitude of purposes. . . . The units often have built-in microphones, videocassette recorders, and batteries for completely self-contained operation (Fig. 2). These compact and lightweight camcorders can be easily handled by one person.

Id. at 212, 216 (emphasis added). While JVC argues that this authority distinguishes television cameras from camcorders, we agree with the government that this reference source supports the view that a camcorder is a type of television camera — one with a built-in videocassette recorder.

Having thus concluded that camcorders are *prima facie* classifiable under heading 8525 of the HTSUS, the only remaining issue is whether camcorders should nonetheless be classified under some alternative heading. JVC contends that its camcorders are described under headings 8543 and 8479, and therefore should be classified under either subheading 8543.80.90 or 8479.89.90. We disagree for the following reasons. First, as we noted earlier, the Explanatory Notes to heading 8525 explicitly state that "[t]his heading covers television cameras. . . . Cameras for underwater work and portable cameras with or without a built-in video recorder are also classified here." Explanatory Notes, Section XVI, 85.25(c), at 1375 (1986); *see also Carl Zeiss*, 195 F.3d at 1378 n. 1 (explaining that although the Explanatory Notes are not legally binding or dispositive, they may be consulted for guidance and are generally indicative of the proper interpretation of the various HTSUS provisions). Moreover, while heading 8543 ("Electrical machines and apparatus, having individual functions, not specified or included elsewhere") and heading 8479 ("Machines and mechanical appliances having individual functions, not specified or included elsewhere") may arguably describe camcorders, they should not be classified under these headings because heading 8525 ("television cameras") is more specific.

Better Home Plastics Corp. v. United States
United States Court of Appeals, Federal Circuit, 1997
119 F.3d 969

RICH, Circuit Judge.

The shower curtain sets in question comprise an outer textile curtain, an inner plastic magnetic liner, and plastic hooks. The outer textile curtain typically has a decorative pattern, and being semi-transparent, it permits the color of the plastic liner to show through. The inner plastic liner prevents water from escaping the shower and prevents the fabric curtain from being soiled with mildew or soap. The liner is opaque, and thereby also contributes to the decorative and privacy-maintaining functions of the set. The hooks attach the liner and the curtain to the overhead curtain rod found at the entrance to most domestic showers. The sets are at the low end of the shower curtain market: plaintiff, Better Home Plastics, sells the sets to discount stores for $5-$6 per set; they are resold to consumers for $9-$12 per set.

The General Rules of Interpretation (GRI) of the Harmonized Tariff Schedule of the United States (HTSUS) help determine which subheading should govern the duty to be assessed on imports of these sets. According to GRI 3(a), when "goods are, *prima facie*, classifiable under two or more headings," the court must choose the heading providing the most specific description. This is the so-called relative specificity test. GRI 3(a) provides an exception to the applicability of this test, however, when "two or more headings each refer . . . to only part of the items in a set." Pursuant to GRI 3(b), goods not classifiable under GRI 3(a) are classified by the "component which gives them their essential character." This is the so-called essential character test. GRI 3(c) provides a default rule for goods not classifiable after resort to either GRI 3(a) or (b). GRI 3(c) directs that such goods be classified "under the heading which occurs last in numerical order among those which equally merit consideration."

Two subheadings of the HTSUS are in issue. The sets might be classified on the basis of the textile curtain, pursuant to subheading 6303.92.000 of the HTSUS, resulting in a duty of 12.8%. Alternatively, they might be classified on the basis of the plastic liner, pursuant to subheading 3924.90.1010 of the HTSUS, resulting in a duty of 3.36%.

[Customs classified the sets on the basis of the textile curtain. Plaintiff challenged the ruling in the Court of International Trade, which held that sets should have been classified based on the plastic liner. The United States has appealed the decision to the court of appeals.]

ANALYSIS

On appeal, there is extensive argument about presumptions and deference that can be quickly addressed. Acknowledging the procedural importance of presumptions, the Court of International Trade is nonetheless charged with the duty to "reach the correct decision." *Rollerblade*, 112 F.3d at 484 (quoting 28 U.S.C. §2643(b)). On appeal, we review the findings of that court—not those of Customs—for clear error; while we decide questions of law *de novo*.

We turn, then, to the merits of the arguments presented. The United States argues that the Court of International Trade erred in its application of the essential character test because, according to the United States, the fabric curtain provides the essential character of the sets. In the alternative, the United States argues that the essential character cannot be determined and the default rule of GRI 3(c) should apply. We disagree with both arguments.

The Court of International Trade carefully considered all of the facts, and, after a reasoned balancing of all the facts, concluded that Better Home Plastics offered sufficient evidence and argument to overcome the presumption of correctness. The court concluded that the indispensable function of keeping water inside the shower along with the protective, privacy and decorative functions of the plastic liner, and the relatively low cost of the sets *all combined* to support the decision that the plastic liner provided the essential character of the sets. Contrary to the argument offered by the United States, we are not persuaded that the court erred in looking to analogous areas of law concerning "indispensability" for guidance in analyzing "essential character." The court's decision did not rely solely, or even hinge, on the indispensability of the water-retaining function. The decision was substantially based on the importance of the other functions as well as the cost of the entire set. Therefore, we see no error in the court's ultimate conclusion of essential character in this case. As a result, we also see no error in this case in the court's refusal to reject the essential character test in favor of the default rule of GRI 3(c).

NOTES AND QUESTIONS

1. Should the courts on judicial review accord deference to rulings of the U.S. Customs Service?

2. The three principal cases set forth above illustrate the basic rules of interpretation applied to determine the classification of a product. Make a list of these rules.

PROBLEM 2-16

Importer A imports several models of battery-operated toothbrushes. These have (1) one to four interchangeable plastic toothbrush heads, (2) a detachable plastic handle containing a battery-operated motor, and (3) a stand that incorporates a battery recharger.

The classification alternatives are:

9603   Brooms, brushes (including brushes constituting parts of machines, appliances or vehicles) . . .
9603.21.00   Toothbrushes (duty rate 1 percent *ad valorem*)

or

8509   Electromechanical domestic appliances, with self-contained motor
8509.80.00   Other appliances (duty rate 4.2 percent *ad valorem*)

Importer A argues that the proper classification is 9603.21 on the ground that it is more specific under GRI 3(a) than 8509.80. Note that in order for 9603.21 to apply the mechanical toothbrush must first satisfy 9603, the category heading. Importer A argues that a mechanical toothbrush falls within the phrase in heading 9603 "brushes (including brushes constituting parts of machines, appliances or vehicles)." However, if the mechanical toothbrush satisfies 9603, what prevents a street sweeper or a vacuum cleaner from also from falling within this heading? How would you interpret 9603 to avoid this result and what is the applicable rate of duty? *See Bausch & Lomb, Inc. v. United States*, 148 F.3d 1363 (Fed. Cir. 1998).

In many cases, the classification determination is of importance only to the importers who are trying to pay a lower tax. In the following two principal cases, *Marubeni America Corp. v. United States* involving imports of automobiles and *Heartland By-Products v. United States* involving sugar, however, the classification issue had important societal implications.

Marubeni America Corp. v. United States
United States Court of Appeals, Federal Circuit, 1994
35 F.3d 530

RICH, Circuit Judge.

The merchandise at issue is a two-door, two-wheel or four-wheel drive, dual-purpose or multipurpose passenger vehicle, generally referred to as a compact sports utility vehicle. The Pathfinder does not have a cargo box or bed like a truck. Instead, its body is one unit that is configured much like an ordinary station wagon in that it has rear seats that fold forward, but not flat, for extra cargo space. These seats, however, are not removable. The spare tire is housed within the cargo space or alternatively, it may be attached outside the vehicle on the rear hatch. The rear hatch operates like those on a station wagon; it has a window that may be opened to place small packages in the cargo area without opening the tailgate. The Pathfinder is mechanically designed for both on- and off-road use.

The Pathfinder was classified by the United States Customs Service (Customs) under 8704.31.00 (8704) of the HTSUS as a "motor vehicle for the transport of goods." Pursuant to 9903.87.00 of the HTSUS, a 25% *ad valorem* duty was assessed.

Nissan administratively protested this decision, pursuant to 19 U.S.C. §1514, claiming that the Pathfinder should be classified as "motor cars and other motor vehicles principally designed for the transport of persons . . . including station wagons" under 8703 HTSUS. This protest was denied. Nissan then brought an action in the CIT. The CIT concluded that Customs' classification of the Pathfinder under 8704 HTSUS, "motor vehicle for the transport of goods," was incorrect, and that the correct classification was under 8703 HTSUS, "motor vehicle principally designed for the transport of persons." The duty assessed under 8703 HTSUS is 2.5% *ad valorem*. The United States now appeals from the judgment of the CIT.

A. PROPER MEANING

It is well settled that "[t]he ultimate issue, whether particular merchandise has been classified under an appropriate tariff provision, necessarily depends on the meaning of the terms of that provision, which is a question of law subject to *de novo* review."

The two competing provisions of the HTSUS are set forth below.

8703 Motor cars and other motor vehicles principally designed for the transport of persons (other than those of heading 8702), including station wagons and racing cars.

8704 Motor vehicles for the transport of goods.

There are no legally binding notes to these headings that are relevant to the classification of dual-purpose vehicles such as the Pathfinder; therefore, we need only look to the common meaning of the terms as they appear above.

By the express language of 8703, "motor vehicles principally designed for the transport of persons," it is clear that the vehicle must be designed "more" for the transport of persons than goods. *Webster's Third New International Dictionary of the English Language*, Unabridged (1986) defines "principally" as "in the chief place, chiefly;" and defines "designed" as "done by design or purposefully opposed to accidental or inadvertent; intended, planned." Thus, if the vehicle is equally designed for the transport of goods and persons, it would not be properly classified under 8703 HTSUS. There is nothing in the legislative history that indicates a different meaning.

The government argues that "the correct standard to be utilized in determining the principal design of any vehicle must be its construction—its basic structure, body, components, and vehicle layout—and the proper question to be asked is whether that construction is uniquely for passenger transportation." This standard is clearly at odds with Customs' interpretation in its March 1, 1989, memorandum providing guidance in applying these headings to sports utility vehicles. Customs stated:

> *Design features*, whether they accommodate passenger transport or cargo transport, or both, *are of two types both of which are relevant in determining the proper classification of a sports-utility vehicle*. First are what may be regarded as *structural, or integral design features* such as basic body, chassis, and suspension design, . . . style and structure of the body [control access to rear]. The second type of design features, *auxiliary design*

features, are also relevant when determining whether, on the whole, the transport of persons was the principal design consideration. *Neither type by itself can be considered determinative on the issue of the purpose for which the vehicle was principally designed.* (emphasis added).

Thus, "requir[ing] that the resulting product be uniquely constructed for the purpose of transporting persons," to the exclusion of any other use, is a constrictive interpretation of the terms with which we cannot agree.

There is nothing in the statute, legislative history, or prior Customs decisions that would indicate that "principally designed" refers only to a vehicle's structural design as asserted by the government. To answer the question, whether a vehicle is principally designed for a particular purpose, not uniquely designed for a particular purpose, one must look at both the structural and auxiliary design features, as neither by itself is determinative.

The government's exclusionary construction fails on another point. Heading 8703 HTSUS specifically includes "station wagons," which are not uniquely designed for transport of persons, rather, they are designed as dual-purpose vehicles for the transport of goods and persons. The Pathfinder, like a station wagon, is a vehicle designed with a dual-purpose — to transport goods and persons.

In summary, we find that the proper meaning of "motor vehicle principally designed for the transport of persons" to be just that, a motor vehicle principally designed for the transport of persons. While we find it unnecessary to assign a quantitative value to "principally," the statutory language is clear that a vehicle's intended purpose of transporting persons must outweigh an intended purpose of transporting goods. To make this determination, we find that both the structural and auxiliary design features must be considered. This construction comports with Customs' interpretations and the CIT's analysis; and it is equally consistent with the common and popular meaning of the terms.

B. PROPER CLASSIFICATION

While the meaning of a classification term is a question of law, the issue of whether merchandise comes within the definition of a classification term is a question of fact subject to the clearly erroneous standard of review.

The CIT conducted a three week trial *de novo*, pursuant to 28 U.S.C. §2640, to determine whether the Pathfinder was principally designed for the transport of persons or goods. The CIT looked at both design intent and execution, evaluating both structural and auxiliary design features. The CIT limited evidence to the vehicle models in the entries currently under consideration with the exception of evidence that was provided for comparison with vehicles that were readily accepted as trucks or passenger cars. These included the Nissan Hardbody truck and the Nissan Maxima sedan.

It is evident that the CIT carefully applied the proper standards in making its decision. In reaching its conclusion, the CIT evaluated the marketing and engineering design goals (consumer demands, off the line parts availability, etc.), the structural design necessary to meet both cargo and passenger carrying requirements for both on- and off-road use, as well as interior passenger amenities.

The CIT also recognized that the Pathfinder was basically derived from Nissan's Hardbody truck line yet, the Pathfinder was based upon totally different design concepts than a truck. The CIT correctly pointed out these differences and more importantly, the reasons behind the design decisions, including the need for speed and economy in manufacturing to capture the changing market, a market into which Nissan was a late entrant. Specifically, the designers decided to adopt the Hardbody's frame side rails and the cab portion from the front bumper to the frame just behind the driver's seats so that they could quickly and economically reach the market. The front suspension system was also adopted from Nissan's truck line but the rear suspension was not. The fact that a vehicle is derived in-part from a truck or from a sedan is not, without more, determinative of its intended principal design objectives which were passenger transport and off-road capability.

Substantial structural changes were necessary to meet the design criterion of transporting passengers. The addition of the rear passenger seat required that the gas tank be moved to the rear and the spare tire relocated. This effectively reduces the cargo carrying capacity. Of particular importance was the design of a new rear suspension that was developed specifically to provide a smooth ride for passengers. New and different cross beams, not present on the Hardbody frame, were added to the Pathfinder's frame to accommodate the above changes. Other design aspects that point to a principal design for passengers include: the spare tire and the rear seat when folded down intrude upon the cargo space; the cargo area is carpeted; a separate window opening in the pop-up tailgate accommodates passengers loading and unloading small packages without having to lower the tailgate. In contrast, the Hardbody truck bed can accommodate loading with a fork lift, clearly a design feature for cargo. The CIT also found that the cargo volume is greatly reduced when the rear seat is up to accommodate passengers. Moreover, the axle and wheel differences are minor and consistent with the Pathfinder's off-road mission, particularly in the loaded condition. The Pathfinder has the same engine size as the Maxima passenger car.

Auxiliary design aspects, in addition to those merely relating to the structural derivation of the Pathfinder, that indicate passenger use over cargo use include: vehicle height was lowered 50 millimeters; the seat slides were improved yet similar to those on two door passenger sedans. Other auxiliary design features that point to transport of passengers include: rear seats that recline, are comfortable, and fold to make a fairly flat cargo bed but are not removable; rear seat stereo outlets, ashtrays, cubbyholes, arm rests, handholds, footwells, seat belts, child seat tie down hooks and operable windows. The CIT noted that there is not much more that can be done to accommodate passengers in the rear seat. Moreover, the testimony of the three primary design engineers as well as the contemporaneous design development documents support the finding that the Pathfinder was principally designed for the transport of persons.

The non-tariff regulations (NHTSA and EPA regulations) are not dispositive for purposes of tariff classification. The government concedes this point. Nonetheless, the government goes on to argue that "the fact that safety, emission and fuel design changes required by those regulations are an element of the design process . . . should afford greater import to Nissan's decisions of what features to incorporate under the . . . regulatory schemes" and that these regulations are in accord with the motor vehicle industry. As noted by the CIT, the government's assessment that these regulatory schemes contain language that is substantially the same as the statutory language in the HTSUS, therefore affording these regulations greater relevance, is misplaced. The reasoning is baseless because those regulations include a category for Multipurpose Passenger Vehicles (MPV), a category that is not specifically delineated in the HTSUS.

In its March 1, 1989, memorandum referred to above, Customs has drawn what appears to be a line between two door and four door versions of sports utility vehicles. Customs' conclusion, however, that vehicles that lack rear side passenger access doors are to be classified under 8704, is *de facto* affording determinative weight to this feature. This line, classifying two door dual-purpose vehicles for the transport of goods while classifying the four door version as principally designed for transport of persons, appears to be arbitrary.

Passenger cars with two doors also have restricted entry into the rear seat but this fact does not take these vehicles out of 8703 classification. Two door passenger cars are equipped with a seat slide mechanism that effectively slides the front seat forward to provide easier access to the rear seat. The doors of two door passenger cars are generally wider as well. The CIT found that the Pathfinder has both of these features so that passengers can be easily accommodated. Therefore, the two door Pathfinder accommodates passengers in the rear seat as well as two door passenger cars, if not as easily as four door sports utility vehicles. Consequently, the number of doors on a vehicle should not be determinative.

CONCLUSION

We hold that the court applied the correct legal standards, and that the evidence of record supports the CIT's decision that the Pathfinder is principally designed for the transport of persons.

Affirmed.

Heartland By-Products v. United States
United States Court of Appeals, Federal Circuit, 2001
264 F.3d 1126

SCHALL, Circuit Judge.

[Heartland By-Products (Heartland), a Michigan company, imports sugar syrup from Canada. The import of certain types of sugar syrup into the United States is governed by a tariff rate quota (TRQ), which sets two different duties. For products entering under the quota, there is one rate of duty and for products entering above the quota there is a higher rate of duty. The reason for the TRQ is to protect the domestic U.S. sugar industry from foreign competition. Certain types of sugar syrups are not subject to the TRQ but other types are subject to the TRQ because they are considered to be directly competitive with sugar. The types of syrups that are subject to the TRQ under HTSUS 1702.90 are those that contain "soluble non-sugar solids (excluding foreign substances that may have been added or developed in the product) equal to 6 percent or less by weight of the total soluble solids." Those syrups that contained more than 6 percent of soluble nonsugar solids, however, were classified under HTSUS 1702.40 and were not subject to the TRQ. In other words, a syrup had to contain a certain minimum level of nonsugar substances in order to be deemed to be a product that did not compete directly with sugar and not subject to the TRQ. If a syrup's nonsugar substances did not meet a certain level, then it was considered to be a direct competitor of sugar and subject to the TRQ. The test was whether the nonsugar substances exceeded 6 percent of the syrup. However, in order to be within the meaning of 1702.90 and outside of the scope of the TRQ, the nonsugar substances must constitute a certain minimum percentage — more than 6 percent — of the syrup *excluding any foreign substances*.

On May 15, 1995, Heartland got an advance ruling (N.Y. Ruling Letter 810329) from Customs that the syrup it wanted to import from Canada fell under HTSUS 1702.90.40 and was thus not subject to the TRQ. With this ruling in hand, Heartland began to import sugar from Canada. In mid-1997, a source from the sugar industry alerted Customs that Heartland was importing sugar syrup in circumvention of the TRQ, and Customs investigated the complaint but did not take any action. On January 18, 1998, the United States Cane Sugar Refiner's Association, the United States Beet Sugar Association, and their member companies (together the Sugar Industry) filed an action with Customs seeking reclassification of Heartland's sugar syrup as being subject to the TRQ. In making its determinations, Customs received many comments both in support of and against the revocation. Those supporting the revocation were members of the U.S. Sugar Industry. Those opposing the revocation were largely trade associations engaged in the import and export business. Customs agreed with the Sugar Industry and reclassified the syrup as subject to the TRQ.

Customs found that molasses had been added to the syrup prior to its importation to the United States and that once the syrup entered the United States the molasses was then extracted. The molasses introduced into the syrup contained enough impurities to assure that nonsugar substances in the syrup exceeded the 6 percent limitation so that the syrup was not subject to the TRQ. Customs then found that the molasses with its impurities was a "foreign substance" and so thus could not be included when determining the soluble content of nonsugar solids in the syrup. Once the molasses was excluded from the syrup, the nonsugar substances in the syrup did not exceed the 6 percent limit and thus the syrup was subject to the TRQ. Customs also found that the addition of the molasses was an artifice or disguise and not a genuine step in the manufacturing process.

Heartland filed a complaint in the Court of International Trade, challenging the revocation and reclassification by Customs. The court agreed with Heartland and held (1) the molasses was not a foreign substance because the molasses is made from cane or beet sugar and that molasses and other ingredients "all have the same chemical ingredients, including impurities that naturally occur in sugar" and should not have been excluded in determining the 6 percent minimum nonsugar content; and (2) adding the molasses was not an artifice or disguise but was used to adjust the purity of the product during the manufacturing process. The Sugar Industry appealed to the Federal Circuit Court of Appeals. The court of appeals decided that the molasses was a foreign substance and thus did not reach or decide the second issue of whether adding the molasses was an artifice or disguise.]

I.

In reviewing a decision of the Court of International Trade, this court usually applies anew the statutory standard of review applied by that court to the agency's decision. *Inland Steel Indus. v. United States*, 188 F.3d 1349, 1359 (Fed. Cir. 1999). Pursuant to 28 U.S.C. §2640(e), the court applied the APA standard of review to Customs' classification of Heartland's sugar syrup, determining whether the revocation ruling was "'arbitrary, capricious, an abuse of discretion, or otherwise not in accordance with law.'" *Heartland*, 74 F. Supp. 2d at 1329 (quoting 5 U.S.C. §706(2)(A)). Subsequent to the court's decision, however, the Supreme Court issued *United States v. Mead Corp.*, 533 U.S. 218, 121 S. Ct. 2164, 150 L. Ed. 2d 292 (2001), in which it held that Customs classification rulings may merit deference under *Skidmore v. Swift & Co.*, 323 U.S. 134, 65 S. Ct. 161, 89 L. Ed. 124 (1944). We therefore will evaluate Customs' classification of Heartland's sugar syrup under the standards required by *Mead* and *Skidmore*, as discussed in more detail below.

II.

The issue before the Supreme Court in *Mead* was "whether a tariff classification ruling by the United States Customs Service deserves judicial deference." *Mead*, 533 U.S. at 221, 121 S. Ct. at 2168. The Court determined that Customs "classification rulings are best treated like 'interpretations contained in policy statements, agency manuals, and enforcement guidelines.' They are beyond the *Chevron* pale." *Id.* at 2175 (quoting *Christensen v. Harris County*, 529 U.S. 576, 587, 120 S. Ct. 1655, 146 L. Ed. 2d 621 (2000)). The Court continued,

> To agree . . . that Customs ruling letters do not fall within *Chevron* is not . . . to place them outside the pale of any deference whatever. *Chevron* did nothing to eliminate *Skidmore*'s holding that an agency's interpretation may merit some deference whatever its form, given the "specialized experience and broader investigations and information" available to the agency, and given the value of uniformity in its administrative and judicial understandings of what a national law requires.

Id. Commenting on the highly detailed nature of the applicable regulatory scheme and Customs' specialized experience in classifying goods, the Court determined that "[a] classification ruling . . . may . . . at least seek respect proportional to its 'power to persuade.'" *Id.* at 2175-76. The Court stated that "[s]uch a ruling may surely claim the merit of its writer's thoroughness, logic and expertness, its fit with prior interpretations, and any other sources of weight." *Id.* at 2176.

Although the classification ruling before the Court in *Mead* was not issued pursuant to 19 U.S.C. §1625(c) and, therefore, was not subject to a public notice and comment procedure, we read the Court's holding as applying to all Customs classification rulings. We therefore will review the classification of Heartland's sugar syrup in accordance with *Mead* and *Skidmore*.

III.

Mead indicates that the following factors are to be evaluated when determining the degree of deference to accord a Customs classification ruling: "its writer's thoroughness, logic and expertness, its fit with prior interpretations, and any other sources of weight." *Mead*, 533 U.S. at 235, 121 S. Ct. at 2176. Those factors echo the factors set forth in *Skidmore* for determining the weight to accord an administrative ruling, interpretation, or opinion: "the thoroughness evident in its consideration, the validity of its reasoning, its consistency with earlier and later pronouncements, and all those factors which give it power to persuade." *Skidmore*, 323 U.S. at 140, 65 S. Ct. 161. Applying these factors to the classification of Heartland's sugar syrup, we determine that the revocation ruling is entitled to deference because of its persuasiveness.

The revocation ruling was issued pursuant to a notice and comment process, during which numerous members of the sugar industry, including the United States Beet Sugar Association and Heartland, submitted comments in support of and in opposition to the ruling. Customs responded to the two main legal issues raised by the comments when it issued the ruling. *Revocation of Ruling Letter*, 33 Cust. Bull. No. 35/36 at 42-47. We therefore conclude that Customs gave thorough consideration to the ruling.

The revocation ruling is supported by a logical and well-reasoned explanation published in the Customs Bulletin. *Id.* at 42-54. Specifically, on the issue of whether the term "foreign substances" encompasses the molasses Heartland adds to raw sugar to make its sugar syrup, Customs explained:

> The addition of the molasses to the sugar is a foreign substance [sic] containing impurities in producing the sugar syrup and, therefore, we exclude the molasses with impurities in calculating the 6% rule. . . .
>
> There is a view that since the molasses is naturally found in sugar cane or sugar beets, it meets the requirements of subheadings 1702.90.10/20 HTSUS, in that it (molasses) is derived also from sugar cane or sugar beets. As stated above, molasses is derived as a by-product from the refining of sugar cane or sugar beets and it is not derived as sugar from the refining of sugar cane or sugar beets. Thus, molasses syrups are classified in heading 1703, HTSUS, and not in heading 1702, HTSUS.

Id. at 53.

We also note that Customs has "specialized experience" in classifying goods, *Mead*, 533 U.S. at 235, 121 S. Ct. at 2175, which lends further persuasiveness to its ruling.

The only factor that weighs against giving deference to the revocation ruling is the ruling's lack of consistency with an earlier pronouncement, the New York Ruling Letter. The revocation ruling, of course, changed the classification of Heartland's sugar syrup. However, because §1625(c) permits Customs to revoke a prior classification of goods, inconsistency with a prior ruling is not itself a basis for denying all deference to a revocation ruling. Moreover, the New York Ruling Letter was not issued pursuant to a notice and comment process and did not address the specific issue addressed in the revocation ruling—whether the molasses Heartland adds to raw sugar is a foreign substance within the meaning of 1702.90.10/20 HTSUS.

Under these circumstances, we conclude that the revocation ruling has "power to persuade." *Mead*, 533 U.S. at 235, 121 S. Ct. at 2176; *Skidmore*, 323 U.S. at 140, 65 S. Ct. 161. As discussed above, the relevant provision of the HTSUS does not indicate to what a substance must be "foreign" in order to be a "foreign substance" excluded from the solids content calculation of 1702.90.10/20 HTSUS. Customs therefore had to interpret the term "foreign substances" in order to classify

Heartland's sugar syrup. Customs determined that the term refers to substances that are foreign to the sugar syrup at the relevant stage of the refining process. Customs concluded that, while molasses is a by-product of the sugar refining process, "[t]he mix[ing] of molasses with sugar is not a refining process for raw sugar." *Revocation of Ruling Letter*, 33 Cust. Bull. No. 35/36 at 53. Customs therefore determined that the molasses Heartland adds to raw sugar to make its sugar syrup is a foreign substance that must be excluded from the solids content calculation of 1702.90.10/20 HTSUS.

The Court of International Trade went too far when it determined that, because 1702.90 HTSUS encompasses sugar syrups "'derived from sugar cane or sugar beets,'" any substance that also is "'derived from sugar cane or sugar beets' . . . cannot be 'foreign' to HTSUS 1702.90." *Id.* at 1334–35 (quoting 1702.90 HTSUS). The explanatory notes cited by the court do not support its narrow construction. Explanatory Note 17.02(B)(3), which provides examples of sugar syrups that fall under 1702 HTSUS, states that "golden syrup" falls under 1702 HTSUS. The court noted that golden syrup is a table syrup made from molasses, and considered that the inclusion of golden syrup under 1702 HTSUS undermined Customs' determination that molasses is a "foreign substance" under 1702.90.10/20 HTSUS. *Id.* at 1332-33. However, the note's discussion of golden syrup does not shed light on the issue before us because the note addresses classification under heading 1702 in general, not classification under subheading 1702.90.10/20 specifically. Moreover, the note does not address a syrup made by combining raw sugar with molasses; instead, golden syrup is described in the note as being "'made from the syrup remaining during sugar refining after crystallization and separation of refined sugar, or from cane or beet sugar, by inverting part of the sucrose or by the addition of invert sugar.'" *Id.* at 1333 (quoting HTSUS Explanatory Note 17.02(B)(3)).

The court also cited Explanatory Note 17.02(B)(2), which states that "[j]uices and syrups obtained during the extraction of sugars from sugar beet, sugar cane, etc.," fall under 1702 HTSUS, and that these syrups "may contain pectin, albuminoidal substances, mineral salts, etc., as impurities." *Id.* at 1335. The court determined that because this note permits products with the same impurities as molasses to be classified under 1702 HTSUS, it undermines Customs' determination that molasses is a foreign substance. *Id.* This note, however, does not indicate whether the molasses added to raw sugar to make Heartland's sugar syrup is a "foreign substance" under 1702.90.10/20 HTSUS because it does not set forth under which subdivision of 1702 HTSUS the described sugar syrups are classified. Moreover, the impurities described in the note are naturally present in the juices and sugar syrups, not added to raw sugar like the molasses at issue in this case.

Heartland does not argue that its sugar syrup contains less than 6 percent by weight of soluble nonsugar solids when the weight of the molasses solids is excluded. For the foregoing reasons, the decision of the Court of International Trade declaring the revocation ruling unlawful and ordering that Heartland's sugar syrup be classified under 1702.90.40 HTSUS is *REVERSED*.

FRIEDMAN, Senior Circuit Judge, concurring.

I reach the same result [as the majority] but get there by a different route.

The syrup Heartland imported from Canada had molasses added to it before importation. Upon receiving the syrup in the United States, Heartland first removed the molasses and then refined the remaining syrup. The removed molasses was returned to Canada but was again used the same way by adding it to other sugar syrup. As far as appears, this chain continued indefinitely.

Heartland makes no claim that the presence of the molasses in the sugar during the syrup's journey from Canada to the United States in any way aided, improved or facilitated the refining of the sugar syrup after the molasses had been removed. It does not state, or even suggest, that if the sugar syrup it had imported had not contained the molasses, it would temporarily have added molasses in the United States and then removed it prior to processing.

Since the addition and removal of the molasses from the sugar served no manufacturing or commercial purpose, the conclusion is irresistible that the only purpose of this strange arrangement was to create a fictitious product that, because of the temporary presence of the molasses, qualified for the lower rate of duty on sugar imports containing specified amounts of nonsugar solids.

NOTES AND QUESTIONS

1. *Marubeni* was the culmination of a long battle between Japanese and U.S. automobile manufacturers. If the U.S. Customs' classification had been upheld, Nissan would have had to pay a 25 percent ad valorem tariff on the Pathfinder. What effect would this have had on Nissan's ability to compete with U.S. automobile manufacturers? How would consumers have fared? What strategy do you think Nissan would have adopted had the Pathfinder been found subject to a 25 percent tariff?

2. The *Heartland* case culminates a bitter dispute between U.S. sugar product importers and U.S. sugar producers. Customs' reclassification decision was made in response to a petition by U.S. producers. Why did the importer add molasses to the syrup only to remove it once the syrup entered the United States? Why did the majority refuse to address the issue of whether the importers engaged in an artifice or disguise?

3. In both the *Marubeni* and the *Heartland* cases, the U.S. Customs Service advocated a position that benefited domestic producers of automobiles and sugar at the expense of foreign competition. Had Customs prevailed in the *Marubeni* case, Nissan's vehicles would have been subject to a 25 percent duty. Customs' reclassification of the syrup was upheld by the court of appeals in *Heartland* and the syrup in question became subject to the tariff rate quota, greatly benefiting the domestic sugar industry. Is the U.S. Customs Service protectionist?

B. VALUATION ISSUES

Century Importers, Inc. v. United States
United States Court of Appeals, Federal Circuit, 2000
205 F.3d 1308

RADER, Circuit Judge.

Century is a wholly owned importing subsidiary of the Miller Brewing Company of Milwaukee, Wisconsin (Miller). On January 14, 1993, Miller entered an agreement (the Beer Agreement) with Molson Breweries of Toronto, Ontario, Canada (Molson), which covered the importation, sale, advertising, and distribution of beer. Exhibit 9(j) of the Beer Agreement, titled "Calculation and Payment of Transfer Prices," set the formula for calculating the price of Molson's beer. This price — the "transfer price" — included production, overhead, packaging, and shipping costs. Exhibit 9(j) also included tariffs, levies, taxes, and duties under "packaging costs" to be invoiced separately. The parties to the agreement treated these tariffs and duties as Molson's costs, which Molson would invoice separately to Miller. Because these tariff and duty costs appeared on a separate invoice, the parties did not count the duties in the price of the beer.

When Molson and Miller began to negotiate the Beer Agreement, the duty for beer imported from Canada was a specific (i.e., volume-based) rate under one cent per liter. During the negotiations, however, as a result of a trade dispute, the United States replaced the specific duty rate for beer imported from the Province of Ontario with a rate based upon value. This ad valorem rate was fifty percent of the value of the imported product. Molson and Miller agreed, in a side letter headed "Import Duties" accompanying the Beer Agreement, that Molson would "pay or reimburse" Miller and its affiliates for the cost of these duties.

When Century later imported Molson beer, Customs assessed fifty per cent ad valorem duties based on the price stated on the invoices or bills. The invoices did not contain any statements about subsequent duty reimbursements. Customs assessed the duty based on the sales invoice price. Century paid the duty to Customs. Later Miller billed Molson for the duties, and Molson reimbursed Miller (and Century) the billed amount.

Century brought an action in the Court of International Trade seeking a refund of part of the duties it paid, contending that Customs, in calculating the duties on the imported beer, should have deducted the reimbursed duties from the invoice price. In essence, Century argued that Molson had in reality reduced the price of its beer by agreeing to reimburse Miller for the duties. Molson had recovered, Century argued, only the invoice price minus the reimbursed duties. Therefore, Century contends that this reduction in the invoice reflects the value of the transaction.

Customs contends that it calculated the duty on the basis of 19 U.S.C. §1401a(b)(1) which sets the "transaction value," the basis for the duty calculation, at "the price actually paid or payable for the merchandise." Customs contended that the price "actually paid" for the beer was the invoice price. According to Customs, Molson's reimbursement was a rebate. Customs treated this alleged rebate according to the statutory formula: a "rebate of, or decrease in, the price actually paid . . . after the date of the importation . . . shall be disregarded in determining the transaction value." §1401a(b)(4)(B). Customs acknowledges that the transaction value would not include customs duties "if identified separately from the price actually paid." 19 U.S.C. §1401a(b)(3)(B). Customs notes, however, that neither Molson nor Century separately identified at importation the customs duties later reimbursed by Molson.

Century and Customs cross-moved for summary judgment. The Court of International Trade granted Century's motion, holding that the invoice price included a component for duties which Customs should have deducted before it assessed duties. Further, the trial court reasoned that repayment of duties to the importer after importation is not a "rebate in price" within the meaning of the statute. *See Century*, 19 F. Supp. 2d at 1126. Therefore, the Court of International Trade held that Molson's failure to identify separately the reimbursement agreement was a ministerial error which the parties could later correct. See id. at 1127. The Government now appeals the decision of the Court of International Trade.

Title 19 authorizes Customs to determine the value of imported merchandise. See 19 U.S.C. §1500(a) (1999). According to title 19, Customs appraises imports "on the basis of . . . (A) The transaction value provided for under subsection (b) of this section." §1401a(a)(1). Transaction value is the "price actually paid or payable for the merchandise." §1401a(b)(1). Two further provisions inform the meaning of the "price actually paid or payable." Title 19 uses that phrase again in excluding rebates from the transaction value: "any rebate of, or other decrease in, the price actually paid or payable that is made or otherwise effected between the buyer and seller after the date of the importation . . . shall be disregarded in determining the transaction value. . . ." §1401a(b)(4)(B) (emphasis supplied). Again, title 19 uses the phrase in excluding from transaction value several items when identified separately from the price: "the transaction value . . . does not include any of the following, if identified separately from the price actually paid or payable. . . . (B) The customs duties . . . currently payable on the imported merchandise by reason of its importation. . . ." §1401a(b)(3)(B).

These provisions show that title 19 makes the transaction value a touchstone for valuation of imports. Transaction value or "the price actually paid or payable" is "the total payment . . . made, or to be made, for imported merchandise by the buyer to . . . the seller." §1401a(b)(4)(A). From this touchstone, title 19 authorizes deductions "for transportation, insurance, and related services incident to the international shipment of the merchandise." Id. Those deductions are not at issue in this case. Title 19 also enumerates other costs that Customs must exclude from transaction value, but only if they were identified separately from the price actually paid or payable. These costs include "the customs duties and other Federal taxes currently payable on the imported merchandise." §1401a(b)(3)(B). According to title 19, the transaction value, the touchstone of duty calculation, does not include customs duties payable upon importation, if identified separately from the price actually paid.

Applying the statutory formula to this case, §1401a(b)(3) explicitly excludes customs duties from the transaction value if identified separately to Customs. Therefore, because the record shows that the parties did not identify these duties separately, Customs has no authorization to deduct them from the price calculation. Beyond this straightforward application of the statute to this case, title 19 supplies further confirmation for Customs' refusal to deduct the duties from the transactional value. Because Molson reimbursed the duties after the date of importation, that post-importation action was in fact a rebate. See Black's Law Dictionary 1266 (6th ed. 1990). Section 1401a(b)(4)(B) directs Customs to disregard rebates after the date of importation. Thus Customs properly appraised the merchandise at the invoiced unit prices.

In the declaration of its Import Specialist, Customs acknowledges that it might well have reached a different appraisal if it had been informed of the duty rebates at the time of importation. The Court of International Trade considered this omitted notice a simple error in the preparation of the entry papers and thus considered it remediable under 19 U.S.C. §1520I(1) (1994), which states:

> [A] clerical error, mistake of fact, or other inadvertence . . . not amounting to an error in the construction of a law, adverse to the importer and manifest from the record or established by documentary evidence, in any entry, liquidation, or other customs transaction, [may give rise to a refund] when the error, mistake, or inadvertence is brought to the attention of the Customs Service within one year after the date of liquidation.

The Court of International Trade read §1520 to give Miller a year to correct its failure to identify the "duty paid" invoice at the time of importation. To the contrary, §1520 does not apply to this case.

Century's repeated failure to mark its documents "duty paid" falls outside the allowance for correction under §1520I(1). Section 1520 extends a correction chance to "a clerical error, mistake of fact, or *other inadvertence*." (Emphasis supplied.) A correctable inadvertence under §1520I(1) is easy to recognize because it is commensurate with, as the statute states, a "clerical error" or a "mistake of fact." Century's course of conduct with respect to the entries that occurred both before and after the entries at issue is relevant in demonstrating that its error is one of law. The repetition of "inadvertence" may indicate an advertent misunderstanding of the law. In this case, Century's repeated failures to provide notice of the duty arrangements over a period of at least four months do not qualify as inadvertent clerical errors or as inadvertent mistakes of fact. Century might well have known that it was not marking its import documents "duty paid," but not have known it was operating under a misapprehension of the law. To use an alternative label, Century acted negligently. "Inadvertence does not stretch so far as to encompass intentional or negligent inaction." *Ford Motor Co. v. United States*, 157 F.3d 849, 860 (Fed. Cir. 1998). Century's failure to provide notice falls outside the scope of inadvertence correctable under 19 U.S.C. §1520I(1).

Correction is not possible if the error is one in the construction of law. Mistakes of law occur where the facts are known but their legal consequences are not, or are believed to be different than they really are. Thus, misunderstanding or ignorance of the law does not qualify as a correctable inadvertence under §1520.

Because the Court of International Trade mistakenly interpreted the Century's import transactions to be duty-paid imports, improperly assessed by Customs due to remediable error on the part of the importer, it erred in its grant of summary judgment. This court therefore vacates the grant of summary judgment to Century and reverses the denial of summary judgment to the United States.

NOTES AND QUESTIONS

1. Why was Century so careless in filling out the proper paperwork to get an accurate assessment of duties, which seems to be a simple, straightforward task? Who do you think discovered the error, Century or Molson?

2. There are two alternative methods to calculate value if the transaction value method is not applicable: Deductive value and computed value. The reasons for the alternative methods is that in some cases, as in transactions between affiliated parties, the actual price paid may not be an accurate measure of the value of the merchandise. The deductive value method also recognizes that in some cases the product may be processed or finished by a related importer and contains complex rules for determining the value of the product. *See* 19 C.F.R. §152.105. When deductive value does not apply, Customs will apply the computed value method, which is essentially a constructed value of the product based on its costs of production, profit, and general expenses. *See* 19 C.F.R. §152.106.

3. If the U.S. importer and the foreign exporter are related companies, charge-backs and commissions paid by the importer to the exporter may be included in the transaction value of the goods. *See VWP of America v. United States*, 259 F. Supp. 2d 1289 (CIT 2003).

PROBLEM 2-17

A U.S. importer B imports glassware from its parent company in Italy. The parent company bills B an extra charge of 1.25 percent above the invoice price per month as interest. U.S. Customs has issued guidelines that it will not include interest as part of dutiable value where, among other conditions, the parties have their financing arrangement in writing. B and its parent company have a written agreement under which B is to pay accrued interest charges on a quarterly basis and the principal on the invoices within 90 days of billing. In practice, however, B has been paying interest charges every 6 to 12 months and also frequently pays the outstanding invoices up to 22 days after the expiration of the 90-day period. B says that the parties have contractually modified the agreement by their practices and by oral agreement. Should the interest charges be treated as dutiable value? Why would the parties have such an arrangement? *See Luigi Bormioli Corp., Inc. v. United States*, 304 F.3d 1362 (Fed. Cir. 2002).

C.   RULES OF ORIGIN

Zuniga v. United States
United States Court of Appeals, Federal Circuit, 1993
996 F.2d 1203

ARCHER, Circuit Judge.

[Refractarios Monterrey, S.A. (Refractarios) produced kiln furniture in Mexico using raw materials from the United States. Customs classified the kiln products as refractory articles under TSUS 531.39 subject to a 7.5 percent duty. Refractarios and F.F. Zuniga, the importer of record, sought to have the products enter the United States duty free under the general system of preferences under which Mexico is a beneficiary developing country. Under the GSP rules of origin, products could enter the United States duty free only if the sum of the cost or value of the materials and production in Mexico were at least 35 percent of the appraised value of the product. In order to reach this 35 percent level, however, the parties had to be able to include the value of raw materials from the United States as being originating materials from Mexico. Refractarios and Zuniga argued that the raw materials were "substantially transformed" into a new and different article of commerce in the manufacturing process and could be considered to be of Mexican origin. Customs denied duty-free status to the kiln products. The CIT agreed with Customs and the parties appealed to the court of appeals.]

Before United States starting materials can be regarded as "materials produced" in Mexico, "[t]here must first be a substantial transformation of the [United States] material into a new and different article of commerce which becomes 'materials produced,' and these materials produced in [Mexico] must then be substantially transformed into a new and different article of commerce." *Azteca*, 890 F.2d at 1151. A substantial transformation occurs "when an article emerges from a manufacturing process with a name, character, or use which differs from [that] of the original material subjected to the process." *Torrington Co. v. United States*, 764 F.2d 1563, 1568 (Fed. Cir. 1985). Thus Refractarios must show first that the dry components processed into kiln furniture were, at an intermediate stage in the process, "substantially transformed . . . into a new and different article of commerce." 19 C.F.R. §10.177(a)(2); *see Azteca*, 890 F.2d at 1151. The determinative issue in this case is whether the casting slip is such a new and different article of commerce.

In this case, the trial court found that making the casting slip required only a simple addition of water and dispersing agents to the dry ingredients and that the slip did not lose the identifying characteristics of the dry components. It concluded that the "casting slip remained clearly recognizable as a simple blend of its dry ingredients, and was not substantially transformed." Although Refractarios contests these findings, it does not point to any evidence to the contrary. Instead, Refractarios merely argues that the process is more than a mere dilution and that performing it requires a considerable degree of experience. Because Refractarios points to no evidence that distinguishes the character of the casting slip from the dry components, we are not persuaded that the trial court clearly erred in finding no substantial transformation.

In addition to being substantially transformed, the intermediate product must also be an "article of commerce." *See* 19 C.F.R. §10.177(a)(2). In *Torrington*, this court said:

> By emphasizing that the article must be "of commerce," the Customs regulation imposes the requirement that the "new and different" product be commercially recognizable as a different article, i.e., that the "new and different" article be readily susceptible of trade, and be an item that persons might well wish to buy and acquire for their own purposes of consumption or production. . . .
>
> . . . [A]n "article of commerce" — for the purposes of the pertinent Customs regulation — is one that is ready to be put into a stream of commerce, but need not have actually been bought-and-sold, or actually traded, in the past.

Torrington, 764 F.2d at 1570.

The trial court held that Refractarios' casting slip is not an article of commerce and that it is not "readily susceptible of trade." Refractarios contends however that it demonstrated that the casting slip is an article of commerce based on (1) testimony of a competitor's employee, that the competitor would buy the slip if it were economically feasible; (2) evidence that other casting slip is sold in the market and (3) testimony by Mr. Turk, former president and chief executive officer of Refractarios, that he had once been asked to sell casting slip (though no actual sales were ever made). These same contentions were made at trial and were specifically considered and rejected by the trial court. Employees of Refractarios' competitor testified without contradiction that the confidential formula of Refractarios' kiln furniture could be ascertained if its casting slip was sold. Moreover, in their view the slip could not be sold at prices that would be economical for a competitor to purchase. Because of the potential disclosure of confidential information and the uncompetitive price at which the slip would have to be sold, the trial court concluded that Refractarios' casting slip is not "susceptible of trade." As to the sale of other slip, unrebutted testimony demonstrated that it is not comparable to Refractarios' casting slip in kind or quality. It is comprised of different ingredients and cannot be used in the making of kiln furniture. Rather, it is a lower quality product that is sold to hobbyists. By the same token, the evidence indicates that kiln furniture casting slip is not suitable for hobbyists because it contains excessive ingredients and the products made from it have an unattractive rough texture.

Accordingly, we affirm the judgment of the Court of International Trade that Refractarios is not entitled to duty free importation of the kiln furniture at issue.

Affirmed.

NOTES AND QUESTIONS

1.   *Zuniga* was decided prior to NAFTA. If the case arose today, there would not be an origin issue as all of the originating materials and the production costs of the product are attributable to NAFTA countries (the United States and Mexico) and the kiln furniture would pass duty free from Mexico into the United States. A determination of origin using rules of origin and the substantial transformation test discussed in *Zuniga*, however, continues to be applicable to goods coming from other beneficiary developing countries under the GSP or to goods from other free-trade zones.

2.   With the tremendous proliferation of preference trade agreements all over the world, origin determination has become an issue of paramount importance. How clear are the rules? What is the definition of "substantial transformation"? Is this test easy to apply?

3.   There is a WTO Agreement on Rules of Origin (1994), but this is essentially an agreement-to-agree in the future, and little progress has been made on harmonization of rules of origin.

4.   Two categories of problems arise in this area: (1) the proliferation and difficulty of applying the many rules of origin of domestic law and (2) lack of international standardization. Is this an argument for more trade agreements on a global scale?

PROBLEM 2-18

Fish are caught by a Spanish-flag vessel in the exclusive economic zone (EEZ), a band 200 miles offshore that is subject to Canadian sovereignty. Assume that the Spanish vessel has received permission from Canadian authorities to fish in the EEZ. The fish are beheaded, detailed, eviscerated, and cut into fillets on the Spanish vessel, then transported to South Korea where they are treated with preservatives and flavoring and then packaged into cans before being imported into the United States. What country is the origin of the fish? Is it Canada, Spain, or South Korea? In a situation like this involving multiple jurisdictions each with a connection to the product, U.S. Customs will use a default rule that is easy to apply. *See* 19 C.F.R. §102.11(d).

D.   MARKING

Bestfoods v. United States
United States Court of Appeals, Federal Circuit, 2001
260 F.3d 1320

ARCHER, Circuit Judge.

[Bestfoods makes Skippy Peanut Butter in Arkansas using peanut slurry, a gritty peanut-based paste. Most of the paste is from the United States but 10 to 40 percent of the peanut slurry is made in Canada. In 1993, Bestfoods sought a ruling from Customs that it was not required to indicate under the federal marking statute, 19 U.S.C. §1304(a), that its peanut butter was partially of Canadian origin. The federal marking statute requires "article[s] of foreign origin . . . imported into the United States [to] be marked in a conspicuous manner . . . to indicate to an ultimate purchaser the English name of the country of origin of the article." 19 U.S.C. §1304(a) (1994). However, 19 C.F.R. §102.13(b) (2000), a subsection of the federal marking statute, contained a de minimis rule that excepts from the marking requirement products that contain foreign materials that make up less than 7 percent of the overall value of the good (or 10 percent of the value for a good of Chapter 22, Harmonized System).[29] This de minimis exception is not applicable, however, to most agricultural products, as set forth in 19 C.F.R. §102.13(b). Bestfoods argued that the exclusion of agricultural products, such as its peanut butter, from the de minimis exception was arbitrary and capricious and, therefore, invalid. The Court of International Trade agreed with Bestfoods and entered judgment invalidating 19 C.F.R. §102.13(b), effectively extending the de minimis rule of 19 C.F.R. §102.13 to agricultural products such as Bestfoods' peanut butter. *Bestfoods v. United States*, 110 F. Supp. 2d 965 (Ct. Int'l Trade 2000). The United States now appeals.]

We review the Court of International Trade's consideration of Customs' regulations, a pure question of law, de novo. The federal marking statute expressly delegates to the Secretary of the Treasury the authority to promulgate regulations implementing the marking statute, in general, and as it specifically applies to goods imported from a NAFTA country. 19 U.S.C. §§1304(a) and 1304(j) (1994); 19 U.S.C. §3314(b) (1994). In reviewing the regulations promulgated pursuant to this grant of authority, we must defer to the administrative agency and, under the APA standard of judicial review, we must uphold these regulations unless they are "arbitrary, capricious, an abuse of discretion, or otherwise not in accordance with law." 5 U.S.C. §706 (1994).

The regulation at issue, 19 C.F.R. §102.13(b), is not arbitrary, capricious, an abuse of discretion, or otherwise not in accordance with law. Neither the federal marking statute, 19 U.S.C. §1304(a), nor the NAFTA marking rules, set out in Annex 311 of the NAFTA, requires a de minimis exception for agricultural products. Indeed, the federal marking statute does not provide specifically for any such de minimis exceptions. In general, it requires that "every article of foreign origin . . . be marked." 19 U.S.C. §1304(a). The marking statute then sets out certain circumstances where a foreign product need not be marked. For example, no

---

29. §102.13 provides in pertinent part:

§102.13 De Minimis
I. I.(a) Except as otherwise provided in paragraphs (b) and (c) of this section, foreign materials that do not undergo the applicable change in tariff classification set out in §102.20 or satisfy the other applicable requirements of that section when incorporated into a good shall be disregarded in determining the country of origin of that good if the value of those materials is no more than 7% of the value of the good or 10% of the value of a good of Chapter 22, Harmonized System.
(b) Paragraph (a) of this section does not apply to a foreign material incorporated in a good provided for in Chapter 1, 2, 3, 4, 7, 8, 11, 12, 15, 17, or 20 of the Harmonized System.

19 C.F.R. §102.13.

marking is required when the article cannot be marked (§1304(a)(3)(A)) or the article was produced more than 20 years before its import (§1304(a)(3)(I)) or where marking of the article in question would be economically prohibitive (§1304(a)(3)(K)). In view of the broad statutory language requiring marking of all articles, except for the listed exceptions, we cannot conclude that Customs was required to allow further exceptions from the marking requirement.

As the United States points out, Customs' treatment of agricultural products under the NAFTA marking rules codifies its past practice of strictly enforcing the marking statute with respect to such articles. For example, in 1985, Customs determined that orange juice manufacturers were required to mark their products to identify every source of foreign concentrate included in their juice. C.S.D. 85-47, 19 Cust. B. & Dec. No. 593 (1985); *Nat'l Juice Prods. Ass'n v. United States*, 628 F. Supp. 978 (Ct. Int'l Trade 1986) (affirming Customs' decision on appeal).[30]

In addition, withholding the de minimis exception from agricultural products tends to harmonize the country of origin rules for marking purposes with the country of origin rules for preferential tariff treatment under the NAFTA. The country of origin rules for preferential tariff treatment, while providing a de minimis exception for components comprising less than 7 percent of the value of the overall good, withhold this treatment from agricultural products. These rules withhold de minimis treatment from various other products as well. Customs' action in establishing a de minimis rule, for purposes of the NAFTA marking rules, that closely tracks the de minimis rule for preferential tariff treatment under the NAFTA is not arbitrary.

We also reject Bestfoods' arguments that the regulations at issue are based on inappropriate health and safety concerns and lead to absurd results. Pointing to published comments concerning the regulation at issue, Bestfoods contends that Customs improperly withheld the de minimis exception from agricultural products out of a misplaced concern for consumer safety. See 61 Fed. Reg. 28,932 (June 6, 1996). Bestfoods argues that it is not the role of Customs to address food safety issues and, therefore, this was an inappropriate justification for Customs' regulation. We do not agree. Customs has the discretion to promulgate regulations to implement the federal marking statute, 19 U.S.C. §1304(a), as further directed by the NAFTA marking rules, for products from NAFTA countries. As noted above, the purpose of marking products under the marking statute is to inform consumers of the origin of foreign goods. It was surely within Customs' discretion to determine that consumers might be more concerned about foreign materials in agricultural products, including foods. Thus, Customs' reference to "health and food safety concerns" does not necessarily indicate that Customs has improperly taken on a role assigned to other federal agencies that are directly responsible for ensuring food safety. Rather, Customs was merely exercising its discretion to craft rules that would best inform consumers.

---

30. Customs subsequently relaxed this requirement, following a showing by the juice manufacturers that the marking was economically prohibitive. Treas. Dec. 89-66 (1989), reprinted in 54 Fed. Reg. 29,540 (July 13, 1989). Bestfoods argues that this subsequent decision indicates that Customs' past practice was not to enforce strictly the marking requirement. We disagree. Customs' decision to relax the marking requirement for juice manufacturers was based on a specific showing of economic harm, which is an enumerated exception to the general rule set out in the statute. *See* 19 U.S.C. §1304(a)(3)(K) (1994).

We similarly reject Bestfoods' arguments that the regulation leads to absurd results. Bestfoods points out that under the marking regulations consumers are not informed about any quantity of foreign ingredients, if such ingredients are substantially transformed (so as to undergo a shift in tariff classification) during manufacturing of the final product. Further, Bestfoods argues that potentially toxic foreign non-agricultural additives are subject to the de minimis exceptions, and the foreign origins of such additives need not be indicated if less than 7 percent. Again, we do not find Bestfoods' contentions persuasive. Although the marking regulations will not always indicate to consumers the foreign origin of certain components, we cannot conclude that it was arbitrary or capricious for Customs to consider substantially-transformed ingredients to be products of the country of manufacture, even if the raw materials come from some foreign location. Indeed, this was exactly the conclusion that the NAFTA Marking Rules required. See NAFTA Annex 311, 32 I.L.M. 289 (1993). As for Bestfoods' contention concerning non-agricultural additives, it is simply incorrect. The de minimis exception is withheld for foreign material incorporated into any agricultural product identified in §102.13(b), no matter whether the incorporated foreign material is an agricultural product or non-agricultural food additive. See 19 C.F.R. §102.13(b).

We conclude that the regulations, when properly interpreted, do not lead to any absurd results.

Reversed.

NOTES AND QUESTIONS

1.   Why was Bestfoods so concerned about marking its label to indicate that its peanut butter included Canadian peanuts?

2.   Origin marking requirements are a battleground between importers and domestic producers. A basic requirement of the WTO is the principle of national treatment requiring that imported products receive treatment equal to that of domestic products. As a result, nations are not allowed to impose restrictions and conditions on imported products that do not also apply to domestic products. An exception, however, is made under GATT Article IX for marks of origin. Should this be changed? Is origin marking necessary? Helpful?

3.   Does origin marking really influence consumers to "buy American"?

4.   Formerly, a domestic manufacturer could request the U.S. Customs Service to issue an interpretive "letter ruling" on whether foreign origin marking was required. This practice was overturned in *Norcal/Crosetti Foods, Inc. v. United States*, 963 F.2d 356 (Fed. Cir. 1992). Now a petition under 19 U.S.C. §1516 must be filed with the Customs Service, invoking an administrative procedure. *See* 19 C.F.R. §175. Failure to mark allows the assessment of additional duties.

PROBLEM 2-19

The State of Hawaii is particularly vulnerable to penetration by imported products because of its isolation and location, creating a need for many products not available locally. In order to satisfy the demands of domestic producers, the Hawaii legislature has enacted a law: All retail stores that sell eggs produced outside the United States must display a sign in a conspicuous place in their shops in letters at least 3 inches high stating, "WE SELL FOREIGN EGGS." A local supermarket that imports eggs from Australia objects to this new law. If federal law requires that the foreign origin of the eggs must be marked on the package anyway, why should there be an issue with this sign? Is this lawful? *See Hawaii v. Ho*, 41 Haw. 565 (1957).

NOTE ON INTERNATIONAL TRADE LAW AND THE IMPORT/EXPORT SALES TRANSACTION

As we explained in Chapter 1, this book concerns the laws governing international business transactions, and our treatment of international trade law will only be introductory. Nevertheless, we wish to emphasize that in the "real world" international trade law is important. In the preceding section, we explored the principal effects of trade law concepts on import/export transactions, that is, the international sale of goods. Now we wish to summarize and present the "big picture."

International trade laws exist on both the national and the international levels. The public international law of international trade operates to inject a necessary discipline into national laws that otherwise would be free to differ and conflict, impeding trade. Thus, the international law of trade consists of internationally agreed rules of conduct that must be observed by individual states. Of course, not all national trade laws come within the discipline of the international rules, but most important concerns are addressed.

As we have seen, international trade law rules are agreed upon by states on a global level through the World Trade Organization and on a regional or bilateral basis through free-trade and other international economic agreements. In the preceding section, the impacts of some of these rules were explored. An interesting initial question is: Are the global and the subglobal rules complementary?

The answer is "yes and no." The GATT Article XXIV sets out very flexible criteria for compatibility of free trade and customs unions with the global trading system, so, at least legally, these can be compatible. The GATT takes the view that trade liberalization is the purpose of both categories of regimes so they may coexist. In reality, however, there may be problems. Only three will be mentioned here. First, a fundamental rule of WTO/GATT is the most-favored-nation principle—that no advantage or preference can be given to one trade partner that is not automatically extended to all. Regional and bilateral free-trade regimes are considered allowable exceptions to and obviously bypass the most-favored-nation principle. Second, from the point of view of the individual buyer/seller or importer/exporter, the proliferation of free-trade regimes makes international business decisions more complex and increases paperwork and expense. For example, the businessperson must keep in mind and comply with multiple rules of origin. Third, free-trade areas have a double edge—they not only create trade they also divert trade from nonparty states. On a macroeconomic basis, they are successful only if trade creation is more important than trade diversion. But this is not always the case. In the 1990s, the World Bank concluded that MERCOSUR, the free-trade agreement between Brazil, Argentina, Uruguay, Paraguay, and Chile, was having a negative economic effect through trade diversion.

As the preceding section indicated, the primary impact of international trade rules for the exporter/importer will be with respect to the tariff that applies to the particular transaction. International norms place limits on tariffs that can be charged and set out rules and standards for the tariff calculation and collection process. These are very important to the security and predictability of access to foreign markets. International rules also ensure the integrity of the system by banning (with limited exceptions) market access impediments other than tariffs, such as quantitative restrictions on imports. Additional nontariff market access barriers are addressed as well through international agreements on such matters as import licensing, product standards and technical requirements, and preshipment inspection.

The law of international trade concerns other matters as well. These include:

- Rules on treatment that must be accorded to imported products once they clear customs and border formalities. "National treatment" is required that generally prohibits any measure or internal tax that puts imports at a competitive disadvantage with respect to domestic products.
- Rules on how imports can be subject to extra duties if they are unfairly traded. These concern the ability of states to levy antidumping and countervailing duties.
- Rules on "safeguards" — the ability of a state to limit fairly traded imports that are causing a serious adverse impact on a domestic industry.

The law of international trade also has processes for the periodic review, revision, and renegotiation of tariffs and trade matters. The WTO and several other trade agreements contain important dispute settlement systems as well. For complete treatment of these and international trade law issues, *see* Mitsuo Matsushita, Thomas J. Schoenbaum, and Petros C. Mavroidis, *The World Trade Organization: Law, Practice and Policy* (Oxford 2003).

3 *The Sales Contract*

In the preceding chapter, we provided an overview of the entire international sales transaction and the myriad issues involved. In this chapter and the next, we focus on two of the most important topics in the international sale: The sales contract itself, the subject of the present chapter, and the letter of credit, the subject of the next. We begin our study of the sales contract with some preliminary issues concerning choice of law and then turn to an examination of the sales contract under the United Nations Convention on Contracts for the International Sale of Goods.

I. Choice of Law

We begin with a basic issue: How is the determination made on what substantive law governs the international sales contract? The case below examines choice of law for a sale of goods in an international context. As you read the case, keep in mind the following questions: What choice of law approach will courts use in determining the applicable law in a case involving a choice between domestic and foreign law? What factors will the court consider in making the choice of law determination and what problems or issues do you see with such an approach?

Kristinus v. H. Stern Com. E. Ind. S.A.
United States District Court, Southern District of New York, 1979
463 F. Supp. 1263

LASKER, District Judge.

While visiting Rio de Janeiro in December, 1974, Rainer Kristinus, a Pennsylvania resident, purchased three gems from H. Stern Com. E Ind. S.A. (H. Stern) for $30,467.43. According to Kristinus, a flyer advertising H. Stern's wares had been slipped under the door of his hotel room in Brazil. The flyer contained the following statement (in English) in red type:

> "Every sale carries Stern's one-year guarantee for refund, credit or exchange either here or in your own country. H. Stern Jewelers New York, (681 Fifth Avenue) are at your disposal for help and service."

Kristinus asserts that when he purchased the gems, a vice-president of H. Stern assured him that he would be able to return them for a complete refund in New York.

In January, 1975, Kristinus tendered the gems to H. Stern Jewelers, Inc. in New York City and requested a refund. His request was denied, and this suit for specific performance of the alleged oral promise to refund the purchase price followed.

H. Stern moves to dismiss the complaint on the ground that the alleged oral promise is unenforceable under the laws of Brazil, which H. Stern contends govern the transaction in question.

The provisions of Brazilian law on which H. Stern relies are Articles 141 and 142 of the Brazilian Civil Code, which provide:

> "Article 141. Except in cases specifically provided for to the contrary, evidence which is solely by testimony is only admitted as to Contracts whose value does not exceed Cr $10.000,00 (ten thousand cruzeiros).
> Sole Paragraph. Whatever the amount of the Contract, evidence by testimony is admissible as a subsidiary to or complement of evidence in writing.
> Article 142. There cannot be admitted as witnesses:
> IV. The person interested in the object of the litigation, as well as the ancestor and the descendant, or collateral relative, through the third degree of one of the parties, whether by blood or by affiliation."[1]

The question presented at this juncture is not whether H. Stern has properly stated Brazilian law, but whether a New York court would apply that law or the law of the state of New York in the circumstances of this case. *See Klaxon Co. v. Stentor Electric Manufacturing Co.*, 313 U.S. 487, 496, 61 S. Ct. 1020, 85 L. Ed. 1477 (1941). We conclude that a New York court would apply the law of New York, and accordingly we deny H. Stern's motion to dismiss.

In deciding choice of law questions, the rule in New York is that "the law of the jurisdiction having the greatest interest in the litigation will be applied and that the facts or contacts which obtain significance in defining State interests are those which relate to the purpose of the particular law in conflict." *Miller v. Miller* 22 N.Y.2d 12, 15-16, 290 N.Y.S.2d 734, 737, 237 N.E.2d 877, 879 (1968). In short, New York courts balance New York's interest in having New York law apply against a foreign state's interest in having foreign law apply.

An examination of the provisions of the Brazilian Civil Code on which H. Stern relies suggests that those provisions promote two interests. First, they protect the integrity of the judicial process in Brazil against the taints of perjured and biased testimony, by 1) requiring that testimony regarding a contract be corroborated by written evidence (Article 141), and 2) barring testimony from interested parties (Article 142). This interest is not implicated in the present case, since the integrity of the Brazilian judicial process is not threatened in a suit in the United States District Court for the Southern District of New York.

Second, Article 141 protects persons who transact business in Brazil from unfounded contractual claims by requiring that such claims, to be enforceable, be supported by a writing. This interest of Brazil does have a bearing on this case, since presumably Brazil seeks to provide this protection to anyone who

---

1. H. Stern's expert on Brazilian law states that the statement in the flyer that Kristinus received in Brazil would not "be sufficient under Brazilian law to constitute a written contract or even a writing sufficient to enable plaintiff, or his wife, to testify as to the Contract." Affidavit of Paul Griffith Garland, Exhibit B to Defendant's Notice of Motion, P. 4.

transacts business there, regardless of where suit on the transaction is brought. The question, then, is whether this interest is greater than any interest that New York may have in applying its own law (which we assume, for the purposes of this motion, would permit enforcement of the contract alleged by Kristinus) to the transaction involved here.

Although Kristinus is not a New York resident, New York may nonetheless assert an interest on his behalf. New York's contacts with this case are 1) that H. Stern transacts business in New York through its franchisee and agent, H. Stern Jewelers, Inc., and 2) that the alleged promise that Kristinus seeks to enforce was to refund the purchase price of the gems in New York through that franchisee. New York has some interest in ensuring that persons who transact business within its borders (and thus subject themselves to some extent at least to the authority of the state) honor obligations, including contracts made elsewhere. Usually, of course, this interest must bow to the paramount interest of the state or country where the contract is made in regulating the conduct of those within its territory. When the contract is to be performed in New York, however, New York's interest is heightened, since its ability to regulate business affairs and the rights and obligations of those within its territory is then directly implicated. In such circumstances, we conclude that a New York court would decline to apply foreign law where, as here, that law would foreclose enforcement of a contract valid under New York law. In short, a New York court would not permit H. Stern of Brazil to contract in Brazil to refund Kristinus' purchase price in New York, and then rely on the laws of Brazil to avoid its obligation under the contract. Accordingly, New York law should be applied. This is an equitable result, since it simply preserves the dispute between the parties for resolution on the merits.

For the reasons stated, H. Stern's motion to dismiss is denied.

NOTES AND QUESTIONS

1. The choice of law materials in this section concern the many issues that arise in attempting to identify a substantive law to apply to the sales contract. Choice of law on general issues, of course, is also important in dispute resolution and needs to be considered in conjunction with choice of forum, jurisdiction, and other related issues, which we cover in Chapter 8 on dispute resolution.

2. In *Kristinus*, the parties could have agreed on a contractual choice of law clause that designated the applicable law. Where the parties have freely entered into a choice of law clause, most courts will recognize and uphold the clause on the basis of the freedom of the parties to contract although some jurisdictions will require that the law chosen bears a reasonable relationship to the transaction. Such a choice would have avoided the expenditure of resources by the parties and the courts in litigating this issue, but many parties do not have the foresight (or the benefit of advice from their lawyers) to make an effective choice of law.

3. In *Kristinus*, the plaintiff, a Pennsylvania resident, brought suit against a Brazilian defendant in a federal district court in New York City. The federal court, exercising diversity jurisdiction, applied the choice of law approach of the New York state courts under the rule established by *Erie Railroad Co. v. Tompkins*, 304 U.S. 64 (1941) and *Klaxon Co. v. Stentor Electric Manufacturing Co.*, 313 U.S. 487 (1941). In making a choice between New York and Brazilian law, the court is involved in an application of the rules of private international law, as we

have discussed in Chapter 1. If the case were brought in Brazil, then the Brazilian courts would apply their own version of private international law rules to decide whether Brazilian or New York law governed this transaction. Brazil follows a civil law system that is heavily influenced by the continental law traditions of its European settlers. Suppose that Brazil follows the continental law rule that the validity of a contract is governed by the law of the place where it was formed. Under this approach, if the case had been brought in Brazil the Brazilian court might well have chosen Brazilian law to govern the case. What problems of perception might arise if it appeared that, depending on where the case was brought, a Brazilian court would apply the law of Brazil and a New York federal court would apply the law of New York to govern the case?

4. §1-105 of the Uniform Commercial Code (UCC) provides that parties may agree on a choice of law where a transaction bears "a reasonable relation to this state and also to another state or nation." In the absence of such an agreement, "this Act applies to transactions bearing an appropriate relation to this state." UCC §1-105. This last clause has been called the "Imperial Clause" because it allows the application by a U.S. court of U.S. law in any case where the court in its judgment deems the transaction to have an appropriate connection to the state. What issues for the international legal system might arise from this type of choice of law approach?

5. Approaches to choice of law analysis differ among nations, and in the United States, the analysis can differ among the 50 states, all of which have their own choice of law rules. These different approaches can lead to an unfortunate lack of predictability in results. In an effort to promote uniformity in choice of law analysis and the rules of private international law, a number of attempts have been made in the United States and Europe to promote a uniform approach. The Restatement Conflicts of Law (Second) (1971) provides in relevant part for the following choice of law approach in the case of contracts:

§188. Law Governing in Absence of Effective Choice by the Parties

(1)   The rights and duties of the parties with respect to an issue in contract are determined by local law of the state which, with respect to that issue, has the most significant relationship to the transaction and the parties. . . .

(2)   In the absence of an effective choice of law by the parties (see §187), the contacts to be taken into account . . . to determine the law applicable to an issue include:

(a)   the place of contracting;

(b)   the place of negotiation of the contract;

(c)   the place of performance;

(d)   the location of the subject matter of the contract, and

(e)   the domicile, residence, nationality, place of incorporation and place of business of the parties.

These contracts are to be evaluated according to their relative importance with respect to the particular issue.

Note that the Restatement creates a heavy burden on courts as it requires the above analysis to be made with regard to each issue concerning the contract. The Convention on the Law Applicable to Contractual Obligations (1980) applicable within certain states of the European Union provides in Article 4(1) that the contract is to be governed by the law of the country "with which it is most closely connected." This approach appears quite similar to the Restatement approach focusing on the state with "the most significant relationship" to the contract. Under the convention, the contract is presumed to be "most closely connected with the country where the party who is to effect the performance which is characteristic of the contract has, at the time of conclusion of the contract, his habitual residence, or, in the case of a body corporate or unincorporate, its central administration." *Id.* at Article 4(2).

How predictable do you think the Restatement and the EU approach would be in deciding international choice of law cases such as *Kristinus*?

6. In *Kristinus*, the court engaged in a detailed analysis of Brazilian law in order to demonstrate why in its view Brazilian law was inapplicable to the case and why therefore Brazil did not have a significant interest in the case. The court also indicated why New York's interests would support the application of New York law. The federal district court was applying New York state choice of law rules. In other cases, New York courts have not hesitated to examine foreign laws in some detail in order to weigh the interests of the foreign nation against the interests of New York in having its law applied to a particular case. *See, e.g., J. Zeevi & Sons, Ltd. v. Grindlays Bank*, 37 N.Y.2d 220, 330 N.E.2d 168, 371 N.Y.S.2d 892, *cert. denied*, 423 U.S. 1866 (1975) (refusing to apply Uganda national exchange law that would cancel a letter of credit opened in favor of Israeli companies and payable in New York); *see also Stillman v. Nickel Odeon, S.A.*, 608 F. Supp. 1050 (S.D.N.Y. 1985) (applying New York choice of law rules and finding Spain had no valid interests in a dispute over a film distribution contract). Note that each of the 50 states applies its own choice of law rules in an international context giving rise to the possibility of many different regimes in state courts and in federal courts exercising diversity jurisdiction in determining international choice of law issues. The use of state choice of law rules in international cases continues to be commonplace even though one might argue that the interests of foreign states ought to be a federal rather than a state matter and that a federal approach would promote uniformity in the international choice of law context. *See* Daniel C.K. Chow, *Limiting Erie in a New Age of International Law: Toward a Federal Common Law of International Choice of Law*, 74 Iowa L. Rev. 165 (1988).

7. The discussion above indicates that there are three areas of concern in an international choice of law situation: (1) the perception that states may sometimes assert nationalistic interests in choosing their own law as opposed to foreign law, (2) lack of predictability in results in applying the rules of private international law, and (3) the intrusion of the states in an area that may implicate federal interests through the use of state choice of law rules in cases involving the interests of foreign sovereign nations. Added to these three concerns is the need for harmonization and uniformity of national substantive contract laws that we introduced in Chapter 1. All of these concerns are addressed to some extent by the promulgation of the Convention for the International Sale of Goods, the subject of the remainder of this chapter. The CISG is a uniform substantive law that applies in many cases without the need for a choice of law analysis. As more and more states become contracting parties, the CISG will soon apply to the bulk of international contracts for the sale of goods. The time will soon come when all of the major trading nations of the world are parties to the CISG. Can you explain how the CISG addresses each of the concerns set forth above?

II. The United Nations Convention on Contracts for the International Sale of Goods

We turn now to the United Nations Convention on Contracts for the International Sale of Goods. The CISG is a multilateral convention drafted and promulgated under the auspices of the United Nations Commission on International Trade Law to which 56 nations, including the United States, are parties. (For a discussion of UNCITRAL, see Chapter 1 at pp. 32-33; for a discussion of treaties, see Chapter 1 at p. 36.) The UN convention entered into force on January 1, 1988. The CISG is a self-executing treaty that applies directly within its contracting states without the need for domestic implementing legislation.

The CISG is one of the most important instruments of harmonization in the area of international commercial law in the twentieth century. The major goal of the CISG is to promote uniformity in the treatment of contracts in the light of international commercial usage and practice. We will be exploring the meaning of this statement in the materials that follow. Note that in the materials that follow we will not examine the substantive provisions of the Uniform Commercial Code in detail, although we highlight some significant differences between the CISG and the UCC and examine the relationship between the two laws. We leave a detailed consideration of the UCC, however, to other courses in the law school curriculum. Our focus is on the CISG.

When the CISG applies, it displaces domestic law. In the case of the United States, the CISG often displaces the UCC in international sales contracts. Note that the CISG only applies to *international* sales contracts so the UCC and other domestic laws are not disturbed in their internal application. But where the contract is international and the CISG applies, a growing number of nations, including most of the major trading powers, have agreed to displace their domestic law in favor of a uniform substantive international contract law. This is a remarkable achievement.

As of this writing, the following nations were parties to the convention: Argentina, Australia, Austria, Belarus, Belgium, Bosnia and Herzegovina, Bulgaria, Burundi, Canada, Chile, China, Croatia, Cuba, Czech Republic, Denmark, Ecuador, Egypt, Estonia, Finland, France, Georgia, Germany, Greece, Guinea, Hungary, Iraq, Italy, Kyrgyzstan, Latvia, Lesotho, Lithuania, Luxembourg, Mexico, Moldova, Mongolia, Netherlands, New Zealand, Norway, Peru, Poland, Romania, Russia, Singapore, Slovakia, Slovenia, Spain, Sweden, Switzerland, Syria, Uganda, Ukraine, United States, Uruguay, Uzebekistan, Yugoslavia, and Zambia.

A. Basic Features of the CISG

There are several basic features of the CISG that need emphasis. First, the CISG is not a mandatory public law but a supplementary private one; the parties can exclude the application of the CISG, vary the effect of its provisions, and the terms of the contract will override any conflicting terms in the convention. In other words, the CISG, like domestic contract law, plays a supporting role in resolving questions that the parties have not themselves already agreed on. Second, the CISG is not a comprehensive contract law, and there are important areas that are excluded from its coverage. The CISG governs two basic aspects of the contract: Part I governs the formation of the contract and Part II governs the obligations of the parties to the contract. Contracting states can exclude either part by a specific declaration under Article 92. Note also that important issues such as validity of the contract, third-party rights, and property rights in the goods are not governed by the CISG. The result is that these important excluded issues must be governed by another substantive law, usually the domestic law of the one of the parties. Where the parties have not explicitly agreed on a domestic law to govern issues that are excluded from the CISG, the court must engage in a choice of law analysis. Thus, although the CISG is an important tool of harmonization, it does not avoid the need for the use of private international law analysis or the use of domestic law or both in any given case. Both of these matters will continue to play a major role in international contracts for the sale of goods in addition to the CISG.

B.   Historical Origins

Although the CISG came into effect in 1988, its origins can be traced to the work of UNIDROIT that was launched in the 1930s. (For an introduction to UNIDROIT, see Chapter 1 at pp. 33-35.) Work on drafting a uniform law under the auspices of UNIDROIT continued, interrupted by war, until two conventions, a Uniform Law for the International Sale of Goods and a Uniform Law on the Formation of Contracts for the International Sale of Goods, were finalized at a diplomatic conference held at the Hague in 1964. Most of the states that ratified these conventions were European, reflecting the Western European orientation of the drafters. When it became clear that widespread global adoption of the Hague conventions was unlikely due to their Western European origins, UNCITRAL began the process of drafting a more universally acceptable convention, culminating in the CISG. Many of the solutions adopted in the CISG, however, reflect those of the Hague conventions and the legislative history of the Hague conventions continues to be useful in shedding light on the interpretation of the CISG.

C.   Cases on the CISG

States that have implemented the CISG and other UNCITRAL uniform laws have been requested to designate national correspondents whose role is to send decisions applying the CISG (and other uniform laws) to the UNCITRAL secretariat. As many of these cases are too long for multilingual translations, the correspondents have also been asked to prepare one-page abstracts of such cases. UNCITRAL has established a clearinghouse in its Vienna office that publishes abstracts of cases decided under the CISG and its other uniform laws. The cases are published under the acronym CLOUT (Case Law on UNCITRAL Texts) and are available on the Internet. The address is *http://www.uncitral.org* then access "Case Law (CLOUT)."

Professor Michael J. Bonnell, University of Rome, and his staff have developed a comprehensive list of CISG decisions that are compiled in a two-volume loose-leaf service that is widely considered to be authoritative: UNILEX: International

Case Law & Bibliography on CISG (Transnational Publishers, New York). The cases are arranged according to date, country, and issue. Full texts of the decisions of the cases are available in their original languages in Volume II. The decisions have also been abstracted in English in Volume I. In the materials that follow, we will use materials from both CLOUT and UNILEX.

NOTE ON THE UNIDROIT PRINCIPLES

The UNIDROIT Principles of International Commercial Contracts is another important source of law for international commercial contracts. The principles were the result of 20 years of work, culminating in their adoption by UNIDROIT in May 1994. Unlike the CISG, the principles are not a binding legal instrument; rather, the principles are a type of international restatement of contracts, but, as set forth in the preamble, the principles can have legal effect in the following circumstances, when: (1) the parties expressly agree that the contract shall be governed by them, (2) the parties agree that the contract shall be governed by general principles of international commercial law such as the *lex mercatoria*, (3) domestic law is unable to provide a solution, and (4) international instruments need supplementation or interpretation. By all accounts, the UNIDROIT principles are an outstanding achievement and they are highly influential.

There are several reasons why the UNIDROIT principles and the CISG may complement each other and are not in conflict. The CISG applies only to sales contracts whereas the principles apply to all international commercial contracts. In an IBT, the parties may not only need to contract for the sale of goods but may also need to engage in contracts related to agency, distribution, marketing, personnel issues, and other services. It is possible that in some transactions, some of the contracts are governed by the CISG while others are subject to the principles. In addition, even where the CISG applies, the principles may be used to supplement the CISG under Article 7, which provides that in interpreting the CISG regard shall be given to its "international character and to the need to promote uniformity in its application." The principles, as they are a distillation of international practice, may be used as a source of interpretation to promote uniformity. As the focus of this chapter is on the international sales contract most of our attention will be squarely on the CISG, but we introduce the UNIDROIT principles where appropriate.

D.   Sphere of Application of the CISG: Articles 1-6

Articles 1-6 of the CISG define its sphere of application. The most important provisions delimiting the scope of application of the CISG are contained in the first article:

Article 1

(1) This Convention applies to contracts of sale of goods between parties whose places of business are in different States:
   (a) when the States are Contracting States; or
   (b) when the rules of private international law lead to the application of the law of a Contracting State.

(2) The fact that the parties have their places of business in different States is to be disregarded whenever this fact does not appear either from the contract or from any dealings between, or from information disclosed by, the parties at any time before or at the conclusion of the contract.

(3) Neither the nationality of the parties nor the civil or commercial character of the parties or of the contract is to be taken into consideration in determining the application of this Convention.

1. Article 1(1)(a) and the Test of Internationality

Note that the CISG applies only to contracts for the sale of goods that are international. Of the three elements of its subject matter, the CISG defines only one: Internationality. The test of whether a contract is international under Article 1(1)(a) is whether the parties have their places of business in different contracting states.

Illustration 1a. In a contract for the sale of goods, seller has its place of business in country A and buyer has its place of business in country B. Both country A and country B are parties to the CISG. Unless the parties expressly exclude the application of the CISG, an action to resolve a dispute under the sales contract that is brought either in country A or country B is governed by the CISG under Article 1(1)(a).

Suppose that the action were brought in a third nation country C, a contracting state. What law should country C apply? Country C need look no further than Article 1(1)(a) for a clear answer: The CISG governs the contract so long as the parties have their places of business in two contracting states and the parties have not expressly excluded the CISG. The more difficult question occurs when country C is a noncontracting state. Note that in many, if not most cases, country C would apply the CISG because the practical result should be the same whether country C recognizes the effect of subparagraph (1)(a) or if C applies a choice of law analysis. If country C recognizes subparagraph (1)(a), it applies the CISG; if C applies its own choice of law rules that result in a choice of either the law of country A or the law of country B, then the CISG applies as the CISG is part of the domestic law of both countries.

The most difficult situation occurs when country C's choice of law analysis results in the choice of country C's domestic law (e.g., suppose that delivery of the goods was to occur in C). What law should C apply in this case, the CISG or country C's domestic law? Note that even in this case, country C should apply the CISG unless the application of the CISG violates a basic public policy of the forum. The entry into the CISG by countries A and B is a type of implicit choice of law, and country C should give effect to the choice of law by parties; otherwise, country C would nullify the effect of Article 1(1)(a).

In this age of the multinational enterprise with multiple places of business around the world, it is not always easy to determine whether the parties have their places of business in different states as required by Article 1(1)(a). Consider the following problem.

PROBLEM 3-1

Microtel is a multinational enterprise engaged in the manufacture and sale of computer equipment with offices in five continents and headquarters in the

United States. Microtel's wholly owned foreign subsidiary in Japan manufactures microprocessors and enters into a contract to sell microprocessors to a Ugandan company. All of the early negotiations concerning the contract occur between in-house lawyers from the Japanese subsidiary and several executives of the Ugandan company. During these negotiations, the in-house lawyers for the Japanese subsidiary repeatedly asked for and received instructions from management in the U.S. headquarters. When the negotiations reached a critical stage, two senior executives from the U.S. headquarters traveled to Uganda, rented a suite of rooms in a hotel for a week, and worked out the final details of the contract. Most of the final negotiations with the Ugandans occurred in the hotel suite with the two senior U.S. executives as active participants. When the final details were worked out, the CEO of the Japanese subsidiary traveled to Uganda and signed the contract in a ceremony held in the hotel suite. Is this contract governed by the CISG? See Article (1)(a) and (2); *see also* Article 10(a).

2. Article 1(1)(b)

If the CISG applies by virtue of Article 1(1)(a), it is unnecessary to apply the choice of law approach of Article 1(1)(b). If subparagraph (1)(a) is not applicable, then the CISG may apply as a result of subparagraph (1)(b):

> *Illustration 1b.* In a contract for the sale of goods, the seller is from country A, a contracting state to the CISG, and the buyer is from a noncontracting state. As country B is a noncontracting state, the CISG cannot apply by virtue of Article 1(1)(a). In a dispute brought in the courts of either country A or country B, the court must then make a choice of law decision applying the forum's choice of law rules or its rules of private international law. If the court chooses the law of country B, then the domestic law of country B will govern the contract. If the court chooses the law of country A, then under Article 1(1)(b) the CISG governs the contract as the CISG is part of the law of country A.

Article 95 of the CISG allows a party to make a reservation at the time of ratification that it will not be bound by Article 1(1)(b). The United States has made such a reservation. In fact, the United States and several other nations had attempted to have subparagraph (1)(b) deleted from the working drafts of the CISG, but this attempt was defeated. The compromise that was reached was the opt-out mechanism of Article 95. In explaining its position to exclude subparagraph (1)(b), the United States offered this rationale:

> [S]ubparagraph 1(b) would displace our own domestic law more frequently than foreign law. By its terms, subparagraph 1(b) would be relevant only in sales between parties in the United States (a Contracting State) and a *non*-Contracting State. Under subparagraph 1(b), when private international law points to the law of a foreign *non*-Contracting State the Convention will not displace that foreign law, since subparagraph 1(b) makes the Convention applicable only when "the rules of private international law lead to the application of the law of a *Contracting* State." Consequently, when those rules point to United States law, subparagraph 1(b) would normally operate to displace United States law (the Uniform Commercial Code) and would not displace the law of foreign *non*-Contracting States.

U.S. State Department, *Legal Analysis of the UN Convention on Tracts for the International Sale of Goods* (1990), Appendix B.

NOTES AND QUESTIONS

1. Why did the United States declare a reservation under Article 95 to exclude the application of Article 1(1)(b)? The American Bar Association supported the reservation on the grounds that the use of subparagraph (1)(b) might be disadvantageous to U.S. commercial lawyers and their clients. As an illustration of the U.S. concern, take the following situation of a sales contract where the parties are from the United States and a noncontracting state, such as Japan. In a dispute between the parties brought either in a U.S. court or in a Japanese court, Article 1(1)(a) of the CISG would be inapplicable as the parties do not have their places of business in two contracting states. Assume that the United States did not exclude Article 1(1)(b), and that the court engaged in an international choice of law analysis. What are the possible outcomes in the choice of law analysis? Is the application of the Uniform Commercial Code a possibility?

2. Note that the application of subparagraph (1)(b) increases the application of the CISG as it will apply even when one of the parties is from a noncontracting state if a private international law analysis chooses the law of the contracting state. Reservations such as that made by the United States result in fewer applications of the CISG as any contracts between the United States and a noncontracting state will now be governed by the domestic law of either the United States or the other state. In making a reservation under Article 95, has the United States put its own interests ahead of the interests of promoting harmonization through the broadest possible application of the CISG?

3. Return to *Kristinus, supra*, p. 187. That case was decided in 1979 before the CISG became effective on January 1, 1988. Suppose that the CISG were in effect when the case was decided and assume hypothetically that both the United States and Brazil are contracting parties. Would the CISG apply to govern the case? To determine the answer to this question, several questions need to be answered. First, was there a contract for the *international* sale of goods? Note that the sale and purchase occurred in Brazil. Would that fact remove that case from the scope of CISG Article 1(1)(a)? *See also* CISG Article 10(b). Also, does this case fall within Article 1(2)? Second, do any other exclusions apply? *See* CISG Article 2(a). As of October 2004, the United States is a contracting party to the CISG, but Brazil is not. Under this scenario, Article 1(1)(a) would not apply and as the United States would not be bound by subparagraph (1)(b), courts would need to apply a private international choice of law analysis.

4. So far, we have seen fairly straightforward applications of Article 1(1)(a) and (1)(b). When both parties are from contracting states, the CISG applies under subparagraph (1)(a); when only one party is from a contracting state, either the CISG applies or the domestic law of the noncontracting state applies under subparagraph (1)(b); when only one party is from a contracting state and the state has excluded subparagraph (1)(b) through a declaration under Article 95, then the domestic law of one of the states will apply. We now come to a more complex issue: What law applies when a contracting state has excluded Article 1(1)(b) but the dispute, between the contracting state and a noncontracting state, is brought in a third contracting state? What effect will the third state give to the Article 95 declaration? The following problem requires you to work through the analysis of these issues.

PROBLEM 3-2

A U.S. computer company has a foreign subsidiary in Germany that services the European Union markets. The U.S. company makes a contract with a Japanese corporation for the sale of memory chip sets. The U.S. company buys the chip sets and then supplies them to its German subsidiary, among its other foreign subsidiaries. Suppose a dispute has arisen and the U.S. company decides to bring an action against the Japanese supplier in a German court. The United States and Germany are contracting parties to the CISG while Japan is not, and the United States has made an Article 95 declaration excluding the application of Article 1(1)(b). Germany has not made an Article 95 declaration but has made the following statement:

> The Government of the Federal Republic of Germany holds the view that parties to the Convention that have made a declaration under article 95 of the Convention are not considered Contracting States within the meaning of subparagraph 1(b) of Article 1 of the Convention. Accordingly, there is no obligation to apply—and the Federal Republic of Germany assumes no obligation to apply—this provision when the rules of private international law lead to the application of the law of a Party that has made a declaration to the effect that it will not be bound by subparagraph 1(b) of Article 1 of the Convention. Subject to this observation the Government of the Federal Republic of Germany makes no declaration under Article 95 of the Convention.

After the U.S. exclusion of Article 1(1)(b) and the German statement, what possible laws can the German court apply to this transaction? Why would Germany take this position? A leading commentator believes that the German position is the correction interpretation of Article 1(1)(b). *See* John O. Honnold, *Uniform Law for International Sales Under the 1980 United Nations Convention* 43 (3d ed. 1999).

3. Other Issues Relating to Scope

Articles 1-3 identify the transactions that are subject to the CISG, while Articles 4 and 5 define the issues that are governed by the CISG. We have already examined the scope of Article 1. The following problems and cases require you to work through the exclusions in Articles 2-5 and the opt-out provisions of Article 6.

PROBLEM 3-3

The Brasilia Metals Company of Brazil (Brasilia) enters into a joint venture with Akron Steel (Akron), located in Ohio, for the manufacture, distribution, and sale of steel in Brazil and South America. Under the joint venture contract entered into between Brasilia and Akron Steel, the new joint venture company, Akron-Brasilia Steel, promised to use "its best efforts in light of market conditions" to purchase up to $2 million in steel in the first two years of the contract and serve as Akron Steel's Brazilian distributor. In return, Akron Steel promised to purchase chromium from the joint venture, which would comprise 35 percent of the ingredients used by Akron Steel to manufacture the steel that would be sold to the joint venture. During the first year, the joint venture submits a purchase order with Akron for $350,000 in steel, which Akron fills. Later, Akron Steel argues that the joint venture has breached it good-faith purchasing obligations under the joint venture contract and has also failed to secure various Brazilian government approvals as required by the contract. Is this issue governed by the CISG? What about the $350,000 purchase of steel? See *American Meter infra* and CISG Article 2.

PROBLEM 3-4

Suppose that in Problem 3-3 above the joint venture agreement contains a provision allowing the parties to enter into corollary agreements necessary to support the operations of the joint venture. The following separate agreements were entered into by the joint venture with Akron Steel and annexed to the joint venture agreement as appendixes:

(1) Indemnification Agreement: The joint venture promised to hold Akron harmless for any death or injury caused by the use of Akron's products in Brazil;

(2) Technology Transfer Agreement: Within two years after the entry into the joint venture agreement, Akron Steel will then sell a ten-year license to the patents in the steel manufacturing process plus all supporting computer software and know-how needed to implement the patents to the joint venture, which would begin to manufacture steel directly in Brazil; Akron promised to indemnify the joint venture in the event that any third party asserted superior rights in the patent or software;

(3) Stock Sale Agreement: Within seven years after the entry into the joint venture agreement, Brasilia Metals will sell 100 percent of the common stock in its steel manufacturing subsidiary to Akron steel (including several buildings with western-style housing for Akron's managers and a small fleet of automobiles made by a German-Brazilian joint venture for use by the managers); the name of the subsidiary will be changed to Akron Steel (Brazil), S.A., the joint venture will terminate, and Akron Steel will thereafter operate Akron Steel (Brazil), S.A. as a wholly owned subsidiary. A separate clause in the contract provides that the sale of stock is expressly made subject to the CISG by the parties; and

(4) Utilities Agreement: Once the Akron Steel wholly owned subsidiary is established in Brazil, Brasilia Metals will sell electricity to the subsidiary.

Which of the agreements set forth above (or parts of such agreements) are governed by the CISG? See CISG Articles 2, 3, 4, 5, and 6, the *American Meter* case *infra*, and CLOUT Cases 131 and 122 *infra*.

Amco Ukrservice & Prompriladamco v. American Mctcr Company

United States District Court, Eastern District of Pennsylvania, 2004
312 F. Supp. 2d 681

DALZELL, District Judge.

Plaintiffs Amco Ukrservice and Prompriladamco are Ukrainian corporations seeking over $200 million in damages for the breach of two joint venture agreements that, they contend, obligated defendant American Meter Company to provide them with all of the gas meters and related piping they could sell in republics of the former Soviet Union.

After extensive discovery, American Meter and Prompriladamco filed the cross-motions for summary judgment now before us. American Meter asserts that it is entitled to judgment against both plaintiffs as a matter of law because the joint venture agreements are unenforceable under both the United Nations Convention on Contracts for the International Sale of Goods ("CISG") and Ukrainian commercial law. Prompriladamco claims that its agreement is enforceable, that there is no genuine issue of material fact as to whether American Meter is in breach of that agreement, and that the only remaining issue is the extent of the damages it has sustained.

Upon consideration of this complex web of law, we conclude that American Meter is not entitled to summary judgment because the CISG does not apply to the joint venture agreements.

I. FACTUAL AND PROCEDURAL HISTORY

The origins of this action lie in the collapse of the Soviet Union and the newly-independent Ukraine's fitful transition to a market economy. American Meter began to explore the possibility of selling its products in the former Soviet Union in the early 1990s, and in 1992 it named Prendergast as Director of Operations of C.I.S. [Commonwealth of Independent States] Projects. Sometime in 1996, a Ukrainian-born American citizen named Simon Friedman approached Prendergast about the possibility of marketing American Meter products in Ukraine.

Ukraine was a potentially appealing market for American Meter at that time. During and immediately after the Soviet era, Ukrainian utilities had not charged consumers for their actual consumption of natural gas but instead had allocated charges on the basis of total deliveries to a given area. That system penalized consumers for their neighbors' wastefulness and saddled them with the cost of leakage losses. In 1997, the Ukrainian government enacted legislation requiring utilities to shift toward a usage-based billing system. Prendergast's early prediction was that implementation of the legislation would require the installation of gas meters in millions of homes and apartment buildings.

After some investigation, Prendergast and his superiors at American Meter concluded they could best penetrate the Ukrainian market by forming a joint venture with a local manufacturer. To this end, American Meter Vice-President Andrew Watson authorized Friedman on June 24, 1997 to engage in discussions and negotiations with Ukrainian organizations, and the corporation also hired a former vice-president, Peter Russo, to consult on the project. Prendergast, Russo, and Friedman began to identify potential joint venture partners, and by late 1997, they had selected Promprilad, a Ukrainian manufacturer of commercial and industrial meters based in Ivano-Frankivsk, the industrial capital of western Ukraine. On December 11, 1997, Prendergast (representing American Meter), Friedman (representing his firm, Joseph Friedman & Sons, International, Inc.), and representatives of Promprilad and American-Ukrainian Business Consultants, L.P. ("AUBC") met in Kyiv (the current preferred transliteration of "Kiev") and entered into the first of the agreements at issue here.

The agreement provided for the establishment of a joint venture company, to be called Prompriladamco, in which the four signatories would become shareholders. Prompriladamco would work in conjunction with its principals to develop the market for American Meter products in the former Soviet Union and, most important for the purposes of this action, the agreement committed American Meter to the following obligations:

9. AMCO shall grant Joint Venture PrompryladAmco exclusive rights to manufacture and install Meters within the former Soviet Union . . .
10. AMCO shall grant Joint Venture PrompryladAmco exclusive rights to distribute the products manufactured by PrompryladAmco and all products manufactured by AMCO in the former Soviet Union . . .
13. AMCO will deliver components and parts for Meters taking into account 90% assembly.
14. PrompryladAmco (at the first stage) shall perform 10% of the work required to assemble the Meters using components and parts delivered by AMCO.
15. AMCO will deliver the components and parts for Meters by lots in containers, payments for the delivery being subject to at least a 90-day grace period.
16. The number of the components and parts for Meters to be delivered to Ukraine shall be based on demand in the former Soviet Union.
17. Orders for the components and parts for Meters, with the quantities and prices according to paragraph 16 above shall be an integral part of this Agreement.

After executing the agreement, the parties incorporated Prompriladamco in Ukraine, and Friedman became its Chief Executive Officer. The new corporation set out to obtain Ukrainian regulatory approval for American Meter products, which required bringing Ukrainian officials to the United States to inspect American Meter's manufacturing process, and it sponsored a legislative measure that would give those products a competitive advantage in the Ukrainian market.

On April 20, 1998, Friedman and a representative of AUBC executed a second joint venture agreement for the purpose of marketing the gas piping products of Perfection Corporation, a wholly-owned subsidiary of American Meter. Again, the parties agreed to create and fund a corporation, this one to be called Amco Ukrservice, and American Meter committed itself to deliver, on credit, a level of goods based on demand in the former Soviet Union. The parties duly formed Amco Ukrservice, and Friedman became its Chief Executive Officer.

By early summer, Prompriladamco and Amco Ukrservice had begun submitting product orders to American Meter. In late June or early July, however, American Meter President Harry Skilton effectively terminated the joint ventures by stopping a shipment of goods that was on its way to Ukraine and by refusing to extend credit to either Prompriladamco or Amco Ukrservice. *See* Skilton Dep. at 123-24 admitting that, as a result of his decisions, the project "died a natural death from then on out." Finally, at a meeting on October 27, 1998, American Meter Vice-President Alex Tyshovnytsky informed Friedman that the corporation had decided to withdraw from Ukraine "due to unstable business conditions and eroding investment confidence in that country." Letter from Tyshovnytsky to Friedman of 10/29/98.

On May 23, 2000, Prompriladamco and Amco Ukrservice filed parallel complaints claiming that American Meter had breached the relevant joint venture agreement by refusing to deliver the meters and parts that the plaintiffs could sell in the former Soviet Union. Prompriladamco's complaint alleges that the breach caused it to lose $143,179,913 in profits between 1998 and 2003, and Amco Ukrservice claims lost profits of $88,812,000 for the same period. We consolidated the actions on August 18, 2000.

II. AMERICAN METER'S MOTION FOR SUMMARY JUDGMENT

American Meter argues that summary judgment is warranted here because the joint venture agreements are invalid under the CISG and Ukrainian law. It also contends that it is entitled to summary judgment because the plaintiffs' claims for damages are based on nothing but "rank speculation." We consider each of these arguments in turn.

A. THE CISG

The United States and Ukraine are both signatories to the CISG, which applies to contracts for the sale of goods where the parties have places of business in different nations, the nations are CISG signatories, and the contract does not contain a choice of law provision. American Meter argues that the CISG governs the plaintiffs' claims because, at bottom, they seek damages for its refusal to sell them goods and that, under the CISG, the supply provisions of the agreements are invalid because they lack sufficient price[2] and quantity terms. Apart from a handful of exclusions that have no relevance here, the CISG does not define what constitutes a contract for the sale of goods. See CISG art. 2, reprinted in 15 U.S.C.A. App., at 335 (West 1998). This lacuna has given rise to the problem of the Convention's applicability to distributorship agreements, which typically create a framework for future sales of goods but do not lay down precise price and quantity terms.

In the few cases examining this issue, courts both here and in Germany have concluded that the CISG does not apply to such contracts. In *Helen Kaminski PTY. Ltd. v. Marketing Australian Prods.*, 1997 U.S. Dist. LEXIS 10630 (S.D.N.Y. July 23,

---

2. It is not entirely clear whether an open price term invalidates a contract for the sale of goods under the CISG. Article 14(1) of the Convention provides that a proposal is sufficiently definite to constitute an offer if "it indicates the goods and expressly or implicitly fixes or makes provision for determining the quantity and the price." However, Article 55 states that "where a contract has been validly concluded but does not expressly or implicitly fix or make provision for determining the price, the parties are considered . . . to have impliedly made reference to the price generally charged at the time of the conclusion of the contract for such goods sold under comparable circumstances in the trade concerned." The relationship between Articles 14 and 55 is the subject of a long-simmering academic controversy. Some commentators claim that Article 55 obviates the need for a specific price term. Others argue that this approach begs the question whether the parties have "validly concluded" a contract — a question that can only be answered by reference to Article 14 — and surmise that Article 55 applies where a Contracting State has opted out of the CISG's provisions on contract formation. *See* generally Paul Amato, *U.N. Convention on Contracts for the International Sale of Goods — The Open Price Term and Uniform Application: An Early Interpretation by the Hungarian Courts*, 13 J.L. & Com. 1, 9-11 (1993) (discussing the controversy and comparing the views of Professors Farnsworth and Honnold).

1997), the court held that the CISG did not govern the parties' distributorship agreement, but it suggested in dictum that the CISG would apply to a term in the contract that addressed specified goods. Id. at *3. Three years later, Judge DuBois of this Court followed *Helen Kaminski* and held that the CISG did not govern an exclusive distributorship agreement, an agreement granting the plaintiff a 25% interest in the defendant, or a sales commission agreement. *Viva Vino Import Corp. v. Farnese Vini S.r.l.*, 2000 U.S. Dist. LEXIS 12347, No. 99-6384, 2000 WL 1224903, [**11] at *1-2 (E.D. Pa. Aug. 29, 2000). Two German appellate cases have similarly concluded that the CISG does not apply to distributorship agreements, which they termed "framework agreements," but does govern sales contracts that the parties enter pursuant to those agreements. *See OLG Dusseldorf*, UNILEX, No. 6 U 152/95 (July 11, 1996); *OLG Koblenz*, UNILEX, No. 2 U 1230/91 (Sept. 17, 1993).

American Meter argues that this line of cases is inapplicable here because the plaintiffs do not claim damages for breach of what it terms the "relationship" provisions of the joint venture agreements,[3] but instead seek to enforce an obligation to sell goods. In other words, American Meter claims that the supply and credit provisions are severable and governed by the CISG, even if the Convention has no bearing on the remainder of the two agreements.

There are a number of difficulties with this argument, both in its characterization of the plaintiffs' claims and its construction of the CISG. To begin with, Prompriladamco and Amco Ukrservice are not seeking damages for American Meter's refusal to fill particular orders. Instead, they are claiming that American Meter materially breached the joint venture agreements when it refused to sell its products on credit, and as the ad damnum clauses of their complaints make clear, they seek damages for their projected lost profits between 1998 and 2003.

American Meter's construction of the CISG is equally problematic. It is premised on an artificial and untenable distinction between the "relationship" and supply provisions of a distributorship agreement—after all, what could be more central to the parties' relationship than the products the buyer is expected to distribute? American Meter's rhetorical view would also render it difficult for parties to create a general framework for their future sales without triggering the CISG's invalidating provisions. Such a construction of the Convention would be particularly destabilizing, not to mention unjust, in the context of the joint venture agreements at issue here. On American Meter's reading of the CISG, it could have invoked ordinary breach of contract principles if the plaintiffs had failed to exercise their best efforts to promote demand for its products, all the while reserving the right to escape its obligation to supply those products by invoking Article 14's price and quantity requirements. The CISG's provisions on contract formation do not compel such an expectation-defeating result.

We therefore join the other courts that have examined this issue and conclude that, although the CISG may have governed discrete contracts for the sale of goods that the parties had entered pursuant to the joint venture agreements, it does not apply to the agreements themselves. [The court went on to find that Pennsylvania law, not Ukrainian law, governed the joint venture agreements and denied

---

3. In this category, American Meter would place terms dealing with such matters as quality control, the use of registered trademarks, and the parties' advertising and marketing obligations.

Prompriladamco's motion for summary judgment on the liability issue on the ground that there is a genuine issue of material fact as to whether C. Douglas Prendergast, the American Meter employee who signed the Prompriladamco joint venture agreement, had actual or apparent authority to make the commitments on behalf of American Meter. This portion of the opinion is contained in Chapter 8 at p. 670.]

UNCITRAL CLOUT Case 131
Germany: Landgericht München I (February 8, 1995)

The German defendant ordered a computer programme from the French plaintiff. The programme was delivered and installed. The parties also intended to conclude a second contract concerning the use of the programme, but the negotiations on that contract failed. The defendant then refused to pay the purchase price of the programme, which was delivered and installed.

The court held that the CISG was applicable as the parties had their place of business in different CISG Contracting States and as the CISG applies to standard software. The court further found also that the parties had agreed on all particulars of the sale of the programme and therefore had concluded a sales contract.

It was held that the defendant could not rely on a possible lack of conformity of the software programme, since it had not effectively given notice of the defect but had only asked for assistance in addressing the problems identified. As a result, the court ordered the defendant to pay the purchase price and interest at the rate of 5%.

UNCITRAL CLOUT Case 122
Germany: Oberlandesgericht Köln (August 26, 1994)

The plaintiff, a Swiss market research institute, had elaborated and delivered a market analysis, which had been ordered by the defendant, a German company. The defendant refused to pay the price alleging that the report did not comply with the conditions agreed upon by the parties.

The court held that the CISG was not applicable, since the underlying contract was neither a contract for the sale of goods (article 1(1) CISG) nor a contract for the production of goods (article 3(1) CISG). Noting that the sale of goods is characterized by the transfer of property in an object, the court found that, although a report is fixed on a piece of paper, the main concern of the parties is not the handing over of the paper but the transfer of the right to use the ideas written down on such paper. Therefore, the court held that the agreement to prepare a market analysis is not a sale of goods within the meaning of articles 1 or 3 CISG.

NOTES AND QUESTIONS

1. One of the reasons why the CISG provides a strong legal regime for international sales contracts and enjoys the strong allegiance of a large contingent of contracting states is that it is limited in its scope of application to an area that

states felt was amenable to international legislation and does not (1) govern areas that states might view as difficult to legislate or (2) intrude in areas viewed as important to their sovereign interests. As an example of the former, the CISG excludes sales by auction under Article 2(b), which present some unique problems with respect to contract formation as the seller may not know who the buyer is until the sale is concluded; sales on execution are excluded under Article 2(c) as these transactions are fundamentally different from other transactions because of the inability of the parties to negotiate the contract. As an example of the latter concern with avoiding conflict with state interests, Article 2(a) provides that certain consumer purchases are excluded from the CISG. A number of states have developed national legislation and case law designed to protect consumers and the drafters of the CISG agreed that the convention should not supersede these rules. Ships and vessels are excluded under Article 2(e) as such vessels are often subject to registration requirements under national legislation. Under Article 4, the CISG does not displace domestic rules on the validity of the contract or prejudice the rights of third parties. Thus, the ability of states to prohibit certain types of contracts as against public policy is not compromised by the CISG. Article 5 excludes issues of the liability of the seller for death or injury caused by the goods to any person on the grounds that these issues are more appropriately treated under domestic legislation.

   2. Article 2(d) excludes stocks, other securities, and negotiable instruments from the CISG, illustrating that the CISG is concerned with physical, tangible things and not intangible rights. The exclusion of "negotiable instruments" refers to instruments calling for the payment of money and does not refer to documents that allow the bearer to control goods, such as the negotiable bill of lading. *See* J. Honnold, *supra*, at 54.

   3. Article 6 provides:

> The parties may exclude the application of this Convention or, subject to Article 12, derogate from or vary the effect of any of its provisions.

Article 6 reflects the supplementary nature of the CISG by allowing the parties to opt out of the convention. Note that the parties are also allowed to change the effect of any of the convention's provisions, recognizing the primacy of the contract. Thus, the parties can vary the effect of Parts II and III of the CISG regarding the formation of the contract and rights and obligations of the parties. If the parties can opt out of the convention, can they also opt in by altering the effect of Articles 1-5 so that the CISG governs contracts that would otherwise be outside of its scope? In considering this question, note that Articles 1-5 strike a balance between domestic and international law: Contracting states have agreed to allow the CISG to displace domestic law for certain transactions and issues while preserving others for domestic control. Article 6 now introduces a third interest: The intent of the contracting parties and the primacy of the contract. Can this third interest change this balance by making an additional displacement of domestic law? Note that the only explicit limit that Article 6 imposes on the parties' right to vary the convention is the recognition of the privilege of a contracting state under Articles 12 and 96 to maintain its domestic law requiring a writing. Does this mean that other than this limitation, the parties can vary any other provisions even those affecting the balance struck between domestic law and the CISG, that is, Articles 1-5? We believe that the answer is "yes" but a qualified one and one that depends on a case-by-case analysis. Can you see why? Would it depend on whether the contact attempts to opt in an area that (1) is difficult to legislate or (2) is considered to be an area of state sovereignty? Now consider CISG Article 1. Should parties be able to "opt in" by varying the effect of Article 1? What is the underlying purpose of Article 1?

4. Interpreting the CISG: Articles 7-13

Articles 7-13 concern the interpretation of the CISG. Note that while the CISG is a major step forward in harmonization, there will continue to be a need for choice of law analysis and the application of domestic law to international contracts for the sale of goods. We have already seen the continuing need for private international law analysis under Article 1(1)(b) but Article 7 provides another reason. The reason for this need is that the scope of the CISG is limited; it covers (1) the formation of contracts and (2) the rights and obligations of the parties. There are many issues that fall within a gap in the CISG or an exclusion that is outside the scope of coverage of the CISG.

It is important to distinguish between a gap, which can be filled without any choice of law, and an exclusion, which requires a choice of law determination. A gap refers to an issue that is governed by the CISG but on which the CISG is silent, whereas an exclusion refers to an issue that is not governed by the CISG but which must be governed by some other substantive law.

> *Illustration 7a.* Article 78 of the CISG provides that a party that fails to pay a money obligation on time must pay interest. However, nothing in the CISG specifies the interest rate or how it is to be determined. The issue of interest is a subject that is clearly governed by the CISG but the rate of interest is specified. The interest rate issue falls into a gap or is an interstitial issue.
>
> *Illustration 7b.* Article 4 of the CISG provides that only the rights and obligations of the seller and buyer are covered by the CISG; third-party rights are excluded. Article 4 also provides that matters concerning the validity of the contract and the effect that the contract may have on the property in the goods sold are also excluded from the CISG. Article 5 provides that the convention does not apply to liability for death or personal injury caused by the goods sold. All of these issues are not governed by the CISG. These are excluded from the CISG scope of coverage.

The treatment of gaps and exclusions is quite different under the CISG. Article 7 provides "[q]uestions concerning matters governed by this Convention, which are not expressly settled in it are to be settled in conformity with the general principles on which it is based, or in the absence of such principles, in conformity with the law applicable by virtue of the rules of private international rule." Under this prescription, a gap, such as that involved in Illustration 7a, should be filled first through the use of principles upon which the CISG is based before a resort to a private international choice of law analysis, which will result in the choice of a domestic national law. Where are these general principles? A number of commentators believe that the general principles must be found within the CISG itself either by extracting these principles from specific articles of the CISG or by applying existing articles by analogy to a specific case. As an example of a general principle, one need look no further than Article 7(1): The CISG should be interpreted so as "to promote . . . the observance of good faith in international trade." An additional norm is a reasonableness standard: Under Article 8(2) and (3), statements, conduct, and the intent of parties are to be interpreted according to the understanding of a reasonable person. The requirements of good faith and reasonableness underlie numerous other articles of the CISG. *See* Henry Mather, *Choice of Law for International Sales Issues Not Resolved by the CISG*, 20 J. L. & Com. 155, 157-158 (2001). In Illustration 7a above concerning the determination of interest rates, Professor Mather suggests that Article 74 requiring full compensation in the case of breach leads to a conclusion that the rate should be the average prime lending rate in the aggrieved party's country. *See id.* at 158. Additional important general principles derived from the specific provisions of the CISG and applicable by analogy are the primacy of the contract and freedom of contract (Article 6), a general rule that international sales contracts should not be subject to writing requirements and other formal requirements (Article 11), and a general presumption that the parties have formed a binding contract (Articles 16, 18(1), 19(2), and 21). *See* Mather, *supra*, at 158. Only if an appeal to general principles fails to find a basis for resolving the gap should the court then resort to private international law and domestic law.

The treatment of the exclusions in Illustration 7b is quite different. Here these are issues that are not governed by the CISG — in other words, these are matters normally covered by a substantive contract law that are completely outside the scope of the CISG. As a result, these matters will be governed by a different substantive contract law to be determined by a private international choice of law analysis (absent a choice of law clause in the contract). Under Article 7, exclusions are to be treated by a direct appeal to domestic law and there is no need to first attempt to find general principles of international law.

NOTES AND QUESTIONS

1. Aside from the general rules of interpretation set forth under Article 7 above, the policy orientation of the CISG against the use of excessive formalities in the contract may also provide a useful interpretive guide for those who come to a study of the CISG from a common law tradition. Various provisions under the CISG demonstrate a policy decision by the drafters to avoid the formalities associated with the Anglo-American approach to contract law as typified by American common law and the Uniform Commercial Code. Some examples of such formalities are the statute of frauds, the parol evidence rule, and rules requiring consideration for enforceable promises. The following materials will highlight some of the major differences between the approach to formalities in the CISG and the UCC.

2. The parol evidence rule has been used in the United States to bar consideration of any contemporaneous oral agreement or prior agreement (whether oral or in writing) that contradicts a subsequent writing intended by the parties as the final expression of their agreement. *See* UCC §2-202 (2003). CISG Article 8(3) provides that in interpreting the contract "due consideration is to be given to all relevant circumstances of the case." Does this provision of the CISG override a domestic parol evidence rule? *See MCC-Marble Ceramic Center, Inc. v. Ceramica Nuova D'Agostino*, 144 F.3d 1384 (11th Cir. 1998) (stating that "The CISG precludes the application of the parol evidence rule, which would otherwise bar the consideration of evidence concerning a prior or contemporaneous negotiated oral agreement"); *cf. Beijing Metals & Minerals Import/Export Corp. v. American Business*

Center, Inc., 993 F.2d 1178 (5th Cir. 1993) (court applied Texas parol evidence in a suit between a Chinese seller and a U.S. buyer for payment under a sales contract, noting that the parol evidence rule applied regardless of whether Texas law or the CISG applied). Which decision do you think is correct?

PROBLEM 3-5

A U.S. seller and a Mexican buyer meet at a trade fair and enter into negotiations for the sale of power tools. The seller and the buyer have discussions at the fair and then exchange various e-mail messages and phone calls. During one phone call, the Mexican buyer says, "Okay, can you send me 450 power drills and 500 power saws CIF Mexico for $19,600?" The seller says, "I can do it for $22,000." The buyer says, "You sure drive a hard bargain. Throw in extra parts for the drills and we have a deal." The seller sends the buyer an e-mail stating, "As you requested, we have included extra spare drill parts and will ship via truck tomorrow." The buyer calls the seller and leaves a message on the seller's voice mail, "Hey, got your e-mail. Sounds good." The seller then ships the tools to Mexico whereupon the buyer refuses to accept delivery on the grounds that no contract was ever entered into by the parties. The seller sues the buyer for breach of contract. The buyer moves to dismiss on the ground that no contract ever existed because of failure to satisfy the statute of frauds contained in UCC §2-201, which provides in relevant part that "a contract for the sale of goods for the price of $5,000 or more is not enforceable by way of action or defense unless there is some writing sufficient to indicate that a contract for sale has been made between the parties and signed by the party against whom enforcement is sought or by his authorized agent or broker. . . ." What result? See CISG Articles 1(1)(a) and 11; see also *GPL Treatment infra.*

UNCITRAL CLOUT Case 137
GPL Treatment, Ltd. v. Louisiana-Pacific Corp.
Oregon Supreme Court, 1996
113 Or. App. 633, 894 P.2d 470, *aff'd*, 323 Or. 116, 914 P.2d 682

Plaintiffs, three Canadian manufacturers and sellers of raw shakes (long wooden shingles), sued a U.S. corporation to recover damages for breach of alleged contracts for the sale and purchase of truckloads of cedar shakes. Defendant denied entering into these contracts. Defendant moved *in limine* for dismissal on the ground that plaintiffs failed to satisfy the writing requirement of the "statute of frauds" of the Uniform Commercial Code (UCC) as enacted in Oregon. The trial court denied the motion. During the trial, the plaintiffs attempted to raise the issue of whether the CISG, rather than the UCC, governed, but the trial court ruled that plaintiffs' attempt was untimely and that they had waived reliance on that theory. The jury returned a verdict awarding lost profits to the plaintiffs and the trial court entered judgment on the verdict.

Defendant appealed to an intermediate appellate court on the ground, inter alia, that the trial court had erred when it denied defendant's motion *in limine*. A majority of the three-judge appellate court found that plaintiffs had satisfied the UCC statute of frauds. The dissenting judge disagreed with the majority's analysis of the UCC as applied to the facts in the case. In a final footnote, the dissenting judge also stated that he would have addressed the issue of whether the trial court abused its discretion in its ruling on the applicability of the CISG.

On appeal to the Oregon Supreme Court, the decisions of the trial and intermediate courts were affirmed. The majority, concurring, and dissenting opinions do not address the issue of whether the CISG governed or whether the trial court abused its discretion.

NOTES AND QUESTIONS

1. In *GPL Treatment*, why did the plaintiffs wait until the trial had already begun to raise the argument that the contract was governed by the CISG rather than the UCC?

2. Article 12 provides that a contracting state can preserve its writing requirement by making a declaration under Article 96 that Article 11 does not apply in any case where one of the parties has a place of business in that state. The parties cannot derogate or vary the effect of Article 12. The United States has not made declarations under Articles 12 and 96.

3. As Canada and the United States are both parties to the CISG, there is little doubt that the CISG would have applied in *GPL Treatment* if the issue had been timely raised. But why does the plaintiff have to raise the issue in a timely fashion or at all? After all, as the CISG is a treaty to which both Canada and the United States are parties shouldn't the court take judicial notice of this fact and apply the CISG notwithstanding the failure of the plaintiff to raise the issue in a timely fashion? *See* CISG Article 6.

4. Plaintiffs were able to prevail on the statute of frauds issue in *GLP Treatment*. Suppose that the court had found that the contract did not satisfy the statute of frauds and had dismissed the plaintiffs' case. In that case, would the failure of the plaintiffs' lawyers to timely raise the applicability of the CISG constitute malpractice? Recall our earlier discussion of the responsibility of the lawyer to be knowledgeable about the CISG. See Chapter 1, *supra*, pp. 41-42.

5. Part II of the CISG: Formation of the Contract

Part II of the CISG, Formation of the Contract, is subject to the rules of Part I (Articles 1-13) on the interpretation of the contract but is independent of Part III dealing with the obligations and rights of the parties (Articles 25-88). The structure of the CISG reflects its historical antecedents, the Uniform Law on the Formation of Contracts for the International Sale of Goods and the Uniform Law for the International Sale of Goods, both of which were finalized under the auspices of UNIDROIT at the Hague in 1964. The CISG reflected UNCITRAL's decision to promulgate a single convention but allows contracting parties to make a declaration under Article 92 excluding Part II on formation or Part III on the obligations and rights of the parties.

Articles 14-17 of Part II deal with the offer, including the minimum prerequisites for an effective offer (Article 14), withdrawal (Article 15), revocation (Article 16), and termination of an offer (Article 17). Articles 18-22 deal with the acceptance, including the form of the acceptance (Article 18), the effect of an acceptance that varies the terms of the offer (Article 19), time allowed for acceptance (Articles 20-21), and withdrawal of the acceptance (Article 22). Articles 23 and 24 deal with the time when a contract is concluded. For a common law lawyer trained to expect a comprehensive and detailed code such as the UCC, the CISG, which follows a civil law model, may appear to be brief and general in nature. In addition, the CISG does not contain some provisions usually found in a common law code: There is no statute of frauds, no provision for the modification of contracts, and consideration is not required for a contract. The following materials will provide an overview of the articles relating to contract formation.

A. THE OFFER

Article 14 sets forth the basic criteria for an offer. The CISG recognizes that many sales transactions today can occur in a casual and rapid way rather than through the formal model of a negotiation, an offer, and an acceptance. For an effective offer, the key issue is whether the offeror intended to be bound by the offer. This issue is affected by two corollary issues: The number of people to whom the offer is addressed and the definiteness of the proposal.

> *Illustration 14a.* A German seller sends out a sales catalogue for hand-held electronic organizers to persons on a mailing list that the seller has obtained from a consumer research company that identifies American buyers who have purchased high-end electronic goods within the past two years. The catalogue lists the organizers at $55 each. An American buyer sends in an order for 50 organizers. No contract has been made as there was no offer. The offer has not been addressed to specific persons.
> *Illustration 14b.* The German seller tells the American buyer, "We will give you a nice discount if you order a large quantity of the organizers." The buyer responds by sending in an order for 100 organizers at $50 each. The proposal is addressed to a specific person but unless the parties have a prior course of dealing that would indicate the quantity and price referred to by the seller (see Article 9), no contract has been made as the offer was insufficiently definite as to quantity and price.

B. ACCEPTANCE, WITHDRAWAL, AND REVOCATION OF AN OFFER

Article 15 provides that the seller has the power to withdraw an offer at any time before the offer reaches the offeree, even if it purports to be irrevocable.

> *Illustration 15a.* The German seller sends the American buyer a letter by next-day delivery with an offer to sell 150 organizers at $50 each, offer good for 10 days. Later the same day, the seller telephones the buyer and says, "I hereby withdraw the offer sent to you by my letter." The buyer receives the letter the next day and writes back, "I accept your offer as it is good for 10 days." No contract has been made as the offer was withdrawn before it reached the buyer. As the offer never reached the buyer prior to the withdrawal and the buyer was never aware of the offer, the buyer cannot suffer any harm by its withdrawal.

Article 15 empowers the seller to withdraw an offer before it reaches the seller. In contrast, Article 16 deals with the power of the seller to revoke an offer after it has reached the buyer and has become an effective offer. Note that Article 16(a) and (b) provide that certain offers are irrevocable even though they are not supported by consideration. This is a departure from the traditional common law approach in the United States that a promise is not irrevocable unless the offeree has given a payment or some other thing or act in consideration for the promise to hold the offer open. For example, under the common law approach, a seller who makes an offer to a buyer and who promises to hold the offer open for 15 days is free to revoke the offer at any time. The offer is revocable despite the explicit statement that it is irrevocable unless there is some consideration given such as a payment by the buyer to the seller. If the buyer gives the seller a payment to hold the offer open, then the offer is irrevocable for the 15 days (under the common law, this becomes an option contract).

> *Illustration 16a*. The seller telephones the buyer and offers to sell the buyer 50 live chickens for $45, offer good for 15 days. The next day the seller calls the buyer and revokes the offer. Under Article 16(2), the seller cannot revoke the offer and it remains irrevocable for the period fixed as open for acceptance.

The common law rule requiring consideration has been limited by some important exceptions. One is the famous mailbox rule established by the celebrated case of *Adams v. Linsell*, 1 B. & Ald. 681 (1818), which provides that if the offeror has impliedly authorized the offeree to respond by mail, the power of the offeror to revoke an offer without consideration is cut off once the offeree dispatches a letter. Article 16(1) of the CISG has adopted a significance aspect of the mailbox rule. How is the CISG mailbox rule different from the common law rule?

In addition, the Uniform Commercial Code has modified the common law by providing that some offers are irrevocable even if not supported by consideration:

Uniform Commercial Code §2-205. Firm Offers

> An offer by a merchant to buy or sell goods in a signed record that by its terms gives assurance that it will be held open is not revocable, for lack of consideration, during the time stated or if no time is stated for a reasonable time, but in no event may the period of irrevocability exceed three months. Any such term of assurance in a form supplied by the offeree must be separately signed by the offeror.

PROBLEM 3-6

A German seller telephones an American buyer and says, "I will sell you 150 hand-held organizers at $50 each, but you must respond in writing within ten days."

(1) The next day, the seller telephones the buyer and says, "Sorry, I have to withdraw the offer as I am having inventory problems." The buyer replies, "I hereby accept your offer. As you telephoned me yesterday with this offer, the offer received by me became effective and by its own terms the offer was irrevocable for a period of ten days. As the acceptance was within the ten days you held the offer open, a contract has been formed." Was the seller's second phone call an attempted withdrawal or revocation? *See* Articles 15 and 16. Was the buyer's oral acceptance effective or does the buyer have to respond in writing? *See* Article 11. Neither Germany nor the United States has made a declaration under Articles 12 and 96. *See also* Article 6.

(2) Suppose that after receiving the initial telephone call in which the seller makes the offer, the buyer calls back the same day and says, "Sorry, the price is too

high and I can't accept your offer." The next day, the buyer calls the seller and says, "Hey, I talked it over with the finance department and it's a go. We accept the offer and I am having a written acceptance delivered to you within the hour." The seller says, "Sorry, but you already rejected the offer yesterday so no deal." The buyer says, "You promised to hold the offer open for ten days and my written acceptance will be received by you within this period." Is there a contract? *See* Article 17.

PROBLEM 3-7

An English seller meets an American buyer at a trade fair in London. During their conversation, the seller offers to sell the buyer a specified quantity of tea at a specified price. The buyer is interested but needs to review the offer with head-quarters in Atlanta. The seller ends the discussion by saying, "Okay, but if you want the tea, you need to let me know in three business days before you head back to the U.S. Hope to hear from you. Call me." The next day, the buyer sends a letter by express mail accepting the offer but before it reaches the seller, the seller calls and says, "I take back the offer." The buyer immediately replies, "I've already dis-patched an acceptance by mail but I now also add my oral acceptance of your offer." The United Kingdom is not a contracting state to the CISG.

(1)   What is the result under the common law?
(2)   What is the result under UCC §2-205?
(3)   What is the result under the CISG? *See* Article 16.

C. ACCEPTANCE

The first four articles of Part II deal with the offer; the last six articles deal with the acceptance. Of these, Articles 18 and 19 are the most basic and important. Article 18 provides that there are two elements to an acceptance: Assent to the offer and communicating that assent to the offeror. *See* Article 18(1) and (2). Once the assent of the offeree reaches the offeror, acceptance of the offer becomes effective and a contract is formed. *See* Article 18(2). While this might seem straightforward enough, there can be a number of complications. The offeror might withdraw or revoke the offer before the offeree can communicate the accep-tance to the offeror or the offeree may exceed the time limits on the offer set by the offeror. Article 18 deals with the issue of communication of the assent to the offeror. We further examine the application of Article 18 in Problem 3-8.

Article 19 deals with an assent that contains alterations or modifications of the terms of the offer. A reply to an offer may contain additional terms that add to or are inconsistent with the terms of the offer. Such a situation is commonplace in today's commercial marketplace that is marked by high-speed communications and rapid transactions that often involve the use of preprinted and standard offer sheets, orders, and sales acknowledgment forms. Many businesses now use pre-printed forms in international sales transactions. The front of the form will contain blank spaces regarding quantity, delivery, and price that one party will fill in while the back of the form may contain a dense collection of standard clauses on issues such as liability, warranties, dispute resolution, and remedies. The seller's forms will be drafted with the purpose of protecting the seller's rights and the buyer's forms will be drafted to protect the buyer's rights. Note that no problem arises if an offer on a preprinted form is rejected by the offeree. The problem that usually arises is when the offeree purports to accept an offer on a preprinted form with a reply on a preprinted form of its own that contains additions or modifications specifically added by the offeree or that contains different or additional standard terms on the back of the form. Note that the use of different forms or exchanges containing conflicting or discrepant terms is in most instances not a problem in ordinary commercial life. Business is routinely conducted by sellers and buyers using different forms containing different terms and no issue arises because the seller supplies the goods and the buyer pays for them without incident. Only when there is some problem that arises in the performance of the contract will the parties then need to resolve the problem of whether a contract was formed and which of the conflicting or discrepant terms were incorporated into the contract. This problem has been known to generations of lawyers and law students as the so-called "battle of the forms."

The approach of Article 19 to the "battle of the forms" problem reflects the pre–Uniform Commercial Code practice of the common law. Article 19(1) provides that a reply to an offer must be a precise "mirror image" of the offer; there can be no deviations in the terms of the response to an offer if that response is to operate as an acceptance. If the reply contains additional terms, the reply is treated as a rejection and a counteroffer. Article 19(2) qualifies this rule by providing that the alterations or additions must "materially alter the terms of offer" to constitute a rejection and counteroffer. Otherwise, the new terms become part of the contract unless the offeror objects without undue delay. Article 19(3) provides some examples of terms that are "material" such as terms relating to price, payment, quality and quantity of the goods, delivery, liability, and dispute settlement.

Illustration 19a. A German seller sends an offer on a preprinted form to an American buyer for the sale of screws at a specific price for a specified quantity. The American buyer uses its own order form in sending back a reply that purports to accept the seller's offer. Standard clauses on the back of the buyer's form subject the contract to the jurisdiction of U.S. courts and contains other material alterations. On the advice of counsel, the buyer draws the seller's attention to the choice of forum clause. The seller does not respond and no goods are shipped. No contract has been made as the acceptance contains terms that materially alter the offer. The buyer's reply is a rejection and a counteroffer under Article 19(1) that the seller has failed to accept.

Illustration 19b. A Chinese seller sends an offer on a preprinted form to an American buyer for the sale of Republican Period (1912-1949) Chinese furniture and art. The back of the form contains a clause providing for shipment in "commercial furniture crates designed for the safe shipment of art objects and antiques." The buyer sends back a reply purporting to accept the seller's offer. On the front of the buyer's form, the buyer has added a clause providing, "All furniture and art to be separately packaged and shipped in separate crates." The seller receives the form, reads the buyer's clause, and does not object. A contract has been formed as the buyer's clause does not materially alter the terms of the offer. The buyer's clause is part of the contract.

Note that if the reply contains any terms that are not identical to the terms of the offer, even if they are nonmaterial, the offeror has the power to avoid making a contract by objecting to the discrepancy under Article 19(2). As the offeror has objected to the discrepancy, the offeree's reply is treated as a rejection and counteroffer under Article 19(1) and as the offeror has not accepted the counteroffer, no contract is formed.

> *Illustration 19c.* Under the same facts in Illustration 19b, the seller immediately objects to the buyer's reply with the following notice, "We cannot agree to separately package and ship furniture and art without a modest increase in price." Although the buyer's clause is not a material alteration under Article 19(3), the result of the seller's timely objection to the buyer's modification is that the buyer's response is treated as a rejection and a counteroffer and no contract is formed under Article 19(1).

Note that in Illustration 19a if the seller ships the goods and the buyer pays the price, a contract may be formed by the conduct of the parties under Article 18(3). If so, what are the terms of the contract? Is the German seller subject to the jurisdiction of U.S. courts? Under Article 19(1), the buyer's reply is treated as a rejection and counteroffer. As the buyer has specifically called the seller's attention to the forum selection clause, the seller cannot claim surprise. Under the approach of the "last shot theory," a corollary to the mirror image approach, when the seller shipped the goods, the act constituted an acceptance of the buyer's counteroffer. *See* Article 18(3). The parties formed a contract by their conduct and the contract was governed by the terms of the only valid offer that existed between the parties, that is, the buyer's counteroffer with the clause subjecting the contract to the jurisdiction of U.S. courts.[4] We further examine the application of Article 19 in Problem 3-9.

PROBLEM 3-8

On September 1, an American buyer sends the following telex to a French seller, "I will buy from you 500 four-ounce bottles of your perfume at $35 per bottle. As this offer is $5 over the wholesale price per bottle, I am sure that you will accept. If we do not hear otherwise from you by September 5th, we will expect delivery by September 10th."

(1) The seller does not respond by September 5. Is there a contract? *See* Article 18(1). No

(2) The seller ships the bottles on September 2. On September 3, the buyer calls the seller and says, "I revoke my offer." The bottles arrive on September 10. The buyer refuses to accept the shipment on the grounds that the offer was revoked before an indication of assent — the shipment — by the seller reached the buyer. Is the buyer in breach? *See* Article 18(2) and (3).

(3) Suppose that the buyer had put in the telex, "Any disputes under this agreement will be settled by arbitration in the United States. Payment by

---

4. What happens if the buyer does not specifically call the seller's attention to the forum selection clause printed on the back of the form? Is the seller still bound under the "last shot approach"? In this situation, it might seem unfair to hold the seller to a standard clause printed on the back of the buyer's form when neither the seller nor the buyer paid any attention to the boilerplate clauses on the backs of each other's forms. Under these circumstances, the resolution of the dispute as to the terms of the contract might be resolved in light of Article 8 where the surrounding circumstances and the course of dealing between the parties provide an indication of the parties' intent to be bound by the discrepant clause.

confirmed irrevocable letter of credit." On September 6, the seller notifies the buyer by e-mail, "Okay we can do the shipment. I will draw up a written confirmation and send it to you with the shipment." The buyer establishes the letter of credit and the shipment arrives, but the seller's written confirmation mentions nothing about arbitration. Is there a contract? Is the arbitration part of the contract? See Article 18(3) and the *Chilewich* case *infra*.

Filanto, S.P.A. v. Chilewich International Corp.
United States District Court, Southern District of New York, 1992
789 F. Supp. 1229

BRIEANT, Chief Judge.

By motion fully submitted on December 11, 1991, defendant Chilewich International Corp. moves to stay this action pending arbitration in Moscow. Plaintiff Filanto has moved to enjoin arbitration or to order arbitration in this federal district.

Plaintiff Filanto is an Italian corporation engaged in the manufacture and sale of footwear. Defendant Chilewich is an export-import firm incorporated in the state of New York with its principal place of business in White Plains. On February 28, 1989, Chilewich's agent in the United Kingdom, Byerly Johnson, Ltd., signed a contract with Raznoexport, the Soviet Foreign Economic Association, which obligated Byerly Johnson to supply footwear to Raznoexport. Section 10 of this contract — the "Russian Contract" — is an arbitration clause, which reads in pertinent part as follows:

> "All disputes or differences which may arise out of or in connection with the present Contract are to be settled, jurisdiction of ordinary courts being excluded, by the Arbitration at the USSR Chamber of Commerce and Industry, Moscow, in accordance with the Regulations of the said Arbitration." [sic]

The next document in this case, and the focal point of the parties' dispute regarding whether an arbitration agreement exists, is a Memorandum Agreement dated March 13, 1990. This Memorandum Agreement, number 9003002, is a standard merchant's memo prepared by Chilewich for signature by both parties confirming that Filanto will deliver 100,000 pairs of boots to Chilewich at the Italian/Yugoslav border on September 15, 1990, with the balance of 150,000 pairs to be delivered on November 1, 1990. Chilewich's obligations were to open a Letter of Credit in Filanto's favor prior to the September 15 delivery, and another letter prior to the November delivery. This Memorandum includes the following provision:

> "It is understood between Buyer and Seller that USSR Contract No. 32-03/93085 [the Russian Contract] is hereby incorporated in this contract as far as practicable, and specifically that any arbitration shall be in accordance with that Contract."

Chilewich signed this Memorandum Agreement, and sent it to Filanto. Filanto at that time did not sign or return the document. Nevertheless, on May 7, 1990, Chilewich opened a Letter of Credit in Filanto's favor in the sum of

$2,595,600.00. The Letter of Credit itself mentions the Russian Contract, but only insofar as concerns packing and labeling.

Then, on August 7, 1990, Filanto returned the Memorandum Agreement, sued on here, that Chilewich had signed and sent to it in March; though Filanto had signed the Memorandum Agreement, it once again appended a covering letter, purporting to exclude all but three sections of the Russian Contract.

According to the Complaint, what ultimately happened was that Chilewich bought and paid for 60,000 pairs of boots in January 1991, but never purchased the 90,000 pairs of boots that comprise the balance of Chilewich's original order. It is Chilewich's failure to do so that forms the basis of this lawsuit, commenced by Filanto on May 14, 1991.

Against this background based almost entirely on documents, defendant Chilewich on July 24, 1991 moved to stay this action pending arbitration, while plaintiff Filanto on August 22, 1992 moved to enjoin arbitration, or, alternatively, for an order directing that arbitration be held in the Southern District of New York rather than Moscow, because of unsettled political conditions in Russia.

JURISDICTION/APPLICABLE LAW

This Court finds [as a] basis for subject matter jurisdiction chapter 2 of the Federal Arbitration Act, which comprises the Convention on the Recognition and Enforcement of Foreign Arbitral Awards. The United States, Italy and the USSR are all signatories to this Convention, and its implementing legislation makes clear that the Arbitration Convention governs disputes regarding arbitration agreements between parties to international commercial transactions. The Arbitration Convention specifically requires courts to recognize any "agreement in writing under which the parties undertake to submit to arbitration. . . ." The term "agreement in writing" is defined as "an arbitral clause in a contract or an arbitration agreement, signed by the parties or contained in an exchange of letters or telegrams".

This Court concludes that the question of whether these parties agreed to arbitrate their disputes is governed by the Arbitration Convention and its implementing legislation. That Convention, as a treaty, is the supreme law of the land and controls *any* case in any American court falling within its sphere of application. Thus, any dispute involving international commercial arbitration which meets the Convention's jurisdictional requirements, whether brought in state or federal court, must be resolved with reference to that instrument.

In this case, [t]he central disputed issue [under the Arbitration Convention] is whether the correspondence between the parties, viewed in light of their business relationship, constitutes an "agreement in writing".

[A]s plaintiff correctly notes, the "federal law of contracts" to be applied in this case is found in the United Nations Convention on Contracts for the International Sale of Goods (the "Sale of Goods Convention"). This Convention, ratified by the Senate in 1986, is a self-executing agreement which entered into force between the United States and other signatories, including Italy, on January 1, 1988. Since the contract alleged in this case most certainly was formed, if at all, after January 1, 1988, and since both the United States and Italy are signatories to the Convention, the Court will interpret the "agreement in writing" requirement of the Arbitration Convention in light of, and with reference to, the substantive international law of contracts embodied in the Sale of Goods Convention.

Not surprisingly, the parties offer varying interpretations of the numerous letters and documents exchanged between them. The Court will briefly summarize their respective contentions.

Defendant Chilewich contends that the Memorandum Agreement dated March 13 which it signed and sent to Filanto was an offer. It then argues that Filanto's retention of the letter, along with its subsequent acceptance of Chilewich's performance under the Agreement — the furnishing of the May 11 letter of credit — estops it from denying its acceptance of the contract. Although phrased as an estoppel argument, this contention is better viewed as an acceptance by conduct argument, e.g., that in light of the parties' course of dealing, Filanto had a duty timely to inform Chilewich that it objected to the incorporation by reference of all the terms of the Russian contract. Under this view, the return of the Memorandum Agreement, signed by Filanto, on August 7, 1990, along with the covering letter purporting to exclude parts of the Russian Contract, was ineffective as a matter of law as a rejection of the March 13 offer, because this occurred some five months after Filanto received the Memorandum Agreement and two months after Chilewich furnished the Letter of Credit. Instead, in Chilewich's view, this action was a proposal for modification of the March 13 Agreement. Chilewich rejected this proposal, by its letter of August 7 to Byerly Johnson, and the August 29 fax by Johnson to Italian Trading SRL, which communication Filanto acknowledges receiving. Accordingly, Filanto under this interpretation is bound by the written terms of the March 13 Memorandum Agreement; since that agreement incorporates by reference the Russian Contract containing the arbitration provision, Filanto is bound to arbitrate.

Plaintiff Filanto's interpretation of the evidence is rather different. While Filanto apparently agrees that the March 13 Memorandum Agreement was indeed an offer, it characterizes its August 7 return of the signed Memorandum Agreement with the covering letter as a counteroffer. While defendant contends that under Uniform Commercial Code §2-207 this action would be viewed as an acceptance with a proposal for a material modification, the Uniform Commercial Code, as previously noted, does not apply to this case, because the State Department undertook to fix something that was not broken by helping to create the Sale of Goods Convention which varies from the Uniform Commercial Code in many significant ways. Instead, under this analysis, Article 19(1) of the Sale of Goods Convention would apply. That section, as the Commentary to the Sale of Goods Convention notes, reverses the rule of Uniform Commercial Code §2-207, and reverts to the common law rule that "A reply to an offer which purports to be an acceptance but contains additions, limitations or other modifications is a rejection of the offer and constitutes a counter-offer". Although the Convention, like the Uniform Commercial Code, does state that non-material terms do become part of the contract unless objected to, Sale of Goods Convention Article 19(2), the Convention treats inclusion (or deletion) of an arbitration provision as "material", Sale of Goods Convention Article 19(3). The August 7 letter, therefore, was a counteroffer which, according to Filanto, Chilewich accepted by its letter dated September 27, 1990. Though that letter refers to and acknowledges the "contractual obligations" between the parties, it is doubtful whether it can be characterized as an acceptance.

More generally, both parties seem to have lost sight of the narrow scope of the inquiry required by the Arbitration Convention. All that this Court need do is to determine if a sufficient "agreement in writing" to arbitrate disputes exists between these parties.

Since the issue of whether and how a contract between these parties was formed is obviously related to the issue of whether Chilewich breached any contractual obligations, the Court will direct its analysis to whether there was objective conduct evidencing an intent to be bound with respect to the arbitration provision. The Court is satisfied on this record that there *was* indeed an agreement to arbitrate between these parties.

There is simply no satisfactory explanation as to why Filanto failed to object to the incorporation by reference of the Russian Contract in a timely fashion. As noted above, Chilewich had in the meantime commenced its performance under the Agreement, and the Letter of Credit it furnished Filanto on May 11 *itself* mentioned the Russian Contract. An offeree who, knowing that the offeror has commenced performance, fails to notify the offeror of its objection to the terms of the contract within a reasonable time will, under certain circumstances, be deemed to have assented to those terms. The Sale of Goods Convention itself recognizes this rule: Article 18(1) provides that "A statement made by or other conduct of the offeree indicating assent to an offer is an acceptance". Although mere "silence or inactivity" does not constitute acceptance, Sale of Goods Convention Article 18(1), the Court may consider previous relations between the parties in assessing whether a party's conduct constituted acceptance, Sale of Goods Convention Article 8(3). In this case, in light of the extensive course of prior dealing between these parties, Filanto was certainly under a duty to alert Chilewich in timely fashion to its objections to the terms of the March 13 Memorandum Agreement—particularly since Chilewich had repeatedly referred it to the Russian Contract and Filanto had had a copy of that document for some time.

REMEDY

Having determined that the parties should arbitrate their disputes in accordance with their agreement, the Court must address the question of remedy. As this action is governed by the Convention and its implementing legislation, the Court has specific authority to order the parties to proceed to arbitration in Moscow. Defendant has not sought this remedy, since it would likewise be the defendant in the arbitration. However, it would be clearly inequitable to permit the party contending that there is an arbitration agreement to avoid arbitration. In the interests of justice, the Court will compel the parties to arbitrate in Moscow.

So ordered.

QUESTION

Suppose that in *Chilewich*, Filanto had replied on March 15 by express mail to Chilewich's March 13 memorandum agreement and that the reply contained the same contents as the August 7 reply that was actually sent in the case.

Under these facts, would the arbitration clause be a part of the contract? *See* Article 19(2).

there were no K [handwritten margin note]

PROBLEM 3-9 (skip)

A Czech buyer contacts an American seller for the purchase of replacement parts for heavy industrial production equipment in the buyer's factory. As part of the negotiations, the seller sent a team of engineers and business officials to the Czech Republic for several weeks to get an understanding of the intended uses of the parts by the buyer. They visited the buyer's headquarters, examined the buyer's factory, and reviewed the buyer's business operations. After several more weeks of negotiations, the buyer sends the seller a purchase order for the parts for a total price of $1 million with delivery in the Czech Republic by October 10 and payment against documents by confirmed irrevocable letter of credit. The purchase order is a single one-page printed form. On the page in large bold letters is a printed clause stating, "Seller will be responsible for damages caused by any defects in the replacement parts, including consequential damages."

The seller replies with a standard order acknowledgment form confirming the quantity of engines, price, delivery, and payment terms. The seller's form is also a short one-page form. On the front of the seller's order acknowledgment form is a handwritten clause in large bold letters stating, "Seller will repair or replace any defective parts, but Seller is in no event liable for any other damages including consequential damages."

The seller ships the parts, which arrive in the Czech Republic by October 10. The buyer pays the price against documents while the parts are en route to the Czech Republic. By November 1, the parts have been installed in the buyer's factory but a malfunction in the parts causes serious damage to the buyer's production facilities, requiring total replacement of all of the production equipment. The buyer also misses several big production orders, is facing several irate customers who are threatening to sue, and now faces bankruptcy. The buyer brings an action against the seller in the Czech Republic for recovery of the purchase price of $1 million plus $10 million in damages. Assume that, under Czech law, consequential damages are an available remedy. The seller argues that the buyer is limited to replacement costs. What is the result under the CISG? *See* Article 19(1), (2) and (3) and Article 18(3).

NOTES AND QUESTIONS

1. Suppose that in Problem 3-9 the seller's counsel, an experienced U.S. commercial lawyer, was able to convince the Czech buyer to opt out of the CISG and have the dispute governed by U.S. law. How would the issues in Problem 3-9 be resolved using the UCC? Work through the analysis using the proposed revised UCC §§2-206 and 2-207 set forth in note 2 below. Is the seller better off under the CISG or the UCC?

2. The American Law Institute has proposed amendments and revisions to the current Article 2 sections of the UCC that concern the "battle of the forms." Although these amendments have not yet been adopted by any state, it is expected that these provisions will soon be adopted on a widespread basis and

will replace the existing provision UCC §2-207,[5] which has proved difficult to apply in practice as there are a number of complex and unsettled issues concerning its interpretation and application. The new provisions, designed to simplify the "battle of the forms" analysis, are set forth below in two articles, §§2-206 and 2-207:

§2-206. Offer and Acceptance in Formation of Contract.

. . . (3) A definite and seasonable expression of acceptance in a record operates as an acceptance even if it contains terms additional to or different from the offer.

§2-207. Additional Terms of Contract;
Effect of Confirmation.

Subject to Section 2-202, if (i) conduct by both parties recognizes the existence of a contract although their records do not otherwise establish a contract, (ii) a contract

---

5. UCC §2-207, the current "battle of the forms" provision, provides:

§2-207. Additional Terms in Accceptance and Confirmation

(1) A definite and seasonable expression of acceptance or a written confirmation which is sent within a reasonable time operates as an acceptance even though it states terms additional to or different from those offered or agreed upon, unless acceptance is expressly made conditional on assent to the additional or different terms.

(2) The additional terms are to be construed as proposals for addition to the contract. Between merchants such terms become part of the contract unless:

    (a)   the offer expressly limits acceptance to the terms of the offer;
    (b)   they materially alter it; or
    (c)   notification of objection to them has already been given or is given within a reasonable time after notice of them is received.

(3) Conduct by both parties which recognizes the existence of a contract is sufficient to establish a contract for sale although the writings of the parties do not otherwise establish a contract. In such case the terms of the particular contract consist of those terms on which the writings of the parties agree, together with any supplementary terms incorporated under any other provisions of this Act.

UCC §2-207 rejects the common law mirror image rule in favor of an approach that would specifically recognize the creation of a contract even though the offeror and the offeree exchanged less than identical terms so long as the parties intented a contract to exist. *See* UCC §2-207(1). While the common law approach operated upon a presumption that no contract exists unless the exchanges of the offeror and offeree were identical, the UCC reversed this presumption by providing that even though the exchanges were not identical, the contract is formed. Any additional discrepant terms, if material (e.g., a limitation on liability), do not become part of the contract. See UCC §2-207(2)(b). Nonmaterial additional discrepant terms in the reply are incorporated into the contract unless the offer expressly limits acceptance to its terms or the offeror objects in a timely fashion. See UCC §2-207(2)(a) and (c). Note that the effect of an objection to a nonmaterial discrepancy in the reply is also treated differently in the CISG and the UCC. While Article 19(2) gives the offeror the power to reject any reply that is not identical to the offer and avoid the making of a contract under Article 19(1), the effect of an objection to a nonmaterial discrepancy under §2-207 is that the contract exists but the discrepant term falls out. The drafters of the UCC wanted to create a legal framework in which parties could not welsh on a contract due to technical differences in the terms of the offer and acceptance so long as the parties otherwise intended a contract to be formed. As a result, the drafters rejected the common law mirror image rule embodied in Article 19(1), adopting instead an approach that explicitly recognized a contract despite differences in terms.

is formed by an offer and acceptance, or (iii) a contract formed in any manner is confirmed by a record that contains terms additional to or different from those in the contract being confirmed, the terms of the contract, are:

    (a)   terms that appear in the records of both parties;

    (b)   terms, whether in a record or not, to which both parties agree; and

    (c)   terms supplied or incorporated under any provision of this Act.

On the issue of seller's liability for consequential damages to buyer, see UCC §2-715 ("[c]onsequential damages resulting from seller's breach include . . . any loss resulting from general or particular requirements and needs of which the seller at the time of contracting had reason to know and which could not reasonably be prevented by cover or otherwise").

3. The UNIDROIT Principles of International Commercial Contracts provides in relevant part:

Article 2.1.22

(Battle of Forms)

Where both parties use standard terms and reach agreement except on those terms, a contract is concluded on the basis of the agreed terms and of any standard terms which are common in substance unless one party clearly indicates in advance, or later and without undue delay informs the other party, that it does not intend to be bound by such a contract.

The UNIDROIT also rejects the mirror image approach of the CISG. Similar to the proposed revised UCC provisions, the principles will result in the formation of a contract on the basis of the agreed terms and any standard terms that are similar in substance. Moreover, any additional terms that are different in substance from the original terms that concern the same issue cancel each other out. The difference between the approaches of UNIDROIT and CISG is that the former may lead to the formation of a contract in a greater number of cases.

How would Problem 3-9 be resolved under the principles? In order to answer this question, you need to also consider UNIDROIT Article 2.1.21: "In case of conflict between a standard term and a term which is not a standard term the latter prevails."

D.   FORMATION OF THE COMPLEX SALES CONTRACT UNDER THE CISG

So far, we have considered contracts for simple sales transactions in which the quantity and price of the goods are straightforward items that the parties can readily agree on in the course of negotiations. The buyer wishes to purchase a specific quantity of goods and the seller is willing to sell them for a specific price. Once the parties exchange goods and payment, the transaction has concluded and the parties go their separate ways. The sale of shoes, perfume, and furniture are some examples of these straightforward transactions and these types of contracts fall neatly within the framework of the CISG.

At the other end of the spectrum, there are some complex sales transactions that are subject to many issues and variations that could take months to work out. Questions of exact price and quantity may also be difficult to determine. These transactions also contemplate performance over a long period such as several months or years and thus envision a continuing business relationship between the parties. In some of these transactions, the buyer may be seeking to obtain some overall result but is not quite sure what quantity and combination of goods and services will be necessary to achieve the desired result. For its part, the seller is willing to sell to the buyer but is not sure what the price will be and cannot determine the price until well into the negotiations or until the project itself is underway. What types of contracts are these and how would such contracts fare under the CISG? The following problem explores these issues.

PROBLEM 3-10

The Telecommunications Bureau of Argentina (TBA) is negotiating to purchase a telecommunications system from General Telecom (GT), a multinational enterprise with its headquarters in Chicago. Argentine officials have made clear that they need a system that brings telephone, Internet, and television access to an entire region of Argentina. The preliminary negotiations take several months and involve numerous visits by GT's engineers and other representatives to Argentina. After studying Argentina's situation in some depth, GT's representatives tell TBA that there are different options involving various levels of service that would result in (a) basic, (b) sophisticated, or (c) state-of-the-art telecommunications service that will meet the country's needs for the foreseeable future. Each of these options will also involve extended training programs for maintenance, upkeep, and upgrade of the systems. GT's engineers and finance managers have various estimated figures for each of the options, but these estimates are rough figures only. There is no "market price" for the installation of entire telecommunications systems as each situation is different. The engineers also stated that the total cost of any of the options will vary as the project is actually implemented over a five-year period as there are always unexpected developments, problems, and issues on the ground in installing a complete system such as this. For its part, the TBA says that it is studying the needs of the region and has unofficially told GT representatives that it is sure that it will purchase a system from GT over its rival Western Electronics but is unsure which of the options makes the most sense. The TBA has asked for detailed presentations from GT on each of the options and has asked GT to send a senior management team to Buenos Aires for a two-week stay at a hotel to make these presentations and to engage in discussions.

GT has the following concern: Negotiations have already gone on for several months and as this is a major project, management would like to sign a binding contract with the TBA as soon as possible. GT is concerned that these negotiations are consuming large amounts of resources in time and money and two weeks is a significant commitment of senior management's time. GT is nervous that all of these negotiations may finally lead to nowhere. GT has heard rumors that TBA is using the negotiations with GT as leverage to get a better deal from Western Electronics. GT's engineers have been reluctant to propose specific figures for each of the options, stating that it is up to the lawyers to come up with a binding agreement. Can a binding contract be structured now with the three options with final prices to be determined during the five-year period it will take to install the whole system? Can you advise GT on how to structure a binding contract? What issues exist under the CISG? *See* Article 14(1) and the case involving Pratt Whitney *infra*. What about using the UCC?

United Technologies International Pratt & Whitney Commercial Engine Business v. Malev Hungarian Airlines

The Supreme Court of the Republic of Hungary GF. I. 31 349/1992/9
Translated in 13 Journal of Law and Commerce 31-47 (1993)

[In the fall of 1990, Pratt & Whitney Commercial Engine Business (PW) began negotiating with Malev Hungarian Airlines (MHA) about the sale of replacement engines for MHA's Soviet-made aircraft and for the purchase of new aircraft engines, the PW 4000 series. Concerned that the negotiations had already lasted several months, PW asked MHA to sign a nonbinding letter of intent. In the letter, the parties agreed that the signing of a final agreement would depend on MHA's acceptance of a support offer (a service contract) for the new PW 4000 engines that would be part of new aircraft to be purchased by MHA. PW also attempted at various times to make the sale of replacement engines conditional upon MHA's purchase of new engines. At the time, MHA was also separately negotiating with two aircraft companies to purchase two or three airplanes and was choosing from among different aircraft companies. Under the practice of the industry, a buyer would not select an engine until it chose the aircraft that it would purchase. Subsequently, PW submitted two purchase-support offers dated December 14, 1990 to MHA, one for each of type of plane, that replaced an earlier November 9 purchase-support offer. According to the offers, depending on which plane MHA chose, MHA would then purchase a different PW engine that would then come installed in the aircraft. For example, if MHA decided to purchase the Boeing 767, MHA would also purchase a PW 4056, which had a base price of $5.84 million (MHA could also select the PW 4060 engine or two replacement engines for the Boeing but no base price was included for these other engines); if MHA decided to purchase the Airbus 310-300 aircraft, MHA would then purchase a PW 4152, which had a base price of $5.55 million, or the PW 4156 for $5.84 million and two spare engines. The Airbus was slightly different from the Boeing in that while the Boeing could receive the installation of the engines without any further modification, the Airbus had to be further modified and additional parts such as a gondola had to be installed. As a result, the Airbus was to receive a "jet engine system" as opposed to a simple engine as in the case of the Boeing planes. (The offer for the Airbus engines, however, did not include a price for the engine system, but just for the engine.) Under these types of arrangements, MHA would pay the aircraft manufacturer for the cost of a complete plane and the aircraft manufacturer would then pay PW for the cost of the engine. The support offers from PW also offered financing to MHA.

Both of the purchase-support offers contained a place where MHA was to sign, but rather than signing the offers, MHA composed a letter on December 21, 1990 stating that it had selected the PW 4000 engine for the new fleet of aircraft. MHA also mentioned in the letter that it was looking forward to cooperating with PW on the replacement engines as well. The letter also mentioned that it was wholly based on the conditions contained in the December 14, 1990 purchase-support offers. In February 1991, PW sent a letter adding a $65,000 advertising budget and stated that PW would come to Budapest to continue discussions on the replacement engines and to finalize the contract for the new PW 4000 engines. MHA then chose the Boeing aircraft but notified PW that it would not choose the

PW engines. PW countered that MHA had committed to purchase the Boeing aircraft and the PW 4000 engines and asked MHA to immediately notify Boeing about its selection and to make a public announcement.

When MHA refused to do so, PW brought suit in Hungary. As both Hungary and the United States are contracting parties to the CISG, the contract was governed by the CISG. PW claimed that the purchase-support offers of December 14, 1990 constituted offers within the meaning of Article 14 of the CISG because they clearly stated the product, the quantity, and data on which the price could be determined precisely. According to PW, the offers were definite because the parties could determine, based on the aircraft type, the number of engines and the price. Further, MHA's declaration of December 21, 1990 operated as an acceptance of PW's offer. MHA argued that the December 14, 1990 offers were not definite within the meaning of CISG Article 14. The price and quantity of the engines all depended on the type of plane that MHA was to purchase and could not be determined through the December 14, 1990 offers alone. Once MHA chose a certain type of aircraft, then the type of engine and the cost of the engine could be determined with precision. Here neither the quantity nor the price could be determined through the December 14, 1990 offers alone. MHA also argued that in its February 11, 1991 letter, PW referred to the finalization of the contract and did not transfer a $1 million U.S. payment as a dollar premium for signing. This was a contractual premium given to the buyer in case the buyer signed the contract within the deadline.

The lower court found that a contract had been established under the CISG. The court found that the December 1990 offers were sufficiently definite because once MHA selected the aircraft the quantity and price of the engines could be determined concretely. MHA's December 21, 1990 declaration was the acceptance of the offer. The court treated the February 11 letter as a later addition or modification of the contract. On appeal, MHA's argument was that the December 14, 1990 purchase support offers were not definite offers but still part of the process of negotiations. The court of appeals agreed with MHA and reversed. The court of appeals noted that in the case of the Airbus as the engines were to be built into the planes, MHA was really buying a "jet engine system" and not merely the base engine. The jet engine system included additional parts—in the case of the Airbus the jet engine system included the engine, other parts, and the gondola as well. The court found that if the offers were to be definite under CISG Article 14, the offers had to include the price of all of the products, engines, and jet engine systems. In the case of the Boeing, the engine only was needed as Boeing planes included all of the other parts that otherwise had to be supplied for the Airbus. PW then appealed to the Hungarian Supreme Court, which rendered the decision below.]

It clearly follows from the above, that none of Plaintiff's offer, neither the one for the Boeing aircraft's engines, nor the one for the Airbus aircraft's jet engine systems, complied with the requirements stipulated in Paragraph 1, Section 14 of the Agreement, for it did not indicate the price of the services or it could not have been determined.

Plaintiff's parallel and alternative contractual offers should be interpreted, according to the noticeable intention of the offer's wording and following common sense, so, that Plaintiff wished to provide an opportunity to Defendant to select one of the engine types defined in the offer at the time of the acceptance of the offer.

For according to the wording of Section Y of the offers:

- Defendant, following the acceptance of the proposal, immediately notifies the aircraft manufacturer about the selection of one of the numerically defined engines (jet engine systems) for use on the wide bodied aircrafts;
- Plaintiff sells the selected engine (jet engine system) to Defendant according to a separate agreement made with the aircraft manufacturer;
- Thereby (that is, with the acceptance of the proposal) Defendant sends a final and unconditional purchase order to Plaintiff for the delivery of the spare engines of the determined type.

In addition to grammatical interpretation, the assumption of Plaintiff granting "power" to Defendant, made by the court of first instance, essentially entitling Defendant to make its selection until some undetermined point of time or even during performance from the services offered alternatively, goes against economic reasoning as well. For the legal consequences of this would be that Plaintiff should manufacture the quantity, stipulated in the contract, of all four types — two engines and two jet engine systems — and prepared with its services wait for Defendant to exercise its right to make its selection with no deadline.

It follows from this all that Plaintiff provided was an opportunity to choose a certain type of engine or jet engine system at the time of the acceptance of its offer.

Plaintiff's offers were alternative, therefore Defendant should have determined which engine or jet engine system, listed in the offers, it chose. There was no declaration made, on behalf of Defendant, in which Defendant would have indicated the subject of the service, the concrete type of the engine or jet engine system, listed in the offers, as an essential condition of the contract. Defendant's declaration, that it had chosen the PW 4000 series engine, expresses merely Defendant's intention to close the contract, which is insufficient for the establishment of the contract.

Therefore, the court of first instance was mistaken when it found that with Defendant's December 21, 1990 declaration the contract was established with the "power" — or, more precisely stipulation — according to which Defendant was entitled to select from the indicated four types (PW 4056 or PW 4060 engine and spare engine, PW 4152 or PW 4156 jet engine system and spare engine) with a unilateral declaration later, after the contract had been closed. The opportunity to choose after closing the contract does not follow from the offer. If perhaps such a further condition would have been intended by Defendant, then this should have been regarded as a new offer on its behalf.

Lacking an appropriately explicit offer from Plaintiff and not having a clear indication as to the subject of the service in Defendant's declaration of acceptance, no sales contract has been established between the Parties.

It is a different issue, whether the series of discussions and Defendant's declaration of acceptance created such a special atmosphere of confidence, where Plaintiff could seriously count on closing the contract and failing that Plaintiff suffered economic and other disadvantages. With this question and with its legal grounds, no suit being initiated, the court of appeals was not entitled to deal with.

The stipulation of the contract, that the validity of the offer's acceptance depended on the approval of the United States or of the Hungarian Government, could bear with any significance only if the acceptance of the offer would have resulted in a contract, however, since a contract was not established, the above-mentioned uncertain future circumstances bear with no significance in relation to the judgment passed in this present suit.

The degree to which the discussions between the Parties about the replacement of the TU-154 aircrafts' engines were related to the acceptance of the offers involved in the suit also had no significance, although Defendant's letter of December 21, 1990 and Plaintiff's letter of February 11, 1991 clearly proves that the Parties, besides the present offers, were continuously negotiating and that Defendant's understanding of the cooperation with Plaintiff included the replacement of the engines.

Plaintiff has lost the case, therefore, according to Paragraph 1, Section 78 of the Civil Procedure, in addition to bearing its own costs, it is obligated to reimburse all costs that emerged during the first and the appeal procedure to Defendant. Defendant's costs consist of legal fees, determined on the basis of Point B, Paragraph 1 of the Decree of the Minister of Justice of 12/1991 (IX.29.), and a HUF 150,000 appeal duty. Plaintiff indicated more than 2 billion forints as the subject of the suit, the court has determined the court fee, which amounts to 0.5% of the above sum for the proceedings of the first instance, while in the appeal proceeding half of that amount.

NOTES AND QUESTIONS

1. In the preceding case, Pratt & Whitney and the prospective buyer signed a letter of intent, which is often the case where long and complex negotiations are involved and where months or even years of negotiations are required before the parties are able to agree to a binding contract or a series of legally binding agreements. The purpose of the letter is for both parties to evidence their good-faith commitment to enter into a binding agreement so that each party has some assurance that the other party is serious about the transaction and is not wasting the other party's time and resources. The letter of intent, however, is not intended to be a binding legal document and both parties can walk away from the transaction with legal impunity. The reason that the parties may not want a binding commitment is that there are cases where although the parties wish to consummate a deal, the details just cannot be worked out in a satisfactory way to both sides despite the earnest efforts of the parties. In most cases, parties who enter into a letter of intent do take the commitment seriously and are less likely to simply abandon the transaction over some minor detail. Letters of intent are often used in negotiations on foreign investment enterprises, such as joint ventures, which often take 18 months to two years of negotiations before binding documents are executed. In complex contract transactions, such as those involved in the attempted sale of Pratt & Whitney engines, letters of intent are also often used.

2. Why did the Hungarian Supreme Court find that there was no contract in the principal case? Does the *Pratt & Whitney* case stand for the proposition that offers that contain open price and open quantity terms are not "offers" within the meaning of Article 14(1) and that an acceptance of such "offers" will not form a contract?

3. Does this also mean that the CISG refuses to recognize open price and open quantity contracts? Consider the following: The key issue under Article 14(1)

is whether the offeror intends to be bound by an acceptance of the offer. Offerors do not usually intend to be bound by offers that are indefinite as to price and quantity. Rather, offerors usually intend to be bound when a proposal is addressed to specific persons containing definite terms on price and quantity. Thus, a final or definite price and quantity function as an indication of the intent of the offeror to be bound by an acceptance. The key issue is the intent of the offeror to be bound and the reasonable expectation of the offeree that an answer of "yes" creates a binding contract. Usually, this requires a final price and final quantity but there are many instances when a long-term or complex contract is involved and the parties intend to be bound when there is a provisional price and quantity that may need to be adjusted as the contract is being performed.

4. Suppose that Pratt & Whitney and the buyer had inserted the following clause into their contract: "The parties hereby exercise their power under CISG Article 6 to derogate from the requirements of CISG Article 14(1) providing a proposal must be sufficiently definite as to quantity and price in order to constitute an offer. The parties hereby declare their intention to be bound by this open price and open quantity contract despite the lack of agreement on a final price and final quantity." Would such a statement be effective to create a binding contract without details as to a final price and quantity? Is it a sufficient response to this query to simply note that Article 14(1) provides that a proposal that is not sufficiently definite is not an offer and so thus a response of "I accept" cannot conclude a contract because there was no offer to accept?

In considering this question, note the following points. First, recall that the CISG is not concerned with the validity of the contract but only with contract formation and the rights and obligations of the parties. Issues of validity are governed by another source of substantive law, which would most likely be domestic law. To suggest that a proposal without concrete terms on quantity and price cannot be a valid offer under Article 14(1) is raising the issue of the validity of the contract, which is not within the scope of Article 14(1) or any other provision of the CISG. Open price and open quantity contracts are valid under both the common law and the Uniform Commercial Code. Second, the creation of a contract through the model of a formal offer and an acceptance under Article 14(1) is not the only way that a binding contract can be created under the CISG. Article 18(3) provides that a binding contract can be created by the conduct of the parties. Consider also Article 55, which provides in part:

> Where a contract has been validly concluded but does not expressly or implicitly fix or make provision for determining the price, the parties are considered . . . to have impliedly made reference to the price generally charged at the time of the conclusion of the contract for such goods sold under comparable circumstances in the trade concerned.

After considering these materials, what is your answer?

rank around

6. *Performance of the Contract*

Once a valid contract is formed, the parties must then carry out their obligations under the contract: The seller must deliver conforming goods and the buyer must pay the purchase price. The materials below focus on these three elements: Delivery, conformity of the goods, and payment. *3 elements*

A. DELIVERY BY SELLER (Art. 30, 31, 33)

While delivery may seem straightforward enough where the parties are involved in a face-to-face cash for goods transaction where the seller can hand over the goods to the buyer, these types of transactions are very rare in any context today, but especially so in the context of an international sale. When the seller and buyer are in different countries, what does the seller have to do to satisfy its delivery obligation? While the parties may look to the terms of the contract, the contract may be silent on these matters, especially if the contract is formed through casual contracts.

PROBLEM 3-11

The buyer, a manufacturer of auto parts in Cleveland, Ohio, calls the seller, a supplier of machine parts, in Toronto, Canada, and says, "Hey, I saw your Web site and you've got just what we need. Can you sell me 6,000 widgets for $15,000?"

(1) The seller responds, "Sorry, my costs have gone up recently. I can't do it for any less than $16,500." The buyer then says, "Okay, let's do it." What must the seller do to satisfy its obligation to deliver the goods? *See* Articles 30 and 31. When must the seller deliver the goods? *See* Article 33.

(2) Suppose instead that the seller responds, "I can do it for $17,000 inland freight by truck. I'll have the trucker's bills of lading waiting for you in my office." What must the seller do to satisfy its delivery obligations with respect to the goods and the documents under these circumstances? *See* Articles 31 and 34. Suppose that during the course of transport the truck is involved in a traffic accident and the goods are damaged. Who bears the risk of loss? *See* Article 67. Were there any obligations concerning insurance? *See* Article 32.

NOTES

1. Recall that the CISG is a supplementary law that is meant to interpret the contract, which remains primary. In Problem 3-11, the parties could have explicitly agreed on place of delivery, insurance, and risk of loss. In contracts that are formed through casual contacts, however, it is not unusual for the parties to omit some or all of these terms. The CISG serves to supply these obligations in the absence of an agreement by the parties.

2. While the parties can set out in detail the delivery obligations of the seller, this can be time consuming and misunderstandings and disagreement about the meaning of terms can also arise between the parties. In Chapter 2, we introduced the ICC Incoterms, which are standard terms for delivery obligations that the parties can incorporate by contract. Incoterms help to define the terms of the contract and the use of Incoterms is entirely consistent with the CISG. Incoterms offer a short-cut through the incorporation of a set of agreed-on definitions that reflect international commercial practice. Once the contract is formed, it is then governed by the CISG. In Problem 3-11, the parties could have supplemented the CISG through an explicit agreement incorporating Incoterms. The parties could have agreed, for example, on a contract "CIF Cleveland (Incoterms 2000)." Article 32 details the seller's obligations where the seller is

bound to arrange for carriage of the goods, leaving it up to the parties to decide whether to place the burden for arranging carriage on the seller. The incorporation of the CIF term now explicitly places the obligation on the seller to arrange for transport of the goods, and Article 32 is now applicable and the seller must comply with its requirements. If the parties had not agreed on Incoterms or otherwise specified that the seller was to arrange for the carriage contract, then Article 32 is not applicable unless such an obligation can be inferred from the circumstances. In the case of casual contracts, such as that involved in Problem 3-11, the parties may not refer to Incoterms and the CISG will be applied in the absence of such details in the contract.

B. CONFORMING GOODS

A seller not only has the obligation to deliver the goods but also to deliver goods that meet the reasonable expectations of the buyer. At a minimum, the buyer expects the seller to deliver goods that conform to the contract, that is, of the same quality, quantity, and condition as expressed in the contract. There are often cases, however, where the contract may be silent or does not expressly resolve an issue relating to the conformity of the goods. Even where the contract is silent, however, the buyer may have reasonable expectations that the law wishes to protect. Domestic U.S. law has dealt with these obligations of the seller through three types of warranties: An express warranty (UCC §2-313), an implied warranty of merchantability relating to the quality of the goods (UCC §2-314), and an implied warranty of fitness for a particular purpose (UCC §2-315). The most significant difference between express and implied warranties is that the latter can be disclaimed under UCC §2-316(2) while the former cannot. The approach of the CISG is to combine all of the seller's obligations concerning the conformity of the goods into Article 35.

PROBLEM 3-12

A South Korean manufacturer of plasma flat-screen high-definition televisions contracts to sell a large quantity of televisions to a U.S. wholesale distributor. The contract called for Model H-1. The seller has a surplus of H-2s, which exceed the performance standards of the H-1 and actually have a higher retail market value. The seller ships the H-2 instead. Has the seller met its obligations under Article 35?   *It's an edge.*   *No.*

PROBLEM 3-13

In Problem 3-12 above, the seller ships the H-1 sets.

(1) Because of some minute differences in the U.S. satellite system, the TV cannot display a picture at the high-definition level but only at the level of ordinary television. The buyer refuses to accept the goods. Has the seller met its obligation under Article 35(2)(b) and (c)?   *depends on if there is a specific purpose*

(2) The goods are packaged in wooden crates that are used for ordinary TVs and are damaged en route to the United States. The contract is silent on the type of packaging that needs to be used. Has the seller met its obligation under Article 35(2)(d) and *Medical Marketing infra*?   *depends on industry norms*

(3) When the TVs arrive at U.S. Customs, Customs officials will not allow the TVs entry into the United States because their electrical wiring systems do not meet U.S. safety standards. Is it the seller's responsibility to know about U.S. electrical safety standards or is it the buyer's responsibility? *See* Article 35(2) and *Medical Marketing infra*.

(4) Assume that the contract calls for delivery to the buyer in the port of Los Angeles. Before the seller ships the goods, the buyer engages a South Korean company to check the TVs for use in the United States. The South Korean company reports that the goods satisfy U.S. safety standards but upon their arrival in the United States the goods are refused entry by U.S. Customs. The seller argues that the buyer has waived the right to assert any nonconformity. The buyer argues that as delivery is to occur in the United States, the buyer has the right to defer examination until the goods have arrived and to assert the nonconformity upon inspection of the goods in the United States. What is the result? *See* Articles 36, 38 and 39. Suppose the seller knew that the TVs did not satisfy U.S. safety standards? *See* Article 40. See also *Medical Marketing* and *BP Oil infra*.

Medical Marketing International, Inc. v. Internazionale Medico Scientifica, S.r.l.

United States District Court, Eastern District of Louisiana, 1999
1999 WL 311945

DUVAL, District Judge.

Before the court is an Application for Order Confirming Arbitral Award and Entry of Judgment, filed by plaintiff, Medical Marketing International, Inc. ("MMI"). Having considered the memoranda of plaintiff, and the memorandum in opposition filed by defendant, Internazionale Medico Scientifica, S.r.l. ("IMS"), the court grants the motion.

FACTUAL BACKGROUND

Plaintiff MMI is a Louisiana marketing corporation with its principal place of business in Baton Rouge, Louisiana. Defendant IMS is an Italian corporation that manufactures radiology materials with its principal place of business in Bologna, Italy. On January 25, 1993, MMI and IMS entered into a Business Licensing Agreement in which IMS granted exclusive sales rights for Giotto Mammography H.F. Units to MMI.

In 1996, the Food and Drug Administration ("FDA") seized the equipment for noncompliance with administrative procedures, and a dispute arose over who bore the obligation of ensuring that the Giotto equipment complied with the United States Governmental Safety Regulations, specifically the Good Manufacturing Practices (GMP) for Medical Device Regulations. MMI formally demanded mediation on October 28, 1996, pursuant to Article 13 of the agreement. Mediation was unsuccessful, and the parties entered into arbitration, also pursuant to Article 13, whereby each party chose one arbitrator and a third was agreed upon by both.

An arbitration hearing was held on July 13-15, July 28, and November 17, 1998. The hearing was formally closed on November 30, 1998. The arbitrators rendered their decision on December 21, 1998, awarding MMI damages in the amount of $357,009.00 and legal interest on that amount from October 28, 1996. IMS moved for reconsideration on December 30, 1998, and this request was denied by the arbitrators on January 7, 1999. Plaintiff now moves for an order from this court confirming the arbitral award and entering judgment in favor of the plaintiff.

ANALYSIS

IMS has alleged that the arbitrators' decision violates public policy of the international global market and that the arbitrators exhibited "manifest disregard of international sales law." Specifically, IMS argues that the arbitrators misapplied the United Nations Convention on Contracts for the International Sale of Goods, commonly referred to as CISG, and that they refused to follow a German Supreme Court Case interpreting CISG.

MMI does not dispute that CISG applies to the case at hand. Under CISG, the finder of fact has a duty to regard the "international character" of the convention and to promote uniformity in its application. CISG Article 7. The Convention also provides that in an international contract for goods, goods conform to the contract if they are fit for the purpose for which goods of the same description would ordinarily be used or are fit for any particular purpose expressly or impliedly made known to the seller and relied upon by the buyer. CISG Article 35(2). To avoid a contract based on the nonconformity of goods, the buyer must allege and prove that the seller's breach was "fundamental" in nature. CISG Article 49. A breach is fundamental when it results in such detriment to the party that he or she is substantially deprived of what he or she is entitled to expect under the contract, unless the party in breach did not foresee such a result. CISG Article 25.

At the arbitration, IMS argued that MMI was not entitled to avoid its contract with IMS based on nonconformity under Article 49, because IMS's breach was not "fundamental." IMS argued that CISG did not require that it furnish MMI with equipment that complied with the United States GMP regulations. To support this proposition, IMS cited a German Supreme Court case, which held that under CISG Article 35, a seller is generally not obligated to supply goods that conform to public laws and regulations enforced at the buyer's place of business. *Entscheidunger des Bundersgerichtshofs in Zivilsachen* (BGHZ) 129, 75 (1995). In that case, the court held that this general rule carries with it exceptions in three limited circumstances: (1) if the public laws and regulations of the buyer's state are identical to those enforced in the seller's state; (2) if the buyer informed the seller about those regulations; or (3) if due to "special circumstances," such as the existence of a seller's branch office in the buyer's state, the seller knew or should have known about the regulations at issue.

The arbitration panel decided that under the third exception, the general rule did not apply to this case. The arbitrators held that IMS was, or should have been, aware of the GMP regulations prior to entering into the 1993 agreement, and explained their reasoning at length. IMS now argues that the arbitration panel refused to apply CISG and the law as articulated by the German Supreme Court. It is clear from the arbitrators' written findings, however, that they carefully considered that decision and found that this case fit the exception and not the rule as articulated in that decision. The arbitrators' decision was neither contrary to public policy nor in manifest disregard of international sales law. This court therefore finds that the arbitration panel did not "exceed its powers" in violation of the FAA. Accordingly,

It is ordered that the Application for Order Confirming Arbitral Award is hereby Granted.

BP Oil International, Ltd. v. Empresa Estatal
Petroleos de Ecuador
United States Court of Appeals, Fifth Circuit, 2003
332 F.3d 333

SMITH, Circuit Judge.

Empresa Estatal Petroleos de Ecuador ("PetroEcuador") contracted with BP Oil International, Ltd. ("BP"), for the purchase and transport of gasoline from Texas to Ecuador. PetroEcuador refused to accept delivery, so BP sold the gasoline at a loss. BP appeals a summary judgment dismissing PetroEcuador and Saybolt, Inc. ("Saybolt"), the company responsible for testing the gasoline at the port of departure. We affirm in part, reverse in part, and remand.

I.

PetroEcuador sent BP an invitation to bid for supplying 140,000 barrels of unleaded gasoline deliverable "CFR" to Ecuador. "CFR," which stands for "Cost and Freight," is one of thirteen International Commercial Terms ("Incoterms") designed to "provide a set of international rules for the interpretation of the most commonly used trade terms in foreign trade." Incoterms are recognized through their incorporation into the Convention on Contracts for the International Sale of Goods ("CISG").

BP responded favorably to the invitation, and PetroEcuador confirmed the sale on its contract form. The final agreement required that the oil be sent "CFR La Libertad-Ecuador." The contract further specifies that the gasoline have a gum content of less than three milliliters per one hundred milliliters, to be determined at the port of departure. PetroEcuador appointed Saybolt, a company specializing in quality control services, to ensure this requirement was met.

To fulfill the contract, BP purchased gasoline from Shell Oil Company and, following testing by Saybolt, loaded it on board the M/T TIBER at Shell's Deer Park, Texas, refinery. The TIBER sailed to La Libertad, Ecuador, where the gasoline was again tested for gum content. On learning that the gum content now exceeded the contractual limit, PetroEcuador refused to accept delivery. Eventually, BP resold the gasoline to Shell at a loss of approximately two million dollars.

BP sued PetroEcuador for breach of contract and wrongful draw of a letter of guarantee. After PetroEcuador filed a notice of intent to apply foreign law pursuant to Fed. R. Civ. P. 44.1, the district court applied Texas choice of law rules and determined that Ecuadorian law governed. BP argued that the term "CFR" demonstrated the parties' intent to pass the risk of loss to PetroEcuador once the goods were delivered on board the TIBER. The district court disagreed and held that under Ecuadorian law, the seller must deliver conforming goods to the agreed destination, in this case Ecuador. The court granted summary judgment for PetroEcuador.

BP also brought negligence and breach of contract claims against Saybolt, alleging that the company had improperly tested the gasoline. Saybolt moved for summary judgment, asserting a limitation of liability defense and waiver of claims based on the terms of its service contract with BP. The court granted Saybolt's motion, holding that BP could not sue in tort, that BP was bound by the waiver provision, and that Saybolt did not take any action causing harm to BP. Pursuant to Fed. R. Civ. P. 54(b), the court entered final judgment in favor of PetroEcuador and Saybolt.

[The court of appeals held that the CISG, not Ecuadorian domestic law, governed the contract, then turned to a discussion of the CISG.] The CISG incorporates Incoterms through article 9(2), which provides:

> The parties are considered, unless otherwise agreed, to have impliedly made applicable to their contract or its formation a usage of which the parties knew or ought to have known and which in international trade is widely known to, and regularly observed by, parties to contracts of the type involved in the particular trade concerned.

CISG art. 9(2). Even if the usage of Incoterms is not global, the fact that they are well known in international trade means that they are incorporated through article 9(2).

PetroEcuador's invitation to bid for the procurement of 140,000 barrels of gasoline proposed "CFR" delivery. The final agreement, drafted by PetroEcuador, again specified that the gasoline be sent "CFR La Libertad-Ecuador" and that the cargo's gum content be tested pre-shipment. Shipments designated "CFR" require the seller to pay the costs and freight to transport the goods to the delivery port, but pass title and risk of loss to the buyer once the goods "pass the ship's rail" at the port of shipment. The goods should be tested for conformity before the risk of loss passes to the buyer. In the event of subsequent damage or loss, the buyer generally must seek a remedy against the carrier or insurer.

In light of the parties' unambiguous use of the Incoterm "CFR," BP fulfilled its contractual obligations if the gasoline met the contract's qualitative specifications when it passed the ship's rail and risk transferred to PetroEcuador. CISG art. 36(1). Indeed, Saybolt's testing confirmed that the gasoline's gum content was adequate before departure from Texas. Nevertheless, in its opposition to BP's motion for summary judgment, PetroEcuador contends that BP purchased the gasoline from Shell on an "as is" basis and thereafter failed to add sufficient gum inhibitor as a way to "cut corners." In other words, the cargo contained a hidden defect.

Having appointed Saybolt to test the gasoline, PetroEcuador "ought to have discovered" the defect before the cargo left Texas. CISG art. 39(1). Permitting PetroEcuador now to distance itself from Saybolt's test would negate the parties' selection of CFR delivery and would undermine the key role that reliance plays in international sales agreements. Nevertheless, BP could have breached the agreement if it provided goods that it "knew or could not have been unaware" were defective when they "passed over the ship's rail" and risk shifted to PetroEcuador. CISG art. 40.

Therefore, there is a fact issue as to whether BP knowingly provided gasoline with an excessive gum content. The district court should permit the parties to conduct discovery as to this issue only.

IV.

BP raises negligence and breach of contract claims against Saybolt, alleging that the company improperly tested the gasoline's gum content before shipment. These claims amount to indemnification for BP's losses suffered on account of PetroEcuador's refusal to accept delivery. Our conclusion that PetroEcuador is liable so long as BP did not knowingly provide deficient gasoline renders these claims moot. Summary judgment was therefore proper, though we need not review the district court's reasoning.

If PetroEcuador improperly refused CFR delivery, it is liable to BP for any consequential damages. In its claims against Saybolt, BP pleaded "in the alternative"; counsel also acknowledged, at oral argument, that beyond those damages stemming from PetroEcuador's refusal to accept delivery, BP has no collateral claims against Saybolt. If Saybolt negligently misrepresented the gasoline's gum content, PetroEcuador (not BP) becomes the party with a potential claim.

Even if PetroEcuador is not liable because BP knowingly presented gasoline with an inadequate gum content, BP's claims drop out. BP alleges that Saybolt "negligently misrepresented the quality" of the gasoline before its loading in Texas; it also claims that Saybolt's improper testing was "a proximate cause of the gasoline to be refused by PetroEcuador and/or the gum content to increase which caused BP to suffer pecuniary loss." BP's claims depend on the fact that Saybolt misrepresented the quality of the gasoline. It goes without saying, however, that if BP knew that the gasoline was deficient, it could not have relied on Saybolt's report to its detriment.

The judgment dismissing PetroEcuador is reversed and remanded for proceedings consistent with this opinion. The judgment dismissing Saybolt is affirmed.

NOTES AND QUESTIONS

1. In *BP Oil*, the Fifth Circuit held that, under CISG Article 9(2), Incoterms applied to the contract because the parties "impliedly made applicable to their contract or its formation a usage of which the parties knew or ought to have known." The court then noted that even if the use of Incoterms "is not global, the fact that they are well known in international trade means that they are incorporated through article 9(2)." See *BP Oil, supra*, 332 F.3d at 337-338. Is the effect of the court's decision to incorporate Incoterms into all CISG contracts?

2. The issue of disclaimer of warranties is given extensive treatment in the UCC, but is an issue on which the CISG is silent. Are the UCC disclaimer provisions applicable to a contract governed by the CISG and, if not, what standards are applicable?

The issue would arise in only one context: Where a contract is governed by the CISG and U.S. law may be used to decide on an issue excluded from the scope of the CISG. For example, a U.S. seller contracts with a buyer from a CISG country for the sale of goods. The contract is governed by the CISG but the U.S. seller attempts to disclaim the seller's obligations under CISG Article 35(2)(a) and (b). What standards govern the disclaimer of these obligations? In particular, must the seller specifically mention Article 35 or quote the language of the obligations that the seller is attempting to waive and must the waiver be one that cannot fail to draw the buyer's attention? The CISG is silent on this issue. UCC §2-316(2) provides that "to exclude . . . the implied warranty of merchantability . . . the language must mention merchantability and in case of a record must be conspicuous." An exclusion of the implied warranty of fitness for a particular purpose does not need to mention the warranty and can be done by general language but the disclaimer must be in writing and conspicuous. *See id*. Must the seller comply with the requirements of UCC §2-316 in disclaiming its Article 35 obligations? The resolution of this issue depends on whether UCC §2-316 establishes a rule of validity or a rule of interpretation; that is, is UCC §2-316 concerned about the validity of the disclaimer or is it merely intended to provide an interpretative guide to language purporting to be a disclaimer? If §2-316 concerns validity, then any disclaimer that fails to satisfy §2-316 has no legal effect; if the rule concerns interpretation, the disclaimer, even if it does not satisfy §2-316, may still be effective if supported by other evidence of the understanding of the parties.

Can you see why the applicability of §2-316 to our CISG contract depends on whether it is a rule of validity or a rule of interpretation? Review CISG Article 4(2) concerning rules of validity and Article 8 concerning rules of interpretation. The debate has not yet been settled. The different views are represented by John O. Honnold, *Uniform Law for International Sales Under the 1980 United Nations Convention* 310-313 (1982) [UCC §2-316 is a rule of interpretation and is superseded by CISG rules of interpretation in Article 8(2)] and Laura E. Longobardi, *Disclaimers of Implied Warranties: The 1980 United Nations Convention on Contracts for the International Sale of Goods*, 53 Fordham L. Rev. 863, 878-884 (1985) [mandatory character of UCC §2-316 indicates that it is a rule of validity and applies to CISG contracts as issues of validity are excluded from the scope of the CISG under Article 4(a)].

C.   PAYMENT BY BUYER

The buyer's obligation is to pay against delivery but if the transaction is not a face-to-face one, questions arise as to under what conditions, when, and where payment is to be made.

PROBLEM 3-14

A wholesale distributor in Mexico City sends a fax to a grain dealer in Indiana with the following message, "I need 1,000 bushels of corn. Can you get them to me by June 15th?" The seller responds with a reply by fax, "Yes, we accept your offer. We can make delivery on or before June 15th in Mexico City at the market price of $3 per bushel." The buyer responds, "Sorry, but our fax was one of several inquiries sent out and not an offer. We have already concluded a contract with another dealer so we cannot agree to accept delivery." The seller responds, "Our lawyers have reviewed our communications and have advised us that when we accepted your offer a valid contract was formed. We intend to hold you to the contract." Is there a valid contract and must buyer pay for the goods? *See* Article 14(1).

PROBLEM 3-15

Suppose that under the same facts above the Mexican distributor states in the fax, "I am in urgent need of 1,000 bushels of corn at market price." The buyer immediately ships 1,000 bushels and the next day sends a fax, "We have shipped 1,000 bushels of corn at the low price of $6 per bushel." Must the buyer pay for the goods and at what price? *See* Article 18(3) and Article 55 and the case below.

sufficiently definite – 14(1)   depends on fair market price

acceptance – 18(3)

Unilex, D. 1995-1
France: Cour de Cassation (April 1, 1995)

A French buyer ordered electronic components from a German seller. The order specified that the final purchase price, previously indicated by the seller, would have to be revised taking into account a possible decrease in market prices, and that the goods would be delivered at certain dates, upon confirmation by the seller. The seller replied, specifying that the purchase price would have to be revised according to both the increase and decrease in market prices. Later, the buyer cancelled the order involving some other components. The seller objected to such partial cancellation, alleging that it had already dispatched the goods concerned for delivery. Upon delivery the buyer rejected the goods in excess and requested the seller to take back the said goods. The seller refused to take back the goods rejected by the buyer and demanded payment.

As to the buyer's argument that the offer was not sufficiently definite (Art. 14(1) CISG), the appellate court held that the revision of price according to the market trends indicated in the buyer's original offer did make the price determinable.

Upon the buyer's appeal, the Supreme Court affirmed the appellate court decision.

PROBLEM 3-16

A Kentucky farmer sells a large quantity of paddlefish caviar to a buyer in the Ukraine. The contract called for carriage of the goods by sea and a negotiable bill of lading. As for the price, the parties had orally agreed to a price of $250,000 but did not agree on currency or a place of payment. Both parties assumed that they would work out these details eventually but the caviar is now en route. The seller is reluctant to part with the bill of lading until several payment issues are resolved. The buyer insists that payment is to be made in the Ukraine in local currency after it receives a formal written request for payment from the seller. This presents several problems for the seller. Banks in the United States will not convert Ukrainian currency into U.S. dollars. One option for the seller is to accept payment by the buyer in local Ukrainian currency and then convert the currency into U.S. dollars through local banks in the Ukraine. However, although Ukrainian banks will convert local currency into U.S. dollars, the exchange of such a large sum and the removal of such a large quantity of U.S. dollars from the Ukraine requires government approval. As the Ukraine wants to build up its foreign currency reserves of U.S. dollars, it is not at all certain whether the government will give its approval and, in any event, the approval process takes up to a year and involves all types of fees. The seller wants payment in U.S. dollars in the United States. Where does the buyer need to make payment and in what currency? *See* Articles 57 and 58.

Should the seller consider a confirmed letter of credit in this case? How would a confirmed letter of credit help the seller resolve the payment issues?

The buyer also insists on inspection of the goods before payment, saying that it is not sure that the paddlefish roe will be suited to local tastes. Does the buyer have the right to inspect the goods before payment? *See* Article 58.

D.   EXCUSED PERFORMANCE

In the course of a contract, any number of unexpected difficulties can arise that prevent its performance: War, government prohibitions, the unavailability of transportation routes such as the closing of a well-known route such as the Suez Canal, strikes, fire, and economic conditions. The situations themselves can be the subject of endless variations but the narrow legal issue remains the same: Under what conditions will the performance of the contract by the parties be excused due to some unexpected event or difficulty that prevents performance? If non-performance is excused, then the nonperforming party is not liable to the disappointed party for breach of contract. Domestic courts deal with this issue through the various doctrines of frustration, impossibility, and force majeure.

(1)   ARTICLE 79

Excused performance is governed by Article 79, the first clause of which provides:

Article 79

(1) A party is not liable for a failure to perform any of his obligations if he proves that the failure was due to an impediment beyond his control and that he could not reasonably be expected to have taken the impediment into account at the time of the conclusion of the contract or to have avoided or overcome it or its consequences.

Note that Article 79(1) consists of three elements: (1) The failure to perform must be due to an impediment beyond the control of the nonperforming party; (2) the nonperforming party could not reasonably be expected to take the impediment into account; and (3) the nonperforming party could not overcome the impediment.

Illustration 79a. In a contract for the sale of widgets, the seller's operating costs unexpectedly go up and the seller will suffer serious financial hardship if it performs the contract. The seller is not excused under Article 79. An "impediment" to performance connotes a barrier that prevents performance, not an event that makes performance more difficult or costly.

Illustration 79b. In a contract for the sale of widgets, the seller's factory is destroyed by a fire caused by faulty wiring. The city had inspected the factory in the prior month and had given the seller a warning that the factory's electrical wiring did not satisfy city fire code standards. The seller is not excused. In this case, the destruction of the factory by fire is an impediment under Article 79 but it is one that the seller should have taken into account under the circumstances of the case.

Illustration 79c. In a contract for the sale of widgets, the seller's factory is destroyed by a fire even though the seller's factory had just passed a city fire inspection and had no history of fire problems. The contract calls for the delivery of widgets but did not specify that the widgets were to be produced in the seller's factory. The seller is not excused. Although the seller's nonperformance is caused by an impediment that the seller could not reasonably be expected to take into account, the seller can overcome the impediment by purchasing substitute widgets on the market and delivering them to the buyer.

If a party fulfills all of the conditions under Article 79 and is excused from performance, the exemption provided by Article 79 is a narrow one. Assuming that the nonperforming party is exempt, Article 79(5) provides "Nothing in this Article prevents either party from exercising any right other than to claim damages." The most important consequence of this limitation is the disappointed party's ability to avoid the contract is not impaired. (Avoidance is governed by Articles 25, 49, 64, 72, and 73, which we take up in the following section on remedies.) Suppose that the seller is excused from performance under Article 79; the buyer cannot sue the seller for damages but the buyer can avoid the contract and does not have to pay the contract price. The buyer is also entitled to restitution [Article 81(2)] of whatever the buyer may have paid to the seller. The same holds true if the nonperforming party is the buyer: The seller does not have to deliver the goods.

PROBLEM 3-17

An Ecuadorian seller enters into a sales contract with a U.S. buyer for goods. The contract does not specify the route but simply states, "delivery to occur in Miami by the most economically available route." The seller arranges for the contract of carriage to set sail through the Panama Canal to reach Miami. The buyer knows that the route through the Panama Canal is the usual and customary shipping route for merchants in Ecuador and all of its immediately adjacent neighboring countries. While the carrier is en route to the Panama Canal, however, a military coup breaks out in the region and the Panama Canal is closed. The alternative route is to sale around the southern end of South America and then up to Miami but the trip will take an additional two months and will add 75 percent to the cost of carriage.

(1) Two weeks after the ship returns to Ecuador, the seller tells the buyer that its performance is prevented by an impediment under Article 79. Has the seller fulfilled its obligations under Article 79(4)? NO

(2) The contract is for the sale of Ecuadorian fruit. If the seller takes the trip around the southern tip of South America, the goods will perish. But upon return of the ship to port, the seller can ship the goods via air but this would cost 20 times as much and may force the seller into bankruptcy. What is the result under Article 79(1)? Does it make a difference whether the contract is construed as a contract for goods from Ecuador to Miami or as a contract for goods from Ecuador to Miami via the Panama Canal?

(3) The contract is for the sale of Ecuadorian-made shoes. What is the result under Article 79(1)? *See also Tsakiroglou infra.*

Tsakiroglou & Co. Ltd. v. Noblee Thorl G.m.b.H.
House of Lords
[1962] A.C. 93

[In an arbitration between Tsakiroglou & Co. Ltd., sellers, and Noblee Thorl G.m.b.H., buyers, the arbitrators awarded the buyers the sum of £5,625 against the sellers as damages for breach of contract. Diplock J. upheld the award and his decision was affirmed by the court of appeal. The sellers (appellants) appealed the decision of the court of appeal to the House of Lords.]

VISCOUNT SIMONDS.

[Under the contract, the sellers] agreed to sell to the respondents 300 tons of Sudanese groundnuts at £50 per 1,000 kilos including bags c.i.f. Hamburg, shipment during November/December, 1956. No goods were shipped by the sellers.

All groundnuts exported from the Sudan to Europe are shipped from Port Sudan, which is the only suitable port. At the date of the contract (October 4, 1956), the usual and normal route for the shipment of Sudanese groundnuts from Port Sudan to Hamburg was via the Suez Canal. Both parties then contemplated that shipment would be made by that route. It would have been unusual and rare for any substantial parcel of Sudanese groundnuts from Port Sudan to Europe to be shipped via the Cape of Good Hope. Before the closure of the Suez Canal the appellants acquired 300 tons of Sudanese groundnuts in shell which were held to their order in warehouses at Port Sudan as from November 1, 1956. They also, before the closure, booked space for 300 tons of nuts in one or other of four vessels scheduled to call at Port Sudan between November 10 and December 26, 1956. The shipping company cancelled these bookings on November 4, 1956. British and French armed forces began military operations against Egypt on October 29, 1956. The Suez Canal was blocked on November 2 and remained closed for effective purposes until at least April 9, 1957. But the appellants could have transported the goods from Port Sudan to Hamburg via the Cape of Good Hope during November and December, 1956.

The distance from Port Sudan to Hamburg via the Suez Canal is about 4,386 miles, and via the Cape about 11,137 miles. The freight ruling at the time of the contract for the shipment of groundnuts from Port Sudan to Hamburg via the Canal was about £7 10s. per ton. After the closure of the Canal the Port Sudan United Kingdom Conference imposed the following surcharges for goods supplied on vessels proceeding via the Cape, namely, as from November 10, 1956, 25 per cent., and as from December 13, 1956, 100 per cent. The market price of Sudanese nuts in shell shipped from Port Sudan c.i.f. Hamburg was £68 15s. per ton between January 1 and 13, 1957. [The sellers] did not ship any nuts. They claimed that they were entitled to consider the contract as cancelled.

The contract provided by clause 6 that "In case of prohibition of import or export, blockade or war, epidemic or strike, and in all cases of force majeure preventing the shipment within the time fixed, or the delivery, the period allowed for shipment or delivery shall be extended by not exceeding two months. After that, if the case of force majeure be still operating, the contract shall be cancelled."

The award was in these terms: "So far as it is a question of fact we find and as far as it is a question of law we hold:

"(i) There were hostilities but not war in Egypt at the material time:

"(ii) Neither war nor force majeure prevented shipment of the contract goods during the contract period if the word 'shipment' means placing the goods on board a vessel destined for the Port of Hamburg:

"(iii) If the word 'shipment' includes not only the placing of the contract goods on board a vessel but also their transportation to the contract destination then shipment via the Suez Canal was prevented during the contract period of shipment by reason of force majeure but shipment via the Cape was not so prevented:

"(iv) It was not an implied term of the contract that shipment or transportation should be made via the Suez Canal:

"(v) The contract was not frustrated by the closure of the Suez Canal:

"(vi) The performance of the contract by shipping the goods on a vessel routed via the Cape of Good Hope was not commercially or fundamentally different from its being performed by shipping the goods on a vessel routed via the Suez Canal."

The first three of these findings relate to the claim of the [sellers] that the exceptions clause (clause 6 of the contract) absolved them from performance of the contract. I will deal with this at once and shortly.

Similar words to those in clause 6 fell to be construed in *In re Comptor Commercial Anversois and Power, Son & Co.*[6] Bailhache J. said: "Now, if I give to the word 'shipment' the widest meaning of which it is capable, it cannot mean more than bringing the goods to the shipping port and then loading them on a ship prepared to carry them to their contractual destination." His judgment on this point was affirmed in the Court of Appeal. It has never been questioned and I see no reason for questioning it.

I come then to the main issue and, as usual, I find two questions interlocked: (1) What does the contract mean? In other words, is there an implied term that the goods shall be carried by a particular route? (2) Is the contract frustrated?

It is convenient to examine the first question first, though the answer may be inconclusive. It is put in the forefront of the appellants' case that the contract was a contract for the shipment of goods via Suez. This contention can only prevail if a term is implied, for the contract does not say so. To say that that is nevertheless its meaning is to say in other words that the term must be implied. For this I see no ground. It has been rejected by the learned trial judge and each of the members of the Court of Appeal; and in two other cases, *Carapanayoti & Co. Ltd. v. E.T. Green Ltd.*[7] and *Gaon (Albert D.) & Co. v. Societe Interprofessionelle des Oleagineux Fluides Alimentaires,*[8] where the same question arose, it was rejected by McNair J. and Ashworth J. respectively. A variant of this contention was that there should be read into the contract by implication the words "by the usual and customary route" and that, as the only usual and customary route at the date of the contract was via Suez, the contractual obligation was to carry the goods via Suez. Though this contention has been viewed somewhat differently, I see as little ground for the implication for it seems to me that there are precisely the same grounds

---

6. [1920] 1 K.B. 868.
7. [1959] 1 Q.B. 131.
8. [1960] 2 Q.B. 318.

for rejecting the one as the other. Both of them assume that sellers and buyers alike intended and would have agreed that, if the route via Suez became impossible, the goods should not be shipped at all. Inasmuch as the buyers presumably wanted the goods and might well have resold them, the assumption appears wholly unjustified. Freight charges may go up or down. If the parties do not specifically protect themselves against change, the loss must lie where it falls.

I turn now to what was the main argument for the appellants: that the contract was frustrated by the closure of the Canal from November 2, 1956, till April 1957. Were it not for the decision of McNair J. in *Green's* case I should not have thought this contention arguable and I must say with the greatest respect to that learned judge that I cannot think he has given full weight to the decisions old and new of this House upon the doctrine of frustration. He correctly held that "where *frustration rule* a contract, expressly or by necessary implication, provides that performance, or a particular part of the performance, is to be carried out in a customary manner, the performance must be carried out in a manner which is customary at the time when the performance is called for." But he concluded that the continued availability of *seller's argument* the Suez route was a fundamental assumption at the time when the contract was made and that to impose upon the sellers the obligation to ship by an emergency route via the Cape would be to impose upon them a fundamentally different obligation which neither party could at the time when the contract was performed have dreamed that the sellers would be required to perform. Your Lordships will observe how similar this line of argument is to that which supports the implication of a term that the route should be via Suez and no other. I can see no justification for it. We are concerned with a c.i.f. contract for the sale of goods, not a contract of affreightment, though part of the sellers' obligation will be to procure a contract of affreightment. There is no evidence that the buyers attached any importance to the route. They were content that the nuts should be shipped at any date in November or December. There was no evidence, and I suppose could not be, that the nuts would deteriorate as the result of a longer voyage and a double *Buyer's argument* crossing of the Equator, nor any evidence that the market was seasonable. In a word, there was no evidence that the buyers cared by what route or, within reasonable limits, when the nuts arrived. What, then, of the sellers? I recall the well-known passage in the speech of Lord Atkinson where he states the obligations of the vendor of goods under a c.i.f. contract, and ask which of these obligations is "fundamentally" altered by a change of route. Clearly the contract of affreightment will be different and so may be the terms of insurance. In both these respects the sellers may be put to greater cost: their profit may be reduced or even disappear. But it hardly needs reasserting that an increase of expense is not a ground of frustration.

Nothing else remains to justify the view that the nature of the contract was "fundamentally" altered. . . . [or] "radically different." Whatever expression is used, the doctrine of frustration must be applied within very narrow limits. In my opinion this case falls far short of satisfying the necessary conditions. In my opinion the appeal should be dismissed with costs.

(2) PERFORMANCE DELEGATED TO A THIRD PARTY

In some cases, a party, usually the seller, will subcontract with a third party to perform the contract. What happens when the seller's failure to perform is due to the nonperformance of the third party? Article 79(2) addresses this situation:

Article 79

. . . (2) If the party's failure is due to the failure of a third person whom he has engaged to perform the whole or a part of the contract, that party is exempt from liability only if:

(a) he is exempt under the preceding paragraph; and

(b) the person whom he has so engaged would be so exempt if the provisions of that paragraph were applied to him.

Article 79(2) contemplates a two-step analysis under subparagraphs (2)(a) and (b). Under subparagraph (2)(a), the issue is whether the failure of the third party is an impediment to performance by the seller of its contract with the buyer within the meaning of Article 79(1), *supra*, p. 237.

> *Illustration 79d.* In a contract for the sale of hand tools, the seller, a manufacturer of tools, subcontracts the manufacture to T, a third-party manufacturer. The seller is already working at near capacity and the production of tools for the buyer would require higher costs in overtime pay. T's factory is destroyed by a fire. The seller is not exempt under Article 79(2). Under subparagraph (2)(a), T's failure is not an "impediment" to the seller's performance within the meaning of Article 79(1). The seller can produce the tools at a higher cost.

The key to Article 79(2) is subparagraph (2)(b): Would the third party be exempt from liability to the seller under Article 79(1)?

> *Illustration 79e.* The seller, a distributor, enters into a contract to sell specialty farm equipment to the buyer. The seller subcontracts the manufacture of the equipment to T, a well-known manufacturer with a good reputation for reliability. In this case, however, T makes several errors in the manufacturing process and is unable to deliver the equipment on time. The seller is unable to procure substitute equipment. The seller takes the position that under Article 79(2)(a) it is exempt because its nonperformance is due to "an impediment" beyond its control under Article 79(1), namely, the failure of T to deliver the equipment. The seller is not excused for nonperformance of the contract with the buyer. The seller is excused from nonperformance of its contract with the buyer only if under Article 79(2)(b) T is excused from nonperformance of its contract with the seller. Here T is not excused as T made errors in the manufacturing process.

PROBLEM 3-18

A U.S. buyer enters into a contract with an Italian seller for the sale of silk dresses to be delivered in the United States in time for the peak summer season. The Italian seller subcontracts the production of the dresses to a manufacturer in Pakistan. The production by the third party is disrupted by several government decrees imposing curfews that shorten the workday. The government decrees are mandatory laws and failure to comply would result in government sanctions. As a result, the third party is unable to deliver the dresses to the seller who, in turn, cannot deliver the dresses to the U.S. buyer in time for the summer season and it is now too late to find a substitute manufacturer. The seller pleads excuse under Article 79(2). What is the result? See the following case.

Unilex, D. 1996-3.4
Germany: Schiedsgericht der Handelskammer–Hamburg

A German buyer concluded two separate but substantially identical framework agreements with two Hong Kong companies (sellers), concerning delivery of goods produced in the People's Republic of China. Further to the agreements the buyer placed several orders on behalf of its customers. Price and time of delivery varied each time, taking into account that the buyer needed the goods at short notice. Payment had to take place within 90 days of delivery but in individual cases the buyer paid in advance on delivery.

In the course of the business relationship the buyer ordered 10,000 units of product from one of the sellers. The latter asked for advance payment; later on it informed the buyer that its own Chinese supplier was undergoing serious financial and personal difficulties, and refused to deliver the goods unless the buyer paid all outstanding debts. The buyer refused. The seller brought an action before the Arbitral Court. The buyer declared the sales contract avoided and asked for damages deriving from breach of the individual sales contract in dispute and breach of the framework agreement.

In the opinion of the court, the buyer was entitled to avoid the sales contract pursuant to Arts. 49(1)(b) and 47(1) CISG because the seller refused to deliver without receiving payment for all outstanding debts deriving from past deliveries to the buyer. Such a request was inconsistent with a term in the sales contract providing for advance cash payment by the buyer, which by its nature implied that delivery should not be conditioned on payment of any amount due under previous contracts.

Moreover, the seller was not exempted for non-performance under Art. 79 CISG. According to Art. 79 CISG, a party is not liable for failure to perform its obligation if it provides that the failure was due to an impediment beyond its control and that it could not reasonably be expected to have taken it into account. As a rule, difficulties in delivery due to the seller's financial problems, or to financial problems of the seller's supplier (even when connected to the act of public authority in the supplier's country) are not to be considered an impediment beyond the seller's control but belong to the seller's area of risk.

NOTES AND QUESTIONS

1. Suppose that in Problem 3-18 the Pakistani government issued a decree prohibiting the export of products to the United States or Italy under pain of serious civil and criminal sanctions. In this case, what is the result under Article 79(2)?

2. In any situation where the seller delegates performance of the contract to a third party (T), there are four different possibilities concerning liability of T to seller (S) and of seller to buyer (B):

    (1)   T is not exempt from liability to S; S is not exempt from liability to B;

    (2)   T is not exempt from liability to S; S is exempt from liability to B;

    (3)   T is exempt from liability to S; S is not exempt from liability to B; and

    (4)   T is exempt from liability to S; S is exempt from liability to B.

How many of these possibilities are permitted under Article 79? Can you go through each one of the possibilities permitted by Article 79 and give a policy reason why the possibility is permitted? If any of these possibilities are not permitted, can you give a policy rationale justifying the exclusion?

3. Recall that the CISG is a supplementary law and that the parties are free to derogate from its provisions. Article 79 applies when the parties have not themselves allocated the risk of nonperformance due to unforeseen circumstances. In the problems discussed, we have assumed that the parties have not contracted to allocate the risk of loss in the event of unforeseen circumstances that lead to nonperformance. If the parties have a force majeure clause in their contract of sale, then the clause, if it applies, will supersede Article 79. Note that *Tsakiroglou* involved a contract that contained a standard force majeure or war clause, but the court held that the clause did not apply because the hostilities initiated by the British and French forces did not amount to war.

7. Remedies

The CISG specifies extensive remedies for both buyers and sellers in international sales transactions. We will consider each in turn. This will be followed by a consideration of remedies in the case of an anticipatory breach or an installment contract, for which the CISG gives similar options to a buyer and to a seller.

We start with the basic approach of the CISG to remedies, which is to view the relationship between most buyers and sellers in commerce as a cooperative relationship and one that the parties will often seek to preserve and maintain. For example, when faced with a dissatisfied buyer, sellers often do not need to be coerced into repairing a defective performance but rather are usually anxious to "make things right." Sellers seek out opportunities to meet the buyer's expectations at least so long as they are commercially reasonable. Buyers also have an interest in maintaining relationships with dependable sellers and will rarely allow a single mishap to result in the termination of the relationship. When sellers are faced with a buyer who is a regular customer but who cannot meet payment on a particular order, sellers usually seek to accommodate the buyer and to work out a reasonable solution. Given that both parties have a stake in preserving the business relationship, the CISG remedial system provides many mechanisms that serve as tools of cooperation that can be used to remedy, repair, or cure a defective performance rather than as weapons that can be used by an aggrieved party to punish a breaching party. Of course, there will be failures in performance and genuine breakdowns that result in litigation that will require drastic remedies that will likely result in the termination of the business relationship. In these cases, the CISG's remedial system allows for a set of remedies to put the aggrieved party in as good a position as if the breaching party fully performed.

Keep this general approach in mind as you think about options for the various aggrieved sellers and buyers in the problems that follow.

A. REMEDIES OF THE SELLER

Articles 61-65 govern the seller's remedies for breach by the buyer. Article 61 provides an overview of the remedial system and the relationship of each of the provisions to each other. The heart of the remedial system for the seller is contained in Articles 62-64. The seller is allowed to compel performance (Article 62), to extend the time for performance by the buyer (Article 63), to avoid the contract (Article 64), and to sue for damages under Articles 74-76. Article 65 deals with the right of the seller under some circumstances to provide specifications for the goods.

PROBLEM 3-19

A seller in Japan receives an order from a French company for 16,000 uniball, fine-point pens. Since this model comes in several colors, the seller e-mails the French company asking for guidance on which colors to supply. There is no response. The Japanese company then e-mails the buyer that the order will be filled with 16,000 black-ink models. The e-mail concludes, "Kindly inform us whether this specification meets your requirements. We plan to ship to you in 14 days."

There is no response and two weeks later the pens are shipped by air freight.

The day after the pens are received in France by the buyer, the seller receives a nastily worded e-mail that says the shipment does not conform to the contract, that the buyer will not pay the agreed price, and that all of the pens will be returned at the seller's expense only if the seller forwards payment for shipment fees in advance. The buyer explains that the pens are "nonconforming" because in France only blue-ink pens are marketed because "black after all is the color of death." The seller contends that the pens conform to the contract and that the buyer must accept delivery.

What should the seller do? Consider Articles 62, 63, and 64 of the CISG. Which party is in the right concerning whether the pens are nonconforming and whether the buyer must accept delivery? Consider Article 65. *65(1)—buyer needs to accept*

NOTES AND QUESTIONS

1. Articles 62-64 provide three options to the seller. Go through and discuss each of these options and what purpose they are designed to serve. Which should the seller choose? How realistic or practicable is the first option of compelling performance by the buyer under Article 62? Are there are any limitations on the power of the court to compel specific performance under the CISG? Consider Article 28.

2. Suppose that in this case the seller is allowed to compel performance by the buyer in a French court. Would you recommend this option?

3. Suppose the seller has in hand an irrevocable letter of credit authorized by the buyer and issued by a Paris bank. How would this affect the seller's situation? What does this suggest about the utility of letters of credit, which we consider in the next chapter, in the international sale of goods?

4. Suppose that the price has not been paid and that the sale was made on open account. Should the seller declare the contract avoided under Article 64? Article 64 provides that an aggrieved seller can declare a contract avoided where (1) the buyer has committed a fundamental breach and (2) the buyer has not paid the price or accepted delivery of the goods within the additional time period fixed by the seller. What constitutes a fundamental breach and what is the effect of an avoidance? Consider the following additional provisions of the CISG.

Article 25

A breach of contract committed by one of the parties is fundamental if it results in such detriment to the other party as substantially to deprive him of what he is entitled to expect under the contract, unless the party in breach did not foresee and a reasonable person of the same kind in the same circumstances would not have foreseen such a result.

Article 26

A declaration of avoidance of the contract is effective only if made by notice to the other party. *need notice*

Article 81

(1) Avoidance of the contract releases both parties from their obligations under it, subject to any damages which may be due. Avoidance does not affect any provision of the contract for the settlement of disputes or any other provision of the contract governing the rights and obligations of the parties consequent upon the avoidance of the contract.

5. Can the seller in Problem 3-19 avoid the contract?

6. The articles governing damages under the CISG are Articles 74-76. What is the basic general principle of damages that is set forth in Article 74 and what is the relationship of Article 74 to Articles 75 and 76? What is the difference between the methods of determining damages under Articles 75 and 76? Consider these questions in light of the following problems.

PROBLEM 3-20

A Japanese seller has contracted with an English buyer to manufacture 3,000 lawn mower engines for $150,000. After the Japanese seller has shipped the engines by ocean carrier, the buyer runs into financial problems and apologizes profusely but says it cannot go through with the order. The seller avoids the contract under Article 64 and sues for damages. Similar engines sell in England for $60 each and the seller has found another buyer who is willing to buy the entire shipment for $120,000. What should the seller do? Consider CISG Articles 74-76.   *75 - recover difference in price*

PROBLEM 3-21

Suppose that in Problem 3-20 the buyer cancels before the seller begins production of the motors. Due to limitations in production capacity, the seller had turned down an order for 2,500 lawn mower engines from a French buyer to accept the English order. The French buyer found a South Korean manufacturer to make the motors. The English buyer says, "Sorry, but you never told me that you were turning down the French offer to accept ours. Anyway, these are the breaks of the business. As you didn't manufacture the goods, you have suffered no damages. So please accept our most heartfelt apologies." Can the seller recover anything for the French order?   *reliance damages   should be   yes*

B. REMEDIES OF THE BUYER

The remedies available to the buyer under Articles 46-49 mirror the remedies available to the seller under Articles 62-64. We start with Article 45, which provides a general overview of the remedies available to the buyer and the relationship of each of the remedies to each other. Like the seller, the buyer has the right to compel performance (Article 46), to fix an additional time for the seller to perform (Article 47), and to avoid the contract and sue for damages (Article 49). Mirroring Article 64, Article 49 allows the buyer to avoid the contract where the seller has committed a fundamental breach or has failed to deliver the goods within the additional time period fixed by the buyer. Article 48 provides for a restricted right on the part of the seller to cure defects in performance even after delivery of the goods. Articles 50-52 deal with three special situations: The buyer's right to reduce the price, the applicability of remedies to only part of the goods, and deliveries that are early or excessive in quantity. Articles 74-77, which we reviewed in connection with our discussion of the seller's right against a breaching buyer, apply equally to govern the rights of an aggrieved buyer to damages against a breaching seller.

PROBLEM 3-22

A seller in Japan agrees to deliver 1,000 special high-speed photomax printers of the latest design to a buyer in the United Kingdom. The delivery date is April 25, and the UK buyer inserts a clause into the contract that "time is of the essence" since the buyer has a resale contract with a major retail marketer-customer.

On April 15, the Japanese seller telephones the UK buyer and apologizes profusely — a major subcontractor is in financial difficulty, and the delivery of the printers will be delayed.

The UK buyer calls his customer and is told that the customer needs the machines without fail on April 27 for a promotion already announced.

What options does the UK buyer have under the CISG?

Suppose, alternatively, that the UK buyer's customer is agreeable to waiting until May 15 for the delivery. What then? Consider CISG Articles 46, 47, and 49 and apply them to this problem. What about damages under Articles 74-76?

PROBLEM 3-23

A U.S. buyer contracts with a Japanese seller for the sale of laptop computers. The contract calls for one battery and one spare battery for each laptop. The computers arrive with only one battery instead of two. The buyer immediately informs the seller of this deficiency and sends the seller an e-mail in April, which states, "We must have the additional spare battery for all of the computers by no later than May 31, 2005. We will not accept delivery after that date." Under Article 47, the buyer "may fix an additional period of time of reasonable length for performance by the seller of his obligations." Article 49(1) allows the buyer to declare the contract avoided if the seller does not deliver within the additional period fixed under Article 47. The buyer can sell the laptops with one battery without difficulty on the market as most other laptops sold on the market have only one battery. The seller cannot deliver the spare batteries in time. Under Article 49, can the buyer avoid the contract?

+9 possibly

PROBLEM 3-24

A seller in Japan fills an order from a German customer for 2,000 room air conditioners. By an oversight, the electric plugs on the air conditioners are small gauge, North American models. When notified, the Japanese seller offers to send a representative to the buyer's place of business to swap out the correct plugs for the incorrect ones. Consider Article 48.

Should the buyer accept this offer?

Does the buyer have the right to refuse this offer?

In considering the second question, note that the exercise of the seller's right to cure under Article 48(1) is explicitly made subject to the buyer's right to avoid the contract under Article 49. Suppose that after the seller offers to cure the buyer quickly avoids the contract by declaring a fundamental breach under Article 49. Has the seller committed a fundamental breach within the meaning of Article 25, which requires that all circumstances be considered?

PROBLEM 3-25

A seller in Japan has an order for 3,000 punch presses from a Canadian buyer for $60,000. Demand for the punch presses soars unexpectedly in Japan, and the seller runs short. He ships 2,000 to Canada and e-mails the Canadian buyer apologies that he can supply no more.

What is the buyer's remedy under Articles 50 and 51?

C.   ANTICIPATORY BREACH AND INSTALLMENT CONTRACTS

So far, we have considered the remedies available to a buyer and seller when one party fails to perform at the time the performance is due. Suppose, however, that *before* the time that performance is due, it appears or becomes certain that one of the parties will be unable to perform either the entire contract or one portion or installment of the contract. This, of course, is the problem of anticipatory breach. What remedies are available to the aggrieved party in these cases? Consider Articles 71, 72, and 73 in solving the problems below.

PROBLEM 3-26

A Japanese seller has a contract to sell 1,000 computers to a customer in Germany. Two weeks before the shipment date, the buyer e-mails the seller that, due to circumstances beyond his control, he must cancel the order. What remedies are available to the seller?

PROBLEM 3-27

A Japanese buyer has an installment contract with a Canadian seller for delivery of 1,000 cubic tons of wood chips on the first of each month. On April 1, there is no delivery. The buyer is concerned, but wants to continue the arrangement, which has been conducted faithfully for over two years. What should the buyer do in this situation?

NOTES AND QUESTIONS

1. Articles 71 and 72 offer two different approaches that would be available to our seller in Problem 3-26. What is the purpose of Article 71? Between Articles 71 and 72, which is the most drastic remedy and which article contains the higher standard?

2. Must an aggrieved party elect between Articles 71 and 72 and does the exercise by the aggrieved party of its rights under Article 71 preclude the later exercise of rights under Article 72?

3. Compare the approach under Article 51 that we examined in Problem 3-25 and the approach under Article 73. Both of these articles share a common approach. What is this approach? Both of these articles can also be considered tools of cooperation consistent with the general approach of the CISG. Can you explain why?

4   *Letters of Credit*

In this chapter, we turn to a detailed consideration of the letter of credit, the third of the three contracts involved in a typical documentary sale of goods together with the sales contract, which we covered in Chapter 3, and the contract of carriage, which we discussed in Chapter 2. This chapter is the last in the unit of Chapters 2, 3, and 4 that considers the international sales transaction.

The letter of credit has a long history in the law merchant and is international in its origins, traceable to practices in the twelfth century. European merchants used credits in the form of drafts or bills of exchange to make payment in the international sale of goods. The bill was a request or order for payment that through mercantile usage became well established and accepted as a method of payment. The use of the bills allowed merchants to avoid the risky practice of carrying large amounts of gold or silver and to solve the problem of the unavailability of large amounts of currency to make large and frequent payments. *See* John F. Dolan, *Letters of Credit* ¶3.02 (2004).

In international commerce today, the role of the letter of credit in the documentary sale is to provide a mechanism for payment. This type of credit is referred to as the *documentary credit* and it is the subject of the first part of this chapter. We then turn the *standby letter of credit*, which is used to guarantee the performance of some obligation.

I.   Sources of Letter of Credit Law

Unlike in the case of contracts for the sale of goods, there is no comprehensive multilateral treaty that serves as a source of law for letters of credit. The principal sources of law for the international letter of credit that we will be considering below are the Uniform Customs and Practice for Documentary Credits (UCP 500) issued by the International Chamber of Commerce in 1993 (for more on the ICC, see Chapter 1 at p. 35) and Article 5 of the Uniform Commercial Code (2003). The UCP and the UCC are in general agreement. Standby letters of credit have additional sources of law that we shall consider in a later section.

The Uniform Customs provide in Article 1 that they apply to all credits "where they are incorporated into the text of the Credit" and are "binding on all parties thereto, unless otherwise expressly stipulated in the Credit." UCC §5-103(c) provides, with some exceptions, that "the effect of this article may be varied by agreement or by a provision stated or incorporated by reference in an undertaking." Thus, the UCC explicitly recognizes that parties to a letter of credit that is otherwise governed by the UCC may exclude the UCC in favor of the UCP. As the UCP is designed for use in international letters of credit, most U.S. credits that are not international in character are governed by the UCC. Note that even where the UCP applies there is an important area in which the UCP is completely silent that must be decided by domestic law: The issue of fraud as a defense to payment of the letter of credit. (On other issues that fall within an exclusion in the UCP, resort must also be had to a domestic law.) The UCP drafters took the position that the fraud issue, developed by common law courts that share the same language and commercial culture, was best left to domestic law as international regimes do not have the same advantages. UCC Article 5 has an extensive fraud provision and jurisprudence. Our focus in these materials shall be on the UCP except on the issue of fraud, where we examine the UCC.

H.   Letter of Credit Basics

Recall that in a typical letter of credit transaction that is part of a documentary sale, the letter of credit is a separate undertaking between the buyer of goods and its bank that the bank will pay the seller against the presentation of certain documents. The letter of credit is an undertaking (i.e., a contract) by the issuing bank to honor drafts [see below (8)] drawn on it if the draft is accompanied by specified documents. You should now review Figure 2-7 on p. 72 of Chapter 2.

We now set forth some letter of credit basics, consistent with both the UCP and the UCC, that you will need to master. The discussion below applies primarily to the documentary credit but also to the standby letter of credit where applicable. As the latter serves different purposes, we postpone detailed coverage of standby letters of credit until later in this chapter. You need to review these materials carefully to answer the problems that follow at the end of this section.

(1) *Applicant and Beneficiary.* The party establishing the credit is the *applicant* and the party entitled to payment under the credit is the *beneficiary* of the credit. In a documentary credit, the buyer is usually the applicant and the seller is the beneficiary.

(2) *Issuing Bank.* The applicant's bank is the *issuing bank*, which undertakes to honor the letter of credit against the presentation of a specified set of documents. The issuing bank will receive reimbursement (plus a fee) for the amount of the credit from the applicant. In the documentary credit, the seller will usually present a bill of lading, commercial invoice, insurance certificate, packing list, and other documents required in the letter of credit agreement to the issuing bank. The absolute obligation of the issuing bank to pay against the documents provides the seller with the assurance of payment. If the issuing bank pays, then it is protected from liability and is entitled to get reimbursement of the credit from the buyer-applicant. If the issuing bank refuses to honor a demand for payment that complies with the terms of the credit, then the issuing bank may be liable to the presenter of the draft for wrongful dishonor. On the other hand, if the issuing bank makes an improper payment, that is, pays the letter of credit against nonconforming documents in violation of the terms of the letter of credit agreement, then the issuing bank will lose its right to receive reimbursement from the buyer-applicant. Many of the disputes that arise in letter of credit law concern attempts by the applicant to prevent the issuing bank from paying under the letter of credit because of some issue with the underlying sales transaction.

(3) *Revocable and Irrevocable Credits*. Letters of credit can be *revocable* or capable of termination at any time by the applicant or *irrevocable*. Note that under an irrevocable letter of credit, the credit will be subject to expiration if not exercised within a stated period. An irrevocable credit is required in most modern commercial transactions.

(4) *Straight and Negotiation Credits*. Similar to the distinction drawn earlier between a straight and negotiable bill of lading (see Chapter 2 at p. 68), a letter of credit can also be a straight or negotiation credit. If the issuing bank issues a straight letter of credit, the credit is an undertaking from the bank that runs only to the seller-beneficiary and not to any other endorser or purchaser of the draft and documents from the seller. Note that the draft itself, or an order for payment, is normally a negotiable instrument but the negotiability of the draft must be distinguished from the obligation of the issuing bank to honor a negotiated draft. Although the draft itself may be negotiated and purchased from the seller-beneficiary, under a straight letter of credit the issuing bank has no obligation to honor the draft from the purchaser. If the credit is a negotiation credit, however, the issuing bank has undertaken to purchase the drafts from the beneficiary, or any authorized bank that negotiates or purchases the credit. The negotiation credit may authorize any bank to negotiate or a single bank. Note that the bank authorized to negotiate the credit does not have an obligation to the seller to negotiate the credit but will normally do so to earn a fee.

(5) *Advising Bank*. The issuing bank may engage another bank, usually one within the beneficiary's locality, to notify the beneficiary of the establishment and terms of the credit. An advising bank has an obligation to make reasonable efforts to check the authenticity of the credit that it advises but has no obligation to make payment under the credit.

(6) *Confirming Bank*. An issuing bank will sometimes engage a second bank to serve as a *confirming bank*. The use of a confirming bank is usually due to the insistence of the seller-beneficiary of the credit and the confirming bank is usually situated in the beneficiary's locality and may be an institution with which the beneficiary is familiar. The confirming bank independently assumes all of the obligations of the issuing bank by adding its own undertaking that it will pay the seller upon presentation of documents. Now the seller has a letter of credit that is backed by the credit of two banks. If the confirming bank has properly paid the credit against conforming documents, then the issuing bank must reimburse the confirming bank. If the issuing bank refuses to pay under these conditions, then the issuing bank is liable for wrongful dishonor. On the other hand, if the confirming bank has made a wrongful payment, then the confirming bank loses the right to receive reimbursement from the issuing bank.

(7) *Nominated Bank*. An issuing bank may authorize another bank to pay under the letter of credit. The bank so authorized is the *nominated bank*. Unless the nominated bank is also a confirming bank, the former undertakes no obligation to pay under the letter of credit but may choose to do so for a fee.

(8) *Settlement*. There are four different methods of settlement: Payment, acceptance, negotiation, or deferred payment. The first three methods all involve the use of a draft (or a bill of exchange), which the beneficiary will submit along with any required documents. The draft is an unconditional order in writing addressed from one person to another requiring the person to whom it is addressed to make payment on demand or on some future date to or to the order of a specific person or to bearer. The beneficiary stands in the position

of the *drawer*, the bank (or sometimes the applicant) is the *drawee*, and the beneficiary is also the *payee*.

(a) *Payment Credit*. A payment credit requires the bank to honor the draft on sight. The beneficiary submits a *sight draft* payable immediately (on sight). Article 13(b) of the UCP allows the bank seven banking days in which to pay the credit. The drawee of the draft is usually the issuing bank or a nominated bank.

(b) *Acceptance Credit*. An acceptance credit is payable within a stipulated period, such as 60 days. The beneficiary submits a *time draft*, which requires payment by the date specified in the draft. When the bank accepts the draft, the acceptance becomes a banker's acceptance, which entails the obligation of the bank to pay the draft at maturity. After the drawer presents the draft, the bank will usually stamp the time draft as accepted with a signature of a bank official and will return it to the drawer.

(c) *Negotiation Credit*. Under a negotiation credit, the beneficiary submits a draft to a nominated bank. The draft will usually be drawn on the issuing bank (not the negotiating bank) and will be made payable to the beneficiary. The nominated bank will purchase the draft from the beneficiary who endorses it to the nominated bank. At this point, the bank may also acquire the rights of a holder in due course. See p. 286 *infra*. The nominated bank will then forward the draft and documents to the issuing bank. Under a negotiation credit, the issuing bank must purchase the drafts from the nominated bank if the documents conform with the terms of the credit. Note that negotiation can occur in any credit situation as the drafts themselves are normally negotiable instruments. Thus, under a straight letter of credit calling for an acceptance draft, a seller may decide to take an acceptance draft to its local bank and ask its bank to negotiate the draft. The local bank may decide to do so in order to earn a fee; the bank then forwards the draft and documents to the issuing bank. Note that there are two crucial differences between this situation and a negotiation credit. In this situation, the issuing bank is under no obligation to purchase the draft but may do so, whereas in a negotiation credit the issuing bank is bound to purchase the negotiated documents. In addition, under a negotiation credit, the submission by the beneficiary of the draft and documents to the nominated bank before the expiry of the credit satisfies the presentation requirements of the credit and will trigger the issuing bank's engagement to honor the draft. Where the credit is a straight credit and the beneficiary chooses to negotiate the draft with a negotiating bank, presentation, which must occur before the expiry of the credit, does not occur until the negotiating bank presents the documents to the issuing bank. In these cases, the beneficiary must be careful to ensure that there is enough time for the drafts to reach the issuing bank before the expiry of the credit.

(d) *Deferred Payment*. Under a deferred payment credit, payment is required within some fixed period of time after a specified date (e.g., 60 days after seller's presentation of the bill of lading). In this respect, the deferred payment credit is similar to the acceptance credit but the former does not require a draft or an acceptance. Rather, the deferred payment credit is usually evidenced by a letter, advice, or some other undertaking. The deferred payment credit was created to avoid the regulations on drafts and banker's acceptances that some jurisdiction have enacted. Note that the deferred payment credit is a nonnegotiable undertaking.

(9) *Transfer and Assignment of Credit*. If the credit expressly so provides, it may be transferred. A *transfer* of the credit means that the transferee acquires the right to perform all or some of the obligations of the credit, to receive all or a portion of the payments due under the credit, and to enforce the right of payment under the credit. An *assignment* of the credit means that the assignee acquires only the right to receive all or some portion of the payment under the credit after all of the conditions for payment under the credit have been satisfied by the assignor or another party who is entitled to satisfy the conditions for payment under the credit such as a purchaser of the draft from the assignor. Unlike a transferee, the assignee does not have the right to enforce payment against a party obligated to pay such as an issuing bank or confirming bank. Unlike a transfer, an assignment does not have be expressly authorized by the terms of the credit. The party seeking a transferable credit is usually a seller who intends to fulfill the buyer's purchase by subcontracting the sale to a third party. Suppose that under a contract for the sale of goods CIF buyer's port, the buyer has its issuing bank open a transferable letter of credit in favor of the seller in the amount of $100,000. The seller may decide to engage a third party to manufacture the goods for $80,000. The seller then transfers the credit to the third party who presents a draft for $80,000, an invoice, a bill of lading, and other documents required by the letter of credit to the issuing bank. Meanwhile, the seller has submitted a draft for $100,000 to the issuing bank. If the issuing bank finds the documents to be in order, the issuing bank will pay the seller's draft for $100,000 to the order of seller's account and then charge that account $80,000 to pay the draft drawn by the third party. The issuing bank then charges the buyer's account in the amount of $100,000 and forwards the bill of lading and other documents to the buyer.

(10) *Back-to-Back Credits*. In the case of the transferable credit, the buyer and the third party will have knowledge of the seller's arrangements. For business reasons, the seller may wish to keep the identity of the buyer and third-party supplier confidential so as to avoid the possibility that they will deal directly with each other in the future. In addition, the seller may also wish to maintain greater control of the transaction or use the payment from the buyer to satisfy a number of third-party suppliers. Finally, the seller may wish to use the proceeds from the letter of credit to pay for the goods acquired from the third party. For these reasons, the seller may wish to set up a back-to-back credit by using the credit established by the buyer as the basis for a second letter of credit. This can be done as follows. Suppose that in our example discussed in (9) above, the seller takes the letter of credit opened in its favor by the buyer to a local bank in the seller's country. The seller then assigns the right to receive the proceeds under the prime letter of credit to the seller's bank and gives the bank a security interest in the credit. On the strength of the assignment of the prime letter of credit by the seller, the seller's bank now issues a second letter of credit in the amount of $80,000 naming the third-party supplier as the beneficiary. It is crucial that the documents required by the second letter of credit be tailored to meet the requirements under the first letter of credit so that once the third-party supplier provides the documents required for payment under the second letter of credit, the seller's bank is now assured that it has the all of the documents that will

trigger payment under the prime letter of credit. There will be some differences, however, between the documents required for payment under the second and the prime letter of credit and the seller's bank must be careful to assure that these differences can be reconciled. For instance, the draft submitted by the third-party supplier will most likely be drawn on the seller's bank and will name the third party as the beneficiary. On the other hand, it is likely that the prime letter of credit will require a draft drawn by the seller on the issuing bank. In addition, if a negotiable bill of lading is required, the bill supplied by the third party will most likely not satisfy the prime letter of credit, but the bill will allow the seller to unload the goods and reload them on a different carrier that will issue a new bill of lading to the seller that will satisfy the requirements of the prime letter of credit. In other cases, there is only one shipment (i.e., the seller and the third party are in the same location) and the bill of lading will identify the third party as the shipper. In these cases, the seller can ask the carrier to "switch" the bill, that is, reissue the original bill of lading with the same information but substituting the name of seller for the name of the third-party supplier. As back-to-back credits are now common, an experienced bank should be able to structure the transaction so that it can obtain the proper documents for payment under the prime letter of credit. Once this is worked out, the back-to-back credit transaction would proceed as follows: The third-party supplier presents a draft, bill of lading, and other documents to the seller's bank, which will pay $80,000, the amount of the back-to-back credit, to the supplier; the seller's bank then forwards a draft drawn by the seller, a substituted bill of lading, and other documents to the issuing bank and receives payment in the amount of $100,000 under the prime letter of credit. The seller's bank will then credit the seller's account in the amount of $20,000 minus a fee.

(11) *Revolving Credits*. In the credit industry, there are many commercial relationships that involve ongoing or revolving loans. In the case of a revolving documentary credit, the credit allows the beneficiary to draw up to a certain amount for a given period. For example, a grain distributor in Belgium asks its bank to issue a credit to a London grain merchant that allows the merchant to draw up to a certain amount each month upon presentation of documents. Such a revolving documentary credit can be established in the amount of $20,000 per month for a period of six months. Under this credit, $20,000 is automatically available each month regardless of whether any sum was drawn the previous month. A revolving credit can be cumulative or noncumulative. If the credit is cumulative, any amount that is not used during a given month carries over and may be used in a subsequent period. If the credit is noncumulative, the failure to draw on the credit during any given month means that the amount or any portion remaining is not carried over to a subsequent month. In our example, the total obligation of the bank is for $120,000, that is, $20,000 per month for six months. So while the face value of the credit may be given at $20,000, the total undertaking of the bank under the six-month revolving credit is for $120,000.

QUESTIONS

1. Review the sample letter of credit that we included in Chapter 2 at p. 69. Is the letter of credit revocable or irrevocable? Confirmed or unconfirmed?

2. Does the sample letter of credit establish a straight or a negotiation credit? How do you know? *negotiated*

PROBLEM 4-1

At the request of the seller, the buyer in a CIF contract for the sale of goods obtains a straight letter of credit from its issuing bank requiring payment against documents. The issuing bank then asks a local bank in the seller's jurisdiction to be an advising bank on the credit. The seller loads the goods, receives a bill of lading from the carrier, and presents the bill of lading, other documents, and a draft drawn on the issuing bank to the advising bank.

(1) Does the advising bank have an obligation to pay on the letter of credit? *No* *See* UCP Article 7; see also §II(5) in the discussion of the letter of credit basics above.

(2) If the advising bank does not have an obligation to pay on the letter of credit, can the advising bank purchase the draft if it wishes to do so and obtain reimbursement from the issuing bank? See §II(4). Would you counsel the advising bank to purchase the draft? If so, what measures would you advise the bank to first undertake? *Yes but not a good idea* *Not really since bank isn't under an obligation to pay*

PROBLEM 4-2

In a confirmed letter of credit transaction, the seller ships the goods and obtains the necessary documents for payment under the letter of credit. Rather than presenting the documents to the confirming bank, which is experiencing some unexpected financial difficulties, the seller forwards the documents directly to the issuing bank. The issuing bank refuses to pay on the grounds that the seller must first submit the documents to the confirming bank. What is the result? *See* UCP Article 9(b); see also §II(6). *liable for wrongful dishonor*

PROBLEM 4-3

In a documentary sale, an issuing bank establishes an unconfirmed letter of credit in favor of the seller. On July 30, 2005, the seller goes to its local bank and submits a draft and documents. The local bank purchases the drafts and documents from the seller and then forwards them to the buyer's bank. The documents arrive on August 2. The buyer's bank refuses to honor the letter of credit on the grounds that it has expired. What is the result under each of the following scenarios?

(1) The language of the credit provides: "We hereby engage with drawers, endorsers, and bona fide purchasers of drafts drawn under the terms of this credit shall be paid. All drafts must be presented not later than August 1, 2005." *See* UCP Article 10(a); see also §II(8)(c). *submission triggered obligation*

(2) The language of the credit provides: "We hereby undertake to honor the beneficiary's drafts if submitted not later than August 1, 2005." *See* UCP Article 10(a) and §§II(4) and II(8)(c). *straight credit? art as check*

PROBLEM 4-4

[handwritten: Issuing bank is drawee / ntl. bank / A-payee & drawer]

A is the beneficiary of a negotiation credit. The issuing bank has nominated National Bank, a large and well-known bank in A's locality, to be the negotiating bank. A comes to your law office with the following questions:

(1) "Who is the drawer, who is the drawee, and who is the beneficiary of the draft that I need to submit to the local bank for payment?" See §II(8)(c).

[handwritten left margin: advising bank. senons]

(2) "I don't like dealing with National Bank. Can I submit the draft to my own bank for negotiation?" See UCP Article 10(b); see also §II(4).

[handwritten left margin: nominating bank is auth. but not obligated, so No.]

(3) "Must the nominated bank pay the draft or can it lawfully refuse to do so?" *See* UCP Article 10(c); see also §II(7).

(4) "Are there any circumstances in which a nominated bank under a negotiation credit is obligated to negotiate the credit?" *[handwritten: Yes, but only if nominating becomes confirming]*

PROBLEM 4-5

The seller, the beneficiary under a confirmed letter of credit, assigns the letter of credit to the confirming bank to establish a back-to-back credit for the purpose of paying T, a third-party manufacturer of goods that the seller has contracted to sell to the buyer. The seller uses the back-to-back credit because the seller does not want the buyer or T to know each other's identities. The prime letter of credit provides for payment against a draft drawn on the issuing bank, a negotiable bill of lading, and a commercial invoice. T produces the goods and has them loaded on board the carrier for shipment to the buyer. T gives the confirming bank (1) a bill of lading naming T as the shipper consigned to order, (2) a draft drawn on the confirming bank and naming T as the payee, (3) and a commercial invoice from T to the seller detailing the quantity of the goods and the price. The confirming bank pays T under the back-to-back credit and asks you the following question: "Can we simply forward these documents to the issuing bank for payment under the prime letter of credit? If not, why not? How would you suggest that we get the documents that we need?" *See* §II(10).

III. Basic Principles of Letter of Credit Law

In this section, we turn to two of the most basic principles of letter of credit law: (1) the independence principle holding that the letter of credit is independent from the underlying sales contract and (2) the strict compliance principle requiring that documents submitted for payment must conform to the terms of the credit.

A. The Independence Principle

UCP Article 3(a) provides:

> Credits by their nature, are separate transactions from the sales or other contract(s) on which they may be based and banks are in no way concerned with or bound by such contracts(s), even if any reference whatsoever to such contract(s) is included in

the Credit. Consequently, the undertaking of a bank to pay, accept and pay Draft(s) or negotiate and/or fulfill any other obligation under the Credit, is not subject to claims or defences by the Applicant resulting from his relationships with the Issuing Bank or the Beneficiary.

UCP Article 4 provides:

> In Credit operations all parties concerned deal with documents, and not with goods, services and /or other performances to which the documents may relate.

PROBLEM 4-6

A Kuwaiti buyer enters into a contract with a U.S. seller for the purchase of medical devices in three shipments at $100,000 each. The sales contract called for the seller to sterilize the medical devices so that they are safe for human implantation and to provide with each shipment a certification that each device in the shipment has been sterilized. The contract also included the following provision:

> Payment is to be made by documentary credit subject to UCP 500. Buyer shall open a credit in favor of seller at the Kuwaiti National Bank (KNB) in the amount of $300,000. KNB shall make payment to seller upon the presentation of a bill of lading, commercial invoice, packing list, insurance certificate, and a written certification by seller that the delivered devices have been sterilized and are safe for human implantation. Seller acknowledges the importance of the sterilization procedure and that failure to perform this procedure shall be treated as a breach of the contract. Seller further acknowledges that in the case that it fails to test the devices buyer shall have the right to test the devices and deduct the costs of the tests from the purchase price of the goods.

The seller makes the first shipment of the devices to the buyer and includes the certification specified in the contract. The buyer learns from industry sources that the seller's tests may have been conducted by untrained staff and has expensive and time-consuming tests done on the devices at its own expense and finds that they are marginally unsuitable. The buyer then has the devices sterilized at its own expense. Meanwhile, the seller has sent the second shipment and has forwarded the documents to KNB for both shipments for payment under the letter of credit. The buyer then sends a written instruction to KNB instructing KNB to pay on the first shipment minus a set-off for the costs of the tests and sterilization procedure and to refuse payment on the second shipment unless the seller retests the devices with trained staff.

(1) Must KNB pay the entire amount of the credit for the first two shipments ($200,000) or can KNB make the first payment minus a set-off for the costs of testing and sterilization and refuse payment for the second shipment?

(2) The buyer's concern is that it will receive medical devices that are not suitable for use. The certificate of inspection by the seller did not adequately address this concern. How would you advise the buyer to structure the letter of credit transaction to alleviate these concerns? Will your suggestion ensure that the devices are safe to use?

(3) Can the buyer simply revoke the credit? *See* UCP Article 6.

(4) If KNB must pay and has failed to do so, KNB is liable for wrongful dishonor. What damages can the seller recover? Can the seller recover damages against the bank for the third shipment, which has not yet been sent?

In addition to the UCP, consider *Urquhart* and *Maurice O'Meara infra*.

Urquhart Lindsay and Company, Ltd. v. Eastern Bank, Ltd.
King's Bench Division
[1921] 1 King's Bench 318

The plaintiffs were manufacturers of machinery, and the defendants were bankers with various branches in the East, including Calcutta. In December, 1919, the plaintiffs agreed to manufacture for the Benjamin Jute Mills Co., Ltd., who were customers of the defendants, a quantity of machinery for delivery f.o.b. Glasgow to the amount of 64,942£.

This contract contained (inter alia) the following terms: (1.) that in the event of any increase taking place in wages or cost of materials or transit rates or any further reduction taking place in working hours, the plaintiffs' prices would be correspondingly increased; and (2.) that the Benjamin Jute Co., Ltd., should open in this country a confirmed irrevocable banker's credit to the extent of 70,000 pounds.

On February 14, 1920, the defendants wrote to the plaintiffs the following letter:

"4 Crosby Square, London.

TO MESSRS. URQUHART LINDSAY & CO., DUNDEE.

DEAR SIRS,

We beg to advise you that under instructions received from our Calcutta branch we are prepared to pay you the amounts of your bills on B.N. Elias, managing agent, the Benjamin Jute Mills Co., Ltd., Calcutta, to the extent of, but not exceeding 70,000 pounds in all (say seventy thousand pounds). The bills are to be accompanied by the following complete documents covering shipments of machinery to Calcutta, are to be drawn payable 30 days after sight, and are to be received by us for payment on or before April 14, 1921:

Signed Invoices in duplicate.
Complete sets of bills of lading made out 'to order' indorsed in blank and marked by the shipping company 'freight paid.'
Policies of insurance against marine or war risks.

This is to be considered a confirmed and irrevocable credit, and the bills should bear a clause to the effect that they are drawn under credit No. 102 dated Calcutta, January 15, 1920.

Kindly acknowledge receipt.

Yours faithfully,
M. HARKNESS, Manager"

The plaintiffs thereupon bought raw material and in 1920 began to manufacture the goods. They made two shipments under the contract in February and March, 1921, and tendered to the defendants bills of exchange together with shipping documents, which the defendants duly paid. On February 18, 1921, the defendants wrote to the plaintiffs, in reference to their former letter of February 14, 1920, a further letter advising them that they had heard from Calcutta that should it be necessary for the plaintiffs to include in their invoice for extra cost of labor, this extra amount must be referred to the buyers, before they (the defendants) would be at liberty to pay the same. The defendants then refused to meet the bills of exchange presented by the plaintiffs on the third shipment, and only did so, under protest on May 9, 1921, when the confirmed credit had expired.

The plaintiffs meantime on April 12, 1921, issued a writ in the action, and in their points of claim, dated June 29, 1921, alleged that the defendants' letter of February 18, 1921, was a breach of the contract contained in their letter of February 14, 1920, and that they (plaintiffs) had suffered damage, and lost the profit which they would otherwise have made, and that there was no available market for the goods.

The defendants in their points of defense (July 30, 1921) alleged that it was a term or condition in the contract between the plaintiffs and the Benjamin Jute Mills Co., Ltd., that the plaintiffs should not draw bills of exchange for more than shippers' current prices in December, 1919, and in particular that they should not include in such bills any increased cost over the price in 1919 on which the agreed credit of 70,000£. was calculated. They contended that the plaintiffs had acted in breach of this term or condition; and further that the damage (if any) was too remote and was not recoverable.

ROWLATT, J.

This credit was by its terms to be irrevocable and the invoices were to be for machinery. There can be no doubt that upon the plaintiffs acting upon the undertaking contained in this letter of credit consideration moved from the plaintiffs, which bound the defendants to the irrevocable character of the arrangement between the defendants and the plaintiffs; nor was it contended before me that this had not become the position when the circumstances giving rise to this action took place.

In my view the defendants committed a breach of their contract with the plaintiffs when they refused to pay the amount of the invoices as presented. Mr. Stuart Bevan contended that the letter of credit must be taken to incorporate the contract between the plaintiffs and their buyers; and that according to the true meaning of that contract the amount of any increase claimed in respect of an alleged advance in manufacturing costs was not to be included in any invoice to be presented under the letter of credit, but was to be the subject of subsequent independent adjustment. The answer to this is that the defendants undertook to pay the amount of invoices for machinery without qualification, the basis of this form of banking facility being that the buyer is taken for the purposes of all questions between himself and his banker or between his banker and the seller to be content to accept the invoices of the seller as correct. It seems to me that so far from the letter of credit being qualified by the contract of sale, the latter must accommodate itself to the letter of credit. The buyer having authorized his banker to undertake to pay the amount of the invoice as presented, it follows that any adjustment must be made by way of refund by the seller, and not by way of retention by the buyer.

There being thus in my view a breach of contract, the question arises what damages the plaintiffs can recover. The point is a new one, and not free from difficulty. It is, of course, elementary that as a general rule the amount of damages for non-payment of money is only the amount of the money itself. If, for instance, the defendants had merely undertaken to pay the price of goods as and when shipped, nothing being said about the undertaking being irrevocable within limits of time and amount, such undertaking would become binding only in respect of each shipment upon its being made, the successive shipments being the separable considerations for the separable undertakings referring to them respectively; and the engagement could be revoked at any time as to future shipments. In such a case the damages in case of a refusal to pay for any shipment made before revocation would be merely the amount owing in respect of the shipment. In the present case, however, the credit was irrevocable; and the effect of that was that the bank really agreed to buy the contemplated series of bills and documents representing the contemplated shipments just as the buyer agreed to take and pay for by this means the goods themselves. Now, if a buyer under a contract of this sort declines to pay for an installment of the goods, the seller can cancel and claim damages upon the footing of an anticipatory breach of the contract of sale as a whole. These damages are not for non-payment of money. It is true that non-payment of money was what the buyer was guilty of; but such non-payment is evidence of a repudiation of the contract to accept and pay for the remainder of the goods; and the damages are in respect of such repudiation. I confess I cannot see why the refusal of the bank to take and pay for the bills with the documents representing the goods is not in the same way a repudiation of their contract to take the bills to be presented in future under the letter of credit; nor, if that is so, why the damages are not the same. Mr. Stewart Bevan argued that the sellers should go on shipping and sue the bank toties quoties. Why should they be put in this position as against the bank any more than as against the seller? What is the difference for this purpose between the obligation to take the goods and pay the invoice, and the obligation to take bills and documents representing the goods and pay the invoice? The whole purpose of the arrangement is that the seller shall have a responsible paymaster in this country to protect him against the very contingency which has occurred and the very damages which he claims.

The damages to which the plaintiffs are entitled are the difference between on the one hand the value of the materials left on their hands and the cost of such as they would have further provided, and, on the other hand, what they would have been entitled to receive for the manufactured machinery from the buyers, the whole being limited to the amount they could in fact have tendered before the expiry of the letter of credit.

NOTES AND QUESTIONS

1. In *Urquhart*, the sellers sought to build in some flexibility in their transaction with the buyers. The contract allowed the sellers to increase the sales price when necessary to reflect increases in their costs. No issue arose as to the first two

shipments as no increased costs were involved and the sellers received payment from the bank against documents. The sellers' costs, however, had increased with regard to the third shipment and the sellers had increased their price to reflect the increased costs. The bank advised the sellers that it would not pay on the third shipment until the buyers first approved the increase in price. The sellers treated this as a breach of the letter of credit and brought suit.

2. Review the February 14 letter from the bank advising the sellers of the credit. Note that the letter provides that the sellers will be paid under the credit if the sellers submit a commercial invoice, a bill of lading, and an insurance policy. The buyers argued, however, that the sellers could not lawfully draw on the credit if the sellers increased their prices beyond those that existed for the goods as of December 1919. Is there anything in the February 14 letter that gives the buyers this right? If not, what was the source of the buyers' right to refuse payment? Note that in most cases banks feel compelled to pay on letters of credit if all of the terms of the credit have been met by the beneficiary. In this case, the buyers were likely valuable customers of the bank and the bank decided to consult the buyers before payment.

3. The buyers argued that the letter of credit had incorporated the terms of the sales contract under which buyers were entitled to a price for the goods set as of December 1919. The result of incorporating the sales contract into the letter of credit is that the letter of credit will not be paid if there is some nonperformance of the sales contract. This result would abrogate the independence principle. What was the court's response to this argument?

4. The buyers wanted to protect themselves against an increase in price for the goods by having the bank pay under the letter of credit for the third shipment only up to the price of the goods as of December 1919 and not the full amount of the bills of exchange, which included an added charge for increased labor costs. The buyers were not very skillful in protecting their interests. If you were advising the buyers, what would you suggest to the buyers to protect against increases in the price of the goods due to increased costs of the sellers?

Maurice O'Meara Co. v. National Park Bank of New York
Court of Appeals of New York, 1925
239 N.Y. 386, 146 N.E. 636

McLaughlin, J.

This action was brought to recover damages alleged to have been sustained by the plaintiff's assignor, Ronconi & Millar, by defendant's refusal to pay three sight drafts against a confirmed irrevocable letter of credit. The letter of credit was in the following form:

"The National Park Bank of New York.
Our Credit No. 14956

October 28, 1920.

Messrs. Ronconi & Millar, 49 Chambers Street, New York City, N.Y. — Dear Sirs: In accordance with instructions received from the Sun-Herald Corporation of this city, we open a confirmed or irrevocable credit in your favor for account of themselves, in amount of $224,853.30, covering the shipment of 1,322 2/3 tons of newsprint paper in 72 1/2″ and 36 1/2″ rolls to test 11-12, 32 lbs. at 8 1/2 cents per pound net weight-delivery to be made in December, 1920, and January 1921.

Drafts under this credit are to be drawn at sight on this bank, and are to be accompanied by the following documents of a character which must meet with our approval:

Commercial invoice in triplicate.
Weight returns.
Negotiable dock delivery order actually carrying with it control of the goods.
This is a confirmed or irrevocable credit, and will remain in force to and including February 15, 1921, subject to the conditions mentioned herein.
When drawing drafts under this credit, or referring to it, please quote our number as above.

Very truly yours,

R. Stuart, Assistant Cashier.

(R. C.)"

The complaint alleged the issuance of the letter of credit; the tender of three drafts, the first on the 17th of December, 1920, for $46,301.71, the second on January 7, 1921, for $41,416.34, and the third on January 13, 1921, for $32,968.35. Accompanying the first draft were the following documents:

> "1. Commercial invoice of the said firm of Ronconi & Millar in triplicate, covering three hundred (300) thirty-six and one-half (36 1/2) inch rolls of newsprint paper and three hundred (300) seventy-two and one-half (72 1/2) inch rolls of newsprint paper, aggregating a net weight of five hundred and forty-four thousand seven hundred and twenty-six pounds (544,726), to test eleven (11), twelve (12), thirty-two (32) pounds.
> 2. Affidavit of Elwin Walker, verified December 16, 1920, to which were annexed samples of newsprint paper, which the said affidavit stated to be representative of the shipment covered by the accompanying invoices and to test twelve (12) points, thirty-two (32) pounds.
> 3. Full weight returns in triplicate.
> 4. Negotiable dock delivery order on the Swedish American Line, directing delivery to the order of the National Park Bank of three hundred (300) rolls of newsprint paper seventy-two and one-half (72 1/2) inches long and three hundred (300) half rolls of newsprint paper."

The documents accompanying the second draft were similar to those accompanying the first, except as to the number of rolls, weight of paper, omission of the affidavit of Walker, but with a statement: "Paper equal to original sample in test 11/12-32 pounds;" and a negotiable dock delivery order on the Seager Steamship Company, Inc. The complaint also alleged defendant's refusal to pay, a statement of the amount of loss upon the resale of the paper due to a fall in the market price, expenses for lighterage, cartage, storage, and insurance amounting to $3,045.02, an assignment of the cause of action by Ronconi & Millar to the plaintiff, and a demand for judgment.

The answer denied, upon information and belief, many of the allegations of the complaint, and set up (a) as an affirmative defense, that plaintiff's assignor was required by the letter of credit to furnish to the defendant "evidence reasonably satisfactory" to it that the paper shipped to the Sun-Herald Corporation was of a bursting or tensile strength of 11 to 12 points at a weight of paper of 32 pounds; that neither the plaintiff nor its assignor, at the time the drafts were presented, or at any time thereafter, furnished such evidence; (b) as a partial defense, that, when the draft for $46,301.71 was presented, the defendant notified the plaintiff there had not been presented "evidence reasonably satisfactory" to it, showing that the newsprint paper referred to in the documents accompanying said drafts was of the tensile or bursting strength specified in the letter of credit; that thereupon an agreement was entered into between plaintiff and defendant that the latter should cause a test to be made of the paper represented by the documents then presented, and, if such test showed that the paper was up to the specifications of the letter of credit, defendant would make payment of the draft; (c) for a third separate and distinct defense that the paper tendered was not, in fact, of the tensile or bursting strength specified in the letter of credit; (d) for a fourth separate and distinct defense that on or about January 15, 1921, and after the respective drafts referred to in the complaint had been presented to defendant for payment and payment refused, and at a time when the paper was owned and possessed by plaintiff or Ronconi & Millar, the Sun-Herald Corporation, in accordance with whose instructions and for whose account the letter of credit was issued, offered to the plaintiff that it would accept the newsprint paper referred to and pay for the same at a price of 8 1/2 cents per pound, provided the plaintiff or its assignor would promptly and reasonably satisfy the Sun-Herald Corporation that the newsprint paper tested as much as 11 points to 32 pounds as specified in the letter of credit, and was of the sizes specified therein; that the plaintiff refused to accept said offer; and (e) as a fifth separate and partial defense, all of the allegations of the fourth defense were repeated.

After issue had been joined the plaintiff moved, upon the pleadings and affidavits, pursuant to rule 113 of the Rules of Civil Practice, to strike out the answer and for summary judgment.

The claim for damages for the nonpayment of the third draft was, apparently, abandoned at or prior to the time the motion was made. It is unnecessary, therefore, to further consider that and it will not be again referred to in the discussion as to the first two drafts.

The motion for summary judgment was denied and the defendant appealed to the Appellate Division, where the order denying the same was unanimously affirmed, leave to appeal to this court granted, and the following question certified: Should the motion of the plaintiff for summary judgment herein have been granted?

I am of the opinion that the order of the Appellate Division and the Special Term should be reversed and the motion granted. The facts set out in defendant's answer and in the affidavits used by it in opposition to the motion are not a defense to the action.

The bank issued to plaintiff's assignor an irrevocable letter of credit, a contract solely between the bank and plaintiff's assignor, in and by which the bank agreed to pay sight drafts to a certain amount on presentation to it of the documents specified in the letter of credit. This contract was in no way involved in or connected with, other than the presentation of the documents, the contract for the purchase and sale of the paper mentioned. That was a contract between buyer and seller, which in no way concerned the bank. The bank's obligation was to pay sight drafts when presented if accompanied by genuine documents specified in the letter of credit. If the paper when delivered did not correspond to what had been purchased, either in weight, kind or quality, then the purchaser had his remedy against the seller for damages. Whether the paper was what the purchaser contracted to purchase did not concern the bank and in no way affected its liability. It was under no obligation to ascertain, either by a personal examination or otherwise, whether the paper conformed to the contract between the buyer and seller. The bank was concerned only in the drafts and the documents accompanying them. This was the extent of its interest. If the drafts, when presented, were accompanied by the proper documents, then it was absolutely bound to make the payment under the letter of credit, irrespective of whether it knew, or had reason to believe, that the paper was not of the tensile strength contracted for. This view, I think, is the one generally entertained with reference to a bank's liability under an irrevocable letter of credit of the character of the one here under consideration.

The defendant had no right to insist that a test of the tensile strength of the paper be made before paying the drafts; nor did it even have a right to inspect the paper before payment, to determine whether it in fact corresponded to the description contained in the documents. The letter of credit did not so provide. All that the letter of credit provided was that documents be presented which described the paper shipped as of a certain size, weight, and tensile strength. To hold otherwise is to read into the letter of credit something which is not there, and this the court ought not to do, since it would impose upon a bank a duty which in many cases would defeat the primary purpose of such letters of credit. This primary purpose is an assurance to the seller of merchandise of prompt payment against documents.

It has never been held, so far as I am able to discover, that a bank has the right or is under an obligation to see that the description of the merchandise contained in the documents presented is correct. A provision giving it such right, or imposing such obligation, might, of course, be provided for in the letter of credit. The letter under consideration contains no such provision. If the bank had the right to determine whether the paper was of the tensile strength stated, then it might be pertinent to inquire how much of the paper must it subject to the test. If it had to make a test as to tensile strength, then it was equally obligated to measure and weigh the paper. No such thing was intended by the parties and there was no such obligation upon the bank. The documents presented were sufficient. The only reason stated by defendant in its letter of December 18, 1920, for refusing to pay the draft, was that —

> "There has arisen a reasonable doubt regarding the quality of the newsprint paper. . . . Until such time as we can have a test made by an impartial and unprejudiced expert we shall be obliged to defer payment."

This being the sole objection, the only inference to be drawn therefrom is that otherwise the documents presented conformed to the requirements of the letter of credit. All other objections were thereby waived.

Some criticism is made as to the statement contained in the documents when the second draft was presented. The criticism, really, is directed towards the expressions "in test 11/12, 32 lbs." and "paper equal to original sample in test 11/12, 32 pounds." It is claimed that these expressions are not equivalent to "rolls to test 11-12, 32 lbs." I think they are. I do not see how any one could have been misled by them or misunderstood them. The general rule is that an obligation to present documents is complied with if any of the documents attached to the draft contain the required description. The purpose, obviously, was to enable defendant to know that dock delivery orders had been issued for the paper.

The alleged oral agreement for a test was unenforceable against plaintiff. It is not alleged that Ronconi & Millar, the beneficiaries of the letter of credit, were parties to this alleged modification of it. They did not assign it to the plaintiff until May 25, 1921, five months after the agreement is alleged to have been made. The letter of credit could not have been modified in this way by parol. Since the defendant was already bound by its letter of credit to pay the drafts on presentation of the documents, without any inspection of the goods, there was no consideration for the alleged new promise and the same, even if made, was invalid.

Finally, it is claimed that the plaintiff was not entitled to a summary judgment since there was an issue raised as to the amount of damages. It appears from the affidavits in support of the motion that after the defendant had refused to pay the drafts, due notice was given to it by the plaintiff of its intention to sell the paper for the best price possible, although no notice of such resale was necessary. No attention was paid to the notice and the paper was sold as soon as practicable thereafter and for the best price obtainable, which represented the fair market value at the time of the sale. The plaintiff's damages were, primarily, the face amount of the drafts. Plaintiff, of course, was bound to minimize such damage so far as it reasonably could. This it undertook to do by reselling the paper, and for the amount received, less expenses connected with the sale, it was bound to give the defendant credit. There was absolutely no statement in defendant's affidavits to the effect that the plaintiff did not act in the utmost good faith or with reasonable care and diligence in making the resale. The only reference thereto is that defendant did not get the best price possible. The defendant gave no evidence, however, of a market value at the time and the plaintiff submitted the affidavits of three dealers in paper that the paper was sold at the fair market value at the time of the sale. Plaintiff's damages were therefore liquidated by a resale on notice. This is the rule which has long prevailed between seller and buyer. The only requirement is that the resale must be a fair one.

There was a loss on the resale of the paper called for under the first draft of $5,447.26, and under the second draft of $14,617.53, making a total loss of $20,064.79, for which amount judgment should be directed in favor of the plaintiff.

The orders appealed from should therefore be reversed and the motion granted, with costs in all courts. The question certified is answered in the affirmative.

CARDOZO, J. (dissenting).

I am unable to concur in the opinion of the court.

I assume that no duty is owing from the bank to its depositor which requires it to investigate the quality of the merchandise. I dissent from the view that, if it chooses to investigate and discovers thereby that the merchandise tendered is not in truth the merchandise which the documents describe, it may be forced by the delinquent seller to make payment of the price irrespective of its knowledge. We are to bear in mind that this controversy is not one between the bank on the one side and on the other a holder of the drafts who has taken them without notice and for value. The controversy arises between the bank and a seller who has misrepresented the security upon which advances are demanded. Between parties so situated payment may be resisted if the documents are false.

I think we lose sight of the true nature of the transaction when we view the bank as acting upon the credit of its customer to the exclusion of all else. It acts not merely upon the credit of its customer, but upon the credit also of the merchandise which is to be tendered as security. The letter of credit is explicit in its provision that documents sufficient to give control of the goods shall be lodged with the bank when drafts are presented. I cannot accept the statement of the majority opinion that the bank was not concerned with any question as to the character of the paper. If that is so, the bales tendered might have been rags instead of paper, and still the bank would have been helpless, though it had knowledge of the truth, if the documents tendered by the seller were sufficient on their face. A different question would be here if the defects had no relation to the description in the documents. In such circumstances it would be proper to say that a departure from the terms of the contract between the vendor and the vendee was of no moment to the bank. That is not the case before us. If the paper was of the quality stated in the defendant's answer the documents were false.

I think the conclusion is inevitable that a bank which pays a draft upon a bill of lading misrepresenting the character of the merchandise may recover the payment when the misrepresentation is discovered, or at the very least, the difference between the value of the thing described and the value of the thing received. If payment might have been recovered the moment after it was made, the seller cannot coerce payment if the truth is earlier revealed.

We may find persuasive analogies in connection with the law of sales. One who promises to make payment in advance of delivery and inspection may be technically in default if he refuses the promised payment before inspection has been made. Nonetheless, if the result of the inspection is to prove that the merchandise is defective, the seller must fail in an action for the recovery of the price. The reason is that "the buyer would have been entitled to recover back the price if he had paid it without inspection of the goods." 2 Williston on Sales [2d ed.] §§479-576.

I think the defendant's answer and the affidavits submitted in support of it are sufficient to permit a finding that the plaintiff's assignors misrepresented the nature of the shipment. The misrepresentation does not cease to be a defense, partial if not complete, though it was innocently made.

The order should be affirmed and the question answered "No."

NOTES AND QUESTIONS

1. The independence of the letter of credit means that the performance of the letter of credit contract is separate and independent of the performance of the sales contract and that breach or nonperformance of the sales contract alone is

no defense to payment under the letter of credit. The documents that must be submitted for payment under the letter of credit are linked to the performance of the sales contract because they evidence that conforming goods have been shipped but it is the documents themselves not the underlying performance of the sales contract that they evidence that is essential for payment under the terms of the credit. Once documents complying with the terms of the credit are presented by the seller to the confirming or issuing bank as the case may be, the bank must pay regardless of nonperformance of the sales contract and the buyer-applicant must reimburse the bank. The remedy of the buyer is to sue the seller for breach of the underlying sales contract and not to withhold payment under the letter of credit. As the bank is bound to pay only when the seller presents conforming documents, the standard determining when the documents are conforming is a crucial part of letter of credit law and is an issue that we will be exploring in the next section of this chapter.

2. Note that the independence principle serves at least two important functions in the area of international banking that promote the commercial utility of the letter of credit. First, the seller is provided an assured method of prompt payment so long as the seller presents conforming documents. The seller does not need to be concerned that the bank will become embroiled with issues relating to the performance of the underlying contract, which can be complex and time consuming, as a defense to payment. The simple, mechanistic role of the bank in dealing only with the documents means that the seller enjoys a reliable method of payment and can be confident of payment once the seller ships the goods. Second, the independence principle simplifies the task for banks, which act as "document merchants." Banks need not concern themselves with the performance of the underlying contract in making payment; banks need only examine the documents to determine whether they comply with the terms of the credit. This is a relatively straightforward and simple task. If banks had to determine whether the underlying contract had been performed before they could pay on the letter of credit, this task would create significant burdens on banks and add costs to international credit transactions. While bankers may be expected to examine and handle documents, requiring bankers to examine whether contracts outside their area of experience and expertise have been properly performed is another matter. Limiting banks to an examination of documents helps to assure that letters of credit will be paid expeditiously and at minimal expense, facilitating international commerce.

3. Judge Cardozo's dissent brings up the need to set limits on the independence principle when faced with an undeserving beneficiary. He argues why should a seller who submits documents that misrepresent the goods be entitled to payment if the bank discovers that the goods are not those described in the documents. Judge Cardozo argues that while the bank has no duty to investigate whether the goods match the description in the documents if the bank does so and discovers that the goods are not those described in the documents, the bank may refuse to pay on the letter of credit. Judge Cardozo's argument foreshadows the landmark case of *Sztejn v. J. Henry Schroder Banking Co.*, 31 N.Y.S.2d 631 (Sup. Ct. 1941), which established the fraud exception to the independence principle, which we take up in detail in §C *infra*.

4. While we agree with Judge Cardozo that the legitimate purposes of the independence principle can be subverted by an undeserving beneficiary, we

take some issue with his rationale and with the scope of the exception that he proposes. He argues that the bank has a security interest in the goods that is put at risk when the quality of the goods does not match the description in the documents. Note that if a bank pays the seller-beneficiary against conforming documents, the buyer-applicant of the credit is bound to reimburse the bank for the amount of the credit. Judge Cardozo's argument as to the bank's security interest being compromised by goods that do not match the documents would apply only when the buyer-applicant refuses to reimburse the bank and the bank must look to the goods to recoup its losses caused by the buyer's breach of its reimbursement obligation. In addition, Judge Cardozo does not make a distinction between the unscrupulous seller out to intentionally defraud the buyer and the well-meaning seller who may have interpreted the contract differently from the buyer. For example, suppose that the seller genuinely believed that the paper met the tensile strength requirements under the contract and that a genuine commercial dispute arose when the buyer did not agree with the seller's interpretation of the contract. Under Judge Cardozo's view, if the bank had investigated the goods and agreed with the buyer that they did not conform to the documents, should the bank withhold payment? In other words, should a bank withhold payment where there is a genuine contract dispute between the buyer and the seller? If so, would this approach undermine the independence principle and the commercial utility of the letter of credit?

B. Strict Compliance

Banks must pay against documents that comply with the requirements of the letter of credit. What constitutes compliance? UCP Article 13 provides in relevant part:

Standard for Examination of Documents

(a) Banks must examine all documents stipulated in the Credit with reasonable care, to ascertain whether or not they appear, on their face, to be in compliance with the terms and conditions of the Credit. Compliance of the stipulated documents on their face with the terms and conditions of the Credit shall be determined by international standard banking practice as reflected in these Articles. Documents which appear on their face to be inconsistent with one another will be considered as not appearing on their face to be in compliance with the terms and conditions of the Credit.

Documents not stipulated in the Credit will not be examined by banks. If they receive such documents, they shall return them to the presenter or pass them on without responsibility.

PROBLEM 4-7

A U.S. buyer purchases computer chips from Sine-Tech, a manufacturer in Taiwan, under a contract calling for payment by letter of credit. The buyer's bank advises the Taiwanese manufacturer of the credit as follows:

Payment against the letter of credit will be made upon the submission of a commercial invoice, full set original on board bills of lading in triplicate, commercial invoice, certificate of insurance, and inspection certificate. All documents to refer to Altima III Central Processing Units at 750 Megahertz and 512 Random Access Memory Chips shipped from Sine-Tech. All documents must strictly conform with the terms of this credit in light of standard international banking practices.

The buyer's senior vice president for sales stops by Sine-Tech while on a business trip to Asia and is able to inspect the shipment of chips. The vice president signs the inspection certificate and writes a handwritten note on the certificate: "Samples fit our contract specifications precisely. Note to bank: Please pay seller without delay."

Sine-Tech subsequently ships the chips and submits the documents, including the inspection certificate signed by the buyer's vice president, to its own bank in Taiwan. The seller's bank then forwards the documents to the buyer's bank in the United States along with a sight draft. The bill of lading refers to:

Altima III CPUs @ 750 MHz and 512 RAM memory chips shipped from Sino-Tech.

The examiner in the credit department of the buyer's bank looks at the documents and writes a memo to the head of the credit department: "I have two master's degrees in computer science and I know for a fact that the terms that are being used in the documents (e.g., CPU, MHz, RAM) are well-known technical equivalents that completely match the terms under the letter of credit. The documents are conforming and we should pay." Is he right? Are there any other compliance issues?

Is it safe for the bank to pay the credit on the basis of the vice president's endorsement of the inspection certificate and does that constitute a waiver of discrepancies by the applicant under Article 14(c)?

In addition to Articles 13 and 14, see also *Rayner* and *Hanil Bank infra.*

J.H. Rayner and Company, Ltd. v. Hambro's Bank, Ltd.
Court of Appeal
[1943] 1 King's Bench 37

Appeal from ATKINSON J.

On March 29, 1940, the defendants, Hambro's Bank, Ltd., received a cable from correspondents in Denmark, which was not then in enemy occupation, requesting them to open an irrevocable sight credit expiring June 1, 1940, in favour of J.H. Rayner & Co., the plaintiffs. The material words of this cable were: ". . . account Aarhus Oliefabrik for about £16,975 against invoice full set straight clean bills of lading to Aarhus Oliefabrik dated Madras during April, 1940, covering about 1400 tons Coromandel groundnuts in bags at £12 2s. 6d. per ton f.o.b. Madras shipment motorship *Stensby* to Aarhus." On April 1, the defendants issued a letter of credit to the plaintiffs in these terms.

"Confirmed credit No. 14597.

We beg to inform you that a confirmed credit has been opened with us in favour of yourselves for an amount of up to about £16,975 account of Aarhus Oliefabrik available by drafts on this bank at sight to be accompanied by the following documents—invoice, clean on board bills of lading in complete set issued to order

Aarhus Oliefabrik, dated Madras during April, 1940, covering a shipment of about 1400 tons Coromandel groundnuts in bags at £12 2s. 6d. per ton f.o.b. Madras per m.s. *Stensby* to Aarhus.

This credit is valid until June 1, 1940. All drafts drawn here against must contain the clause 'Drawn under confirmed credit No. 14597.' We undertake to honour drafts on presentation, if drawn in conformity with the terms of this credit."

On April 15, the plaintiffs presented to the defendant bank a draft, accompanied by an invoice of the same date for "17,724 bags Coromandel groundnuts. Bill of lading dated 2.4.40" and three bills of lading, differing only as to the number of bags, which totalled 17,724, in each of which the goods were described in these terms: In the margin were the marks

"O.T.C. C.R.S. Aarhus,"

and in the body of the bill

". . . bags machine-shelled groundnut kernels, each bag said to weigh 177 lb. net. Country of origin, British India. Country of final destination, Denmark. Goods are Danish property."

Those documents having been presented to the defendants, they refused to accept the draft, on the ground that the terms of the letter of credit called for an invoice and bill of lading both covering a shipment of "Coromandel groundnuts" whereas the bills of lading presented described the goods as "machine shelled groundnut kernels. Country of origin, British India." The plaintiffs thereupon brought this action, alleging that the defendants' refusal to honour their draft was wrongful, and a breach of the undertaking in the letter of credit. At the trial before Atkinson J. evidence was given and accepted by him that "machine-shelled groundnut kernels" were the same commodity as "Coromandel groundnuts" and would be universally understood to be so in the trade in London, and, further, that the marginal mark "C.R.S." was short for "Coros" or "Coromandels" and would be so understood in the trade. Atkinson J. gave judgment for the plaintiffs, and the defendants appealed.

MACKINNON L.J.

The legal result of a banker issuing a letter of credit has been considered in various cases to which I do not think it is necessary to refer, but two passages which have been mentioned by Goddard L.J. seem to me to sum up the position in general terms with the greatest accuracy. In *English, Scottish and Australian Bank, Ltd. v. Bank of South Africa*,[1] Bailhache J. said:

"It is elementary to say that a person who ships in reliance on a letter of credit must do so in exact compliance with its terms. It is also elementary to say that a bank is not bound or indeed entitled to honour drafts presented to it under a letter of credit unless those drafts with the accompanying documents are in strict accord with the credit as opened."

---

1. (1922) 13 Ll. L. Rep. 21, 24.

Lord Sumner in *Equitable Trust Co. of New York v. Dawson Partners, Ltd.*,[2] said:

> "It is both common ground and common sense that in such a transaction the accepting bank can only claim indemnity if the conditions on which it is authorized to accept are in the matter of the accompanying documents strictly observed. There is no room for documents which are almost the same, or which will do just as well. Business could not proceed securely on any other lines. The bank's branch abroad, which knows nothing officially of the details of the transaction thus financed, cannot take upon itself to decide what will do well enough and what will not. If it does as it is told, it is safe; if it declines to do anything else, it is safe; if it departs from the conditions laid down, it acts at its own risk."

The defendant bank were told by their Danish principals to issue a letter of credit under which they were to accept documents—an invoice and bills of lading—covering "Coromandel groundnuts in bags." They were offered bills of lading covering "machine-shelled groundnut kernels." The country of origin was stated to be British India. The words in that bill of lading clearly are not the same as those required by the letter of credit. The whole case of the plaintiffs is, in the words of Lord Sumner, that "they are almost the same, or they will do just as well." The bank, if they had accepted that proposition, would have done so at their own risk. I think on pure principle that the bank were entitled to refuse to accept this sight draft on the ground that the documents tendered, the bill of lading in particular, did not comply precisely with the terms of the letter of credit which they had issued.

Atkinson J., however, in his judgment says:

> "A sale of Coromandel groundnuts is universally understood to be a sale of machine-shelled kernels that is, dry decorticated, and there is a standard form of contract, No. 37, used in the trade. The marking C.R.S. is short for 'Coros,' which is itself an abbreviation for 'Coromandels.' If a bag of kernels is marked 'C.R.S.,' it means that it is a bag of Coromandel groundnuts."

That is stating the effect of evidence given by persons who deal in groundnuts in Mincing Lane, and when Atkinson J. says that it is "universally understood," he means that these gentlemen from Mincing Lane have told him:

> "We dealers in Mincing Lane all understand these things. We understand that 'Coromandel groundnuts' are machine shelled groundnut kernels, and we understand when we see 'C.R.S.' that that means 'Coromandels.'"

It is suggested that as a consequence the bank, when this bill of lading for machine-shelled groundnut kernels with C.R.S. in the margin was brought to them, ought to be affected with this special knowledge of those witnesses who deal in these things on contracts in Mincing Lane. I think that is a perfectly impossible suggestion. To begin with, this case does not concern any transaction in Mincing Lane. It is a transaction with Denmark, and for aught I know and for aught the evidence proved, the people in Denmark know nothing about this business usage of Mincing Lane. Moreover, quite apart from that special application of the relevant considerations, it is quite impossible to suggest that a banker is to be

---

2. (1927) 27 Ll. Rep. 49, 52.

affected with knowledge of the customs and customary terms of every one of the thousands of trades for whose dealings he may issue letters of credit. A homely illustration is suggested by the books in front of me. If a banker were ordered to issue a letter of credit with respect to the shipment of so many copies of the "1942 Annual Practice" and were handed a bill of lading for so many copies of the "1942 White Book," it would be entirely beside the mark to call a lawyer to say that all lawyers know that the "1942 White Book" means the "1942 Annual Practice." It would be quite impossible for business to be carried on, and for bankers to be in any way protected in such matters, if it were said that they must be affected by a knowledge of all the details of the way in which particular traders carry on their business. For these reasons, I think that this appeal succeeds, that the judgment in favour of the plaintiffs must be set aside, and judgment entered for the defendants with costs, here and below.

GODDARD L.J.

I agree. It seems to me that Atkinson J. has based his judgment on the consideration that the bank was affected in some way by this custom of the trade, and, secondly, that he has considered whether what the bank required was reasonable or unreasonable. I protest against the view that a bank is to be deemed affected by knowledge of the trade of its various customers, but, quite apart from that, even if the bank did know of this trade practice by which "Coromandel groundnuts" can be described as "machine-shelled groundnut kernels," I do not think that would be conclusive of the case.

There are three parties concerned in a banker's credit — the person who requests the bank to establish the credit, the bank which establishes it, and the beneficiary who can draw on it. The person who requests the bank to establish the credit can impose what terms he likes. If he says to the bank: "I want a bill of lading in a particular form," he is entitled to it. If the bank accepts the mandate which its customer gives it, it must do so on the terms which he imposes. The bank, as between itself and the beneficiary, can impose extra terms if it likes. For instance, in this case, the bank imposes a term: "All drafts drawn here against must contain the clause: 'Drawn under confirmed credit No. 14597.'" The bank can say to the beneficiary: "These are the terms on which the bank will pay," and if it has only been authorized by its customer to pay on certain terms it must see that those terms are included in the notification which it gives to the beneficiary, and it must not pay on any other terms. If it does pay on any other terms, it runs the risk of its customer refusing to reimburse it. It does not matter whether the terms imposed by the person who requires the bank to open the credit seem reasonable or unreasonable. The bank is not concerned with that. If it accepts the mandate to open the credit, it must do exactly what its customer requires it to do. If the customer says: "I require a bill of lading for Coromandel groundnuts," the bank is not justified, in my judgment, in paying against a bill of lading for anything except Coromandel groundnuts, and it is no answer to say: "You know perfectly well that 'machine-shelled groundnut kernels are the same as Coromandel groundnuts.'" For all the bank knows, its customer may have a particular reason for wanting "Coromandel groundnuts" in the bill of lading. At any rate, that is the instruction which the customer has given to the bank, and if the bank wants to be reimbursed and remunerated by its customer, it must show that it has performed his mandate.

In my opinion, in this case, whether the bank knew or did not know that there was this trade practice to treat "Coromandel groundnuts" and "machine-shelled groundnut kernels" as interchangeable terms, is nothing to the point. They were told to establish a credit, and to pay against a bill of lading describing particular goods, and the beneficiary under that credit presented a bill of lading which was not what they had promised to pay against. Therefore, it seems to me, whether it is reasonable or unreasonable for their principals to say that they want a bill of lading for "Coromandel groundnuts," or whether the bank had or had not knowledge of some of the trade practices which are referred to, is not the question. The question is "What was the promise which the bank made to the beneficiary under the credit, and did the beneficiary avail himself of that promise?" In my opinion, in the present case, he did not, and, therefore, I think that the bank was justified in refusing to pay. The other matters are, in my opinion, quite irrelevant, though the judge seems to have paid particular attention to them. I agree that this appeal should be allowed.

Hanil Bank v. PT. Bank Negara Indonesia
United States District Court, Southern District of New York, 2000
No. 96 Civ. 3201, 41 U.C.C. Rep. Serv. 2d 618

KEENAN, District Judge.

Before the Court are cross-motions for summary judgment, pursuant to Fed. R. Civ. P. 56. For the reasons discussed below, the Court grants Defendant's motion for summary judgment and denies Plaintiff's motion for summary judgment.

THE PARTIES

Plaintiff Hanil Bank ("Hanil") was, at all times relevant to this action, a banking corporation organized under the laws of the Republic of Korea, with an agency in New York, New York.

Defendant PT. Bank Negara Indonesia (Pesero) ("BNI") is a banking corporation organized under the laws of Indonesia, with an agency located in New York, New York.

BACKGROUND

On July 27, 1995, PT. Kodeco Electronics Indonesia ("Kodeco") applied to BNI to issue a letter of credit (the "L/C") for the benefit of "Sung Jun Electronics Co., Ltd." ("Sung Jun"). On July 28, 1995, BNI issued the L/C, No. IM1MHT0272.95, in the amount of $170,955.00 but misspelled the name of the beneficiary as "Sung Jin Electronics Co. Ltd." The beneficiary did not request amendment of the L/C to change the name of the beneficiary. On August 2, 1995 Sung Jun negotiated the L/C to Hanil. Hanil purchased the L/C and the documents submitted by Sung Jun thereunder from Sung Jun for $157,493.00, the face amount of the draft, less Hanil's commission. On August 2, 1995, Hanil submitted the documents, a draft, a commercial invoice, bill of lading, insurance policy, a packing list, and a fax advice, to BNI for payment. On August 16, 1995, BNI rejected the documents tendered by Hanil and refused to pay under the L/C. BNI alleges that it compared the documents with the L/C and identified four discrepancies, and based upon those discrepancies, refused the documents and demand for payment. The alleged discrepancies are as follows:

(1)   The Name of the Beneficiary: The L/C identifies the beneficiary as Sung Jin Electronics Co. Ltd. instead of Sung Jun Electronics Co. Ltd.
(2)   The Packing List: BNI claims that the packing list did not show the contents of each carton as required by the L/C.
(3)   "Export Quality": BNI claims that the packing list also fails to specify that the goods were of "export quality."
(4)   The Bill of Lading: BNI claims that Hanil supplied a "Freight Bill of Lading" instead of the required "Ocean Bill of Lading."

BNI alleges that before it issued its notice of refusal on August 16, 1995, it contacted Kodeco to ask whether it would accept the discrepancies and approve the requested payment, but Kodeco declined to do so. BNI further alleges that it continued to ask Kodeco to waive the discrepancies after August 16, but that Kodeco continued to refuse to waive the discrepancies. BNI then returned the entire original package of documents back to Hanil on September 4, 1995.

Hanil contends that BNI decided to reject the documents presented by Hanil after consulting with, and on the instructions of, Kodeco. In support of this contention, Hanil points to a letter from BNI to Hanil, dated October 4, 1995, which stated that "we are acting at the request and on the instruction of the applicant, i.e., PT. Kodeco Electronics Indonesia. We will, anyhow make a final attempt to have the applicant reconsider their determination and to accept the discrepancies and give as the approval [sic] for payment of the documents." BNI denies the contention that it acted on the instructions of Kodeco when BNI refused to pay because of the alleged discrepancies.

Plaintiff brought suit in New York State court on April 19, 1996, asserting claims for breach of contract, breach of the Uniform Customs and Practice for Documentary Credits (1993 Revision) International Chamber of Commerce Publication No. 500 (the "UCP"), unjust enrichment, and breach of an implied covenant of good faith and fair dealing, and seeking $157,493 in damages, plus interest. Defendant then removed the case to this Court. Both parties now move for summary judgment.

SUMMARY JUDGMENT STANDARDS

In this case, both parties argue that summary judgment is appropriate because there is no genuine issue of material fact. Hanil argues that the documents it presented to BNI complied with the terms of the L/C and that, as a result, Hanil is entitled to judgment enforcing the L/C. BNI, however, contends that each of the four discrepancies it identified justified rejection of Hanil's presentation under the L/C and the refusal to pay and that the Complaint should therefore be dismissed.

LETTERS OF CREDIT AND THE UCP

The principles of letter of credit law are embodied in the Uniform Customs and Practice for Documentary Credits (1993 Revision) International Chamber of Commerce Publication No. 500 (the "UCP"). The UCP is a compilation of internationally accepted commercial practices. Although it is not law, the UCP commonly governs letters of credit by virtue of its incorporation into most letters of credit. See id. In this case, the L/C provides that it is governed by the UCP and both parties agree that the provisions of the UCP govern the L/C in this case. The New York Uniform Commercial Code (the "U.C.C.") provides that if a letter of credit is subject in whole or part to the UCP, as in this case, the U.C.C. does not apply.

A fundamental tenet of letter of credit law is that the obligation of the issuing bank to honor a draft on a credit is independent of the performance of the underlying contract. "The duty of the issuing bank to pay upon the submission of documents which appear on their face to conform to the terms and conditions of the letter of credit is absolute, absent proof of intentional fraud. . . ." *E & H Partners*, 39 F. Supp.2d at 280. Because the credit engagement is concerned only with documents, "[t]he essential requirements of a letter of credit must be strictly complied with by the party entitled to draw against the letter of credit, which means that the papers, documents and shipping description must be as stated in the letter." *Marino Indus.*, 686 F.2d at 114. "There is no room for documents which are almost the same, or which will do just as well." *Alaska Textile*, 982 F.2d at 816. Even under the strict compliance rule, however, "some variations . . . might be so insignificant as not to relieve the issuing or confirming bank of its obligation to pay," for example, if there were a case where "the name intended is unmistakably clear despite what is obviously a typographical error, as might be the case if, for example, 'Smith' were misspelled 'Smithh.'" *Beyene*, 762 F.2d at 6. The Court will now consider the alleged discrepancies in this case.

THE NAME OF THE BENEFICIARY

As set out above, the name of the beneficiary in this case was Sung Jun. Kodeco's application to BNI for the issuance of the L/C requested that the L/C be issued to Sung Jun. BNI, however, issued the L/C identifying the beneficiary as Sung Jin. BNI argues that under *Beyene v. Irving Trust Co.*, 762 F.2d 4 (2d Cir. 1985) and *Mutual Export Corp. v. Westpac Banking Corp.*, 983 F.2d 420 (2d Cir. 1993), this discrepancy was a proper basis to reject the letter of credit presentation. Hanil argues, however, that the strict compliance rule does not permit an issuing bank to dishonor a letter of credit based on a discrepancy such as the misspelling in this case which could not have misled or prejudiced the issuing bank. For the reasons discussed below, the Court agrees with BNI.

In *Beyene*, Plaintiffs brought suit seeking damages for the alleged wrongful refusal of the defendant trust company, Irving Trust Co. ("Irving"), to honor a letter of credit. The district court granted Irving's motion for summary judgment because the bill of lading presented to Irving misspelled the name of the person to whom notice was to be given of the arrival of the goods, listing the name of the party as Mohammed Soran instead of Mohammed Sofan. As a result, the district court found that the bill of lading failed to comply with the terms of the letter of credit and that Irving was under no obligation to honor the letter of credit. The Second Circuit agreed, finding that "the misspelling in the bill of lading of Sofan's name as 'Soran' was a material discrepancy that entitled Irving to refuse to honor the letter of credit" and stating that "this is not a case where the name intended is unmistakably clear despite what is obviously a typographical error, as might be the case if, for example, 'Smith' were misspelled 'Smithh.'" 762 F.2d at 6. The Second Circuit also noted that it was not claimed that in the Middle East, where the letter of credit was issued, that "Soran" would be obviously recognized as a misspelling of the surname "Sofan." The Court finds the misspelling in the present case to be similar to the misspelling in *Beyene* and notes that Hanil likewise does not claim that Sung "Jin" would be obviously recognized as a misspelling of Sung "Jun."

Plaintiff argues that *Beyene* is distinguishable from the present case because in *Beyene* the beneficiary made the error, while in the present case, the issuing bank made the error. However, the Second Circuit has made it clear that under letter of credit law, "[t]he beneficiary must inspect the letter of credit and is responsible for any negligent failure to discover that the credit does not achieve the desired commercial ends." *Mutual Export*, 983 F.2d at 423. Thus, in *Mutual Export*, even though the issuing bank had issued a letter of credit with an incorrect termination date, the Second Circuit reversed the district court's finding that the letter of credit should be reformed to reflect the appropriate date, and held that the beneficiary was responsible for failure to discover the error. The *Mutual Export* court explained that this rule is important because

> [t]he beneficiary is in the best position to determine whether a letter of credit meets the needs of the underlying commercial transaction and to request any necessary changes. . . . "[i]t is more efficient to require the beneficiary to conduct that review of the credit before the fact of performance than after it, and the beneficiary that performs without seeing or examining the credit should bear the costs." . . .

See *id.* Pursuant to *Beyene* and *Mutual Export*, this Court concludes that BNI properly rejected payment on the ground that the documents improperly identified the beneficiary of the letter of credit. Although Hanil contends that BNI should have known that the intended beneficiary was Sung Jun, not Sung Jin, based on the application letter in BNI's own file, the Second Circuit has stated that in considering whether to pay, "the bank looks solely at the letter and the documentation the beneficiary presents to determine whether the documentation meets the requirements in the letter." *See Marino Indus.*, 686 F.2d at 115.

Although Plaintiff argues that *Bank of Montreal v. Federal Nat'l Bank & Trust Co.*, 662 F. Supp. 6 (W.D. Okla. 1984), allowed recovery when the error was greater than the misspelling of a single letter, in *Bank of Montreal*, the letter of credit contained two, internally inconsistent, statements of the name of one of the entities whose indebtedness was secured. The letter of credit referred to "Blow Out Products, Ltd." in its first paragraph and to "Blow Out Prevention, Ltd." in its second paragraph. Based on this inconsistency on the face of the letter of credit itself, the court found that the letter of credit was ambiguous and resolved the ambiguity against the issuer. There is no internal inconsistency or ambiguity in the L/C at issue in the present case, however.

Having found that BNI properly refused payment based on the improper identification of the beneficiary of the L/C, the Court need not address the three remaining alleged discrepancies.

Finally, as to Hanil's argument that BNI dishonored the L/C at the instruction of Kodeco and thereby violated its duty of good faith and fair dealing, the Court again disagrees. As noted above, the issuing bank's obligation under the letter of credit is independent of the underlying commercial transaction. Thus, BNI had an obligation to independently review Hanil's submissions to determine if there were any discrepancies. However, under the UCP, BNI is permitted to approach the payor of the letter of credit, in this case Kodeco, for a waiver of any discrepancies with or without the beneficiary's approval. See UCP, Art. 14(c). In this case there is no evidence that BNI communicated with Kodeco other than to ask whether Kodeco would accept the discrepancies and approve the requested payment. As a result, the Court finds that Hanil has not set forth facts showing there is a genuine issue as to whether BNI breached its duty of good faith and fair dealing by dishonoring the L/C. Summary judgment for BNI is therefore appropriate.

For the reasons discussed above, the Court grants BNI's motion for summary judgment and denies Hanil's motion for summary judgment. The Court orders this case closed and directs that it be removed from the Court's active docket.

So ordered.

NOTES AND QUESTIONS

1. *Hanil* followed *Beyene v. Irving Trust Co.*, 762 F.2d 4 (2d Cir. 1985) in finding that unless the name of the intended beneficiary is unmistakably clear despite an obvious typographical error, any difference in the name constitutes noncompliance. In *Voest-Alpine Trading USA Corp. v. Bank of China*, 167 F. Supp. 2d 940 (S.D. Tex. 2000), *aff'd*, 288 F.3d 262 (5th Cir. 2002), the district court held that although documents naming the beneficiary "Voest-Alpine USA Trading Corp." did not conform to the letter of credit requiring documents identifying the beneficiary as "Voest-Alpine Trading USA Corp.," the discrepancy did not justify dishonor. Looking at other documents and the transaction as a whole, the court concluded that the documents did not appear to come from a beneficiary other than that named in the credit. On appeal, the Fifth Circuit held that the issuing bank was required to pay as it had waived its right to reject payment of the letter of credit because the bank did not give a proper notice of refusal within seven banking days as required by the UCP and did not address the discrepancy issue. *See* 288 F.3d at 266. In general, typographical errors occur with some regularity in letter of credit transactions and in documents presented under credits, especially when foreign names are involved that use combinations of the alphabet that are not found in the English language. "[L]eading figures in the U.S. LC community support the *Voest-Alpine* approach and regard as too narrow the approach taken in *Hanil* and its forerunner, *Beyene v. Irving Trust Co.* The LC community has no interest in inviting reformation of LCs, but it does wish the courts to take a more practice oriented view with respect to typographical errors." James G. Barnes and James E. Byrne, *Letters of Credit: 2000 Cases*, 56 Bus. Law 1805 (2001).

2. In *Rayner*, the sellers emphasized that it was universally understood in the trade that "Coromandel groundnuts" are machine-shelled groundnut kernels and that "C.R.S." means "Coromandels." On this basis, the sellers argued that documents referring to "machine-shelled groundnut kernels" and "C.R.S." are conforming documents. The court of appeals rejected this argument and emphasized that bankers cannot be charged with knowledge of the customs of merchants even if such customs are universally known among the merchants. The purpose of the strict compliance principle is to reduce the bank's task to the mechanical one of comparing the documents on their face with the terms of the credit. A mechanical examination would assure the seller of expeditious payment and relieve the burden on banks of being charged with extraneous knowledge or having to engage in research of unfamiliar topics. But what about terms that are now generally if not universally known such as "C.O.D." for "cash on delivery"? These are terms that are not peculiar to a trade but have become widely known throughout all trades and channels of commerce. Should banks be charged with knowledge of such widely accepted terms?

3. *Rayner* held that banks cannot be charged with knowledge of customs among London merchants. What about customs among banks? Should banks be charged with knowledge of well-known and standard practices among other banks? In *Dixon, Irmaos & CIA., Ltda. v. Chase National Bank of City of New York*, 144 F.2d 759 (2d Cir. 1944), *cert. denied*, 324 U.S. 850 (1945), the seller submitted only one of the two sets of original bills of lading that were required by the letter of credit. In lieu of the other original set, which was being sent by mail, the seller submitted, as was the custom among New York banks, a letter of guaranty from a reputable New York bank that would indemnify Chase National Bank, the issuing bank, in the event that the original set did not arrive safely. The sellers brought an action to enforce payment when the defendant Chase National Bank refused to honor the letter of credit on the ground that the submission of the letter of guarantee in lieu of the second set of original bills of lading did not conform to the terms of the credit. In rejecting this argument, the Second Circuit Court of Appeals stated:

> It is true, as the defendant argues, that the law requires strict compliance with the terms of a letter of credit. It is likewise true that numerous cases, several of which are cited by the defendant, declare that evidence of a custom is not admissible to contradict the unambiguous terms of a written contract. But it is also well settled "that parties who contract on a subject-matter concerning which known usages prevail, incorporate such usages by implication into their agreements, if nothing is said to the contrary." . . . In our opinion the custom under consideration explains the meaning of the technical phrase "full set of bills of lading" and is incorporated by implication into the terms of the defendant's letters of credit. The reasonableness and utility of the local New York custom is obvious. It is absolutely essential to the expeditious doing of business in overseas transactions in these days when one part of the bill of lading goes by air and another by water. Unless an indemnity can be substituted for the delayed part, not only does quick clearance of such transactions become impossible but also the universal practice of issuing bills of ladings in sets and sending the different parts by separate mails loses much of its purpose. We conclude therefore that the defendant's ground for dishonor of the drafts was not a valid reason.

144 F.2d at 762. *See also* UCC §5-108(e) ("An issuer shall observe standard practice of financial institutions that regularly issue letters of credit. Determination of

the issuer's observance of the standard practice is a matter of interpretation for the court. The court shall offer the parties a reasonable opportunity to present evidence of the standard practice.").

4. *Rayner* is the landmark case establishing the principle of strict compliance. The leading case for a less stringent standard is *Banco Espanol de Credito v. State Street Bank and Trust Co.*, 385 F.2d 230 (1st Cir. 1967). The letter of credit required an inspection certificate but did not name the inspector or the wording of the certificate. A later amendment named the inspector and required the certificate to specify that "the goods were in conformity with the order." The inspector submitted a certificate that the goods were in conformity as required by the letter of credit but added a statement that the certificate was delivered "under reserves," which nullified the statement required by the credit. The First Circuit Court of Appeals held that the certificate complied with the letter of credit *See* 385 F.2d at 237. The official comment to UCC §5-108 provides that *State Street Bank* applied a "substantial compliance" standard but that this standard is rejected in favor of the standard of strict compliance. UCC §5-108(a) provides: "[A]n issuer shall honor a presentation that . . . appears on its face strictly to comply with the terms and conditions of the letter of credit." The Official Comment further provides:

> Strict compliance does not mean slavish conformity to the terms of the letter of credit. For example, standard practice (what issuers do) may recognize certain presentations as complying that an unschooled layman would find as discrepant. By adopting standard practice as a way of measuring strict compliance, this article indorses the conclusion of the court in *New Braunfels Nat'l. Bank v. Odiorne*, 780 S.W.2d 313 (Tex. Ct. App. 1989) (beneficiary could collect when draft requested payment on "Letter of Credit No. 86-122-5" and letter of credit specified "Letter of Credit No. 86-122-S" holding strict compliance does not demand oppressive perfectionism). The section also indorses the result in *Tosco Corp. v. Federal Deposit Insurance Corp.*, 723 F.2d 1242 (6th Cir. 1983). The letter of credit in that case called for "drafts Drawn under Bank of Clarksville Letter of Credit Number 105." The draft presented stated "drawn under Bank of Clarksville, Clarksville, Tennessee letter of Credit No. 105." The court correctly found that despite the change of upper case "L" to a lower case "l" and the use of the word "No." instead of "Number," and despite the addition of the words "Clarksville, Tennessee" the presentation conformed. Similarly a document addressed by a foreign person to General Motors as "Jeneral Motors" would strictly conform in the absence of other defects.

UCC §5-108, Official Comment note 1.

PROBLEM 4-8

On February 17, the National Bank of Cleveland (NBC) received drafts and documents from a Danish seller for payment under a letter of credit issued by NBC. Upon examining the documents, NBC noticed that the bills of lading were not marked "clean on board" as required by the terms of the credit. NBC notified the seller by fax on February 23 of the discrepancy, informing the seller that it could not pay on the letter of credit due to the discrepancy and that it was holding the documents to the disposal of the seller. Later the same day, NBC's documents examiners notice an additional discrepancy: The commercial invoice was not issued in the name of the seller as required by the credit but was in the name of a third party. On February 24, NBC notified the seller of this additional discrepancy. Is the notice by NBC effective as to both discrepancies under UCP Article 14(d) because both were given within the seven banking day notice period? What is the purpose of the notice requirement of Article 14(d)?

PROBLEM 4-9

Mid-America Bank (MAB) receives drafts and documents from a Swiss seller for payment under a letter of credit. MAB examines the documents and notices no discrepancies and sends the following e-mail to the buyer-applicant of the credit: "We have examined the documents and have found that they are conforming. We are forwarding the documents for your review for discrepancies." Upon examining the documents, the buyer tells MAB that the seller did not submit an inspection certificate as required by the credit. MAB thereafter sends a fax within the seven banking day period of UCP Article 14 to the seller stating that it will not pay as the documents are discrepant and that it is holding the documents to the disposal of the seller. Is this notice effective under UCP 14(b)-(e)?

NOTE ON ELECTRONIC COMMUNICATIONS

Electronic communications have become a significant part of letter of credit practice, but, at least for the present, there are a number of limitations on the use of an electronic system to fully replicate the traditional documentary credit transaction that relied on paper documents.

The most significant hurdle in accommodating the letter of credit transaction within electronic commerce is related to the bill of lading. As we have previously noted, in a documentary sale of goods using letters of credit, the negotiable bill of lading serves the vital function of being a document of title entitling the bearer to physical possession of the goods. In a typical documentary sale, the seller will present a paper bill of lading (and other documents) to the buyer's bank, which will pay against presentation and then transfer the bill properly endorsed to the buyer who will then present the bill of lading to the carrier to recover possession of the goods. Traditionally, of course, the bill of lading has been a paper document, which is physically transferred from one party to another, and it is the physical transfer of the paper document, accompanied by a proper endorsement, which creates legal rights in the person to whom the bill is transferred. The electronic letter of credit will only work successfully if somehow the characteristics of the physical transfer normally associated with such a transaction, in particular the physical transfer of the bill of lading, can be successfully replicated in electronic form. So far, these attempts have met with only limited success. The best known and most successful to date of all of these electronic systems is Bolero (Bills of Lading Electronic Registry Organization), which maintains a central registry of ownership of title operated by a company called Bolero International Limited, founded in part by SWIFT, the Society for Worldwide Interstate Financial Telecommunications, a not-for-profit organization established in Belgium by banks for the purpose of facilitating the flow of financial transactions information. Under Bolero, an electronic bill of lading is registered with Bolero International Limited and transfer is then effected by the registered holder (party A) sending a message to the central title registry indicating that the

Bolero bill of lading has been transferred to a new holder (party B) who is now the official registered holder.

One of the major problems with Bolero is that the system will work effectively only if all parties to the transaction subscribe to the Bolero framework and are members of the Bolero Association. Consider the limitations of Bolero where the carrier, a Bolero member, faces competing claims for goods from a holder of a Bolero bill of lading and a person who claims to be the rightful owner of the goods but who is not a Bolero member. Under the traditional system, a long history of accumulated mercantile and legal convention provides that the carrier would be fully protected if it delivered the goods to the holder of the paper bill of lading and the holder of the bill would have the unquestioned right to the delivery of the goods. In the situation just described, however, it is far from clear that the accumulated conventions of the traditional system would apply to the electronic transaction and protect the carrier. This example illustrates the technological limitations of attempting to fully replicate the physical bill of lading in electronic form. In addition to the problems of technological limitations, the future of the Bolero system or any form of electronic bill also depends on the further development of a mature legal regime that confers incidents on the electronic bill that are identical to that of the paper bill.

While there are limitations to the use of electronic communications to fully replicate the documentary sale, two areas in which electronic communications have become quite commonplace is in bank-to-bank communications and in the initiation by beneficiaries of the letter of credit application process. Most bank-to-bank communications about letter of credit transactions occur via the dedicated network operated by SWIFT, which provides for a specific format for all messages, message types, and message space. Thus, an issuing bank will often notify an advising or confirming bank about a letter of credit established by the buyer in favor of the seller via electronic communications. In addition, the initial establishment of the letter of credit by the buyer can also be done through electronic commerce. However, while electronic communications are frequently used to initiate the letter of credit application and to communicate its terms, most seller-beneficiaries usually want a "hard copy" or a letter of credit in the traditional form of a paper document that commits the bank to paying upon certain conditions. Where the initiation of the letter of credit has been done electronically, the issuing or confirming bank will need to convert the SWIFT electronic message creating the letter of credit into a paper form. One issue that has arisen in the age of electronic communications is the risk of errors in the transmission of messages or the conversion of electronic messages into paper documents. The following problem explores these issues.

PROBLEM 4-10

A New York tea merchant contracts to buy a large quantity of English tea from a London seller. The buyer asks its New York bank to open a confirmed letter of credit in favor of the seller. The Merchants' Bank of New York uses the dedicated SWIFT network to contact the London Commercial Bank and asks it to add its confirmation and advise the London seller that a confirmed letter of credit has been issued in favor of the seller by the New York buyer. The electronic message calls for "Payment against documents for English Green Tea in bulk. Details to follow by mail."

As the London seller insists on a hard copy of the letter of credit, the New York bank sends the confirming bank the following message, "To save time, please print out our electronic letter of credit and forward to the seller." However, as the London bank is printing out the electronic letter, a glitch occurs in the computer software program that converts the message in the SWIFT electronic format to a word processing format. The glitch results in the deletion of the word "Green" so the hard copy of the letter of credit printed out by the London bank refers to "Payment against documents for English Tea in Bulk." As this problem had never occurred before, the London bank simply forwards the documents to the London seller. The seller subsequently submits documents for English tea to the London bank and receives payment under the letter of credit. The London bank forwards the documents to the New York bank, which notifies the London bank, "We cannot reimburse you as documents refer to 'English Tea' instead of 'English Green Tea' as per our SWIFT instructions on the letter of credit. We hold these documents at your disposal."

The London bank discovers the computer software problem but argues that the operative document is not the electronic message but as per the instructions from the New York bank the printed-out hard copy, which requires documents relating to "English Tea." The operative document called for documents relating to English Tea and such documents were submitted that strictly complied with the terms of the credit as fixed by the hard copy. The London bank argues that its payment was therefore proper and that the New York bank must now reimburse or the London bank will sue for wrongful dishonor. The New York bank argues that the operative letter of credit is contained in the SWIFT electronic message that required documents for English Green Tea and that as the documents for English Tea are nonconforming the New York bank has no obligation to reimburse the London bank. Who is right and how should this dispute be decided under UCP 500? *See* UCP Articles 11 and 16.

C. The Fraud Exception to the Independence Principle and Enjoining the Letter of Credit

1. *The Problem of Fraud*

While the purpose of the independence principle is to provide the seller an assured method of payment, courts soon realized that an overly rigid extension of the independence rule could result in the unjust enrichment of an undeserving and fraudulent beneficiary and undermine the very commercial utility that the independence principle was designed to promote. The problem arises as follows:

Illustration 4-1. A seller contracts to sell new bristles (or brushes) to a buyer. Instead of shipping new bristles, the seller ships worthless discarded materials and submits fraudulent documents such as a commercial invoice and bills of lading covering new bristles to the issuing bank for payment under a letter of credit. The buyer discovers the fraud before the payment under the letter of credit. A strict application of the independence principle, one which does not allow the bank to look behind the documents, might result in the bank paying the letter to an unscrupulous beneficiary in an obvious fraud situation.

These were essentially the facts in the landmark pre–Uniform Commercial Code case of *Sztejn v. J. Henry Schroder Banking Co.*, 31 N.Y.S.2d 631 (Sup. Ct. 1941), which established the fraud exception and was foreshadowed by Judge Cardozo's dissent in *O'Meara v. National Park Bank*, *supra*. As the court in *Sztejn* recognized, an overly rigid application of the independence principle to require payment to an unscrupulous seller-beneficiary who intentionally provides forged documents for the purpose of defrauding the buyer would undermine the legitimate purposes of the letter of credit. For this reason, the court established an exception to the independence principle for fraud; that is, in some cases the nonperformance of the underlying contract due to fraud will constitute grounds for nonpayment of the letter of credit.

In *Sztejn*, the Schroder bank issued a commercial letter of credit for its customer, Charles Sztejn, in favor of the beneficiary, Transea Traders, Ltd., a company doing business in India. The letter of credit was to finance the sale of 50 cases of bristles and could be drawn upon the presentation of an invoice and a bill of lading. The sellers presented documents to their bank in India, Chartered Bank, which acted as a collection agent by forwarding the documents to the Schroder bank for payment. Before payment, the buyers learned that the sellers had instead shipped cowhair and other worthless material to simulate genuine merchandise and that the documents presented by the sellers were fraudulent. The buyers brought suit against the Schroder bank to declare the letter of credit void and to enjoin payment. In holding for the buyers, the court stated:

> It is well established that a letter of credit is independent of the primary contract of sale between the buyer and the seller. The issuing bank agrees to pay upon presentation of documents, not goods. This rule is necessary to preserve the efficiency of the letter of credit as an instrument for the financing of trade. One of the chief purposes of the letter of credit is to furnish the seller with a ready means of obtaining prompt payment for his merchandise. It would be a most unfortunate interference with business transactions if a bank before honoring drafts drawn upon it was obliged or even allowed to go behind the documents, at the request of the buyer and enter into controversies between the buyer and the seller regarding the quality of the merchandise shipped. If the buyer and the seller intended the bank to do this they could have so provided in the letter of credit itself, and in the absence of such a provision, the court will not demand or even permit the bank to delay paying drafts which are proper in form. . . . Of course, the application of this doctrine presupposes that the documents accompanying the draft are genuine and conform in terms to the requirements of the letter of credit. . . . [A] different situation is presented in the instant action. This is not a controversy between the buyer and seller concerning a mere breach of warranty regarding the quality of the merchandise. . . . [T]he seller has intentionally failed to ship any goods ordered by the buyer. In such a situation, where the seller's fraud has been called to the bank's attention before the drafts and documents have been presented for payment, the principle of the independence of the bank's obligation under the letter of credit should not be extended to protect the unscrupulous seller. It is true that even though the documents are forged or fraudulent, if the issuing bank has already paid the draft before receiving notice of the seller's fraud, it will be protected if it exercised reasonable diligence before making such payment. . . . However, in the instant action Schroder has received notice of Transea's active fraud before it accepted or paid the draft. The Chartered Bank, which under the allegations of the complaint stands in no better position than Transea, should not be heard to complain because Schroder is not forced to pay the draft accompanied by documents covering a transaction which it has reason to

believe is fraudulent. . . . The distinction between a breach of warranty and active fraud on the part of the seller is supported by authority and reason. As one court has stated: "Obviously, when the issuer of a letter of credit knows that a document, although correct in form, is, in point of fact, false or illegal, he cannot be called upon to recognize such a document as complying with the terms of a letter of credit." *Old Colony Trust Co. v. Lawyer's Title & Trust Co.*, 2d Cir., 297 F.152 at page 158 . . . On this motion only the complaint is before me and I am bound by its allegation that the Chartered Bank is not a holder in due course but is a mere agent for collection for the account of the seller charged with fraud. Therefore the Chartered Bank's motion to dismiss the complaint must be denied.

31 N.Y.S.2d at 633-636. Note that as set forth in *Stzejn* the fraud exception is rather narrow. The issuing bank had discovered the fraud before payment and only the fraudulent party and no innocent third party, such as a confirming bank or a negotiating bank, had relied on the letter of credit (see the last two sentences of the quotation from *Stzejn*). Because *Stzejn* was rather limited in scope, many unresolved questions relating to the fraud exception were left unanswered as we shall see shortly in the principal cases below.

2. *Sources of Law*

What is the law governing fraud in international letters of credit? As we noted earlier, the UCP is silent on the issue of fraud as the drafters of the UCP believed that fraud should be left to domestic law. The doctrine of fraud that was established by *Stzejn* has been codified in §5-109 of the Uniform Commercial Code and an extensive case law has arisen concerning the interpretation of this provision and its predecessors. Many of the fraud cases involving a U.S. party under an international letter of credit will be governed by the UCC.

For reasons that will become apparent in the discussion below, the issue of fraud usually arises in the context of the buyer-applicant of the letter of credit seeking to enjoin the issuing bank from paying against fraudulent documents submitted by the seller-beneficiary. The UCC treats the issue of fraud and enjoining letters of credit together in the following article:

§5-109. *Fraud and Forgery.*

(a) If a presentation is made that appears on its face strictly to comply with the terms and conditions of the letter of credit, but a required document is forged or materially fraudulent, or honor of the presentation would facilitate a material fraud by the beneficiary on the issuer or applicant:

(1) the issuer shall honor the presentation, if honor is demanded by (i) a nominated person who has given value in good faith and without notice of forgery or material fraud, (ii) a confirmer who has honored its confirmation in good faith, (iii) a holder in due course of a draft drawn under the letter of credit which was taken after acceptance by the issuer or nominated person, or (iv) an assignee of the issuer's or nominated person's deferred obligation that was taken for value and without notice of forgery or material fraud after the obligation was incurred by the issuer or nominated person; and

(2) the issuer, acting in good faith, may honor or dishonor the presentation in any other case.

(b) If an applicant claims that a required document is forged or materially fraudulent or that honor of the presentation would facilitate a material fraud by the beneficiary on the issuer or applicant, a court of competent jurisdiction may temporarily or permanently enjoin the issuer from honoring a presentation or grant similar relief against the issuer or other persons only if the court finds that:

(1) the relief is not prohibited under the law applicable to an accepted draft or deferred obligation incurred by the issuer;

(2) a beneficiary, issuer, or nominated person who may be adversely affected is adequately protected against loss that it may suffer because the relief is granted;

(3) all of the conditions to entitle a person to the relief under the law of this State have been met; and

(4) on the basis of the information submitted to the court, the applicant is more likely than not to succeed under its claim of forgery or material fraud and the person demanding honor does not qualify for protection under subsection (a)(1).

§5-109(a) divides cases involving fraud into two categories: Where the honor is demanded by (1) certain third parties who have given value in good faith and without notice of the fraud and (2) all other cases. In the first category, the issuing bank *must* honor the presentation even if forgery or a material fraud exists within the meaning of §5-109(a). In all other cases, the bank *may*, acting in good faith, choose to honor or dishonor. What is the purpose of making this distinction? We now turn to this issue.

3. Different Types of Innocent Parties

In fraud cases, the UCC will, if possible, impose the loss on the wrongdoer. However, that is not always possible as the wrongdoer may have disappeared or be unavailable as a defendant for other reasons. At this juncture, it may become necessary to impose the loss on an innocent party, but as between innocent parties not all are treated equally. The rationale for requiring honor in the case of certain third parties is that where there are two innocent parties subject to the fraud — the buyer-applicant and a third party who has given value in good faith — it is the buyer-applicant who has voluntarily chosen to deal with the fraudulent party (the seller-beneficiary) and who has brought the third party into contact with the fraudulent party. An illustration follows.

Illustration 4-2. A buyer enters into a sales contract with an unscrupulous seller and at the behest of the seller asks its issuing bank to open a confirmed letter of credit engaging a local bank in the seller's jurisdiction to add its confirmation. The seller submits fraudulent documents to the confirming bank, which pays the seller without notice of the fraud. The confirming bank forwards documents for reimbursement from the issuing bank, which in the meanwhile has been alerted to the fraud by the buyer-applicant.

Of the two innocent parties in our illustration, the confirming bank and the buyer-applicant, the UCC drafters decided that it is the buyer-applicant who should bear the higher risk. Under §5-109(a)(1)(ii), the issuing bank must reimburse the confirming bank and the buyer-applicant must, in turn, reimburse the issuing bank. As a result, the loss is imposed on the buyer. The buyer's remedy is to sue the seller for fraud. If the buyer recovers, then the loss is imposed on the wrongdoer, but if not, then the buyer-applicant must bear the loss.

Note that §5-109(a)(1) does not protect *all* innocent third parties who give value but only certain third parties, that is, nominated persons [§5-109(a)(1)(i)], a confirmer [§5-109(a)(1)(ii)], a holder in due course of a draft drawn under a letter of credit which was taken *after* acceptance by the issuer [§5-109(a)(1)(iii)], or an assignee of the issuer or nominated person's deferred obligation [§5-109(a)(1)(iv)]. Note that what all of these innocent third parties have in common is that they were brought into contact directly or indirectly with the wrongdoer by the applicant of the credit. Where there is an innocent third party that is not brought into contact directly or indirectly by the applicant, then that third party would *not* be protected. For example, suppose that the fraudulent seller sells or negotiates the drafts to a third-party financial institution. Even if the third party takes without notice of the fraud and pays value, this third party is not protected under §5-109(a)(1). This is because this third party voluntarily chose to deal with the seller or wrongdoer in the stream of commerce presumably in order to make a profit. In this case, the drafters of the UCC decided that the loss will stay where it falls, that is, on the third party whose only remedy is to sue the wrongdoer. However, if the third party takes up the drafts *after* the drafts were accepted by the issuer or a nominated person [§5-109(a)(1)(iii)], then that third party is protected as that party should be able to rely on the credit of solvent banks and the banks (and the third party indirectly) were brought into contact with the wrongdoer by the applicant in having the letter of credit issued by the issuing bank.

4. *Fraud Cases Not Involving Innocent Third Parties*

Under §5-109(a)(2) where honor is demanded in all other cases that do not involve third parties falling within §5-109(a)(1), the bank is protected if it chooses in good faith either to honor or dishonor. This situation arises as follows.

> *Illustration 4-3.* In a contract for the sale of goods financed by a letter of credit authorized by the buyer, the seller submits fraudulent documents to the issuing bank. Before payment, the buyer learns of the fraud and asks the bank to withhold payment. The bank may at its option honor or dishonor the demand for payment from the seller.

Note that in most cases banks will choose to honor as this is the less burdensome course of action and involves fewer risks. If the bank chooses to honor the letter of credit in the face of allegations of fraud by the buyer, the bank is entitled to receive reimbursement of the letter of credit from the buyer-applicant so long as the bank acts in good faith. The bank also has the option of dishonor but this course of action may involve considerably more risk and expense to the bank. If the bank chooses to dishonor and the seller-beneficiary then brings a lawsuit against the bank for wrongful dishonor, the bank must defend its dishonor in the litigation by proving forgery or material fraud as set forth in UCC §5-109(a). In many cases, the facts surrounding the fraud are not within the bank's knowledge so proving fraud will may be difficult and time consuming. In addition, note that as fraud is treated as an affirmative defense, the bank has the burden of proof that fraud existed and will lose the lawsuit if it cannot sustain its burden. Faced with the option of simply honoring the demand for payment and receiving reimbursement from the buyer-applicant and facing a claim of wrongful dishonor and a lawsuit, most banks will presumably choose to honor in the face of allegations of fraud.

Faced with a fraudulent seller and a bank that intends to pay on the credit, the buyer-applicant's recourse under §5-109(b) is to sue for an injunction against the bank prohibiting payment. The bank is, of course, protected against any claims of wrongful dishonor by the seller-beneficiary if it is prevented from payment by an injunction issued by a competent court. If the applicant fails to obtain an injunction and the bank pays despite allegations of fraud, the applicant will have recourse against the bank only in the rare cases where the applicant can prove that the bank did not act in good faith, that is, intended to perpetuate a fraud on the applicant.

PROBLEM 4-11

Maxwell & Associates, a car distributor based in Columbus, Ohio, enters into negotiations with Chincotti, an Italian automobile manufacturer, for rights to become the sole U.S. distributor of a new high-end sports car. Maxwell believes that the sports car will do well in its market, which encompasses most of the midwestern United States. Chincotti is in the process of reorganizing its image from a staid manufacturer of family sedans to a new-age manufacturer of sleek luxury cars. Chincotti tells Maxwell that in order to receive the exclusive rights to sell Chincotti sports cars, Maxwell must first buy a large shipment of its sedans. Maxwell believes that the sedans will face a lot of stiff competition in the U.S. market but is so keen on obtaining the rights to the sports car that it agrees to the deal and authorizes a Columbus bank to establish a letter of credit, subject to the UCP, in the amount of $15 million in favor of Chincotti for the purchase of 500 sedans. Maxwell then discovers that Chincotti has already given the exclusive U.S. rights to the sports cars to a competitor in Indiana. In the meantime, Chincotti has presented conforming documents to the Columbus bank for payment under the letter of credit. Maxwell seeks to enjoin the Columbus bank from paying on the letter of credit on the basis of fraud. In its defense, Chincotti argues:

(1) The parties' agreement to have the letter of credit governed by the UCP results in the complete exclusion of the UCC, including its fraud provision, §5-109. The UCP's silence on the issue of fraud means that in cases where the parties have opted for the UCP and excluded the UCC, the fraud defense is not available at all unless the parties also explicitly provided that UCC §5-109 applies.

(2) Even if the fraud exception applies to this case, the fraud defense to payment under the letter of credit fails for two reasons: (a) The fraud doctrine, as established in *Stzejn* and codified in the UCC, requires fraud in the letter of credit transaction and fraud in the underlying sales transaction is not sufficient unless the fraud is also manifested in the letter of credit transaction. In *Stzejn*, the seller presented fraudulent documents. Here the documents are genuine as they are for the 500 sedans and strictly conform to the requirements of the letter of credit. In cases where there is fraud in the underlying transaction that does not manifest itself in the letter of credit transaction itself, the independence principle insulates the letter of credit from the fraud defense. Maxwell's recourse is to pay the letter of credit and to sue Chincotti directly for breach of contract; and (b) Chincotti's actions did not amount to fraud. This was a simple breach of contract.

How should these issues be decided? See UCC §5-109 at pp. 286-287 *supra* and *Mid-America Tire* below.

Mid-America Tire, Inc. v. PTZ Trading Ltd.
Supreme Court of Ohio, 2002
95 Ohio St. 3d 367, 768 N.E.2d 619

RESNICK, J.

PARTIES AND PARTICIPANTS

Given the multilateral nature of the negotiations and arrangements in this case, it is beneficial to provide a working list of the various parties and key participants and their relationships to one another and the transactions at hand.

The American parties and participants are as follows:

(1) Plaintiff-appellant and cross-appellee, Mid-America Tire, Inc. ("Mid-America"), is an Ohio corporation doing business as a tire wholesaler. Mid-America provided the financing for the purchase of the tires in this case and was the named applicant by whose order and for whose account the LC was issued.

(2) Arthur Hine is the president of Mid-America and signatory to the LC application.

(3) Plaintiff-appellant and cross-appellee, Jenco Marketing, Inc. ("Jenco"), is a Tennessee corporation doing business as a tire wholesaler. Jenco formed a joint venture with Mid-America to purchase the tires at issue.

(4) Fred Alvin "F.A." Jenkins is the owner of Jenco and also acted as Mid-America's agent in the underlying negotiations.

(5) Paul Chappell is an independent tire broker who resides in Irvine, California. Chappell works as an independent contractor for Tire Network, Inc., a company owned by his wife, and acted throughout most of the negotiations as an agent for Jenco.

(6) First National Bank of Chicago ("First National"), on behalf of NBD Bank Michigan, is the issuer of the LC in this case. First National was a defendant below, but is not a party to this appeal.

The European parties and participants are as follows:

(1) Defendant-appellee and cross-appellant, PTZ Trading Ltd. ("PTZ"), is an offshore import and export company established in Guernsey, Channel Islands. PTZ is the seller in the underlying transaction and the beneficiary under the LC.

(2) Gary Corby is an independent tire broker operating as Corby International, a trading name of Corby Tyres (Wholesale) Ltd., in Wales, United Kingdom. Corby was the initiator of the underlying negotiations. The trial court's findings with regard to Corby's status as PTZ's agent form the subject of PTZ's cross-appeal.

(3) John Evans is the owner of Transcontinental Tyre Company located in Wolverhampton, England, and PTZ's admitted agent in the underlying negotiations.

(4) Aloysius Sievers is a German tire broker to whom PTZ owed money from a previous transaction unconnected to this case. Sievers, also an admitted agent for PTZ, procured and shipped the subject tires on behalf of PTZ, and signed and presented the draft for payment under the LC.

(5) Patrick Doumerc is the son of the proprietor of Doumerc SA, a French company that is authorized to sell Michelin overstock or surplus tires worldwide.

Doumerc is the person from whom Sievers procured the mud and snow tires for sale to Jenco and Mid-America.

(6) Barclays Bank PLC in St. Peter Port, Guernsey, is the bank to which Sievers presented the invoice and shipping documents for payment under the supporting LC. Barclays Bank was a defendant below, but is not a party to this appeal.

EVENTS LEADING TO THE ISSUANCE OF THE LC

In October 1998, Corby approached Evans about obtaining large quantities of Michelin winter tires. Evans contacted Sievers, to whom PTZ owed money. Evans knew that Sievers had a relationship with a sole distributor of Michelin surplus tires out of France. Eventually, an arrangement was worked out under which Sievers would buy the tires from Doumerc's warehouse in France and Evans would sell them on behalf of PTZ through Corby to an American purchaser.

Meanwhile, Corby contacted Chappell in California and asked whether he was interested in importing Michelin tires on the gray market for sale in the United States. "Gray imports" are tires that are imported without the knowledge or approval of a manufacturer into a market that the manufacturer serves, at a greatly reduced price. Corby told Chappell that he had a large client who negotiated an arrangement directly with Michelin to handle all of its overstock blem tires from France and who could offer 50,000 to 70,000 Michelin tires per quarter at 40 to 60 percent below the United States market price on an exclusive and ongoing basis. Chappell contacted Jenkins in Tennessee, who called Hine in Ohio, and it was arranged that Jenco and Mid-America would pursue the deal through Chappell.

On October 28, 1998, Corby faxed Chappell a list of Michelin mud and snow tires that were immediately available for shipment and Chappell forwarded the list to Jenkins. The list was arranged in columns for quantity, size, pattern, and other designations applicable to the European market with which Chappell and Jenkins were unfamiliar. In particular, many of the tires on the list bore the designation "DA/2C." Chappell and Jenkins understood that DA meant "defective appearance," a European marking for a blem, but they were not familiar with the "/2C" portion of the designation. When they asked for clarification, Corby told Chappell that "DA/2C" means the same thing as "DA," but since all of the listed tires are not warehoused at a single location, "/2C" is used merely to indicate that those blemished tires are located in a different warehouse.

Chappell also asked Corby whether he could procure and offer summer or "highway" tires, along with the winter tires. Chappell, Jenkins, and Hine had no interest in purchasing strictly snow tires, as it was already too late in the season to market them profitably. However, they would have an interest in buying both winter and highway tires and marketing them together as a package deal.

Corby told Chappell that 50,000 to 70,000 highway tires would be made available on a quarterly basis at 40 to 60 percent below the United States market price. However, when Chappell received another list of available tires from Corby on November 11, 1998, he complained to Corby that this list contained no summer tires and nowhere near 50,000 units. Corby responded that Michelin was anxious to get rid of these tires first, as the market for snow tires in Europe was coming to a close, that a list of summer highway tires would be made available over the next few weeks, and that Chappell and appellants would not have an oppor-tunity to procure the highway tires unless they first agreed to purchase the snow tires. Corby explained that Michelin does not list available summer tires in the mid-month of a quarter. Instead, it waits for these tires to accumulate in a ware-house and then puts out the list at the end of the month. Thus, a list of summer tires would be available over the next few weeks.

In a transmission dated November 13, 1998, Corby wrote to Chappell:

"The situation is as I explained yesterday, there are no summer tyres available at all but, if, and a very big if, this deal goes ahead we will get all surplus stocks at the end [of] each qu[arter] from now on, but if this deal does not go, then I know we can kiss any future offers good buy [sic]."

On November 20, 1998, Corby faxed Chappell a list of summer tires available for immediate shipment, but the listed units were not priced, were composed of many small "odd ball sizes" unmarketable in the United States, and did not approach the 50- to 70,000-range in aggregate quantity. In his cover letter, Corby assured Chappell that "I have of course been in contact with Michelin regarding the list of summer tyres" and "they have confirmed that in the next three/four weeks we have exclusive to us the new list of Michelin summer tyres, quantity unknown as yet, but they believe to be anything from 50,000/70,000 tyres, which would not be too bad for Jan sales." The letter also stated that Michelin was offering the tires at "the price of $1.50 per tyre more than the M & S tyres . . . based on taking the whole lot."

On November 23, 1998, Corby faxed the following letter to Jenkins:

"Subject: Michelin Tyre Programme.

"Dear F.A.

"I would just like to confirm our current position with the Off-Shore market-ing company that have been authorised to sell all Michelin factory 'Over Stock' tyres. That is, from now on the tyres will only be offered for sale to us through PTZ Trading Ltd., these tyres will come available every two/three months which I have been informed by my contact the next large consignment (not including the current stock of winter/summer tyres) will be in the next three/four weeks time of around 50,000/70,000 tyres.

"If our business with the winter tyres goes well, then I see this as [an] ex-tremely excellent opportunity to tap into large consignments of tyres direct from the factory on a regular long term basis.

"Just to confirm once again, I have been assured by PTZ Trading who are acting on behalf of the factory that we will have exclusivity to all tyres that come available from now on."

On December 1, 1998, Evans faxed a letter and "pro forma invoice" (an invoice that sets out in rough terms what the eventual invoice will look like) to Jenkins. The letter stated, "We understand from Gary Corby that you are now about to open the Letter of Credit for the Michelin M&S Tyres."

However, Chappell and Jenkins were hesitant to have Hine proceed with the financing for the winter tires because they had not yet received concrete informa-tion as to the cost and availability of the initial 50,000 to 70,000 summer tires. As Chappell and Jenkins held out for the list of summer tires, Corby and Evans pressed for the LC. While continually assuring Chappell and Jenkins that large stocks of Michelin summer tires will be made available in a short time, Corby and Evans became increasingly insistent about conditioning the offer of summer tires upon the issuance of an acceptable LC in favor of PTZ for the winter tires.

From early December 1998, through late January 1999, Corby made repeated, often daily, telephone calls to Chappell insisting that Jenkins confirm the issuance of the LC or forfeit the deal entirely. During this time, Corby also sent a number of faxes to Chappell, each one proclaiming that without confirmation of the LC by the end of the day, the offer for the winter tires would be withdrawn and there would be no future offers for winter or summer tires.

In addition, Evans faxed two messages to Jenkins on January 7, 1999. In the first, Evans wrote:

"There are large stocks of Michelin summer pattern tyres being made available within the next 7/10 days and we will be pleased to offer these to you when an acceptable Letter of Credit is received for the winter pattern tyres. We will be very happy to work with you on Michelin tyres on a long term basis and give you first option on offers.

"May we once again stress the urgency of letting us have the Letter of Credit for the Michelin winter tyres so that we can commence business on a long term basis."

In the second message, Evans informed Jenkins:

"Further to our fax of today we understand that you would like clarification on future offers made by PTZ Trading Ltd. of Michelin tyres.

"As we have already indicated we wish to commence a long term business relationship with Jenco Marketing Ltd. [Sic]. We assure you that we will not offer any Michelin tyres that we obtain to any other party in the United States of America provided Jenco Marketing Inc. agree[s] to purchase in a reasonable time."

THE ISSUANCE OF THE LC

By the end of January 1999, Jenkins and Hine were convinced that they had to open the LC for the winter tires as a show of good faith towards the quarterly acquisition of summer tires and that, upon doing so, PTZ would honor its end of the bargain.

Effective February 1, 1999, and expiring in Guernsey, Channel Islands, on April 2, 1999, First National issued an irrevocable credit at Hine's request in favor of PTZ and for the account of Mid-America in the amount of $517,260.33. The LC provided, among other things:

"COVERING SHIPMENT OF:

"14,851 MICHELIN TYPES AT USD 34.83 PER TIRE IN ACCORDANCE WITH SELLER'S PROFORMA INVOICE 927-98 DATED 11-19-98

"SHIPPING TERMS: EXWORKS ANY EUROPEAN LOCATION . . .

"THE CREDIT IS SUBJECT TO THE UNIFORM CUSTOMS AND PRACTICE FOR DOCUMENTARY CREDITS (1993 REVISION), INTERNATIONAL CHAMBER OF COMMERCE-PUBLICATION 500."

EVENTS FOLLOWING THE ISSUANCE OF THE LC

Over the next month, Corby and Evans pushed for shipping arrangements under the supporting LC for the winter tires, while Chappell and Jenkins continued to insist on a conforming price list for the summer tires. As the final LC shipping date approached, and several nonconforming lists of summer tires emerged, the negotiations grew increasingly volatile until they were hostilely terminated.

A week after the issuance of the LC, Chappell wrote to Corby, "Without the list and pricing [for the summer tires], we are at a standstill with the clock ticking on the winters. Please make every effort to send list during your workday, so we can compile our list for combined sales of both winter and summer units." Corby then faxed Chappell a list of summer tires but, as before, this list contained no prices and fell considerably short of 50,000 units. When Chappell complained, Corby sent another list, which he noted to be six out of 15 sheets of an "original list from Michelin." The other nine sheets, however, were never sent. In any event, this list once again failed to contain the promised quantities of tires, and a considerable number of the listed units were snow tires. Although this list did set forth unit prices, those prices were represented in French francs, and when the French francs were converted into United States dollars, it became apparent that the prices for these units were equal to or in excess of the maximum market prices for a like product in the United States.

On the morning of February 17, 1999, Evans telephoned Jenkins to inform him that no price list for summer tires would be sent until Barclays Bank received the LC for the winter tires. This caught Jenkins by surprise, as the LC had been in place since the first of the month and all information pertaining thereto had previously been sent to Evans, but Jenkins nevertheless faxed Evans the LC confirmation number. Throughout that day, Evans made repeated requests for Jenkins to provide him with shipping instructions and orders to release the winter tires. Jenkins responded with several letters that he faxed to Evans on February 17. In these letters, Jenkins informed Evans that he would not authorize the shipment of any winter tires in the absence of a conforming list of summer tires, that any attempt by Evans to ship the winter tires without Jenkins's written consent would be met with legal action, and that the deal would be voided and the LC recalled unless a complete list of competitively priced summer tires arrived in Jenkins's office by February 19.

On February 19, 1999, Evans faxed the following message to Jenkins:

"We appreciate your feeling of frustration at the delay in giving you the price for the Summer Tyres but assure you it is only in your best interests to obtain the most favourable prices. . . .

"Further urgent negotiations are due to take place with Michelin on Monday February 22nd 1999 to see if we can arrive at an acceptable packaged price but of course the final desission [sic] is yours.

"In the meantime in the interests of all concerned please do not give a specific time for completion if you want us to obtain the most favourable price."

On February 23, 1999, Corby faxed Chappell another list of summer tires, but this list was illegible in places and irreconcilable with the previous list. Chappell complained and Corby sent another list the following day. However, once again, this list fell well short of 50,000 units, contained many European sizes not used in the United States and various tires not manufactured by Michelin, and stated prices that were often higher than the cost of purchasing the tires one at a time from most United States dealers. The list also provided that, in addition to the stated prices, appellants were required to pay all shipping, handling, duty, and freight charges. Moreover, Jenkins was now informed that he could no longer pick and choose from among the listed tires, but instead must purchase the entire lot or none at all.

On March 1, 1999, Jenkins wrote to Evans, "We are with drawing [sic] our offer effective immediately to purchase the snow package, as PTZ has failed to meet their agreed commitment on the Michelin summer tire offer." Jenkins stated that the listed prices for the tires are "not competitive" and "TOTALLY UNACCEPTABLE," and that "[w]e have gone from a reported 50,000 tires to a total offer of about 12,000 tires of which approximately 2,500 of those are TRX tires not sold in this country."

Between March 1 and March 5, 1999, Chappell and Jenkins discovered that it was Doumerc, not PTZ, who all along had the direct and exclusive relationship with Michelin to sell all of its overstock and blem tires. They also discovered that Corby had misrepresented the "DA/2C" designation, which attached to many of the tires on the summer lists as well as on the original winter list. Rather than indicating the warehousing location for those tires, "/2C" actually meant that the Department of Transportation serial numbers had been buffed off those units, rendering them illegal for import or sale in the United States.

During this time, Jenkins informed Evans that he would notify the United States Customs Service if the DA/2C tires were shipped, and Evans confirmed that he would not ship those tires to the United States. Also, Chappell informed Doumerc of the entire course of events, and Doumerc agreed not to ship the tires until Chappell and Jenkins had the opportunity to come to France, inspect the tires, and resolve the situation.

Chappell and Jenkins made arrangements to fly to France, but when they called Doumerc on March 11, Sievers answered the phone. They explained the entire matter to Sievers and offered to extend the LC expiration date in order to allow for a peaceful resolution. Sievers rejected the offer, however, stating that the winter tires belonged to him, not Doumerc, that he did not care what Doumerc had agreed to, and that "I have a letter of credit and I am shipping the tires."

The following day, Mid-America instituted the present action to enjoin payment under the LC. The complaint was later amended to add Jenco as a plaintiff. The trial court granted a temporary restraining order on March 16, 1999, and a preliminary injunction on April 8, 1999.

On July 14 and 15, 1999, a trial was held on appellants' motion for a permanent injunction. In a final judgment entry dated October 8, 1999, the trial court granted a permanent injunction against honor or presentment under the LC pursuant to R.C. 1305.08(B).[3] In its separate findings of fact and conclusions of law, the trial court found that the documents presented to Barclays Bank on behalf of PTZ appeared on their face to be in strict compliance with the terms and conditions of the LC. However, the court also found by clear and convincing evidence that PTZ, acting through Evans and Corby, fraudulently induced appellants to open the LC, and that such fraud was sufficient to vitiate the LC. In this regard, the trial court was "satisfied that fraud in the inducement of the issuance of

---

3. Ohio Revised Code Chapter 1305 is Ohio's version of Article 5 of the Uniform Commercial Code. R.C. 1305.08(B) provides:

> If an applicant claims that a required document is forged or materially fraudulent or that honor of the presentation would facilitate a material fraud by the beneficiary on the issuer or applicant, a court of competent jurisdiction may temporarily or permanently enjoin the issuer from honoring a presentation.

This provision is substantially equivalent to UCC §5-109(b). — EDS.

a letter of credit is grounds for a court to grant injunctive relief against the payment of such letter of credit to the beneficiary who perpetrated such fraud."

In a split decision, the court of appeals reversed the judgment of the trial court. In so doing, the majority noted that the LC in this case is expressly made subject to the Uniform Customs and Practice for Documentary Credits (Rev. 1993), International Chamber of Commerce, Publication No. 500 ("UCP"). Thus, in this case the UCP's terms replace those of R.C. 1305(B) with respect to the issues of whether and under what circumstances honor may be enjoined on the basis of fraud. The majority then found that the UCP embodies the "independence principle," under which the issuing bank's duty to honor a conforming presentment is independent of the underlying transaction. Because the UCP is silent as to any fraud exception to the independence principle, the majority concluded that the UCP necessarily precludes the enjoinment of LC honor on the basis of fraud in the underlying transaction.

The appeals court also examined cases decided under former UCC 5-114, which provided an exception to the independence principle where "there is fraud in the transaction." Based on these decisions, the court of appeals recognized that LC honor may be enjoined by a court when the beneficiary commits a fraud so extensive as to vitiate the entire transaction. However, the majority felt that this exception should be narrowly construed to require that the beneficiary's fraud occur in the credit transaction. Thus, the court decided that injunctive relief may be granted on the basis of a beneficiary's presentation of forged or fraudulent documents under an LC, but that such relief may not be granted on the basis of the beneficiary's commission of fraud solely in the underlying sales transaction. After finding that the invoice and shipping documents presented to Barclays Bank on behalf of PTZ conformed strictly to the LC in this case, the majority held the exception inapplicable and injunctive relief inappropriate.

ISSUES FOR REVIEW

The issue generally presented by both appeals is whether the trial court abused its discretion in granting a permanent injunction against LC honor under the facts and circumstances of this case.

The specific questions that arise under the appeal brought by Mid-America and Jenco are as follows:

1. Is the absence of an adequate legal remedy one of the prerequisites for injunctive relief under R.C. 1305.08(B)?

2. With regard to the availability and scope of a fraud exception to the independence principle, is the LC in this case governed by the UCP or R.C. 1305.08(B)?

3. Under the governing law, is there any fraud exception to the independence principle beyond the situation involving the beneficiary's presentation of forged or fraudulent documents? In particular, does the governing law recognize an exception for fraud in the inducement of the underlying contract and the supporting LC?

4. Are the trial court's factual findings sufficient to support the application of a recognized exception to the independence principle?

INADEQUATE LEGAL REMEDY

PTZ argues, and the court of appeals held, that appellants should be denied injunctive relief under R.C. 1305.08(B) because they have an adequate remedy at law. It is well settled that an injunction will not issue where there is an adequate remedy at law.

In the present case, an action to recover damages for fraud would not be an adequate legal remedy because it would not be as prompt, efficient, and practical as the injunction issued by the trial court, and would not provide appellants with certain and complete relief in a single action. The pursuit of such a remedy would likely entail a multiplicity of suits against a number of defendants in several jurisdictions. The damages that appellants might seek to recover in an action for fraud would be difficult to estimate because of the near impossibility of determining the quantity of winter and summer tires that could or would have been seasonably marketed together and separately, the quantity of the "DA/2C" and other tires not marketable in the United States that could have been sold overseas, and the appropriate market conditions, cost/price differential, and quantity of offered or promised units. While it may be true, as PTZ argues, that appellants accepted some risk of pursuing damages in another nation's courts, it cannot be found that appellants assumed the risk of having to pursue an inadequate legal remedy.

GOVERNING LAW

R.C. Chapter 1305 is Ohio's version of Article 5 of the Uniform Commercial Code ("UCC"). It was enacted in its current form, effective July 1, 1998, to reflect the 1995 revision of Article 5, and is applicable to any LC that is issued on or after its effective date.

The parties in this case have specifically adopted the UCP as applicable to the present undertaking. The question that naturally arises from such an incorporation is whether and to what extent R.C. Chapter 1305 will continue to apply to the undertaking. In other words, when a particular LC states that it is subject to the UCP, what is the resulting relationship between the UCP and R.C. Chapter 1305 with regard to that transaction?

The court of appeals took the approach that the entirety of R.C. Chapter 1305 is displaced whenever the UCP is incorporated into a particular transaction.

This is not a situation where one complete set of rules is substituted for another. The scope of the UCP is basically different from that of Article 5. Because of their different scope, Article 5 [of the UCC] covers some important areas not covered by the UCP, and the UCP covers some important areas not covered by Article 5. Each of these bodies of rules will apply to govern the undertaking in their respective areas of coverage, and both will apply concurrently in the event of any overlapping consistent provisions. It is only when the UCP and R.C. Chapter 1305 contain overlapping inconsistent provisions on the same issue or subject that the UCP's terms will displace those of R.C. Chapter 1305.

Thus, the fact that the credit in this case was expressly made subject to the UCP is not dispositive. Instead, the determinative issue is whether a direct conflict exists between the UCP and R.C. Chapter 1305 as to the availability of injunctive relief against honor where fraud is claimed.

The court of appeals found essentially that the UCP's silence on the issue of fraud precludes the applicant from obtaining relief under R.C. 1305.08(B). We disagree.

In adopting the UCP, "the International Chamber of Commerce undertook to fill in operational details for documentary letter of credit transactions by stating a consensus view of the customs and practice for documentary credits." Because "the UCP 'is by definition a recording of practice rather than a statement of legal rules,' [it] does not purport to offer rules which govern the issuance of an injunction against honor of a draft." Thus, the UCP's silence on the issue of fraud "should not be construed as *preventing* relief under the 'fraud in the transaction' doctrine, where applicable law permits it."

In fact, the overwhelming weight of authority is to the effect that Article 5's fraud exception continues to apply in credit transactions made subject to the UCP. These courts hold, in one form or another, that the UCP's failure to include a rule governing injunctive relief for fraud does not prevent the applicant from obtaining such relief under Article 5. Stated variously, these courts recognize that there is no inherent conflict between the UCP's statement of the independence principle and Article 5's remedy against honor where fraud is charged. Instead, this is merely a situation where Article 5 covers a subject not covered by the UCP.

PTZ concedes that these cases were correctly decided under former UCP Publication No. 400 (1983), which was silent on the issue of fraud. According to PTZ, however, "UCP 500 art. 3, which controls this action, is no longer silent on the fraud exception." Instead, PTZ argues that the last sentence in Article 3 of UCP 500, which did not appear in UCP 400, "specifically speaks to the fraud exception, [and provides that] a fraud claim may not be interposed to bar the collection of [an] L/C." In fact, relying on Documentary Credits, UCP 500 & 400 Compared, International Chamber of Commerce Publication No. 511 (1993), PTZ contends that Article 3 was amended in 1993 for the express purpose of breaking the UCP's long-standing silence on the issue of fraud in order to counteract the effect of the foregoing decisions.

[T]he official comments to UCP [500] do not support the notion that Article 3 has now addressed the issue of fraud. The word "fraud" does not even appear in the commentary quoted by PTZ. To the contrary, the Working Group states specifically that the new text of Article 3 operates to deter "the Applicant's demand that payment should be stopped because of the Beneficiary's *breach of his contractual obligations* to the Applicant." (Emphasis added.) Reporting further, the Working Group explains, "This new language in UCP 500 Article 3 clarifies that neither the Beneficiary nor the Applicant can avail himself of any underlying *contractual relationship*." (Emphasis added.)

The UCP has been amended approximately every ten years since 1962. If the current version had finally broken the UCP's longstanding silence on the issue of fraud, one would expect at least a mention of that fact somewhere in the amendatory text or commentary.

We hold, therefore, that when a letter of credit expressly incorporates the terms of the UCP, but the UCP does not contain any rule covering the issue in controversy, the UCP will not replace the relevant provisions of R.C. Chapter 1305.

Since the UCP does not contain any rule addressing the issue of injunctive relief where fraud occurs in either the credit documents or the underlying transaction, R.C. 1305.08(B) remains applicable in credit transactions made subject to the UCP.

Accordingly, the rights and obligations of the parties in this case are governed by R.C. 1305.08(B), and the judgment of the court of appeals is reversed as to this issue.

ESTABLISHING FRAUD UNDER R.C. 1305.08(B)

Having determined the applicability of R.C. 1305.08(B), we must now consider its boundaries. In this regard, we have been asked to decide whether an issuer may be enjoined from honoring a presentation on the basis of beneficiary's fraud in the underlying transaction and to characterize the fraudulent activity justifying such relief.

FRAUD IN THE UNDERLYING TRANSACTION

May the issuer be enjoined from honoring a presentation under R.C. 1305.08(B) on the basis of the beneficiary's fraudulent activity in the underlying transaction? The short answer is yes, since R.C. 1305.08(B) authorizes injunctive relief where "honor of the presentation would facilitate a material fraud by the beneficiary on the . . . applicant." To fully appreciate the import of this language, however, it is necessary to review some of the history leading to its adoption.

Before the independence principle was ever codified, its parameters were set in the seminal case of *Sztejn v. J. Henry Schroder Banking Corp.* In that case, the applicant-buyer contracted to purchase a quantity of bristles from the beneficiary-seller, but the seller shipped 50 crates of cow hair and other rubbish. The court concluded that these facts, if established, could support an injunction against honor. In so doing, the court explained that the independence principle applies "in cases concerning alleged breaches of warranty," but does not extend to a case "involving an intentional fraud on the part of the seller." In other words, the fraud defense actually " 'marks the limit of the generally accepted principle that a letter of credit is independent of whatever obligation it secures.' "

As originally drafted in 1955, UCC 5-114 provided that a court of appropriate jurisdiction may enjoin honor only if there was forgery or fraud in a required document. In 1957, the drafters added language providing that the court may enjoin such honor where "a required document . . . is forged or fraudulent *or there is fraud in the transaction*." (Emphasis added.) UCC 5-114(2). This rule represents a codification of the *Sztejn* case.

One of the major disputes surrounding former UCC 5-114(2) centered on whether the "transaction" meant only the credit transaction per se or encompassed the underlying transaction as well.

R.C. 1305.08(B) (UCC 5-109[b]) now provides that a court of competent jurisdiction may grant injunctive relief where "honor of the presentation would facilitate a material fraud by the beneficiary on the issuer or applicant." In so doing, R.C. 1305.08(B) refocuses the court's attention away from the particular transaction in which the fraud occurred and toward the level of fraud committed.

It clarifies that the beneficiary's fraud in either transaction will suffice to enjoin the issuer from honoring a presentation, provided the fraud is material.

We hold, therefore, that material fraud committed by the beneficiary in either the letter of credit transaction or the underlying sales transaction is sufficient to warrant injunctive relief under R.C. 1305.08(B). Accordingly, the judgment of the court of appeals is reversed as to this issue.

MEASURE OF FRAUD

Another controversy that surrounded the "fraud in the transaction" language of UCC 5-114(2) involved the degree or quantity of fraud necessary to warrant injunctive relief. However, UCC 5-109(b) (R.C. 1305.08(B)) clarifies that only "material fraud" by the beneficiary will justify an injunction against honor.

As another court adhering to this standard explained, the applicant must show that the letter of credit was, in fact, being used by the beneficiary "as a vehicle for fraud," or in other words, that the beneficiary's conduct, if rewarded by payment, "would deprive the [applicant] of any benefit of the underlying contract and . . . transform the letter of credit . . . into a means for perpetrating fraud." *GATX Leasing Corp.*, 657 S.W.2d at 183.

Thus, we hold that "material fraud" under R.C. 1305.08(B) means fraud that has so vitiated the entire transaction that the legitimate purposes of the independence of the issuer's obligation can no longer be served.

The court of appeals did establish its so-called "vitiation exception," but construed the exception so narrowly as to preclude relief where the beneficiary's fraudulent conduct occurs solely in the underlying transaction. As a consequence, the court of appeals declined to address the issues of agency and fraud in the underlying contract, holding instead that the trial court should not even have taken evidence on these issues.

Accordingly, the judgment of the court of appeals is reversed on this issue as well.

PTZ'S ACTIONS

The trial court found the following facts to have been established by clear and convincing evidence:

"6. Gary Corby represented to F.A. Jenkins that PTZ Trading, Ltd. was in fact the sole distributor for surplus Michelin tires and that there was a direct relationship between PTZ Trading, Ltd. [a]nd Michelin. Corby further represented to Jenkins that there would be 50,000 to 70,000 summer tires available to Jenco per quarter at a price 40 to 60 percent below the U.S. market price within weeks of Jenco showing good faith by purchasing in excess of five hundred thousand dollars worth of mud and snow tires currently offered by PTZ Trading, Ltd.

"7. The Court further finds that John Evans, as agent for PTZ Trading, Ltd., was aware that Corby was making such representations to Jenco and that such representations were false. Mr. John Evans, as an agent for PTZ, knew that Jenco considered the purchase of the summer tires to be necessary in order to make the winter snow and mud tires saleable in the U.S. market. Mr. Evans did nothing to correct Mr. Corby's misrepresentations. Mr. Evans affirmed the misrepresentations and attempted to buttress them in correspondence with Jenco.

"8. Mr. Evans conveyed this information to Mr. Sievers who also acknowledged that he understood that the purchase of the summer tires by Jenco was critical to the conclusion of the sale of the mud and snow tires and without which the winter tire sale would not occur.

"9. John Evans and Aloysius Sievers also knew that a large portion of the mud and snow tires they were attempting to sell were not capable of being imported into the United States or sol[d] here because the United States Department of Transportation identification number had been 'buffed' off of such tires. Both Sievers and Evans knew that Jenco and Mid America Tire intended to sell the snow tires in the United States, but neither advised Jenco or Mid America Tire of the existence of the 'buffed' tires.

"10. Prior to the issuance of the letter of credit, John Evans knew Mid America Tire, Inc. and Jenco were operating under intentionally false and inaccurate representations made by Corby and reinforced by John Evans. . . .

"12. The Court finds, specifically, that the representation that PTZ had a direct relationship with Michelin Tire, the representation that PTZ was the exclusive distributor for surplus Michelin Tires, the representation that a substantial quantity of between fifty and seventy thousand tires would be available quarterly on an exclusive basis to Jenco and Mid America Tire, Inc. at 40 to 60 percent of the U.S. market price were all material statements inducing Plaintiffs to issue the underlying letter of credit and were in fact false and made with knowledge of their falsity."

Whether or not this court would have made the same factual findings is irrelevant. This court does not resolve questions of fact. We are constrained to accept these facts as established because the trial court sat as factfinder in this case and because the record contains ample evidence to support them.

Given these facts, we are compelled to conclude that PTZ's actions in this case are sufficiently egregious to warrant injunctive relief under the "material fraud" standard of R.C. 1305.08(B). The trial court's findings demonstrate that PTZ sought to unload a large quantity of surplus winter tires on appellants by promising a large number of bargain-priced summer tires, without which the winter tires would be virtually worthless to appellants. Keenly aware that appellants would not agree to purchase the winter tires without the summer tires, PTZ made, participated in, and/or failed to correct a series of materially fraudulent promises and representations regarding the more lucrative summer tires in order to induce appellants to commit to purchasing the winter tires and to open an LC in PTZ's favor to secure payment. Dangling the prospect of the summer tires just beyond appellants' reach, PTZ sought first the issuance of the LC, and then shipping instructions, in an effort to cash in on the winter deal before appellants could discover the truth about the "DA/2C" tires and PTZ's lack of ability and intention ever to provide summer tires at the price and quantity represented. Indeed, when appellants learned of PTZ's fraud after opening the LC, and PTZ was no longer able to stall for shipping instructions with nonconforming lists of summer tires, Sievers proclaimed, "I have a letter of credit and I am shipping the tires."

Under these facts, it can truly be said that the LC in this case was being used by PTZ as a vehicle for fraud and that PTZ's actions effectively deprived appellants of any benefit in the underlying arrangement. In this sense, PTZ's conduct is comparable to the shipment of cow hair in *Sztejn*, [and] the shipment of old, ripped, and mildewed boxing gloves in [*United Bank Ltd. v. Cambridge Sporting Goods Corp.*, 41 N.Y.2d. 254, 392 N.Y.S.2d 265, 360 N.E.2d 943 (1976)].

PTZ's demand for payment under these circumstances has absolutely no basis in fact, and it would be pointless and unjust to permit PTZ to draw the money. PTZ's conduct has so vitiated the entire transaction that the only purpose served by invoking the independence principle in this case would be to transform the LC into a fraudulent seller's Holy Grail, which once obtained would provide cover for fraudulent business practices in the name of commercial expedience. Accordingly, we reverse the court of appeals' judgment as it bears on this issue.

Based on all of the foregoing, the judgment of the court of appeals is hereby reversed, and the permanent injunction as granted by the trial court is reinstated.

NOTES AND QUESTIONS

1. As the Ohio Supreme Court noted, a prior version of UCC §5-109 — the former §5-114 — referred to "fraud in the transaction" giving rise to a long debate on whether the "transaction" was limited to the letter of credit transaction or also encompassed the underlying sales transaction. *American Bell International, Inc. v. Islamic Republic of Iran*, 474 F. Supp. 420 (S.D.N.Y. 1979), which we include in the materials on standby letters of credit in the following section, gives an indication of the many authorities arrayed on both sides of this issue under former §5-114. Proponents of either view could point to *Stzejn* for support as there was fraud in both transactions in that case: The seller committed fraud in the letter of credit transaction by submitting forged documents to the bank and also committed fraud in the sales contract by shipping worthless merchandise and rubbish instead of the contracted-for goods. Note that if the "transaction" referred only to the letter of credit transaction, then it would appear that the UCC codification of fraud as a defense to payment under the credit is unnecessary as fraud is an equitable defense that should have been available to the issuing bank in any event even in the absence of codification in the Uniform Commercial Code. Moreover, a narrow fraud doctrine that is limited to fraud in the letter of credit transaction would not constitute an exception to the independence principle. Can you see why?

2. What clarification does UCC §5-109 provide on whether fraud must be in the letter of credit or underlying sales transaction?

3. *Mid-America Tire* also, in our view, correctly states the relationship between the UCP and the UCC. Where the parties have opted for the UCP, the UCC may still apply on issues where the UCP is silent. Fraud is one major area where the UCP is silent and thus the parties must look to another source of substantive law, but it is not the only issue that is not covered by the UCP. The Ohio Supreme Court appears to have assumed that Ohio law would govern these other issues as well but that may not always be the case. Can you see why? If you were advising a U.S. buyer on how to ensure that the UCC would govern in all areas in which the UCP is silent, what measures would you suggest?

5.   Enjoining the Standby Letter of Credit

We turn now to the standby letter of credit. As most of the U.S. cases involving standby letters of credit occur in the context of an attempt to enjoin payment under the credit based on fraud under UCC §5-109 (and its predecessor), we treat the standby letter along with the materials that we have already introduced on these topics.

A.   THE STANDBY LETTER OF CREDIT

Unlike the commercial letter of credit, which is usually a method used by the buyer to pay the seller under a contract for the sale of goods, the standby letter of credit is generally used to secure the obligation by the seller to perform the sales contract for the benefit of the buyer. In the cases that we examine below, the sales contract is typically a long-term contract for equipment and consulting services. As the buyer is relying on the seller to perform a contract that will take several years to complete, the buyer may feel that it is in a vulnerable position if the seller is unable to complete the contract. Not only has the buyer lost a great deal of time in relying on the seller and now must find a substitute seller but the subject matter of the contract may involve an essential service or product that the buyer needs urgently. In order to protect itself from the risk of nonperformance by the seller, the buyer requires the following arrangement to secure performance: The seller must establish a standby letter of credit in favor of the buyer that is payable upon the submission of a pro forma declaration by the buyer that the seller has failed to perform the contract. In some cases, the buyer will also obtain an obligation from its own bank to pay upon presentation of documents. The buyer's bank stands in a position analogous to that of a confirming bank in a documentary letter of credit. Once the buyer's bank pays the buyer, the bank then forwards the documents to the seller's bank for payment under the standby letter of credit. To distinguish the obligation of the

FIGURE 4-1

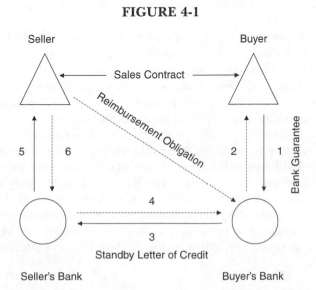

buyer's bank from that of the standby letter of credit, we refer to the commitment of the buyer's bank as a bank guarantee.

Payment under the standby letter of credit would occur as follows:

(1) Buyer submits a pro forma declaration and a demand for payment (such as a sight draft) to Buyer's Bank;
(2) Buyer's Bank pays Buyer upon the Bank Guarantee;
(3) Buyer's Bank forwards the documents and a demand for reimbursement to Seller's bank;
(4) Seller's Bank reimburses Buyer's Bank under the Standby Letter of Credit;
(5) Seller's Bank forwards the documents to Seller;
(6) Seller reimburses Seller's Bank.

Note that where the seller has agreed to open a standby letter of credit that is confirmed by a local bank guarantee, the primary reimbursement obligation exists between the seller and the buyer's bank. If for some reason the buyer's bank decided to submit the documents directly to the seller, the seller would be obligated to reimburse the buyer's bank on the bank guarantee.

Compare payment under the commercial letter of credit on p. 73 *supra*, where the payment obligations run in the reverse direction. There are several other notable differences between the standby letter of credit and the commercial letter of credit.

First, while the commercial letter of credit is payable upon performance of the sales contract, the standby letter is payable upon some nonperformance. For this reason, the standby letter has been called the "psychological opposite" of the commercial credit. *See* Henry Harfield, *The Increasing Domestic Use of the Letter of Credit*, 4 U.C.C. L.J. 251, 258 (1972). Whereas the applicant-buyer of the commercial letter of credit wishes to see the credit paid as this would represent success of the transaction, the applicant-seller of the standby letter does not wish for the standby letter to be paid for this would signal some failure of the transaction. The seller under the standby letter of credit is also more likely to oppose payment by way of injunctive relief.

Second, in a commercial letter of credit, the documents submitted for payment will often include documents issued by third parties, such as the negotiable bill of lading. These documents provide some indicia that the goods have been shipped and that the underlying contract has been performed. A standby letter of credit will typically call for the submission only of a pro forma declaration by the buyer that the seller has breached the underlying contract. As the independence principle applies to standby and commercial letters of credit alike, the bank is under no duty to investigate the underlying facts to determine whether in fact the seller has breached. Rather, as the strict compliance principle applies to the standby letter of credit as well, the bank is required only to determine whether the declaration complies on its face with the terms of the credit. For this reason, the documentary requirement in a standby letter of credit does not function as much of a safeguard against an undeserving beneficiary. At the most, the requirement of a pro forma declaration may prevent an obvious forgery.

Third, issuers are exposed to greater risks in the case of standby letters because the documents required for payment are not documents of title. In the case of a commercial letter of credit, in the event that the banks are unable to receive reimbursement for payment under the credit, the banks can recover possession of the goods through presentation of the negotiable bill of lading and then sell the goods to recoup their losses. Banks that pay under a standby letter of credit or a bank guarantee do not have a security interest in the goods to protect their interest. Banks must rely solely on the credit of the applicant (or in the case of a confirming bank on the credit of the issuing bank) and for this reason, banks have an incentive to conduct a full credit evaluation of the customer.

B.   SOURCES OF LAW FOR THE STANDBY CREDIT

As we previously noted, standby letters of credit are also subject to UCC Article 5 and the UCP 500 to the extent applicable. In addition, there are several other possible sources of law: The United Nations Convention on Independent Guarantees and Standby Letters of Credit; the Uniform Rules for Demand Guarantees (URDG) (I.C.C. Pub. No. 455, 1992); and the International Standby Practices (ISP98) (I.C.C. Pub. No. 590, 1998).

The United States is a signatory to the UN Convention on Independent Guarantees and Standby Letters of Credit, but it does not have legally binding effect because the United States has not yet ratified the convention. The UN Convention is in force only for a handful of contracting states. Like many other UN conventions in the area of private law, the parties are allowed to opt out of the convention in favor of some other source of law.

The URDG was promulgated by the International Chamber of Commerce to provide guidance on all forms of bank guarantees, which include standby letters of credit. The ICC decided that special rules were needed for standby letters of credit and promulgated the ISP in 1998. At present, the ICC intends the UCP 500 to apply primarily to commercial letters of credit and to standby letters of credit to the extent applicable, the URDG to apply to all forms of bank guarantees, and the ISP to apply specifically to standby letters of credit. As we have earlier noted, the ICC rules and practices are not laws but become legally effective through incorporation by contract. Thus, the three separate sets of ICC rules are available for incorporation by parties to govern the three principal forms of primary obligor/independent issuer undertakings that are in current use in the banking industry.

NOTES AND QUESTIONS

1. While the standby letter of credit is used to guarantee some performance by the seller, it should be distinguished from a similar device such as a surety contract or performance bond, which serves a similar function but involves higher costs and is usually payable only after a factual determination of default rather than upon an examination of documents. In the case of a surety contract guaranteeing performance by the seller, the surety usually undertakes to complete the performance of the seller (by hiring a third party to complete the seller's contract) but the surety will first need to make a factual determination whether the seller has defaulted. Performance bonds also require a factual investigation into the nonperformance

of the contract before payment, which can involve a lengthy investigation. The advantage of the standby letter is that it is inexpensive and efficient as payment is based on an examination of the documents alone not on a breach of the underlying sales contract.

2. While the standby letter of credit may have the advantage of efficiency, it also carries higher risk for the issuer and the seller than a performance bond or surety contract. The standby letter of credit is often referred to as a "suicide" credit because the buyer often has to do nothing more than submit a declaration that the seller has breached the contract. Establishing a surety contract or performance bond would entail higher costs for the parties but would afford the seller protection against the possibility of a baseless demand for payment by the beneficiary. The risks associated with the standby or suicide letter of credit, however, have not diminished their popularity. Why are sellers willing to assume such risks?

The following is an actual example of a standby letter of credit. The credit is similar to the credit described in Figure 4-1 except that it does not involve a guarantee by a local bank:

> "*** TO: THE PRESIDENT OF INDIA
> India
> BY ORDER OF: ELECTRONICS SYSTEMS DIVISION OF DYNAMICS CORPORATION OF AMERICA ***
> For account of same
> GENTLEMEN:
> WE HEREBY ESTABLISH OUR IRREVOCABLE CREDIT IN YOUR FAVOR, FOR THE ACCOUNT INDICATED ABOVE, FOR A SUM OR SUMS NOT EXCEEDING IN ALL FOUR HUNDRED TEN THOUSAND FOUR HUNDRED SEVENTY TWO AND 60/100 US DOLLARS (US$410,472.60)- AVAILABLE BY YOUR DRAFT(S) AT sight,
> DRAWN ON: us
> Which must be accompanied by:
> 1. Your signed certification as follows: 'The President of India being one of the parties to the Agreement dated March 14, 1971 signed and exchanged between The President of India and the Dynamics Corporation of America for the license to manufacture, purchase and supply of radio equipment as per Schedule I thereof for the total contract value of $1,368,242.00, does hereby certify in the exercise of reasonable discretion and in good faith that the Dynamics Corporation of America has failed to carry out certain obligations of theirs under the said Order/Agreement. ***"

Dynamics Corporation of America v. Citizens and Southern National Bank, 356 F. Supp. 991, 994 (N.D. Ga. 1973).

The buyer-beneficiaries in *Dynamics* and in the cases set forth below were foreign sovereign governments and the sums involved in the underlying contracts and letters of credit were very large. What does this suggest to you about the bargaining power of the parties and why sellers would agree to accept the risks of a standby letter of credit?

PROBLEM 4-12

World Telecom (WT), a U.S.-based multinational enterprise, enters into a contract with the National Television and Radio Ministry (NTRM) of a South

American country to supply consulting services and telecommunications equipment. Under the terms of the contract, WT would receive $80 million over three years during the performance of the contract. As required by the contract, NTRM paid WT an advance payment of $10 million. The contract also provided that NTRM would be entitled to return of the $10 million plus an additional $40 million representing NTRM's damages if WT failed to fulfill the contract. The $50 million in total payments to NTRM were secured by a standby letter of credit issued by Chase Manhattan Bank in New York City naming NTRM as the beneficiary. The terms of the standby letter of credit called for the submission of a declaration by the director of the NTRM that "World Telecom has breached its contract with NTRM." Three months later, a radical group overthrows the reigning government and has now established a new Revolutionary People's Government. Chase Manhattan Bank notifies WT that it has received a declaration from the director of the People's Telecommunications Ministry, the renamed NTRM, that "World Telecom has breach its contract with the People's Telecommunications Ministry" and a sight draft for $50 million.

WT argues:

(1) The beneficiary of the standby letter of credit is NTRM and only NTRM is allowed to draw on the credit as the letter of credit is nonassignable and nontransferable. As events have occurred that have caused NTRM to cease to exist, the letter of credit is terminated as a matter of force majeure or impossibility.

(2) The documents fail to satisfy the terms of the credit under the strict compliance principle as the credit calls for documents from NTRM and the present documents are from the People's Telecommunications Ministry.

(3) If the People's Telecommunications Ministry were to resubmit a declaration and demand for payment under the NTRM name, this would be a document that is "forged or materially fraudulent" within the meaning of UCC §5-109(a) and would be sufficient to constitute a fraud that prevents payment under the letter of credit.

How should each of these claims be resolved? *See American Bell* and *Harris infra.*

American Bell International, Inc. v. Islamic Republic of Iran
United States District Court, Southern District of New York, 1979
474 F. Supp. 420

MacMahon, District Judge.

Plaintiff American Bell International Inc. ("Bell") moves for a preliminary injunction pursuant to Rule 65(a), Fed. R. Civ. P. enjoining defendant Manufacturers Hanover Trust Company ("Manufacturers") from making any payment under its Letter of Credit No. SC 170027 to defendants the Islamic Republic of Iran or Bank Iranshahr or their agents, instrumentalities, successors, employees and assigns. We held an evidentiary hearing and heard oral argument on August 3, 1979. The following facts appear from the evidence presented:

The action arises from the recent revolution in Iran and its impact upon contracts made with the ousted Imperial Government of Iran and upon banking arrangements incident to such contracts. Bell, a wholly-owned subsidiary of

American Telephone & Telegraph Co. ("AT & T"), made a contract on July 23, 1978 (the "Contract") with the Imperial Government of Iran Ministry of War ("Imperial Government") to provide consulting services and equipment to the Imperial Government as part of a program to improve Iran's international communications system.

The Contract provides a complex mechanism for payment to Bell totalling approximately $280,000,000, including a down payment of $38,800,000. The Imperial Government had the right to demand return of the down payment at any time. The amount so callable, however, was to be reduced by 20% of the amounts invoiced by Bell to which the Imperial Government did not object. Bell's liability for return of the down payment was reduced by application of this mechanism as the Contract was performed, with the result that approximately $30,200,000 of the down payment now remains callable.

In order to secure the return of the down payment on demand, Bell was required to establish an unconditional and irrevocable Letter of Guaranty, to be issued by Bank Iranshahr in the amount of $38,800,000 in favor of the Imperial Government. The Contract provides that it is to be governed by the laws of Iran and that all disputes arising under it are to be resolved by the Iranian courts.

Bell obtained a Letter of Guaranty from Bank Iranshahr. In turn, as required by Bank Iranshahr, Bell obtained a standby Letter of Credit, No. SC 170027, issued by Manufacturers in favor of Bank Iranshahr in the amount of $38,800,000 to secure reimbursement to Bank Iranshahr should it be required to pay the Imperial Government under its Letter of Guaranty.

The standby Letter of Credit provided for payment by Manufacturers to Bank Iranshahr upon receipt of:

> "Your (Bank Iranshahr's) dated statement purportedly signed by an officer indicating name and title or your Tested Telex Reading: (A) 'Referring Manufacturers Hanover Trust Co. Credit No. SC170027, the amount of our claim $____ represents funds due us as we have received a written request from the Imperial Government of Iran Ministry of War to pay them the sum of ____ under our Guarantee No.____ issued for the account of American Bell International Inc. covering advance payment under Contract No. 138 dated July 23, 1978 and such payment has been made by us' . . .".

In the application for the Letter of Credit, Bell agreed — guaranteed by AT & T — immediately to reimburse Manufacturers for all amounts paid by Manufacturers to Bank Iranshahr pursuant to the Letter of Credit.

Bell commenced performance of its Contract with the Imperial Government. It provided certain services and equipment to update Iran's communications system and submitted a number of invoices, some of which were paid.

In late 1978 and early 1979, Iran was wreaked with revolutionary turmoil culminating in the overthrow of the Iranian government and its replacement by the Islamic Republic. In the wake of this upheaval, Bell was left with substantial unpaid invoices and claims under the Contract and ceased its performance in January 1979. Bell claims that the Contract was breached by the Imperial Government, as well as repudiated by the Islamic Republic, in that it is owed substantial sums for services rendered under the Contract and its termination provisions.

On July 25 and 29, 1979, Manufacturers received demands by Tested Telex from Bank Iranshahr for payment of $30,220,724 under the Letter of Credit, the remaining balance of the down payment. Asserting that the demand did not conform with the Letter of Credit, Manufacturers declined payment and so informed Bank Iranshahr. Informed of this, Bell responded by filing this action and an application by way of order to show cause for a temporary restraining order bringing on this motion for a preliminary injunction. Following argument, we granted a temporary restraining order on July 29 enjoining Manufacturers from making any payment to Bank Iranshahr until forty-eight hours after Manufacturers notified Bell of the receipt of a conforming demand, and this order has been extended pending decision of this motion.

On August 1, 1979, Manufacturers notified Bell that it had received a conforming demand from Bank Iranshahr. At the request of the parties, the court held an evidentiary hearing on August 3 on this motion for a preliminary injunction.

CRITERIA FOR PRELIMINARY INJUNCTIONS

The current criteria in this circuit for determining whether to grant the extraordinary remedy of a preliminary injunction are:

"(T)here must be a showing of possible irreparable injury And either (1) probable success on the merits Or (2) sufficiently serious questions going to the merits to make them a fair ground for litigation And a balance of hardships tipping decidedly toward the party requesting the preliminary relief."

We are not persuaded that the plaintiff has met the criteria and therefore deny the motion.

A. IRREPARABLE INJURY

Plaintiff has failed to show that irreparable injury may possibly ensue if a preliminary injunction is denied. Bell does not even claim, much less show, that it lacks an adequate remedy at law if Manufacturers makes a payment to Bank Iranshahr in violation of the Letter of Credit. It is too clear for argument that a suit for money damages could be based on any such violation, and surely Manufacturers would be able to pay any money judgment against it.

Bell falls back on a contention that it is without any effective remedy unless it can restrain payment. This contention is based on the fact that it agreed to be bound by the laws of Iran and to submit resolution of any disputes under the Contract to the courts of Iran. Bell claims that it now has no meaningful access to those courts.

There is credible evidence that the Islamic Republic is xenophobic and anti-American and that it has no regard for consulting service contracts such as the one here. Although Bell has made no effort to invoke the aid of the Iranian courts, we think the current situation in Iran, as shown by the evidence, warrants the conclusion that an attempt by Bell to resort to those courts would be futile. However, Bell has not demonstrated that it is without adequate remedy in this court against the Iranian defendants under the Sovereign Immunity Act which it invokes in this very case.

Accordingly, we conclude that Bell has failed to demonstrate irreparable injury.

B. PROBABLE SUCCESS ON THE MERITS

Even assuming that plaintiff has shown possible irreparable injury, it has failed to show probable success on the merits.

In order to succeed on the merits, Bell must prove, by a preponderance of the evidence, that either (1) a demand for payment of the Manufacturers Letter of Credit conforming to the terms of that Letter has not yet been made or (2) a demand, even though in conformity, should not be honored because of fraud in the transaction. It is not probable, in the sense of a greater than 50% likelihood, that Bell will be able to prove either nonconformity or fraud.

As to nonconformity, the August 1 demand by Bank Iranshahr is identical to the terms of the Manufacturers Letter of Credit in every respect except one: it names as payee the "Government of Iran Ministry of Defense, Successor to the Imperial Government of Iran Ministry of War" rather than the "Imperial Government of Iran Ministry of War." It is, of course, a bedrock principle of letter of credit law that a demand must strictly comply with the letter in order to justify payment. Nevertheless, we deem it less than probable that a court, upon a full trial, would find nonconformity in the instant case.

At the outset, we notice, and the parties agree, that the United States now recognizes the present Government of Iran as the legal successor to the Imperial Government of Iran. That recognition is binding on American Courts. Though we may decide for ourselves the consequences of such recognition upon the litigants in this case, we point out that American courts have traditionally viewed contract rights as vesting not in any particular government but in the state of which that government is an agent.

Accordingly, the Government of Iran is the successor to the Imperial Government under the Letter of Guaranty. As legal successor, the Government of Iran may properly demand payment even though the terms of the Letter of Guaranty only provide for payment to the Government of Iran's predecessor and a demand for payment under the Letter of Credit reciting that payment has been made by Bank Iranshahr to the new government is sufficient.

Finally, an opposite answer to the narrow question of conformity would not only elevate form over substance, but would render financial arrangements and undertakings worldwide wholly subject to the vicissitudes of political power. A nonviolent, unanimous transformation of the form of government, or, as this case shows, the mere change of the name of a government agency, would be enough to warrant an issuer's refusal to honor a demand. We cannot suppose such uncertainty and opportunity for chicanery to be the purpose of the requirement of strict conformity.

If conformity is established, as here, the issuer of an irrevocable, unconditional letter of credit, such as Manufacturers normally has an absolute duty to transfer the requisite funds. This duty is wholly independent of the underlying contractual relationship that gives rise to the letter of credit. Nevertheless, both the Uniform Commercial Code of New York, which the parties concede governs here, and the courts state that payment is enjoinable where a germane document is forged or fraudulent or there is "fraud in the transaction." Bell does not contend that any documents are fraudulent by virtue of misstatements or omissions. Instead, it argues there is "fraud in the transaction."

The parties disagree over the scope to be given as a matter of law to the term "transaction." Manufacturers, citing voluminous authorities, argues that the term refers only to the Letter of Credit transaction, not to the underlying commercial transaction or to the totality of dealings among the banks, the Iranian government and Bell. On this view of the law, Bell must fail to establish a probability of success, for it does not claim that the Imperial Government or Bank Iranshahr induced Manufacturers to extend the Letter by lies or half-truths, that the Letter contained any false representations by the Imperial Government or Bank Iranshahr, or that they intended misdeeds with it. Nor does Bell claim that the demand contains any misstatements.

Bell argues, citing equally voluminous authorities, that the term "transaction" refers to the totality of circumstances. On this view, Bell has some chance of success on the merits, for a court can consider Bell's allegations that the Government of Iran's behavior in connection with the consulting contract suffices to make its demand on the Letter of Guaranty fraudulent and that the ensuing demand on the Letter of Credit by Bank Iranshahr is tainted with the fraud.

There is some question whether these divergent understandings of the law are wholly incompatible since it would seem impossible to keep the Letter of Credit transaction conceptually distinct. A demand which facially conforms to the Letter of Credit and which contains no misstatements may, nevertheless, be considered fraudulent if made with the goal of mulcting the party who caused the Letter of Credit to be issued. Be that as it may, we need not decide this thorny issue of law. For, even on the construction most favorable to Bell, we find that success on the merits is not probable. Many of the facts alleged, even if proven, would not constitute fraud. As to others, the proof is insufficient to indicate a probability of success on the merits.

Bell sets forth five contentions which, in its view, support the issuance of an injunction. Bell asserts that (1) both the old and new Governments failed to approve invoices for services fully performed; (2) both failed to fund contracted-for independent Letters of Credit in Bell's favor; (3) the new Government has taken steps to renounce altogether its obligations under the Contract; (4) the new Government has made it impossible to assert contract rights in Iranian courts; and (5) the new Government has caused Bank Iranshahr to demand payment on the Manufacturers Letter of Credit, thus asserting rights in a transaction it has otherwise repudiated.

As to contention (4), it is not immediately apparent how denial of Bell's opportunity to assert rights under the Contract makes a demand on an independent letter of credit fraudulent.

Contentions (1), (2), (3) and the latter part of (5) all state essentially the same proposition that the Government of Iran is currently repudiating all its contractual obligations with American companies, including those with Bell. Again, the evidence on this point is uncompelling.

Bell points to (1) an intragovernmental order of July 2, 1979 ordering the termination of Iran's contract with Bell, and (2) hearsay discussions between Bell's president and Iranian officials to the effect that Iran would not pay on the Contract until it had determined whether the services under it had benefited the country. Manufacturers, for its part, points to a public statement in the Wall Street Journal of July 16, 1979, under the name of the present Iranian Government, to the effect that Iran intends to honor all legitimate contracts. Taken together, this evidence does not suggest that Iran has finally and irrevocably decided to repudiate the Bell contract. It suggests equally that Iran is still considering the question whether to perform that contract.

Even if we accept the proposition that the evidence does show repudiation, plaintiff is still far from demonstrating the kind of evil intent necessary to support a claim of fraud. Surely, plaintiff cannot contend that every party who breaches or repudiates his contract is for that reason culpable of fraud. The law of contract damages is adequate to repay the economic harm caused by repudiation, and the law presumes that one who repudiates has done so because of a calculation that such damages are cheaper than performance. Absent any showing that Iran would refuse to pay damages upon a contract action here or in Iran, much less a showing that Bell has even attempted to obtain such a remedy, the evidence is ambivalent as to whether the purported repudiation results from nonfraudulent economic calculation or from fraudulent intent to mulct Bell.

Plaintiff contends that the alleged repudiation, viewed in connection with its demand for payment on the Letter of Credit, supplies the basis from which only one inference fraud can be drawn. Again, we remain unpersuaded.

Plaintiff's argument requires us to presume bad faith on the part of the Iranian government. It requires us further to hold that that government may not rely on the plain terms of the consulting contract and the Letter of Credit arrangements with Bank Iranshahr and Manufacturers providing for immediate repayment of the down payment upon demand, without regard to cause. On the evidence before us, fraud is no more inferable than an economically rational decision by the government to recoup its down payment, as it is entitled to do under the consulting contract and still dispute its liabilities under that Contract.

While fraud in the transaction is doubtless a possibility, plaintiff has not shown it to be a probability.

C. SERIOUS QUESTIONS AND BALANCE OF HARDSHIPS

If plaintiff fails to demonstrate probable success, he may still obtain relief by showing, in addition to the possibility of irreparable injury, both (1) sufficiently serious questions going to the merits to make them a fair ground for litigation, and (2) a balance of hardships tipping decidedly toward plaintiff. Both Bell and Manufacturers appear to concede the existence of serious questions, and the complexity and novelty of this matter lead us to find they exist. Nevertheless, we hold that plaintiff is not entitled to relief because the balance of hardships does not tip decidedly toward Bell, if indeed it tips that way at all.

To be sure, Bell faces substantial hardships upon denial of its motion. Should Manufacturers pay the demand, Bell will immediately become liable to Manufacturers for $30.2 million, with no assurance of recouping those funds from Iran for the services performed. While counsel represented in graphic detail the other losses Bell faces at the hands of the current Iranian government, these would flow regardless of whether we ordered the relief sought. The hardship imposed from a denial of relief is limited to the admittedly substantial sum of $30.2 million.

But Manufacturers would face at least as great a loss, and perhaps a greater one, were we to grant relief. Upon Manufacturers' failure to pay, Bank Iranshahr could initiate a suit on the Letter of Credit and attach $30.2 million of Manufacturers' assets in Iran. In addition, it could seek to hold Manufacturers liable for consequential damages beyond that sum resulting from the failure to make timely payment. Finally, there is no guarantee that Bank Iranshahr or the government, in retaliation for Manufacturers' recalcitrance, will not nationalize additional Manufacturers' assets in Iran in amounts which counsel, at oral argument, represented to be far in excess of the amount in controversy here.

Apart from a greater monetary exposure flowing from an adverse decision, Manufacturers faces a loss of credibility in the international banking community that could result from its failure to make good on a letter of credit.

CONCLUSION

Finally, apart from questions of relative hardship and the specific criteria [for a preliminary injunction], general considerations of equity counsel us to deny the motion for injunctive relief. Bell, a sophisticated multinational enterprise well advised by competent counsel, entered into these arrangements with its corporate eyes open. It knowingly and voluntarily signed a contract allowing the Iranian government to recoup its down payment on demand, without regard to cause. It caused Manufacturers to enter into an arrangement whereby Manufacturers became obligated to pay Bank Iranshahr the unamortized down payment balance upon receipt of conforming documents, again without regard to cause.

Both of these arrangements redounded tangibly to the benefit of Bell. The Contract with Iran, with its prospect of designing and installing from scratch a nationwide and international communications system, was certain to bring to Bell both monetary profit and prestige and good will in the global communications industry. The agreement to indemnify Manufacturers on its Letter of Credit provided the means by which these benefits could be achieved.

One who reaps the rewards of commercial arrangements must also accept their burdens. One such burden in this case, voluntarily accepted by Bell, was the risk that demand might be made without cause on the funds constituting the down payment. To be sure, the sequence of events that led up to that demand may well have been unforeseeable when the contracts were signed. To this extent, both Bell and Manufacturers have been made the unwitting and innocent victims of tumultuous events beyond their control. But, as between two innocents, the party who undertakes by contract the risk of political uncertainty and governmental caprice must bear the consequences when the risk comes home to roost.

Accordingly, plaintiff's motion for a preliminary injunction is denied. So ordered.

Harris Corporation v. National Iranian Radio
& Television
United States Court of Appeals, Eleventh Circuit, 1982
691 F.2d 1344

HILL, Circuit Judge.

I. THE FACTS

On February 22, 1978, the Broadcast Products Division of Harris Corporation entered into a contract with NIRT ("the contract") to manufacture and deliver 144 FM broadcast transmitters to Teheran, Iran, and to provide related training and technical services for a total price of $6,740,352. Harris received an advance payment of $1,331,470.40, which was to be amortized over the life of the contract by deducting a percentage of the payment due upon shipment of the equipment or receipt of the services and training from the balance of the advance.

Pursuant to the contract, Harris obtained a performance guarantee in favor of NIRT from Bank Melli, an agency of the State of Iran. The guarantee provides that Melli is to pay NIRT any amount up to $674,035.20 upon Melli's receipt of NIRT's written declaration that Harris has failed to comply with the terms and conditions of the contract. The contract between Harris and NIRT makes the guarantee an integral part of the contract and provides that NIRT must release the guarantee upon termination of the contract due to force majeure. Before Melli issued the guarantee it required that Harris obtain a letter of credit in Melli's favor. Continental Bank issued this standby, which provides that Continental is to reimburse Melli to the extent that Melli pays on the guarantee it issued. Harris, in turn, must indemnify Continental Bank to the extent that Continental pays Melli.

From August 1978 through February 1979, Harris shipped to Iran 138 of the 144 transmitters (together with related equipment for 144 transmitters) and also conducted a 24-week training program in the United States for NIRT personnel. In February 1979, the Islamic Republic of Iran overthrew the Imperial Government of Iran. After the overthrow, one shipment of goods which Harris sent could not be delivered safely in Iran. Harris notified NIRT, by telex dated February 27, that those goods were taken to Antwerp, Belgium, and Sharjah, United Arab Emirates.

Frank R. Blaha, the Director of Customer Products and Systems Operations of the Broadcast Products Division of Harris Corporation, met with NIRT officials in Teheran in early May, 1979, to help them obtain the goods in Antwerp, to discuss amendments to the contract, and to discuss a revised delivery schedule made necessary by Iranian events. Harris, offering Blaha's affidavit, contends that all parties at those meetings acknowledged the existence of force majeure as defined in the contract.

Blaha worked in May to obtain the Antwerp goods for NIRT, then returned to Teheran to continue discussions with NIRT officials. At these discussions, NIRT agreed to delay shipment of the final six transmitters until the fall of 1979 due to the conditions in Iran.

Negotiations on contract modifications continued during the summer and fall of 1979. On August 18, 1979, Harris formally advised NIRT of the additional costs it had incurred with respect to the goods that had been reshipped from Antwerp, and Harris requested payment for the additional amount in accordance with the contract's force majeure clause and with a letter from NIRT authorizing Harris to reship the goods.

On November 4, 1979, Iranian militants took 52 hostages at the United States Embassy in Teheran. Harris received no further communications from NIRT after the seizure of the hostages.

Harris completed the remaining six transmitters in November 1979 and inventoried them for future delivery. Harris, supported by Blaha's affidavits, has argued that disruptive conditions created by the Iranian revolution initially prevented shipment of the final six transmitters. Subsequently, Harris contends, it was unable to ship the materials as a result of the Iranian Assets Control Regulations effective November 14, 1979. In particular, Harris points out, the Treasury voided all general licenses to ship to Iran and required sellers to obtain special license on a case-by-case basis before exporting goods. An affidavit submitted by Blaha states that Harris's counsel was advised by the Office of Foreign Assets Control that special licenses would be issued only in emergency situations or for humanitarian reasons and would not be issued for the transmitters. This request is not documented, and Harris did not inform NIRT of its inability to ship. On April 7, 1980, Treasury Regulation 535.207 became effective and prohibited the shipment of nonessential items to Iran.

On June 3, 1980, Continental Bank received a telex from Melli reporting that NIRT had presented Melli with a written declaration that Harris had failed to comply with the terms of the contract and stating that NIRT had demanded that Melli extend or pay the guarantee. Melli demanded that it be authorized to extend the guarantee and that Continental Bank extend its corresponding letter of credit to Melli, or else Melli would pay the guarantee and demand immediate payment from Continental.

In response to the demand by Melli, Harris sought and obtained the preliminary injunction at issue in this case. On July 11, 1980, Harris filed a verified complaint against NIRT and Melli in the United States District Court for the Middle District of Florida, seeking to enjoin payment and receipt of payment on the guarantee and receipt of payment on the letter of credit. The complaint also sought a declaratory judgment that the contract underlying the guarantee and the letter of credit had been terminated by force majeure. The court granted a temporary restraining order on June 13, 1980, pending a hearing on Harris's motion for a preliminary injunction.

On June 16, 1980, a copy of the TRO was mailed to Melli's counsel and on the following day was hand-delivered to Melli's branch office in Manhattan. On June 20, 1980, three days after receipt of the June 13th TRO at its Manhattan branch office, and despite the restraint against payment contained in the TRO, Melli telexed Continental Bank that it had paid the full amount of the guarantee "after receipt of a demand for payment from the National Iranian Radio and Television stating that there has been a default by Harris Corporation, Broadcast Products Division[,] to comply with the terms and conditions of contract F-601-1." The telex also demanded that Continental pay Melli by crediting Melli's London office with the amount of the letter of credit. After a hearing on August 15, 1980, the district court issued the preliminary injunction at issue here.

IV. The Preliminary Injunction

A. THE FRAMEWORK FOR REVIEW

The appellants contend that the district court erred in entering the preliminary injunction against payment or receipt of payment on the NIRT-Melli guarantee letter of credit and against receipt of payment on the Melli-Continental letter of credit. The four prerequisites for the injunction are: (1) a substantial likelihood that the plaintiff will prevail on the merits; (2) a substantial threat that the plaintiff will suffer irreparable injury if the injunction is not granted; (3) threatened injury to the plaintiff must outweigh the threatened harm that the injunction may cause to the defendant; and (4) granting the preliminary injunction must not disserve the public interest.

B. SUBSTANTIAL LIKELIHOOD OF SUCCESS ON THE MERITS

The merits of this case involve letter of credit law. Harris asserts that the existence of force majeure terminated its obligations under the contract with NIRT, making illegitimate NIRT's subsequent attempt to draw upon the performance guarantee issued by Melli. The appellants respond by relying upon a fundamental principle of letter of credit law: the letter of credit is independent of the underlying contract. Harris advanced two ways to overcome this barrier to enjoining a letter of credit transaction.

First, Harris asserts that the independence principle was modified by the parties here. It points to those paragraphs of its contract with NIRT which make "the bank guarantees" an "integral part" of the contract and which state that NIRT shall release all guarantees upon termination of the contract due to force majeure. Harris contends that it has demonstrated a substantial likelihood that force majeure occurred and terminated both the contract and the guarantee.

We choose not to rely upon Harris's first line of argument, for we hesitate to hold that the letters of credit were automatically terminated by the operation of the contractual provisions. Accepting Harris's first argument would create problems; a bank could honor a letter of credit only to find that it had terminated earlier. While parties may modify the independence principle by drafting letters of credit specifically to achieve that result there is no assertion by Harris that the performance guarantee or the letter of credit contain provisions (conditions) which would modify the independence of the banks' obligations. Since the banks were not parties to the underlying contract, it would appear that the contractual provisions relied upon by Harris would have the same effect as a warranty by NIRT that it would not draw upon the letter of credit issued by Melli if the contract were to terminate due to force majeure.

The second avenue pursued by Harris is the doctrine of "fraud in the transaction." Under this doctrine, a court may enjoin payment on a letter of credit, despite the independence principle, where there is shown to be fraud by the beneficiary of the letter of credit. Unfortunately, one unsettled point in the law is what constitutes fraud in the transaction, i.e., what degree of defective performance by the beneficiary justifies enjoining a letter of credit transaction in violation of the independence principle?

Contending that a narrow definition of fraud is appropriate, the appellants assert that an injunction should issue only upon a showing of facts indicating egregious misconduct. They argue that fraud in the transaction should be restricted to the type of chicanery present in the landmark case of *Sztejn v. Henry Schroder Banking Corp.* where a seller sent fifty crates of "cowhair, other worthless material, and rubbish with intent to simulate genuine merchandise and defraud [the buyer]."

The appellants further contend that Harris does not and cannot allege conduct on the part of NIRT or Melli that would justify a finding of fraud under *Sztejn*. The egregious conduct, they assert, was by Harris. They state that it was Harris which failed to ship the remaining goods, unreasonably refused to extend the letter of credit obtained from Continental, and deliberately abandoned and destroyed the underlying contract. In contrast, they point out that they informed Continental that they would have been satisfied if the letter of credit had been extended long enough for Harris to complete performance. According to the view of NIRT and Melli, all that Harris has — taking its assertions as true — is an impossibility defense to an action on the underlying contract.

Appellants' arguments are not persuasive in the context of this case. *Sztejn* does not offer much direct guidance because it involved fraud by the beneficiary seller in the letter of credit transaction in the form of false documentation covering up egregiously fraudulent performance of the underlying transaction. That does not mean that the fraud exception should be restricted to allegations involving fraud in the underlying transaction, nor does it mean that the exception should be restricted to protecting the buyer in the framework of the traditional letter of credit. The fraud exception is flexible and it may be invoked on behalf of a customer seeking to prevent a beneficiary from fraudulently utilizing a standby (guarantee) letter of credit.

Thus, the independent contracts rule does not make a fraudulent demand completely irrelevant to a bank's obligation to honor a standby. The differences between the allegations in this case and those in *Sztejn* merely require us to focus on the conduct of the buyer rather than the seller as we evaluate the beneficiary's conduct in light of the terms of the particular documents involved in the demand.

In order to collect upon the guarantee letter of credit, NIRT was required to declare that Harris had failed to comply with the terms and conditions of the contract. Harris contends that NIRT intentionally misrepresented the quality of Harris's performance; Harris thus asserts fraud as it has been defined traditionally.

We find that the evidence adduced by Harris is sufficient to support a conclusion that it has a substantial likelihood of prevailing on the merits. The facts suggest that the contract in this case broke down through no fault of Harris's but rather as a result of problems stemming from the Iranian revolution. NIRT apparently admitted as much during its negotiations with Harris over how to carry out the remainder of the contract. Nonetheless, NIRT sought to call the performance guarantee. Its attempt to do so necessarily involved its representation that Harris had defaulted under the contract. Yet the contract explicitly provides that it can be terminated due to force majeure. Moreover, NIRT's demand was made in a situation that was subtly suggestive of fraud. Since NIRT and Bank Melli had both become government enterprises, the demand was in some sense by Iran upon itself and may have been an effort by Iran to harvest undeserved bounty from Continental Bank. Under these circumstances, it was within the district court's discretion to find that, at a full hearing, Harris might well be able to prove that NIRT's demand was a fraudulent attempt to obtain the benefit of payment on the letter of credit in addition to the benefit of Harris's substantial performance.

C. IRREPARABLE INJURY

The district court did not abuse its discretion in finding a substantial like-lihood of irreparable injury to Harris absent an injunction. Harris has sufficiently demonstrated that its ability to pursue a legal remedy against NIRT and Melli (*i.e.*, to recover the proceeds of the standby) has been precluded. It is clear that the Islamic regime now governing Iran has shown a deep hostility toward the United States and its citizens, thus making effective access to the Iranian courts unlikely. Similarly, the cooperative response of agencies of Iran to orders of a United States court would be unlikely where the court's order would impose a financial obliga-tion on the agencies. Harris's possible resort to the Iran–United States Claims Tribunal does not, in our eyes, ameliorate the likelihood of irreparable injury for purposes of this requirement for preliminary relief.

D. THE BALANCE OF HARMS

Neither appellant argues that the preliminary injunction has caused or will cause it any harm. Since there would otherwise be a likelihood that Harris would suffer irreparable injury, the balance of harms weighs heavily in Harris's favor.

E. THE PUBLIC INTEREST

In a Statement of Interest filed with the district court on July 16, 1982, the United States indicated that new amendments to the Iranian Assets Control Regulations governing letter of credit claims still permit American litigants to proceed in United States Courts and to obtain preliminary injunctive relief. The supplementary information explaining the changes provides a good indication that preliminary injunctions such as the one entered here are in the public interest:

> Iran filed more than 200 claims with the Iran-U.S. Claims Tribunal (the "Tribunal") based on standby letters of credit issued for the account of United States parties. United States nationals have filed with the Tribunal a large number of claims related to, or based on, many of the same standby letters of credit at issue in Iran's claims. Other United States nationals have litigation pending in United States courts concerning some of these same letters of credit.
>
> The purpose of the amendment is to preserve the status quo by continuing to allow U.S. account parties to obtain preliminary injunctions or other temporary relief to prevent payment on standby letters of credit, while prohibiting, for the time being, final judicial action permanently enjoining, nullifying or otherwise permanently dis-posing of such letters of credit.
>
> Preservation of the status quo will provide an opportunity for negotiations with Iran regarding the status and disposition of these various letter of credit claims.

Preservation of the status quo for a period of time also permits possible resolution in the context of the Tribunal of the matters pending before it. The amendment will expire by its terms on December 31, 1982.

Melli has charged, however, that the entry of a preliminary injunction here would threaten the function of letters of credit in commercial transactions. Admittedly, that has given us pause, for it would be improper to impose relief contrary to the intentions of parties that have contracted to carry out their business in a certain manner. Some might contend that the use of the fraud exception in a case such as this damages commercial law and that Harris could have chosen to shift the risks represented in this case. Under the circumstances, however, we disagree. First, the risk of a fraudulent demand of the type which Harris has demonstrated a likelihood of showing is not one which it should be expected to bear in light of the manner in which the documents in this transaction were structured. Second, to argue that Harris could have protected itself further by inserting special conditions in the letters of credit and should be confined to that protection is to ignore the realities of the drafting of commercial documents. Third, unlike the first line of argument presented by Harris, the issuance of a preliminary injunction based on a showing of fraud does not create unfortunate consequences for a bank that honors letters of credit in good faith; it is up to the customer to seek and obtain an injunction before a bank would be prohibited from paying on a letter of credit. Finally, foreign situations like the one before us are exceptional. For these reasons, the district court's holding is not contrary to the public interest in maintaining the market integrity and commercial utility of guarantee letters of credit.

V. Conclusion

[T]he requirements for preliminary injunctive relief have been met. Accordingly, the decision of the district court is affirmed.

NOTES AND QUESTIONS

1. The situations in *American Bell* and *Harris* were similar but the seller was able to sustain an allegation of fraud only in *Harris*. What events occurred in the intervening time between these two cases that might have had an influence on the courts involved?

2. Review these cases and examine the approach taken by the sellers in each case in asserting its allegations of fraud. The sellers took very different approaches in each of these cases. In *American Bell*, the approach was unsuccessful whereas the approach in *Harris* was successful in surviving the defendant's motion to dismiss. How would you characterize the differences in approach taken by the sellers in alleging fraud in these two cases? What lessons can you draw from these two cases?

3. Both *American Bell* and *Harris* were decided under former UCC §5-114, a prior version of UCC §5-109. The current standard of fraud under §5-109(a) requires that "a document is forged or material required fraudulently, or honor of the presentation would facilitate a material fraud by the beneficiary on the issuer or applicant."

PROBLEM 4-13

A multinational computer company comes to your law office and tells you that it has entered into a major contract with a foreign sovereign government to provide computer equipment, software, and consulting services. The foreign sovereign has asked the client for a standby letter of credit securing the return of its 10 percent down payment and a payment of $80 million dollars in the event that the client fails to fulfill its contract obligations. The client has made it clear that it wishes to enter into the sales and consulting contract and does not want to be talked out of the standby letter. Rather, the client asks for your advice on how to structure the standby letter of credit transaction to control and minimize its risks. What is your advice?

5

Nonestablishment Forms of International Business: Agency and Distributorships, Technology Transfer, Contract Manufacturing, and Franchising

In Chapters 2-4, we examined the basic sales transaction of goods across national boundaries. The direct export sales transaction remains the simplest form of international business and is the method by which many business entities first enter the international business transactions arena. Exports transactions have become common because in the modern age of electronic communications, information about products and services may reach large numbers of potential international customers and manufacturers of goods and service providers may receive unsolicited purchase orders from customers around the world. However, waiting for buyers to visit a Web site, to respond to advertising, or to visit annual trade fairs may not be sufficient to satisfy the aspirations of some sellers. A seller may wish to take more active steps and be more aggressive in penetrating a certain targeted market. What steps are available to the seller beyond the international sale? This is the subject of this chapter and the next.

Beyond the Sales Transaction

This chapter and the next chapter are interrelated and can be seen as a progression for the seller, a U.S. corporation, from actions that are least integrated in the foreign operation to the most integrated. In this chapter, we discuss "nonestablishment" forms of doing business abroad, whereas the next chapter involves "establishment" forms of doing business. In nonestablishment forms of doing business, the seller or U.S. corporation exercises greater control in the foreign market than can be achieved through direct sales alone by hiring an entity in the foreign market in which the seller has no ownership interest such as an agent, distributor, or contract manufacturer, that is, a third party authorized by the U.S. seller to manufacture the seller's products for sale abroad. These nonestablishment forms allow the U.S. corporation to achieve greater control than possible through direct selling but much less control than if the U.S. corporation actually acquired a permanent or lasting presence in the foreign market in the form of partial or total ownership of a business entity in the foreign market that will manufacture the seller's products. The movement from various forms of nonestablishment to establishment forms of doing business abroad marks an increasing progression in the amount of control, integration, and commitment for the U.S. corporation. This is a theme that will underline all of the topics that we cover in this chapter and the next.

Note that while this progression is a useful concept in an academic setting such as this textbook, it is one that is also openly acknowledged in the real world. Many U.S. corporations and foreign parties enter into agency arrangements or distributorships with the explicit understanding that a successful relationship may lead to contract manufacturing. The parties may further provide that if the contract manufacturing relationship is successful, the parties will move forward and further deepen their business relationship by forming a joint venture. Note that many foreign entities are often eager and want more of a business relationship with the U.S. corporation and will openly acknowledge that they see an agency or distributorship as a stepping stone to a joint venture. Alternatively, the U.S. corporation may wish to acquire a foreign manufacturer or set up its own wholly owned foreign subsidiary. Many U.S. corporations find this progression useful as it allows them to "test the waters" with small steps along the way and does not involve one huge leap into the unknown.

This leap or last step — forming a joint venture, foreign subsidiary, or acquiring a foreign company — is what is generally known as foreign direct investment and allows the U.S. corporation the greatest control in the foreign market, but, as you can imagine, it also involves the greatest level of commitment and risk. These topics are so complex and FDI is such an important decision that many U.S. corporations regard FDI as a fundamental turning point in the life of any corporation. However, while the level of risk and commitment is much greater in FDI than in the topics covered in this chapter, FDI can and should be understood as a progression from the present topics.

Of course, FDI is not appropriate for some U.S. corporations at all or may not be appropriate at certain points in their corporate lives. The U.S. corporation may not wish to undertake the substantial commitment of investing in and establishing a business entity abroad in which it is the sole or partial owner. Or the U.S. corporation may not wish to undertake this commitment without some preliminary steps involving less risk to test the foreign market. What are the initial steps that a seller can take in moving beyond the simple sales transaction but short of establishing a business abroad? This is the subject of this chapter.

Nonestablishment Forms of Business Abroad

There are two methods that we will examine in this chapter. First, the seller can engage a person or business entity in the foreign market to serve as its sales representative. Having a representative in the foreign market will allow the seller to have on the ground knowledge and expertise and a representative that will actively market its products and seek out customers. Second, if the sales representative proves to be successful, the seller may wish to take the additional step of contract manufacturing, that is, licensing a foreign entity to manufacture its products in the foreign market. By having its products manufactured by a local manufacturer under authorization in the foreign market, the seller can save on the costs of transportation and storage. In addition, as products sold in a foreign market require different packaging and may require certain physical alterations, the use of a local manufacturer with expertise in these areas may also create greater efficiencies.

Contract manufacturing is a form of licensing under which the seller or owner will authorize a third party to use its intellectual property and other proprietary information in order to manufacture its products. In the area of the trade in services, franchising is another form of licensing under which the owner will allow a third party to use its intellectual property to provide services or a combination of services and products. In the case of both contract manufacturing for products and franchising for services (or services and products), the transfer of technology and other forms of intellectual property becomes a critical issue. There is often tension between the owner-licensor and the licensee on access to proprietary technology. The licensee typically wishes to have greater access whereas the owner wishes to allow sufficient access but at the same time protect its proprietary property. How these technology transfer issues and issues concerning the protection of intellectual property are handled in the various agreements are among the most important topics that we consider in this chapter.

I. Agency and Distributorships

Suppose that a seller in Ohio with little knowledge or expertise about Germany has been able to generate enough business through trade fairs to have several steady years of direct sales to several customers in Germany. The seller is confident that other companies in Germany would be interested in purchasing its products and wishes to adopt a more aggressive strategy to penetrate further into German markets and generate higher sales. In many cases, one of the most difficult problems that sellers encounter is how to get the product to the customer. In some instances, the seller may have a complete distribution network in the foreign country, but this is frequently not the case. Sellers, like the one in our hypothetical, that have limited their activities to direct exports may have little knowledge or contact with the foreign market except for the few customers with whom the seller has developed a business relationship. To compensate for its lack of knowledge about Germany, the seller can choose to engage a German party in the target foreign market to sell its products. This is the first step in developing a distribution network in Germany. If the seller is a small company, the seller may choose to retain a representative that handles many different products for different customers. A large company may establish its own foreign agent or distributor. In most cases, it is more likely that the U.S. seller will hire some local entity for the distribution of its products.

In choosing a local person or entity to distribute its products, the seller or exporter generally has two options. The seller can engage (1) an independent foreign agent or sales representative or (2) an independent foreign distributor. Note, however, that while the seller usually has the option to choose either of these forms, in some cases, especially in developing countries, the seller may not have a choice of the form of distribution as the form may be mandated by local law.

An independent foreign agent is a person or entity in a foreign country that solicits orders for the goods but does not take title to the goods. As the agent does not take title to the goods, the agent does not bear the risk that the local buyer will not pay. Rather, this risk remains with the seller. The agent will obtain sales orders on behalf of the seller in the foreign country and forward those orders to the seller. The seller completes the transaction by selling directly to the buyer so there is no need to store the goods in the foreign country. The buyer usually pays the seller directly and some portion of the sales price will be given to the agent as a commission in addition to a regular salary. The foreign agent usually does not have the power to bind the seller, but as the relationship between the seller and the agent is that of a principal-agent relationship whether the agent can bind the principal may depend on the law of the foreign jurisdiction. In some cases, the foreign agent may have the implied power to do so and in all cases the seller may expressly confer such power upon the agent.

An independent foreign distributor, unlike an agent, buys the goods from the seller for resale in the foreign country. As the foreign distributor then takes title to the goods once they have been purchased from the seller, the distributor assumes the risk of being unable to resell the goods and the distributor must usually arrange for a place of storage for the goods. As the seller has already sold the goods to the distributor, buyers of the products are buying directly from the distributor. Unlike the uncertainty on this issue in the case of the foreign agent, a distributor usually has no power to bind the seller. This is because the distributor is essentially buying the products from the seller for resale in the foreign nation and the relationship between the seller and the distributor is that of principal and independent contractor or principal to principal. Note that it is possible for the distributor to also act as an agent for goods not already obtained from the seller. It is also possible for the seller to explicitly confer a power on the distributor to bind the seller. A foreign distributor must usually make a greater financial commitment than a foreign agent. While an agent may be a small company or even an individual, a distributor is usually a larger, more established company with more substantial resources.

A.   Control

As the role of the agent is to find a buyer and not to set the terms of the sale, the agency relationship allows the seller-principal to control the price of the goods and the parties to whom the products are distributed. By contrast, an independent distributor takes title to the goods for resale and so the seller may lose control over the sales price and the customers to whom the products are sold. The seller can attempt to limit the powers of the independent distributor by contract but as this will be an attempt to inhibit inherent features of the distributor relationship, the seller may encounter resistance in contract negotiations with the distributor. Local laws may also restrict the ability of the seller to limit the freedom of the distributor.

Another element of control concerns the ability to appoint subagents or subdistributors without the prior consent of the seller. An agent normally does not have the power to appoint a subagent but a distributor, as a principal in its own right, can enter into its own arrangements with third parties for distribution unless the contract provides otherwise.

While the seller will usually wish for greater control over the agent/distributor, there are some downside risks. In general, the greater the degree of control the more likely the seller will be subject to liability under the laws of the foreign nation. If the agent is an actual employee of the seller, then the seller will be able to exert the greatest possible degree of control allowed by law. However, if the seller actually hires the agent as an employee, then the seller may become subject to the labor and tax laws of the foreign nation. As we shall further discuss below, the termination of agents or distributors is an important issue to consider in any event, but the termination of an employee, as opposed to an independent contractor, is usually subject to stricter requirements. For example, local labor laws might restrict the seller from terminating the agent without first satisfying requirements such as review by a labor bureau or some other onerous requirements. Some national labor laws might require the employee to belong to a labor union and the seller-employer to contribute to social welfare, insurance, and health care funds for employees. None of these requirements would generally apply to an independent contractor such as an agent or distributor.

An additional consideration is that where the agent/distributor is an employee, the sale of the product by the employee might subject the seller to the income tax laws of the foreign nation. The sale of the product by a local employee might be deemed to be income earned in the foreign nation by the seller. Local tax laws are less likely to apply in the case of an independent agent and distributor as the seller's connection with the foreign nation is more tenuous, but, in this matter, the seller would be well advised to review all tax issues with local foreign counsel as laws vary from jurisdiction to jurisdiction.

One other consideration concerns the seller's liability for the actions of the sales representative. Where the representative is an employee of the seller, the actions of the employee may not only be imputed to the seller for purposes of tort or contract liability but the presence of the employee in the foreign nation may be a basis for the assertion by the foreign courts of territorial jurisdiction over the seller in a lawsuit. The costs in time and resources of defending a lawsuit in a foreign nation is a substantial burden that most sellers will wish to avoid and should be a major consideration in choosing the form of sales representation in the foreign nation. It is less likely that the seller will be liable for the actions of an independent agent and even less so in the case of an independent distributor but the precise determination of these issues is a matter of local law that the seller would be well advised to review with local counsel.

A final issue concerning control relates to the conduct of the agent/distributor that may implicate the seller in illegal activity. This problem arises more often that you might think, and the issue is an especially serious one in developing countries. Foreign agents and distributors have been known to make illegal payments to government officials in order to obtain business, engage in tax evasion, use company funds for personal purposes, or use other improper means to advance business interests. In many developing countries without strong legal systems, illegal or questionable activities by business enterprises are common practices and often go ignored or unpunished but there is always the possibility for the seller of being implicated in illegal acts in the foreign nation. For a U.S. seller, there is also the specter of the Foreign Corrupt Practices Act (FCPA), which would expose the seller to criminal or civil liability for making or causing improper payments to foreign government officials. The seller should carefully screen potential candidates and should include an explicit provision in the agency/distributorship agreement that prohibits any act that violates the laws of the host nation. We consider the FCPA in detail in Chapter 6 on foreign direct investment, but the issue of illegal bribes is also a common problem in the case of agents and distributors.

B.   Antitrust and Anticompetition Issues

In many cases, the agent/distributor will wish to have exclusive rights for a particular territory and an exclusive arrangement may even be required by local law. As the agent/distributor will expend a considerable amount of time and resources in selling the products, it should not be surprising that the agent/distributor will seek to obtain exclusive rights to the territory.

Exclusive agreements involving a distributor, as opposed to an agent, may create antitrust or anticompetition issues. The distributorship agreement is an agreement between two independent business entities; if the agreement provides for exclusive territorial rights for the distributorship, this may be considered to be an agreement to divide markets that may run afoul of local antitrust laws. Outside of the United States, the European Union has the most advanced antitrust laws in the world and the seller must be aware of the possible antitrust implications of doing business in the EU. The EU has specific anticompetition rules that deal with exclusive distribution agreements that differ from those in the United States. It is important to note that the EU considers the territories of all of its member nations to be a single territory for competition purposes and so arrangements that might not appear on their face to be anticompetitive from a U.S. perspective might violate EU law. For example, a prohibition against selling outside of an EU country, such as Germany, may not be recognized as it is considered to restrict competition within all of the EU territories as a whole. As antitrust issues are important considerations in using distributorships in the EU, we consider this topic in further detail in the materials that follow.

A similar anticompetition issue may arise if the distributor is prohibited from selling competing or similar products. Such an arrangement may create issues both under the extraterritorial application of U.S. antitrust law, as the arrangement may prevent other U.S. companies from entering the foreign market, and under local anticompetition laws.

C.   Termination Issues

How and when an agency or distributorship may be terminated can be very important to both the seller and the agent/distributor. For this reason, it is essential for the seller to be familiar with the laws governing the termination of an agency or distributorship in the host nation. Many nations have laws that impose extensive costs upon the seller-principal upon the termination of an agency or distributorship. A number of nations, especially developing nations, are concerned about what they perceive to be attempts by sellers to exploit the local agent/distributor. Some sellers may use an agent/distributor to establish a distribution network and to make contacts with local customers. Once the seller becomes familiar with the customers and is able to establish direct contacts with the customers, the seller can then terminate the agency/distributorship relationship and sell directly to the customers or can install its own sales representative in the host nation. Many nations find this type of conduct to be unfair and predatory and have enacted laws to protect the agent/distributor.

The seller must bear in mind that the termination of the agency/distributorship relationship is rarely a happy event except in those cases where the parties proceed to form a joint venture. In most cases, the termination also signals a permanent end to the business relationship between the parties and usually signals some business failure in the relationship and disappointment on the part of the seller-principal or both parties. In addition to disappointment, there may even be some acrimony between the parties if the agent/distributor believes that it was unfairly treated and may seek to vindicate its rights under the protection afforded by local law. For these reasons, the seller must consider the choice of the agent/distributor carefully and provide for a detailed treatment of the termination issues in the agreement before the relationship is established. While the parties may not wish to consider termination issues during the flush of goodwill and optimism that usually accompanies the establishment of an agency/distributorship, these issues need to be carefully considered at the outset because the relationship between parties usually deteriorates significantly by the time of termination, making negotiations far more difficult.

In the bulk of national laws governing termination, a distinction is usually drawn between termination with cause and termination without cause. The distinction is important because the most onerous penalties for the seller-principal usually accompany termination without cause. The laws themselves may define just cause but regardless of whether such definitions exist, it is usually advisable for the seller to list in the agreement the reasons that justify termination for cause. The agreement should also provide for other contingencies that automatically terminate the agreement, such as bankruptcy or insolvency of the agent/distributor, nationalization of the property of the agent/distributor by the host nation, or other events that will terminate the agreement by way of force majeure. The most difficult termination issue in most cases is usually whether the agent/distributor's failure to reach stated sales quotas or minimum performance goals will constitute just cause for termination. In some countries, such a failure may not constitute just cause. Even where such failure may constitute just cause, it is usually advisable for the agreement to provide the agent/distributor with ample opportunities to cure defects in performance after fair notification. The seller would be well advised to be scrupulously fair in its treatment of the agent/distributor in nations that have restrictive laws protecting agents/distributors.

In the event of a termination that is deemed to be without cause, the agent/distributor may have extensive rights against the seller. The agent/distributor is usually entitled to a monetary settlement, which may be extensive and calculated as a percentage of the seller's gross sales during the entire period of the agreement or as a multiple of the agent/distributor's earnings during the term of the agreement. The seller may be required to pay the agent/distributor for any goods still in its possession, for the cost of any goodwill created by the agent/distributor with customers in connection with the seller's product, and for any advertising and promotional expenses incurred by the agent/distributor. Where there is a dispute between the parties about the rights of the agent/distributor, the seller may need to have its claims decided in a local court. The court may enjoin the seller from terminating the agency/distribution agreement pending the resolution of the dispute and prevent the seller from engaging another sales representative until the dispute is resolved. The foreign nation may also deny any import privileges for the seller for any additional products until the terminated agent/distributor has been fully compensated and all termination issues have been finally resolved.

D. Intellectual Property Issues

It is imperative that the seller protect its intellectual property rights in the products and other proprietary information involved in the agency/distributorship. Before entering into any agency/distribution agreement, the seller must first comply with the laws of the host nation to obtain local protection for its trademarks, patents, copyrights, trade secrets, and other forms of intellectual property. We will be examining the procedures for obtaining local protection of intellectual property in greater detail in a subsequent section in this chapter on licensing and technology transfer but for now we can simply note that many nations require the intellectual property owner to register its trademarks, patents, and copyrights under local law. The seller must ensure that all of these protections for its intellectual property are in place before doing business in the foreign nation.

Note that in this chapter and in Chapter 6 on foreign direct investment, we focus on what planning and preventive measures the seller can undertake to protect its intellectual property rights. Most of our attention will be on what procedures the seller or intellectual property owner must follow under international and national laws to obtain recognition of its patents, trademarks, and copyrights. We also examine the basic principles and types of contractual provisions the seller should include in the various agreements with the agent/distributor, licensee, or franchisee. We return to intellectual property in Chapter 7 where our focus shifts to what can be done after a theft has already occurred, which concerns the growing problem of commercial piracy. Another way to differentiate between our approach here is that we focus on prophylactic measures whereas Chapter 7 focuses on enforcement.

The agreement between the seller and the agent/distributor must make clear that the seller is the sole and exclusive owner of the intellectual property rights in the product and that the agent/distributor only has the right to obtain sales orders or to sell the products under the authority of the seller. The agreement should provide that the agent/distributor will not make any claims to the intellectual property in the products and must not copy, alter, develop, or use any of the intellectual property rights in the products for its own purposes or to promote its own businesses. The agent/distributor should also agree to notify the seller of any violations of its intellectual property rights in the territory and to assist the seller in enforcing its rights.

The seller will also likely disclose other confidential business information that may not qualify as intellectual property under applicable law that it will need to protect. Such information can be protected only by contract that imposes confidentiality obligations upon the agent/distributor and its employees. Many agreements provide that the confidential obligations survive the termination of the business relationship for a period of years or even indefinitely. Examples of confidential business information include the seller's corporate structure, financial information about the seller, the seller's marketing plans and business strategies, lists of customers, and information about the seller's personnel. The agreement should provide that the agent/distributor will share confidential information with its own employees on a need-to-know basis and to keep this information confidential from third parties.

E. Other Considerations

While the discussion above has drawn a number of distinctions between agents and distributors, in many cases it may not be clear whether the foreign party is an agent or a distributor under foreign law. Many foreign nations use these terms interchangeably or without precision. In some countries, laws regulating agency agreements have been extended by analogy to distribution agreements and laws regulating distributorships have extended to agency agreements. In the case of both agents and distributors, foreign laws may regulate these relationships far more extensively than laws in the United States. It is usually advisable that the seller have local counsel examine foreign laws closely and that the agreement between the parties is carefully drafted to make as clear as possible what type of relationship is being created. In general, language associated with an independent contractor should be used in connection with an independent distributor.

In the case of both the agency and the distributorship, it is essential that the parties reduce their agreement into a writing prior to entering into a business relationship. While this may seem evident, you may be surprised at the number of instances where parties do not have a written agreement at all, have an agreement that is not drafted by an experienced lawyer, or orally agree on a business relationship and leave it to their lawyers to draft the agreement later. Note that any agency or distribution agreement requires an understanding of U.S. law, the law of the distributor or agent's country, and any applicable international law, including regional international law that applies to agency/distributorships as in the case of the European Union. Like the sales contract that we considered in previous chapters, there can also be choice of law issues unless the parties agree to an applicable law, and even in the case of such agreement there can continue to be choice of law issues on matters that are not explicitly covered by the agreement. We provide a sample of a distribution agreement below.

PROBLEM 5-1

Worthington Superabrasives manufactures high-technology industrial diamonds and other abrasives under the trademark "Superabrasives" for use in drills and other industrial tools. Unlike other industrial abrasives, the products manufactured by Worthington have a much higher capacity for drilling through tough substances. Worthington has secured a U.S. patent for its products. Worthington, based in Ohio, has had only limited success in selling its products directly in Germany for several years and is seeking a sales representative in Germany for its products. Worthington is considering the use of an independent agent or a distributor and its general counsel has a number of questions for your law firm.

For the purposes of answering these questions, review the introductory materials on agents and distributors set forth above. You are also to assume that general principles of German law on issues such as jurisdiction and liability are similar to U.S. law.

(1) Worthington would like to pay the sales representative on a salary and commission basis rather than a salary.

(2) In the event that a person using tools that contain products manufactured by Worthington is injured in Germany, which form of business arrangement will more likely lead to jurisdiction over the company in a lawsuit filed in Germany?

(3) In a personal injury lawsuit in Germany, which form of business arrangement will more likely lead to a finding of liability on the part of the company?

(4) It is important for the company to maintain price controls over the products sold so that its pricing structure in Germany is similar to its pricing structure in other European markets. Which business relationship will allow the company to maintain stricter control over pricing?

(5) It is also important for Worthington to maintain strict control over customer lists. For various reasons, the company wishes for its products to be used by high-end, qualified customers and does not wish for its products to be used in low-end manufacturing. Which business relationship will allow the company to maintain stricter control over the customers who buy its products?

After examining these questions and further considering the issue, which form of business arrangement, independent agent or distributor, would you recommend to Worthington?

PROBLEM 5-2

One of the sales representatives that is being considered by Worthington is an upstart, aggressive German company with strong connections to industrial suppliers for the German government. The German company has asked to be paid in sales commissions and has asked that Worthington make all payments to its account in a Luxembourg bank. The German company says that it has kept the account for years to service all of its operations in Europe. Advise Worthington.

PROBLEM 5-3

Worthington has entered into the distribution agreement below with Berens, a small Germany company that manufactures and distributes industrial abrasives in Germany and several other European nations. The products manufactured and sold by Berens are not as advanced as those sold by Worthington. Several issues have arisen on which Worthington would like your advice.

(1) As part of its promotional activities, Berens intends to take out a number of advertisements in newspapers and industrial journals stating that "Berens is proud to offer a new line of industrial abrasives under the

brand name 'Superabrasives' that will meet the world's highest standards for your industrial uses. Contact Wolfgang Schmidt for a demonstration of our exciting new products and to place your order." Should Worthington take issue with this advertisement? See Articles 4 and 6 of the distribution agreement. If you were advising Worthington, what language would you suggest for the Berens advertisement?

(2) Berens has given some of the Worthington diamonds that it purchased but was unable to sell to its research and development laboratory, which has discovered that through a process of polishing and refining, the Worthington industrial diamonds can be transformed into diamonds that are suitable for use in expensive watches and clocks. Berens now seeks to obtain a German patent on the refining process. Berens claims that the process could have been developed using any industrial diamonds. Worthington does not compete in any diamond industries related to uses for watches or clocks. Have any of Worthington's rights under the agreement been violated? See Article 4. What remedies are available to Worthington under the agreement? Can Worthington assert any rights to the patent for the refining process or prevent Berens from obtaining the patent?

Distribution Agreement

This Agreement is made by and between:
Worthington Superabrasives (hereinafter "MANUFACTURER/SELLER"), a corporation formed under the laws of the State of Ohio, United States of America
- and -
Berens, GmbH (hereinafter "DISTRIBUTOR"), a corporation formed under the laws of the Federal Republic of Germany.
WITNESSED:
WHEREAS:
I.   MANUFACTURER/SELLER is engaged in the business of manufacturing industrial diamonds and other abrasives (the "Products") and selling the Products in the United States; is the owner of the trademark "Superabrasives" in the United States, the Federal Republic of Germany, and other countries around the world; is also the owner of German patent No. 6,820-1564 for the Products and the owner of patents for the Products in the United States and other countries around the world;
II.   DISTRIBUTOR has the means and experience to market and distribute the products in the Federal Republic of Germany; and
III.   MANUFACTURER/SELLER and DISTRIBUTOR have reached an agreement as hereinafter set forth.
In consideration of the mutual covenants and agreements herein contained, the Parties hereto, intending to be legally bound hereby, covenant and agree as follows:

Article 1.   Appointment

MANUFACTURER/SELLER hereby appoints DISTRIBUTOR and DISTRIBUTOR hereby accepts appointment as exclusive distributor of the Products (as detailed in Exhibit A hereto) in the Federal Republic of Germany (the "TERRITORY") subject to the terms and conditions of this Agreement.

Article 2.   Independent Contractor Status

DISTRIBUTOR is an independent contractor, and this Agreement does not constitute DISTRIBUTOR the agent or legal representative of MANUFACTURER/ SELLER for any purpose whatsoever. DISTRIBUTOR is not granted any right or authority to assume or to create an obligation or responsibility, expressed or implied, on behalf of or in the name of MANUFACTURER/SELLER or to bind MANUFACTURER/ SELLER in any manner.

Article 3.   Performance by DISTRIBUTOR

3.1   DISTRIBUTOR agrees to use its best good-faith efforts to achieve the highest possible sales volume in the Territory with a goal of purchasing no less than $75,000 worth of the Products from the MANUFACTURER/SELLER in each one-year period of this Agreement.

3.2   DISTRIBUTOR hereby agrees not to sell, develop, or manufacture any product that competes with the Products or to distribute any of the products by a competitor of the MANUFACTURER/SELLER that competes with the Products as set forth in Exhibit A attached hereto. This agreement shall not apply to any products that the DISTRIBUTOR may offer for sale as of the date of execution of this agreement.

non-compete

Article 4.   Intellectual Property and Other Proprietary Rights of the MANUFACTURER/SELLER

4.1   DISTRIBUTOR hereby acknowledges that any patents, trademarks, copyrights, trade secrets, know-how, or any other forms of intellectual property (collectively "Intellectual Property") in the Products are the sole and exclusive property of the MANUFACTURER/SELLER. Any use by DISTRIBUTOR of the Intellectual Property in the Products for promotional, advertising, or any other purposes must be in furtherance of the purposes of this Agreement. DISTRIBUTOR shall not make, assert, or cause any third parties to make or assert any claim to the Intellectual Property of the MANUFACTURER/SELLER. DISTRIBUTOR further acknowledges that it shall not provide access to such intellectual property to any third parties without the prior written authorization of the MANUFACTURER/SELLER.

4.2   DISTRIBUTOR shall immediately notify MANUFACTURER/SELLER of any violations or infringements upon MANUFACTURER/SELLER's Intellectual Property rights in the Products within the territory and shall assist MANUFACTURER/SELLER in the protection and enforcement of its Intellectual Property within the territory. However, in no event shall DISTRIBUTOR seek to enforce the Intellectual Property rights in the Products in its own name but shall act at all times on behalf of MANUFACTURER/SELLER. All expenses incurred in connection with the protection of the Intellectual Property within the territory shall be borne by MANUFACTURER/SELLER.

4.3   DISTRIBUTOR further acknowledges that it shall be given access to other valuable and confidential information of the MANUFACTURER/SELLER including, but not limited to, confidential business and financial information, marketing plans, developmental designs and information, processes, procedures, addresses, telephone numbers, customers lists, information about personnel, and other confidential information and data relating to the business of MANUFACTURER/ SELLER (hereinafter "Proprietary Information"). DISTRIBUTOR further acknowledges that MANUFACTURER/SELLER has valid reasons to protect such Proprietary Information and DISTRIBUTOR hereby agrees to take the following steps: (1) keep all Proprietary Information confidential and secret by not disclosing such information to any third parties without the prior written authorization of MANUFACTURER/SELLER; (2) use such Proprietary Information only in accordance with the purposes of this Agreement; (3) provide such Proprietary Information only to employees of the DISTRIBUTOR who have the need to know such information; and (4) take all steps to protect the confidentiality of such Proprietary Information in accordance with the laws of the Federal Republic of Germany. The obligations set forth in this Article shall survive the termination of this Agreement indefinitely.

Article 5.   Purchase Price and Payment

5.1   Each order for the Products shall be placed by DISTRIBUTOR by a written purchase order at the offices of the MANUFACTURER/SELLER or at such other place as the MANUFACTURER/SELLER may designate by notice to the DISTRIBUTOR. The order shall become effective upon the DISTRIBUTOR's receipt of an order acknowledgment from MANUFACTURER/SELLER.

5.2   Unless otherwise agreed to by the parties in writing, prices for all products shall be C&F Hamburg (as per Incoterms 2000) and the Products shall be shipped by ocean freight on board a vessel to be nominated by Berens. The prices for the Products shall be the wholesale prices established by the MANUFACTURER/SELLER in the price list attached as set forth in Exhibit A attached hereto plus cost and freight. Each order shall be placed at least ninety days in advance of delivery to DISTRIBUTOR.

5.3   Unless otherwise agreed by the parties in writing, MANUFACTURER/SELLER shall invoice DISTRIBUTOR within thirty days after delivery of the products to DISTRIBUTOR. DISTRIBUTOR shall pay by bill of exchange within thirty business days from the date of the invoice.

Article 6.   Marketing

6.1   DISTRIBUTOR shall use its best efforts to actively promote the sale of the Products in the Territory. Best efforts include the use of appropriate advertising levels to support the sale of the Products according to the change of market conditions.

6.2   DISTRIBUTOR hereby agrees to submit to MANUFACTURER/SELLER a marketing plan within thirty days from the date of execution of this agreement and, on a quarterly basis, which shall include such information as sales projections, marketing objectives, and achievement of those objectives.

6.3   All expenses incurred in advertising and promoting the Products in the Territory shall be the responsibility of the DISTRIBUTOR. The marketing and advertising spending plan shall be developed by DISTRIBUTOR. MANUFACTURER/SELLER shall be given an opportunity to review the plan and to provide comments.

Article 7.   Service and Marketing Assistance

7.1   MANUFACTURER/SELLER shall provide to DISTRIBUTOR at no cost, operation, instruction, and service manuals that DISTRIBUTOR shall provide to customers.

7.2   MANUFACTURER/SELLER agrees to sell DISTRIBUTOR replacement or spare parts for the Products in accordance with the prices set forth in Exhibit A attached hereto. The sale of spare parts shall occur in accordance with the terms and conditions set forth in Article 5.

Article 8.   Warranties and Liability

8.1   MANUFACTURER/SELLER hereby warrants that the Products sold by MANUFACTURER/SELLER to DISTRIBUTOR shall be free from any defects in materials and workmanship for a period of twelve months from the date of shipment by DISTRIBUTOR to its customer. This warranty shall not apply to any defects caused by normal wear and tear, improper or unreasonable use, or improper installation.

8.2   MANUFACTURER/SELLER's sole obligation under the warranty set forth in this section is expressly limited to providing replacement or repair of defective Products or parts thereof.

8.3   The warranty in this Article is expressly in lieu of any other express or implied warranty, including any implied warranty of merchantability or fitness for any particular purpose, with respect to any of the Products sold by MANUFACTURER/SELLER under this Agreement.

Article 9.   Compliance with Laws and Regulations

DISTRIBUTOR shall at all times in the conduct of the distribution and sale of the Products strictly comply with all laws and regulations in force in the Territory pertaining to the Products distributed hereunder. DISTRIBUTOR shall also comply with all laws and regulations in force in the Territory pertaining to the proper and lawful conduct of business activity, including laws applicable to improper and illegal payments to government officials for the purpose of obtaining or retaining business. DISTRIBUTOR also acknowledges that it is familiar with the U.S. Foreign Corrupt Practices Act (FCPA) and that it shall not perform or cause to be performed any act that would result in any liability of the MANUFACTURER/SELLER under the FCPA. DISTRIBUTOR shall be solely responsible for any penalties occasioned by the act or failure to act of DISTRIBUTOR.

Article 10.   Term and Termination

10.1   Subject to the termination provisions herein, the Term of this Agreement shall begin on the date of execution set forth below; and shall continue thereafter for successive periods of three years unless and until either party shall give the other not less than ninety (90) days written notice prior to the next expiration date of its decision not to renew. At the end of the first three-year period, the parties shall enter in good faith in discussions concerning the formation of a joint venture in the Federal Republic of Germany for the production and sale of the Products.

(a)   In the event that a Party hereto defaults in the observance or performance of any of its obligations hereunder the other Party shall have the right to terminate this Agreement on thirty (30) days' prior written notice, provided, however, that such notice shall be without effect if such default is remedied within the thirty (30) days' notice period. Defaults in the observance or performance of any obligations under this Agreement shall constitute grounds for termination with cause.

(b)   If DISTRIBUTOR fails to make timely payment of any amounts due to MANUFACTURER/SELLER hereunder, MANUFACTURER/SELLER may notify DISTRIBUTOR in writing, of its intention to terminate this Agreement, and if payment in full is not received within thirty (30) days after the giving of such notice, MANUFACTURE/SELLER may terminate this Agreement immediately.

(c)   If either Party shall cease to do business or be adjudicated as bankrupt or insolvent, or shall make an assignment for the benefit of its creditors or a composition with its creditors, or shall file a voluntary bankruptcy petition, or shall consent to such involuntary petition, or shall commit an act of bankruptcy pursuant to any applicable law of the Federal Republic of Germany, or if an order is entered appointing a receiver or trustee of either Party or of a substantial portion of the property of either Party, or if either Party applies for or consents to the appointment of any such receiver or trustee, then and in every such event the other Party shall be entitled to terminate this Agreement at any time with written notice.

(d)   Upon termination of this Agreement for any cause whatsoever, all amounts owing hereunder between the Parties hereto shall become immediately due and payable.

(e)   Upon termination of this Agreement for any reason, MANUFACTURER/SELLER shall be entitled to repurchase and take possession of any Products previously purchased by DISTRIBUTOR that are not committed under a prior business arrangement for sale to customers of the DISTRIBUTOR. The parties shall negotiate a price for the repurchase of such products but in no case shall the repurchase price exceed the price paid by the DISTRIBUTOR. DISTRIBUTOR shall also return any instruction manuals, brochures, installation manuals, or any other written materials provided by MANUFACTURER/SELLER to DISTRIBUTOR in connection with the performance of this Agreement.

(f)   Upon termination of this Agreement for any reason other than the non-renewal of the Agreement by MANUFACTURER/SELLER without cause, DISTRIBUTOR shall not demonstrate, promote, sell, distribute, or service any products that are similar to or compete with the Products for a period of one year. The MANUFACTURER/SELLER shall have the sole right to determine which products are similar to or compete with the Products.

10.2   Within the first 21 days of the first quarter of each year MANUFACTURER/SELLER shall pay to DISTRIBUTOR an amount equal to 5% of the gross annual purchases for the prior year of the products by DISTRIBUTOR from MANUFACTURER/SELLER. This payment shall be considered an advance payment of any claims to compensation by DISTRIBUTOR in the event of termination by MANUFACTURER/SELLER of the business relationship between the parties. DISTRIBUTOR hereby acknowledges that it shall not receive and that it shall not seek any additional compensation from MANUFACTURER/SELLER in the event of termination by MANUFACTURER/SELLER.

Article 11.   General

11.1   Force Majeure: In the event that either Party is prevented, interrupted, or delayed in the performance of its obligations hereunder by riots, wars, acts of war, acts of God, fires, floods, accidents, strikes, labor disputes, embargoes, governmental orders or regulations (whether valid or invalid and including, without limitation, priorities, requisitions, allocations and price adjustment restrictions), delays of carriers, lack of transportation facilities, inability to obtain raw materials, curtailment of or failure in obtaining fuel or electrical power, or by any other similar or dissimilar occurrence beyond the reasonable control of such Party, the said Party shall be excused from the performance of its obligations hereunder while and to the extent that it is so prevented, interrupted and/or delayed; provided, that the Party so affected shall use its best efforts to avoid or remove such causes of nonperformance and shall continue performance hereunder with the utmost dispatch whenever such causes are removed.

11.2   Governing Law: The Parties agree that this Agreement and their respective rights and obligations hereunder shall be governed by and construed in accordance with the laws of the State of Ohio, United States of America.

11.3   Dispute Resolution: In the event of any controversy or claim arising out of or relating to this contract, the parties hereto shall consult and negotiate with each other and, recognizing their mutual interests, attempt to reach a solution satisfactory to both parties. If they do not reach settlement within 60 days, then either party may, upon notice to the other party and the International Centre for Dispute Resolution, demand mediation under the International Mediation Rules of the International Centre for Dispute Resolution. If settlement is not reached within 60 days after service of a written demand for mediation, any unresolved controversy or claim arising out of or relating to this contract, or the breach, termination, or invalidity thereof, shall be settled by arbitration under the UNCITRAL Arbitration Rules in effect on the date of this contract. The appointed authority shall be the International Centre for Dispute Resolution. The case shall be administered by the International Centre for Dispute Resolution under its Procedures for Cases under the UNCITRAL Arbitration Rules.

11.4   Waiver: The failure of either Party to assert any of its rights hereunder or to exercise any remedy available to it shall not constitute a waiver of such right or remedy and no waiver shall be made except in writing. The waiver of any term or provision hereof shall not constitute a waiver of such term or provision for the future unless expressly so provided.

11.5   Assignment: No Party may assign this Agreement or any rights granted hereunder without the prior written consent of the other Party.

11.6   Language: The English language version of this Agreement shall be the authorized text for all purposes.

IN WITNESS WHEREOF, the Parties hereto have executed this Agreement on the dates mentioned below.

* * *

1.   *Local and Regional Legal Requirements*

The distribution agreement set forth above is subject to various sources of both private and public law. It is subject to the substantive private law of contracts and any specific laws relating to agency and distributorships of the United States and Germany. We have included the German Commercial Code in the materials below as an example of a private law governing agency and distribution agreements in a foreign nation. Note that German contract law and general civil law provisions may also apply to this contract. In addition to German law, the law of the European Union may also apply to the agreement. While German law will apply to the private law issues (e.g., contract), European Union law in the form of the Treaty of Rome and related regulations will apply to the mandatory public law issues of antitrust and anticompetition law regulation. Under the hierarchy of sources of law, EU law applies directly to activity in Germany and will supersede German law in case of a conflict.

A. GERMAN LAW

The distribution agreement set forth above is subject to regulation under the German Commercial Code, which contains a number of provisions designed to protect the appointed agent. Note that the provisions of the German Commercial Code apply to agents as opposed to independent distributors. The concept of an independent distributor is relatively recent under German law and there are currently no distinct rules that apply to independent distributors. However, German courts have held that certain provisions of the law of agency set forth below, including §§86, 86a, 88, 89, 89a, 90, and 90a, apply to independent distributors by analogy. *See Koller/Roth/Morek*, Handelgesetzbuch (1996).

PROBLEM 5-4

Two years after the execution of the distribution agreement set forth above, Worthington becomes dissatisfied with Berens' performance. Berens has purchased $100,000 worth of products from Worthington during this period and has been able to earn a profit during this period from its resale of the products to consumers in Germany. Berens' purchases of products from Worthington for resale in Germany are much higher than Worthington's previous direct sales to Germany but having examined Berens' customer lists, having attended sales meetings with Berens' customers, and doing some additional research, Worthington believes that Berens is not aggressively pursuing sales among its existing customers and a number of potential new customers. Worthington believes that it could easily double Berens' sales if Worthington were able to market these products directly to customers in Germany. Worthington now wants to terminate the agreement with Berens but has several questions:

(1) Can Worthington sell into Germany on its own? See Article 1 of the distribution agreement. If Worthington does so, what rights will Berens have?

(2) Can Worthington terminate for cause? See Article 3.1. How much notice must Worthington give Berens? See Article 10; see also German Commercial Code §§89 and 89a. Suppose instead that Berens had been selling competing products made by a Swiss competitor of Worthington. Could Worthington terminate for cause? How much notice would Worthington have to give Berens in this case?

(3) What is the advantage to Worthington of terminating for cause as opposed to terminating without cause? See German Commercial Code §89b(3).

(4) If Worthington terminates because of unsatisfactory performance, is Berens entitled to compensation after termination? See Article 10.2; see also German Commercial Code §89b(4). If Berens is entitled to compensation, what is the maximum amount that Berens can receive?

(5) Should Worthington even be concerned about compensation after termination? Assume that Ohio law is silent on this issue. See Article 11.2; but cf. German Civil Code Article 6 and note 2 in the Notes and Questions on p. 346 *infra*.

(6) After Worthington terminates the distributorship, Berens begins selling industrial abrasives that are of average or ordinary capacity as opposed to the super-hard abrasives sold by Worthington. Can Worthington prohibit Berens from selling these products? See Article 10.1(f); see also German Commercial Code §90a.

German Statutes Relating to Agency Agreements

COMMERCIAL CODE SECTION 84

(1) A commercial agent is anyone who, as an independent person pursuing a trade, is regularly entrusted to negotiate business transactions for another entrepreneur or to conclude business transactions in his name. A person is independent if he is essentially free to arrange his activity and specify his hours of work.

(2) Anyone who, without being independent within the meaning of Subsection 1, is regularly entrusted to solicit business transactions for an entrepreneur or to conclude business transactions in his name is deemed an employee.

COMMERCIAL CODE SECTION 89

(1) Where the contractual relationship has been concluded for an indefinite duration, it can be terminated in the first year of the agreement on one month's notice, in the second year of the agreement on two months' notice and in the third to fifth years on three months' notice. Where another termination notice period is agreed to, it must be at least one month; termination can only be as of the close of a calendar month. After a contractual duration of five years, the contract may be terminated on six months' notice. Notice shall only take effect at the end of a calendar month, unless otherwise agreed.

(2) The notice periods according to Subsection 1 Sentences 1 and 2 may be extended by agreement; the notice period may not be shorter for the entrepreneur than for the agent. Where a shorter period is agreed for the entrepreneur, then the notice period agreed for the agent shall apply instead.

(3) Where a contractual relationship concluded for a definite duration is continued by both parties after expiration of the agreed duration it shall be deemed to be extended indefinitely. For determining the notice periods under Subsection 1 Sentences 1 and 2, the cumulative duration of the relationship shall be controlling.

COMMERCIAL CODE SECTION 89A

(1) The contractual relationship can be terminated without notice by either party for good cause. This right cannot be excluded or limited.

(2) Where termination results from conduct of the other party, this party is obligated to compensate for damages resulting from the termination of the contractual relationship.

COMMERCIAL CODE SECTION 89B

(1) The commercial agent can, after expiration of the contractual relationship, demand from the entrepreneur reasonable compensation if and in so far as

1. the entrepreneur obtained substantial advantages, after expiration of the contractual period, from the business relations with new customers solicited by the commercial agent;
2. the commercial agent lost, by reason of termination of the contractual relationship, rights to commissions relating to concluded business transactions or business transactions to be concluded in the future with those customers he had solicited, which he would have had the contractual relationship continued; and
3. the payment of compensation is equitable, in consideration of all circumstances.

Where the commercial agent has so significantly expanded business with a customer that this commercially corresponds to solicitation of a new customer, it shall be considered to be the solicitation of a new customer.

(2) Compensation may amount to no more than the average of the annual commission or other annual compensation over the last five years of the activity of the commercial agent; in the event that the contractual relationship has lasted less than five years, the average during the period of activity is applicable.

(3) The right does not exist if

1. the commercial agent has terminated the contractual relationship, unless conduct of the entrepreneur provided reasonable cause therefore or the commercial agent cannot be reasonably expected to continue because of age or ill health, or
2. the entrepreneur terminated the contractual relationship for serious cause based upon the fault of the commercial agent, or
3. based on an agreement between the entrepreneur and the commercial agent, a third party succeeds the commercial agent in the contractual relationship; the agreement may not be concluded before the termination of the contractual relationship.

(4) The right to compensation cannot be excluded in advance. It must be asserted within one year following termination of the contractual relationship.

COMMERCIAL CODE SECTION 90A

(1) An agreement by which a commercial agent is restricted in his commercial activity following termination of the contractual relationship (agreement prohibiting competition) must be in writing and the document containing the conditions

agreed to signed by the entrepreneur must be provided to the commercial agent. The agreement can be made for no longer than two years following the termination of the contractual relationship; it may only relate to the region or group of customers allocated to the commercial agent, and only to the objects regarding which the commercial agent is to strive to solicit or conclude business transactions for the entrepreneur. The entrepreneur is obligated to pay reasonable compensation to the commercial agent for the duration of the prohibition of competition. . . .

(3) Where the commercial agent terminates the contractual relationship for cause based on the fault of the entrepreneur, he can, in writing within one month following the termination, declare himself unrestricted by the prohibition of competition.

(4) Agreements differing from these provisions to the detriment of the commercial agent cannot be made.

COMMERCIAL CODE SECTION 92c

(1) Where it is intended that the commercial agent will not perform his activities for the entrepreneur under the contract within the territory of the European Community or other Contracting State of the Agreement on the European Economic Area, then all provisions of this Part can be altered by agreement.

CIVIL CODE ARTICLE 6

The application of any foreign law is excluded if its application could obviously not be reconciled with basic principles of German Law. In particular the application is excluded, if this could not be reconciled with the basic constitutional rights.

B. EUROPEAN UNION ANTICOMPETITION LAW

We have also set forth below the basic anticompetition provisions of the Treaty of Rome, which formally established the European Economic Community on January 1, 1958, one of the first institutions of European unity. [The European Economic Community was renamed the European Community after the Treaty of Maastricht in 1993 to emphasize the centrality of the community's noneconomic goals.] At the end of the Second World War, a number of Western European countries believed that it was necessary to establish unity among European states to overcome the disastrous effects of the war and to achieve the benefits of harmonization and economies of scale in order to bring a higher standard of living to Europe as a whole. There were three different basic organizations of states or "communities" that were established in the period following the war. In addition to the European Economic Community, the European Coal and Steel Community was established by the Treaty of Paris in 1952,[1] and the European Atomic Energy

---

1. The origin of the European Coal and Steel Community can be traced to the end of the Second World War. The French occupied the iron- and coal-rich Saar terrritory, which was to be reunited with Germany. The French were concerned with its return to Germany, as its previous return to Germany at the end of the First World War helped to fuel Nazi

Community was established by the Euroatom Treaty also on January 1, 1958. Although these three communities began with separate administrative structures, the three eventually unified their administrative organizations into a single European parliament, a consultative body with control over budget issues; a council of ministers, a legislative body; and a European commission, an executive body. These three communities continue to exist as legal entities but now form the economic "pillar" of the European Union, a political entity established by the Treaty of Masstricht signed on February 7, 1992, and the Treaty on European Union signed on October 29, 1993, which sought to deepen the economic and political integration of Europe. We will consider the EU in greater detail in Chapter 6.

The major provisions in the field of anticompetition law (what we would call antitrust law in the United States) are Articles 85 and 86 of the Treaty of Rome (now renumbered as Articles 81 and 82, respectively), which are often said to be related to Articles 1 and 2 of the Sherman Act. Article 85, similar to Article 1 of *Art. 85* the Sherman Act, prohibits agreements, decisions by associations, and concerted practices that have as their object or effect the prevention, reduction, or distortion of competition that may affect trade between the member states. Article 86, similar *Art. 86* to Article 2 of the Sherman Act, addresses the issue of monopolization or abuse of a dominant position. These provisions may be relevant to distributorships and licensing agreements.

The Treaty of Rome is a form of primary legislation or constitutional law that has direct effect within the territories of member states and is applied in national courts. There are also two forms of secondary legislation: Regulations, which also *reg. &* have direct effect; and directives to the member states directing them to amend *directives* their legislation to conform with community laws. Although the council of ministers (so named because it consists of ministers from each of the member states) is a law-making body, the council has delegated law-making authority to the European Commission in the field of competition law that is governed by Articles 81 and 82 the Treaty of Rome. The commission has the power to issue regulations that create exemptions from the broad prohibitions of certain types of activities by the Treaty of Rome. The commission has done so in the areas of distribution, patent and know-how licensing, and franchising, which we shall consider below.

Note that the structure of Article 81 of the Treaty of Rome, which we set forth below, is to set out a very broad prohibition [Article 81(1)]; to provide that all such agreements, decisions, or concerted practices violating the prohibitions are void *void* [Article 81(2)]; and then to authorize the European Commission to issue exemptions to the prohibitions [Article 81(3)]. The basic justification for these *exemptions* exemptions is that some types of anticompetitive conduct that would otherwise be void should be exempted and permitted because the benefits of the conduct outweigh the harm.

European Commission Regulation No. 2790/1999, set out below following Article 81, is an example of a block exemption to the prohibitions contained in

---

expansionism but long-term French occupation also seemed implausible as the territory's population was mostly German. The Saar was returned to German control in 1957. In the meantime, six principal countries in Western Europe (France, Germany, Italy, Belgium, Netherlands, and Luxembourg) established a community to "Europeanize" the coal and steel industries in Europe through the Paris Treaty of 1952, a precursor to the Rome Treaty establishing the European Economic Community in 1958.

Article 81. Since a block exemption exempts an entire category of agreements and activities, it must be issued in the form of a regulation. The 1999 block exemption is a single provision that unifies and replaces earlier block exemptions issued by the EC in the areas of exclusive distribution (No. 1983/83), exclusive purchasing (No. 1984/83), and franchising (No. 4087/88). The approach of the 1999 block exemption departs from those of its predecessors in that it does not use an approach based on the so-called "black lists" and "white lists." Rather, the approach under the 1999 block exemption is that everything that is not prohibited is permitted. The 1999 block exemption is also an economics-based approach that departs from the more formalistic approach of its predecessors. As long as the parties involved do not cross certain thresholds of market share, their agreements, decisions, or concerted practices, even if anticompetitive, are permitted as they are deemed to lack a sufficient impact on the market.

In addition to block exemptions, the commission also has the authority to issue individual exemptions to the proscriptions contained in Article 81(1) and in Article 82, which prohibits abuse of a dominant market position. An individual exemption may be granted only upon an application to the commission made in the form of a notification under Articles 4 and 5 of Regulation 17. Since the grant of an individual exemption may affect the rights of third parties, the commission will give public notice to interested third parties who may make their objections known to the commission or who may challenge the exemption if it is later granted with the European Court of Justice. A proceeding to obtain an individual exemption usually takes up to one year. Parties who are in doubt as to whether their agreements fall within a block exemption can also notify the commission and request a formal clearance, which is then treated similarly to a request for an individual exemption. An individual exemption gives the parties legal certainty and binds national courts as to the application of European Community law to the agreement in question.

Parties can also request a negative clearance, which is a declaration by the commission that it sees no grounds to take action under either Article 81(1) or 82 on the facts before it. Unlike an exemption, a negative clearance does not provide legal certainty and is not binding on national courts. A negative clearance, however, can be obtained more quickly than an individual exemption. The commission can also issue "comfort letters," which informally confirm that the parties have not violated Article 81, meet the requirements for an individual exemption, or satisfy a block exemption. Comfort letters may be issued in a considerably quicker period of time than individual exemptions or negative clearances but provide less legal certainty. When submitting their notices to the commission, parties are now asked to specify whether they would be satisfied with a comfort letter instead of a formal exemption or a negative clearance.

PROBLEM 5-5

Worthington Superabrasives is considering a renewal and extension of the distribution agreement with some amendments but is concerned about whether any of the existing provisions or proposed amendments might run afoul of antitrust issues under European Union law. In answering the following questions, assume that Berens has annual total revenues of $50 million and has a 30 percent market share and that Worthington has a 25 percent market share in Germany. Worthington has the following questions:

(1) Is the distribution agreement, as written, subject to the prohibition contained in Article 81(1) of the Treaty of Rome set forth below? If so, the agreement is void under Article 81(2) unless there is an applicable exemption under Article 81(3). Does the exemption contained in Article 2 of Commission Regulation No. 2790/1999 apply? What about Article 3? *Ar. 2(b) seems to allow it.*

falls under exemption

Art. 3 – no prob.

(2) Worthington would like to add a provision that requires Berens to sell its products at no less than 90 percent of the sales price of the product in the United States. Is this lawful? See Article 4(a) of the regulation. *seems unlawful – pressure*

(3) Worthington would like to add a provision that restricts Berens from selling the products in France and Italy. Worthington wishes to sell directly to customers in those two countries. Would such a provision be lawful? See Article 4(b). *seems ok*

(4) Does the noncompetition clause contained in Article 10.1(f) of the distribution agreement violate EU law? What about the nondisclosure clause in Article 4.3 of the distribution agreement? On both questions, see Article 5(b) of EC Regulation No. 2790/1999. *possibly ok*

Treaty Establishing the European Community

ARTICLE 81 (EX ARTICLE 85)

1. The following shall be prohibited as incompatible with the common market: all agreements between undertakings, decisions by associations of undertakings and concerted practices which may affect trade between Member States and which have as their object or effect the prevention, restriction or distortion of competition within the common market, and in particular those which:

(a) directly or indirectly fix purchase or selling prices or any other trading conditions;

(b) limit or control production, markets, technical development, or investment;

(c) share markets or sources of supply;

(d) apply dissimilar conditions to equivalent transactions with other trading parties, thereby placing them at a competitive disadvantage;

(e) make the conclusion of contracts subject to acceptance by the other parties of supplementary obligations which, by their nature or according to commercial usage, have no connection with the subject of such contracts.

2. Any agreements or decisions prohibited pursuant to this Article shall be automatically void.

3. The provisions of paragraph 1 may, however, be declared inapplicable in the case of:

- any agreement or category of agreements between undertakings;
- any decision or category of decisions by associations of undertakings;
- any concerted practice or category of concerted practices, which contributes to improving the production or distribution of goods or to

promoting technical or economic progress, while allowing consumers a fair share of the resulting benefit and which does not:

(a) impose on the undertakings concerned restrictions which are not indispensable to the attainment of these objectives;

(b) afford such undertakings the possibility of eliminating competition in respect of a substantial part of the products in question.

Commission Regulation (EC) No. 2790/1999 of 22 December 1999 on the Application of Article 81(3) of the Treaty to Categories of Vertical Agreements and Concerted Practices

ARTICLE 2

1. Pursuant to Article 81(3) of the Treaty and subject to the provisions of this Regulation, it is hereby declared that Article 81(1) shall not apply to agreements or concerted practices entered into between two or more undertakings each of which operates, for the purposes of the agreement, at a different level of the production or distribution chain, and relating to the conditions under which the parties may purchase, sell or resell certain goods or services ("vertical services").

This exemption shall apply to the extent that such agreements contain restrictions of competition falling within the scope of Article 81(1). . . .

4. The exemption provided for in paragraph 1 shall not apply to vertical agreements entered into between competing undertakings;[2] however, it shall apply where competing undertakings enter into a non-reciprocal vertical agreement and:

(a) the buyer has a total annual turnover not exceeding EUR 100 million,[3] or

(b) the supplier is a manufacturer and a distributor of goods, while the buyer is a distributor not manufacturing goods competing with the contract goods, or

(c) the supplier is a provider of services at several levels of trade, while the buyer does not provide competing services at the level of trade where it purchases the contract services.

ARTICLE 3

1. Subject to paragraph 2 of this Article, the exemption provided in Article 2 shall apply on condition that the market share held by the supplier does not exceed 30% of the relevant market on which it sells the contract goods or services.

---

2. Article 1(a) of the Treaty of Rome provides:

"competing undertakings" means actual or potential suppliers in the same product market; the product market includes goods or services which are regarded by the buyer as interchangeable with or substitutable for the contract goods or services by reason of the products' characteristics, their prices and their intended use.

— EDS.

3. As of this writing, the conversion rate is 1 euro (EUR) = 1.17 U.S. dollars (USD).

— EDS.

2. In the case of vertical agreements containing exclusive obligations, the exemption provided for in Article 2 shall apply on condition that the market share held by the buyer does not exceed 30% of the relevant market on which it purchases the contract goods or services.

ARTICLE 4

The exemption provided for in Article 2 shall not apply to vertical agreements which, directly or indirectly, in isolation or in combination with other factors under the control of the parties, have as their object:

(a) the restriction of the buyer's ability to determine its sale price, without prejudice to the possibility of the supplier's imposing a maximum sale price or recommending a sale price, provided that they do not amount to a fixed or minimum sale price as a result of pressure from or incentives offered by, any of the parties;

(b) the restriction of the territory into which, or of the customers to whom, the buyer may sell the contract goods or services, except:

- the restriction of active sales into the exclusive territory or to an exclusive customer group reserved to the supplier or allocated by the supplier to another buyer, where such a restriction does not limit sales by the customers of the buyer,
- the restriction of sales to end users by a buyer operating at the wholesale level of trade,
- the restriction of sales to unauthorized distributors by the members of a selective distribution system, and
- the restriction of the buyer's ability to sell components, supplied for the purposes of incorporation, to customers who would use them to manufacture the same type of goods as those produced by the supplier.

ARTICLE 5

The exemption provided for in Article 2 shall not apply to any of the following obligations contained in vertical agreements:

(a) any direct or indirect non-compete obligation, the duration of which is indefinite or exceeds five years. A non-compete obligation which is tacitly renewable beyond a period of five years is to be deemed to have been concluded for an indefinite duration. However, the time limitation of five years shall not apply where the contract goods or services are sold by the buyer from premises and land owned by the supplier or leased by the supplier from third parties not connected with the buyer, provided that the duration of the non-compete obligation does not exceed the period of occupancy of the premises and land by the buyer;

(b) any direct or indirect obligation causing the buyer, after termination of the agreement, not to manufacture, purchase, sell or resell goods or services, unless such obligation:

- relates to goods or services which compete with the contract goods or services, and
- is limited to the premises and land from which the buyer has operated during the contract period, and
- is indispensable to protect know-how transferred by the supplier to the buyer

and provided that the duration of such non-compete obligation is limited to a period of one year after termination of the agreement; this obligation is without prejudice to the possibility of imposing a restriction which is unlimited on the use and disclosure of know-how which has not entered the public domain;

(c)   any direct or indirect obligation causing the members of a selective distribution system not to sell the brands of particular competing suppliers.

NOTES AND QUESTIONS

1. Article 2 of the 1999 block exemption makes clear that it only applies to certain types of agreements. Does an exclusive territorial agreement between a U.S. distributor and a German distributor fall within this exemption? What is the difference between this type of agreement and the ones that are covered and what is the rationale for this distinction?

2. Article 8 of the distribution agreement deals with one of the most important issues in any distributorship agreement: Warranties and the waiver of express and implied warranties. Article 8 was clearly drafted with UCC §§2-313 through 2-315 in mind. Will the UCC govern this agreement or is the agreement governed by the Convention on Contracts for the International Sale of Goods as both Germany and the United States are parties to the CISG? Under existing authority, the CISG does not apply to this agreement as it is a distribution agreement and not a contract for the sale of goods. *See Helen Kaminski Pty. Ltd. v. Marketing Australian Products, Inc.*, 1997 U.S. Dist. LEXIS 10630 (S.D.N.Y. 1997). (Note that although a distribution agreement is not covered by the CISG, it is probably covered under the UCC, which is not limited to sales contracts but applies to transactions in goods.) In addition, although the agreement has a choice of law provision choosing Ohio law that provision may not be effective to exclude the CISG as the CISG is a part of Ohio law. Moreover, a court might find that German law applies to the agreement despite the choice of law clause. *See Southern International Sales Co., Inc. v. Potter & Brumfield Division of AMF Inc.*, 410 F. Supp. 1339 (S.D.N.Y. 1976) (refusing to apply Indiana law to distributorship despite a choice of law clause on the grounds that contacts with Puerto Rico justified an application of Puerto Rican law that included protections for distributors not present under Indiana law). What if there were no express choice of law provision or the choice of law provision was not effective to exclude the CISG? If the CISG did apply to this agreement, then Articles 35 and 36 of the CISG covering warranties would apply to the agreement. Note that the language of CISG Article 35 is similar to that of UCC §§2-313 through 2-315, except that the CISG does not draw an explicit distinction between implied and express warranties. Despite these similarities, however, in a situation where the CISG warranty provisions do apply, a U.S. lawyer cannot rely on foreign courts to interpret the CISG using the U.S. jurisprudence that has been developed under the UCC. Foreign courts would seek to promote uniformity in the

application of the CISG. If a U.S. lawyer is really intent on having the UCC warranty provisions apply to the distribution agreement, do you think that the choice of law provision presently contained in Article 11.2 of the agreement is sufficient to ensure this result?

3. Note that even if the CISG were found to govern the agreement, the choice of law issue would continue to be an important one. Article 4(a) of the CISG expressly excludes issues of the substantive validity of the contract from its scope so these issues will be governed by some other substantive law, most likely the law of the United States or Germany. If the agreement did not have a choice of law clause, the court would have to apply the rules of private international law to find the applicable law.

4. Under German law, the purpose of providing compensation to an agent or distributor when the principal terminates the contractual relationship is neither to compensate the agent for any damage suffered as a result of the termination nor to compensate him for the loss of a right or protected position as in the case of a terminated employee. It is also not the intent of German law to discourage principals from exploiting agents who establish successful distribution networks only to have the principal discharge the agent and take over once the principal has been able to achieve a foothold in the marketplace. Rather, compensation serves a remunerative purpose. The award of compensation recognizes that the principal will likely receive further orders from customers solicited by the agent, for which the agent would have otherwise received commissions. The agent will now lose these commissions since a prerequisite of a right to a commission is that the principal accepted the order during the existence of the agency relationship. As a result, it is considered unfair for the agent not to receive any compensation. Since allowing the agent to collect commissions after the termination of the agency would continue the principal-agent relationship for an indefinite period, would create burdens in the administration of claims, and would likely lead to disputes, it was decided under German law to award the agent a lump sum in the form of compensation to resolve all of the agent's claims to future commissions.

Some countries have compensation provisions that are more stringent than those in Germany. For example, unlike German law which provides that the agent/distributor has no right to compensation if the principal terminates for cause, Colombian law provides for compensation even if the termination is for cause. The amount of compensation is one-twelfth of the average commission received by the agent over the last three years multiplied by the duration of the agreement or if the agreement lasted for less than three years then compensation shall equal one-twelfth of the average commission received by the agent while the agreement was in force. *See* Colombia Code of Commerce, Article 1324. Where the termination is without cause, the principal has to pay in addition to any compensation any indemnity to be fixed by experts who shall take into account the agent's activities in enhancing the principal's line of services or products. The right to compensation is nonwaivable under Colombian law. *See id.* In Costa Rica, the principal must pay an indemnity equal to four months' average gross profits for each year or fractional year that the distributorship agreement has been in existence if the principal terminates or refuses to renew the agreement. The indemnity can be as high as nine years' average gross profit of the distributor and the principal may also be required to buy back the inventory purchased by the distributor at government-set prices. The distributor's right to an indemnity cannot be waived. *See* Costa Rican Law No. 6209 of April 3, 1978. If you were representing a U.S.

company that sought to engage a distributor in a country such as Colombia or Costa Rica with extensive protections for distributorships, what types of provisions or clauses would you include in the distribution agreement? lots of clauses

5. Tax issues are another important consideration in distributorships. Worthington Superabrasives would not wish to have its sales subject to double taxation under German and U.S. tax law. To avoid this problem, the United States has entered into treaties with a number of foreign nations to avoid the problem of double taxation. Under the Convention Between the United States and the Federal Republic of Germany for the Avoidance of Double Taxation with Respect to Taxes on Income, signed at Washington, D.C., July 22, 1954, U.S.T. & O.I. 2768, T.I.A.S. No. 3133, a U.S. entity would be subject to German taxation only if the entity had a permanent establishment in Germany and an agent or distributor is not deemed to be a permanent establishment.

II. *Technology Transfer and Licensing*

Suppose that Worthington decides that the market in Germany and Europe for its products offers so much potential that it needs to move beyond the distributorship into other forms of doing business that will allow additional penetration into these markets. The agency/distributorship form has a number of limitations for Worthington or any principal.

First, in many cases the agent/distributor is engaged in other businesses. In the problems that we considered in the previous section, the U.S. principal chose a German company that was engaged in the production and sale of a similar product although at a lower level of technology. In most cases, a principal will seek to find an agent/distributor that is engaged in the same industry as the agent/distributor will need to have knowledge about the product in order to promote and sell it to customers and may also need to provide technical and support services to customers using the product in the foreign market. In many cases, the agent/distributor may sell its own products or similar products that compete with the products of the foreign principal. The distribution agreement included a noncompetition clause to deal with this issue. However, the problem with many distributorships is that the distributor may be engaged in a number of other business activities and the sale of the principal's products may not receive the priority or attention that would satisfy the principal.

A second limitation is created by the manufacture of the product in the United States and the need to ship the product from Worthington's manufacturing plant in the United States to Germany. To get an idea of the costs in time and resources, let's review the entire transaction. Suppose that a customer in Germany places an order for certain industrial abrasives with Berens. For various reasons, Worthington does not have an inventory of the products ordered but must manufacture the products. It may be that it is too inefficient and costly to keep large stockpiles of industrial diamonds or it may be the case that the customer has a specific need for a certain product that is not in Worthington's inventory but which must be manufactured. Worthington now must manufacture the product, ship the product to Germany where Berens must pay any customs duties on the importation of the products, and place the products in a warehouse owned or leased by

Berens for storage. The product is then delivered by Berens to the customer at the end of a lengthy process. Like most sellers, Berens will likely pass these costs on to its customers by raising the price for the products. The costs in time and additional expenses can create competitive pressures for Berens and Worthington. Note that in the previous problems we have assumed that Worthington has a product with leading-edge technology. But let us now suppose that a German competitor is able to invent a product that is of equivalent or similar technological capability. In this case, Worthington and Berens are now at a disadvantage as the German competitor is not burdened with the same costs that Worthington must face in doing business in the German market. Not only is the German market in jeopardy for Worthington, but Worthington's other European markets will also come under competitive pressure. Even if there is no current competitor offering a similar product, is it a sound business strategy and planning for Worthington to simply assume that, in a highly competitive business, no competitor will come along with a similar product of an equivalent level of technology? How many businesses can you think of that are always able to maintain a significant gap in technology between themselves and their competitors? What can Worthington do to meet this concern and new challenge?

Beyond the Agency/Distributorship to Technology Transfer

One response is for Worthington to establish a manufacturing subsidiary in Germany, but suppose that Worthington is not yet convinced that the potential revenues in the German or European markets justify the significant commitment of resources of capital and personnel that is involved in a foreign direct investment. As we shall see in the next chapter, a foreign direct investment is a major undertaking and represents a fundamental policy decision for Worthington. For now, Worthington has decided that it will be able to meet some of the concerns and challenges discussed above by contract manufacturing or by *licensing* Berens to manufacture Worthington Superabrasives in Germany. Licensing is a form of technology transfer.

A.   What Is Technology Transfer and Why Is It Important?

We have now come to the topic of technology transfer. We will explore this topic in this section, and in the next section we take up the topic of the international legal framework for the transfer and protection of intellectual property (IP) rights.

What do we mean by technology transfer? By technology, we are referring to intellectual property rights such as patents, trademarks, copyrights, trade secrets, and other forms of intellectual property that are given statutory protection by both domestic and international law. In addition, by technology we also mean know-how or valuable business information that may or may not receive statutory protection or recognition as intellectual property. Examples of know-how that may not qualify as intellectual property are confidential financial information and marketing and business strategies. Support services for recognized intellectual property rights might also qualify as know-how. While this information may be commercially valuable and many others would be willing to pay substantial sums for this knowledge, it does not fall into any of the recognized categories of intellectual property. Commercially valuable information that does not qualify as intellectual property is usually protected by contract or by keeping the information secret.

All of these intellectual property rights are what we mean by technology in this context. Technology transfer refers to the process by which an owner of technology gives access to its technology to another. Access can consist of the transfer of complete ownership through a sale or assignment of the technology or the transfer of a more limited right such as a limited authorized use of the technology through a licensing agreement.

Technology Transfer in International Business

Before we turn to a more technical review of the international and domestic frameworks protecting intellectual property rights, we want to emphasize the importance of technology transfer in modern international business transactions. In the modern world, knowledge and information of all kinds have become increasingly important to international commerce. Some of the world's most valuable business property today consists of intellectual property and other forms of knowledge. Our hypothetical company, Worthington Superabrasives, possesses a technological advantage over its competitors and its most important asset is its advanced technology. The German distributor seeks to promote Worthington's products because they are technologically superior to the products of Worthington's competitors in Germany. Even where a company does not have a clear technological advantage over its competitors, a company's intellectual property in the form of patents, trademarks, and copyrights is among its most valuable properties. Think of patents for pharmaceuticals owned by Pfizer, Merck, and Bristol-Meyers Squibb; patents and copyrights for computer software owned by IBM, Microsoft, and Cisco Systems; and trademarks owned by Coca-Cola, Johnson & Johnson, Procter & Gamble, and other consumer products companies. The Coca-Cola trademark is among the most valuable commercial properties in the world, worth hundreds of billions of dollars at the very least. One indication of the value of intellectual property rights is the dramatic surge in copyright piracy and trademark counterfeiting around the world. We explore these topics in a subsequent chapter on the protection of intellectual property and for present purposes we simply note that theft of intellectual property by commercial pirates has become a major business problem for IP owners.

As the discussion above suggests, the bulk of the world's most valuable intellectual property is owned by MNEs. The creation or development of almost all commercially valuable intellectual property rights requires the investment of a significant amount of resources in research and development and in marketing. In most cases, only MNEs have these types of resources. For every pharmaceutical that is successfully brought to market, hundreds of millions of dollars are spent in research and development. The costs for developing a successful business software program can also involve similar sums. In the case of trademarks, MNEs spend millions of dollars annually in advertising and marketing the trademark in order to create goodwill, brand image, and identity with consumers.

The licensing of these valuable intellectual property rights is a complex issue and one with many risks and pitfalls. In most cases, the licensee wishes to acquire the latest possible technology and to obtain as much access as possible to the intellectual property and other supporting information. The IP owner seeks to provide sufficient access for the purposes of the licensing agreement but also seeks to protect its rights. As the intellectual property rights are often the most valuable business property owned by the business entity, the entity is taking a number of risks in providing access to a third party. Among these risks are the licensee will make improper use of the intellectual property, will use the technology to become a competitor to the licensor, or will allow the property to get into the hands of a counterfeiter or pirate. For this reason, the IP owner often refuses to allow access to its core technology but will license only its nonessential technology. The licensee, of course, seeks access to the core technology. We examine the complex issues involving a licensing agreement in the following section.

Intellectual Property and World Economic Development

Not only is intellectual property more valuable than ever in international business, but intellectual property and technology of all kinds play a central role in international economic development and implicates larger political issues. As we begin the twenty-first century, more and more developing countries have shifted the focus of their national energies on closing the gap between the developing and developed world. It is a national priority for many developing countries to modernize and industrialize their economies and achieve a higher standard of living for their constituents. These twin goals will also allow many developing countries to eventually compete in international commerce as opposed to being outsiders who must depend on the largesse of developed countries. A critical tool for modernization and industrialization is advanced technology, most of which is now owned and created by a few advanced industrialized nations. The leading nation in the creation and export of advanced technology and intellectual property of all kinds is the United States. Developed nations, and advanced industrialized countries, the United States in particular, feel constant pressure from developing nations to share the fruits of their advanced technology. Of course, access by developing nations to technology is a political issue and is not often of direct concern in an international business transaction. But the topic is of considerable concern in the area of international regulation of economic relations and within international institutions such as the World Trade Organization and it is an issue that we shall touch upon in our discussion of the public law international regulatory issues in Chapter 7 on protecting intellectual property.

Intellectual Property and Related Topics

The materials in the next section concern a topic that anyone interested in setting up a licensing agreement must consider: The international and national legal frameworks that have been established for the protection of intellectual property rights.

However, before we examine the international intellectual property system, we wish to place these materials in the larger context of topics that we have already covered and those yet to come. First, although the materials below concern international intellectual property laws, technology transfers may also be subject to national export controls where the materials are sensitive and may pose national security concerns, which is frequently the case when advanced technology is involved. We examined this topic in Chapter 2 on export trade law matters at p. 131. These are a set of controls external to the intellectual property system but are very important when sensitive technology may be involved, and you should keep these export controls in mind as you work through the materials below. Second, the materials on the international intellectual property system below focus on laws creating substantive rights and the procedures that must be followed to acquire those rights. In Chapter 7, we focus on a separate set of international and national laws targeted at the enforcement of those rights when they have been breached. The enforcement regime has a very different set of laws relating to intellectual property. We treat the topic of enforcement separately as it has grown in complexity and detail corresponding to the rise in the theft of intellectual property.

After reviewing the international intellectual property system, we turn to specific issues in the drafting of a patent licensing agreement and a business format franchise agreement.

NOTES AND QUESTIONS

1. Some types of intellectual property require relatively little investment of capital by comparison and are owned by individuals or small groups of individuals such as authors of successful works of art, books, or music. But these are not the types of intellectual property rights that are most sought after by developing nations or importers of intellectual property rights. Why?

2. One of the authors once heard the CEO of one of the world's largest MNEs in the consumer products industry claim that his company's people, not its brands or capital, were the key to the company's success. "Take away all of our brands, our capital, and our resources," he said, "but leave our people and we can rebuild our business in one generation." What do you think of this statement?

3. Developing countries are most eager to obtain technology that results in production processes that maximize the use of labor and natural resources to make products that are competitive in the world marketplace. They are less interested in technology that requires significant capital investment unless the IP owner is also willing to make a significant portion of the capital investment in the form of foreign direct investment. One issue for the IP owner is whether developing countries eager for advanced technology has the capability to absorb it. Suppose, for example, that a developing country with a weak system of education and poorly educated labor force sought to license the patent technology from Worthington Superabrasives and to manufacture its products for export. Can you see what the issues might be? Why would a country without the capability to absorb advanced technology seek it?

B. The International Intellectual Property Legal System

The international intellectual property legal system can be divided into two categories: Individual national legal systems and international treaties, including regional treaties such as those for the European Union and North America. In general, most substantive laws that directly create, recognize, and protect intellectual property rights are those that belong to domestic legal systems. International treaties generally serve two purposes: They establish legal standards that its members must implement through domestic legislation, and they establish certain principles and procedures regarding the treatment of foreign intellectual property rights by its members. With some exceptions, however, international treaties do not directly create intellectual property rights.

As a general matter, intellectual property rights are territorial in nature and are independent creatures of the domestic law of the nation that has created or recognized those rights. For example, when an IP owner obtains a trademark from the U.S. Patent and Trademark Office, it is a U.S. trademark effective within the territory of the United States only and, in the absence of a treaty, has no legal effect in any other country. When the same IP owner obtains a German or Chinese trademark for the same mark, it is a German trademark or a Chinese trademark with rights created by German and Chinese law and is a different and independent legal entity from the U.S. trademark. In the absence of an international treaty, an IP owner must comply with the procedures for obtaining intellectual property rights of every country that the owner seeks intellectual property protection. For MNEs, this would mean complying with the application procedures in every country in which the MNE seeks to do business. Note that a particular product or brand of goods is likely to have trademarks in many different languages. In the case of the trademark owner discussed previously, the owner will likely have to apply for a German language trademark and a Chinese language trademark that will be different from the U.S. trademark. Even where the foreign trademark itself is identical in language and appearance to a U.S. trademark, for example, where a U.S. owner also owns a trademark in England or Australia, these are legally discrete trademarks. The same principle of territoriality also holds for patents and copyrights, so an IP owner will have a U.S., German, and Chinese patent for the same product and so on. As you can well imagine, some MNEs hold hundreds, or even thousands, of foreign patents, trademarks, and copyrights.

Turning now to international and regional treaties, as we noted above most of these legal regimes serve two purposes. One purpose is to harmonize legal standards by creating minimum legal standards for intellectual property rights protection for all of its members. Prior to the establishment of the World Trade Organization in 1995, two of the most important instruments of harmonization were the International Convention for the Protection of Industrial Property originally signed in Paris in 1883 and revised most recently in Stockholm in 1967 (the Paris Convention), which applies to patents and trademarks, and the Berne Convention for the Protection of Literary and Artistic Works originally signed in 1886 and most recently revised in Paris in 1971 (the Berne Convention), which applies to copyrights. Both of these treaties will be discussed below in connection with a more detailed treatment of patents, trademarks, and copyrights, but for now it is important to note that they established minimum substantive legal standards for their members. Neither of these treaties had direct legal effect within the territory of a member, but each member gave effect to the Paris and Berne Conventions by enacting domestic legislation that embodied their requirements. Both treaties are administered by the World Intellectual Property Organization, a specialized agency of the United Nations.

After the establishment of the WTO, the most important intellectual property treaty is now the Agreement on Trade Related Intellectual Property Rights (TRIPS), which is one of the essential disciplines to which all WTO members must submit. TRIPS incorporates the major provisions of the Paris and Berne Conventions. In the area of patent and trademark, TRIPS goes beyond the Paris Convention by providing that patent and trademark protection must be provided by all WTO members. (The Paris Convention does not require patent and trademark protection but sets forth the type of rights and protections required if a Paris member decided to provide patent and trademark rights.) TRIPS is also the first international treaty to set forth the minimal substantive standards for all seven major categories of rights: Copyright, trademarks, geographical indications, industrial designs, patents, integrated circuit designs, and trade secrets. In addition, TRIPS is also the first international intellectual property treaty to recognize the importance of effective enforcement of laws and explicitly incorporates enforcement obligations in Part III of the treaty.

A second major purpose served by international treaties is to provide a procedural mechanism that allows IP owners to enjoy protections and benefits across national boundaries and which simplifies and facilitates the process of obtaining intellectual property rights within national legal systems. On a regional level, the European Union has created procedures whereby a single application decided by a single authority can result in a patent or trademark that has the same effect as a national patent or trademark in each participating country. The North American Free Trade Agreement incorporates the major provisions of TRIPS and goes beyond TRIPS in some areas such as enforcement. We shall examine these procedural protections in further detail in connection with our discussion of patents, trademarks, and copyrights.

Patents (novelty)

Under U.S. law, patents are granted to inventions or processes that are novel, useful, and nonobvious. *See* 35 U.S.C. §101. The term of patent protection under U.S. law is 20 years, the minimum required under Article 33 of TRIPS. Although the terms used to describe the requirements for patents may vary from nation to nation, the three requirements set forth under U.S. law for patents or their equivalents are found in TRIPS and most patents laws in nations around the world. This does not mean, however, that every product or process that receives patent protection in one country will receive similar protection in another country. The promulgation of TRIPS and its wide acceptance by developing countries has now resulted in greater harmonization of all patent eligibility issues, but there are still variations among nations in the application of their own laws and implementation of TRIPS; therefore, you should not assume that patentability standards are uniform even among TRIPS members.

Examples of products that receive patents are machines, fabricated products such as pharmaceuticals, and new compositions such as a new chemical invention. A patent issued by the U.S. Patent and Trademark Office (PTO) gives the patentee a limited monopoly for 20 years that will allow the patentee to exclude others from making, using, or selling the patented invention without the patentee's permission. The patentee can enforce these rights against an infringer in U.S. courts and obtain damages and injunctive relief. In addition, the patentee can also prevent the importation into the United States of foreign-made goods that violate the patent by obtaining an exclusion order from the International Trade Commission under §357 of the Tariff Act of 1930. These orders are enforced by the U.S. Customs Office.

In determining priority between competing patent applications, the United States follows a "first to invent" approach as opposed to a "first to file" approach as is followed by many other countries. As these terms suggest, the "first to invent" approach will award a patent to the inventor who was prior in time but who lost in the race to file the application with the patent authority. The "first to file" approach rewards the swiftest to file regardless of whether the applicant was the first inventor or not. Many countries follow the first to file approach as it draws a bright line and is easier to administer than a first to invent approach.

There are two basic systems for the granting of patents in the world: The examination system followed by the United States and the registration system followed by countries such as France. The difference between the two systems is that the examination system requires a determination on the validity of the patent prior to granting the patent whereas the registration system does not. Under the examination system, the patent-granting authority will examine the prior art and the statutory criteria to determine whether the patent application qualifies for patent protection. The patent authority will also provide public notice of the application in order to permit an opposition to the patent. A patent granted under the examination system is more likely to survive a subsequent challenge to its validity. In most cases, the challenge arises in the context of an infringement action. The patentee will file an action against an alleged infringer and the infringer will assert as a defense that the patent is invalid. Although the United States follows the examination system, many U.S. patents are subsequently held to be invalid, leading to criticism that the PTO is not sufficiently rigorous in its examination of patent applications.

Under the registration system, a patent is issued when the application, with accompanying documents and fees, is registered. The issuance of the patent occurs without a determination of its validity. The validity of the patent is determined when and if there is a challenge to the patent. The merits of the registration system are its low costs and speed of the issuance process. As you can imagine, the examination system involves a much longer period before a patent is issued, a much higher demand on the resources of the patent authority, and higher costs to the applicant in the form of attorney's fees and processing costs.

International Patent Treaties

The major international treaties governing patents are the Paris Convention discussed previously and the Patent Cooperation Treaty (PCT) of June 19, 1970. Article 2 of TRIPS expressly incorporates the bulk of the substantive provisions of the Paris Convention. As a result, the Paris Convention now applies among its members, which numbers over 100 countries (including the United States) and its main obligations also apply among all members of the WTO, which now numbers over 136 countries, many of which are not signatories to the Paris Convention.

The two most important rights created by the Paris Convention are the right of national treatment and the right of priority. Article 2 of the Paris Convention sets forth the right of national treatment, which holds that a nation cannot discriminate against foreign holders of patents or trademarks but must provide them with treatment equal to that received by domestic owners. For example, a French holder of a German patent or trademark must receive all of the rights that a German holder would receive and also cannot be subjected to additional burdens. If Germany were to require higher fees for the processing of the French patent, such a requirement would violate the national treatment principle. The Paris Convention also prohibits countries from requiring a foreign applicant to set up an establishment or domicile in the country as a condition for patent or trademark protection.

The second principle established by the Paris Convention is the right of priority. Under Article 4(C)(1) of the Paris Convention, a person who receives a patent or registers a trademark in a member country will receive priority over any other person for the same invention or who seeks to register the same trademark in any other member country if the patent or trademark owner files in the latter country within the period of priority, that is, 12 months in the case of patents and 6 months in the case of trademarks.

While the Paris Convention sets forth important procedural rights, it does not affect the basic principle of territoriality of patent rights and thus does not obviate the necessity for the inventor to file a patent application in every country in which the inventor seeks to obtain patent protection. A second major treaty administered by the World Intellectual Property Organization (WIPO), the Patent Cooperation Treaty (PCT), consisting of 117 parties, including the United States, provides procedures to facilitate international patent filings. Under Chapter I of the PCT, an applicant can file an international application that has the effect of a national application in each of the PCT's member countries. The application can be filed with the national patent authorities of the United States, Japan, Sweden, the European Patent Office at Munich, or any of the other designated international search authorities. The countries in which the applicant seeks patent protection are called the "designated states." The search authority will then conduct a novelty search and forward the results of the search along with a copy of the patent application to the national patent authorities of each of the designated states. The applicant can also arrange for a preliminary examination report in which the search authority will issue a nonbinding opinion on whether the application has met the requirements of novelty, utility, and nonobviousness (or their equivalents). The applicant can then decide whether it wishes to amend, withdraw, or proceed with the application process in each of the designated states. The applicant has a 20-month period of priority as compared with a 12-month period under the Paris Convention.

Note that the PCT does not create a truly international patent system. While the PCT facilitates the novelty search, offers a preliminary examination, and reduces the paperwork involved, the final decision on whether to grant the patent continues to be made by each national patent office. While no international patent system now exists, the European Patent Convention (EPC) of October 5, 1973, offers a regional patent system. The EPC provides a procedure whereby an applicant can file a single application in a single language, have it subjected to a single examination procedure carried out by the European Patent Office (EPO) located in Munich, Germany, and the Hague, Netherlands, and obtain a patent that has the effect of a national patent in all of the EPC countries designated by the applicant. No national patent authorities participate in the patent approval process. The European patent has a term of 20 years from the date of filing and confers upon its holder the same rights as a national patent. Note, however, that the EPC does not replace national patent systems in Europe. Each nation continues to have its own patent system and its own substantive laws that may conflict with the EPC and an applicant can choose to apply for a single national patent as opposed to a European patent. Americans filing in Europe can apply for a European patent under the Patent Cooperation Treaty by designating all of the member countries of the EPC as "designated states" and the EPO as the international search authority. Under the PCT, the patent application then becomes a European patent application.

The proposed European Community Patent Convention, if and when it comes into effect, will go beyond the EPC in creating a truly unitary European patent. While patents under the EPC have the same effect as a national patent within each of the EPC member countries and the scope of the rights conferred and remedies available may vary from country to country depending on its substantive law, the European Community Patent Convention will create a unitary European patent that will have the same effect in every country regardless of the country's national law. Due to internal legal issues, it is unclear when the European Community Patent Convention will come into effect.

Although it may come, the day seems to be far off in the future when the world will have a truly international patent system in which a single patent application will be decided by a single authority resulting in a patent that will have effect in every country in the world that chooses to be part of the international system. There are many advocates for this approach, but there are also many unresolved issues. For example, take the issue of language. To be a truly effective international system, the patent application must use a single language. The most likely candidate would be English, the most widely used business and scientific language in the world. What cultural, legal, and political issues can you foresee in the adoption of English as the universal language for an international patent system?

Trademarks (distinctiveness)

Under the U.S. trademark law, the Lanham Act, a trademark is any word, name, symbol, or device or any combination thereof that is capable of distinguishing goods from those of another. *See* 15 U.S.C.A. §1127. While novelty is the hallmark of a patent, distinctiveness is the hallmark of a trademark. Trademarks may be a word or words or a design or logo. In some cases, sounds and colors can also qualify as a trademark. Many countries draw distinctions among trademarks applied to goods; "service marks" applied to services; "collective marks" applied by a group or organization; "certificate marks" designating a certain quality, standard, or origin; and "trade names" that designate the name of a business or entity. All of these different categories are treated as trademarks. The United States follows a "first to use" rule in establishing priority to trademarks whereas some other countries use a "first to register" approach.

Traditionally, a trademark served an origin and a guarantee function: The trademark served to indicate the source of origin of the goods as being produced by a certain manufacturer or provider and also served as an indication of the quality of the product. For instance, all goods with the same trademark indicated that the product was from the same company and that the goods were of a certain quality. Note that the guarantee function of a trademark did not have to be an indication of high quality just similar quality; that is, all goods bearing the same trademark were also of a similar quality whether the quality was that of a luxury brand, a mid-tier brand, or an economy brand. The origin and guarantee functions also meant that trademark rights were *appurtenant* rights, not *in gross*. The trademark always had to be associated with some product, service, or commercial activity to indicate origin and quality and could not be obtained on its own.

[margin note: 3 function of Tm]

Today, trademarks also serve a third function: A marketing and advertising function. Most of the world's most commercially valuable trademarks are owned by MNEs, which in many cases have invested millions of dollars annually in advertising and promotion, creating a significant amount of prestige and goodwill associated with their trademarks. In the case of some of the world's most successful trademarks, the marketing function and goodwill of the trademark may now be more important than the trademark's traditional origin and guarantee functions. Think of "Nike" for example. When the "Nike" brand name is used, is it always used to sell athletic apparel or does it stand for a certain type of lifestyle, image, or attitude that transcends the goods to which the brand name is applied? The success of MNEs in creating highly valuable trademarks is one reason for the surge in worldwide trademark counterfeiting and infringement.

Unlike other intellectual property rights, trademarks must be used in connection with some commercial activity and cannot exist independently of such activity. Accordingly, a trademark cannot be obtained by mere adoption but only through use. So long as the trademark continues to be used, it can remain valid indefinitely unlike patents and copyrights, which have limited duration.

[margin note: unlimited duration]

In the United States, unlike patent which is exclusively governed by federal law, trademark is a creature of both state and federal law. Unlike the case of patents, which enjoy the protection of the Patent Clause, there is nothing specific in the Constitution relating to trademarks, and common law remains the source of substantive trademark rights. Based on the Interstate Commerce Clause, Congress passed the Lanham Act in 1946, 15 U.S.C.A. §§1051-1127, but the act neither created new trademark rights nor codified common law rights. Rather the Lanham Act provides a framework in which common law trademark can be enforced at the federal level. Under the Lanham Act, the U.S. Patent and Trademark Office keeps a register of trademarks. The proper registration of a trademark with the PTO allows the trademark owner to assert remedies in federal courts, which are empowered to issue injunctions or award monetary relief. In addition, §526 of the Tariff Act of 1930, 19 U.S.C. §1526, allows the U.S. Customs Service to seize goods entering the United States that bear a counterfeit or infringing version of a registered U.S. trademark. We examine the remedies available to a trademark owner in enforcing its rights against counterfeiters and infringers in further detail in Chapter 7.

International Treaties

The Paris Convention discussed earlier in connection with patents is also one of the major multilateral conventions applicable to trademarks. As in the case of patents, Article 2 of TRIPS incorporates all of the major substantive provisions of the Paris Convention concerning trademarks. The principle of national treatment and the right of priority (six months in the case of trademarks) discussed in connection with patents under the Paris Convention apply as well to trademarks.

The 1957 Nice Agreement Concerning the International Classification of Goods and Services for the Purposes of the Registration of Marks (to which the United States became a party in 1984) provides a single classification system for the registration of trademarks. As trademarks are always used in connection with goods (or services), the applicant for registration needs to identify the class of goods to which the trademark applies. For example, an applicant seeking registration for the trademark must identify the products (e.g., clothing, eyeglasses, handbags, etc.) to which the trademark will be used, and the trademark, once

[margin note: Tm's must have connection w/ goods]

registered, will receive legal protection only if used in connection with these goods. In some countries, the use of a registered trademark with a different class of goods is illegal and can lead to the cancellation of the mark. Note that it is possible that the same sign or mark that is applied to two or more different classes of goods might result in multiple trademarks for multiple owners (e.g., "Grand Luxe" for automobiles and chocolates). Prior to the Nice Agreement, different countries had different classification systems for goods and some countries had no classification systems at all. The Nice Agreement brought unification and order to the field by providing a single classification for goods and services.

The Protocol Relating to the Madrid Agreement Concerning the International Registration of Marks (the "Madrid Protocol"), effective as of April 1, 1996, establishes a system for the international registration of trademarks. Under the Madrid system, any person or entity based in a member country can file a single application that will allow the applicant to obtain trademark protection in all of the protocol's other member countries. Under this system, the applicant is allowed to file an application for the international registration of the mark at any time after it has registered or filed an application in its home country for that mark as applied to the same goods or services. An international registration is valid for ten years from the date of issue of the applicant's home country registration. *See* Madrid Protocol, Article 6(1). The registration can be renewed indefinitely for additional ten-year periods by the payment of fees. *See id.*, Article 7. On August 2, 2003, the United States joined the Madrid Protocol, and the PTO began accepting Madrid filings on November 2, 2003.

The Trademark Law Treaty of October 28, 1994, negotiated under the auspices of the WIPO, is an ambitious treaty that sought to harmonize trademark laws around the world. The treaty has come into effect and the United States is party to the treaty but the treaty has so far been limited to harmonizing procedures concerning trademark application and recording changes in names and addresses of trademark owners, changes in ownership, and trademark renewals.

On a regional level, the Council of the European Community adopted Council Regulation No. 40/94 on December 23, 1993, which establishes a unitary European Community trademark that is uniformly valid in the entire territory of the European Union independent of any existing national laws and regulations. The European Community trademark may be obtained through the filing of a single application and registration proceeding through the Office for Harmonization in the International Market in Alciante, Spain. The term of the trademark is ten years and can be renewed indefinitely. In North America, the United States is a party with several Latin American countries to the General Inter-American Convention of 1920, which is closely modeled after the Paris Convention.

Copyright (originality)

Under the U.S. Copyright Act of 1976, copyright protection is available for all original works fixed in a tangible medium of expression. As novelty is to patent and distinctiveness is to trademarks, originality is to copyright. The requirement of originality, however, is easily met as long as the author created the work and did not copy it from any other source. The author has fixed the work in a tangible medium of expression when the work is permanently embodied in a copy or a phonorecord. A U.S. copyright is valid for the life of the author and extends for 70 years after the death of the author.

Categories of copyrightable material recognized under U.S. law include: (1) Literary works; (2) musical works, including any accompanying words; (3) dramatic works, including any accompanying music; (4) pantomimes and choreographic works; (5) pictorial, graphic, and sculptural works; (6) motion pictures and other audiovisual works; (7) sound recordings; and (8) architectural works. *See* 17 U.S.C.A. §102. The owner of a U.S. copyright has the exclusive rights "to do and authorize" (1) reproduction, (2) adaptation, (3) public distribution, (4) public performance, and (5) public display of the copyrighted matter. *See* 17 U.S.C.A. §106. The basic right of copyright ownership is the right to prevent unauthorized copying without permission. There is a limited exception for educators, librarians, critics, and news reporters who are allowed limited copying for educational and archival purposes under the common law "fair use doctrine" now codified in the 1976 Copyright Act.

In order to obtain a U.S. copyright, no formal procedures are necessary and it is not necessary to publish the work. Copyright exists in the work so long as it is original and fixed in a tangible medium of expression. However, to retain a U.S. copyright, the author must provide a formal notice reserving the copyright when publishing the work or the work becomes dedicated to public use. While registration of the copyright with the U.S. Copyright Office in Washington, D.C., is not required in order to obtain copyright protection, registration is required in order to make use of federal copyright infringement remedies, which include criminal penalties, civil damages, and injunctive relief. A U.S. copyright owner has the right to exclude copies of copyrighted materials from entering the United States without the permission of the copyright owner under §602(a) of the Copyright Act of 1976.

International Treaties

Aside from TRIPS, the most important international treaty concerning copyright is the Berne Convention. Similar to the Paris Convention, the basic features of the Berne Convention are the national treatment principle and the requirement of minimum substantive standards of protection. Among the rights established by the Berne Convention are a minimum term of protection of the life of the author plus 50 years, translation, reproduction, public broadcasting, adaptation, arrangement, and other alterations. The Berne Convention also prohibits the requirement of any formalities such as registration for the enjoyment of copyright. The United States joined the Berne Convention in 1989. As in the case of patents and trademarks, TRIPS incorporates the major substantive provisions of the Berne Convention.

Under the Berne Convention, a work that is first published in a signatory country is entitled to receive the same copyright protection in every other signatory country that nationals of the signatory country receive in addition to rights specifically granted by the convention.

One area in which the Berne Convention has differed from U.S. law is in the area of moral rights. U.S. copyright law has traditionally viewed copyright as consisting of economic rights, that is, the rights to profit from and exploit the copyrighted work. In addition to economic rights, European nations have traditionally also associated copyright with a set of moral rights, which are essentially rights that are personal to the author. Moral rights include the right to be known as the author of the work; the right to prevent others from distorting, mutilating, or modifying the work; the right to prevent others from using the work in such a derogatory way that may prejudice the author's good name and professional standing; and the right to withdraw the work. Article 6 of the Berne Convention guarantees the recognition of moral rights and this requirement was one of the reasons the United States resisted accession to the Berne Convention for many years. Note that Article 6bis of the Berne Convention also provides that moral rights, as opposed to economic rights, are nonassignable. As a result, an author retains moral rights even after the transfer of his or her economic rights. Why would U.S. corporations object to moral rights?

Article 9 of TRIPS incorporates Articles 1-21 of the Berne Convention, the bulk of its substantive provisions, but expressly excludes Article 6bis of the Berne Convention relating to moral rights. Does the United States have a current legal obligation to recognize moral rights?

During its long history, the Berne Convention has been extended to recognize new technologies in the form of radio, cinematography, and television, but the emergence of new computer and Internet technologies has raised new issues about copyright protection that appear to be more difficult to accommodate than technological challenges in the past. One issue concerned whether computer software was eligible for copyright protection as computer software has both an expressive function associated with copyright and a utilitarian function associated with patent. Rather than permit each nation to decide on the scope of protection for computer software, Article 10 of TRIPS expressly provides that computer programs shall be protected by copyright. Other types of *sui generis* forms of intellectual property protection have been recently created for semiconductor chip designs and, in Europe, for the content of certain types of electronic databases that are not eligible for copyright protection.

The Universal Copyright Convention (UCC) was created as an alternative to the Berne Convention largely by the United States and is administered by the United Nations Educational Scientific and Cultural Organization, a specialized agency of the United Nations located in Paris. With the accession of countries such as the United States, China, and Russia to the Berne Convention and TRIPS, the UCC has been largely eclipsed in importance. The UCC required little more than national treatment and allowed its members to impose formal requirements such as notice and registration.

Know-How and Trade Secrets (commercially valuable knowledge)

Know-how is commercially valuable knowledge. It may or may not be entitled to protection as a patent, as a trade secret, or through any other form of intellectual property. Where know-how does not qualify as intellectual property, it is protected primarily through contract and tort. Contracts can impose confidentiality obligations on the recipient of the know-how and its employees or agents. Tort law includes the law of unfair competition, which would prevent third parties from misappropriating valuable commercial information. In some cases, even where know-how qualifies for intellectual property protection, the owner may opt to forgo such protection because of a desire to prolong the commercial exploitation of the know-how. For example, an owner may decide to apply for a patent to protect its know-how but the patent expires after 20 years and the know-how then enters the public domain. Rather than risk losing the know-how, some owners may simply protect the know-how by keeping it closely guarded.

In the United States, know-how may qualify for patent protection or for protection as a trade secret. Until 1996, the regulation of trade secrets was governed solely by state law. Over 40 states and the District of Columbia have adopted the definition of a trade secret under §1(4) of the Uniform Trade Secrets Act of 1979, which provides: *Fed. law*

> "Trade Secret" means information, including a formula, pattern, compilation, program device, method, technique, or process that (i) derives independent economic value, actual or potential, from not being generally known to, and not being readily ascertainable by proper means by, other persons who can obtain economic value from its disclosure or use; and (ii) is the subject of efforts that are reasonable under the circumstances to maintain its secrecy.

def. of trade secret

In 1996, the United States passed the Economic Espionage Act of 1996 (EEA), 18 U.S.C.A. §§1831-1839, which creates federal criminal penalties for the misappropriation of trade secrets for the benefit of foreign governments and others. Trade secrets are defined as "all forms and all types of financial, business, scientific, technical, economic or engineering information whether tangible or intangible if the information derives independent economic value, actual or potential, from not being generally known to, and not being readily ascertainable through proper means by, the public." 18 U.S.C. §1839(3). The EEA applies to all products "produced or placed in interstate or foreign commerce" [18 U.S.C.A. §1832(a)] and to foreign crimes committed by citizens and resident aliens of the United States as well as to acts in furtherance to such offense committed by any persons within the United States.

International Treaties

TRIPS is the first international treaty that recognizes trade secrets. Article 39 of TRIPS provides that its members shall provide procedures to protect "undisclosed information" from being acquired by others in "a manner contrary to honest commercial practices," so long as such information is secret, has commercial value, and has been subject to reasonable steps by the person in control of the information to keep it secret.

NOTES AND QUESTIONS

1. The goal of countries such as the United States is the standardization and harmonization of all substantive intellectual property laws and procedures. TRIPS represents a major achievement toward these goals. Harmonization, of course, implies that one set of standards is to be adopted on a global basis. In the area of intellectual property, what or whose standards are these? Who might object to these goals and why?

2. As an example of the types of changes brought about by TRIPS, consider that some countries have historically imposed "local working requirements" as a condition for obtaining a local patent. The idea behind this requirement was to

prevent a patent owner from simply manufacturing the products in its own home country and exporting them to the foreign nation where the owner has obtained the patent. The foreign owner had to obtain the patent in the foreign nation before introducing its product in the foreign market in order to prevent infringement and counterfeiting. But some nations found that once the foreign owner obtained the patent, many owners would simply export the patented products to the foreign nation and not use the patent locally. As a result, many countries required as a condition of granting or maintaining the patent that the patent owner had to use the patent in the foreign nation by establishing a foreign subsidiary that used the patent or by licensing the patent to a local manufacturer. Why do some countries object to granting patents to owners who intend to manufacture the product in their home nation and then simply export the patented products to the foreign nation? Why is a patent that is locally worked viewed as creating a mutually beneficial economic relationship? The relevant article of TRIPS applicable to local working requirements is set forth below.

Article 27
Patentable Subject Matter

[P]atents shall be available for any inventions, whether products or processes, in all fields of technology, provided that they are new, involve an inventive steps and are capable of industrial application. . . . [P]atents shall be available and patent rights enjoyable without discrimination as to the place of invention the field of technology and whether the products are imported or locally produced.

no local working req's

What is the TRIPS position on local working requirements and who stands to benefit?

3. Article 10 of TRIPS provides that computer programs shall receive copyright protection. Without this provision, it would arguably be left to each country to determine whether computer programs received copyright, patent, or no protection. Why would the United States favor copyright protection for computer programs as opposed to patent or trade secret protection?

4. Only a handful of people in the world know the formula for Coca-Cola, one of the world's most valuable pieces of know-how. Coca-Cola made the decision not to obtain a U.S. patent for the formula, which would expire after 20 years. Why do pharmaceutical companies apply for patent protection for their drugs, which confers a monopoly for 20 years, which many consider to be a rather short period considering that these companies invest millions or hundreds of millions of dollars in developing some of these drugs? Why don't pharmaceutical companies follow the example of Coca-Cola and protect their know-how by keeping it closely guarded in perpetuity and forgo patent protection?

5. State trade secrets law is designed to protect national companies from having their trade secrets stolen by each other. Most states provide only civil remedies for breach of trade secrets. Although some states provide criminal penalties, they differ in the area of criminal conduct covered. In passing the EEA, the United States decided that the present system did not adequately address certain additional international commercial and political concerns. What other concerns do you think the U.S. government had in mind in passing the EEA? Compare the definition of a trade secret in the Uniform Trade Secrets Act and in the EEA. What differences can you see?

III. Selected Issues in Licensing: The Patent License Agreement

Suppose that, for some of the reasons we discussed earlier, Worthington has decided to move forward with a contract manufacturing agreement that will permit Berens to manufacture the products in Germany and serve as a base for the German market. Worthington has a U.S. patent for its products. Set forth below is a patent license agreement.

PROBLEM 5-6

Worthington has a U.S. patent for its products but in order to do business in Germany, Worthington must obtain a German patent by filing an application in Germany and a trademark registration for its mark "Superabrasives." Berens has proposed the following: Rather than having Worthington apply for a German patent and then license it to Berens as would be the normal procedure that Worthington would follow, Berens can file the patent application and trademark registration for the Worthington products in its own name in Germany and then assign the patent and trademark to Worthington at the end of the contract manufacturing period. Berens will assume all of the paperwork and costs of the filing procedures and will save Worthington substantially on legal fees and other costs to do it this way. The duty to assign can be explicitly included in the contract manufacturing agreement. Such a clause is enforceable under applicable law by damages and specific performance. Based on the general principles discussed in §II on the value of intellectual property, what advice do you have for Worthington?

not a good idea

PROBLEM 5-7

Suppose that, after the patent agreement goes into effect, Worthington sets up a factory on its own in Germany and begins to use the patent in manufacturing and selling Superabrasives. Berens now brings an action in German court, seeking to enforce its patent and trademark rights against Worthington. In its defense, Worthington moves to dismiss the action on the grounds that, under a patent and trademark license agreement, the licensee cannot sue the licensor for breach of patent and trademark rights. Carefully review Articles 2 and 3 of the patent agreement. What types of rights were granted to Berens? Can Berens prevent Worthington using the patent and trademark rights and, if so, on what basis?

PROBLEM 5-8

In the agreement below, Worthington sought to address a major concern about its long-term marketing plans for the European Union. Worthington has entered into two other licensing agreements for the patent with a company in France and one in the United Kingdom and is also considering entering into similar agreements with other countries in the European Union. To protect these other markets, Worthington would like to prevent Berens from

manufacturing, using, promoting, or selling the products in France and the
United Kingdom or any other countries where Worthington enters into an exclusive licensing agreement with a licensee. The agreement sets forth these
obligations, but Worthington is still concerned about whether these arrangements
will violate any antitrust laws in the European Union. Compare Article 2 of the
draft agreement with Articles 1.1 and Article 3 of Commission Regulation No. 240/
96 on p. 372 *infra*. Worthington has included a noncompetition clause in Article 4
of the agreement. Is this clause lawful under Article 3 of Regulation No. 240/96?
What advice do you have for Worthington?

PROBLEM 5-9

Worthington is also concerned about protecting its intellectual property
rights. In particular, Worthington does not want to get into a dispute with
Berens over who owns the patent rights for the products. The agreement licenses
the German patent rights to Berens, but Worthington knows that it is common for
licensees to make some changes and improvements to the patented product as the
product is adapted for the local market or as a result of the licensee's using the
patent in the manufacturing process. As the patent covers only the technology
described in the patent application, any improvements by the licensee will
be outside the scope of the existing patent. Often, there will then arise some
dispute over who owns the improvements to the original patent. Many licensors
take the position that they own the basic technology covered by the patent and that
without access to the patent and the licensor's proprietary technology in the first
place, the licensee will be unable to create any improvements. Licensees, on the
other hand, often take the position that as they have invested the resources in
making the improvements, they should be the owner of the improvements, not the
licensor. In order to avoid such disputes, Worthington has added a "grant back
clause" in the license agreement that makes clear that it is the owner of any
improvements by Berens. See Article 12 of the patent license agreement. Is the
grant back clause lawful? See Articles 2(4) and 3(6) of Regulation No. 240/96. If
there are problems with the grant back clause, can you give Worthington some
suggestions on language it could use to deal with this issue? Can Worthington
simply prohibit Berens from making any improvements?

Patent License Agreement

THIS AGREEMENT is made this 1st day of January 2005 between
Worthington Superabrasives, a corporation organized and existing under the
laws of the State of Ohio, having a place of business at 59 Scots Brook Road,
Worthington, Ohio, United States of America (Licensor), and Berens, GmbH, a
company duly incorporated under the Laws of the Federal Republic of Germany
whose Registered Office is at 35 Wilheimstrasse, Munich, Federal Republic of
Germany (Licensee).
WHEREAS:
(1) Licensor is the owner of German Patent No. 6,820-1564 on certain industrial abrasives and of patents and patent applications in other countries relating
thereto;

(2) Licensor is the owner of the trademark SUPERABRASIVES in the Federal Republic of Germany and the trademark SUPERABRASIVES in other countries; and

(3) Licensee is interested in the manufacture and sale of industrial abrasives in the Federal Republic of Germany (the Territory), and in that connection seeks to avail itself of said German Patent No. 6,820-1564.

Now, THEREFORE, in consideration of the covenants and agreements herein contained, it is agreed as follows:

ARTICLE 1
DEFINITIONS

(1) The "Products" shall mean and include any industrial abrasive that is manufactured, used, or sold making use of German Patent No. 6,820-1564 in the Territory.

(2) "Sales" will mean: the sale, rental, lease, or other transfer of the Products by Licensee to parties other than its subsidiaries and affiliates; the sale, rental, lease, or other transfer of the Products by a subsidiary or affiliate of Licensee to a third party for use or consumption; the use or consumption of the Products by Licensee in its own business; the use or consumption of the Products by a subsidiary or affiliates of Licensee in its own business.

(3) The "selling price" will mean the price paid to Licensee by the party to whom the Products are transferred. Licensee shall establish the selling price in consultation with Licensor.

(4) "License Year" will mean each twelve (12) month calendar period commencing with January 1 and beginning with the year 2005 and continuing during the existence in force of the exclusive licenses.

ARTICLE 2
GRANTS

(1) Licensor hereby agrees to grant to Licensee exclusive licenses to manufacture, use, and sell in the Territory industrial abrasives as described in and covered by German Patent No. 6,820-1564 subject to any and all provisions and conditions of this Agreement. This grant is subject to the following conditions:

(a) Licensee shall not manufacture, use, or sell the Products in France, the United Kingdom, or any other country within the European Union in which Licensor enters into an exclusive licensing agreement for the Products with another licensee.

(b) Licensee shall not sell the Products to users in the Territory who are known to resell the Products in France, the United Kingdom, or any other country within the European Union in which Licensor enters into an exclusive licensing agreement for the Products with another licensee.

(c) Licensee shall not advertise or promote the Products in France, the United Kingdom, or any other country within the European Union in which Licensor enters into an exclusive licensing agreement for the Products with another licensee.

(d) Licensee shall not solicit any orders from France, the United Kingdom, or any other countries within the European Union in which Licensor enters into an exclusive licensing agreement for the Products and shall not sell any Products on the basis of any orders, solicited or unsolicited, to customers in any of these countries.

(2) Licensor hereby agrees to grant to Licensee the right to use, and will appoint Licensee a Registered User or Licensee of the registered German trademark "SUPERABRASIVES" within the Territory. Licensee shall place the trademark "SUPERABRASIVES" in a prominent location on all Products that are sold under this Agreement.

ARTICLE 3
OWNERSHIP OF INTELLECTUAL PROPERTY RIGHTS

(1) Licensee hereby acknowledges that Licensor is the sole and exclusive owner of German Patent No. 6,820-1564, the registered German trademark "SUPERABRASIVES," know-how, and other proprietary business information ("intellectual property") to which Licensee shall have access.

(2) Licensee shall make use of all intellectual property only for the purposes of this Agreement.

(3) Licensee shall not assert or assist any third parties in asserting a claim to the intellectual property of the Licensor. If Licensee shall make or assist any third parties in making a claim to the intellectual property of the Licensor, Licensor shall be entitled to terminate this Agreement upon thirty (30) days' written notice.

ARTICLE 4
NONCOMPETITION

During the term of this Agreement, Licensee shall not manufacture, sell, promote, or distribute any products that compete directly or indirectly with the Products. This obligation does not apply to any products that the Licensee was manufacturing, selling, promoting or distributing at the time that this Agreement was signed. A list of products that compete directly or indirectly with the Products is included in Appendix A attached hereto. If the Licensee is in violation of this Article, the Licensor shall have the right to grant licenses to other licensees within the Territory and the Licensor shall also have the right to manufacture and sell the Product within the Territory.

ARTICLE 5
SUPPLY OF KNOW-HOW, TECHNICAL ASSISTANCE, AND ENGINEERING DEVELOPMENT

(1) From time to time as Licensor shall deem reasonably necessary for the performance of this Agreement, Licensor shall provide any know-how, technical information, and knowledge that will assist Licensee in the manufacture, operation,

installation, repair, maintenance, and sale of the Products. Licensee shall pay any out-of-pocket costs in connection with any training, meetings, and travel incurred in connection with this technical assistance.

(2) Licensor and Licensee may enter into separate written agreements from time to time as both parties deem appropriate for the separate development of special engineering projects or research and development concerning the Products.

ARTICLE 6
CONFIDENTIALITY

(1) Licensee acknowledges that it shall be given access to valuable commercial information in the form of patents, trademarks, know-how, and other proprietary business information. Licensee shall undertake all measures in conformity with German law to keep such valuable commercial information confidential by limiting access to such information only to employees who must have access to this information in order to perform this Agreement.

(2) Licensee shall be bound by this confidentiality obligation after the termination of this Agreement. If this Agreement were to terminate, Licensee shall immediately return to Licensor any brochures, pamphlets, instructional manuals, computer disks, or any other physical or written materials relating to the Products and any other proprietary business information received by Licensee from Licensor in connection with this Agreement.

ARTICLE 7
ROYALTIES

(1) Licensee, in consideration of the grant of the licenses hereunder, will pay to Licensor the sum of fifty thousand United States dollars (US $50,000) (in the manner provided in paragraph (5) below) within one month of the date hereof, less any taxes assessed against Licensor on said payment which Licensee may be required by law to deduct. In the absence of any clearly defined legal restrictions, Licensor will have the right to determine how any taxes will be paid.

(2) During the continuance of these licenses, Licensee will pay to Licensor on all sales by it of the Products a royalty of ten percent (10%) of the selling price for each Product manufactured by or on behalf of Licensee and sold by Licensee, its affiliates, and subsidiaries.

(3) Royalties are to be paid in quarterly installments (less taxes as aforesaid) within thirty (30) days after the close of each quarter of the License Year. Any payment (less taxes as aforesaid) (hereinafter referred to as a Deficiency Payment) required to be made by Licensee to ensure that the aggregate royalties paid in respect of any License Year are equal to the minimum royalty for that License Year will become due and payable by Licensee with the quarterly installment of royalties due and payable for the quarter ending on December 31 of that License Year.

Each of these installment or Deficiency Payments will be converted to U.S. dollars by reference to the official exchange rates between German Deutsche Marks and U.S. dollars prevailing at the close of the last day of the quarter for which the payment is due and will be paid at Licensor's office in Worthington,

Ohio, USA, or at such other places as Licensor may specify from time to time, in United States dollars and through a New York bank designated by Licensor.

(4) Each Royalty payment shall be accompanied by a statement of the number of Products sold, the date of sale, and the selling price.

(5) For as long as royalties are due under this Agreement, Licensee will keep true and accurate records adequate to permit royalties due to Licensor to be computed and verified, which records will be open, at all reasonable times during business hours, for inspection by a chartered accountant or, alternatively, another independent accountant acceptable to Licensee duly authorized in writing by Licensor to the extent necessary for the determination of the accuracy of the reports made hereunder. Licensor's accountants will have the right to make copies of the relevant records. These records will be kept in a manner permitting determination of production, use, shipping, pricing, sales, and royalties. If in any of these audits there is an error in the reports or payments by Licensee to Licensor of five percent (5%) or more in the royalty paid or payable to Licensor, Licensee will forthwith reimburse Licensor the cost of that audit and all other costs of the collection of the unpaid royalty, including, but not limited to, reasonable attorney's fees and court fees. Upon request by Licensor, Licensee will have the independent accountant that is auditing its books for the benefit of its shareholders provide Licensor with an auditor's certificate as to the accuracy of the royalty statements and payments made hereunder for the two (2) years immediately preceding such a request.

ARTICLE 8
BEST EFFORTS

Licensee agrees to be diligent and to use its best endeavors to manufacture, promote, and develop the sale of and the market for the Products within the Territory. Licensee shall provide Licensor with a promotional and marketing plan for the Products on a semi-annual basis for comment.

ARTICLE 9
MANUFACTURE AND MARKETING

(1) Licensee agrees to manufacture the Products in accordance with the designs, specifications, drawings, and other information supplied or approved by Licensor, in accordance with standards set by Licensor. Licensor will not unreasonably withhold approval of improvements suggested by Licensee.

(2) Licensor will have the right to inspect the production facilities and processes used by Licensee in manufacturing the Products and to test the finished Products sold under any trademark of Licensor.

(3) Licensee agrees to mark the Products and the packages or containers in which the Products are sold and shipped in a manner which conforms with the patent and trademark law of the Territory with respect to notice or other matters relating to patent and trademark ownership license and infringement.

(4) Licensee agrees to use the trademark SUPERABRASIVES or other trademark selected by Licensor on all the Products within the Territory in accordance with the provisions of paragraph (3) under "Trademarks" of this Agreement.

ARTICLE 10
TERM

(1) This Agreement shall have a term of ten (10) years. The licenses granted pursuant to Article 2 "Grants" of this Agreement shall be in effect for the term of this Agreement and shall terminate at the end of the term of this Agreement or upon the earlier termination of this Agreement. If for any reason, German Patent No. 6,820-1564 shall terminate before the expiration of the 10-year term of this Agreement, this Agreement and the licenses granted hereunder shall automatically terminate.

(2) At the conclusion of five (5) years, the parties shall enter into good faith negotiations for a joint venture partnership for the manufacture and sale of the Products and other products or services within the Federal Republic of Germany.

(3) If Licensee defaults in making royalty payments in pursuance to the provisions of paragraph (3) under "Royalties" or commits any other material breach of the terms of this Agreement, Licensor, at its option (to be exercised within thirty (30) days of knowledge of occurrence of said breach), can give written notice of its intention to terminate to Licensee, specifying the default or breach and a termination date not earlier than thirty (30) days from the date of the mailing of that notice, in the case of default in making royalty payments, and not earlier than ninety (90) days from the date of mailing of that notice for any other breach.

If Licensee fails to repair the default or breach prior to the specified date of termination, the licenses hereunder will then terminate. No failure by Licensor to exercise the option hereunder upon any occurrence therefore will be a waiver of Licensor's right to exercise the option respecting a subsequent default or breach.

(4) In the event either party commits any act of bankruptcy, becomes insolvent, enters into any arrangement with creditors, or goes into liquidation (other than for purposes of amalgamation or reconstruction), the other party will be entitled to terminate this Agreement forthwith by notice in writing without prejudice to the rights and remedies of either party against the other accrued prior thereto.

(5) The licenses under this Agreement cannot be terminated because either Licensor or Licensee undergoes reorganization, provided that the obligations under this Agreement are fulfilled.

(6) Subject to the royalty provisions of this Agreement, Licensor, for a period of one hundred and twenty (120) days upon termination of the licenses hereunder for cause by Licensor, can sell all Products in inventory and finish and sell all thereof in the process of manufacture. Upon termination for reasons other than cause by Licensor, the period will be one (1) year.

ARTICLE 11
INFRINGEMENT AND WARRANTY

If any infringement or threatened infringement of any patents and trademarks licensed hereunder comes to the notice of Licensee, it will forthwith notify Licensor giving particulars thereof. Licensee shall provide all reasonable aid and assistance to Licensor in enforcing the patent and trademark rights of the Licensor. Licensor shall be responsible for all costs in connection with the enforcement and protection of its patent and trademark rights in Germany.

ARTICLE 12
GRANT BACK OF IMPROVEMENTS

(1) Licensor agrees to promptly notify Licensee of any improvements or inventions relating to the Products developed or in the process of development by Licensor. Licensee will have the right to use those improvements. In the event that Licensor secures patents on any of these improvements within the Territory, Licensee will have the right, at its option, to include those patents within the terms of the present Agreement. Only one (1) royalty per Product will be due regardless of the number of patents involved in a Product.

(2) Licensee agrees to promptly notify Licensor of any improvements or inventions relating to the Products developed or in the process of development by Licensee, and of any such inventions or improvements which may be acquired by or come under the control of Licensee, its officers, or employees. Licensor shall be entitled to seek patents for such improvements in any country in the world. Licensee will execute or cause to be executed, delivered, or filed, as Licensor may direct, all papers, documents, and assignments as Licensor, at its sole expense, prepares in order to vest effectively in Licensor full right, title, and interest in and to the applications and patents resulting therefrom.

ARTICLE 13
TRADEMARKS

(1) Licensor agrees to register and maintain, at its expense, in the Territory any Licensor trademarks relating to the Products in use during the continuance of this Agreement if so requested by Licensee from time to time.

(2) Licensee agrees to use the trademark SUPERABRASIVES or other trademark selected by Licensor on all the Products within the Territory. This marking will be conspicuous on all manufactured products, advertising media brochures, and other technical data transmitted to customers regarding the Products. Licensee will be entitled, at its own discretion, to use in addition its own name, provided that the ownership by Licensor of the trademark SUPERABRASIVES or other trademarks is made distinct. Upon termination of the licenses under this Agreement, Licensee will cease to use the word SUPERABRASIVES or other Licensor mark as soon as reasonably practicable for it to do so.

(3) The term of use of any trademark licensed in connection with this Agreement will be coincident with the life of this Agreement.

ARTICLE 14
MISCELLANEOUS

(1) The terms and provisions of this Agreement will be construed in accordance with the laws of the United States.

U.S. law

(2) Any dispute or difference arising between the parties hereto will be resolved by consultation between the parties. If such consultation cannot resolve the dispute, such dispute shall be submitted to arbitration in Columbus, Ohio.

forum - arbitration

(3) Licensee covenants that at any time hereafter, it will not contest, nor assist others in contesting, (a) the validity of the patents and patent applications which

are the subjects of this Agreement, (b) the title of Licensor thereto, nor (c) the novelty, utility, or patentability of any subject matter of any of the patents. The patents, throughout their respective terms and for all purposes, will be deemed in force and valid unless declared invalid by a court of last resort or by any court from the decision of which an appeal is not taken within the time provided by law.

ARTICLE 15
TRANSFER

This Agreement and the rights hereunder cannot be assigned by any party without the prior written consent of the other party except to an assignee of the entire business of the transferring party. This Agreement has been drawn up in triplicate and all copies duly signed by all parties, as witness the signatures of the parties the date and year first above written.

* * *

Commission Regulation (EC) No. 240/96 of 31 January 1996 on the Application of Article 85(3) of the Treaty to Certain Categories of Technology Transfer Agreements

ARTICLE 1

1. Pursuant to Article 85(3)[4] of the Treaty and subject to the conditions set out below, it is hereby declared that Article 85(1) of the Treaty shall not apply to pure patent licensing or know-how licensing agreements and to mixed patent and know-how licensing agreements, including those agreements containing ancillary provisions relating to intellectual property rights other than patents, to which only two undertakings are party and which include one or more of the following obligations:

(1)   an obligation on the licensor not to license other undertakings to exploit the licensed technology in the licensed territory;

(2)   an obligation on the licensor not to exploit the licensed technology in the licensed territory himself;

(3)   an obligation on the licensee not to exploit the licensed technology in the territory of the licensor within the common market;

(4)   an obligation on the licensee not to manufacture or use the licensed product, or use the licensed process, in territories within the common market which are licensed to other licensees;

(5)   an obligation on the licensee not to pursue an active policy of putting the licensed product on the market in the territories within the common market which are licensed to other licensees, and in particular not to engage in advertising specifically aimed at those territories or to establish any branch or maintain an distribution depot there;

---

4. Article 85 (now renumbered as Article 81) is set forth on p. 343 *supra*.

(6)   an obligation on the licensee not to put the licensed product on the market in the territories licensed to other licensees within the common market in response to unsolicited orders;

(7)   an obligation on the licensee to use only the licensor's trademark or get up to distinguish the licensed product during the term of the agreement, provided that the licensee is not prevented from identifying himself as the manufacturer of the licensed products;

(8)   an obligation on the licensee to limit his production of the licensed product to the quantities he requires in manufacturing his own products and to sell the licensed product only as an integral part of or a replacement part for his own products or otherwise in connection with the sale of his own products, provided that such quantities are freely determined by the licensee.

2. Where the agreement is a pure patent licensing agreement, the exemption of the obligations referred to in paragraph 1 is granted only to the extent that and for as long as the licensed product is protected by parallel patents, in the territories respectively of the licensee (points (1), (2), (7) and (8)), the licensor (point (3)) and other licensees (points (4) and (5)). The exemption of the obligation referred to in point (6) of paragraph 1 is granted for a period not exceeding five years from the date when the licensed product is first put on the market within the common market by one of the licensees, to the extent that and for as long as, in these territories, this product is protected by parallel patents. . . .

ARTICLE 2

1. Article 1 shall apply notwithstanding the presence in particular of any of the following clauses, which are generally not restrictive of competition:

(1)   an obligation on the licensee not to divulge the know-how communicated by the licensor; the licensee may be held to this obligation after the agreement has expired;

(2)   an obligation on the licensee not to grant sublicenses or assign the license;

(3)   an obligation on the licensee not to exploit the licensed know-how or patents after termination of the agreement in so far and as long as the know-how is still secret or the patents are still in force;

(4)   an obligation on the licensee to grant to the licensor a license in respect of his own improvements to or his new applications of the licensed technology, provided:
   •   that, in the case of severable improvements, such a license is not exclusive, so that the licensee is free to use his own improvements or to license them to third parties, in so far as that does not involve disclosure of the know-how communicated by the licensor that is still secret,
   •   and that the licensor undertakes to grant an exclusive or nonexclusive license of his own improvements to the licensee;

(5)   an obligation on the licensee to observe minimum quality specifications, including technical specifications, for the licensed product or to procure goods or services from the licensor or from an undertaking designated

by the licensor, in so far as these quality specifications, products or services are necessary for:

(a) a technically proper exploitation of the licensed technology; or

(b) ensuring that the product of the licensee conforms to the minimum quality specifications that are applicable to the licensor and other licensees;

and to allow the licensor to carry out related checks;

(6) obligations:

(a) to inform the licensor of misappropriation of the know-how or of infringements of the licensed patents; or

(b) to take or to assist the licensor in taking legal action against such misappropriation or infringements;

(7) an obligation on the licensee to continue paying the royalties:

(a) until the end of the agreement in the amounts, for the periods and according to the methods freely determined by the parties, in the event of the know-how becoming publicly known other than by action of the licensor, without prejudice to the payment of any additional damages in the event of the know-how becoming publicly known by the action of the licensee in breach of the agreement;

(b) over a period going beyond the duration of the licensed patents, in order to facilitate payment;

(8) an obligation on the licensee to restrict his exploitation of the licensed technology to one or more technical fields of application covered by the licensed technology or to one or more product markets;

(9) an obligation on the licensee to pay a minimum royalty or to produce a minimum quantity of the licensed product or to carry out a minimum number of operations exploiting the licensed technology;

(10) an obligation on the licensor to grant the licensee any more favorable terms that the licensor may grant to another undertaking after the agreement is entered into;

(11) an obligation on the licensee to mark the licensed product with an indication of the licensor's name or of the licensed patent;

(12) an obligation on the licensee not to use the licensor's technology to construct facilities for third parties; this is without prejudice to the right of the licensee to increase the capacity of his facilities or to set up additional facilities for his own use on normal commercial terms, including the payment of additional royalties;

(13) an obligation on the licensee to supply only a limited quantity of the licensed product to a particular customer, where the license was granted so that the customer might have a second source of supply inside the licensed territory; this provision shall also apply where the customer is the licensee, and the license which was granted in order to provide a second source of supply provides that the customer is himself to manufacture the licensed products or to have them manufactured by a subcontractor;

(14) a reservation by the licensor of the right to exercise the rights conferred by a patent to oppose the exploitation of the technology by the licensee outside the licensed territory;

(15)   a reservation by the licensor of the right to terminate the agreement if the licensee contests the secret or substantial nature of the licensed know-how or challenges the validity of licensed patents within the common market belonging to the licensor or undertakings connected with him;

(16)   a reservation by the licensor of the right to terminate the license agreement of a patent if the licensee raises the claim that such a patent is not necessary;

(17)   an obligation on the licensee to use his best endeavors to manufacture and market the licensed product;

(18)   a reservation by the licensor of the right to terminate the exclusivity granted to the licensee and to stop licensing improvements to him when the licensee enters into competition within the common market with the licensor, with undertakings connected with the licensor or with other undertakings in respect of research and development, production, use or distribution of competing products, and to require the licensee to prove that the licensed know-how is not being used for the production of products and the provision of services other than those licensed.

2. In the event that, because of particular circumstances, the clauses referred to in paragraph 1 fall within the scope of Article 85 (1), they shall also be exempted even if they are not accompanied by any of the obligations exempted by Article 1.

3. The exemption in paragraph 2 shall also apply where an agreement contains clauses of the types referred to in paragraph 1 but with a more limited scope than is permitted by that paragraph.

ARTICLE 3

Article 1 and Article 2 (2) shall not apply where:

(1)   one party is restricted in the determination of prices, components of prices or discounts for the licensed products;

(2)   one party is restricted from competing within the common market with the other party, with undertakings connected with the other party or with other undertakings in respect of research and development, production, use or distribution of competing products without prejudice to the provisions of Article 2(1)(17) and (18);

(3)   one or both of the parties are required without any objectively justified reason:

   (a)   to refuse to meet orders from users or resellers in their respective territories who would market products in other territories within the common market;

   (b)   to make it difficult for users or resellers to obtain the products from other resellers within the common market, and in particular to exercise intellectual property rights or take measures so as to prevent users or resellers from obtaining outside, or from putting on the market in the licensed territory products which have been lawfully put on the market within the common market by the licensor or with his consent;

or do so as a result of a concerted practice between them;

(4) the parties were already competing manufacturers before the grant of the license and one of them is restricted, within the same technical field of use or within the same product market, as to the customers he may serve, in particular by being prohibited from supplying certain classes of user, employing certain forms of distribution or, with the aim of sharing customers, using certain types of packaging for the products, save as provided in Article 1(1)(7) and Article 2(1)(13);

(5) the quantity of the licensed products one party may manufacture or sell or the number of operations exploiting the licensed technology he may carry out are subject to limitations, save as provided in Article (1)(8) and Article 2(1)(13);

(6) the licensee is obliged to assign in whole or in part to the licensor rights to improvements to or new applications of the licensed technology;

(7) the licensor is required, albeit in separate agreements or through automatic prolongation of the initial duration of the agreement by the inclusion of any new improvements, for a period exceeding that referred to in Article 1(2) and (3) not to license other undertakings to exploit the licensed technology in the licensed territory, or a party is required for a period exceeding that referred to in Article 1(2) and (3) or Article 1(4) not to exploit the licensed technology in the territory of the other party or of other licensees.

NOTES AND QUESTIONS

1. Are the confidentiality obligations contained in Article 6 of the patent licensing agreement lawful under European Community law? See Article 2 of Regulation No. 240/96.

2. Commission Regulation No. 240/96 (the 1996 block exemption) is another example of a block exemption to the prohibitions contained in Article 81(1) of the Treaty of Rome. We have already seen an example of a block exemption issued by the commission, namely, No. 2790/1999 (the 1999 block exemption), which applied to vertical agreements, including distributorships. The 1996 block exemption applies specifically to technology transfer agreements, including patent and know-how licenses and some types of mixed licenses. Note that while the 1999 block exemption was based on the principle that everything that is not prohibited is allowed, the 1996 block exemption on technology licensing uses a "white list" contained in Article 2 specifying the types of clauses that are permitted and a "black list" contained in Article 3. An agreement that contains a provision violating Article 3 is not entitled to an exemption from Article 81(1) of the Treaty of Rome, which means that the entire agreement is void. What about clauses that do not fall within either the white list or the black list but fall within the "gray list"? Article 4 of the 1996 block exemption, which we have not reproduced above, allows for an opposition procedure under which an applicant can formally notice a clause to the commission. If the commission does not object within four months, the clause is permitted. Although the block exemption is a type of general exception, Article 7 of the 1996 block exemption allows the commission to withdraw the benefit of the exemption for an agreement where the commission finds that the agreement results in certain specified anticompetitive effects.

IV. Business Format Franchising

In both of the topics we have considered so far in this chapter, selling overseas through an agent/distributor or by contract manufacturing, the U.S. corporation is able to establish deeper penetration of the foreign market. In both cases, the U.S. corporation does not establish a business entity overseas but works through a third party that is authorized to sell or manufacture its products. While these two methods may allow greater penetration by the product of the foreign market, there are limitations to how effective these methods will be in establishing the identity and business reputation of the U.S. corporation overseas. In the distribution agreement that we considered earlier in this chapter, the distributor is an independent contractor and is required to avoid creating any confusion on the part of consumers that the distributor owns the products or is authorized to act on behalf of the U.S. corporation. One intended purpose of this approach is to create a separation between the distributor and the U.S. corporation in the minds of consumers. Similar provisions also exist in the patent licensing agreement. The limitation created by this approach is that while the U.S. corporation's product may achieve a greater penetration of the foreign market, the U.S. corporation is unable to achieve a broader international recognition of its trade name, business reputation, and identity in the foreign market.

Suppose that our U.S. corporation wishes not only to sell its products overseas but also to achieve international recognition for its trademarks, trade name, and business identity and reputation. We are, of course, now inching ever closer to the topic of foreign direct investment, the subject of the next chapter, as one clear way of achieving this goal is to invest capital and establish a business entity overseas in the form of a wholly or partially owned foreign subsidiary. But this method is the subject of the next chapter, and the question we wish to consider now is how a U.S. corporation can expand its international reputation without the investment of capital overseas or by using a nonestablishment form of overseas expansion consistent with the other topics covered in this chapter. For these purposes, the U.S. corporation should consider the last topic in this chapter: The business format franchise, a nonestablishment form of doing business that moves the progression of penetrating foreign markets even closer to the final step of FDI.

In a business format franchise, the franchisee operates its business under the franchisor's trade name and under the franchisor's business identity. The franchisee is identified as part of a select group of dealers and is generally required to assume a standard appearance and to follow standardized methods of operation. A wide variety of products and services can be offered through this format. Note that the advantage of the franchise is that the franchisor is able to achieve international trademark and trade name recognition within a short time without the outlay of capital and the franchisee is able to obtain status as an independent business and the use of valuable trademarks, trade names, business methods, and knowledge, all under the guidance of an experienced company. Because of its advantages, the franchising concept has now become a major factor in both the U.S. and the global economy. According to the U.S. Department of Commerce:

> Franchising is one of the most creative of the various marketing techniques that have emerged in this century. Today, the key to a successful franchise operation is a strong

system. It is the system that provides the appearance that all outlets belong to a chain; it is the system that all franchisees can follow; it is the system that provides the know-how to franchisees to keep one step ahead of the competition; and it is the system that will continue to provide abundant opportunities to all that want to fulfill the dream of owning one's own business.[5]

While the patent licensing agreement primarily concerned the licensing of patents, the franchise agreement concerns primarily the licensing of trademarks and trade names as these are essential to establish business identity and reputation. Other important considerations in a franchise agreement concern ensuring the quality of the services offered by the franchisee and the protection of the goodwill of the trademarks and the reputation of the trademark owner.

In the United States, both federal and state laws govern the franchise relationship. The Federal Trade Commission has promulgated legislation setting forth disclosure requirements and prohibitions.[6] Other examples of federal legislation are the Automobile Dealer's Day in Court Act, 15 U.S.C. §1221 *et seq.*, and the Petroleum Marketing Practices Act, 15 U.S.C. §2801 *et seq.* Many states also have statutes governing the franchise relationship. On an international level, some nations do not have specific laws governing franchise agreements but apply general principles of contract law. Others, such as Canada, have laws governing issues such as misrepresentation in the franchise prospectus and providing the franchisee with a period in which the agreement can be canceled without penalty. Other laws, such as EU anticompetition laws, may also apply as we shall see in the materials below.

NOTES AND QUESTIONS

1. Authorizing an independent entity to sell the franchisor's product, as in a distributorship, or licensing a franchisee to manufacture the franchisor's product, as in contract manufacturing, can also be considered franchising, although in a more limited form. Our focus in this section is on the business format franchise.

2. Business format franchise agreements usually impose requirements on the uniformity of the product, decor of the restaurant, and services. Think of the case of successful fast-food franchises such as McDonald's. Why?

3. Culture, not usually an issue in international patent licensing, can present some significant issues in international franchise agreements. Again, think of successful international franchises such as Pizza Hut or Friday's. Why?

PROBLEM 5-10

Hamburger Heaven (HH), an Ohio corporation, is a fast-food restaurant specializing in wholesome, hearty American food. HH's menu consists mostly of

---

5. U.S. Department of Commerce, *Franchising in the Economy 1984-86.*
6. Franchising and Business Opportunity Ventures Disclosure Requirements and Prohibitions, 16 C.F.R. Part 436.

hamburgers and chicken. It owns several U.S. service marks and trademarks for its foods, each using alliterative sounds, for example "Harry's Heartland Hamburger," "Betty's Buckeye Breakfast," and "Charlie's Cleveland Club." HH is considering overseas franchises in Germany, including in some old historical cities near some famous landmarks to attract the tourist crowd, and would like to maintain the same business approach. HH also has a distinctive decorative scheme and includes the use of an outdoor sign featuring a 25-foot tall representation of Brutus Buckeye, the Ohio State University mascot. (Brutus wears a football jersey and has a very large buckeye, a nut that is the state symbol, for a head.)

(1)   Review the discussion in §B above on the international intellectual property system (p. 353) and the subsection on trademarks at p. 357. What must HH do to protect its trademarks in Europe? Are there any preliminary issues that you see that need to be resolved before submitting the marks for registration?

(2)   HH has asked you to review the franchise agreement below, which HH uses for its franchises in the United States. HH asks whether the agreement is suitable for an international franchisee. In particular, HH asks you whether any additional issues and concerns in the case of an international franchise might require changes to Article 2 (Development and Opening of Restaurant), Article 3 (Training and Operating Assistance), and Article 4 (Restaurant Image and Operating Standards). What other provisions need to be adapted for an international franchise?

Franchise Agreement

THIS AGREEMENT is made and entered into this _____ day of _____, 20_____, by and between Hamburger Heaven, an Ohio corporation, with its principal office at 2436 Heartland Drive, Toledo, Ohio (the Company), and _____, a _____ corporation, whose principal address is _____ (the Franchisee). The parties hereby agree as follows:

ARTICLE 1
GRANT AND RENEWAL OF FRANCHISE

(1) *Grant of Franchise.* Subject to the provisions of this Agreement, the Company hereby grants to the Franchisee a franchise to operate a Company Restaurant at premises identified, or to be identified, in Exhibit 1 or a substitute premises hereafter approved by the Company (the Restaurant), and to use the Names and Marks in the operation thereof, for a term of ten (10) years commencing on the date of this Agreement (the Franchise). Termination or expiration of this Agreement shall constitute a termination or expiration of the Franchise.

(2) *Exclusive Territory.* The Company agrees that during the term of the Franchise, provided that the Franchisee is in substantial compliance with this Agreement, the Company will not operate or grant a franchise for the operation

of a Company Restaurant within the area described in Exhibit 2 as Franchisee's exclusive territory.

ARTICLE 2
DEVELOPMENT AND OPENING OF RESTAURANT

(1) *Lease or Purchase of Premises of Restaurant.* Franchisee, contemporaneously with the execution of this Agreement, will lease or purchase the premises of the Restaurant identified in Exhibit 1, provided that if a premises have not then been selected or approved by the Company, the Franchisee agrees to lease or purchase suitable premises, reasonably acceptable to the Company, within ninety (90) days after the execution of this Agreement. The Company will reasonably assist Franchisee in site evaluation and lease or purchase negotiations. If Franchisee fails to lease or purchase suitable premises within ninety (90) days after execution of this Agreement, the Company shall have the right to terminate this Agreement, effective upon delivery of written notice of termination to Franchisee.

(2) *Required Lease Provisions.* The lease for the premises of the Restaurant shall provide that upon termination or expiration of the Franchise for any reason, other than a termination by Franchisee for cause, the Company shall have the right to assume the Franchisee's status and replace the Franchisee as lessee.

(3) *Development of Restaurant.* The Company will furnish to the Franchisee standard basic plans and specifications for a Company Restaurant, including requirements for dimensions, exterior design, interior layout, building materials, equipment, signs, and color scheme.

(4) *Equipment, Fixtures, and Signs.* The Franchisee agrees to use in the operation of the Restaurant only those brands and models of equipment, fixtures, and signs that the Company has approved for Company Restaurants. The Franchisee further agrees to place or display at the premises of the Restaurant (interior and exterior) only such signs, emblems, lettering, logos, and display materials that are from time to time approved in writing by the Company. The Franchisee may purchase or lease approved brands and models of equipment, fixtures, and signs from any supplier. If the Franchisee proposes to purchase or lease any brand and/or model of equipment, fixture, or sign which is not then approved by the Company, the Franchisee shall first notify the Company and obtain the Company's written consent.

(5) *Restaurant Opening.* The Franchisee agrees to open the Restaurant for business and commence the conduct of its business within fifteen (15) days after the Company's determination that it is in suitable condition.

ARTICLE 3
TRAINING AND OPERATING ASSISTANCE

(1) *Training.* Prior to the opening of the Restaurant, the Company shall train the Franchisee and the manager of the Restaurant in the operation of a Company Restaurant.

(2) *Completion of Training/Termination.* The Franchisee shall complete training in the operation of a Company Restaurant to the satisfaction of the Company. If the Company reasonably determines that the Franchisee is unable to satisfactorily complete such training, this Agreement shall terminate.

ARTICLE 4
RESTAURANT IMAGE AND OPERATING STANDARDS

(1) *Condition and Appearance of Restaurant.* The Franchisee agrees to maintain the condition and appearance of the Restaurant consistent with the image of a Company Restaurant as an attractive, modern, sanitary, convenient, and efficiently operated restaurant selling high-quality products and service.

(2) *Alterations to Restaurant.* The Franchisee shall make no material alterations to the leasehold improvements or appearance of the Restaurant, nor shall the Franchisee make any material replacements of or alterations to the equipment, fixtures, or signs of the Restaurant without prior written approval by the Company.

(3) *Authorized Products and Services.* The presentation of a uniform image to the public and the furnishing of uniform products and services is an essential element of a successful franchise system. The Franchisee therefore agrees that the Restaurant will offer all hamburgers, sandwiches, chicken, beverages, ice cream flavors and dishes, and all other products and services that the Company from time to time authorizes for Company Restaurants. The Franchisee further agrees that the Restaurant, without prior written approval by the Company, will not offer any other products or services, nor shall the Restaurant or the premises which it occupies be used for any purpose other than the operation of a Company Restaurant.

(4) *Food and Beverage Products, Supplies, and Materials.* The reputation and goodwill of the Company Restaurant is based upon, and can be maintained and enhanced only by, the sale of high-quality products and the rendering of fast, efficient, and high-quality service. The Franchisee therefore agrees that all food and beverage products, cooking materials, containers, packaging materials, other paper and plastic products, glassware, utensils, uniforms, menus, forms, cleaning and sanitation materials, and other supplies and materials used in the operation of the Restaurant shall conform to the specifications and quality standards established by the Company and shall be purchased from suppliers approved by the Company. If the Franchisee proposes to use in the operation of the Restaurant any product, supply, or material not theretofore approved by the Company, the Franchisee shall submit to the Company sufficient specifications, photographs, and/or other information or samples for examination and/or testing and for a determination by the Company of whether such product, supply, or material, and/or such supplier, meets the Company's specifications and standards. . . .

(6) *Standards of Service.* The Restaurant shall at all times give prompt, courteous, and efficient service to its customers. The Restaurant shall in all dealings with its customers, suppliers, and the public adhere to the highest standards of honesty, integrity, fair dealing, and ethical conduct.

(7) *Specifications, Standards, and Procedures.* The Franchisee agrees to comply with all mandatory specifications, standards, and operating procedures relating to the operation of a Company Restaurant.

(8) *Compliance With Laws and Good Business Practices.* The Franchisee shall secure and maintain in force all required licenses, permits, and certificates relating to the operation of the Restaurant and shall operate the Restaurant in full compliance with all applicable laws, ordinances, and regulations. The Franchisee agrees to refrain from any business or advertising practice which may be injurious to the business of the Company and the goodwill associated with the Names and Marks and other Company Restaurants.

(9) *Prices to Be Determined by Franchisee*. The Company may from time to time advise or offer guidance to the Franchisee relative to menu prices for Company Restaurants. The Franchisee shall not be obligated to accept any such advice or guidance and shall have the sole right to determine the prices and charges to be charged by the Restaurant. . . .

(11) *Insurance*. The Franchisee shall at all times during the term of the Franchise maintain in force at his sole expense comprehensive public and product liability against claims for bodily and personal injury, death and property damage caused by or occurring in conjunction with the operation of the Restaurant. Such insurance coverage shall be maintained under one or more policies of insurance containing minimum liability protection of two million dollars ($2,000,000) for bodily and personal injury and death and two hundred thousand dollars ($200,000) for property damage. All such liability insurance policies shall name the Company as an additional insured and shall provide that the Company shall receive ten (10) days prior written notice of termination, expiration, or cancellation of any such policy.

ARTICLE 5
OPERATING MANUAL

The Company will loan to the Franchisee during the term of the Franchise one or more copies of an operating manual for Company Restaurants containing mandatory and suggested specifications, standards, and operating procedures. The operating manual contains proprietary information of the Company and the Franchisee agrees to keep the operating manual confidential at all times during and after the term of the Franchise.

ARTICLE 6
TRADE SECRETS OF COMPANY

The Franchisee acknowledges that its knowledge of the operation of a Company Restaurant will be derived from information disclosed by the Company and that certain of such information, including without limitation that contained in the operating manual, is proprietary, confidential, and a trade secret of the Company. The Franchisee agrees that it will maintain the absolute confidentiality of all such information during and after the term of the Franchise, and that it will not use any such information in any other business or in any manner not specifically authorized or approved in writing by the Company.

ARTICLE 7
ADVERTISING AND PROMOTION

(1) *By Company*. The Company will develop, prepare, and furnish to the Franchisee fliers, posters, ad formats, and other direct mail, point of sale, and media advertising materials for Company Restaurants and will implement advertising and promotion programs in such form and media as it determines to be

most effective and economical. The Franchisee agrees to pay to the Company as its share of the cost of the development and preparation of such advertising ... four percent (4%) of the net revenues of the Restaurant, payable monthly with the royalty and service fee hereinafter described.

(2) *By Franchisee.* The Company shall have the right to require the Franchisee to submit for prior approval by the Company any or all advertising and promotional materials prepared by the Franchisee, and the Franchisee shall not use any disapproved advertising or promotional materials.

ARTICLE 8
RESTAURANT RECORDS AND REPORTING

(1) *Bookkeeping, Accounting and Records.* The Franchisee shall establish a book-keeping, accounting, and record keeping system conforming to the requirements prescribed by the Company.

(2) *Reports and Tax Returns.* The Franchisee shall furnish monthly reports on the gross and net revenues of the Restaurant and federal and state income tax returns to the Company in the form as prescribed by the Company. If the Company reasonably believes that any monthly report, financial statement, or tax return or schedule furnished by the Franchisee understates the net revenues of the Restaurant, distorts any other information, or is unclear or misleading, the Company shall have the right to require the Franchisee to furnish audited annual financial statements thereafter.

ARTICLE 9
NAMES AND MARKS

(1) *Ownership of Names and Marks.* The Franchisee acknowledges that the Company is the owner of all Names and Marks licensed to the Franchisee by this Agreement, that the Franchisee's right to use the Names and Marks is derived solely from this Agreement, is limited to the operation of the Restaurant in compliance with this Agreement at the location and premises identified in Exhibit 1. The Franchisee agrees that all usage of the Names and Marks by the Franchisee and any goodwill established thereby shall inure to the exclusive benefit of the Company. The Franchisee further agrees that after the termination or expiration of the Franchise, it will not directly or indirectly at any time or in any manner identify himself, any restaurant, or any other business as a Company Restaurant, a former Company Restaurant, or as a franchisee of or otherwise associated with the Company.

(2) *Limitations on Franchisee's Use of Names and Marks.* The Franchisee agrees to use the Names and Marks as the sole service mark and trade name identification of the Restaurant. The Franchisee shall not use any Name or Mark as part of any corporate name or with any prefix, suffix, or other modifying words, terms, designs, or symbols (other than logos licensed to the Franchisee hereunder), or in any modified form, nor may the Franchisee use any Name or Mark in connection with the sale of any unauthorized product or service, or in any other manner not explicitly authorized in writing by the Company.

ARTICLE 10
INITIAL FRANCHISE FEE

The Franchisee shall pay to the Company a nonrecurring and nonrefundable initial franchise fee for the Franchise in the amount of one hundred thousand dollars ($100,000), payable upon the execution of this Agreement.

ARTICLE 11
ROYALTY AND SERVICE FEE

(1) *Amount and Payment of Royalty and Service Fee.* The Franchisee agrees to pay to the Company a royalty and service fee of four percent (4%) of the net revenues of the Restaurant, payable by the fifteenth (l5th) day of each month on net revenues for the preceding month.

ARTICLE 12
INSPECTIONS AND AUDITS

(1) *Company's Right to Inspect Restaurant.* To determine whether the Franchisee is complying with this Agreement, the Company shall have the right, at any time during business hours and without prior notice to the Franchisee, to inspect the Restaurant and the business records, and to take or supervise a physical inventory of the food products and ingredients, beverages and other products, materials, and supplies of the Restaurant.

(2) *Company's Right to Audit.* The Company shall have the right, at any time during business hours and without prior notice to the Franchisee, to audit or cause to be audited the monthly reports, financial statements, tax returns and schedules, and other forms, information, and supporting records which the Franchisee is required to submit to the Company hereunder, and the books and records of the Restaurant and of any corporation or partnership which owns or operates the Restaurant.

ARTICLE 13
TERMINATION OF FRANCHISE

(1) *By Franchisee.* If the Franchisee is in substantial compliance with this Agreement and the Company breaches this Agreement and fails to cure such breach within thirty (30) days after written notice thereof is delivered to the Company, the Franchisee may terminate this Agreement effective ten (10) days after delivery to the Company of notice thereof.

(2) *By Company.* The Company may terminate this Agreement effective upon delivery of notice of termination to the Franchisee, if the Franchisee or the Restaurant:

(a)   Makes an assignment for the benefit of creditors or an admission of its inability to pay its obligations as they become due;

default

(b) Files a voluntary petition in bankruptcy or any pleading seeking any *bankruptcy* reorganization, liquidation, or dissolution under any law or is adjudi- *insolvency* cated bankrupt or insolvent, or a receiver is appointed for a substantial part of the assets of the Franchisee or the Restaurant;

(c) Abandons, surrenders, or transfers control of the operation of the Restaurant, or fails to actively operate the Restaurant, unless precluded from doing so by damage to the premises of the Restaurant, war or civil disturbance, natural disaster, labor dispute, or other event beyond the Franchisee's reasonable control;

(d) Suffers cancellation of, fails to renew or extend the lease for, or otherwise fails to maintain possession of the premises of the Restaurant;

(e) Submits to the Company on two (2) or more separate occasions a monthly report, financial statement, tax return or schedule, or other information or supporting records that understates the net revenues of the Restaurant for any period by more than three percent (3%);

(f) Consistently fails or refuses to submit when due monthly reports, quarterly and annual financial statements, tax returns, schedules, or other information or supporting records, to pay when due the royalty and service fees, advertising contributions, amounts due for any products purchased from the Company, or other payments due to the Company, or otherwise repeatedly fails or refuses to comply with this Agreement;

(g) Operates the Restaurant in a manner that presents a health or safety hazard to its customers, employees, or the public;

(h) Makes an unauthorized assignment of the Franchise or ownership of the Franchisee;

(i) Fails or refuses to pay any amount owed to the Company for royalty and service fees, advertising contributions, products purchased from the Company, or any amounts otherwise due to the Company, or fails or refuses to comply with any mandatory specification, standard, or operating procedure prescribed by the Company and does not correct such failure or refusal within seven (7) days after written notice thereof; or

(j) Fails to comply with any other provision of this Agreement or any other mandatory specification, standard, or operating procedure prescribed by the Company, and does not correct such failure within thirty (30) days after written notice of such failure to comply is delivered to the Franchisee.

ARTICLE 14
FRANCHISEE'S OBLIGATION UPON TERMINATION OR EXPIRATION

(1) *Payment of Amounts Owed to Company*. The Franchisee agrees to pay to the Company within fifteen (15) days after the effective date of termination or expiration of the Franchise such royalty and service fees, advertising contributions, amounts owed for products purchased by the Franchisee from the Company, and all other amounts owed to the Company which are then unpaid.

(2) *Return of Manuals*. The Franchisee further agrees that upon termination or expiration of the Franchise, it will immediately return to the Company all copies of the operating manual for Company Restaurants that have been loaned to it by the Company.

(4) *Company Has Right to Purchase Restaurant*. If this Agreement is terminated prior to its expiration by the Company in accordance with the provisions of this Agreement, or by the Franchisee without cause, the Company shall have the right to purchase from the Franchisee the assets of the Restaurant (including the premises of the Restaurant if owned by the Franchisee) and to an assignment of the Franchisee's lease for the premises of the Restaurant. . . .

(5) *Covenant Not to Compete*. If this Agreement is terminated prior to its expiration by the Company in accordance with the provisions of this Agreement, or by the Franchisee without cause, the Franchisee agrees that for a period of two (2) years it will not have any interest as an owner, partner, director, officer, employee, consultant, representative, or agent, or in any other capacity, in any restaurant serving hamburgers, sandwiches, chicken, or ice cream and located within the metropolitan area wherein the Restaurant is located.

ARTICLE 15
ASSIGNMENT, TRANSFER, AND ENCUMBRANCE

The Franchise is personal to the Franchisee, and neither the Franchise nor any part of the ownership of the Franchise may voluntarily, involuntarily, directly, or indirectly be assigned, subdivided, subfranchised, or otherwise transferred by the Franchisee or its owners without the prior written approval of the Company.

PROBLEM 5-11

Based on the agreement set forth above, Hamburger Heaven has entered into a franchise with Schmidt, a German franchisee. The franchisee has opened up a restaurant called "Schimdt's Hamburger Heaven." The franchisee also wishes to conduct an extensive advertising campaign in the German television and print media. Schmidt would also like to add a few menu items such as "Schimdt's Bavarian Burger," "Schimdt's Bratwurst Blast," and a few kinds of German beer because such items are more suited to local tastes. Finally, Schmidt would like to move his restaurant five miles to a location near a new shopping center development.

(1) Under the franchise agreement is the franchisee allowed to use his own name in the trade name of the restaurant? See Article 9 of the franchise agreement. *9(2) - no modified form of title or mark*

(2) Can Schmidt add the menu items? See Articles 4 and 9. Suppose that Hamburger Heaven's own marketing research shows that these items will be popular with German consumers. What advice would you have for Hamburger Heaven on these items? *→ get German tm's for them*

yes w/ written permission

(3) Can Schmidt proceed with his advertising campaign? Who controls the advertising for the franchise and why? See Article 7.

7(2)

(4) Can Schmidt move his restaurant? See Article 1. Suppose that Hamburger Heaven opposes the move. Why might Hamburger Heaven do so?

w/ exclusive area

(5) Are the restrictions established by Articles 1, 7, and 9 consistent with European Community law? Evaluate each of these restrictions in light of the *Pronuptia* case below.

Pronuptia de Paris GmbH v. Pronuptia de Paris
European Court of Justice[7]
1986 Eur. Comm. Rep. 353 (Jan. 28, 1986)

[Q]uestions arose in proceedings between Pronuptia de Paris GmbH, Frankfurt am Main (hereinafter referred to as "the franchisor"), a subsidiary of the French company of the same name, and Mrs Schillgalis, who carries on business in Hamburg under the name Pronuptia de Paris and is referred to herein after as "the franchisee", regarding the franchisee's obligation to pay to the franchisor arrears of royalties on her turnover for the years 1978 to 1980. [Mrs. Schillgalis argued no royalties were due because the franchisee agreement was void.]

The franchisor's French parent company distributes wedding dresses and other articles of clothing worn at weddings under the trade-mark "Pronuptia de Paris". In the Federal Republic of Germany those products are distributed through shops operated directly by its subsidiary and through shops belonging to independent retailers under franchise contracts concluded by the subsidiary in its own name and in the name of the parent company.

In the court of its first instance judgment was given against the franchisee in the amount of DM 158,502 for arrears of royalties on her turnover for the years 1978 to 1980; the franchisee appealed to the Oberlandesgericht Frankfurt am Main, where she argued, in order to avoid payment of the arrears, that the contracts were contrary to Article 85(1) of the EEC Treaty and were not covered by the block exemption granted to certain categories of exclusive dealing agreements under Regulation No 67/67 of the Commission. By judgment of 2 December 1982 the Oberlandesgericht upheld the franchisee's argument. It held that the mutual obligations of exclusivity constituted restrictions on competition within the Common Market, since the franchisor could not supply any other dealers in the contract territory and the franchisee could not purchase and resell other goods from other Member States only to a limited extent. Since they were not eligible for exemption under Article 85(3) the contracts must, in its view, be regarded as void under Article 85(2). With regard to the issue of exemption, the Oberlandesgericht considered that it was not obliged to decide whether franchise contracts are in principle excluded from the scope of Regulation No 67/67 of the Commission. In its view, the agreements in question in any event contain undertakings which go well beyond those described in Article 1 of the regulation and give rise to restrictions of competition not covered by Article 2.

The franchisor appealed against that judgment to the Bundesgerichtshof, arguing that the judgment of the trial court should be upheld. The Bundesgerichtshof considered that the outcome of the appeal depended on the interpretation of Community law. It therefore asked the Court to give a preliminary ruling on the following questions:

"1. Is Article 85(1) of the EEC Treaty applicable to franchise agreements such as the contracts between the parties, which have as their object the establishment of a special distribution system whereby the franchisor provides to the franchisee, in

---

7. The Court of Justice of the European Community, with its seat in Luxembourg, was created by the Treaty of Rome and given responsibility for its interpretation and application. Among its other powers, the Court is authorized by Article 177 to render preliminary decisions on questions of European Community law when so requested by a court of a member state as in *Pronuptia*. — EDS.

addition to goods, certain trade names, trade-marks, merchandising material and services?"

Pronuptia de Paris GmbH, Frankfurt am Main, the franchisor, argues that a system of franchise agreements makes it possible to combine the advantages offered by a form of distribution which presents a uniform image to the public (such as a system of subsidiaries) with the distribution of goods by independent retailers who themselves bear the risks associated with selling. The system is made up of a network of vertical agreements intended to ensure uniform presentation to the public and reinforces the franchisor's competitive power at the horizontal level, that is to say, with regard to other forms of distribution. It makes it possible for an undertaking which would not otherwise have the necessary financial resources to establish a distribution network beyond the confines of its own region, a network which enables small undertakings to participate as franchisees while retaining their independence. In view of those advantages Article 85(1) does not apply where the franchise agreements do not include restrictions on the liberty of the contracting parties which go beyond those which are the necessary concomitants of the franchise system. Exclusive delivery and supply obligations, in so far as they are intended to ensure a standard selection of goods, uniform advertising and shop lay-out and a prohibition on selling goods supplied under the contract in other shops, are inherent in the very nature of the franchise contract and are outside the scope of Article 85(1).

Mrs Schillgalis, the franchisee, submits that the first question should be answered in the affirmative. The most significant characteristic of the contracts in question is the territorial protection given to the franchisee. They cannot be compared with agency agreements, since franchisees, unlike agents, act in their own name and on their own account and bear all trading risks. The system of franchise agreements at issue gives rise to significant restrictions of competition, having regard to the fact that Pronuptia is, as it itself asserts, the world's leading French supplier of wedding dresses and accessories.

In a system of distribution franchises of that kind an undertaking which has established itself as a distributor in a given market and thus developed certain business methods grants independent traders, for a fee, the right to establish themselves in other markets using its business name and the business methods which have made it successful. Rather than a method of distribution, it is a way for an undertaking to derive financial benefit from its expertise without investing its own capital. Moreover, the system gives traders who do not have the necessary experience access to methods which they could not have learned without considerable effort and allows them to benefit from the reputation of the franchisor's business name. Franchise agreements for the distribution system, which do not involve the use of a single business name, involve the application of uniform business methods or the payment of royalties in return for the benefits granted. Such a system, which allows the franchisor to profit from his success, does not in itself interfere with competition. In order for the system to work two conditions must be met. First, the franchisor must be able to communicate his know-how to the franchisees and provide them with the necessary assistance in order to enable them to apply his methods, without running the risk that that know-how and assistance might benefit competitors, even indirectly. It follows that provisions that are essential in order to avoid that risk do not constitute restrictions on competition for the purpose of Article 85(1). That is also true of a clause prohibiting the franchisee, during the period of validity of the contract and for a reasonable period after its expiry, from opening a shop of the same or a similar nature in an area where he may compete with a member of the network. The same may be said of the franchisee's obligation not to transfer his shop to another party without the prior approval of the franchisor; that provision is intended to prevent competitors from indirectly benefiting from the know-how and assistance provided.

Secondly, the franchisor must be able to take the measures necessary for maintaining the identity and reputation of the network bearing his business name or symbol. It follows that provisions which establish the means of control necessary for that purpose do not constitute restrictions on competition for the purposes of Article 85(1).

The same is true of the franchisee's obligation to apply the business methods developed by the franchisor and to use the know-how provided.

That is also the case with regard to the franchisee's obligation to sell the goods covered by the contract only in premises laid out and decorated according to the franchisor's instructions, which is intended to ensure uniform presentation in conformity with certain requirements. The same requirements apply to the location of the shop, the choice of which is also likely to affect the network's reputation. It is thus understandable that the franchisee cannot transfer his shop to another location without the franchisor's approval.

The prohibition of the assignment by the franchisee of his right and obligations under the contract without the franchisor's approval protects the latter's right freely to choose the franchisees, on whose business qualifications the establishment and maintenance of the network's reputation depend.

By means of the control exerted by the franchisor on the selection of goods offered by the franchisee, the public is able to obtain goods of the same quality from each franchisee. It may in certain cases — for instance, the distribution of fashion articles — be impractical to lay down objective quality specifications. Because of the large number of franchisees it may also be too expensive to ensure that such specifications are observed. In such circumstances a provision requiring the franchisee to sell only products supplied by the franchisor or by suppliers selected by him may be considered necessary for the protection of the network's reputation. Such a provision may not however have the effect of preventing the franchisee from obtaining those products from other franchisees.

Finally, since advertising helps to define the image of the network's name or symbol in the eyes of the public, a provision requiring the franchisee to obtain the franchisor's approval for all advertising is also essential for the maintenance of the network's identity, so long as that provision concerns only the nature of the advertising.

It must be emphasized on the other hand that, far from being necessary for the protection of the know-how provided or the maintenance of the network's identity and reputation, certain provisions restrict competition between the members of the network. That is true of provisions that share markets between the franchisor and franchisees or between franchisees or prevent franchisees from engaging in price competition with each other.

In that regard, the attention of the national court should be drawn to the provision which obliges the franchisee to sell goods covered by the contract only in the premises specified therein. That provision prohibits the franchisee from opening a second shop. Its real effect becomes clear if it is examined in conjunction with the franchisor's undertaking to ensure that the franchisee has the exclusive use of his business name or symbol in a given territory. In order to comply with that undertaking the franchisor must not only refrain from establishing himself within that territory but also require other franchisees to give an undertaking not to open a second shop outside their own territory. A combination of provisions of that kind results in a sharing of markets between the franchisor and the franchisees or between franchisees and thus restricts competition within the network. As is clear from the judgment of 13 July 1966 (Joined Cases 56 and 58/64, *Consten* and *Grundig v Commission* [1966] ECR 299), a restriction of that kind constitutes a limitation of competition for the purposes of Article 85(1) if it concerns a business name or symbol which is already well-known. It is of course possible that a prospective franchisee would not take the risk of becoming part of the chain, investing his own money, paying a relatively high entry fee and undertaking to pay a substantial annual royalty, unless he could hope, thanks to a degree of protection against competition on the part of the franchisor and other franchisees, that his business would be profitable. That consideration, however, is relevant only to an examination of the agreement in the light of the conditions laid down in Article 85(3).

Although provisions which impair the franchisee's freedom to determine his own prices are restrictive of competition, that is not the case where the franchisor simply provides franchisees with price guidelines, so long as there is no concerted practice between the franchisor and the franchisees or between the franchisees themselves for the actual application of such prices. It is for the national court to determine whether that is indeed the case.

Finally, it must be added that franchise agreements for the distribution of goods which contain provisions sharing markets between the franchisor and the franchisees or between the franchisees themselves are in any event liable to affect trade between Member States, even if they are entered into by undertakings established in the same Member State, in so far as they prevent franchises from establishing themselves in another Member State.

In view of the foregoing, the answer to the first question must be that:

1. The compatibility of franchise agreements for the distribution of goods with Article 85(1) depends on the provisions contained therein and on their economic context.

2. Provisions that are strictly necessary in order to ensure that the know-how and assistance provided by the franchisor do not benefit competitors do not constitute restrictions of competition for the purposes of Article 85(1).

3. Provisions which establish the control strictly necessary for maintaining the identity and reputation of the network identified by the common name or symbol do not constitute restrictions of competition for the purposes of Article 85(1).

4. Provisions that share markets between the franchisor and the franchisees or between franchisees constitute restrictions of competition for the purposes of Article 85(1).

5. The fact that the franchisor makes price recommendations to the franchisee does not constitute a restriction of competition, so long as there is no concerted practice between the franchisor and the franchisees or between the franchisees themselves for the actual application of such prices.

6. Franchise agreements for the distribution of goods which contain provisions sharing markets between the franchisor and the franchisees or between franchisees are capable of affecting trade between Member States.

[The court went on to hold that as franchise agreements differ in some significant ways from exclusive dealing agreements the block exemption granted to certain categories of exclusive dealing agreements under Regulation No. 67/67 of the commission did not apply to franchise agreements.]

NOTES

1. In *Pronuptia*, the European Court of Justice (ECJ) reasoned that franchise systems provided valuable economic benefits to the parties involved and to the customers of the systems. As a result, franchise systems should be permitted and should not be considered to be anticompetitive within the meaning of Article 85(1) [now Article 81(1)] of the Treaty of Rome. The ECJ distinguished between two types of restrictions: Those necessary to maintain a franchise system and those restrictions that are not. The restrictions protecting know-how and other intellectual property rights of the franchisor and those restrictions necessary to maintain the common identity and reputation of the franchise network are deemed to be necessary and thus outside the prohibitions of Article 85(1) of the Treaty of Rome. Mutually exclusive territorial restrictions, however, are not considered by the ECJ to be absolutely necessary to maintain a franchise system and run afoul of the restriction against market sharing. These restrictions, unless they fall within an exemption under Article 85(3) [now Article 81(3)], would render the entire franchise agreement void. The ECJ agreed with the German appeals court that the 1967 block exemption for exclusive purchasing agreements did not apply to the franchise agreement in the case and therefore did not exempt the agreement from the scope of Article 85(1).

2. After *Pronuptia* was decided, the EC issued Regulation No. 4087/88 in 1989 that was specifically directed at distribution and service franchises. The 1989 block exemption exempted the types of territorial restrictions involved in *Pronuptia*, that is, (1) an exclusive right to the franchisee to operate a franchise in a particular territory from the contract premises and (2) a prohibition against the sale of competing goods and services by the franchisee. EC Regulation No. 4087/88 has since been superseded by EC Regulation No. 2790/1999, which is the block exemption applicable to vertical undertakings that we examined in connection with the distribution agreement at the beginning of this chapter. The 1999 block exemption has been construed to include most distribution and service franchises within its scope and will permit the types of exclusive territory restrictions that were recognized by its predecessor and that were involved in *Pronuptia*.

6   *Foreign Direct Investment*

I.   *Introduction: The Decision to Invest*

Suppose that you are fortunate enough to have a client, Medtech, whose founders have developed very innovative and advanced medical technology and equipment. Medtech has its corporate offices and manufacturing facilities in the United States, and business is booming. Medtech equipment has an impressive market share domestically and, with a minimum of effort, foreign sales orders are also coming in. Every year for the past five years, Medtech's foreign sales have increased by an average of over 20 percent. Despite appearances, however, not all is well.

For the past five years, Medtech has been servicing what it considers to be its most important foreign markets, Europe, Asia, and South America, through the use of foreign distributors and contract manufacturers. Because its products are so successful and attractive, Medtech has already secured a significant market share in these markets that is growing each year but there has been a recent slowdown and Medtech's management is concerned. After healthy double-digit growth in market share in its three major markets abroad for the first three years, growth has begun to slow down considerably in the past two years. Medtech's growth in its foreign markets averaged 25 percent during the first three years of its expansion abroad but dipped to 15 percent during the fourth year and was just 10 percent last year. First- and second-quarter receipts from the current fiscal year indicate that growth will likely be in single digits for the current year. Medtech's management believes that this slowdown is due to increasing competition in its foreign markets by Medtech's domestic competitors and by foreign competitors native to the foreign markets. Another factor appears to be the growing number of counterfeits and infringements of Medtech's products in its foreign markets, especially in Asia (but Medtech's executives will delay consideration on this issue as it is the topic of Chapter 7).

Medtech is generally considered to be a "star" in the medical technology field in the United States. But Medtech executives know that they must take steps now to anticipate future market developments because it has become clear that foreign growth cannot be sustained using its current strategies. Although Medtech is still doing very well, its executives, using the foresight that made Medtech successful in the first place, are now very concerned about Medtech's future and there is a growing feeling within the company that it has reached a critical point in its corporate life.

At a corporate retreat for senior management, several new strategies were discussed. One strategy that was proposed was to abandon its foreign markets and to concentrate just on the U.S. market. Medtech has reached the same point that many companies that sell overseas through the use of distributors and contract manufacturers also find themselves: Use of nonestablishment forms of doing business abroad has limits in expanding business abroad and may not be a viable strategy against aggressive local competition. While some companies may be satisfied with continuing to use nonestablishment forms of business, that may not be true for all companies, particularly those such as Medtech that are in competitive and fast-growing industries vulnerable to foreign competition. However, the suggestion to abandon foreign markets was quickly rejected. All of Medtech's domestic competitors have foreign operations and Medtech believes that it cannot survive if it concentrates just on the U.S. market. While Medtech is about the same size as some of its competitors, Medtech's executives realize that a few domestic competitors are likely to double in size within the next decade through foreign expansion. The larger companies will be able to put intense competitive pressure on the smaller companies as those with greater resources will have an advantage in research and development and pricing. Medtech also realizes that although there are several competitors in the field now not all of these companies will survive as the industry grows and consolidates and that some will face business failure or will be vulnerable to being acquired by more aggressive and successful competitors. Although a market leader now, Medtech fully realizes that its position could completely change in several years and is well aware that some of today's "stars" will disappear in a few years in the intensively competitive global marketplace. Another set of strategies concerns geographical expansion into the Middle East and Africa. These strategies struck a responsive chord and a subcommittee was established to study this prospect further and to report to senior management. However, Medtech executives soon turned to a discussion of the more basic topic that was on everyone's mind: Whether it will continue its plan of using nonestablishment forms of doing business abroad under directions from its U.S. headquarters or whether it will set up a foreign subsidiary or joint venture company to manufacture medical equipment in an important foreign market. Medtech has thoroughly studied the probable costs and revenues likely to result from each alternative. Its analysis depends on estimates and suppositions, but Medtech is ready to make a calculated leap into the unknown: Foreign direct investment.

A useful definition refers to FDI as an "investment that is made to acquire a lasting interest in an enterprise operating in an economy other than that of an investor, the investor's purpose being to have an effective choice in the management of the enterprise."[1] FDI is usually a fundamental policy decision for a domestic business entity that may affect its identity for the future. Why?

FDI usually entails a major long-term commitment of capital and other resources. MNEs can invest hundreds of millions or even billions of dollars to establish successful FDI projects. Not only can the capital expenditures be significant, but successful FDI projects usually involve a significant commitment of senior management time and require long-term overseas assignments for the company's key personnel. The costs of extended assignments abroad for employees and their families and the collateral labor issues of managing foreign local employees are often significant. In addition, while the termination of a distributorship or licensing agreement due to business failure may involve costs, the legal issues tend to be relatively straightforward. Unwinding a foreign business establishment and

---

1. International Monetary Fund, *Balance of Payments Manual*, para. 408 (1980).

repatriating all employees can present complex legal issues that will take years to resolve. Withdrawing an FDI is also often perceived as a significant business failure. The costs and the level of commitment required for an FDI suggest that the decision to make an FDI is a watershed event in a company's life.

As Medtech expands into foreign markets through FDI, the character of the company will also change. If its foreign expansion resumes its double-digit growth as a result of FDI, then in a few years, Medtech will need to establish independent management headquarters in its major overseas markets. The more successful Medtech's foreign expansion abroad becomes, the more likely Medtech's identity will be transformed. The U.S. market, once its most important market, may become only one of several important markets, and its U.S. headquarters, once the center of the entire company, may become a national or regional office on par with similar offices in other regions. Although the CEO may still be housed in the U.S. office, the CEO may be a European who has made a reputation by successfully running Medtech's European operations. In other words, once Medtech decides to plunge into the world of FDI, it has started on a path that may one day lead to a change in its identity from a U.S. company to a multinational enterprise.

As you can see, the decision to make an FDI is an important one for Medtech and the stakes are high. What leads a U.S. business concern to make a foreign direct investment?

A.   Market Penetration

The business concern may decide that the nonestablishment forms of doing business abroad do not result in a sufficient degree of market penetration for a number of reasons. We have already seen that direct sales to a foreign market are often limited by the seller's lack of knowledge of the foreign market and a lack of a local distribution network. In the case of licensing of patents and trademarks, considered in the last chapter, the licensor is sharing the foreign market with the licensee by receiving royalties, commissions, or a percentage of sales from the licensee while the licensee keeps the revenues that it earns from the sales of the product. A U.S. business entity that is attracted by the size and potential of a foreign market may not be satisfied with the limited returns available through licensing fees and sharing the market and may wish to enter the market directly. Note, however, that a preliminary consideration for the MNE, at least for developing countries, is whether the host nation has in place a basic logistics system that will allow for the delivery of products to market and travel and communication by the MNE's employees.

B.   Management and Control

An additional consideration is the desire to exercise greater management and control over the foreign market. A local distributor, sales agent, or licensee may not have the capability, resources, or desire to manage an aggressive penetration of the foreign market. Many agents, distributors, and licensees will have other products, including their own, that they are seeking to promote and may not wish to devote the bulk of their time and resources to the one product sold under authority of the U.S. business entity. The U.S. business entity may wish

to develop a marketing strategy and long-term business plan for the foreign
market and surrounding countries. A major component of any long-term business
plan is an advertising strategy in television, the print media, and electronic media.
Even where a local entity has the capability and resources to develop some market
penetration, the U.S. business entity is unlikely to entrust the marketing of its
proprietary trademarks and brands to any independent third-party agents, distributors, or licensees. In order to exercise significant management and control
over market penetration, the U.S. business entity may decide that it needs to have
a presence in the foreign market.

C. Intellectual Property

The U.S. business concern may also be reluctant to license its patents, trademarks,
copyrights, and other intellectual property to foreign entities. For many U.S.
business concerns, the commercial value of their brands and the goodwill associated with those brands constitute the most valuable part of their businesses. This
is increasingly true in a global marketplace where consumer demand for well-
known brands and leading-edge technology continues to be on the rise. How
those brand names are presented and marketed on a global basis are of vital
importance to the U.S. business concern, which is in the best position to market
its brands and technology while maintaining consistency with the product's image
on a worldwide basis. The U.S. business concern may not wish to cede such control
over its intellectual property to a foreign business entity.

The U.S. business concern may also wish to directly control and protect its
intellectual property and forgo licensing to a third party altogether. As we noted
previously, providing access to one's own proprietary technology to a third party
always creates some risks of breaches of security, improper use, infringement, and
piracy. No matter how well drafted the licensing agreement, effective enforcement
of these agreements can be difficult and time consuming. Some companies deal
with these risks by licensing only their secondary technologies. Many licensees,
especially in developing nations, complain that companies never license their
most advanced and valuable intellectual property. But licensing only secondary
technology also presents limitations for the U.S. business concern as it will not be
able to market its leading-edge products. These considerations have led some U.S.
business owners to take a total or partial ownership interest in the foreign business
entity that is given access to its proprietary technology. By being the owner of the
foreign business entity, the U.S. business concern is in a better position to exercise
greater control and to protect its most valuable technology.

D. Research and Development Abroad

Another concern closely related to the previous topic, intellectual property, is
research and development abroad. A U.S. business concern that is manufacturing
and selling products in a foreign market may soon find it necessary to establish
research and development capabilities to service that market and other markets in
the region. For many U.S. business concerns, the first stage of a foreign investment
enterprise (FIE) involves establishing basic capabilities and reapplying techniques

and the fruits of research and development developed in the U.S. market to the foreign market. For example, a particular advertising campaign that worked successfully in the United States may be adapted to the foreign market. After this initial stage, the FIE may move beyond reapplication to create and implement innovations particular to the foreign market. The FIE may begin to develop advertising specifically for the foreign market and make adjustments to the products to suit the needs of the foreign consumer. For example, one well-known consumer products company found that certain European consumers were less fond of high-sudsing laundry detergents than their U.S. counterparts and created a low-sudsing formula more suited to local tastes. Where the product is a high-technology product such as cellular phones, switching devices, or electronic products, the U.S. concern may need to make technical adjustments to the products to meet the different technical requirements of a foreign system. Many foreign countries also have their own special national quality standards and approval procedures for new products and technologies. These requirements would suggest that establishing a local research and development facility may be more efficient than relying on global research and development in the United States and then adapting the technology to comply with local quality standards.

Where the U.S. business concern begins to achieve significant market penetration and its business abroad begins to mature, the research and development facilities abroad will need to focus on innovations for the particular foreign markets rather than reapply or adapt global research and development results. This further allows the FIE to meet the particular needs of the foreign market. At some point, the foreign research and development facility may become a platform for meeting the needs of the entire region. For example, a research and development facility established in Germany, Brazil, or China may become the platform for supporting all of the European, South American, or Southeast Asian markets. At the end of this cycle, the FIE moves from a business dependent on the U.S. concern's domestic business centers for research and development support to a regional business center with research and development capabilities of its own that support other regional and national markets.

Of course, research and development often involves the company's cutting-edge and core technologies, and there will be a great need to protect the company's intellectual property rights. To accomplish these long-term objectives, the U.S. business concern will find it necessary to establish a wholly or partially owned FIE engaged specifically in research and development for the foreign markets. Research and development of core technologies is of such strategic importance that most U.S. business concerns will insist on total or substantial control through ownership of the foreign facility, which can be accomplished by establishing an FIE. Independent, regional research and development facilities dedicated to foreign markets are a hallmark of a mature international business.

E. Global Competition

The last impetus that we wish to touch upon for the expansion into FDI is increasing global competition. As companies are under increasing pressure to find new markets and to increase revenues and as new technologies reduce the barriers of time and distance, many business concerns and most MNEs find that FDI is no longer an option but a necessary long-term strategy. Competition for foreign markets is becoming increasingly fierce and, particularly, in developing countries early entry can create a sizeable advantage. Early entry by Coca-Cola into the China market, for example, has created a significant advantage that competitors are finding difficult to overcome. Many developing countries also provide preferential treatment in the form of tax incentives, currency exchange, rebates of fees, and land incentives to foreign investors that enter the market early. As markets mature, these preferential incentives are gradually reduced and later entrants may find themselves faced with higher entry requirements.

incentives to enter early

II.   *Global Trends in Foreign Direct Investment*

A.   Recent Growth

Growth in FDI has been one of the defining features of the world economy and globalization over the past 20 years. FDI has grown at an unprecedented rate in the past two decades with only a slight retrenchment during the global economic downturn in the 1990s. As we noted in Chapter 1, the growth in FDI can be traced to increased liberalization in laws and practices pertaining to foreign trade and investment, technological change, and growing competition.[2] An additional factor is political reform leading to the opening up of hereto closed markets in such major destinations of FDI such as China and parts of Eastern Europe.[3] The 1990s also witnessed the removal of domestic barriers through widespread regulatory reform.

The growth of FDI in the past two decades has been exceptional. In 2000, the total dollar value of world FDI inflows reached $1.3 trillion up from just over $200 billion in 1993, a growth of over 600 percent in less than a decade. In 1980, total FDI stock represented only 6 percent of world GDP, while this percentage had almost tripled to 17 percent by the end of the 1990s. The tremendous growth in FDI has been propelled and dominated by MNEs. Today, there are about 65,000 MNEs with about 850,000 foreign affiliates in countries around the world. In 2001, foreign subsidiaries totaled 54 million employees as compared to 24 million in 1990; their sales of about $19 billion were double the world's exports in 2001 as compared to 1990 when sales and exports were approximately equal. The stock of FDIs increased from $1.7 trillion to $6.6 trillion in the same period.

The vast majority of world investment still takes place among the advanced industrialized countries of the OECD.[4] More than 90 percent of world FDI outflows originate in OECD countries and OECD countries receive over 70 percent of FDI inflows as well. Two-thirds of OECD outflows to non-OECD countries were concentrated in Latin America and Asia. Outflows to non-OECD countries has accelerated in recent years, reaching nearly 30 percent by the end of 2001 from an average of about 18 percent in the previous two years. This trend indicates the

---

2. See pp. 20-21 *supra*.
3. See pp. 16-17 *supra*.
4. See pp. 55-56 *supra*.

growing importance of FDI in developing countries. For the first time since UNCTAD began to collect data on MNEs, a record five MNEs located in developing economies entered in the list of the world's 100 largest publicly traded companies: Hutchinson Whampoa (Hong Kong, China), Petronas (Malaysia), Cemex (Mexico), Petroleos de Venezuela (Venezuela), and LG Electronics (South Korea).

FDI has become strongly oriented toward the services sector. In 1999, more than half of all OECD outflows involved the services sector with banks and other financial institutions accounting for the bulk of these investments. FDI in electricity, gas and water, and telecommunications enjoyed the largest percentage increases, reflecting the widespread privatization and deregulation of the public utilities on a worldwide basis in the past decade.

B. Role of FDI in Economic Development

For all recipient countries, FDI means an infusion of capital and technology transfer but these benefits are most important to developing countries as FDI represents the fastest route to economic growth. FDI is usually the best source of finance for domestic capital needs. Other types of private capital inflows are portfolio equity from foreign investors who purchase domestic stocks for investment purposes and debt flows, which involve lending by private entities such as investment banks and financial companies. Portfolio equity tends to be more volatile than FDI as investors may liquidate or shift their investments in accordance with market performance or portfolio needs. Debt requires payments of principal and interest that restrict short-term economic growth. Compared to these other forms of private capital flows, FDI is more stable and long term.

While the benefits of FDI in creating a capital base for the recipient nation may stimulate economic growth, the role of FDI in technology transfer may be even more important for long-term economic development. In general, FDI is the most effective form of technology transfer. Some of the technologies available through FDI are simply not available through other channels, including licensing. Technology transfer, including the sharing of managerial knowledge and skills, can lead to increased productivity by the recipient nation, which, in turn, leads to greater competitiveness in the world market for exports of goods and services, all of which results in economic growth and development and higher standards of living for the recipient country. While the effects of technology transfer and the spillover on productivity and economic development are still being debated and studied and there continue to be many strident opponents of globalization, most studies conclude that technology transfer has a positive impact on productivity and economic growth. However, the impact of FDI varies from country to country and from industry to industry. Some countries, such as China, have enjoyed spectacular success in exploiting FDI, while other similarly situated countries, such as India, have enjoyed only modest success up to the present. Capturing the benefits of FDI appears to require, among other things, that the host country reach a certain level of development so that there is not too large of a "technology gap" between the MNE and the local firms as reflected in their technical capabilities. The host country must also have an acceptable general level of human capital and other infrastructures in place to effectively exploit the benefits of FDI.

NOTES AND QUESTIONS

1. In the past, due to a lack of business experience and mistrust of MNEs, many developing countries placed restrictions on FDI that had the effect of discouraging it altogether. For example, some countries required that the foreign investor establish joint ventures in which the local partner would have a mandatory majority ownership regardless of capital contribution; other practices included requirements that all foreign trademarks had to be used in connection with a local trademark or trade name (i.e., "Rohit's Coca-Cola)." India had such onerous demands that Coca-Cola decided to withdraw altogether from India. This trend has been reversed in the past decade, however, as many developing countries have come to realize the role of FDI in increasing productivity and economic development. Many developing countries have also become members of the WTO, have eliminated discriminatory laws, and have passed laws to encourage foreign direct investment. Competition for FDI among developing countries is now fierce. Coca-Cola has since returned to India.

2. FDI is generally a more effective means of technology transfer than licensing for two reasons: The level of technology acquired is higher and the absorption and assimilation of the technology by the recipient nation is more effective. Can you explain why the level of technology acquired is higher? As for the second reason, why does FDI result in a more effective absorption of technology than licensing? In considering this question, note that a great deal of FDI in developing countries occurs through joint ventures in which an MNE partners with a local company but even where the MNE sets up a wholly owned subsidiary, the technology transfer can be far more easily absorbed than in licensing. Why?

3. One of the major problems for developing countries is that they may not have the capacity to absorb or fully exploit the advanced technology that they are seeking. How does technology transfer through FDI address this concern?

4. Although FDI can address some of the concerns about capacity to absorb foreign technology, there are limits to how effective FDI can be if the host nation has not reached a minimum level of development, which is the case for many of the least developed and poorest nations of the world. An important consideration for the foreign investor is whether the host country has an educated workforce, universities, and research and development institutions that are capable of absorbing the advanced technology. This type of structure usually takes decades to develop and the investment of substantial resources. What resources are available to the least developed nations, which stand at the margins of world trade, to create conditions that will attract FDI?

5. Given all of the complex issues and risks involved in planning an FDI, foreign investors need to come prepared with a general legal opinion that provides an overview of how to assess and manage the risks. This topic is explored in the reading below.

David D. Bradlow & Alfred Escher (Eds.), Legal Aspects of Foreign Direct Investment, 20-21, 35 (1999)

[A] foreign investor has to know the rules to build up, run and secure his business abroad. The legal dimension, which is explored in more detail below, concerns:

(1)   the protection against possible risks,

(2)   the facilitation of an individual investment and
(3)   the means of dispute avoidance and dispute resolution.

In addition to the normal commercial risks, a foreign investor typically faces certain non-commercial risks. One obvious risk is the clash of legal and economic cultures. For example, lawyers in many host countries are not used to dealing with Anglo-American style legal documentation. A joint venture between a western corporation and a privatised company of a former socialist country or a patriarchal family business in Asia or Latin America may lead to cultural clashes. From a legal point of view, the non-commercial risks of FDI may be summarised as follows:

- The approval and monitoring process relating to the necessary licenses is not transparent and reasonably fast.
- The investment climate is unstable; incentives, tax rates, conditions of export producing zones, import duties and disguised administrative costs change rapidly and are unpredictable.
- The banking system is not well developed. The procedures for wiring and exchanging money are too burdensome. The imposition of exchange and repatriation restrictions is unforeseeable.
- The existing judicial system is not effective, independent and reliable when it comes to the enforcement of contractual and property rights.
- A new administration may not honour the investment contract which was concluded with the old administration, and thus deprive an investor of existing contractual rights.
- A radical political change may occur leading to nationalisation, outright and creeping expropriation and civil unrest.
- Reality may not conform to the written laws and regulations; corruption may take place in various forms at the different agencies which are in charge of granting approvals, licenses, and incentives to foreign investors.

This list is not complete. However, it highlights the need that lawyers both from the host and home state should be involved from the beginning of a foreign investment transaction. The legal work may be divided into administrative work and contractual arrangements. In the following, we provide an overview on common legal issues which may arise in this regard.

A foreign investment has its own life cycle which includes the planning stage, a feasibility study, the implementation and operating stage. From the viewpoint of the legal counsel to foreign investors, one can distinguish the following documents and proceedings which are related to those stages:

- legal statement about the host state, the home country and the project
- letters of intent with domestic partners and state agencies involved
- applications to protect the relevant intellectual property in the host country
- setting up of corporate or contractual joint ventures with local partners and/or establishing of domestic subsidiaries
- if applicable, due diligence investigation of the acquisition target
- if applicable, entering into construction and related financing contracts
- if applicable, conclusion of long-term state contracts with the host government

- obtaining the necessary registrations, admission approvals, sector-specific and environmental licences
- labour contracts with domestic and foreign personnel
- entering into business-specific contracts like international and domestic supply or distributions agreements
- conclusion of risk insurance and financing contracts with private and public institutions.

The legal analysis of a foreign investment transaction is undertaken by the legal counsel to the investor in the home and host state. It can be regarded as a means of risk management. The result is the legal statement or legal opinion. The legal statement sets out the relevant legal situation in the host country, the home state, and the project. The statement should accompany the transaction from its inception to the implementation stage, and consequently requires updating.

Regarding the host country, a legal statement has to explore the national investment law and the relevant administrative procedures which are necessary for implementing and operating the foreign investment. It also has to consider whether a host state complies with its applicable international obligations. For example, the NAFTA contains obligations regarding state enterprises and monopolies. It demands from its signatories the abolition of performance requirements. A foreign investor from a NAFTA signatory could invoke the arbitration provisions by claiming that the host state has not complied with these obligations. Other multilateral agreements contain certain protection and liberalisation standards which can only be enforced by the contracting parties. For example, no individual can claim before the Dispute Settlement Body of the WTO that a member state has violated its obligations under the Agreement on Trade-Related Investment Measures (TRIMs). However, foreign investors may use the international obligations of a host country as arguments in their negotiations with officials. Although not legally enforceable by private parties, these international commitments may leverage the bargaining power of foreign investors.

Concerning the law of the home state, the legal statement has to review applicable export controls for capital and sensitive technology. Further, the legal statement has to investigate the national laws on export financing and risk insurance, taxation and transfer pricing arrangements between affiliates, and the extraterritorial application of antitrust laws. Similarly, the lawyer must investigate anti-corruption laws which apply to the bribery of foreign officials by nationals. The importance of these laws will most likely grow in the future as a result of recently concluded international conventions.

The legal opinion has to deal with the various contractual arrangements. One may distinguish at least four kinds of contracts related to foreign investment. The first type consists of normal commercial contracts like labour, supply and distribution agreements. The second type concerns specific investment arrangements such as joint ventures between foreign and domestic enterprises. The third type embraces insurance and financing agreements. State contracts between the foreign investor and the domestic government fall into the fourth type. Since many FDI transactions are unique, sample drafts of these four types of contracts may not be readily available. Even if such samples exist, it is always necessary to adapt those forms to the individual circumstances.

In general, it is in the interests of both parties that the contract itself be as comprehensive as possible. In each contract that is part of a foreign investment project, one has to decide such basic issues as the applicable law, the choice of forum including the means of dispute resolution, liability for breach of contract, and its duration and termination.

It is important to realise that even in FDI transactions, many contracts are judged by the law of the host state. International standards and the law of the home state have limited application. Labour contracts with the domestic work force, local supply and distribution agreements normally have to follow the law of the host state. If the key personnel in a foreign affiliate conclude a contract with the head-quarters of a multinational corporation, such an agreement may be governed by the law of the home country. Insurance and financing arrangements with domestic institutions, either public or private ones, will most likely follow the domestic law.

PROBLEM 6-1

Based on the readings so far in this chapter, consider the following:

An MNE that produces and sells daily-use products such as shampoos, soaps, skin cream, and laundry detergent is considering FDI in a developing country but is concerned about whether the country has reached a minimum level of development adequate for FDI. The MNE's products are world famous and involve many patents, trademarks, and trade secrets. About 80 percent of the country's population is concentrated in two regions: The north and south. The rest of the country lives in large rain forests located in the middle of the country. The plan calls for the building of a manufacturing facility and a corporate headquarters in the southern region with a distribution center in the north that will together serve markets throughout the north and south with plans to establish smaller distribution centers in the middle regions to reach the remaining population. The headquarters will house some of the MNE's senior and midlevel employees and their families who will spend up to five years abroad setting up the business and operating the facility. A major responsibility of the ex-patriate employees will be to train their replacements from the local workforce. After five years, the plan is to repatriate all of the MNE's employees who will be replaced on a permanent basis with local employees. The MNE consults with you and asks that you make a list of the minimum "hard" (e.g., physical structures) and "soft" (e.g., social structures and institutions) infrastructures that must be in place before the MNE can proceed with its plans.

III. *International Investment Law*

In the last 20 years, great strides have been made to establish an international law framework that governs foreign direct investment as well as to provide forums for the resolution of international investment disputes. This international law has come about through the conclusion of various types of treaties:

(1) bilateral investment treaties,
(2) regional economic treaties such as the North American Free Trade Agreement,

(3)   sectoral-specific treaties such as the Energy Charter Treaty,
(4)   ad hoc tribunals such as the Iran-U.S. Claims Tribunal, and
(5)   multilateral treaties such as the Convention on the Settlement of
        Investment Disputes Between States and Nationals of Other States.

In §A, we explore the older, traditional international law reflected in cases decided by the International Court of Justice (ICJ). One of the obstacles to the use of the ICJ to protect foreign investment is that private parties have no standing to appear before the ICJ. This limitation, along with others described by Professor Lowenfeld below, severely hampered the ICJ's usefulness as an arbiter of private investment disputes. For this reason, the modern law of international investment, as described in §§B-D, was developed.

In §B, we cover the law as reflected by multilateral and bilateral investment treaties; in §C, we turn to NAFTA; and in §D, we cover the investment rules of the multilateral trading system administered by the World Trade Organization.

A.   The International Court of Justice

Andreas F. Lowenfeld, International Economic Law, 432-438 (Oxford University Press, 2000)

Three cases involving claims of expropriation of foreign investment have come before the post-War International Court of Justice. In each case the claim was dismissed, but in each case the Court has avoided pronouncing on the underlying question of the responsibility of the host state to the foreign investors.

(A) THE ANGLO-IRANIAN CASE (1952)[5]

The Anglo-Iranian Oil Company, a company incorporated in the United Kingdom (later British Petroleum), held a concession in Iran, originally negotiated in 1933. In March 1951, the Iranian parliament adopted a law nationalizing the oil industry and creating a state-owned National Iranian Oil Company (NIOC). Anglo-Iranian first invoked an arbitration clause, which Iran rejected. The British government then took up the case, first seeking interim measures of protection, and subsequently relief on the merits.

The Court "indicated" interim measures without prejudice to the question of its jurisdiction. In the plenary phase, Britain invoked a Declaration made by Iran in 1930 accepting, on conditions of reciprocity, the jurisdiction of the Court "in any disputes arising after the satisfaction of the present declaration with regard to situations or facts relating directly or indirectly to the application of treaties or conventions accepted by Persia and subsequent to the ratification of this declaration." The Court had to decide whether "subsequent" referred to "situations or facts" as Britain contended, or to "treaties or conventions" as Iran contended. This was significant because Britain sought to rely on treaties between Iran and

---

5. *Anglo-Iranian Oil Co.* case (*United Kingdom v. Iran*), [1952] *I.C.J. Rep.* 93.

Denmark and between Iran and Turkey in both of which Iran had undertaken to treat the nationals of those countries in accordance with the principles and practice of ordinary international laws. Though both of those treaties had been concluded in the 1930s, i.e. subsequent to Iran's acceptance of the jurisdiction of the Court, Britain claimed the benefit of those treaties by virtue of most-favoured-nation clauses in treaties with Iran (Persia) of 1857 and 1903. The Court held (by 9 to 5) that the text of Iran's Declaration referred to treaties concluded after its ratification. Accordingly, the United Kingdom could not invoke the MFN provisions of its earlier treaties with Iran, which formed the sole connection with the treaties between Iran and Denmark and Turkey.

Thus the Court arrived at the conclusion that it lacked jurisdiction. Case dismissed.

(B) THE BARCELONA TRACTION CASE (1970)[6]

Barcelona Traction, Light and Power Company Limited was a holding company incorporated in Toronto, Canada in 1911 to develop a system to produce and distribute electric power in Catalonia (Spain). According to the government of Belgium, the shares of the company came to be very largely held by Belgian nationals — both natural and juristic persons. Barcelona Traction issued a series of bonds payable in British pounds and Spanish pesetas, secured by mortgages on assets of various subsidiaries in Spain. In 1948 three Spanish holders of bonds of Barcelona Traction petitioned a Spanish Court for a declaration of bankruptcy for Barcelona Traction. A judgment of bankruptcy was entered several days later, and the Court ordered seizure of the assets of Barcelona Traction. The Spanish court appointed a receiver, and the Traction Company lost the capacity to administer any of its properties. The principal managers of the company were dismissed, new directors were appointed, new shares were issued of the Spanish subsidiaries of Barcelona Traction, and these shares were sold by public auction to a newly founded Spanish company.

Following several years of diplomatic representations on behalf of Barcelona Traction, also by Canada, Great Britain, and the United States, Belgium initiated proceedings against Spain in the World Court, alleging essentially "creeping expropriation" and claiming some $90 million in reparations, or 88 percent of this sum representing the Belgian share interest in the company. Belgium asserted jurisdiction on the basis of a 1927 Treaty of Conciliation, Judicial Settlement and Arbitration between Spain and Belgium. Spain objected to the Court's jurisdiction, on the basis that the Barcelona Traction Company was not a Belgian company, and that Belgium had no right to exercise diplomatic protection, including standing in the World Court, on behalf of mere shareholders. The Court began its analysis by distinguishing among the obligations of host states:

> When a State admits into its territory foreign investments or foreign nationals, whether natural or juristic persons, it is bound to extend to them the protection of the law and assumes obligations concerning the treatment to be afforded them. These obligations, however, are neither absolute nor unqualified. In particular, an essential

---

6. *Case concerning the Barcelona Traction, Light and Power Company Limited* (New Application: 1962) (*Belgium v. Spain*) Second Phase, [1970] *I.C.J. Rep.* 3.

distinction should be drawn between the obligations of a State towards the international community as a whole, and those arising vis-a-vis another State in the field of diplomatic protection. By their very nature the former are the concern of all states. In view of the importance of the rights involved, all States can be held to have a legal interest in their protection; they are obligations *erga omnes*.

Such obligations derive, for example, in contemporary international law, from the outlawing of acts of aggression, and of genocide, as also from the principles and rules concerning the basic rights of the human person, including protection from slavery and racial discrimination. . . .

Obligations the performance of which is the subject of diplomatic protection are not of the same category. It cannot be held, when one such obligation in particular is in question, in a specific case, that all States have a legal interest in its observance. In order to bring a claim in respect of the breach of such an obligation, a State must first establish the rights to do so. . . . In the present case it is therefore essential to establish whether . . . a right of Belgium [has] been violated on account of its nationals having suffered infringements of their rights as shareholders of a company not of Belgian nationality.[7]

The Court sought the answer to its question in corporate law:

Seen in historical perspective, the corporate personality represents a development brought about by new and expanding requirements in the economic field, an entity which in particular allows of operation in circumstances which exceed the normal capacity of individuals.

It is a basic characteristic of the corporate structure that the company above, through its directors or management acting in its name, can take action in respect of matters that are of a corporate character. . . . Ordinarily, no individual shareholder can take legal steps, either in the name of the company or in his own name.[8]

If the shareholders had no rights independent from the company, it followed, as the Court saw it, that a state with links only to the shareholders had no rights of diplomatic protection, and therefore no standing before the International Court. The Court conceded that the measures complained of, although taken with respect to Barcelona Traction and causing it direct damage, also caused damage to the Belgian shareholders.

Canada, of course, could have exercised diplomatic protection on behalf of Barcelona Traction, and as the Court pointed out, it had done so for several years. The fact that no link of compulsory jurisdiction existed between Canada and Spain did not confer standing on Belgium:

It follows from what has already been stated above that where it is a question of an unlawful act committed against a company representing foreign capital, the general rule of international law authorizes the national State of the company alone to make a claim.[9]

One might have thought that the Court would stop there, having found that the claimant lacked standing. But the Court seems to have felt that something more

---

7. *Barcelona Traction* Judgment, paras. 33-5.
8. Id., paras. 39, 42.
9. Id., para. 88.

should be said about the substance of protection for foreign investments, in view of the wide attention given to the *Barcelona Traction* case in twelve years of litigation.

What the Court said could hardly have pleased those who were looking for an affirmative pronouncement from the World Court about protection of foreign investment.

> Considering the important developments of the last half century, the growth of foreign investments and the expansion of the international activities of corporations, in particular of holding companies, which are often multinational, and considering the way in which the economic interests of States have proliferated, it may at first sight appear surprising that the evolution of law has not gone further and that no generally accepted rules in the matter have crystallized on the international plane. Nevertheless, a more thorough examination of the facts shows that the law on the subject has been formed in a period characterized by an intense conflict of systems and interests. . . .
>
> [I]n the present state of the law, the protection of shareholders requires that recourse be had to treaty stipulations or special agreements directly concluded between the private investor and the State in which the investment is placed. States ever more frequently provide for protection, in both bilateral and multilateral relations, either by means of special instruments or within the framework of wider economic arrangements. . . . No such instrument is in force between the Parties to the present case.[10]

In other words, special agreements could provide substantive protections or avenues for dispute settlement. But customary law would not be built from these arrangements, or at least had not been built. [T]he International Court of Justice saw "an intense conflict of systems and interests" and decided to get out of the way.

(C) THE ELSI CASE[11]

Elettronica Sicula S.p.A. (ELSI) was an Italian company engaged in manufacturing sophisticated electronic equipment in its plant in Palermo, Sicily. ELSI was owned by the Raytheon Manufacturing Company, a major American manufacturer of electronic equipment, and ELSI's business depended largely on patents, licenses, and technical assistance from Raytheon. ELSI never became economically self-sufficient, and never paid any dividends. In March 1968, after more than fifteen years of investment in ELSI, Raytheon decided not to invest any more capital in its Italian subsidiary. ELSI developed a plan for the orderly shutdown of its operations; existing orders would be completed, efforts would be made to sell the plant, and employees not needed during the liquidation were sent notices of dismissal. Two days after the dismissal letters were sent out, the mayor of Palermo "requisitioned" the plant, pursuant, as he said, to an 1865 law that authorized disposal of private property for reasons of "grave public necessity".

---

10. Id., paras. 89-90.
11. Case concerning *Elettronica Sicula S.p.A. (Ew)* (*United States v. Italy*), [1989] *I.C.J. Rep.* 15, reproduced in 28 *I.L.M.* 1109 (1989).

ELSI's management surrendered control of the plant, but petitioned the mayor to lift his order. The mayor did not respond, and ELSI appealed to the Prefect of Palermo, contending that the order of requisition was illegal, arbitrary, and *ultra vires*. The Prefect ultimately allowed the appeal, but only sixteen months later. Three weeks after giving up control of the plant, ELSI's directors voted to file for bankruptcy, and three weeks later the court in Palermo adjudged ELSI bankrupt and appointed a trustee.

For six years ELSI sought before various Italian courts and officials to recover its plant or secure compensation.[12] Eventually, Raytheon, the parent company, sought help from the US government. In February 1974, the State Department submitted a diplomatic note to Italy espousing Raytheon's claim, alleging illegal actions and interferences by Italian authorities with ELSI's management, contrary to treaty provisions, Italian law, and international law. It took four years for Italy to give its answer, denying the claim on the ground that even if unlawful, the seizure of the ELSI plant did not cause damage to the shareholders. After close to a further decade of diplomatic exchanges, the two countries agreed to submit the dispute to a chamber of the World Court. Following two rounds of written pleadings and three weeks of oral hearings, a five-member Chamber presided over by the President of the World Court and including both the Italian and the American judge of the Court, issued its judgment on July 20, 1989, 21 years after the events giving rise to the dispute.[13]

The Chamber ultimately rejected the claim, essentially on the ground that the United States had not proven that the ELSI plant had substantial value before the action of the mayor, and that the shareholder (i.e. Raytheon) had been damaged by the requisition. But while the finding of facts went against the United States, several legal rulings, some explicit, others by implication, went in favour of the United States, and added to the picture of the World Court as a source of the international law of international investment.

First, Italy pleaded failure by ELSI to exhaust its local remedies. This had been a successful defense by the United States in the *Interhandel* case on the ground that the controversy was still in active litigation in the United States.[14] In *ELSI*, the Chamber rejected the defense. While it was true that the [Friendship, Commerce, and Navigation (FCN)] Treaty on which the United States founded its international claim had not been litigated in Italy, the Chamber, having reviewed the proceedings in Italy, concluded:

> With such a deal of litigation in the municipal courts about what is in substance the claim now before the Chamber, it was for Italy to demonstrate that there was nevertheless some local remedy that had not been tried; or at least exhausted. . . .

---

12. For the details, see *ELSI* case judgment, paras. 27-45.

13. One may wonder why the United States brought just this case to the World Court, so long after the event and involving a relatively small amount of money — $6-8 million before interest. A clue may be that the United States wanted to demonstrate its continued support for the Court, on the same day that it announced that it was terminating its acceptance of the compulsory jurisdiction of the Court, following its withdrawal from participation in the Nicaragua case.

14. See *Interhandel* Case (*Switzerland v. United States*) (Preliminary Objections), Judgment of 21 Mar. 1959, [1959] *I.C.J. Rep.* 6, esp. 26-30.

It is never easy to decide, in a case where there has in fact been much resort to the municipal courts, whether local remedies have been truly "exhausted". But in this case Italy has not been able to satisfy the Chamber that there clearly remained some remedy which Raytheon . . . independently of ELSI, and of ELSI's trustee in bankruptcy, ought to have pursued and exhausted. Accordingly, the Chamber will now proceed to consider the merits of the case.[15]

Second, what about the holding in *Barcelona Traction* that shareholders had no rights cognizable in international law independent of the corporation? Here ELSI was an Italian corporation, and the United States was bringing a claim on behalf of ELSI's shareholder Raytheon. To Judge Oda, writing separately, *Barcelona Traction* and the fundamental distinction between the rights of a corporation (here ELSI) and its shareholders (here Raytheon) were fatal to the claim of the United States. In not adopting Judge Oda's view and addressing the claim on the merits, it seems fair to say that the Chamber retreated from that position, as Judge Schwebel pointed out in his dissent.

Third, as in *Barcelona Traction*, the claim was not for an overt taking, but for a disguised or "creeping" expropriation. Italy contended that the FCN Treaty and Protocol did not cover the claim because the term used in the Italian version of the treaty, *espropriazone*, was narrower than the term *taking* in the English version, both texts being equally authentic. The Chamber wrote

> neither this question of interpretation of the two texts of the Protocol, nor the questions raised as to the possibilities of disguised expropriation or of a "taking" amounting ultimately to expropriation have to be resolved in the present case, because it is simply not possible to say that the ultimate result was the consequence of the acts or omissions of the Italian authorities, yet at the same time to ignore the most important factor, namely ELSI's financial situation, and the consequent decision of its shareholders to close the plant and put an end to its activities.[16]

One may regard this statement as an acknowledgement of creeping expropriation, which has figured in a number of more recent controversies.

NOTES AND QUESTIONS

1. The *Anglo-Iranian, Barcelona Traction,* and *ELSI* cases each illustrates a different hurdle for foreign investors who seek relief before the International Court of Justice for dispute over FDI with the host nation. Describe each one.

2. Why did the ICJ avoid reaching the merits of the disputes in each of these three cases?

3. *State Responsibility to Foreign Investors.* The traditional U.S. view of the law of state responsibility toward foreign investors is that no government is entitled to expropriate private property, for whatever purpose, without payment of prompt, effective, and adequate compensation. This is known as the "Hull formula," as it was relied on by U.S. Secretary of State Cordell Hull, who was embroiled in controversies with Mexico in the 1930s over a series of agrarian expropriations. This principle was articulated as well by the Permanent Court of International Justice in

---

15. *ELSI* case judgment, paras. 59, 63.
16. Id., para. 119.

the *Chozow Factory* case [*Case Concerning German Interests in Upper Silesia*, P.C.I.J. Series A, Nos. 7, 9, 17, 19 (1926-29)], which involved the taking of a nitrogen factory by the government of Poland. The World Court declared the taking unlawful and stated that "reparation must, as far as possible, wipe out all the consequences of the illegal act and reestablish the situation which would have existed if that act had met been committed." *Id.*, No. 17, at 47.

4. *The Calvo Doctrine.* The Hull formula was criticized and disputed by many developing countries and socialist countries in the twentieth century. It was contended that a sovereign nation has a right to nationalize property and to assert control over its natural resources. Many constitutions, especially in Latin America, recognize that property has a social welfare function. Therefore, compensation need not be prior or prompt, and the amount may be determined by the law of the expropriating state, which may take into account the equities of the situation. This is known as the "Calvo doctrine" after the Argentine jurist who expounded these views. *See* Donald R. Shea, *The Calvo Clause* (1955).

5. What is the current law on expropriation? Consider the formulation of the Restatement (Third) of the Foreign Relations Law of the United States (1987):

Section 712. State Responsibility for Economic Injury to Nationals of Other States

A state is responsible under international law for injury resulting from:

(1)   a taking by the state of the property of a national of another state that

(a)   is not for a public purpose, or
(b)   is discriminatory, or
(c)   is not accompanied by provision for just compensation.

For compensation to be just under this subsection, it must, in the absence of exceptional circumstances, be in an amount equivalent to the value of the property taken and be paid at the time of taking, or within a reasonable time thereafter with interest from the date of taking, and in a form economically usable by the foreign national.

B.   Multilateral and Bilateral Treaties

Andreas F. Lowenfeld, International Economic Law
456-460, 473-492 (Oxford University Press 2002)

The ICSID Convention

(A) ORIGINS AND PURPOSE OF THE CONVENTION

By the early 1960s, following the wave of decolonization in Africa and parts of Asia, and a wave of take-overs of foreign investments throughout the Third World, it had become apparent that it would be very difficult to achieve consensus on the obligations of host countries toward alien investors (read multinational corporations). The leading international aid institution, the World Bank, began to consider how, on the one hand, it could avoid becoming embroiled in controversies between home and host states concerning expropriation, and on the other hand, how it could assist the resolution of such controversies so as to further its overall purpose of promoting economic development in the world's poor countries.

Of course, every dispute between an investor and a host state does not involve expropriation, nor is right always on one side. The World Bank came up with a plan for settlement of disputes not between states, but between private parties on one side, host states on the other, under the auspices of an institution to which almost every state outside the Soviet bloc belonged, and which could be seen as a neutral umpire. The result, which took several years of negotiations to achieve, was the Convention on the Settlement of Investment Disputes Between States and Nationals of Other States.[17] The Convention established the International Centre for Settlement of Investment Disputes (ICSID) within the World Bank, and the Convention became known generally as the ICSID Convention.

(B) The Scheme of the Convention and the Question of Consent

The scheme of the ICSID Convention is quite simple. First, both the home country of the investor — say the United States or France — and the host state — say Morocco — must have been parties to the Convention. Second, in order for the Convention to be applicable, a given investment dispute must be the subject of a consent to arbitrate under the auspices of ICSID, which may be given in an investment agreement at the time the project in question is undertaken, or in an ad hoc agreement after the dispute arises. A consent once given is not subject to revocation (Art. 25(1)).

To avoid the problems with the Calvo doctrine in its various versions, as well as requirements in many states that a corporation be established under the law of the state where it operates, Article 25(2)(b) defines "National of Another Contracting State" to include not only a foreign corporation or other juridical entity but also "any juridical person, which, because of foreign control, the parties have agreed should be treated as a national of another Contracting State for the purposes of the Convention." Article 26 provides that, unless otherwise stated, consent of the parties to arbitration under the Convention shall be deemed to exclude any other remedy. A Contracting State may make a reservation to require the exhaustion of local administrative or judicial remedies, but typically host states have not done so. Correspondingly, home states of an investor are precluded from giving diplomatic protection or bringing an international claim in connection with a dispute subject to the Convention (Art. 27(1)).

Normally, an arbitral tribunal under the ICSID Convention consists of three persons, one selected by each party to the dispute (i.e. the host state and the investor), and the presiding arbitrator selected either by the parties or, if they cannot agree, by the Chairman of ICSID, who is ex officio the President of the World Bank. Thus the pattern of choosing an arbitral tribunal follows the pattern of other international arbitration — commercial or state-to-state — except that Article 39 provides that the majority of arbitrators shall be nationals of States other than the host state or of the home state of the investor.

(C) The Convention and International Law

The Convention is addressed to investment disputes. That term was deliberately not defined, but efforts to limit the scope of the Convention, for instance to

17. 17 U.S.T. 1270, 575 U.N.T.S. 159, entered into force 16 Oct. 1966.

claims of denial of justice or discrimination, or to claims of violation of investment promotion laws, were rejected. The key question in drafting the Convention was what law an arbitral tribunal should apply when it had an investment dispute before it. The resolution adopted in the Convention, was to avoid all attempts to define the substantive obligations between host state and foreign investor, but to provide the following in Article 42(1):

> The Tribunal shall decide a dispute in accordance with such rules of law as may be agreed by the parties. In the absence of such agreement, the Tribunal shall apply the law of the Contracting State party to the dispute (including its rules on the conflict of laws) and such rules of international law as may be applicable.

Aron Broches, who as General Counsel of the World Bank and first Secretary-General of ICSID may be said to be the founding father of the Convention, explained the provision as follows:

> The Tribunal will first look at the law of the host State and that law will in the first instance be applied to the merits of the dispute. Then the result will be tested against international law. That process will not involve the confirmation or denial of the host State's law, but may result in not applying it where that law, or action taken under that law, violates international law. In that sense . . . , international law is hierarchically superior to national law under Article 42(1).

Broches explains further that four situations may be envisioned in which an ICSID Tribunal will have occasion to apply international law.

    (i)   where the parties have so agreed;
    (ii)   where the law of the host state calls for the application of international law, including customary international law;
    (iii) where the subject-matter or issue is directly regulated by international law, for instance a treaty between the host state and the home state of the investor;
    (iv)   where the law of the host state or action taken under that law violates international law. In this instance, international law could operate as a corrective to national law.

[C]ategory (iii) has been the most useful category, as hundreds of Bilateral Investment Treaties have set out substantive provisions concerning the obligations of host states, and have provided for adjudication pursuant to the ICSID Convention as at least one available option for resolution of disputes.

Bilateral Investment Treaties

(A) Introduction: The Spread of BITs

A striking illustration of the changing perception of the rules of international investment has been the growth of bilateral investment treaties or BITs. The first such treaty was concluded between the Federal Republic of Germany and Pakistan in 1959. Since then Germany has entered into over 90 BITs; France and Switzerland soon followed with similar programs, and all the Western European states as well as the United States have made BITs an element of their foreign economic policy.

(B) THE CONTENT OF BITs

Considering the large number of BITs in force, they are remarkably similar. BITs generally start with a preamble that recites the desire to promote greater economic cooperation between the parties, and to encourage the flow of private capital and create conditions conducive to such flow. The definitions article typically contains a broad definition of investment or covered investment, and makes clear that whether or not the investment is held by an entity incorporated in the host country, if it is owned or controlled by nationals of the other party, it is entitled to the protections afforded by the treaty.

1. ADMISSION OF THE INVESTMENT

All the BITs appear to cover admission or entry into the host country. Some treaties, including all those entered into by the United States, require national treatment on conditions for entry, with the possibility of reserving certain sectors, such as airlines, telecommunications, and financial institutions from the national treatment undertaking. Those treaties that do not contain a national treatment requirement for entry typically provide that investments of the other contracting party will be admitted in accordance with each party's legislation, rules, and regulations.

Some BITs, notably the recent treaties concluded by the United States, including the NAFTA, have introduced a new element into the international law of investment — a prohibition, or partial prohibition, of so-called performance requirements. The recent US BITs provide that neither Party shall mandate, as a condition for the establishment, acquisition, expansion, or operation of a covered investment, any of six performance requirements:

(a) to achieve a particular level or percentage of local content or to give a preference to products of services of domestic content or source;

(b) to limit imports in relation to a particular volume of production, exports, or foreign exchange earnings;

(c) to export a particular level or percentage of products or services;

(d) to limit sales in the Party's territory in relation to a particular volume or value of production, exports, or foreign exchange earnings;

(e) to transfer technology to a national company in the Party's territory; or

(f) to carry out a particular type, level or percentage of research and development in the party's territory.

2. FAIR AND EQUITABLE TREATMENT

Whether or not the entry requires special permission once an investment is admitted, it is entitled under virtually all the treaties to "fair and equitable treatment" and "full protection and security." The United States BITs, including the Investment Chapter of the North American Free Trade Agreement, add "as required by [or no less favourable than required by] international law." At a minimum, "fair and equitable treatment" means no discrimination by nationality or origin, in respect to such matters as access to local courts and administrative bodies, applicable taxes, and administration of governmental regulations. But the reason for the clause, separate from the MFN and national treatment requirements, is to make clear that a minimum international standard of behaviour applies to treatment of foreign investment even if no discrimination can be shown. For instance, in an arbitration under the North American Free Trade Agreement between a US-based firm and Mexico, the investor had received a permit from the national government to construct a facility for disposal of hazardous waste, and had spent 13 months and 20 million dollars constructing the plant when the local authorities announced that their permission was required and would not be forthcoming. The arbitral tribunal concluded:

> Mexico failed to assure a transparent and predictable framework for [the investor's] business planning and investment. The totality of these circumstances demonstrates a lack of orderly process and timely disposition in relation to an investor of a party acting in the expectation that it would be treated fairly and justly in accordance with the NAFTA.[18]

Accordingly, the Tribunal held that Mexico had violated the requirement of fair and equitable treatment in Article 1105 of the NAFTA.

3. "FULL PROTECTION AND SECURITY"

BITs seem to require the government of the host state not only not to attack the facilities or personnel of the investor, but to defend the investor or investment against others, including, for instance, rebel forces. In an ICSID arbitration initiated under the BIT between the United Kingdom and Sri Lanka, claimant asserted that its shrimp farm was destroyed during a military operation conducted by the security forces of Sri Lanka against installations reported to be used by local rebels. Following an evidentiary hearing, the tribunal was unable to conclude that the government security forces were themselves the actors of the destruction. But a majority of the tribunal did conclude that the governmental authorities failed to take the appropriate precautionary measures in view of fighting in the area.

> Therefore, and faced with the impossibility of obtaining conclusive evidence about what effectively caused the destruction of the farm premises during the period in which the entire area was out of bounds under the exclusive control of the government security force, the Tribunal considers the State's responsibility established . . . under international law.[19]

4. EXPROPRIATION

All of the Bilateral Investment Treaties contain provisions on expropriation, in closely parallel, if not identical wording. Expropriation is lawful and not

---

18. *Metalclad Corporation v. United Mexican States*, Final Award, 30 Aug. 2000, para. 99 ICSID Case No. ARB(AF)/97/1.

19. *Asian Agricultural Products Ltd. v. Republic of Sri Lanka*, Award of 27 June 1990, paras. 85-6, 30 I.L.M. 577 (1991), 4 ICSID Rep. 246 (1997).

inconsistent with the BITs if it (i) is carried out for a public purpose; (ii) is non-discriminatory; (iii) is carried out in accordance with due process; and (iv) is accompanied by payment of compensation—in some treaties qualified by the word "just", in most other recent treaties by the traditional "Hull formula—prompt, adequate and effective". Many of the treaties speak also of "expropriation or nationalization", of "expropriation direct or indirect", or "expropriation through measures tantamount to expropriation" or variations of these terms.

The reason for including "direct or indirect", "similar to", or "tantamount to expropriation" is to confirm or establish that so-called "creeping expropriation" is included within the provisions on expropriation. The use of these terms, however, has caused major controversy, particularly in disputes brought under the investment chapter of NAFTA, in which investors cite the expropriation text "No Party [i.e. no host state] may directly or indirectly . . . take a measure tantamount to nationalization or expropriation" to challenge what the host state regards as an exercise of regulatory or police powers. Investors have argued, in effect, that they are not challenging the state's power to regulate, but if the regulation results in closing down or significantly impairing the investor's business, then compensation is required. The state Parties have replied that while they committed themselves not to expropriate except under the conditions set out in the treaty, they have not agreed to place their regulatory authorities—particularly in connection with management of the environment—under the treaty regime.

5. COMPENSATION

The subject of compensation has been at the center of the debate about the rights and responsibilities related to foreign direct investment. Since virtually all statements of the law recognize the right of host states to expropriate or nationalize, subject to stated conditions, and since the requirement of public purpose is generally a tautology because it is the state that has acted for what it considers its benefit, the critical question has been whether compensation is due to the investor, and if so, how much, in what form, and in what period of time.

Most, though not all BITs adopt the "Hull formula" for compensation for takings; many of the BITs—notably the German and the American treaties—elaborate at least somewhat on the meaning of "prompt", "effective", and "adequate". Adequacy is typically defined as "market value" or "fair market value" before the expropriation took place, and is supposed to exclude any change in value occurring because the plan to expropriate had become known before the actual taking. The object is spelled out most clearly in the BIT between Japan and China of 1988. Article 5(3) states:

> The compensation . . . shall be such as to place the nationals and companies [of the other Contracting Party] in the same financial position as that in which the nationals and companies would have been if expropriation, nationalization or any other measures the effects of which would be similar to expropriation or nationalization . . . had not been taken. Such compensation shall be paid without delay. It shall be effectively realizable and freely transferable at the exchange rate in effect on the date used for the determination of the amount of compensation.

Prompt need not mean immediate. Indeed it is generally contemplated in the BITs that there may be disputes about the amount of compensation, and provision is made for resolution of those disputes. But "prompt" means that interest shall accrue from the date of the expropriation and shall be included in any agreement, or any arbitral award, concerning the amount of compensation. Some agreements, including the United States model agreement, state that interest shall be paid at a "commercially reasonable rate" for the currency (assuming it is freely usable) in which the compensation is paid. Some other BITs refer expressly to the London Interbank rate (LIBOR). Still other BITs say nothing about interest or provide for interest but say nothing about the rate.

Effective means in a form usable by the investor. The currency of payment must be freely usable or convertible into a freely usable currency, without restrictions on transfer. Marketable bonds are acceptable, provided their actual value, as contrasted with their nominal value, is equal to the compensation determined to be payable.

The most difficult problem—with or without BITs—is how to establish "market value", "fair market value", or "genuine value" all of which are essentially synonymous, or even just compensation, which usually is as well. If the value of the investment can be defined—for instance if the shares of the entity in question have been traded on a stock exchange, the price of the shares on the relevant date may be used to determine the market value of the investment. If the investment is unique—for instance a mine or a large manufacturing entity—it may be hard to find comparable assets or a hypothetical willing buyer, and thus establishment of market value may be difficult. The BITs generally do not give guidance for such cases, but if the enterprise has a record of earnings over a representative period, negotiators or a disputes panel may attempt to establish going concern value, i.e. the present value of the expected future earnings. When an investment is expropriated or destroyed before it has been able to establish an earnings experience, or when it has failed to make a profit in the period prior to the expropriation or destruction, arbitral tribunals tend to be skeptical about claims of prospective earnings, and to found their awards rather on the actual funds invested in the enterprise.

6. DISPUTE SETTLEMENT

Every modern BIT makes provision for settlement of disputes between the investor and the host state. The ICSID Convention, it will be recalled, requires consent by the parties to arbitration under a particular investment agreement or in respect to a particular dispute, but provides that the consent once given may not be withdrawn. The BITs go a significant step further, by providing in nearly all of the treaties that the host state gives its consent to arbitration of any investment dispute subject of the treaty, generally by reference to the rules or arbitral institutions provided for in the treaty. If the treaty provides for arbitration pursuant to the ICSID Convention, the consent given in the BIT satisfies the requirement of Article 25(1) of that Convention; if the treaty provides for arbitration under the UNCITRAL rules or under some other set of rules, the consent by the state satisfies those rules as well as the requirements of the United Nations Convention on the Recognition and Enforcement of Foreign Arbitral Awards (the New York Convention).

The Multilateral Investment Guarantee Agency (MIGA)

(A) INTRODUCTION

In the early 1980s, the staff of the World Bank, urged by its new President, A. W. Clausen of the United States, launched a project for a Bank-sponsored multinational agency that would "enhance the flow to developing countries of capital and technology for productive purposes" by improving the conditions for direct foreign investment and reducing — and insuring against — the political risks of such investment. The promoters of MIGA had two purposes in mind. One, of course, was to create a multilateral investment guarantee agency linked in some way to the World Bank. Beyond this, by involving all member states of the World Bank in serious debate and information exchange, the sponsors of MIGA sought to change the "investment climate" in developing countries.

(B) COVERED RISKS

Eligible investors can purchase insurance against risks of inconvertibility of local currency; expropriation; breach of contract; and war and civil disturbance, including politically motivated acts of sabotage or terrorism. To be an eligible investor, a person must be a national of a member country other than the host country, a corporation organized or established in such a country, or, if it is incorporated in the host country, a corporation the majority of whose capital is owned by nationals of member countries. Two interesting additional classes of investors are stated to be eligible for coverage by MIGA. *First*, state-owned enterprises are eligible if they operate on a commercial basis. Thus, for instance, the Norwegian Statoil, the Mexican Pemex, and numerous enterprises of the People's Republic of China, would qualify as investors if they undertook a project in another eligible country. *Second*, upon agreement of the host country and the investor, the MIGA Board may extend eligibility to an investor (natural or juridical) from the host country that seeks to engage in so-called "round-tripping," i.e. to invest assets left abroad back to the host country, thus reversing prior capital flight.

Eligible projects can include new investments as well as expansion, modernization, restructuring, and privatization of existing investments, and in some circumstances loans made or guaranteed by holders of equity in the enterprise in question.

(C) MIGA AND INTERNATIONAL LAW

If the practice of states and international organizations is evidence of prevailing thinking about international law, the MIGA Convention — adhered to by more than 150 states — developed and developing — makes several contributions to international law and to the receptivity of foreign direct investment loosely referred to as investment climate. Not only does it state explicitly the objective "to encourage the flow of investment for productive purposes among member countries, and in particular to developing member countries" (Art. 2), Article 12 concerning investments eligible for a MIGA guarantee states, in paragraph (d):

> In guaranteeing an investment, the Agency shall satisfy itself as to . . .
>   (iv) the investment conditions in the host country, including the availability of fair and equitable treatment and legal protection for the investment.

A promise of the host country addressed only to the particular investment is not sufficient. The Agency must be satisfied with the "investment conditions".

Further, Article 23, which is directed to Investment Promotion, i.e. not explicitly to issuance of investment guarantees, states in section (b):

> The Agency also shall:
>   (i) encourage the amicable settlement of disputes between investors and host countries;
>   (ii) endeavor to conclude agreements with developing member countries, and in particular with prospective host countries, which will assure that the Agency, with respect to investment guaranteed by it, has treatment at least as favorable as that agreed by the member concerned for the most favored investment guarantee agency or State in an agreement relating to investment, such agreements to be approved by special majority of the Board; and
>   (iii) promote and facilitate the conclusion of agreements, among its members, on the promotion and protection of investments.

Thus, far from maintaining the traditional neutrality of international agencies toward investment in developing countries, the MIGA Convention requires the agency to encourage developing countries to enter into Bilateral Investment Treaties; to join the ICSID Convention, or adopt other indicia of an investor-friendly legal regime. The official Commentary to the MIGA Convention confirms that in case no protection is assured under the laws of a host country or a BIT, the Agency will issue a guarantee only after it reaches agreement with the host country pursuant to Article 23(b)(ii), in which investments guaranteed by the host country will receive MFN treatment.

Finally, as pointed out in the preceding section, there has been and continues to be a debate about the contours of expropriation, which requires compensation (and almost always triggers an investment guarantee if one is applicable), and regulation, which does not call for compensation and generally does not engage international law unless it is discriminatory or violates fair and equitable treatment. The MIGA Convention adopts a fairly broad definition of "expropriation and similar measures", and makes clear that the focus is on the loss to the investor, not on the gain to the host government:

> any legislative action or administrative action or omission attributable to the host government which has the effect of depriving the holder of a guarantee of his ownership or control of, or a substantial benefit from, his investment, with the exception of non-discriminatory measures of general application which the governments normally take for the purpose of regulating economic activity in their territories.[20]

---

20. MIGA Convention, Art. 11(a)(ii).

There can be little doubt that these various provisions, and their broad acceptance by countries all around the globe, reflect and contribute to a relatively warm investment climate.

NOTES AND QUESTIONS

1. *A New Era of Investment Protection.* The international community has clearly bypassed the ICJ as a forum for dealing with investment disputes in favor of a range of alternative forums that are more friendly to investors. Not only has ICSID been used, but also more particular regimes have been created, such as the Iran-United States Claims Tribunal, which was created in 1980 to deal with expropriation and other commercial claims growing out of the Islamic Revolution in Iran. The United Nations Compensation Commission was established by the Security Council in 1991 to deal with claims growing out of the invasion of Kuwait by Iraq. The Energy Charter Treaty of 1994 provides a forum for energy investor claims against states. Clearly, we are in a new era as far as protection of international investor rights is concerned.

[handwritten margin note: ways to protect investments other than ICJ]

2. *Investment Guaranty Programs.* Today, the private sector, such as Lloyds of London, offers political risk insurance to investors as well as export credit insurance, which protects against a private buyer's failure to pay for goods or services. In addition, government programs are designed to complement the coverage of private insurance. In the United States, insurance against a wide variety of international investment and commercial risks is offered by the Overseas Private Investment Corporation (OPIC). The Multilateral Investment Guarantee Agency was established, in part, to provide incentives to increase foreign direct investment to developing countries. The MIGA is designed to complement national and private investment schemes.

3. *Creeping Expropriation.* This term is used for unreasonable interference with an investment that is not a physical taking. How is "creeping expropriation" to be distinguished from economic regulation of property or property taxation? Section 712, Comment g of the Restatement (Third) of the Foreign Relations Law of the United States (1987) defines "creeping expropriation" as subjecting

> alien property to taxation, regulation, or other action that is confiscatory, or that prevents, unreasonably interferes with, or unduly delays, effective enjoyment of an alien's property or its removal from the territory [of] a state. A state is not responsible for loss of property or for other economic disadvantage resulting from bona fide general taxation, regulation, forfeiture for crime, or other action of the kind that is commonly accepted as within the police power of states, if it is not discriminatory and is not designed to cause the alien to abandon the property to the state or sell it at a distress price. As under United States constitutional law, the line between "taking" and regulation is sometimes uncertain.

[handwritten margin note: def of creeping expropriation]

4. *Prompt, Adequate, and Effective Compensation.* What is the measure of adequate compensation? There are at least three common methods of business valuation. First, the present "going concern" value of a business can be measured by estimating future earnings based on the past and present earnings. Second, the replacement value of the assets of the business can be determined. Third, the book value (original cost) of the assets may be used. Which is best?

[handwritten margin note: 3 ways]

Would payment of the fair market value mean payment in convertible currency without restriction as to repatriation? Would bonds be acceptable if they bear interest at an economically reasonable rate?

PROBLEM 6-2

In 1995, the Province of Tucuman in Argentina decided to privatize its water and sewerage facilities. Accordingly, Tucuman signed a concession contract with Puritech Corporation, an Ohio utility company. The concession contract committed Puritech to make investments for the improvement and expansion of the water and sewerage system and for its operation.

Argentina is a party to a bilateral investment treaty signed in 1994 with the United States. Both Argentina and the United States are also parties to the ICSID Convention. The BIT commits contracting parties to "fair and equitable treatment" to investors and protection against expropriation or nationalizing measures. Argentina was not a party to the concession contract.

Puritech has recently filed with ICSID a request for arbitration against the Argentine Republic under the ICSID Convention. Puritech alleges that between 1995 and 1999 it was subjected to a steady stream of decrees and laws passed by the government of Tucuman designed to undermine the concession contract. Tucuman authorities made public verbal attacks on Puritech and encouraged customers not to pay their bills and otherwise interfered with the operation of the water and sewerage system. It claims $63 million in damages.

A provision of the concession contract states that the resolution of all contract disputes concerning both the interpretation and the application of the contract are to be submitted to the exclusive jurisdiction of the administrative courts of Tucuman. Puritech has never brought any challenge to the acts of the government of Tucuman in the administrative courts. Argentina argues that the forum selection clause deprives ICSID of jurisdiction and also argues that it was not a party to the concession agreement. What is the result? Consult *Lanco infra*.

Lanco International, Inc. v. Argentine Republic
December 8, 1998
40 I.L.M. 457 (2001)
ICSID Case No. ARB/97/6

FACTUAL BACKGROUND

[Lanco International, Inc. owns 18.3 percent of the shares in an Argentine corporation formed for the purpose of bidding to build and operate a port terminal in Buenos Aires. The bid was successful and a concession agreement was signed between the Argentine Ministry of Economy, Public Works, and Services and the Grantee Argentine corporation on June 6, 1994. Article 12 of the concession agreement provided as follows:

> For all purposes derived from the agreement and the BID CONDITIONS, the parties agree to the jurisdiction of the Federal Contentious-Administrative Tribunals of the Federal Capital of the ARGENTINE REPUBLIC.

A dispute has arisen and Lanco argues that the dispute should be resolved by ICSID arbitration under Article VII(3)(i) of the Treaty Concerning the Reciprocal Encouragement and Protection of Investment by nationals and companies of one party in the territory of the other party (the ARGENTINA-U.S. Treaty). Argentina argues that the forum selection clause in the concession agreement deprives ICSID of jurisdiction and that as a shareholder in the Argentine corporation that won the bid, Lanco is not a party to the concession agreement and has no standing to bring an arbitration action. The ICSID Tribunal, in the opinion below, examined and resolved these jurisdictional issues.]

A. APPLICABILITY OF THE BILATERAL TREATY BETWEEN THE UNITED STATES OF AMERICA AND THE ARGENTINE REPUBLIC CONCERNING THE RECIPROCAL ENCOURAGEMENT AND PROTECTION OF INVESTMENT

To determine whether the ARGENTINA-U.S. Treaty applies, this Tribunal must analyze (a) whether LANCO's involvement in the Argentine Republic can be characterized as an investment; (b) whether there is an investment dispute, as defined in Article VII *ab initio*; and (c) whether the conditions established in Article VII for access to ICSID arbitration have been met.

(A) THE EXISTENCE OF AN INVESTMENT FOR THE PURPOSES OF THE ARGENTINA-U.S. TREATY

This Tribunal must analyze the definition of the term "investment" in the ARGENTINA-U.S. Treaty, set forth in its Article I(1) as follows:

(a) "investment" means every kind of investment in the territory of one Party owned or controlled directly or indirectly by nationals or companies of the other Party, such as equity, debt, and service and investment contracts; and includes without limitation:

(i) tangible and intangible property, including rights, such as mortgages, liens and pledges;

(ii) a company or shares of stock or other interests in a company or interests in the assets thereof;

(iii) a claim to money or a claim to performance having economic value and directly related to an investment;

(iv) intellectual property which includes, inter alia, rights relating to:
literary and artistic works, including sound recordings,
inventions in all fields of human endeavor,
industrial designs,
semiconductor mask works,
trade secrets, know-how, and confidential business information, and
trademarks, service marks, and trade names; and

(v) any right conferred by law or contract, and any licenses and permits pursuant to law.

[A]s regards shareholder equity, the ARGENTINA-U.S. Treaty says nothing indicating that the investor in the capital stock has to have control over the administration of the company, or a majority share; thus the fact that LANCO holds an equity share of 18.3% in the capital stock of the Grantee allows one to conclude that it is an investor in the meaning of Article I of the ARGENTINA-U.S. Treaty.

[A]s LANCO is [also] a party to this agreement as awardee and guarantor, LANCO is liable to the Argentine State not only because of its direct equity ownership in the Grantee company, but also by reason of its direct liability to the Grantee and to all of its co-awardees in their liability to the State, in the event of a default by any of them. From this liability, it can be concluded that LANCO is a party to the Concession Agreement, in its own name and right, and in its capacity as a foreign investor; and for the purposes of Article VII(1) of the ARGENTINA-U.S. Treaty, it can be considered that the Concession Agreement is in effect an investment agreement.

(B) THE EXISTENCE OF AN INVESTMENT DISPUTE FOR THE PURPOSES OF ARTICLE VII(1) OF THE ARGENTINA-U.S. TREATY

The ARGENTINA-U.S. Treaty requires the existence of an investment dispute in order for its dispute-settlement provisions to be applicable.

Article VII of the ARGENTINA-U.S. Treaty provides:

> For the purposes of this Article, an investment dispute is a dispute between a Party and a national or a company of the other Party arising out of or relating to:
>   (a) an investment agreement between that Party and such national or company;
>   (b) an investment authorization granted by that Party's foreign investment authority (if any such authorization exists) to such national or company; or
>   (c) an alleged breach of any right conferred or created by this Treaty with respect to an investment.

Article I of the ARGENTINA-U.S. Treaty does not require, as the Argentine Republic alleges, that the investment agreement refer to an exclusively foreign investment. Nor can this Tribunal agree with the definition offered by the Argentine Republic of an investment agreement, according to which "a concession agreement that does not contain specific clauses referring to foreign investments is not an investment contract in the terms and scope of the BIT, not even under the assumption that the Concession Agreement had been entered into by a State Party and a national or company of the other Party controlled 100% by foreigners" (Respondent's Rejoinder of November 9, 1998, page 2) (Translation).

It should be recalled here that the Bid Conditions do provide for foreign companies to come forth as bidders, as arises from the reference it makes to the legislation regulating foreign investment; thus, Article 8 of the Bid Conditions specifically indicates:

> This bidding is national and international in character. It shall be governed by the laws of the Argentine Republic and the provisions of these Bid Conditions, its Circulars, the accepted Bid, and the Agreement signed with the awardee. . . . With respect to foreign investments, the Laws . . . shall apply along with their regulatory decrees.

[T]he Argentine Republic having included the awardees in their own name and right (in our case, LANCO) to ensure the sound completion of the project, the

Argentine Republic should bear in mind that the ARGENTINA-U.S. Treaty applies to its relationship with LANCO.

(C) COMPLIANCE WITH THE REQUIREMENTS OF ARTICLE VII
OF THE ARGENTINA-U.S. TREATY

Article VII establishes:

2. In the event of an investment dispute, the parties to the dispute should initially seek a resolution through consultation and negotiation. If the dispute cannot be settled amicably, the national or company concerned may choose to submit the dispute for resolution:

(a) to the courts or administrative tribunals of the Party that is a party to the dispute; or

(b) in accordance with any applicable, previously agreed dispute-settlement procedures; or

(c) in accordance with the terms of paragraph 3.

3. (a) Provided that the national or company concerned has not submitted the dispute for resolution under paragraph 2 (a) or (b) and that six months have elapsed from the date on which the dispute arose, the national or company concerned may choose to consent in writing to the submission of the dispute for settlement by binding arbitration:

(i) to the International Centre for Settlement of Investment Disputes ("Centre") established by the Convention on the Settlement of Investment Disputes between States and Nationals of other States, done at Washington, March 18, 1965 ("ICSID Convention"), provided that the Party is a party to such Convention; or

(ii) to the Additional Facility of the Centre, if the Centre is not available; or

(iii) in accordance with the Arbitration Rules of the United Nations Commission on International Trade Law (UNCITRAL); or

(iv) to any other arbitration institution, or in accordance with any other arbitration rules, as may be mutually agreed between the parties to the dispute.

(b) Once the national or company concerned has so consented, either party to the dispute may initiate arbitration in accordance with the choice so specified in the consent.

4. Each Party hereby consents to the submission of any investment dispute for settlement by binding arbitration in accordance with the choice specified in the written consent of the national or company under paragraph 3. Such consent, together with the written consent of the national or company when given under paragraph 3 shall satisfy the requirement for:

(a) written consent of the parties to the dispute for purposes of Chapter II of the ICSID Convention (Jurisdiction of the Centre) and for purposes of the Additional Facility Rules; and

(b) an "agreement in writing" for purposes of Article II of the United Nations Convention on the Recognition and Enforcement of Foreign Arbitral Awards, done at New York, June 10, 1958 ("New York Convention").

(1) Article VII(2): Dispute-settlement mechanisms at the option of the investor.

[Under Article VII(2)(b) of the BIT the parties are to resolve a dispute in accordance with "any . . . previously agreed dispute-settlement procedures." Under

Article VII(3)(a) if the parties have not submitted the dispute to agreed-on dispute settlement procedures and six months have elapsed from the time the dispute arose, the parties can submit the dispute to ICSID arbitration. Argentina argued, however, that when Article VII(2)(b) refers to "previously agreed dispute-settlement procedures," it is referring to agreements entered into prior to the BIT. Agreements entered into after the BIT, such as the concession agreement in this case, fall outside the scope of Article VII(2)(b) altogether. As a result, the provision in the concession agreement providing for settlement of disputes in the courts of Argentina is controlling and provides the exclusive method for resolving all disputes between the parties. The ICSID panel therefore had no jurisdiction over this case. The Tribunal turns to consider this argument below.]

This Tribunal shares the view of the Claimant that the expression "previously agreed" means prior to the moment that the dispute arises, consistent with Article VII(2) *ab initio* where it specifies: "In the event of an investment dispute . . . the national or company concerned may choose" among dispute-settlement procedures.

This Tribunal understands that the stipulation of Article 12 of the Concession Agreement, according to which the parties shall submit to the jurisdiction of the Federal Contentious-Administrative Tribunals of the City of Buenos Aires, cannot be considered a previously agreed dispute-settlement procedure. The Parties could have foreseen submission to domestic or international arbitration, but the choice of a national forum could only lead to the jurisdiction of the contentious-administrative tribunals, since administrative jurisdiction cannot be selected by mutual agreement. In this regard, the Parties could not have selected the jurisdiction of the Federal Contentious-Administrative Tribunals of the City of Buenos Aires because it would hardly be possible to select the jurisdiction of courts whose own jurisdictions are, by law, not subject to agreement or waiver, whether territorially, objectively, or functionally. As the contentious-administrative jurisdiction cannot be selected or waived, submission to the contentious-administrative tribunals cannot be understood as a previously agreed dispute-settlement procedure.

Nor can this Tribunal agree with the interpretation of the Argentine Republic, according to which Article VII(2)(b) makes reference to agreements entered into between the Parties prior to the entry into force of the ARGENTINA-U.S. Treaty, and consequently agreements concluded after the entry into force of the ARGENTINA-U.S. Treaty are not subsumed by this Article, and therefore are not an option for the investor, but rather prevail.

The Argentine Republic forgets that Article XIV of the ARGENTINA-U.S. Treaty clearly establishes that it "shall apply to investments existing at the time of entry into force as well as to investments made or acquired thereafter." Therefore, it applies to all investments, and their respective agreements, whether prior or subsequent to entry into force of the Treaty.

(2) Article VII(3): Submission to binding international arbitration

According to Article VII(3)(a):

Provided that the national or company concerned has not submitted the dispute for resolution under paragraph 2(a) or (b) and that six months have elapsed from the date on which the dispute arose, the national or company concerned may choose to consent in writing to the submission of the dispute for settlement by binding arbitration:

(i) to the International Centre for the Settlement of Investment Disputes ("Centre") established by the Convention on the Settlement of Investment Disputes between States and Nationals of other States, done at Washington, March 18, 1965 ("ICSID Convention"), provided that the Party is a party to such Convention.

The investor has not submitted the dispute to the Federal Contentious-Administrative Tribunals of the Argentine Republic nor to any other previously agreed dispute-settlement system. In addition, aside from the efforts to reach agreement, more than six months have elapsed since the letter sent on March 18, 1997, by the President of LANCO to the Minister of Economy and Public Works and Services setting forth the dispute that had arisen, such that the letter of September 17, 1997, sent by LANCO's attorney to the Minister expresses the written consent of the national for the purposes of the ARGENTINA-U.S. Treaty to submit to the arbitration provided for at Article VII(3)(i).

B. THE REQUIREMENTS OF ARTICLE 25 OF THE ICSID CONVENTION

The Tribunal shall now proceed to consider its jurisdiction to decide the dispute in the instant case. The general rule that determines the jurisdiction of ICSID, and consequently that of this Tribunal, is established in Article 25 of the ICSID Convention[, which] enumerates several requirements to determine ICSID's jurisdiction, among which the fundamental and central consideration is the consent given by the parties to the dispute to submit their dispute to ICSID. This consent must be in writing, and once given it may not be withdrawn unilaterally.

(A) CONSENT TO JURISDICTION

In the case before us the consent of the Argentine Republic arises from the ARGENTINA-U.S. Treaty, in which the Argentine Republic has made a generic offer for submission to ICSID arbitration.

In effect, Article VII(3) provides: "Once the national or company concerned has so consented, either party to the dispute may initiate arbitration in accordance with the choice so specified in the consent." And Article VII(4) provides: "Each Party hereby consents to the submission of any investment dispute for settlement by binding arbitration in accordance with the choice specified in the written consent of the national or company under paragraph 3. Such consent, together with the written consent of the national or company when given under paragraph 3 shall satisfy the requirement for: (a) written consent of the parties to the dispute for purposes of Chapter II of the ICSID Convention (Jurisdiction of the Centre) and for purposes of the Additional Facility Rules."

The investor's consent, as noted, has been given by the investor LANCO and it has been so expressed unequivocally, such that this will, together with that of the Argentine Republic expressed in the ARGENTINA-U.S. Treaty, creates the consent necessary for conferring jurisdiction on ICSID, and therefore on this Tribunal.

The written consent by the Argentine Republic is set forth in the ARGENTINA-U.S. Treaty; as concerns the investor, as indicated supra, such consent was set forth in its letter of September 17, 1997, and in the request for arbitration, which was filed with ICSID on October 1, 1997.

(B) PERSONAL JURISDICTION

The requirement of Article 25 in terms of the nature of the parties is not at issue, since on the one hand we have the Argentine State, and on the other a corporation constituted under laws of the State of Illinois, in the United States, both the United States and the Argentine Republic being parties to the ICSID Convention.

(C) SUBJECT-MATTER JURISDICTION

Article 25 establishes that the dispute must be legal in nature and arise directly from an investment. In the instant case, LANCO understands that the Argentine Republic has breached its obligations established in the ARGENTINA-U.S. Treaty; it thus seeks to have the Tribunal rule on the following points: (i) the Argentine Republic has breached the obligations it assumed in Article II(2)(c) of the ARGENTINA-U.S. Treaty with respect to investments, and (ii) those assumed in Article II(2)(a) to the effect that it must accord fair and equitable treatment to investments; in addition, (iii) its breach constitutes a deprivation of a right conferred on the Claimant by the Concession Agreement, and therefore under Article IV(1) it should receive compensation; and (iv) finally, its breach also constitutes conduct equivalent to an expropriation, because it is responsible for the damages incurred by the Claimant. All of these are points indicative of a legal dispute.

legal dispute present

PRELIMINARY DECISION

In view of the foregoing, from the documents and arguments made by the Parties, this Arbitral Tribunal must decide, as a preliminary matter — and its decision shall be included in its final award — that it has jurisdiction to examine the merits of the dispute that has arisen, pursuant to the provisions of the Convention on the Settlement of Investment Disputes between States and Nationals of Other States, done at Washington, D.C. on March 18, 1965.

NOTES AND QUESTIONS

1. In the *Lanco* case, the U.S. investor was part of a consortium that had been granted the right to operate a port terminal in Argentina. The investor claimed that Argentina had damaged its investment by giving more favorable treatment to a competitor operating another terminal in the same port. What substantive investment requirements does this allegedly violate?

2. What were the two objections to jurisdiction raised by Argentina? How were they resolved?

Wena Hotels, Ltd. v. Arab Republic of Egypt
May 25, 1999
41 I.L.M. 881 (2002)
ICSID Case No. ARB/98/4

I. THE PROCEEDINGS

The present arbitration was initiated on July 10, 1998 when Claimant, Wena Hotels Limited ("Wena"), filed a request for arbitration with the Secretary-General of the International Centre for Settlement of Investment Disputes ("ICSID"). The request was filed against Respondent, the Arab Republic of Egypt ("Egypt"), and asserted that "as a result of Egypt's expropriation of and failure to protect Wena's investment in Egypt, Wena has suffered enormous losses leading to the almost total collapse of its business."[21] Wena requested the following relief:

> (a) a declaration that Egypt has breached its obligations to Wena by expropriating Wena's investments without providing prompt, adequate and effective compensation, and by failing to accord Wena's investment in Egypt fair and equitable treatment and full protections and security;
> (b) an order that Egypt pay Wena damages in respect of the loss it has suffered through Egypt's conduct described above, in an amount to be quantified precisely during this proceeding but, in any event, no less than USD 62,820,000; and
> (c) an order that Egypt pay Wena's costs occasioned by this arbitration including the arbitrators' fees and administrative costs fixed by ICSID, the expenses of the arbitration, the fees and expenses of any experts, and the legal costs incurred by the parties (including fees of counsel).

In accordance with Article 36 of the ICSID Convention and Rule 6(1) of the ICSID Institution Rules, the Acting Secretary-General of ICSID registered the request for arbitration on July 31, 1998, and invited the parties to constitute an Arbitral Tribunal.

The Tribunal was constituted on December 18, 1998 and held its first session, at the Permanent Court of Arbitration in The Hague, on February 11, 1999. During this first session, Egypt objected to the request for arbitration filed by Wena and raised objections as to the Tribunal's jurisdiction to hear the dispute.

For the reasons discussed below, the Tribunal has concluded that Respondent's objections should be denied and jurisdiction exercised over the dispute.

II. THE FACTS

This dispute arose out of agreements to develop and manage two hotels in Luxor and Cairo, Egypt.

On August 8, 1989, Wena and the Egyptian Hotels Company ("EHC"), "a company of the Egyptian Public Sector affiliated to the General Public Sector Authority for Tourism"[22] entered into a 21 year, 6 month "Lease and Development Agreement" for the Luxor Hotel in Luxor Egypt. Pursuant to the Agreement,

---

21. Claimant's Request for Arbitration, at 1 (submitted on July 10, 1998) ("Request").

22. As explained during oral argument, the Egyptian government holds all of the shares of EHC, but the company is considered a separate legal entity.

K details

1st

Wena was to "operate and manage the 'Hotel' exclusively for [its] account through the original or extended period of the 'Lease,' to develop and raise the operating efficiency and standard of the 'Hotel' to an upgraded four star hotel according to the specifications of the Egyptian Ministry of Tourism or upgrade [sic] it to a five star hotel if [Wena] so elects. . . . " Wena also agreed to make certain "additions to and expansion of the 'Hotel,'" including "at least forty additional guest rooms, a coffee shop, fast food shops, a children's swimming pool, a recreation center" and other improvements.

2d

On January 28, 1990, Wena and EHC entered into a similar, 25-year agreement for the El Nile Hotel in Cairo, Egypt. Wena also entered into an October 1, 1989 Training Agreement with EHC and the Egyptian Ministry of Tourism "to train in the United Kingdom . . . Egyptian Nationals in the skills of hotel management. . . ."[23]

Shortly after entering into the agreements, disputes arose between EHC and Wena concerning their respective obligations. Wena claims that it "found the condition of the Hotels to be far below that stipulated in the lease [and] withheld part of the rent, as the lease permitted."[24] In turn, Egypt claims that Wena "failed to pay rent due to EHC on May 15 and August 15, 1990, and EHC in turn liquidated the performance security posted by Claimant."[25]

According to Egypt, Wena subsequently instituted arbitration proceedings in Egypt against EHC. The Tribunal has not seen copies of the resulting arbitration decision; however, Wena, so far, has not contested Egypt's summary of the award as requiring Wena "to pay rental due," but denying "EHC's request to revoke the Luxor Lease."[26]

On April 1, 1991, large crowds attacked the Luxor and Nile Hotels and the staff and guests were forcibly evicted [Both parties agree that EHC participated in these attacks and subsequently took control of the hotels.] As Egypt notes, "it has been recognized by the authorities in Egypt that the repossession by EHC of the Luxor and Nile Hotels and EHC's eviction of the Claimant from the Hotels on April 1, 1991 was wrong."[27] The Tribunal expects that both parties will present additional information about these attacks—and Egypt's role, if any—as part of their submissions on the merits.

In January 1992, the Chief Prosecutor of Egypt ruled that the attack on the Nile Hotel was illegal and, on February 25, 1992, the hotel was returned to Wena's control. Similarly, on April 28, 1992, the Chief Prosecutor of Egypt ruled that the attack on the Luxor Hotel was illegal and Wena resumed control of the hotel sometime thereafter.

On November 24, 1993 EHC requested that a receiver be appointed for the Luxor Hotel because of Wena's alleged failure to pay rent. Soon thereafter, on December 2, 1993, Wena initiated arbitration in Egypt against EHC for damages from the Nile Hotel invasion. Similar arbitration was initiated by Wena regarding the Luxor Hotel.

---

23. An Agreement between His Excellency Fouad Sultan Minister of Tourism for the Egyptian Government jointly with Mr. Kamal Kandil of the Egyptian Hotels Company and Wena Hotels Limited (October 1, 1989).

24. Request, at 8.

25. Respondent's Memorial on its Objections to Jurisdiction, at 4 (submitted March 4, 1999) ("Memorial").

26. Id.

27. Id., at 9.

On April 10, 1994, an arbitration award of LE 1.5 million for damages from the invasion of the Nile Hotel was issued in favor of Wena. However, the award also required Wena to surrender the Nile Hotel to EHC's control. On June 21, 1995, Wena was evicted from the Nile Hotel.

The Luxor Hotel arbitration panel also found in favor of Wena, awarding the company, in a September 29, 1994 decision, nearly LE 18 million for damages from the invasion. However, this award subsequently was nullified by the Cairo Appeal Court on December 20, 1995. On August 14, 1997, Wena was evicted from the Luxor Hotel and, according to Egypt, the hotel was turned over to a court-appointed receiver requested by EHC. Again, the Tribunal expects that both parties will present additional information about Wena's eviction from the two hotels, and Egypt's responsibility, if any, for the evictions.

In addition to the disputes regarding the two hotels, Wena also has alleged a "campaign of continual harassment of Wena," including the following allegations: "in 1991 the Minister of Tourism made defamatory statements about Wena that were reproduced in the media; in 1992 Egypt revoked the Nile Hotel's operating license without reason; in 1995 Egypt imposed an enormous, but fictitious, tax demand on Wena; in 1996 Egypt removed the Luxor Hotel's police book, effectively rendering it unable to accept guests; and, last but not least, in 1997 Egypt imposed a three-year prison sentence and a LE 2000,000 bail bond on the Managing Director of Wena based on trumped-up charges."[28] With the exception of the 1997 conviction of Mr. Nael El-Farargy, the Managing Director of Wena, the parties have discussed none of these allegations in detail before the Tribunal. The Tribunal looks forwards to the parties' elaboration on these issues. . . .

IV. OBJECTION 1: "THE RESPONDENT HAS NOT AGREED TO ARBITRATE WITH THE CLAIMANT AS IT IS, BY VIRTUE OF OWNERSHIP, TO BE TREATED AS AN EGYPTIAN COMPANY."

The Arab Republic of Egypt's principal objection is that, "although the claimant is an English company, it is, by virtue of Mr. El-Farargy's ownership and his Egyptian nationality, to be treated as an Egyptian company pursuant to Article 8(1)" [of the Agreement between the Arab Republic of Egypt and the United Kingdom of Great Britain and Northern Ireland for the Protection and Promotion of Investments, June 11, 1975 (IPPA)]. Accordingly, "as the respondent has not consented under the IPPA, to arbitrate with companies, such as the claimant, that are to be treated as Egyptian thereunder, it therefore follows from the IPPA's express terms that the respondent has not consented to the present arbitration."[29]

A. ARTICLE 8(1) OF THE IPPA AND ARTICLE 25 OF THE ICSID CONVENTION

Consent of the parties is the "cornerstone of the jurisdiction of the Centre."[30] In its deliberations, the Tribunal gave considerable attention to the instrument in

---

28. Request, at 16.

29. Respondent's Reply on Jurisdiction, at 2 (submitted on April 8, 1999) ("Reply").

30. Report of the Executive Directors on the Settlement of Investment Disputes between States and Nationals of Other States, ICSID Document No. 2 (March 18, 1965) [Annex ARE23, at 5]. . . .

which Egypt expressed its consent to ICSID arbitration — Article 8(1) of the IPPA between Egypt and the United Kingdom. The first sentence of this article contains a general consent to arbitration between a contracting State to the IPPA and a juridical person of the other contracting State to the IPPA, the situation in this case:

> Each Contracting Party hereby consents to submit to the International Centre for the [sic] Settlement of Investment Disputes . . . any legal dispute arising between that Contracting Party and a national or party of the other Contracting Party concerning an investment of the latter in the territory of the former.

Of considerable importance to this arbitration, however, is the second sentence of Article 8(1), which states that:

> Such a company of one Contracting Party in which before such a dispute arises a majority of shares are owned by nationals or companies of the other Contracting Party shall in accordance with Article 25(2)(b) of the Convention be treated for the purposes of the Convention as a company of the other Contracting Party.

Article 25(2)(b) of the ICSID Convention, which the second sentence expressly references, provides that, for purposes of jurisdiction under Article 25(1) of the Convention, "National of another Contracting State" means:

> (b) any juridical person which had the nationality of the Contracting State other than the State party to the dispute on the date on which the parties consented to submit such dispute to conciliation or arbitration and any juridical person that had the nationality of the Contracting State party to the dispute on that date and which, because of foreign control, the parties have agreed should be treated as a national of another Contracting State for the purposes of this Convention.

B. THE PARTIES' INTERPRETATION OF ARTICLE 8(1)

Egypt contends that the second sentence of Article 8(1) of the IPPA "reverses the nationality of a company incorporated in the United Kingdom but majority owned by Egyptian nationals."[31] Thus, "a company such as the Claimant, in which the majority of shares are held by an Egyptian national, is to be treated as an Egyptian company, not a United Kingdom company."[32] Because the first sentence of Article 8(1), quoted above, requires diversity of nationality between the "Contracting Party" and the "national or party of the other Contracting Party," Egypt argues that the second sentence of Article 8(1) has the effect of "excluding jurisdiction in cases, such as this one, where a company is majority-owned by shareholders having the nationality of the State with which the company has a dispute."[33]

In contrast, Wena argues that "Egypt has completely misconstrued the meaning of Article 8(1): it is a provision allowing companies incorporated in a state to

---

31. Memorial, at 12.
32. Id., at 11.
33. Reply, at 7.

sue that state where local companies are under foreign control; it does not prevent companies incorporated in that state from suing the other state."[34] In other words, "Wena's construction of this provision is that it applies not in every case, but only to a company which has the 'nationality of the Contracting State party to the dispute,' in accordance with Article 25(2)(b) of the ICSID Convention . . . to which the second sentence of Article 8(1) cross-refers."[35] Thus, according to Wena, the "second sentence of Article 8(1) . . . does not apply to Wena, a company which does not have the nationality of Egypt, the Contracting State party to this dispute."[36]

C. THE TRIBUNAL'S ANALYSIS

[T]he Tribunal agrees with Wena's interpretation that the purpose of the sentence is to expand jurisdiction in cases where a company incorporated in the host State is controlled by nationals of the non-host State, "in accordance with Article 25(2)(b) of the [ICSID] Convention."

The literature rather convincingly demonstrates that Article 25(2)(b) of the ICSID Convention—and provisions like Article 8 of the United Kingdom's model bilateral investment treaty—are meant to expand ICSID jurisdiction by "permitting parties to a dispute to stipulate that a subsidiary of a 'national of another contracting state' which is incorporated in the host state (and therefore arguably a 'local national') will be treated as itself a 'national of another contracting state.'"[37] In the absence of any direct evidence of the intent of the Arab Republic of Egypt and the United Kingdom in negotiating Article 8(1), the Tribunal was strongly convinced by this common academic interpretation.

The purpose of Article 25(2)(b) is "to account for the rather common situation in which a host government insists that foreign investors channel their investment through a locally incorporated company. In the absence of this qualification to the general rule, such a company could not resort to ICSID facilities. . . ."[38] As every commentator cited by the parties explains, Article 25(2)(b) was specifically "designed to accommodate this problem by creating an exception to the diversity of nationality requirement."[39] Thus, the article acts to expand the Convention's normal jurisdiction—allowing a "juridical person incorporated in the host State [to] be regarded as the national of another Contracting state if 'because of foreign control,' the parties have agreed that it should be treated as such for the purposes of the Convention."[40]

---

34. Response, at 25.

35. Claimant's Rejoinder on Jurisdiction (submitted on April 22, 1999), at 21-22.

36. Id., at 22.

37. Aron Broches, Bilateral Investment Protection Treaties and Arbitration of Investment Disputes, in The Art of Arbitration edited by Jan C. Schultz (1982) [Annex W38, at 70].

38. Georges R. Delaume, ICSID Arbitration: Practical Considerations, Journal of International Arbitration, vol. 1 (1984) [Annex W33, at 112].

39. Christoph Schreuer, Commentary on the ICSID Convention, 12 ICSID Review—FILJ (1997) [Annex ARE24, at 94].

40. Georges R. Delaume, ICSID Arbitration: Practical Considerations, Journal of International Arbitration, vol. 1 (1984) [Annex W33, at 112].

VI. Objection: "There Is No Legal Dispute Between the Claimant and the Respondent."

Egypt's [other] objection is that there is no "legal dispute" between Wena and Egypt. Specifically, Egypt contends that Wena has attempted to "make a succession of disputes arising out of a series of private relations into something larger than the sum of its parts—a dispute with Respondent. . . ."[41] According to Egypt, Wena's disputes actually are with the Egyptian Hotel Company ("EHC"), with whom Wena entered its original lease agreements and whose employees allegedly attacked the two hotels. As Egypt concluded, "Claimant has not demonstrated, and cannot, that there is any dispute between it and the Respondent."[42]

Wena, of course, disagrees. During the second session, Wena's counsel argued that Claimant actually has two separate disputes. One dispute, Wena acknowledges, is with EHC for violating its agreements with Wena. As the parties agree, this dispute with EHC has been the subject of at least four domestic arbitrations in Egypt. However, Wena also contends that it has a separate dispute with Respondent for "expropriating Wena's investments without providing prompt, adequate and effective compensation, and by failing to accord Wena's investments in Egypt fair and equitable treatment and full protection and security."[43]

From a jurisdictional perspective, the Tribunal believes that Wena has satisfied [its] burden. Wena has raised allegations against Egypt—of assisting in, or at least failing to prevent, the expropriation of Wena's assets—which, if proven, clearly satisfy the requirement of a "legal dispute" under Article 25(1) of the ICSID Convention. In addition, Wena has presented at least some evidence that suggests Egypt's possible culpability.[44]

VIII. Conclusion

In sum, the Tribunal concludes that it has jurisdiction under the IPPA and the ICSID Convention for this matter to proceed to the merits of this case.

NOTES AND QUESTIONS

1. In *Wena Hotels*, is the Egyptian government responsible for the actions of the private parties who attacked the hotels? In what sense?

Under principles of the international law of state responsibility, the actions of a subdivision of a federal or central government are attributable to the federal or central government in question.

2. In a subsequent arbitration on the merits of the case, the tribunal held that Egypt had violated its duties of "fair and equitable treatment" and "full protection and security" as required by Article 2(2) of the IPPA. Compensation was awarded as measured by the standard: "the market value of the expropriated property immediately before the expropriation." See 41 I.L.M. 892 (2002).

---

41. Memorial, at 26.
42. Id., at 20.
43. Request, at 18.
44. See, e.g., "British tourists are beaten and thrown out of Egypt hotels," Daily Telegraph (April 4, 1991) [Annex W7].

C. The North American Free Trade Agreement

In Chapter 1, we provided a brief overview of NAFTA and its objectives at pp. 49-52, which we suggest that you review now. In this section, we focus on NAFTA Chapter 11, which provides a special regime to facilitate investment. The key provisions of Chapter 11 are as follows:

Article 1102: National Treatment

1. Each Party shall accord to investors of another Party treatment no less favorable than that it accords, in like circumstances, to its own investors with respect to the establishment, acquisition, expansion, management, conduct, operation, and sale or other disposition of investments.

2. Each Party shall accord to investments of investors of another Party treatment no less favorable than that it accords, in like circumstances, to investments of its own investors with respect to the establishment, acquisition, expansion, management, conduct, operation, and sale or other disposition of investments.

3. The treatment accorded by a Party under paragraphs 1 and 2 means, with respect to a state or province, treatment no less favorable than the most favorable treatment accorded, in like circumstances, by that state or province to investors, and to investments of investors, of the Party of which it forms a part.

Article 1103: Most-Favored-Nation Treatment

1. Each Party shall accord to investors of another Party treatment no less favorable than that it accords, in like circumstances, to investors of any other Party or of a non-Party with respect to the establishment, acquisition, expansion, management, conduct, operation, and sale or other disposition of investments.

2. Each Party shall accord to investments of investors of another Party treatment no less favorable than that it accords, in like circumstances, to investments of investors of any other Party or of a non-Party with respect to the establishment, acquisition, expansion, management, conduct, operation, and sale or other disposition of investments.

Article 1104: Standard of Treatment

Each Party shall accord to investors of another Party and to investments of investors of another Party the better of the treatment required by Articles 1102 and 1103.

Article 1105: Minimum Standard of Treatment

1. Each Party shall accord to investments of investors of another Party treatment in accordance with international law, including fair and equitable treatment and full protection and security.

2. Without prejudice to paragraph 1. . . , each Party shall accord to investors of another Party, and to investments of investors of another Party, non-discriminatory treatment with respect to measures it adopts or maintains relating to losses suffered by investments in its territory owing to armed conflict or civil strife.

Article 1106: Performance Requirements

1. No Party may impose or enforce any of the following requirements, or enforce any commitment or undertaking, in connection with the establishment, acquisition, expansion, management, conduct or operation of an investment of an investor

of a Party or of a non-Party in its territory:

>   (a) to export a given level or percentage of goods or services;

>   (b) to achieve a given level or percentage of domestic content;

>   (c) to purchase, use or accord a preference to goods produced or services provided in its territory, or to purchase goods or services from persons in its territory;

>   (d) to relate in any way the volume or value of imports to the volume or value of exports or to the amount of foreign exchange inflows associated with such investment;

>   (e) to restrict sales of goods or services in its territory that such investment produces or provides by relating such sales in any way to the volume or value of its exports or foreign exchange earnings;

>   (f) to transfer technology, a production process or other proprietary knowledge to a person in its territory, except when the requirement is imposed or the commitment or undertaking is enforced by a court, administrative tribunal or competition authority to remedy an alleged violation of competition laws or to act in a manner not inconsistent with other provisions of this Agreement; or

>   (g) to act as the exclusive supplier of the goods it produces or services it provides to a specific region or world market.

2. A measure that requires an investment to use a technology to meet generally applicable health, safety or environmental requirements shall not be construed to be inconsistent with paragraph 1(f). For greater certainty, Articles 1102 and 1103 apply to the measure.

3. No Party may condition the receipt or continued receipt of an advantage, in connection with an investment in its territory of an investor of a Party or of a non-Party, on compliance with any of the following requirements:

>   (a) to achieve a given level or percentage of domestic content;

>   (b) to purchase, use or accord a preference to goods produced in its territory, or to purchase goods from producers in its territory;

>   (c) to relate in any way the volume or value of imports to the volume or value of exports or to the amount of foreign exchange inflows associated with such investment; or

>   (d) to restrict sales of goods or services in its territory that such investment produces or provides by relating such sales in any way to the volume or value of its exports or foreign exchange earnings.

4. Nothing in paragraph 3 shall be construed to prevent a Party from conditioning the receipt or continued receipt of an advantage, in connection with an investment in its territory of an investor of a Party or of a non-Party, on compliance with a requirement to locate production, provide a service, train or employ workers, construct or expand particular facilities, or carry out research and development, in its territory.

5. Paragraphs 1 and 3 do not apply to any requirement other than the requirements set out in those paragraphs.

6. Provided that such measures are not applied in an arbitrary or unjustifiable manner, or do not constitute a disguised restriction on international trade or investment, nothing in paragraph 1(b) or (c) or 3(a) or (b) shall be construed to prevent any Party from adopting or maintaining measures, including environmental measures:

>   (a) necessary to secure compliance with laws and regulations that are not inconsistent with the provisions of this Agreement;

>   (b) necessary to protect human, animal or plant life or health; or

>   (c) necessary for the conservation of living or non-living exhaustible natural resources. . . .

Article 1110: Expropriation and Compensation

1. No Party may directly or indirectly nationalize or expropriate an investment of an investor of another Party in its territory or take a measure tantamount to nationalization or expropriation of such an investment ("expropriation"), except:

(a) for a public purpose;

(b) on a non-discriminatory basis;

(c) in accordance with due process of law and Article 1105(1); and

(d) on payment of compensation in accordance with paragraphs 2 through 6.

2. Compensation shall be equivalent to the fair market value of the expropriated investment immediately before the expropriation took place ("date of expropriation"), and shall not reflect any change in value occurring because the intended expropriation had become known earlier. Valuation criteria shall include going concern value, asset value including declared tax value of tangible property, and other criteria, as appropriate, to determine fair market value.

3. Compensation shall be paid without delay and be fully realizable. . . .

Article 1114: Environmental Measures

1. Nothing in this Chapter shall be construed to prevent a Party from adopting, maintaining or enforcing any measure otherwise consistent with this Chapter that it considers appropriate to ensure that investment activity in its territory is undertaken in a manner sensitive to environmental concerns.

* * *

Chapter 11 of NAFTA provides for a choice by the investor between arbitration under UNCITRAL rules or under ICSID in investment disputes. Since 1978, ICSID has operated a so-called additional facility which is open to arbitrations where either of the host countries are parties to ICSID. The United States is a party to ICSID, but Mexico and Canada are not.

The following case deals with the particular aspects of the investment law of NAFTA.

Martin Feldman v. Mexico
December 16, 2002
42 I.L.M. 625 (2003)
ICSID CASE NO. ARB(AF)99/1

[Corporacion de Exportaciones Mexicanas, S.A. de V.C. (CEMSA), a corporation organized under the laws of Mexico and controlled by the Claimant Marvin Feldman, a U.S. citizen and its sole investor, was engaged in the purchase and export of American branded cigarettes produced under license in Mexico to the United States. CEMSA purchased cigarettes from retailers in Mexico such as Wal-Mart and Sam's Club because cigarette producers and their wholly owned distributors refused to sell to CEMSA or other exporters. Mexico imposed a tax on the production and sale of cigarettes in Mexico (139.5 percent from 1990 through 1994 and 85 percent from 1995 through 1997) under the Impuesto Especial Sobre Produccion y Servicios (IESP) but provided a rebate on those cigarettes when they were exported, which resulted in an effective tax rate of 0 percent on all exported cigarettes. The tax was collected and rebated by the Mexican Ministry of Finance and Public Credit (Secretaria de Hacienda y Credito Publico or SHCP). CEMSA began exporting cigarettes in 1990 and received rebates on its cigarettes by SHCP. According to the Claimant, in 1991, one of the producers of cigarettes in Mexico, Carlos Slim, protested against CEMSA's exports with Mexican authorities and influenced the authorities to pass a law in 1991 that denied the tax rebates to resellers of cigarettes such as CEMSA. The Claimant subsequently challenged the 1991 law in Mexican courts on the grounds that it violated the constitutional principle of the "equity of taxpayers" by excluding exports by resellers from the possibility of obtaining the 0 percent tax rate. After the lawsuit was filed, the Mexican Congress amended the IEPS law effective January 1, 1992, to allow the IEPS rebates to all cigarette exporters, and CEMSA was able to export cigarettes with rebates that year. However, in January 1993, the Mexican authorities shut down the Claimant's cigarette export business for a second time because the Claimant could not produce tax invoices in accordance with legal requirements. Under the IEPS tax law, the tax on cigarettes must be stated "separately and expressly in their invoices." However, only producers of cigarettes had access to such itemized invoices. As CEMSA purchased its cigarettes from retailers such as Wal-Mart and Sam's Club, CEMSA did not receive invoices that separately stated the tax. As a result, CEMSA could not comply with the IEPS tax law.

In August 1993, the Supreme Court of Mexico ruled on CEMSA's lawsuit brought in 1991 and held that the IEPS measures allowing rebates only to producers and their distributors violated constitutional law.

From 1993 to 1995, Mexican authorities recognized that as a taxpayer CEMSA was entitled to receive a 0 percent tax rate on cigarette exports but continued to demand that the Claimant meet the tax invoice requirements. CEMSA also claims that from 1995 to 1996 it received oral assurances from Mexican authorities that they would permit CEMSA to export cigarettes in large quantities and receive rebates. In 1996-1997, CEMSA continued to receive rebates and by late 1997, CEMSA accounted for almost 15 percent of Mexico's cigarette exports.

On December 1, 1997, however, the SHCP terminated rebates to CEMSA and refused to pay rebates of U.S.$2.35 million on exports made by CEMSA in October and November 1997. On December 1, 1997, the IEPS law was amended again to bar tax rebates to cigarette resellers such as CEMSA, limiting rebates to the "first sale" in Mexico. As CEMSA purchased its cigarettes from retailers who had already completed the first sale in Mexico, CEMSA was not entitled to any rebates under the "first sale" rule. In addition, the amendments also imposed an obligation on exporters of certain goods, including cigarettes, of registering with Mexican authorities in order to apply for the 0 percent tax rate on exports. CEMSA was refused registration as a cigarette exporter.

On July 14, 1998, SHCP began an audit of CEMSA and demanded that CEMSA repay the approximately $25 million that it received during the 21-month period from January 1996 to September 1997. CEMSA challenged this assessment in the Mexican courts, which challenge was still pending at the time of the ICSID arbitration.

CEMSA was not the only reseller and exporter of cigarettes in Mexico. Two other firms, Mercados I and Mercados II, both owned by Mexican nationals, also purchased cigarettes from Mexican volume retailers such as Wal-Mart for export. These Mexican firms were allowed to obtain tax rebates for the exports during the same period that such rebates were denied to CEMSA even though these other exporters were also resellers and also lacked tax invoices.

The Claimant thereafter challenged Mexico's refusal to rebate excise taxes on cigarettes exported by CEMSA in an abritral proceeding before ICSID on the grounds that the actions of the Mexican government amounted to a nationalization and expropriation of Claimant's investment in violation of NAFTA Article 1110 and violated the national treatment principle embodied in NAFTA Article 1102.

In the first part of the opinion below, the ICSID panel examines whether an expropriation has occurred, and in the second part, the panel examines whether the national treatment principle has been violated.]

[Expropriation: NAFTA Article 1110]

Expropriation under Chapter 11 is governed by NAFTA Article 1110, although NAFTA lacks a precise definition of expropriation. That provision reads in pertinent part as follows:

> 1. No Party may directly or indirectly nationalize or expropriate an investment of an investor of another Party in its territory or take a measure tantamount to nationalization or expropriation of such an investment ("expropriation"), except:
>   (a) for a public purpose;
>   (b) on a non-discriminatory basis;
>   (c) in accordance with due process of law and article 1105(1); and
>   (d) on payment of compensation in accordance with paragraphs 2 through 6.

The key issue, in general and in the instant case, is whether the Respondent's actions constitute an expropriation.

This Tribunal's rationale for declining to find a violation of Article 1110 [is as follows:]

MANY BUSINESS PROBLEMS ARE NOT EXPROPRIATIONS

First, the Tribunal is aware that not every business problem experienced by a foreign investor is an indirect or creeping expropriation under Article 1110, or a denial of due process or fair and equitable treatment under Article 1110(1)(c). Governments, in their exercise of regulatory power, frequently change their laws and regulations in response to changing economic circumstances or changing political, economic or social considerations. Those changes may well make certain activities less profitable or even uneconomic to continue.

Here, it is undeniable that the Claimant has experienced great difficulties in dealing with SHCP officials, and in some respects has been treated in a less than reasonable manner, but that treatment under the circumstances of this case does not rise to the level of a violation of international law under Article 1110. Unfortunately, tax authorities in most countries do not always act in a consistent and predictable way. The IEPS law on its face (although not necessarily as applied) is undeniably a measure of general taxation. As in most tax regimes, the tax laws are used as instruments of public policy as well as fiscal policy, and certain taxpayers are inevitably favored, with others less favored or even disadvantaged.

GRAY MARKET EXPORTS AND INTERNATIONAL LAW

Second, NAFTA and principles of customary international law do not, in the view of the Tribunal, require a state to permit cigarette exports by unauthorized resellers (gray market exports). A prohibition to this effect may rely on objective reasons. Such reasons include discouragement of smuggling (of cigarettes purportedly exported back into Mexico), which may deprive a government of substantial amounts of tax revenue, maintenance of high cigarette taxes to discourage smoking (as in Canada) and, as a Mexican government official has suggested, assisting producers in complying with trademark licensing obligations under private agreements (*see* statement of Ismael Gomez Gordillo, App. 6045-6054). It is undeniable, as both parties in this proceeding have recognized, that smuggling of cigarettes is a serious problem not only for Mexico but for many other nations.

CONTINUING REQUIREMENTS OF ARTICLE 4(III) OF IEPS LAW

Third, in the present case, a per se government ban on reseller exports of cigarettes (or other products) from Mexico was not in force during the entire 1990-1997 period. The Respondent's efforts to impose such a ban legislatively in 1990 were held unconstitutional by the Supreme Court in a 1993 *Amparo* decision. In a narrow interpretation of that decision—that it required both producers and resellers be offered the zero percent tax rate for exports, but no more—it was legally possible for the Claimant to export cigarettes at the 0% rate if the Claimant could meet the other requirements of the IEPS law. However, the Claimant was effectively prevented from benefiting from the 0% rate, and therefore from exporting cigarettes, unless he could also obtain a rebate of the taxes reflected (but not separately stated) in the price that the Claimant paid to large retailers—Walmart and Sam's—for his cigarettes. This problem resulted from the fact that Mexican cigarette producers—particularly Cigatam, the Mexican licensee of the Marlboro brand—refused to sell to him because they wanted to maintain an export monopoly or perhaps for other reasons, a refusal which was apparently within their right under Mexican law. In economic terms, it would have been impossible for the Claimant to pay the price of the cigarettes in Mexico, including the 85% excise tax required under the IEPS law, and then sell the cigarettes in any foreign country. (Once the foreign nation added its own excise taxes upon importation, the Mexican cigarettes with both tax amounts included would have been priced far out of the market.)

In his efforts to obtain the rebates, the Claimant was stymied by a longstanding requirement of the IEPS law, the requirement in Article 4(III) that when seeking rebates he, as non-taxpayer, present invoices showing that the IEPS tax had been separately transferred to the taxpayer. The Claimant could not obtain the information from the retailers who supplied his cigarettes (since they did not know the tax amounts themselves), and the producers of the cigarettes were unwilling to provide the information.

[A] finding of expropriation here depends in significant part on whether under the circumstances the Article 4 invoice requirements are inconsistent with the Claimant's rights under NAFTA Article 1110. On the basis of the evidence presented to the Tribunal, the Tribunal is not persuaded that they are. The Article 4 invoice requirements have been part of the IEPS law at least since 1987, that is, for at least three years before CEMSA was first registered as an export company in 1991. Since the operation of its export business depended substantially on the terms of the IEPS law, the Claimant was or should have been aware at all relevant times that the separate invoice requirement existed, as there has been no *de jure* change in it at any time relevant to this dispute. Equally important, the Tribunal is reluctant to find an expropriation based largely on the failure of Mexican government officials to comply with an agreement in which those officials allegedly waived an explicit requirement of a tax law, even though there is some evidence, albeit contested by the Respondent, that the requirement was *de facto* ignored at some times both for the Claimant and for other cigarette resellers, including but not limited to members of the [so-called] Poblano group. This, however, is not in the view of the Tribunal evidence of expropriatory action and will be dealt with below in the section on national treatment.

National Treatment (NAFTA Article 1102)

[CEMSA also argued that it was denied national treatment under NAFTA.] In the present case, there are only a handful of relevant investors, one foreign (the Claimant) and one domestic (the Poblano-Guemes Group), each engaged in the business of purchasing Mexican cigarettes and marketing those cigarettes abroad. These investors cannot purchase the cigarettes from Mexican cigarette producers because the producers (and their wholly owned distributors) refuse to sell to them. Therefore, the Claimant or the Poblano Group firms must purchase their cigarettes from volume retailers, Walmart and Sam's Club. Since Walmart and Sam's Club are retailers and not IEPS taxpayers, they do not have available to them the precise amounts of the IEPS taxes included in the price paid first by the retailers in the transaction with the producers or distributors, and then by the Claimant and other reseller/exporters. Accordingly, neither the Claimant nor the Poblano Group companies can comply with the requirement of the IEPS law, Article 4(III), which makes it a condition of obtaining tax rebates upon export that the applicant be a taxpayer who possesses invoices showing the tax amount stated separately.

[Although the Poblano Group did not comply with the IEPS law, Article 4(III), its members were able to obtain tax rebates during 1998-2000 and 1996-1997. In addition, in order to receive tax rebates, an exporter had to register under Mexican law as an export trading company. CEMSA was denied registration as an export trading company, while members of the Plobano group were able to register. CEMSA also argued that while Mexico recouped rebates given to CEMSA, no similar effort was made to recoup rebates given to the members of the Poblano group.]

ANALYSIS BY THE TRIBUNAL

The national treatment/non-discrimination provision is a fundamental obligation of Chapter 11. Despite its deceptively simple language, the interpretative hurdles for Article 1102 are several. They include (a) which domestic investors, if any, are in "like circumstances" with the foreign investor; (b) whether there has been discrimination against foreign investors, either *de jure or de facto*; [and] (c) the extent to which differential treatment must be demonstrated to be a *result of* the foreign investor's nationality.

IN LIKE CIRCUMSTANCES

In this instance, the disputing parties agree that CEMSA is in "like circumstances" with Mexican owned resellers of cigarettes for export, including the two members of the Poblano Group, Mercados Regionales and Mercados Extranjeros.

Accordingly, the Tribunal holds that the companies which are in like circumstances, domestic and foreign, are the trading companies, those in the business of purchasing Mexican cigarettes for export, which for purposes of this case are CEMSA and the corporate members of the Poblano Group.

EXISTENCE OF DISCRIMINATION

The limited facts made available to the Tribunal demonstrate on balance to a majority of the Tribunal that CEMSA has been treated in a less favorable manner than domestically owned reseller/exporters of cigarettes, a *de facto* discrimination by SHCP, which is inconsistent with Mexico's obligations under Article 1102. The only confirmed cigarette exporters on the limited record before the tribunal are CEMSA, owned by U.S. citizen Marvin Roy Feldman Karpa, and the Mexican corporate members of the Poblano Group, Mercados I and Mercados II. According to the available evidence, CEMSA was denied the rebates for October-November 1997 and subsequently; SHCP also demanded that CEMSA repay rebate amounts initially allowed from June 1996 through September 1997. Thus, CEMSA was denied IEPS rebates during periods when members of the Poblano Group were receiving them.

The evidence also shows that CEMSA was denied registration as an export trading company, apparently in part because this action was filed, and in part as a result of the ongoing audit of the rebates for exports during 1996 and 1997, even though three other cigarette export trading companies had been granted registration. An unsigned memorandum which reasonably could have been generated only in SHCP indicates that registration was being denied on the basis of the audit of the Claimant's rebate payments. There is no evidence that any domestic reseller/exporter has been denied export privileges in this manner. Moreover, there appears to have been differential treatment between CEMSA and Mr. Poblano with regard to registration issues as well. According to the Claimant's witness, Mr. Carvajal, taxpayer CEMSA filed its application for export registration status on June 30, 1998; information was still being requested in writing seven months later. For taxpayer Mr. Poblano, information was requested by SHCP orally within 14 days of the date of Poblano's application, and any questions were apparently resolved.

DISCRIMINATION AS A RESULT OF NATIONALITY

It is clear that the concept of national treatment as embodied in NAFTA and similar agreements is designed to prevent discrimination on the basis of nationality, or "by reason of nationality." (U.S. Statement of Administrative Action, Article 1102.) However, it is not self-evident, as the Respondent argues, that any departure from national treatment must be *explicitly* shown to be a result of the investor's nationality. There is no such language in Article 1102. Rather, Article 1102 by its terms suggests that it is sufficient to show less favorable treatment for the foreign investor than for domestic investors in like circumstances.

However, in this case there is evidence of a nexus between the discrimination and the Claimant's status as a foreign investor. In the first place, there does not appear to be any rational justification in the record for SHCP's less favorable *de facto* treatment of CEMSA other than the obvious fact that CEMSA was owned by a very outspoken foreigner, who had, prior to the initiation of the audit, filed a NAFTA Chapter 11 claim against the Government of Mexico. Certainly, the action of filing a request for arbitration under Chapter 11 could only have been taken by a person who was a citizen of the United States or Canada (rather than Mexico), i.e., as a result of his (foreign) nationality. While a tax audit in itself is not, of course, evidence of a denial of national treatment, the fact that the audit was initiated shortly after the Notice of Arbitration (first Feldman affidavit, paras. 85-86) and the existence of the unsigned memo at SHCP noting the filing of the Chapter 11 claim in the context of the Claimant's export registration efforts, at minimum raise a very strong suspicion that the events were related, given that no similar audit action was taken against domestic reseller/exporter taxpayers at the time.

On the basis of this analysis, a majority of the Tribunal concludes that Mexico has violated the Claimant's rights to non-discrimination under Article 1102 of NAFTA.

DECISION

For these reasons, the Tribunal:

Finds that the Respondent has not violated the Claimant's rights or acted inconsistently with the Respondent's obligations under NAFTA Article 1110;

Finds that the Respondent has acted inconsistently with the Claimant's rights and the Respondent's obligations under NAFTA Article 1102;

Orders the Respondent to pay immediately to the Claimant the sum of $9,464,627.50 Mexican pesos as principal, plus interest generated at the time of signature of this award, in the amount of $7,496,428.47 Mexican pesos, which interest shall accrue until the date the payment is effectively made. [The Tribunal found that the Claimant proved only that it was entitled to rebates due in the period of October-December 1997.]

NOTES AND QUESTIONS

1. Are you convinced by the tribunal's analysis and rejection of the claimant's "creeping expropriation" argument?

2. Is the tribunal correct in its interpretation of discrimination based on national treatment? Does the discrimination point make it easy to find some discrimination in every case?

3. Because of the controversy over NAFTA investment decisions, Canada and Mexico have allowed review of awards in annulment proceedings to be conducted by principal courts at the seat of arbitration. For an argument against such review, *see* Charles H. Brower II, *Investor-State Disputes Under NAFTA: The Empire Strikes Back*, 40 Colum. J. Trans. L. 43 (2001).

PROBLEM 6-3

New Life Corp. is a U.S. company that manufactures biotechnology products. New Life has a Canadian subsidiary company that manufactures and markets a variety of such products, including a genetically modified potato plant that is engineered to produce a poison to kill the plant's chief predator insects. Canada has recently enacted a law that makes the sale of this seedplant illegal on the basis of evidence that the plant may have a deleterious effect on certain beneficial insects, such as the monarch butterfly. Is this a violation of NAFTA Chapter 11?

D. Investment and the World Trade Organization

Mitsuo Matsushita, Thomas J. Schoenbaum, & Petros C. Mavroidis, The World Trade Organization, Law, Practice, and Policy
522-525 (Oxford University Press, 2003)

1. INTRODUCTION TO THE TRADE AND INVESTMENT DEBATE

International trade and investment go hand in hand. Market access through trade can lead to foreign investment, which can, in turn, lead to additional trade. Global sourcing of components means that multinational companies may wish to establish operations in many different markets or countries. Investment can be for exporting as well as for selling in a domestic market. Businesses established with foreign investment can, in turn, import components in the course of their operations. In some cases, too, investment can substitute for trade as companies establish in a market to circumvent trade barriers. Investment can go hand in hand with trade in services as well, as one of the modes of delivering services is through a commercial presence in a foreign country.

In the 1990s, a serious effort was made to negotiate a comprehensive treaty on investment, known as the Multilateral Agreement on Investment (MAI). Negotiated by the OECD, the MAI was intended for transfer to the WTO, where it would have completed triumvirate global liberalization agreements covering goods, services, and investment. The MAI would have removed barriers to investment, provided protection against expropriation and measures diminishing its value, and instituted a dispute settlement system. Yet, the MAI negotiations failed in late 1998 and were abandoned. This defeat was due to an unprecedented coalition of anti-globalists who feared the impact of the MAI on society, including workers and the environment. Over 600 nongovernmental organizations (NGOs) from 70 countries were reportedly involved in opposing the MAI.

The debate involving the MAI focused on several issues. First, although investment creates jobs, foreign firms can, it is charged, exert too much influence on or dominate economic sectors, especially in developing countries, unless they are subject to some controls. Second, there are fears that investment liberalization can lead to economic crisis when, in times of trouble, foreign investors pull their money out. However, empirical research has shown that the withdrawal of foreign investment is a problem only with portfolio investment, bank deposits, and loans, not with foreign direct investment (FDI). For example, during both the Mexican peso devaluation of 1994-95 and the Asian economic crisis of 1997-98, FDI was largely stable; there was little capital flight in this sector.

Third, investment liberalization is opposed because NGOs argue that multilateral companies will use FDI to exploit workers in low-wage countries with inadequate labour standards. Similarly, NGOs charge that companies will invest in countries with low environmental standards and use their influence to attack efforts in these countries to improve environmental standards. As evidence, they cite the impact of NAFTA, Chapter 11, which has been used by companies to recover damages when new, higher environmental standards frustrate investment expectations.[45]

2. THE LEGAL FRAMEWORK OF TRADE-RELATED INVESTMENT MEASURES IN THE GATT/WTO REGIME

INTRODUCTION TO THE TRIMS AGREEMENT

The TRIMs Agreement applies to investment measures related to trade in *goods*. The TRIMs Agreement prohibits Members from applying any such investment measure that is inconsistent with GATT Article III (national treatment) or Article XI (prohibition on quotas and other measures prohibiting or restricting the importation, exportation or sale for export of any product, except for duties, taxes and other charges). An Illustrative List annexed to the TRIMs Agreement provides examples of measures that are inconsistent with Article III:4 or Article XI:1. This List cites the following as examples of host-country investment measures that either restrict imports or exports or require imports or exports: local content requirements, export performance requirements, trade balancing requirements, foreign exchange balancing restrictions, and restrictions on an enterprise's export or sale for export of products. Such measures are prohibited, but a transition period allows WTO Members to phase out WTO-inconsistent measures that were notified to the WTO under the TRIMs Agreement. A different transition period is stipulated for developed and developing countries. During the transition period, the TRIMs Agreement imposes a "standstill" obligation. [Selected TRIM provisions follow.]

AGREEMENT ON TRADE-RELATED INVESTMENT MEASURES

Members,

Considering that Ministers agreed in the Punta del Este Declaration that "Following an examination of the operation of GATT Articles related to the trade restrictive and distorting effects of investment measures, negotiations should elaborate, as appropriate, further provisions that may be necessary to avoid such adverse effects on trade";

Desiring to promote the expansion and progressive liberalisation of world trade and to facilitate investment across international frontiers so as to increase the economic growth of all trading partners, particularly developing country Members, while ensuring free competition;

---

45. *E.g.*, *Metalclad Corp. v. United Mexican States*, 40 I.L.M. 36 (2001) (awarding damages when company's investment in a hazardous waste treatment facility approved by the federal government of Mexico was blocked by local Mexican authorities).

Taking into account the particular trade, development and financial needs of developing country Members, particularly those of the least developed country Members;

Recognizing that certain investment measures can cause trade-restrictive and distorting effects;

Hereby *agree* as follows:

Article 1
Coverage

This Agreement applies to investment measures related to trade in goods only (referred to in this Agreement as "TRIMs").

Article 2
National Treatment and Quantitative Restrictions

1. Without prejudice to other rights and obligations under GATT 1994, no Member shall apply any TRIM that is inconsistent with the provisions of Article III or Article XI of GATT 1994.

2. An illustrative list of TRIMs that are inconsistent with the obligation of national treatment provided for in paragraph 4 of Article III of GATT 1994 and the obligation of general elimination of quantitative restrictions provided for in paragraph 1 of Article XI of GATT 1994 is contained in the Annex to this Agreement.

Annex
Illustrative List

1. TRIMs that are inconsistent with the obligation of national treatment provided for in paragraph 4 of Article III of GATT 1994 include those which are mandatory or enforceable under domestic law or under administrative rulings, or compliance with which is necessary to obtain an advantage, and which require:

(a) the purchase or use by an enterprise of products of domestic origin or from any domestic source, whether specified in terms of particular products, in terms of volume or value of products, or in terms of a proportion of volume or value of its local production; or

(b) that an enterprise's purchases or use of imported products be limited to an amount related to the volume or value of local products that it exports.

2. TRIMs that are inconsistent with the obligation of general elimination of quantitative restrictions provided for in paragraph 1 of Article XI of GATT 1994 include those which are mandatory or enforceable under domestic law or under administrative rulings, or compliance with which is necessary to obtain an advantage, and which restrict:

(a) the importation by an enterprise of products used in or related to its local production, generally or to an amount related to the volume or value of local production that it exports;

(b) the importation by an enterprise of products used in or related to its local production by restricting its access to foreign exchange to an amount related to the foreign exchange inflows attributable to the enterprise; or

(c) the exportation or sale for export by an enterprise of products, whether specified in terms of particular products, in terms of volume or value of products, or in terms of a proportion of volume or value of its local production.

Mitsuo Matsushita, Thomas J. Schoenbaum, & Petros C. Mavroidis, The World Trade Organization, Law, Practice, and Policy
228-239 (Oxford University Press, 2003)

TRADE IN SERVICES

1. INTRODUCTION

The agreement to liberalize trade in services is probably the single most important achievement of the Uruguay Round negotiations. At the domestic level, services represent the overwhelming majority of the GDP of OECD countries. At the international level, however, services did not represent a majority of the GDP of most industrialized countries until after World War II. This explains why services were not on the ITO agenda in the 1940s. Before the Uruguay Round, liberalization of trade in services took place on a bilateral basis (the [European Community] being the only full-fledged regional example before the NAFTA entered into force). Gradual liberalization of investment (mostly on a bilateral basis) led to liberalization of non-tradable service sectors, such as distribution. As a result, there was enough impetus to discuss liberalization of trade in services at the international level.

The Uruguay Round negotiations resulted in the first multilateral agreement on trade in services, namely, the General Agreement on Trade in Services (GATS). The GATS was inspired by the structure of the GATT but also displays elements of its own.

2. OVERVIEW OF THE GENERAL AGREEMENT ON TRADE IN SERVICES

The GATS covers all manner of services except those supplied in the exercise of government authority.[46] Four modes[47] of trade in services are identified: (1) "cross border" services where both provider and user remain in their home territory (*e.g.*, services provided generally by facsimile, e-mail, phone, or other means of communication); (2) services provided to the user who travels to the territory of the provider (*e.g.*, tourism); (3) services provided where the provider establishes a commercial presence in the territory of the user (*e.g.*, a UK bank, insurance, or financial services company establishes a branch or subsidiary in Japan); and (4) services provided when a natural person provider temporarily travels to the territory of the user (*e.g.*, an attorney, interpreter, or teacher travels to another country to consult or lecture).

The GATS applies to any "measure" taken by governmental bodies or non-governmental associations exercising delegated authority affecting any of these modes of trade in services.[48]

The broad scope of the GATS outlined above poses certain conceptual problems. First, the outer boundary of what is "services" for purposes of the

---

46. GATS Arts. I and XIII.
47. *Id.* Art. I:2.
48. *Id.* Art. I:1.

GATS is not sharply defined. Services trade is defined more in terms of categories of transactions (the modes of supply) rather than substantive categories. Thus, although services can in most cases be distinguished from goods based upon the idea that services are simultaneously provided and consumed, whereas goods are storable for later use or enjoyment, there may be overlap between the international rules for services and those for goods, especially given that GATS applies to all measures that "affect" services. Second, because trade in services is defined in terms of transactions, services trade under the GATS will inevitably involve more than just the bare services supplied. The transactional notion of services in the GATS means that services trade will also implicate in some instances certain international factor flows, notably (1) information; (2) technology; (3) capital or investment; and (4) labour or immigration.

The core of the GATS is the national treatment provision. As far as services are concerned, national treatment extends only to service sectors inscribed in an individual WTO Member's Schedule of Specific Commitments, and even commitments with respect to these service sectors can be conditioned and qualified. Thus, so-called national treatment is distinctly limited under the GATS. A WTO Member may protect certain service sectors or modes of supply from national treatment by omitting it from its Schedule. However, with respect to market access in those sectors liberalized under a particular Member's Schedule, six measures are, in principle, prohibited:

1. Limits on the number of service suppliers,
2. Limits on the value of transactions or assets,
3. Limits on the total quantity of service output,
4. Limits on the number of natural persons that can be employed,
5. Limits on the type of legal entity that can be used and
6. Limits on participation of foreign capital or investment.

In addition, WTO Members may negotiate commitments with respect to service sectors not covered by national treatment or market access Schedule commitments.

Most-favoured-nation treatment is also highly qualified under the GATS. A WTO Member can list exemptions to MFN in the GATS Annex on Article II Exemptions. These exemptions can be maintained for up to ten years, although they are subject to periodic review and negotiation. This means that MFN in the GATS is conditioned to prevent "free-riding" in the markets of more open WTO Members.

The GATS also contains a set of general obligations that apply to measures affecting trade in services. First, there is an obligation of transparency — the prompt publication of "all relevant measures"; however, certain confidential information may be withheld. Furthermore, WTO Members must administer domestic regulations affecting services in a "reasonable, objective and impartial manner". A Council on Trade in Services is authorized to establish "disciplines" to ensure that regulations are objective, transparent and not more burdensome than necessary. Mutual recognition (national agreements to recognize each others' approvals) and harmonization (adoption of similar standards) of domestic regulation are encouraged. Service monopolies and exclusive service providers must not abuse their monopoly position or act inconsistently with a Member's commitments. Business practices that restrain competition must be addressed through "full and sympathetic consideration" with a "view to eliminating" the practice. Payments and transfers of capital must be open with respect to a Member's commitments. Subsidies affecting services are subject to negotiation with a view to eliminating their trade distorting affects.

GATS contains a number of qualifications and exemptions. Economic and market-to-market integration agreements are permitted to operate within the context of a Member's GATS commitments. There is provision for emergency safeguard measures and restrictions to safeguard balance of payments. Government procurement is exempt, and there are general exceptions to protect public morals, human, animal, plant life, or health and to protect against fraud and invasion of privacy. There is also an exemption for certain issues of national security.

The GATS also provides for progressive liberalization of services trade through future negotiations. The increasing participation of developing countries is encouraged. A Member's Schedule of Specific Commitments is intended to be progressively liberalized, but commitments may also be modified and withdrawn. Disputes are resolved according to the WTO Dispute Settlement Understanding.

4.2 The concept of "services"

The GATS "applies to measures by Members affecting trade in services".[49] The term "services" is defined to include "*any service in any sector* except services supplied in the exercise of governmental authority".[50]

The scope of the GATS is, therefore, not limited to any list of covered sectors. There is, however, no agreement on an exhaustive list of services. This problem became apparent during the negotiations in the WTO on electronic commerce.[51] The legal implications of this lack of agreement are surmountable: the general obligations in GATS apply to all services, but WTO Members may impose restrictions when scheduling their specific commitments.

A "Services Sectoral Classification List"[52] was developed during the Uruguay Round and is largely based on the UN Central Product Classification System (CPC). The List classifies services by sector. Although the use of the Services Sectoral Classification List is not mandatory, most WTO Members have adopted it as basis for scheduling their commitments under the GATS.[53] This classification could be revised in the future.

4.3 Modes of supply

The term "trade in services" is defined in terms of so-called modes of supply of services[54]:

1. Mode 1 is the supply of a service "from the territory of one Member into the territory of any other Member".[55] Mode 1 is known as cross-border

---

49. GATS Art. I:1.

50. *Id.* Art. 1:3(b) (emphases added). The phrase "a service supplied in the exercise of governmental authority" is defined as "any service which is supplied neither on a commercial basis nor in competition with one or more service suppliers". *Id.* Art. 1:3(c).

51. *See* Marc Bacchetta et al., WTO, ELECTRONIC COMMERCE AND THE ROLE OF THE WTO (Special Study No. 2, 1998).

52. *See* WTO, Services Sectoral Classification List, MTN.GNS/W/120, 10 July 1991.

53. GATS Arts. XVI, XVII and XVIII.

54. GATS Art. I:2. *See* Bernard M. Hoekman, *Market Access Through Multilateral Agreement: From Goods to Services*, 15 WORLD ECONOMY 707 (1992).

55. GATS Art. I:2(a).

supply. Cross-border supply occurs when neither the service supplier nor the service consumer has to travel, such as a lawyer in Italy sends advice by facsimile to a person in Canada.

2.   Mode 2 is the supply of a service "in the territory of one Member to the service consumer of any other Member".[56] Mode 2 is known as consumption abroad. Consumption abroad occurs when the consumer travels to the country where the service is supplied, such as with tourism.

3.   Mode 3 is the supply of a service "by a service supplier of one Member, through commercial presence in the territory of any other Member".[57] Mode 3 is known as commercial presence.[58] The commercial presence mode of supply occurs when the service supplier establishes commercial presence in the country in which he supplies the service, such as when a U.S. bank establishes a subsidiary in Japan.

4.   Mode 4 is the supply of a service "by a service supplier of one Member, through presence of natural persons of a Member in the territory of any other Member".[59] Mode 4 is known as presence of natural persons. Presence of natural persons occurs when the service supplier (a natural person in this case and not a legal person like in mode 3) is established in a different country, such as when a lawyer who is a national of Costa Rica establishes himself as a lawyer in the United Kingdom.

The GATS disciplines, therefore, are relevant for not only services but also service suppliers (both natural and legal persons). Viewed from this angle, mode 3 essentially amounts to an international agreement to liberalize investment: by allowing foreign banks, for example, to sell banking services under mode 3, a WTO Member is *de facto* opening up to foreign investment in the banking sector.

NOTES AND QUESTIONS

1. Given the tremendous upsurge in international protection of investments, is there an appropriate role for the WTO? How does the WTO TRIMS Agreement compare with ICSID and NAFTA?

2. At the 2001 WTO Ministerial Conference in Doha, Qatar, it was agreed to begin negotiations on a comprehensive WTO Agreement on Investment in 2003. At the 2003 WTO Ministerial Conference in Cancun, Mexico, however, there was no agreement, and the conference failed. Should a comprehensive investment agreement be concluded at a future WTO meeting?

IV.   Limits on Corporate Conduct in International Investment: The Foreign Corrupt Practices Act

In §V, we will turn to the transactional aspects of establishing a foreign investment enterprise and the many collateral issues involved. One of these issues is so

---

56. *Id.* Art. I:2(b).
57. *Id.* Art. I:2(c).
58. The term "commercial presence" is defined in Article XXVIII(d) of the GATS.
59. GATS Art. I:2.

common and of such importance, however, that it is the subject of this entire section: The demand for bribes, payments, gifts, and other favors from government officials in the foreign host nation. The corrupt payment issue is one that involves serious legal consequences, and U.S. companies must be fully prepared to deal with this issue. Recent accounts indicate that government corruption involving foreign companies exists in every corner of the world ranging from advanced developed countries such as those in the European Union to developing countries such as Brazil and China. Some of these accounts tell lurid tales of avarice and personal indiscretions on the part of both foreign government officials and U.S. companies. Some examples of the types of payments and machinations involved are detailed in the three principal cases below.

While companies need to be vigilant about government corruption in every host nation, the problem of corruption appears to be especially serious in developing countries for several reasons. In many cases, a strict government regulatory regime empowers a few local government officials, who are largely unaccountable to the general populace, with the discretion to control the fate of wealthy MNEs. A local government official in a developing country who earns a salary equivalent to several hundred dollars per month may be in a position to decide whether to approve a foreign investment project involving tens of millions of dollars — or more — by one of the world's leading companies. This type of power structure leads to demands of exchanges of money for the exercise of power. In addition, many developing countries appear to be resigned to accept that some corruption on the part of government officials is unavoidable and must be tolerated. As many developing countries have weak legal systems, corrupt government officials are often able to act without fear of punishment. The vesting of significant power in low-paid officials in combination with a weak legal regime and a culture that tolerates "squeeze" among government officials in many developing countries has combined to create a business environment where demands for payments, gifts, and favors are all too common. Each of the three principal cases below involves a developing country.

Of course, not every U.S. corporation that pays bribes does so because it feels pressured or compelled by the host nation to do so. Rather, some companies and individuals like an environment of corruption and seek out opportunities to make bribes and gifts and to lure government officials into improper situations to secure an advantage. An atmosphere of corruption allows a company with an inferior product to make a bribe and overcome a competitor's superior product and the effect of market forces. The fruits of an improper payment may also result in personal gain and professional advantage for the individual business officials in the company making the payment. On the other hand, corruption can harm the company and its shareholders. In developing countries, government corruption harms the public by diverting public funds. These are some reasons why governments have become increasingly concerned about corruption in international business. What are the limits on corporate conduct concerning improper payments, gifts, and favors? An answer to this question must begin with an examination of the Foreign Corrupt Practices Act (FCPA), 15 U.S.C. §78 *et seq.*

We begin our examination of these issues with the following problems. To solve these problems, consider the discussion of the FCPA in §A below and the notes and questions following. You will also need to carefully review §§78m(b), 78dd-1, 78dd-2, and 78dd-3 of the FCPA.

One final note: As FCPA issues often arise in the context of foreign invest-ment, we have chosen to study it in the context of FDI. However, the FCPA can also apply to the sales contract, agency/distributorships, and licensing.

PROBLEM 6-4

Medtech is a publicly traded company located in Atlanta, Georgia. Medtech wishes to establish a foreign subsidiary to manufacture and sell its products in a developing country but has been warned by a local business consultant that it is customary to pay "substantial" fees for a business license. In addition, Medtech has been told that it is expected for new companies to make an additional payment of a "closing fee" of $1 million to the minister of trade. The consultant says, "Don't worry, this is all part of the business and legal culture here — everybody knows that it is legal and no one ever gets into trouble. It's been done in the open for years and the ministry has even said that the practice will be codified in a new law. All of your foreign competitors are making payments and you don't want to lose out to them do you? I'll handle everything for you and you won't need to concern yourself with details. Just send payments to me when I ask for them. Also, if you are worried about your shareholders, you can file these payments under 'Closing Costs.' In fact, I'll be in the U.S. on another matter next week and I can come and pick up the first payment from you at your head office." What issues are involved? *See* 15 U.S.C. §§78m, 78dd-1, and 78dd-3.

PROBLEM 6-5

Medtech is one of several companies that has applied to establish a $30 million joint venture in Chile. Before Medtech submitted its joint venture project applica-tion, several officials from Medtech's U.S. headquarters flew to Chile and invited various officials of the national bureau on foreign investment, which will decide whether to approve Medtech's application for the project, out for an evening's get together in order to get acquainted with Medtech's business and its plans for Chile and South America. The government officials were first treated to a World Cup soccer match between Chile and Germany, then a lavish champagne dinner at an expensive restaurant, and, finally, an extravagant evening at an exclusive nightclub, all paid for by Medtech. The whole evening cost more than a year's salary of the chief of the investment bureau. As the evening concluded, the chief of the invest-ment bureau asked Medtech where he can find a scholarship for his daughter to attend a prestigious university in California. A Medtech official later sends the following e-mail message to Medtech's finance department in Atlanta, "Can you look into the scholarship? There must be a way so let's find it." What are the legal issues involved? *See* 15 U.S.C. §78dd-1(c)(2).

PROBLEM 6-6

Medtech has been approached by Sino-Med, a privately owned medical com-pany in China, to be its joint venture partner for the Chinese market. The president of Sino-Med has mentioned that it is customary for a foreign investor such as Medtech to give him $250,000 cash in "lucky money" as a gesture of goodwill and mutual friendship. Is this unlawful under the FCPA or any other relevant laws? What if 60 percent of the shares of Sino-Med were owned by the Supervision Bureau of Pharmaceuticals, a local regulatory agency? Would you advise Medtech to make the payment? *See* 15 U.S.C. §§78dd-1(a)(1)-(2) and 78dd-1(f)(1)(A).

A.   Overview of the FCPA

The Foreign Corrupt Practices Act was enacted in 1977 to deal with the rising problem of foreign corrupt payments. We do not examine the history of the FCPA in detail here as *United States v. Kay*, one of the principal cases below, offers an excellent summary of its legislative history. Rather, we offer an overview of its major substantive provisions.

The FCPA provides for two sets of obligations contained in its antibribery provisions and books and records provisions. The antibribery provisions proscribe the making of improper payments to foreign government officials and certain other persons. The books and records provision applies only to entities qualified as issuers under the Securities and Exchange Act of 1934 and requires that such issuers keep accurate records that do not disguise improper payments as something innocuous. As the antibribery provisions are the centerpiece of the FCPA, we focus on these provisions below.

The antibribery provisions of the FCPA, 15 U.S.C. §§78dd-1, 78dd-2, and 78dd-3, prohibit:

(1)   Issuers, domestic concerns, and any person
(2)   from making use of interstate commerce
(3)   corruptly
(4)   in furtherance of an offer or payment of anything of value
(5)   to a foreign official, foreign political party, or candidate for political office
(6)   for the purpose of influencing any act of that foreign official in violation of the duty of that official or to secure any improper advantage in order to obtain or retain business.

Enforcement of the FCPA is divided between two federal agencies: The Securities and Exchange Commission has civil and administrative authority over issuers, and the Justice Department has civil and criminal authority over all covered persons. A criminal violation of the antibribery provisions by a corporation can result in a statutory fine of up to $2 million. *See* 15 U.S.C. §78ff(c). Officers, directors, shareholders, employees, or agents may also be subject to fines of up to $10,000 and five years' imprisonment. *See id.* There is no private cause of action under the FCPA.

Each of the six elements of a violation of the FCPA is further discussed below.

1.   Persons Subject to the FCPA

"Issuers"—who are subject to both the antibribery and books and records provisions—include any U.S. or foreign corporation that has a class of securities registered, or that is required to file reports, under the Securities and Exchange

Act of 1934. In other words, the FCPA applies to any U.S. or foreign corporation with publicly traded securities in the United States.

"Domestic concerns" refer to any individual who is a citizen, national, or resident of the United States and any corporation and other business entity organized under the laws of the United States or having its principal place of business in the United States. The term domestic concern does not cover foreign subsidiaries of U.S. companies. Company officials such as officers, directors, employees, or agents of issuers and domestic concerns are also covered by the FCPA.

"Any person" covers both enterprises and individuals. Foreign entities that do not have publicly traded securities are included within this term as well as foreign nationals so long as they commit an act within the territory of the United States. An issuer, domestic concern, or any covered person cannot circumvent the FCPA by having the payment made through an intermediary, such as a sales agent, distributor, or business consultant. It is unlawful for a covered person to make a payment to any person "while knowing that all or a portion of the payment will be offered, given or promised, directly or indirectly, to any foreign official, foreign political party or official thereof." 15 U.S.C. §78dd(3).

2. Nexus with Interstate Commerce

As the FCPA is a federal statute, there must be a nexus with interstate commerce to justify federal jurisdiction. However, this requirement is easily met. Any connection with interstate commerce, such as a single phone call, a single e-mail, or the posting of a letter will satisfy this requirement.

3. Corrupt Intent

The FCPA has a scienter requirement that the covered person made the payment with an evil motive, intent, or purpose in order to wrongfully influence the recipient to abuse his or her official position or to influence someone else to do so for the purpose of wrongfully directing business to the payor or to wrongfully obtain favorable legislation or a preferential regulation. *See United States v. Liebo*, 923 F.2d 1308, 1312 (8th Cir. 1991). Corrupt intent is also discussed in *Schreiber*, one of the principal cases below.

4. Proscribed Payments

The FCPA defines corrupt payments to include acts "in furtherance of any offer, payment, promise to pay, or authorization of the payment of any money, gift, promise to give, or authorization of the giving of anything of value." 15 U.S.C. §78dd-1(a). Not only are payments prohibited but any acts "in furtherance" of payments are also proscribed. In addition, any person who participates in or even authorizes such a payment can be held liable. A U.S. company that plans to make a corrupt payment and takes some concrete steps toward the making of such a payment may also be held liable under the FCPA even though the payment is never made.

The FCPA contains a so-called "grease payment" exception when the payment is a facilitating payment to secure the performance of a routine government action. *See* 15 U.S.C. §78dd-1(b). In addition, the FCPA contains an affirmative defense for payments that are lawful under the written laws of the foreign official's country or are for "bona fide expenditures" such as travel and lodging incurred by a foreign government official for the purpose of promoting the payor's products or services. *See* U.S.C. §78dd(c)(1)-(2).

5. *Persons to Whom Payments Are Made*

The FCPA does not apply to payments made to private persons but covers only payments made to foreign officials, foreign political parties, party officials, or candidates for political office. An officer or employee of a foreign government or any instrumentality thereof acting in an official capacity will qualify as a foreign official. In a transition economy such as China where it is difficult to distinguish between private and public sectors, the issue of persons to whom payments are prohibited can be difficult to determine.

6. *Purpose of the Payment* (business purpose test)

To violate the FCPA, the payment must be made in order to assist the payor in obtaining, retaining, or directing business to any person. This is the so-called "business purpose test." Note that under the FCPA the recipient of the payment must be a foreign government official, party official, or candidate for political office but the business gained does not have to be with the foreign government. The scope of the business purpose test is the subject of *United States v. Kay*, one of the principal cases below.

NOTE ON THE OECD BRIBERY CONVENTION AND OTHER INTERNATIONAL TREATIES

On December 17, 1997, 28 of the 29 members of the Organization for Economic Cooperation and Development, including the United States, signed the OECD Convention on Combating Bribery of Foreign Public Officials in International Business Transactions. This represented a victory for the United States, which had long been a proponent of promulgating international legal standards proscribing bribery. The convention was ratified in 1998 by ten countries and entered into force on February 15, 1999. As of 2004, 35 countries have ratified the convention. Most ratifying states have complied with the convention by enacting legislation prohibiting transnational bribery. The elements of the transnational bribery offense are slightly more narrow but otherwise track those of the FCPA. In 1998, the United States enacted changes to the FCPA that have expanded the jurisdictional scope of the act as it applies to foreign persons.

The convention requires that contracting states enact domestic criminal laws that prohibit the making of payments directly or through an intermediary to a foreign government official for the purpose of inducing that official to act or refrain from acting in an official capacity in order to retain or obtain business or obtain some other improper advantage. Unlike the FCPA, the convention does not apply to payments to political parties, party officials, or candidates for political office. When it was enacted, the convention was broader than the FCPA because it also proscribed payments to secure an "improper advantage." The FCPA has since been amended to incorporate this language. The effect of this new language on the business purpose test is discussed in *United States v. Kay* below.

On October 31, 2003, the General Assembly of the United Nations approved the United Nations Convention Against Corruption. The UN convention goes beyond the FCPA and the OECD convention in that it also proscribes commercial bribery, trading in influence, and "laundering" of the proceeds of corruption. The UN convention also breaks new ground in providing for asset recovery. This feature was of particular importance to developing countries as they often suffer the most harm when public funds are diverted for personal gain. The UN convention has been signed by over 110 countries, including the United States, and will come into force 90 days after deposit of the thirtieth instrument of ratification. As of this writing, four ratifications have been deposited with the UN.

The United States has also signed the 1996 Inter-American Convention Against Corruption, 35 I.L.M. 724 (1996), and the Council of Europe's 1999 Criminal Law Convention on Corruption.

NOTES AND QUESTIONS

1. Prior to the OECD Convention on Transnational Bribery, it appears that the United States was the only nation in the world that had laws prohibiting payments to *foreign* government officials. Most nations had laws against the making of payments to domestic government officials but the United States was for a time alone in proscribing payments to the government officials of another nation. Some U.S. businesses complained that the FCPA created a competitive disadvantage as paying bribes to government officials is a common part of doing business in many host countries. Businesses from other countries were not prohibited from making bribes in the host country and some nations even allowed tax deductions for bribes. As not all nations will join the OECD and enact domestic legislation, there will continue to be some competitors of U.S. businesses that will not be restricted in making bribes. What national interests of the United States are furthered by prohibiting improper payments to government officials in a foreign country that outweigh any business disadvantages? In the view of the United States, why is controlling corruption in international business transactions in the best interests of U.S. businesses even if it creates a possible short-term competitive disadvantage?

2. Note that the FCPA prohibits bribery of foreign *government officials*. Commercial bribery in the form of payments or kickbacks given to foreign private buyers and other foreign customers to obtain business is not covered by the FCPA or any other U.S. laws. Note that commercial bribes, while not prohibited by the FCPA, may be illegal under the domestic laws of some foreign countries. Why does the United States draw a distinction between official and commercial bribery?

3. Most U.S. companies are quite vigilant about the FCPA. Should they be as concerned with local laws against commercial bribery in the host nation, especially if, as is often the case, the host nation, because of a weak legal system, does not regularly enforce such laws?

4. The FCPA provides for an exception for "grease payments." *See* 15 U.S.C. §78dd-1(b). What is the rationale for this exception? See *United States v. Kay* below.

5. The FCPA also provides for an affirmative defense for certain other types of payments as discussed in §A above. *See* 15 U.S.C. §78dd-1(c). From the standpoint of the payor, the difference between an exception, as for grease payments, and an affirmative defense can be significant. Why?

6. Are foreign companies or individuals subject to the FCPA? If so, under what conditions and how can the United States justify its regulation of foreign entities? *See* 15 U.S.C. §§78dd-1 and 78dd-3.

B. Cases Under the FCPA

United States v. King
United States Court of Appeals, Eighth Circuit, 2003
351 F.3d 859

BEAM, Circuit Judge.

On June 27, 2001, a grand jury indicted Richard King for conspiring to violate the Foreign Corrupt Practices Act ("FCPA") and for violating the FCPA and the Interstate Travel in Aid of Racketeering Act ("Travel Act") by agreeing to bribe Costa Rican officials to obtain valuable land concessions needed to develop a Costa Rica project. A jury later convicted King of one count of conspiracy and four counts under the FCPA. The district court sentenced King to thirty months' imprisonment and fined him $60,000.

King appeals claiming [that] the evidence was insufficient to support the convictions [and] the trial court erred by denying King's motion to dismiss the indictment prior to trial due to the government's overreaching conduct. For the reasons set forth below, we affirm. *disp.*

I. BACKGROUND

This case involves an FBI investigation into the dealings between certain individuals who hoped to develop a port in Limon, Costa Rica. The focus of the investigation concerned the planned payment of a $1 million bribe (a.k.a. "kiss payment" or "closing cost" or "toll") to senior Costa Rican officials and political parties to obtain concessions for the land on which the new development was to be built.

Much of the investigation centered around the dealings of Owl Securities and Investments, Ltd. ("OSI"), a company based in Kansas City, and its employees and contributors. Several individuals attempted to raise funds from investors through OSI for the multi-faceted project in Costa Rica involving a large land and port development. The project had many components including a port, a salvage station, development of recreational facilities, housing, light manufacturing, warehouses, and an airport. During the investigation, the FBI encountered several individuals including Stephen Kingsley, President and CEO of OSI; Richard Halford, OSI's CFO; Albert Reitz, OSI's VP; Pablo Barquero, an agent of OSI in the Costa Rican office; and Defendant King, one of OSI's largest investors. FBI Special Agent Robert Herndon led the inquiry, originally investigating Kingsley and OSI. Ultimately, Agent Herndon sought the cooperation of both Kingsley and Reitz to obtain recordings of conversations between alleged conspirators, including King.

II. DISCUSSION

A. SUFFICIENCY OF THE EVIDENCE

At trial, the government presented six witnesses. Two of those witnesses, Richard Halford and Albert Reitz, testified on behalf of the government pursuant to a plea agreement wherein each pleaded guilty to certain offenses in exchange for the possibility of a more lenient sentence. The government questioned each of the six witnesses about King's involvement with and knowledge of the planned bribe. The government also published portions of several taped conversations between King and others, which Stephen Kingsley recorded at the FBI's request. These taped conversations involving King occurred between May 26, 2000, and August 17, 2000.

To prove conspiracy, the government must show an agreement between at least two people and that the agreement's objective was a violation of the law. *United States v. Jackson*, 345 F.3d 638, 648 (8th Cir. 2003). "Proof of a formal agreement is unnecessary; a tacit understanding is sufficient, and can be proved by direct or circumstantial evidence." Id.

For King's remaining FCPA convictions, the plain language of the FCPA prohibits the use of "any means or instrumentality of interstate commerce corruptly in furtherance of an offer, payment, promise to pay, or authorization of the payment of any money, or offer, gift, promise to give, or authorization of the giving of anything of value to any foreign official for purposes of influencing any act or decision of such foreign official in his official capacity." 15 U.S.C. §78dd-1(a)(1)(A).

Viewing the evidence in the light most favorable to the verdict, there was ample evidence in the record to support the jury's convictions. The tape recordings, alone, support the jury's verdict.

For example, the following exchanges are just a small sample of what the jury heard:

May 26, 2000:

> Kingsley: Well you've always known about the closing cost fees and that.
> King: I've known what?
> Kingsley: You've known about the closing costs.
> King: The one million dollars?
> Kingsley: Yeah.
> King: I've known about that for five years, yeah, . . .

June 1 and 2, 2000:

> King: You see when they walk into the bank, you know, the bank is going to be curious as to what they're putting up a million-dollars for . . .
> Kingsley: Well do they . . .
> King: . . . If they do a letter of credit.
> Kingsley: . . . do the bank . . . do . . .
> King: Ah, my own bank does not ask for that. My own bank is going to take the Falcon. But if I go with these other people, a letter of credit, and the reason I may go to them for a letter of credit instead of my own letter of credit is that it's, it's going to get them involved in this.
> Kingsley: Yeah. Do
> King: And we don't, we don't want just a million-dollars, we want a hundred thirty-five million.
> Kingsley: Yeah. Do they know what the million[']s for though?
> King: Ah, probably . . . I think I told them yeah.
> Kingsley: Yeah. Well
> King: They didn't bat an eye.
> Kingsley: (coughs)

King: I put it in this letter as a closing cost.

Kingsley: Yeah, that's what Dick likes to call it, is a closing cost.

June 28, 2000:

Kingsley: Well, look, what.

Halford: He irritated a lot of people.

Kingsley: Yeah, what, um, what Pablo had said, was why just pay, pay off the current politicians. Pay off the future ones.

King: That's right. Because we're gonna have to work with them anyway.

Kingsley: And so what he was saying was double, you know, give them more money. Buy the opposition. If you buy the current party and the opposition, then it doesn't matter who's in because there's only two parties.

King: The thing that really worries me is that, uh, if the Justice Department gets a hold of. Finds out how many people we've been paying off down there. Uh, or even if they don't. Are we gonna have to spend the rest of our lives paying off these petty politicians to keep them out of our hair? I can just see us, every, every day some politician on our doorstep down there wanting a hand out for this or that.

Kingsley: Well, I mean,

King: I'd like to

Kingsley: I

King: Think we could pay the top people enough, that the rest of the people won't bother us any. That's what I'm hoping this million and a half dollars does. I'm hoping it pays enough top people . . .

August 17, 2000:

Kingsley: Now Pablo's continued to talk to the politicians. They know about the toll, closing costs call it what you will. So he's still our biggest asset in place.

King: What do they know about the closing costs?

Kingsley: Who?

King: Does everybody agree to what we talked about recently?

Kingsley: Yeah, a million into escrow for the toll.

King: And then we get the property and then we do the (unintelligible)?

Kingsley: Um-hum. Yeah now let me I'll, I'll, I'll come on to that because I'll explain how we work through that. Uh, essentially once the politicians see the money in escrow, they'll move. That's what it comes down to (clears throat). Pablo's gonna send a list, an e-mail with a list of politicians already paid off and the ones he's gonna pay off.

King: Isn't that awfully dangerous?

Kingsley: No e-mail's probably the most secure form of communication.

King: From what I read it's not, number one and number two, there's got to be a better way.

Barquero: We have to make the politicians sure that they are going to get that. That is one thing that we have to make them feel comfortable that uh, we would get the full support.

King: I (unintelligible)

Barquero: What

King: I'm more concerned about

Barquero: (unintelligible)

King: Not getting caught.

There was sufficient evidence to prove King's knowledge of the proposed payment long before Kingsley became an informant for the government. Moreover, the recordings show King's knowing participation in, approval of, and subsequent actions in furtherance of the conspiracy to offer the bribe. In addition, the testimony of six witnesses conducted over a five-day period, and the remaining exhibits support the jury's conviction of King for conspiracy and substantive violations under the FCPA.

D. MOTION TO DISMISS

King's final argument is that the district court erred in refusing to dismiss the indictment due to the government's alleged outrageous misconduct. King claims that the government allowed its informant Kingsley to target King for prosecution and essentially manufactured the crimes for which King was convicted.

After our thorough review of the evidence presented at the hearing on the motion to dismiss, we find no evidence of conscience-shocking behavior on the part of the government. That the evidence was "contrived" or that trickery was involved is simply not supported by the evidence. We do not dispute that it was quite likely that Kingsley's character was flawed, but we recognize that the use of unsavory informants is quite often the nature of the beast in police investigations. Such realities do not rise to the level of outrageousness needed to support a due process violation.

Accordingly, we affirm the district court's dismissal of King's motion to dismiss.

PROBLEM 6-7

Hyde Chemical Industries, a Delaware corporation, has established a wholly owned subsidiary in the Congo Republic (CR). Under the CR's foreign investment laws, foreign invested companies are eligible to receive one of three designations: Level 1 for state-of-the-art technology, Level 2 for advanced technology, and Level 3 for high technology. Each designation carries a number of benefits. A Level 1 designation exempts the company from the CR's onerous environmental laws for a period of twenty years. Under the CR's laws, any foreign invested company can apply to the government for a review for a fee of $500,000. Most companies that pay for the review obtain a technology designation. In 2003, Hyde donated $5 million to CR's environmental protection bureau in order to allow the bureau to purchase and install a new computer system. In 2004, Hyde applied for a review and received a Level 1 designation. Later that year, the Justice Department charged Hyde with a violation of the FCPA. In its defense, Hyde argued that the donation was not for the purpose of obtaining new business. Hyde's plant was already established and Hyde had no intention of establishing any new businesses in the CR or in expanding its present operations. Does Hyde have a good argument? Consult *United States v. Kay* below. What other arguments would you suggest for Hyde? See *Schrieber* below following *Kay*.

United States v. Kay
United States Court of Appeals, Fifth Circuit, 2004
359 F.3d 738

WIENER, Circuit Judge.

Plaintiff-appellant, the United States of America ("government"), appeals the district court's grant of the motion of defendants-appellees David Kay and Douglas Murphy ("defendants") to dismiss the Superseding Indictment ("indictment") that charged them with bribery of foreign officials in violation of the Foreign Corrupt Practices Act ("FCPA"). In their dismissal motion, defendants contended that the indictment failed to state an offense against them. The principal dispute in this case is whether, if proved beyond a reasonable doubt, the conduct that the indictment ascribed to defendants in connection with the alleged bribery of Haitian officials to understate customs duties and sales taxes on rice shipped to Haiti to assist American Rice, Inc. in obtaining or retaining business was sufficient to constitute an offense under the FCPA. Underlying this question of sufficiency of the contents of the indictment is the preliminary task of ascertaining the scope of the FCPA, which in turn requires us to construe the statute.

The district court concluded that, as a matter of law, an indictment alleging illicit payments to foreign officials for the purpose of avoiding substantial portions of customs duties and sales taxes to obtain or retain business are not the kind of bribes that the FCPA criminalizes. We disagree with this assessment of the scope of the FCPA and hold that such bribes could (but do not necessarily) come within the ambit of the statute. Concluding in the end that the indictment in this case is sufficient to state an offense under the FCPA, we remand the instant case for further proceedings consistent with this opinion.

I. FACTS AND PROCEEDINGS

American Rice, Inc. ("ARI") is a Houston-based company that exports rice to foreign countries, including Haiti. Rice Corporation of Haiti ("RCH"), a wholly owned subsidiary of ARI, was incorporated in Haiti to represent ARI's interests and deal with third parties there. As an aspect of Haiti's standard importation procedure, its customs officials assess duties based on the quantity and value of rice imported into the country. Haiti also requires businesses that deliver rice there to remit an advance deposit against Haitian sales taxes, based on the value of that rice, for which deposit a credit is eventually allowed on Haitian sales tax returns when filed.

In 2001, a grand jury charged Kay with violating the FCPA and subsequently returned the indictment, which charges both Kay and Murphy with 12 counts of FCPA violations. As is readily apparent on its face, the indictment contains detailed factual allegations about (1) the timing and purposes of Congress's enactment of the FCPA, (2) ARI and its status as an "issuer" under the FCPA, (3) RCH and its status as a wholly owned subsidiary and "service corporation" of ARI, representing ARI's interest in Haiti, and (4) defendants' citizenship, their positions as officers of ARI, and their status as "issuers" and "domestic concerns" under the FCPA. The indictment also spells out in detail how Kay and Murphy allegedly orchestrated the bribing of Haitian customs officials to accept false bills of lading and other documentation that intentionally understated by one-third the quantity of rice shipped to Haiti, thereby significantly reducing ARI's customs duties and sales taxes. In this regard, the indictment alleges the details of the bribery scheme's machinations, including the preparation of duplicate documentation, the calculation of bribes as a percentage of the value of the rice not reported, the surreptitious payment of monthly retainers to Haitian officials, and the defendants' purported authorization of withdrawals of funds from ARI's bank accounts with which to pay the Haitian officials, either directly or through intermediaries all to produce substantially reduced Haitian customs and tax costs to ARI.

Although it recites in great detail the discrete facts that the government intends to prove to satisfy each other element of an FCPA violation, the indictment recites no particularized facts that, if proved, would satisfy the "assist" aspect of the business nexus element of the statute, i.e., the nexus between the illicit tax savings produced by the bribery and the assistance such savings provided or were intended to provide in obtaining or retaining business for ARI and RCH. In other words, the indictment recites no facts that could demonstrate an actual or intended cause-and-effect nexus between reduced taxes and obtaining identified business or retaining identified business opportunities.

P.P.

In granting defendants' motion to dismiss the indictment for failure to state an offense, the district court held that, as a matter of law, bribes paid to obtain favorable tax treatment are not payments made to "obtain or retain business" within the intendment of the FCPA, and thus are not within the scope of that statute's proscription of foreign bribery. The government timely filed a notice of appeal.

II. ANALYSIS

A. STANDARD OF REVIEW

We review de novo questions of statutory interpretation, as well as "whether an indictment sufficiently alleges the elements of an offense." Because an offense under the FCPA requires that the alleged bribery be committed for the purpose of inducing foreign officials to commit unlawful acts, the results of which will assist in obtaining or retaining business in their country, the questions before us in this appeal are (1) whether bribes to obtain illegal but favorable tax and customs treatment can ever come within the scope of the statute, and (2) if so, whether, in combination, there are minimally sufficient facts alleged in the indictment to inform the defendants regarding the nexus between, on the one hand, Haitian taxes avoided through bribery, and, on the other hand, assistance in getting or keeping some business or business opportunity in Haiti.

Issues

B. WORDS OF THE FCPA

FCPA
Rule

None contend that the FCPA criminalizes every payment to a foreign official: It criminalizes only those payments that are intended to (1) influence a foreign official to act or make a decision in his official capacity, or (2) induce such an official to perform or refrain from performing some act in violation of his duty, or (3) secure some wrongful advantage to the payor. And even then, the FCPA criminalizes these kinds of payments only if the result they are intended to produce their quid pro quo will assist (or is intended to assist) the payor in efforts to get or keep some business for or with "any person." Thus, the first question of statutory interpretation presented in this appeal is whether payments made to foreign officials to obtain unlawfully reduced customs duties or sales tax liabilities can ever fall within the scope of the FCPA, i.e., whether the illicit payments made to obtain a reduction of revenue liabilities can ever constitute the kind of bribery that is proscribed by the FCPA.

The principal thrust of the defendants' argument is that the business nexus element, i.e., the "assist . . . in obtaining or retaining business" element, narrowly limits the statute's applicability to those payments that are intended to obtain a foreign official's approval of a bid for a new government contract or the renewal of an existing government contract. In contrast, the government insists that, in addition to payments to officials that lead directly to getting or renewing business contracts, the statute covers payments that indirectly advance ("assist") the payor's goal of obtaining or retaining foreign business with or for some person. The government reasons that paying reduced customs duties and sales taxes on imports, as is purported to have occurred in this case, is the type of "improper advantage" that always will assist in obtaining or retaining business in a foreign country, and thus is always covered by the FCPA.

policy arg.

C. FCPA LEGISLATIVE HISTORY

As the statutory language itself is amenable to more than one reasonable interpretation, it is ambiguous as a matter of law. We turn therefore to legislative history in our effort to ascertain Congress's true intentions.

1. 1977 Legislative History

Congress enacted the FCPA in 1977, in response to recently discovered but widespread bribery of foreign officials by United States business interests. Congress resolved to interdict such bribery, not just because it is morally and economically suspect, but also because it was causing foreign policy problems for the United States.[60] In particular, these concerns arose from revelations that United States defense contractors and oil companies had made large payments to high government officials in Japan, the Netherlands, and Italy. Congress also discovered that more than 400 corporations had made questionable or illegal payments in excess of $300 million to foreign officials for a wide range of favorable actions on behalf of the companies.

In deciding to criminalize this type of commercial bribery, the House and Senate each proposed similarly far-reaching, but non-identical, legislation. In its bill, the House intended "broadly [to] prohibit[ ] transactions that are corruptly intended to induce the recipient to use his or her influence to affect any act or decision of a foreign official. . . ." Thus, the House bill contained no limiting "business nexus" element. Reflecting a somewhat narrower purpose, the Senate expressed its desire to ban payments made for the purpose of inducing foreign

---

60. The House Committee stated that such bribes were "counter to the moral expectations and values of the American public," "eroded public confidence in the integrity of the free market system," "embarrassed friendly governments, lowered the esteem for the United States among the citizens of foreign nations, and lended credence to the suspicions sown by foreign opponents of the United States that American enterprises exert a corrupting influence on the political processes of their nations." H.R. Rep. No. 95-640, at 4-5 (1977); S. Rep. No. 95-114, at 3-4 (1977), reprinted in 1977 U.S.C.C.A.N. 4098, 4100-01.

officials to act "so as to direct business to any person, maintain an established business opportunity with any person, divert any business opportunity from any person or influence the enactment or promulgation of legislation or regulations of that government or instrumentality." In the end, Congress adopted the Senate's proposal to prohibit only those payments designed to induce a foreign official to act in a way that is intended to facilitate ("assist") in obtaining or retaining of business.

Congress expressly emphasized that it did not intend to prohibit "so-called grease or facilitating payments,"[61] such as "payments for expediting shipments through customs or placing a transatlantic telephone call, securing required permits, or obtaining adequate police protection, transactions which may involve even the proper performance of duties."[62] Instead of making an express textual exception for these types of non-covered payments, the respective committees of the two chambers sought to distinguish permissible grease payments from prohibited bribery by only prohibiting payments that induce an official to act "corruptly," i.e., actions requiring him "to misuse his official position" and his discretionary authority,[63] not those "essentially ministerial" actions that "merely move a particular matter toward an eventual act or decision or which do not involve any discretionary action."[64]

In short, Congress sought to prohibit the type of bribery that (1) prompts officials to misuse their discretionary authority and (2) disrupts market efficiency and United States foreign relations, at the same time recognizing that smaller payments intended to expedite ministerial actions should remain outside of the scope of the statute. The Conference Report explanation, on which the district court relied to find a narrow statutory scope, truly offers little insight into the FCPA's precise scope, however; it merely parrots the statutory language itself by stating that the purpose of a payment must be to induce official action "so as to assist an issuer in obtaining, retaining or directing business to any person."

To divine the categories of bribery Congress did and did not intend to prohibit, we must look to the Senate's proposal, because the final statutory language was drawn from it, and from the SEC Report on which the Senate's legislative proposal was based. In distinguishing among the types of illegal payments that United States entities were making at the time, the SEC Report identified four principal categories: (1) payments "made in an effort to procure special and unjustified favors or advantages in the enactment or administration of the tax or other laws" of a foreign country; (2) payments "made with the intent to assist the company in obtaining or retaining government contracts"; (3) payments "to persuade low-level government officials to perform functions or services which they are obliged to perform as part of their governmental responsibilities, but which they may refuse or delay unless compensated" ("grease"), and (4) political contributions. The SEC thus exhibited concern about a wide range of questionable payments (explicitly including the kind at issue here) that were resulting in millions of dollars being recorded falsely in corporate books and records.

As noted, the Senate Report explained that the statute should apply to payments intended "to direct business to any person, maintain an established business

---

61. H.R. Rep. No. 95-640, at 4; S. Rep. No. 95-114, at 10.
62. S. Rep. No. 95-114, at 10.
63. H.R. Rep. No. 95-640, at 7-8; S. Rep. No. 95-114, at 10.
64. H.R. Rep. No. 95-640, at 8. Similarly, when the House defined "foreign official" it excluded those individuals "whose duties are essentially ministerial or clerical." Id.

opportunity with any person, divert any business opportunity from any person or influence the enactment or promulgation of legislation or regulations of that government or instrumentality."[65] We observe initially that the Senate only loosely addressed the categories of conduct highlighted by the SEC Report. Although the Senate's proposal picked up the SEC's concern with a business nexus, it did not expressly cover bribery influencing the administration of tax laws or seeking favorable tax treatment. It is clear, however, that even though the Senate was particularly concerned with bribery intended to secure new business, it was also mindful of bribes that influence legislative or regulatory actions, and those that maintain established business opportunities, a category of economic activity separate from, and much more capacious than, simply "directing business" to someone.

The statute's ultimate language of "obtaining or retaining" mirrors identical language in the SEC Report. But, whereas the SEC Report highlights payments that go toward "obtaining or retaining government contracts," the FCPA, incorporating the Senate Report's language, prohibits payments that assist in obtaining or retaining business, not just government contracts. Had the Senate and ultimately Congress wanted to carry over the exact, narrower scope of the SEC Report, they would have adopted the same language. We surmise that, in using the word "business" when it easily could have used the phraseology of SEC Report, Congress intended for the statute to apply to bribes beyond the narrow band of payments sufficient only to "obtain or retain government contracts." The Senate's express intention that the statute apply to corrupt payments that maintain business opportunities also supports this conclusion.

For purposes of deciding the instant appeal, the question nevertheless remains whether the Senate, and concomitantly Congress, intended this broader statutory scope to encompass the administration of tax, customs, and other laws and regulations affecting the revenue of foreign states. To reach this conclusion, we must ask whether Congress's remaining expressed desire to prohibit bribery aimed at getting assistance in retaining business or maintaining business opportunities was sufficiently broad to include bribes meant to affect the administration of revenue laws. When we do so, we conclude that the legislative intent was so broad.

Congress was obviously distraught not only about high profile bribes to high-ranking foreign officials, but also by the pervasiveness of foreign bribery by United States businesses and businessmen. Congress thus made the decision to clamp down on bribes intended to prompt foreign officials to misuse their discretionary authority for the benefit of a domestic entity's business in that country. This observation is not diminished by Congress's understanding and accepting that relatively small facilitating payments were, at the time, among the accepted costs of doing business in many foreign countries.

In addition, the concern of Congress with the immorality, inefficiency, and unethical character of bribery presumably does not vanish simply because the tainted payments are intended to secure a favorable decision less significant than winning a contract bid. Obviously, a commercial concern that bribes a foreign government official to award a construction, supply, or services contract violates the statute. Yet, there is little difference between this example and that of a corporation's lawfully obtaining a contract from an honest official or agency by submitting the lowest bid, and either before or after doing so bribing a different

---

65. S. Rep. No. 95-114, at 17 (emphasis added).

government official to reduce taxes and thereby ensure that the under-bid venture is nevertheless profitable. Avoiding or lowering taxes reduces operating costs and thus increases profit margins, thereby freeing up funds that the business is otherwise legally obligated to expend. And this, in turn, enables it to take any number of actions to the disadvantage of competitors. Bribing foreign officials to lower taxes and customs duties certainly can provide an unfair advantage over competitors and thereby be of assistance to the payor in obtaining or retaining business. This demonstrates that the question whether the defendants' alleged payments constitute a violation of the FCPA truly turns on whether these bribes were intended to lower ARI's cost of doing business in Haiti enough to have a sufficient nexus to garnering business there or to maintaining or increasing business operations that ARI already had there, so as to come within the scope of the business nexus element as Congress used it in the FCPA. Answering this fact question, then, implicates a matter of proof and thus evidence.

In short, the 1977 legislative history suggests that Congress intended for the FCPA to prohibit all other illicit payments that are intended to influence nontrivial official foreign action in an effort to aid in obtaining or retaining business for some person. The congressional target was bribery paid to engender assistance in improving the business opportunities of the payor or his beneficiary, irrespective of whether that assistance be direct or indirect, and irrespective of whether it be related to administering the law, awarding, extending, or renewing a contract, or executing or preserving an agreement. In light of our reading of the 1977 legislative history, the subsequent 1988 and 1998 legislative history is only important to our analysis to the extent it confirms or conflicts with our initial conclusions about the scope of the statute.

2. 1988 Legislative History

After the FCPA's enactment, United States business entities and executives experienced difficulty in discerning a clear line between prohibited bribes and permissible facilitating payments. As a result, Congress amended the FCPA in 1988, expressly to clarify its original intent in enacting the statute. In this effort to crystallize the scope of the FCPA's prohibitions on bribery, Congress chose to identify carefully two types of payments that are not proscribed by the statute. It expressly excepted payments made to procure "routine governmental action" (again, the grease exception),[66] and it incorporated an affirmative defense for payments that are legal in the country in which they are offered or that constitute bona fide expenditures directly relating to promotion of products or services, or to the execution or performance of a contract with a foreign government or agency.[67]

We agree with the position of the government that these 1988 amendments illustrate an intention by Congress to identify very limited exceptions to the kinds of bribes to which the FCPA does not apply. A brief review of the types of routine governmental actions enumerated by Congress shows how limited Congress wanted to make the grease exceptions. Routine governmental action, for instance, includes "obtaining permits, licenses, or other official documents to qualify a person to do business in a foreign country," and "scheduling inspections associated with contract performance or inspections related to transit of goods

---

66. 15 U.S.C. §§78dd-1(b) & (f)(3)(A).
67. 15 U.S.C. §78dd-1(c).

across country."[68] Therefore, routine governmental action does not include the issuance of every official document or every inspection, but only (1) documentation that qualifies a party to do business and (2) scheduling an inspection — very narrow categories of largely non-discretionary, ministerial activities performed by mid- or low-level foreign functionaries. In contrast, the FCPA uses broad, general language in prohibiting payments to procure assistance for the payor in obtaining or retaining business, instead of employing similarly detailed language, such as applying the statute only to payments that attempt to secure or renew particular government contracts. Indeed, Congress had the opportunity to adopt narrower language in 1977 from the SEC Report, but chose not to do so.

3. 1998 Legislative History

In 1998, Congress made its most recent adjustments to the FCPA when the Senate ratified and Congress implemented the Organization of Economic Cooperation and Development's Convention on Combating Bribery of Foreign Public Officials in International Business Transactions (the "Convention"). Article 1.1 of the Convention prohibits payments to a foreign public official to induce him to "act or refrain from acting in relation to the performance of official duties, in order to obtain or retain business or other improper advantage in the conduct of international business."[69] When Congress amended the language of the FCPA, however, rather than inserting "any improper advantage" immediately following "obtaining or retaining business" within the business nexus requirement (as does the Convention), it chose to add the "improper advantage" provision to the original list of abuses of discretion in consideration for bribes that the statute proscribes. Thus, as amended, the statute now prohibits payments to foreign officials not just to buy any act or decision, and not just to induce the doing or omitting of an official function "to assist . . . in obtaining or retaining business for or with, or directing business to, any person,"[70] but also the making of a payment to such a foreign official to secure an "improper advantage" that will assist in obtaining or retaining business.[71]

The district court concluded, and defendants argue on appeal, that merely by adding the "improper advantage" language to the two existing kinds of prohibited acts acquired in consideration for bribes paid, Congress "again declined to amend the 'obtain or retain' business language in the FCPA."[72] In contrast, the government responds that Congress's choice to place the Convention language elsewhere merely shows that Congress already intended for the business nexus requirement to apply broadly, and thus declined to be redundant.

The Convention's broad prohibition of bribery of foreign officials likely includes the types of payments that comprise defendants' alleged conduct. The commentaries to the Convention explain that " 'other improper advantage' refers to something to which the company concerned was not clearly entitled, for example, an operating permit for a factory which fails to meet the statutory

---

68. 15 U.S.C. §78dd-1(f)(3)(A).

69. Convention on Combating Bribery of Foreign Public Officials in International Business Transactions, Dec. 17, 1997, art. 1.1, S. Treaty Doc. No. 105-43, 37 I.L.M. 1, 4 (1998) (emphasis added).

70. *See* 15 U.S.C. §78dd-1(a)(1).

71. Id.

72. Kay, 200 F. Supp. 2d at 686.

requirements."[73] Unlawfully reducing the taxes and customs duties at issue here to a level substantially below that which ARI was legally obligated to pay surely constitutes "something [ARI] was not clearly entitled to," and was thus potentially an "improper advantage" under the Convention.

4. Summary

Given the foregoing analysis of the statute's legislative history, we cannot hold as a matter of law that Congress meant to limit the FCPA's applicability to cover only bribes that lead directly to the award or renewal of contracts. Instead, we hold that Congress intended for the FCPA to apply broadly to payments intended to assist the payor, either directly or indirectly, in obtaining or retaining business for some person, and that bribes paid to foreign tax officials to secure illegally reduced customs and tax liability constitute a type of payment that can fall within this broad coverage. [W]e conclude that bribes paid to foreign officials in consideration for unlawful evasion of customs duties and sales taxes could fall within the purview of the FCPA's proscription. We hasten to add, however, that this conduct does not automatically constitute a violation of the FCPA: It still must be shown that the bribery was intended to produce an effect here, through tax savings that would "assist in obtaining or retaining business."

III. CONCLUSION

We are satisfied that for purposes of the statutory provisions criminalizing payments designed to induce foreign officials unlawfully to perform their official duties in administering the laws and regulations of their country to produce a result intended to assist in obtaining or retaining business in that country an unjustified reduction in duties and taxes can, under appropriate circumstances, come within the scope of the statute.

Reversed and remanded.

Stichting Ter behartiging Van de Belangen Van Oudaandeelhouders in Het Kapitaal Van Saybolt International B.V. v. Schreiber
United States Court of Appeals, Second Circuit, 2003
327 F.3d 173

SACK, Circuit Judge.

The plaintiff, Stichting ter behartiging van de belangen van oudaandeelhouders in het kapitaal van Saybolt International B.V. (Foundation of the Shareholders' Committee Representing the Former Shareholders of Saybolt International B.V.), appeals from a decision of the United States District Court for the Southern District of New York (Jed S. Rakoff, Judge) granting the defendants' motion for summary judgment. *See Stichting Ter behartiging Van de Belangen*

---

73. Commentaries on the Convention on Combating Bribery of Foreign Public Officials in International Business Transactions, 37 I.L.M. at 8.

Van Oudaandeelhouders in Het Kapitaal Van Saybolt International B.V. v. Schreiber, 145 F. Supp. 2d 356 (S.D.N.Y. 2001) ("Stichting"). The plaintiff claims that the erroneous legal advice given by defendant Philippe E. Schreiber caused a United States–based corporation that was a subsidiary of a Dutch company to violate the Foreign Corrupt Practices Act, 15 U.S.C. §§78dd-1, et seq. ("FCPA"). The corporation pleaded guilty in a Massachusetts federal district court to violating the FCPA, and its former chief executive officer ("CEO") was convicted of violating the FCPA by a New Jersey federal district court jury.

In the case at bar, the district court concluded that the guilty plea and the conviction collaterally estop the plaintiff, as the corporation's assignee, from claiming that Schreiber caused the corporation to think that its acts would not violate the FCPA. We disagree with the district court's conclusion that the corporation's guilty plea is inconsistent with the plaintiff's theory of how Schreiber misled the corporation. We also disagree with the district court's conclusion that the corporation was in privity with its former CEO at the time of his trial and therefore is bound by the trial's outcome. We vacate the judgment and remand for further proceedings consistent with this opinion. In so doing, we do not question the validity of either the plea or the conviction.

BACKGROUND

This appeal is from the district court's grant of the defendants' motion for summary judgment. The facts we adduce here are undisputed except as otherwise noted.

THE BRIBE

In 1995, Saybolt International was a private Dutch limited-liability company whose various worldwide subsidiaries were engaged in "the business of performing quantitative and qualitative testing of bulk commodities such as oil, gasoline, and other petrochemicals, as well as grains [and] vegetable oils." Am. Compl. P 20. Saybolt International owned Saybolt North America, Inc., a Delaware corporation with principal offices in Parsippany, New Jersey. All directors and officers of Saybolt North America were also directors or officers of Saybolt International. One such person was David H. Mead, who served as chief executive officer of Saybolt North America and as an officer and director of Saybolt International. Mead also served as the de facto head of all operations under the control of Saybolt International in the Western Hemisphere.

Beginning in late 1994 or early 1995, Saybolt de Panama S.A. ("Saybolt de Panama"), a subsidiary of Saybolt International under Mead's supervision, sought to acquire property in Panama for the construction of a laboratory and office complex. Sometime in 1995, Mead was told that Saybolt de Panama had identified suitable property in the Panama Canal Zone but that the lease could be acquired only if the company would first pay a $50,000 bribe to a Panamanian government official.

Mead raised the issue of the bribe in a Saybolt North America board meeting held in New Jersey on November 9, 1995. Schreiber, a lawyer admitted to practice in New York State, was present at the meeting. In addition to serving as a director of Saybolt North America, Schreiber occasionally provided legal services to the corporation. At the meeting, Schreiber advised those present that Saybolt North America could not pay the proposed bribe to the Panamanian official without subjecting the corporation and its officers and directors to potential liability. Then and in the weeks that followed, however, Schreiber allegedly led Mead and others to believe that "the bribe payment could legally be made under U.S. law by [their] Dutch affiliate," Saybolt International. Am. Compl. P 13. Allegedly on this basis, on December 17, 1995, an employee of Saybolt North America traveled by commercial airline from New Jersey to Panama for purposes of arranging the bribe. On December 21, 1995, Saybolt International wired $50,000 from the Netherlands to a bank account controlled by Saybolt de Panama. The Saybolt North America employee then directed an employee of Saybolt de Panama to deliver the $50,000 to an individual acting as an intermediary for the Panamanian official.

THE CRIMINAL PROCEEDINGS

On November 20, 1996, United States officials investigating possible environmental crimes by Saybolt North America executed a search warrant at its offices in New Jersey. The search uncovered evidence of the Panama bribe.

Shortly thereafter, on May 12, 1997, Core Laboratories, N.V. ("Core") purchased Saybolt International and its controlling interest in Saybolt North America. Pursuant to the purchase agreement, Saybolt International's former shareholders placed $6 million in escrow to cover any criminal liability that might arise from the company's activities in Panama. In exchange, Core assigned the former shareholders all causes of action for any legal malpractice related to the Panama incident.

United States prosecutors decided to bring separate criminal proceedings against Saybolt North America and its officers. Mead was arrested in January 1998, at which point he stopped actively working for the various Saybolt entities, which were by then part of Core. On April 20, 1998, a federal grand jury in the District of New Jersey returned an indictment charging Mead with, inter alia, violating the FCPA, 15 U.S.C. §78dd-2(a)(3), and conspiring to violate the FCPA, 18 U.S.C. §371.

At about that time, the United States Attorney for the District of Massachusetts and the United States Attorney for the District of New Jersey jointly issued an information charging Saybolt North America with substantially the same offenses charged in Mead's indictment: violating, and conspiring to violate, the FCPA. On August 18, 1998, officers of Core caused Saybolt North America to enter into a plea agreement in which Saybolt North America promised to "cooperate truthfully and completely with the United States . . . in any trial or other proceedings arising out of this investigation of [Saybolt North America] and any of [its] present and former officers and employees." On December 3, 1998, Saybolt North America pleaded guilty to the charges in the information before the United States District Court for the District of Massachusetts. In the plea colloquy, the court instructed John D. Denson, the Core officer representing Saybolt North America, as follows:

> You understand that before the corporation or corporations can be found guilty of [violating the FCPA], the government would have to prove beyond a reasonable doubt

that an agent of the corporation, acting for the corporation and so situated with respect to the management of the corporation[] that the act or acts can properly be considered the acts of the corporation itself, has to have entered into a corrupt, that is, a bribe-like transaction in the international commerce of the United States. It has to be not just that there was a mistake, that this agent or agents of the corporations knew what they were doing.

Do you understand that?

Denson answered "Yes, sir." The court then entered judgment against the corporation.

Unlike his former employer, Mead decided to fight the charges against him. His case went to trial before the United States District Court for the District of New Jersey (Anne E. Thompson, Judge) in early October 1998. At trial, Mead presented evidence that, Mead contended, suggested that Schreiber led Mead to believe that "the bribe payment could legally be made," Am. Compl. P 13, if the bribe of the Panamanian official were paid by a non–United States entity. The court instructed the jury that "if the evidence shows you that the defendant actually believed that the transaction was legal, he cannot be convicted." Mead Trial Tr. at 6.131. The jury convicted Mead on both charges, and the district court sentenced him to four months' imprisonment and a $20,000 fine.

THE MALPRACTICE SUIT

Saybolt International's former shareholders assigned their legal malpractice causes of action to the plaintiff, which brought this diversity action in the United States District Court for the Southern District of New York on November 18, 1999. In its amended complaint, the plaintiff alleged that Schreiber, and through him Walter, Conston, Alexander & Green, P.C., defendant-third-party-plaintiff, a law firm with which Schreiber was affiliated, committed legal malpractice by failing to advise Saybolt North America that "the bribe payment as proposed to be paid by a Dutch company to Panamanian officials would violate the FCPA." Am. Compl. P 110. Without Schreiber's malpractice, the amended complaint alleged, "the bribe payment would not have been made, even at the cost of the entire Panama deal." Am. Compl. P 111. The plaintiff further alleged that by committing such malpractice, Schreiber also breached his lawyer's fiduciary duty to Saybolt North America and breached his contract to provide competent professional services. Finally, the plaintiff alleged that Schreiber's malpractice cost the former Saybolt International shareholders $4.2 million, mostly in criminal fines.

In a June 12, 2001, Memorandum Order, the district court granted the defendants' motion for summary judgment on all claims. *Stichting,* 145 F. Supp. 2d at 359. The court noted that the plaintiff alleged that Schreiber's erroneous advice led Saybolt North America to act without the knowledge that its conduct violated United States law. *Id.* at 357. The court then held that this allegation necessarily contradicts Saybolt North America's guilty plea to the charges that it violated the FCPA:

> To enter such a plea Saybolt [North America] had to affirm, as it did, that it undertook the misconduct in question with knowledge of the corruptness of its acts. Since, if it had in fact relied on Schreiber's allegedly erroneous and misleading advice, Saybolt [North America] would not have believed at the time that its misconduct was unlawful

or corrupt, it could never have made this admission at its allocution or, indeed, entered its guilty plea at all.

Id. On this basis, the district court concluded that under the doctrine of collateral estoppel, Saybolt North America's guilty plea forecloses the plaintiff's theory of causation. "Since Saybolt did . . . plead guilty and admit its criminal intent, it is bound by those admissions, and therefore cannot now contend either that it relied on Schreiber's alleged advice or that that advice, even if erroneous, . . . proximately caused whatever damages . . . were incurred by Saybolt." *Id.* at 357-58.

The district court also held that Mead's criminal convictions are an independent basis for entering judgment against the plaintiff. *Id.* at 358. The court observed that the plaintiff's theory of how Schreiber misled Saybolt North America had been "squarely put before, and rejected by, the jury that convicted Mead." *Id.* The court then held that "Mead was indicted and convicted for criminal activity he undertook for [the corporation's] benefit in his capacity as chief executive officer . . . , and his intent is therefore directly imputable" to the corporation. *Id.* at 358-59. On this basis, the district court concluded that the plaintiff is collaterally estopped from relitigating the issue of Saybolt North America's reliance on Schreiber's legal advice. *Id.*

The plaintiff appealed.

DISCUSSION . . .

II. THE GUILTY PLEA

As indicated, the district court held that Saybolt North America's guilty plea constituted an admission that the corporation acted with knowledge that its conduct was "unlawful or corrupt." *Stichting*, 145 F. Supp. 2d at 357. For this reason, the district court concluded that the plaintiff is collaterally estopped from arguing that Schreiber led Saybolt North America to believe that its acts would not violate the FCPA. The plaintiff challenges this conclusion on appeal. We agree with the plaintiff.

A. THE ELEMENTS OF THE CRIME

[The court sets forth the six elements of the crime discussed at p. 451 above.]

As the district court described it, the plaintiff's claim in its civil suit is that its lawyer, Schreiber, "advised Saybolt [North America] that a bribe payment by a foreign affiliate might be legal but also failed to advise Saybolt [North America] that any involvement by Saybolt [North America] or its officers in arranging the affiliate's payment could result in criminal liability." *Stichting*, 145 F. Supp. 2d at 357. "[I]f Saybolt [North America] had in good faith relied on Schreiber's advice, Saybolt [North America] would have believed that its arranging the bribe through a foreign affiliate was permissible." *Id.*

By pleading guilty, Saybolt North America admitted the six elements of the FCPA crime. But by pleading guilty, Saybolt North America did not admit that at the time of the criminal act it knew that the act of arranging, rather than paying, such a bribe was criminal. Knowledge by a defendant that it is violating the

FCPA — that it is committing all the elements of an FCPA violation — is not itself an element of the FCPA crime. Federal statutes in which the defendant's knowledge that he or she is violating the statute is an element of the violation are rare; the FCPA is plainly not such a statute. Saybolt North America did not, therefore, by pleading guilty, preclude an assertion in a subsequent civil action — the case at bar — that it did not know it was violating the FCPA at the time of the violation.

The plaintiff is thus not collaterally estopped by Saybolt North America's criminal plea from arguing in this civil suit that, even though Saybolt North America admittedly did commit a violation of the FCPA, it did not know that it was committing a violation of the FCPA at the time; that it did not know it was committing such a violation because Schreiber negligently told it that it was not committing a violation by causing a foreign entity to pay the bribe; and that it suffered damages as a result of the negligent advice.

We therefore conclude that the case should be remanded to the district court to permit the plaintiff to attempt to establish what the district court identified as its claim: that the defendant advised Saybolt North America that a bribe payment by a foreign affiliate might be legal, but failed to advise Saybolt North America that any involvement by Saybolt North America or its officers in arranging the affiliate's payment could result in criminal liability, i.e., as stated in the Complaint, that "Schreiber erroneously advised [Saybolt North America] that the bribe payment could legally be made under U.S. law by a Dutch affiliate," Am. Compl. P 13; and that, as stated by the district court, Saybolt North America "in good faith relied on Schreiber's advice" that "arranging the bribe through a foreign affiliate was permissible," *Stichting*, 145 F. Supp. 2d at 357.

B. THE "CORRUPTLY" ELEMENT

To be sure, by pleading guilty, Saybolt North America admitted that it acted "corruptly" in its actions related to the Panamanian bribe. The defendants see in this admission a collateral bar to the plaintiff's assertion that Saybolt North America did not know that it was violating the FCPA at the relevant time and, indeed, was misled into believing that it was acting legally. The district court apparently agreed. *See Stichting*, 145 F. Supp. 2d at 357. We do not. We conclude that an admission that an act was done "corruptly" in this context is not equivalent to an admission that the person committing it knew that it violated the particular law at the time the act was performed.

It is difficult to determine the meaning of the word "corruptly" simply by reading it in context. We therefore look outside the text of the statute to determine its intended meaning.

The Senate Report for the FCPA explains the statute's use of the term "corruptly" as follows:

> The word "corruptly" is used [in the FCPA] in order to make clear that the offer, payment, promise, or gift, must be intended to induce the recipient to misuse his official position in order to wrongfully direct business to the payor or his client, or to obtain preferential legislation or a favorable regulation. The word "corruptly" connotes an evil motive or purpose, an intent to wrongfully influence the recipient.

S. Rep. No. 95-114, at 10 (1977), reprinted in 1977 U.S.C.C.A.N. 4098, 4108.

The Senate's explanation of the term "corruptly" tracks closely our interpretation of that term in 18 U.S.C. §201(b). We have repeatedly held in that context that "a fundamental component of a 'corrupt' act is a breach of some official duty owed to the government or the public at large." *United States v. Rooney*, 37 F.3d 847, 852 (2d Cir. 1994). Our case law defining the term "corruptly" in federal bribery statutes thus parallels the Senate Report's explanation of the term as denoting an evil motive or purpose and an intent to induce an official to misuse his position.

We thus conclude that the word "corruptly" in the FCPA signifies, in addition to the element of "general intent" present in most criminal statutes, a bad or wrongful purpose and an intent to influence a foreign official to misuse his official position. But there is nothing in that word or any thing else in the FCPA that indicates that the government must establish that the defendant in fact knew that his or her conduct violated the FCPA to be guilty of such a violation.

Finally in this connection, we note that had Saybolt North America gone to trial, it would have been allowed to present evidence that it relied on Schreiber's advice that the benefit sought from the Panamanian official would not require the official to misuse his position or breach his duties — i.e., that it did not act corruptly — precisely because "corruptly" is an element of the offense. Saybolt North America also would have been allowed a jury instruction on this allegation. By pleading guilty, Saybolt North America effectively admitted that it could not factually support such a theory of reliance.

But Saybolt North America would not properly have been entitled to a jury instruction on an allegation that Schreiber led it to believe that its acts did not violate the FCPA. A defense of reliance on advice of counsel is available only to the extent that it might show that a defendant lacked the requisite specific intent and specific intent to violate the FCPA is not an element of an FCPA violation. Thus, Saybolt North America's guilty plea does not constitute an admission that it could not factually support the theory of reliance on counsel that is the basis of the plaintiff's malpractice action.

C. CONCLUSION

We conclude that the question whether Saybolt North America acted with knowledge that its conduct violated the FCPA was not answered by its guilty plea, and thus that the plea does not collaterally estop the plaintiff from litigating the issue in its claim against Schreiber and the law firm with which he was affiliated. *See N.L.R.B.* v. Thalbo Corp., 171 F.3d 102, 109 (2d Cir. 1999) (collateral estoppel applies only to issues "actually decided" in the previous proceeding).

III. THE CONVICTION OF MEAD

[The court went on to hold that the conviction of Mead, the former CEO of Saybolt North America, did not bar the plaintiff from relitigating the issue of malpractice against Schreiber. Mead had argued at his trial that he relied on the advice of Schreiber that the payments were lawful. The trial court had instructed the jury to convict only if the jury found that Mead knew that the transactions were illegal. The district court then found that because the jury convicted Mead, it must have concluded that Mead knew that the transactions were illegal and was not misled by Schreiber. The district court then held that plaintiff was collaterally estopped to challenge this finding. However, as neither the plaintiff nor Saybolt North America was a party to Mead's trial, the plaintiff would be barred by collateral estoppel only if at the time of Mead's trial, Mead was in privity with Saybolt North America. The court of appeals found that no such privity existed as Mead was released from his duties for all of the Saybolt entities before the trial and Saybolt North America, by then Mead's former employer, did not exercise any degree of actual control over his defense. As no privity existed between Mead and Saybolt North America, plaintiff was not barred by collateral estoppel in pursuing its claims against Schreiber.]

CONCLUSION

For the foregoing reasons, the judgment of the district court is vacated, and the case remanded for further proceedings consistent with this opinion.

NOTES AND QUESTIONS

1. Does *Schreiber* stand for the proposition that a company is not protected if it acts after receiving an opinion of counsel that a particular act is not in violation of the FCPA? If so, does this create a "chilling effect" on international business?

2. The Justice Department provides an opinion procedure under which a company may request an opinion regarding whether the proposed conduct violates the antibribery provisions of the FCPA. The request must describe an actual — not a hypothetical — transaction and must be based on full and true disclosure of all relevant facts. *See* 28 C.F.R. Part 80 (1995). The Department of Justice must provide an opinion within 30 days after a complete request is submitted. So far, this procedure, available since 1992, has been rarely used. In *Schreiber*, why didn't Mead use this procedure instead of getting an opinion from Schreiber?

3. Most U.S. companies are keenly aware of the FCPA and wish to avoid the public scandal and embarrassment of an FCPA problem as well as the negative impact that such a problem may have on their economic interests. Most companies have promulgated their own internal company guidelines on corporate behavior that are meant to comply with and in many cases exceed the requirements of the FCPA. Companies are also vigilant in their dealings with third-party contractors in foreign states. In addition to performing due diligence on prospective third-party contractors, many companies also include explicit covenants in their contracts that a contractor will not make payments or violate any local laws. Some companies include provisions of the FCPA in their contracts and include provisions that the contractor is aware and understands the FCPA. However, despite these precautions, U.S. corporations must be vigilant as situations that might trigger the FCPA continue to arise in many IBTs.

V.   The Transactional Aspects of FDI: Establishment in the European Union, China, and Brazil

A.   Introduction

Despite the growing importance of international investment law, the lawyer's most crucial role is to handle the *transactional* aspects of an investment decision. These will vary with each business deal and will be vastly different in differing countries and areas of the world. Legal counsel will, therefore, require a familiarity with the legal system and laws of the country that is the target of the investment, as well as a good understanding of the political, economic, and cultural conditions of that country. Obviously, no one person possesses this knowledge with respect to every country in the world. Thus, an association with local counsel will be crucial in most cases.

In every foreign direct investment, several categories of issues arise. Consider the example of Medtech, Inc., the medical technology company detailed at the outset of this chapter. First, Medtech must decide where to establish its investment. Second, it must decide whether to establish a joint venture, a wholly owned foreign subsidiary, or to purchase the stock or assets of an existing company. Third, the requisite legal form must be decided—this will normally be a stock company, but in exceptional cases may be a branch office or a partnership. Fourth, relevant government approvals must be secured; these may involve approvals from competition law authorities or government investment agencies. Fifth, a list of the required different contracts should be compiled and each must be negotiated and carefully drafted in meetings with other parties to the venture. Sixth, careful attention should be given to financial planning, present and future financing and tax matters. Seventh, government regulatory standards that must be met should be studied, particularly those dealing with environmental protection, labor rights, consumer issues, land use, and construction matters. Finally, a plan should be prepared for the dissolution or liquidation of the project if and when the decision is made to terminate the venture.

The following materials that focus on foreign investment in three countries and regions—the European Union, China (Asia), and Brazil (Latin America)—are designed to provide an analysis of the aforementioned set of issues in very different settings, each a very important one for international business. We have selected the European Union for its obvious importance as an economic power. The materials on the EU also illustrate the issues of an investment in advanced industrialized countries and in the most important customs union in the world. We have also selected China and Brazil as they are developing countries and are the world's largest and second largest recipients, respectively, of FDI among developing countries in the world (China, in fact, is the world's largest recipient of FDI among all countries having surpassed the United States as the largest recipient in 2002). The United States is also the largest foreign investor in Brazil and in the view of many the most important foreign investor in China. Both countries also play prominent and leading roles in their regions. China has begun to dominate Asia and Brazil has a leading role in South America.

China and Brazil also offer important contrasts. Although the countries are in many ways in similar stages of economic development as first emerging economies, they take very different approaches to FDI. Both China and Brazil also differ from the EU in their approach as to whether FDI requires a special legal regime that is distinct from the general legal rules regulating business activity:

- European Union member nations have few special national legal rules regulating FDI but instead generally subject FDI to the same rules governing domestic investment. Some states have filing and disclosure requirements. Any laws of each member that attempt to regulate FDI are subject to the superseding laws of the EU.
- China has a special mandatory legal regime for FDI and subjects FDI to extensive regulation.
- Bazil has an optional FDI regime based on an incentive system of sticks and carrots.

There are, of course, fundamental differences in the political, economic, and legal systems of these regions and countries. An examination of all of these differences is beyond the scope of this book, but one major difference that we wish to highlight is that the EU has a developed legal system and is governed by the rule of law whereas China and Brazil cannot be said to be subject to the rule of law, at least not in the sense that this term is commonly used in the United States. Any foreign investor who enters China or Brazil must keep this caution firmly in mind. An example of the types of major problems that exist in China and Brazil traceable to a weak legal system is commercial piracy, the focus of Chapter 7, but other problems, such as government corruption that is often tolerated and unpunished, examined in §IV, are also serious and common. In addition, while it is possible to assume that laws in the EU will be applied and enforced by courts on a consistent and predictable basis and that judgments of courts will be regularly enforced, the same cannot be assumed in China or Brazil. These cautions about the weakness of the legal system apply in varying degrees to all foreign investment in developing countries and our materials on China and Brazil are intended as examples of such issues. Moreover, while China and Brazil, as developing countries, share some similarities, there are also some fundamental differences between them. China is a socialist country under a one-party rule, and its markets are still under extensive state control although there are now significant free-market elements. China also shares traditions that are very different from the Western traditions of countries like the United States. On the other hand, after a period of authoritarian rule under a military government from 1964 to 1985, Brazil now operates under a democratic system of government with free markets. Although Brazil is an ethnic melting pot, it was also under European rule for a long period and shares some traditions associated with its European settlers, including a civil law legal system. Each country faces different challenges, some unique but also representative of challenges faced by other developing countries in Asia and South America. We will point out how China and Brazil can serve as examples for other countries in their regions in the materials below.

Note that while the area with the strongest legal system, the EU, has relatively few special laws governing FDI, China, the country with arguably the least developed legal system, has the most comprehensive legal regime governing FDI, with Brazil somewhere in between. What explains this?

While we do not wish to minimize the differences of doing business in these three areas, there are, of course, also some common issues. We offer a brief conceptual outline of investment issues.

CONCEPTUAL OUTLINE AND CHECKLIST OF FOREIGN DIRECT INVESTMENT ISSUES

1. In what country will the investment be made?

This will be determined primarily by business considerations, but legal provisions will also be important.

A. Is there a treaty on friendship, commerce, and navigation and/or a bilateral investment treaty that creates a legal right to establishment and legal protections?

B. Is there an applicable free-trade agreement, such as NAFTA, that grants the right of establishment as well as national treatment and protects the investor against arbitrary and discriminatory conduct and against expropriation?

C. Investment in a free-trade area or a customs union may give the investor access to the entire multicountry market. For example, a U.S. investor in Mexico or Canada may obtain free movement of products to be sold in all three NAFTA countries. Even a non-NAFTA investor in a NAFTA country may obtain free-movement access by complying with NAFTA rule of origin requirements so as to obtain a NAFTA Certificate of Origin.

Another example is that an investor in the European Union may obtain the right under the Treaty Establishing the European Community to free movement of goods, services, and capital and the right of further establishment throughout the EU.

2. Will the investment be made by (1) establishing a joint venture, (2) establishing a wholly owned subsidiary, or (3) acquiring an existing company?

In most cases, this necessitates the formation of a foreign stock company. There may be a choice of form — for example, in Germany there is a form called the Aktiengesellschaft (AG) for ordinary companies and the Gesellschaft mit beschrankter Haftung (GmbH) form for closely held companies.

Acquiring a substantial equity interest in an existing foreign company may be suitable in a particular case. This can be done through a purchase of assets, a purchase of stock, or an exchange of a foreign company's stock for the stock of a U.S. company. In all but the latter case, the investor is best advised to incorporate a local (foreign) company to effect the acquisition. Tax considerations will be paramount here.

3. What host country government approvals are necessary?

A. Even in OECD countries relatively open to investment, certain disclosure and reporting forms must be filed with government agencies. In some cases, advance approval may be required. For example, the Investment Canada Act restricts acquisitions in certain sectors such as natural resources, transportation, financial, and cultural industries.

B. In the United States, foreign investors must contend with reporting requirements under such federal statutes as the International Investment

Survey Act, 22 U.S.C. §§3101-3108; the Agricultural Foreign Investment Disclosure Act, 7 U.S.C. §§3501-3508; and the Foreign Investment in Real Property Tax Act (codified in scattered sections of the Internal Revenue Code). In addition, the so-called Exon-Florio amendment, 19 U.S.C. §2901, authorizes the President to investigate mergers, acquisitions, and takeovers of U.S. companies by foreign parties and to suspend or prohibit investment that could impair "national security."

4. What steps must be taken to secure and protect intellectual property rights?

5. What immigration permits and visas are necessary to allow personnel from the investor's country to live and work in the host country?

6. What competition law disclosures, permits, or approvals are required? For example, in the EU under Regulation (EC) 4064/89 joint ventures, mergers, and acquisitions over a certain size (250 million euros) must be notified and cleared by the EU Commission.

7. What environmental and labor laws must be observed?

8. If financing is to come in whole or in part from the host country, what are the securities laws aspects of the deal?

9. Will tax treaties ameliorate the tax aspects of the venture?

B. Foreign Investment in the European Union

We now turn to FDI in the European Union, which is the largest and most important customs union in the world (for a discussion of customs unions, see pp. 157-158). The free movement of goods, services, capital, and people is a fundamental feature at the forefront of doing business in any EU nation. As you work through these materials, keep in mind that the lessons learned in the context of the EU can also be applied to the customs unions that are being developed around the world or, with some qualifications, to free-trade areas, such as NAFTA.

The EU today is the result of over 50 years of negotiations and a series of landmark treaties and international understandings. Beginning as an international union of the coal and steel industries in six European countries (Belgium, France, Germany, Italy, the Netherlands, and Luxembourg), the Europeans then agreed to form a customs union (a free-trade area with a common external tariff), the European Economic Community, under the Treaty of Rome (the EC Treaty), in 1957. In 1986, the decision was taken to form the Common Market, a single economic area. In the 1990s, a series of treaties created the EU itself, a political, social, and monetary union. Periodic enlargements have expanded the number of participating states to 25. Now a "Constitution for Europe" is proposed, which must be ratified by all member states to become effective.

A salient characteristic of European Union–United States economic relations is the extensive flow of foreign direct investment in both directions. Each is the most significant investment host for the other. Despite recent economic and political tensions, this is likely to continue. As a result of EU enlargement in 2004, investment in the EU is now more attractive than ever. With 10 new members, the EU consists of 25 nations with a total population of 455 million and an $11 trillion economy, 28 percent of world GDP, and a 20 percent share of world trade. The EU is also effectively a single internal market so that goods, services, capital, and, to a great extent, people can move freely throughout the area. This presents opportunity for foreign as well as European companies. The EU and its member states have completed negotiations on friendship, commerce, and navigation treaties, bilateral investment treaties, and treaties on taxation with most of the states of the world, including the United States and Japan. Moreover, through its commitments to the World Trade Organization, the EU permits extensive trade and establishment in service sectors, including financial services, insurance, and telecommunications.

1. *The Historical Development of the EU*

James Hanlon, European Community Law, 1-19 (2003)

THE BEGINNING

At the end of the Second World War mainland Europe was devastated. Many millions of lives had been lost. The misery of the six war years had induced in the people of Europe the idea that this carnage must never be allowed to happen again. The peoples of Europe were receptive to the idea that the nation-state was not the best structure for the future and that the path of integration was the path to follow. The first move towards this end, and the first of the integrative measures, was taken by two men, Robert Schuman, the French Foreign Minister, and Jean Monnet, an administrator in the French civil service. In May 1950 in what has become known as the "Schuman Declaration", the French Foreign Minister said:

> the French government proposes to take action immediately on one limited but decisive point. It proposes to place Franco-German production of coal and steel as a whole under a common higher authority within the framework of an organization open to the participation of the other countries of Europe.

In 1951, six states, Germany, France, Italy, the Netherlands, Belgium and Luxembourg, signed the Treaty of Paris. This established the European Coal and Steel Community (the ECSC Treaty).

The essential feature of the ECSC Treaty was the creation of a new entity (the "Community") with international legal status and separate and autonomous institutions. This also made the Treaty very different from a traditional intergovernmental organization. The vital step towards integration was the transfer of legislative and administrative powers to the institutions of the Treaty. From now on, the six signatories to the Treaty pooled their sovereignty for defined, although limited, purposes. All aspects of the production and distribution of coal and steel were brought under the control of a High Authority, which had the power to make legally binding "decisions" and "recommendations". The other institutions were the Assembly, a body representing the people of Europe, brought together in a "parliament", with some supervisory powers; a Council of Ministers representing the Member States, with some legislative and some consultative powers; and the Court of Justice whose function was to "ensure that in the interpretation and application of this Treaty . . . the law is observed".

In 1955 an inter-governmental conference of the original six states of the ECSC met at Messina under the leadership of Paul Henri Spack, the Belgium foreign minister. The conference and the report it produced on the attractions of economic integration led, in 1957, to the signing of two Treaties of Rome. These treaties established the European Atomic Energy Community (Euratom) and the European Economic Community (EEC). The immediate purpose of Euratom was to create "the conditions necessary for the speedy establishment and growth of nuclear industries". The purpose of the EEC was to establish a "common market". However, it must be remembered that the founding fathers of the treaties had longer term political aims and aspirations. The Schuman Declaration referred to "common foundations of economic development as a firm step towards a European federation"; the Preamble to the Treaty of Paris stated that the parties were "resolved to substitute for age-old rivalries the merging of their essential interests". The Preamble to the EEC Treaty resolved that Member States will "lay the foundations of an ever closer union among the peoples of Europe." Certainly, the views of the founding fathers of the Communities were that the aim of the Treaties was to achieve political ends through economic means. They thought that integration in one economic sector would "snowball" into integration in other sectors. They also believed that modern states were so closely interdependent that any element of cooperation would tend to induce further cooperation. Coal and steel were the start as they were "the basic elements of industrial production". Atomic energy, then in its infancy, was seen as the principal future source of new energy. By bringing these activities, as well as economic activity generally, under common rules and common institutions, there would be economic interdependence and eventually, political integration between the Member States. This view might now seem naive as subsequent events have shown that even economic integration has proved difficult to achieve. As the debates of the last decade have demonstrated, political integration is not even on the agenda of some Member States.

After the passing of the Treaties of Rome, there were three Communities each with a set of autonomous institutions having the power to develop new structures independently of the participating Member States. Each community had an Assembly, a Council and Court of Justice. Whereas the ECSC had a High Authority, the Treaties of Rome had established a Commission. The Commission's powers under Euratom and the EEC were more limited than the High Authority and the Commission was ranked after the Council and Assembly in order of precedence. However, the members of these institutions were the same people, albeit wearing different "caps". In order to rationalise their administration, a Merger Treaty was completed in 1967. The Merger Treaty established a single Council, a single Assembly, and the High Authority of the ECSC was merged with the EEC and Euratom Commission, to be known as the Commission. Nevertheless, although the three communities now have common institutions (although the ECSC expired in 2002) they remain legally distinct and the powers and functions of the institutions depend on the terms of the treaty under which they act.

During the 1960s France and more particularly de Gaulle became dissatisfied with the workings of the Community and in 1965 France absented herself from Council meetings thereby effectively bringing the legislative machinery of the Community to a halt. This became known as the "policy of the empty chair". The crisis was resolved by the so-called "Luxembourg Accord". Although this had no legal status, it was an agreement that allowed any member-state to veto any legislation that it thought might affect its "very important interests".

The effect of this agreement was to halt any movement of importance on the political front for almost 20 years.

THE FIRST ENLARGEMENT

A Treaty of Agreement was signed on January 22, 1972 and the United Kingdom became a member of the EEC with effect from January 1, 1973. Also joining at the same time were Ireland and Denmark. Norway had also been accepted into membership but did not take up the opportunity because a majority of the people voted "no" in a referendum on the subject.

The period between the United Kingdom accession and 1986 was a time of inactivity in the Community. There was little progress towards either economic or political union. This was caused mainly by the impasse of the Luxembourg Accord. One important development to be noted during this period was the beginning of the process of political cooperation by the Member States. This took the form of a series of meetings of the heads of states and government. The "summits" or as they became known, meetings of the European Council, did not have legal status within the framework of the Community, nor did they have any power to make binding decisions. Nevertheless, the European Council increasingly assumed overall policy making authority, thereby changing the balance of power in the Community away from the supranational body (the Commission) and towards the intergovernmental body (the Council of Ministers). The meetings of the European Council are those which are most widely reported in the media. It is a separate body from, and should not be confused with, the Council of Ministers or the Council of Europe. The existence of the European Council was officially recognised in the Single European Act 1986 and subsequently reaffirmed by the Treaty on European Union 1992 (Maastricht).

Although the voice of the peoples of Europe was called the Assembly, it was increasingly referred to as the "European Parliament". At first it consisted of nominees of the parliaments of the Member States. However, in 1979 the first direct elections to the European Parliament were held. In 1981 Greece became the tenth member of the Community, joined in 1986 by Spain and Portugal.

THE SINGLE EUROPEAN ACT

The stagnation in the decision making process following the Luxembourg Accord brought about considerable dissatisfaction at the slow pace at which Community goals were being achieved. Naturally, attempting to obtain the unanimous agreement of all Member States was almost impossible; and those agreements which were reached were at the "lowest common denominator" level. Thus, it was recognised that some change had to be brought about. The original Treaty of Rome had survived without major amendment for almost thirty years. There had been many and various attempts to improve the Treaty all of them failing, probably because they were too ambitious. Nevertheless, they helped to establish the climate for the eventual changes that were to be brought about by the Single European Act (SEA) of 1986. In 1985 the Dooge Committee proposed an intergovernmental conference "to negotiate a draft European Union Treaty". The conference was to discuss the decision making of the Council of Ministers, the legislative powers of the parliament, the executive powers of the Commission, and new policy areas of Community competence. The outcome of the conference was a summit meeting in Milan which brought into being the above mentioned Single European Act, which came into force on July 1, 1987. The Preamble of the Act says that it is "a step towards European union". The Act amended the EEC Treaty in a number of important ways. A major change was the different method to be adopted in the legislative process affecting ten Treaty articles. The SEA replaced the requirement for unanimity in the Council by qualified majority voting. This meant that one single state did not have the ability to block legislation. This was an important change because it applied to the legislation concerning the new date for completion of the internal market, *i.e.* the end of 1992. The need to complete the internal market (which should have been completed by January 1, 1970) was identified in a White Paper published by Lord Cockfield, the Commissioner with responsibility for the internal Community market, encouraged by the new President of the Commission, Jacques Delors. The SEA incorporated these recommendations and set "1992" as the date by which the internal market was to be achieved. The Commission had identified almost three hundred areas in which directives, or other measures, were considered necessary to complete the internal market. Measures concerning the internal market were now subject to qualified majority voting, and it says much for the efficiency of this process that by the end of 1992, all but 18 of the three hundred measures had been adopted by the Council. To all intents and purposes the internal market was completed on time.

The SEA officially recognised the Assembly as the European Parliament. In addition it introduced some changes to the legislative process which enhanced to a small extent the powers of the Parliament. Prior to the SEA, Parliament had only the right to be "consulted" on various legislative measures passed by the Council. The SEA introduced the "cooperation procedure", whereby if the procedure applies, Parliament had a "second reading" of proposed legislation. If Parliament rejected the legislation at this point, it could only be taken forward by the Council if that body was unanimous in its view. Parliament did not yet have positive powers and it could not assert its own views, and a unanimous Council could still pass legislation. However, the influence of Parliament had been increased. It can form an alliance with the Commission and one, even small, Member State. Thus the Council will often have to accommodate Parliament's view and introduce a compromise solution.

The SEA also introduced new Community competencies. One such competence was in the area of economic and social cooperation. This is not to say that the EEC had not previously introduced initiatives in this area, but rather the Act placed them on a formal footing. In this area it was provided that the Community should develop and pursue actions leading to the strengthening of its economic and social cohesion. It would attempt this by reducing disparities between the regions of the Community by setting up various funds, such as the European Regional Development Fund and the Social Fund and the European Investment Bank, all of which would provide money for projects which had the support of the Community.

Other new areas of Community competence were in research and technology, and in environmental protection. This latter competence is particularly apt for the Community, as environmental problems (especially pollution) of a particular Member State do not stop at national borders, but impact on neighbouring states.

The achievement of the internal market was an economic success. Yet the Commission was aware that the social repercussions had not been sufficiently addressed by the SEA. To address this problem it published a Community Charter of Fundamental Social Rights of Workers, which became known as the Social Charter. This more or less self-explanatory Charter was adopted by 11 of the 12 Member States in December 1989. The United Kingdom refused to sign it. Although it had no legal force it was intended to be the blue-print for social legislation in the Community.

THE TREATY ON EUROPEAN UNION

The signing of the SEA and the accompanying package of the "1992" programme quickened the pace of Community action. It was soon realised that even further action was needed to bring about further institutional change, and the adoption of common monetary and fiscal policies. To this end an intergovernmental conference (IGC) was held in 1991 that resulted in the signing on February 2, 1992 of the Treaty on European Union (TEU) (or the "Maastricht Treaty"). Following some difficulties in ratification in some Member States, notably the United Kingdom, Denmark and Germany, the Treaty came into force on November 1, 1993.

The TEU created the "European Union". It consists of three "pillars". In the middle are three existing Communities (*i.e.* the ECSC, Euratom and the EC). These three Communities will be known collectively as the European Communities. It will be noted here that the TEU officially changed the name to EC, dropping the "Economic" from the title. On either side of this central "pillar" is the Common Foreign and Security Policy (CFSP) and Cooperation in Justice and Home Affairs (JHA). These three "pillars" support the over-arching constitutional order of the Union. However, only the central pillar, the EC, is governed by Community law. The CFSP pillar and the JHA pillar are governed by intergovernmental cooperation. This means they are outside the jurisdiction of the Community institutions, particularly the Court of Justice. Neither will any of the Articles of the outside pillars be enforceable, or challengeable, in national courts. Thus, although the Union is wider than the European Community it has its roots in the Community.

The objectives of the Union are set out in Article 2 of the TEU. This Article reflects the activities to be pursued under the three pillars. In addition the Union is to maintain and build on the *"acquis communautaire"*. This expression means the body of EC law as found in the founding treaties and the case law of the Court of Justice. The main changes are set out as objectives in Articles 1-45 of the TEU. These represent an increase in, and further development of, policy areas. The most important, and controversial, developments are set out in Article 8 which adds to Article 3 of the EC Treaty the following:

> . . . in accordance with the timetable set out . . . these activities shall include the irrevocable fixing of exchange rates leading to the introduction of a single currency . . .

The single currency (now known as the "Euro") was to be achieved in three stages by 1999. The United Kingdom, Sweden and Denmark have to date opted out of the third and final stage. The other 12 Member States continued with their arrangements for the single currency and on January 1, 2002 the new banknotes and coins were introduced.

There was the realisation at Maastricht that the Community was dynamic and still evolving. For some Member States it was going too fast, and in the wrong direction; for others it was not moving fast enough. The debate was a continuing one. What sort of Community did these new citizens of Europe want? Was it a common market club of co-operating sovereign states, or was it an emerging political federation?

Also, in 1993, Austria, Finland, Norway and Sweden applied to become members of the Community. The negotiations for entry were completed relatively quickly and the treaty of Accession was signed in June 1994. However, as in 1972, the Norwegian people decided in a referendum against joining. Therefore, on January 1, 1995, Austria, Finland and Sweden became members of the European Union. The Union now had fifteen Member States.

THE AMSTERDAM TREATY

It was decided at Maastricht to review the TEU. This review was to take place at the sixth Intergovernmental Conference (IGC) to be held in the history of the Community. The remit for the IGC was far reaching, and was agreed at the Brussels European Council meeting of the December 10-11, 1993. The major subjects to be discussed at the IGC were as follows:

- to examine the legislative role of the European Parliament and other matters outlined in the Maastricht Treaty;
- to review the number of commissioners;
- to review the weighting of Member States votes in the Council of Ministers; and
- to consider measures needed to facilitate the work and smooth running of the EU institutions.

The aim of the IGC was to supply answers to some important questions. How can the Union be made more efficient, democratic and transparent? How can the Union contribute to the stability of the continent in the present international context? How can a dilution of the Community be avoided when it is expected to include more than 20 members after the year 2003?

The need for reform was largely driven by the enlargement process. The current unwieldy processes would become unworkable with the expected influx of new members. Enlargement itself was not on the agenda (neither was EMU), but issues that needed to be discussed were institutional reform, decision making, flexibility, employment provisions, the abolition of border controls, the common foreign and security policy, subsidiarity, transparency and the western European Union.

The outcome of the IGC and subsequent negotiations was the Treaty of Amsterdam. This was agreed by the Heads of State and Government on June 19, 1997 and concluded on October 2, 1997. The Treaty was to be ratified by the Member States, according to their constitutional traditions. Three Member States, Denmark, Ireland and Portugal each held a referendum, which confirmed their people's support for the new Treaty. The Treaty came into force on May 1, 1999. This was a few months behind the third stage of Economic and Monetary Union, which took place on January 1, 1999.

To cope with the expected influx of new Member States it was considered necessary to reform the institutional structure of the Community. Three areas in particular were said to be in need of reform. First it would be necessary to simplify the complex procedures for passing legislation. Secondly it was thought that qualified majority voting would become too ponderous with twenty or more Member States, and third, it was held that the number of commissioners would need to be controlled. The outcome in the Treaty was mere tinkering! Despite a proposal to give the larger Member States more power in terms of the votes they had for Qualified majority voting (QMV), the eventual Treaty left matters as they were. There was very little change to the process of legislation, and it was agreed to limit the number of commissioners to the current Treaty. A Protocol was added to the Treaty of Amsterdam providing that on the next enlargement of the Community the Commission will be made up of one national of each Member State. But even this small rearrangement is dependent on an agreement between the Member States to an acceptable weighting of votes within the Council. The protocol also provides that a Member State that has to give up a second Commissioner will need to be compensated, presumably by some increase in its votes in the Council.

There were also some small changes to the complex range of legislative procedures (44 different procedures). The "cooperation" procedure of Article 252 [ex 189c] has been abolished, except for monetary policy provisions. The vast majority of Articles are now subject to the "co-decision" procedure (Article 251 [ex 189b]). This will help to increase the power and influence of the European Parliament. This is a real, if modest, reform.

It was mentioned earlier that the TEU had created a three "pillar" European Union. One of the pillars was called Cooperation and Justice in Home Affairs (JHA). It will be remembered that this pillar (and the other pillar, Common Foreign and Security Policy (CFSP)) are outside the jurisdiction of the European Community, in particular the Court of Justice. However, the Treaty of Amsterdam introduced changes in respect of the JHA. It has now been renamed Police and Judicial Cooperation in Criminal Matters (Title VI TEU). But, more importantly, the provisions on visas, asylum, immigration and other policies relating to the free movement of persons are brought into the EC in Articles 61-69 [ex 73i-73q]. This means that these provisions are now justiciable before the Court of Justice.

THE TREATY OF NICE

The Treaty of Amsterdam left a certain number of "left-over" issues. These issues concerned the balance of power between the European Union and the Member States and between the Member States themselves. It was fairly obvious that these issues would become more problematical with the proposed enlargement of the Union.

It was therefore agreed by the Member States that the year 2000 should see yet another IGC, the primary task of which was to ensure institutional reform in order that the Union can work efficiently with a membership comprising twenty-five states. The Union's institutions had been created with just six Member States in mind. It was obvious that these institutions were experiencing difficulties with 15 Member States. The need for reform was pressing. It was decided that the new

IGC would consider the following issues:

- the size and composition of the Commission;
- the weighting of votes in the Council;
- the extension of qualified majority voting in the Council.

The IGC was convened on February 14, 2000. Negotiations were concluded in time for the meeting of the Council in Nice (France) on December 11, 2000. The result was the Treaty of Nice. The Treaty came into force on February 1, 2003.

The Treaty, as passed, indicates that reaching agreement on many of the issues was difficult and there is an element of postponing changes and decisions to a later date. The Treaty of Nice limits the Commission to one member per Member State with effect from 2005. A ceiling on the number of Commissioners will be imposed once the Union has 27 Member States. At that point the Council will have to take a unanimous decision on the exact number of Commissioners, which must be less than 27. The nationality of the Commissioners will then be determined by a system of rotation. There is no requirement for the Council to consult either the Commission or the European Parliament. The rotation system has yet to be devised but it will be "based on the principle of equality" and will reflect demography and geography.

The Treaty also increased the power of the president of the Commission. Under the revised Article 217 EC the president will decide on the allocation of portfolios and may reassign responsibilities in the course of a Commissioner's term of office, albeit with the approval of the other members of the Commission.

NOTES AND QUESTIONS

1. What was the original purpose of European integration? Was it a means to an end? How did the purposes change over time? What is the predominant reason today?

2. A number of discrete phases in the integration process can be identified. In the beginning, the process was dominated by those, like Jean Monnet, who believed in a federalist Europe. This gave way to the functionalism of the 1950s, the idea that European integration could best be served by focusing on discrete economic sectors, which could be managed by supranational rather than intergovernmental institutions. Such institutions could operate efficiently and technocratically away from the political spotlight. Functionalism is based on the premise that promoting functional cooperation between states will deter them from more aggressive action to settle disputes over scarce resources. The way to prevent war between states with a history of mutual hostility is not to keep them apart, but to require them to engage in cooperative ventures, in functionally specific agencies.

In the early 1960s, scholars such as E.B. Haas [*Beyond the Nation State* (Stanford University Press, 1964)] coined the term "neofunctionalism" to refer to the idea that economic integration is a process based on spillover from noncontroversial economic sectors to more sensitive political issues, otherwise too hot to handle. Is this what happened in the EC/EU?

Neofunctionalism was challenged by neorealism in the late 1960s and 1970s, and intergovernmentalism began to predominate. In the 1980s, there was a neofederalist and "constructivist" revival leading to the creation of the EU itself and economic and monetary union.

2. *Jurisdictional Competence, Institutions, and Lawmaking in the EU: The Proposed Constitution for Europe*

In June 2003, as a result of the European Convention on the Future of Europe, a draft constitution for Europe was submitted for approval by member states of the EU. The new constitution, which must be approved by all member states to take effect, is viewed as a response to a growing crisis of legitimacy that began with the creation of the EU in 1992. While it is beyond the scope of this casebook to explore this topic in depth, we offer a brief overview of the issues surrounding the debate leading to the constitution as it is a hotly contested issue of fundamental importance in Europe and is relevant to any business or company seeking to invest in Europe.

The Maastricht Treaty of 1992, which created the European Union, moved Europe beyond the previous "economic community" limited to the enhancement of trade and economic welfare into a full blown union that had explicit political ambitions. The EU was created based on three "pillars." The three existing European communities (the European Coal and Steel Community, the European Atomic Energy Community, and the European Economic Community), the product of the first three decades of economic integration, were renamed collectively as the European Communities and constituted one of the pillars. The two other pillars, the Common Foreign and Security Policy and the Cooperation in Justice and Home Affairs, moved the EU well beyond the economic sphere into fundamental political integration with explicit political aims and goals. For many, the new political nature of the EU required more popular support and legitimacy than could be obtained through the process of passive consensus that marked the first three decades of economic integration. During this period, the population of Europe was deemed to have passively consented to the formation of a common market by their national governments and to the ceding of significant governmental functions to the European Economic Community in pursuit of trade and economic welfare. As these functions were related to the relatively noncontroversial issues of enhanced trade and increased economic welfare, however, the passive consent of the governed was deemed to be sufficient. The new EU established in 1992, however, was a different entity as it now proclaimed bold ambitions in the area of foreign policy, security, and justice. As these ambitions signaled a move beyond economic integration into the more fundamental area of political integration, it was believed that a more explicit popular support of the governed was necessary to support the legitimacy of the EU and a move was begun to draft a constitution for Europe that would address this need.

The initial impetus for the constitution discussed above can be characterized as an internally focused rationale that was based on the need to address issues of internal legitimacy, popular support by the governed, and democracy. This rationale also encompassed a need to clarify the internal organization, structure, and procedures of the institutions of the EU as well as a perceived need to "rein in" the EU's creeping powers so that it would not usurp the power of individual nations. While the internally focused rationale might have been the impetus for developing a constitution, it became clear during the drafting process that there was a second, competing rationale that can be characterized as an externally focused rationale based on the need to strengthen the external identity, unity, representation, and capacity for action of the EU. A strong and complete sovereign entity, with its own legal personality, not merely another internally divided international organization and loose confederation of bickering states, will considerably strengthen the EU's external economic and political role in the world. In the economic sphere, a strong and unified EU will enhance its effectiveness as an economic power as it will be able to better represent its interests on trade issues where the EU is often at odds with its principal trading partners, including the United States and Japan. In the political sphere, a unified EU might also serve as a counterweight to the United States on important international political issues such as war and the use of force.

We have included selected provisions of the proposed EU constitution below. As you review these materials, can you identify which of the provisions support the internally focused rationale and which support the externally focused rationale? As you conduct your review, we wish to highlight several changes: The proposed EU constitution confers a single legal personality on the EU (Article 2), creates a new position for a foreign minister of the EU (Article 27), creates a more permanent nonrotating president of the European Council (Article 21), and clarifies how a qualified majority is determined (Article 24) for purposes of the existing co-decision legislative process depicted on p. 495 *infra*. Based on your review of the highlighted changes above and the provisions set forth below, which rationale do you believe is more strongly supported by the text of the proposed constitution? Which rationale is better suited for doing business in the EU?

Treaty Establishing a Constitution for Europe (2003)

TITLE I. DEFINITION AND OBJECTIVES OF THE UNION

ARTICLE 1. ESTABLISHMENT OF THE UNION

1. Reflecting the will of the citizens and States of Europe to build a common future, this Constitution establishes the European Union, on which the Member States confer competences to attain objectives they have in common. The Union shall coordinate the policies by which the Member States aim to achieve these objectives, and shall exercise in the Community way the competences they confer on it.

2. The Union shall be open to all European States which respect its values and are committed to promoting them together.

TITLE III. UNION COMPETENCES

ARTICLE 9. FUNDAMENTAL PRINCIPLES

1. The limits of Union competences are governed by the principle of conferral. The use of Union competences is governed by the principles of subsidiarity and proportionality.

2. Under the principle of conferral, the Union shall act within the limits of the competences conferred upon it by the Member States in the Constitution to attain

the objectives set out in the Constitution. Competences not conferred upon the Union in the Constitution remain with the Member States.

3. Under the principle of subsidiarity, in areas which do not fall within its exclusive competence the Union shall act only if and insofar as the objectives of the intended action cannot be sufficiently achieved by the Member States, either at central level or at regional and local level, but can rather, by reason of the scale or effects of the proposed action, be better achieved at Union level.

4. Under the principle of proportionality, the content and form of Union action shall not exceed what is necessary to achieve the objectives of the Constitution.

ARTICLE 10. UNION LAW

1. The Constitution, and law adopted by the Union's Institutions in exercising competences conferred on it, shall have primacy over the law of the Member States.

2. Member States shall take all appropriate measures, general or particular, to ensure fulfillment of the obligations flowing from the Constitution or resulting from the Union Institutions' acts.

ARTICLE 11. CATEGORIES OF COMPETENCE

1. When the Constitution confers on the Union exclusive competence in a specific area, only the Union may legislate and adopt legally binding acts, the Member States being able to do so themselves only if so empowered by the Union or for the implementation of acts adopted by the Union.

2. When the Constitution confers on the Union a competence shared with the Member States in a specific area, the Union and the Member States shall have the power to legislate and adopt legally binding acts in that area. The Member States shall exercise their competence to the extent that the Union has not exercised, or has decided to cease exercising, its competence.

3. The Union shall have competence to promote and coordinate the economic and employment policies of the Member States.

4. The Union shall have competence to define and implement a common foreign and security policy, including the progressive framing of a common defence policy.

5. In certain areas and in the conditions laid down in the Constitution, the Union shall have competence to carry out actions to support, coordinate or supplement the actions of the Member States, without thereby superseding their competence in these areas.

ARTICLE 12. EXCLUSIVE COMPETENCE

1. The Union shall have exclusive competence to establish the competition rules necessary for the functioning of the internal market, and in the following areas:

- monetary policy, for the Member States which have adopted the euro,
- common commercial policy,
- customs union,
- the conservation of marine biological resources under the common fisheries policy.

2. The Union shall have exclusive competence for the conclusion of an international agreement when its conclusion is provided for in a legislative act of the Union, is necessary to enable the Union to exercise its competence internally, or affects an internal Union act.

Title IV. The Union's Institutions

Chapter I. Institutional Framework

ARTICLE 18. THE UNION'S INSTITUTIONS

1. The Union shall be served by a single institutional framework which shall aim to:

- advance the objectives of the Union,
- promote the values of the Union,
- serve the interests of the Union, its citizens and its Member States,

and ensure the consistency, effectiveness and continuity of the policies and actions which it undertakes in pursuit of its objectives.

2. This institutional framework comprises:

The European Parliament,
The European Council,
The Council of Ministers,
The European Commission,
The Court of Justice.

ARTICLE 19. THE EUROPEAN PARLIAMENT

1. The European Parliament shall, jointly with the Council of Ministers, enact legislation, and exercise the budgetary function, as well as functions of political control and consultation as laid down in the Constitution. It shall elect the President of the European Commission.

2. The European Parliament shall be elected by direct universal suffrage of European citizens in free and secret ballot for a term of five years. Its members shall not exceed seven hundred and thirty-six in number. Representation of European citizens shall be degressively proportional, with a minimum threshold of four members per Member State.

3. The European Parliament shall elect its President and its officers from among its members.

ARTICLE 20. THE EUROPEAN COUNCIL

1. The European Council shall provide the Union with the necessary impetus for its development, and shall define its general political directions and priorities. It does not exercise legislative functions.

2. The European Council shall consist of the Heads of State or Government of the Member States, together with its President and the President of the Commission. The Union Minister for Foreign Affairs shall take part in its work.

3. The European Council shall meet quarterly, convened by its President. When the agenda so requires, its members may decide to be assisted by a minister and, in the case of the President of the Commission, a European Commissioner. When the situation so requires, the President shall convene a special meeting of the European Council.

4. Except where the Constitution provides otherwise, decisions of the European Council shall be taken by consensus.

ARTICLE 21. THE EUROPEAN COUNCIL CHAIR

1. The European Council shall elect its President, by qualified majority, for a term of two and a half years, renewable once. In the event of an impediment or serious misconduct, the European Council can end his or her mandate according to the same procedure.

2. The President of the European Council:

- shall chair it and drive forward its work,
- shall ensure its proper preparation and continuity in cooperation with the President of the Commission, and on the basis of the work of the General Affairs Council.
- Shall present a report to the European Parliament after each of its meetings.

The President of the European Council shall at his or her level and in that capacity ensure the external representation of the Union on issues concerning its common foreign and security policy, without prejudice to the responsibilities of the Union Minister for Foreign Affairs.

3. The President of the European Council may not hold a national mandate.

ARTICLE 22. THE COUNCIL OF MINISTERS

1. The Council of Ministers shall, jointly with the European Parliament, enact legislation, exercise the budgetary function and carry out policy-making and coordinating functions, as laid down in the Constitution.

2. The Council of Ministers shall consist of a representative of each Member State at ministerial level for each of its formations. Only this representative may commit the Member State in question and cast its vote.

3. Except where the Constitution provides otherwise, decisions of the Council of Ministers shall be taken by qualified majority.

ARTICLE 23. FORMATIONS OF THE COUNCIL OF MINISTERS

1. The Legislative and General Affairs Council shall ensure consistency in the work of the Council of Ministers.

When it acts in its General Affairs function, it shall, in liaison with the Commission, prepare, and ensure follow-up to, meetings of the European Council.

When it acts in its legislative function, the Council of Ministers shall consider and, jointly with the European Parliament, enact European laws and European framework laws, in accordance with the provisions of the Constitution. In this function, each Member State's representation shall include one or two representatives at ministerial level with relevant expertise, reflecting the business on the agenda of the Council of Ministers.

2. The Foreign Affairs Council shall, on the basis of strategic guidelines laid down by the European Council, flesh out the Union's external policies, and ensure that its actions are consistent. It shall be chaired by the Union Minister for Foreign Affairs. . . .

4. The Presidency of Council of Ministers formations, other than that of Foreign Affairs, shall be held by Member State representatives within the council of Ministers on the basis of equal rotation for periods of at least a year. The European Council shall adopt a European decision establishing the rules of such rotation, taking into account European political and geographical balance and the diversity of Member States.

ARTICLE 24. QUALIFIED MAJORITY

1. When the European Council or the Council of Ministers takes decisions by qualified majority, such a majority shall consist of Member States, representing at least three fifths of the population of the Union.

2. When the Constitution does not require the European Council or the Council of Ministers to act on the basis of a proposal of the Commission, or when the European Council or the Council of Ministers is not acting on the initiative of the Union Minister for Foreign Affairs, the required qualified majority shall consist of two thirds of the Member States, representing at least three fifths of the population of the Union.

3. The provisions of paragraphs 1 and 2 shall take effect on 1 November 2009, after the European Parliament elections have taken place, according to the provisions of Article 19. . . .

5. Within the European Council, its President and the President of the Commission do not vote.

ARTICLE 25. THE EUROPEAN COMMISSION

1. The European Commission shall promote the general European interest and take appropriate initiatives to that end. It shall ensure the application of the Constitution, and steps taken by the Institutions under the Constitution. It shall oversee the application of Union law under the control of the Court of Justice. It shall execute the budget and manage programmes. It shall exercise coordinating, executive and management functions, as laid down in the Constitution. With the exception of the common foreign and security policy, and other cases provided for in the Constitution, it shall ensure the Union's external representation. It shall initiate the Union's annual and multiannual programming with a view to achieving interinstitutional agreements.

2. Except where the Constitution provides otherwise, Union legislative acts can be adopted only on the basis of a Commission proposal. Other acts are adopted on the basis of a Commission proposal where the Constitution so provides.

3. The Commission shall consist of a College comprising its President, the Union Minister of Foreign Affairs/Vice-President, and thirteen European Commissioners selected on the basis of a system of equal rotation between the Member States. This system shall be established by a European decision adopted by the European Council on the basis of the following principles:

(a) Member States shall be treated on a strictly equal footing as regard determination of the sequence of, and the time spent by, their nationals as Members of the College; consequently, the difference between the total number of terms of office held by nationals of any given pair of Member States may never be more than one;

(b) subject to point (a), each successive College shall be so composed as to reflect satisfactorily the demographic and geographical range of all the Member States of the Union.

The Commission President shall appoint non-voting Commissioners, chosen according to the same criteria as apply for Members of the College and coming from all other Member States.

These arrangements shall take effect on 1 November 2009.

4. In carrying out its responsibilities, the Commission shall be completely independent. In the discharge of their duties, the European Commissioners and Commissioners shall neither seek nor take instructions from any government or other body.

5. The Commission, as a College, shall be responsible to the European Parliament. The Commission President shall be responsible to the European Parliament for the activities of the Commissioners. Under the procedures set out in Article III-243, the European Parliament may pass a censure motion on the Commission. If such a motion is passed, the European Commissioners and Commissioners must all resign. The Commission shall continue to handle everyday business until a new College is nominated.

ARTICLE 26. THE PRESIDENT OF THE EUROPEAN COMMISSION

1. Taking into account the elections to the European Parliament and after appropriate consultations, the European Council, deciding by qualified majority, shall put to the European Parliament its proposed candidate for Presidency of the Commission. This candidate shall be elected by the European Parliament by a majority of its members. If this candidate does not receive the required majority support, the European Council shall within one month put forward a new candidate, following the same procedure as before.

2. Each Member State determined by the system of rotation shall establish a list of three persons, in which both genders shall be represented, whom it considers qualified to be a European Commissioner. By choosing one person from each of the proposed lists, the President-elect shall select the thirteen European Commissioners for their competence, European commitment, and guaranteed independence. The President and the persons so nominated for membership of the College, including the future Union Minister for Foreign Affairs, as well as the persons nominated as non-voting Commissioners, shall be submitted collectively to a vote of approval by the European Parliament. The Commission's term of office shall be five years.

3. President of the Commission shall:

- lay down guidelines within which the Commission is to work;

- decide its internal organisation, ensuring that it acts consistently, efficiently and on a collegiate basis;
- appoint Vice-Presidents from among the members of the College.

A European Commissioner or Commissioner shall resign if the President so requests.

ARTICLE 27. THE UNION MINISTER FOR FOREIGN AFFAIRS

1. The European Council, acting by qualified majority, with the agreement of the President of the Commission, shall appoint the Union Minister for Foreign Affairs. He shall conduct the Union's common foreign and security policy. The European Council may end his tenure by the same procedure.

2. The Union Minister for Foreign Affairs shall contribute by his proposals to the development of the common foreign policy, which he shall carry out as mandated by the Council of Ministers. The same shall apply to the common security and defence policy.

3. The Union Minister for Foreign Affairs shall be one of the Vice-Presidents of the Commission. He shall be responsible there for handling external relations and for coordinating other aspects of the Union's external action. In exercising these responsibilities within the Commission, and only for these responsibilities, the Union Minister for Foreign Affairs shall be bound by Commission procedures.

ARTICLE 28. THE COURT OF JUSTICE

1. The Court of Justice shall include the European Court of Justice, the High Court and specialised courts. It shall ensure respect for the law in the interpretation and application of the Constitution.

Member States shall provide rights of appeal sufficient to ensure effective legal protection in the field of Union law.

2. The European Court of Justice shall consist of one judge from each Member State, and shall be assisted by Advocates-General.

The High Court shall include at least one judge per Member State: the number shall be fixed by the Statute of the Court of Justice.

The judges and the Advocates-General of the European Court of Justice and the judges of the High Court, chosen from persons whose independence is beyond doubt and who satisfy the conditions set out in Articles 1II-260 and 1II-261, shall be appointed by common accord of the governments of the Member States for a term of six years, renewable.

3. The Court of Justice shall:

- rule on actions brought by a Member State, an Institution or a natural or legal person in accordance with the provisions of Part III;
- give preliminary rulings, at the request of Member State courts, on the interpretation of Union law or the validity of acts adopted by the Institutions;
- rule on the other cases provided for in the Constitution.

TITLE V. EXERCISE OF UNION COMPETENCE

CHAPTER I. COMMON PROVISIONS

ARTICLE 32. THE LEGAL ACTS OF THE UNION

1. In exercising the competences conferred on it in the Constitution, the Union shall use as legal instruments, in accordance with the provisions of Part III, European laws, European framework laws, European regulations, European decisions, recommendations and opinions.

A European law shall be a legislative act of general application. It shall be binding in its entirety and directly applicable in all Member States.

A European framework law shall be a legislative act binding, as to the result to be achieved, on the Member States to which it is addressed, but leaving the national authorities entirely free to choose the form and means of achieving that result.

A European regulation shall be a non-legislative act of general application for the implementation of legislative acts and of certain specific provisions of the Constitution. It may either be binding in its entirety and directly applicable in all Member States, or be binding, as regards the result to be achieved, on all Member States to which it is addressed, but leaving the National authorities entirely free to choose the form and means of achieving that result.

A European decision shall be a non-legislative act, binding in its entirety. A decision which specifies those to whom it is addressed shall be binding only on them.

Recommendations and opinions adopted by the Institutions shall have no binding force.

NOTES AND QUESTIONS

1. Consider the jurisdictional competence of the EU. Are most decisions that affect international business within the competence of the EU or the member states?

2. Will the EU have a strong executive branch of government?

3. Consider the lawmaking power. At present, most laws that affect business and commercial policy are passed using a complex process known as the "Co-Decision Procedure" (see Figure 6-1 on the following page), which generally requires the Council and the Commission to negotiate and coordinate with the European Parliament, which is granted veto power over any proposal. The reform (Article 24) proposed by the new constitution would improve the EU's legislative efficiency, but is predicted to greatly increase the power of the four largest members: Germany, France, the United Kingdom, and Italy. Why? The Commission would also gain; its monopoly over legislative proposals operates as a kind of legislative "pre-veto." The Parliament would gain because parliamentary approval would be required for most EU laws. The Council's influence would perhaps be lessened. How would these reforms affect international business operations?

3. Access to the Internal Market of the EU: The Four Freedoms

The key advantage for businesses operating in the EU is access to all 25 member countries as a single economic area. This is due to the fact that the various

FIGURE 6-1
The Co-decision Procedure in the EC

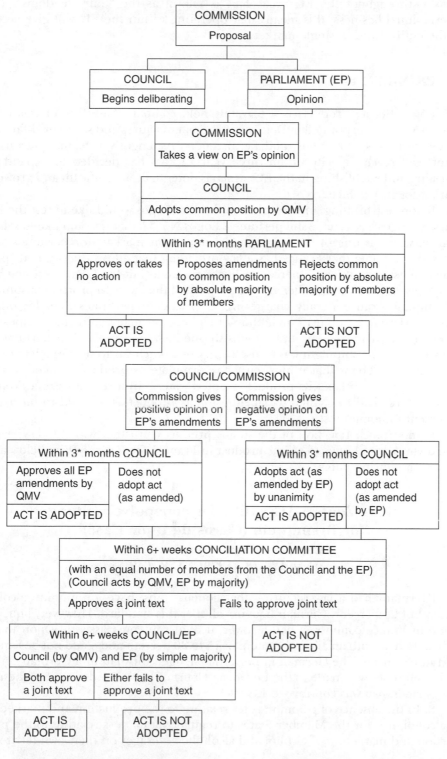

* May be extended by one month
\+ May be extended by two weeks

legal instruments that created the EU mandate free movement of four elements — goods, services, capital, and persons (including legal persons such as corporations) — throughout the EU area. This is known as the "four freedoms." For international business, this means that operating within the EU will give access to the entire EU as a single market.

PROBLEM 6-8

Logos Beauty Products is a privately held company based in Kansas City, Missouri, and incorporated in Delaware, that manufactures and sells world-famous soaps, cosmetics, shampoos, and facial toners. As Logos's U.S. manufacturing plants will reach capacity within three years, Logos has decided to expand by investing and establishing in the EU, which is potentially a significant and growing market for its products.

Before establishing an enterprise in the EU, Logos would like to test the EU market. Logos has a successful perfume, "Logos No. 3," that it would like to sell in France, which is one of the world's most important markets for perfumes and cosmetics. Assume that France has a law providing that all products called "perfumes" must have at least 5 percent active ingredients but the Logos perfume has only 3 percent active ingredients. The purpose of the law is to protect consumers as companies can generally charge higher prices for perfumes than for other scented fragrances. France's neighbors, Belgium, Germany, and Italy, impose a 3 percent active ingredient limit. Logos shipped a large supply of its perfume to France where the shipment was refused entry by French Customs. French authorities have told Logos that it must either reformulate its product to meet French standards or it can label its product "scented water." In a recent case, a French manufacturer had to change its labeling for its product as it failed to meet the 5 percent minimum test.

Is the French rejection of the Logos product consistent with EU law? How would you advise Logos to sell its product in France? *See Casis de Dijon* below and the accompanying notes.

Rewe-Zentral AG v. Bundesmonopolverwaltung für Branntwein (Cassis de Dijon Case)
European Court of Justice, 1979
Case 120/78, [1979] E.C.R. 649

[Germany had a law requiring that liqueurs must have a minimum alcohol content of 25 percent. German liqueurs all met this standard. However, liqueurs made in France commonly had a lower alcohol content. Cassis de Dijon was a French liqueur with an alcohol content of 15 to 20 percent and could not be legally sold in Germany. The German importer challenged this ban in a German court, and a reference was made to the European Court of Justice to determine whether the German ban was contrary to EC law].

8. In the absence of common rules relating to the production and marketing of alcohol, it is for the Member States to regulate all matters relating to the production and marketing of alcohol and alcoholic beverages on their own territory.

Obstacles to movement within the Community resulting from disparities between the national laws relating to the marketing of the products in question must be accepted insofar as those provisions may be recognized as being necessary in order to satisfy mandatory requirements relating in particular to the effectiveness of fiscal supervision, the protection of public health, the fairness of commercial transactions and the defence of the consumer.

9. The Government of the Federal Republic of Germany put forward various arguments which, in its view, justify the application of provisions relating to the minimum alcohol content of alcoholic beverages, adducing considerations relating on the one hand to the protection of public health and on the other to the protection of the consumer against unfair commercial practices.

10. As regards the protection of public health the German government states that the purpose of the fixing of minimum alcohol content by national legislation is to avoid the proliferation of alcoholic beverages on the national market, in particular alcoholic beverages with a low alcohol content, since, in its view, such products may more easily induce a tolerance towards alcohol than more highly alcoholic beverages.

11. Such considerations are not decisive since the consumer can obtain on the market an extremely wide range of weakly or moderately alcoholic products and furthermore a large proportion of alcoholic beverages with a high alcohol content freely sold on the German market is generally consumed in a diluted form.

12. The German government also claims that the fixing of a lower limit for the alcohol content of certain liqueurs is designed to protect the consumer against unfair practices on the part of producers and distributors of alcoholic beverages.

This argument is based on the consideration that the lowering of the alcohol content secures a competitive advantage in relation to beverages with a higher alcohol content, since alcohol constitutes by far the most expensive constituent of beverages by reason of the high rate of tax to which it is subject.

Furthermore, according to the German government, to allow alcoholic products into free circulation wherever, as regards their alcohol content, they comply with the rules laid down in the country of production would have the effect of imposing as a common standard within the Community the lowest alcohol content permitted in any of the Member States, and even of rendering any requirements in this field inoperative since a lower limit of this nature is foreign to the rules of several Member States.

13. As the Commission rightly observed, the fixing of limits to the alcohol content of beverages may lead to the standardization of products placed on the market and of their designations, in the interest of greater transparency of commercial transactions and offers for sale to the public.

However, this line of argument cannot be taken so far as to regard the mandatory fixing of minimum alcohol contents as being an essential guarantee of the fairness of commercial transactions, since it is a simple matter to ensure that suitable information is conveyed to the purchaser by requiring the display of an indication of origin and of the alcohol content on the packaging of the products.

14. It is clear from the foregoing that the requirements relating to the minimum alcohol content of alcoholic beverages do not serve a purpose which is in the general interest and such as to take precedence over the requirements of the free movement of goods, which constitutes one of the fundamental rules of the Community.

In practice, the principal effect of requirements of this nature is to promote alcoholic beverages having a high alcohol content by excluding from the national market products of other Member States which do not answer that description.

It therefore appears that the unilateral requirement imposed by the rules of a Member State of a minimum alcohol content for the purposes of the sales of alcoholic beverages constitutes an obstacle to trade which is incompatible with the provisions of Article [28] of the Treaty.

There is therefore no valid reason why, provided that they have been lawfully produced and marketed in one of the Member States, alcoholic beverages should not be introduced into any other Member State; the sale of such products may not be subject to a legal prohibition on the marketing of beverages with an alcohol content lower than the limits set by the national rules.

NOTES AND QUESTIONS

1. The ECJ ruling in the *Cassis de Dijon* case is the leading case interpreting Article 28 of the Treaty Establishing the European Community, as amended (2003). This article provides as follows:

Article 28

Quantitative restrictions on imports and all measures having equivalent effect shall be prohibited between Member States.

Article 29 of the Treaty establishes the same rule with respect to exports. Note that the German measure was not discriminatory, yet it was contrary to Article 28.

2. Article 30 of the EC Treaty contains an exception to Articles 28 and 29: Member States may justify a restriction on grounds of "public morality, public policy or public security; the protection of life or health of humans, animals or plants; the protection of national treasures possessing artistic, historic, or archaeological value; or the protection of industrial and commercial property. Such prohibitions or restrictions shall not, however, constitute a means of arbitrary discrimination or a disguised restriction on trade between Member States." Why was this not applied in the *Cassis de Dijon* case?

3. What if it is found that one of the goals of Article 30 could be accomplished by a less restrictive means than a trade ban?

4. Can an EU nation ban imported products under Article 30 without also banning domestic production of the same category of goods?

PROBLEM 6-9

As Logos is considering a strategy for penetrating all of the key markets of the EU, it needs an overall corporate structure for its European operations. Logos has identified ten key markets; it would ideally like to have a corporate presence in each market. Logos is currently exploring the following approach proposed by its local counsel in Kansas City: In each key market, Logos should set up subsidiaries that will be wholly owned by the Logos parent company in Kansas City. This is the same strategy proposed by Kansas counsel for expansion of Logos operations in the United States and it seems logical to Logos management to extend this approach in Europe. An issue that Logos has encountered, however, is that it has set aside a capital fund for investment in the EU and the minimum capital requirements of a number of EU nations will exhaust the capital fund set aside and will limit the number of subsidiaries that Logos can establish. Logos's Kansas counsel has advised Logos that it will have to abandon its plans to set up subsidiaries in all ten member countries (as there is not sufficient capital to do so) but should decide instead which two or three countries will be most strategically important and set up subsidiaries in those countries that can serve the rest of the EU market. Do you agree with this advice? What approach would you suggest? *See Centros* and the accompanying notes below.

Centros Ltd. v. Erhvervs-og Selskabsstyrelsen
European Court of Justice, 1999
Case 212/97, [1999] E.C.R. 1-1459

[In this case, Mr. and Mrs. Bryde, who were Danish citizens living in Denmark, wanted to set up a company in Denmark. However, Danish Company Law required a minimum share capital of DKK 200,000 (about $30,000). The Brydes thus set up a company in the UK, where there was no minimum capital requirement, and established a "branch office" in Denmark. The company did no business in the UK, and a friend of the Brydes agreed that his home would be their registered office in the UK. The Brydes brought suit after the Danish Companies Board rejected the application for a branch office.]

21. Where it is the practice of a Member State, in certain circumstances, to refuse to register a branch of a company having its registered office in another Member State, the result is that companies formed in accordance with the law of that other Member State are prevented from exercising the freedom of establishment conferred on them by Articles 52 and 58 of the Treaty.

22. Consequently, that practice constitutes an obstacle to the exercise of the freedoms guaranteed by those provisions.

23. According to the Danish authorities, however, Mr and Mrs Bryde cannot rely on those provisions, since the sole purpose of the company formation which they have in mind is to circumvent the application of the national law governing formation of private limited companies and therefore constitutes abuse of the freedom of establishment. In their submission, the Kingdom of Denmark is therefore entitled to take steps to prevent such abuse by refusing to register the branch.

24. It is true that according to the case-law of the Court a Member State is entitled to take measures designed to prevent certain of its nationals from attempting, undercover of the rights created by the Treaty, improperly to circumvent their national legislation or to prevent individuals from improperly or fraudulently taking advantage of provisions of Community law . . .

25. However, although, in such circumstances, the national courts may, case by case, take account — on the basis of objective evidence — of abuse or fraudulent conduct on the part of the persons concerned in order, where appropriate, to deny them the benefit of the provisions of Community law on which they seek to rely, they must nevertheless assess such conduct in the light of the objectives pursued by those provisions.

26. In the present case, the provisions of national law, application of which the parties concerned sought to avoid, are rules governing the formation of companies and not rules concerning the carrying on of certain trades, professions or businesses. The provisions of the Treaty on freedom of a establishment are intended specifically to enable companies formed in accordance with the law of a Member State and having their registered office, central administration or principal place of business within the Community to pursue activities in other Member States through an agency, branch or subsidiary.

27. That being so, the fact that a national of a Member State who wishes to set up a company chooses to form it in the Member State whose rules of company law seem to him the least restrictive and to set up branches in other Member States cannot, in itself, constitute an abuse of the right of establishment. The right to form a company in accordance with the law of a Member State and to set up branches in other Member States is inherent in the exercise, in a single market of the freedom of establishment guaranteed by the Treaty. . . .

29. In addition, . . . the fact that a company does not conduct any business in the Member State in which it has its registered office and pursues its activities only in the Member State where its branch is established is not sufficient to prove the existence of abuse or fraudulent conduct which would entitle the latter Member State to deny that company the benefit of the provisions of Community law relating to the right of establishment.

30. Accordingly, the refusal of a Member State to register a branch of a company formed in accordance with the law of another Member State in which it has its registered office on the grounds that the branch is intended to enable the company to carry on all its economic activity in the host State, with the result that the secondary establishment escapes national rules on the provision for and the paying-up of a minimum capital, is incompatible with Articles 52 and 58 of the Treaty, in so far as it prevents any exercise of the right freely to set up a secondary establishment which Articles 52 and 58 are specifically intended to guarantee.

NOTES AND QUESTIONS

1. The *Centros* case referred to several articles of the Treaty of Rome. Article 43 (ex Article 52) provides in relevant part:

> [R]estrictions on the freedom of establishment of nationals of a Member State in the territory of another Member State shall be prohibited. Such prohibitions should also apply to restrictions on the setting-up of agencies, branches, or subsidiaries by nationals of any Member State established in the territory of any Member State.

Article 48 (ex Article 58) provides in relevant part that

> [C]ompanies or firms formed in accordance with the law of a Member State and having their registered office, central administration or principal place of business within the Community shall, for the purposes of this Chapter, be treated in the same way as natural persons who are nationals of Member States.

2. In *Centros,* how was it possible to override Danish authorities? The ECJ was careful to point out that measures may be taken by national authorities to protect creditors and to combat fraud. However, such measures will be scrutinized against

four requirements: They must (1) be applied in a non-discriminatory manner; (2) be justified by imperative requirements relating to the public interest; (3) be suitable for securing the attainment of their objective; and (4) not go beyond what is necessary.

NOTE ON PROTECTION OF INTELLECTUAL PROPERTY IN THE EU

Protection of intellectual property in the EU also benefits from the establishment of a single market. Through the EC Patent Convention concluded in 1975 and its implementing regulations, it is now possible to apply for and obtain patent protection throughout the EU area. Under EU trademark law (Commission Regulation 40/94, 1994 O.J. (L 11) 1), an applicant may now register a mark for the EU as a whole. In the field of copyright, EU directives and regulations have harmonized the laws of Member States concerning cable and satellite technology, computer software, e-commerce, and other matters. *See* Council Directive 92/100, 1992 O.J. (L 346) 61; Council Directive 93/83, 1993 O.J. (L 248) 15; Council Directive 96/9, 1996 O.J. (L 77) 20.

Legal questions concerning the interpretation of these directives and regulations will be referred to the ECJ. For example, in the case of *Lloyd Schuhfabrik Meyer v. Klijsen Handel,* Case C-342/97, [1999] E.C.R. 1-3819, the ECJ laid down EU law standards for determining whether there is confusion in a trademark matter:

> 22. In determining the distinctive character of a mark and, accordingly, in assessing whether it is highly distinctive, the national court must make an overall assessment of the greater or lesser capacity of the mark to identify the goods or services for which it has been registered as coming from a particular undertaking, and thus to distinguish those goods or services from those of other undertakings.
>
> 23. In making that assessment, account should be taken, in particular, of:
>
> - the inherent characteristics of the mark, including the fact that it does or does not contain an element descriptive of the goods or services for which it has been registered;
> - the market share held by the mark;
> - how intensive, geographically widespread and long-standing use of the mark has been;
> - the amount invested by the undertaking in promoting the mark;
> - the proportion of the relevant section of the public which, because of the mark, identifies the goods or services as originating from a particular undertaking; and
> - statements from chambers of commerce and industry or other trade and professional associations.
>
> 24. It follows that it is not possible to state in general terms, for example by referring to given percentages relating to the degree of recognition attained by the mark within the relevant section of the public, when a mark has a strong distinctive character.
>
> 25. In addition, the global appreciation of the likelihood of confusion must, as regards the visual, aural or conceptual similarity of the marks in question, be based on the overall impression created by them, bearing in mind, in particular, their distinctive and dominant components. [T]he perception of marks in the mind of the average consumer of the category of goods or services in question plays a decisive role in the global appreciation of the likelihood of confusion. The average consumer normally perceives a mark as a whole and does not proceed to analyse its various details.

26. For the purposes of that global appreciation, the average consumer of the category of products concerned is deemed to be reasonably well-informed and reasonably observant and circumspect. However, account should be taken of the fact that the average consumer only rarely has the chance to make a direct comparison between the different marks but must place his trust in the imperfect picture of them that he has kept in his mind. It should also be borne in mind that the average consumer's level of attention is likely to vary according to the category of goods or services in question.

27. In order to assess the degree of similarity between the marks concerned, the national court must determine the degree of visual, aural or conceptual similarity between them and, where appropriate, evaluate the importance to be attached to those different elements, taking account of the category of goods or services in question and the circumstances in which they are marketed.

4. Establishment in the EU

Once the decision is made to invest in the EU, many additional considerations will arise.

- Which EU Member State is the best place to do business?
- Should the investment be a branch office or a corporate or other business entity?
- Should the investment be in the form of a joint venture? If so, a good business partner will have to be found. If not a joint venture, then a wholly owned subsidiary company might be best.
- Should the investment be a new one ("Greenfield Investment"), or can an existing company be acquired as the core, at least, of the new business? If the decision is made to acquire an existing business, what form should the acquisition take — (1) a purchase of assets, (2) a purchase of stock, or (3) a merger. The latter would typically involve the formation of a shell company into which the acquired company can be merged under local law.

Keep these and other factors in mind as you read the following materials.

PROBLEM 6-10

Logos has narrowed its locations where it will establish its first foreign subsidiary in Europe to one of three countries, France, Germany, or England (the United Kingdom). Logos has asked your law firm to recommend which of these three jurisdictions it should choose. As previously mentioned, Logos is a privately held company and is not interested in a public ownership structure in Europe although Logos is open to forming a joint venture with a suitable partner. For example, Logos is considering as a potential partner an old-line UK company, Boats, PLC, with its headquarters in Newcastle Upon Tyne, and a line of beauty products and soaps that it markets throughout the UK through an established distribution network. Another potential partner is La Jeunesse, an up-and-coming Marseilles manufacturer, and Renata, a large, well-established Munich company. Logos is also open to the idea of acquiring a foreign company in France, Germany, or England. An acquisition will likely lead to the layoff of some workers of the acquired company.

Logos is owned by the Jackson family of Kansas City with the patriarch, James Sr., heading up a small group of his family members who form an inner management circle. James is known to be very shrewd but also somewhat eccentric. Although he "retired" many years ago and has no official title, he continues to run management meetings and is consulted on all important strategic decisions. One of James' most eccentric habits is that he often travels unannounced to the various subsidiaries of Logos around the United States and will stay for weeks at a time to review production and management. When some of these subsidiaries first complained to James Jr., the current CEO, James Jr. replied that he fully supports whatever his father wishes to do. James Sr. also cherishes the warm family-like atmosphere of his company and is viewed as a benevolent patriarch by Logos employees. He will often spend hours on the plant floor chatting with employees and will regularly treat a large group of employees and their families to a steak dinner. James has also always championed generous compensation and vacation packages for his employees who seem to be content and have had little interest in organizing a labor union or demanding a voice in management affairs.

The Jackson family would like to use the same flexible "approach" to management in Europe. In fact, James Sr. has already mentioned how much he is looking forward to spending time in his plants in Europe.

Where should the Jacksons establish their EU company? What about an acquisition?

What about setting up a European Company, which is a creature of EU law and not subject to the laws of any individual EU nation? Consult the three readings below, on business forms in France, Germany, and the United Kingdom and the accompanying notes.

James R. Silkenat & Jeffrey M. Aresty, Eds., The ABA Guide to International Business Negotiations at pp. 425-430, 447-455, 667-672 (American Bar Association 2000)

International Business Negotiations in France
Philippe Sarrailhé

THE LEGAL ENVIRONMENT

Unlike its Anglo-Saxon neighbors, France chose to adopt a Civil Code instead of the case law system that is the foundation of common law practice. The development of the civil law system followed from this decision. The system of choice of numerous countries, particularly countries influenced by France, civil law is based chiefly on a series of codes and bodies of rules that lay down the major principles interpreted in court decisions.

The civil law system offers the advantages of standardization and stability, whereas the common law system is characterized to a great extent by creativity and hence, uncertainty, resulting in the need for exhaustive negotiations. The disadvantage of standardization is the heavy burden of rules and regulations and government intervention that foreign negotiators find so surprising.

In France, the state exercises a determining influence on business and is sometimes an active party in negotiations (for instance, in connection with the extensive privatization programs which are still on-going).

Principal Relevant Laws and Regulations

Since the Civil Code is the fundamental basis for law in France, parties to negotiations may find it helpful to refer to the Civil Code, and in particular to its Title II, Contracts and Contractual Obligations in General; Title VI, Sales; and Title IX, the Company.

Business and Corporate Law. The Commercial Companies Law of July 24, 1966, establishes the bases for the rules and regulations governing the organization of companies in France. There are two types of companies: commercial and non-commercial (*sociétés commerciales* and *sociétés civiles*).

Commercial companies include partnerships (*sociétés de personnes*), which are characterized by a personal relationship and by unlimited liability of the partners, and stock companies (*sociétés de capitaux*), characterized by limited liability of the stockholders. The corporation (*société anonyme,* or S.A.) is the most common type of stock company. The limited liability company (*société a responsibilité limitée,* or SARL) combines features of the partnership and the stock company.

There is no restriction on direct French investments in other countries, and direct foreign investments in France. The only requirement is prior filing of a declaration that contains the information indicated below (authorization procedure). The investor must request an authorization from the Treasury Department (a division of the Ministry of Finance, the Economy, and the Budget). The declaration, in the French language, may be filed on a form supplied by the Treasury Department, but an ordinary letter is sufficient.

This authorization request, which is a condition precedent to the finalization of the investment, must contain the following information: description of the investor and of the company in which the investment is to be made (name, nationality, address); administrative, legal (including identification of the major shareholder of the investor), financial, economic, and technical information concerning both companies; a description of the terms and conditions of the investment; and a description of the reasons for the effects of the investment. Prior authorization by the Minister for the Economy is presumed to have been granted after a 30-day period has expired following the receipt of the declaration.

Employee-Rights Issues. Traditionally, French law has always been highly protective of employees' rights. The Labor Code provides that "If there is any change in the legal status of the employer, particularly through succession, sale, merger, transformation of the business, or conversion to a company, all employment contracts in effect on the date of the change shall remain in existence as between the new employer and the company personnel." Participants in the operation that do not wish to retain all employees must comply scrupulously with the dismissal procedure.

In an individual dismissal, the employer must base the decision on reasons having to do with the person or the employee or with the economic condition of the company. Regardless of the personal reasons for the dismissal, before making any decision the employer must schedule a meeting with the person concerned, by registered letter or by personally delivered letter. When the reconciliation phase produces no result, the employee may be dismissed, subject to certain conditions as to manner and time. In the case of dismissal for economic reasons, the procedure is considerably more cumbersome. The works council, which represents the employees, must be consulted in companies with more than 50 employees; conversion agreements must be implemented, and the appropriate government agency must be notified of the dismissal. The procedure is similar in the case of general layoffs.

The severance pay is the one established by law, by collective-bargaining agreement, or by the individual employment contract. In all cases, the indemnity may not be less than a legal minimum representing a sum calculated per year of employment. Unless otherwise agreed, the purchaser of the company must bear the cost of the dismissal.

The Labor Code also provides that "the works council [composed of employees] shall be informed and consulted on changes in the economic organization or legal status of the company," particularly in cases of merger, sale, major changes in production structures, acquisition or sale of subsidiaries, or investment. The works council must prepare a report indicating the grounds for its opinion. For this purpose it must furnished with specific written information, and must be accorded sufficient time (at least three days) to examine it. It must also be given a copy of the answer to its observations, with the grounds of the answer. The government requires two consultation procedures, one concerning the reorganization project, the other concerning the measures planned with respect to the employees.

The role of the works council is merely consultative: it has no veto power. However, hindrance of its operations, that is, the ignoring of the legal powers of the council and the resulting obligations of the employer carries criminal penalties of one year of imprisonment and/or a fine of 25,000 francs.

International Business Negotiations in Germany
Thomas O. Verhoeven

LEGAL ENVIRONMENT

Germany is a civil law country, where the main task of the courts can be described as interpretation of statutes by developing the purpose and meaning of the law. Case law is of growing importance, and the courts at the local level tend to follow the interpretation of the laws by the federal supreme courts or the courts of appeal, but there is still great freedom to decide and interpret independently.

MAJOR COMMERCIAL AND CORPORATE STATUTES

The Stock Corporation Law (*Aktiengesetz*, or AktG) governs the German stock corporation (*Aktiengesellschaft*), as well as the limited liability partnership on shares (*Kommanditgesellschaft auf Aktien*, or KgaA), which is a corporation on stock with fully liable general partners. In addition, the Stock Corporation law regulates affiliated enterprises and determines the level of liability among parent companies and subsidiaries.

The Limited Liability Company Law sets the rules for the *Gesellschaft mit beschränkter Haftung* (GmbH), which is a corporation similar to limited liability companies in other jurisdictions.

CORPORATE LEGAL ISSUES

The GmbH is very easy to establish, and only a minimum of formalities must be met. It has only two statutory bodies, namely, the shareholders' meeting and the managing directors, and a supervisory board need only be established if it has more than 500 employees. The stock corporation has a three-tier system including the stockholders' meeting, the management board, and the supervisory board. One of the major differences between a stock corporation and a GmbH is that a management board runs the stock corporation independently of the stock-holders, and the supervisory board is not allowed to give any kind of directions, but rather only to supervise management. This gives the management board of a stock corporation great power, although in practice majority shareholders and the supervisory board may exercise a high level of influence on the management board as well, but this is purchased with the risk of additional liabilities as described below. Because of this more lenient legal environment, GmbH's make up more than 90 percent of all German corporations. The statistics showed until recently only about 2,000 stock corporations, and only some of those are listed on the stock exchange.

The limitation of liability by using a stock corporation, a GmbH, or a GmbH & Co, KG is achieved in principle, but the "piercing of the corporate veil" has created some specific developments in German law. In 1985, the German Federal Supreme Court in Civil Matters (*Bundesgerichtshof,* or BGH) rendered a decision to the effect that a business entity that is running a corporation, not as a separate legal entity but merely as a branch, must assume that subsidiary's balance-sheet losses. This applies not only to parent companies and holding corporations, but also to businesspersons who are running separate businesses having one or more in the legal form of a corporation, so that the effect of this judgment may reach even the pocket of majority shareholders. The great uproar of criticism directed toward this and similar judgments by almost the whole judicial world in Germany and, of course, the business world, seems to have caused a reversion to retaining the limitation of liability for corporations. In a judgment in March 1993, the Court set additional, and to some extent new, standards when this kind of indirect piercing of the corporate veil takes place, namely, that the shareholder directs the subsidiary in a way that individual disadvantages and losses caused by such shareholders' direction cannot be indi-vidually determined. This movement is of great interest for international investment in Germany because American corporate structures with reporting systems differing from the management-to-management reporting system, but disregarding the separate legal entities along the lines of functional responsi-bilities, as well as the tendency to cash-pooling arrangements among affiliated enterprises, bear the risk of falling under the standards of the judgments, caus-ing full liability for balance-sheet losses of subsidiaries.

LABOR LAWS

The basic issues of German labor law are governed by the Civil Code, for example, employment contracts and their statutory notice periods. In addition, the German Law Against Unfair Dismissal (*Kündigungschutzgesetz*) and the Labor Management Relations Law (*Betriebsverfassungsgesetz*), which governs the establishment of works councils and their rights, the codetermination laws, working-hour laws, holiday laws, and so forth, are all federal laws.

The statutory notice period for salaried and for blue-collar employees is four weeks, becoming effective either on the 15th or at the end of a calendar month. By agreement, the statutory notice period can be shortened for the trial period to a minimum of two weeks. Such statutory notice periods are extended by law after two years of services with a notice period of one month to the end of a calendar month up to a notice period of seven months to the end of a calendar month for at least 24 years of service, but the services rendered before the age of 25 do not count. Especially in employment agreements for managers, such notice periods are often extended even longer. During the notice period, an employee can claim full salary, even if that employee has been relieved earlier from his or her duties. A termination without notice is only available if a so-called cogent reason exists, and then only within 14 days from the time the employer became aware of such a cogent reason. Since German constitutional law generally grants a "right to work," employees may claim such right to work until the settlement of a termination dispute by injunction of the labor court unless the interests of the employer to relieve employees earlier from their duties prevail.

The works council (if established by the employees) must be notified of each termination for its approval, and only after a period specifically determined in the law may the employer serve the notice to the employee, even if such approval has not been received. If the notification to the works council has not been made properly, the termination is null and void.

Any termination is valid only if it is socially justified within the meaning of Section 1 of the Law Against Unfair Dismissals. Every employee of a shop with more than five regular employees and with a service of more than six months can challenge a termination by filing a suit in the local labor court within three weeks. A termination is socially justified if motivated by good cause, either due to the performance or the behavior of the employee, or to business reasons. The burden of proof is with the employer. In the case of the business reasons, the employer must first terminate those employees with the lowest-ranking social protection and seniority. Handicapped employees can only validly be terminated after obtaining the consent of local authorities. The termination of a pregnant woman is null and void unless, within a very narrow scenario, the approval of local authorities has been given.

Mass dismissals must be notified to several labor authorities and impose some waiting periods. In addition, a social plan as part of a compromise of interests between employer and employees must be negotiated in enterprises where a works council exists. The social plan determines that amount of severance to be paid to the employees to be dismissed. If such an agreement cannot be reached between the employer and the works council, a mediation procedure applies.

International Business Negotiations
in the United Kingdom
John Davidson

The United Kingdom is principally a common law jurisdiction hence the process of negotiating, structuring, and documenting an international business transaction involving a U.K. party tends to be more familiar to U.S. companies and their legal advisors than might be the case in a continental European civil law jurisdiction. However, in business negotiations, as well as in many cultural areas, there is still force in the old saying that the United States and the United Kingdom remain two cultures (or two legal systems) divided by a common language, and it is important to appreciate some of the differences in U.K. assumptions, expectations, and practices before setting out on the cross-border acquisition trail or launching into a new international joint venture.

CORPORATE ORGANIZATION IN THE UNITED KINGDOM

PUBLIC AND PRIVATE COMPANIES

It is technically incorrect to refer to a "U.K. company." Companies registered under the Companies Act 1985 must be incorporated in England and Wales or in Scotland (or in Northern Ireland under the equivalent statutory provisions). Although the United Kingdom is by no means a federal system, the division of its legal systems into these separate jurisdictions will be familiar to U.S. business people used to dealing with companies incorporated in different U.S. states. Then, leaving aside some minor exceptions, companies in the United Kingdom are further categorized as public limited companies (or PLCs) and private limited companies (usually abbreviated to public and private companies, respectively). A public company is not necessarily a listed company, and may indeed be privately or even closely held, but is usually large and draws its working capital from the public (both as investing shareholders and as debenture-holding creditors). Private companies vary greatly in size, from local subsidiaries of multinationals to small, family-run "mom and pop" businesses.

The name of a public company must end with the words *public limited company* (although it may use the abbreviation PLC) and the name of a private company must end with the word *limited* (although it may use the abbreviation Ltd.), or the Welsh equivalents if the company's registered office is in Wales. Only public companies can apply for a listing on the London Stock Exchange or on the Alternative Investment Market, and only public companies can offer their shares to the public.

MANAGEMENT

U.K. companies are not required by law to appoint officers — president, treasurer, and secretary — as U.S. corporations typically are, although a U.K. company is required to have a secretary whose functions are broadly equivalent to those of the secretary of a U.S. company.

The directors of the company are charged with the management of its affairs. They are appointed by the shareholders (or *members* as they are referred to in the

Companies Act) of the company in accordance with the procedures laid down in the company's articles of association. In large, usually public, companies, an important distinction exists in practice between executive and nonexecutive directors. In legal terms, however, directors have the same fiduciary and other duties to the company whether they are executives or not.

The primary decision-making body in a U.K. company is the members in general meeting, to which certain matters are reserved either by statute or by the articles of association. However, the articles of association will almost invariably provide that the company's business is to be managed by the directors, who will exercise all the powers of the company. It is presumed by the law that in exercising their functions, the directors make collective decisions and are collectively responsible for those decisions. Specific delegations of power are often made to a managing director, whose role is such that he or she may often be regarded as a third organ of the company in addition to the shareholders and the board of directors. The larger the company, the more likely it will be that management functions are undertaken by a small class of executive directors and senior management employees.

DIRECTORS' DUTIES AND AUTHORITY

In principle, authority to exercise the powers of the company is vested in the board of directors, and express powers may be delegated to a managing director or other individual directors or senior managers. English law also recognizes the implied agency of a managing director in the general conduct of the affairs of the company, or of individuals such as a finance director in connection with financial responsibilities, as well as the concept of "apparent" or ostensible" authority, where a company has expressly or by implication held out a person having authority to bind the company. However, even where directors purport to negotiate and to sign documents "for and on behalf of" the company, it is not uncommon in major transactions for third parties to require some proof of specific board authority, for example, by the provision of a copy of the relevant board resolution certified by the company secretary.

AVAILABLE INFORMATION

English law prides itself on its extensive disclosure provisions. These aim to ensure that as much commercial information about the company as possible is publicly available without jeopardizing commercial confidences. The Companies Act requires all U.K. limited companies, whether public or private, to file certain documents with the registrar of companies and these documents are then available for public inspection. These include the company's constitution (that is, the memorandum of association and the articles of association, equivalent to the articles of incorporation and bylaws of a U.S. company); the company's annual audited financial statements (which include the profit and loss account and balance sheet, the directors' report, the auditors' report, and if the company has subsidiaries, consolidated group accounts); the company's annual return (which includes a statement of its directors, secretary, shareholders and respective shareholdings, the type of company, and its principal business activities); and details of any legal encumbrances created by the company over specified classes of its assets.

NOTE ON EMPLOYEE CO-DETERMINATION IN MANAGEMENT ISSUES

Like some other European countries, both France and Germany recognize the right of workers to participate in management. Participation in management can occur at either the plant level or the enterprise level. Both France and Germany recognize worker participation at the plant level in the form of works councils, consisting of employees, which have a right of co-determination with shareholders on a number of issues such as the formal conditions of work, including work hours, time, place and form of payment, and measures to prevent accidents. Works councils also have a right of co-determination on personnel issues that relate to layoffs, dismissals, and proposed organizational changes that may adversely affect workers.

Germany goes beyond France in recognizing co-determination rights at the enterprise level involving issues of the business management of the company itself. In Germany, workers participate in the management of the enterprise through representation on the supervisory board, a management body found in both the AG and the GmbH. Under Germany's various co-determination laws, workers have a potential voice in naming the managing directors, declaring dividends, and other strategic business decisions involving the enterprise. German unions have taken the position that they need to participate at the enterprise level on an equal level with shareholders. The Codetermination Act of 1976 greatly expanded the number of businesses that are potentially subject to the principle of parity co-determination. The 1976 act mandates the formation of a supervisory board composed of 50 percent shareholders and 50 percent employees or their representatives for each business organization regularly employing more than 2,000 members. For this reason, many companies in Germany have adopted the GmbH form, which is more flexible and allows management to limit the role of the supervisory board and have reorganized subsidiaries with limited workforces to fall outside the scope of the 1976 act. However, while there is some resistance to co-determination, German employers accept the principle in theory although they often disagree on whether workers should be entitled to "parity" in decision making and what constitutes "parity."

Unlike all other EU members, the United Kingdom refused to sign the Charter of the Fundamental Social Rights of Workers, commonly known as the Social Charter, promulgated in 1989 in the form of a non-legally binding declaration creating "moral obligations" to recognize certain workers' rights. One of the main factors that led the United Kingdom government to refuse to agree to the EU Social Charter is that it contained articles that established participation rights for workers. The UK has taken the position that worker participation in management issues should be a matter for industry to determine on a country-by-country basis. As a result, no legislation exists at the present in the UK that requires any degree of worker participation in the decision-making process of management.

NOTES AND QUESTIONS

1. Suppose, after carefully considering all options, the Logos Company has decided to set up a joint venture. An attraction of the joint venture for Logos is the expertise and experience of a European partner as well as the existing, ready-made distribution network. Joining forces with a European partner will also allow

the new joint venture company to undertake to market and establish its brand name and products throughout the EU.

What steps, decisions, and legal documents are necessary to form and operate the joint venture? Consider the following:

- A letter of intent or memorandum of understanding
- The Joint Venture Agreement
- A Shareholders' Agreement
- A Nondisclosure Agreement
- A Trademark Licensing Agreement

2. A key document will be the Joint Venture Agreement. This must be carefully considered, drafted, and tailored to the particular business operations. Some of the issues that must be addressed include

- Objectives
- Nature of the company or companies to be formed
- Capital and financing
- Percentage ownership shares of the parties
- Transfers of shares
- Minority rights clauses, quorums for voting, dividend policy, voting rights
- Management clauses covering membership on the board of directors and management policies and responsibilities
- Taxation
- General relationship issues (e.g., disclosure, representations, warranties, noncompetition promises)
- Dispute resolution and applicable law
- Deadlock and dissolution
- Duration and termination
- Due diligence and comfort letter requirements
- Intellectual property rights

3. *Societas Europaea.* Under Council Regulation 2157/2001, 2001 O.J. (L 294) 1, it is now possible to establish in the EU incorporating as a European Company or Societas Europaea (SE). The advantage is that an SE is a creature of EU law, not member state law, and its functioning will be largely determined by EU norms. An SE can be set up to function as a European holding company with subsidiaries as national law companies or subsidiary SE companies. Perhaps the greatest disadvantage is that an SE must comply with Council Directive 2001/86, 2001 O.J. (L 294) 22, which requires including workers of the company as members of the managing board.

If the Logos joint venture is successful in penetrating the entire EU market, it may be wise to form an SE or to employ the UK company as a holding company with subsidiary operating companies in various EU member states. An EU directive known as the Parent-Subsidiary Directive, Council Directive 90/435, 1990 O.J. (L 225) 6, eliminates withholding and double taxation and facilitates capital transfers between related corporations doing business in the EU.

What will be the tax consequences for Logos and its U.S. operations? Taxation is beyond the scope of this book, but generally speaking, while a U.S. corporation is taxed on its worldwide income, a foreign corporation is taxed on its taxable

income effectively connected with a U.S. trade or business. *See* I.R.C. §11 (2000).
Foreign source income may generally be shielded from U.S. tax through careful
planning, but Logos will not be able to avoid taxation on intercompany export
sales from its U.S. operations. Intercompany pricing is carefully regulated by the
Internal Revenue Service. *See* I.R.C. §482 (2000).

4. *EU Company Law Harmonization.* Logos must be aware that, under EC Treaty
Article 44(g), the EU has the authority to issue directives requiring the harmoni-
zation of the company law of the EU member states. This is an ongoing process.
Several directives have been issued and implemented by the EU member states.
Logos must realize that future directives from Brussels may have an impact on its
European business operations.

5. Competition Law Considerations

For U.S. and foreign companies operating in the EU, an important consideration is EU competition law as contained in the EC Treaty and associated
regulations and decisions.

PROBLEM 6-11

After several years, Logos has established several subsidiaries and a holding
company in Europe and all are doing well. At a week-long annual meeting of all of
the European managers held at the Jackson estate in Kansas City, James Jackson
Sr. gave a long speech after the closing dinner that was short on detail but long on
inspiration and pride. He discussed the virtues of collegiality, friendly relations,
and above all the need to be loyal to one's consumer base. Jackson also discussed
the virtues of leadership, loyalty, and the need to follow a well-established leader.
Several months after the meeting, each of the Logos European subsidiaries
increased their sales in their home markets but their export sales into neighboring
EU markets declined. All of the prices of Logos products are also within 5 percent
of the U.S. sales price converted into local currency. Are there any competition law
issues involved? Is Logos U.S.A. subject to EU competition law for any of its
actions? Consult the readings below.

James Hanlon, European Community
Law, 260-265 (2003)

(i)   Article 81 [ex 85] restricts trading agreements between otherwise inde-
       pendent business undertakings which may affect trade between Member
       States and which distort competition within the common market.
(ii) Article 82 [ex 86] restricts the abuse of a dominant market position by
       large undertakings.
(iii) Regulation 4064/89 attempts to control mergers of undertakings which
       may result in the abuse of a dominant position.

The main piece of secondary legislation is Regulation 17/62. It is important,
at this point, to know that it is the Commission which has the task of ensuring that

competition in the Community is not distorted by companies making their own agreements which might be obstacles to trade.

DECISIONS BY ASSOCIATIONS OF UNDERTAKINGS

The most usual type of "association" covered by Article 81(1) [ex 85(1)] is the trade association. In *Vereringing van Cementhandelmen v. Commission* (8/72) the Court of Justice held that a non-binding recommendation made by a trade association may amount to a decision. If compliance with the recommendation by the undertaking to which it is addressed has an appreciable influence in the market then that recommendation will amount to a decision. In *AROW v. BNlC* ([1982] O.J. L379/1) the Bureau National Interprofessional de Cognac had fixed a minimum distribution price for cognac, arguing that this was necessary to guarantee quality. The Commission decided that this argument could not be sustained, as there were other quality control measures in the cognac industry.

CONCERTED PRACTICES

Once again, this term has been widely interpreted. The term means some kind of co-ordinated action which, although it may fall short of an agreement, knowingly substitutes practical cooperation for competition. In *ICI v. Commission (Dyestuffs)* (48/69), ICI was the first of a number of businesses to raise the price of aniline dye in Italy. Other producers of this product, accounting for 85 percent of the market quickly followed this rise. A similar pattern of price increases had occurred previously. The companies argued that the price co-ordination was simply a reflection of parallel behaviour in an oligopolistic market, where each producer followed the leader. When the matter came before the Court of Justice the Commission was able to demonstrate collusion. Four of the parent companies had sent telex messages indicating price rises to their subsidiaries within an hour of each other, and each message was similarly worded. This had happened on more than one occasion. The Court of Justice held that this behaviour amounted to a "concerted practice" arising out of co-ordination.

PREVENTION, RESTRICTION OR DISTORTION OF COMPETITION

The major point of European law is to prevent an altering or distortion of the competitive balance between undertakings. This distinction of competition is most clearly seen in horizontal agreements, that is an agreement between undertakings on the same level, *e.g.* two producers or two distributors who agree to the same price rise or agree to give each other exclusive rights in specific natural territories. It is relatively easy to see that these agreements partition what should be a single market. It is also easy to see that trade is affected and consumers are denied the benefit of competitive producers from other Member States. However, a vertical agreement, that is one between a manufacturer and a distributor may be more difficult to determine as inimical to competition. Indeed, some vertical agreements can work to a consumer's advantage.

This issue of vertical agreements was examined by the Court of Justice in the important case of *Consten and Grundig v. Commission* (56/64). The German manufacturer of electronic goods, Grundig, entered into an exclusive dealing agreement with Consten, a French distributor. By the agreement, Consten had the sole right to distribute Grundig products in France, and also had the exclusive rights to use Grundig's trademark (GINT) in France. In return, Consten agreed not to re-export Grundig products to any other Member State, effectively banning parallel imports and exports. However, another French distributor, UNEF, bought Grundig products in Germany, and sold them in France, at a lower price than Consten. Because of this, Consten brought an action against UNEF in the French court for infringement of the trademark. However, UNEF applied to the Commission who held that the Grundig/Consten agreement contravened Article 81(1) [ex 85(1)]. The argument found its way to the Court of Justice. The Court found that the agreement did contravene Article 81(1) [ex 85(1)]:

"... the contract between Grundig and Consten, on the one hand by preventing undertakings other than Consten from importing Grundig products into France, and on the other hand by prohibiting Consten from re-exporting those products to other countries of the common market, indisputably affects trade between Member States."

WITHIN THE EUROPEAN COMMUNITY

It would seem to be logical to suggest that Community law had no jurisdiction outside the boundaries of the Member States of the Community. However, this is not the case with European competition law. Competition law is founded on an *effects doctrine*, and if the effects of an agreement, wherever made, are felt within the Community then the agreements are within the scope of Article 81 [ex 85]. In the *Aniline Dye* case four of the parties were established outside the Community. As the effects of their concerted practices were felt within the Community the Court of Justice found them liable for infringements of Article 81(1) [ex 85(1)].

This issue was decided definitively in *Ahlstrom v. Commission (Wood Pulp)* (89, 104, 114, 116, 117, 125-129/85). None of the wood pulp producers in this case was established in a Member State of the Community. Nevertheless, they supplied two-thirds of the wood pulp in the common market. The Court of Justice held that the undertakings had been in breach of Article 81(1) [ex 85(1)]. The key factor, according to the Court, was the place where the agreement or concerted practice was *implemented*.

THE LIST OF AGREEMENTS LIKELY TO BREACH ARTICLE 81(1) [EX 85(1)]

Article 81(1) [ex 85(1)] contains a list, paras (a)-(e), of the kinds of agreement which will be prohibited. This list is not exhaustive and provides no more than a guide to the sort of agreements that will fall foul of the prohibition. The examples include the following:

- price fixing;
- control of production markets or technical developments;

- exclusive distribution agreements;
- franchise agreements.

If they are found to be in breach of Article 81(1) [ex 85(1)] they are, by virtue of Article 81(2) [ex 85(2)], automatically void. This means that they cannot be enforced in law, or used as a defence before a national court. It should be remembered though, that even if an agreement is in breach of Article 81(1) [ex 85(1)] it may be granted exemption by the Commission under Article 81(3) [ex 85(3)].

EXEMPTIONS FROM ARTICLE 81(1) [EX 85(1)]

The main exemptions are set out in Article 81(3) [ex 85(3)] which provides that Article 81(1) [ex 85(1)] does not apply to any agreement or category of agreement between undertakings, or any decision or category of decisions by associations of undertakings which contribute to improving the production or distribution of goods or to promoting technical or economic progress, while allowing consumers a fair share of the resulting benefits, provided the agreement does not:

(a) impose on the undertaking concerned restrictions which are not indispensable to the attainment of these objectives;

(b) afford such undertakings the possibility of eliminating competition in respect of a substantial part of the products in question.

To obtain an individual exemption the party must apply to the Commission. The procedure is set out in Regulation 17/62L. Article 4(1) of the Regulation provides that full notification of the agreement must be given to the Commission. This is the only method by which exemption can be granted. By Article 19(1) of the Regulation, all parties to the agreement have the right to be heard, and any third party also has such a right if they can establish "sufficient interest". This could mean that a competitor, who might be affected by an agreement, could put their case to the Commission. The decision to grant exemption must be published in the Official Journal.

A careful reading of Article 81(3) [ex 85(3)] will indicate that there are four conditions to be satisfied before an exemption may be granted under Article 81(3) [ex 85(3)]; two of them are positive, two are negative. The two positive conditions are that an agreement must contribute to improving the production or distribution of goods or to promoting technical or economic progress and the agreement must allow consumers a fair share of the resulting benefit. The negative conditions are that there must be no unnecessary restrictions, and there must be no elimination of competition.

The formal process by which the Commission has avoided the necessity of a long involved investigation before issuing an individual exemption is the practice of issuing a "block exemption". This process came about because of the burden placed on the Commission by the large number of applications for individual exemptions. The delays caused obvious difficulties for business and the Commission has increasingly relied on its powers to issue block exemptions. A series of regulations has been issued in areas where agreements are generally beneficial rather than anti-competitive. The advantage of the block exemption process is that the undertakings can make their own assessment as to whether or not their agreement falls within a particular block exemption. Indeed, they can tailor the terms of their agreement so that their agreement matches the terms set out in the block exemption. If an agreement marches the terms of the block exemption there is no need for the agreement to be notified to the Commission. Block exemptions have been issued in the following categories:

(a) exclusive distribution;
(b) exclusive purchasing;
(c) specialisation;
(d) research and development;
(e) motor vehicle distribution;
(f) franchising.

Each block exemption contains its own individual rules, which must be satisfied in every respect. Each of the exemptions contains "white" clauses. These are clauses that are specifically permitted. There are also "black" clauses. These are clauses that are expressly forbidden because they would restrict or distort competition. Any agreement which contained a "black" clause would be outside the scope of a block agreement.

NOTE ON THE EXTRATERRITORIAL APPLICATION OF EU COMPETITION LAW

For many years, the European Court of Justice used the "economic entity" theory to found jurisdiction over foreign companies. The economic entity theory asserts jurisdiction on the basis that a company doing business in the EU may be a part of the same economic enterprise as a foreign company even though they are legally separate entities. *See, e.g., ICI v. Commission,* [1972] E.C.R. 619.

A new basis for extraterritorial jurisdiction was announced, however, in the *Wood Pulp* case, *Ahlstrom v. Commission,* [1988] E.C.R. 5193. This case involved Kraft Export Association, a U.S. membership cartel of wood pulp producers benefiting from antitrust immunity under the U.S. Webb Pomerene Act of 1918. The ECJ upheld the commission's application of Article 85 (now Article 81) of the Treaty of Rome, stating: "The decisive factor [in this case] is . . . the place where [a price fixing undertaking] is implemented. The producers in this case implemented their pricing agreement within the common market. It is immaterial in that respect whether or not they had recourse to subsidiaries, agents, sub-agents, or branches within the Community in order to make their contacts within the Community." Compare this holding to the statement by the U.S. Supreme Court in *Hartford Fire Ins. Co. v. California,* 509 U.S. 764, 796 (1993) that "it is well established . . . that the Sherman Act applies to foreign conduct that was meant to produce and did in fact produce some substantial effect in the United States."

On the basis of the *Wood Pulp* case, the commission has asserted jurisdiction over U.S. companies, not only under Article 81, but also under the Merger Regulation (Council Regulation 4064/89, 1989 O.J. (L 395) 1) and Article 82. For example, in *Boeing/McDonnell Douglas v. Commission,* Case IV/M, 1997 O.J. (L 336) 16, the Merger Regulation was applied to prohibit Boeing from enforcing exclusive arrangements to sell aircraft to several airlines and from leveraging its relationships with suppliers to pressure the suppliers into giving Boeing preferential treating and into refusing to deal with Boeing's competitors.

In 2004, the European Commission acted to block General Electric's $43 billion acquisition of Honeywell. The commission's case, which is on appeal to the ECJ, is based on the theory that GE would be able to shut out competitors by bundling its aircraft engines with Honeywell's in-flight electronic systems.

In May 2004, the commission also objected to a proposed deal between Japan's Sony Corp. and Germany's Bertelsmann, AG, a 50-50 joint venture to be called Sony BMG, on the basis that the deal might "create or strengthen a collective dominant position in the world music market." The joint venture would hold about 25 percent of the global music market and would be the second ranking entity behind only Universal Music Group, a U.S. company. The deal was later approved only after the parties accepted conditions recommended by the commission.

In March 2004, the commission levied a $600 million fine on Microsoft Corporation, accusing it of abusing a dominant position in the EU. Abuse of a dominant position under Article 82 depends on a finding that an enterprise is dominant in the "relevant market," which can be a product market, a geographical market, or a temporal market. *See Commission Decision of 24 March 2004 Relating to a Proceeding Under Article 82 of the EC Treaty*, Case Comp/C-3/37.792. The latter term refers to the time during which supply conditions are uniform; therefore, dominance may occur in temporary or seasonal markets. Dominance is the power to behave to an appreciable extent independently of competitors, customers, and consumers. *See United Brands Co. v. Commission,* [1978] E.C.R. 207. The idea of abuse is flexible; it can include both exploitative and anticompetitive conduct. The commission also ruled that Microsoft must begin offering in the EU market versions of its Windows operating system without the media player software (which displays video and sound) and must also disclose complete and accurate data on Windows to allow work-group servers — computers that control office networks — to be fully compatible with Windows computers on the desks of network customers. Microsoft is appealing this ruling to the ECJ.

The European Commission decision is similar to the remedy sought by several states and by Microsoft competitors in the case brought by the U.S. Department of Justice in 1998. The solution adopted in the settlement of that case, which was approved by the court, was to require Microsoft to allow masking of access to Microsoft programs bundled with Windows, though consumers are free to turn them back on. Is there any problem with inconsistent decisions by regulators in the United States and the EU? In 1998, the United States and the EU signed an agreement to share information and to cooperate on competition matters. *See* 37 I.L.M. 1070 (1998).

C. Foreign Direct Investment in China

We move now to a consideration of FDI in China. Keep in mind as you review these materials that although many FDI issues in China are unique there are some issues common to FDI in other developing countries in Asia and elsewhere: Different goals and expectations of the foreign investor and its local joint venture partner, conflicts in management styles and approaches and the need to resolve them, labor issues involving local employees, and the need to protect intellectual property rights in the FDI project from theft and misappropriation.

Japanese Capital and Jobs Flow into China
New York Times, p. C1 (Feb. 17, 2004)

The qualms are gone. Now even Japan's pride and joy, its top-end electronics manufacturers, are coming to China. They are building immense new plants and research centers here to take advantage of abundant Chinese labor, doing nearly every kind of job their Japanese work force does. Cost pressures are driving them to forget old fears of having their best technology stolen or of harsh publicity at home from moving high-paying jobs out of the country.

"We hesitated in the past, but we cannot say that any more," said Hiroyuki Mineta, chairman of the Pioneer Corporation's Shanghai subsidiary, as he stood on the factory floor where hundreds of Chinese workers were building 11 types of DVD recorders. "We have to overcome our fear or we won't be able to survive in the market."

"Our top management is afraid of exporting brain jobs to China," Mr. Matsuo said. "But comparing Chinese and Japanese engineers on a cost-performance basis, Chinese are superior. They are hungrier. Most Japanese are no longer hungry." For a Japanese manager to say such a thing would have been unthinkable a few years ago. The Japanese electronics giants have for decades been national symbols of know-how and corporate might, with globally famous brands, well-paid work forces and sales in the billions. "Japanese manufacturers are only doing what's rational" by moving to China, said Masaki Yabuuchi, who tracks Japanese manufacturers in Asia for the external trade organization.

The interweaving of East Asia's two giants shows no sign of slowing. At the back of Pioneer's factory, Mr. Mineta takes visitors to the loading docks. From there, beyond the parking lot filled with hundreds of workers' bicycles, the view is of flat, mud-caked fields and a few rough-hewn huts that seem lost in time. For now, farmers still work that land, but Pioneer has an option to lease it and nearly double its production space. Though headquarters has not given a final go-ahead, Mr. Mineta said it was only a matter of time. "We want to expand as quickly as possible," he said.

NOTES AND QUESTIONS

1. A word of caution: The optimism of the report above needs be tempered with an awareness that foreign investors continue to confront formidable and intimidating challenges in doing business in China. Among the most serious are concerns about the theft of intellectual property as we will detail in Chapter 7.

2. According to some estimates, China is on track to have the largest economy in the world early in the first decades of the twenty-first century. Japan currently has the second largest economy in the world and is deepening its economic integration with China begun in the 1990s even though Japan and China were bitter enemies for long stretches during the twentieth century. A similar process of economic integration has been long underway between Taiwan, itself an economic power, and China for over a decade. In 1997, Hong Kong, the bastion of unbridled capitalism on China's front door step under British rule for a century and a half, was returned to Chinese sovereignty and was promised autonomy to run its own affairs. These developments signal a rising role and perhaps, for the first time in modern history, a leadership role for Asia in the world economy during the twenty-first century.

3. Because of China's growing economic power and its role in Asia, many U.S. foreign policy experts believe that the relationship between the United States and China will be the most important country-to-country relationship in the twenty-first century.

4. Do the economic developments in Asia pose a threat for U.S. businesses? An opportunity?

1. *China's Economic System*

As China's economic and social system may be unfamiliar to you, we first introduce the Chinese economic system and the background environment for FDI.

Daniel C.K. Chow, The Legal System of the People's Republic of China in a Nutshell, 20-34 (2003)

[1.] CHINA'S ECONOMY, 1949-78

Although never subject to the type of overwhelming central control exercised by such countries as the Soviet Union, the economy of the [People's Republic of China or] PRC for most of the period since its founding until economic reforms begun in 1978 was a command economy. Under this system, the state owned all property and all enterprises were essentially administrative units of the state. The state received all revenues from industrial and agricultural enterprises, redistributed revenues in accordance with state goals, and subsidized or absorbed all losses. Production targets for all enterprises were set in accordance with a five-year economic plan promulgated by the State Council, the executive arm of the PRC government. The plans set forth production quotas for commodities, set prices for products, and allocated products for distribution. Although economic reforms have relaxed state control over the economy and China no longer sets production quotas for as many sectors of the economy, China still continues to use state sponsored economic plans. China is now in the midst of its Tenth Five Year Plan covering 2001-2006.

A. THE COLLECTIVIZATION OF AGRICULTURE

Early in its history, from 1953-54, the PRC implemented a system of collectivization of agriculture in which private ownership of farmland and crops was abolished. The state confiscated lands owned by landlords, many of who were killed in the process, and redistributed the lands to large collectives of workers who farmed the land communally. By the 1960s, the collectives were reorganized into massive communes with responsibility for meeting government quotas set forth in the state sponsored five-year economic plans.

All crops grown and harvested by agricultural communes were sold to the state at government fixed prices. Government units then distributed revenues to the individual workers of the communes in accordance with a set of guidelines that awarded workers a number of work points for their daily work. In many cases, workers would accumulate the same number of work points whether they worked industriously or not, creating little incentive for effective performance. Many of these communes were massive in size. For example, on the eve of reforms in 1978 that would dismantle the collective system of agriculture, Guangdong province's

9.2 million farm families were organized into approximately 2,000 communes, each containing 46,000 farm families.

B. INDUSTRY AND THE STATE ENTERPRISE SYSTEM

In the industrial sector, the foundation of China's pre-reform economy was the state-owned enterprise system. A state-owned enterprise (SOE) is owned by the state as opposed to any private entity, individual, or group of individuals. An SOE was expected to meet state production targets, to turn over all of its revenues to the state, and to have all of its losses subsidized or absorbed by the state. The state also controlled all of the enterprise's business and management functions including matters that fell within the business scope of the firm. While many governments, including the United States, regulate enterprise matters that affect the public interest, pre-reform China went far beyond this limited scope of government regulation and exerted control over all matters of the firm, including business strategies, marketing, distribution, and sales. Because the state also owned the enterprise, the state served both as regulator and entrepreneur in many cases.

SOEs were subject to the control and supervision of government departments at all levels. For example, a local chemicals factory would report to the local bureau of light industry, which would have supervisory authority over all enterprises engaged in the light industry sectors. Because of a massive and complex bureaucracy, however, complicated lines of authority resulted in a number of government bureaus exerting some control over the enterprise. For example, the planning departments at all levels of government determined how much capital investment was required for enterprises. The economic and trade committees determined the use of technology by enterprises in their operations. Labor and financial departments determined wages of employees. No single government bureau was completely responsible for all facets of the operations of the enterprise, but rather many entities had uncoordinated input into the management of the enterprise. This chaotic supervisory structure resulted in enterprises that were inefficiently managed and performed poorly. For most of the history of the PRC, SOEs have operated with chronic losses even during the period since economic reforms began in 1978 and even though the overall economy of the PRC has grown consistently during this same period.

Since 1949, the state sector has played a major role in the PRC industrial economy. Prior to economic reform, the percentage of China's industrial output from SOEs stood at 83%. Since reforms in 1978, the state sector has experienced a diminishing role. By 1994, SOEs accounted for 38% of industrial output. The state sector rebounded to account for 48.3% of industrial output in 2000. These figures reflect a growing role for private enterprises, in which foreign investment plays a major role, in China's changing economy. A shift in production also reflects attempts by the PRC to reform the state sector and its continuing losses. Despite the diminishing role of the state sector, China's rulers claim that the SOEs will continue to be the mainstay of China's economy. The continuing reform of the state sector remains one of China's most significant challenges in the years ahead.

C. SOCIAL WELFARE FUNCTIONS OF SOES

A primary reason for the inefficiency of SOEs is their social welfare role. Prior to reform, workers in SOEs found their professional, personal, and family lives to be inseparable and that all revolved around the work unit. Social services that are provided by the private sector or government social welfare agencies in the United States were all provided by the work unit in pre-reform China. SOEs not only provided employment, but also housing, schooling, medical care, and pension benefits. In a typical case, an SOE worker would live in a dormitory or housing provided by the SOE, work in the adjacent SOE factory or plant, send his children to the nearby school operated by the SOE, shop at the nearby markets owned by the SOE, visit the doctor at the nearby SOE hospital, watch movies at a theater operated by the SOE, and receive pension benefits supplied by the SOE upon retirement. Workers' personal lives became inseparable from their professional lives. For example, a worker was expected to seek permission from supervisors for marriage and other personal decisions. Seeking permission from the work unit supervisors was required because marriage meant that the new spouse and any children would create additional demands for employment, housing, and other services. The SOE work unit came to be viewed as a social net that provided its employees with a basic level of guaranteed social services. Typically, an SOE would not discharge workers for unsatisfactory work, and all workers received a common salary regardless of performance.

The role of the SOE as a provider of social welfare services meant that there was constant pressure to absorb more workers and their families. Some SOEs are the size of the world's largest multi-national enterprises. For example, the Capital Iron and Steel Corporation in western Beijing employs approximately 150,000 workers, more than most of the largest private companies in the world. Some SOEs have compounds that resemble small towns. The Wuhan Iron & Steel Corporation was considered to be a "company run society" and was known as "Red Steel Town." As many as one-third or more of SOE workers were redundant.

Given the social welfare role of SOEs, the main goals of such enterprises were not profits, efficiency, and productivity. When an enterprise lost money or faced bankruptcy, the state would intervene and grant it another subsidy or exemption because failure of the SOE would result in significant social costs. While this system served important social welfare goals, the inefficient and poorly managed state sector resulted in the bulk of China's economy operating at a loss, a situation that needed to be remedied if China was to step into the modern industrial age.

[2.] China's Reforms, 1978

With Mao's death marking the end of the Cultural Revolution in 1976, the Chinese Communist Party (CPC) turned its attention to rebuilding the nation's long neglected economy. Party elders were shocked and embarrassed by China's backwardness and poverty by comparison to some of its Asian neighbors such as Hong Kong and Japan. In 1978, the CPC, under the leadership of Deng Xiaoping, announced that the focus of its work would shift from class struggle to economic development.

To implement this shift, the CPC endorsed the development of some free markets and a limited role for private enterprise within an overall framework of socialism, creating a mixed economic system. This shift represented a relaxation of the command economy approach of the PRC that had been in place for most of the period since 1949. Under China's reforms, the private sector is viewed as an adjunct or complement to the state sector, which remains dominant, despite its many problems. Some free markets and some private ownership of wealth will be developed, but the economy will continue to be state-owned and controlled. Consistent with Marxist-Leninist principles, the state will continue to own all real property and the means of production.

China's policy is to create a socialist market economy, as distinguished from a market economy based upon liberal capitalism, such as that of the United States, which contemplates private ownership of property and the means of production. As long as China's political commitment to socialism remains firm, there will be limits on the private ownership of wealth and the state sector will continue to be a dominant portion of the economy. For example, complete privatization of most state-owned enterprises will not be an option under the present approach. The state continues to own SOEs — in principle at least. In the view of China's rulers, the nation is undergoing economic, not political, reform.

A. REFORMS IN THE AGRICULTURAL SECTOR

The 1978 reforms met with immediate and dramatic success in the agricultural sector. While the collectivization of agriculture was trumpeted with great fanfare, the dismantling of the system was done quietly and unobtrusively. In addition to disbanding the communes, the reforms instituted a basic shift in responsibility within the production system. Under the new system, responsibility for meeting production quotas was shifted from the massive commune organizations down to the family household unit. Once households met the assigned government quotas, they were free to sell any excess product at market prices and to keep the proceeds. In another major shift, fixed government quotas were gradually replaced by contracts between the state and local collectives, composed of individual households. The collectives in turn contracted with household units. These seemingly minor changes created a basic change in incentives. Farming households now had incentive to maximize production because they were allowed to keep revenues above certain levels. Under the old system of assigning work points, hard work or indolence was rewarded in the same way. The new household responsibility system was immediately popular with farming households and agricultural production soared in the years after the reforms.

B. REFORMS IN THE STATE SECTOR

By contrast with reforms in the agricultural sector, effective reform of the state sector has been difficult to achieve and continues to be one of China's most significant challenges. Reforms have reflected two policy goals. First, China enacted legislation early in the reform era that granted SOEs independent legal status and the right to make their own managerial decisions. Subsequent legislation provided greater details about the types of decision-making authority that state-owned enterprises would enjoy, including greater independence to import and export, make investment and production decisions, hire and manage workers, and set prices and wages. This shift represented an attempt to protect SOEs from government intrusion into their business operations that would hamper their efficient operation.

Second, these reforms also attempted to wean SOEs from dependence upon state subsidies. For example, one fundamental change of the reform movement is that government funds are no longer given as free capital grants or investment subsidies, but are now treated as low-interest bank loans. SOEs are required to pay charges on their fixed assets and working capital. Equally important, SOEs are no longer eligible in principle to be rescued by state subsidies in the event of losses. In theory, SOEs are now in principle fully responsible for their own profits and losses. To create further incentives for enterprises to improve their economic performance, the reformers also enacted the Enterprise Bankruptcy Law (1986), requiring chronically mismanaged and inefficient enterprises to be closed down.

One of the obstacles faced by reformers in the state sector are the broader social and political consequences of reform. As previously discussed, state-owned enterprises create a system of integrated social welfare institutions. Any reform of the enterprise system will affect the delivery of essential social services to industrial workers. Under this system, China cannot simply announce that SOEs will now be governed by principles of profit and loss and that unprofitable enterprises will be closed under the Bankruptcy Law. Closing an unprofitable enterprise will not only result in the loss of employment for workers, many of whom will be unable to find new jobs, but will also result in a family catastrophe. The family loses housing, medical care, and schooling upon separation from the SOE. The costs of unemployment can be so severe that desperate workers use threats, demonstrations, and even violence against managers to avoid losing their jobs. Effective reform of the state sector involves creating alternative means for providing social services for the employable industrial worker as well as for the unemployable and redundant workers for whom the state-owned enterprise has traditionally served as a caretaker. These are fundamental long-term reforms.

Some of China's reforms in the state sector have been bold. One reform involves restructuring state enterprises using international capitalist models of the corporate form. Recent legislation now allows for the "corporatization" of state-owned enterprises, which involves the reorganization of the SOE as a stock corporation, with the stock of some companies trading on public stock exchanges. The state maintains a controlling interest by owning a majority of the shares once the enterprise has been reorganized into a stock corporation. Other reforms include reorganizing and merging state-owned enterprises into mega-enterprise conglomerates. Not long ago, the very notion of state enterprises as corporations with stock openly traded on public stock exchanges and available for private ownership would have been regarded by China's leaders as repugnant to socialism. These new directions indicate China's willingness to experiment and its receptivity to western corporate and business law concepts.

Other sweeping changes are underway. In recent years China has been able to create a substantial private housing market and has now largely removed cost-free housing as a benefit of the SOE. The booming construction of high-rise apartment buildings in the teeming cities of Shanghai and Guangzhou serve as a testament to the new private housing industry. Efforts are under way to establish an independent social welfare system in order to decrease the social welfare role of SOEs so that they can be further subjected to the pressures of the competitive marketplace. Re-employment centers have been established to help retrain and find new jobs for workers who have been terminated from SOEs undergoing reform. Basic pension programs and general health care programs are all in the process of being established outside of the SOE system.

Despite more than a decade of reforms, however, effective reforms have been difficult to achieve because of the complex and interrelated issues involved in reforming this fundamental sector of the economy, which continues to operate with chronic losses. New and even greater challenges may await this sector with

China's entry into the WTO, as China will need to open protected areas of industry to international competition.

[3.] CHINA'S ECONOMY SINCE 1978

Since economic reforms began in 1978, China has achieved unprecedented economic growth for an economy of its size. From 1978-97, China experienced an average annual GDP growth rate of 9.8%. Despite the recent economic retrenchment in Asia, China has reported an average annual growth rate of 7.5% for 1999-2001 and a 7.6% growth rate in 2002. In 1997, China had the seventh largest economy in the world measured by GDP with $1.05 trillion and is only slightly behind Italy, France, and the United Kingdom. Given present trends, China will become the third largest economy in the world behind the United States and Japan early in the twenty-first century. This will stand as a remarkable achievement for a nation that was mired in poverty and backwardness and caught in upheaval and turmoil for the bulk of the twentieth century.

GDP of Top Ten Countries

Country	1980 US$m	Rank	1985 US$m	Rank	1990 US$m	Rank	1995 US$m	Rank	1997 US$m	Rank
USA	2,587,100	1	3,946,600	1	5,392,200	1	6,952,020	1	7,690,100	1
Japan	1,039,980	2	1,327,900	2	2,942,890	2	5,108,540	2	4,772,300	2
Germany	819,140	3	624,970	3	1,488,210	3	2,415,764	3	2,319,500	3
France	651,890	4	510,320	4	1,190,780	4	1,536,089	4	1,526,600	4
U.K.	522,850	5	454,300	5	975,150	6	1,105,822	5	1,220,200	5
Italy	393,950	6	358,670	6	1,090,750	5	1,086,932	6	1,155,400	6
Canada	253,350	7	346,030	7	570,150	7	568,928	9	583,900	9
China	252,230	8	265,530	8	364,900	10	697,647	7	1,055,400	7
Brazil	237,930	9	188,250	9	414,060	9	688,085	8	773,400	8
Spain	198,320	10	164,250	11	491,240	8	558,617	10	570,100	10
Mexico	166,700	11	177,360	10	237,750	13	250,038	13	348,600	16

Source: PRC State Council Research and Development Center.

In foreign trade, China has been able to become a world leader in the span of just two decades. China's foreign trade rose from twenty-seventh in the world with $20.6 billion in 1978 to sixth in the world in 2001 at $510 billion, an increase of almost 25 fold. China now has the second largest foreign currency reserves in the world behind only Japan, with reserves increasing from $167 million in 1978 to $250 billion in 2001.

A. THE ROLE OF FOREIGN INVESTMENT IN CHINA'S DEVELOPMENT

The pace of foreign investment has increased dramatically within the past decade and has played a major role in the nation's rising economy. Ninety percent of China's foreign investment has occurred since 1992 when Deng Xiaoping's southern tour of China helped to propel his reform policies forward. Since 1992, China has been the world's second largest recipient of foreign capital

behind the United States with foreign investment reaching $47 billion in 2001 up from an average of $11.7 billion during 1985-1995. Foreign direct investment in China accounted for 23% of all FDI in developing countries in 2001.

Foreign investment enterprises, such as joint ventures and wholly foreign-owned enterprises, have now assumed a major role in China's economy. According to China's most recent official statistics, foreign investment enterprises accounted for approximately one-fifth of all of China's industrial output and for 13% ($12 billion) of all annual tax revenues in the industrial and commercial sector and are one of the fastest growing sources of tax revenue for the PRC government. At present there are 145,000 foreign investment enterprises in operation employing 18 million people or approximately 10% of the entire non-rural labor population. There are now approximately 200 multi-national enterprises with foreign investments in China, including seventeen of Japan's largest companies, and nine out of ten of Germany's largest companies. Some of the largest companies in the United States, such as Coca-Cola, General Motors, General Electric, McDonald's, Motorola, Boeing, and Procter & Gamble, all have sizeable business operations in China.

NOTES AND QUESTIONS

1. While private enterprises in China are starting to became a more important part of the economy, for the most part the largest and most powerful companies in the most critical industrial sectors continue to be state-owned enterprises. Critical sectors of the PRC economy (e.g., steel, gas, electricity, telecommunications, automotive) are all controlled by state-owned enterprises. For most MNEs investing in joint ventures in China, from General Motors to Procter & Gamble, there is little choice but to partner with a state-owned enterprise as they are the only business entities with the resources and capacity necessary for the joint venture project.

2. Prior to economic reforms, most state-owned enterprises were not primarily concerned with profits and losses. Why not?

3. In most state-owned enterprises, there are many "redundant workers," that is, many more workers than are necessary to operate the SOE at full efficiency. In a typical SOE, up to a third or more of all workers are redundant. Why? Why would a worker in an SOE need to seek permission from the work unit for personal decisions such as marriage and children?

4. Are the economic reforms in China designed to transform China's economy from a command economy to a market economy and from a socialist system to a capitalist one?

5. Economic reforms in Russia have focused on privatizing the state-owned enterprises of the former Soviet Union by selling these enterprises to private entrepreneurs. Is China's state sector undergoing a similar process of privatization?

2. China's FDI Legal Regime and Foreign Investment Business Vehicles

Like many developing countries, China has specific laws that apply to FDI. Developing countries believe that while FDI is crucial to their economic development it also poses many risks for their growing economic systems. As a result, special attention in the form of separate legal rules must be applied. In China, FDI is considered a matter of national policy and is considered to play a vital role in the nation's continued economic development.

All FDI projects must be approved by PRC government authorities. FDI in China is a privilege, not a right, and a foreign investor has no recourse if government authorities refuse to approve an FDI project.

There are three standard business vehicles available for FDI: The equity joint venture, the contractual joint venture, and the wholly foreign-owned enterprise. As there are many similarities between the two joint venture forms, the materials below will focus on the equity joint venture. Although the contractual joint venture offers the parties more flexibility to determine their rights and obligations, most MNEs prefer the stability of the equity joint venture, and it is generally used when large sums of capital are invested.

A. THE JOINT VENTURE

A joint venture in China is a business entity formed by a combination of two or more business entities into a third separate entity. A joint venture should be distinguished from other business arrangements such as mergers or acquisitions. In a joint venture, both of the original partners continue to maintain their existence as separate legal entities while forming a third legal entity, the joint venture. For example, when Company A (a foreign company) and Company B (a PRC company) form a joint venture, Company C (a PRC company), the end result is three separate corporate entities: A, B, and C. In a merger, A and B combine to form a new Company C, but neither A nor B continues to exist after the merger. In an acquisition, A absorbs B, which ceases to exist as a separate legal entity and the sole surviving entity would be Company A.

The joint venture was the overwhelming investment vehicle of choice in the 1980s and continues to be popular. The advantage of this investment form is that it offers the foreign investor the opportunity to partner with a local entity that is familiar with the local environment and the labyrinth of local regulations and politics. A local partner is able to help obtain initial government approvals for the joint venture and to help navigate the constant complex of additional government approvals for taxation, customs, and other matters that are part of the daily existence of foreign investment enterprises (FIEs) in China. Finding a suitable local partner is usually the single most important decision for an MNE. The wrong partner can lead to conflict, turmoil, and, in some cases, the premature termination of the joint venture itself.

In general, PRC authorities view the joint venture as a temporary measure to introduce advanced technology and management skills into China. Although PRC law no longer imposes mandatory maximum limits on the duration of the joint venture, government authorities usually require the joint venture contract or articles of association to include a term limit of between ten and fifty years. The local partner will be exposed to these benefits and at the termination of the joint venture, the foreign partner will depart the scene and the Chinese partner will have the opportunity to acquire the assets of the joint venture and to continue to operate the company as an ongoing concern.

B. THE WHOLLY FOREIGN-OWNED ENTERPRISE

Unlike the joint venture, the wholly foreign-owned enterprise (WFOE) is a foreign investment vehicle that is owned entirely by the foreign investor and there is no participation by a Chinese entity. The advantage of a WFOE is that there is no possibility of a conflict with a local partner. In addition, the WFOE will provide the MNE with greater control over technology and intellectual property than will a joint venture as there will be no local partner who may misuse or misappropriate the technology of the foreign investor. The disadvantage of the WFOE is the absence of a local partner who can serve as an intermediary with PRC government authorities. A local partner also creates an image that the joint venture is an entity with local participation and this may be politically and tactically advantageous. The WFOE, while technically a Chinese legal entity, is sometimes viewed as foreign by local authorities, which may result in less favorable treatment in some circumstances.

Recent trends indicate that the WFOE is becoming increasingly popular. In 1997, the number of WFOEs approved exceeded for the first time the number of equity joint ventures approved by PRC authorities. *See* 1997 Bulletin of the PRC Ministry of Foreign Trade and Economic Cooperation, at 12.

NOTES AND QUESTIONS

1. In the past, China has placed greater restrictions on the WFOE than on the joint venture. For example, PRC law banned the use of WFOEs in certain industries and restricted their use in other industries. Until recently, a WFOE was also required to import advanced technology and to export at least 50 percent of its products per year, restrictions that did not apply to joint ventures. China has since relaxed some of these restrictions as a result of its entry into the WTO, but as a practical matter approvals of WFOEs continue to be more difficult to obtain than approvals for joint ventures. Why would China favor joint ventures over WFOEs?

2. If China favors joint ventures over WFOEs, why permit the WFOE at all?

3. Suppose that you were advising an MNE on the best business form for a research and development center in China to support its manufacturing operations. Which form would you suggest and why?

NOTE ON A GAMBLE BY AN MNE THAT PAID OFF

During the initial stages of FDI in China in the 1980s and early 1990s, some MNEs, such as Procter & Gamble, made a strategic decision not to form a joint venture directly with a Chinese local entity. Rather, some MNEs formed an offshore joint venture with large diversified companies in Hong Kong or Singapore and the new off-shore joint venture became the foreign investor that partnered with local entities in China. For example, in the 1980s, P&G formed a joint venture with Hutchinson-Whampoa, a large diversified multinational Hong Kong company involved in many businesses such as real estate, hotels, and telecommunications in Hong Kong and China. The new joint venture, based in Hong Kong, was called Procter & Gamble-Hutchinson (PGH). PGH, a Hong Kong company, then served as the foreign investor in a number of joint ventures with different partners in China. The reasoning behind such a strategic move is that companies like Hutchinson, with Hong Kong executives with facility in both Chinese and English as well as training and education in Western countries, would be able to advise P&G and other MNEs on the suitability of potential venture partners and locations in China as well as on doing business in China generally. By the late 1980s, Hutchinson had already established a long track record of investing in China well ahead of Western companies, many of which were just entering the China market. P&G felt that Hutchinson would be instrumental in helping to find a suitable location for the new joint venture and a suitable joint venture partner, which is probably the single most important factor in the success or failure of any joint venture. Many MNEs did not believe that they were in a good position to make a judgment about potential partners and did not trust the many business consultants who held themselves out as "old China hands" but who were little more than charlatans. Hutchinson, a sophisticated MNE in its own right, would be accustomed to Western business practices and would be in a good position to work with P&G's Western executives. At the same time, Hutchinson's Hong Kong executives had no language or cultural problems in dealing with China and, in addition, had strong ties with the PRC government and could help to open doors. With the help of Hutchinson, P&G was one of the earliest MNEs to enter the Chinese market and was able to secure a sizeable market share and competitive advantage over its global rivals such as Unilever, Colgate, and Johnson & Johnson.

When P&G entered China in 1988, China was just beginning to open up to the West and to shed the Mao suits and nondescript work uniforms in favor of more freedom in dress. In addition, China was just emerging from the culture of fervent self-sacrifice and asceticism that had marked its history since the founding of the PRC in 1949. P&G struck a responsive chord when it introduced high-quality shampoos into China in the late 1980s through the use of television commercials. Most shampoos in China at the time were coarse and hardly different from detergents used to wash clothes, as personal luxury was not viewed as a priority in China. The high quality and perfume of P&G's shampoos immediately differentiated them from local brands, but it was the image created by P&G or the "branding" of its products that was its real success. One of P&G's earliest and most effective television shampoo advertisements featured glamorous and stylishly dressed young Chinese airline flight attendants walking through airports with lustrous black hair. For many of China's female audience at the time, a job as a flight attendant represented a life of travel, adventure, and opportunity and P&G's advertisement immediately struck a responsive chord. P&G's products quickly came to stand for Western sophistication and glamour and offered a bit of luxury into ordinary lives. The timing and message were right and P&G products were a resounding success with Chinese consumers. By the mid-1990s, P&G had become well known as a rare success story in China and had built a business generating over $1 billion in annual revenues. P&G brands have been able to obtain a level of recognition and prestige in China that far exceeds their levels in the United States.

3. *Establishing the Joint Venture*

A. APPROVAL PROCESS

Establishing a joint venture in China usually involves three levels of approvals: (1) a preliminary approval by the government department supervising the local Chinese enterprise, (2) final approval by the PRC authorities with jurisdiction over foreign trade and economic planning, and (3) the issuance of a business license by the appropriate government entities with authority over the regulation of industry and commerce. Equity joint ventures are governed by the PRC Equity Joint Venture Law (1979, revised 1990 & 2001) and the PRC Equity Joint Venture Law Implementing Regulations (1983, amended 1986, 1987, & 2001).

Before the Chinese partner, usually a state-owned enterprise, can proceed with the project, it must obtain the preliminary approval of its supervisory department, a government bureau. All economic and industrial sectors are subject to the supervision of a particular supervisory authority and all entities operating with these sectors, including the joint venture that is later established, must report to the supervisory authority — although, by law, joint ventures are entitled to operate independently. To obtain this approval, the Chinese partner must submit a preliminary feasibility report that demonstrates the economic viability of the joint venture.

After the preliminary approvals have been obtained, final approvals must be obtained from the appropriate foreign trade and economic planning authorities. To obtain final approval, the applicant must submit the joint venture application, the joint venture contract, articles of association, and ancillary documents. PRC approval authorities will scrutinize all of the documents carefully. Approval authorities will examine these documents line by line and raise specific objections and suggest detailed changes. In most cases, it is advisable to submit drafts well in advance to the approval authorities for comment. Note that the approval process is, in reality, a process of negotiation with the approval authorities. Thus, there are three parties to any joint venture negotiation in China: The foreign investor, the local partner, and the approval authorities.

The appropriate authority for approval depends on the size of the investment in the joint venture. If the registered capital (discussed in the next section) in the joint venture exceeds $30 million, approval must be obtained at the central level from the Ministry of Foreign Trade and Economic Cooperation. If the total registered capital of the joint venture does not exceed $30 million, then approvals can be obtained at the provincial or local levels. Under Article 10 of the Equity Joint Venture Law Implementing Regulations, the approval authorities must make a decision within three months of submission of the application. Once approval is granted, the authorities will issue an approval certificate.

The last step in this process is the submission of the approval certificate to the appropriate Administration of Industry and Commerce, which will issue a business license. The scope of the business license will reflect the scope of business approved for the joint venture by the approval authorities as set forth in the joint venture contract. The issuance of the business license should be routine as long as there are no improprieties in the approval process, but the business license itself is essential as no enterprise can lawfully operate in China without one. With the approval certificate and business license in hand, the joint venture is now able to lawfully commence operations.

Based on the readings so far consider the following:

PROBLEM 6-12

The whole process of negotiating the joint venture contract, articles of association, and related documents and obtaining the needed approvals and business license usually takes between 18 months and two years. Negotiating the joint venture documents will require the significant expenditure of senior management time in travel and meetings and other significant costs in the form of legal fees as law firms are often engaged to draft the legal documents and assist in the negotiations. MNEs are, of course, reluctant to invest such significant resources in this whole process if the application is eventually rejected by the approval authorities. How can an MNE address these concerns? What role can the local partner play?

B. CAPITAL INVESTMENT

A basic issue for the foreign investor is deciding on the amount of capital to invest in the joint venture and the related issue of management structure as management control is usually determined by the ratio of capital investment of the parties. Under PRC laws, the initial capital investment in the joint venture is called its "registered capital." The concept of registered capital refers to the amount of capital needed (sometimes referred to as "basic construction funds") for the start-up costs of the company to become operational and is used mainly to meet the physical needs of the joint venture. It is referred to as "registered" capital because the initial amount of the capital contributed is recorded or registered with PRC authorities and cannot be reduced without official authorization. What are some of these basic start-up costs? Every business venture in China must start out with certain basic physical needs such as land, buildings, equipment, and access to utilities. In many cases, existing buildings and equipment must be refurbished or renovated to suit the needs of the joint venture. Other common start-up costs for the joint venture are payments to the MNE in order to license its patents, trademarks, and copyrights. The joint venture will also need to make payments to the local partner to obtain the assignment or license of its intellectual property rights. In most cases, registered capital is invested in fixed assets such as land and buildings, but some of the start-up costs such as required fees for access to electricity are not reflected in the acquisition of a permanent physical asset. Unlike the United States where businesses can be established with minimal start-up costs, PRC approval authorities will usually require a substantial investment of start-up capital as a condition of approval of the joint venture. The amount of registered capital must be approved by PRC approval authorities and is stated in the joint venture contract and articles of association. The amount of registered capital also represents the value of the investor's equity interest or ownership in the joint venture company.

Registered capital cannot take the form of debt but can consist of cash or physical assets. It is common for the foreign investor to contribute cash and for the local partner to contribute assets to satisfy a part or all of its capital requirements. The joint venture can assume debt to provide working capital used to pay for salaries, raw materials, and supplies. The joint venture's registered capital plus the amount of any debt is referred to under PRC law as its total investment. PRC laws prescribe specific limits on the debt to equity ratio in all FIEs.

C. MANAGEMENT STRUCTURE

By law, the management structure of a joint venture consists of a board of directors, the highest authority within the company, a general manager, and one or more deputy general managers. The board of directors is jointly appointed by the foreign investor and the local partner as prescribed by law. The board appoints the general manager who runs the day-to-day affairs of the joint venture.

PROBLEM 6-13

Company B, an MNE with its headquarters in the United States, wishes to establish an 80 percent equity ownership interest in a PRC joint venture with Company A, a state-owned enterprise. The joint venture will have a total investment of $40 million, $10 million of which is debt used to finance working capital.

(1) How much registered capital must B contribute? See Articles 17 and 18 of the Equity Joint Venture Law Implementing Regulations (EJVLIR) below.

(2) How much registered capital must the local partner contribute?

(3) How many members of a five-member board can B appoint? See EJVLIR, Article 31, below.

(4) What percentage of profits or dividends from the joint venture must be paid to A? See Article 4 of the Equity Joint Venture Law (EJVL) below.

(5) After the equity contributions are made, what legal document serves as the evidence of ownership by each of the joint venture partners? See the Joint Venture Contract (JV Contract) below, Article 6.9.

PROBLEM 6-14

A fundamental issue for a U.S. corporation in any joint venture in China, Brazil, or any other country in the world concerns ownership and management control. In considering the ownership ratio of the joint venture between A and B, B considered three options: 51/49, 60/40, and 80/20. Assume that the local partner A has enough capital to contribute its share under each of these options so that the total amount of registered capital of the joint venture under each of these options remains the same and will be sufficient to meet start-up costs but that each party's contribution will be more or less in accordance with the option chosen. Under each of these options, B will be a majority owner and will be entitled to appoint a majority of the board of directors of the joint venture. As the board is the highest authority within the joint venture, control of the board is, in theory, equivalent to control of the joint venture. One of B's priorities is management control of the joint venture.

(1) Why should B consider any ownership ratio other than the 51/49 option, which would give B majority control without the requirement of investing additional capital of its own? In answering this question, consider the following: Although B has control of the board and, in theory, can vote down any dissent by A under any of these options, board resolutions as a practical matter are invariably passed unanimously in joint venture companies operating in China (as well as in corporations everywhere). Why? In light of this practical reality, which of these options would you advise B to choose?

(2) The local partner A argues that if B controls the board then A should be allowed to appoint the general manager. A argues that this will save B in costs as well as A will appoint one of its own employees. As the general manager is under the authority of the board, this should not compromise the control by B. Should B agree? In answering this question, consider the role of the board and the general manager described in Articles 12 and 13 of the JV Contract below and in Articles 30-36 of the EJVLIR. The board of directors is required to meet once a year under law and most boards in China meet no more than twice a year. What

does this suggest on how much authority the board must delegate to the general manager?

PROBLEM 6-15

One of the most important issues for a joint venture not just in China but anywhere in the world has to do with how intellectual property rights are treated. As the joint venture is a new and distinct legal entity in China that is formed by Acme (the foreign investor) and its local partner, the joint venture at its inception owns no intellectual property rights at all. Rather Acme, the MNE, owns its trademarks and Seagull, the local partner, is the owner of its trademarks. As the new joint venture company will manufacture detergents and sell them in China using the trademarks of both Acme and Seagull, the joint venture must somehow acquire the rights to do so.

(1) How are these rights to use these trademarks acquired by the joint venture and who owns the trademarks in China? In answering this question, distinguish between the treatment of the trademarks owned by Seagull and Acme under Articles 10.1(a) and 10.1(b) of the JV contract, respectively. What bedrock principle concerning its intellectual property rights must Acme follow in dealing with the joint venture in China or anywhere in the world? We saw this same basic principle applied to the distribution agreement (Article 4.1 at p. 332), the patent license agreement (Article 3 at p. 367), and the franchise agreement (Article 9 at p. 383).

(2) Note that Acme should insist that the Seagull trademarks are to be treated differently under Article 10.1(a) of the JV contract. The joint venture will manufacture and sell products under both the Acme trademark and the Seagull brands. Acme brands will be premium products designed for the high-end market, whereas Seagull brands will be economy brands offered at a lower price. Seagull, the local partner, will no longer manufacture any brands using the Seagull trademarks. The reason why Article 10.1(a) is so important is because without such a clause Seagull may be able to continue to produce some laundry detergent products or related products such as household cleansers and soaps using the Seagull trademarks. Under this scenario, the joint venture manufactures detergent sold under Acme's trademarks while Seagull continues to manufacture and sell detergent and related products under its own brands. Note that the local partner is given access to the advanced technology of the foreign investor used in the manufacture of detergent. This situation creates significant risks for the foreign investor and may also jeopardize the continuing working relationship between the parties. What are these risks and how does Article 10.1(a) address them? Does it make sense for the joint venture to buy all of Seagull's trademarks even if the joint venture never intends to use them?

(3) Why are these intellectual property issues with local partners also commonly found by MNEs in other developing countries? Are these issues also likely to exist to the same extent with a joint venture partner in a developed country?

PROBLEM 6-16

The local partner's capital contribution to the joint venture is also a common issue in joint ventures in developing countries. The problem arises because the local partner is often short on cash. For example, one of the basic issues that the parties must resolve relates to basic physical requirements: A site for the joint venture, buildings, equipment, and utilities. Although all land in China is owned by the state, business entities and individuals are allowed to acquire and transfer land use rights. Access to utilities must be authorized by state authorities in exchange for payments of fees.

(1) A is eager to locate the joint venture on a plot of land within its grounds used for its own operations. Why? See Article 6.2 of the JV Contract and EJVLIR, Article 45.

(2) How will the joint venture be supplied with electricity, water, steam, and other utilities? See Article 9 of the JV Contract.

(3) Why would B agree to this arrangement for land and utilities?

(4) The arrangement proposed by the local partner A is popular in China although it involves locating the joint venture on a plot surrounded by other lands owned by A and accessible only by crossing roads owned by A. This arrangement also makes the joint venture dependent on the local partner for utilities. Do you see any long-term problems with this arrangement for B?

PROBLEM 6-17

After several years, Acme, the foreign investor in the joint venture governed by the JV Contract below, decides to expand into the manufacture and sale of shampoo and body soaps in China. Acme will need to inject additional capital into the existing joint venture to expand the present plant and to add new production lines.

(1) Can Acme expand its product lines using the existing joint venture? See Article 5.2 of the JV Contract below.

(2) If Acme uses the existing joint venture to manufacture shampoo and soap, what might be the consequences?

(3) Advise Acme on what procedures it should undertake internally and with PRC authorities to accomplish these goals. For internal procedures, see JV Contract, Article 12.3, and EJVLIR, Article 33. For steps that Acme must take with PRC authorities, see EJVL, Article 3, and EJVLIR, Article 20.

PRC Equity Joint Venture Law (2001)

ARTICLE 2

The Chinese government shall, according to the law, protect the investment of foreign parties, the profits due them and their other lawful rights and interests in an equity joint venture, pursuant to the agreements, contracts and articles of association approved by the Chinese government.

All activities of an equity joint venture shall comply with the provisions of the laws, decrees, and pertinent regulations of the People's Republic of China.

The State shall not nationalize or expropriate any equity joint venture. Under special circumstances, when public interests require, equity joint ventures may be expropriated by following legal procedures and appropriate compensation shall be made.

ARTICLE 3

The equity joint venture agreement, contract and articles of association concluded by the parties to the venture shall be submitted to the state's competent department for foreign economic relations and trade. When approved, the equity joint venture shall register with the state's competent department in charge of industry and commerce, and acquire a business license and start operations.

ARTICLE 4

An equity joint venture shall take the form of a limited liability company. The parties to the venture shall share the profits, risks, and losses in proportion to their contributions to the registered capital.

Equity Joint Venture Law Implementing Regulations (2001)

ARTICLE 1

These regulations are formulated with a view to facilitating the implementation of the People's Republic of China, Sino-Foreign Equity Joint Venture Law (hereinafter, "Equity Joint Venture Law").

ARTICLE 2

Sino-Foreign equity joint ventures (hereinafter, "joint ventures") established within China's territory in accordance with the Equity Joint Venture Law are legal persons in China and are subject to the jurisdiction of Chinese laws and enjoy protection thereof. . . .

ARTICLE 6

Unless otherwise stipulated, the government department in charge of the Chinese party to the venture shall be the department in charge of the joint venture (hereinafter, "the department in charge"). If a joint venture has two or more Chinese parties, which are under different departments or regions, the departments and regions concerned shall, through consultation, designate a department in charge.

Departments in charge shall be responsible for providing guidance and assistance and exercising supervision over the joint venture.

ARTICLE 7

A joint venture has the right to independently conduct business operation and management within the scope prescribed by Chinese laws and regulations, and by the agreement, contract and articles of association of the joint venture. The departments concerned shall provide support and assistance. . . .

ARTICLE 17

The total amount of investment (including loans) of an equity joint venture means the total sum of basic construction funds and operating funds invested in accordance with the contract and articles of association of the equity joint venture.

ARTICLE 18

The registered capital of an equity joint venture shall be the total sum of all capital subscribed by all parties to the equity joint venture. . . .

ARTICLE 20

Increase or reduction of registered capital of an equity venture shall be adopted by the meeting of the board of directors [and] shall be reported to the examining and approving authority for approval. . . .

ARTICLE 30

The board of directors is the highest authority in an equity joint venture, and decides on all important issues of the equity joint venture.

ARTICLE 31

Members of the board of directors of an equity joint venture shall not be less than three. Allotment of quota of directors shall be determined by all parties to the equity venture with reference to their respective capital subscription.

ARTICLE 32

The board meeting shall be convened once a year at least and the board chairman shall be responsible for convening and presiding over the meeting.

ARTICLE 33

Decisions shall be made on the following issues upon unanimous adoption of all directors who attend the board meeting:

(1)   Revision of the articles of the equity joint venture;
(2)   Dissolution or termination of the equity joint venture;
(3)   Increase or reduction of the registered capital of the equity joint venture; and
(4)   Merger or division of the equity joint venture.

Decisions on other issues may be made in accordance with rules of procedures as specified by articles of the equity joint venture.

ARTICLE 35

An equity joint venture shall set up a business operation and management organ, which is responsible for routine business operation and management of the equity joint venture. The business operation and management organ consists of one general manager and several vice general managers. Vice general managers assist the general manager.

ARTICLE 36

The general manager shall execute all decisions of the board meeting and organize and lead the routine business operation and management of the equity joint venture. Within the limits of authorization of the board of directors, the general manager represents the equity joint venture externally, shall appoint and dismiss subordinates internally, and exercise other authority awarded by the board of directors. . . .

ARTICLE 45

Where the right to use a site needed by an equity joint venture is owned by a Chinese party to the joint venture, the Chinese party may take the site as its capital subscription to the equity joint venture, the evaluated amount shall be the same as the fees payable to obtain the right to use the site. . . .

Joint Venture Contract Between Beijing Seagull Detergent Group and Acme (China), Ltd.

This Joint Venture Contract ("Contract") is made on this day of December 10, 2005 between Beijing Seagull Detergent Group Corp. ("Party A"), a limited liability company established and existing under the laws of the People's Republic of China (PRC or "China"), and Acme (China), Ltd., a wholly foreign-owned investment company incorporated and existing under the laws of the PRC ("Party B").

ARTICLE 1 GENERAL PROVISIONS

1.1 PRELIMINARY STATEMENT

Party A is a limited liability company producing laundry detergents and other cleansing products in its factory in Beijing, China. Party B, a WFOE incorporated and existing under the laws of the PRC, is a wholly owned subsidiary of Acme-Henderson, Ltd., which is a company incorporated and existing under the laws of Hong Kong, and also is an affiliated corporation of the Acme Company, an internationally well-known producer of detergents and other products ("Acme").

Henderson is a diversified Hong Kong company with interests in real estate, hotels, and telecommunications. The Parties wish to establish a joint venture company for the production of detergents and other cleansing products which will utilize Acme's advanced technology and the well recognized trademarks pertaining to detergents of both Parties, and the facilities, plant, equipment, assets and business to be contributed by Party A and Party B.

Therefore, after friendly consultations conducted in accordance with the principles of equality and mutual benefit, Party A and Party B have agreed to establish an equity joint venture enterprise for the production of detergents and other cleansing products in accordance with the Law of the People's Republic of China on Joint Ventures Using Chinese and Foreign Investment (the "Joint Venture Law"), the implementing regulations issued thereunder (the "Joint Venture Regulations"), other relevant laws and regulations of China, and the provisions of this Contract. . . .

ARTICLE 2 PARTIES TO THE CONTRACT

2.1 PARTIES

The parties to the Contract are as follows:

1. Beijing Seagull Detergent Group Corp. (Party A), a limited liability company, established and existing under the laws of the PRC, registered with the Beijing Municipal Administration of Industry and Commerce, Beijing, PRC (Business License No. 13638555-2-1) and with its legal address at Meng Jia Gou, Beijing, China.

    The Legal Representative Person of Party A is:

    Name: Yu Heyi
    Position: General Manager
    Nationality: Chinese

2. Acme (China), Ltd. (Party B), a company incorporated and existing under the laws of China, with its registered office at 15/F Yuehai Building, No 472, Huanshi East Road, Guangzhou, China (Business License No. 221).

    The Legal Representative Person of Party B is:

    Name: Dennis Smith
    Position: Chairman
    Nationality: United States

Party A and Party B are collectively referred to herein as the "Parties", and individually as a "Party." . . .

ARTICLE 4 ESTABLISHMENT OF THE JOINT VENTURE COMPANY

4.1 ESTABLISHMENT OF THE JOINT VENTURE COMPANY

In accordance with the Joint Venture Law and relevant Chinese laws and regulations, the Parties hereby agree to establish the Company pursuant to the terms of this Contract.

4.2 NAME AND ADDRESS OF THE COMPANY

(a) The name of the Company shall be _____ in Chinese and Acme Seagull (Beijing), Ltd., in English. In the event that Party B ceases to own more than 50% of the registered capital of the Company, the Parties shall, unless ACME specifically agrees otherwise in writing, ensure that the name of the Company is changed to delete the words "Acme" in English and _____ in Chinese.

(b) The legal address of the Company shall be Meng Jia Guo, Beijing, China.

4.3 LIMITED LIABILITY COMPANY

The Company shall be a limited liability company. The liability of each Party to the Company shall be limited to the amount of its respective subscribed capital contributions required to be made pursuant to this Contract and neither Party shall have any liability to the Company in excess of such amount. Neither Party shall have any liability to any third party jointly or severally in respect of the debts or obligations of the Company. The Parties shall share the profits and bear risks and losses in accordance with the ratio of their respective capital contributions as set forth in Article 6.2.

4.4 LEGAL PERSON

The Company shall be a legal person under the laws of China. . . .

ARTICLE 5 THE PURPOSE, SCOPE AND SCALE OF PRODUCTION AND BUSINESS

5.1 PURPOSE OF THE COMPANY

The purpose of the Parties to this Contract, in accordance with their desire to strengthen economic cooperation and technical exchange, and to adopt advanced and appropriate technology and scientific management methods, is:

(a) to utilize both Parties' advanced technology and the well recognized Trademarks of both Parties to produce and sell laundry detergent and other cleansing products as well as to produce related raw materials and packaging materials;

(b) to apply Acme's advanced technology and management expertise to upgrade existing Chinese manufacturing entities;

(c) to develop, manufacture and market high quality consumer products to meet the growing demands of consumers inside and outside China;

(d) to further improve living standards and spur faster development of China's consumer industry, so as to enable the Parties to achieve satisfactory economic benefits.

5.2 SCOPE OF BUSINESS OF THE COMPANY

The scope of business of the Company is:

(a) to produce and sell laundry detergents and other cleansing products used for laundry (collectively, the "JV Products"); and

(b) to produce related raw materials and packaging materials.

5.3 ESTIMATED SCALE OF PRODUCTION

The total productive capacity of the Plant with intended modifications should be _____ metric tons of JV Products in ten years.

The Parties agree that the Board of Directors will regularly review the operations and economic performance of the Company. . . .

ARTICLE 6 TOTAL AMOUNT OF INVESTMENT AND REGISTERED CAPITAL

6.1 TOTAL INVESTMENT

The total amount of investment of the Company shall be US$ _____ (_____ Million United States Dollars).

6.2 REGISTERED CAPITAL

The total amount of the registered capital of the Company shall be US$ _____ (_____ Million United States Dollars).

Party A's contribution to the Company shall be the equivalent of US$ _____ (_____ Million United States Dollars) in the form of facilities, buildings and equipment, as set forth on Schedule 1, which is _____% of the total registered capital of the Company.

Party B's contribution to the Company shall be US$ _____ (_____ Million United States Dollars) or the equivalent in RMB in the form of cash, which shall be _____% of the total registered capital.

6.3 USE OF REGISTERED CAPITAL

The cash contribution of Party B shall be used in part by the Company to obtain the ownership of Party A's Trademarks as set out in Article 10.1, and land use rights, to buy equipment and to renovate the Company's equipment and production facilities. . . .

6.5 ADDITIONAL FINANCING

(a) In addition to the registered capital, the Company may borrow any necessary funds from domestic or international banks or other financial institutions on terms and conditions approved by the Board of Directors. . . .

(b) In the event that pursuant to Article 6.6 below, the Board of Directors approves an increase in the registered capital of the Company and the Approval Authority grants its approval to such increase, but either Party is unable to contribute its pro-rata share, the other Party may contribute its and the aforesaid Party's pro-rata share (or a portion thereof), resulting in an increase of the contributing Party's share of the registered capital of the Company.

6.6 INCREASE OF REGISTERED CAPITAL

During the term of the Company, any increase in the registered capital of the Company shall require the unanimous approval of the Board of Directors and the approval of the Approval Authority.

6.7 TRANSFER OF REGISTERED CAPITAL

(a) Subject to the provisions of paragraphs (b) and (c) below, either Party may assign all or part of its registered capital contribution to the Company to any third party, provided it first obtains the unanimous approval of the Board of Directors and the approval of the Approval Authority.

(b) When a Party (the "Disposing Party") wishes to assign, sell or otherwise dispose of all or part of its registered capital contribution to a third party (a "Transfer"), it shall notify the other Party (the "Non-Disposing Party") in writing of its wish to make the Transfer, the capital contribution it wishes to transfer, the terms and conditions of the Transfer and the identity of the proposed transferee (the "Notice"). The Non-Disposing Party shall have a preemptive right to purchase the whole of such capital contribution on terms and conditions no less favorable than those specified in the Notice.

Notwithstanding the provisions of this Article 6.7 and subject to requisite Chinese government approvals, Party B may transfer all of its interest in the Company to another Acme Affiliate or Henderson Affiliate, and Party A hereby agrees to such transfer. Such transfer may be made in either case only if the nature of the Company will not be affected by the transfer. In the event of such a transfer as contemplated herein, Party B's transferee shall undertake all of the responsibilities and obligations of Party B hereunder.

6.8 ENCUMBRANCE OF REGISTERED CAPITAL

No Party shall mortgage or otherwise encumber all or any part of its contribution to the registered capital of the Company without the prior written consent of the other Party hereto.

6.9 INVESTMENT CERTIFICATES

After the Parties have made their capital contributions, the Joint Venture Company shall engage an accountant registered in China to verify the contributions. Upon the issuance of a verification report by such an accountant, the Joint Venture Company shall issue an investment certificate to each of the Parties as required by the Joint Venture Law.

ARTICLE 7 RESPONSIBILITIES OF THE PARTIES

7.1 RESPONSIBILITIES OF PARTY A

In addition to its other responsibilities under this Contract, Party A shall:

(a) be responsible for handling all matters relating to the establishment of the Company, including the submission of applications for approval of this

Contract to the Approval Authority and any other governmental authority whose approval is required, registration of the Company and issuance of a business license and assist in the opening of Renminbi and foreign exchange bank accounts;

(b) assist the Company, if requested to do so, in the submission of applications for, and the grant of, all necessary approvals, permits, certificates and licenses required in connection with safety, environmental matters and other matters regulated by governmental authorities; enter into the Land Use Transfer Agreement pursuant to article 9.1(a); and handle all other necessary procedures in relation thereto to ensure that the Company has the right to use the Site in conformity with the scope of its operations for 50 years;

(c) assist the Company in contracting for and obtaining the electricity, water and other necessary utilities required by the Company and conforming to the specifications and conditions set forth in the Feasibility Study on a continuous uninterrupted basis and in quantities sufficient to meet the full operational requirements of the Company;

(d) assist directors and foreign personnel of Party B and the Company to obtain all necessary entry visas, travel documents and work permits;

(e) assist the Company with the smooth transfer of employees from Party A that are recruited by the Company, with handing over employee files, and with other employment-related matters and with the recruitment of other qualified Chinese management personnel, technical personnel, workers and other needed personnel;

(f) assist the Company and Party B in applying for, and use its best efforts to assist the Company and Party B to obtain tax reductions and exemptions and any other investment incentives available to the Company and Party B, and assist the Company to liaise with the relevant tax authorities in order to assist the Company to obtain tax reductions or exemptions and access to cost effective raw material;

(g) generally assist the Company in its relations with local government authorities and Chinese domestic companies, including the customers of Party A;

(h) assist the Company to buy raw materials, and in sourcing, purchasing or leasing local equipment, means of transportation, articles for office use and communication facilities;

(i) assist the Company in processing import customs declarations for the machinery, equipment, vehicles, and telecommunications systems purchased within the amount of the Company's total capital and in going through customs declaration procedures for the importation into China of such other machinery, equipment, materials, supplies, and raw materials as are required by the Company (including applying for and procuring any approval documents for the import of the same) as well as assisting in arranging for the inland transportation of the same to the Company's Site;

(j) assist the Company in obtaining Renminbi and foreign exchange loans from financial institutions in China;

(k) assist the Company in qualifying for the status of "Technologically Advanced Enterprise", to ensure that the Company is charged the most favorable rates for land use and for utilities;

(l) be responsible for any damage to the environment prior to the date the Joint Venture begins operations and to indemnify the Company and Party B for any such damages in respect to environmental pollution, worker injuries and other related hazards; and

(m) handle other matters entrusted to it by the Company.

7.2 RESPONSIBILITIES OF PARTY B

In addition to its other responsibilities under this Contract, Party B shall:

(a) assist the Company, if requested, to procure from abroad equipment, supplies and raw materials which are not otherwise available within China or which the Company considers should be imported;

(b) assist the Company as requested to recruit appropriate management and senior technical personnel and assist the Company in the provision of training for employees of the Company;

(c) procure that Acme, or its subsidiaries or other Affiliates, enters into (i) an agreement to license the use of the Trademarks to the Company in the form of Annex E2 hereto and (ii) an agreement to provide management and technical assistance to the Company in the form of Annex D hereto;

(d) provide technical assistance to the extent possible to upgrade the manufacturing process of Party A's own brand products manufactured in its existing factory;

(e) assist the Company to become familiar with international market conditions;

(f) assist the Company in obtaining foreign exchange loans from financial institutions outside China;

(g) provide technical assistance to the Company in relation to packaging and product quality of JV Products; and

(h) handle other matters entrusted to it by the Company.

ARTICLE 8 PURCHASE OF MATERIALS AND SUPPLIES

8.1 LOCALLY SOURCED MATERIALS

Party A shall ensure that all raw materials required by the Company are available through the existing channels of supply currently utilized by Party A for its detergent factory. The purchase of all such items from Chinese suppliers shall be paid for in RMB and, to the extent possible, at the equivalent price levels to those enjoyed by state-owned enterprises. Attached to this Contract as Schedule 2 is a list of raw materials required by the Company that are available locally in Beijing and their current stated prices in RMB.

8.2 IMPORTED MATERIALS

To the extent that the Company's specifications with respect to quality, quantity, price, and delivery terms and dates cannot be met from sources within China, the Company may procure such materials and supplies from abroad. For items purchased from abroad, the Company shall give preference to procurement from Party B or its Affiliates and suppliers recommended by Party B or its Affiliates if the quality, quantity, price and delivery terms are competitive.

ARTICLE 9 RIGHT TO USE SITE; UTILITIES

9.1 RIGHT TO USE THE SITE

(a) Party A shall enter into a Land Use Transfer Agreement substantially in the form attached hereto as Annex B which shall be valid for the Joint Venture Term, and grant to the Company the exclusive right to use the Site, as more particularly set forth on the Site Map attached as Annex C (inclusive of all necessary and sufficient easements over adjacent property to the nearest public roads to enable the Company fully and freely to access the Site and to conduct thereon the activities contemplated by this Contract, irrespective of whether or not such easements presently vest in the Site). The actual boundaries of the Site will be verified by an independent certified surveyor chosen by Party B. The Land Use Transfer Agreement shall guarantee that the Company shall have the exclusive right to use the Site for fifty years from the Establishment Date. The Land Use Transfer Agreement should be recorded with the Land Management Bureau. In the event of a dispute between the Parties on this issue either Party may submit the question to arbitration before the China International Economic Trade Arbitration Commission for resolution.

(b) The total fee payable by the Company to Party A for the exclusive right to use the Site shall be RMB _____ which amount shall be payable in one lump sum during _____.

(c) Party A warrants that the Site to be provided to the Company by Party A shall be as set forth in the Site Map attached as Annex C.

9.2 UTILITIES

Party A shall supply to the Company all water, electricity and steam required by the Company at the favorable prices and on the favorable terms and conditions to be agreed by the Parties. Payment for all such services shall be made in RMB. Attached to this Contract as Schedule 3 is a list of the utility services to be supplied by Party A and their current prices in RMB. The Parties shall ensure that the Company supplies to Party A all sewerage services and waste water treatment services required by Party A on terms to be agreed by the Parties.

ARTICLE 10 TRADEMARK ASSIGNMENT AND LICENSE; TECHNICAL ASSISTANCE

10.1 TRADEMARK ASSIGNMENT AND LICENSE

(a) Party A covenants that within _____ days after the Establishment Date, the Seagull Trademark Assignment Agreement shall be signed between the Company and Party A so as to ensure that the Company obtains the ownership and the exclusive right to use the Seagull Trademarks needed for marketing and sale of the JV Products. The Company shall pay to Party A a one time lump sum payment of RMB 45,000,000 (Forty-five Million RMB) within ninety (90) days after the assignment of Seagull trademarks to the Company. In consideration of the payment referred to above, Party A agrees not to produce nor permit any other party to produce any laundry detergent products to compete with the Company.

(b) The Parties agree that within thirty (30) days after the Establishment Date, the ACME Trademark License Agreement shall be signed between the Company and ACME or its relevant Affiliate so as to ensure that the Company obtains the right to use the Trademarks needed for marketing and sale of the JV Products.

10.2 TECHNICAL ASSISTANCE

The Parties agree that within thirty (30) days after the Establishment Date, the Technical Assistance Agreement (Annex D) shall be signed between the Company and ACME so that the Company will receive management and technical assistance from ACME or its relevant Affiliate, including production techniques, product and equipment design and training of personnel. Considering the technical assistance provided to the Company by both Parties and the Distribution Agreement (Annex A) between the Company and Acme (China) Ltd., both Parties agree that no technical assistance fee shall be charged to the Company.

ARTICLE 11 SALE OF JV PRODUCTS

11.1 GENERAL PRINCIPLES

In accordance with relevant Chinese regulations, the Company shall have the right to price and sell its products at its own discretion on the domestic market and shall develop other sales-related services.

11.2 DOMESTIC SALES

The Company shall appoint Party B as its exclusive agent to sell and distribute the products of the Company on the Chinese domestic market. Party B shall in addition to selling and distributing the JV Products, market the JV Products and provide ancillary services in relation thereto pursuant to the Distribution Agreement. The price charged to domestic purchasers of the Company's products shall be denominated in RMB. The sales prices of products sold on the domestic market shall be determined by the General Manager.

11.3 EXPORT SALES

JV Products sold by the Company in the export market shall also be handled by Party B. Export price decisions shall be made by the General Manager in the light of market conditions.

ARTICLE 12 BOARD OF DIRECTORS

12.1 ESTABLISHMENT

The Board of Directors of the Company shall be established on the Establishment Date. The first meeting of the Board of Directors shall be held after the Establishment Date.

12.2 COMPOSITION

The Board of Directors of the Company shall consist of _____ directors, as follows:

(a) _____ to be appointed by Party A, one of whom shall be appointed by Party A to be the vice Chairman of the Board for the first term; and

(b) _____ to be appointed by Party B, one of whom shall be appointed by Party B to be the Chairman of the Board for the first term.

The term of office of the Board of Directors shall be four (4) years and directors may serve consecutive terms if reappointed by the appointing party.

The first set of officers of the Company shall be appointed at the first Board of Directors' meeting. Each Party shall have the right, at any time, to remove or replace any director appointed by it by providing prior written notice to the other Party, the Company, and the other Directors.

12.3 AUTHORITY

The Board of Directors shall be the highest authority of the Company and shall decide all major issues of the Company. The following matters shall require the unanimous approval of the Board of Directors:

(a) The amendment of the Articles of Association of the Company;
(b) The termination or dissolution of the Company;
(c) The increase or assignment of the registered capital of the Company;
(d) The merger of the Company with any other economic organization.

Decisions with respect to all other matters shall be adopted if they receive the affirmative votes of a simple majority of the directors present and voting in person or by proxy, or in the case of a resolution in writing, by a simple majority of the directors.

12.4 LEGAL REPRESENTATIVE

The Chairman of the Board shall be the legal representative of the Company but may not bind the Company beyond the scope of the express authorization of the Board of Directors. If the Chairman of the Board is unable to perform his duties for any reason he may authorize the Vice Chairman to perform his duties. If the Vice Chairman is also unable to perform such duties, the Board of Directors shall authorize another director to perform such duties.

12.5 COMPENSATION AND EXPENSES

Directors shall serve the Company without compensation except when a director is also an officer or employee of the Company. Expenses incurred by directors in connection with attending meetings of the Board of Directors shall be deemed to be regular expenditures of the Company.

12.6 MEETINGS

The quorum for all Board of Directors' meetings shall be _____ of the directors present in person or by proxy. Meetings of the Board of Directors shall be held at least once a year to review the operations of the Company. Board meetings shall be convened and presided over by the Chairman of the Board.

12.7 MEETINGS BY TELEPHONE

The Board may, in lieu of meeting in person, conduct any meeting by means of telephone, provided that each Director present at the meeting is able to hear and speak to all other Directors present at all times.

In lieu of a meeting of the Board of Directors, a written resolution may be adopted by the Board of Directors if such resolution is sent to all members of the Board and signed and affirmatively adopted by the number of directors necessary to make such a decision as stipulated in Article 12.3 hereof.

12.8 FURTHER POWERS AND PROCEDURES

The detailed powers and procedures of the Board of Directors shall be as set forth in the Articles of Association.

ARTICLE 13 BUSINESS MANAGEMENT

13.1 BUSINESS MANAGEMENT

The day-to-day operation and management of the Company shall be under the direction of the General Manager of the Company, who shall be assisted by two (2) Deputy General Managers and such other officers as may be appointed by the Board of Directors as necessary. On important issues, the General Manager shall consult with the Deputy General Managers. The General Manager shall have the right to decide all such issues.

13.2 APPOINTMENT OF GENERAL MANAGER, THE DEPUTY GENERAL MANAGERS AND OTHER OFFICERS

The General Manager shall be nominated by Party _____ and shall be appointed by the Board. Party A and Party B each shall nominate one Deputy General Manager and the Deputy General Managers shall be appointed by the Board. As requested by the General Manager, the Board shall appoint other senior officers to assist the General Manager in the performance of his duties. Any such senior officer shall report to and be under the direction of the General Manager.

13.3 TERM OF OFFICE

The General Manager and the Deputy General Managers shall, unless they become incapacitated, retire or are removed from office earlier by the Board of Directors, hold office for a term of four years each and are eligible for reappointment for further terms.

13.4 RESPONSIBILITIES OF GENERAL MANAGER AND THE DEPUTY GENERAL MANAGERS

The General Manager shall have overall responsibility for the management and operations of the Company. The principal responsibilities of the General Manager shall be (a) to exercise his best efforts to achieve the business objectives of the Company set forth in the Feasibility Study; (b) to carry out the various decisions of the Board and (c) to organize and manage the daily business of the Company. The responsibility of the Deputy General Managers shall be to assist the General Manager to carry out various decisions of the Board and to organize and manage the daily business of the Company as instructed by the General Manager. The powers and duties of the General Manager are set forth in the Articles of Association.

ARTICLE 14 PERSONNEL AND LABOR MANAGEMENT

14.1 PERSONNEL

(a) All matters relating to the selection, appointment, retirement, dismissal, wages, benefits, labor insurance, labor protection, labor discipline of the Company's employees and so on shall be handled in accordance with the Regulations of the People's Republic of China on Labor Management in Chinese-Foreign Joint Ventures. The Company shall in principle have the right to recruit and dismiss its own employees freely in accordance with applicable Chinese laws and regulations. In the initial period, the Company shall give priority to employing current employees of Party A, provided that the Company will employ only those employees of Party A who have suitable qualifications determined pursuant to examination by the Company. Such employees shall be placed on a six (6) month probation period at the end of which the Company will, in its sole discretion, decide whether to offer the employee permanent employment. Any such employee who is not offered permanent employment with the Company will be the responsibility of Party A and shall be treated as those not employed by the Company pursuant to sub-paragraph (b) below.

(b) Party A shall be solely responsible for wages, salaries, benefits, pensions, termination payments and any other remuneration of any Party A employees who are not employed by the Company, provided, however that the Company shall pay Party A a one-time payment of RMB 50,000 for any Party A employee who is not employed by the Company except as set forth below. Any such payment by the

Company to Party A may only be used for the purposes described in the Redundancy Payment Policy.

(c) In the event that the Company does not offer permanent employment to a Party A employee offered probationary employment (the "Probationary Employee") pursuant to paragraph (a), the Company shall decide whether or not to offer probationary employment to another employee of Party A. If the Company does offer probationary employment to another employee of Party A, the Company shall not be required to make any payment in respect of the Probationary Employee. If the Company does not offer probationary employment to an employee of Party A in place of the Probationary Employee, the Company shall make a one-time payment of RMB 50,000 in respect of such Probationary Employee, and shall not be required to make any further offer of employment to an employee of Party A in the place of such Probationary Employee. Notwithstanding the above, the Company shall not be required to make any such payment in respect of an employee, or to accept another employee of Party A in place of an employee, who resigns voluntarily from the Company or is dismissed for disciplinary reasons.

(d) It is currently contemplated by the Parties, as set forth in the Feasibility Study, that the complement of salaried employees from Party A will not be less than _____ workers. . . .

14.3 LABOR CONTRACTS

The Company shall enter into individual labor contracts between the Company and individual employees in the form agreed by the Parties. All local employees shall be paid in RMB. The Company shall only employ those who pass the physical examination based on the relevant Chinese regulations and Acme standards. . . .

14.5 CONTRIBUTING FUNDS

The Company shall pay an amount equal to:

(a) two (2%) percent of the actual wages received by local Chinese employees of the Company into the Company's trade union fund for such trade union's use in accordance with the applicable laws of China on the management of trade union funds; and

(b) the percentage of the actual wages received by local Chinese employees of the Company required by applicable law to be paid into the insurance, welfare, pension, housing and other statutory funds for the benefit of the employees and any other employee allowance required by applicable law.

The General Manager shall approve the disbursement of amounts from the funds referred to in paragraph (b).

ARTICLE 15 FINANCIAL AFFAIRS AND ACCOUNTING

15.1 ACCOUNTING SYSTEM

(a) The chief financial officer of the Company, under the supervision of the General Manager, shall be responsible for the financial management of the Company.

(b) The standard bookkeeping currency of the Company shall be Renminbi. The accounting system and procedures to be adopted by the Company shall be drafted in accordance with the Accounting System of the People's Republic of China for Foreign Investment Enterprises and other relevant rules and regulations ("Accounting System"). The internationally used debit and credit method, as well as the accrual basis of accounting, shall be adopted as the methods and principles for keeping accounts.

15.2 AUDIT

(a) An independent auditor (the "Independent Auditor") registered in China who is capable of performing accounting work meeting both Chinese domestic accounting standards and international standards shall be engaged by the Company, as its auditor, to examine and verify the Annual Accounts, and submit its report to the Board of Directors and the General Manager. The Company shall submit to the Parties and to each director the audited Annual Accounts within 60 days after the end of the fiscal year, together with the audit report of the Independent Auditor. . . .

15.6 DIVIDENDS DECLARATION

Considering the cash flow and financial position at the end of each fiscal year, the Board of Directors shall determine if dividends shall be distributed to the Parties in Renminbi in proportion to their respective shares in the registered capital. If the Board of Directors determines that dividends should be distributed to a Party or the Parties in foreign exchange, the Company shall convert Renminbi into the relevant foreign exchange at the official rate announced by the Bank of China on the date the distribution is made and payment shall be made in foreign exchange. Such dividends shall, unless the Board of Directors decides otherwise, be distributed once a year and the plan of dividends distribution shall be determined by the Board of Directors within sixty (60) days after the receipt of the audited Annual Accounts referred to in paragraph (a) of Article 15.2 above.

ARTICLE 16 TAXATION AND INSURANCE

16.1 INCOME TAX, CUSTOMS DUTIES AND OTHER
TAXES—REQUESTS FOR PREFERENTIAL TREATMENT

(a) The Company shall pay tax in accordance with the relevant laws and regulations of China and local regulations applicable in Beijing Municipality. Chinese and foreign employees shall pay individual income tax in accordance with applicable Chinese law and regulations.

(b) The Parties shall assist the Company to apply for the Company the benefits of all applicable tax exemptions, reductions, privileges and preferences which are available.

16.2 INSURANCE

(a) Insurance will, as required by applicable Chinese law, be obtained in China and such policies will be denominated in RMB and/or foreign currencies, as appropriate.

(b) The Company shall maintain third party liability insurance and other relevant insurance coverage in order to protect the Company, its employees, agents and other appropriate parties from claims. . . .

ARTICLE 18 FAIR DEALING

18.2 NON-COMPETITION

Each Party agrees that it will not enter into any joint venture, contract manufacturing agreement or other production arrangement (each, a "Transaction") in the Area of Beijing with any of the competitors of Party A or Party B or with any other company whose business is connected with the competitors unless such Party has first given a notice in writing (the "Notice") to the other Party setting forth the name, address and ownership information of the third Party, (b) summarizing the terms on which the Party proposes to enter into the Transaction, and (c) offering the other Party the preferential right to participate in the Transaction on terms no less favorable than those offered to the third Party. If the other Party fails to commence good faith negotiations with such Party to enter into the Transaction within three (3) months after receiving the Notice, such Party may enter into the Transaction with the third Party on the terms set forth in the Notice no later than one year after the date of the Notice.

ARTICLE 19 JOINT VENTURE TERM

19.1 EFFECTIVE DATE

This Contract and its Annexes shall be submitted to the Approval Authority for approval and shall come into force on the day on which the Approval Authority issues its certificate of approval, provided that, in the event that this Contract is not approved within four (4) months of the date set forth on the first page of this Contract, both Parties will take the necessary steps to effectuate the termination of this Contract.

19.2 JOINT VENTURE TERM

The term of the Company (the "Joint Venture Term") shall be 50 years from the Establishment Date.

19.3 EXTENSION OF JOINT VENTURE TERM

At least two (2) years prior to the expiration of the Joint Venture Term, the Parties shall hold consultations to discuss the extension of the Joint Venture

Term. If both Parties agree to extend the Joint Venture Term, an application for such extension shall be submitted to the Approval Authority for approval not less than six (6) months prior to the expiration of the Joint Venture Term.

ARTICLE 20 TERMINATION; DISPOSAL OF ASSETS ON DISSOLUTION

20.1 TERMINATION OR DISSOLUTION

The Company shall be dissolved and the Contract terminated in accordance with the Joint Venture Law, the Joint Venture Regulations and the Articles of Association of the Company (i) upon expiration of the Joint Venture Term (if not extended) or any extension thereof, or (ii) if any of the conditions or events set forth below shall occur and be continuing, in which case the Parties shall cause their representatives on the Board of Directors, upon written notice by any Party, to unanimously adopt a resolution to dissolve the Company:

(a) The Company sustains significant losses in three (3) consecutive years and, after consultations, the Parties are unable to agree on a method to improve the economic situation of the Company to the extent satisfactory to both Parties;

(b) The Company is unable to continue operations for six (6) months or more because of an Event of Force Majeure;

(c) The Seagull Trademark Exclusive Licensing Agreement, the Acme Trademark License Agreement or Technical Assistance Agreement or the Foreign Exchange Services Agreement are not entered into within six (6) months after the Establishment Date or are terminated early;

(d) The Company is unable to continue operations because of the failure of any Party to perform its obligations under the Contract if, in the reasonable opinion of the non-breaching Party, such non-performance defeats the economic objectives of the Contract and of the establishment of the Company or creates a material risk of loss to such non-breaching Party or materially and adversely affects the value of its interest in the Company;

(e) Either Party fails to make its contributions in accordance with the provisions of Article 6 of this Contract, where such failure continues for a period of more than three months and is not waived by the other Party;

(f) A material portion of the assets or property of the Company or the interest of either Party in the Company is subject to expropriation or requisition or the Chinese or other personnel of the Company are subject to reassignment or withdrawal with the effect that the operations of the Company are, in the reasonable opinion of either of the Parties, adversely affected;

(g) Any law or regulation is imposed by the Chinese government which controls the export or sale for foreign exchange of the products of the Company, the effect of which will render the Company unable to carry out its normal operation; or

(h) The Parties mutually agree to dissolve the Company.

After the Board of Directors resolves to dissolve the Company, it shall apply to the Approval Authority for approval of such dissolution. . . .

ARTICLE 23 LAWS APPLICABLE

23.1 APPLICABLE LAW

The formation, validity, interpretation, execution, amendment, settlement of disputes and termination of this Contract shall be governed by the laws of the PRC. In the event that there is no relevant provision of Chinese law, international practices may be used as a reference. . . .

ARTICLE 24 SETTLEMENT OF DISPUTES

24.1 ARBITRATION

(a) Any dispute arising from, out of or in connection with the Contract shall be settled through friendly consultations between the Parties. Such consultations shall begin immediately after one Party has delivered to the other Party a written request for such consultation. If within 30 days following the date on which such notice is given, the dispute cannot be settled through consultations, the dispute shall be submitted to arbitration in Beijing under the China International Economic Trade and Arbitration Commission ("CIETAC") upon the request of any Party with notice to the other Party.

(b) There shall be three (3) arbitrators. Each Party shall select one arbitrator within thirty (30) days after giving or receiving the demand for arbitration.

(c) The arbitration proceedings shall be conducted in English.

(d) Each Party shall cooperate with the other Party in making full disclosure of and providing complete access to all information and documents requested by the other Party in connection with such proceedings, subject only to any confidentiality obligations binding on such Party.

(e) The arbitral award shall be final and binding upon all Parties. The costs of the arbitration shall be as fixed by the arbitration tribunal.

ARTICLE 25 MISCELLANEOUS

25.4. LANGUAGE

This Agreement is written in English and Chinese and the two versions shall have equal weight and validity. In case of any inconsistency between the English version and Chinese version, the Parties shall enforce the version that is more consistent with their intent as evidenced by the context of the entire agreement. Where there is a discrepancy between the two interpretations, such a question may be submitted for arbitration as provided herein. . . .

25.6 ANNEXES

The Annexes and Schedules attached hereto are hereby made an integral part of this Contract and are equally binding with these Articles 1 to 25. The Annexes and Schedules are as follows:

Annex A   Distribution Agreement
Annex B   Land Use Transfer Agreement

NOTES AND QUESTIONS

1. In addition to the joint venture contract set forth, the parties must also agree to articles of association for the new company. The JV contract set forth the rights and obligations of the two parties to the venture whereas the articles of association set forth the basic organization of the joint venture itself. Annexes A-H and Schedules 1-3 described in Article 25.6 above give you an idea of the types of ancillary documents that must accompany the joint venture contract. All of these joint venture documents form part of the package that must be submitted to PRC authorities for approval.

2. Review Articles 1 and 2 of the JV contract. Who are the parties to the joint venture? Why did Acme set up the joint venture this way?

3. Local partners will generally attempt to transfer as large a number of its workers to the joint venture as possible. Why? How does the JV contract deal with this issue? See Article 14 in the JV contract.

The number of workers to be transferred from the local partner to the joint venture tends to be one of the most contentious issues in negotiations. This is an issue that is unrelated to the actual operations or business of the joint venture but will consume substantial energies of the foreign investor during the setup process and likely throughout the life of the joint venture. This is an example of peripheral issues in China and other developing countries that are generally not encountered in the United States but which require significant attention in running a business enterprise. In addition to a disagreement over the number of workers from the local partner needed to run the joint venture, there are also many issues relating to conflicts in the workplace caused by the collection of a diverse workforce usually consisting of many nationalities and backgrounds. An expatriate foreign manager from the United States or Hong Kong (still treated equivalent to a foreign nation) may have a salary that is ten times higher than the salary for a local manager who works at the next desk even though both have the same position and responsibility within the company. As China is viewed as a "hardship" assignment, expatriate workers often receive other amenities such as company-provided housing, subsidies for international schools for their children, and company-provided chauffeured automobiles. There are often perceived (as well as real) issues of superiority, arrogance, and condescension among foreign employees, including those from Hong Kong and Taiwan toward local employees that result in tensions at the workplace. Some practices by MNEs did not help in alleviating these perceptions of superiority. In the 1990s at Procter & Gamble (China), Ltd., for example, P&G's Western executives lived in company-provided housing in Hong Kong and commuted to P&G's China headquarters in nearby Guangzhou (about 100 miles inland) during the week. A typical schedule would have the executive work at P&G's Hong Kong office on Monday, take a flight on Tuesday morning and arrive at P&G's China headquarters by noon, stay in a hotel, and work in the China offices until Thursday at about 3 p.m. when they would fly back to Hong Kong and work at the Hong Kong office on Friday. The policy was based on the view that it was too much of a "hardship" to live in Guangzhou on a full-time basis. As you can imagine, many of P&G's local employees viewed this arrangement as an example of Western condescension and arrogance (not to mention extravagance) as they had to live in the "hardship" environment of China every day of their lives. P&G eliminated this practice of commuting in the late 1990s, but as a cost-cutting measure.

Despite the many efforts of MNEs to combat perceptions of inequality, there is still a widespread perception that there is an unspoken hierarchy on issues of rank and salary with U.S. or European expatriates at the top, followed by overseas Chinese from Hong Kong, Singapore, and Taiwan in the second tier, and followed at the bottom by local PRC employees. There is also often a perceived "glass ceiling" for local workers who feel that they can never obtain a certain level of professional achievement and salary without a degree from a Western university and foreign citizenship. Many local employees in MNEs in China aspire to obtain the salaries, benefits, and perks given to Western expatriate managers but this is usually impossible under company policy as these arrangements are available only as temporary inducements to expatriates to work in China. The theory of many companies is that foreign expatriate managers are to remain in China only for a short period of time in order to train local employees to be their permanent replacements. The local employees would then be paid at local wages, which are high in comparison to other jobs in China, but only a small fraction of the cost of an expatriate manager. However, many companies, such as Procter & Gamble, found that they had to keep foreign expatriate managers in China far longer than expected and some on a permanent rotating basis. As a result, a perception arose of a permanent hierarchy and vast differentials in pay and benefits at the workplace for foreigners and locals. It is often said in China that the "dream" of many local workers is to study abroad, acquire foreign citizenship, and return to China as an expatriate to live among friends and relatives under conditions provided for expatriate managers.

The types of labor issues described above are also pervasive in other developing countries. Why? Why are these issues less likely to exist in a developed country?

4. Although foreign investors entered into joint ventures in great numbers during the first phase of foreign investment in China in the 1980s, many MNEs soon found that there were many conflicts with the local partner. There are many areas of conflict but we focus on two major areas in this note. First, in many cases, the parties had different goals and expectations. (A popular expression in China is "Same Bed, Different Dreams.") The foreign investor usually had a long-term horizon and during the initial years of operation often wanted to reinvest its profits into building the business. The local partner, however, often wanted profits to be paid out as soon as possible in the form of dividends as it was under pressure from local supervisory authorities to demonstrate profits and to pay taxes on those profits to local governments. A second major area of contention is that the local partner often saw the joint venture as a means to improve its own operations. The

local partner often saw nothing wrong with using technology acquired from the foreign investor used for the joint venture to improve its own operations and upgrade its products. After all, this was one of the reasons why the local partner entered into the joint venture in the first place. If the two companies were in the same business (such as Acme and Seagull in our hypothetical case), the local partner was actually using the foreign investor's technology to make itself into a better competitor with the joint venture. This use of technology would usually incense the foreign investor who saw this as misappropriation of technology and, more important, a breach of trust. Many foreign investors found that managing conflicts with the local partner consumed significant time and resources that could have otherwise been devoted to operating the business. These and other issues have led many foreign investors to seek out the WFOE as an investment vehicle and is one reason for their increasing popularity. This experience in China mirrors that of many MNEs in other developing countries as well.

D.   Foreign Direct Investment in Brazil

We now turn to an examination of FDI in Brazil. Keep in mind when you review these materials that although there are some aspects of FDI in Brazil that are unique to that country, there are also some larger issues of strategic importance to the foreign investor involving the region as well as some issues that are common among other developing countries, including other countries in South America. What are some of these issues?

First, a foreign investor making an initial foray into FDI in a South American country will not only consider the issue of which country will serve as a good target of FDI in the present but will also ponder the obvious issue of which country can also act as a base for expanding business into other countries in the region. Even the largest MNEs are unlikely, at least initially, to enter two or more countries in South America simultaneously but will choose the country that offers them the best prospect for business success in the present as well as a strategic position for future expansion. Keep in mind whether Brazil can serve these purposes or whether another country will be a better option.

Second, like many other developing countries, Brazil has a long history of a shortage of foreign currency and problems related to its balance of payments obligations, that is, the obligation to repay loans or other monetary obligations using foreign currency. Like many developing countries, Brazil's currency, the real, cannot be freely converted into a hard currency such as U.S. dollars. As it has a shortage of hard currency, Brazil must carefully regulate the exodus of hard currency because its limited stores of hard currency are needed for most types of international monetary obligations and transactions, including the repayment of loans, as few, if any, foreign creditors will accept reals. Note that while Brazil and other countries will regulate the exodus of foreign currency, like many other countries, Brazil will allow foreign investors to repatriate the foreign capital that they have brought into Brazil for the purpose of making a foreign direct investment and will also authorize, under certain conditions, the exodus of foreign currency for the purpose of repatriating profits and for other types of payments. Without such an exception for the repatriation of foreign capital brought into Brazil and an allowance for the repatriation of profits in foreign currency, Brazil would be able to attract few foreign investors. How, and under what conditions, capital, profits, and other payments can be repatriated in foreign currency, that is, U.S. dollars, is a fundamental issue for foreign investors in Brazil and many other developing countries.

As we have suggested, obtaining foreign currency is a common problem in developing countries. How common? Until just several years ago, China also had strict currency exchange controls but these have been relaxed as China now boasts the second largest foreign currency reserves in the world. Similarly, Argentina subjected foreign currency to strict controls for four decades but lifted the controls in 1989, allowing foreign exchange to be freely sold and transferred in and out of the country. But while some developing countries eliminate their foreign currency controls once they have reached a stage of development where they are no longer burdened by chronic shortages of hard currency, many other developing countries in the world did not find themselves in this fortunate position. Other South American countries, such as Chile, continue to maintain foreign currency controls and, like Brazil, Chile also maintains a registration system under which foreign capital and loans brought into the country must be registered with central banking authorities. Keep in mind that foreign currency issues, which are of fundamental importance for foreign investors in Brazil, are common problems for foreign investors in developing countries and that the management of these issues in Brazil, explored in the problems below, offers lessons for dealing with the same problem in other countries in the world.

1. Brazil's Approach to FDI

Brazil's approach to FDI differs from the approach that some developing nations have adopted, which is to create a specific legal regime regulating FDI and to designate certain government authorities to screen foreign investment. A useful comparison is that of Brazil with China. As we have seen, China's laws recognize a certain class of business entities called foreign investment enterprises that are specifically designed as vehicles for foreign capital. In addition, PRC law requires that all foreign investment enterprises must be approved by PRC authorities and continue to be subject to regular supervision in the form of regular reporting requirements. By contrast, Brazilian law has not created a special class of business vehicles for FDI but allows foreign investors to participate freely in the general group of business vehicles available to all investors in Brazil. No special permission or screening is required in Brazil for a foreign investor to buy or establish a Brazilian company. Rather, foreign investors follow the laws governing the establishment of business entities as if they were no different from domestic investors. In Brazil, FDI is chiefly regulated through the Profits Remittance Law and Brazilian tax laws, which operate together to create a system of sticks and carrots relating to the repatriation of capital and profits. Moreover, while China's FDI laws are mandatory, compliance with Brazil's Profit Remittance Law is optional as foreign investors are not required to register their capital with the Central Bank. As you review the materials in this section, keep in mind the different approaches taken by Brazil and China, two countries in a similar stage of economic development, and consider the merits and disadvantages of each approach from the perspective of the foreign investor.

The rationale for Brazil's approach is that screening FDI at the point of entry into the market involves the making of judgments by government agencies on what are meritorious FDI projects, which is a difficult task that government agencies may not be qualified to handle and often results in erroneous conclusions.

In addition, the type of pervasive regulation of FDI typical of some developing countries can deter foreign investors who may find such regulation to be intrusive. Brazil's approach is to allow market forces and the foreign investor to decide what are meritorious projects and to limit government oversight in all areas except for repatriation of capital and profits. Regulation of FDI will not occur at the point of entry and continue throughout the life of the foreign invested business entity as it does in some countries but at the other end of the process when the foreign investor seeks to repatriate capital or profits.

To be sure, the issue of repatriation of capital and profits is a crucial issue and if a nation were to regulate any one aspect of FDI, repatriation of capital and profits is the most logical choice. For example, once a U.S. company has established a successful business abroad, the U.S. foreign investor will seek to reap the benefits of its success by returning the profits earned to the United States. If capital and profits cannot be easily repatriated to the foreign investor's home country, then the investor (and its shareholders) will not be able to enjoy the full fruits of its success. How and under what conditions such repatriation occurs is of crucial importance to the foreign investor.

We include the main provisions from the Profits Remittance Law and summarize some of the key aspects of Brazilian tax law in the materials that follow but we turn first to a closer examination of the policies behind those laws.

A. POLICY OBJECTIVES

The regulation of FDI in Brazil through the Profits Remittance Law and various tax laws is based on two basic policy goals: (1) The need to regulate and control the exodus of foreign hard currency that is used to repatriate foreign capital and to make payments such as dividends, interest, and royalties to a foreign investor located in a foreign nation, such as the United States; and (2) the need to ensure that foreign companies pay their share of taxes on any payments that are remitted to a foreign nation so that foreign investors do not exploit Brazil by earning unfairly high profits. At times in tension with these two policy goals is a third objective of providing a legal environment that can attract and retain FDI. The recent history of FDI in Brazil indicates that the first two policies have been in conflict with the third objective and have at times, especially in the decades preceding the 1990s, discouraged FDI. After its adoption of a democratic form of government in the latter half of the 1980s, Brazil made a number of changes in the 1990s, which have indicated that the balance has been shifted in favor of fewer harsh controls and more liberal laws that are designed to implement the two policy objectives in favor of greater incentives for foreign investment.

B. SOME BACKGROUND ECONOMIC HISTORY AND CONSIDERATIONS

To understand the first policy goal, which is largely driven by a need to protect the Brazilian currency against devaluation and to prevent depletion of Brazil's store of foreign currency reserves, it is necessary to review Brazil's recent economic history during the latter half of the twentieth century. For much of this period, Brazil's currency, the real, came under severe inflationary pressure caused by a number of Brazilian fiscal policies that led to hyperinflation and a drastic depreciation of the value of the real. The depreciation within Brazil of the value of the real, in turn, created pressures on Brazil's Central Bank to devalue the

Brazilian currency against a basket of hard currencies, including the U.S. dollar, on the foreign exchange market. The economic policy that led to severe internal inflation was primarily a long-standing policy of deficit spending by the Brazilian government. Deficit spending exists when a government spends beyond what it has the capacity to pay for with funds in the government treasury. Beginning in the 1950s, Brazil, which has also long viewed itself as being on the cusp of a first world country, embarked on an aggressive campaign of government spending to catch up to advanced industrialized countries. As government corruption and patronage were also common, the demands for government largesse were further increased by an endless amount of unnecessary spending for phantom projects in the form of "pork" that was required to garner legislative support among Brazil's many political parties for any type of government expenditure.

Brazil's deficit spending was not in itself the cause of the country's inflation woes. A common method used by governments to cover the deficit is to raise funds through the use of credit, such as by borrowing money to pay its debts through the issuance of government bonds, which are essentially debts owed by the government to the bondholder. The bondholder buys the bond at a discount from the face amount of the bond to the government. The bond is treated as a loan and the government pays interest on the bond to the borrower (which is interest on the loan) and then pays off the face amount of the bond at maturity, which represents the repayment of the principal of the loan usually plus some amount that was discounted when the bond was originally purchased. Bonds and other debt instruments raise short-term cash that the government can use to cover its expenses but do not address the long-term issues of how to eliminate the budget deficit through economic growth and, as a result, are usually used as part of an overall economic stimulus package. In Brazil's case, however, the government covered its deficit spending not by using credit (in the form of government bonds or otherwise) but by printing more money and encouraging the use of "near money" such as U.S. dollars, which only led to additional spending. As a fiscal policy, moreover, the issuance of more paper money to cover the deficit was a disastrous policy as it led directly to chronic hyperinflation. As there was an ever-increasing oversupply of Brazilian reals in the economy, it took more reals to buy the same goods and services as the value of each real was worth less, resulting in a severe depreciation of the currency. Other policies that led to hyperinflation included a decision by the Central Bank to cover all loans made by state banks, creating an incentive for local banks to issue ill-advised, worthless, and unrepayable loans as the banks knew that they were protected by the Central Bank. The issuance of unrepayable loans resulted in an even higher increase in the amount of money in circulation and also encouraged irresponsible spending, which also contributed to inflation. The depreciation of the real caused by chronic inflation also meant that the real was depreciating in value in the foreign exchange market against such currencies as the U.S. dollar. As the value of the real declined and was worth less in Brazil, the real was devalued in relation to other currencies such as the dollar and an ever higher number of reals were needed to be exchanged for each U.S. dollar.

By 1993, the inflationary pressures had reached critical levels. The annual inflation rate had reached 2,703 percent, threatening to destabilize the Brazilian economy. In 1994, the Brazilian government introduced the Real Plan to stabilize the currency and to bring inflation under control. A key feature of the Real Plan was to peg the real against the U.S. dollar based on a one-to-one exchange rate to keep domestic prices in check. The one-to-one exchange rate had the psychological effect of creating stabilization and confidence in the real for the Brazilian consumer as the consumer knew that the real would not be devalued. Pegging the real to a high exchange rate in relation to the U.S. dollar, however, did not curb the inflation that continued to create depreciation pressure on the real at home and devaluation pressure on the real in the foreign exchange market. To control some of the excessive spending at home, the Central Bank raised interest rates up to as high as 45 percent in order to increase the cost of borrowing money and to limit spending. The Central Bank also used its reserves of foreign hard currency in the form of U.S. dollars to buy up reals on the open market in order to decrease the amount of reals in circulation to support the value of the real at home and in the foreign exchange market. While these measures did check inflation in the 1990s, it came at a high cost as by some estimates the Central Bank used $60 billion in foreign currency reserves to buy reals on the open market and to prop up the value of its currency.

As these fiscal policies began to prop up the value of the real, it began to appreciate against other hard currencies. Appreciation of the real through government intervention rather than through the growth of the Brazilian economy had the unintended side effect of making Brazilian goods more expensive for foreign consumers as the consumer had to pay more in domestic currency to exchange for the same amount of reals. For example, goods sold from Brazil to the United States were expensive because the U.S. importer had to pay the same amount in U.S. dollars for the goods as they cost in reals, even though the goods did not have an equivalent value on the market as the currency exchange did not reflect market forces but was due to the intervention of the Brazilian government. As you can imagine, the increase in the price of Brazilian goods led to a decline in global demand for the goods and to a decrease in total exports from Brazil in the 1990s to 0.86 percent of total global exports, the lowest figure in three decades. The high interest rates also had the effect of increasing the costs of doing business in Brazil. In the meantime, the use of such a large amount of foreign currency reserves to support the real in the foreign exchange market left Brazil dangerously low on foreign currency reserves. Having a sufficient amount of foreign hard currency was essential for Brazil's balance of payments obligations. As the real was not a freely convertible currency, Brazil had to use hard currencies, such as the U.S. dollar, in buying products from countries, in repaying credit, or in satisfying any other monetary obligations as few countries would accept the real. In addition, hyperinflation caused a constant and continuing depreciation of the real so it was quite risky to accept reals for payment even if one were able to go to the thriving black market in Brazil to exchange reals for hard currency. To deal with these pressures, Brazil borrowed $41 billion, $15.7 billion, and $30 billion in U.S. dollars from the International Monetary Fund in 1998, 2000, and 2001 to replenish its stores of hard currency and to restore confidence in the Brazilian economy. The result of these somewhat painful measures is that Brazil appears to have stabilized its economy and to have eliminated the hyperinflation of the preceding decades through the Real Plan, but at the cost of imposing a heavy burden on the country's economic growth and development. A comparison between Brazil and China, for example, shows the marked difference between their economic growth in the 1990s. Brazil's GDP grew from $465 billion in 1990 to $504 billion in 2001, an 8 percent increase, while China's GDP grew from $387 billion to $1.1 trillion during the same period, a 199 percent increase.

C. THE ENACTMENT OF THE PROFITS REMITTANCE LAW

Against this background of inflationary pressure and pressure on the value of the real, the Profits Remittance Law was first enacted in 1962 and has been continuously amended up to the present. During the beginning of this period, the Brazilian government was of two minds about foreign direct investment. While the government wanted the benefits of FDI, it was also concerned that foreign investors would exploit Brazil by making unconscionably high profits and by contributing to Brazil's balance of payments problems. One way in which foreign investors would potentially harm Brazilian interests would be to bring in foreign capital in the form of foreign investment and then suddenly repatriate all of the original foreign capital as well as additional foreign currency in the form of capital appreciation and profits. As these funds would need to be taken out of Brazil in foreign currency, such a swift departure of foreign capital could intensify Brazil's problems by suddenly depleting Brazil's foreign currency reserves, further exacerbating Brazil's chronic balance of payment problems. Nationalistic pressure led to the enactment of the Profits Remittance Law, which contained a number of harsh provisions limiting the repatriation of foreign currency. For example, as originally enacted, Articles 31 and 32 placed an annual limitation on capital repatriation of 20 percent of registered capital and 10 percent of registered capital on profit remittances. Registered capital refers to the original amount of the foreign capital that was brought into Brazil by the foreign investor and that was recorded or registered with Brazilian authorities. In addition, the Profits Remittance Law limited remittances for patent and trademark royalties and fees for technical assistance to 5 percent of gross sales for a maximum term of five years. These harsh restrictions have all been relaxed or eliminated as we shall examine in detail in a subsequent section.

The Profits Remittance Law worked in tandem with Brazil's tax and customs laws to control the outflow of foreign currency. A foreign investor had to submit proof that all taxes had been properly paid before any remittance in foreign currency could be lawfully permitted. If the foreign investor had the required documentary proof, the foreign investor could then apply to certain designated banks authorized to deal in foreign exchange for remittance in foreign currency to its home jurisdiction. To further discourage the remittance of large amounts of foreign capital, the tax laws imposed prohibitive taxes on certain types of payments. For example, prior to its repeal in 1991, existing Brazilian tax law provided that repatriated dividends that do not exceed 12 percent of registered capital were subject to a withholding tax of 15 percent, but dividends that exceeded 12 percent were subject to a prohibitive supplementary tax of between 40 and 60 percent. The requirement that proof of payment of all taxes before repatriation was also designed to ensure that foreign investors did not take advantage of Brazil by disguising profits as other types of payments and evading Brazilian taxes that were due on profits earned. This feature of the Profits Remittance Law requiring proof of tax payments still exists although much of the harsher tax obligations have also been relaxed.

2. The Business Climate in Brazil

PROBLEM 6-18

Acme, a U.S. company in the consumer products industry, is considering establishing or acquiring a subsidiary in Brazil. Acme manufactures and sells premium-brand shampoos, soaps, toothpaste, and other daily-use consumer products aimed at the upper echelon of the consumer market. Acme's CEO asks you to prepare a report on Brazil as a target market and has the following questions:

(1) What are the main strengths of Brazil, such as demographics and consumer markets, that would support establishing an Acme subsidiary there as opposed to another country in South America such as Chile, which is also being considered?

(2) What are the main problems with the consumer market for Acme's products? Can Acme adapt to these issues?

(3) Where should Acme locate the subsidiary in Brazil?

(4) Is Brazil a potential platform for the export of Acme products to other countries in South America?

(5) Acme wants to develop a line of organic body soaps and lotions, herbal teas, natural vitamin supplements, and biotechnology products (including pharmaceuticals) in Brazil and export these products to North America. Is this a good plan?

Consider the following reading from Professor Gouvea and the accompanying notes.

Raul Gouvea, Brazil: A Strategic Approach
46 Thunderbird International Business Review 165 (April 2004)

[Located in the southern cone of Latin America, the Federative Republic of Brazil is the fifth largest country in the world by area, comprising 8,514,215 square kilometers or 3,286,000 square miles, with the sixth largest population in the world at 172.6 million. Brazil occupies nearly one-half of the entire South American continent, is larger than the continental United States, and is slightly smaller than all of the European countries put together. Brazil borders all South American countries except Chile and Ecuador. The coastline runs for more than 5,700 miles, most of it along the South Atlantic Ocean.]

The country offers a mosaic of climates, flora, fauna, and geological formations. For example, Brazil is home to the largest rainforest in the world, with the Amazon region accounting for 60% of Brazilian territory. Brazilian climates range from equatorial in the Amazon region to subtropical in the Southern region. Temperatures can reach above 40°C in the Amazon region during the summer and below freezing during the winter in the South. Brazil shares its borders with every South American country except Chile and Ecuador.

The Portuguese ruled the country of Brazil for more than three centuries, ranging from 1500 to 1822. Although Brazil gained its independence from Portugal in 1822, many Portuguese influences can still be found, including Brazil's national language, Portuguese. In 1889, the Federal Republic of Brazil was proclaimed. Brazil is comprised of five major regions: North, Northeast, Southeast, South, and Central West. These regions encompass 26 states, the Federal District, and 5,561 municipalities.

Brazil is a melting pot of diverse ethnic groups and religions. It offers a unique mix of European, African, Arab, Asian, and native Brazilian populations. Brazil received waves of European and Asian immigrants in the nineteenth century. The blend of these different cultures makes Brazil a very unique country in Latin America, resulting in a distinguished literary and musical heritage.

The Federal Republic of Brazil is a late-emerging economy, with most of its manufacturing development occurring in the period from 1950 to the 1970s. The Brazilian labor force migrated from the agriculture sector to manufacturing and services over the last 50 years. In the 1940s, close to 66% of the Brazilian labor force was employed in the agricultural sector, 9.4% in the industrial sector, and 24.6% in the service sector. Now, in the early 2000s, 24% of the Brazilian labor force is in the agricultural sector, 20% in manufacturing, and 56% in the service sector. These numbers illustrate some of the changes that have been transforming the Brazilian economy over the last 50 years.

A major shift in Brazil has been the migration of Brazilians from rural areas and coastal cities to urban centers. A majority — 81.7% — of the Brazilian population is now located in urban centers. Brazil has developed more than 31 metropolitan centers with populations exceeding 1 million. Nineteen of these metropolitan centers are in the interior; this inward migration is having a strong impact on the strategies of Brazilian companies. In 1970, only 20% of Brazil's top 500 companies had operations in the interior of Brazil. By 2001, this number had doubled to 40%. Brazil has been a member of Mercosur (Common Market of the South) since 1995. Mercosur's other members are Argentina, Uruguay, and Paraguay. In addition, Brazil has joined with the United States to create a Western Hemispheric free trade area called the FTAA (Free Trade Agreement for the Americas). The FTAA aims to create a free trade area spanning 34 countries in North, Central, and South America.

ECONOMY AND ECONOMIC FACTORS

Table 1 offers an overview of the key economic indicators of Brazil, comparing them to Mexican and Chilean economic indicators.

As shown in Table 1, in 2001, Brazil had the second largest economy in Latin America, with a GDP of US$502.5 billion. The service industry accounted for 56% of the Brazilian GDP, followed by industry with 35% and agriculture with 8%. The economy is still not as open as the Chilean or Mexican economies as measured by the share of imports and exports in the country's GDP. In addition, Brazilian export performance has been less than stellar for the past two decades. Between 1980 and 2000, global trade expanded by 12%-15% annually. In contrast, Brazilian exports in the same period expanded by only 8.6%. In 2001, Mexico exported US$171 billion, compared to Brazil's US$61 billion. Brazil's share of high-tech exports over total exports is also well below Mexico's. In addition, the Brazilian economy shows a very high degree of external fragility as measured by the size of its external debt, US$223.8 billion, one of the world's highest, and by the total debt service ratio, about 90.7%, also the highest in our sample of countries. Brazil's small export volume and high level of debt aggravates the country's global standing.

TABLE 1. Economic Indicators for Brazil, Mexico, and Chile

Economic Indicator	Brazil	Mexico	Chile
GDP (US$billions)	502.5	617.8	63.5
GDP % Growth Last 5 Years	1.5	4.4	3.2
Real Interest Rate	11.8	3.5	2.9
Inflation GDP Deflator (annual %)	7.4	5.5	3.8
Share of Sectors/GDP:			
Agriculture	8.0	4.4	10.5
Industry	35.8	26.8	33.5
Service	56.2	68.9	56.0
Exports (US$billions)	61.7	171.2	16.1
Exports Growth Rate, 1994-2001 (%)	5.6	12.5	7.6
Exports of Goods and Services/GDP	13.4	27.6	31.8
Imports of Goods and Services/GDP	14.4	30.0	30.8
High Tech. Exports/Manufactured Exports	18.6	22.4	3.4
Present Value of External Debt (US$billions)	223.8	157.0	34.9
Total Debt Service (% of Exports of Goods and Services)	90.7	30.2	26.0

BRAZIL'S GLOBAL COMPETITIVENESS

One source of information for Brazil's global competitiveness ranking is "The Global Competitiveness Report," published by the World Economic Forum. The report offers two approaches to the analysis of a country's competitiveness: a) the Growth Competitiveness Index (GCI) and b) the Microeconomic Competitiveness Index (MICI). The Growth Competitiveness Index offers a proxy for the underlying prospects for growth. The index is made of three variables that tend to drive economic growth in the medium and long term, such as technology, public institutions, and macroeconomic environment. The Microeconomic Competitiveness Index reflects the degree of a country's company sophistication and the quality of the country's business environment. Combined, these two indexes offer a broader picture of a country's competitiveness.

Tables 2a and 2b illustrate how Brazil compares with other countries on Growth Competitiveness and Microeconomic Competitiveness.

The 2002 Growth Competitiveness Index shows Brazil ranked forty-sixth. Brazil needs to pay heed to indigenous technology development, something Korea has done. For instance, in 2002, Brazil was not listed as a core innovator, like other emerging economies such as Taiwan, Hong Kong, South Korea, and Singapore. These countries were not listed as core innovators in the 1980s; however, 20 years later they became core innovators. In addition, the country needs to strive to maintain more stable and predictable business policies and strengthen its public institutional environment.

On the Microeconomic Competitiveness Index, Brazil shows an upside potential, ranking thirty-third. The market-oriented reforms introduced in the 1990s created a more competitive business environment, leading Brazilian companies to develop more sophisticated operations and strategies.

Brazil's source of competitiveness can be broken down into four major categories: factor endowments, firm strategy and rivalry, related and supporting industry, and local demand conditions.

TABLE 2A. Growth Competitiveness Index, Components Index (GCI), 2002

Country	GCI Rank	Technology Index Rank	Public Institutions Rank	Macroeconomy Env. Index Rank
United States	1	1	16	2
Korea	21	18	32	10
Chile	20	33	19	13
Mexico	45	47	58	21
Brazil	46	35	45	67
Argentina	63	44	66	65

TABLE 2B. Microeconomic Competitiveness Index, Components Index (MCI), 2002

Country	MICI Rank	Company Operations and Strategy Rank	Quality of National Business Environment Rank
United States	1	1	1
Korea	23	21	23
Chile	31	35	31
Mexico	33	28	36
Brazil	55	45	60
Argentina	65	57	68

FACTOR ENDOWMENTS

Brazil is rich in basic factors (natural resources, climate, location, and demographics), as well as rich in advanced factors (communication infrastructure, skilled labor, indigenous technology, and know-how).

For instance Brazil a) is the world's richest biodiverse country, an "El Dorado" for the rising biotechnology industry; b) accounts for 20% of the world's fresh water, a vital input in agricultural production for the coming decades; c) is rich in minerals, allowing Brazil to be a leading producer of aluminum and steel in the Americas; and d) has a population that is predominantly young and increasingly more educated. This fact points to a growing domestic market and an increasing supply of skilled labor. In 2002, 250,000 Brazilians were enrolled in graduate-level programs such as MBA programs. In addition, the privatization program introduced in the 1990s helped improve the country's infrastructure, especially the telecommunications industry. Brazil's increasing importance as a producer of jet commuter planes (Embraer) also points to a growing and solid expansion of Brazilian know-how and indigenous technology ability.

FIRM STRATEGY AND RIVALRY

Trade liberalization policies introduced in the early 1990s made the Brazilian business environment more competitive and dynamic. Local companies have invested in new technologies and also demanded more qualified labor. The entrance of foreign players in the Brazilian retailing industry has forced a number of local chains to improve the quality and technological content of their services. For instance, in the 1980s, Brazilian consumers found 20,000 different items on supermarket shelves. By 2003, this number had increased to about 70,000. In the auto industry, the number of models increased from 40 in the 1980s to about 400 in 2003. In another example, the existence of a competitive Brazilian engineering industry environment favored the later expansion of Brazilian engineering companies overseas. Companies such as Norberto Odebrecht are operating in North America, Europe, and Latin America.

RELATED AND SUPPORTING INDUSTRY

Brazil's import substitution strategy led to the creation of a diversified manufacturing industry. Brazil's auto industry largely benefits from a very competitive steel, glass, rubber, and auto parts industry. The existence of diversified and competitive suppliers, seeds, agricultural equipment, fertilizers, and insecticides has made the Brazilian agribusiness industry competitive on a global scale.

DEMAND CONDITIONS

Brazilian consumers are sophisticated and demanding. The trade liberalization strategies implemented in the early 1990s further exposed Brazilian consumers to products of higher quality and a greater variety. Several local companies, such as the media giant TV Globo, were responsive to Brazilian TV viewers' demanding standards. TV Globo's increasing attention to quality and product innovation for the Brazilian market turned it into a competitive advantage for the company's global operations. TV Globo's soap operas are sold in Latin American, North American, European, and Asian markets. TV Globo is the world's fourth largest TV network.

THE ROLE OF FOREIGN DIRECT INVESTMENT

In the period of 1995-2000, the country received US$117 billion, second only to China among emerging economies. Several factors have contributed to position Brazil as an important and strategic site for foreign direct investment:

a) *Market Size.* Brazil has the world's sixth largest population, 63% under 29 years old. The size of the Brazilian middle class is estimated at 63 million people. Increasing improvements in income distribution point to a very promising market. In 2001, consumer expenditure on household goods and services was at US$31 billion, the largest in South America, second only to Mexico in Latin America. Total consumer expenditure for 2001 was estimated at US$341 billion, the largest in South America, once again second only to Mexico in Latin America.

b) *Ease and Compatibility of Operations.* Brazil's treatment of foreign direct investment has been quite liberal. Its legislation does not discriminate against foreign companies. In addition, the Constitutional Reform of 1995 abolished a number of state monopolies and made the operations of foreign companies easier for a number of industries.

c) *Cost and Resource Availability.* Brazil's low wages, coupled with increasing labor quality and productivity, make the country a very attractive site for manufacturing and exporting. Along with its rich minerals and farming land, the country is also becoming an important producer of software, reflecting Brazil's increasing labor skills and quality.

d) *Red Tape.* Brazil's market reforms introduced during the Collor administration and followed by the Cardoso administration reduced the level of red tape and introduced more transparency into the Brazilian business environment. More predictable and transparent rules make investing in Brazil an appealing proposition.

e) *Risks.* Brazil has established a solid democratic regime. Since 1994, Brazil has achieved higher levels of economic stability with increasingly lower levels of inflation. In addition, Brazil's laws are also increasingly protecting patents and trademarks. Brazil's risk-reduced environment has made it an attractive country for FDI.

Foreign direct investment has been an important element in Brazil's quest for economic development and growth. The United States became an important source of foreign direct investments for Brazil after World War II. By the early 1950s, the United States had taken over as the largest investor in Brazil, accounting for more than 40% of all FDI. In addition, implementation of the Import Substitution Industrialization economic strategy in the 1950s diversified sources of FDI for the Brazilian economy. German, French, Italian, and Japanese investments joined U.S. FDI in developing the Brazilian manufacturing sector.

Multinational corporations (MNCs) were also largely responsible for Brazil's export drive in the late 1960s and early 1970s. At that time, the large majority of manufactured products exported from Brazil were produced by multinationals established in Brazil. Multinationals also played a main role in diversifying Brazil's industrial sector. By the mid 1990s, foreign direct investment was increasingly being diverted to the Brazilian service industry. Brazil's privatization program opened a number of service industries to MNCs, such as telecommunications, energy generation, transportation, and financial services.

For the past five decades the Brazilian government has promoted, given incentives to encourage, and controlled the role of FDI in the Brazilian economy. The government has monitored remittances of profits and payments for technology transfer. It has also protected some sectors from foreign competition. Accordingly, the relationship between the Brazilian economy and foreign direct investment is largely controlled by the administration in control of the government at that particular time. For instance, Brazil's attitude toward FDI changed considerably in the 1990s when the market-oriented reforms and policies implemented by the Collor government opened a number of industries to foreign direct investment. The Collor administration understood the need to attract foreign direct investment to Brazil in order to promote higher levels of competition in the Brazilian economy, bring in technology, create jobs, and introduce new managerial styles and strategies. The Real Plan also had an impact on attracting FDI. A more stable and open economy attracted investors from around the globe. For instance, in 2002, Brazil had 15 car manufacturers; this made Brazil the world's fourth largest manufacturer of small-size vehicles.

Changes in the Brazilian Constitution eliminating discriminations against MNCs also had a positive impact on flows of FDI to Brazil. Additional changes have been implemented to further attract FDI. For instance, in 2002, multinationals were allowed to control up to 30% of the voting capital in the Brazilian media industry. This was a high percentage compared to pre-1990.

Table 3 shows the recently increasing share of MNCs and the declining share of state companies in Brazil's total sales. In the period from 1978 to 2000, MNCs increased their share from 35.4% to 45.6% of total Brazilian sales. This reflects the market-oriented reforms implemented in the 1990s, which caused the share of state-controlled companies to decline from 29.7% to about 18.7%. Between 1994 and 2000, close to 1,070 domestic companies were acquired by MNCs.

Foreign direct investment increased from US$0.28 billion in 1990 to US$33.4 billion in 2000 and then declined to US$16.5 billion by 2002. The decline in FDI is a reflection of the global economic recession and macroeconomic instabilities in the Brazilian economy, which were compounded by the Argentine economic and political crisis of 2001-2002.

Brazil's market-oriented reforms, as introduced in the 1990s, had a dramatic impact on FDI attraction to the Brazilian market. In the late 1990s, Brazil was ranked fifth among the world's largest recipients of FDI flows and ranked eighth in the world for its volume of stock of FDI (US$156.8 billion). Brazil increased its share of global FDI from 0.7% in the early 1990s to about 4.5% by early 2000. In the late 1990s, Brazil was second only to China amongst emerging economies for its stock of FDI. This increase in FDI can be translated to the entrance of 80% of the world's top 500 companies into Brazil by 2002.

In the 1990s, FDI targeted the Brazilian service industry. The privatization of sectors of the Brazilian service industry received the lion's share of FDI flowing into the Brazilian economy. For instance, in the period from 1994 to 2001, the share of foreign banks in the Brazilian market increased from 8.4% to 33.7%. Table 4 shows the breakdown of FDI in the Brazilian economy by main sectors. This tabe shows the drastic change in the profile of FDI flowing to Brazil. In 2000, 69% of all FDI flows were concentrated in the service sector, or nontradables with emphasis on infrastructure and financial services, compared to a 30.77% share in 1995.

TABLE 3. Evolution of Sales: Share of MNCs, State Companies, and Domestic Companies

	1978	1989	1995	2000
Multinational Corporations	35.4%	30.8%	33.3%	45.6%
Domestic Companies	34.9%	44.0%	43.6%	35.7%
State Companies	29.7%	25.2%	23.1%	18.7%

TABLE 4. FDI in the Brazilian Economy, Main Sectors, 1995-2000 (percentage of total FDI invested by section)

	1995	2000
Agriculture & Mining	4.49%	2.50%
Manufacturing	64.74%	28.00%
Services	30.77%	69.50%

FOREIGN TRADE

In 1990, Brazil made radical changes in its trade policies, substantially reducing trade barriers along its borders. In 1997, Brazil implemented a computerized trade documentation system, Siscomex, which facilitates import and export processing by adding more transparency and speed to the import process. In 1990, the average tariff was 32%; by 2002, the average tariff fell to 14%. Currently, tariffs range from 5% to 32%. Customs clearance can still be cumbersome and time consuming. On average, customs clearance takes 150 hours. In addition, importers need to register with the Foreign Trade Secretariat–SECEX Export & Import Registry.

Brazil has, however, drastically reduced the list of prohibited imported products, but importation of used equipment and machinery, automobiles, clothing, and other consumer products remain prohibited. In addition, the country still applies a number of trade restrictions including: a) a number of sanitary and phytosanitary (SPS) restrictions; b) the enforcement of reference prices; c) the Ministry of Health requirement that imported processed food receive product registration from the Ministry; d) government procurement policies that are biased toward Brazilian products; e) import controls on genetically modified food products; and f) import restrictions on service exports.

Brazil is currently taking an active role in several trading blocks. It is a cofounder of Mercosur, the common market of the south. However, Mercosur is currently under severe strain caused by the Argentine economic crisis, which is challenging the future of the trading block. Brazil is also an important player in the creation of the Free Trade Agreement for the Americas (FTAA), which is scheduled for implementation in 2005. The FTAA will liberalize trade and investment throughout the Americas and create the world's largest trading block. Implementation of the FTAA is extremely important to Brazil, which sells 50% of its total exports and 70% of its manufactured products within the Americas.

In 2002, Brazil exported US$60 billion. Brazil's leading exporting products included transport equipment, soy beans, steel products, chemicals, frozen meat, footwear, paper and pulp, coffee, and frozen orange juice.

Brazil is a global trader; its main markets are the United States, the European Union, and Latin America. The U.S. market accounts for 24% of Brazil's total exports, followed by Argentina with 10%, and Germany with 4.6%. In 2002, Brazil accounted for 0.9% of global trade, a substantial market share loss compared to the late 1970s and early 1980s, when Brazil accounted for about 1.5% of global trade.

INFRASTRUCTURE

The Brazilian infrastructure shows different degrees of quality and sophistication. The quality of Brazil's roads, railroads, waterways, ports, telecommunications, and energy supply follows the country's regional income disparities. Brazil's most sophisticated and best quality infrastructure is located in the Southeast and Southern regions of Brazil. The privatization of the Brazilian infrastructure has promoted the introduction of higher levels of quality and efficiency. The Brazilian transportation industry is strongly biased toward road transportation, accounting for 63% of freight transportation. Airfreight accounts for only 0.3%, waterway 11.7%, rail 21%, and pipeline 3.9%.

PORTS

The large majority of Brazil's imports & exports reach the Brazilian market through Brazil's 13 major seaports, but its antiquated and inefficient ports increase the cost of doing business with Brazil. The government has launched the Reporto project, aimed at increasing port efficiency and updating the ports with the latest technology. The current quality of Brazilian ports causes delays and a low speed of merchandise processing, which is costing the country US$2.5 billion a year. In addition, the Brazilian longshoremen's union has fought to keep a virtual monopoly, thereby blocking attempts to hire nonunion workers.

ROAD TRANSPORTATION

Brazil developed its transportation industry around highways. The national highway network is around 1.7 million kilometers, of which only 10% are paved roads. Transportation by truck is not the most efficient mode of transportation and the cost of fuel is high.

RAILROAD TRANSPORTATION

The construction and expansion of the Brazilian railroad network has not been a main concern for Brazilian policymakers. The network is small for a country the size of Brazil, reaching only 28,000 kilometers.

WATERWAYS

Waterways are becoming a major mode of transportation, especially for grains. Waterways are now being developed and expanded in the areas around the Pantanal and Amazon region. Currently they extend 50,000 kilometers. Environmental concerns have been the main impediments to further expansion of waterways in environmentally sensitive areas of the country.

AIRPORTS

Brazil has 3,264 airports, but only 570 with paved runways. Airfreight is not very widespread and accounts for only a small fraction of Brazil's freight volume.

TELECOMMUNICATIONS

The Brazilian telecommunications industry has been the subject of aggressive privatization programs. As a result of these privatization moves, the sector has shown high growth rates. Recent emphasis has been placed on cellular services and increasing access to public telephone services. In 2000, Brazil had 909,000 public access phone lines compared to 740,000 in 1999. The ratio of conventional telephones per 100 inhabitants is proof that Brazil is getting closer to countries such as Chile and Argentina. Cellular technology has made phones more accessible to the average Brazilian. In 1994, Brazil had 755,000 cell phones, and by 2001 this number had increased to 29.2 million.

INTERNET

The Internet is also expanding rapidly in Brazil even though less than 3% of the Brazilian population has access. The digital divide poses a major challenge for further Internet expansion. In 2000, the government released two national programs, the Information Society Program and the Electronic Government, that will boost investment in the industry and expand the role of the Internet in Brazil. E-commerce is, however, developing slowly. In a 2002 survey of 100 Brazilian companies from different sectors, 90% stated that they have a Web site; however, Internet sales accounted for only 5% of total sales.

ENERGY

The Brazilian energy production capacity is estimated at 65,000 megawatts, and it is largely dependent on hydroelectric power plants. Lack of investment in the sector led to a nationwide energy crisis in 2001 and consequently, Brazil is currently trying to diversify its energy matrix. In 2002, gas-powered plants were being built to supply some of the country's energy needs. It is expected that by 2005 gas will account for 10% of the country's energy needs. Ethanol, a sugar cane–derived fuel, is also receiving more attention. Unless new investments are made in the sector, Brazil may suffer additional energy shortages in the near future.

MARKET CONSUMPTION DYNAMICS

Brazil has a dynamic and growing consumer market. For 2002, Brazil's total consumer expenditure was estimated at US$298 billion, the largest in South America. According to Table 5, the Southeast region is Brazil's largest urban and rural consumer markets. As shown by Figure 1, in the Southeast region, the state of São Paulo is Brazil's largest urban market, estimated at US$95.8 billion, followed by the state of Rio de Janeiro with US$34.8 billion.

One of the main problems restricting the further growth of Brazil's consumer market is Brazil's unequal income distribution. Nonetheless, Brazil's middle class is a profitable market for a number of industries. For instance, foreign credit card companies targeting the Brazilian middle class profited US$2.7 billion in 2001. Banks, on the other hand, are negatively affected by the small middle class; only 30 million Brazilians have bank accounts, or 17.4% of the Brazilian population.

TABLE 5. Regional Urban and Rural Consumption Potential, 2001 (US$billions)

Regions	Urban Consumption Potential	Rural Consumption Potential
North	11.8	1.3
Northeast	45.0	3.4
Southeast	165.5	3.4
South	54.3	2.5
Midwest	21.7	0.8
Brazil	298.2	11.5

FIGURE 1.   Brazil's Main State Urban Markets, 2001 (US$billions)

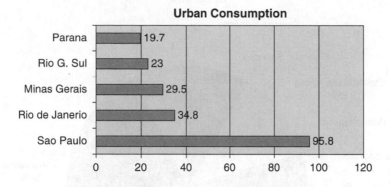

The Brazilian socioeconomic situation, with its large populace of poor people, is leading to the development of new brands and business strategies. These new brands and strategies are designed to explore the poorest segments of the Brazilian market, a segment of the market that has been ignored by local companies over the past few decades. Historically, Classes A and B, with incomes higher than ten minimum wages, accounted for 52% of Brazil's total consumption of goods and services. Class C, with incomes between four and ten minimum wages, accounted for 28% of Brazil's total consumption and Classes D and E, with incomes between one and three minimum wages, accounted for 20% of Brazil's total consumption. Now, with a 37% increase in the size of Class C between 1992 and 2000, new companies and new brands have been introduced specifically to cater to Class C. These new brands (called "B-brands") and companies are taking market share from well-established domestic and multinational companies. For instance, Kellogg used to control 72% of the Brazilian cereal market; by 2002, its market share was reduced to 47% as a result of the introduction of cheaper domestic brands. In 2002, out of 100 boxes of cereal, 32 were accounted for by nontraditional brands. Nestle used to control 62% of chocolate mixes, but in 2002 its share dropped to 52% as a result of increasing competition from new cheaper B-brands. It is estimated that B-brands now account for 30% of the Brazilian market.

PRIVATIZATION

Privatization is a fashionable policy strategy for developed and developing economies around the globe. Brazil has been no exception to this global trend. State-led industrialization was the vogue in Brazil between the 1950s and 1980s. However, by the mid-1980s, state intervention was increasingly becoming a hindrance for the further growth and expansion of the past few decades. In 1990, Brazil unleashed a bold privatization program. Contrary to previous programs, this time privatization was included within the framework of a deregulation project. Thus, the government would no longer act as an entrepreneur, but rather as a rule maker and promoter of growth and development.

In the period from 1990 to 2002, the Brazilian privatization program generated US$105 billion in revenues. State companies generated US$34 billion and federal companies took in US$71 billion. The early years of privatization were largely concentrated in the manufacturing sector, such as steel mills. In the second

FIGURE 2.   Brazilian Privatization Program, Relative Share of Total Revenues
by Sectors

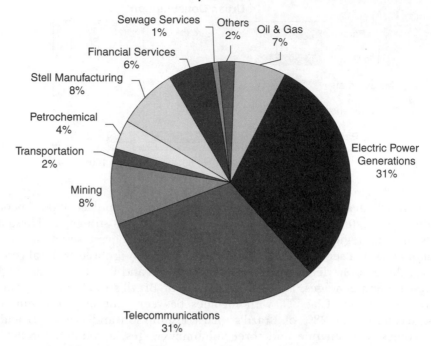

half of the 1990s, the service sector became the main focus of attention. Figure 2
illustrates the relative share of the different sectors that were the focus of the
Brazilian privatization program in the period from 1991 to 2002.

INTELLECTUAL AND INDUSTRIAL PROPERTY RIGHTS

Brazil was late to adopt and implement regulations for intellectual and property rights. In the early 1990s, the first steps were taken to modernize the Brazilian
business environment, laws, and regulations. The Brazilian National Institute of
Industrial Property (INPI) oversees the protection of intellectual and industrial
property rights in Brazil. The following points are important facts to keep in mind
when bringing foreign intellectual property into Brazil:

a) Trademarks: Foreign trademarks should be registered with the INPI.
Nonregistered trademarks run the risk of not being protected by local legislation.
In Brazil, well-known trademarks are given special protection that is aimed at
protecting these globally recognized trademarks from local piracy. Trademarks
must be registered every ten years. If a trademark is not used for five years, its
registration will be voided.

b) Patents: The INPI also controls patents. Companies seeking patent protection need to register their patents with the INPI. Patents must be used within
3 years of their registration or they will be forfeited.

c) Franchising: The INPI also controls franchising agreements. Law number
8955 created the Franchise Law, which oversees the relationship between franchisees and franchisors. According to the 2002 International Planning and
Research Corporation Report (IPR), Brazil continues to be plagued by business
software piracy. However, since 1996, business software piracy shows a declining

trend; piracy rates declined from 68% in 1996 to 56% in 2001. According to the IPR 2002 Report, Brazilian retail software revenues lost to piracy amounted to US$346 million in 2001.

"Hot" Sectors

The Brazilian economy offers a number of opportunities for companies willing to invest in Brazil. Recent market-oriented reforms opened a number of industries to foreign direct investment. The following paragraphs will list some of these sectors.

OIL AND GAS

In 1998, the Brazilian government opened this industry to the private sector and consequently, Petrobras, the Brazilian oil company, no longer has a monopoly. In 2002, Petrobras had a share of 49% of all exploration, while domestic companies and multinationals accounted for the other 51%. The share of industry in the country's GDP increased from 2.7% in 1997 to about 5.5% in 2001. Increasing competition is making the industry more efficient. The sector is expected to grow at 15% per year for the next five years. Offshore petroleum services, offshore production equipment and onshore exploration services offer a number of business opportunities for foreign companies. In 2000, the Brazilian markets for gas and oil equipment and machinery were estimated at US$6 billion.

BANKING AND FINANCIAL SECTOR

Brazil's market-oriented reforms have also led to an increasing exposure of the Brazilian banking industry to foreign competition. The Brazilian banking industry has seen a decreasing participation of state banks, the result of an aggressive privatization program. During the period of 1994-2001, Brazil saw an increasing participation of foreign banks in the Brazilian banking industry. Among Brazil's top 15 banks, six are foreign banks from Europe and the United States: HSBC, ABN, Santander, Bank of Boston (Fleet Bank), and Citibank. The share of foreign banks in the Brazilian banking industry has expanded consistently in the period of 1994-2001. In 1994, foreign banks accounted for 8.2% of the Brazilian banking industry assets. By 2001, this share expanded to 33.7% of the Brazilian banking industry. In 2002, the banking industry accounted for 8.6% of the Brazilian GDP, up from 6.58% in 2001. Increasing inflation rates and high levels of interest rates increased the banking revenues. In 2001, Brazil had 63.2 million bank accounts, up from 50 million in 1999. Internet banking is expanding rapidly, increasing from 8.3 million users in 2000 to 13 million in 2001. Increasing disposable income coupled with improving income distribution should keep the Brazilian banking industry appealing to foreign banks.

AUTO PARTS

This sector generated US$11 billion in revenues for 2001. In 2002, this sector was predicted to expand by 8%, with revenues of US$11.7 billion. Multinationals' share of the Brazilian auto parts industry was a hefty 69% in 2002. The main markets are in gears and friction wheels, rubber products, ball axles, and rollers.

DRUGS AND PHARMACEUTICALS

In 2001, this industry generated US$5.7 billion in revenues. Brazil is the largest Latin American market for the drug and pharmaceutical industry. In 1999, Brazil imported US$2.5 billion worth of pharmaceutical products. Generic drug products are increasingly gaining market share in the Brazilian market, accounting for 6%. It is estimated that by 2005 generic drugs will account for 30% of drug company revenues. Consequently, a number of multinationals are being attracted to the Brazilian market to manufacture generic products.

ELECTRICAL POWER SYSTEMS

Brazil went through an energy crisis from 2001 to 2002. The crisis revealed the sector's need for investment and technology. The Brazilian market for electrical power equipment is estimated at US$2 billion. The Brazilian government is pursuing the diversification of the Brazilian energy matrix. Thermal power generation and renewable energy (excluding hydro) is expected to grow in the next few years. Photovoltaic products and services will be in high demand in the upcoming years. Natural gas power generation also will create demand for equipment and services over the next few years.

TELECOMMUNICATIONS

Privatization and open market competition revolutionized Latin America's largest telecommunication sector. The market is currently estimated at US$8 billion. In the period from 2000 to 2005, it is estimated that US$64 billion will be invested in the industry. The combination of privatization and open market policies has increased the number of fixed phones lines from 10 million in 1990 to 40 million in 2001. Cellular phones increased from thousands of phones in 1992 to 29 million cellular phones in 2001. These numbers show a rapidly growing industry.

COMPUTER HARDWARE AND INFORMATION TECHNOLOGY

Brazil is increasingly investing in computers, software, and information technology. Brazil's computer and peripheral industry has been expanding at rates higher than the rest of Latin America. The number of computers has increased since the early 1990s, as has the number of Internet users. In 1990, the country had 1.6 million computers. This number increased to 11.8 million by 2001. The number of Internet users also expanded from 700,000 in 1996 to 11 million in 2001. Still, these numbers show that Brazil is lagging far behind a number of other emerging economies in terms of computers per capita and the share of the Brazilian population with access to the Internet.

Information technology investments in Brazil were expected to reach US$14 billion by 2002. Expenditures on security software should expand in 2003.

Internet data centers are also expected to expand their operations in the Brazilian market.

MEDIA

The Brazilian media industry was opened to foreign direct investment in 2002. Foreign direct investment in the industry could reach 2.5% of the Brazilian GDP by 2005. The industry reaches 90% of Brazilian households. It is expected that the introduction of Digital TV to the Brazilian market will require US$500 million; most of this investment will be undertaken by multinationals.

RETAILING

Brazil has a sophisticated retailing industry, increasingly adopting self-service formats. In the past decade, the Brazilian retailing industry saw dramatic moves toward the concentration of the industry, a response to the increasing competition in the industry. In addition, this sector has upgraded the technological content of its operations. The Brazilian retailing industry has also attracted global players, such as Wal-Mart and Carrefour. In 2000, the industry received US$1.6 billion in foreign direct investment, reflecting foreigners' perceptions of Brazil's retailing market potential. The Brazilian food-retailing segment has followed general retailing trends, with an increasing participation of foreign companies. According to the Brazilian Association of Supermarkets (ABRAS), the French retailer Carrefour, and the American retailer Wal-Mart are among Brazil's top ten largest national food retailers based on gross revenues.

NOTES

1. As Professor Gouvea notes, Brazil is a member of Mercosur (Common Market of the South), along with Argentina, Uruguay, and Paraguay. Chile and Bolivia are associate members, allowing them to have some of the benefits of Mercosur. Mexico and Cuba have indicated that they wish to join Mercosur. (As you can imagine, Cuba's inclusion in Mercosur is controversial.) Mercosur represents a total population of approximately 200 million people, living in an area of 7,452,000 square miles, twice the size of the continental United States. In recent years, the total GDP of the four principal members of Mercosur was approximately 1 trillion U.S. dollars. In theory, the movement of goods among all members of Mercosur, as a free-trade area (FTA), is free from any customs duties. However, Argentina, with severe economic problems of its own, has adopted a practice of imposing customs duties on imports from Brazil. Argentina's practices are creating a severe strain on Mercosur and if other members of Mercosur retaliate by imposing customs duties of their own on goods from Argentina and these practices spread, this could have the effect of undermining the FTA altogether. Note that Mercosur is an FTA not a customs union although Mercosur has some ambitions of developing itself into a customs union. If that ever occurs, then the lessons learned in the process of establishing an FDI in the European Union may apply to Mercosur as well. For a further discussion of FTAs and customs unions, see pp. 157-158 *supra*.

2. Brazil has also taken the lead in the negotiations for the Free Trade Area of the Americas (FTAA), an ambitious plan to create an FTA among the 34 democracies in the Americas. The original plan called for the establishment of the FTAA by December 2005, but Brazil may also be responsible for creating some of the most significant stumbling blocks to the completion of the FTAA. In negotiating with the United States for the conditions of the FTAA, Brazil (and Argentina) are demanding unrestricted rights to export agricultural products to the United States and the elimination of all government subsidies provided by the U.S. government to U.S. farmers. U.S. policy, however, has long supported the granting of subsidies to the agricultural sector and the elimination of these subsidies altogether will meet with fierce political resistance. The dispute over the agricultural sector has created an impasse that renders it unlikely that the FTAA will be completed by 2005 as originally intended. Rather, it appears that the FTAA will proceed on a piecemeal basis with the United States negotiating free-trade agreements with individual countries. If these and other hurdles can eventually be overcome, the FTAA will create the world's largest free-trade zone.

3. Brazil and the United States also have been at loggerheads over intellectual property rights. We return to the disputes between Brazil and the United States in Chapter 7.

3. Brazilian Laws Relating to Foreign Direct Investment and Business Organizations

The Brazilian legal system is basically modeled on the civil law system and may be compared to the French, Italian, and Spanish systems, all of which have exerted influence on the development of the Brazilian legal system. Brazil has a federal constitution that extensively regulates the entire legal system, defining the powers of the federal, state, and municipal administrations, the Brazilian legislature, and the courts. Business organizations, to which we turn below, are regulated by civil and commercial codes, both part of Brazil's federal law.

A. BRAZILIAN BUSINESS ORGANIZATIONS

As we noted in the introductory materials, Brazil does not create specialized business forms for foreign capital and investment. Rather, the foreign investor will choose one of the Brazil business organization forms. As these business forms were created for domestic use, however, the foreign investor may need to be creative and adapt them for use as vehicles for FDI. The question remains which form of business entity should the foreign investor use and how can the foreign investor adapt it to suit its purposes such as establishing a joint venture with a local Brazilian company? An overview of these forms is set forth below.

PROBLEM 6-19

Pharma, Inc., is considering forming a joint venture with Medico do Brasil, a large state-owned pharmaceutical company. The joint venture is to be a separate legal entity formed and jointly owned by Pharma and Medico. Both joint venture partners also want to manage the new company as it enters into the pharmaceutical industry. Pharma will bring its technology and research and development capabilities and Medico will bring its knowledge of the Brazilian pharmaceutical industry and market to the joint venture. Pharma wants to structure the joint venture so that Pharma has a 60% ownership interest and Medico has a 40% ownership interest. All of Pharma's senior officials work at the company headquarters in Chicago and are all needed at headquarters to run Pharma's U.S. operations and to plan Pharma's international expansion. Pharma asks you to describe which business form you would recommend for the joint venture and how the joint venture should be set up to accomplish Pharma's ownership interests and other goals. Unlike China, Brazil has no special laws governing joint ventures between foreign companies and local Brazilian companies, so Pharma will have to be creative in using Brazil's existing business laws to achieve its goals. Will setting up a consortium with Medico work? Consider the reading from Professor Rosenn below.

Keith S. Rosenn, Overview of Brazilian Business Forms (2004)

A large variety of business organizations are available in Brazil. By far the most common is the sole proprietorship. A sole proprietorship is widely used for small business ventures because of its simplicity, but it has the serious disadvantage of exposing all the proprietor's individual assets to potential liability for the debts of the firm. For medium and large ventures, investors normally utilize a limited liability company or a stock corporation. One should never forget, however, that Brazilian law permits a wide variety of business organization. Occasionally, it makes sense to utilize one of the more exotic forms of business organization to structure a Brazilian operation.

(1) Limited Liability Company (Sociedade Limitada)

The limited liability company, popularly known as the *limitada,* is one of the most commonly used vehicles for investment in Brazil. The Brazilian subsidiaries of large multinationals such as Ford, Pfizer, and Wal-Mart, are organized as *limitadas*. A basic reason for the popularity of the *limitada* has been its extraordinary flexibility. Like the limited liability company in U.S. law, it is a hybrid that combines the limited liability of corporations with the flexibility of partnerships. Prior to the entry into force of the new Civil Code in January 2003, few charter provisions were required by the Limitada Law,[74] giving the organizers virtually *carte blanche*. Today, however, the *limitada* is governed by the Articles 1052 et seq. of the new Civil Code, which has made the *limitada* much less flexible and more costly.

Ownership in a *limitada* is represented only by quotas designated in the charter. A quota, unlike a share of stock, is not represented by a certificate. A quota can be transferred only by changing the charter and filing a copy of the amendment with the Commercial Registry.[75]

The amount of capital of the *limitada* must be set out in the charter and must be subscribed to by two or more persons, who may be either individuals or legal

---

74. Decree No. 3.708 of Jan. 10, 1919.

75. Failure to file the amendment may result in a court's imposing unlimited liability on the quotaholders. See *e.g.*, Mandado de Segurance No. 26.147-1, 285 R. For. 181 (T.J.S.P. 1982).

entities. Brazilian law imposes no minimum capital for a *limitada,* nor does it require that a minimum percentage of subscribed capital be paid in. The *limitada* must have at least one manager, either designated in the charter or in a separate act. If the charter permits the manager to be someone who does not own quotas in the *limitada,* unanimous approval of the quotaholders is required if the capital is not fully paid in, or a minimum of two-thirds must approve if the capital is fully paid in. (Art. 1061). An administrator nominated in a separate act may assume that role only after designation in the book in which the administrative acts are registered.

The Civil Code permits the charter to create a Fiscal Council of three or more members, who do not have to be quotaholders but must be residents of Brazil. Members of the Council are to be elected at the annual quotaholders' meeting. In addition to powers conferred on it by the charter, the Fiscal Council has the power to examine the company's books at least three times per annum, present an annual report to the quotaholders' meeting, denounce fraud or errors, or convene a quotaholders' meeting.

Quotaholders are now required to decide societal matters by formal meeting or assembly. If there are more than ten quotaholders, deliberation in an assembly is mandatory. Annual financial statements, which must include an inventory, a balance sheet, and the economic results of the operations during the year, are mandatory. The notice of the assembly has to be thrice published in the press unless all quotaholders are present at the meeting and acknowledge in writing the place, date, hour and object of the meeting, or vote in writing. Minutes of the meetings must be recorded in the proper minute book and signed. No longer may decisions be taken by informal understanding.

Unless the charter provides otherwise, resolutions of the *limitada* are normally by majority vote. Nevertheless, transformation of the limitada into a different kind of company requires a unanimous vote, unless the charter permits a lower figure. Appointment of managers who are quotaholders in the charter requires a three-fourths vote, as do amendments to the charter, merger, amalgamation and dissolution. Appointment of non-quotaholder managers (after capital is fully paid in) requires a two-thirds vote, as does removal of a quotaholder manager appointed in the charter, unless otherwise agreed upon by contract.

As the name *limitada* implies, quotaholders are generally not responsible for the liabilities of the company. If, however, the amount of subscribed capital has not been fully paid in, each quotaholder is jointly and severally liable for the entire amount of the company's unpaid capital as well as any portion of his own quota that remains unpaid. Once a *limitada's* capital has been fully paid, individual quotaholders will be held personally liable for the company's debts only if the company is irregularly wound up or if the quotaholder violates the charter or commits an unlawful act.[76] But Article 1059 obligates quotaholders to pay back all profits and sums withdrawn from the *limitada,* even if authorized by the charter, whenever such profits or withdrawals reduce the capital.

A *limitada* is automatically dissolved if there are fewer than two quotaholders. To avoid this often undesired result, at least three quotaholders are commonly used unless two of the quotaholders are legal entities.

Unless the charter provides to the contrary, a quotaholder may assign his or her quotas, either wholly or in part, to another quotaholder without permission of

---

76. Appeal No. 105.599-5 of the Supreme Federal Tribunal.

any other quotaholder; however, quotas may not be assigned to a non-quotaholder if holders of more than one-fourth of the capital object.

The *limitada* has three principal advantages over the stock corporation as a vehicle for foreign investors to establish subsidiaries or to set up joint ventures in Brazil. One is that the *limitada* is less expensive to organize and to maintain. Two is that even though characterized as a corporation under Brazilian law, the *limitada* can be either a partnership or a corporation for U.S. tax purposes. All one need to do is file an election with the U. S. Internal Revenue Service as to which status one prefers.[77] Three is that unlike directors of stock corporations, the managers of a *limitada* do not have to be residents of Brazil.[78] In practice, however, at least one of the managers is almost always a Brazilian resident. Generally, management of a *limitada* is entrusted to one or more of the quotaholders, as provided in the charter. Depending upon how the charter is drafted, unanimity, a super majority, or a bare majority of the votes of quotaholders can be required for approval of various kinds of actions, or a particular quotaholder can be empowered to make certain kinds of decisions by himself. Some of the quotaholders can be managers, while others can be mere investors. The drafter of the charter has enormous freedom to structure control arrangements.

The *limitada* has two other advantages over stock corporations. It does not have to maintain the legal reserve required for stock corporations.[79] Moreover, the *limitada* is exempt from a 25 percent tax levied upon corporate reserves and retained earnings to the extent that such reserves exceed paid in capital.[80]

The principal disadvantage of the *limitada* is that its form precludes public participation. The *limitada* cannot issue stock or debentures.

Artificial names, or the names of quotaholders (not all) followed by "e companhia" or "e cia," can be used in organizing a *limitada*. If one uses an artificial name, it must suggest the business activity. Unless the company's name ends with *limitada* or *ltda*, quotaholders have unlimited liability.

(2) STOCK CORPORATION (SOCIEDADE ANONIMA)

The stock corporation (S.A.) most closely resembles the United States corporation. The S.A.'s capital is divided into shares of stock, and the liability of each shareholder is limited to the issue price of the shares to which he has subscribed but not paid in.[81] Preliminarily, all shares must be subscribed to by two or more persons. At least 10 percent of the capital must be paid in cash and deposited with the Banco do Brasil or some other commercial bank before one can incorporate.[82]

---

77. Reg., 61 FR 21989, 26 CFR Part 301 (May 13, 1996). Formerly, one had to draft the bylaws in such a way as to make the *limitada* more like a corporation or a partnership. Rev. Rul. 73-254, 1973-1 C.B. 413; IRS LTR 8019112, Feb. 15, 1980; IRS LTR 8003072, Oct. 25, 1979.

78. See Corporation Law, art. 146. The managing quotaholders do not have to be Brazilian residents. Instead they may exercise their managerial functions through authorized representatives, but these representatives must be Brazilian residents. PINHEIRO NETO, DOING BUSINESS IN BRAZIL (2000), at §§3.126.

79. THOMAS FELSBERG, FOREIGN BUSINESS IN BRAZIL 20 (1976). See also Corporation Law, art. 193.

80. Braz. Tax Reg.s, art. 551.

81. Corp. Law, art. 1.

82. *Id.*, art. 80.

The S.A. must have at least two shareholders. It may, however, be temporarily owned by a single shareholder until the next shareholder's meeting. At that time, the corporation will be dissolved unless the number of shareholders is increased to the legal minimum of two.[83]

Regardless of its objectives, an S.A. is always deemed to be a commercial entity.[84] It must file its charter with the Commercial Registry and publish its acts of incorporation and minutes of annual meetings in the Official Gazette and one other widely distributed newspaper.[85] All financial statements and balance sheets must be similarly published at least once a year.[86]

The Corporation Law permits great flexibility in types of shares that can be issued. An S.A. can issue a wide variety of shares, including registered, treasury, endorsable, no par, book, and founders shares.[87] It can have different classes of stock, such as preferred and common. An S.A. can issue debentures with a floating charge on assets, as well as convertible debentures with or without monetary correction.[88] Up to one-half of the S.A.'s capital can be in the form of preferred shares without the right to vote.[89] Unlike the *limitada*, the S.A.'s name does not have to indicate its principal business activity. A corporation must include "S.A." or "sociedade anonima" at the end of its name, or place "companhia" at the beginning.

Corporations can be either closely held or publicly held. If its capital is open to the public, the S.A. must register its shares with the Securities Commission (CVM).[90]

The S.A. is administered by a board of directors made up of at least two directors. The S.A. may also be governed by an administrative council, consisting of at least three members elected by the shareholders. An administrative council is optional, unless the S.A. has "authorized capital" or is a public corporation.[91] In Brazil, the directors discharge most of the management functions of officers of U.S. corporations, while the administrative councils perform the general policy-making functions of U.S. boards of directors. The board of directors is elected either by the stockholders or by the administrative council.[92] The members of the administrative council are always elected by the stockholders. All members of the board of directors and administrative council must be Brazilian residents but need not be Brazilian nationals.[93] This requirement has created problems for some foreign-controlled corporations, for it used to be common practice for members of their administrative councils to be nonresidents. Corporations with closely held capital can dispense with an administrative council, but corporations whose capital is open to the public must either move certain key personnel to Brazil or operate with straw representatives on the council.

---

83. *Id.*, art. 206(I)(d).
84. *Id.*, art. 2, para. 1.
85. *Id.*, arts. 94, 134(5), and 289.
86. *Id.*, art. 176(1).
87. *Id.*, arts. 11, 20, 31-34, and 46.
88. *Id.*, arts. 52, 54, 57, and 58.
89. *Id.*, art. 15(2), as modified by Law No. 10.303 of Oct. 31, 2001.
90. *Id.*, art. 4.
91. Corporation Law, arts. 138, 140 and 143. A corporation with "authorized capital" simply has authorized the issuance of more shares than have been subscribed.
92. *Id.*, art. 143.
93. *Id.*, arts. 140, 145, and 146.

Brazil's Corporation Law requires an annual shareholder's meeting within four months after the close of the company's fiscal year. At this meeting, management's accounts and balance sheets are reviewed and a dividend distribution policy is adopted. In addition, the shareholders elect the management and the audit committee.[94] The audit committee is supposed to examine the corporate books every quarter and to report its findings to the stockholders. In practice, however, most audit committees simply go through the motions.[95]

Corporate charters usually provide for a minimum mandatory dividend. If there is no such provision, Brazilian law mandates that 50 percent of net profits, less appropriations for reserves, be distributed as dividends.[96]

Five percent of net profits must be placed in a legal reserve to protect the integrity of the corporation's capital. This reserve can be used only to offset losses or to increase capital. If the reserve reaches 20 percent of the corporation's capital, additional appropriations are no longer necessary.[97] If the reserve exceeds the corporation's capital, the excess will be subject to a 25 percent tax unless it is capitalized or distributed as dividends.[98]

(3) BRANCH OFFICE

A foreign corporation can operate in Brazil as a branch, but few companies other than banks organize themselves as branches. Opening a branch requires a decree issued by the President of the Republic.[99] Substantial delays in issuing such decrees are common; occasionally, the President has refused to issue a requested decree. Setting up a branch is considerably more time-consuming and costly than organizing a *limitada* or an S.A. because one has to file many more documents and secure presidential action. The application for the decree must show that a Brazilian resident has been appointed as the foreign parent's representative with unrestricted authority to perform any and all acts and to accept service of process.[100] As Paul Garland has observed: "As a result, such a person almost certainly has more power to commit the company than any other executive."[101]

Branch organization also has significant tax disadvantages. Like any other business organization, a branch is considered to be a legal entity separate from its foreign parent and is taxed on its net profits.[102] In addition, the after-tax profits of the branch are then conclusively presumed to be immediately distributed to the parent, irrespective of whether they are actually credited to the parent or remitted abroad. Thus, branch profits are automatically subject to the 15 percent withholding tax on Brazilian source income of foreign residents or domiciliaries.[103]

---

94. *Id.*, art. 132.

95. P. GARLAND, DOING BUSINESS IN AND WITH BRAZIL 164 (3d ed. 1978).

96. Corporation Law, arts. 109(I) and 202.

97. *Id.*, art. 193.

98. Braz. Tax Regs., art. 551.

99. Decree-Law No. 2.627 of Sept. 26, 1940, arts. 64 and 65. These provisions were explicitly maintained in force by Article 300 of the Corporation Law.

100. Civil Code, art. 1138.

101. P. GARLAND, *supra* note 95, at 167.

102. Braz. Tax Regs., arts. 95 and 96(II).

103. Braz. Tax Regs., arts. 554 and 555, ¶9; Law No. 4.131 of Sept. 3, 1962, as amended, arts. 41-43. *See* Parecer Normativo CSL No. 05 of Mar. 6, 1974.

(4) JOINT VENTURES

Brazilian law has no systematic treatment of joint ventures. Nor does Brazil have legislation formally requiring foreign companies to form joint ventures with Brazilian firms. Nevertheless in a few areas, such as petrochemicals, engineering and mining, the joint venture has often been a *de facto* requirement for a foreign company's doing business in Brazil.[104] Joint ventures can be organized by contract, but the contractual joint venture usually takes the form of a silent partnership *(sociedade em conta de participção)*. In such cases the Civil Code requires that one party be an active participant and the other a passive participant.[105] If this form of business organization is unsuitable, joint venturers usually organize a new company or buy shares of an existing corporation. The most common vehicles for joint ventures are the *limitada* and the S.A.

The principal advantage of using the *limitada* is that the joint venture rules can be set out in the charter. Since alterations of the charter cannot be registered without the signature of each quotaholder, barring a provision to the contrary in the charter,[106] joint venturers have some assurance that their agreement will be respected. Nevertheless, if the agreement is not respected, Brazilian law contains no mechanism for securing specific performance of the obligations stipulated in the *limitada* charter. To a limited extent, this remedial gap in Brazilian law can be bridged by use of a liquidated damages clause.

This remedial gap can also be bridged by use of the corporate form for a joint venture. Brazil's Corporation Law makes shareholders' agreements concerning share transfers and voting specifically enforceable, provided that such agreements are registered on the books of the S.A. and noted on the share certificates.[107] Creative drafting of such shareholders' agreements may bring joint venture arrangements within this rare opportunity for specific performance.

Some mechanism is needed to break deadlocks should the venturers disagree. The S.A. operates on the majority vote principle, but the bylaws of an S.A. with closed capital can stipulate that extraordinary majorities are required on certain issues.[108] Controlling stockholders must take into account a substantial body of law requiring them to act for the benefit of the corporation and to respect the rights of the minority.[109]

(5) CONSORTIA

Brazilian law permits consortia, but does not recognize the consortium as a separate legal entity either for tax purposes or for purposes of liability.[110] Foreign

---

104. P. EVANS, DEPENDENT DEVELOPMENT: THE ALLIANCE OF MULTI-NATIONAL, STATE AND LOCAL CAPITAL IN BRAZIL 228-49 (1979); P. GARLAND, *supra*, at 170-71.

105. Civil Code, art. 991.

106. Decree No. 57.651 of Jan. 19, 1966, art. 71(V).

107. Corporation Law, art. 118.

108. Corporation Law, arts. 129 para. 1 and 136.

109. *Id.*, arts. 116 and 117.

110. Corporation law, art. 278, para. 1. *See generally*, A. ANDRADE JÚNIOR, CONCEITOS JURÍDICOS PARA O DESENVOLVIMENTO DAS EMPRESAS NO BRASIL 13-64 (1982).

companies or foreign-owned national companies are permitted to participate in consortia. In Brazil, a consortium is organized by an agreement in which two or more companies agree to participate in a common activity or specific project. The Corporation Law directs that the consortium agreement, at a minimum, cover the following matters:

(a) the name of the consortium;
(b) the objective;
(c) period of duration;
(d) location of the principal place of business;
(e) responsibilities and duties of each participant;
(f) rules for receipt of income and allocation of profits and losses;
(g) rules for operating the consortium, accounting system, representation of participants, and management fees, if any;
(h) number of votes to which each participant is entitled;
(i) the contribution of each participant to expenses.[111]

The consortium agreement must be filed with the Commercial Registry, and the certificate of filing must be published.

Each participant in a consortium is responsible for its agreed-upon share of the debts. There is no presumption of joint and several liability. Bankruptcy of one of the participants does not affect any of the other participants, who are free to continue the consortium.[112] The consortium is commonly used in Brazil for large construction projects.

B. BRAZILIAN LAWS APPLICABLE TO FOREIGN DIRECT INVESTMENT

PROBLEM 6-20

Advanced Precision Tools (APT), a Delaware corporation in the industrial tool and machine industry, has been under pressure from its shareholders to increase earnings and dividend payouts and has decided on a strategy of global expansion to address these concerns. APT is interested in establishing a manufacturing facility in Brazil and is considering several options. One option is to purchase the Brazilian subsidiary of a Canadian company, Worktools do Brasil, which has a capital investment of $50 million dollars and has earned a steady stream of profits for the past ten years. Worktools Canada has mentioned in passing that the capital of Worktools do Brasil is not registered with the Central Bank of Brazil but that registration is not required by law. Worktools' asking price for its subsidiary is $75 million. Another option is for APT to establish its own subsidiary but this would require an investment of at least $75 million and will take several years in order to become operational. Which option would you recommend for APT? See Profits Remittance Law, Articles 1, 3, 5, and 9. See also the following accompanying notes discussing the Profits Remittance Law and the Brazilian tax laws. If you were advising Worktools Canada, the parent company of the Brazilian subsidiary, would you ask for payment in Canada in Canadian dollars or payment in Brazil? Worktools Canada is really intent on selling its Brazilian subsidiary. What type of buyer should Worktools be looking for?

---

111. Corporation Law, arts. 278 and 279.
112. *Id.*, art. 278, §§1 and 2.

PROBLEM 6-21

Pharma, Inc., an Illinois company, has established a subsidiary in Brazil to manufacture various pharmaceuticals for sale in Brazil and other countries in South America. As the Brazilian subsidiary must use Pharma's technology in the manufacturing process, Pharma has entered into three separate patent, trademark, and know-how licensing agreements with the subsidiary. Under the terms of the licensing agreements, Pharma's Brazilian subsidiary is to make annual royalty payments to Pharma's Chicago bank account equal to 12 percent of the subsidiary's total annual revenues of the products in Brazil. Pharma's patent division has forwarded all of the documentation needed to register Pharma's U.S. patents to Pharma's Brazilian subsidiary, but due to organization changes in the legal department, no one has forwarded trademark or know-how documentation to Brazil. Will Pharma receive its annual royalty payments under each of the licensing agreements and for how much? See Profits Remittance Law, Articles 11, 12, 13, 43, 44, the accompanying notes, and Professor Gouvea's article at pp. 572-573 *supra*.

Profits Remittance Law
Law No. 4.131 of September 3, 1962

(Annotated translation, as originally enacted and as amended by Law No. 4.390 and other enactments)[113]

ART. 1.

For the purposes of this Law, foreign capital shall mean assets, machinery and equipment entering Brazil without an initial outlay of foreign exchange, destined for the production of goods or services, as well as financial or monetary resources brought into the country for investment in economic activities, provided that, in either case, they belong to individuals or legal entities resident, domiciled, or headquartered abroad.

ART. 2.

Foreign capital invested in the country shall be accorded identical legal treatment with that granted to nation capital, under equal conditions, prohibiting any discrimination not provided for in this Law.

OF THE REGISTRATION OF CAPITAL, REMITTANCE AND REINVESTMENT

ART. 3.

A special service for the registration of foreign capital, regardless of its form of entry into the country, as well as for foreign financial operations, is

---

113. Subsequent amendments are placed in brackets.

hereby instituted in the Superintendency of Money and Credit,[114] which shall register:

(a)   foreign capital entering the country in the form of a direct investment or a loan, whether in money or in physical assets;

(b)   foreign remittances as a return of capital or as capital earnings, profits, dividends, interest, amortization, as well as royalties, payments for technical assistance, or any other type of payment that involves the transference of income out of the country;

(c)   reinvestment of earnings from foreign capital;

(d)   changes in the monetary value of the capital of companies, effectuated in accordance with the legislation in force.

Sole Paragraph. Registration of the reinvestments referred to in letter (c) above shall also be made for legal entities headquartered in Brazil when affiliated with foreign companies or controlled by a majority of shares belonging to individuals or legal entities resident or headquartered abroad.

ART. 4.

Registration of foreign capital shall be made in the currency of the country of origin and that of reinvested profits in national currency. Registration of foreign capital shall be made in the currency of the country of origin, and reinvestment of profits shall be made simultaneously in national currency and the currency of the country to which it could have been remitted, with the conversion being carried out at the exchange rate of the period during which it was proven that the reinvestment was actually made.

Sole Paragraph. If the capital is in the form of physical assets, the registration shall be made at their value in the country of origin or, in the absence of satisfactory substantiation, in accordance with the value carried on the books of the company receiving the capital or by valuation according to criteria to be determined in appropriate regulations.

ART. 5.

Registration of foreign investment shall be applied for within 30 (thirty) days from the date of its entry into the country and shall be free from payment of any charge or fee. Registration of reinvested profits shall be made within the same period, starting from the date of approval of the respective accounting entry by the proper department of the company.

Sole Paragraph. Foreign capital and respective reinvested profits already present in the country are also subject to registration, which shall be requested by its owners or the parties responsible for the companies in which they have been invested, within the period of 180 (one hundred and eighty) days from the date of publication of this law.

---

114. The Superintendency of Currency and Credit (SUMOC) was transformed into the Central Bank of Art. 8 of Law No. 4.595 of Dec. 31, 1964.

[§18 Foreign capital and respective reinvested profits already present in the country are also subject to registration, which shall be requested by its owners or those responsible for the firms in which they have been invested, within a period of 180 (one hundred and eighty) days from the date of publication of this law.]

[§28 The Council of the Superintendency of Currency and Credit shall determine that proof shall be required for concession of registration of capital dealt with in the prior paragraph.] . . .

ART. 7.

For the purposes of registration, reinvestment is considered to be those amounts which could have been legally remitted abroad as profits but, were instead reinvested into the same company that generated them, or were invested in another sector of the national economy.

[There shall be considered as reinvestment, for the purposes of this law, income derived from companies established in the country and attributed to residents and domiciliaries abroad and which was invested in the same companies from which it was derived or in another sector of the national economy.]

OF THE REMITTANCE OF INTEREST, ROYALTIES AND TECHNICAL ASSISTANCE PAYMENTS

ART. 8.

To the extent that remittance of interest on loans, credits and financing exceeds the interest rate noted in the respective contract and in the respective registration, it shall be considered as amortization of capital. SUMOC is entitled to contest and reject that part of the rate that exceeds the interest charged in the financial market from which the loan, credit or financing originated for operations made at the same time and in similar conditions.

ART. 9.

Individuals and legal entities wishing to make transfers abroad for profits, dividends, interest, amortization, royalties, technical, scientific or administrative assistance or the like, must submit the contracts and documents considered necessary to justify the remittance to the proper departments of SUMOC and the Income Tax Division.

Sole Paragraph. Remittances abroad depend upon registration of the company with SUMOC and upon proof of payment of any income tax owed.

[§18 Remittances abroad depend upon registration of the company with SUMOC and proof of payment of any income tax owed.] . . .

ART. 11.

Transfers for the payment of royalties for patents of invention, industrial and commercial trademarks, or other similar rights, require proof from the interested party that the respective rights have not expired in the country of origin.

[Requests for registration of contracts for the purpose of financial transfers for payment of royalties owed for the use of patents, industrial and commercial trademarks or other similar types of property, shall be accompanied by a certificate proving the existence and effectiveness in Brazil of the respective privileges granted by the National Department of Industrial Property, as well as an appropriate document showing that they have not expired in the country of origin.]

ART. 12.

The total amounts due for royalties for the exploitation of patents of invention or for the use of industrial or commercial trademarks or for technical, scientific, administrative or similar assistance, that may be deducted on income tax returns for the purposes of Article 37 of Decree No. 47.373 of December 7, 1959, shall be limited to a maximum of 5% (five percent) of the gross receipts from the product manufactured or sold.

§18 The percentage coefficients permitted for the deductions referred to in this article shall be set and periodically revised by acts of the Finance Ministry, taking into consideration the types of production or activities, classified by groups, according to the degree to which they are essential.

§28 The deductions referred to in this article shall be permitted when the expenses for technical, scientific, administrative or similar assistance have been proven, provided that such services have been effectively rendered, and that a contract for the assignment or license of the use of the trademarks and patents of invention has been properly registered in the country in accordance with the prescriptions of the Code of Industrial Property.

§38 Expenses for technical, scientific, administrative or similar assistance may only be deducted during the first 5 (five) years of the functioning of the firm or the introduction of the special process of production, when its necessity has been demonstrated. This period may be extended up to 5 (five) more years by authorization of the Council of the Superintendency of Currency and Credit.

ART. 13.

The sums owed for royalties for the exploitation of patents of invention or for technical, scientific, administrative or similar assistance that do not satisfy the conditions or exceed the limits provided for in the prior article shall be considered as distributed profits and taxed in accordance with Arts. 43 and 44.

Sole Paragraph. The total of the amounts owed to individual or legal entities resident or headquartered abroad for the use of industrial or commercial trademarks shall also be taxable in accordance with Articles 43 and 44. . . .

ART. 28.

Whenever a serious disequilibrium in the balance of payments occurs, or when there are serious reasons to foresee that such a situation is imminent, the Council of the Superintendency of Currency and Credit may impose restrictions for a limited period on imports and the remittance of profits on foreign capital, and for this purpose, it may grant the Bank of Brazil a total or partial monopoly on foreign exchange operations.

§1º In the case provided for in this article, remittances for the return of risk capital are prohibited and profit remittances are limited to 10% (ten percent) of registered capital, in accordance with Articles 3 and 4.

[In the case provided for in this article, remittances for the return of capital are prohibited and remittance of profits shall be limited to 10% (ten percent) per annum upon capital and reinvestments registered in the currency of origin in accordance with articles 3 and 4 of this Law.]

§2º Earnings that exceed 10% (ten percent) of capital shall be communicated to SUMOC, which, in the event the restriction referred to in this article is extended for more than one financial year, may authorize the remittance, in the next fiscal year, of the quantities relating to the excess when the profits earned then do not reach that limit.

[Earnings that exceed the percentage fixed by the Council of the Superintendency of Currency and Credit, in accordance with the prior paragraph, shall be communicated to the Superintendency, which, in the event that the restriction referred to in this article is extended for more than a year, may authorize the remittance in the following fiscal year of amounts that represent the excess when the profits realized in that year did not reach that limit.]

§3º In the same cases in this article, the Council of the Superintendency of Currency and Credit may limit the remittance of quantities for the payment of royalties and technical, administrative or similar assistance up to the maximum cumulative annual limit of 5% (five percent) of the gross receipts of the firm.

§4º Also, in the cases described in this article, the Council of SUMOC is authorized to issue instructions limiting exchange expenses for "International Travel."

§5º Restrictions shall not be imposed, however, on the remittance of interest and amortization quotas contained in duly registered foreign loan agreements.

ART. 29.

Whenever it becomes advisable to economize the use of foreign exchange reserves, the Executive is authorized to demand temporarily, via an instruction from the Council of the Superintendency of Currency and Credit, a financial charge of a strictly monetary character which shall be imposed upon the importation of merchandise and upon financial transfer up to a maximum limit of 10% (ten percent) on the value of imported products and up to 50% (fifty percent) on the value of any financial transfer including "International Travel."

ART. 30.

Amounts collected from the financial charge provided for in the preceding article shall constitute a cruzeiro monetary reserve to be maintained by the Superintendency of Currency and Credit in a separate account, and shall be utilized, whenever deemed opportune, exclusively for the purchase of gold and foreign exchange to reinforce the foreign exchange reserves and capabilities....

FISCAL PROVISIONS

ART. 41.

The following earnings shall be subject to income tax withholding in the terms of this Law:

(a) dividends from bearer shares payments attributed thereto;

(b) interest and any other earnings and benefits from bearer securities denominated participation Shares" or "Founder's Shares";

(c) the profits, dividends, and any other benefits and interest from registered shares or any other securities in registered form from legal entities, received by individuals or legal entities resident, domiciled or headquartered abroad, or by the branches or subsidiaries of foreign firms.

ART. 42.

Legal entities with a predominance of foreign capital, or which are branches or subsidiaries of firms headquartered abroad, are subject to the rules and rates of income tax established in the legislation for this tax.

ART. 43.

The profits and dividends attributed to individuals or legal entities, resident or headquartered abroad, are subject to payment of income tax withholding at the rates in force for dividends on bearer shares.

ART. 44.

The tax referred to above shall be collected with a 20% (twenty percent increase) in the case of firms engaged in activities of lesser interest for the national economy also taking into account their geographic location as defined in an executive decree, after consultation with the National Economic Council and the Council for the Superintendency of Currency and Credit.

NOTES AND QUESTIONS

1. *The Profits Remittance Law.* The fundamental feature of the Profits Remittance Law (PRL) is the registration of foreign capital, reinvestment, and payments such as dividends, profits, and royalties. Despite the language of the PRL in Article 5, registration is not mandatory. However, there are several features of the PRL that create strong incentives for registration:

(1) All registered capital can be repatriated in foreign currency in its entirety at any time without penalty or restriction.

(2) Payments of dividends, profits, interest, and royalties can be repatriated in foreign currency if they have been properly registered under

the PRL and proof is submitted that all taxes due have been withheld or paid.

(3) Capital or payments that are not registered cannot be lawfully repatriated in foreign currency.

Repatriation in the form of hard currency is crucial to the foreign investor because Brazilian currency, which can be removed from Brazil without restrictions, is not a freely convertible currency. However, a thriving black market and various schemes have arisen to funnel unregistered foreign capital and payments in foreign currency out of Brazil to other countries. The real can be exchanged for U.S. dollars through various unauthorized vendors in the black market and ferreted out of Brazil. These schemes are commonly used by some foreign companies doing business in Brazil and it appears that there is a fairly high level of tolerance and acceptance for these schemes among Brazilian officials, especially as some of them benefit through various payoffs. Should a U.S. company be concerned about using any of these black-market schemes as they are widespread and tolerated?

2. *Brazilian Tax Laws.* As the PRL works in tandem with Brazilian tax laws, we summarize several key current features of the tax laws below. Tax is payable at the following rates:

(1) 15% on all corporate income plus a surtax based on portions of income above a certain level;

(2) 15% on the remittance of interest payments on loans;

(3) 15% on the payment of royalties and technical assistance payments on all technology transfer contracts that exceed 5% of gross receipts from the product manufactured or sold;

(4) 0% on all dividends and profits earned from Brazilian sources as of January 1, 1996;

(5) 0% on all dividends and profits that are reinvested as registered capital; and

(6) 0% on the remittance of registered capital but if the registered capital that is remitted is larger than the original amount registered then the excess is treated as capital gains subject to a 15% withholding tax. Note that capital gains tax on capital appreciation is due only if the sale of the capital occurs in Brazil. Under current Brazilian tax laws, sale of registered capital in Brazil that occurs entirely overseas is not subject to the capital gains tax.

One of the recent changes in the Brazilian tax regime is the exemption of dividends and profits earned after January 1, 1996, from withholding. Prior to this change, dividends were subject to the general withholding rate of 15%. This tax structure created incentives for the foreign investor to reinvest profits in registered capital, which were then not subject to taxation, rather than pay out profits in the form of dividends, which was a taxable event. Under the current tax structure, however, the foreign investor no longer has a tax-driven incentive to reinvest profits as the payout of dividends is also tax free.

3. One of the original purposes of the PRL was to protect Brazil from the sudden flight of foreign currency through repatriation that might endanger Brazil's foreign currency reserves. As previously discussed, some of the harshest limitations on the exodus of foreign currency that set a ceiling on how much

capital could be repatriated on an annual basis have now been revoked. Under the current PRL, what mechanisms are available to protect Brazil against foreign currency flight? See Profits Remittance Law, Articles 28–30.

4. To be successful, Brazil's legal regime governing FDI depends on the strict observance of the Profits Remittance Law and the tax laws. What problems do you see with the current system?

7 *Protecting Intellectual Property Rights*

In Chapters 5 and 6, we examined the three principal forms of IBTs (agency/distributorship, contract manufacturing, and FDI) beyond the sales transaction that was the focus of Chapters 2, 3, and 4. In all of these forms of IBTs, intellectual property (IP) rights have played a significant role. But as a U.S. corporation moves deeper into the progression of doing business abroad from the sales transaction, the least involved form of IBTs, to foreign direct investment, the most involved form, the issue of protecting intellectual property rights becomes more important. The progression of international business transactions to FDI generally requires providing greater access to intellectual property rights, which at the same time also creates greater risks to the foreign investor. In previous chapters, we have examined the types of legal procedures and precautionary steps under the international intellectual property system that a U.S. corporation must undertake in order to protect its IP, which includes following the filing and registration requirements for its IP abroad. We also examined how a U.S. corporation should attempt to structure the licensing and FDI transactions through contract to protect its IP while at the same time providing appropriate access to those rights to third parties, which is now such an important part of international business. However, no matter how careful the planning of a transaction and thorough the precautions taken by a foreign investor, there is a limit to how effective prophylactic measures can be when there are pirates and profiteers who are intent upon the theft of IP. While the previous chapters discussed how to take the appropriate steps in the planning stages to protect IP from misuse and theft, the bulk of this chapter focuses on what happens after a theft has occurred and on the enforcement and protection of rights that have been breached. This brings us to the growing problem of commercial piracy, which refers to the unauthorized copying of copyrights, trademarks, patents, and trade secrets. Why is commercial piracy a growing problem for all IP owners?

The rise in commercial piracy can be directly traced to the growing importance and value of IP. We are now in an age where information and intellectual property of all kinds are increasingly integral to success in business and for the economic development of nations. As IP has become increasingly valuable, its theft by pirates has also become an increasingly lucrative criminal activity. In fact, as we detail below, commercial piracy has become, in many cases, one of the most significant business problems for IP owners, many of them multinational enterprises. In this chapter, we will consider the problem of commercial piracy and the strategies and methods that intellectual property owners, in most cases MNEs and their lawyers, can undertake to enforce their rights. As you will see, this is a complex and controversial topic and a problem for which we are far from having clear solutions. After an overview of the problem, we will take a closer look at commercial piracy in China. It is no coincidence that China, one of the largest recipients of foreign direct investment and one of the fastest growing economies in the world, also has one of the world's most serious commercial piracy problems. While in certain respects unique, commercial piracy in China also illustrates some of the common and daunting challenges for IP owners that exist in many other developing countries.

While commercial piracy exists in all countries to some extent, some of the worst problems are in developing countries due to the lack of mature legal systems and differences in social values. Modern IP rights, as embodied in TRIPS, have been primarily developed by Western nations and reflect a Western legal culture. In contrast, many developing countries do not have a tradition of recognizing property rights in individuals to knowledge and information. While many developing countries may have adopted laws modeled on Western IP laws, the basic social institutions and values underlying many of these societies do not support a Western-style legal regime protecting IP. As a result, commercial piracy often pits MNEs and their home countries, advanced industrialized countries, against developing countries and their constituencies. This alignment of interests has resulted in a number of controversial issues. For example, one debate concerns whether public health needs can justify the disregard of patents by some countries that are without the resources to pay for patented drugs that are needed to treat serious diseases such as AIDS that threaten their populations. Is it commercial piracy for countries to disregard patents when doing so helps to make medicines available to treat major problems of public health that might otherwise lead to a social crisis? We will take a look at the access to medicines debate.

Commercial piracy, moreover, is not the only type of piracy that we shall be examining. In this chapter, we shall also look at the current controversy concerning "biopiracy," which is a term used by some to describe the attempts by MNEs to obtain intellectual property rights in forms of traditional knowledge indigenous to many developing countries rich in biological resources without sharing any profits with these countries.

In the final section of this chapter, we explore the means available to IP owners to combat the import of "gray market" goods, that is, genuine goods intended for sale in a foreign market but which find their way into the United States.

I. Overview of Commercial Piracy

Commercial piracy is a broad term that encompasses copyright piracy, trademark counterfeiting, and patent infringements. This section begins with an overview of the size and scope of all forms of commercial piracy and the following sections will examine each specific type of piracy in more detail.

A. Rise in Commercial Piracy

In the past few decades, commercial piracy has increased dramatically around the world. In 1982, the U.S. International Trade Commission estimated that commercial piracy resulted in losses of $5.5 billion. A similar study by the ITC in 1988 estimated losses at over $60 billion. Today, industry groups estimate that losses to U.S. companies exceed $200 billion and that worldwide losses for all IP owners exceed $350 billion.[1]

In subsequent sections of this chapter, we set forth some more detailed information on the size and scope of this problem. In this section, we discuss some of the causes for this trend. This sharp rise is tied directly to some of the basic themes that were discussed in Chapter 1: The process of globalization that has been accompanied by a dramatic rise in trade in goods and services; the increase in foreign direct investment in the past several decades; and the increasing importance of information, technology, and IP as a tool for economic development. One way to understand the rise in commercial piracy is to view it as the illegal by-product of the development of legitimate commercial and economic activity. As lawful commercial activity has increased dramatically so has unlawful economic activity. For example, in some countries the growth of the market in legitimate products is mirrored by the growth of an underground economy selling pirated versions of the same products. In certain parts of Asia, it is well-known that some sections of cities trade in genuine products through large well-known department stores while other sections of town offer knock-offs and smuggled versions of the same products in open-air street markets, small stores, and stalls.

There are several specific factors that we wish to highlight:

(1) *Access to Materials and Technology*. The relatively free flow of products and information across national borders and the availability of inexpensive high-quality copy technology have been major contributors to the rise in commercial piracy. In the area of copyright, the use of the Internet to download copyrighted materials and the availability of cheap computer technology means that individuals can make massive amounts of copies at a low cost. A common practice is to use handheld digital cameras to copy first-run movies during a showing in a movie theater and then to churn out massive numbers of DVDs that are then sold while the movie is still in its first run. In some cases, copies of movies are available on the street before the movie is publicly available. In the area of trademark counterfeiting, high-quality, low-cost technology such as color copiers and printers have made it easier than ever to duplicate labels, packaging, and symbols with accuracy and speed.

(2) *Increasing Importance of Trademarks and Brands*. As competition becomes increasingly sharp on a global basis, companies are spending more on advertising, promotion, and marketing to further distinguish their trademarks or brands and to create a clearly identifiable image. The issue of creating a brand image or "branding" has become more important as competition becomes ever more acute and brand owners are looking for every possible avenue to distinguish themselves from their competitors. In many instances, as technology advances, the only difference between products is brand image as competitors offer products that are indistinguishable in quality. As a result, IP owners are spending millions of dollars on advertising and other promotional activities (including sponsorship of sporting events, educational programs, charitable events) to create

---

1. George W. Abbott, Jr. & Lee S. Sporn, Trademark Counterfeiting §1.03 pp. 1-11 (2000 Supp.).

differences between what are essentially similar products through the creation of an identifiable image and goodwill with consumers. As brands become more valuable and brand image becomes a more valuable commercial good, the incentive to counterfeit these brands also increases. To some extent, the sharp increase in counterfeiting and piracy is a reflection of the success of IP owners in increasing the value of their brands.

(3) *Technology Transfer Through FDI.* The increase of FDI in countries around the world has led to an unprecedented rate of technology transfer and has created widespread access to all forms of intellectual property that were simply unavailable before. FDI also encourages the development of an infrastructure to support the absorption of advanced technology by the host countries. Offering advanced training for employees, sponsoring employees for education at universities abroad, and establishing research and development centers are some of the ways in which FDI helps host countries to increase their capabilities to absorb technology. One of the main benefits of licensing and foreign direct investment is the authorized transfer of technology to the recipient, but such transfers also carry the risk of the unauthorized use of the technology by the recipient or by third parties. It is no coincidence that in many cases as the level of technology transfer increases to a recipient country so does the level of the unauthorized use of that technology. As FDI is often the most effective form of technology transfer, some of the countries that are receiving large amounts of FDI also have some of the world's most serious commercial piracy problems. In many developing countries, the areas where goods are manufactured by authorized factories are also the same areas where the bulk of pirated and counterfeit goods are produced.

PROBLEM 7-1

Acme Company, a U.S.-based MNE engaged in the consumer products business, has entered into a joint venture in Argentina with a local company to manufacture and sell shampoo. As is consistent with Acme's global business practices, the Acme joint venture sources its bottles from a third-party supplier and its raw materials, such as enzymes and perfumes, from third parties and then combines these raw materials using its own special formula and manufacturing process to make its world-famous shampoo. Acme has discovered that within a week of the launch of a new product with all new packaging, its heavily advertised and promoted 2-in-1 shampoo and conditioner, counterfeits in large quantities have appeared on the market. The counterfeits are of such high quality in both packaging and content that Acme must have the counterfeits tested in its laboratories to distinguish them from the real product. In fact, the counterfeits were so clever that at first Acme thought that they were real but then discovered that they contained a layer of real Acme shampoo that occupied the top third of the bottle so Acme scientists started taking some of the shampoo from the bottom of the bottles, which contained only some minor blemishes and other imperfections. Acme's CEO is incensed and has called upon you — Acme's general counsel — to fix the problem. According to the CEO, the first order of business is for you to meet with the Buenos Aires authorities and ask them to locate and shut down the underground factories making these counterfeits. Do you agree with this approach? What would you suggest?

B. Categories of Commercial Piracy

1. Copyright Piracy

Copyright piracy refers to the unauthorized copying of a fixed content of a medium of expression such as books, films, musical recordings, and computer software that are contained in print, audio- and videotapes, compact disks, digital video disks, or computer diskettes. Copyright piracy, the focus of this section, refers to the exact duplication of a copyrighted work as opposed to copyright infringement, which refers to the partial copying of a work. In many instances, copyright infringement may involve a legitimate business dispute between two business entities that is resolved in a civil litigation. Issues of liability on the part of the offender are usually clear in the case of copyright piracy, which may also be a criminal offense.

In the case of copyright piracy, there is not necessarily any attempt to convince the customer that the pirated product was manufactured and distributed by the original copyright owner. Many consumers knowingly purchase a product that they know is pirated because the consumer wants the content of the product and is not concerned that it is not manufactured by the copyright owner. As modern technology makes it possible to provide exact or high-quality duplicates of original material, the quality of the pirated product may not be a major concern to the consumer.

Studies by government and industry groups show that losses from copyright piracy on a global basis are in the tens of billions of dollars.

FIGURE 7-1

Worldwide Losses from Copyright Piracy[2] (in millions of U.S. dollars)

	Motion Pictures		Records & Music		Business Software Applications		Entertainment Software		Books		Total Losses	
	2002	2001	2002	2001	2002	2001	2002	2001	2002	2001	2002	2001
Asia	455.0	427.5	473.5	420.3	2583.5	1829.5	1024.4	1147.6	289.8	376.2	4826.2	4201.1
Europe[3]	495.0	494.5	813.7	662.4	1041.7	633.4	648.5	387.5	77.8	89.8	3076.7	2267.6
North & South America[4]	303.0	283.0	1232.4	1247.1	799.8	792.1	0.0 (NA)	202.5	101.7	114.2	2436.9	2638.9
Middle East & Africa	148.3	139.5	81.7	66.7	141.7	126.2	17.2	232.0	87.7	97.7	476.6	662.1
World Totals	1401.3	1344.5	2601.3	2396.5	4566.7	3381.2	1690.1	1969.6	557.0	677.9	10816.4	9769.7

---

2. This table is derived from partial data based on trade loss estimates for 2003 by the office of the United States Trade Representative in making "Special 301" decisions and on the International Intellectual Property Alliance (IIPA) estimated U.S. trade losses due to copyright piracy. Special 301 of the Omnibus Trade and Development Act of 1988 requires the USTR to notify Congress of those countries that fail to adequately protect U.S. intellectual property rights. IIPA is an industry group composed of IP owners.
3. Includes states of the former Soviet Union.
4. Excludes the United States.

The figures above do not include losses within the United States, where losses from the piracy of business software alone totaled almost $2 billion in 2002. We will take a closer look at the methods used to measure the level of piracy and losses at the end of this section but for now we present an overview picture of the world piracy problem.

Some of the worst copyright piracy problems are in the area of business software. As the following chart indicates, although world software piracy rates have recently declined, it is still about 40 percent today.

FIGURE 7-2[5]

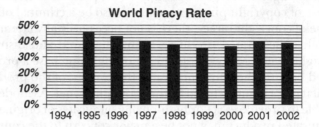

Eastern Europe is the region with the highest piracy rate (71%), followed by Latin America (57%), Asia (55%), Middle East/Africa (50%), Western Europe (33%), and North America (25%).

Measured by the amount of losses rather than by the piracy level, Asia is by far the leading region in the world.

FIGURE 7-3[6]

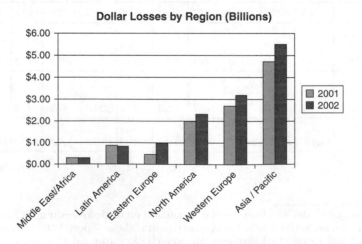

5. Source: 2003 Business Software Alliance Global Software Piracy Study.
6. *Id.*

Most experts believe that the piracy level is a more reliable indicator of the seriousness of the problem than the amount of losses. For example, losses in the United States are the second highest in the world at almost $2 billion but the piracy level for software in the United States is about 23 percent. U.S. losses are large because of the size of the U.S. economy. As a result, the piracy problem in the United States is considered mild by comparison to a country such as Vietnam where more than nine in ten software applications are pirated. If we take piracy level as a more accurate measure of the severity of the problem, then China stands out in the area of copyright piracy. Not only does China have the second highest world piracy rate at 92 percent, but with losses at $2.4 billion, China also has the highest loss total for any single country in the world. Losses from China alone account for 44 percent of the total in Asia.

NOTES AND QUESTIONS

1. For all forms of commercial piracy, there appears to be a widespread perception on the part of some consumers that it is not a serious offense as the only "harm" involved is that wealthy multinational enterprises may earn fewer profits. The perception that the offense is harmless especially appears to apply to copyright piracy, which, unlike trademark counterfeiting and patent infringements involving drugs, generally involves no issues of consumer health and safety. Pirated business and entertainment software, music, and movies flood some markets, particularly in Asia, where Western tourists eagerly flock to look for "bargains." Many consumers also eagerly buy certain types of counterfeit goods, such as copies of famous watches, handbags, and clothing. Some well-known public figures, including a former U.S. trade representative, have been reported in the media as having knowingly purchased pirated products while in China negotiating the conditions of China's entry into the WTO. During one overseas trip to visit the legal system of a developing country, one state supreme court justice purchased counterfeit luxury watches as gifts for each member of the high court. Many tourists have been known to specifically seek out pirated products while on trips abroad as souvenirs. Some consumers seem to find buying pirated products at home or abroad to be fun, exciting, and harmless. How would you respond to the assertion there is really nothing wrong with buying pirated goods?

2. Is the only consequence of commercial piracy that wealthy MNEs make smaller profits?

3. Looking at Figure 7-4 on the following page, how would you characterize the developmental stage of these countries. Is piracy being used as a tool of economic development?

4. Some have argued that commercial piracy of IP owned in most part by developed countries and their constituents benefits developing countries, many of which were colonized by developed countries and were set back in their development through years of exploitation and oppression. What these developing countries, many liberated from colonization only within the past several decades, need most is advanced technology to modernize and industrialize their economies. Can commercial piracy be viewed as free technology transfer and a form of justified retribution or compensation exacted by developing countries upon developed countries for past wrongs?

FIGURE 7-4[7]
25 Countries with the Highest Software Piracy Rates

Country	2001	2002
Vietnam	94%	95%
China	92%	92%
Other CIS[8]	88%	90%
Indonesia	88%	89%
Russia	87%	89%
Ukraine	86%	89%
Pakistan	83%	80%
Nicaragua	78%	77%
Thailand	77%	77%
Bahrain	77%	76%
Qatar	78%	76%
Bolivia	77%	74%
Lebanon	79%	74%
Kuwait	76%	73%
Paraguay	72%	71%
India	70%	70%
Oman	77%	70%
Romania	75%	70%
Zimbabwe	68%	70%
Other Asia/Pacific	70%	69%
Bulgaria	75%	68%
El Salvador	73%	68%
Malaysia	70%	68%
Philippines	63%	68%
Nigeria	71%	67%

2. *Trademark Counterfeiting*

While copyright piracy is a serious problem that causes losses in the tens of billions of dollars, industry groups claim that trademark counterfeiting accounts for losses in the hundreds of billions on a worldwide annual basis. Copyright piracy is usually limited to software, movies, music, and books, but counterfeiting today can occur in an almost unlimited array of products from all different sectors. Counterfeiters not only target consumer products but also fake industrial products such as automobiles, aircraft engines, and airplane parts and agricultural products such as fertilizers. The International Chamber of Commerce estimates that 5-7 percent of global commerce consists of counterfeit goods. The bulk of the $350 billion of total worldwide losses caused by commercial piracy previously quoted can be attributed to trademark counterfeiting.

Counterfeiting refers to the unauthorized act by one party of producing and passing off exact duplicates of authentic products with trademarks owned by another

---

7. *Id.*
8. CIS are the former states of the Soviet Union.

party. In contrast to copyright piracy discussed in the previous section, counterfeiters often attempt to pass off the counterfeit as the genuine product through making copies that are often indistinguishable from the authentic product and that will often bear the registered or unregistered trademark of another party along with the company name, address, and trade dress of the lawful manufacturer or trademark owner. In many cases, the trademark or brand owner cannot distinguish between the counterfeit and genuine product without subjecting the product to detailed laboratory testing and analysis.

While many copyright pirates may make little or no attempt to convince the consumer that the product is a genuine one, consumer deception is a more serious issue in the case of trademark counterfeiting. However, not all consumers who buy counterfeits are deceived. Consumers tend to be willing to buy counterfeit goods where product quality is not a major issue. With "high involvement" products that consumers ingest or put on their skin or hair, most consumers do not tend to knowingly buy counterfeits. However, many consumers knowingly purchase counterfeits of "low involvement" products that are worn such as clothing, shoes, or watches or carried such as handbags and luggage. In these cases, consumers are less concerned with product quality and more concerned about the prestige of the brand. In any case, consumer deception is always a possibility in the case of counterfeits that are passed off as genuine goods.

Consumer health and safety, not usually an issue in the area of copyright piracy, can also be a problem in dealing with counterfeit goods. As many, although not all, counterfeit goods are of an inferior quality, they can cause harm to consumers. For example, counterfeit airplane and car parts and counterfeit consumer products, such as fake liquor and medicines, have resulted in injury or death to consumers.

A recent trend is that criminal organizations around the world have been drawn to commercial piracy—particularly counterfeiting—by high profit and the relatively low risk nature of the crime as an easy source of revenue and money laundering. In order to coordinate the manufacture, export, import, distribution, and sale of counterfeit goods in international markets, the participation of criminal organizations of considerable size and with considerable resources is necessary. Take the growing problem of counterfeit cigarettes that are being smuggled into the United States, which is estimated to exceed $1 billion per year. A single entity must be able to coordinate the supply of tobacco plants, the production of the counterfeit cigarettes in underground factories, the export of the cigarettes to the United States, the clearance of the counterfeits through Customs under false documentation (using names of importers acquired through identity theft making them untraceable), and the distribution of the product to weak links in the distribution chain of the brand owner. As most legitimate brand owners deal only with qualified large-scale distributors who will not deal in counterfeits, the counterfeiters must identify the "soft" spots in the distribution network, that is, those sub-jobbers or sub-distributorships who purchase goods from the qualified distributors but who are also willing to purchase counterfeits to mix in with the supply of genuine product. The sub-jobbers then sell the counterfeit product to small retail stores. This type of organization must have the capability of dealing with all of these issues and must have a large number of "foot soldiers" in the United States and abroad to handle all of these operations. At the first sign of trouble, these "foot soldiers" board a plane leaving the United States and disappear. According to Los Angeles

Customs officials, the Asian criminal gangs involved in the trade in counterfeit cigarettes are every bit as well organized, ruthless, and violent as Colombian gangs involved in narcotics.

A comparison between the trade in narcotics and the trade in counterfeit cigarettes illustrates the attraction of counterfeiting to criminal gangs. At a profit margin of more than ten to one, the trade in counterfeit cigarettes is highly lucrative and rivals that for narcotics but with lower risks. While the trade in counterfeit cigarettes is most likely the most profitable, trade in counterfeit luxury items such as handbags and clothing and counterfeit and pirated software is also extremely lucrative. The maximum jail sentence for counterfeiting under the Trademark Counterfeiting Act of 1984 (see note on p. 622) is ten years in prison, but trafficking in narcotics will routinely result in much stiffer jail sentences. In addition, there is the issue of priorities for law enforcement entities. The U.S. Customs Service, part of the Department of Homeland Security, has stated that its first priority is detecting and preventing terrorism. The FBI places priority on targeting terrorism, violent crimes, and narcotics. With thousands of containers arriving every day at the port of Los Angeles alone, it is not possible for Customs officials to do a detailed inspection of every container, which involves opening the container and going through its contents. Customs will target specific containers but only on the basis of specific intelligence, which is usually supplied by brand owners but is difficult to obtain. When Customs has seized containers with counterfeits, it often discovers that the name of the importer has been obtained through identity theft, making it difficult to trace those involved. It appears that counterfeiters have decided that as some containers will inevitably be seized they simply abandon those that are seized as a cost of doing business, given the large number of containers that do go through undetected. Tracing the seized containers involves setting up a "sting" operation that would allow a pass-through of the counterfeit goods into commerce through the use of federal agents assuming false identities to penetrate the criminal gangs. This usually involves months of work and a substantial commitment of resources from Customs, the FBI, and the United States Attorney.

Industry groups have provided evidence that some organizations are selling counterfeit products to finance terrorist activities. However, it has been difficult to prove a systematic link between terrorist organizations and commercial piracy, although industry groups are continuing to try to make this connection.

The high profits involved combined with the low risk nature of the crime have prompted some law enforcement officials to call counterfeiting the crime of the twenty-first century.

NOTES AND QUESTIONS

1. Not only are profits high, but costs in the trade in counterfeit cigarettes and other goods are also lower than costs in drug trafficking. Counterfeit goods can be moved undetected through normal channels of commerce in plain sight in trucks or trains, can be stored in common warehouses, and can be sold through normal retail channels in public stores. Why do these attributes result in lower costs than those in drug trafficking?

2. One of the problems with counterfeits that does not generally exist in the case of copyright piracy is harm to the reputation of the brand owner and its

goodwill with consumers. Suppose a consumer inadvertently buys a counterfeit product and soon discovers it to be of inferior quality. How might this harm the reputation of the brand owner?

3. Consumers who later discover that they have been deceived into purchasing a counterfeit are often angry and wish to voice their complaints. Which person or what entity are these consumers most likely to contact in order to complain? How might this process affect the reputation of the brand owner?

3. Patent Infringements

Patent infringements in this context refer to the unauthorized copying of a registered patent. In many cases, patent infringements tend to be complex matters because determining whether a patent has been infringed can involve detailed scientific and technical analysis. In the United States, patent infringements are often legitimate business disputes that are highly esoteric and involve expert testimony. On a global scale, patent infringements are not usually grouped together with other forms of commercial piracy with the notable exception of pharmaceuticals where the unauthorized copying of patents is widespread. For example, the World Health Organization estimates that over 7 percent of the medicines sold around the world are fakes with the number rising as high as 60 percent in some developing countries. As you can well imagine, pharmaceutical companies and industry groups are seeking more effective enforcement of their rights. Companies point out that unauthorized copies do not allow them to recoup the exceptionally high cost of research and development, which is now estimated to be $802 million for each new pharmaceutical product brought to market. *See* Tufts Center for the Study of Drug Development, Press Release (Nov. 30, 2001). The pharmaceutical industry is particularly vulnerable to unauthorized copies because while it takes the expenditure of hundreds of millions of dollars to invent a new drug, the drug can in many cases be easily reversed engineered and a serviceable copy can be made at low cost. Unlike the area of counterfeit products where issues of liability tend to be clear, however, drug patents and the unauthorized copying of pharmaceuticals have a public health dimension that raises complex public policy issues on an international level. We return to a more detailed examination of this issue in a later section.

NOTES AND QUESTIONS

1. In setting forth the different types of commercial piracy, we do not mean to imply that they are mutually exclusive. To the contrary, one product may involve different types of commercial piracy. Can you give an example of a single product that (1) involves both copyright piracy and trademark counterfeiting, (2) involves both patent infringement and trademark counterfeiting, and (3) involves all three types of commercial piracy?

2. When faced with a pirated product that violates multiple rights, IP owners usually assert a counterfeiting claim because of issues of proof. Why? How do you prove a claim of counterfeiting, copyright piracy, or patent infringement?

3. We have included a number of tables with statistics and other information on piracy. Most of this information is provided by MNEs who have formed industry groups to deal with piracy, such as the International Anti-Counterfeiting

Coalition and the Business Software Alliance. These statistics are impressive, but what methods do MNEs use in arriving at some of these statistics on the level of piracy and the losses involved? MNEs calculate the level of commercial piracy using some variant of the following method: For example, in the area of trademark counterfeiting, MNEs first calculate the demand for their product by determining how much product overall there is in any given market. This can be done through market surveys. The MNE will hire a marketing company to do an on-site survey of how much of their products are available for sale in a given location through store visitations. The MNE will then determine how much genuine product is shipped to the particular market through its own legitimate distribution channels. The difference between the amount of total product and the amount of legitimate product shipped by the MNE equals the amount of counterfeits on the market. For example, if there are 100,000 bottles of shampoo sold in a particular city and the MNE has shipped 80,000 units to that city, then 20,000 units are counterfeit. Owners of software use a similar method. The difference between the number of applications supplied to a particular location, which represents demand, and the number of genuine applications shipped, which represents supply, equals the estimate of software applications pirated. What assumptions must these methods make about the amount and type of control exercised by MNEs over the distribution of their products? Do you find these assumptions to be sound?

4. MNEs calculate losses from commercial piracy using a variant of the following method. Sometimes, MNEs appear to assume that the presence or availability on the market of a pirated product equals a lost sale of a genuine product. More often, they claim that a lost sale occurs for each pirated or counterfeit product that is purchased by a consumer. For example, if a consumer purchases a bottle of counterfeit shampoo, the manufacturer will consider that purchase to result in the loss of a purchase of a bottle of authentic shampoo at the retail price that the consumer would have otherwise made but for the counterfeit. Using the estimate of the amount of counterfeit and pirated products that exist in any given market under the methods set forth in note 3 above, MNEs then claim that the amount of pirated products valued at the retail price of the genuine product represents their losses. For example, if 20 percent of the shampoo on the market in a given location is counterfeit, the MNE will then calculate that it has lost 20 percent of sales revenue of the genuine shampoo at retail prices. If the total sales for the location is $100,000 and 20 percent of the product on the market is counterfeit, then MNEs will claim that their losses for that market are $20,000. A similar method is used in the case of software applications by copyright owners. Assume that a genuine bottle of shampoo costs $5 and that a counterfeit costs $1.50. Assume also that a genuine software application costs $85 and that a pirated copy costs $5. Using these figures, which reflect the actual differences between real and pirated products in many markets, do you agree with the position of the MNEs that each purchase of a pirated product represents the loss of a sale of a genuine product? Why do MNEs make these claims?

5. Some MNEs will privately admit that some piracy of their products is beneficial at the early stages of the product's introduction in a developing market. The reason is that in developing markets there is often the lack of a sophisticated distribution system. As in all cases, success in a market requires a strong distribution system as such a system is necessary to deliver the product to the end-use consumer. To fully exploit a product that is in high demand requires providing convenient access to the product to the consumer. If consumers cannot find the product in a

market, store, or retail outlet, the manufacturer will lose sales even if the product is in high demand. In many developing countries, the lack of transportation, roads, and a sophisticated logistics system results in a limited number of markets where legitimate and qualified distributors can deliver their products. Pirated products, however, do not rely on legitimate distributors but travel through underground channels using the same illegal distributors that also bring smuggled products to consumers who want them. Pirated products can reach a larger number of end-use consumers in some developing markets, creating brand and name recognition for the IP owner. As the developing market matures and distribution systems are established, the legitimate product can further penetrate into these more remote areas and benefit from the brand recognition established by the pirated product. Are MNEs exaggerating the seriousness of the commercial piracy problem?

6. Established distribution systems are also important because counterfeits and pirated products tend to flourish where the legitimate products are not available. Where legitimate products are not available, consumers are more likely to be confused into thinking that a pirated product is a genuine one as there is no way for consumers to make a comparison. In addition, where there is strong consumer demand for a good, consumers are more likely to purchase counterfeits where no genuine goods are available. In developing countries, there are often "soft spots" in the market where logistical problems prevent distribution of the genuine products and where pirated products fill consumer demand. Brand owners often place a priority on developing distribution channels in developing countries as one strategy for controlling the proliferation of counterfeits and pirated products. In some of the least developed countries, such as those in Eastern Europe and Asia that border on China's western front, there is no market for some genuine products at all and, as a result, there is a flourishing market in cheap pirated goods of all kinds.

C.   Counterfeiting in China

In this section, we take a closer look at trademark counterfeiting in China to get a sense of the complexity of the problem and the challenges facing government policy and lawmakers, enforcement authorities, and brand owners. Although many aspects of counterfeiting in China are unique, there are some common aspects that appear in various degrees in most other developing countries involved in counterfeiting and commercial piracy: Government corruption and local protectionism, weak enforcement of IP rights by the legal system, lack of education about the importance of intellectual property rights, and the extensive involvement of international criminal organizations. Many observers have also predicted that as other ambitious Asian countries such as Vietnam develop, similar counterfeiting problems, sharing many of the characteristics in China, will also arise.

Trademark counterfeiting is now considered by many multinational enterprises doing business in China to be their most serious business problem in China as well as a threat to their businesses overseas. In a study published in 2001, the PRC State Council Research and Development Center reported that the PRC economy was flooded with $19-24 billion in counterfeit products. The study did not include pharmaceuticals and tobacco, which are two of the most heavily pirated industries so the total amount of counterfeits is likely to be much higher. China has also become a platform for the export of counterfeit and pirated products to other countries in Asia, Eastern Europe, and other territories in the world.

In 2003, U.S. Customs seized $62,468,018[9] in counterfeit and pirated products at ports of entry in the United States that were exported from China, the single largest source of these illegal products. Of course, the amount of counterfeits seized can represent only a tiny fraction of what actually enters the U.S. market.

Many observers believe that, overall, the commercial piracy problem in China is not only the most serious in the world today but in world history. Recent industry estimates indicate that 80 percent of all counterfeiting on a global basis can be traced to China.

Richard Behar, Beijing's Phony War on Fakes, Fortune Magazine, p. 188 (October 30, 2000)

China produces more fakes than any other nation—everything from autos to aircraft parts, beer to blades, soap to shampoo, TVs to toilets. Moreover, exports of fakes are rising (72% of the counterfeit Beanie Babies seized in the U.S. last year were from China), and crime syndicates are entering the racket. "The problem is getting worse rather than better," says David Holloway, who until October ran Kroll's Asian operation.[10]

It's impossible to know what percentage of China's manufacturing base is dependent on fakes and other illegal knockoffs—estimates range from 10% to as high as 30%—but Beijing is surely not going to decimate its economy if it doesn't need to. Even in Guangdong, a showcase province, one need only ride the train between Shenzhen and Guangzhou to glimpse the poverty that helps fuel the counterfeiting trade. Rickety homes, slapped together with boards and sheet metal, line the tracks. The shantytowns are separated by factories. "One in five factories along the train from Hong Kong to Guangzhou is infringing at one time or another," says Kroll's Holloway. "There are thousands and thousands of them—those are just the ones you can see."

Despite its rapid development, China remains a land of 800 million peasants. Unemployment is estimated at more than 150 million people, many of whom float around the nation as temporary migrant workers or counterfeiters. According to People's Daily, the main Communist Party newspaper, illegal economic activity grew at a faster pace than the nation's legitimate economy in the first half of this year. With entrance into the WTO sure to attract yet more foreign competition, and more unemployment, piracy will probably grow, at least for the near future. "If you're a small-business man in China, will you really spend money on R&D, or just copy someone else's design, patent, or copyright work?" asks Barry Yen, an intellectual-property lawyer in Hong Kong.

The inclination to copy is also cultural. If imitation really is the highest form of flattery, then China has been the Land of the Laud for nearly 2,000 years. Counterfeiting is so ingrained that many Chinese view it as harmless—or at least not the same as stealing. For Chinese consumers, most of whom can't afford the genuine articles, an almost fetishistic obsession with Western brands is fueling the racket. Toss in a long history of foreign incursions, and copying has morphed into a sport. "Most Chinese are aware that this country was bullied and carved up

---

9. *See* U.S. Customs, *http://www.customs.ustreas.gov/xp/cgov/import/communications_to_industry/statistics/seizure/china.xml*.

10. Kroll is a private investigation company. — EDS.

by aggressors, and there's a backlash against it with counterfeiting," says Peter Humphrey, who manages Kroll's China operations. "There's a sense of humiliation and a national getting-even going on here."

The horror stories go on and on. Toilets? A survey found that 35% of the American Standard toilets purchased in Shanghai in 1999 were fake. Drugs? Pfizer only began selling Viagra in China in July. But by last year three local producers had already introduced ripped-off versions of the erection pill, and more than 30 enterprises have since pirated it. There are Viagra wines, Viagra soup, even Viagra clothes.

Personal-care-product giants like Germany's Henkel and America's P&G estimate that about a quarter of the goods bearing their names in China are fake. (Henkel has identified more than 300 counterfeits of its brands.) China produces nearly half of the world's 14 billion batteries, most of them fake versions of Panasonic, Gillette (sometimes artfully called "Gillelle"), and other big brands. In the footwear market, Nike's potential annual losses in China resulting from fakes "approach the size of our legitimate business here," says company lawyer Nina Chen.

In the auto market the situation is so bad that Beijing Jeep, a joint venture with Chrysler, can barely sell its own parts because of a cottage industry of knockoff vendors. In Guangzhou, says Victor Kho, an investigator with Quest IPR, 99% of Suzuki motorcycles are fake. Even whole vehicles are being cloned: Earlier this year 22 fake Audis were discovered in Hubei province, and experts say that look-alike Mercedes are being assembled in the south.

Nobody knows how many Chinese are employed making fakes, but some experts put the figure well into the millions. Most work at small to midsized factories, but many stay at home, doing things like filling Head & Shoulders shampoo bottles from large vats in their living rooms. Last year 10,000 bottles of fake Evian water were found inside a building controlled by Beijing's correctional department, while investigators for Yale, the U.S. lockmaker, found a factory producing knockoffs inside a Chinese army compound. (The People's Liberation Army had rented the space to the counterfeiter, a not uncommon arrangement.) Fakes are also produced by state-owned enterprises trying to survive in the wake of having their subsidies cut.

To be fair, China has adopted most of the international treaties that frown on counterfeits. And China's leaders are finally spouting the right rhetoric. In a letter to a business conference last November, Premier Zhu Rongji wrote, "If we tolerate fake and shoddy commodities, there will be no hope for the state." Similarly, a committee of the National People's Congress notes that "the most serious issue is the production and selling of poor-quality and fake commodities, which has become rampant despite unceasing bans and crackdowns." But China has failed to enact the tough laws and rigid enforcement that are needed to get the job done. In fact, one of the ironies of China is that it is a police state with a lack of basic policing.

The reluctance of China's rulers to rock the boat is chillingly obvious in the city of Shenzhen, a one-hour train ride from downtown Hong Kong. A six-story, glass-enclosed building, Luo Hu Commercial City, sits defiantly at the border crossing. It is a monument to crime, a glistening Oz of fictional merchandise. Every day, 20,000 to 50,000 people (mostly day-trippers from Hong Kong) stream into the mall to buy cheap fakes in hundreds of shops and stalls — Hermes bags, Rolex watches, Fendi baguettes, Sony microphones. "In this district, the mall is the main source of income, taxes, and employment," concedes a senior official at the TSB, one of the enforcement units that regulates the mall. Adds the official, who agreed to a lunch interview on the condition he not be named: "If they're top-quality counterfeits, and they're not hurting the consumer, the government in China tends to take it easier on enforcement."

Luo Hu certainly has it easy. Since 1997, more than 300 shops in the mall have been raided, but most of the operators are back in action within a week, often under new business names. The mall's manager is not held accountable, nor are the various lease owners who rent out the units. Today the counterfeiters have developed an elaborate system of lookouts and security monitors to warn them when enforcers are on the way. The bulk of their goods are kept hidden in ceilings or in nearby unmarked warehouses. Last winter, a survey by luxury-goods maker Louis Vuitton found more than 100 shops at the mall selling Vuitton fakes. But a visit by government officials 11 days later — news of which leaked in advance — turned up only five such shops. In June, a memo from Beijing stressed that enforcement at Luo Hu "must be handled more strictly and quickly" in order to "enhance our international image" in light of the WTO drive.

It sounds good, but why not begin with Silk Alley, a massive counterfeiting market just ten steps from the U.S. Embassy in Beijing? "It's like China is doing this to the U.S.," says a private investigator, holding up his middle finger. Rather than bulldoze the place, the Chinese authorities have built a fancy entranceway. At Booth 35, Section Two, a jeans peddler with spiked hair explains that a 1,000-pair order of Levi's jeans (with "Made in the U.S.A." labels) will take 20 days and cost $10 apiece. The sand-washing is done in south China, he explains, while the pants and labels are made in Beijing. He wants a 30% cash deposit. At Booth 55, a bulk order of 5,000 pairs of fake Timberland boots can be had for less than $25 a pair but may take time because "the factory is very busy." Also available: Guess, Fila, Adidas, Nike, and Wrangler. Nearby, a Rolex faker named Huang Nan Mei promises 500 real gold watches from his Guangzhou factory at a price of just $300 apiece.

[PRC] authorities act more forcefully when consumers are hurt. Last year, after dozens of people were blinded, and ten killed, by counterfeit rice wines, the factory owner was executed. (More than 1,000 people overall have been injured by such "wine," which is usually just coloring added to industrial alcohol.) According to official figures, cases involving "serious harm" from fake or inferior goods are growing at an 80% annual clip. They include dozens who are maimed or killed each year by exploding fake beer bottles. One phony Johnson & Johnson baby oil has been causing rashes. Sometimes fakes are responsible for serious harm overseas: In 1996 a counterfeit cough syrup, made in China and shipped through Germany, killed 88 children.

Indeed, one of the most alarming trends in Chinese counterfeiting is the rapid rise in exports. Until the mid-1990s, foreign brand owners could stomach some fakes in China as an unofficial tax for doing business there — as long as the knock-offs stayed on the mainland. But now their overseas markets (and brand goodwill) are being chipped away. Last year Mattel broke up a counterfeiting ring that stretched from China to the Netherlands, and Oakley smashed a ring in South Africa, seizing 200,000 fake sunglasses, lens-cutting and frame-molding machines, and sample frames originating in China. Unilever says that fake Dove soap is making its way from China into Europe. Bose, a maker of high-end audio systems, is finding Chinese fakes in overseas markets. And in August, Brazilian authorities shredded 45,000 pairs of Nike sneakers — all fakes from China.

In the U.S., China is the leading country of origin for fakes confiscated by customs (30% of all seized imports). Since 1997, seizures have more than tripled in size. "There are zigzag routes, through three or four territories, for getting the goods into the U.S.," says Kroll's Humphrey. "It's a bit like money laundering." Indeed, when investigators seized seven million counterfeit CDs in 1998 at a Panama airport, they were shocked to trace them back to factories in China, as well as to a freight company in Florida. One of the ring's masterminds was a major courier for moving heroin from Hong Kong to New York. "He was using very similar routes and tactics with CDs," says Robert Youill, a music industry investigator who helped crack the case. Similarly, a new British intelligence report says that organized crime groups in Britain are raising money to finance drug deals through the burgeoning trade in counterfeit toys, clothing, and music, much of which arrives by the container-load from China.

The simple reason for the explosion in counterfeits is the big money and low risk involved. A Chinese counterfeiter knows he'll get a slap on the wrist if caught, while a drug trafficker will get a bullet in the head. "There's so much money to be made, it's beyond your imagination," says Curlewis. "If you run a [fake] video CD production line, you can recoup a $1 million investment by the seventh month." A counterfeiter who invests 2 cents making a low-grade zinc battery can retail it as a high-grade, brand-name alkaline battery for 60 cents—a return of 2,900%.

Some firms are taking off the kid gloves. Last year Gillette hired ex-U.S. Army Special Forces expert Philip Yang to lead its anticounterfeiting crusade. Working almost nonstop from his base in Shanghai, Yang is approaching China like a war zone. He has divided the country into sections and given his soldiers quotas. At least 25% of Gillette's products in China are fake—from razorblades and Duracells to Parker pens—and Yang wants to cut that to 5%.

It's a bold goal, and nearly every foreign brand owner is rooting from the sidelines. Yang's raid results are certainly impressive: In the first half of this year, he seized 2.4 million batteries, 25 million blades, and 140,000 pens, nearly the total seized by Gillette in the past seven years combined. (He says most of those goods were bound for overseas markets.) But even Yang is exasperated. "The more we raid them, the more there are," he says. The situation is so bad that Yang often ignores the retailers, focusing on the "capture of the masterminds." Among them: state-owned foreign trade companies, which Yang calls the "lifelines of the Chinese export economy."

Yang estimates there are thousands of fake blade factories in China. Last year, he stumbled on tellers inside a bank wrapping counterfeit blades during their spare time. More recently, he discovered a prison camp in Guangzhou making blades for export. "How do I raid them?" he asks, his eyes bugging. Batteries are another nightmare. On the Internet, Yang found several outfits falsely advertising themselves as makers or suppliers of Duracells; one required a minimum order of a container-load. "Blank batteries are usually stored in warehouses, and then middlemen will take a million batteries and divide them among a dozen villages," says Yang. The batteries are labeled by families in the village, then collected and sent to another location for blister-plastic wrapping. "You need damn good intelligence," he adds. "It's a war, the worst we've ever seen. Counterfeiting is now a way of life in China."

NOTES AND QUESTIONS

1. How would you respond to arguments that Western IP owners need to understand that counterfeiters in China do not think that what they are doing

is wrong because under China's cultural traditions copying is not wrongful but is a means to propagate knowledge and culture? The solution to the counterfeiting problem lies in educating the general population that copying IP rights that have commercial value is wrong and should be stopped. Do you agree?

2. Gillette's hiring of ex-Special Forces expert Philip Yang to head up its security department illustrates a trend in the industry. Many companies and private investigation agencies involved in anti-counterfeiting in China are hiring retired or former military commandos, FBI, Customs, and police officials as part of a "get tough" approach. If you were in-house counsel at an MNE doing business in China, what concerns might you have with hiring a private investigation agency that treats China like a "war zone" and refers to its investigators as "commandos" and "soldiers" who are given quotas?

3. The description of the counterfeiting problem in China in the Fortune Magazine article excerpted above paints a daunting problem. What are brand owners in China to do? Most brand owners take matters into their own hands through aggressive action in pursing counterfeiters. Brand owners hire private investigation companies to track down counterfeiters. Once the counterfeiter is located, brand owners have the option of bringing a lawsuit in court or seeking redress through PRC administrative authorities, which have concurrent jurisdiction to enforce the PRC Trademark Law (2002). With information in hand, almost all brand owners choose to go to PRC administrative authorities, such as the Administration of Industry and Commerce (AIC), which has administrative authority (but no police powers) to enforce trademark rights and seek an enforcement action in the form of a raid and seizure. Compared with a court action, the procedure for obtaining a raid is much faster, simpler, and more straightforward. All most brand owners need to do is to have one of their representatives appear at the local AIC office and file a one-page written complaint. The experience of most brand owners in China is that the AICs are quite eager to conduct enforcement actions. In most cases, AIC officials will leave shortly with the brand owner, sometimes in as little as 15 minutes, after the filing of the complaint. The private investigator and the brand owner will then lead the AIC officials to the site of the suspected counterfeiter. As noted in the Fortune article, most brand owners will not reveal the location in advance but usually insist on leading the authorities to the suspect premises to avoid tip-offs. The AICs will then raid the site of the suspected counterfeiter with the brand owner present and have the power to seize all illegal product, equipment, and funds. *See* Article 53, PRC Trademark Law. The products are later destroyed or sold after the counterfeit marks are obliterated and equipment is auctioned off at a public auction if it can be used for lawful purposes.

The AICs have authority to impose a fine and to order compensation to the brand owner. They also have the authority to award expenses incurred by the brand owner in the enforcement action. Where evidence of large sales of counterfeits is found, AICs also have discretion to transfer cases to judicial authorities for criminal prosecution.

Set forth in Figure 7-5 is a summary of the enforcement results of the AICs for a recent period.

4. After reviewing the statistics in Figure 7-5, what issues do you see with current levels of enforcement against counterfeiting in China?

5. Note that in addition to having powers to award damages based on proof by the brand owner, PRC courts also have the power under Article 56 of the Trademark Law to award statutory damages of up to 500,000 RMB or about

FIGURE 7-5
AIC Trademark Enforcement Activity, 1997-2000

Year	Cases	Average Fine	Average Damages	Criminal Prosecutions
1997	15,321	$679	$40	57 total or 1 in 268 cases
1998	14,216	$699	$41	35 total or 1 in 406 cases
1999	16,938	$754	$40	21 total or 1 in 806 cases
2000	22,001	$794	$19	45 total or 1 in 489 cases

Source: State Administration of Industry and Commerce Annual Statistics.

$60,000 in cases where damages are difficult to prove. Thus, it appears that PRC courts have adequate powers to provide for adequate compensation. Why don't brand owners just sue counterfeiters in court and obtain full compensation, which, if large enough, should serve as a deterrent?

6. Another troublesome issue that brand owners have encountered in enforcement is described below:

> One thing [private] investigators have mastered is the Chinese art of guan xi, or relationship building. The wining and dining of AIC agents, who earn about $200 a month, is today the stuff of karaoke legend. "They [AIC officers] are very busy," laughs [a private investigator] in Beijing. "They go from banquet to banquet." AIC officials, she adds, "have bought nice apartments and new cars with cash from corporations," and "holiday bonuses to division chiefs are distributed." The local branches of raiding agencies, often lacking in resources such as mobile phones and copy machines, typically extract "case-handling fees" from the corporations. For American firms, such gifts and payments could violate the Foreign Corrupt Practices Act. But that law normally applies to making payments to government officials in order to get business, rather than to greasing the wheels of an agency to get it to perform its mandated tasks. "It's a sensitive issue," says Ohio State Professor Chow. "The higher the fees, the more doubtful that it's legal."

Behar, *Beijing's Phony War on Fakes*, Fortune Magazine, *supra*, p. 198. Should U.S. corporations be concerned about payments of "case fees" to enforcement officials?

7. The total annual costs of enforcement against counterfeiting for MNEs in China can be quite high. Many MNEs in China spend more than $1 million just on enforcement actions against counterfeiting on an annual basis. Other expenses, such as lobbying of the PRC government, and litigation in courts are additional. Many MNEs believe that it is necessary to be vigilant with independent contractors such as private investigators, but some MNEs have taken the attitude that they don't need to know all the details. Is this advisable from a legal standpoint? Is this prudent from a business standpoint?

PROBLEM 7-2

An MNE has asked you to analyze the damage done to two of its brands in China based on the following two graphs (based on two actual cases involving real brands). In the graphs, the vertical axis represents the percentage of the market share for the product category. The vertical bar represents the total amount of all products, authentic and counterfeit, at any given time. The jagged line represents all genuine products in the market, which is determined according to the amount of actual shipments by the brand owner to its distributors to that market. If all products sold in the market are genuine, then the amount of products actually supplied by the brand owner should closely approximate the total amount of the product available. The horizontal axis is a time line beginning in August-September 2002 and ending in April-May 2005.

Beijing Case Study

Actual Shipment Versus Volumes Share Data

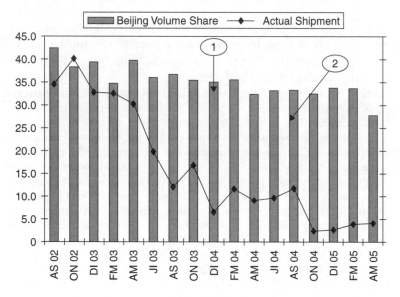

Guangdong Case Study

Actual Shipment Versus Volumes Share Data

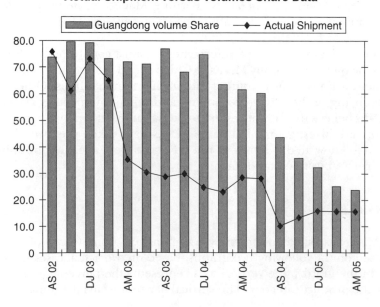

(1) What was the total market share of the product, real and counterfeit, in Beijing (top graph) in August-September 2002? What was the market share of the genuine product in August-September 2002? What was the total market share of the brand, both genuine and counterfeit, in April-May 2005? What was the total market share of the genuine product?

(2) What was the market share of the product, real and counterfeit, in Guangdong (bottom graph) in August-September 2002? What was the market share of the genuine product in August-September 2002? What was the total market share of the brand, real and counterfeit, in April-May 2005? What was the total market share of the genuine product?

(3) In the second case, counterfeits have greatly damaged the market position of the brand while in the first case, counterfeits have harmed the market less substantially. Assuming that in both cases the counterfeits were of low quality but that the first case involved a "low involvement" product whereas the second case involved a "high involvement" product (see p. 601), can you explain why?

(4) What must the brand owner in the second case study do to recover its market share? What lessons do you draw from this case on the harm from counterfeiting to brands?

PROBLEM 7-3

An MNE brand owner that has a manufacturing facility in north China finds that large quantities of counterfeits have recently appeared in parts of south China. Through the use of a private investigation agency, the brand owner has identified the counterfeiter and has located its factory. Aware of the difficulties of law enforcement in China, an intellectual property law expert in the United States has advised the brand owner to seek out the counterfeiter and to discuss the possibility of forming a joint venture together. The brand owner can qualify the counterfeiter to help produce the genuine product. As the brand owner does not have a manufacturing facility in the south and has been seriously considering an expansion in that area, forming a joint venture can help achieve two goals at once: Eliminate the counterfeiting problem and secure a manufacturing base in the south. Should the brand owner follow this advice? Consider the article below by Professor Chow and the accompanying notes.

PROBLEM 7-4

For the past several years, Mrs. Johnson, a flight attendant for a U.S.-based airline, has been holding "Purse Parties" at her home in an upscale neighborhood in a city in the Midwest. During these parties, attended mostly by professional women and wealthy homemakers, Mrs. Johnson gives the participants an opportunity to order counterfeits from catalogs of genuine handbags. She begins each party by telling the customers at the outset that the handbags are counterfeits so that no one is deceived about what they are buying. She says, "These are not genuine products but they are the highest quality fakes that we can find. There's nothing illegal about what we are doing. So everybody enjoy yourselves." The customers then pick genuine handbags from catalogs of products from famous brand owners. Mrs. Johnson will then buy counterfeit versions of their selections during her trips to visit her regular contacts in China. After buying the bags, she will carry them into the United States in her luggage and will also send the bags to some friends in New York where they enter the United States. No one seems to be very concerned that the bags are counterfeit, and Mrs. Johnson promotes these parties as "harmless fun" and offers part of the proceeds as a donation to a nearby children's hospital. Are any laws being violated by these "Purse Parties" and who, if anyone, might be liable? What about Mrs. Johnson's "customers"? Do you think that Mrs. Johnson has a connection to organized crime in China? Consider the article below and the accompanying notes.

Daniel C.K. Chow, Organized Crime, Local Protectionism, and the Trade in Counterfeit Goods in China
14 China Economic Review 473-484 (2003)

This paper examines the role of organized crime and local protectionism in promoting and protecting the trade in counterfeit goods in the People's Republic of China ("PRC" or "China"). By "organized crime," this paper refers to a group of persons or entities acting in concert to engage in criminal conduct within an overall organizational structure and under the direction of an individual or group of individuals. "Local protectionism" refers to the role of local governments in protecting illegal activity by failing to fully enforce the law. Note that under the definitions set forth above some forms of local protectionism may also be considered forms of organized crime.

THE ROLE OF ORGANIZED CRIME AND LOCAL PROTECTIONISM

The illegal trade in counterfeit goods in China can be divided into two components: manufacture and distribution. Criminal organizations play a significant role in the manufacturing side whereas local governments are involved in the distribution side. Local governments also protect the illegal but useful economic activity of counterfeiters through the imposition of light fines and penalties, which do not serve as a deterrent to further counterfeiting by the same offender.

A. MANUFACTURE AND ORGANIZED CRIME

The manufacture of counterfeits appears to be concentrated in the southeastern region of China, mostly in Fujian and Guangdong Provinces. Fujian, located across the China Straits from Taiwan, is the ancestral home of many Taiwanese. Guangdong Province is adjacent to Hong Kong and the ancestral home of many Hong Kongese. Both Guangdong and Fujian Provinces were some of the first areas opened to foreign investment in China and were some of the first locations for sino-foreign joint ventures and wholly foreign owned enterprises engaged in the manufacture of famous international brands of consumer products. Both of these areas were among the first areas in China to legally acquire foreign technology used in the production and manufacture of famous brands. Some of this technology and know-how has been acquired for illegal purposes. In a pattern that appears throughout other parts of China, an area where legitimate manufacturing is concentrated has given rise to illegal underground factories manufacturing counterfeits of the genuine products that are manufactured in nearby factories under the authority of the intellectual property owner.

Criminal organizations based in Hong Kong and Taiwan who have maintained connections with their ancestral homelands often provide the financing for the underground factories that manufacture illegal counterfeits in Guangdong and Fujian province. Anecdotal evidence indicates that these are the same criminal organizations that are involved in smuggling products into China, narcotics, prostitution, and pornography.

These criminal organizations promoting the counterfeit trade in China benefit from the jurisdictional and legal issues that are created by the international borders that separate Hong Kong and Taiwan from mainland China. As Hong Kong is an autonomous administrative unit of China, it continues to maintain its own police force, system of courts, and laws. As a result, police in China must work together with police in Hong Kong to pursue Hong Kong criminal organizations that support counterfeiting in Guangdong. The involvement of more than one set of enforcement authorities, laws, and legal systems create practical and logistical problems that impede law enforcement. In the case of Taiwan-based criminal organizations, the political problems that continue to divide China and Taiwan result in little or no law enforcement cooperation across the China Straits and Taiwan enforcement authorities have shown little interest in pursuing Taiwan persons or corporations for illegal activity on mainland China. Many Taiwan organizations feel that they can act with relative impunity in China.

(1) Exports: Counterfeit Cigarettes

Recent investigations by U.S. tobacco companies have revealed that these criminal organizations are heavily involved in the export of counterfeit cigarettes made in China to the United States. . . .

A carton of genuine premium cigarettes sells in the United States for about $35.00 in many states; a high quality carton of counterfeits produced in China can sell for as much as $30.00 in the U.S. while the cost of producing a counterfeit carton is $3.00. [A]t a recent meeting, U.S. Customs officials reported that every day containers of counterfeit cigarettes produced in China are unloaded from ships in Los Angeles port and enter the United States under false import documents as U.S. officials are unable to detect and seize all of these containers. Each container that is seized has a street value of $1-1.5 million yet the cost of producing the counterfeit product in the container to the manufacturer is about $80,000. In the same meeting, U.S. Customs officials estimated that as many as 8-10 containers pass through Los Angeles Customs undetected everyday. On the basis of the street value of each container at $1-1.5 million, the trade in counterfeit cigarettes produced in China and exported to the United States through Los Angeles port alone likely exceeds $1 billion per year. Criminal organizations with entities active in the United States, China, and Hong Kong are known to be behind this highly successful trade.

B. DISTRIBUTION AND LOCAL PROTECTIONISM

The manufacture of counterfeit products is of little use if the products cannot be delivered to the end use consumer. For this reason, the distribution of counterfeit products to retail levels of commerce is crucial to the counterfeit trade in China as elsewhere in the world. Large, legitimate wholesale distributors deliver products to state-owned stores or foreign-owned chain stores. Counterfeits cannot enter retail markets through these regular channels.

In China, the distribution of counterfeit products occurs through a series of large open air or partially enclosed wholesale markets located in densely populated areas with convenient transportation access. These markets are often massive in size and can contain more than one thousand outlets, each a wholesale distributor, occupying a stall or a semi-finished storefront. In the author's experience there is no wholesale market in China that does not carry counterfeit and infringing goods for sale. Many wholesale dealers have counterfeit goods on open display while others will display genuine products but have counterfeits in a back room or under the counter and available for the asking. In the heart of Beijing, hundreds of small retail vendors swarm the Tianyi wholesale market everyday and use three wheel bicycles, lorries, and small trucks to furnish the street stalls, open air kiosks, and small retail stores with abundant supplies of counterfeit and infringing products.

These wholesale markets are established and regulated by the local Administration of Industry and Commerce (AIC), a branch of the local government responsible for promoting, regulating, and policing commercial activity. In a typical situation, AICs will invest their own funds in establishing the wholesale market and will collect rent from each of the individual wholesale distributors. In addition, AICs will issue business licenses for a fee to each individual proprietor. Once the business is in operation, AICs will also collect a management fee from each individual proprietor. In a large wholesale market such as Tianyi, the operating revenues to the local AIC can easily exceed $100,000 per year. As noted above, many if not most of these wholesale distributors deal in counterfeit goods. As AICs are also one of the primary government entities in China charged with the enforcement against counterfeiting, AICs are faced with a conflict of interest as they are charged with policing and enforcing the very markets in which AICs and the local government have a substantial investment and financial interest. Shutting down these wholesale markets would not only result in a direct loss of revenue to the AIC but would also have many repercussions as many retail businesses, hotels, restaurants, and nightclubs are all supported by the trade in counterfeit goods. In some cities, such as Yiwu discussed below, the entire local economy is connected to the trade in counterfeits.

[T]here are at least five major wholesale markets in China: Hanzhen Jie in Wuhan City, Hubei Province; Linyi Market in Linyi, Shandong Province; Nansantiao Market in Shijiazhuang in Hebei Province; China Small Commodities City in Yiwu City, Zhejiang Province; and Wuai Market in Shenyang, Liaoning Province. Together these markets serve the entire coastal region of China and its most populous urban areas including Guangzhou in the south, Shanghai in the east and Beijing and Tianjin in the northeast. A branch of the China Small Commodities City market of Yiwu located in Wulumuqui in Xinjiang Province serves as an export post for the Middle East and Eastern Europe. These markets (represented by circles) and their relationship to the manufacturing centers (shaded areas) are set forth in the map opposite.

Major Distributors and Manufacturers of Counterfeit Goods in China

1. The Zhejiang China Small Commodities City Group, Ltd.

A sense of the formidable size, scope, organization, and resources of these wholesale markets is provided by a review of the China Small Commodities City wholesale market in Yiwu, Zhejiang Province, one of the most highly organized and successful wholesale markets for counterfeit and infringing goods in China.

In 1982, the Yiwu Administration of Industry and Commerce ("AIC") established the Zhejiang China Small Commodities City Group, Ltd. (hereinafter "CSCG"), a wholesale market specializing in trading small commodities.[11] By its own estimates, the Yiwu City AIC invested US$10 million to establish this market, which immediately experienced rapid and sustained growth. Recognizing the potential for further growth and the potential for expanding into related businesses, the Yiwu City AIC and related government entities decided to privatize the management and operation of the wholesale markets by forming the CSCG as a limited liability stock company in 1993. Privatization extended to management only but not to ownership of the CSCG. A majority interest in the CSCG continues to be held by state and collective enterprises and a substantial minority interest is held by individuals.

---

11. The information in this section was gathered through the course of several weeks of investigation in Yiwu by the author working with a private investigation company.

a. Privatization.   Privatization has served a critical strategic purpose for the CSCG. Under previous practice so long as the markets were under the direct management of the AIC or other local government entities, all revenues derived from such operations had to be transferred to the national government treasury with some portion of the funds returned as a type of rebate to the local government. After privatization, the company became responsible for its own profits and losses and company revenues and profits can be distributed in any manner in accordance with management directives. An additional advantage of privatization is that the company can now branch out into other related businesses that are beyond the scope of the AIC's jurisdiction, which is limited to regulating markets. This allows the privatized company to form a conglomerate of different businesses and to benefit from the synergy that such a combination creates. Forming a conglomerate of different businesses was far more difficult to accomplish so long as the markets were directly under the management of the AIC with its circumscribed jurisdiction. Privatization has served the key function of allowing the shareholders of the company direct access to the substantial wealth generated by the company and has created the framework for aggressive expansion.

The CSCG is unique among the wholesale markets in China described in this paper in that it is the only distribution center to the author's knowledge to have privatized its operations.

b. Ties with Local Government.   Although ostensible efforts were made to sever direct connections between government entities and the business operations of the CSCG, there are still strong ties between the CSCG and local government. In practice, the process of privatization meant that many of the same government officials responsible for forming and operating the CSCG left their government posts and assumed leadership roles within the corporation as private citizens. The lines between government and private spheres, however, continue to be blurred. The CSCG Chairman is a former vice mayor of Yiwu who continues to maintain office space in the Yiwu city government building. The Director of the Yiwu City AIC was also at the same time the legal representative of the CSCG's largest corporate shareholder. The Director is said to have resigned from all CSCG offices and is currently a director of one of Yiwu's four municipal offices, but his name continues to be listed second on a list of the CSCG's top executives in the CSCG's internal documents. The Vice-Director of the Yiwu City Government Municipal offices uses a name card that also bears the logo and the name of the China Small Commodities City Group. It appears to be a common practice for Yiwu government officials to use name cards with the China Small Commodities City Group logo. In practice, the CSCG conducts its affairs as if it carries government authority. In the case of the CSCG, as in many other instances in China, the line between a private enterprise and government authority is blurred.

Given the historical and present links between the Yiwu government and the CSCG and the CSCG's importance to the local economy, it is reasonable to assume that there is a *de facto* partnership between the Yiwu government and the CSCG. This partnership is likely to be a significant cause of the CSCG's remarkable growth from US$470,000 in sales in 1982 to US$2.2 billion in 1996 — a growth of 4,700% in 14 years. It is also reasonable to assume that the CSCG and the Yiwu City government are well aware of the size and magnitude of the traffic in counterfeit goods in the CSCG markets and elsewhere in Yiwu.

c. Shareholding and Corporate Structure. With a total registered capital of US$14 million, the CSCG currently has six corporate shareholders, all state owned or collectively owned enterprises, which own 55.59% of all shares. The shareholders and their respective shareholder's interest in percentage terms and value in RMB are:

(1) Zhejiang Yiwu China Small Commodities City Hengda Development Corp.
   Capital Contribution: RMB 43,211,300 (37%);
(2) Yiwu City Financial Development Corp.
   Capital Contribution: RMB 6,600,000 (5.7%);
(3) Zhejiang Province International Trust Investment Corp.
   Capital Contribution: RMB 5,500,000 (4.7%);
(4) Zhejiang Province Financial Development Corp.
   Capital Contribution: RMB 5,500,000 (4.7%);
(5) Zhongxin Trading Corp.
   Capital Contribution: RMB 2,200,000 (1.9%);
(6) Shanghai Shenyin Bond Corp.
   Capital Contribution: RMB 2,200,000 (1.9%).

Individual shareholders own 41% of all total shares worth RMB 47,401,200[12] and employees of the CSCG own 2.5% of all total shares worth RMB 2,887,500.

The CSCG operates through a board of directors, with a president, and a CSCG parent holding company that has a president's office, and separate departments for marketing, development, finance and securities. The CSCG parent holding company operates through a series of 14 wholly owned subsidiaries that have expanded into other businesses, most of which directly or indirectly support its trading operations through its wholesale markets, which seems to remain the CSCG's core business. These subsidiaries are as follows:

(1) China Small Commodities Market ("CSCM") Management Company
(2) CSCM Property Management Company
(3) CSCM Information Internet Company
(4) CSCM Hengda Development Company
(5) CSCM Trading Development Company
(6) Yindu Hotel Limited Liability Company
(7) Shangcheng Hotel
(8) Yiwu City Finance Development Company
(9) CSCM Real Estate Company
(10) CSCM Advertising Company
(11) Shangcheng Urban Credit Cooperative
(12) Yiwu City Property Right Exchange
(13) CSCM Highway Construction Co., Ltd.
(14) CSCM Exhibition Company

One CSCG subsidiary, the CSCM Management Company, actually engages in the trading of counterfeit goods and serves a major role in distribution of these products to the CSCG's branch markets. The CSCM internet company has set up a

---

12. The exchange rate is approximately 8.3 RMB = 1 U.S. dollar.

website advertising numerous small commodities for sale, creating worldwide access to goods sold in Yiwu and attracting buyers worldwide. Notable among the other subsidiaries is the Yindu Hotel Limited Liability Company, which operates a four star hotel that is by far the best hotel in Yiwu and that is part of a complex also housing the corporate headquarters of the CSCG, which includes a nightclub and karaoke bar in the lower level of the hotel. The CSCG has also set up a trade development subsidiary that has been exploring the establishment of representative branches in countries abroad, although the recent economic downturn seems to have curtailed these expansion efforts for the time being.

d. The CSCG Yiwu Wholesale Markets. The CSCG manages the China Small Commodities City, which has been by far the largest wholesale market in the PRC for the past six successive years. In 1996, the last year for which statistics published by the Yiwu City AIC are available, the market reached a floor space of over 500,000 square meters and had over 24,000 booths. The CSCG rents these booths to individual proprietors who hold individual business licenses. Over 50,000 business people operate in this market and over 200,000 people visit the market each day to conduct business. Based upon the author's own experience, at least 90% of the products sold in the China Small Commodities City are either counterfeit or infringing products.

During a four year period in the 1990's, the wholesale market grew at a rate of over 100% annually and its average annual growth rate through the entire history of the market is 90%. From 1991 to 1996, total volume of business in the market grew 22 times from US$100 million in 1991 to US$2.2 billion in 1996. No official data are available after 1997, but even assuming a modest growth rate, total sales for the China Small Commodities City wholesale market should reach nearly US$3 billion in 2003. Revenues at this level would place the CSCG above most of the largest multi-national enterprises doing business in China.

Given its rapid growth, the China Small Commodities City has quickly assumed a major role in supporting the entire local economy. In the 1990's, the tax revenues from the wholesale market operations have averaged 26% of the entire tax revenues for the city of Yiwu. The CSCG's total annual revenue from rental fees alone paid by the 30,000 wholesalers and 3,500 stores is about US$55 million. Total annual management fees paid by individual businesses to the local AIC are about US$6 million. Total local taxes paid by individual businesses in the CSCG wholesale markets to the Yiwu city government are approximately US$8 million. The CSCG appears to be involved in virtually every aspect of the local economy with over 50 pages of listings in the local 112 page phone book related to the CSCG. The remarkable growth of the CSCG's trade in counterfeit goods and the growth of other wholesale markets parallel the recent sharp rise in the amount of counterfeiting in the PRC.

e. Role of Yiwu in Distribution. Yiwu serves as a central distribution center for counterfeit goods to markets around the country. At the center of town, two large transportation companies occupy two open area transport areas, both the size of football fields. Around the perimeter of these areas are representative local transport offices from cities and towns all over China. Operating continuously day and night, trucks and lorries unload counterfeit products made in southern China in factories financed by criminal organizations in Hong Kong and Taiwan in one open transport area for storage and sale in Yiwu's wholesale markets. In the other open transport area, other trucks and lorries load

15-Year Development of China Small Commodities City Wholesale Market

	Number of Booths	Business Area (m^2 in 1000's)	Business Volume (RMB, million)	Business Volume Annual Growth (%)	Tax Volume (RMB, 1000)	Tax Volume Annual Growth (%)	% of Total YIWU Tax Revenues
1982	750	4.252	3.92	—	160	—	0.64
1983	1,050	4.252	14.44	268	380	137	1.12
1984	1,874	4.252	23.21	61	640	68	1.02
1985	2,874	13.59	61.90	167	1,290	102	2.03
1986	5,500	13.59	100.29	62	2,840	120	5.24
1987	5,600	57	153.8	54	5,650	99	9.45
1988	6,130	57	265	72	9,360	66	11.09
1989	8,400	57	390	47	14,870	59	17.45
1990	10,500	57	606	55	19,760	33	24.1
1991	10,500	57	1,025	67	42,050	113	28
1992	13,910	103	2,054	99	42,350	0.7	31
1993	13,910	103	4,515.2	120	55,750	32	25.14
1994	22,731	269	10,212	126	52,100	−0.7	24.69
1995	15,747	269	15,200	49	61,640	18	23.8
1996	24,069	500.1	18,468	21.5	—	—	—

counterfeit products already purchased from these wholesale markets for delivery to all parts of China.

e. Importance of the CSCG to the Local Economy. As this brief examination of the CSCG indicates, the trade in counterfeit goods has become an integral part of the Yiwu economy. Businesses that engage in the sale of counterfeit products pay taxes to the local government, which support public services for the local economy. This point is worth emphasizing because brand owners have argued that China suffers from a loss of tax revenues on counterfeit goods that otherwise would be paid by legitimate manufacturers on sales that are lost to counterfeiting. In Yiwu, local businesses operating within the CSCG markets negotiate a flat tax rate that becomes a substantial portion of the tax revenue of the city, thus helping to integrate the economic benefits of counterfeiting into the local economy. The myriad other businesses operated by the CSCG all depend directly or indirectly on the robust trade in counterfeit goods. The second point worth emphasizing is the close link between the CSCG, composed of former or current government officials, and the Yiwu government. This link suggests that the operations of the CSCG will be strongly defended at local levels.

NOTES AND QUESTIONS

1. Based on the discussion above, what do you think is the single most serious problem in the effective enforcement against counterfeiting in China? Is this an issue of intellectual property rights?

2. Review the bottom category of the chart on p. 621 on the percentage of total tax revenues paid by the CSCG, the corporate conglomerate that operates the wholesale market in counterfeit goods in Yiwu City, for the five-year period from 1991 to 1995. How important is the corporate group and the trade in counterfeit goods for the tax revenues of the city? What would happen if the trade in counterfeit goods were shut down?

3. In response to the serious problem of the smuggling of counterfeit goods into the United States by organized crime, Congress has made counterfeiting a predicate offense under RICO, the federal organized-crime statute. *See* 18 U.S.C. §§1961-1968. Congress has also passed the Trademark Counterfeiting Act of 1984, Pub. L. No. 98-473, 98 Stat. 2178 (1984), which provides in relevant part that "[w]hoever intentionally traffics or attempts to traffic in goods or services and knowingly uses a counterfeit mark on or in connection with such goods shall, if an individual, be fined not more than $2,000,000 or imprisoned not more than 10 years, or both, and, if a person other than an individual, be fined not more than $5,000,000." 18 U.S.C.S. §2320(a). The term "traffic" here means to "transport, transfer, or otherwise dispose of, to another, as consideration for anything of value." *Id.*, §2320(3)(2). Importing counterfeit merchandise under false documentation into the United States is a violation of 18 U.S.C.S. §545 (2003), the anti-smuggling statute which provides in relevant part that "whoever knowingly and willfully . . . smuggles, or clandestinely introduces or attempts to smuggle or clandestinely introduce into the United States any merchandise which should have been invoiced, or makes out or passes, or attempts to pass through the customhouse any false, forged, or fraudulent invoice, or other document or paper . . . [s]hall be fined under this title or imprisoned not more than five years, or both." In addition, other federal laws such as those relating to money laundering and the use of interstate commerce to transport smuggled and illegal goods may also be applicable.

Civil remedies are also available against counterfeiting under federal law. A plaintiff in a civil action against a counterfeiter is entitled to recover "(1) defendant's profits, (2) any damages sustained by the plaintiff, and (3) the costs of the action." 15 U.S.C. §1117(a) (West Supp. 1999). In cases where the act of counterfeiting is intentional, courts are required, in the absence of attenuating circumstances, to enter judgment for three times such profit or damages, whichever is higher, along with an award to the plaintiff of reasonable attorney's fees. *See* 15 U.S.C. §1117(b). In addition, the plaintiff may elect, at any time before a final judgment is entered by the court, to recover statutory damages instead of actual damages and profits. *See* 15 U.S.C. §1117(c). Statutory damages range from $500 to $100,000 where the actions were not willful up to $1,000,000 where the counterfeiting was willful. *See id.* In addition to federal laws, the states may have their own criminal and civil laws that apply to counterfeiting.

NOTE ON THE INDUSTRY RESPONSES BY MNES AND THE U.S. GOVERNMENT

Faced with the many challenges and obstacles of enforcement in China, IP owners have formed industrial coalitions to lobby the PRC government for reform. In 1998, representatives from Procter & Gamble, Johnson & Johnson, and SC Johnson formed the China Anti-Counterfeiting Coalition. The name of the group was later changed at the request of the PRC government to the less threatening Quality Brands Protection Committee (QBPC). The mission of the QBPC is to work with the PRC government in a cooperative and nonconfrontational style to promote long-term reform of laws and the legal system to improve the enforcement environment in China. At present, more than 80 of the largest MNEs in China are members of the QBPC.

One option that the QBPC and other brand owners are not anxious to pursue is seeking out the help of the U.S. Trade Representative (USTR) and threatening China with trade sanctions. Early in the trading relationship between the parties, tensions over intellectual property nearly caused a trade war on several occasions. Under the 1979 trade agreement between China and the United States that was part of establishing diplomatic relations between the two nations, China had agreed to provide protection for copyrights, trademarks, and patents to U.S. companies and persons on a reciprocal basis equal to the protections provided by U.S. law to Chinese parties. By 1989, both U.S. companies and the U.S. government believed that China's intellectual property protections were inadequate, and the USTR placed China on the "priority watch list" of Special 301 of the Omnibus Trade and Competitiveness Act of 1988, Pub. L. No. 100-418, §1342, 102 Stat. 1107, 1212-16 (1988). Based on §301 (also known as "Super 301") of the Trade Act of 1974, Pub. L. No. 93-618, §314(a), 88 Stat. 1978, 2053 (1975), which was a general statute applicable to all areas of trade, Special 301 requires the USTR to notify Congress on a regular basis of "priority foreign countries" that fail to adequately protect U.S. intellectual property rights and to undertake all required remedial measures within a mandated period. A designation as a priority foreign country triggered a series of actions that could culminate in retaliatory trade sanctions imposed by the United States on the offending country. To increase the effectiveness of Special 301, the USTR created two other categories, a "priority watch list," and a "watch list," to put nations that had not quite crossed the "priority foreign country" threshold on notice that they might fall in that dreaded category if their protections did not improve. Special 301, like its predecessor Super 301, has been called the "nuclear bomb" of trade relations, better used as a threat than in practice because its use can escalate trade tensions into a trade war.

To avoid U.S. sanctions, China agreed in 1989 to a memorandum of understanding (MOU) that set out a series of steps that would improve China's intellectual property protection. Among other steps, China agreed to study the possibility of joining various international intellectual property treaties, to pass a copyright law by the end of the year, and to amend its patent law by extending the period of protection to 20 years in accordance with international practice. In January 1992, China entered into a second MOU with the United States under which China agreed to join the Berne Convention for the Protection of Literary and Artistic Works by October 1992 and to make other changes to its existing copyright legislation. By 1994, the USTR determined that the situation in China had not improved and once again placed China on the Special 301 priority watch list. Although China had made significant progress in upgrading its laws, the USTR and U.S. companies felt that enforcement of the laws was inadequate. The USTR set a deadline by which China had to respond to U.S. demands or face retaliatory 100 percent tariffs on $1.1 billion of Chinese imports into the United States. China responded by threatening 100 percent tariffs on U.S. imports into China and also threatened to cut off negotiations with U.S. automakers on joint ventures in China to build minivans and passenger cars. Just

hours before the deadline, China and the United States signed the Agreement
Regarding Intellectual Property, which included an action plan for enforcement of
intellectual property rights calling for the creation of new enforcement bodies,
including task forces, and special provisions for the protection of compact disks,
laser disks, and CD ROMs. By May 1996, the United States was once again dissatisfied with China's efforts and again threatened China with retaliatory tariff
sanctions on Chinese imports, causing China to respond within the hour with
its own threats of sanctions of a similar amount on U.S. imports into China.
The parties reached a new agreement, the 1996 Accord, just before the deadline.

Unlike the agreements reached in 1992 and 1995, the 1996 Accord, perhaps
indicating China's growing negotiating power with the United States, did not
specify new commitments that China had to undertake. Rather, the 1996
Accord mainly reaffirmed China's previous commitments to protect intellectual
property rights. Since 1996, China has continued to upgrade its intellectual property laws in response to the 1996 Accord. Most observers agree that China's laws
were substantially in compliance with TRIPS and international standards by the
time of China's formal accession to the WTO in 2000. The issue in China is the lack
of adequate enforcement, not the existence of complying laws. U.S. multinationals, however, have no interest in putting pressure on China to improve its
enforcement efforts through threats of trade sanctions from the U.S. government
and have scrupulously avoided involving the USTR in a public way in this dispute.
Behind closed doors, companies will complain to the USTR and the Commerce
Department but they generally ask that their names not be used in connection with
any informal talks between these agencies and the PRC. U.S. companies are also
adamantly opposed to any formal action by the U.S. government that might lead
to trade sanctions under U.S. law or to a formal dispute settlement proceeding
before the WTO.

PROBLEM 7-5

At a "town meeting" of angry and frustrated MNEs in Beijing, an intellectual
property expert argues that the strategy of bringing waves of enforcement actions
is short sighted and wrong headed. The expert argues that MNEs should convince
the PRC government that respect for IP is in China's own best interests and is
necessary to support the long-term development of its economy. "When you show
China that enforcement against commercial piracy is in its own best interests —
not just in your interests — then you will see real progress." What do you think of
this proposal? Consider the article below.

Daniel C.K. Chow, Counterfeiting in the People's
Republic of China
78 Washington University Law Quarterly 1, 39, 48-49, 53 (2000)

A firm political commitment from the top echelons of the PRC government is
probably necessary before any dramatic progress against counterfeiting can be
made at least in the short term. Certain problems — local protectionism and government involvement in profit-making and commercial activities in particular —

[cannot be addressed] without the political will from the top that is necessary to overcome these internal hurdles and crack down on counterfeiting. Whether this commitment is forthcoming or how this commitment can be obtained remains unclear.

The Future of Counterfeiting in China

Top level PRC authorities publicly acknowledge the severity of the counterfeiting problem and acknowledge that counterfeiting is detrimental to China's national interests. On the other hand, consumer markets continue to grow and consumer wealth and spending continue to increase dramatically. While many consumers are concerned about counterfeit products, there is a less affluent and less educated portion of the population that has an appetite for all types of counterfeit products. Foreign brand owners continue to invest in China's economy, which continues to grow and continues to receive positive forecasts for the future. Most foreign and local brand owners wish to raise the profile of the counterfeiting problem but are wary of offending the Chinese government. Government enforcement entities compete for resources and the prestige associated with power to combat counterfeiting — and then mete out sanctions that in many instances fail to deter counterfeiters from repeating their offenses or that serve as a deterrent for others who wish to enter the trade. For the most part, the United States government and foreign governments — taking their cues from their constituencies — have played a background role and have put little or no pressure on the PRC government. A major campaign against counterfeiting would involve an expenditure of significant political and economic resources that would shift such resources from other pressing concerns and would likely lead to social and political costs that will be unpopular with local governments and constituencies. Given this present scenario, there does not appear to be the internal or external pressures that would prompt the PRC government to undertake a top level political commitment to crack down on counterfeiting and without such a commitment, it is unlikely that there will be a dramatic improvement in the counterfeiting problem in the short term. What this may indicate is that the Chinese government, despite its rhetoric, does not consider counterfeiting to truly imperil its national interests, at least in the short term.

The extent to which counterfeiting harms China's long term national interests is unclear. A popular argument raised by brand owners and other interest groups is that counterfeiting is harmful to China's long term national interests and that it is in China's own best interests to resolve this problem. This argument is appealing and is supported by history and by the general policies behind the protection of intellectual property. After all, [we have always assumed] that no nation can achieve high levels of modernization and industrialization without a strong regime protecting intellectual property rights — but an examination of the present situation in China indicates that this historical lesson appears to be inapplicable to China, at least for the present. A scientific study of the economic impact of counterfeiting on China's economy might reveal that counterfeiting will lead to future harm, but at present all economic indicators of importance to the Chinese — overall growth of the economy, the influx of foreign investment, and the rise in Chinese wealth and spending — show that China continues to be on course despite a counterfeiting problem that has no parallels in world history. For now China has not seen tangible evidence of the harm caused by counterfeiting on a national level. As China continues its journey down the path of modernization and industrialization, it remains to be seen whether China can defy history.

QUESTIONS

1. Is counterfeiting harmful to China?
2. Why are U.S. companies so reluctant to involve the U.S. government?
3. Why should China do anything about counterfeiting?

II. TRIPS and the Protection of Intellectual Property Rights

In Chapter 5, we examined the international intellectual property system and the role of TRIPS in promulgating harmonized substantive legal standards setting forth the types of IP rights that each member nation should make available. In this section, we focus on the impact of TRIPS on the enforcement and protection of IP rights against commercial piracy and other types of infringements. Most of these obligations are contained in Part III of TRIPS, which will be the focus of this section. As we shall see, protecting intellectual property rights under TRIPS has hardly been uncontroversial.

In addition to the application of TRIPS to commercial piracy, we will also examine two of the WTO's most hotly debated current topics: The impact of TRIPS on access to medicines and biopiracy.

A. Intellectual Property, TRIPS, and the WTO

One of the major triumphs of the Uruguay Round of negotiations that led to the establishment of the WTO was the inclusion of intellectual property rights within the world trade framework through TRIPS, one of the treaties administered by the new WTO established in 1995. As we noted in Chapter 1, one of the weaknesses of the GATT system was that contracting states were allowed to pick and choose which treaty obligations to which they were bound. Some called this system "GATT à la carte," which permitted many free-riders, that is, those contracting states that enjoyed GATT trading benefits even though they refused to enact intellectual property laws that met international standards. As a result of the Uruguay Round, this problem has been addressed as membership in the WTO requires adherence to all of the WTO's major treaties, including TRIPS. The new framework meant that developing nations had to accept TRIPS standards as one of the requirements of admission to the WTO.

As TRIPS is a non-self-executing treaty, membership in the WTO obligates each member to enact domestic IP legislation that complies with the minimum standards established by TRIPS. When the WTO agreements took effect on January 1, 1995, all 146 WTO members had to ensure that their laws and practices complied with TRIPS within one year for developed countries, within five years (until 2000) for developing countries, and within eleven years (until 2006) for least developed countries. The result of TRIPS is the eventual widespread promulgation of intellectual property laws on copyright, patent, trademark and other IP rights based on standards established by the United States and a number of other developed countries that were the main proponents of including TRIPS within the WTO framework.

TRIPS member nations not only have obligations to enact comprehensive laws in all IP areas, but under Part III of TRIPS they also have specific obligations to enact laws specifically directed against commercial piracy. TRIPS also imposes specific enforcement obligations on its members. However, while TRIPS has been effective in obtaining the widespread enactment of complying legislation, TRIPS has been less effective in securing enforcement of these laws. In most instances in the world today, the problem is not with the existence of IP laws but with their effective enforcement.

From a larger political perspective, the incorporation of TRIPS into the WTO framework was viewed at the time as a major triumph for advanced industrialized nations and a major shift in the way that intellectual property was viewed in international commerce. Both the Paris Convention on patents and trademarks and the Berne Convention on copyright (see Chapter 5 at p. 353) as well as other major international treaties are administered by the World Intellectual Property Organization (WIPO), a specialized agency of the United Nations located in Geneva. These intellectual property treaties were administered in isolation from other issues concerning trade and commerce, and the WIPO is a largely toothless organization that has little, if any, enforcement power. Many developing nations had sought to keep intellectual property outside of the jurisdiction of the WTO and its predecessor, the GATT, as these organizations were viewed as a "club for rich nations." The incorporation of intellectual property rights into the WTO now means that intellectual property has become a trade issue connected with other trade issues within the WTO framework and can no longer be viewed in isolation. For example, if a developing nation that is a WTO member is not enforcing laws against commercial piracy as required by TRIPS, a nation that is harmed can challenge this deficiency by bringing a petition within the WTO dispute settlement system. Among the remedies available to the petitioning nation would be retaliation in any industrial sector, not limited to intellectual property rights. Returning to our example, a developing nation that failed to provide adequate intellectual property rights protection as required by TRIPS might find, for example, that the petitioning nation is allowed to impose tariffs on agricultural goods imported from the offending nation. The mere threat of this type of remedy (as opposed to its actual implementation), not possible under the WIPO system, has created pressure on all nations to comply with WTO obligations, including TRIPS.

While TRIPS was initially viewed as a triumph for developed nations, TRIPS has more recently come under intense criticism. We will return to other lines of criticism of TRIPS in the biopiracy debate but for now consider the following line of argument. Some critics of TRIPS have argued that there is an explanation from culture that illuminates why problems of commercial piracy can be so difficult to control in developing countries. TRIPS standards are premised upon the values of free-market capitalism. Developing countries are being asked to transplant Western-style IP laws to societies with entirely differently cultural traditions and social institutions. It is one matter to ask a developing country to enact Western-style intellectual property laws but another matter to expect that country to give full effect to those laws if its underlying social institutions and traditions are in tension with those laws. Advanced capitalist democracies such as the United States have a powerful and independent judiciary, a legal profession, and powerful interests groups, all of which support an approach to intellectual property rights that rewards individual creativity and entrepreneurship. All of these social institutions are necessary in addition to IP laws to support a vigorous enforcement of intellectual property rights. However, many developing countries have historically adhered to a different set of social values, which emphasized communal ownership of knowledge and information. In traditional Asian societies, for example, copying the work of another was not seen as wrongful but as a way to spread knowledge and culture, which was viewed as the common heritage of the nation. One cannot simply ask a developing country to fully enforce its TRIPS-compliant IP laws without first developing the social and legal institutions that would support such enforcement. Just as advanced industrialized countries have put pressure on developing and non-Western countries to adopt Western-style intellectual property laws, industrialized countries are now asking developing countries to fully enforce these laws and to implement the rule of law, which means also adopting the Western-style social and legal institutions that underlie free-market capitalism.

QUESTIONS

1. Are developing countries being coerced into rejecting their traditional culture and social institutions and replacing them with their Western counterparts as a price of meeting the standards of TRIPS?

2. Should alternative types of intellectual property laws that respect non-Western cultures be considered by the WTO?

B. Enforcement Obligations Under TRIPS Against Commercial Piracy

1. General Enforcement Obligations

Recognizing that the enactment of laws that meet international standards means little if those laws are not adequately enforced, Part III of TRIPS provides for specific enforcement obligations as follows.

Article 41

1. Members shall ensure that enforcement procedures as specified in this Part are available under their law so as to permit effective action against any act of infringement of intellectual property rights covered by this Agreement, including expeditious remedies to prevent infringements and remedies which constitute a deterrent to further infringements. . . .

2. Procedures concerning the enforcement of intellectual property rights shall be fair and equitable. They shall not be unnecessarily complicated or costly, or entail unreasonable time-limits or unwarranted delays. . . .

Article 45

Damages

1. The judicial authorities shall have the authority to order the infringer to pay the right holder damages adequate to compensate for the injury the right holder has

suffered because of an infringement of that person's intellectual property right by an infringer who knowingly, or with reasonable grounds to know, engaged in infringing activity.

2. The judicial authorities shall also have the authority to order the infringer to pay the right holder expenses, which may include appropriate attorney's fees. In appropriate cases, Members may authorize the judicial authorities to order recovery of profits. . . .

Article 51

Suspension of Release by Customs Authorities

Members shall . . . adopt procedures to enable a right holder, who has valid grounds for suspecting that the importation of counterfeit trademark or pirated copyright goods may take place, to lodge an application in writing with competent authorities, administrative or judicial, for the suspension by the customs authorities of the release into free circulation of such goods. Members may enable such an application to be made in respect of goods which involve other infringements of intellectual property rights. . . .

Article 61

Members shall provide for criminal procedures and penalties to be applied at least in cases of willful trademark counterfeiting or copyright piracy on a commercial scale. Remedies available shall include imprisonment and/or monetary fines sufficient to provide a deterrent, consistently with the level of penalties applied for crimes of a corresponding gravity. In appropriate cases, remedies available shall also include the seizure, forfeiture and destruction of the infringing goods and of any materials and implements the predominant use of which has been in the commission of the offence.

Consistent with TRIPS, U.S. law contains simple procedures for trademark and copyright owners to obtain border enforcement measures against counterfeit and pirated copyright goods. These procedures are set forth in 19 C.F.R. Chap. 1 Subparts C & D. Counterfeit goods are subject to seizure at ports of entry by U.S. Customs under 19 C.F.R. §133.21. Customs is also authorized to detain goods that infringe (but do not counterfeit) a registered U.S. trademark under 19 C.F.R. §133.22. While the trademark owner does not need to record its trademark with Customs in order for Customs to seize counterfeits, Customs will detain infringing (but not counterfeit) goods only if a registered U.S. trademark owner first records the trademark with Customs under the procedures set forth in §§133.1-133.4. (Note the trademark owner must first register the mark with the Patent and Trademark Office then record the registered mark with Customs.) A similar procedure exists for copyrights. U.S. Customs will detain goods that infringe a registered U.S. copyright where the owner has recorded the copyright with Customs under §133.31. Unlike in the case of trademarks, Customs does not distinguish between pirated copyright goods (identical copies) and infringing goods (partial copies). The copyright owner must first record the copyright in all cases. Once the suspect goods have been seized or detained, Customs regulations contain detailed procedures for the forfeiture and destruction of the goods or for their release to the importer (with possible indemnification) if the charges of piracy and infringement cannot be substantiated by the IP owner. U.S. Customs regulations do not contain similar procedures for the protection of U.S. patents against infringing imports. For reasons of history, patent holders are protected from unfair import competition under a different statutory scheme, §337 of the Tariff Act of 1930, §303, ch. 497, 46 Stat. 687 (1930). Unlike the case of trademarks and copyrights, which require only a simple recording procedure with Customs, a patent holder must obtain an exclusion order under §337 before the International Trade Commission, which requires bringing an action and the presentation of evidence at an adversary hearing before the ITC.

NOTES AND QUESTIONS

1. Review the enforcement statistics on China contained in Figure 7-5 on p. 611 *supra* and compare them with China's obligations under the TRIPS provisions set forth above. Is China in compliance with its enforcement obligations concerning deterrence (Article 41(1)), damages (Article 45), and criminal enforcement (Article 61) under TRIPS?

2. After considering question 1 above, what problems do you see with the articles of TRIPS Part III as presently drafted?

3. While the United States appears to have met its TRIPS enforcement obligations, what happens if a WTO member believes that another member has failed to satisfy its TRIPS enforcement obligations? If a dispute arises concerning a nation's compliance with its TRIPS obligations, it is possible for the complaining nation to seek dispute settlement under the WTO Understanding on Dispute Settlement. At the preliminary stages of the dispute settlement process, the parties have opportunities for the informal settlement of the dispute through consultations and mediation. If the informal process does not settle the parties' differences, the parties then undergo a process much like that of civil litigation in which the dispute is first heard by a dispute settlement panel that has fact-finding powers. Review of the report issued by the panel is available through an appellate body with a scope of review that is limited to issues of law. A report can then be adopted by the Dispute Settlement Body (DSB) of the WTO. If the report finds that a measure is inconsistent with the requirements of a covered WTO agreement, the report will recommend that the member bring its measure into conformity with the concerned agreement and may suggest ways that the member concerned can implement the report's recommendations. If a member fails to comply with the recommendations of the DSB or otherwise bring an inconsistent measure into conformity, the complaining party can seek compensation; if compensation cannot be agreed upon, the complaining member can seek authorization for retaliation. For a detailed discussion of the WTO dispute settlement process, *see* David Palmeter & Petros C. Mavroidis, *Dispute Settlement in the World Trade Organization* (1999).

2. Provisional Measures

A major problem that IP owners face is that most counterfeiters and pirates destroy evidence and flee at the first sign of trouble. As a result, it is essential that IP owners preserve the element of surprise in enforcement actions. To address this concern, Part III of TRIPS requires that its members provide provisional (or temporary) measures that can be used against infringers.

A review of the procedures available to an IP owner under U.S. law illustrates how provisional measures can be used effectively against an infringer. Under

Rule 65 of the Federal Rules of Civil Procedure, a plaintiff can appear ex parte before a federal court and apply for a seizure order for counterfeit, pirated, or infringing goods and a temporary restraining order (TRO) against a suspected offender. In the past, some IP owners have encountered some problems in obtaining a TRO as they are sometimes unable to obtain the name and identity of the suspected offender. To accommodate this issue, some federal courts will issue a "John Doe" TRO. If the court decides to grant the plaintiff's application, the plaintiff is then entitled to go to the premises of the suspected infringer accompanied by a federal marshal and serve a copy of the TRO and order on the defendant and seize the goods. (When a federal court issues a TRO and seizure order, a copy is usually sent to the U.S. Attorney's office, which then has the option to consider a criminal prosecution.) If the defendant is not present, the plaintiff can post the order or find other substitute means to provide legally effective notice. The order served by the plaintiff also notices a hearing before the expiration of the TRO at which the plaintiff can seek a preliminary injunction that would prevent the defendant from engaging in additional illegal activity until the case is finally resolved. Where true counterfeiting is involved, the entry of the TRO and the seizure of the goods is usually the final resolution of the case as issues of liability are rarely contested by the counterfeiters, if they appear in court at all. In other instances, the parties agree to settle the case without a trial and the court enters a consent decree. In some instances, the final resolution of the case may involve a permanent injunction, a court order that permanently bars the defendant from engaging in certain activities. The critical feature of these provisional remedies discussed above is that they allow a brand owner to immediately stop a counterfeiter from engaging in additional harmful conduct at the same time (or before) a complaint is filed in civil court. Many IP owners believe that pretrial relief that can be obtained ex parte is essential to preserve the element of surprise and to obtain effective civil action in the United States.

Many of these features available under U.S. provisional measures are now required by Article 50 of TRIPS, which provides in relevant part:

Article 50

    1. The judicial authorities shall have the authority to order prompt and effective provisional measures:

        (a) to prevent an infringement of any intellectual property right from occurring and, in particular to prevent the entry into the channels of commerce in their jurisdiction of goods, including imported goods immediately after customs clearance;

        (b) to preserve relevant evidence in regard to the alleged infringement.

    2. The judicial authorities shall have the authority to adopt provisional measures *inaudita altera parte* where appropriate, in particular where any delay is likely to cause irreparable harm to the right holder, or where there is a demonstrable risk of evidence being destroyed. . . .

    6. [P]rovisional measures taken on the basis of paragraphs 1 and 2 shall, upon request by the defendant, be revoked . . . if proceedings leading to a decision on the merits of the case are not initiated within a reasonable period, to be determined by the judicial authority ordering the measures where a Member's law so permits or, in the absence of such a determination, not to exceed 20 working days or 31 calendar days, whichever is the longer.

    7. Where the provisional measures are revoked or where they lapse due to any act or omission by the applicant, or where it is subsequently found that there has been

no infringement or threat of infringement of an intellectual property right, the judicial authorities shall have the authority to order the applicant, upon request of the defendant, to provide the defendant appropriate compensation.

PROBLEM 7-6

As a new member of the WTO, a developing country has issued several new laws to meet its TRIPS obligations. One set of laws deals with civil enforcement procedures. The key features of the law are as follows:

(1) The plaintiff can obtain injunctive relief against an infringer by (a) filing a complaint against the infringer with a court and (b) serving a copy of the complaint and notice of the hearing on the infringer.
(2) At the hearing, the plaintiff must establish irreparable harm or the threat thereof. The defendant is allowed to offer a defense at the hearing.
(3) If the court decides to issue the injunction, the plaintiff must post a bond to indemnify the defendant.
(4) The preliminary injunction is continued for the duration of the trial at the end of which a permanent injunction can be issued if the defendant is found liable.

Go through each feature of this law and explain whether it is consistent with Article 50 of TRIPS. Is this law an effective measure against commercial piracy?

C. TRIPS and the Access to Medicines Debate

One area where TRIPS helped initially to address some of the concerns of MNEs about commercial piracy and counterfeiting is in the long-standing and heated debate over patents for pharmaceuticals. Prior to joining TRIPS, some developing countries, such as Thailand and India, refused to enact domestic patent legislation. These countries justified this decision on the grounds that public health needs required unrestricted access to essential medicines. As all patents are territorial in nature, a U.S. patent for a drug would have effect within the United States but would have no legal effect in Thailand (in the absence of some international treaty requiring recognition). Rather, the U.S. patent holder would have to apply for a patent under the laws of Thailand in order to receive patent protection within that country. Thailand and other developing countries, however, refused to enact patent legislation in order to allow copying of these drugs. As a result, it was arguably not illegal prior to TRIPS to make inexpensive copies of a U.S. drug in Thailand as it violated no applicable patent law. The effect of TRIPS, however, is that all WTO members must now enact IP laws that meet the minimal substantive standards of TRIPS, which includes patent protection for pharmaceuticals. As a result, Thailand now has a domestic patent law, and the U.S. patent holder can now receive patent protection for its drug within Thailand. Assuming that the U.S. drug company obtains a Thai patent, if unauthorized copies of the U.S. drug are produced in Thailand, these copies are now illegal counterfeits. The U.S. drug maker can now seek assistance from the Thai authorities to shut down the counterfeiters and the Thai authorities would be subject to political pressure from the U.S. government if they did not comply. The U.S. company could also seek to ban the entry of parallel imports into Thailand, that is, less expensive but genuine versions of the drug produced in another country and imported into Thailand.

Soon after the implementation of TRIPS, however, it came under intense criticism for its effect on access to medicines on those in the world who need them the most. The critics of TRIPS argued that (1) increased patent protection leads to higher drug prices, which will cause drugs to be out of reach for many developing countries; (2) enforcement of TRIPS will restrict local manufacturing capacity and remove a source of drugs on which many in the developing world depend; (3) widespread patent protection will further discourage drug companies from undertaking research and development on diseases such as malaria and tuberculosis in developing countries as such activities do not offer enough incentive in the form of profits; (4) TRIPS compliance appears to be only a minimal threshold as many developed countries are putting pressure on developing countries to provide "TRIPS plus" protection by extending patent protection beyond the required 20-year period.

Although TRIPS requires its members to provide patent protection, the drafters of TRIPS did recognize that, in certain cases, host countries should be able to override a patent without having to obtain the consent of the patent holder for reasons of public health. This is the basic concept behind a compulsory license that is the subject of the following article of TRIPS:

Article 31

Other Use Without Authorization of the Right Holder

Where the law of a Member allows for other use of the subject matter of a patent without the authorization of the right holder, including use by the government or third parties authorized by the government, the following provisions shall be respected:

(a) authorization of such use shall be considered on its individual merits;

(b) such use may only be permitted if, prior to such use, the proposed user has made efforts to obtain authorization from the right holder on reasonable commercial terms and conditions and that such efforts have not been successful within a reasonable period of time. This requirement may be waived by a Member in the case of national emergency or other circumstances of extreme urgency or in cases of public non-commercial use. . . . ;

(c) the scope and duration of such use shall be limited to the purpose for which it was authorized. . . . ;

(d) such use shall be non-exclusive;

(e) such use shall be non-assignable, except with that part of the enterprise or goodwill which enjoys such use;

(f) any such use shall be authorized predominantly for the supply of the domestic market of the Member authorizing such use;

(g) authorization for such use shall be liable . . . to be terminated if and when the circumstances which led to it cease to exist and are unlikely to recur. . . . ;

(h) the right holder shall be paid adequate remuneration in the circumstances of each case, taking into account the economic value of the authorization. . . .

Most critics of TRIPS, however, found this provision to be too restrictive and not useful as a tool to address the concerns that TRIPS denied meaningful access to medicines.

The controversy over access to medicines flared and galvanized world opinion against the interests of drug companies due to several well-publicized incidents in the 1990s. In one incident, a group of multinational drug companies brought suit in 1998 against the South African government, arguing that a law that permitted broad access to patented medicines violated TRIPS. Both the United States and the European Commission threatened trade sanctions to put pressure on the South African government to repeal the law. A storm of protest erupted in the United States as AIDS activists argued that the United States valued profits over people. These protests created public pressure and embarrassed government leaders in several well-known incidents to force a change to these policies. By the time the lawsuit came to trial in South Africa, the United States had reversed its policy, and the drug companies, which could no longer count on the support of their governments, dropped the case. In 2001, the United States brought a claim against Brazil with the WTO Dispute Settlement Body, challenging a Brazilian law that imposed a local working requirement on all Brazilian patent holders to manufacture drugs locally or be subject to a compulsory license after three years. As a result of this law, U.S. drug makers could no longer simply export their drugs protected by a Brazilian patent to Brazil but had to establish a factory in Brazil or the Brazilian government would issue a license for the patent to local drug makers without the authorization of the U.S. companies. The Brazilian law was the linchpin of a government AIDS program that had reduced AIDS mortality among the estimated 536,000 people infected with AIDS in Brazil by more than 50 percent between 1996 and 1999. The U.S. action came under fierce criticism from international non-government organizations (NGOs) such as the World Health Organization, which were concerned that the U.S. action would have a negative effect on the efforts by other developing nations to institute government programs to combat AIDS. Faced with mounting international pressure, the United States eventually withdrew its complaint with the WTO.

By the time that the Fourth Ministerial Conference of the WTO was held in Doha in 2001, the access to medicines issue was a key item on the agenda. After much debate, the following declaration, based on a compromise between the United States and Brazil, was adopted by the Ministerial Conference:

Declaration on the TRIPS Agreement and Public Health

Adopted on 14 November 2001

We agree that the TRIPS Agreement does not and should not prevent Members from taking measures to protect public health. Accordingly, while reiterating our commitment to the TRIPS Agreement, we affirm that the Agreement can and should be interpreted and implemented in a matter supportive of WTO Members' right to protect public health and, in particular, to promote access to medicines for all.

In this connection, we affirm the right of WTO Members to use, to the full, the provisions in the TRIPS Agreement, which provide flexibility for this purpose.

Accordingly . . . , while maintaining our commitments in the TRIPS Agreement, we recognize that these flexibilities include:

(a) In applying the customary rules of interpretation of public international law, each provision of the TRIPS Agreement shall be read in the light of the object and purpose of the Agreement as expressed, in particular, in its objectives and principles.

(b) Each Member has the right to grant compulsory licenses and the freedom to determine the grounds upon which such licenses are granted.

(c) Each Member has the right to determine what constitutes a national emergency or other circumstances of extreme urgency, it being understood that public health crises, including those relating to HIV/AIDS, tuberculosis, malaria, and other epidemics, can represent a national emergency or other circumstances of extreme urgency.

(d) The effect of the provisions in the TRIPS Agreement that are relevant to the exhaustion of intellectual property rights is to leave each Member free to establish its own regime for such exhaustion without challenge, subject to the MFN and national treatment provisions of Articles 3 and 4.

6. We recognize that WTO Members with insufficient or no manufacturing capacities in the pharmaceutical sector could face difficulties in making effective use of compulsory licensing under the TRIPS Agreement. We instruct the Council for TRIPS to find an expeditious solution to this problem and to report to the General Council before the end of 2002.

7. We reaffirm the commitment of developed-country Members to provide incentives to their enterprises and institutions to promote and encourage technology transfer to least-developed country Members pursuant to Article 66.2. We also agree that the least-developed country Members will not be obliged, with respect to pharmaceutical products, to implement or apply Sections 5 and 7 of Part II of the TRIPS Agreement or to enforce rights provided for under these Sections until 1 January 2016, without prejudice to the right of least-developed country Members to seek other extensions of the transition periods as provided for in Article 66.1 of the TRIPS Agreement. We instruct the Council for TRIPS to take the necessary action to give effect to this pursuant to Article 66.1 of the TRIPS Agreement.

Note that paragraph 6 of the Declaration on TRIPS and Public Health recognized that the least developed countries in the world have a special problem in the area of access to medicines. Although such countries were given the authority under the Doha Declaration to grant a compulsory license to their domestic companies for the purpose of making inexpensive copies, granting a compulsory license is not much use if the domestic companies lacked the technical ability or resources to manufacture these medicines. Paragraph 6 above recognizes this harsh reality and instructed the Council on TRIPS to address this problem resulting in the following:

Implementation of Paragraph 6 of the Doha Declaration on the TRIPS Agreement and Public Health

Decision of 30 August 2003

The General Council, . . .
Decides as follows:

1. For the purposes of this Decision:
(a) "pharmaceutical product" means any patented product, or product manufactured through a patented process, of the pharmaceutical sector needed to address the public health problems as recognized in paragraph 1 of the Declaration. It is understood that active ingredients necessary for its manufacture and diagnostic kits needed for its use would be included;
(b) "eligible importing Member" means any least-developed country Member, and any other Member that has made a notification to the Council for TRIPS of its intention to use the system as an importer, it being understood that a Member may notify at any time that it will use the system in whole or in a limited way, for example only in the case of a national emergency or other circumstances of

extreme urgency or in cases of public non-commercial use. It is noted that some Members will not use the system set out in this Decision as importing Members[13] and that some other Members have stated that, if they use the system, it would be in no more than situations of national emergency or other circumstances of extreme urgency;

(c) "exporting Member" means a Member using the system set out in this Decision to produce pharmaceutical products for, and export them to, an eligible importing Member.

2. The obligations of an exporting Member under Article 31(f) of the TRIPS Agreement shall be waived with respect to the grant by it of a compulsory licence to the extent necessary for the purposes of production of a pharmaceutical product(s) and its export to an eligible importing Member(s) in accordance with the terms set out below in this paragraph:

(a) the eligible importing Member(s) has made a notification to the Council for TRIPS, that:

(i) specifies the names and expected quantities of the product(s) needed;

(ii) confirms that the eligible importing Member in question, other than a least-developed country Member, has established that it has insufficient or no manufacturing capacities in the pharmaceutical sector for the product(s) in question in one of the ways set out in the Annex to this Decision; and

(iii) confirms that, where a pharmaceutical product is patented in its territory, it has granted or intends to grant a compulsory licence in accordance with Article 31 of the TRIPS Agreement and the provisions of this Decision;

(b) the compulsory licence issued by the exporting Member under this Decision shall contain the following conditions:

(i) only the amount necessary to meet the needs of the eligible importing Member(s) may be manufactured under the licence and the entirety of this production shall be exported to the Member(s) which has notified its needs to the Council for TRIPS;

(ii) products produced under the licence shall be clearly identified as being produced under the system set out in this Decision through specific labeling or marking. Suppliers should distinguish such products through special packaging and/or special colouring/shaping of the products themselves, provided that such distinction is feasible and does not have a significant impact on price; and

(iii) before shipment begins, the licensee shall post on a website the following information:

- the quantities being supplied to each destination as referred to in indent (i) above; and
- the distinguishing features of the product(s) referred to in indent (ii) above;

(c) the exporting Member shall notify the Council for TRIPS of the grant of the licence, including the conditions attached to it. The information provided shall include the name and address of the licensee, the product(s) for which the licence has been granted, the quantity(ies) for which it has been granted, the country(ies) to which the product(s) is (are) to be supplied and the duration of the licence. The notification shall also indicate the address of the website referred to in subparagraph (b)(iii) above. . . .

---

13. Australia, Austria, Belgium, Canada, Denmark, Finland, France, Germany, Greece, Iceland, Ireland, Italy, Japan, Luxembourg, the Netherlands, New Zealand, Norway, Portugal, Spain, Sweden, Switzerland, the United Kingdom and the United States.

5. Members shall ensure the availability of effective legal means to prevent the importation into, and sale in, their territories of products produced under the system set out in this Decision and diverted to their markets inconsistently with its provisions, using the means already required to be available under the TRIPS Agreement. If any Member considers that such measures are proving insufficient for this purpose, the matter may be reviewed in the Council for TRIPS at the request of that Member. . . .

11. This Decision, including the waivers granted in it, shall terminate for each Member on the date on which an amendment to the TRIPS Agreement replacing its provisions takes effect for that Member. The TRIPS Council shall initiate by the end of 2003 work on the preparation of such an amendment with a view to its adoption within six months. . . .

NOTES AND QUESTIONS

1. Drug companies argue that patent protection under TRIPS is necessary to allow them to obtain a fair return in the commercial exploitation of the drug. It now takes on average $802 million to develop a new drug (see p. 603 *supra*). A patent gives the drug company a monopoly for a limited period, that is, 20 years, in which to recoup its expenses and to earn a profit. After the patent period expires, generic versions are allowed to enter the market, which often drastically reduce the future sales of the drug.

2. The Doha Declaration on TRIPS and Public Health and the Implementation Decision, both set forth above, can be used by developing and least developed countries to obtain access to patented drugs owned by multinational drug companies at little or minimal cost. How do you think pharmaceutical companies will respond?

PROBLEM 7-7

For most of its history, Z, a populous developing country, has suffered from several infectious diseases caused by poor sanitation and diet. Although these diseases have a very low mortality rate, thousands of people die needlessly in the country each year as these diseases can be completely cured if antibiotics are used effectively. Others survive these diseases but are permanently affected. After Z joined the WTO, it issued a number of patent laws, but the health minister has recently issued a compulsory license to local manufacturers for a powerful antibiotic and has authorized the payment of a nominal fee to the patent owner, a Swiss pharmaceutical company. The local manufacturers not only produce enough for their own use but have also exported additional supplies to several neighboring countries and to the EU. Z has also begun importing inexpensive copies of the drug made by its neighbors in violation of the patent. The Swiss company claims that there is no national emergency and that the importation of the copies of its drug violates its patent obtained in Z.

    (1)   Are the actions of Z consistent with Article 31 of TRIPS pre-Doha?

    (2)   Are the actions of Z consistent with Article 31 in light of the Doha Declaration on TRIPS and Public Health and the Implementation Decision?

D. TRIPS and the Biopiracy Debate

Another issue that was debated during the Doha Conference in 2001 was a practice that some developing countries have called "biopiracy." While commercial piracy generally pits MNEs and developed countries against developing countries and their constituencies, the array of interests is reversed in biopiracy. Developing countries claim to be owners of traditional knowledge and biological resources and accuse MNEs and developed countries of theft. Biopiracy is also accused of subverting the legitimate purposes of the patent system, which is to protect individual knowledge so that it can be brought out into the public domain for public good. The patenting of indigenous knowledge achieves the opposite effect: It is a legal mechanism through which the commonly shared knowledge and traditions of a community is converted into private property and exploited for the financial gain of a few.

Consider the following illustrations.

Illustration 7-1. An MNE pharmaceutical company is looking for a new treatment for heart disease and sends researchers to a South American country rich in biological diversity and where some indigenous tribes have a long life span and a low incidence of heart disease despite a diet consisting mainly of meat. After interviewing tribe members and being allowed to observe their dietary habits for several months, the researchers discover that one of the few vegetables that tribal members consume is a locally grown plant that helps to create a highly potent form of HDL (high-density lipoprotein) cholesterol that keeps the heart healthy and arteries unclogged. The few weeks spent with the tribe have saved the researchers years in research time and the pharmaceutical company millions of dollars in research and development expenses. Moreover, without tapping into the habits and knowledge of the tribe, the company may never have discovered as effective a heart disease medicine. The researchers return home, isolate and purify the genetic materials that give rise to the super HDL, patent the invention, and produce a highly successful drug that earns hundreds of millions of dollars in its first few years on the market. The indigenous tribe never receives any compensation.

Illustration 7-2. An MNE agricultural and food processing company is looking for a new variety of rice that is disease resistant and with a low starch content. Researchers from the MNE travel to Asia and work with local universities to find a variety of rice grown for hundreds of years in only two Asian countries that has some of these characteristics. The researchers return home and cross-breed the Asian rice with a U.S. variety and produce a new and superior breed of rice. The MNE obtains a patent for the new product, which is a major success in the United States and overseas. The company never shares any profits with the local universities or with the Asian countries. Nationwide outrage erupts when the Asian countries discover that the MNE has patented "their" national product and there is a backlash against intellectual property rights in Western products.

One response to the concerns raised by these illustrations might be to urge the owners of traditional knowledge to protect themselves by acquiring patents of their own. However, the problem is that forms of traditional knowledge do not usually qualify for patent protection under TRIPS standards. For example, U.S. patent law requires three elements for a patent: Novelty, utility, and nonobviousness. A product that is found in nature such as the plant in Illustration 7-1 is not eligible for patent protection because it does not satisfy the novelty requirement.

Rather, in Illustration 7-1, the patentable invention is the isolated and purified genetic material, which is not found in nature, not the plant itself. Similarly, in Illustration 7-2, the patentable product is not the Asian rice but the cross-breed, a newly invented product not found in nature. What about the knowledge itself in Illustration 7-1? Here the knowledge has been publicly available for hundreds of years as part of the cultural heritage of the tribe and does not qualify as novel. Patent laws also require a single act of discovery and do not recognize common knowledge the origins of which are unknown. An applicant for a patent must also normally be an individual not a group. The dilemma is that traditional knowledge does not qualify for intellectual property protection under TRIPS standards. However, these standards, of course, were created by developed nations and did not take into consideration the possibility of rights in traditional knowledge and bioresources.

While TRIPS standards did not appear to accommodate forms of traditional knowledge, another international treaty, the 1992 Convention for Biological Diversity (CBD) negotiated at a United Nations conference in Rio de Janeiro, provides a legal basis for recognizing ownership rights in traditional knowledge. Article 8(j) of the CBD requires its contracting parties "to respect, preserve, and maintain knowledge, innovations and practices of indigenous and local communities embodying traditional lifestyles relevant for the conservation and sustainable use of biological diversity and promote their wider application with the approval and involvement of the holders of such knowledge, innovations and practices and encourage the equitable sharing of the benefits arising from the utilization of such knowledge, innovations, and practices." Until the Doha Conference, however, the CBD was overshadowed by TRIPS, which was far more influential and powerful. By the time of the Doha Conference, however, international controversy over the biopiracy issue sparked by several well-known international incidents had drawn the attention of the ministers. At the Doha Conference, a well-organized and effective lobbying effort by developing countries succeeded in gaining recognition of the problem of traditional knowledge by the conference. The Doha Conference stated as part of its ministerial declaration:

> We instruct the Council for TRIPS . . . to examine, *inter alia*, the relationship between the TRIPS Agreement and the Convention on Biological Diversity, the protection of traditional knowledge and folklore, and other relevant new developments raised by Members. . . . In undertaking this work, the TRIPS Council shall be guided by the objectives and principles set out in Articles 7 and 8[14] of the TRIPS Agreement and shall take fully into account the development dimension.

---

14. Articles 7 and 8 of TRIPS are set out below.

Article 7
Objectives

The protection and enforcement of intellectual property rights should contribute to the promotion of technological innovation and to the transfer and dissemination of technology, to the mutual advantage of producers and users of technological knowledge and in a manner conducive to social and economic welfare, and to a balance of rights and obligations.

The TRIPS Council is currently working with the World Intellectual Property Organization and the CBD in addressing these issues.

PROBLEM 7-8

Brazil is rich in rain forests and biological resources and has become a fertile ground for developing new drugs, organic consumer products, and herbal medicines. Brazil has grown increasingly concerned about "bioprospecting" by various aggressive multinational pharmaceutical companies that are actively exploring various local plant and animal species as sources of new medicines. Suppose that the legislature is considering a new national law recognizing *sui generis* intellectual property rights in traditional knowledge in its indigenous communities and also property rights in the nation's biological resources. Will this new law fully protect the interests of the country? What is required?

III. *Gray-Market Goods and Parallel Imports*

As we have seen, IP owners have serious concerns about pirated and infringing products. While IP owners consider commercial piracy to be a far more serious problem, they are also concerned about the unauthorized distribution of their genuine goods or "gray-market goods." In this section, we turn to the issue of protection against imports of gray-market goods and parallel imports.

A. What Are Gray-Market Goods and Parallel Imports?

We have already been introduced to the concept of gray-market goods in an international context in *Feldman v. Mexico* in Chapter 6 at p. 435. We turn now to a consideration of gray-market goods in the United States.

Consider the following illustration.

Illustration 7-3. A consumer goes to a large discount department store to buy a new consumer electronics product. The consumer sees the same product by a famous manufacturer on two different shelves with two prices. The packaging

---

Article 8
Principles

1. Members may, in formulating or amending their laws and regulations, adopt measures necessary to protect public health and nutrition, and to promote the public interest in sectors of vital importance to their socio-economic and technological development, provided that such measures are consistent with the provisions of this Agreement.

2. Appropriate measures, provided that they are consistent with the provisions of this Agreement, may be needed to prevent the abuse of intellectual property rights by right holders or the resort to practices which unreasonably restrain trade or adversely affect the international transfer of technology.

of one set of goods has English language labeling that appears to have been later pasted on top of a foreign language printed on the package itself. This product sells for about 30 percent less and carries a store warranty rather than a manufacturer's warranty. Aware of the global problem of commercial piracy and concerned that the less expensive product may be a counterfeit, the customer asks a sales manager for an explanation. The manager assures the consumer that the product is not a counterfeit or pirated product but a genuine product produced abroad by the manufacturer and originally intended for a foreign market. The department store was able to take advantage of currency fluctuations and a strong dollar to buy the products in the foreign market at a discount and import them into the United States to pass the savings on to the consumer. The consumer is satisfied and buys the less expensive item. The consumer has just bought a "gray-market good." When the U.S. manufacturer finds out about the sale, the manufacturer seeks to prevent any further imports of the gray-market electronics goods into the United States.

Gray-market goods and parallel imports are terms that are often used interchangeably and there is probably no harm in this usage, but a gray-market good is not necessarily a parallel import. A true parallel import situation arises as follows.

Illustration 7-4. Because of less expensive labor costs abroad, a U.S. trademark owner licenses the right to manufacture products under the U.S. registered trademark to a foreign company. The company manufactures the goods for import into the U.S. market to the U.S. trademark owner, which, in turn, will distribute the goods for sale in the United States. The foreign manufacturer is also authorized to sell the products to foreign markets. A foreign distributor buys a quantity of goods manufactured by the foreign licensee for sale in foreign markets at a discount and finds a large U.S. discount department store that is willing to buy the goods for import into the United States. These are "parallel" imports because they are a second channel of imports into the United States that is not authorized by the U.S. trademark owner.

Note that, unlike counterfeits and pirated goods, gray-market goods[15] are genuine products and the market for these goods is lawful. Gray-market goods are also allowed to enter the United States under some circumstances without or despite the wishes of the U.S. trademark owner.

Although some brand owners object to gray-market goods, note that these goods can often still represent a sale to the trademark owner. Illustrations 7-3 and 7-4 are such examples because in each case a foreign distributor has purchased the goods at the wholesale level overseas, taking advantage of currency fluctuations to buy the goods at a favorable exchange rate and to sell the goods on the U.S. market. These overseas transactions represent sales to the U.S. trademark owner.

---

15. In the materials that follow unless otherwise indicated, "gray market goods" also includes parallel imports.

QUESTIONS

1. Many consumers view gray-market goods to be a benefit as they offer consumers more choice and better prices. Why should the U.S. manufacturer be concerned if consumers are happy?

2. If a gray-market good imported into the United States usually represents a sale abroad to the U.S. manufacturer, why would the U.S. company ever object to gray-market goods? Hint: Assume that you are the U.S. sales and marketing director of the U.S. manufacturer.

3. If gray-market goods are genuine and lawful, why should Customs ever want to exclude them?

4. Given that gray-market goods provide some benefits but that trademark owners also have some legitimate concerns, should Customs enforce a total ban or a partial ban on the imports of gray-market goods? The following materials address this issue.

B. Gray-Market Goods Under U.S. Law

In Illustration 7-3, we explained the concept of a gray-market good but the illustration did not explain how a gray market arises or how the gray-market goods were obtained by the U.S. department store. The gray market may have been created through a number of different scenarios that we set forth below. How the gray market is created is important because U.S. law treats gray-market goods differently depending on which of the following situations has given rise to the gray market.

In general, a gray market in goods arises from one of three prototypical situations. In each of the cases set forth below, A is a U.S. company that seeks to ban the importation of the gray-market goods and B is a foreign company that manufactures the gray-market goods.

(1) *U.S. Owner of a Foreign Trademark.* A, a U.S. company, purchases the U.S. rights to a foreign trademark from B, a foreign company and trademark owner, and registers the mark as a U.S. trademark. For example, suppose that B has a famous brand of perfume that is protected by a foreign trademark. A purchases the U.S. trademark rights for the perfume from B, registers the mark as a U.S. trademark, and begins to manufacture and sell the perfume in the United States. After B sells the trademark rights to A, however, B begins to import the perfume into the United States, creating a gray-market for the goods that compete with A's products. This has been called the "classic" gray-market-goods case.

(2) *Affiliated Companies Under a Common Ownership.* A and B are related companies and have a parent-subsidiary relationship or are otherwise subject to a common ownership and control. There are two variants of this situation:

    (a) A is a U.S. subsidiary of B, the foreign parent company and the owner of the foreign trademark. B has incorporated A in the United States for the purpose of controlling and serving the U.S. market. B is the owner of the foreign trademark for the goods but A is the registered owner of the U.S. trademark for the goods. A manufactures and sells the goods on the U.S. market but the goods are also imported into the United States by B or by a third party who has purchased the goods overseas from B.

(b)   A is a U.S. parent company and has established B in a foreign country as a subsidiary, a foreign branch, or an unincorporated foreign department. The goods are manufactured abroad by B for import into the United States and also for sale abroad. A third-party distributor purchases the goods abroad from B and then imports them into the United States.

(3)   *Licensed Manufacturing Abroad.* A, a U.S. company and trademark owner, licenses the manufacture of its product in a foreign country to B, a foreign company. B then imports the goods into the United States or sells the products to a third-party distributor who imports the goods into the United States.

Prior to 1922, the United States did not regulate gray-market goods at all and, as a result, they were permitted free entry into the United States. At that time, U.S. trademark law only protected trademark owners from the importation of infringing or counterfeit goods, and as gray-market goods bore a genuine trademark, they were permitted to be imported into the United States despite the protests of trademark owners. In 1922, as the direct result of the storm of protest that arose in reaction to *A. Bourjois & Co. v. Katzel*, 275 F. 539 (2d Cir. 1921), *rev'd*, 260 U.S. 689 (1923), Congress enacted legislation that imposed a ban on the importation of gray-market goods. In *Katzel*, a U.S. citizen purchased the U.S. trademark rights from a French powder manufacturer. After the purchase was completed, the French manufacturer sold the powder to a U.S. druggist who began to import the product into the United States. The purchaser sued the druggist, seeking injunctive relief to protect the value of its trademark. You should recognize that the situation in *Katzel* involved the first of the three prototypical situations set forth above giving rise to a gray market.

The Second Circuit found that the trademark owner could exclude the goods only if they infringed upon his trademark. Finding that the importation of genuine goods was not trademark infringement, the court allowed the imports. The decision incensed U.S. trademark owners who viewed the actions of the French company as an underhanded attempt to undermine the U.S. purchaser's investment. They appealed directly to Congress to enact legislation that would overturn the Second Circuit decision. Before the U.S. Supreme Court could hear the appeal from the Second Circuit, Congress enacted §526, a last-minute legislative amendment to the Tariff Act of 1922. §526 provided that a U.S. trademark owner had to give its prior consent before the importation into the United States of "any merchandise of foreign manufacture if such merchandise . . . bears a trademark owned by a citizen of, or by a corporation . . . created" within the United States.

As §526 was enacted to overturn the result of the Second Circuit decision in *Katzel*, it is clear that §526 prohibited the importation of gray-market goods under the *Katzel* facts or in case (1) above. However, did Congress intend to create a total ban of all gray-market goods and not just those that arise as a result of case (1) or out of the *Katzel* facts? In other words, were gray-market goods that arose as a result of cases (2) and (3) above also included within the scope of the prohibition of §526?

As Congress acted swiftly and under pressure from trademark owners, §526 was hastily and poorly drafted and left these questions unanswered. Note that the language of §526 is sufficiently ambiguous that resort to the text of §526 alone cannot answer these questions. For example, take case (2)(a) above. In this case, A, the U.S. subsidiary of B, the foreign parent, is the owner of the registered U.S. trademark and is faced with gray-market importation. Whether or not A can prevent the importation under §526 depends on whether the trademark is "*owned by* a citizen" of the United States. In this case, A owns the U.S. trademark but as B, the foreign parent, owns A, it is possible to argue that B, not A, is actually the owner of the U.S. trademark. If B, the foreign parent, is deemed to be the owner of the U.S. trademark, then the gray-market goods do not bear a trademark owned by a citizen of the United States and thereby fall outside the prohibition of §526 and are permitted entry into the United States.

A similar ambiguity exists with respect to case (2)(b) above. In this case, A is the U.S. parent and B is a foreign subsidiary that manufactures the goods. §526 prohibits importation of merchandise of *foreign manufacture*. However, although B is located in a foreign country and the goods are manufactured abroad, B is a subsidiary owned by A, the U.S. parent company. As A is the owner of B, it is arguable that the goods manufactured by B are not goods of foreign manufacture and fall outside the prohibition of §526. As for case (3), licensing arrangements were not common when §526 was enacted and it was also unclear whether Congress intended to include case (3) within the scope of the prohibition set forth in §526.

As this discussion indicates, while it was clear that case (1) was included within the prohibition of §526, it was unclear from the text or legislative history of the statute whether cases (2) and (3) were included. In other words, it was unclear whether Congress intended to enact a total ban on the importation of gray-market goods (without the permission of the trademark owner) or only a partial ban. Left to enforce §526 and without clear answers to these questions, the U.S. Customs Service enacted a series of regulations that interpreted these ambiguities in §526 to result in a partial ban. As §526 on its face and at first glance appears to create a total ban and as Customs interpreted §526 to create a partial ban, Customs styled its regulations as creating "exceptions" to §526. At the time that the following principal case, *K-Mart Corp. v. Cartier*, was decided, Customs regulations interpreted §526 to ban case (1) only and contained exceptions that took cases (2) and (3) outside the prohibition of §526.

This was the situation that existed when *K-Mart Corp. v. Cartier*, the principal case below, came before the Supreme Court. *K-Mart* concerns the Supreme Court's review of whether the U.S. Customs regulations recognizing a partial ban were a reasonable interpretation of §526. The revised Customs regulation and the two other principal cases trace the development of the law relating to gray-market goods after *K-Mart*.

PROBLEM 7-9

A U.S. manufacturer licenses its foreign affiliate in Canada to produce a soft drink for the Canadian market. In addition to selling the product in the Canadian market, the Canadian affiliate also exports the soft drink into the United States. The U.S. manufacturer objects to the imports because the soft drink contains less carbonation than its U.S. soft drinks as Canadians are less fond of highly carbonated drinks than Americans. Can the U.S. company exclude the soft drink? Consider the issues in this problem in the following order: (1) The license, (2) the affiliation between the two companies, and (3) the differences in the products. See *K-Mart* and *Lever Bros.* below and the current 19 C.F.R. §133.23 following *Lever Bros.* in the accompanying notes.

K-Mart Corp. v. Cartier, Inc.
United States Supreme Court, 1988
486 U.S. 281, 108 S. Ct. 1811, 100 L. Ed. 2d 313

JUSTICE KENNEDY announced the judgment of the Court and delivered the opinion of the Court with respect to Parts I, II-A, and II-C, and an opinion with respect to Part II-B, in which WHITE, J., joined.

A gray-market good is a foreign-manufactured good, bearing a valid United States trademark, that is imported without the consent of the United States trademark holder. These cases present the issue whether the Secretary of the Treasury's regulation permitting the importation of certain gray-market goods, 19 CFR §133.21 (1987), is a reasonable agency interpretation of §526 of the Tariff Act of 1930 (1930 Tariff Act), 46 Stat. 741, as amended, 19 U.S.C. §1526.

I

A

The gray market arises in any of three general contexts. The prototypical gray-market victim (case 1) is a domestic firm that purchases from an independent foreign firm the rights to register and use the latter's trademark as a United States trademark and to sell its foreign-manufactured products here. Especially where the foreign firm has already registered the trademark in the United States or where the product has already earned a reputation for quality, the right to use that trademark can be very valuable. If the foreign manufacturer could import the trademarked goods and distribute them here, despite having sold the trademark to a domestic firm, the domestic firm would be forced into sharp intrabrand competition involving the very trademark it purchased. Similar intrabrand competition could arise if the foreign manufacturer markets its wares outside the United States, as is often the case, and a third party who purchases them abroad could legally import them. In either event, the parallel importation, if permitted to proceed, would create a gray market that could jeopardize the trademark holder's investment.

The second context (case 2) is a situation in which a domestic firm registers the United States trademark for goods that are manufactured abroad by an affiliated manufacturer. In its most common variation (case 2a), a foreign firm wishes to control distribution of its wares in this country by incorporating a subsidiary here. The subsidiary then registers under its own name (or the manufacturer assigns to the subsidiary's name) a United States trademark that is identical to its parent's foreign trademark. The parallel importation by a third party who buys the goods abroad (or conceivably even by the affiliated foreign manufacturer itself) creates a gray market. Two other variations on this theme occur when an American-based firm establishes abroad a manufacturing subsidiary corporation (case 2b) or its own unincorporated manufacturing division (case 2c) to produce its United States trademarked goods, and then imports them for domestic distribution. If the trademark holder or its foreign subsidiary sells the trademarked goods abroad, the parallel importation of the goods competes on the gray market with the holder's domestic sales.

In the third context (case 3), the domestic holder of a United States trademark *authorizes* an independent foreign manufacturer to use it. Usually the holder sells to the foreign manufacturer an exclusive right to use the trademark in a particular foreign location, but conditions the right on the foreign manufacturer's promise not to import its trademarked goods into the United States. Once again, if the foreign manufacturer or a third party imports into the United States, the foreign-manufactured goods will compete on the gray market with the holder's domestic goods.

B

Until 1922, the Federal Government did not regulate the importation of gray-market goods, not even to protect the investment of an independent purchaser of a foreign trademark, and not even in the extreme case where the independent foreign manufacturer breached its agreement to refrain from direct competition with the purchaser. That year, however, Congress was spurred to action by a Court of Appeals decision declining to enjoin the parallel importation of goods bearing a trademark that (as in case 1) a domestic company had purchased from an independent foreign manufacturer at a premium. See *A. Bourjois & Co.* v. *Katzel*, 275 F. 539 (CA2 1921), rev'd, 260 U.S. 689, 43 S. Ct. 244, 67 L. Ed. 464 (1923).

In an immediate response to *Katzel*, Congress enacted §526 of the Tariff Act of 1922, 42 Stat. 975. That provision, later reenacted in identical form as §526 of the 1930 Tariff Act, 19 U.S.C. §1526, prohibits importing

> "into the United States any merchandise of foreign manufacture if such merchandise . . . bears a trademark owned by a citizen of, or by a corporation or association created or organized within, the United States, and registered in the Patent and Trademark Office by a person domiciled in the United States . . . , unless written consent of the owner of such trademark is produced at the time of making entry." 19 U.S.C. §1526(a).

The regulations implementing §526 for the past 50 years have not applied the prohibition to all gray-market goods. The Customs Service regulation now in force provides generally that "foreign-made articles bearing a trademark identical with one owned and recorded by a citizen of the United States or a corporation or association created or organized within the United States are subject to seizure and forfeiture as prohibited importations." 19 CFR §133.21(b) (1987). But the regulation furnishes a "common-control" exception from the ban, permitting the entry of gray-market goods manufactured abroad by the trademark owner or its affiliate:

> "(c) *Restrictions not applicable.* The restrictions . . . do not apply to imported articles when:
>> "(1) Both the foreign and the U.S. trademark or trade name are owned by the same person or business entity; [or]

"(2) The foreign and domestic trademark or trade name owners are parent and subsidiary companies or are otherwise subject to common ownership or control. . . ."

The Customs Service regulation further provides an "authorized-use" exception, which permits importation of gray-market goods where

"(3) the articles of foreign manufacture bear a recorded trademark or trade name applied under authorization of the U.S. owner. . . ." 19 CFR §133.21(c) (1987).

Respondents, an association of United States trademark holders and two of its members, brought suit in Federal District Court in February 1984, seeking both a declaration that the Customs Service regulation, 19 CFR §§133.21(c)(1)-(3) (1987), is invalid and an injunction against its enforcement. *Coalition to Preserve the Integrity of American Trademarks* v. *United States*, 598 F. Supp. 844 (DC 1984). They asserted that the common-control and authorized-use exceptions are inconsistent with §526 of the 1930 Tariff Act. Petitioners K mart and 47th Street Photo intervened as defendants.

The District Court upheld the Customs Service regulation, but the Court of Appeals reversed [,] holding that the Customs Service regulation was an unreasonable administrative interpretation of §526. We granted certiorari, 479 U.S. 1005 (1986), to resolve a conflict among the Courts of Appeals. . . .

A majority of this Court now holds that the common-control exception of the Customs Service regulation, 19 CFR §§133.21(c)(1)-(2) (1987), is consistent with §526. See *post*, at 309-310 (opinion of BRENNAN, J.). A different majority, however, holds that the authorized-use exception, 19 CFR §133.21(c)(3) (1987), is inconsistent with §526. See *post*, at 328-329 (opinion of SCALIA, J.). We therefore affirm the Court of Appeals in part and reverse in part.

II

A

In determining whether a challenged regulation is valid, a reviewing court must first determine if the regulation is consistent with the language of the statute. "If the statute is clear and unambiguous 'that is the end of the matter, for the court, as well as the agency, must give effect to the unambiguously expressed intent of Congress.' . . . The traditional deference courts pay to agency interpretation is not to be applied to alter the clearly expressed intent of Congress." *Board of Governors, FRS v. Dimension Financial Corp.*, 474 U.S. 361, 368, 88 L. Ed. 2d 691, 106 S. Ct. 681 (1986).

Following this analysis, I conclude that subsections (c)(1) and (c)(2) of the Customs Service regulation, 19 CFR §§133.21 (c)(1) and (c)(2) (1987), are permissible constructions designed to resolve statutory ambiguities. All Members of the Court are in agreement that the agency may interpret the statute to bar importation of gray-market goods in what we have denoted case 1 and to permit the imports under case 2a. . . . As these writings state, "owned by" is sufficiently ambiguous, in the context of the statute, that it applies to situations involving a foreign parent, which is case 2a. This ambiguity arises from the inability to discern, from the statutory language, which of the two entities involved in case 2a can be said to "own" the United States trademark if, as in some instances, the domestic subsidiary is wholly owned by its foreign parent.

A further statutory ambiguity contained in the phrase "merchandise of foreign manufacture," suffices to sustain the regulations as they apply to cases 2b and 2c. This ambiguity parallels that of "owned by," which sustained case 2a, because it is possible to interpret "merchandise of foreign manufacture" to mean (1) goods manufactured in a foreign country, (2) goods manufactured by a foreign company, or (3) goods manufactured in a foreign country by a foreign company. Given the imprecision in the statute, the agency is entitled to choose any reasonable definition and to interpret the statute to say that goods manufactured by a foreign subsidiary or division of a domestic company are not goods "of foreign manufacture."

Subsection (c)(3), 19 CFR §133.21(c)(3) (1987), of the regulation, however, cannot stand. The ambiguous statutory phrases that we have already discussed, "owned by" and "merchandise of foreign manufacture," are irrelevant to the proscription contained in subsection (3) of the regulation. This subsection of the regulation denies a domestic trademark holder the power to prohibit the importation of goods made by an independent foreign manufacturer where the domestic trademark holder has authorized the foreign manufacturer to use the trademark. Under no reasonable construction of the statutory language can goods made in a foreign country by an independent foreign manufacturer be removed from the purview of the statute.

We hold that the Customs Service regulation is consistent with §526 insofar as it exempts from the importation ban goods that are manufactured abroad by the "same person" who holds the United States trademark, 19 CFR §133.21(c)(1) (1987), or by a person who is "subject to common . . . control" with the United States trademark holder, §133.21(c)(2). Because the authorized-use exception of the regulation, §133.21(c)(3), is in conflict with the plain language of the statute, that provision cannot stand.

It is so ordered.

Lever Brothers Co. v. United States
United States Court of Appeals, D.C. Circuit, 1993
981 F.2d 1330

SENTELLE, Circuit Judge.

Lever Brothers Company ("Lever US" or "Lever"), an American company, and its British affiliate, Lever Brothers Limited ("Lever UK"), both manufacture deodorant soap under the "Shield" trademark and hand dishwashing liquid under the "Sunlight" trademark. The trademarks are registered in each country. The products have evidently been formulated differently to suit local tastes and circumstances. The U.S. version lathers more, the soaps smell different, the colorants used in American "Shield" have been certified by the FDA whereas the colorants in British "Shield" have not, and the U.S. version contains a bacteriostat that enhances the deodorant properties of the soap. The British version of "Sunlight" dishwashing soap produces less suds, and the American version is formulated to work best in the "soft water" available in most American cities, whereas the British version is designed for "hard water" common in Britain.

The packaging of the U.S. and U.K. products is also somewhat different. The British "Shield" logo is written in script form and is packaged in foil wrapping and contains a wave motif, whereas the American "Shield" logo is written in block form, does not come in foil wrapping and contains a grid pattern. There is small print on the packages indicating where they were manufactured. The British "Sunlight" comes in a cylindrical bottle labeled "Sunlight Washing Up Liquid." The American "Sunlight" comes in a yellow, hourglass-shaped bottle labeled "Sunlight Dishwashing Liquid."

Lever asserts that the unauthorized influx of these foreign products has created substantial consumer confusion and deception in the United States about the nature and origin of this merchandise, and that it has received numerous consumer complaints from American consumers who unknowingly bought the British products and were disappointed.

Lever argues that the importation of the British products was in violation of section 42 of the Lanham Act, 15 U.S.C. §1124 which provides that with the exception of goods imported for personal use:

> No article of imported merchandise which shall copy or simulate the name of the [sic] any domestic manufacture, or manufacturer . . . or which shall copy or simulate a trademark registered in accordance with the provisions of this chapter . . . shall be admitted to entry at any customhouse of the United States.

Id. The United States Customs Service ("Customs"), however, was allowing importation of the British goods under the "affiliate exception" created by 19 C.F.R. §133.21(c)(2), which provides that foreign goods bearing United States trademarks are not forbidden when "the foreign and domestic trademark or trade name owners are parent and subsidiary companies or are otherwise subject to common ownership or control."[16]

In *Lever I*, we concluded that "the natural, virtually inevitable reading of section 42 is that it bars foreign goods bearing a trademark identical to the valid U.S. trademark but physically different," without regard to affiliation between the producing firms or the genuine character of the trademark abroad. 278 U.S. App. D.C. 166, 877 F.2d 101, 111 (D.C. Cir. 1989).

After reviewing the submissions of the parties, the District Court found that Customs' administrative practice was "at best inconsistent" and, in any event, had "never addressed the specific question of physically different goods that bear identical trademarks." *Lever Bros. Co. v. United States,* 796 F. Supp. 1, 5 (D.D.C. 1992). The District Court concluded that "section 42 . . . prohibits the importation of foreign goods that . . . are physically different, regardless of the validity of the foreign trademark or the existence of an affiliation between the U.S. and foreign markholders." *Id.* The court accordingly concluded that "neither the legislative history of the statute nor the administrative practice of the Customs Service clearly contradicts the plain meaning of section 42" and granted summary judgment against the government. *Id.* at 13.

Customs' main argument from the legislative history is that section 42 of the Lanham Act applies only to imports of goods bearing trademarks that "copy or simulate" a registered mark. Customs thus draws a distinction between "genuine" marks and marks that "copy or simulate." A mark applied by a foreign firm subject to ownership and control common to that of the domestic trademark owner is by definition "genuine," Customs urges, regardless of whether or not the goods are

---

16. This case does not involve a dispute between corporate affiliates. Neither Lever US nor Lever UK has authorized the importation, which is being conducted by third parties. *See Lever I,* 877 F.2d at 103.

identical. Thus, any importation of goods manufactured by an affiliate of a U.S. trademark owner cannot "copy or simulate" a registered mark because those goods are *ipso facto* "genuine."

This argument is fatally flawed. It rests on the false premise that foreign trademarks applied to foreign goods are "genuine" in the United States. Trademarks applied to physically different foreign goods are not genuine from the viewpoint of the American consumer. As we stated in *Lever I:*

> On its face . . . section [42] appears to aim at deceit and consumer confusion; when identical trademarks have acquired different meanings in different countries, one who imports the foreign version to sell it under that trademark will (in the absence of some specially differentiating feature) cause the confusion Congress sought to avoid. The fact of affiliation between the producers in no way reduces the probability of that confusion; it is certainly not a constructive consent to importation.

877 F.2d at 111.

There is a larger, more fundamental and ultimately fatal weakness in Customs' position in this case. Section 42 on its face appears to forbid importation of goods that "copy or simulate" a United States trademark. Customs has the burden of adducing evidence from the legislative history of section 42 and its administrative practice of an exception for materially different goods whose similar foreign and domestic trademarks are owned by affiliated companies. At a minimum, this requires that the specific question be addressed in the legislative history and administrative practice. The bottom line, however, is that the issue of materially different goods was not addressed either in the legislative history or the administrative record. It is not enough to posit that silence implies authorization, when the authorization sought runs counter to the evident meaning of the governing statute. Therefore, we conclude that section 42 of the Lanham Act precludes the application of Customs' affiliate exception with respect to physically, materially different goods.

For the foregoing reasons, we affirm the District Court's ruling that section 42 of the Lanham Act, 15 U.S.C. §1124, bars the importation of physically different foreign goods bearing a trademark identical to a valid U.S. trademark, regardless of the trademark's genuine character abroad or affiliation between the producing firms.

So ordered.

NOTES AND QUESTIONS

1. Review the discussion of cases (1)-(3) on pp. 642-643. After *K-Mart*, which of these cases are within the ban of §526 and which are outside the ban of §526?

2. In *Lever Bros.*, plaintiff Lever US invoked §42 of the Lanham Act to exclude the gray-market goods and decided not to invoke §526 of the Tariff Act of 1930. Why?

3. After the decisions in *K-Mart* and *Lever Bros.*, the Customs Service amended its regulations. The current regulation, 19 C.F.R. §133.23, provides:

> (a) *Restricted gray market articles defined.* "Restricted gray market articles" are foreign made articles bearing a genuine trademark or trade name identical with or substantially indistinguishable from one owned and recorded by a citizen of the United States or a corporation or association created or organized within the United States

and imported without the authorization of the U.S. owner. "Restricted gray market goods" include goods bearing a genuine trademark or trade name which is:

(1) *Independent licensee*. Applied by a licensee (including a manufacturer) independent of the U.S. owner, or

(2) *Foreign owner*. Applied under the authority of a foreign trademark or trade name owner other than the U.S. owner, a parent or subsidiary of the U.S. owner, or a party otherwise subject to common ownership or control with the U.S. owner . . . from whom the U.S. owner acquired the domestic title, or to whom the U.S. owner sold the foreign titles(s); or

(3) *"Lever Rule."* Applied by the U.S. owner, a parent or subsidiary of the U.S. owner or a party otherwise subject to common ownership or control with the U.S. owner . . . to goods that the Customs Service has determined to be physically and materially different from the articles authorized by the U.S. trademark owner for importation or sale in the U.S.

(b) *Labeling of physically and materially different goods*. Goods determined by the Customs Service to be physically and materially different [and] bearing a genuine mark applied under the authority of the U.S. owner, a parent or subsidiary of the U.S. owner, or a party otherwise subject to common ownership or control with the U.S. owner . . . shall not be detained . . . where the merchandise or its packaging bears a conspicuous and legible label designed to remain on the product until the first point of sale to a retail consumer in the United States stating that: "This product is not a product authorized by the United States trademark owner for importation and is physically and materially different from the authorized product."

(c) *Denial of Entry*. All restricted gray market goods imported into the United States shall be denied entry and subject to detention. . . .

PROBLEM 7-10

Microtel licenses its wholly owned subsidiary in England to manufacture its latest office software under the "Microtel" trademark. In a separate agreement, Microtel also licenses its copyright in the software to the subsidiary. The British subsidiary has been exporting large quantities of the software to the United States. Microtel's British subsidiary has also sold the software to a French distributor, which has also been exporting to the United States.

(1) Can Microtel use trademark rights to exclude the software? Consider §526 of the Tariff Act of 1930 quoted and discussed in *K-Mart* above, 19 C.F.R. §133.23 above, and §42 of the Lanham Act, 15 U.S.C. §1124 quoted and discussed in *Lever Bros.* above.

(2) Can Microtel exclude the software under copyright law? Consider the Copyright Act of 1976 as interpreted and applied by *Quality King* below.

Quality King Distributors, Inc. v. L'anza
Research International, Inc.
United States Supreme Court, 1998
523 U.S. 135, 118 S. Ct. 1125, 140 L. Ed. 2d 254

Justice Stevens delivered the opinion of the Court.

Section 106(3) of the Copyright Act of 1976 (Act), 17 U.S.C. §106(3), gives the owner of a copyright the exclusive right to distribute copies of a copyrighted work.

That exclusive right is expressly limited, however, by the provisions of §§107 through 120. Section 602(a) gives the copyright owner the right to prohibit the unauthorized importation of copies. The question presented by this case is whether the right granted by §602(a) is also limited by §§107 through 120. More narrowly, the question is whether the "first sale" doctrine endorsed in §109(a) is applicable to imported copies.

I

Respondent, L'anza Research International, Inc. (L'anza), is a California corporation engaged in the business of manufacturing and selling shampoos, conditioners, and other hair care products. L'anza has copyrighted the labels that are affixed to those products. In the United States, L'anza sells exclusively to domestic distributors who have agreed to resell within limited geographic areas and then only to authorized retailers such as barber shops, beauty salons, and professional hair care colleges. L'anza has found that the American "public is generally unwilling to pay the price charged for high quality products, such as L'anza's products, when they are sold along with the less expensive lower quality products that are generally carried by supermarkets and drug stores." L'anza promotes the domestic sales of its products with extensive advertising in various trade magazines and at point of sale, and by providing special training to authorized retailers.

L'anza also sells its products in foreign markets. In those markets, however, it does not engage in comparable advertising or promotion; its prices to foreign distributors are 35% to 40% lower than the prices charged to domestic distributors. In 1992 and 1993, L'anza's distributor in the United Kingdom arranged the sale of three shipments to a distributor in Malta; each shipment contained several tons of L'anza products with copyrighted labels affixed. The record does not establish whether the initial purchaser was the distributor in the United Kingdom or the distributor in Malta, or whether title passed when the goods were delivered to the carrier or when they arrived at their destination, but it is undisputed that the goods were manufactured by L'anza and first sold by L'anza to a foreign purchaser.

It is also undisputed that the goods found their way back to the United States without the permission of L'anza and were sold in California by unauthorized retailers who had purchased them at discounted prices from Quality King Distributors, Inc. (petitioner). There is some uncertainty about the identity of the actual importer, but for the purpose of our decision we assume that petitioner bought all three shipments from the Malta distributor, imported them, and then resold them to retailers who were not in L'anza's authorized chain of distribution.

After determining the source of the unauthorized sales, L'anza brought suit against petitioner and several other defendants. The complaint alleged that the importation and subsequent distribution of those products bearing copyrighted labels violated L'anza's "exclusive rights under 17 U.S.C. §§106, 501 and 602 to reproduce and distribute the copyrighted material in the United States." App. 32. The District Court rejected petitioner's defense based on the "first sale" doctrine recognized by §109 and entered summary judgment in favor of L'anza. Based largely on its conclusion that §602 would be "meaningless" if §109 provided a defense in a case of this kind, the Court of Appeals affirmed.

II

This is an unusual copyright case because L'anza does not claim that anyone has made unauthorized copies of its copyrighted labels. Instead, L'anza is primarily interested in protecting the integrity of its method of marketing the products to which the labels are affixed. Although the labels themselves have only a limited creative component, our interpretation of the relevant statutory provisions would apply equally to a case involving more familiar copyrighted materials such as sound recordings or books. Indeed, we first endorsed the first sale doctrine in a case involving a claim by a publisher that the resale of its books at discounted prices infringed its copyright on the books. *Bobbs-Merrill Co. v. Straus*, 210 U.S. 339, 52 L. Ed. 1086, 28 S. Ct. 722 (1908).

In that case, the publisher, Bobbs-Merrill, had inserted a notice in its books that any retail sale at a price under $1.00 would constitute an infringement of its copyright. The defendants, who owned Macy's department store, disregarded the notice and sold the books at a lower price without Bobbs-Merrill's consent. We held that the exclusive statutory right to "vend"[17] applied only to the first sale of the copyrighted work:

> "What does the statute mean in granting 'the sole right of vending the same'? Was it intended to create a right which would permit the holder of the copyright to fasten, by notice in a book or upon one of the articles mentioned within the statute, a restriction upon the subsequent alienation of the subject-matter of copyright after the owner had parted with the title to one who had acquired full dominion over it and had given a satisfactory price for it? It is not denied that one who has sold a copyrighted article, without restriction, has parted with all right to control the sale of it. The purchaser of a book, once sold by authority of the owner of the copyright, may sell it again, although he could not publish a new edition of it.
>
> "In this case the stipulated facts show that the books sold by the appellant were sold at wholesale, and purchased by those who made no agreement as to the control of future sales of the book, and took upon themselves no obligation to enforce the notice printed in the book, undertaking to restrict retail sales to a price of one dollar per copy." 210 U.S. 339 at 349-350, 28 S. Ct. 722, 52 L. Ed. 1086.

The statute in force when *Bobbs-Merrill* was decided provided that the copyright owner had the exclusive right to "vend" the copyrighted work. Congress subsequently codified our holding in *Bobbs-Merrill* that the exclusive right to "vend" was limited to first sales of the work. Under the 1976 Act, the comparable exclusive right granted in 17 U.S.C. §106(3) is the right "to distribute copies . . . by sale or other transfer of ownership." The comparable limitation on that right is provided not by judicial interpretation, but by an express statutory provision. Section 109(a) provides

> "Notwithstanding the provisions of section 106(3), the owner of a particular copy or phonorecord lawfully made under this title, or any person authorized by such owner,

---

17. In 1908, when *Bobbs-Merrill* was decided, the copyright statute provided that copyright owners had "the sole liberty of printing, reprinting, publishing, completing, copying, executing, finishing, and *vending*" their copyrighted works. Copyright Act of 1891, §4952, 26 Stat. 1107 (emphasis added).

is entitled, without the authority of the copyright owner, to sell or otherwise dispose of
the possession of that copy or phonorecord. . . ."

The *Bobbs-Merrill* opinion emphasized the critical distinction between statutory rights and contract rights. In this case, L'anza relies on the terms of its
contracts with its domestic distributors to limit their sales to authorized retail
outlets. Because the basic holding in *Bobbs-Merrill* is now codified in §109(a) of
the Act, and because those domestic distributors are owners of the products that
they purchased from L'anza (the labels of which were "lawfully made under this
title"), L'anza does not, and could not, claim that the statute would enable L'anza
to treat unauthorized resales by its domestic distributors as an infringement of its
exclusive right to distribute copies of its labels. L'anza does claim, however, that
contractual provisions are inadequate to protect it from the actions of foreign
distributors who may resell L'anza's products to American vendors unable to
buy from L'anza's domestic distributors, and that §602(a) of the Act, properly
construed, prohibits such unauthorized competition. To evaluate that submission,
we must, of course, consider the text of §602(a).

III

The most relevant portion of §602(a) provides:

"Importation into the United States, without the authority of the owner of copyright
under this title, of copies or phonorecords of a work that have been acquired outside
the United States is an infringement of the exclusive right to distribute copies or
phonorecords under section 106, actionable under section 501. . . ."[18]

It is significant that this provision does not categorically prohibit the unauthorized importation of copyrighted materials. Instead, it provides that such importation is an infringement of the exclusive right to distribute copies "under section
106." Like the exclusive right to "vend" that was construed in *Bobbs-Merrill*, the
exclusive right to distribute is a limited right. The introductory language in §106
expressly states that all of the exclusive rights granted by that section — including,

---

18. The remainder of §602(a) reads as follows:

"This subsection does not apply to —
   "(1) importation of copies or phonorecords under the authority or for the use of
the Government of the United States or of any State or political subdivision of a State,
but not including copies or phonorecords for use in schools, or copies of any audiovisual work imported for purposes other than archival use;
   "(2) importation, for the private use of the importer and not for distribution, by any
person with respect to no more than one copy or phonorecord of any one work at any
one time, or by any person arriving from outside the United States with respect to
copies or phonorecords forming part of such person's personal baggage; or
   "(3) importation by or for an organization operated for scholarly, educational, or
religious purposes and not for private gain, with respect to no more than one copy of
an audiovisual work solely for its archival purposes, and no more than five copies or
phonorecords of any other work for its library lending or archival purposes, unless the
importation of such copies or phonorecords is part of an activity consisting of systematic reproduction or distribution, engaged in by such organization in violation of
the provisions of section 108(g)(2)."

of course, the distribution right granted by subsection (3)—are limited by the provisions of §§107 through 120. One of those limitations, as we have noted, is provided by the terms of §109(a), which expressly permit the owner of a lawfully made copy to sell that copy "notwithstanding the provisions of section 106(3)."

After the first sale of a copyrighted item "lawfully made under this title," any subsequent purchaser, whether from a domestic or from a foreign reseller, is obviously an "owner" of that item. Read literally, §109(a) unambiguously states that such an owner "is entitled, without the authority of the copyright owner, to sell" that item. Moreover, since §602(a) merely provides that unauthorized importation is an infringement of an exclusive right "under section 106," and since that limited right does not encompass resales by lawful owners, the literal text of §602(a) is simply inapplicable to both domestic and foreign owners of L'anza's products who decide to import them and resell them in the United States.

V

The parties and their *amici* have debated at length the wisdom or unwisdom of governmental restraints on what is sometimes described as either the "gray market" or the practice of "parallel importation." In *K mart Corp. v. Cartier, Inc.*, 486 U.S. 281, 100 L. Ed. 2d 313, 108 S. Ct. 1811 (1988), we used those terms to refer to the importation of foreign-manufactured goods bearing a valid United States trademark without the consent of the trademark holder. *Id.*, at 285-286. We are not at all sure that those terms appropriately describe the consequences of an American manufacturer's decision to limit its promotional efforts to the domestic market and to sell its products abroad at discounted prices that are so low that its foreign distributors can compete in the domestic market. But even if they do, whether or not we think it would be wise policy to provide statutory protection for such price discrimination is not a matter that is relevant to our duty to interpret the text of the Copyright Act.

The judgment of the Court of Appeals is reversed.

NOTES AND QUESTIONS

1. L'anza used a copyright theory to attempt to exclude its shampoo. Why didn't L'anza attempt to use a trademark theory and exclude the items as a restricted gray-market good? Review §526 of the Tariff Act of 1930 and 19 C.F.R. §133.23. What didn't L'anza attempt to exclude the goods under Section 42 of the Lanham Act, 15 U.S.C. §1124?

2. What can L'anza do to protect its interests in light of *Quality King*?

8   *Dispute Resolution*

I.   *Introduction*

A party entering into an international business relationship may not wish to think about the possibility that something might go awry, and an amicable business venture might turn into a dispute. But it is inevitable that disputes arise in international business transactions, and it is best to be prepared. The time for dealing with the possibility of a dispute is usually at the outset of the relationship, not after the dispute erupts. Provisions for dealing with a dispute should be a feature of any international contract but not every one will have the foresight to plan ahead. Despite the many advantages of agreeing upon a dispute resolution procedure during business negotiations, many international disputes continue to arise without any prior planning.

When lawyers think about dispute resolution, they usually assume litigation will occur. In international business, this is usually not the case. Alternative methods of dispute settlement — arbitration, mediation, and conciliation — are more frequently employed rather than the courts. But these alternative methods must be chosen by agreement of the parties; otherwise, litigation may be the only option.

International dispute resolution is a vast topic, and entire casebooks are devoted to it. Our focus below, of course, is not on the entire field of international dispute resolution but the more specialized topic of the resolution of international business disputes. All of the cases that we have chosen in this chapter involve disputes in an international business context.

As the topic is a complex one, we begin this chapter by providing an overview of the issues involved in an international business dispute and how these issues might differ from its domestic counterpart. We introduce some of the main issues in the overview below, and we will return to them in detail during the course of the chapter. Of course, the variations on the issues in an international business dispute are potentially infinite. But there are some main issues and recurring themes, and the emphasis in this chapter is on advance planning to prevent problems from arising.

Overview of International Business Dispute Resolution Issues

In the discussion below, we will assume that there is a business dispute between a U.S. corporation and a foreign business entity. We will also assume that you represent the U.S. corporation either as a plaintiff or as a defendant. The business dispute can involve any of the forms of IBTs that we have considered in Chapters 2-6: Contracts, agency/distributorships, technology transfer, and foreign direct investment.

In this overview and in this chapter, we will focus on the use by the U.S. corporation of the U.S. legal system in international business disputes. We do not attempt to examine in any detail how disputes will be resolved in a foreign legal system as each system is different and unique.

Preliminary Issues

Let us begin by supposing that a business dispute has arisen and that the parties have not planned ahead by agreeing upon a dispute resolution procedure by contract. The parties are unable to settle the dispute informally and amicably. Although the U.S. corporation fully realizes that the bringing of a lawsuit will likely terminate the business relationship with the foreign entity, it is now reluctantly considering that possibility.

Choice of Forum

A threshold question is: in which forum should the lawsuit be brought? One aspect of an international business dispute is that there may be any number of forums in which an action can be brought. An IBT can involve many different countries and each is a potential forum in which a lawsuit can be brought. However, although there may be many options, in many cases where the U.S. corporation is acting as a plaintiff the preference is to bring the action in a federal or state court in the United States. The reasons are clear: Familiarity with the legal system and applicable law, a world-class legal system with sophisticated judges, the ability to conduct all proceedings in English, convenience, and costs. At the same time, compelling a foreign defendant to appear in a U.S. court could create a strong strategic advantage. The lawsuit may be inconvenient and expensive for the foreign defendant, creating additional pressures on the defendant that may add to the plaintiff's bargaining power. By contrast, where the litigation occurs in a foreign country, the interests are reversed. It is now the U.S. corporation that may have to suffer all of the disadvantages that come with proceeding in a distant location, under a different legal system, and in a foreign language.

In some cases, securing a forum in the home nation is such an advantage that there may be a race to the courthouse by the parties. Even where the plaintiff has already filed a lawsuit in a foreign court, the defendant may, instead of appearing in the foreign court, file an action in its home nation against the plaintiff. A race can sometimes lead to situations in which there are multiple proceedings going forward simultaneously in courts of different countries. When such situations occur, one issue that U.S. courts must decide is whether to defer to foreign courts by dismissing or staying the U.S. action. These issues involve the doctrines of international comity and _forum non conveniens_. Other issues involve whether a U.S. or foreign court might wish to enter an "anti-suit" injunction, that is, an order prohibiting a party from suing in a foreign jurisdiction. As you can imagine, this can lead to tensions between international legal systems and can even lead to political conflict. We will cover all of these issues in this chapter.

Where the U.S. corporation is a defendant in a lawsuit, the interests may be quite different. In this case, the corporation might prefer for the litigation to proceed in a foreign jurisdiction, especially if the foreign forum is in a developing country with a weak legal system. Relegating the lawsuit to a country with a weak legal system may result in damage awards that may be lower than those in the United States and it may be difficult for the foreign plaintiff to enforce the judgment due to weaknesses in the legal system. In a number of cases, a U.S.

corporation that is sued in the United States will attempt to have the case dismissed in order to compel the foreign plaintiff to sue in a foreign court. We will return to a number of cases in Chapter 9 on corporate social responsibility where a U.S. corporation is a defendant in an action for wrongful conduct brought by a foreign plaintiff. While a U.S. corporation may prefer a U.S. forum in many cases where it is the plaintiff and may prefer a foreign court in some cases where it is the defendant, in both cases the U.S. corporation usually has a clear preference for a forum in which the dispute should be resolved. Rarely will the U.S. corporation be indifferent between forums. The choice of forum, one of the first issues that need to be decided by the parties, is also usually a key consideration in international business dispute resolution.

Choice of Law

Let us assume that our hypothetical U.S. company is a plaintiff in a business dispute and has chosen its forum by filing an action in federal district court against the defendant. A second threshold issue that will arise concerns what law governs the transaction. Again assuming that the parties have not agreed to a choice of law by contract, the U.S. court will need to engage in a choice of law analysis in order to determine the applicable law. In an international business dispute, there are often at least three possible sources of law, the domestic laws of either the plaintiff's nation (here the United States), the law of the defendant's home nation, and an international law usually embodied in a treaty. If the transaction is one that has connections with many different countries, the choice of law analysis may be even more complex as the domestic laws of each nation with which the IBT has a connection are potentially applicable to different aspects of the litigation. Note that the choice of law issue becomes much more complex in an international as opposed to a domestic U.S. setting where the choice usually involves the laws of different states, which do not differ in fundamental ways. In an international context, however, the choice of law among the competing alternatives may involve differences that are far greater than those in a domestic U.S. context.

The choice of law determination, which we introduced as private international law in Chapter 1, will need to be done by the court using a statute or treaty if one is applicable or by judicially created doctrines of choice of law. As you can imagine, this analysis can be complex and burdensome.

Jurisdiction

As we noted, most parties in an international business dispute will have a clear preference for the forum in which the dispute is to be resolved as the decision will often create strong advantages for one party while simultaneously creating disadvantages for the other. We have already noted that a U.S. corporation that is a plaintiff will often prefer to file a lawsuit in a business dispute in the United States. However, whether the plaintiff will be able to effectively choose a forum depends on whether the tribunal can assert jurisdiction over the defendant. Of course, there are many different types of jurisdictions but in an international business dispute involving foreign defendants, the most important issue is often whether the court can assert territorial jurisdiction over the defendant. Whether a U.S. court can assert jurisdiction over a foreign defendant depends on whether the defendant has the minimum contacts with the United States in accordance with a long line of classic U.S. cases, including *International Shoe Co. v. State of Washington*, 326 U.S. 310 (1945) and its progeny. We will examine how this jurisdictional analysis is made in an international business context.

In the era of the multinational enterprise with entities and affiliations around the globe, a related jurisdictional issue that also often arises is whether the activities of one corporate entity, such as a subsidiary, which meet the tests for territorial jurisdiction can serve as the basis of jurisdiction over a related entity, such as a holding company or the parent corporation. Special judicial doctrines have been created to determine when the assertion of jurisdiction over affiliated entities is appropriate.

Sovereign Immunity and the Act of State Doctrine

So far, we have examined issues that may be familiar to you from a course on civil procedure or civil litigation. Most of these issues, choice of forum, choice of law, and jurisdiction, are similar to issues that arise in domestic litigation and dispute settlement although the issues might be more complex in an international setting. In the area of territorial jurisdiction, for example, the same basic concepts developed in a domestic context can be applied without much modification to an international setting. In an international business dispute, however, there is another set of jurisdictional issues that a U.S. corporation will encounter that it will rarely find in a domestic setting: Sovereign immunity and related issues.

Unlike the issue of territorial jurisdiction, which concerns the power of the court over the defendant, sovereign immunity is related to the court's subject matter jurisdiction. Even where a court has territorial jurisdiction over a foreign sovereign defendant, the court may be deprived of subject matter jurisdiction to hear the dispute.

As multinational enterprises dominate international business today, it is not unusual for a transaction to involve foreign sovereign parties, either foreign government entities that are acting in a commercial capacity or state-owned companies that involve a mix of both public and private interests. One reason is that MNEs now routinely engage in transactions involving tens or even hundreds of millions of dollars or more. MNEs are also intimately involved in providing products and services that are of vital importance for the economic development of whole nations. Government entities, especially in developing countries, often need to be involved directly or indirectly when the sums and stakes are this large. For example, think of cases in which an MNE is engaged to mine the production of gas and oil, to install an entire telecommunications system, or to build a port or a terminal. All of these projects not only involve significant sums but also implicate significant public interests of a nation. As a result, a U.S. corporation may find itself dealing directly with a government or state-owned entity in the business transaction. In other cases, even when only foreign private parties are ostensibly involved, foreign governments may be lurking not too far behind.

In such cases, there are special concerns, including the potential immunity of such entities from jurisdiction in U.S. courts under the Foreign Sovereign Immunities Act (FSIA), 28 U.S.C. §§1602-1611 (1976). A threshold issue in such cases is whether a particular entity is qualified for immunity under the

FSIA. If the entity is so qualified, then it is immune from the jurisdiction of U.S. courts unless one of the exceptions to the FSIA applies to the case.

In addition to FSIA issues, disputes involving foreign sovereigns might implicate broader political issues not usually found when purely private parties are involved. For example, suppose that our hypothetical U.S. corporation has entered into a transaction with a foreign sovereign government and a business dispute erupts. Suppose further that the U.S. corporation sues the foreign government in a U.S. court and the court decides to exercise jurisdiction under some exception to sovereign immunity. Such a lawsuit by a private party against a foreign government might have an adverse impact on the foreign relations of the United States. Even though U.S. courts might have jurisdiction over the foreign sovereign, the courts might decline to exercise such jurisdiction on policy grounds as they do not wish to interfere with the foreign relations of the United States, a subject matter that is within the exclusive competence of the executive branch. Such cases also implicate issues of institutional competence and doctrines of judicial deference to the executive branch. To deal with these issues, the U.S. Supreme Court in *Banco Nacional de Cuba v. Sabbatino*, 376 U.S. 398 (1964), set forth the modern act of state doctrine, which precludes U.S. courts from examining the acts of foreign sovereigns within their own territories. As the result of the application of the act of state doctrine is that a court will decline to adjudicate an issue implicating the foreign relations of the United States, the doctrine is often asserted as a defense in a lawsuit by the defendant.

Resolving Preliminary Issues by Agreement

The discussion of the types of issues involved in an international business dispute has proceeded so far based on the assumption that the parties have not agreed on a resolution of any of these issues by contract. When this is the case, the only option to resolving these issues may be by way of litigation. For example, when the parties have not agreed to a choice of forum or choice of law, then what often occurs is that the U.S. corporation will bring a case in a U.S. court and the defendant will appear for the purpose of contesting the jurisdiction of the court and the choice of law issues. As you can imagine, this can be time consuming and costly. Issues of choice of forum, choice of law, and jurisdiction can often be complex, even when they are uncontested, but when the parties battle over these issues, a great deal of time and expense will be consumed in resolving these issues — and these are only preliminary issues and are not generally issues related to the merits of the dispute. Litigation is obviously a less than optimal way of resolving these issues so parties now will often reach an agreement on these issues before a dispute arises by agreeing to a forum selection clause, choice of law clause, and consent to jurisdiction in the contract that structures the international business transaction in question. While U.S. courts will usually uphold these agreements, interesting issues concerning the enforceability of such clauses do occasionally arise. We examine some of these issues in the cases below.

Dispute Resolution Other Than by Litigation

While parties may agree on preliminary issues to a business dispute and reduce the time and expense involved in settling these issues in court, litigation through the court system can still be a time-consuming process because of all of the formalities that must be followed in any court-based process of litigation. In addition, litigation is often inflexible as it is based on a formal model that is heavily governed by rules and procedures. An additional disadvantage is that as litigation is also adversarial in nature, the business relationship between the parties may be unable to survive after a lawsuit even if the dispute itself is a minor business problem. Adversarial litigation over a small dispute might poison or destroy a more valuable long-term business relationship between the parties.

As a result, some parties today may wish to forgo litigation altogether by agreeing at the outset on forms of alternative dispute resolution (ADR) as a way of handling difficulties. ADR can be chosen by agreement at any time, even after a dispute has arisen, but it is best to choose it at the outset. ADR refers to certain informal methods of dispute settlement. Of course, negotiation is always an option, and many disputes, especially minor ones, are settled this way. Negotiation does not require the assistance of a third party. Mediation, however, requires an impartial third party who seeks to reconcile the parties' positions and to suggest solutions. The level of active involvement of the mediator will depend on the situation and the parties' wishes, but in any case the mediator has no power to impose a binding decision. Conciliation and arbitration are two additional methods of ADR. Conciliation is more formal than mediation; the conciliator hears evidence, perhaps conducts an investigation, makes findings of fact and law, and gives a proposed solution. Unlike arbitration, however, the conciliator's decision is not binding, so many attorneys think it is a waste of time and money. UNCITRAL has developed and published conciliation rules. The final method is arbitration, which, in the context of international business, usually refers to a private and voluntary dispute resolution process that is final and binding upon the parties. We have already seen the choice of arbitration before the International Centre for the Settlement of Investment Disputes as a dispute resolution method concerning foreign direct investment issues in Chapter 6. In this chapter, we offer a broad treatment of arbitration as it is now the preferred method of dispute resolution in international business. Although agreements to arbitrate disputes are now generally enforceable, there can still be some interesting issues that arise.

Other Issues

The discussion above has reviewed some of the major issues in an international business dispute that we will cover in this chapter but there are also many ancillary issues as well. Among those that we will cover in this chapter are

- enforcement of U.S. court judgments abroad and enforcement of foreign judgments in the United States
- enforcement of arbitral awards
- evidence
- discovery
- service of process

We now turn to a closer examination of the issues introduced in this context through the problems, cases, and materials below.

II. *Choice of Forum and Choice of Law*

A. Choice of Forum

PROBLEM 8-1

A U.S. company buys an electric generator from a seller in a South American country under a sales contract providing that all disputes under the contract are governed by U.S. law and that the courts of the seller have exclusive jurisdiction over all disputes. The U.S. buyer installs the generator in its manufacturing plant, but when a problem with the generator develops, the plant is shut down for several weeks, causing the U.S. buyer to miss delivery on certain goods that the company was to produce for a major client. Failure to meet the order has cost the U.S. company $500,000 dollars in lost sales. The U.S. buyer sues the seller in federal district court for the faulty generator and for $500,000 in damages. The seller appears and moves to dismiss the action on the basis of the forum selection clause in the contract. In opposing the motion, the U.S. buyer argues:

(1) U.S. courts are far more familiar with handling complex contract cases of the type involved in this case and have a far greater expertise applying complex U.S. contract law, here the Uniform Commercial Code;

(2) All issues of proof concerning the faulty generator and lost sales are located in the United States and it would be seriously inconvenient to introduce this evidence in a foreign court in a foreign language;

(3) Courts of the foreign country do not recognize consequential damages even when they apply foreign law. The refusal to recognize consequential damages is based on the grounds of local public policy. The buyer would be severely prejudiced if it were limited to the replacement cost or repair of the faulty generator; and

(4) A recently issued decree in the South American country places a $500,000 maximum limit on all damage awards issued by its courts in favor of foreign plaintiffs against domestic companies.

Review each of these arguments and discuss whether any of them will allow the U.S. buyer to proceed in its litigation in the United States despite the forum selection clause. Consult *The Bremen* below.

M/S Bremen v. Zapata Off-Shore Company
United States Supreme Court, 1972
407 U.S. 1, 92 S. Ct. 1907, 32 L. Ed. 2d 513

MR. CHIEF JUSTICE BURGER delivered the opinion of the Court.

We granted certiorari to review a judgment of the United States Court of Appeals for the Fifth Circuit declining to enforce a forum-selection clause governing disputes arising under an international towage contract between petitioners and respondent. The circuits have differed in their approach to such clauses. For the reasons stated hereafter, we vacate the judgment of the Court of Appeals.

In November 1967, respondent Zapata, a Houston-based American corporation, contracted with petitioner Unterweser, a German corporation, to tow Zapata's ocean-going, self-elevating drilling rig *Chaparral* from Louisiana to a point off Ravenna, Italy, in the Adriatic Sea, where Zapata had agreed to drill certain wells.

Zapata had solicited bids for the towage, and several companies including Unterweser had responded. Unterweser was the low bidder and Zapata requested it to submit a contract, which it did. The contract submitted by Unterweser contained the following provision, which is at issue in this case:

"Any dispute arising must be treated before the London Court of Justice."

In addition the contract contained two clauses purporting to exculpate Unterweser from liability for damages to the towed barge.[1]

After reviewing the contract and making several changes, but without any alteration in the forum-selection or exculpatory clauses, a Zapata vice president executed the contract and forwarded it to Unterweser in Germany, where Unterweser accepted the changes, and the contract became effective.

On January 5, 1968, Unterweser's deep sea tug *Bremen* departed Venice, Louisiana, with the *Chaparral* in tow bound for Italy. On January 9, while the flotilla was in international waters in the middle of the Gulf of Mexico, a severe storm arose. The sharp roll of the *Chaparral* in Gulf waters caused its elevator legs, which had been raised for the voyage, to break off and fall into the sea, seriously damaging the *Chaparral*. In this emergency situation Zapata instructed the *Bremen* to tow its damaged rig to Tampa, Florida, the nearest port of refuge.

On January 12, Zapata, ignoring its contract promise to litigate "any dispute arising" in the English courts, commenced a suit in admiralty in the United States District Court at Tampa, seeking $3,500,000 damages against Unterweser *in personam* and the *Bremen in rem*, alleging negligent towage and breach of contract. Unterweser responded by invoking the forum clause of the towage contract, and moved to dismiss for lack of jurisdiction or on *forum non conveniens* grounds, or in the alternative to stay the action pending submission of the dispute to the "London Court of Justice." Shortly thereafter, in February, before the District Court had ruled on its motion to stay or dismiss the United States action, Unterweser commenced an action against Zapata seeking damages for breach of the towage contract in the High Court of Justice in London, as the contract provided. Zapata appeared in that court to contest jurisdiction, but its challenge was rejected, the English courts holding that the contractual forum provision conferred jurisdiction.

---

1. The General Towage Conditions of the contract included the following:

"1. . . . [Unterweser and its] masters and crews are not responsible for defaults and/or errors in the navigation of the two.
"2. . . .
"b) Damages suffered by the towed object are in any case for account of its Owners."

In addition, the contract provided that any insurance of the *Chaparral* was to be "for account of" Zapata. Unterweser's initial telegraphic bid had also offered to "arrange insurance covering towage risk for rig if desired." As Zapata had chosen to be self-insured on all its rigs, the loss in this case was not compensated by insurance.

In the meantime, Unterweser was faced with a dilemma in the pending action in the United States court at Tampa. The six-month period for filing action to limit its liability to Zapata and other potential claimants was about to expire,[2] but the United States District Court in Tampa had not yet ruled on Unterweser's motion to dismiss or stay Zapata's action. On July 2, 1968, confronted with difficult alternatives, Unterweser commenced an action to limit its liability in the District Court in Tampa. That court entered the customary injunction against proceedings outside the limitation court, and Zapata refiled its initial claim in the limitation action.

It was only at this juncture, on July 29, after the six-month period for filing the limitation action had run, that the District Court denied Unterweser's January motion to dismiss or stay Zapata's initial action. In denying the motion, that court relied on the prior decision of the Court of Appeals in *Carbon Black Export, Inc. v. The Monrosa*, 254 F.2d 297 (C.A.5 1958), cert. dismissed, 359 U.S. 180 (1959). In that case the Court of Appeals had held a forum-selection clause unenforceable, reiterating the traditional view of many American courts that "agreements in advance of controversy whose object is to oust the jurisdiction of the courts are contrary to public policy and will not be enforced." 254 F.2d, at 300-301. Apparently concluding that it was bound by the *Carbon Black* case, the District Court gave the forum-selection clause little, if any, weight. Instead, the court treated the motion to dismiss under normal *forum non conveniens* doctrine applicable in the absence of such a clause, citing *Gulf Oil Corp. v. Gilbert* (1947). Under that doctrine "unless the balance is strongly in favor of the defendant, the plaintiff's choice of forum should rarely be disturbed." The District Court concluded: "the balance of conveniences here is not strongly in favor of [Unterweser] and [Zapata's] choice of forum should not be disturbed."

Thereafter, on January 21, 1969, the District Court denied another motion by Unterweser to stay the limitation action pending determination of the controversy in the High Court of Justice in London and granted Zapata's motion to restrain Unterweser from litigating further in the London court. The District Judge ruled that, having taken jurisdiction in the limitation proceeding, he had jurisdiction to determine all matters relating to the controversy.

On appeal, a divided panel of the Court of Appeals affirmed, and on rehearing *en banc* the panel opinion was adopted, with six of the 14 *en banc* judges dissenting. As had the District Court, the majority rested on the *Carbon Black* decision, concluding that " 'at the very least' " that case stood for the proposition that a forum-selection clause " 'will not be enforced unless the selected state would provide a more convenient forum than the state in which suit is brought.' " From that premise the Court of Appeals proceeded to conclude that, apart from the forum-selection clause, the District Court did not abuse its discretion in refusing to decline jurisdiction on the basis of *forum non conveniens*.

We hold, with the six dissenting members of the Court of Appeals, that far too little weight and effect were given to the forum clause in resolving this controversy. For at least two decades we have witnessed an expansion of overseas commercial activities by business enterprises based in the United States. The barrier of distance that once tended to confine a business concern to a modest territory no longer does so. Here we see an American company with special expertise contracting with a foreign company to tow a complex machine thousands of miles

---

2. 46 U.S.C. §§183, 185.

across seas and oceans. The expansion of American business and industry will hardly be encouraged if, notwithstanding solemn contracts, we insist on a parochial concept that all disputes must be resolved under our laws and in our courts. Absent a contract forum, the considerations relied on by the Court of Appeals would be persuasive reasons for holding an American forum convenient in the traditional sense, but in an era of expanding world trade and commerce, the absolute aspects of the doctrine of the *Carbon Black* case have little place and would be a heavy hand indeed on the future development of international commercial dealings by Americans. We cannot have trade and commerce in world markets and international waters exclusively on our terms, governed by our laws, and resolved in our courts.

Forum-selection clauses have historically not been favored by American courts. Many courts, federal and state, have declined to enforce such clauses on the ground that they were "contrary to public policy," or that their effect was to "oust the jurisdiction" of the court. Although this view apparently still has considerable acceptance, other courts are tending to adopt a more hospitable attitude toward forum-selection clauses. This view, advanced in the well-reasoned dissenting opinion in the instant case, is that such clauses are prima facie valid and should be enforced unless enforcement is shown by the resisting party to be "unreasonable" under the circumstances. We believe this is the correct doctrine to be followed by federal district courts sitting in admiralty.

The argument that such clauses are improper because they tend to "oust" a court of jurisdiction is hardly more than a vestigial legal fiction. It appears to rest at core on historical judicial resistance to any attempt to reduce the power and business of a particular court and has little place in an era when all courts are overloaded and when businesses once essentially local now operate in world markets. It reflects something of a provincial attitude regarding the fairness of other tribunals. No one seriously contends in this case that the forum-selection clause "ousted" the District Court of jurisdiction over Zapata's action. The threshold question is whether that court should have exercised its jurisdiction to do more than give effect to the legitimate expectations of the parties, manifested in their freely negotiated agreement, by specifically enforcing the forum clause.

There are compelling reasons why a freely negotiated private international agreement, unaffected by fraud, undue influence, or overweening bargaining power, such as that involved here, should be given full effect. In this case, for example, we are concerned with a far from routine transaction between companies of two different nations contemplating the tow of an extremely costly piece of equipment from Louisiana across the Gulf of Mexico and the Atlantic Ocean, through the Mediterranean Sea to its final destination in the Adriatic Sea. In the course of its voyage, it was to traverse the waters of many jurisdictions. The *Chaparral* could have been damaged at any point along the route, and there were countless possible ports of refuge. That the accident occurred in the Gulf of Mexico and the barge was towed to Tampa in an emergency were mere fortuities. It cannot be doubted for a moment that the parties sought to provide for a neutral forum for the resolution of any disputes arising during the tow. Manifestly much uncertainty and possibly great inconvenience to both parties could arise if a suit could be maintained in any jurisdiction in which an accident might occur or if jurisdiction were left to any place where the *Bremen* or Unterweser might happen to be found. The elimination of all such uncertainties by agreeing in advance on a forum acceptable to both parties is an indispensable element in international trade, commerce, and contracting. There is strong evidence that the forum clause was a vital part of the agreement, and it would be unrealistic to think that the parties did not conduct their negotiations, including fixing the monetary terms, with the consequences of the forum clause figuring prominently in their calculations. Under these circumstances, as Justice Karminski reasoned in sustaining jurisdiction over Zapata in the High Court of Justice, "[t]he force of an agreement for litigation in this country, freely entered into between two competent parties, seems to me to be very powerful."

Thus, in the light of present-day commercial realities and expanding international trade we conclude that the forum clause should control absent a strong showing that it should be set aside. Although their opinions are not altogether explicit, it seems reasonably clear that the District Court and the Court of Appeals placed the burden on Unterweser to show that London would be a more convenient forum than Tampa, although the contract expressly resolved that issue. The correct approach would have been to enforce the forum clause specifically unless Zapata could clearly show that enforcement would be unreasonable and unjust, or that the clause was invalid for such reasons as fraud or overreaching. Accordingly, the case must be remanded for reconsideration.

We note, however, that there is nothing in the record presently before us that would support a refusal to enforce the forum clause. The Court of Appeals suggested that enforcement would be contrary to the public policy of the forum under *Bisso v. Inland Waterways Corp.*, 349 U.S. 85 (1955), because of the prospect that the English courts would enforce the clauses of the towage contract purporting to exculpate Unterweser from liability for damages to the *Chaparral*. A contractual choice-of-forum clause should be held unenforceable if enforcement would contravene a strong public policy of the forum in which suit is brought, whether declared by statute or by judicial decision. It is clear, however, that whatever the proper scope of the policy expressed in *Bisso*, it does not reach this case. *Bisso* rested on considerations with respect to the towage business strictly in American waters, and those considerations are not controlling in an international commercial agreement. Speaking for the dissenting judges in the Court of Appeals, Judge Wisdom pointed out:

> "[W]e should be careful not to overemphasize the strength of the [*Bisso*] policy. . . . [T]wo concerns underlie the rejection of exculpatory agreements: that they may be produced by overweening bargaining power; and that they do not sufficiently discourage negligence. . . . Here the conduct in question is that of a foreign party occurring in international waters outside our jurisdiction. The evidence disputes any notion of overreaching in the contractual agreement. And for all we know, the uncertainties and dangers in the new field of transoceanic towage of oil rigs were so great that the tower was unwilling to take financial responsibility for the risks, and the parties thus allocated responsibility for the voyage to the tow. It is equally possible that the contract price took this factor into account. I conclude that we should not invalidate the forum selection clause here unless we are firmly convinced that we would thereby significantly encourage negligent conduct within the boundaries of the United States." 428 F.2d, at 907-908.

The judgment of the Court of Appeals is vacated and the case is remanded for further proceedings consistent with this opinion.

MR. JUSTICE DOUGLAS, dissenting.

Respondent is a citizen of this country. Moreover, if it were remitted to the English court, its substantive rights would be adversely affected. Exculpatory provisions in the towage control provide (1) that petitioners, the masters and the crews "are not responsible for defaults and/or errors in the navigation of the tow" and (2) that "[d]amages suffered by the towed object are in any case for account of its Owners."

Under our decision in *Dixilyn Drilling Corp. v. Crescent Towing & Salvage Co.*, 372 U.S. 697, 698 "a contract which exempts the tower from liability for its own negligence" is not enforceable, though there is evidence in the present record that it is enforceable in England.

Moreover, the casualty occurred close to the District Court, a number of potential witnesses, including respondent's crewmen, reside in that area, and the inspection and repair work were done there. The testimony of the tower's crewmen, residing in Germany, is already available by way of depositions taken in the proceedings.

I would affirm the judgment below.

NOTES AND QUESTIONS

1. After *The Bremen*, choice of forum clauses are now commonly upheld. What are the criteria for their validity set out by the Supreme Court? For a rare case refusing to uphold a choice of forum clause, *see McDonnell Douglas Corp. v. Islamic Republic of Iran*, 758 F.2d 341 (8th Cir. 1985).

2. The Supreme Court has reaffirmed and expanded the holding in *The Bremen*. In *Carnival Cruise Lines, Inc. v. Shute*, 499 U.S. 585 (1991), the Court upheld a forum selection clause printed on the back of a passenger ticket issued by a cruise line. As long as a passenger cannot prove bad faith, fraud, or over-reaching by the cruise line, such clauses will be upheld. Similarly, in *Vimar Seguros y Reaseguros, S.A. v. M/V Sky Reefer*, 515 U.S. 528 (1995), the Supreme Court upheld a forum selection clause contained in a bill of lading issued by a sea carrier for the shipment of goods.

3. Note that *The Bremen* was a case that arose under the Admiralty Jurisdiction Clause of the U.S. Constitution and the corresponding statute, 18 U.S.C. §1333. The holding has been uniformly followed, however, in nonadmiralty cases in federal and state courts.

PROBLEM 8-2

In a contract for the sale of a collating machine to a U.S. buyer, a Japanese seller inserts a clause that expressly incorporates the regulations of a Japanese business organization that promulgates model contract provisions for incorporation by parties. The regulations contain a forum selection clause providing that, in case of a dispute, all lawsuits must be brought in the same locale as the seller's principal place of business, which is in Osaka. The U.S. buyer's sales department manager signed the contract but the U.S. buyer can show that no one in the U.S. organization read the clause or knew about or had even heard of the Japanese organization. The buyer also argues that the regulations were in Japanese and that no one at the buyer's organization reads or understands Japanese. The buyer further argues that the Japanese seller was well aware that Americans generally lack knowledge of foreign languages and that the Japanese seller's insertion of the clause was an underhanded attempt to sneak the forum selection clause into the contract and amounts to fraud. Under these circumstances, it would be unjust to hold it to the forum selection clause. What is the result? *Cf. Paper Express Ltd. v. Pfankuch Maschinen, GmbH,* 972 F.2d 753 (7th Cir. 1992).

PROBLEM 8-3

In a contract for the sale of goods between a U.S. buyer and an Italian seller, the contract contains the following clauses:

> This agreement shall be construed according to the laws of Italy.
> All disputes arising between the parties shall come within the jurisdiction of the competent Italian courts.

When a dispute arises, the U.S. buyer brings an action in a U.S. federal district court. The Italian seller moves to dismiss on the basis of the forum selection clause. What is the result? *Cf. John Boutari and Son v. Attiki Importers,* 22 F.3d 51 (2d Cir. 1994). What change would you make to the clause above to achieve the intent of the Italian seller?

B.   Choice of Law

In an international business dispute today, choice of law is, of course, a major issue in determining the outcome of the dispute. When the parties have not chosen an applicable law, choice of law questions must be resolved under general choice of law approaches developed by courts or under an applicable statute or treaty; where the parties have provided for a law by contract, the issue becomes whether a court will uphold the choice of law clause. The following sections below deal with both situations

1.   Choice of Law Approaches

Choice of law rules in contract disputes applicable in the absence of agreement by the parties are relatively easy to articulate, but difficult and unpredictable in application. Three approaches are in use in the United States.

First, the *lex loci* (the applicable law is the place of the contract) rule is the traditional approach under the First Restatement of the Conflict of Laws (1931, withdrawn 1971). But what is the place of the contract? Where the initial offer was made? Where the last essential act occurred? In this day of electronic communication, applying this rule is a search for a will-of-the-wisp. And a meaningless search at that. But this rule is still followed by about 15 states. *See, e.g., Sturiano v. Brooks,* 523 So. 2d 1126 (Fla. 1988).

A second approach is the "most significant relationship test" of the Restatement, Conflicts of Law (Second) §188 (1971). This test seeks to balance the diverse interests and expectations of the parties involved in the dispute. Seven factors are important in determining a significant relationship: The needs of the interstate and international systems; the relevant policies of the forum; the policies of interested states; the expectations of the parties; the basic policies underlying the particular field of law; the certainty, predictability, and uniformity of the result; and the ease of applying the law. In applying these factors, the court will consider the place of contracting; the place of negotiation of the contract; the place of performance; the location of the subject matter of the contract; and the domicile, residence, nationality, place of incorporation, and place of business of the parties. *See, e.g., Citizens First Bank v. Intercontinental Express, Inc.*, 77 Or. App. 655, 713 P.2d 1097 (1986). Clearly, this is a flexible test, but one that maximizes uncertainty.

A third approach followed in a few states is "governmental interest analysis." This method requires the court to make a preliminary analysis of the interests of the involved states and a determination of whether the conflict is a true conflict, an apparent conflict, or a false conflict. The last is one where it will be determined that, in reality, only one state has an actual, legitimate interest. If there is only an apparent conflict, the court may be able to resolve it by interpretation. If there is a true conflict, the court will apply the law of the forum with the greatest interest in the dispute. *See, e.g., Clemco Industries v. Commercial Union Insurance Co.*, 665 F. Supp. 816 (N.D. Cal. 1987), *aff'd*, 848 F.2d 1242 (9th Cir. 1988). The following case is an example of a false-conflict situation.

Amco Ukrservice & Prompriladamco v. American Meter Company
United States District Court, Eastern District of Pennsylvania, 2004
312 F. Supp. 2d 681

DALZELL, District Judge.

[The full background facts of this case are set out in Chapter 3 on pp. 199-204. Plaintiffs Amco Ukrservice and Prompriladamco are two Ukrainian corporations that brought an action against defendant American Meter Company, a Pennsylvania company in the business of manufacturing utility meters. Plaintiffs claim that defendant breached two joint venture agreements under which American Meter agreed to supply meters to plaintiffs for sale in the republics of the former Soviet Union. In its defense, American Meter moved for summary judgment, arguing that the joint venture agreements were unenforceable under either the Convention on Contracts for the International Sale of Goods or Ukrainian law. In the first part of its opinion, the federal district court rejected American Meter's argument that the CISG applied to the joint venture agreements (see pp. 202-204 *supra*) and then in the portion of the opinion below turned to the issue of whether the joint venture agreements were unenforceable under Ukrainian law. In order to make that determination, however, the court had to first decide whether Pennsylvania or Ukrainian law applied to the joint venture agreements. As the court was sitting in diversity jurisdiction, the court followed the mandate of *Klaxon Co. v. Stentor Electric Mfg. Co., Inc.*, 313 U.S. 487 (1941), and applied Pennsylvania choice of law rules to decide whether Pennsylvania or Ukrainian law applied to the case.]

1. THE PENNSYLVANIA CHOICE-OF-LAW REGIME

In *Griffith v. United Air Lines, Inc.*, 416 Pa. 1, 203 A.2d 796, 805 (Pa. 1964), the Pennsylvania Supreme Court adopted a flexible choice of law rule that "permits analysis of the policies and interests underlying the particular issue before the court." Our Court of Appeals has explained that the *Griffith* "methodology combines the approaches of both [the Restatement (Second) of Conflict of Laws] (contacts establishing significant relationships) and 'interest analysis' (qualitative appraisal of the relevant States' policies with respect to the controversy)." *Melville v. American Home Assurance Co.*, 584 F.2d 1306, 1311 (3d Cir. 1978).

In applying *Griffith's* hybrid approach, we begin with an "interest analysis" of the policies of all interested states and then, based on the results of that analysis, proceed to characterize the case as a true conflict, false conflict, or unprovided-for case. A true conflict exists "when the governmental interests of both jurisdictions would be impaired if their law were not applied." *Lacey*, 932 F.2d at 187 n. 15. On the other hand, there is a false conflict "if only one jurisdiction's governmental interests would be impaired by the application of the other jurisdiction's law." Id. at 187.

2. Sources of Law

While the plaintiffs and American Meter agree that ordinary breach of contract principles would govern the plaintiffs' claims under Pennsylvania law, they dispute whether the joint venture agreements are invalid under Ukrainian law and, if so, what governmental interests any invalidating laws would serve. We therefore begin with a discussion of Pennsylvania's interest in this action and then turn to the more difficult problems that Ukrainian law presents. Finally, after we have isolated any applicable statutory provisions, we will consider Ukraine's interest in their enforcement.

(A) PENNSYLVANIA LAW

At the threshold, we note that American Meter has disputed whether Pennsylvania has any interest at all in the enforcement of the joint venture agreements because they were negotiated in Ukraine, written in the Ukrainian language, and provide for the creation of Ukrainian corporations. This argument does not withstand close scrutiny because the record amply demonstrates the important contacts between Pennsylvania and both the parties to the joint venture agreements and the obligations those agreements created. All of the American Meter employees who hatched the Ukrainian project worked from corporate headquarters in Horsham, Pennsylvania, and most important of all, the parties to the joint venture agreements contemplated that American Meter would oversee the project, extend credit, and arrange for the shipment of goods from its offices here.

Not only does Pennsylvania have significant contacts with both the parties and the joint ventures, but enforcement of the joint venture agreements would advance the Commonwealth's general interests. As American Meter grudgingly concedes, the vindication of contractual parties' legitimate expectations creates a stable business environment and thereby helps the Commonwealth achieve its commercial potential. Finally, although American Meter asserts that the plaintiffs' claims for damages are too speculative, it does not dispute that, as an abstract proposition, the joint venture agreements create enforceable obligations under Pennsylvania law.

(B) UKRAINIAN LAW

American Meter contends that the joint venture agreements are invalid under three separate statutory schemes and that each advances identifiable and significant state interests.

1. "REGULATIONS ON THE SUPPLY OF INDUSTRIAL GOODS" (1988)

On July 25, 1988, the USSR Council of Ministers promulgated "Regulations on the Supply of Industrial Goods," which remained effective in Ukraine after the collapse of the Soviet Union pursuant to a general reception statute that the Verkovna Rada, the Ukrainian Parliament, enacted in 1991. Under Paragraph 19 of the Regulations, a contract for the supply of goods must identify the goods to be delivered, the time of delivery, and their price, quantity, and quality. American Meter's Ukrainian legal expert has opined that the Regulations were still in force in 1998 and that the joint venture agreements are invalid because their supply provisions lack the terms detailed in Paragraph 19. The plaintiffs' legal expert, however, contends that the Regulations have no relevance here because they were enacted to regulate the Soviet Union's internal market and, in any event, never applied to joint venture agreements.

Although American Meter solicited a supplemental affidavit from its Ukrainian expert, he declined to challenge the plaintiffs' expert's views on the Regulations. In view of the fact that the plaintiffs' contentions appear to have textual support—and in the absence of a counter-argument from American Meter—we must conclude that the plaintiffs' view carries the day on this issue and that the Regulations are inapplicable here.

2. "PROVISIONS ON THE FORM OF FOREIGN ECONOMIC AGREEMENTS" (1995)

American Meter's legal expert has also brought to our attention the "Provisions on the Form of Foreign Economic Agreements," which the Ukrainian Ministry of Foreign Economic Relations and Trade enacted in 1995. The Provisions' preamble states that they "are applicable when concluding sale (purchase) agreements on goods (services, performance of work) and barter agreements among Ukrainian and foreign economic subjects irrespective of their property form and type of activities."

Agreements governed by the Provisions must, inter alia, identify the goods to be sold and specify their quantity and quality. American Meter contends that the joint venture agreements are invalid under the Provisions because they manifestly do not satisfy these requirements. However, as the plaintiffs' legal expert has contended, the Provisions offer no textual support for American Meter's position. Indeed, the text of the Provisions suggests that they do not regulate joint venture agreements and were instead enacted to regularize contracts for the sale of goods and provision of services.

Finally, the plaintiffs' construction of the Provisions gains support from the framers' apparent intention that they be read in pari materia with Ukraine's Foreign Economic Activities Law ("FEAL"). Because the FEAL recognizes joint venture agreements, it is improbable that the Foreign Ministry intended the 1995 enactment to invalidate such agreements, which create long-term relationships and are unlikely to contain price, quantity, and delivery terms that would be sufficiently precise to satisfy the Provisions.

In view of this textual evidence, we conclude that although the Provisions would likely govern a particular sales contract executed pursuant to a joint venture agreement, they do not bear on the validity of the joint venture agreement itself.

3. FOREIGN ECONOMIC ACTIVITY LAW (1991)

Finally, American Meter invites us to consider whether the Ukrainian courts would invalidate the joint venture agreements under Article 6 of the FEAL. At the time the parties entered into these agreements, Article 6 required any contract between a Ukrainian entity and a foreign entity to be executed by two representatives of the Ukrainian signatory, and neither [of the plaintiff Ukrainian corporations] complied with this rule.

Ukraine's two-signature rule was the final incarnation of a policy with deep roots in the history of the Soviet command economy. According to a Stalin-era decree, any contract between a foreign entity and a Soviet foreign trade organization ("FTO") that was executed in Moscow required the signatures of the FTO's chairman or deputy as well as a person possessing the chairman's power of attorney. Contracts executed abroad required the signatures of two persons with powers of attorney.

Whatever its purpose may have been, one might have thought that the two-signature rule would have disappeared after 1990 along with the other legal trappings of the Soviet economy. In 1991, however, the Verkovna Rada enshrined the two-signature rule in the FEAL:

> In the event that the foreign economic agreement is signed by an individual, signature of such individual shall be required. The foreign economic agreement shall be signed on behalf of other subjects of economic activity by two persons: one person who is authorized to sign by virtue of his/her position, in accordance with his/her founding documents, and another person who is solely authorized to sign on the basis of the power of attorney issued under the hand of the directors of the subject of foreign economic activity, unless otherwise provided by founding documents.

FEAL art. 6 para. 2.

Ukrainian businesses, however, did not always comply with the two-signature rule, and a dispute between a Ukrainian pharmaceutical firm and its American trading partner soon forced the courts and Verkovna Rada to clarify the rule's place in Ukrainian commercial law. Armor Pharmaceutical filed a claim in the Ukrainian Arbitration Court against Lubnipharm for the return of partially unpaid pharmaceuticals. On November 22, 1996, the Supreme Arbitration Court of Ukraine ("SACU") invalidated the original contracts on the ground that two representatives of Lubnipharm did not execute them, but on January 11, 1997 the Arbitration Board of the SACU declared that failure to comply with the two-signature rule was not automatic grounds for invalidation and overturned the decision of November 22nd. The Plenary Meeting of the SACU upheld the Arbitration Board's decision, and the dispute ultimately landed in the Constitutional Court of Ukraine. In a decision dated November 26, 1998, the

Court somewhat ambiguously stated that the two-signature rule was "obligatory" but also held that failure to comply "may be the basis for invalidation of the foreign economic agreement in court as not meeting the requirements of laws or international agreements of Ukraine."

The Verkovna Rada and SACU swiftly acted to blunt the Constitutional Court's ruling. The Deputy Prosecutor General of Ukraine filed a submission in the Supreme Arbitration Court to review the Lubnipharm case, but in a ruling issued June 11, 1999, the SACU affirmed its earlier decision to uphold the Lubnipharm contracts. Seizing upon the Constitutional Court's statement that failure to comply with the two-signature rule may be a basis for invalidating a contract, the Court concluded that it retained the discretion to affirm nonconforming contracts and that invalidation would be inappropriate in the Lubnipharm case because both parties had actually performed under the contracts. The Court also noted that, in any event, the Constitutional Court's decision did not state whether it had retroactive effect. Four months later, the Verkovna Rada at last repealed the two-signature rule.

Apparently, however, neither the SACU's narrow construction of the Constitutional Court's ruling nor the amendment to Article 6 has dimmed the lower court's willingness to invoke the two-signature rule in cases involving contracts executed before the repeal. In 2001, for example, Judge Zyrnov of the Kyiv City Commercial Court relied upon the rule to nullify a lease and credit agreement between a Ukrainian corporation and Fortis Bank of the Netherlands, despite the fact that the Bank had rendered performance.

Predicting another judicial system's resolution of an issue is always a perilous business, but we must conclude there is at least a possibility that a Ukrainian court would invalidate the joint venture agreements on the ground that the Ukrainian parties did not comply with the two-signature rule.

3. CHARACTERIZATION OF THE CONFLICT OF LAW PROBLEM

Our conclusion that the courts of Pennsylvania and Ukraine might diverge in their treatment of the joint venture agreements merely poses the conflict of law problem without resolving it. In order to determine whether this case involves a false or true conflict, we must first determine what, if any, governmental interests the two-signature rule advances.

American Meter contends that Ukraine has an interest in the retroactive enforcement of the rule because it protects Ukrainians who enter into contracts with foreigners and promotes certainty, predictability, and uniformity in commercial relationships. American Meter's "argument from paternalism" would bear close scrutiny if we were resolving this conflict of law problem in 1992. After all, the plaintiffs' legal expert had stated that the Verkovna Rada included the rule in the FEAL as a sop to legislators who opposed economic liberalization, and perhaps its proponents believed that requiring two signatures on contracts would protect Ukrainian naifs from more commercially sophisticated (and capitalism-hardened) foreigners. Now that the Verkovna Rada has repealed the two-signature rule, however, we cannot conclude on the record before us that its continued enforcement advances any current social, political, or economic interest of Ukraine. Turning to American Meter's "argument from commercial certainty," we note that this articulation of Ukraine's interest in the rule remains plausible despite the repeal. A hard-and-fast policy that all foreign economic agreements executed between the enactment of the FEAL and the statute's 1999 amendment must comply with the two-signature rule would — like any bright-line rule — have the advantage of letting parties know exactly where they stand. But as the recent decisions of the SACU and Kyiv Commercial Court underscore, the difficulty with this argument is that the two-signature rule is not so much a bright-line rule as it is a controversial repository of judicial discretion that allows courts to invalidate contracts for any reason — or perhaps for no reason at all. Under these circumstances, we cannot discern how the two-signature rule advances any of the procedural or commercial advantages that Ukraine would derive from a predictable body of law governing the validity of contracts.

To summarize, we have concluded that Pennsylvania and Ukraine both have significant relationships with the parties and the transactions. Moreover, we have found that Pennsylvania has a general interest in the enforcement of contracts, and it goes without saying that this interest would be compromised if a Pennsylvania corporation could defeat the expectations of its trading partners in the manner American Meter has proposed here. Finally, we have concluded that American Meter has not identified any governmental interest of Ukraine in the continued enforcement of the repealed two-signature rule.

Because our analysis reveals that Pennsylvania's interest would be harmed by applying Ukraine's law, but that no identified Ukrainian interest will be impaired by enforcing these contracts, this case presents a false conflict. Under the Pennsylvania choice-of-law regime, Pennsylvania law therefore governs the plaintiffs' claims, and American Meter is not entitled to summary judgment on the ground that the contracts are invalid under Ukrainian law.

Defendant's motion for summary judgment is denied.

QUESTIONS

1. What was the purpose of the two-signature rule first established during the Stalin era?

2. Do you think that a Ukrainian court would find this to be a false conflict because the Ukraine has no interest in this case?

3. What issues does this suggest with this approach to choice of law?

2.   Choice of Law Clauses

The parties are, of course, free to insert choice of law clauses in international contracts, which are now widely upheld and seldom litigated. The Uniform Commercial Code, §1-105(1) also specifically authorizes choice of law clauses. Nevertheless, interesting issues sometimes arise.

PROBLEM 8-4

An Ohio company enters into a contract with a German towing company for the towage of a rig owned by the Ohio company from the United States to Argentina. The contract provides that all disputes arising out of the contract are governed by the laws of France. In a subsequent lawsuit for damage to the rig brought by the Ohio company in an Ohio court, the German defendant argues that the issue of risk of loss should be determined by French law pursuant to the contract's choice of law clause. Assume that under French law the risk of loss is on the Ohio company. The Ohio company objects to the use of French law on the grounds that it has no connection with the parties or the transaction. How would this case be resolved under Restatement §187 below?

PROBLEM 8-5

A French company sends an application for a credit card to an Ohio consumer providing for a card with a 60 percent annual interest rate. The credit card contract provides that it is governed by the laws of country Z. Assume that both Ohio and France have laws against usury but that Z does not. In a lawsuit brought by the consumer in an Ohio court against the French company over the amount of a credit card bill, the consumer objects to the application of Z's law on the grounds that it has no connection with the parties or the transaction. How should the Ohio court decide this issue? What if the French company set up a subsidiary in Z for the purpose of serving as the entity on the credit card contract? See Restatement §187 below.

The Restatement (Second) of Conflicts of Laws (1971)

Section 187. Law of the State Chosen by the Parties

(1) The law of the state chosen by the parties to govern their contractual rights and duties will be applied if the particular issue is one which the parties could have resolved by an explicit provision in their agreement directed to that issue.

(2) The law of the state chosen by the parties to govern their contractual rights and duties will be applied, even if the particular issue is one which the parties could not have resolved by an explicit provision in their agreement directed to that issue, unless either:

(a) The chosen state has no substantial relationship to the parties or the transaction and there is no other reasonable basis for the parties' choice, or

(b) Application of the law of the chosen state would be contrary to a fundamental policy of a state which has a materially greater interest than the chosen state in the determination of the particular issue and which, under the rule of Section 188 [relating to the most significant contacts], would be the state of the applicable law in the absence of an effective choice of law by the parties.

(3) In the absence of a contrary indication of intention, the reference is to the local law of the state of the chosen law.

NOTES AND QUESTIONS

1. Can you explain why no substantial relationship of the state of the chosen law is required in Problem 8-4 and Restatement (Second) of Conflicts of Laws §187(1) but is required under Problem 8-5 and §187(2)?

2. Is the Restatement approach too restrictive? In contrast to the U.S. approach, Article 3 of the Rome Convention on the Law Applicable to Contractual Obligations (1980), the applicable law in the European Union, allows

parties to a contract to freely choose the applicable law even if the law chosen has no connection with either the parties or the subject matter of the contract.

3. For a case overturning the parties' choice of law under Restatement §187(2)(b), *see Triad Financial Establishment v. Tumpane Co.*, 611 F. Supp. 157 (N.D.N.Y. 1985). The court refused to apply New York law because Saudi Arabia had a greater interest and application of New York law would have violated a fundamental Saudi Arabian policy.

4. It may be dangerous to simply select a governing law without proper knowledge and planning. In *Volt Information Sciences, Inc. v. Board of Trustees of Leland Stanford Junior University*, 489 U.S. 468 (1989), the parties chose California law and provided that any dispute would be settled by arbitration. When a dispute arose and litigation was filed in California state courts, however, there was no authority under California law that arbitration was exclusive, and the Supreme Court ruled that the selection of California law included California, not federal, arbitration law, and arbitration was stayed pending resolution of the related litigation in the California state courts.

5. How does the attorney prove foreign law in a U.S. court? This question was addressed in *Arbitration Between Trans Chemical Ltd. and China National Machinery Import & Export Corp.*, 978 F. Supp. 266 (S.D.N.Y. 1997) as follows:

> In determining Chinese law the court is not bound by the evidence presented by the parties or by the Federal Rules of Evidence. Pursuant to Fed. R. Civ. P. 44.1 "[t]he court, in determining foreign law, may consider any relevant material or source, including testimony, whether or not submitted by a party or admissible under the Federal Rules of Evidence. The court's determination shall be treated as a ruling on a question of law."
>
> Rule [44.1] permits the court to consider any material that is relevant to a foreign-law issue, whether submitted by counsel or unearthed by the court's own research, and without regard to its admissibility under the rules of evidence.

III. Arbitration

A. Choosing Arbitration

Arbitration is now the normal way to address and resolve international business disputes. Arbitration allows parties engaged in international business to avoid a possible hostile local judicial forum and to resolve differences before a more neutral tribunal. The U.S. courts recognize a strong federal interest in arbitration and will respect parties' written promises to arbitrate even if this means referring the dispute to a tribunal outside the United States and the application of foreign law. The principal centers of international arbitration are the International Chamber of Commerce in Paris, the London Court of Arbitration, and the Stockholm Chamber of Commerce.

The United States and over 70 other nations have acceded to the Convention on the Recognition and Enforcement of Foreign Arbitral Awards, 21 U.S.T. 2517 (June 10, 1958), commonly called the New York Convention. National law, however, gives arbitration its legally binding character. In the United States, the relevant law is the Federal Arbitration Act (FAA), 9 U.S.C. §§1-307 (1994). The

FAA contains three chapters that establish rules for recognizing and enforcing arbitration agreements in both the domestic and the international context. FAA Chapter 1 (9 U.S.C. §§1-16), which is commonly referred to as the "Domestic FAA," authorizes enforcement of arbitration agreements in domestic and foreign commerce. FAA Chapter 2, enacted in 1970, implements the New York Convention and is referred to as the "Convention Act." FAA Chapter 3, enacted in 1990, implements another arbitration convention, the Inter-American Convention on International Commercial Arbitration, 14 I.L.M. 336 (January 30, 1975). Chapter 3 is commonly referred to as the "Panama Convention Act."

A trilogy of international commercial arbitration cases in the U.S. Supreme Court has established the strong federal policy in favor of arbitration. In *Scherk v. Alberto-Culver Co.*, 417 U.S. 506, 516 (1974), which involved a suit by the American purchaser of securities from a German seller, the court upheld a choice of law/forum clause in the agreement between the parties as an "almost indispensable precondition" for the "orderliness and predictability essential to any international business transaction." In *Mitsubishi Motors Corp. v. Soler-Chrysler Plymouth, Inc.*, 473 U.S. 614 (1985), the court held that a claim under the U.S. antitrust laws could be arbitrated in Japan as agreed by the parties. In *Vimar Seguros y Reaseguros, S.A. v. M/V Sky Reefer*, 515 U.S. 528 (1995), the court enforced an arbitration clause in a bill of lading relating to the carriage of goods by sea.

The relationship between the New York Convention and the U.S. FAA has been analyzed in the following article.

Susan Karamanian, The Road to the Tribunal and Beyond: International Arbitration and the United States Courts
34 George Washington International L. Rev. 17, 19-21 (2002)

The New York Convention is republished as a note following section 201 of [the FAA Chapter 2 also known as] the Convention Act. The Convention's requirements as to the arbitral award and arbitration agreement are as follows:

The Arbitral Award. The Convention applies to an arbitral award "made in the territory of a State other than the State where the recognition and enforcement of such awards are sought" and an award "not considered as domestic awards in the State where their recognition and enforcement are sought." The need for the two award categories became apparent during the Convention's drafting sessions. In some civil law countries, whether an award is foreign or domestic does not depend on the territory where an award is made but on the parties' nationalities, the subject of the dispute, the rules of arbitral procedure, or the applicable law. Eight European nations argued that the arbitral award should include a "non-domestic" concept to recognize awards other than those considered domestic "in the country in which they are relied upon." Eventually, the non-domestic concept was narrowed to apply only to the place where recognition and enforcement of the award is sought. The common law countries and certain Eastern European countries, however, were bound to the concept of a foreign award based on territory; thus, article I included both the territorial and non-domestic concepts of the foreign arbitral award.

Enforcement of the Award. The Convention's article III requires a Contracting State to recognize as binding an arbitral award under article I. The award must be enforced under the procedural rules of the territory where the award is relied upon, under the Convention's conditions, and the enforcement conditions must not be substantially more onerous than the conditions for enforcing a domestic award. A Contracting State may "declare that it will apply the Convention to the recognition and enforcement of awards made only in the territory of another Contracting State." The United States made such a reciprocity declaration.

The Arbitration Agreement. Article II addresses the arbitration agreement. Paragraph 1 of article II states as follows:

> Each Contracting State shall recognize an agreement in writing under which the parties undertake to submit to arbitration all or any differences which have arisen or which may arise between them in respect of a defined legal relationship, whether contractual or not, concerning a subject matter capable of settlement by arbitration.

A Contracting State can elect to apply the Convention only to differences arising out of commercial legal relationships. In acceding to the Convention, the United States adopted the commercial declaration. The "agreement in writing" under the Convention "shall include an arbitral clause in a contract or an arbitration agreement, signed by the parties or contained in an exchange of letters or telegrams." A court of a Contracting State, at a party's request, shall order arbitration "unless the agreement is null and void, inoperative or incapable of being performed." Notably, the Convention did not impose article 1's territorial or non-domestic restrictions on the agreement to arbitrate. Also, the Reciprocity Declaration arguably applies only to the arbitration award and not to the arbitration agreement.

Section 202 of the Convention Act. In the Convention Act, the Congress set forth in a single provision, section 202, a definition of both the arbitration agreement and the arbitration award enforceable under the Convention. Section 202 provides, in part, as follows:

> An arbitration agreement or arbitral award arising out of a legal relationship, whether contractual or not, which is considered as commercial, including a transaction, contract, or agreement described in section 2 of this title, falls under the Convention. An agreement or award arising out of such a relationship which is entirely between citizens of the United States shall be deemed not to fall under the Convention unless that relationship involves property located abroad, envisages performance or enforcement abroad, or has some other reasonable relation with one or more foreign states.

In simple terms, section 202 covers any commercial arbitration agreement or award "unless it is between two United States citizens, involves property located in the United States, and has no reasonable relationship with one or more foreign states." Relying on section 202, an arbitral award made in the United States under U.S. law when only one of the parties is domiciled or has its principal place of business outside of the United States has been enforced under the Convention. Section 202 covers an agreement to arbitrate between two non-U.S. citizens, even though the arbitration occurred in the United States. Similarly, courts have held that section 202 is the basis for confirming an award made in the United States involving two U.S. firms when the goods at issue were to be manufactured in the United States but distributed abroad.

The Convention Act and the Federal Courts. Three sections of the Convention Act attempt to steer claims involving the Convention into the federal courts. Section

201 provides that the Convention "shall be enforced in United States courts" in accordance with the Convention Act. Under section 203, an action or proceeding falling under the Convention "shall be deemed to arise under the laws and treaties of the United States." In contrast to the Domestic FAA, under the Convention Act, U.S. district courts have original jurisdiction over an action or proceeding falling under the Convention, regardless of the amount in controversy. Section 205 provides a liberal right to remove a case whose subject matter "relates to an arbitration or award falling under the Convention" from a state court to a U.S. district court. Unlike the general removal statute, removal under the Convention Act may occur "any time before the trial [of the action or proceeding]." Removal is to the U.S. district court for the district and division where the action or proceeding pends. The procedure for removal of causes of action otherwise provided by law applies, except the removal grounds need not appear on the complaint's face but need only be shown in the removal petition.

Venue of cases falling under section 203 rests in any court that would have venue "save for the arbitration agreement" or if the agreement designates a place of arbitration within the United States, then in the court for the district and division which embrace the arbitration site.

Authorization to Compel Arbitration. Section 206 of the Convention Act gives broad authority to the district court to compel arbitration. While the Domestic FAA authorizes a district court to order arbitration in the district where it sits, the district court can, under section 206, order parties to arbitrate under their agreement, which may be outside the United States. Furthermore, the district court can appoint arbitrators per the parties' agreement. But in spite of this, section 206 applies only if the arbitration agreement identifies a place for the arbitration. The district court cannot select an arbitral forum when the agreement to arbitrate fails to do so, nor can a court order the parties to arbitrate in a location they did not designate.

Recognition and Enforcement of an Arbitral Award. Additionally, as with the Domestic FAA, the Convention Act authorizes a district court to confirm an arbitration award. A party has three years after the making of an award to seek confirmation. The district court shall confirm the award unless it finds a ground for refusal or deferral of recognition or enforcement as provided in the Convention. Under article V(1) of the Convention, recognition and enforcement of an award "may be refused" if the party against whom it is invoked furnishes proof that:

(1) the parties to the agreement to arbitrate were under some incapacity under the law applicable to them or the agreement to arbitrate "is not valid under the law to which the parties subjected it or, failing any indication thereon, under the law of the country where the award was made;"

(2) "[t]he party against whom the award is invoked was not given proper notice of the appointment of the arbitrator or of the arbitration proceedings or was otherwise unable to present his case;"

(3) "[t]he award deals with a difference not contemplated by or not falling within the terms of the submission to arbitration, or it contains decisions on matters beyond the scope of the submission to arbitration;"

(4) "[t]he composition of the arbitral authority or the arbitral procedure was not in accordance with the agreement of the parties, or, failing such agreement, was not in accordance with the law of the country where the arbitration took place;" or

(5) "[t]he award has not yet become binding on the parties, or has been set aside or suspended by a competent authority of the country, in which, or under the law of which, that award was made."

[handwritten margin note: not binding]

A competent authority in a country where recognition and enforcement of the arbitral award is sought may also refuse recognition or enforcement if it finds (1) the subject matter is not capable of settlement by arbitration under the law of that country; or (2) recognition or enforcement would be contrary to the public policy of that country.

[handwritten margin note: 1. no SMJ 2. public policy]

Unlike the Domestic FAA, the Convention Act does not expressly authorize a U.S. court to vacate an arbitral award falling under the Convention. Instead, the Convention contemplates that a party can ask a competent authority in the country in which, or under the law of which, the award was made, to set aside or suspend the award. The Convention does not specify grounds for setting aside or suspending the award. The court under whose law the arbitration was conducted has been allowed to apply the law of its country to a motion to set aside or suspend the award.

Finally, article VII(1) provides that the Convention shall not "deprive any interest[ed] party of any right he may have to avail himself of an arbitral award in the manner and to the extent allowed by the law or the treaties of the country where such award is sought to be relied upon." The Convention Act, however, provides no express means of enforcing article VII(1) except through section 201, which recognizes that the Convention is to be enforced in U.S. courts in accordance with the Convention Act.

Now consider the following excerpt, which contains a model arbitration clause.

Jay M. Vogelson, Dispute Resolution, in Negotiating and Structuring International Commercial Transactions
pp. 116-118, 184-185l
(American Bar Association, Section of International Law and Practice, 1991)

ARBITRATION

11.1 DISPUTES

Any and all disputes, controversies, claims and differences arising out of or relating to this Agreement, or any breach thereof, which cannot be settled through correspondence and mutual consultation of the Parties hereto, shall be finally settled by arbitration in accordance with the · Rules of the · Association, in effect on the date of this Agreement, by one or more arbitrators selected in accordance with such rules. In the event of any conflict between these rules and the provisions of this Article, the provisions of this Article shall govern.

11.2 SELECTION OF ARBITRATORS

Upon the written demand of either of the Parties concerned, the Parties shall attempt to appoint a single arbitrator. If they are unable to agree within · days from such demand, then each of the Parties shall appoint one arbitrator and the two nominated shall in turn choose a third arbitrator. If within a period of · days after their nomination no third arbitrator has been nominated, then the third arbitrator shall be appointed by [name of arbitration association].

11.3 SITUS OF ARBITRATION

Arbitration proceedings shall be held in the City of · U.S.A., or such other place as the Parties may mutually agree. The decision of the arbitrator(s) shall be final and binding upon the Parties hereto, not subject to appeal and shall deal with the questions of costs of the arbitration and all matters related thereto. The proceedings, all pleadings, documents, correspondence and the Arbitration Award shall be written in English. Judgment upon the award or decision rendered by the arbitrator(s) may be entered in any court having jurisdiction thereof, or application may be made to such court for a judicial recognition of the Award or an order of enforcement thereof, as the case may be.

11.4 NEW YORK CONVENTION

The Parties acknowledge that this Agreement and any award rendered pursuant to it shall be governed by the 1958 United Nations Convention on the Recognition and Enforcement of Foreign Arbitral Awards.

11.5 ENFORCEABILITY

The Seller represents that an arbitration award reached pursuant to this Article with respect to any dispute, controversy, claim or difference arising out of or relating to this Agreement is enforceable under the laws of [Seller's country].

11.6 ENFORCEABILITY

The Buyer represents that an arbitration award reached pursuant to this Article with respect to any dispute, controversy, claim or difference arising out of or relating to this Agreement is enforceable under the laws of [Buyer's country].

A. The Arbitration Forum

Among the most important issues is the decision regarding the type of arbitration. Parties have a choice between institutional or *ad hoc* arbitration; each has its own characteristics.

The International Chamber of Commerce, the London Court of International Arbitration, and the American Arbitration Association are the most familiar institutional fora, but there are numerous other institutional bodies, most notably the Japan Commercial Arbitration Association, the Stockholm Chamber of Commerce, the Inter-America Commission of Commercial Arbitration, and the International Centre for the Settlement of Investment Disputes. The services of these institutions vary, but they include administration, procedural rules, technical expertise, arbitration experience, and support staff and facilities. *Ad hoc* arbitration is not under the auspices of any institution and requires the parties to agree to procedure rules and to furnish services normally provided by arbitration institutions. In terms of enforcement of an arbitration award, the Arbitration Convention recognizes the validity of both institutional and *ad hoc* arbitration.

The choice between institutional and *ad hoc* arbitration primarily depends on the type of contract involved, the preference of the parties, and the nature of potential disputes. Some firms prefer *ad hoc* arbitration because it is private and frequently is less expensive. The principal advantage of the selection of an institution is that it can provide administrative supervision under established rules, and awards rendered have the imprimatur of an internationally acknowledged institution.

If the parties select *ad hoc* arbitration, they must select the mechanism for appointing the arbitrators and the procedure rules. The parties are free to jointly designate a single arbitrator or a panel of arbitrators, or to agree on the procedure for appointing arbitrators when a dispute arises.

When *ad hoc* arbitration is chosen, it is particularly important to designate the procedural rules which will govern the proceeding. The Arbitration Rules of the United Nations Commission on International Trade Law (UNCITRAL) are readily accepted by parties to *ad hoc* arbitration. It should be noted, however, that parties can select the procedure rules of an institutional arbitration body.

Should the parties prefer institutional arbitration, the selection of the institution is important. Each institution has advantages and disadvantages. These may include cost, location, procedure rule limitations, case administration efficiency, and familiarity with the parties and subject matter of the transaction.

B. Scope of Arbitration

The parties need to consider whether they wish to arbitrate all disputes or only certain disputes. Commercial agreements generally include provisions indicating a preference to submit all disputes to binding arbitration, but that is not required. There has been a great deal of litigation over the "scope" clauses in arbitration agreements and consequently it is important to focus clearly on the explicit language used.

There are certain key expressions, such as "all disputes", "in connection with", and "finally settled." Courts have found these expressions to be pivotal in deciding the scope of arbitration clauses. The purpose of a global, final award provision is to ensure that every conceivable dispute arising out of or in connection with the contract will be settled exclusively by arbitration, and that the award rendered by the arbitrators will be final and enforceable.

It also is useful to consider the possible need for ancillary relief, such as a temporary restraining order to prevent disposition of property or to prevent unlawful conduct pending the arbitration decision. Laws and arbitration rules vary on this subject. For this reason, parties should consider authorizing arbitrators to grant judicially enforceable preliminary relief.

C. Law Applicable to Merits and to Proceeding

In addition to the governing law provision applicable to the contract's interpretation, it is important for the arbitration clause itself to designate the law applicable to the arbitration. There are a host of legal issues which may arise with respect to the interpretation of the arbitration clause, including procedural as well as substantive law issues. If this choice of law clause is not included, then the most likely result will be that the law applicable to arbitration proceedings in the place of arbitration will be applied.

In addition to or instead of the designated governing law on the merits of the dispute, the parties may empower the arbitrators to act as *amiable compositeurs*, that is, authorizing them to decide the dispute on the basis of equity and without necessary reference to any law. This authority is occasionally useful when there are long term contracts and Parties wish arbitrators to fill in contract gaps or renegotiate contract provisions.

D. Place of Arbitration

The choice of law is a matter also tied to the locale selected for arbitration and the choice of arbitrators. The locale should be a place convenient for the parties where sources of the applicable law are readily available. Although not mandatory, it is preferable for the place of arbitration to be in a country which is a party to the Arbitration Convention, in order to facilitate enforcement.

There are some countries where the local law does not favor the ouster of the jurisdiction of courts. For instance, some Middle Eastern countries require supervision of arbitration by the judicial system. In other countries, the complete ouster of court jurisdiction in favor of exclusive arbitration settlement depends upon the execution by the parties of specific waivers. As a consequence, the situs of the arbitration should be where local law will not interfere with the exclusivity of the arbitration process.

E. Other Considerations

There is a decided lack of harmony on relief issues, such as the currency in which an award will be rendered and enforced; whether prejudgment and post judgment interest will be allowed and, if allowed, on what basis and what rate of interest; and costs, including the cost of arbitration, the cost of enforcement procedures, and attorney's fees. These matters should be settled by the arbitration clause.

Finally, special consideration needs to be given where a state, a state agency, or other sovereign entity is a party to the contract. The Foreign Sovereign Immunities Act, 28 U.S.C. §§1602-1611 (1976) provides for immunity from suits under various circumstances. This sovereign immunity, where applicable, prevents judicial enforcement of an arbitration award just as it inhibits the institution of suits against a foreign sovereign. In order to avoid entanglements, the arbitration clause should include a specific, irrevocable waiver of immunity as to the subject matter of the transaction.

NOTES AND QUESTIONS

1. Careful consideration should go into the drafting of the arbitration clause. We only highlight a few of the more obvious matters. First, what is the desired scope of the arbitration—what kinds of disputes will be submitted to arbitration? Are some matters to be excluded? Do the parties wish to try ADR as a first option?

Do the parties wish to choose pre-existing arbitration rules of an arbitral institution or do they want to fashion their own procedures? A checklist of considerations may include the following:

- Broad or narrow clause?
- Location
- Language
- Notice provisions
- Substantive law
- Rules of evidence and extent of discovery
- Arbitrators
- Procedures
- Confidentiality
- Consolidation of claims
- Interim measures
- Waiver of sovereign immunity
- Currency
- Costs and interest
- Finality

2. The choice of law is obviously important. If the parties fail to make a choice, the arbitrator may follow the law of the forum country or may use applicable conflicts of law principles to choose the law. The latter is the solution mandated by the Rome Convention (Article 13) and the UNCITRAL rules (Article 33.1).

3. As for arbitral forums and procedures, parties generally prefer to go to institutions such as the International Chamber of Commerce and the American Arbitration Association. Why? In arbitration, parties may choose a national law, but they may also choose to apply the *lex mercatoria* (law merchant). Another option is to choose "justice and fairness" (*ex aequo et bono*). Why may these options be desirable in a particular case? Consider the following comment.

Andreas F. Lowenfeld, Lex Mercatoria: An Arbitrator's View
6 Arb. Int'l 133, 137-140 (1990)

My own view of *lex mercatoria* is somewhat different from those both of its critics and of its proponents, though closer to the latter. It may be useful to begin with some illustrations and then attempt to resume the doctrinal debate.

First, Professor Lando gives the illustration of the Danish seller who has sold goods to a German buyer but delivered them after the last date specified. Under Article 27 of the Scandinavian Sale of Goods Act as in force in Denmark, a buyer who seeks to make a claim arising out of late delivery must give notice immediately on arrival of the goods. No such rule applies in German or (so far as appears) in other nations. An arbitral tribunal faced with a claim based on late delivery and no law designated in the contract should not devote its energies to the question of whether seller's law (Danish) or buyer's law (German) applies to the controversy: The Scandinavian rule is an internal one, not fit for international sales. Whether Danish or German law applies to other aspects of the contract, the German buyer should not be defeated by failure to give immediate notice, as long as he has complied with the general commercial rule requiring notice within a reasonable period of time. Use of *lex mercatoria* yields the correct solution: the German buyer prevails.

Secondly, a similar case, in which I served as one of the arbitrators, may serve further to illustrate the uses of *lex mercatoria*. A French company [, the claimant,] asserted that it had entered into a contract with an Austrian company for the long-term supply of a commodity produced in a developing country. There had been no performance, but the Austrian company, the respondent, maintained that the contract had not been validly concluded, and that even if it had been, the formalities required to constitute a valid agreement to arbitrate had not been complied with. The document stated that it was to be governed by New York law, and that any disputes that could not be resolved by negotiation were to be submitted to arbitration in Geneva under the rules of the ICC.

[T]he dispute in its preliminary phase — long before issues, such as excuse for non-performance, interpretation of the obligations undertaken, or duty to mitigate damages were addressed — could be governed by the law of three different states: New York, Austria and Switzerland, plus the conflict of laws rules of Switzerland or New York and a question of interpretation of the Austrian law.

As it happened, I do not know whether by coincidence or by design, two of the arbitrators were experts in conflict of laws, and we managed to find our way to what I believe was a principled and technically correct solution. I cannot be certain, however, whether we decided first on the solution and then found a way to achieve it, or whether we set out on a truly unguided journey and ended up with the right result. It is fair to add that the arbitrators had heard testimony and had studied the prior relations of the parties, so that they had some feeling for the transaction beyond the abstract contract and conflict of laws issues they were required to decide.

My feeling is that wholly neutral principles of conflict of laws are an illusion, but that an understanding of reasonable behavior and expectations of major commercial enterprises can be defined with a fair degree of precision, focusing on such issues as the customs of the particular trade, justified expectations of the parties in the light of the prior and current communications between them, the obligation of good faith dealings, and evidence of reliance. Of course these concepts are not precise, but they are everywhere the stuff of contracts, the kinds of issues on which arbitrators, and judges, are competent to pass. The suggestion is that whether or not the two parties before the tribunal had concluded a contract could and probably should have been decided by reference to *lex mercatoria*, rather than by elaborate exercises in comparative conflict of laws.

B. Enforcing the Agreement to Arbitrate

PROBLEM 8-6

Jones works for New Age Products, Inc., a California subsidiary of a People's Republic of China state-owned enterprise in the fiber-optics industry. As a senior executive, Jones spends six months of the year in Beijing and the remainder of the year in San Francisco. When Jones was recruited by New Age, Jones was delighted by the opportunity and signed the standard, nonnegotiable employment contract used by New Age, which provided for settlement of all employment-related claims by arbitration in Beijing. When passed over for a promotion, Jones files a claim in the federal district court for the Northern District of California under Title VII, claiming discrimination on the basis of sex, age, and race. New Age moves to dismiss the claim on the basis of the forum selection clause, arguing that the Title VII claim should be resolved by arbitration in Beijing. In opposing the motion to dismiss, Jones argues that (1) the vital interests of the United States as embodied in Title VII cannot be fully vindicated if the case is decided by a panel of private arbitrators in China and (2) Title VII and the federal antidiscrimination laws that are part of the basic democratic system of the United States are profoundly inconsistent with China's communist system and authoritarian state, which does not give adequate recognition to individual freedom and protection against invidious discrimination. What is the result? Consult *Mitsubishi* below.

Mitsubishi Motors Corp. v. Soler Chrysler-Plymouth, Inc.
United States Supreme Court, 1985
473 U.S. 614, 105 S. Ct. 3346, 87 L. Ed. 2d 444

JUSTICE BLACKMUN delivered the opinion of the Court.

The principal question presented by these cases is the arbitrability, pursuant to the Federal Arbitration Act, and the Convention on the Recognition and Enforcement of Foreign Arbitral Awards (Convention), of claims arising under the Sherman Act, 15 U.S.C. §1 *et seq.*, and encompassed within a valid arbitration clause in an agreement embodying an international commercial transaction.

I

Petitioner–cross-respondent Mitsubishi Motors Corporation (Mitsubishi) is a Japanese corporation which manufactures automobiles and has its principal place of business in Tokyo, Japan. Mitsubishi is the product of a joint venture between Chrysler International, S.A. (CISA), a Swiss corporation registered in Geneva and wholly owned by Chrysler Corporation, and Mitsubishi Heavy Industries, Inc., a Japanese corporation. The aim of the joint venture was the distribution through Chrysler dealers outside the continental United States of vehicles manufactured by Mitsubishi and bearing Chrysler and Mitsubishi trademarks. Respondent–cross-petitioner Soler Chrysler-Plymouth, Inc. (Soler), is a Puerto Rico corporation with its principal place of business in Pueblo Viejo, Guaynabo, Puerto Rico.

On October 31, 1979, Soler entered into a Distributor Agreement with CISA which provided for the sale by Soler of Mitsubishi-manufactured vehicles within a designated area, including metropolitan San Juan. On the same date, CISA, Soler, and Mitsubishi entered into a Sales Procedure Agreement (Sales Agreement) which, referring to the Distributor Agreement, provided for the direct sale of Mitsubishi products to Soler and governed the terms and conditions of such sales. Paragraph VI of the Sales Agreement, labeled "Arbitration of Certain Matters," provides:

"All disputes, controversies or differences which may arise between [Mitsubishi] and [Soler] out of or in relation to Articles I-B through V of this Agreement or for the breach thereof, shall be finally settled by arbitration in Japan in accordance with the rules and regulations of the Japan Commercial Arbitration Association."

Initially, Soler did a brisk business in Mitsubishi-manufactured vehicles. In early 1981, however, the new-car market slackened. Soler ran into serious difficulties in meeting the expected sales volume, and by the spring of 1981 it felt itself compelled to request that Mitsubishi delay or cancel shipment of several orders. About the same time, Soler attempted to arrange for the transshipment of a quantity of its vehicles for sale in the continental United States and Latin America. Mitsubishi and CISA, however, refused permission for any such diversion, citing a variety of reasons, and no vehicles were transshipped. Attempts to work out these difficulties failed. Mitsubishi eventually withheld shipment of 966 vehicles.

The following month, Mitsubishi brought an action against Soler in the United States District Court for the District of Puerto Rico under the Federal Arbitration Act and the Convention.[3] Mitsubishi sought an order, pursuant to 9 U.S.C. §§4 and 201, to compel arbitration in accord with VI of the Sales Agreement. Shortly after filing the complaint, Mitsubishi filed a request for arbitration before the Japan Commercial Arbitration Association.

Soler denied the allegations and counterclaimed against both Mitsubishi and CISA. It alleged numerous breaches by Mitsubishi of the Sales Agreement, raised a pair of defamation claims, and asserted causes of action under the Sherman Act, 15 U.S.C. §1 *et seq.;* the federal Automobile Dealers' Day in Court Act, 70 Stat. 1125, 15 U.S.C. §1221 *et seq.;* the Puerto Rico competition statute, P.R. Laws Ann., Tit. 10, §257 *et seq.* (1976); and the Puerto Rico Dealers' Contracts Act, P.R. Laws Ann., Tit. 10, §278 *et seq.* (1978 and Supp. 1983). In the counterclaim premised on the Sherman Act, Soler alleged that Mitsubishi and CISA had conspired to divide markets in restraint of trade. To effectuate the plan, according to Soler, Mitsubishi had refused to permit Soler to resell to buyers in North, Central, or South America vehicles it had obligated itself to purchase from Mitsubishi; had refused to ship ordered vehicles or the parts, such as heaters and defoggers, that would be necessary to permit Soler to make its vehicles suitable for resale outside Puerto Rico; and had coercively attempted to replace Soler and its other Puerto Rico distributors with a wholly owned subsidiary which would serve as the exclusive Mitsubishi distributor in Puerto Rico.

After a hearing, the District Court ordered Mitsubishi and Soler to arbitrate each of the issues raised in the complaint and in all the counterclaims save two and a portion of a third. With regard to the federal antitrust issues, it recognized that the Courts of Appeals, following *American Safety Equipment Corp. v. J.P. Maguire & Co.,* 391 F.2d 821 (C.A.2 1968), uniformly had held that the rights conferred by the antitrust laws were "'of a character inappropriate for enforcement by arbitration,'" quoting *Wilko v. Swan,* 201 F.2d 439, 444 (C.A.2 1953), rev'd, 346 U.S. 427, 74 S. Ct. 182, 98 L. Ed. 168 (1953). The District Court held, however, that the international character of the Mitsubishi-Soler undertaking required

_____

3. The complaint alleged that Soler had failed to pay for 966 ordered vehicles; that it had failed to pay contractual "distress unit penalties," intended to reimburse Mitsubishi for storage costs and interest charges incurred because of Soler's failure to take shipment of ordered vehicles; that Soler's failure to fulfill warranty obligations threatened Mitsubishi's reputation and goodwill; that Soler had failed to obtain required financing; and that the Distributor and Sales Agreements had expired by their terms or, alternatively, that Soler had surrendered its rights under the Sales Agreement.

enforcement of the agreement to arbitrate even as to the antitrust claims. It relied on *Scherk v. Alberto-Culver Co.*, 417 U.S. 506, 515-520, 94 S. Ct. 2449, 2455-2458, 41 L. Ed. 2d 270 (1974), in which this Court ordered arbitration, pursuant to a provision embodied in an international agreement, of a claim arising under the Securities Exchange Act of 1934 notwithstanding its assumption, *arguendo,* that *Wilko, supra,* which held nonarbitrable claims arising under the Securities Act of 1933, also would bar arbitration of a 1934 Act claim arising in a domestic context.

[A]fter endorsing the doctrine of *American Safety,* precluding arbitration of antitrust claims, the Court of Appeals concluded that neither this Court's decision in *Scherk* nor the Convention required abandonment of that doctrine in the face of an international transaction. Accordingly, it reversed the judgment of the District Court insofar as it had ordered submission of "Soler's antitrust claims" to arbitration. Affirming the remainder of the judgment, the court directed the District Court to consider in the first instance how the parallel judicial and arbitral proceedings should go forward.

II

At the outset, we address the contention raised in Soler's cross petition that the arbitration clause at issue may not be read to encompass the statutory counterclaims stated in its answer to the complaint. Soler reasons that, because it falls within the class for whose benefit the federal and local antitrust laws and dealers' Acts were passed, but the arbitration clause at issue does not mention these statutes or statutes in general, the clause cannot be read to contemplate arbitration of these statutory claims.

We do not agree, for we find no warrant in the Arbitration Act for implying in every contract within its ken a presumption against arbitration of statutory claims. The Act's centerpiece provision makes a written agreement to arbitrate "in any maritime transaction or a contract evidencing a transaction involving commerce . . . valid, irrevocable, and enforceable, save upon such grounds as exist at law or in equity for the revocation of any contract." 9 U.S.C. §2.

Accordingly, the first task of a court asked to compel arbitration of a dispute is to determine whether the parties agreed to arbitrate that dispute. The court is to make this determination by applying the "federal substantive law of arbitrability, applicable to any arbitration agreement within the coverage of the Act." *Moses H. Cone Memorial Hospital*, 460 U.S., at 24. And that body of law counsels

> "that questions of arbitrability must be addressed with a healthy regard for the federal policy favoring arbitration. . . . The Arbitration Act establishes that, as a matter of federal law, any doubts concerning the scope of arbitrable issues should be resolved in favor of arbitration, whether the problem at hand is the construction of the contract language itself or an allegation of waiver, delay, or a like defense to arbitrability." *Moses H. Cone Memorial Hospital*, 460 U.S., at 24-25.

There is no reason to depart from these guidelines where a party bound by an arbitration agreement raises claims founded on statutory rights. Some time ago this Court expressed "hope for [the Act's] usefulness both in controversies based on statutes or on standards otherwise created," *Wilko v. Swan,* and we are well past the time when judicial suspicion of the desirability of arbitration and of the competence of arbitral tribunals inhibited the development of arbitration as an alternative means of dispute resolution. Of course, courts should remain attuned to well supported claims that the agreement to arbitrate resulted from the sort of fraud or overwhelming economic power that would provide grounds "for the revocation of any contract." 9 U.S.C. §2. But, absent such compelling considerations, the Act itself provides no basis for disfavoring agreements to arbitrate statutory claims by skewing the otherwise hospitable inquiry into arbitrability.

That is not to say that all controversies implicating statutory rights are suitable for arbitration. Just as it is the congressional policy manifested in the Federal Arbitration Act that requires courts liberally to construe the scope of arbitration agreements covered by that Act, it is the congressional intention expressed in some other statute on which the courts must rely to identify any category of claims as to which agreements to arbitrate will be held unenforceable. For that reason, Soler's concern for statutorily protected classes provides no reason to color the lens through which the arbitration clause is read. By agreeing to arbitrate a statutory claim, a party does not forgo the substantive rights afforded by the statute; it only submits to their resolution in an arbitral, rather than a judicial, forum. It trades the procedures and opportunity for review of the courtroom for the simplicity, informality, and expedition of arbitration. We must assume that if Congress intended the substantive protection afforded by a given statute to include protection against waiver of the right to a judicial forum, that intention will be deducible from text or legislative history.

In sum, the Court of Appeals correctly conducted a two-step inquiry, first determining whether the parties' agreement to arbitrate reached the statutory issues, and then, upon finding it did, considering whether legal constraints external to the parties' agreement foreclosed the arbitration of those claims.

III

We now turn to consider whether Soler's antitrust claims are nonarbitrable even though it has agreed to arbitrate them. In holding that they are not [arbitrable], the Court of Appeals followed the decision of the Second Circuit in *American Safety Equipment Corp. v. J.P. Maguire & Co.*, 391 F.2d 821 (1968).

At the outset, we confess to some skepticism of certain aspects of the *American Safety* doctrine. As distilled by the First Circuit, the doctrine comprises four ingredients. First, private parties play a pivotal role in aiding governmental enforcement of the antitrust laws by means of the private action for treble damages. Second, "the strong possibility that contracts which generate antitrust disputes may be contracts of adhesion militates against automatic forum determination by contract." Third, antitrust issues, prone to complication, require sophisticated legal and economic analysis, and thus are "ill-adapted to strengths of the arbitral process, *i.e.*, expedition, minimal requirements of written rationale, simplicity, resort to basic concepts of common sense and simple equity." Finally, just as "issues of war and peace are too important to be vested in the generals, . . . decisions as to antitrust regulation of business are too important to be lodged in arbitrators chosen from the business community—particularly those from a foreign community that has had no experience with or exposure to our law and values." See *American Safety*, 391 F.2d, at 826-827.

Initially, we find the second concern unjustified. A party resisting arbitration of course may attack directly the validity of the agreement to arbitrate. Moreover, the party may attempt to make a showing that would warrant setting aside the forum-selection clause — that the agreement was "[a]ffected by fraud, undue influence, or overweening bargaining power"; that "enforcement would be unreasonable and unjust"; or that proceedings "in the contractual forum will be so gravely difficult and inconvenient that [the resisting party] will for all practical purposes be deprived of his day in court." *The Bremen*. But absent such a showing — and none was attempted here — there is no basis for assuming the forum inadequate or its selection unfair.

Next, potential complexity should not suffice to ward off arbitration. In any event, adaptability and access to expertise are hallmarks of arbitration. The anticipated subject matter of the dispute may be taken into account when the arbitrators are appointed, and arbitral rules typically provide for the participation of experts either employed by the parties or appointed by the tribunal. Moreover, it is often a judgment that streamlined proceedings and expeditious results will best serve their needs that causes parties to agree to arbitrate their disputes; it is typically a desire to keep the effort and expense required to resolve a dispute within manageable bounds that prompts them mutually to forgo access to judicial remedies.

For similar reasons, we also reject the proposition that an arbitration panel will pose too great a danger of innate hostility to the constraints on business conduct that antitrust law imposes. International arbitrators frequently are drawn from the legal as well as the business community; where the dispute has an important legal component, the parties and the arbitral body with whose assistance they have agreed to settle their dispute can be expected to select arbitrators accordingly. We decline to indulge the presumption that the parties and arbitral body conducting a proceeding will be unable or unwilling to retain competent, conscientious, and impartial arbitrators.

We are left, then, with the core of the *American Safety* doctrine — the fundamental importance to American democratic capitalism of the regime of the antitrust laws. Without doubt, the private cause of action plays a central role in enforcing this regime. The importance of the private damages remedy, however, does not compel the conclusion that it may not be sought outside an American court.

There is no reason to assume at the outset of the dispute that international arbitration will not provide an adequate mechanism. To be sure, the international arbitral tribunal owes no prior allegiance to the legal norms of particular states; hence, it has no direct obligation to vindicate their statutory dictates. The tribunal, however, is bound to effectuate the intentions of the parties. Where the parties have agreed that the arbitral body is to decide a defined set of claims which includes, as in these cases, those arising from the application of American antitrust law, the tribunal therefore should be bound to decide that dispute in accord with the national law giving rise to the claim. And so long as the prospective litigant effectively may vindicate its statutory cause of action in the arbitral forum, the statute will continue to serve both its remedial and deterrent function.

Having permitted the arbitration to go forward, the national courts of the United States will have the opportunity at the award-enforcement stage to ensure that the legitimate interest in the enforcement of the antitrust laws has been addressed. The Convention reserves to each signatory country the right to refuse enforcement of an award where the "recognition or enforcement of the award would be contrary to the public policy of that country." Art. V(2)(b); see *Scherk, supra* n. 14. While the efficacy of the arbitral process requires that substantive review at the award-enforcement stage remain minimal, it would not require intrusive inquiry to ascertain that the tribunal took cognizance of the antitrust claims and actually decided them.

As international trade has expanded in recent decades, so too has the use of international arbitration to resolve disputes arising in the course of that trade. The controversies that international arbitral institutions are called upon to resolve have increased in diversity as well as in complexity. Yet the potential of these tribunals for efficient disposition of legal disagreements arising from commercial relations has not yet been tested. If they are to take a central place in the international legal order, national courts will need to "shake off the old judicial hostility to arbitration," *Kulukundis Shipping Co. v. Amtorg Trading Corp.*, 126 F.2d 978, 985 (C.A.2 1942), and also their customary and understandable unwillingness to cede jurisdiction of a claim arising under domestic law to a foreign or transnational tribunal. To this extent, at least, it will be necessary for national courts to subordinate domestic notions of arbitrability to the international policy favoring commercial arbitration.

Accordingly, we "require this representative of the American business community to honor its bargain," *Alberto-Culver Co. v. Scherk*, 484 F.2d 611, 620 (C.A.7 1973) (Stevens, J., dissenting), by holding this agreement to arbitrate "enforce[able] . . . in accord with the explicit provisions of the Arbitration Act."

The judgment of the Court of Appeals is affirmed in part and reversed in part, and the cases are remanded for further proceedings consistent with this opinion.

It is so ordered.

JUSTICE POWELL took no part in the decision of these cases.

JUSTICE STEVENS, with whom JUSTICE BRENNAN joins, and with whom JUSTICE MARSHALL joins except as to Part II, dissenting.

The Court assumes for the purposes of its decision that the antitrust issues would not be arbitrable if this were a purely domestic dispute, but holds that the international character of the controversy makes it arbitrable. The holding rests on vague concerns for the international implications of its decision and a misguided application of *Scherk v. Alberto-Culver Co.* The *Scherk* case was an action for damages brought by an American purchaser of three European businesses in which it was claimed that the seller's fraudulent representations concerning the status of certain European trademarks constituted a violation of §10(b) of the Securities Exchange Act of 1934. The Court based its decision on the distinction that the outcome in *Wilko* was governed entirely by American law whereas in *Scherk* foreign rules of law would control and, if the arbitration clause were not enforced, a host of international conflict of laws problems would arise.

[I]n *Scherk*, the Court distinguished *Wilko* because in that case "no credible claim could have been entertained that any international conflict-of-laws problems would arise." That distinction fits this case precisely, since I consider it perfectly clear that the rules of American antitrust law must govern the claim of an American automobile dealer that he has been injured by an international conspiracy to restrain trade in the American automobile market. For that reason, it is especially distressing to find that the Court is unable to perceive why the reasoning in *Scherk* is wholly inapplicable to Soler's antitrust claims against Chrysler and Mitsubishi. The merits of those claims are controlled entirely by American law.

The federal claim that was asserted in *Scherk*, unlike Soler's antitrust claim, had not been expressly authorized by Congress. Indeed, the federal cause of action asserted by *Scherk* would not have been entertained in a number of Federal Circuits because it did not involve the kind of securities transaction that Congress intended to regulate when it enacted the Securities Exchange Act of 1934. The fraud claimed in *Scherk* was virtually identical to the breach of warranty claim; arbitration of such claims arising out of an agreement between parties of equal bargaining strength does not conflict with any significant federal policy.

In contrast, Soler's claim not only implicates our fundamental antitrust policies, but also should be evaluated in the light of an explicit congressional finding concerning the disparity in bargaining power between automobile manufacturers and their franchised dealers. In 1956, when Congress enacted special legislation to protect dealers from bad faith franchise terminations,[4] it recited its intent "to balance the power now heavily weighted in favor of automobile manufacturers." 70 Stat. 1125.

In my opinion, the elected representatives of the American people would not have us dispatch an American citizen to a foreign land in search of an uncertain remedy for the violation of a public right that is protected by the Sherman Act.

NOTES AND QUESTIONS

1. After the *Mitsubishi* case, agreements to arbitrate are routinely enforced in U.S. courts. Will it be possible to avoid enforcement by making a public law claim? If not, is this good policy?

2. A refusal to compel arbitration by a lower court is appealable. *See* 9 U.S.C. §8.

3. There is a split of authority whether pre-award attachment can be ordered by a court. Compare *I.T.A.D. Associates, Inc. v. Podar Bros.*, 636 F.2d 75 (4th Cir. 1981) (no), with *Carolina Power & Light Co. v. Uranex*, 451 F. Supp. 1044 (N.D. Cal. 1977) (yes). What is the proper answer? Is this a reason for covering the matter of provisional measures in the arbitration clause?

C.   Judicial Review and Enforcement of the Award

PROBLEM 8-7

A U.S. seller/shipper asks a shipping office in Louisiana to arrange a charter party with the M/V Liberty, a vessel owned by a New Orleans corporation, for the transport of goods to Marseilles, where the U.S. buyer/distributor will display them at a trade fair. The contract of carriage contains a clause providing for arbitration of all disputes at the International Chamber of Commerce in Paris, but as the parties were in haste the seller/shipper never reads or signs the contract. The shipper then delivers the goods to the M/V Liberty in exchange for a bill of lading,

---

4. Automobile Dealer's Day in Court Act, 15 U.S.C. §§1221-1225.

which contains a standard provision printed on the back of the form stating, "All provisions of the contract of carriage, if any, are hereby incorporated in this agreement." After a dispute later arises between the shipper and the carrier over damage to the cargo, the carrier files for arbitration in Paris and obtains an arbitral award declaring that it is not liable to the shipper for damage. The shipper does not appear in Paris. Later, the shipper files an action in federal district court in New Orleans against the carrier for damage to the cargo but the carrier asserts the Paris arbitral judgment as collateral estoppel on the issue of liability. The carrier argues that the award is entitled to recognition in the court under Chapter 2 of the Federal Arbitration Act implementing the New York Convention. The shipper argues the arbitral award is not entitled to recognition under the convention because there was never a written agreement between the parties to arbitrate and because no international parties were involved. France and the United States are parties to the New York Convention. What is the result? *See Polytek* below.

PROBLEM 8-8

Pursuant to an arbitration agreement, DeLuxe, a British company, sought an arbitration before the International Chamber of Commerce in Paris against Beijing Chemicals Factory (BCF), a Chinese company, for breach of a joint venture agreement to manufacture and sell laundry detergent in China. DeLuxe won an award from the arbitration panel in Paris and then brought an action against BCF in a federal district court under the Federal Arbitration Act to confirm the arbitral award. BCF moves to dismiss the action on the ground that the proper procedure is for Deluxe to first confirm the arbitral award in a French court in Paris, the place of arbitration, and then to seek to enforce the judicial order confirming the award against BCF in France, the United Kingdom, or China. However, as the United States has no connection to the arbitration, the federal district court has no subject matter jurisdiction over the action to confirm the arbitral award. What is the result? Are there any other jurisdictional issues? The United Kingdom, France, China, and the United States are all parties to the New York Convention. *See Glencore* below.

Polytek Engineering Co., Ltd. v. Jacobson Companies
United States District Court, Minnesota, 1997
984 F. Supp. 1238

ROSENBAUM, District Judge.

Plaintiff, Polytek Engineering Co., Ltd. ("Polytek"), asks this Court to confirm a $1,700,367.41 foreign arbitral award granted in its favor, pursuant to Article III of the Convention on the Recognition and Enforcement of Foreign Arbitral Awards and 9 U.S.C. §§201-208. The award was issued on May 26, 1997, by an arbitration panel of the Chinese International Economic and Trade Arbitration Commission ("CIETAC"). The arbitral award was rendered against defendant Jacobson, Inc. ("Jacobson") on a finding that Jacobson breached its contract with Polytek. The Court heard oral argument on October 3, 1997.

I. BACKGROUND

Polytek Engineering Co., Ltd., is a Hong Kong organized corporation with its principal place of business in Hong Kong. Defendant Jacobson, Inc., is a Minnesota corporation with its principal place of business in this state. For the purposes of this motion, the parties agree that Jacobson has never had staff, property, assets, or personnel outside of the United States.

In 1992, Polytek began negotiating with Hebei Import & Export Corp. ("Hebei"), based in the People's Republic of China, to sell rubber recycling equipment for a factory in China's Hebei Province. In November 1992, Polytek contacted Jacobson, a manufacturer of this type of equipment. After this initial contact, however, Polytek and Jacobson forestalled entry into a formal purchase agreement until Polytek concluded its contract with Hebei. In April 1993, Polytek entered into a contract with Hebei to sell the equipment (the "Hebei Contract"). Polytek then turned to Jacobson to obtain the equipment needed to satisfy the Hebei Contract.

To begin its purchase of the rubber recycling equipment, Polytek sent a one-page U.S. $865,000 equipment Purchase Order to Jacobson, dated May 10, 1993. The Purchase Order requested:

> One Set — Rubber Recycling Equipment including spare parts for two years; special tools; commissioning and training charges. For detail specification and terms, please refer to the attached contract.

The Purchase Order contained a section titled "Remarks," which provided that: "All the terms and conditions should conform with the main contract attached." Attached to the Purchase Order was a copy of the Hebei Contract.

Section 19 of the Hebei Contract contained the following arbitration clause:

> All disputes in connection with this contract or the execution thereof shall be settled through friendly negotiations. In case no settlement can be reached through negotiations, the case should then be submitted for arbitration to the Arbitration Commission of the China Council of the Promotion of International Trade[5] in accordance with the rules and procedures promulgated by the said Arbitration Commission. The arbitration shall take place in Beijing, China and the decision of the Arbitration Commission shall be final and binding upon both parties; neither party shall seek recourse to a law court or other authorities to appeal for revision of the decision. The arbitration fee shall be borne by the losing party.

(Polytek Pet., Exh. A).

Subsequent to Polytek's submission of the May 10, 1993, Purchase Order, Polytek and Jacobson discussed the irrevocable letter of guarantee or standby letter of credit, as required by the Hebei Contract. The parties agreed Jacobson would provide a standby letter of credit to Polytek, and Polytek would send Jacobson a deposit. Based upon its agreement with Polytek, Jacobson manufactured and shipped the recycling equipment to China and received payment from Polytek as specified in the Purchase Order.

---

5. Now known as the Chinese International Economic and Trade Arbitration Commission.

In May 1995, Hebei claimed the Jacobson equipment failed to conform to contract specifications, and began a CIETAC arbitration proceeding against Polytek, its seller. On March 29, 1996, the arbitration tribunal awarded Hebei a total of U.S. $1,266,933.85 and 4,762,132.56 RMB, and ordered Polytek to collect the equipment at its cost.

Thereafter, on April 3, 1996, Polytek began its own CIETAC arbitration against Jacobson in Beijing, China, claiming Jacobson breached the Hebei Contract attached to the May 10, 1993, Purchase Order. Polytek claimed Jacobson supplied equipment which did not conform to contract specifications. Jacobson initially ignored the notice given by CIETAC, but ultimately replied to the Chinese arbitral forum in November 1996. Jacobson's reply denied CIETAC's jurisdiction over the matter and the existence of any arbitration agreement between Polytek and Jacobson. CIETAC considered the issue of jurisdiction prior to examining the case on the merits, and, on December 23, 1996, CIETAC issued a decision finding jurisdiction was proper.

Upon rendering its decision, CIETAC wrote to both parties advising them it would hear the trade dispute on March 17, 1997. Jacobson did not appear at the hearing. CIETAC then notified Jacobson that the hearing had taken place and requested objections or further responses by April 20, 1997. CIETAC received nothing from Jacobson. CIETAC issued its decision on May 26, 1997, awarding Polytek U.S. $1,700,367.41, and ordering Jacobson to dismantle and collect the recycling equipment at its own expense.

II. DISCUSSION

A. THE CONVENTION

Chapter 2 of the Federal Arbitration Act grants federal courts the power to affirm foreign arbitral awards. This Chapter enables the Convention on the Recognition and Enforcement of Foreign Arbitral Awards ("Convention"), to which the United States is a signatory. *See* 9 U.S.C. §201. A court must "confirm the award unless it finds one of the grounds for refusal or deferral of recognition or enforcement of the award specified in the . . . Convention." 9 U.S.C. §207.

The Convention compels a court to conduct the following limited, four-part inquiry when deciding whether to confirm an award:

1. Is there an agreement in writing to arbitrate the subject of the dispute?
2. Does the agreement provide for arbitration in the territory of the signatory of the Convention?
3. Does the agreement arise out of a legal relationship whether contractual or not, which is considered as commercial?
4. Is a party to the agreement not an American citizen, or does the commercial relationship have some reasonable relation with one or more foreign states?

The Court does not consider the last three of these questions to be in serious dispute. The answer to the second question is simple: If the Hebei Contract is part of the Polytek/Jacobson agreement, there is a contract to arbitrate. And if the

Hebei Contract is part of the agreement, it provides for arbitration in China, a signatory to the Convention. *See* 9 U.S.C. §201.

The third question asks whether some form of contract or legal contractual relationship existed between Polytek and Jacobson. Both Polytek and Jacobson stipulated in their pleadings that theirs was a legal and contractual relationship. The parties do not deny the commercial nature of the transaction.

As to the fourth question, Polytek is certainly one of the parties to the agreement. It is not an American corporation, and its commercial relationship with Jacobson relates to China, a foreign country. The fourth question is satisfied.

It is the first question — "Is there an agreement in writing to arbitrate the subject of the dispute?" — to which the Court now turns.

B. AN AGREEMENT IN WRITING TO ARBITRATE

The Convention defines an agreement in writing as an "arbitral clause in a contract or an arbitration agreement, signed by the parties or contained in an exchange of letters or telegrams." Convention, Art. II, para. 2, 9 U.S.C. §201. Jacobson claims it never agreed to Chinese arbitration, nor did it manifest an intent to do so.

The Chinese arbitration clause lies within Section 19 of the Hebei Contract attached to Polytek's May 10, 1993, Purchase Order. The Purchase Order twice refers to the attached Hebei Contract, and includes the statement: "All the terms and conditions should conform with the main contract." For the reasons set forth below, the Court finds Section 19 of the Hebei Contract, attached as it was to the Purchase Order, satisfies Article II's definition of an "agreement in writing."

The parties' behavior relative to this Purchase Order and attachment lends credence and support to this determination. Polytek and Jacobson had conducted preliminary negotiations in November, 1992, but waited until April, 1993 — until the Hebei Contract was completed — before entering into their own purchase and manufacture agreement. Jacobson's president, Ivar W. Sorensen, sent a facsimile message to Polytek, dated February 24, 1993, stating: "We hope that you will be able to finish up the contract work this week [with Hebei], as planned. From our discussion, my understanding is that you will then issue us a Polytek Purchase Order, with the official contract attached." The manager responsible for the negotiation on behalf of Polytek, Lau Yiu Chung Reddy, faxed a reply to Mr. Sorensen's message on March 2, 1993, stating: "We'll issue a purchasing order with the contract as attachment to you within this week."

While the exact date the Purchase Order was delivered is in dispute, the date of its arrival is irrelevant. There is no question it arrived and was the document which governed the Polytek/Jacobson relationship. The parties' subsequent conduct decisively illustrates the Hebei Contract's direct influence on each party's transactional behavior.

On May 18, 1993, Mr. Lau asked Jacobson to provide an irrevocable letter of guarantee or a standby letter of credit, as required by Section 10 of the Hebei Contract. Mr. Sorensen declined to provide a standby letter of credit on behalf of Jacobson. After further correspondence, Polytek and Jacobson agreed to a deposit and a standby letter of credit arrangement satisfactory to both sides. This behavior shows that the parties were directly aware of, and were influenced in their contract performance by, the Hebei Contract far beyond the confines of specifications for the manufacture and delivery of rubber recycling equipment.

While Mr. Sorensen indicated initial disagreement with the letter of credit requirement, neither he nor anyone on Jacobson's behalf indicated any problem with the arbitration provision in Section 19 of the Hebei Contract. Mr. Sorensen wrote Polytek on July 21, 1993, indicating "the contract date, . . . will be the date we confirm receipt of the [Polytek] deposit." (Lau's Decl., Exh. 27). Mr. Sorensen then sent a facsimile, dated July 23, 1993, confirming Jacobson's receipt of Polytek's deposit and the commencement of the contract.

All terms of the agreement, with the exception of the compromised change concerning the letter of credit, were thereby adopted, confirming Jacobson's compliance with the Polytek Purchase Order and attached Hebei Contract. Thus, this Court finds that an "agreement in writing," as contemplated by the Convention, existed between Polytek and Jacobson.

III. Conclusion

For the reasons set forth above, it is ordered that:

1. The May 26, 1997, arbitration award issued by the China International Economic and Trade Arbitration Commission is recognized as binding and enforceable, pursuant to the Convention on the Recognition and Enforcement of Foreign Arbitral Awards and 9 U.S.C. §§201-208.
2. Defendant Jacobson shall pay plaintiff Polytek the sum of U.S. $1,700,367.41, plus interest at the rate of nine percent (9%), as specified in the arbitration award.
3. Defendant Jacobson shall dismantle and collect the rubber recycling equipment at its own expense.

Glencore Grain Rotterdam B.V. v. Shivnath Rai Harnarain Co.
United States Court of Appeals, Ninth Circuit, 2002
284 F.3d 1114

TROTT, Circuit Judge.

This case arises out of a series of eleven contracts under which Glencore Grain, a Netherlands corporation with its principal place of business in Rotterdam, agreed to purchase approximately 300,000 tons of rice from Shivnath Rai, a manufacturer and exporter of rice incorporated in India with its principal place of business in New Delhi. The contracts called for the delivery of rice at the Port of Kandla, India. Among the rights and responsibilities set forth in each contract were the following arbitration and choice of law clauses:

11.—Any dispute arising on this Contract shall be referred for settlement to the Arbitration by two Members of [the London Rice Brokers'] Association's Panel of Arbitrators or their Umpire, being also a member of this Panel. Each party to appoint one Arbitrator and having the right to reject one nominee.

14.—Domicile.—The Contract shall be deemed to have been made in England and . . . shall be governed in all respects by English Law. Any dispute arising out

of or in connection therewith shall be submitted to arbitration in accordance with the
Rules of the London Rice Brokers' Association.

A dispute arose between the parties concerning the delivery of rice and was
submitted to arbitration before the London Rice Brokers' Association ("LRBA").
In its written decision from July 1997, the LRBA ruled in favor of Glencore
Grain, awarding it roughly $6.5 million; including interest, the award exceeded
$7 million. Shivnath Rai did not challenge the decision in England, where the
award became final and remains enforceable, nor did Shivnath Rai pay up.

In March 1998, Glencore Grain filed suit in the High Court of Delhi at New
Delhi, India to enforce the unpaid arbitration award. Shivnath Rai objected to the
enforcement of the award on several grounds, including its failure to consent to
the arbitration provisions in the underlying contracts and the arbitrators' allotment of insufficient time to defend its case on the merits. Glencore Grain's
enforcement action remains pending in the High Court of Delhi.

In July 2000, Glencore Grain filed an application in the federal district court
for the Northern District of California, seeking confirmation of the arbitral award
under the [Convention on the Recognition and Enforcement of Foreign Arbitral
Awards]. Shivnath Rai filed a motion to dismiss on six different grounds, including
the absence of personal jurisdiction.

In its motion opposing dismissal, Glencore Grain submitted evidence of
Shivnath Rai's minimum-contacts with California and with the United States as
a whole to justify the exercise of personal jurisdiction. Glencore Grain provided
evidence of the following shipments of rice by Shivnath Rai: a 1987 shipment into
the Port of Los Angeles; seven shipments through East Coast ports from 1993
to 1995; and fifteen shipments into the Port of San Francisco from March 1999 to
March 2000. In addition, Glencore Grain submitted documents indicating that
Alok Mohan, President of Asian Brands, Inc., located in Union City, California,
served as Shivnath Rai's sales agent for its rice sales throughout the United States.
Glencore Grain contended that these contacts supported the exercise of either
specific or general jurisdiction over Shivnath Rai.

Unswayed, the district court dismissed the action for lack of personal jurisdiction. In rejecting the general jurisdiction argument, the district court reasoned:
"[p]etitioner has not asserted that Respondent conducts any business in the [U.S.]
except through this sales agent [*i.e.*, Asian Brands, Inc.]." In addition, the district
court refused to exercise specific jurisdiction because "[Glencore Grain] nowhere
asserts that the cause of action arises out of or relates to [Shivnath Rai's] activities
within the forum."

This timely appeal followed.

DISCUSSION

THE CONVENTION PROVIDES SUBJECT MATTER JURISDICTION
OVER GLENCORE GRAIN'S ACTION TO ENFORCE ITS
ARBITRATION AWARD

In 1970 Congress ratified the New York Convention on the Recognition and
Enforcement of Foreign Arbitral Awards, a multilateral treaty providing for "the
recognition and enforcement of arbitral awards made in the territory of a State

other than the State where the recognition and enforcement of such awards are sought." Convention, art. I(1), 21 U.S.T. 2517. Congress implemented the Convention by passing Chapter II of the Federal Arbitration Act ("FAA"), 9 U.S.C. §§201-208, which provides that

> [a]n action or proceeding falling under the Convention shall be deemed to arise under the laws and treaties of the United States. The district courts of the United States . . . shall have original jurisdiction over such an action or proceeding, regardless of the amount in controversy.

9 U.S.C. §203.

The FAA further provides:

> Within three years after an arbitral award falling under the Convention is made, any party to the arbitration may apply to any court having jurisdiction under this chapter for an order confirming the award as against any other party to the arbitration. The court shall confirm the award unless it finds one of the grounds for refusal or deferral of recognition or enforcement of the award specified in the said Convention.

9 U.S.C. §207.

The Convention governs this action to confirm Glencore Grain's arbitration award because the award was obtained in the United Kingdom (London) within three years of Glencore Grain's suit in district court. *See* Restatement (Third) of Foreign Relations Law §487 cmt. b (1987) ("[T]he critical element is the place of the award: if that place is in the territory of a party to the Convention, all other Convention states are required to recognize and enforce the award, regardless of the citizenship or domicile of the parties to the arbitration.").[6] Thus the district court had subject matter jurisdiction over Glencore Grain's application.

D.C. had SMJ over claim

THE CONVENTION DOES NOT ABROGATE THE DUE PROCESS REQUIREMENT THAT JURISDICTION EXIST OVER THE DEFENDANT'S PERSON OR PROPERTY

Before considering Glencore Grain's arguments for the existence of jurisdiction over Shivnath Rai, we feel it necessary to address briefly Glencore Grain's intimation that the FAA contemplates reduced jurisdictional requirements over a defendant in suits to confirm arbitral awards. For the reasons stated below, we find this position without merit.

The Convention and its implementing legislation have a pro-enforcement bias, a policy long-recognized by the Supreme Court:

> The goal of the Convention, and the principal purpose underlying American adoption and implementation of it, was to encourage the recognition and enforcement of commercial arbitration agreements in international contracts and to unify the standards by which agreements to arbitrate are observed and arbitral awards are enforced in the signatory countries.

---

6. The United Kingdom is a signatory to the Convention. *See* 9 U.S.C.A. §201 note (West 1999).

Scherk v. Alberto-Culver Co., 417 U.S. 506, 520 n. 15, 94 S. Ct. 2449, 41 L. Ed. 2d 270 (1974). The mandatory language of the Convention itself and of the FAA reflects this partiality and leaves the district courts with "little discretion." *Ministry of Def. of the Islamic Republic of Iran v. Gould, Inc.*, 969 F.2d 764, 770 (9th Cir. 1992). Article III of the Convention is illustrative: "Each Contracting State *shall recognize arbitral awards as binding*" without creating conditions or procedures more onerous than those applied to domestic arbitration awards. 21 U.S.T. 2517 (emphasis added). Similarly, the FAA instructs that a federal court "*shall confirm the award* unless it finds one of the grounds for refusal . . . of recognition or enforcement of the award specified in the . . . Convention." 9 U.S.C. §207 (emphasis added).

In light of this mandate to confirm awards, Glencore Grain seems to find significance in what the Convention and the FAA do *not* say: (1) neither the Convention nor its implementing legislation expressly requires personal jurisdiction over the party against whom confirmation is sought; and (2) lack of personal jurisdiction over the defendant in the state where enforcement is sought is not among the Convention's seven defenses to recognition and enforcement of a foreign arbitration award. We do not agree.

It is a bedrock principle of civil procedure and constitutional law that a "statute cannot grant personal jurisdiction where the Constitution forbids it." *Gilson v. Republic of Ir.*, 682 F.2d 1022, 1028 (D.C. Cir. 1982). This precept reflects the idea that a district court must possess authority over the subject matter and over the parties, distinct powers that flow from distinct areas of the Constitution.

The personal jurisdiction requirement "flows . . . from the Due Process Clause . . . [and] represents a restriction on judicial power not as a matter of sovereignty, but as a matter of individual liberty." *Id.* District courts determine the existence *vel non* of personal jurisdiction not by reference to statutory imprimatur, but by inquiring whether maintenance of a suit against the defendant comports with the constitutional notions of due process as outlined in *International Shoe Co. v. Washington*, 326 U.S. 310, 66 S. Ct. 154, 90 L. Ed. 95 (1945), and its progeny. Thus, it is not significant in the least that the legislation implementing the Convention lacks language requiring personal jurisdiction over the litigants. We hold that neither the Convention nor its implementing legislation removed the district courts' obligation to find jurisdiction over the defendant in suits to confirm arbitration awards.

Perhaps because our holding is so unexceptional, we have uncovered relatively little authority squarely addressing the issue. The little authority that exists unequivocally endorses our position. First, we note the following language from the Restatement: "An arbitral award is ordinarily enforced by confirmation in a judgment. . . . As in respect to judgments . . . *an action to enforce a foreign arbitral award requires jurisdiction over the award debtor or his property*." Restatement (Third) of Foreign Relations Law §487 cmt. c (1987) (emphasis added).

Second, we find uniform support from the few courts that have expressly considered the jurisdictional requirements under the Convention. In *Transatlantic Bulk Shipping Ltd. v. Saudi Chartering S.A.*, 622 F. Supp. 25 (S.D.N.Y. 1985), a Liberian plaintiff brought suit under the Convention to confirm its London arbitration award against a Saudi defendant. Addressing the issue of personal jurisdiction, the court concluded:

[A]s to the [FAA] . . . , it authorizes the court to hear a new category of action not previously within its subject matter jurisdiction. It does not, however, give the court power over all persons throughout the world who have entered into an arbitration agreement covered by the Convention. Some basis must be shown, whether arising from the respondent's residence, his conduct, his consent, the location of his property or otherwise, to justify his being subject to the court's power.

Id. at 27.

A final consideration counsels our position. Interpreting the FAA to dispense with the jurisdictional requirements of Due Process in actions to confirm arbitral awards would raise clear questions concerning the constitutionality of the statutes. We avoid such constitutionally questionable constructions whenever fairly possible. [The court of appeals affirmed the district court's dismissal of the case for lack of personal jurisdiction over the defendant.]

NOTES AND QUESTIONS

1. In the United States, there is a strong policy in favor of enforcing arbitration awards. Will judicial review be broad or narrow?

2. Enforcing a foreign arbitration award is much easier than enforcing a foreign judgment because of the New York Convention. After an arbitration award, is it necessary or advisable to get the award confirmed by a court in the place of arbitration? *See Oriental Commercial & Shipping Co. v. Rosseel, N. V.*, 769 F. Supp. 514 (S.D.N.Y. 1991).

IV. Jurisdiction

A. International Law

Jurisdiction is a term with many meanings, especially in the international context. It is important to understand and to distinguish these different meanings.

First, we must understand the international law concept of jurisdiction. In international law, jurisdiction is an aspect of sovereignty. Every sovereign state has the authority to exercise ultimate control over persons and properties in the national sphere through its legislature, police force, and courts. This formulation posits three types of jurisdiction: Prescriptive, enforcement, and adjudicative. The most important of these is prescriptive jurisdiction, which refers to the power of states to prescribe or enact laws that are valid and have binding authority over its objects. It is a well-accepted principle of international law that states have prescriptive jurisdiction over all persons, property, and conduct within their territorial boundaries and over their nationals wherever in the world. However, under certain circumstances, a state also has prescriptive jurisdiction over persons (other than its nationals), property, and conduct outside of its territory. The last aspect of extraterritorial prescriptive jurisdiction is controversial. Another issue is that states must have limits to avoid interference with the legitimate exercise of prescriptive jurisdiction by other states. Consider the following summary of international jurisdiction from the U.S. perspective:

Kathleen Hixson, Extraterritorial Jurisdiction Under the Third Restatement of the Foreign Relations Law of the United States
12 Fordham Int'l L.J. 127 (1988)

A. JURISDICTION: A BASIC APPROACH

B. BASES OF JURISDICTION TO PRESCRIBE

The bases of jurisdiction in the Restatement Second draw upon traditional principles of international law that have found general acceptance abroad; these bases of jurisdiction include territory and nationality. As an offshoot of the traditional territoriality principle, section 18 recognizes the more controversial "effects" doctrine, wherein a state may have prescriptive jurisdiction over conduct occurring outside its territory that causes an effect within.[7] The effects doctrine is limited to rare circumstances when conduct is generally recognized as a crime; the effect within the territory is direct, substantial, and foreseeable; and the rule is consistent with the principles of justice in states that have reasonably developed legal systems.

The Restatement Third enumerates bases of jurisdiction to prescribe in section 402.[8] Within this section, the second and third subsections outline the "nationality" and "protective" principles of jurisdiction. Subsection (1) deals with the principle of territoriality under three approaches: two of these allow a right to prescribe with respect to conduct within the territory or the status of persons or things present within the state; the third allows a state to prescribe law with respect to "conduct outside its territory that has or is intended to have substantial effect within its territory."

---

7. *See* RESTATEMENT SECOND, §18. The effects doctrine receives the following treatment in the Restatement Second:

A state has jurisdiction to prescribe a rule of law attaching legal consequences to conduct that occurs outside its territory and causes an effect within its territory, if either

(a) the conduct and its effect are generally recognized as constituent elements of a crime or tort under the law of states that have reasonably developed legal systems, or

(b) (i) the conduct and its effect are constituent elements of activity to which the rule applies; (ii) the effect within the territory is substantial; (iii) it occurs as a direct and foreseeable result of the conduct outside the territory; and (iv) the rule is not inconsistent with the principles of justice generally recognized by states that have reasonably developed legal systems.

8. RESTATEMENT THIRD, §402.

Subject to §403, a state has jurisdiction to prescribe law with respect to

(1) (a) conduct that, wholly or in substantial part, takes place within its territory;
(b) the status of persons, or interests in things, present within its territory;
(c) conduct outside its territory that has or is intended to have substantial effect within its territory;

(2) the activities, interests, status, or relations of its nationals outside as well as within its territory; and

(3) certain conduct outside its territory by persons not its nationals that is directed against the security of the state or against a limited class of other state interests. *Id.*

Although the Restatement Third takes a traditional approach to territorial jurisdiction generally, this last subsection substantially relaxes the more stringent requirements on the effects doctrine found in the Restatement Second. While the Restatement Second requires direct, substantial, and foreseeable effects under the Restatement Third the effect need not be actual, but merely intended. Actual but unintended effects would also be sufficient to support jurisdiction. And finally, the Restatement Third eliminates the requirement that the conduct in question be generally recognized as a crime in the international community.

C. Limitations on Jurisdiction

Both the Restatement Second and the Restatement Third recognize that conflict may arise when two states concurrently exercise jurisdiction. The Restatement Second approaches this problem, in section 40, as one of the proper exercise of enforcement jurisdiction. While the first prerequisite to enforcement jurisdiction is valid prescriptive jurisdiction, the impact of enforcement jurisdiction is then further ameliorated by section 40. Where the assertion of concurrent jurisdiction by two or more states might require inconsistent conduct, section 40 requires a state to consider in good faith moderating its enforcement jurisdiction. This consideration is stated as an express requirement of international law.

The Restatement Third provides for conflict resolution in section 403 under the heading "Limitations on Jurisdiction to Prescribe."[9] This section states, first,

---

9. Restatement Third, §403. Section 403 reads:

(1) Even when one of the bases for jurisdiction under §402 is present, a state may not exercise jurisdiction to prescribe law with respect to a person or activity having connections with another state when the exercise of such jurisdiction is unreasonable.

(2) Whether exercise of jurisdiction over a person or activity is unreasonable is determined by evaluating all relevant factors, including, where appropriate:

(a) the link of the activity to the territory of the regulating state, *i.e.*, the extent to which the activity takes place within the territory, or has substantial, direct, and foreseeable effect upon or in the territory;

(b) the connections, such as nationality; residence, or economic activity, between the regulating state and the person principally responsible for the activity to be regulated, or between that state and those whom the regulation is designed to protect;

(c) the character of the activity to be regulated, the importance of regulation to the regulating state, the extent to which other states regulate such activities, and the degree to which the desirability of such regulation is generally accepted;

(d) the existence of justified expectations that might be protected or hurt by the regulation;

(e) the importance of the regulation to the international political, legal, or economic system;

(f) the extent to which the regulation is consistent with the traditions of the international system;

(g) the extent to which another state may have an interest in regulating the activity; and

(h) the likelihood of conflict with regulation by another state.

(3) When it would not be unreasonable for each of two states to exercise jurisdiction over a person or activity, but the prescriptions by the two states are in conflict, each state has an obligation to evaluate its own as well as the other state's interest in exercising jurisdiction, in light of all the relevant factors, Subsection (2); a state should defer to the other state if that state's interest is clearly greater.

the so-called "rule of reason," which is the foundation of the Restatement Third balancing test. Under this rule, a state may not exercise prescriptive jurisdiction over persons or things having connections with other states where the exercise of such jurisdiction is unreasonable. Reasonableness, in this provision, is to be measured by evaluating all relevant factors, including certain nonexclusive factors listed in subsection (2). Where the prescriptions by two or more states are both reasonable, but conflict nonetheless, each state must evaluate its own, as well as the other state's, interest and should defer to the other state if that state's interest is clearly greater.

In this area, the Restatement Third has taken perhaps the most radical departure from the Restatement Second. First, under the Restatement Second, the good-faith weighing of interests is presented as a requirement of international law. Under the Restatement Third, however, a state "has an obligation" to evaluate, but "should" defer if the other state's interest is "clearly" greater. The actual moderation of jurisdiction is presented more as an exercise of deference based on principles of comity.

Second, the Restatement Third places less emphasis on territoriality. Instead, it focuses on elements such as the nature of the activity, the effect on the regulating state, and the interests of both the regulating and territorial states, which interests are measured by the amount of regulation generally exercised. These factors are far more difficult to quantify than the narrowly defined factors of the Restatement Second. Thus, they open the door to a substantially broader interpretation of extraterritorial jurisdiction.

Finally, the Restatement Third limitations turn on the concept of reasonableness. This leaves open to the courts the interpretation of the meaning of reasonableness.

NOTES AND QUESTIONS

1. The whole thrust of the Restatement (Third) compared to the Restatement (Second) was to greatly expand concepts of U.S. jurisdiction. Why was this the case? In which areas of law does the United States have an interest in expanding its influence? Does the Restatement (Third) comport with or depart from international law in its expansive notion of jurisdiction?

2. Consider the "effects" doctrine. This is commonly used as a justification for extraterritorial jurisdiction by the United States in the fields of antitrust, securities, and criminal law. Does the effects doctrine go too far?

3. To combat U.S. extraterritorial jurisdiction, many states have enacted blocking statutes that allow authorities to prohibit the production of evidence or compliance with U.S. legal requirements considered inappropriate. *See, e.g., The Protection of Trading Interests Act* 1980 (United Kingdom).

B.   National Law: Territorial Jurisdiction

There are also extensive national law rules on the jurisdiction of courts that are rooted in concepts of order and fundamental fairness. *Subject matter jurisdiction*, the authority of a particular court to decide a given dispute, assigns various subject matters by law to the appropriate courts. In the United States, subject matter jurisdiction is particularly important in maintaining the federal system; thus, the subject matter jurisdiction of the federal courts is generally limited to cases involving a federal question of law, admiralty, and litigation between persons domiciled in different states. In nations such as France and Germany, certain courts are assigned specialty subject matters, such as administrative law cases or labor law cases.

Concerning private international business contracts and transactions, the most important jurisdictional concept will be *territorial jurisdiction*. This topic is important to the domestic as well as the international litigant. In the landmark case of *International Shoe Co. v. State of Washington*, 326 U.S. 310 (1945), the Supreme Court decided that, as an element of constitutional due process, a defendant must have certain minimum contacts with the state of the judicial forum to be subject to the state's adjudicative powers. In *Shaffer v. Heitner*, 433 U.S. 186 (1977), the Supreme Court held that the ownership of property alone in the forum state cannot justify jurisdiction without minimum contacts as required by *International Shoe*. Nevertheless, a so-called quasi-in-rem case based on property ownership can still be brought consistent with due process if the maintenance of property, such as a bank account, constitutes minimum contacts. *See, e.g., Banco Ambrosiano, SPA v. Artoc Bank & Trust Ltd.*, 62 N.Y. 2d 65, 476 N.Y.S. 2d 64, 464 N.E.2d 432 (1984).

Most international business litigation in the United States will concern state-created causes of action in state court or in federal court on the basis of diversity of citizenship. Although these cases will be under state jurisdictional rules, most states provide by statute or judicial interpretation that the jurisdiction of their courts extends to the limits permitted by due process under the U.S. Constitution. Thus, the same constitutional analysis will generally apply to both state and federal law claims in the United States.

Of course, each state or group of states will have its own international jurisdictional rules. In the EU, most international business contracts are subject to two conventions, the Brussels Convention on Jurisdiction and Enforcement of Judgments in Civil and Commercial Matters (1968) (applicable between member states), and the almost identical Lugano Convention on the Jurisdiction and Enforcement of Judgments in Civil and Commercial Matters (1988) (applicable between EU states and members of the European Free Trade Agreement). These two conventions provide that a natural person or a company can be sued in contract in the state of domicile or in the place of performance of the obligation. Non-EU individuals and companies are subject to much more liberal jurisdiction under national laws that differ from state to state. *See generally*, Samuel Cohen, *The EEC Convention and U.S. Law Governing Choice of Law for Contracts*, 13 Md. J. of Int'l L. & Trade 223 (1989).

Many states, including France, Germany, Switzerland, and the United Kingdom, allow suit to be brought *in personam* based on the fact that a defendant owns tangible or intangible assets in the jurisdiction. *See, e.g., Derby & Co., Ltd. v. Weldon* [1989] 2 W.L.R. 276 (Eng. C.A. 1988). Such property-based jurisdiction goes beyond what would be permitted under U.S. due process standards.

In this section, we examine two cases that explore the outer limits of U.S. due process standards in litigation against foreign defendants.

PROBLEM 8-9

Nippon Electronics (NE) is a major Japanese manufacturer of household electronic goods such as high-definition televisions, plasma computer screens and flat-screen televisions, digital cameras, and videocassette, CD, and DVD players. NE sells products that reach the U.S. market in several ways.

(1) Each year, NE participates in a trade fair in Tokyo where buyers from around the world come to see the latest electronics products. Some buyers always take an interest in NE's latest products shown at the fair, and NE will always get large orders for its products after the fair. One year, a purchaser from South Korea buys a large quantity of DVD players for sale in the Korean market; however, as the Korean buyer is unable to sell all of the goods in Korea, the buyer sells the surplus quantities to a distributor in Illinois. A little girl receives some burns on her arms and legs when the DVD player malfunctions as she is inserting a disk. Her mother brings an action against NE in Illinois state court in Chicago.

(2) At the trade fair in Tokyo, NE also sells an order of plasma screens manufactured to specifications to a Sacramento computer company, which incorporates the screens into its state-of-the-art laptop computers back in its California factory. When the screens prove to be defective, the Sacramento computer company sues NE for breach of warranty and breach of contract in California state court.

(3) NE keeps a small office in Texas where it stores some accounting and financial records. Once a month, a representative from NE's Tokyo office flies to Texas en route to NE's subsidiary in Canada and stops in the Texas office for two days to update the records and issue checks. A U.S. tourist from Texas travels to Tokyo and purchases an NE radio and audiocassette recorder and player at the trade fair. The tourist complains about a loss of hearing when the audio player emits a loud and unexpected static noise. When the tourist returns home, he files an action against NE in Texas state court.

Discuss whether the courts in each of these instances have jurisdiction over NE. Consult *Asahi* and *Glencore* below.

Asahi Metal Industry Co., Ltd. v. Superior Court
United States Supreme Court, 1987
480 U.S. 102, 107 S. Ct. 1026, 94 L. Ed. 2d 92

JUSTICE O'CONNOR announced the judgment of the Court and delivered the unanimous opinion of the Court with respect to Part I, the opinion of the Court with respect to Part II-B, in which THE CHIEF JUSTICE, JUSTICE BRENNAN, JUSTICE WHITE, JUSTICE MARSHALL, JUSTICE BLACKMUN, JUSTICE POWELL and JUSTICE STEVENS join, and an opinion with respect to Parts II-A and III, in which THE CHIEF JUSTICE, JUSTICE POWELL, and JUSTICE SCALIA join.

This case presents the question whether the mere awareness on the part of a foreign defendant that the components it manufactured, sold, and delivered outside the United States would reach the forum State in the stream of commerce constitutes "minimum contacts" between the defendant and the forum State such that the exercise of jurisdiction "does not offend 'traditional notions of fair play and substantial justice.'" *International Shoe Co. v. Washington*, 326 U.S. 310, 316 (1945), quoting *Milliken v. Meyer*, 311 U.S. 457, 463 (1940).

I

On September 23, 1978, on Interstate Highway 80 in Solano County, California, Gary Zurcher lost control of his Honda motorcycle and collided with a tractor. Zurcher was severely injured, and his passenger and wife, Ruth Ann Moreno, was killed. In September 1979, Zurcher filed a product liability action in the Superior Court of the State of California in and for the County of Solano. Zurcher alleged that the 1978 accident was caused by a sudden loss of air and an explosion in the rear tire of the motorcycle, and alleged that the motorcycle tire, tube, and sealant were defective. Zurcher's complaint named, *inter alia,* Cheng Shin Rubber Industrial Co., Ltd. (Cheng Shin), the Taiwanese manufacturer of the tube. Cheng Shin in turn filed a cross-complaint seeking indemnification from its codefendants and from petitioner, Asahi Metal Industry Co., Ltd. (Asahi), the manufacturer of the tube's valve assembly. Zurcher's claims against Cheng Shin and the other defendants were eventually settled and dismissed, leaving only Cheng Shin's indemnity action against Asahi.

California's long-arm statute authorizes the exercise of jurisdiction "on any basis not inconsistent with the Constitution of this state or of the United States." Cal. Civ. Proc. Code Ann. §410.10 (West 1973). Asahi moved to quash Cheng Shin's service of summons, arguing the State could not exert jurisdiction over it consistent with the Due Process Clause of the Fourteenth Amendment.

In relation to the motion, the following information was submitted by Asahi and Cheng Shin. Asahi is a Japanese corporation. It manufactures tire valve assemblies in Japan and sells the assemblies to Cheng Shin, and to several other tire manufacturers, for use as components in finished tire tubes. Asahi's sales to Cheng Shin took place in Taiwan. The shipments from Asahi to Cheng Shin were sent from Japan to Taiwan. Cheng Shin bought and incorporated into its tire tubes 150,000 Asahi valve assemblies in 1978; 500,000 in 1979; 500,000 in 1980; 100,000 in 1981; and 100,000 in 1982. Sales to Cheng Shin accounted for 1.24 percent of Asahi's income in 1981 and 0.44 percent in 1982. Cheng Shin alleged that approximately 20 percent of its sales in the United States are in California. Cheng Shin purchases valve assemblies from other suppliers as well, and sells finished tubes throughout the world.

In 1983 an attorney for Cheng Shin conducted an informal examination of the valve stems of the tire tubes sold in one cycle store in Solano County. The attorney declared that of the approximately 115 tire tubes in the store, 97 were purportedly manufactured in Japan or Taiwan, and of those 97, 21 valve stems were marked with the circled letter "A", apparently Asahi's trademark. Of the 21 Asahi valve stems, 12 were incorporated into Cheng Shin tire tubes. The store contained 41 other Cheng Shin tubes that incorporated the valve assemblies of other manufacturers. An affidavit of a manager of Cheng Shin whose duties included the purchasing of component parts stated: "'In discussions with Asahi regarding the purchase of valve stem assemblies the fact that my Company sells tubes throughout the world and specifically the United States has been discussed. I am informed and believe that Asahi was fully aware that valve stem assemblies sold to my Company and to others would end up throughout the United States and in California.'" An affidavit of the president of Asahi, on the other hand, declared that Asahi "'has never contemplated that its limited sales of tire valves to Cheng Shin in Taiwan would subject it to lawsuits in California.'" *Ibid*. The record does not include any contract between Cheng Shin and Asahi.

Primarily on the basis of the above information, the Superior Court denied the motion to quash summons, stating: "Asahi obviously does business on an international scale. It is not unreasonable that they defend claims of defect in their product on an international scale."

The Court of Appeal of the State of California issued a preemptory writ of mandate commanding the Superior Court to quash service of summons. The court concluded that "it would be unreasonable to require Asahi to respond in California solely on the basis of ultimately realized foreseeability that the product into which its component was embodied would be sold all over the world including California."

The Supreme Court of the State of California reversed and discharged the writ issued by the Court of Appeal. The court observed: "Asahi has no offices, property or agents in California. It solicits no business in California and has made no direct sales [in California]." Moreover, "Asahi did not design or control the system of distribution that carried its valve assemblies into California." Nevertheless, the court found the exercise of jurisdiction over Asahi to be consistent with the Due Process Clause. It concluded that Asahi knew that some of the valve assemblies sold to Cheng Shin would be incorporated into tire tubes sold in California, and that Asahi benefited indirectly from the sale in California of products incorporating its components. The court considered Asahi's intentional act of placing its components into the stream of commerce — that is, by delivering the components to Cheng Shin in Taiwan — coupled with Asahi's awareness that some of the components would eventually find their way into California, sufficient to form the basis for state court jurisdiction under the Due Process Clause.

We granted certiorari, and now reverse.

II

A

The Due Process Clause of the Fourteenth Amendment limits the power of a state court to exert personal jurisdiction over a nonresident defendant. "[T]he constitutional touchstone" of the determination whether an exercise of personal jurisdiction comports with due process "remains whether the defendant purposefully established 'minimum contacts' in the forum State." *Burger King Corp. v. Rudzewicz*, 471 U.S. 462, 474 (1985), quoting *International Shoe Co. v. Washington*. Most recently we have reaffirmed the oft-quoted reasoning of *Hanson v. Denckla*, that minimum contacts must have a basis in "some act by which the defendant purposefully avails itself of the privilege of conducting activities within the forum State, thus invoking the benefits and protections of its laws." *Burger King*, 471 U.S., at 475. "Jurisdiction is proper . . . where the contacts proximately result from actions by the defendant *himself* that create a 'substantial connection' with the forum State." *Ibid.*, quoting *McGee v. International Life Insurance Co.* (emphasis in original).

Applying the principle that minimum contacts must be based on an act of the defendant, the Court in *World-Wide Volkswagen Corp. v. Woodson* rejected the assertion that a consumer's unilateral act of bringing the defendant's product into the forum State was a sufficient constitutional basis for personal jurisdiction over the defendant. It had been argued in *World-Wide Volkswagen* that because an automobile retailer and its wholesale distributor sold a product mobile by design and purpose, they could foresee being haled into court in the distant States into which their customers might drive. The Court rejected this concept of foreseeability as an insufficient basis for jurisdiction under the Due Process Clause. The Court disclaimed, however, the idea that "foreseeability is wholly irrelevant" to personal jurisdiction, concluding that "[t]he forum State does not exceed its powers under the Due Process Clause if it asserts personal jurisdiction over a corporation that delivers its products into the stream of commerce with the expectation that they will be purchased by consumers in the forum State." The Court reasoned:

> "When a corporation 'purposefully avails itself of the privilege of conducting activities within the forum State,' *Hanson v. Denckla*, it has clear notice that it is subject to suit there, and can act to alleviate the risk of burdensome litigation by procuring insurance, passing the expected costs on to customers, or, if the risks are too great, severing its connection with the State. Hence if the sale of a product of a manufacturer or distributor . . . is not simply an isolated occurrence, but arises from the efforts of the manufacturer or distributor to serve, directly or indirectly, the market for its product in other States, it is not unreasonable to subject it to suit in one of those States if its allegedly defective merchandise has there been the source of injury to its owners or to others."

In *World-Wide Volkswagen* itself, the state court sought to base jurisdiction not on any act of the defendant, but on the foreseeable unilateral actions of the consumer. Since *World-Wide Volkswagen*, lower courts have been confronted with cases in which the defendant acted by placing a product in the stream of commerce, and the stream eventually swept defendant's product into the forum State, but the defendant did nothing else to purposefully avail itself of the market in the forum State. Some courts have understood the Due Process Clause, as interpreted in *World-Wide Volkswagen*, to allow an exercise of personal jurisdiction to be based on no more than the defendant's act of placing the product in the stream of commerce. Other courts have understood the Due Process Clause and the above-quoted language in *World-Wide Volkswagen* to require the action of the defendant to be more purposefully directed at the forum State than the mere act of placing a product in the stream of commerce.

The reasoning of the Supreme Court of California in the present case illustrates the former interpretation of *World-Wide Volkswagen*. The Supreme Court of California held that, because the stream of commerce eventually brought some valves Asahi sold Cheng Shin into California, Asahi's awareness that its valves would be sold in California was sufficient to permit California to exercise jurisdiction over Asahi consistent with the requirements of the Due Process Clause. The Supreme Court of California's position was consistent with those courts that have held that mere foreseeability or awareness was a constitutionally sufficient basis for personal jurisdiction if the defendant's product made its way into the forum State while still in the stream of commerce.

Other courts, however, have understood the Due Process Clause to require something more than that the defendant was aware of its product's entry into the forum State through the stream of commerce in order for the State to exert jurisdiction over the defendant. In the present case, for example, the State Court of Appeal did not read the Due Process Clause, as interpreted by *World-Wide Volkswagen*, to allow "mere foreseeability that the product will enter the forum state [to] be enough by itself to establish jurisdiction over the distributor and retailer." In *Humble v. Toyota Motor Co.*, 727 F.2d 709 (C.A.8 1984), an injured car passenger brought suit against Arakawa Auto Body Company, a Japanese corporation that manufactured car seats for Toyota. Arakawa did no business in the United States; it had no office, affiliate, subsidiary, or agent in the United States; it manufactured its component parts outside the United States and delivered them to Toyota Motor Company in Japan. The Court of Appeals, adopting the reasoning of the District Court in that case, noted that although it "does not doubt that Arakawa could have foreseen that its product would find its way into the United States," it would be "manifestly unjust" to require Arakawa to defend itself in the United States.

We now find this latter position to be consonant with the requirements of due process. The "substantial connection" between the defendant and the forum State necessary for a finding of minimum contacts must come about by an action of the defendant purposefully directed toward the forum State. The placement of a product into the stream of commerce, without more, is not an act of the defendant purposefully directed toward the forum State. Additional conduct of the defendant may indicate an intent or purpose to serve the market in the forum State, for example, designing the product for the market in the forum State, advertising in the forum State, establishing channels for providing regular advice to customers in the forum State, or marketing the product through a distributor who has agreed to serve as the sales agent in the forum State. But a defendant's awareness that the stream of commerce may or will sweep the product into the forum State does not convert the mere act of placing the product into the stream into an act purposefully directed toward the forum State.

Assuming, *arguendo,* that respondents have established Asahi's awareness that some of the valves sold to Cheng Shin would be incorporated into tire tubes sold in California, respondents have not demonstrated any action by Asahi to purposefully avail itself of the California market. Asahi does not do business in California. It has no office, agents, employees, or property in California. It does not advertise or otherwise solicit business in California. It did not create, control, or employ the distribution system that brought its valves to California. There is no evidence that Asahi designed its product in anticipation of sales in California. On the basis of these facts, the exertion of personal jurisdiction over Asahi by the Superior Court of California exceeds the limits of due process.

B

The strictures of the Due Process Clause forbid a state court to exercise personal jurisdiction over Asahi under circumstances that would offend " 'traditional notions of fair play and substantial justice.' " *International Shoe Co. v. Washington*, quoting *Milliken v. Meyer*.

We have previously explained that the determination of the reasonableness of the exercise of jurisdiction in each case will depend on an evaluation of several factors. A court must consider the burden on the defendant, the interests of the forum State, and the plaintiff's interest in obtaining relief. It must also weigh in its determination "the interstate judicial system's interest in obtaining the most efficient resolution of controversies; and the shared interest of the several States in furthering fundamental substantive social policies." *World-Wide Volkswagen*.

A consideration of these factors in the present case clearly reveals the unreasonableness of the assertion of jurisdiction over Asahi, even apart from the question of the placement of goods in the stream of commerce.

Certainly the burden on the defendant in this case is severe. Asahi has been commanded by the Supreme Court of California not only to traverse the distance between Asahi's headquarters in Japan and the Superior Court of California in and for the County of Solano, but also to submit its dispute with Cheng Shin to a foreign nation's judicial system. The unique burdens placed upon one who must defend oneself in a foreign legal system should have significant weight in assessing the reasonableness of stretching the long arm of personal jurisdiction over national borders.

When minimum contacts have been established, often the interests of the plaintiff and the forum in the exercise of jurisdiction will justify even the serious burdens placed on the filing defendant. In the present case, however, the interests of the plaintiff and the forum in California's assertion of jurisdiction over Asahi are slight. All that remains is a claim for indemnification asserted by Cheng Shin, a Taiwanese corporation, against Asahi. The transaction on which the indemnification claim is based took place in Taiwan; Asahi's components were shipped from Japan to Taiwan. Cheng Shin has not demonstrated that it is more convenient for it to litigate its indemnification claim against Asahi in California rather than in Taiwan, or Japan.

Because the plaintiff is not a California resident, California's legitimate interests in the dispute have considerably diminished. The Supreme Court of California argued that the State had an interest in "protecting its consumers by ensuring that foreign manufacturers comply with the state's safety standards." The State Supreme Court's definition of California's interest, however, was overly broad. The dispute between Cheng Shin and Asahi is primarily about indemnification rather than safety standards. Moreover, it is not at all clear at this point that California law should govern the question whether a Japanese corporation should indemnify a Taiwanese corporation on the basis of a sale made in Taiwan and a shipment of goods from Japan to Taiwan.

World-Wide Volkswagen also admonished courts to take into consideration the interests of the "several States," in addition to the forum State, in the efficient judicial resolution of the dispute and the advancement of substantive policies. In the present case, this advice calls for a court to consider the procedural and substantive policies of other *nations* whose interests are affected by the assertion of jurisdiction by the California court. The procedural and substantive interests of other nations in a state court's assertion of jurisdiction over an alien defendant will differ from case to case. In every case, however, those interests, as well as the Federal interest in Government's foreign relations policies, will be best served by a careful inquiry into the reasonableness of the assertion of jurisdiction in the particular case, and an unwillingness to find the serious burdens on an alien defendant outweighed by minimal interests on the part of the plaintiff or the forum State. "Great care and reserve should be exercised when extending our notions of personal jurisdiction into the international field." *United States v. First National City Bank*, 379 U.S. 378, 404 (1965) (Harlan, J., dissenting). Considering the international context, the heavy burden on the alien defendant, and the slight interests of the plaintiff and the forum State, the exercise of personal jurisdiction by a California court over Asahi in this instance would be unreasonable and unfair.

III

The judgment of the Supreme Court of California is reversed, and the case is remanded for further proceedings not inconsistent with this opinion.
It is so ordered.

JUSTICE BRENNAN, with whom JUSTICE WHITE, JUSTICE MARSHALL, and JUSTICE BLACKMUN join, concurring in part and concurring in the judgment.
[Justice Brennan agrees with Parts I and II-B of the Court's opinion but does do not agree with the interpretation in Part II-A of the stream-of-commerce theory, nor with the conclusion that Asahi did not "purposely avail itself of the California market."]
Part II-A states that "a defendant's awareness that the stream of commerce may or will sweep the product into the forum State does not convert the mere act of placing the product into the stream into an act purposefully directed toward the forum State." Under this view, a plaintiff would be required to show "[a]dditional conduct" directed toward the forum before finding the exercise of jurisdiction over the defendant to be consistent with the Due Process Clause. I see no need for such a showing, however. The stream of commerce refers not to unpredictable currents or eddies, but to the regular and anticipated flow of products from manufacture to distribution to retail sale. As long as a participant in this process is aware that the final product is being marketed in the forum State, the possibility of a lawsuit there cannot come as a surprise. Nor will the litigation present a burden for which there is no corresponding benefit. A defendant who has placed goods in the stream of commerce benefits economically from the retail sale of the final product in the forum State, and indirectly benefits from the State's laws that regulate and facilitate commercial activity. These benefits accrue regardless of whether that participant directly conducts business in the forum State or engages in additional conduct directed toward that State. Accordingly, most courts and commentators have found that jurisdiction premised on the placement of a product into the stream of commerce is consistent with the Due Process Clause, and have not required a showing of additional conduct.

JUSTICE STEVENS, with whom JUSTICE WHITE and JUSTICE BLACKMUN join, concurring in part and concurring in the judgment.
The judgment of the Supreme Court of California should be reversed for the reasons stated in Part II-B of the Court's opinion. While I join Parts I and II-B, I do not join Part II-A for two reasons. First, it is not necessary to the Court's decision. An examination of minimum contacts is not always necessary to determine whether a state court's assertion of personal jurisdiction is constitutional. Part II-B establishes, after considering the factors set forth in *World-Wide Volkswagen*

Corp. v. Woodson, that California's exercise of jurisdiction over Asahi in this case would be "unreasonable and unfair." This finding alone requires reversal.

Second, even assuming that the test ought to be formulated here, Part II-A misapplies it to the facts of this case. The plurality seems to assume that an unwavering line can be drawn between "mere awareness" that a component will find its way into the forum State and "purposeful availment" of the forum's market. Over the course of its dealings with Cheng Shin, Asahi has arguably engaged in a higher quantum of conduct than "[t]he placement of a product into the stream of commerce, without more. . . ." *Ibid*. Whether or not this conduct rises to the level of purposeful availment requires a constitutional determination that is affected by the volume, the value, and the hazardous character of the components. In most circumstances I would be inclined to conclude that a regular course of dealing that results in deliveries of over 100,000 units annually over a period of several years would constitute "purposeful availment" even though the item delivered to the forum State was a standard product marketed throughout the world.

Glencore Grain Rotterdam B.V. v. Shivnath Rai Harnarain Co.
United States Court of Appeals, Ninth Circuit, 2002
284 F.3d 1114

TROTT, Circuit Judge.
[The facts and main issues of this case are set out at p. 698, *supra*.]

THE DISTRICT COURT LACKED JURISDICTION OVER SHIVNATH RAI

A. JURISDICTION UNDER RULE 4(K)(1)(A) AND THE CALIFORNIA LONG-ARM: SHIVNATH RAI LACKS MINIMUM CONTACTS WITH CALIFORNIA

Constitutional due process is satisfied when a non-resident defendant has "certain minimum contacts with [the forum] such that the maintenance of the suit does not offend 'traditional notions of fair play and substantial justice.'" *Int'l Shoe*, 326 U.S. at 316, 66 S. Ct. 154 (quoting *Milliken v. Meyer*, 311 U.S. 457, 463, 61 S. Ct. 339, 85 L. Ed. 278 (1940)). Depending on the nature of a foreign defendant's contacts with the forum, a federal court may obtain either specific or general jurisdiction over him. A court exercises specific jurisdiction where the cause of action arises out of or has a substantial connection to the defendant's contacts with the forum. *Hanson v. Denckla*, 357 U.S. 235, 251, 78 S. Ct. 1228, 2 L. Ed. 2d 1283 (1958). Alternatively, a defendant whose contacts are substantial, continuous, and systematic is subject to a court's general jurisdiction even if the suit concerns matters not arising out of his contacts with the forum.

i. Specific Jurisdiction Is Not Proper over Shivnath Rai

Our Circuit applies a three-part test to evaluate the propriety of exercising specific jurisdiction: (1) whether the defendant purposefully availed himself of the privileges of conducting activities in the forum, (2) whether the claim arises out of or results from the defendant's forum-related activities, and (3) whether the exercise of jurisdiction is reasonable. *Myers,* 238 F.3d at 1072. Glencore Grain's suit fails to clear the second hurdle.

We apply a "but for" test to assess whether Glencore Grain's claims "arise out of" Shivnath Rai's forum conduct: Glencore Grain must show that it would not have been injured "but for" Shivnath Rai's contacts with California. The contracts giving rise to this dispute were negotiated abroad, involved foreign companies, and required performance (*i.e.,* delivery of rice) in India. In short, Glencore Grain's claim does not arise out of conduct directed at or related to California. Thus, due process forbids the exercise of specific jurisdiction.

ii. General Jurisdiction Is Not Proper over Shivnath Rai

We consider, next, the nature of Shivnath Rai's contacts to see whether they constitute the kind of continuous and systematic general business contacts that "approximate physical presence." *Bancroft & Masters, Inc. v. Augusta Nat'l Inc.,* 223 F.3d 1082, 1086 (9th Cir. 2000). Such contacts were found to exist in *Perkins v. Benguet Consol. Mining Co.,* 342 U.S. 437, 448, 72 S. Ct. 413, 96 L. Ed. 485 (1952); the Supreme Court has summarized the circumstances that permitted the exercise of general jurisdiction over the defendant foreign corporation in that case:

> During the Japanese occupation of the Philippine Islands, the president and general manager of a Philippine mining corporation maintained an office in Ohio from which he conducted activities on behalf of the company. He kept company files and held directors' meetings in the office, carried on correspondence relating to the business, distributed salary checks drawn on two active Ohio bank accounts, engaged an Ohio bank to act as transfer agent, and supervised policies dealing with the rehabilitation of the corporation's properties in the Philippines. In short, the foreign corporation, through its president, "[had] been carrying on in Ohio a continuous and systematic, but limited, part of its general business,". . . .

Helicopteros, 466 U.S. at 414-15, 104 S. Ct. 1868 (quoting *Perkins,* 342 U.S. at 438, 72 S. Ct. 413).

Here, Shivnath Rai's contacts with California amount to the presence of an independently employed sales agent who imports and distributes Shivnath Rai's rice, a 1987 rice shipment into Los Angeles, and the fifteen San Francisco shipments from March 1999 to March 2000. There is no evidence that Shivnath Rai owns property, keeps bank accounts, has employees, solicits business, or has designated an agent for service of process in California. Though Shivnath Rai has exported considerable rice through the Port of San Francisco, these contacts seem to "constitute doing business *with* California, but do not constitute doing business *in* California. This is because engaging in commerce with residents of the forum state is not in and of itself the kind of activity that approximates physical presence within the state's borders." *Bancroft & Masters,* 223 F.3d at 1086. Put another way, while it is clear that Shivnath Rai has stepped through the door, there is no indication that it has sat down and made itself at home.

The idea of the foreign defendant making himself at home in the forum was critical in *Perkins,* where the foreign defendant had set up most aspects of its operations in the forum state. Shivnath Rai's San Francisco shipments pale in comparison to the transplanted business operations in *Perkins*. Further, no employee of Shivnath Rai was alleged to have ever stepped foot in California. Granted, Shivnath Rai's sales agent is located in the forum, but it is uncontested that this sales agent, Alok Mohan of Asian Brands, is neither employed by Shivnath Rai nor at liberty to contract on its behalf. Asian Brands's presence, then, does not appreciably magnify Shivnath Rai's California presence under our general jurisdiction analysis. In sum, Shivnath Rai's contacts with California make it, at most, a visitor to the forum; the "physical presence" necessary for an assertion of general jurisdiction requires more. Accordingly, the district court properly refused to exercise general jurisdiction.

iii. The Exercise of Personal Jurisdiction over Shivnath Rai Would Be Unreasonable

Even assuming that Shivnath Rai had the requisite minimum contacts to support the exercise of general jurisdiction, this Court must analyze whether the assertion of jurisdiction is reasonable. *Asahi Metal Indus. Co. v. Superior Court*, 480 U.S. 102, 113, 107 S. Ct. 1026, 94 L. Ed. 2d 92 (1987).

To assess the reasonableness of exercising jurisdiction, we consider seven factors identified by the Supreme Court in *Burger King:*

> (1) the extent of a defendant's purposeful interjection into the forum state's affairs; (2) the burden on the defendant of defending in the forum; (3) the extent of conflict with the sovereignty of the defendant's home state; (4) the forum state's interest in adjudicating the dispute; (5) the most efficient judicial resolution of the controversy; (6) the importance of the forum to the plaintiff's interests in convenient and effective relief; and (7) the existence of an alternative forum.

Even a cursory glance at the factors reveals the unreasonableness of exercising jurisdiction in this case.

(1) Assuming that Shivnath Rai's regular shipments into San Francisco constituted "systematic and continuous" contacts, the extent of its *purposeful interjection* is slight for the reasons given in the previous section.

(2) The burden on Shivnath Rai to defend suit in California appears great, given that it is incorporated in India, owns no property in the forum, and has no employees or persons authorized to act on its behalf there. Moreover, its potential witnesses and evidence are likely half a world away.

(3) As for the potential conflict with India's sovereignty, this Court has noted: "Where, as here, the defendant is from a foreign nation rather than another state, the sovereignty barrier is high and undermines the reasonableness of personal jurisdiction." *Leonis*, 1 F.3d at 852.

(4) The underlying dispute involves foreign parties concerning a contract that was executed in England, that called for rice to be delivered in India, and which provided for English arbitration in the event of a dispute. California's interest in adjudicating this suit appears slight.

(5) The "most efficient resolution" factor "involves a comparison of alternative forums." *Id*. Two alternative forums are readily apparent: (1) India, where a parallel lawsuit is currently pending, and (2) England, where the arbitration award was rendered, is final, and may be sued upon.

(6) Given the foregoing analysis, it is unsurprising that Glencore Grain's interests would seem better served by bringing the action in a different forum. Glencore Grain has provided no evidence that California is particularly convenient for it, a Dutch company. Absent any evidence of assets in the California forum against which Glencore Grain could enforce its award, we find Glencore Grain's interest in "convenient and effective" relief is frustrated, not promoted, by bringing suit there.

(7) As noted above, an alternative forum exists in India where proceedings concerning this same arbitration award are currently pending. Moreover, English courts are also available.

The reasonableness calculus clearly compels the conclusion that the exercise of personal jurisdiction over Shivnath Rai would be unreasonable.

CONCLUSION

Personal jurisdiction must be based on a defendant's person or property. Glencore Grain failed to identify any property of or conduct by Shivnath Rai that might serve as the basis for the court's jurisdiction over it; even if Shivnath Rai's conduct supported the exercise of jurisdiction, that exercise would be unreasonable given the circumstances of this case. Accordingly, the district court properly dismissed this action.
Affirmed.

NOTES AND QUESTIONS

1. There is a distinction between a case in which the cause of action arises out of and is directly related to the contacts with the forum and a case where there are contacts, but unrelated to the cause of action. According to the *Helicopteros* case, discussed in *Glencore Grain*, in the latter case, there is personal jurisdiction only if the contacts are "continuous and systematic." *Helicopteros Nacionales Colombia, S.A. v. Hall*, 466 U.S. at 414-415.

2. In the *Burger King* case, discussed in *Asahi*, a Michigan franchisee had almost no contacts with Florida except that the franchise contract provided that the franchise relationship was established in Miami and was governed by Florida law. This was sufficient for jurisdiction in Florida regarding a cause of action for failure to pay franchise fees. *See Burger King Corp. v. Rudzewicz*, 471 U.S. 462, 478-480 (1985).

3. What different considerations are there for personal jurisdiction in contract and tort actions? What can be done to maximize the possibility of personal jurisdiction when drafting an international business contract?

C. Sovereign Immunity

While the previous section examined territorial jurisdiction in U.S. courts, this section turns to an issue of subject matter jurisdiction that is important in international business transaction. In international business, state sovereign immunity may preclude a court from exercising jurisdiction over a defendant. Sovereign immunity accrues not only to a state itself but also to business entities that are owned by or instrumentalities of a state. Under the law of the United States, the exclusive way of suing an entity with sovereign immunity is under the Foreign Sovereign Immunities Act, 28 U.S.C. §§1602-1611 (1976). The FSIA retains the traditional international law approach that a foreign sovereign is immune from jurisdiction in U.S. courts unless one of the exceptions to immunity found in the FSIA applies.

PROBLEM 8-10

AB-Shanghai Brewing, Ltd., is a joint venture in China formed by AB Industries, a Milwaukee, Wisconsin company, the Shanghai Brewing Company, a state-owned enterprise, and the Shanghai Bureau of Light Industry, a government entity involved in the supervision of the light industrial sector in China. The ownership structure of the joint venture is as follows: Shanghai Brewing owns 30 percent of the joint venture, Shanghai Light Industries owns 30 percent of the joint venture, and AB Industries owns 40 percent. AB-Shanghai's beer is imported into the United States where a consumer in Ohio drinks the beer and is injured. The victim sues AB Industries and AB-Shanghai Brewing, Ltd., in the United States, but AB-Shanghai argues that it is entitled to foreign sovereign immunity on the ground that it is "an instrumentality" of the Chinese government and is therefore not subject to the jurisdiction of the U.S. courts. Plaintiff's lawyer counters that the joint venture is not under the control of the PRC government as Article 7 of the Joint Venture Law provides that "a joint venture has the right to independently conduct business operation and management within the scope prescribed by Chinese laws and regulations." As the law clerk for the judge presiding over the case, you are asked to answer two questions: (1) Does the joint venture qualify as an agent or instrumentality of a foreign state and (2) is the joint venture entitled to foreign sovereign immunity from jurisdiction in U.S. courts? See *Arbitration Between TCL & CNMC* below and the following note on the doctrine of restrictive immunity.

Arbitration Between Trans Chemical Ltd. and China National Machinery Import & Export Corp.
United States District Court, Southern District of Texas, 1997
978 F. Supp. 266

LAKE, District Judge.
[This case involved litigation brought by Trans Chemical Ltd. (TCL) to enforce an arbitration award of over $9.4 million against China National Machinery Import & Export Corp. (CNMC), a Chinese company. The award was enforced by the court under the terms of the New York Convention on the Recognition and Enforcement of Foreign Arbitral Awards. The court had to deal with issues under the FSIA.]

JURISDICTION UNDER THE FOREIGN
SOVEREIGN IMMUNITIES ACT

The FSIA provides that "[s]ubject to existing international agreements to which the United States [was] a party at the time of the enactment of this Act a foreign state shall be immune from the jurisdiction of the courts of the United States and of the States except as provided in sections 1605 to 1607 of this chapter." 28 U.S.C. §1604. Under 28 U.S.C. §1330(a) "[t]he district courts shall have original jurisdiction without regard to amount in controversy of any nonjury civil action against a foreign state as defined in section 1603(a) of this title as to any claim for relief in personam with respect to which the foreign state is not entitled to immunity under sections 1605-1607 of this title or under any applicable international agreement." 28 U.S.C. §1330(a). "Sections 1604 and 1330(a) work in tandem: §1604 bars federal and state courts from exercising jurisdiction when a foreign state *is* entitled to immunity, and §1330(a) confers jurisdiction on district courts to hear suits brought by United States citizens and by aliens when a foreign state is *not* entitled to immunity." *Argentine Republic v. Amerada Hess Shipping Corp.*, 488 U.S. 428, 434, 109 S. Ct. 683, 688, 102 L. Ed. 2d 818 (1989) (emphasis in original).

TCL alleges that CNMC is an "agency or instrumentality of a foreign state" within the meaning of the FSIA. 28 U.S.C. §1603 provides a detailed definition of an "agency or instrumentality of a foreign state:"

> (a) A "foreign state," except as used in section 1608 of this title, includes a political subdivision of a foreign state or an agency or instrumentality of a foreign state as defined in subsection (b).
> (b) An "agency or instrumentality of a foreign state" means any entity —
>   (1) which is a separate legal person, corporate or otherwise, and
>   (2) which is an organ of a foreign state or political subdivision thereof, or a majority of whose shares or other ownership interest is owned by a foreign state or political subdivision thereof, and
>   (3) which is neither a citizen of a State of the United States . . . nor created under the laws of any third country.

TCL bears the burden of showing jurisdiction under the FSIA.

The parties do not dispute that CNMC satisfies the first and last elements of §1603(b). CNMC is a corporation organized under the laws of the People's Republic of China ("China") and is not a citizen of a State of the United States or created under the laws of a third country. Their dispute focuses on the second element. CNMC argues that after its 1992 corporate reorganization it is no longer state-owned by the Chinese government as required by §1603(b)(2). CNMC also argues that the court should require TCL to prove, pursuant to *Edlow Int'l v. Nuklearna Elektrarna Krsko (NEK)*, 441 F. Supp. 827 (D.D.C. 1977), that CNMC discharges a governmental function or that the Chinese government exercises direct control over CNMC's operations in a manner indicating that it owns a controlling interest in CNMC.

Based on the court's analysis of Chinese law and CNMC's documents the court concludes that Chinese industrial enterprises "owned by the whole people," including CNMC, are "state-owned," with proprietary rights exercised by the State Council on behalf of the state. Because CNMC is state-owned the court also concludes that CNMC is an agency or instrumentality of the People's Republic of China within the meaning of 28 U.S.C. §1603(b)(2). Professor Rui's opinion that the 1988 Industrial Enterprises Law somehow converted "ownership by the whole people" from "state ownership" into a form of "social ownership" is not supported by Chinese law. The Constitution, the Civil Law, and the Industrial Enterprises Law and its implementing regulations do not refer to a separate category of "social property" or "social ownership," and do not distinguish between "government property" and "social property."

CNMC argues that adherence to the strict majority ownership test of 28 U.S.C. §1603(b)(2) would render virtually every enterprise in China an agency or instrumentality of the Chinese government under the FSIA. To avoid this result CNMC argues that the court should apply the *Edlow* analysis to determine whether CNMC is an organ of the Chinese government or whether the Chinese government actually exercised control over its operations. In this case, however, the court is not faced with the dilemmas faced by the court in *Edlow*. Private enterprises clearly exist in China, and the Chinese government is encouraging their growth. A Chinese private enterprise would not be an agency or instrumentality of the Chinese state under the FSIA. Moreover, the evidence of state ownership of CNMC in this case goes well beyond the naked presumption based on socialist political ideology offered by the plaintiff in *Edlow*. Because Chinese law makes it clear that CNMC remained a state-owned industrial enterprise even after its 1992 reorganization, the court concludes that an analysis under *Edlow* is unnecessary, even if such an analysis were relevant. CNMC is an agency or instrumentality of the People's Republic of China because it is owned by the Chinese state.

DOES THE COURT HAVE JURISDICTION OVER CNMC UNDER AN EXCEPTION TO IMMUNITY?

The court's conclusion that CNMC is an agency or instrumentality of China does not end the court's inquiry under the FSIA. As a foreign state CNMC is entitled to sovereign immunity from suit in the United States unless the relationship or transaction at issue falls within one of the FSIA's exceptions to immunity enumerated in 28 U.S.C. §1605(a). Section 1605(a) provides in relevant part:

> (a) A foreign state shall not be immune from the jurisdiction of courts of the United States or of the States in any case — . . .
>
> (6) in which the action is brought, either to enforce an agreement made by the foreign state with or for the benefit of a private party to submit to arbitration all or any differences which have arisen or which may arise between the parties with respect to a defined legal relationship, whether contractual or not, concerning a subject matter capable of settlement by arbitration under the laws of the United States, or to confirm an award made pursuant to such an agreement to arbitrate, if (A) the arbitration takes place or is intended to take place in the United States, (B) the agreement or award is or may be governed by a treaty or other international agreement in force for the United States calling for the recognition and enforcement of arbitral awards, (C) the underlying claim, save for the agreement to arbitrate, could have been brought in a United States court under this section or section 1607, or (D) paragraph (1) of this subsection is otherwise applicable.

If one of these exceptions to sovereign immunity applies the court has subject matter jurisdiction.

TCL alleges that the court has jurisdiction under §1605(a)(6)(A) over its claim to confirm the arbitral award pursuant to the FAA. CNMC does not challenge this allegation, and the court agrees that it has jurisdiction over the FAA claim under this subsection.

Section 1605(a)(6) also supplies jurisdiction over TCL's claim under the New York Convention. Section 1605(a)(6)(B) allows the court to exercise jurisdiction over CNMC if the arbitration award "is or may be governed by a treaty or other international agreement in force for the United States calling for the recognition and enforcement of arbitral awards." The Convention falls squarely within the terms of this exception. TCL's claim under the Convention is thus excepted from the immunity provided to CNMC under §1604.

NOTE ON RESTRICTIVE IMMUNITY

The FSIA adopts the doctrine of restrictive immunity under international law, which holds that a state is immune with regard to sovereign or public acts but not with regard to private acts. §1605(a) enumerates six types of claims for which there is no immunity from jurisdiction: A foreign state is amenable to jurisdiction in the United States if (1) the foreign state has waived its immunity, (2) the action is based on commercial activity carried on in the United States or having a direct effect in the United States, (3) the action concerns rights in property taken in violation of international law, (4) the action concerns rights in immovable property located in the United States, (5) the action involves a claim for damages under certain circumstances caused by the tortious activity of the foreign state, and (6) the action is brought in connection with an arbitration agreement with a foreign state. These exceptions may cover nonmaritime as well as maritime claims. §1605(b), however, speaks specifically to maritime claims, stating that "[a] foreign state shall not be immune from the jurisdiction of the courts of the United States in any case in which a suit in admiralty is brought to enforce a maritime lien against a vessel or cargo of the foreign state, which maritime lien is based upon a commercial activity of the foreign state."

D.   The Act of State Doctrine

Disputes in international business can also implicate the act of state doctrine, a judicially created doctrine of deference under which U.S. courts refuse to examine and adjudicate the legality of the acts of a foreign state.

PROBLEM 8-11

While vacationing in Costa Rica, Jones receives a flyer under his hotel door advertising certificates of deposit issued by the Costa Rican branch office of Mid-America Bank, an Ohio banking corporation, payable in 12 months at 50 percent interest at Mid-America's office in Costa Rica. Jones immediately heads down to the nearest branch and buys $500,000 worth of certificates. When Jones returns to Ohio, he reads in the local paper that the Costa Rican government has nationalized the Mid-America branch in Costa Rica and has repudiated the obligation under the certificates. Jones sues Mid-America in Ohio for $750,000, the face amount of the certificates plus the interest due. Mid-America moves to dismiss the case on the basis of the act of state doctrine. What is the result? See *Optopics Laboratories* and *Fogade* below.

Optopics Laboratories Corp. v. Savannah Bank of Nigeria, Ltd.
United States District Court, Southern District of New York, 1993
816 F. Supp. 898

SAND, District Judge.

This case is brought by Optopics Laboratories Corporation, a Delaware corporation, as assignee of Ashford Laboratories, Inc., against Savannah Bank of Nigeria, Ltd. for nonpayment on a letter of credit issued by defendant. Jurisdiction is found under 28 U.S.C. §1330, which provides that district courts shall have original jurisdiction over non-jury civil actions against a foreign state, and also under the Foreign Sovereign Immunities Act. Currently before the Court are cross-motions for summary judgment. Because we find that no genuine issues of material fact are in dispute and that plaintiff is entitled to payment on the Letter of Credit as a matter of law, plaintiff's motion for summary judgment is granted. Defendant's motion for summary judgment is denied.

FACTUAL BACKGROUND

The material facts surrounding the transaction at issue in this lawsuit are undisputed. In October 1982, Ashford Laboratories, Inc. ("Ashford"), a New Jersey corporation, contracted to sell to a Nigerian importer, Mabson Pharmaceuticals, Ltd. ("Mabson"), cold capsules for $32,265. In order to effect payment, Mabson applied for an irrevocable letter of credit with defendant, a government owned bank, Savannah Bank of Nigeria (the "Bank"). On the reverse side of the Application are printed certain "General Terms & Conditions," including one which will be discussed in further detail below, which reads: "This Letter of Credit is subject to the usual terms and conditions operating in the center where the Credit be established."

Subsequent to the submission of the Application to the Bank by Mabson, Bank America International ("Bank America") advised Ashford that a letter of credit known as L-82493 in the amount of $32,265, payable in New York, in United States dollars, had been established by the defendant in Ashford's favor. The Letter of Credit is a two-page document, and is dated November 1, 1982. The Letter of Credit provides that it is subject to the Uniform Customs and Practice for Documentary Credits, 1974 Revision, International Chamber of Commerce Publication No. 290 (the "UCP").

After the Letter of Credit was established and in reliance thereon, Ashford shipped the pharmaceuticals to Mabson. Ashford presented conforming documents in strict compliance with the Letter of Credit on or about November 30, 1982. Each document specifically identified in the Letter of Credit was submitted by Ashford.

The Bank approved the Letter of Credit for payment on December 20, 1982. Both the Application and the Letter of Credit made clear that due to Nigeria's foreign exchange controls, a Form M would have to be filed by the importer, Mabson, through the defendant. A Form M is an application directed to the

Central Bank to purchase foreign exchange. Defendant complied with this requirement on January 20, 1983, with the request that "the Foreign Currency should be paid to Bank of America, New York." The record suggests that Mabson also complied with related procedures regarding the Form M.

The Bank failed to pay on the Letter of Credit, claiming that it was unable to remit United States dollars to Bank America due to the failure of the Central Bank of Nigeria to provide foreign exchange. A June 8, 1983 cable from the Bank advised Bank America that it could negotiate the documents for the Letter of Credit but that Bank America would not be reimbursed by defendant until foreign exchange cover was made available. Similar cables were sent by defendant to Bank America on February 21, 1984, and January 15, 1985. Bank America, justifiably, has not negotiated the payment of the Letter of Credit. Significantly, the defendant has admitted that it would like to pay the Letter of Credit, and has offered to do so in Naira, the Nigerian currency. Plaintiff has rejected that offer.

Sometime subsequent to defendant's acceptance of the Letter of Credit, the Government of Nigeria engaged in a program to reschedule the payment of foreign debt, referred to as the "refinancing exercise." Defendant contends that as part of that refinancing exercise, Nigeria required, as a condition to payment on the Letter of Credit, that Ashford submit a claim form to Chase Manhattan Bank. Defendant further avers that at least as early as April 15, 1985, Ashford received a document entitled "The Central Bank of Nigeria—Circular dated 18th April, 1984," which gave notice that creditors must lodge claims with Chase Manhattan Bank to have debts paid by the Central Bank. Ashford never submitted any such claim form. Defendant asserts that due to Ashford's failure to submit the required document, the conditions of the Letter of Credit were not strictly complied with and the Bank is not required to honor the Letter of Credit.

Two other sets of facts should be noted at this point. In a letter to Mabson dated October 5, 1990, defendant acknowledged receipt of payment from Mabson for the Letter of Credit, and stated that "[w]e have not been able to remit same to the exporters [i.e. Ashford] due to a non-provision of the required foreign exchange cover by the Central Bank of Nigeria." This indicates both that refusal to release funds is not due to any withholding of the money by the bank's customer, and furthermore, that the reason for the refusal is non-provision of foreign exchange, as stated in the cables to Bank America, and not any failure on Ashford's part to strictly comply with the terms of the Letter of Credit.

ACT OF STATE

Defendant argues that the Nigerian exchange controls are governmental policy, and that any adjudication by this Court would be an interference with a sovereign act of state. Although we find that the act of state doctrine is not implicated, it is a claim which is of the utmost seriousness and will be addressed fully.

The act of state doctrine recognizes both that the laws of nations as applied within their own borders are sovereign and should not be passed upon by our courts, and that the judiciary must be restrained from rendering decisions which will affect the United States' foreign policy, a sphere of power constitutionally assigned to the executive and legislative branches. "The act of state doctrine declares that a United States court will not adjudicate a politically sensitive dispute which would require the court to judge the legality of the sovereign act of a foreign state." *International Ass'n of Machinists v. OPEC*, 649 F.2d 1354, 1358 (9th Cir. 1981), *cert. denied*, 454 U.S. 1163, 102 S. Ct. 1036, 71 L. Ed. 2d 319 (1982).

A prerequisite for the application of the act of state doctrine is that the act in question is one which takes effect entirely within the boundaries of the sovereign nation. Where this is not the case, our courts will give extraterritorial effect to the law of another nation, based on comity, only where it does not conflict with the laws and policies of the United States.

Defendant ignores a number of Second Circuit cases which indicate the nature of the pertinent inquiry in determining whether the application of Nigeria's exchange control regulations to the Letter of Credit takes place entirely within the boundaries of Nigeria.

In *Allied Bank Int'l v. Banco Credito Agricola*, 757 F.2d 516 (2d Cir. 1985), the plaintiff brought an action to recover on promissory notes issued by three Costa Rican banks wholly owned by the Government of Costa Rica, which were payable in United States dollars, in New York. The banks defaulted on the notes solely due to the Costa Rican government's suspending all external debt payments. The court explained that the primary concern in applying the act of state doctrine is whether "adjudication would embarrass or hinder the executive in the realm of foreign relations," and that the rule is to be applied flexibly on a case by case basis. 757 F.2d at 521.

The Second Circuit in *Allied* held that the applicability of the act of state doctrine depends on the situs of the debt, defined as the right to receive repayment from the banks in accordance with the loan agreements. The court viewed the Costa Rican government's actions in extinguishing plaintiff's right to receive payment as a "taking," and reasoned that if the taking occurred within the foreign sovereign's territory, then the act of state doctrine would prohibit the courts of this country from adjudicating the matter. The court said that locating the debt "depends in large part on whether the purported taking can be said to have 'come to complete fruition within the dominion of the [foreign] government.'" 757 F.2d at 521.

In applying that standard, the *Allied* court held that "Costa Rica could not wholly extinguish the Costa Rican banks' obligation to timely pay United States dollars to Allied in New York. Thus the situs of the debt was not Costa Rica." 757 F.2d at 521. The court proceeded to state that Costa Rica's

> interest in the contracts at issue is essentially limited to the extent to which it can unilaterally alter the payment terms. Costa Rica's potential jurisdiction over the debt is not sufficient to locate the debt there for the purposes of the act of state doctrine analysis.

757 F.2d at 522.

The *Allied* court further stated that "acts of foreign governments purporting to have extraterritorial effect . . . should be recognized by the courts only if they are consistent with the law and policy of the United States." 757 F.2d at 522. Because the United States would not condone the Costa Rican government's attempt to change unilaterally the terms of the contracts, the court did not give effect to the Costa Rican directives.

Two other Second Circuit cases employ the same analysis and reach the same result. In *Braka v. Bancomber*, 762 F.2d 222 (2d Cir. 1985), a case decided after *Allied*, the plaintiffs, United States citizens, purchased peso and dollar certificates of deposits from a Mexican bank, with the principal and interest payable in Mexico. Subsequently, the Mexican government decreed that all domestic obligations would be paid in pesos and at a devalued exchange rate. Plaintiffs then filed suit in federal district court in New York. The court held that the situs of the debt was Mexico, since the Mexican decree could wholly extinguish the plaintiffs' rights within the dominion of the foreign government. The act of state doctrine therefore barred plaintiffs' recovery.

In *Garcia v. Chase Manhattan Bank, N.A.*, 735 F.2d 645 (2d Cir. 1984), plaintiffs sued over the proceeds of two certificates of deposit which were issued by Chase's Cuba branch prior to the time Cuba seized the assets of the bank. The CDs provided that they were redeemable at any Chase branch worldwide. The Court found that the situs of the debt was wherever it could be collected, and therefore the acts of the Cuban government could not wholly extinguish the plaintiffs' rights. The act of state doctrine was therefore inapplicable.

The application of *Allied, Braka*, and *Garcia* to the case before this Court is clear. The "taking" is plaintiff's right to receive the proceeds of the Letter of Credit in United States dollars at a bank in New York. The act of the Nigerian government in refusing to provide the foreign exchange to defendant is not enough to wholly extinguish the Nigerian bank's obligation to pay on the Letter of Credit in New York. Therefore, the situs of the debt is not Nigeria, and the act of state doctrine is not implicated. Furthermore, because the Nigerian government's attempt to unilaterally modify a private letter of credit contract is against the law and policy of the United States, this Court will not enforce the Nigerian policy extraterritorially.

In response to this caselaw, defendant appears to place reliance on last year's Supreme Court decision in *Republic of Argentina and Banco Central de la Republica Argentina v. Weltover, et al.*, 504 U.S. 607, 112 S. Ct. 2160, 119 L. Ed. 2d 394 (1992). That case however did not address the act of state doctrine at all, but instead dealt with the Foreign Sovereign Immunities Act ("FSIA"), the application of which has not been seriously challenged in this action. *Weltover* makes clear that the FSIA would not bar plaintiff here, as the acts of the defendant clearly fall within the commercial activity exception in the statute and have a direct effect in the United States.

For the foregoing reasons, we find that the act of state doctrine is inapplicable and does not bar plaintiff's suit against the bank.

[Turning to the letter of credit issues, the court held that Ashford had strictly complied with the terms of the letter of credit and was entitled to payment from Savannah Bank and entered judgment in favor of the plaintiff.]

FOGADE v. ENB Revocable Trust
United States Court of Appeals, Eleventh Circuit, 2001
263 F.3d 1274

CARNES, Circuit Judge.
[In early 1994, Venezuela suffered a financial crisis precipitated by the collapse of Venezuela's largest bank. A number of Venezuelan banks were forced to seek assistance from the Fondo de Garantia de Depositos y Proteccion Bancaria (FOGADE), a Venezuelan government agency similar to the Federal Deposit

Insurance Corporation, which provides financial assistance to Venezuelan depository institutions. Among those banks seeking assistance was Bancor, a stock corporation, a majority of whose shares was owned by Corpofin, another bank. Three individuals — Juan Santaella, Julio Leanez, and Oscar Zamora, the defendants in this case — were minority shareholders of Bancor and sat on Bancor's board. These same individuals were also minority shareholders and members of the board of Corpofin. Between March and June of 1994, Bancor received $300 million in financial assistance from FOGADE. On the grounds that Bancor had not repaid its debts or increased its capital, FOGADE caused Bancor to be "intervened," a process similar to placing a company in receivership. In September 1994 upon discovering that Corpofin had large unguaranteed debts with Bancor, FOGADE also placed Corpofin in receivership. As part of the intervention process, FOGADE also removed Santaella, Leanez, and Zamora from the boards of Bancor and Corpofin and appointed new directors. In October 1995, the Venezuelan government ordered Bancor to be liquidated. Corpofin remained in receivership.

Corpofin's interventor subsequently discovered that on May 9, 1994, one day prior to their removal from Corpofin's board, defendants caused Corpofin to engage in a series of transactions that transferred all of Corpofin's ownership of shares of Eastern National Bank (ENB), a U.S. bank chartered in Miami, to several business entities, including the ENB revocable trust, which were directly controlled by defendants. The shares of ENB were worth $30 million but Corpofin received only $870,000 for the shares. On May 9, 1994, Corpofin owed Bancor $16.5 million, which would have been satisfied out of the shares of ENB shares that Corpofin owned.

Plaintiffs FOGADE and Corpofin brought suit in the federal district court for the Southern District of Florida, alleging that the individual defendants and their business entities unlawfully misappropriated ENB shares, which took place primarily in Miami. The district court granted summary judgment in favor of plaintiffs and ordered the shares of ENB be returned to Corpofin. Defendants appealed to the Eleventh Circuit Court of Appeals.]

THE ACT OF STATE ISSUES

Defendants asserted a large number of affirmative defenses [in the district court]. On appeal, defendants have pursued only one of the theories they asserted in their affirmative defenses. In essence, defendants contend that FOGADE illegally confiscated all of their financial interests in Venezuela, including their interest in Corpofin, and then, by causing Corpofin to pursue defendants' ownership interests in Eastern National Bank, sought to extend that unlawful confiscation into U.S. territory. Specifically, defendants argue FOGADE is guilty of confiscation and mismanagement of Corpofin and Bancor and assert RICO, conspiracy, fraud, reclamation of shares, unjust enrichment, accounting, waste, and breach of fiduciary theories. Plaintiffs respond before us, as they did in the district court, that the act of state doctrine bars consideration of the lawfulness of the Venezuelan government's intervention through FOGADE of Corpofin.

The district court agreed with plaintiffs that under the act of state doctrine the intervention of Corpofin must be deemed valid and cannot be subject to review in a United States court. Relying on *Banco Nacional de Cuba v. Sabbatino*, 376 U.S. 398, 428, 84 S. Ct. 923, 940, 11 L. Ed. 2d 804 (1964), the district court concluded that:

> [w]hether FOGADE and others violated Venezuelan law in committing the alleged acts is irrelevant; "the Judicial Branch will not examine the validity of a taking of property within its own territory by a foreign sovereign government . . . even if the complaint alleges that the taking violates customary international law."

Defendants' primary challenge to that reasoning and conclusion is based upon the legislative overruling of *Sabbatino* by passage of the so-called "Second Hickenlooper Amendment," 22 U.S.C. §2370(e)(2). The Second Hickenlooper Amendment provides, in relevant part:

> Notwithstanding any other provision of law, no court in the United States shall decline on the ground of the federal act of state doctrine to make a determination on the merits . . . in a case in which a claim of title or other right to property is asserted . . . based upon (or traced through) a confiscation or other taking after January 1, 1959, by an act of [ ] state in violation of the principles of international law. . . .

22 U.S.C. §2370(e)(2). Thus, defendants argue that the district court should not have applied the act of state doctrine to dismiss their counterclaims because plaintiffs' intervention of Corpofin constituted a confiscation of property in violation of the principles of international law.

The Second Hickenlooper Amendment did overrule, at least with respect to confiscations of property, the *Sabbatino* decision to the extent that it held that the act of state doctrine would apply without regard to whether a foreign state's actions violated international law. The question is how the act of state doctrine and *Sabbatino*, as modified by the Second Hickenlooper Amendment, apply here.

The Second Hickenlooper Amendment has three requirements that must be met before it applies. The Amendment requires: (1) a claim of title or other right to property; (2) based upon or traced through a confiscation or other taking; (3) in violation of international law. 22 U.S.C. §2370(e)(2). Here, the parties do not dispute that the first requirement is met, because the Venezuelan-controlled Corpofin has asserted a claim of right to the shares of ENB. Regarding the second requirement, defendants argue that Corpofin's alleged ownership interest in ENB is "based upon" Venezuela's intervention of Corpofin, which, defendants contend, was an "illegal confiscation or other taking." As for the third requirement, defendants argue that Venezuela's confiscation of Corpofin without payment of compensation to the individual defendants constituted a violation of international law.

Even assuming that FOGADE's intervention of Corpofin constituted a "confiscation or other taking" (the second requirement), we are not persuaded that it was carried out in violation of international law (the third requirement). As a rule, when a foreign nation confiscates the property of its own nationals, it does not implicate principles of international law. None of the decisions that the defendants rely upon are to the contrary. They involve misappropriations by foreign governments of property that belonged to citizens of other countries. Because Venezuela's act of intervening Corpofin, a Venezuelan corporation owned entirely by Venezuelan nationals, does not violate international law, the Second Hickenlooper Amendment does not preclude application of the act of state doctrine.

Seeking to avoid this result, defendants attempt to shift the focus away from the plaintiffs' act of intervening Corpofin to their alleged "extraterritorial confiscation" of ENB, which, defendants stress, was at all times located in the United States. In other words, defendants want to collapse the plaintiffs' intervention of Corpofin and their subsequent "confiscation" of the ENB shares into one long drawn out act, arguing that the intervention of Corpofin was "for the sole purpose of confiscating the ENB shares."

Confiscations by a foreign state of property located in the United States, even if the property belongs to one of the foreign state's own nationals, implicates principles of international law. Moreover, a foreign state's expropriations occur in the jurisdiction in which they are perfected. Defendants' position is that the plaintiffs' actions about which they complain were not perfected in Venezuela with the intervention of Corpofin, but in this country when the ENB shares were "confiscated" by means of this lawsuit. That confiscation, the defendants argue, constituted a violation of international law, thereby precluding application of the act of state doctrine.

We disagree. As previously noted, the Second Hickenlooper Amendment provides that a federal court must not decline on act of state grounds to address the merits in a case when a party asserts a claim of right "*based upon* . . . a confiscation or other taking . . . by an act of state in violation of the principles of international law. . . ." 22 U.S.C. §2370(e)(2) (emphasis added). Thus, the claim to property must be "based upon" — that is, must be derivative of — an act of state that is in violation of international law.

Here the plaintiffs' claim of right to the ENB shares is "based upon" FOGADE's intervention of Corpofin and the defendants' contention that the plaintiffs obtained the ENB shares illegally is also "based upon" FOGADE's intervention of Corpofin. If the plaintiffs legitimately controlled FOGADE, the defendants would have no argument that plaintiffs acted illegally in taking control of ENB. The premise of defendants' position that FOGADE would not have standing to sue on behalf of Corpofin is that FOGADE unlawfully intervened it. So, everything turns on FOGADE's intervention of Corpofin. Thus, the defendants must show that the alleged confiscation of Corpofin was in violation of international law, not that the plaintiffs' subsequent and successful attempt to recapture the ENB shares through Corpofin was. As we have already explained, however, the intervention of Corpofin was purely domestic (to Venezuela) in nature, and does not violate international law. Therefore, because FOGADE's intervention of Corpofin, upon which Corpofin's claim to ENB is based, was not in violation of international law, the Second Hickenlooper Amendment does not apply to preclude the application of the act of state doctrine to defendants' affirmative defenses questioning the standing of plaintiffs to sue because of the alleged illegality of the intervention of Corpofin.

NOTES AND QUESTIONS

1. The act of state doctrine reached a fever pitch of political controversy when in *Banco Nacional de Cuba v. Sabbatino*, 376 U.S. 398 (1964), discussed in the *Fogade* case, the Supreme Court invoked it to refuse to disturb a nationalization of property in Cuba by the Castro government despite the fact there was a clear violation of international law. For a discussion of the historical development of the act of

state doctrine, *see* Daniel C.K. Chow, *Rethinking the Act of State Doctrine: An Analysis in Terms of Jurisdiction to Prescribe*, 62 Wash. L. Rev. 397 (1987).

2. In *Optopics Laboratories v. Savannah Bank*, why did the plaintiffs reject the offer of the Savannah Bank bank to pay in Nigerian currency? Savannah Bank also asked Bank America to negotiate the documents for the letter of credit. Why did Bank America refuse? The court rejected the use of the act of state doctrine as a defense to payment by the Savannah Bank and entered judgment for the plaintiff, but now the plaintiff has a practical problem. What must plaintiff do to collect?

PROBLEM 8-12

Vost Chemical Corporation is a Delaware corporation with its principal offices in New York. Three months ago, Vost entered into an agreement with the Jiang Trading Company (JTC), a Chinese company located in Shanghai, China, for the sale of styrene monomer, a raw material used in the production of automobiles, computers, and a variety of other products. The sales contract required that the styrene had to be delivered in Shanghai and that Vost had to transport and bear the bear the risk of loss of the goods to the port of Shanghai and was obligated to place the goods at the disposal of the buyer, who was responsible for import clearance. To secure payment, JTC obtained an irrevocable letter of credit for the full price of the goods ($1.2 million) from the Shanghai branch of the Bank of China, the government central bank. No place of payment was designated for the letter of credit, but as the Bank of China has a branch office in New York and regularly made payments on its letter of credit business there, Vost assumed that it would submit the documents through that New York branch bank and receive payment there.

Vost shipped the styrene by ocean carrier and forwarded all necessary documents to complete the transaction to the New York branch of the Bank of China, asking that payment be made through the New York branch to Vost's bank account in New York.

The Styrene arrived safely in Shanghai. However, when it was passing through Customs, the cargo was seized by the Chinese Bureau of Customs for nonpayment of past tariff obligations by JTC. As a result, the Bank of China notified Vost that the documents were inadequate, and it was refusing payment on the letter of credit. Advise Vost.

E. International Comity and *Forum Non Conveniens*

DeYoung v. Beddome
United States District Court, Southern District of New York, 1989
707 F. Supp. 132

MUKASEY, District Judge.
[Plaintiffs, individual shareholders of Dome Petroleum Limited (Dome), a Canadian producer of oil and natural gas, brought an action in federal district court to challenge a proposed acquisition of Dome by Amoco Canada Petroleum Company (AC), a Canadian subsidiary of Amoco Corporation (Amoco), an Indiana

corporation with its headquarters in Chicago. Both of the Amoco entities were named as defendants in the case along with two individuals Beddome and MacDonald, officers and directors of Dome. Plaintiffs alleged various state law business tort claims against both the individual and corporate defendants and in addition alleged claims as part of a class action brought on behalf of Dome shareholders that the defendants failed to comply with disclosure requirements of Section 14(a) of the Securities and Exchange Act, 15 U.S.C. §78n(a). Prior to filing the lawsuit in the United States, the plaintiffs had filed a previous action in a Canadian court against the defendants challenging the acquisition on similar grounds under Canadian law, including lack of adequate disclosure. The Canadian action was still pending when the plaintiffs filed the second action in the United States. After the U.S. lawsuit was filed, the Canadian court entered judgment in favor of the defendants, finding that disclosure was adequate. Before the federal district court were the defendants' motions to dismiss the action on the basis of *forum non conveniens* and international comity.]

For the reasons set forth below, I grant the motion to dismiss based on international comity. Accordingly, I do not reach the other grounds for dismissal asserted by defendants.

Hilton v. Guyot, 159 U.S. 113, 16 S. Ct. 139, 40 L. Ed. 95 (1895) provides the basis for applying the doctrine of international comity in federal courts, and defines it as

> the recognition which one nation allows within its territory to the legislative, executive, or judicial acts of another nation, having due regard both to international duty and convenience, and to the rights of its own citizens, or of other persons who are under the protection of its laws.

159 U.S. at 164, 16 S. Ct. at 143.

It is essential that the foreign proceeding or judgment not offend laws or public policy of the forum jurisdiction, or violate the rights of its citizens. Here it is significant that the foreign jurisdiction involved is Canada, "a sister common law jurisdiction with procedures akin to our own." *Clarkson Co. v. Shaheen*, 544 F.2d 624, 630 (2d Cir. 1976). In fact, the procedures adopted by the Court of Queens Bench in Alberta under the CBCA, and affirmed by the Court of Appeal, would seem to be if anything more protective of the rights of the shareholder plaintiffs in this case than procedures they might expect to encounter in this country. Against these considerations plaintiffs place in the balance their claim under Section 14(a) of the Securities Exchange Act, 15 U.S.C. §78n(a) (1981), and Rule 14a-9 promulgated thereunder, and argue that we should not risk compromise of federally protected rights by relegating these plaintiffs to Canadian courts that might not protect them. Furthermore, they argue that the Canadian court's decision should not be accorded comity here because it did not necessarily decide issues of full disclosure.

Although plaintiffs assert that Canadian law is less advantageous to them than the law that would be applied were the case to remain in this Court, they have made no showing that Canadian law does not afford them a cause of action to pursue their claims there.

Rather, plaintiffs' main objection to Canadian case law governing securities class actions and derivative actions seems to be that it does not permit contingent fee arrangements. But even if I were to assume *arguendo* that Canadian procedures are less favorable to the plaintiff than those in this Court, including particularly the unavailability of contingent fees in Canada, such factors have been found, in the context of *forum non conveniens*, not persuasive. There is no reason to accord that minor failing any greater weight in applying principles of international comity.

Accordingly, Canadian law provides causes of action that are the same in all significant respects as those available under United States law. Plaintiffs could have sought relief in Canadian courts, and may still do so, provided of course that Canadian principles of collateral estoppel would not bar such a suit.

Whether the prior judgment satisfies all the requirements of collateral estoppel under Canadian law need not be decided here, however. That decision is best left to the Canadian courts. Nevertheless, I find that the issue of full disclosure was sufficiently considered by the Canadian court so as to invoke international comity principles. Although plaintiffs vigorously dispute this question, my review of the Canadian proceedings convinces me that the issue of full disclosure was actually decided by the Canadian court. I have already described the procedures by which the Canadian court ensured that the corporation provided shareholders with full disclosure. In addition, in its July 14, 1988 judgment, the court specifically stated that it was "satisfied that in the Notice of Special Meeting, Notice Concerning Application and Information Circular and Proxy Statements of Dome dated April 26, 1988 Dome has provided the shareholders of Dome with full, true and plain disclosure of all material facts surrounding the Plan of Arrangement as regards the shareholders of Dome in accordance with the Interim Order." Order at 2. Those are the same disclosure documents challenged in the actions at bar.

When motions to dismiss were first filed, I found compelling defendants' arguments to dismiss on grounds of *forum non conveniens*. Although in the interim the Canadian court's decision has altered the dispositive issue here to one of comity, principles of *forum non conveniens* would support the result here. As defined in *Gulf Oil Corp. v. Gilbert*, 330 U.S. 501, 67 S. Ct. 839, 91 L. Ed. 1055 (1947) and summarized in *Reyno*, 454 U.S. at 241 n. 6, 102 S. Ct. at 258 n. 6, the criteria that doctrine provides for choosing between available forums relate to the private interests of the litigants — primarily convenience in gaining access to documents and witnesses for discovery and trial, and the public interest — including the "local interest in having localized controversies decided at home; the interest in having the trial of a diversity case in a forum that is at home with the law that must govern the action; the avoidance of unnecessary problems in conflict of laws, or in the application of foreign law; and the unfairness of burdening citizens in an unrelated forum with jury duty." *Id.*

[A] plaintiff's choice of forum weighs far less heavily in a case such as this where plaintiffs sue strictly in a representative or derivative capacity. Plaintiffs in such a case have only a small direct interest in a large controversy in which there are many potential plaintiffs, usually in many potential jurisdictions. In such a case, the plaintiffs who actually sue, like Messrs. Beddome and Katz, do not claim to be witnesses to anything other than their ownership of an interest in the dispute and their desire, and that of their lawyers, to represent others similarly situated. Such a case will often turn on events that occurred in a jurisdiction other than where the plaintiff lives, on evidence to be sought from witnesses and documents in such other jurisdiction, and on the law of such other jurisdiction.

Four of the five defendants in this case are domiciled in Canada. The acts of Dome's board challenged by plaintiffs took place in Canada. The agreement being challenged was negotiated between two Canadian corporations, and signed, in Canada. The underlying Dome documents are located in Canada. Indeed, the only location outside Canada where the parties have plausibly suggested any documents might be found is Chicago, where Amoco has its headquarters.

At oral argument, plaintiffs' counsel hypothesized that investment and commercial bankers in New York "controlled and made the decisions, and that is when those decisions were made." 4/18/88 Tr. 49. There is not a single allegation in either complaint to that effect, and not one of those unspecified bankers has been named as a defendant in either action. To the contrary, the gravamen of both complaints is that Dome stockholders are being injured by the misconduct of Dome's board, aided and abetted by Amoco and AC. To the extent that the alleged misconduct involves rejecting bids from likely suitors, the only two identified in the complaints, whose representatives presumably would testify to the advantage they offer over AC, are Trans Canada Pipelines Limited and Imperial Oil Limited — both Canadian entities.

Plaintiffs note also that Dome's transfer agent, the Bank of New York, distributed to stockholders certain interim reports regarding the Dome-AC deal. But even if those reports played some role in the alleged impropriety, there is no suggestion that witnesses whose testimony bears on the content of the reports are to be found in New York. The transfer agent's role in their distribution is utterly insignificant in any evaluation of where the lawsuit should proceed.

Nor can I attach great weight to plaintiffs' claim that Dome's stock is traded on a registered securities exchange in this District and many of its stockholders are U.S. citizens. "'[P]arties who choose to engage in international transactions . . . cannot expect always to bring their foreign opponents into a United States forum when every reasonable consideration leads to the conclusion that the site of the litigation should be elsewhere.'" *Diatronics, Inc. v. Elbit Computers, Ltd.*, 649 F. Supp. 122, 129 (S.D.N.Y. 1986) (quoting *Ionescu v. E.F. Hutton & Co. (France) S.A.*, 465 F. Supp. 139, 145 (S.D.N.Y. 1979)), *aff'd*, 812 F.2d 712 (2d Cir. 1987).

Where the plaintiffs' substantive contribution to the litigation and the evidence to be found in this jurisdiction are both nil, where no potential witness in the litigation who may be unwilling to attend a trial is subject to this Court's process, and where discovery of third parties in Canada (*e.g.* Trans Canada and Imperial) would have to be conducted by cumbersome letters rogatory, it is downright perverse to argue that there is anything close to equal convenience in trying this case here or in Canada, modern communications notwithstanding. The public interest factors present here weigh, if possible, even more heavily in favor of having this case decided in Canada. There is little doubt that, applying New York choice of law rules, *Klaxon Co. v. Stentor Elec. Mfg. Co.*, 313 U.S. 487, 61 S. Ct. 1020, 85 L. Ed. 1477 (1941), Canadian law would govern the common law claims relating to corporate governance of Dome that are at the heart of both complaints. Dome, a Canadian corporation that conducts its operations in Canada, is that country's second largest producer of natural gas and third largest producer of crude oil. Under the governmental interest test that prevails to determine choice of law in New York, Canadian law would control issues of corporate governance here. That would compel this Court to apply an unfamiliar body of law, a prospect that argues strongly for dismissal.

Again, the interest of Canada in having controversies relating to one of its major corporations decided at home is substantial. That consideration, as well, supports dismissal. In this case, Canada's government and courts have already taken an active role over the subject matter of this dispute. Two agencies of the Canadian government approved the transaction, and the Court of Queen's Bench of Alberta, in Calgary, determined, after four days of hearings, just how Dome was to go about securing the approval of its creditors and shareholders before the proposed deal with AC could be consummated. Notably, two-thirds approval by stockholders was necessary before the transaction could be effected. As mentioned above, litigation was commenced in the Canadian courts to challenge the transaction. Finally, the Canadian courts have found that Dome fully disclosed all pertinent information to shareholders and that the transaction was fair. It would be highly intrusive for this Court to involve itself in a matter that has so heavily engaged the attention of both the executive and judicial authorities of Canada.

In addition, although this Court's unfamiliarity with Canadian law extends also to docket conditions in Canadian courts and the parties have offered us no proof on the subject, docket congestion in this Court is a persistent affliction. That, too, is a factor to consider in deciding whether to accept a case that can be litigated elsewhere.

In sum, I find that considerations of international comity mandate dismissal here. Moreover, this result is fully in accord with principles of *forum non conveniens*. Accordingly, defendants' motions for summary judgment are granted, and the complaints are dismissed.

So ordered.

NOTES AND QUESTIONS

1. Why did the plaintiffs bring a second action in the United States?

2. The *forum non conveniens* determination is up to the "sound discretion" of the trial court. It is a "balancing" determination based on a combination of so-called "public interest" factors and "private interest" factors. Did the court in *DeYoung* make the right decision?

3. How does the "comity" determination differ from *forum non conveniens*? Can you isolate the comity factors that are responsible for the court's decision? Is this doctrine even more flexible than *forum non conveniens*?

4. Does dismissal of an action on grounds of *forum non conveniens* or comity mean that the defendant is no longer subject to legal proceedings in the jurisdiction? *See In re Union Carbide Corp. Gas Plant Disaster at Bhopal, India*, 809 F.2d 195 (2d Cir. 1987).

F. Service of Process

Gallagher v. Mazda Motor of America, Inc.
United States District Court, Eastern District of Pennsylvania, 1992
781 F. Supp. 1079

CAHN, District Judge.

On January 1, 1990, John and Judith Gallagher, husband and wife, were traveling with their four children, Gabriella, Yolanda, Laura and Dewi, in their

1989 Mazda MPV motor vehicle when they were involved in an accident. As a result of the accident, Judith, Gabriella and Yolanda were killed, and John, Laura and Dewi were injured. This suit has been brought by John, in his individual capacity and in his capacity as representative for the other Gallagher plaintiffs, against Mazda Motor of America, Inc. ["Mazda of America"] and Mazda Motor Corp. ["Mazda of Japan"]. Mazda of Japan has moved, pursuant to Fed. R. Civ. P. 12(b)(4) and Fed. R. Civ. P. 12(b)(5) to dismiss, or, in the alternative, to quash the plaintiffs' service of process.

According to the pleadings, the plaintiffs attempted to avail themselves of Fed. R. Civ. P. 4(c)(2)(C)(ii) in two ways; by sending a copy of the Notice and Acknowledgement of Receipt of Summons and Complaint, Summons, and Complaint via registered mail to Mazda Motor Corp., 3-1 Sinchi, Funchu-Cho, Aki-Gun Hiroshima 730-91, Japan, and by sending two copies of the above mentioned documents to Mazda Motor Corp., P.O. Box 19735, Irvine, Ca. 92713-0017. All of these documents were in English. The court will discuss the sufficiency of both of these methods of service of process *seriatim*.

I. MAILING TO HIROSHIMA, JAPAN

When process is served abroad, its validity is governed by the Convention on Service Abroad of Judicial and Extrajudicial Documents in Civil and Commercial Matters, 20 UST 361, TIAS No. 6638 ["Hague Convention"].[10] Since the Hague Convention has a preemptive effect, a court need look no further when considering the validity of service abroad. Since the process mailed to Hiroshima, Japan was unquestionably served abroad, its validity must be determined by reference to the Hague Convention, and Mazda of Japan is entitled to insist on strict compliance with its provisions.

The validity of the service of process mailed to Hiroshima, Japan must be determined by reference to Article 10 of the Hague Convention. Article 10 provides:

> Provided the State of destination does not object, the present Convention shall not interfere with —
>
>   (a)   the freedom to send judicial documents, by postal channels, directly to persons abroad.
>
>   (b)   the freedom of judicial officers, officials or other competent persons of the State of origin to effect service of judicial documents directly through the judicial officers, officials or other competent persons of the State of destination.
>
>   (c)   the freedom of any person interested in a judicial proceeding to effect service of judicial documents directly through the judicial officers, officials or other competent persons of the State of destination.

Since Japan has objected to paragraphs (b) and (c) of Article 10, the process mailed to Hiroshima, Japan is valid, if at all, if it was made in accordance with paragraph (a) of Article 10.

---

10. Both the United States and Japan are signatories to the Hague Convention.

There are two distinct lines of cases interpreting the scope of paragraph (a) of Article 10. One line of cases has held that the term "send" in paragraph (a) is equivalent to "serve", and that, absent an objection, paragraph (a) permits the service of process by mail on any foreign party. This line of cases also holds that it is unnecessary to translate the process before serving it.

The second line of cases holds that paragraph (a) of Article 10 only provides for the service of *subsequent* papers after service of process has been effectuated by other means, and does not provide an independent method for the service of process.

Although the Third Circuit Court of Appeals has not yet decided how to interpret paragraph (a) of Article 10, Judge Newcomer has recently visited this area of the law. *See Raffa v. Nissan Motor Co.*, 141 F.R.D. 45 (E.D. Pa. 1991). This court finds his reasoning highly persuasive, and therefore follows him in adopting the rationale behind the second line of cases. Specifically, the court finds it implausible that Japan, which objected to the "less intrusive" paragraphs (b) and (c), and which does not permit service of process by certified mail in domestic cases, would consent to the service of foreign process by mail. This, combined with the fact that the Hague Convention uses the term "service" in all other articles, rather than the term "send", leads this court to hold that paragraph (a) of Article 10 of the Hague Convention does not provide a basis for the service of process on foreign parties to a lawsuit. The process service on Mazda of Japan by mail to Hiroshima, Japan is therefore quashed.

II. Mailing to Irvine, California

Although the Hague Convention controls when process is served abroad, it does not require service to be made abroad whenever a foreign corporation is a party to a lawsuit. For this reason, the process served in Irvine, California does not implicate the Hague Convention. If process was mailed to Mazda of Japan at a California address, the requirements of Fed. R. Civ. P. 4(c)(2)(C)(ii) would have been met, and the service would be valid. It is not clear at this point in time, however, that the process mailed to California was served on Mazda of Japan. Mazda of Japan strenuously argues that the process was mailed to, and therefore served on, Mazda of America.

In order to show that the process mailed to California constituted valid service of process on Mazda of Japan, the plaintiffs will have to show either of two things: 1) that the post office box in Irvine, California belongs to Mazda of Japan, rather than Mazda of America; or 2) that, although the post office box in Irvine, California belongs to Mazda of America, service of process on Mazda of America is effective against Mazda of Japan because the jurisdictional contacts of Mazda of America should be imputed to Mazda of Japan. The court will hold a hearing to establish these jurisdictional facts.

If the plaintiffs are unable to sustain their burden of demonstrating that service of process was validly made upon Mazda of Japan, the court will quash the service and allow the plaintiffs to attempt to re-serve Mazda of Japan in accordance with the Hague Convention. Although the parties will have little trouble deciding what evidence must be presented in order to establish that the Irvine, California post office box belongs to Mazda of Japan, the law is currently unclear as to when the jurisdictional contacts of a subsidiary may be imputed to the parent corporation. In order to provide guidance to the parties, the court will set forth the requirements for imputing such contacts.

While it is clear that the bare parent/subsidiary relationship does not allow a court to impute the jurisdictional contacts of the subsidiary to the parent, there are, in essence, three lines of cases dealing with when imputing jurisdictional contacts is proper. The first line of cases holds that, so long as both the parent and subsidiary corporations observe and respect the corporate form, the jurisdictional contacts of the subsidiary will not be imputed to the parent.

The other two lines of cases set a lower threshold for imputing the jurisdictional contacts of a subsidiary to the parent corporation. One line of cases holds that contacts should be imputed when the parent corporation exercises total control over the affairs and activities of the subsidiary, and can therefore be said to be the subsidiary's alter ego.

The other line of cases holds that contacts should be imputed when the subsidiary was either established for, or is engaged in, activities that, but for the existence of the subsidiary, the parent would have to undertake itself.

The court is persuaded that the last line of cases is the correct one, and that the jurisdictional contacts of a subsidiary corporation should be imputed to the corporate parent when the subsidiary corporation is engaged in functions that, but for the existence of the subsidiary, the parent would have to undertake. If the subsidiary is engaged in activities that are vital to the survival or the success of the parent corporation, the parent will undoubtedly receive notice of any papers served on the subsidiary. Due process will therefore be fulfilled since the party to the lawsuit will know that it has been sued, and that it must mount a defense or suffer the consequences.

The court is also convinced that the parent corporation can truly be said to have "contacts" with a jurisdiction when it has chosen, for its own purposes, to make these contacts through a subsidiary. Put another way, if a parent uses a subsidiary to do what it otherwise would have done itself, it has purposely availed itself of the privilege of doing business in the forum. Jurisdiction over the parent is therefore proper. This contrasts to the case of a holding company. In such a case, the subsidiary is not performing a function that the parent would otherwise have had to perform itself (the holding company could simply hold another type of subsidiary). In such a case, imputing jurisdictional contacts would be improper.

NOTES AND QUESTIONS

1. In order to facilitate service of process outside the United States, Rule 4(f) was added to the Federal Rules of Civil Procedure in 1993. Rule 4(f) states as follows:

> (f) *Service upon Individuals in a Foreign Country.* [S]ervice upon an individual from whom a waiver has not been obtained and filed, other than an infant or an incompetent person, may be effected in a place not within any judicial district of the United States:
>
> > (1) by any internationally agreed means reasonably calculated to give notice, such as those means authorized by the Hague Convention on the Service Abroad of Judicial and Extrajudicial Documents; or

(2) if there is no internationally agreed means of service or the applicable international agreement allows other means of service, provided that service is reasonably calculated to give notice:

(A) in the manner prescribed by the law of the foreign country for service in that country in an action in any of its courts of general jurisdiction; or

(B) as directed by the foreign authority in response to a letter rogatory or letter of request; or

(C) unless prohibited by the law of the foreign country, by

(i) delivery to the individual personally of a copy of the summons and the complaint; or

(ii) any form of mail requiring a signed receipt, to be addressed and dispatched by the clerk of the court to the part to be served; or

(3) by other means not prohibited by international agreement as may be directed by the court.

Would this rule change the result in the *Gallagher* case?

Is it a good policy to search for unilateral methods to serve process or is it better to rely on diplomatic channels?

2. In *Cupp v. Alberto-Culver USA, Inc.*, 308 F. Supp. 2d 873 (W.D. Tenn. 2004), the court stated that service of process abroad by sending a U.S. mail registered letter to the legal department of a French corporation was "questionable." Citing Fed. R. Civ. P. 4(f), the court further stated that (1) the Hague Convention applied and (2) the Hague Convention sets forth procedures for service of process that do *not* include sending documents through the U.S. mail. The court noted that there is a "split of authority" among U.S. federal courts concerning the proper interpretation of the Hague Convention "as to whether Article 10(a) allows service of process abroad by regular mail." The court concluded that the cases holding that service by registered U.S. mail does not comply with the Convention are "persuasive." For a case finding that service by registered mail does not violate the Convention, *see Ackermann v. Levine*, 788 F.2d 830, 839-40 (2d Cir. 1986). For contrary authority, *see Bankston v. Toyota Motor Co.*, 889 F.2d 172, 174 (8th Cir. 1989).

3. In *Brockmeyer v. May*, 361 F.3d 1222 (9th Cir. 2004), the court upheld service by ordinary (not registered or certified) U.S. mail under the Hague Convention, reasoning as follows:

Much of the current controversy concerning the Hague Convention is over the meaning of Article 10(a), which states that "provided the state of destination does not object, the present Convention shall not interfere with — (a) the freedom to *send* judicial documents, by postal channels, directly to persons abroad" (emphasis added). Two lines of cases interpreting the language of Article 10(a) have developed. In the first line of cases, following *Ackermann v. Levine*, 788 F.2d 830 (2d Cir. 1986), the Second Circuit interpreted the word "send" to mean "service." *Ackermann* involved a German plaintiff who filed suit in Germany and served by registered mail an American defendant in the United States. The court held that because the United States did not object to mail service under Article 10(a), service by mail was proper under the Hague Convention.

In contrast, *Bankston v. Toyota Motor Corp.*, 889 F.2d 172, 173-74 (8th Cir. 1989), the Eighth Circuit concluded that the word "send" in Article 10(a) did not mean service of process in a case involving an American plaintiff who served by registered mail a Japanese defendant in Japan. Rather, Article 10(a) provided a method for transmitting judicial documents abroad after service of process had been accomplished. *Id.* at 187. More recently, the Fifth Circuit held in *Nuovo Pignone v. Storman Asia M/V*, 310 F.3d 374, 384 (5th Cir. 2002), that a strict reading of the Hague Convention did not permit an Italian plaintiff who filed suit in the United States to serve an Italian defendant in Italy by Federal Express.

The very purpose of the Convention is to provide the means for service abroad. *See* Hague Convention Preamble. Article 1 states: "the present Convention shall apply in all cases, in civil or commercial matters, where there is occasion to transmit a judicial or extra-judicial document for *service* abroad." (emphasis added). The structure of the Convention and the placement of subsection (a) within Article 10, which lists alternate methods of service to which contracting states must specifically object, suggest that the word "send" was used as a synonym for the word "serve."

361 F.3d at 1225-26. Which view of the Convention is correct?

G. Jurisdiction over Parent and Affiliated Companies

PROBLEM 8-13

Chapman is an Ohio Corporation headquartered in Cleveland. It is engaged in the business of developing, purchasing, fabricating, and selling industrial machine products. In 2000, Chapman developed a process by which it could make a unique, abrasion-resistant steel plate (AR plate) for use in some of its machine products. Because manufacturing costs in the United States would be very expensive, Chapman looked for and found a steel mill in Galatz, Romania, that could produce the AR plate to Chapman's specifications, using the Chapman process.

Because of Romanian economic and legal regulations, however, Chapman could not book orders with the Galatz mill directly; the transaction had to be structured through the Galatz mill's European trading partner, Kirchfeld AG, a German corporation located in Essen, Germany. Kirchfeld AG has partnered with the Galatz mill to sell its products to the European Union. Using Kirchfeld as an intermediary would enable the Galatz mill to obtain payment in Euros from Kirchfeld, thus complying with Romanian regulations.

Accordingly, Chapman booked an order for 10,000 steel plates per month with Kirchfeld USA, a wholly owned subsidiary of Kirchfeld AG. Kirchfeld USA is a California corporation headquartered in Los Angeles and serves as the exclusive conduit for handling all of Kirchfeld AG's business in North America. For the first six months of this business arrangement, all was fine. The steel arrived by ship in Cleveland; Kirchfeld USA invoiced Chapman, who paid the invoice in dollars. When the seventh shipment arrived, however, Chapman discovered some problems. Over 500 AR plates were missing, and the remaining plates were made of lower-grade steel, contrary to Chapman's specifications. Chapman's investigation disclosed that the missing plates may have been consigned in Germany, by mistake or on purpose, to a German competitor. Kirchfeld USA, however, denies all responsibility, and, in an e-mail to Chapman, states that Chapman must pay the invoice as usual, and look to Kirchfeld AG, the Galatz mill, or the carrier of the AR plates for an explanation and liability. What advice do you have for Chapman? Consult Sobin and *Itel Containers* below.

Sturgis M. Sobin, U.S. Courts Can Obtain Jurisdiction Over a Foreign Parent Company
www.ablondifoster.com

While most of the decisions are highly fact specific, recent cases point to the following factors as *supporting* a finding of jurisdiction over a foreign parent:

- A high level of control and involvement by the parent in the day-to-day operations of the U.S. subsidiary;
- A substantial number or percentage of common executives, officers, directors or other key personnel or frequent rotation of such personnel between parent and subsidiary;
- The use of the U.S. subsidiary as essentially a "marketing conduit" through which a significant' percentage of the parent's U.S. sales occur;
- Activities by the U.S. subsidiary that the foreign parent would otherwise have to perform for itself in the U.S.—for example transportation and distribution of the parent's products or services;
- Public and marketing materials that hold the parent and U.S. subsidiary out as a single entity or that do not distinguish between the two;
- The failure to observe corporate and other legal formalities of the separate existence of the two entities; and
- The common and related involvement of the parent and subsidiary in the conduct being challenged (for example, an international price-fixing agreement). Of course, as noted above, if the foreign parent, becomes *directly* involved in a U.S. tort, or directly conducts significant business in the U.S., jurisdiction will be found regardless of the parent/subsidiary relationship.

On the other hand, cases where jurisdiction over the foreign parent is most often *rejected* tend to involve relationships where the parent and its subsidiary act like the separate corporate (legal) entities they are, or where the parent behaves largely as an investor, giving financial support and monitoring performance closely, but not becoming intimately involved in the day-to-day management and operations of the U.S. subsidiary's business.

Itel Containers v. Atlanttrafik Express Service Ltd.
United States Court of Appeals, Second Circuit, 1990
909 F.2d 698

KEARSE, Circuit Judge.

[In 1984, Sea Containers Ltd. (SCL), which was engaged in the business of selling and leasing cargo containers and related equipment to ocean liners, decided to purchase a shipping line (the AES line) and its two carriers. Because SCL did not want to openly compete with its customers, SCL caused to be organized and incorporated a separate legal entity Atlanttrafik Express Service Ltd. (AES Ltd.) under the laws of England for purpose of buying and serving as the holding company of the AES liner service. Another company Atlanttrafik Express Service Inc. (AES Inc.) was formed as a wholly owned subsidiary of AES Ltd. to operate the liner service. SCL advanced the funds to AES Ltd. to purchase the AES line and made loans to

AES Ltd. to finance its operations. Five vessels that were owned or leased by other SCL subsidiaries were then leased or subleased to AES Ltd.

Plaintiffs Itel Containers International Corporation (Itel), Flexi-Van Leasing Inc. (Flexi-Van), and plaintiffs Textainer Inc. and Textainer Special Equipment Ltd. (collectively Textainer) were also in the business of leasing cargo containers to ocean carriers and had leased equipment to the AES line prior to its sale to AES Ltd. When they learned of SCL's involvement in the imminent purchase of the AES line by AES Ltd., they attempted to obtain SCL's guarantee on leases of equipment to the AES line that were being renegotiated, extended, or were being assigned by the AES line to AES Ltd. SCL refused to give its guarantee and the plaintiffs eventually entered into leases directly with AES Ltd.

In 1985, AES Ltd. encountered serious financial difficulty and went into liquidation in England. With AES Ltd. in bankruptcy, plaintiffs brought an action in the federal district court for the Southern District of New York to recover payment on the equipment rentals from SCL. The district court ruled that SCL had no liability for the debts of AES Ltd. and the plaintiffs brought this appeal.]

A. THE CLAIMS AGAINST SCL

Plaintiffs advance three theories in support of their contention that SCL is liable for the damages that resulted when AES Ltd. ceased doing business and thereby breached the container leases. They contend that SCL should have been found liable (1) as a joint venturer with AES Ltd., or (2) as AES Ltd.'s principal, or (3) for such abuse of the corporate form as to warrant piercing the corporate veil. We find no merit in any of these arguments.

1. THE JOINT VENTURE THEORY

Under New York law, which applies to this case, a joint venture "is in a sense a partnership for a limited purpose, and it has long been recognized that the legal consequences of a joint venture are equivalent to those of a partnership." *Gramercy Equities v. Dumont*, 72 N.Y.2d 560, 565, 534 N.Y.S.2d 908, 911, 531 N.E.2d 629 (1988). Thus, for example, one coventurer will be bound by a lease signed by another coventurer, even if the first neither signed nor assented to the lease. Plaintiffs contend that the district court should have found that SCL and AES Ltd. were joint venturers in operating the AES line and that, under the above principles, SCL was liable for the container leases signed by AES Ltd. We conclude that the district court properly found that SCL was not party to a joint venture.

In order to form a joint venture, (1) two or more persons must enter into a specific agreement to carry on an enterprise for profit; (2) their agreement must evidence their intent to be joint venturers; (3) each must make a contribution of property, financing, skill, knowledge, or effort; (4) each must have some degree of joint control over the venture; and (5) there must be a provision for the sharing of both profits and losses. All of these elements must be present before joint venture liability may be imposed. At least two elements were lacking in the present case.

The district court found that SCL did not intend to engage in a joint venture. Plaintiffs have pointed to no evidence to the contrary, and the record fully supports the view that SCL purposely used layers of corporations so that its involvement with the AES line would be remote. Thus the second element listed above was not present. Further, the court found that SCL chose to operate through corporations in order to limit its losses to the amounts it was willing to advance in loans. Though SCL plainly hoped to share in whatever profits the AES line produced, there was no indication that it expected to share in the losses except as a lender to AES Ltd. Thus, the fifth element also was not present. Accordingly, assuming that the AES line was properly to be considered the "venture," the findings of the district court preclude the conclusion that it was an SCL joint venture.

Further, we note that the district court correctly found that AES Ltd. itself was not a joint venture because it was a corporation. A joint venture and a corporation are mutually exclusive ways of doing business. Though business associates may be treated as partners vis-a-vis one another even when they operate through a corporation, the corporate form is to be respected in dealings with third parties.

2. THE AGENCY THEORIES

Plaintiffs also contend that SCL should have been held liable on the leases as a principal for which AES Ltd. was the agent. Though they assert that there was an express agency relationship, their argument appears to rely to a greater extent on the proposition that there was an implied agency.

An express agency is created "by written or spoken words or other conduct of the principal which, reasonably interpreted, causes the agent to believe that the principal desires him so to act on the principal's account." *Restatement (Second) of Agency* §26 (1958) ("*Restatement*"). Whether such an agency is formed depends on the actual interaction between the putative principal and agent, not on any perception a third party may have of the relationship.

Plaintiffs point to various activities of SCL that might perhaps have been thought by others to establish an agency relationship in some respect. There was no evidence, however, that SCL actually authorized AES Ltd. to act as its agent or that it in any way led AES Ltd. to believe AES Ltd. was so authorized. SCL made clear from the start its intention to utilize the corporate form for AES Ltd. so as to limit SCL's liability. SCL did provide financing to AES Ltd., but AES Ltd. was meant to, and did, operate independently. SCL chose not to be a shareholder, and no SCL employee sat on AES Ltd.'s Board of Directors. The record simply would not have supported a finding that SCL authorized AES Ltd. to act on its behalf.

Implied agency, in contrast, depends not on the actual relationship between principal and agent but on the reasonable conclusion of a third party, derived from actions of the principal, that the person acting has authority to do so from the principal. "[A]pparent authority to do an act is created as to a third person by written or spoken words or any other conduct of the principal which, reasonably interpreted, causes the third person to believe that the principal consents to have the act done on his behalf by the person purporting to act for him." *Restatement* §27. Thus, in order to determine whether there was implied authority, the court must focus on the acts of the principal in relation to the third party.

Though plaintiffs argue that the actions of SCL reasonably led them to believe that SCL was AES Ltd.'s principal, the record refutes their claims. Under New York law, "[o]ne who deals with an agent does so at his peril, and must make the necessary effort to discover the actual scope of authority." *Ford v. Unity Hospital*, 32 N.Y.2d at 472, 346 N.Y.S.2d at 244. Whatever the possibility that some of SCL's actions may have given outsiders the impression that AES Ltd. was running the AES line on behalf of SCL, the scope of any such implied authority plainly could not be deemed to have extended to the one set of AES Ltd. actions that is pertinent here, *i.e.*, the execution of the container leases. Both Itel and Flexi-Van, in the course of negotiating the leases with AES Ltd., communicated directly with SCL in an attempt to get SCL to take responsibility for the leases. SCL flatly refused to do so. Neither these plaintiffs nor Textainer (which does not appear to have communicated with SCL when negotiating its leases) point to any action by SCL that they could reasonably have interpreted as authorizing AES Ltd. to enter into the leases on behalf of SCL.

We conclude that the record belies plaintiffs' contentions that SCL actually or impliedly authorized AES Ltd. to enter into the container leases as agent for SCL.

3. THE CORPORATE VEIL

Finally, plaintiffs contend that SCL should have been held liable for AES Ltd.'s debts on the theory that SCL's control over AES Ltd. constituted an abuse of the corporate form that justified piercing the corporate veil. The district court, in rejecting this claim, stated that to succeed on such a theory, plaintiffs would have to show, *inter alia*, (a) that SCL's control over AES Ltd. and/or AES Inc. had been so complete that the latter companies had no separate existence, and (b) that SCL had used that domination to perpetrate a fraud on plaintiffs. Though New York law allows the corporate veil to be pierced *either* when there is fraud *or* when the corporation has been used as an alter ego, we find no basis for reversal.

In *Gartner v. Snyder*, 607 F.2d 582, 586 (2d Cir. 1979), we noted that

> [b]ecause New York courts disregard corporate form reluctantly, they do so only when the form has been used to achieve fraud, or when the corporation has been so domi-nated by an individual or another corporation . . . , and its separate identity so disregarded, that it primarily transacted the dominator's business rather than its own and can be called the other's alter ego.

Similarly, in *Kirno Hill Corp. v. Holt*, 618 F.2d 982, 985 (2d Cir.1980), we stated:

> The prerequisites for piercing a corporate veil are . . . clear . . . : [the defendant] must have used [the corporation] to perpetrate a fraud or have so dominated and disregarded [the corporation's] corporate form that [the corporation] primarily trans-acted [the defendant's] personal business rather than its own corporate business.

Mere use of the corporate form to avoid liability is insufficient to warrant piercing the veil.

The district court's rejection of plaintiffs' claim was consistent with these principles, for the court not only found that plaintiffs had failed to show any fraud by SCL but also found that they had failed to show sufficient control and domination by SCL of AES Ltd. or of AES Inc. to make either of them SCL's alter ego. These findings are not clearly erroneous.

The record shows that AES Inc. was responsible for the everyday affairs of the AES line and that SCL did not interfere. AES Ltd. observed the corporate formalities, including holding board meetings. [P]laintiffs did not show that SCL dominated AES Inc. or AES Ltd. or used its position to have its own loans to AES Ltd. repaid in preference to those of other AES Ltd. creditors. For example, the record includes evidence that AES Ltd. refused, despite SCL's importuning, to give preferential treatment to SCL containers; that in a dispute over whether to retain the president of AES Inc., SCL's view was overruled; and that when AES Ltd. received a $6 million payment from the former owner of the AES line to close a shortfall in the represented working capital, the money was used to pay off some of AES Ltd.'s outstanding bills, including bills from plaintiffs, but no part of the payment was used to reduce the amount owed to SCL.

In sum, we conclude that plaintiffs have presented no tenable theory for holding SCL liable for the debts of AES Ltd. The district court properly dismissed the claims against SCL.

NOTES AND QUESTIONS

1. In light of the foregoing criteria, what steps can or should a parent company take to minimize the possibility of a lawsuit and liability?

2. Compare the factors discussed by the court in *Itel Containers* with the factors enumerated by Sobin. Is there any distinction between the factors necessary for jurisdiction over the foreign parent and the factors necessary for liability?

PROBLEM 8-14

Xenos, an aggressive upstart U.S. computer software company, has established a wholly foreign-owned subsidiary in France to serve as Xenos' holding company for its intellectual property portfolio of patents and copyrights. Xenos assigns the entire portfolio to the French subsidiary, which then grants a license for all of the intellectual property rights back to Xenos for its use in the United States in exchange for royalties. Microtel, a well-established U.S. company and the market leader, brings an action against Xenos and its French subsidiary for breach of one of Microtel's patents in U.S. federal district court. Defendants move to dismiss the case on the grounds that (1) the federal district court has no in personam jurisdiction over the French subsidiary and that (2) as the subsidiary, the owner of the patents and copyrights, is an indispensable party without whom the lawsuit cannot proceed, the action should be dismissed against Xenos as well. Microtel argues that the federal district court has jurisdiction over the French subsidiary on the basis of the actions of Xenos the parent in the United States. What is the result? Can you describe Xenos' strategy? Will it work? *See Dainippon Screen Mfg. Co., Ltd. v. CFMT, Inc.,* 142 F.3d 1266, 1271 (Fed. Cir. 1998).

H. Conflicts of Jurisdiction: Multiple Proceedings in Different Forums

When there is litigation between international parties, the courts in more than one country may have jurisdiction. This means related lawsuits are often filed in more than one forum. This creates conflicts of jurisdiction and the possibility of competing or contradictory rulings in different forums with respect to the same or similar legal issues and parties. Such multiple proceedings take many forms. Among the most common are (1) the aggrieved party to an international transaction may file two lawsuits in two different forums in order to have "two bites of the apple"; (2) the defendant in one forum may file a related claim or a counterclaim against the other party in the defendant's home forum; (3) a party that is subject to ongoing public law or bankruptcy proceedings in one forum may pursue private-claim litigation in another forum; or (4) a party who is sued in a foreign forum may file suit in his home forum, seeking a negative declaratory judgment of nonliability in his home forum.

There are three possible judicial responses in one forum with regard to pending related litigation in another forum. First, a court may grant a motion to dismiss the case before it in whole or in part because of international comity in order to give primacy to the other forum. Second, a court may take a permissive approach and allow both cases to continue. Third, a court can issue an antisuit injunction against the continuance of the foreign litigation (the injunction is issued against a party not the foreign court).

Finanz AG Zurich v. Banco Economico S.A.
United States Court of Appeals, Second Circuit, 1999
192 F.3d 240

STRAUB, Circuit Judge.

[This case involved a "forfaiting" transaction, which is a form type of arrangement for facilitating exports to debt-laden countries. Instead of paying cash for the imports, the importer issues promissory notes payable at some future date to the exporter. The exporter in turn sells the promissory notes to a third party, the forfaiter, who gives the exporter cash, usually at a substantial discount of the face value of the notes. In general, no party is willing to serve as a forfaiter unless the notes are guaranteed by a bank or other substantial guarantor. The importer arranges for the bank to guarantee the note to the forfaiter by providing an endorsement known as an "aval." The forfaiter then presents the notes to the bank at maturity for payment.

In this case, on May 2, 1995, a Brazilian importer Delba Comercio Importacao e Exportacao Ltda (Delba) issued six promissory notes with a face value of over $5.6 million payable in one year to forfaiter Deutsche Morgan Grenfell Trade Finance Ltd. (Morgan Grenfell). The notes were guaranteed by the Cayman Islands branch of Banco Economico S.A. (BESA). Each note stated, however, that it was payable at BESA's New York branch. In a subsequent telex to Morgan Grenfell, BESA's International Division confirmed that the Cayman Branch had guaranteed or "avalized" the notes and that they were payable in New York. On May 24, 1995, Morgan Grenfell sold three of the notes with a total face value of $3 million to Finanz AG Zurich on a non-recourse basis for $2.78 million.

On August 11, 1995, prior to the maturity date of the notes, Brazil's Central Bank caused BESA and all of its branches to be placed into "intervention" (similar to a receivership under U.S. law) and then liquidation, which is similar to a bankruptcy proceeding in the United States. As a result of the Central Bank's intervention, the U.S. Office of the Comptroller of the Currency (OCC) instituted cease-and-desist proceedings against BESA's New York branch, which was licensed by the OCC. The New York branch subsequently entered into an "amended consent order" with the OCC. The order established procedures under which the New York branch would maintain sufficient assets to pay off third-party liabilities and also provided that the branch would voluntarily liquidate and cease operations.

On May 2, 1996, Morgan Grenfell on behalf of Finanz presented the three notes for payment at the New York branch but payment was refused on the basis that the Cayman branch, not the New York branch, had the obligation to pay and that the New York branch served as the "paying agent" only of the Cayman branch. Pursuant to a notice published in the New York Times on May 16, 1997 by the liquidator of BESA describing a claims procedure for creditors, Finanz then filed a claim for the value of the notes in BESA's liquidation proceeding in Brazil.

On December 3, 1997, Finanz filed suit in a New York state court, seeking to recover on the promissory notes. The action was removed to federal district court on the grounds that as BESA was the real party in interest and BESA was an instrumentality of a foreign state, jurisdiction was governed by the Foreign Sovereign Immunities Act. BESA subsequently moved to dismiss the action on the grounds of international comity in deference to the Brazilian liquidation. The district court granted the motion and Finanz brought this appeal.]

DISMISSAL BASED ON INTERNATIONAL COMITY

We review a district court's decision to extend or deny comity to a foreign proceeding for abuse of discretion.

As the Supreme Court explained in *Hilton v. Guyot*, 159 U.S. 113, 16 S. Ct. 139, 40 L. Ed. 95 (1895), comity is "the recognition which one nation allows within its territory to the legislative, executive or judicial acts of another nation, having due regard both to international duty and convenience, and to the rights of its own citizens or of other persons who are under the protection of its laws." *Id*. at 164, 16 S. Ct. 139.

We have repeatedly noted the importance of extending comity to foreign bankruptcy proceedings. Since "[t]he equitable and orderly distribution of a debtor's property requires assembling all claims against the limited assets in a single proceeding," American courts regularly defer to such actions. *Id*. at 713-14. Nonetheless, we will afford comity to foreign bankruptcies only if those proceedings do not violate the laws or public policy of the United States, and if "the foreign court abides by 'fundamental standards of procedural fairness,'" *Allstate Life Ins. Co.*, 994 F.2d at 999.

Accordingly, in this case, deferral to the Brazilian extrajudicial liquidation of BESA is appropriate only if it does not violate United States public policy or principles of due process and fundamental fairness. Finanz argues that both are vitiated by the District Court's decision. Specifically, Finanz contends that (1) the extension of comity violates the United States interest in maintaining New York as a center of commerce and forfaiting; (2) deferral contravenes the United States policy of requiring Federal branches to satisfy all of their liabilities; (3) the Brazilian liquidation offends principles of due process because creditors are not given individualized notice of the bankruptcy; and (4) the Brazilian procedures are fundamentally unfair because the debt is converted into Brazilian reals, thereby forcing the creditor to bear the risk of fluctuations in the value of currency. We consider each of these arguments in turn.

A. PUBLIC POLICY

Finanz first maintains that the District Court failed to consider that since New York is the location where the avals were to be paid, the United States has a special interest in ensuring that the debt remains recoverable in New York to maintain New York's status as a commercial and forfaiting center.

The fact that the forfaiting transaction here required payment in New York does not preclude the granting of comity. Indeed, we have rejected an analogous argument seeking the denial of comity to a foreign bankruptcy proceeding because an indenture agreement contained both a forum selection clause requiring that suit on a contract be brought in New York and a choice of law provision selecting New York law. *See Allstate Life Ins. Co.*, 994 F.2d at 1000 (noting that such clauses "do[ ] not preclude a court from granting comity where it is otherwise warranted"). We do not share Finanz's concern that, as a result of the District Court's decision, "forfaiters will doubt the efficacy of New York as a payment center" and will "choose to make these transactions payable in other commercial centers." Appellant's Brief at 21-22. While forfaiters may require payment in New York because they "expect [ ] . . . regularity in financial dealings," *A.I. Trade Fin., Inc. v. Petra Bank*, 989 F.2d 76, 78 (2d Cir. 1993), if they wish to ensure collection from the New York branch of an international financial institution in circumstances similar to those presented here, they should—and presumably do—take the additional precaution of having the New York entity itself act as a guarantor.

Finanz also asserts that affording comity to the Brazilian liquidation would violate the interest of the United States in enforcing the liabilities of a Federal branch regulated by the OCC. The New York Branch of BESA is currently in voluntary liquidation and is resolving claims of third-party creditors. Finanz is plainly correct that there is a strong United States policy of enforcing the obligations of a Federal branch such as the New York Branch and in ensuring that its liabilities are satisfied as part of its liquidation.

However, like the District Court, we trust the OCC to safeguard this policy interest when it enters into consent orders, and Finanz's argument therefore has merit only if the avals in this case can be deemed a liability of the New York Branch pursuant to the terms of the Amended Consent Order. The Amended Consent Order defines the "Aggregate Amount of Third Party Liabilities" that the branch must pay from its assets in the liquidation as, in pertinent part:

> any liabilities agreed to by the Branch with persons that are neither subsidiaries, Related Parties, Affiliates nor Institution-Affiliated Parties of the Branch or Bank, including checks issued by the Bank or any of its subsidiaries, Affiliates, Related Parties, or Institution-Affiliated Parties, which have been issued outside of the United States and may be presented to the Branch for payment. This term shall also include bankers' acceptances, standby or commercial letters of credit and any other contingent liabilities. This term shall not include . . . accrued expenses and amounts due and other liabilities to the head office of the Bank and any other branch . . . of the Bank or the Branch.

The District Court read this definition to include only those liabilities "agreed to by the Branch," and, since the avals were not liabilities "agreed to by the Branch," they were not its obligations under the Amended Consent Order. Finanz does not challenge the District Court's conclusion that the New York Branch did not "agree[ ] to" the avals. Instead, it relies upon the clause "checks issued *by the Bank* . . . , which have been issued outside of the United States and may be presented to the Branch for payment" (emphasis added). Finanz maintains that the word "checks" should be read to include "any other contingent liabilities," apparently because the next sentence in the definition states, "[t]his term shall also include . . . any other contingent liabilities." According to Finanz, since the Grand Cayman Branch affixed the avals and made them payable at the New York Branch, and the International Division of BESA "confirmed" these facts, the guaranties are contingent liabilities issued by BESA outside of the United States that may be presented to the New York Branch for payment.

However, we conclude that the District Court did not exceed its allowable discretion in reading the Amended Consent Order to include only those liabilities "agreed to by the Branch" within the definition of the New York Branch's third-party liabilities. The District Court's understanding of the Order comports with the plain language of the document. Thus, since the New York Branch did not "agree[ ] to" the avals, it cannot now be held liable for the notes under the terms of the Amended Consent Order.

In sum, we hold that the District Court did not exceed its allowable discretion in concluding that deferral to the Brazilian liquidation would not violate policy interests of the United States.

B. DUE PROCESS AND FUNDAMENTAL FAIRNESS

Finanz next asserts that affording comity to the Brazilian proceeding would violate due process because Brazilian law does not require individualized notice to creditors. To determine whether a foreign bankruptcy proceeding "abide[s] by fundamental standards of procedural fairness," *Cunard S.S. Co.*, 773 F.2d at 457, we have focused on several factors as "indicia of procedural fairness," including:

> (1) whether creditors of the same class are treated equally in the distribution of assets; (2) whether the liquidators are considered fiduciaries and are held accountable to the court; (3) whether creditors have the right to submit claims which, if denied, can be submitted to a bankruptcy court for adjudication; (4) whether the liquidators are required to give notice to the debtor's potential claimants; (5) whether there are provisions for creditors meetings; (6) whether a foreign country's insolvency laws favor its own citizens; (7) whether all assets are marshaled before one body for centralized distribution; and (8) whether there are provisions for an automatic stay and for the lifting of such stays to facilitate the centralization of claims.

Allstate Life Ins. Co., 994 F.2d at 999. As it did in the District Court, Finanz argues that only the fourth factor is not satisfied. However, although the Brazilian proceeding apparently does not require individualized notice, Finanz received actual notice of the Brazilian proceeding from the general manager of the New York Branch and subsequently filed a timely claim. Accordingly, the District Court correctly concluded that there was no due process violation. Furthermore, we disagree with Finanz's contention that *this* action should not be dismissed in favor of the Brazilian liquidation proceeding, simply because *other* creditors might receive inadequate notice of this or another such proceeding.

Finally, we reject Finanz's argument that the Brazilian proceeding is fundamentally unfair because it requires the conversion of Finanz's claims into Brazilian reals. It may well be that this practice places the risk of currency fluctuation on Finanz. Nonetheless, the United States applies a similar practice in its bankruptcy proceedings, and it is not surprising that Brazil would utilize such a procedure to promote the orderly liquidation of claims. Of course, if the early conversion of a creditor's claims into foreign currency would render a debt unenforceable or valueless, we might have cause to conclude that a conversion procedure was fundamentally unfair. However, Finanz does not make this complaint, and that situation is not before us. Accordingly, we agree with the District Court that the conversion procedure in this case is not fundamentally unfair.

Goldhammer v. Dunkin' Donuts, Inc.
United States District Court, Massachusetts, 1999
59 F. Supp. 2d 248

SARIS, District Judge.

I. INTRODUCTION

This action involves a dispute over an agreement to sell donuts in England between Dunkin' Donuts, Inc. ("Dunkin' Donuts"), and DD UK, Ltd. ("DD UK"). Dunkin' Donuts brought an action in English court against DD UK on December 22, 1997. When DD UK and Robert F. Goldhammer, a director and majority shareholder active in management, filed their own action in federal court a year later, Dunkin' Donuts responded with a motion to dismiss or stay the diversity action on international abstention grounds because both actions share overlapping legal and factual issues. After hearing, this Court *DENIES* the defendant's motion to dismiss but stays the proceeding pending the outcome of the parallel first-filed English case.

II. FACTUAL BACKGROUND

Plaintiff, DD UK, is a privately held corporation formed under the laws of England. The shares are owned, in large part, by two Massachusetts trusts. Robert Goldhammer, a Florida resident, is a director of DD UK and is the beneficiary of about two-thirds of the company's shares. He has outstanding loans of $615,000 to DD UK. Dunkin' Donuts is a Delaware corporation with its principal place of business in Randolph, Massachusetts.

In January 1987, DD UK and Dunkin' Donuts entered into a Multiple License Agreement ("MLA"), which authorized DD UK to develop the Dunkin' Donuts brand of donuts and pastries in London, England, and which set up terms for royalty payments and reporting of sales data. The MLA was negotiated and signed in Massachusetts but provides that it will be construed, interpreted, and governed by English law. According to Dunkin' Donuts, DD UK and Dunkin' Donuts later entered into an unwritten agreement, the branded cases agreement ("BCA"), authorizing DD UK to sell Dunkin' Donuts through free-standing product cases in various commercial outlets like convenience stores and gas stations, rather than the traditional stores. In September 1997, Dunkin' Donuts terminated DD UK's rights in the branded cases business. The disputed facts center around whether a branded cases agreement existed, whether Dunkin' Donuts enticed DD UK and Goldhammer to invest as a franchisee in the British market and then purposefully and deceitfully pushed them out, and whether DD UK fulfilled its commitments under the various agreements.

On December 22, 1997, Dunkin' Donuts filed suit in English court against DD UK seeking payment of royalties, interest, and other damages arising from the MLA and the BCA. On February 27, 1998, Dunkin' Donuts filed a second suit in English court seeking the same relief in addition to other unpaid royalties. The English court consolidated the two actions on July 24, 1998, and set up a discovery schedule. Three days later, Dunkin' Donuts amended its complaint with a number of allegations regarding the MLA and the BCA. Dunkin' Donuts argued that the MLA could be terminated on five years' notice and that the BCA existed as a separate agreement, which incorporated the payment and reporting terms of the MLA and which could be terminated on reasonable written notice. Alternatively, Dunkin' Donuts argued, the MLA had been "varied" to include the BCA.

DD UK filed its answer and counterclaims on August 21, 1998. DD UK denied liability for any royalties or damages, the ability to terminate the MLA on five years' notice, the existence of the BCA, and, alternatively, the reasonableness of six months' notice for termination of the BCA. DD UK also denied that it had breached the MLA, the "varied" MLA, or the BCA, arguing that, in fact, Dunkin' Donuts was in repudiatory breach of the MLA. DD UK counterclaimed that Dunkin' Donuts had breached the implied covenant of good faith and fair dealing, and claimed damages, including lost profits through 2016. On October 5, 1998, discovery had been partially completed in the English case.

DD UK and Goldhammer filed the present action in this court, under diversity jurisdiction, on December 17, 1998. Goldhammer asserts claims against Dunkin' Donuts for fraud and deceit, negligent misrepresentation, and promissory estoppel. DD UK asserts claims against Dunkin' Donuts for breach of contract, breach of the implied covenant of good faith and fair dealing, promissory estoppel, quantum meruit, unjust enrichment, fraud and deceit, negligent misrepresentation, and violation of Mass. Gen. L. §93A. These claims arise from the same series of events as those underlying the English claims and counterclaims. Defendant, Dunkin' Donuts, moves to dismiss or stay this action on grounds of abstention based on international comity.

III. DISCUSSION

A. DOCTRINAL FRAMEWORK

Federal courts have the inherent power to stay an action based on the pendency of a related proceeding in a foreign jurisdiction. However, this inherent power to stay parallel litigation must be balanced against the federal courts' "strict duty to exercise the jurisdiction that is conferred upon them by Congress." *Quackenbush v. Allstate Ins. Co.*, 517 U.S. 706, 716, 116 S. Ct. 1712, 135 L. Ed. 2d 1 (1996).

As the Eleventh Circuit recently recognized, "in some private international disputes the prudent and just action is to abstain from the exercise of jurisdiction." *Turner Entertainment Co. v. Degeto Film GmbH*, 25 F.3d 1512, 1518 (11th Cir. 1994). "[I]n the interests of judicial economy and international relations, a federal court may stay an action in favor of pending foreign litigation." *Abdullah Sayid Rajab Al-Rifai & Sons v. McDonnell Douglas Foreign Sales Corp.*, 988 F. Supp. 1285, 1291 (E.D. Mo. 1997). However, the mere fact that there are parallel proceedings in a foreign jurisdiction will not constitute an "exceptional circumstance" which justifies the abdication of federal jurisdiction. *See Neuchatel Swiss Gen. Ins. Co. v. Lufthansa Airlines*, 925 F.2d 1193, 1194-95 (9th Cir. 1991).

The policies underpinning international abstention case law are rooted in concerns about international comity. . . .

Still open is the question whether the federal courts have the power to *dismiss* an action for damages because of parallel foreign litigation. In the abstention context involving parallel state proceedings, federal courts have power to dismiss or remand cases only where relief being sought is equitable or otherwise discretionary, but they may not do so in common law actions for damages. *See Quackenbush*, 517 U.S. at 719-22, 116 S. Ct. 1712.

Quackenbush does not crisply govern in the area of international abstention because the considerations involved in deferring to state court proceedings are different from those involved in deferring to foreign proceedings. Abstention implicates constitutionally rooted considerations of federalism and federal supremacy. International comity is "more a matter of grace than a matter of obligation." *Nippon*, 109 F.3d at 8. The post-*Quackenbush* debate over the power of the federal court to dismiss an action for damages based on international abstention can be somewhat academic because, as a practical matter, in many circumstances a stay is tantamount to dismissal.

The federal trial courts have developed a roster of relevant factors in determining whether to grant a stay because of parallel litigation in a foreign forum: (1) similarity of parties and issues involved in the foreign litigation; (2) the promotion of judicial efficiency; (3) adequacy of relief available in the alternative forum; (4) issues of fairness to and convenience of the parties, counsel, and witnesses; (5) the possibility of prejudice to any of the parties; and (6) the temporal sequence of the filing of the actions.

The overarching concerns for a federal court facing concurrent international jurisdiction are demonstrating a proper level of respect for the acts of other sovereign nations, ensuring fairness to litigants, and efficiently using scarce judicial resources. As will be discussed below, these factors, on the whole, militate in favor of staying the present action pending the outcome of the English action.

B. THE BALANCING

1. Similarity of Parties and Issues

This factor leans in favor of staying the action. The parties are the same in the two actions with two exceptions. The first distinction is that the parties trade places on either side of the "v." DD UK is a defendant in the English suit and a plaintiff here.

This seems to be a distinction without much difference in this case. The titles "plaintiff" and "defendant" have little significance where there are compulsory counterclaims in each suit. The analysis can just as easily rest on whether the counterclaims of the defendant in the first suit are similar to the affirmative claims of the plaintiff in the second.

The second distinction is that Goldhammer is named separately as a plaintiff in the United States action. However, Goldhammer holds a two-thirds interest in DD UK and, thus, has substantially similar interests to those of DD UK. While a shareholder may have claims independent of the corporation, the parties and claims need not be identical in order for one action to be stayed or dismissed in deference to an earlier action.

The factual and legal issues in the two cases overlap, although the stated causes of action are different. Most of the issues require a determination of whether certain agreements existed, whether the terms of agreements were satisfied, and whether parties acted in bad faith in the performance of their contractual duties or in terminating the agreements. The fact that a claim sounds in tort rather than in contract does not mean that the factual issues are so dissimilar that a stay may not be granted.

2. Promotion of Judicial Efficiency

Judicial efficiency militates in favor of staying the action. Allowing this case to go forward in tandem with the English case "would consume a great amount of judicial, administrative, and party resources." *EFCO Corp.*, 983 F. Supp. at 824. Also, "simultaneous adjudications regarding identical facts and highly similar legal issues create the risk of inconsistent judgments." *Id.* While avoidance of duplicative litigation is not dispositive when determining whether to stay a parallel proceeding, it is a key factor to be considered.

3. Adequacy of Relief Available in the Alternative Forum

Plaintiffs claim that the English court cannot provide adequate relief for a number of reasons. Goldhammer claims that he could not have brought some of his claims in the English action. DD UK argues that there are claims in its complaint in the United States action, including a Massachusetts state statutory claim alleging unfair and deceptive business practices under Mass. Gen. L. ch. 93A, that are not included in its counterclaim in the English action. The fact that the Court is staying, rather than dismissing, the federal action provides future opportunity for any relief (like multiple damages) not available to DD UK in the English action or precluded by it. Also, Mr. Goldhammer's individual claims (i.e., fraud) can be litigated here. Therefore, this factor weighs only slightly in favor of plaintiffs.

4. Convenience of the Parties, Counsel, and Witnesses

This factor does not favor either party. On the one hand, DD UK is an English company, the parties transacted business in England, they agreed that English law applied to the agreement, and many of the disputed facts are based on conduct occurring in England. With respect to Goldhammer, he decided to go to England to sell his donuts and actively managed the business there. It is not unfair to require an American party to defend and prosecute a case in England where the party has been engaged in "purposeful activity" there. *Hunt v. BP Exploration Co.*, 492 F. Supp. 885, 896 (N.D. Tex. 1980). On the other hand, Dunkin' Donuts' principal place of business is Randolph, Massachusetts, and Peter Harwood, the key employee who managed its business in Great Britain, is a Massachusetts resident, as are other potential witnesses. This factor is a draw for both sides.

5. Possibility of Prejudice to Any of the Parties

Plaintiffs point out that there are serious differences in discovery rules between the two countries. Most notably, plaintiffs claim that the English court does not permit the taking of depositions. Because the United States and England share the same common law heritage, deference to British proceedings is consistent with notions of international comity. The fact that there is less access to discovery in England than in federal court weighs against staying this action, but only slightly so.

6. Temporal Sequence of the Filing of the Actions

The sequence of these actions heavily favors a stay of the federal action. The plaintiffs' United States action was filed in December of 1998, four months after DD UK's answer and counterclaim were filed in the English action, and a full year after Dunkin' Donuts filed its first English action in December of 1997. While first-filed status is not dispositive on this point, litigation lethargy is an important consideration.

Furthermore, discovery was first exchanged in the English action in October of 1998, and although there are disputes over the production of documents, the case is proceeding toward trial. The parties dispute how quickly a trial is likely to happen. Although there is some support for declining motions to stay when the foreign litigation is in its early stages, the English case has developed significantly enough to tip the scale on this factor in favor of a stay.

A ledger of the factors that guide the Court's discretion in determining whether to proceed in light of the English action leads to a stay in this action. [N]otions of international comity are at an apex when parties inject themselves into the economy of another nation for profit, particularly one as close as Great Britain, and then try to extricate themselves from its jurisdiction.

IV. ORDER

For the foregoing reasons, the Court denies the defendant's motion to dismiss but stays the proceeding pending the outcome of the parallel first-filed English case.

Trevor C. Hartley, Comity and the Use of Antisuit Injunctions in International Litigation
35 Am. J. Comp. L. 487 (1987)

Injunctions requiring a party not to commence, or not to continue, proceedings in a foreign court, or to discontinue them (henceforth "antisuit injunctions") are coming to play an increasingly important role in international litigation. The purpose of this paper is to examine the use of such injunctions and to consider whether they involve a breach of comity or a threat to good relations with foreign countries.

The nature of the problem is apparent from the *Laker Airways*[11] case. Laker Airways, a small British airline hitherto restricted to charter operations, tried to break into the North Atlantic air transportation market by undercutting the established airlines. At first it succeeded, carrying one in seven of all transatlantic passengers at the high-point of its operations. But then things began to go wrong, and it was eventually forced into liquidation when a refinancing deal fell through at the last moment. In 1982 Laker Airways (now in liquidation) brought antitrust suits against a number of airlines which fly the Atlantic route, as well as against Laker's aircraft supplier, McDonnell Douglas, and the latter's financial affiliate, McDonnell Douglas Finance Corporation. The airlines included American, British and Continental European operators. In essence, the allegations were two-fold: first, that the airlines had engaged in predatory pricing to drive Laker out of business and, secondly, that they pressured McDonnell Douglas and Laker's bank, Midland Bank, to withdraw from the planned financial rescue operation. The action was filed in the Federal District Court in Washington D.C. and treble damages of over $1 billion were claimed.

The first response came from the Midland Bank, which was not yet a party to the action. It applied for, and obtained, an antisuit injunction in the English High Court, preventing Laker from adding it to the American proceedings.

Perhaps this gave the airlines the idea. In any event some of the airlines, led by British Airways, then applied in the English High Court, first, for a declaration that they had not engaged in any unlawful conspiracy; secondly, for an antisuit injunction to stop the American proceedings against them; and, thirdly, for an injunction precluding Laker from obtaining an antisuit injunction in the United States to block the English proceedings. This last remedy was something of an innovation, but it is the obvious answer to an imminent antisuit injunction. Henceforth it will be called a "counter-antisuit injunction." Laker then hastily applied to the American court and obtained a counter-antisuit injunction to preclude the remaining defendants from obtaining antisuit injunctions or counter-antisuit injunctions in England.[12] At this time the injunctions on both sides of the Atlantic were on a temporary basis only. In May 1983 the application by British Airways for a permanent injunction was heard. This was dismissed by the High Court,[13] granted by the Court of Appeal[14] (after the British Secretary of State for Trade and Industry had issued an order under the British "blocking statute"[15]

---

11. This case was litigated on both sides of the Atlantic. England: *British Airways Bd. v. Laker Airways* [1985] A.C. 58, *reversing* [1984] Q.B. 169 (C.A.), *reversing* [1984] Q.B. 142. America: *Laker Airways v. Sabena, Belgian World Airlines*, 731 F.2d 909 (D.C. Cir. 1984); *Laker Airways v. Pan Am. World Airways*, 596 F. Supp. 202 (D.D.C. 1984); *Laker Airways v. Pan Am. World Airways*, 577 F. Supp. 811 (D.D.C. 1983); *Laker Airways v. Pan Am. World Airways*, 568 F. Supp. 811 (D.D.C. 1983); *Laker Airways v. Pan Am. World Airways*, 559 F. Supp. 1124 (D.D.C. 1983) *aff'd* 731 F.2d 909 (D.C. Cir. 1984).

12. *See* 559 F. Supp. 1124 (D.D.C. 1983).

13. *See* [1984] Q.B. 142.

14. *See* [1984] Q.B. 169.

15. *The Protection of Trading Interests Act* 1980.

prohibiting the handing over of documents or information to the United States authorities) and finally rescinded by the House of Lords.[16]

In the United States, meanwhile, the counter-antisuit injunctions were upheld on appeals[17] and some thought was given to what should be done if the English courts definitively confirmed their antisuit injunctions. The possibility was mooted of appointing a trustee or receiver to continue the action on Laker's behalf. Such a person, being outside the jurisdiction of the English courts, would be immune from antisuit injunctions. This, of course, proved unnecessary in the end. However, the Midland Bank, whose antisuit injunction was lifted after the House of Lords decision, succeeded in getting it re-imposed by the English Court of Appeal in July 1985. The effect of the lifting of the antisuit injunctions against the defendants in the United States action was to make it possible for that suit to go ahead. The airlines then moved quickly to settle: the injunction battle had proved decisive.

The decision of the Court of Appeal in the *Midland Bank*[18] case (decided after the House of Lords' decision in *Laker*) throws further light on the grant of antisuit injunctions in single-forum cases. It will be remembered that the Midland Bank was never a party to the American proceedings: it obtained an antisuit injunction before it could be joined. In the English proceedings, it issued a writ claiming, first, a declaration that it was not liable under either English or American law for the collapse of Laker; and, secondly, an antisuit injunction. It obtained an inter-locutory antisuit injunction in 1982. After the House of Lords' decision in *Laker*, Leggatt J. discharged the antisuit injunction and struck out the application for a declaration of nonliability under American law.[19] On appeal, the antisuit injunction was reinstated, though the claim for a declaration of nonliability under English law was also struck out.[20] The Court of Appeal's reason for granting the antisuit injunction was that Midland was in a different position from the airlines. The latter had chosen to do business in the United States and the action arose out of their activities there. Midland itself had not done any business there at the time (except on the international interbank market) and its American subsidiaries had done only business which was in no way relevant to the action. Midland subsequently opened up a New York branch, and this presence gave the American courts *in personam* jurisdiction over it, but subject-matter jurisdiction (prescriptive jurisdiction) was lacking. In other words, the Court of Appeal considered that the American action would involve the extraterritorial application of American law; therefore, in the Court of Appeal's view, it was unconscionable for Laker to sue. This was the argument which was unsuccessfully advanced by the airlines in the *Laker* case in the House of Lords. It was rejected because the House of Lords considered that application of American law to *them* would not be extraterritorial.

The *Midland Bank* case therefore adds another ground on which an antisuit injunction will be granted even in a single-forum case: that the foreign proceedings

---

16. *See* [1985] A.C. 58.

17. *See* 731 F.2d 909 (D.C. Cir. 1984).

18. *Midland Bank v. Laker Airways* [1986] 1 All E.R. 526.

19. This was because the House of Lords held in *Laker* that the English courts have no jurisdiction to decide any question of liability under American antitrust law.

20. This left the injunction hanging in mid-air, so to speak without any substantive cause of action at all.

would involve the extraterritorial application of foreign law. As is well known, resistance to what is regarded as the extraterritorial application of American law is a well-established feature of United Kingdom policy.[21] It is probable that antisuit injunctions will also be invoked where other strong policy interests are at stake.

The "role of the judiciary in *any* system [is] the protection of the litigants."[22] The United States judiciary is also expected to protect itself, however, as shown by Article III of the United States Constitution, which grants powers to federal courts which extend to all cases or controversies, and by Congress, which has granted the federal courts the related power to protect their jurisdiction and effectuate their judgments. United States courts have issued anti-foreign suit injunctions for that protective purpose where direct aggressive moves have been made by foreign courts. However, United States courts have generally ignored or have been unaware of the fact that even if their proceedings are concluded without intrusion from a foreign court, their judgments may not be honored due to a double-suit with preemptive effects.[23] They have been mostly concerned about their immediate ability to continue their hearing and render a judgment.[24]

In contrast to these rationales, foreign declarations of nonliability affecting United States plaintiffs and ultimately the power of the United States courts themselves must be viewed from the perspective of their *effects*. When analogized to the recognized effects of antisuit injunctions, their potential for causing harm becomes clear. Antisuit injunctions are correctly understood as

> deny[ing] foreign courts the right to exercise their proper jurisdiction. . . . [and] convey[ing] the message, intended or not, that the issuing court has so little confidence in the foreign court's ability to adjudicate a given dispute fairly and efficiently that it is unwilling even to allow the possibility.[25]

Although foreign declarations of nonliability do not rob United States courts of the opportunity to hear and judge a case, they do strip any resulting judgment of effect in that foreign jurisdiction — the forum in which the defendant most likely holds his or her assets. The result in both foreign declarations of nonliability and foreign antisuit injunctions involving a United States plaintiff is the stymieing of that plaintiff's United States suit at one stage in the action.

---

21. *See The Protection of Trading Interests Act* 1980; *see also British Nylon Spin Imperial Chem. Indus.* [1953] 1 Ch. 19 (C.A.), [1955] 1 Ch. 37; *In re Westinghouse Uranium Contract* [1978] A.C. 547.

22. Julie E. Dowler, *Forging Finality: Searching for a Solution to the International Double Suit Dilemma*, 4 Duke J. of Comp. & Int'l L. 363 (1994).

23. *See, e.g., China Trade*, 837 F.2d at 37 (reversing a district court anti-suit injunction because the possibility that the United States judgment would be unenforceable in Korea was mere speculation and regardless of this, enforcement of the judgment might require relitigation in Korea); *Gau Shan Co., Ltd. v. Bankers Trust Co.*, 956 F.2d 1349, 1356 (reversing a preliminary injunction because Banker Trust's ability to appoint a receiver of its choice for Gau Shan in Hong Kong court, thereby gaining control of Gau Shan, did not threaten the jurisdiction of the United States court, merely Gau Shan's interest in prosecuting the lawsuit).

24. *See, e.g., Gau Shan*, 837 F.2d at 1356; *Laker Airways Ltd. v. Sabena, Belgian World Airlines*, 731 F.2d 909, 938.

25. *Gau Shan*, 956 F.2d at 1355.

Despite the existing judicial disagreement on the importance of the effects of foreign declarations of nonliability, once successful plaintiffs attempt to have their judgments enforced, there is no doubt as to the *actual* harmful effects of a foreign court's negative declaratory judgment on the viability of a United States judgment. Cases that arise under these circumstances clearly demonstrate the impotence of United States judgments abroad if prior domestic declaratory judgments of nonliability have been issued by a foreign court.[26] The *Deutsch v. West Coast Machinery Co.* case and the parallel suit filed in Japan for a negative declaratory judgment, *Marubeni America v. Kansai Iron Works*,[27] provide the best illustration of a United States judgment's ineffectuality in the foreign court which has issued a contrary declaration of nonliability. In the United States case, Deutsch sued West Coast Machinery Company, a Washington corporation; Marubeni-Iida ("Marubeni America"), a New York subsidiary of Marubeni-Iida Co., Ltd. in Japan, importer of the defective power press which caused the injury; and Kansai Iron Works, Ltd. ("Kansai"), a Japanese corporation which manufactured the press. Marubeni America filed a cross-claim for indemnification against Kansai.[28] Kansai attempted to have the cross-claim dismissed, but was denied.[29] The parties entered into a settlement agreement totaling $75,000 in damages for the plaintiff in September 1974. Marubeni America then obtained a Washington State court judgment for the settlement amount and attorneys' fees from Kansai.[30] Marubeni America attempted to enforce the United States judgment in Japan because Kansai had no assets in the United States. However, Kansai had instituted an action and received a declaration in December 1974 from the Osaka District Court that it had no obligation to indemnify Marubeni America. Although this action was entered two months *after* the judgment in the United States for indemnification was secured, it was made final before Marubeni America could secure a judgment in Japan for the recognition and enforcement of its United States judgment.[31]

This case demonstrates that United States courts cannot ignore the international community in which they operate. No positive law exists in this heretofore little-known area of transnational litigation to guide United States courts in formulating uniform approaches to their balancing of issues. The unfortunate result is that far too many cases demonstrate the courts' unresponsiveness to this subtle, though effective, legal tactic.

Where antisuit injunctions are considered ultimately necessary, the potential ramifications lie not only in judicial repercussions, but even in political retaliation. The *Laker Airways* litigation is a dramatic example of the extent to which international politics can be intertwined with judicial action through the thread of

---

26. *See Marubeni America, Inc. v. Kansai Iron Works*, 361 Hanta 127 (Osaka Dist. Ct., Dec. 22, 1977), translated in 23 Jap. Ann. Int'l L. 200, 206-07 (1980) [hereinafter *Kansai Iron Works*]; *Laker Airways v. British Airways Board*, [1984] 3 All E.R. 39; *Laker Airways*, 731 F.2d 909.

27. *Deutsch v. West Coast Machinery Co.*, 497 P.2d 1311 (Wash. 1972).

28. 497 P.2d at 1312-13.

29. *Id*. at 1313.

30. *Id*. at 1318.

31. *Kansai Iron Works, supra*, at 206-07.

international comity. The litigation began when the plaintiff company was forced into liquidation by what it claimed was a price competition conspiracy involving other airlines. A series of conflicting actions issued by English and United States courts initiated a flurry of motions that transformed this litigation into a now infamous confusion of declaratory judgments and injunctions issued from one sovereign court to the next. The effect was that all notions of international comity were ignored and potential relief for the plaintiff from some foreign defendants was denied.

NOTES AND QUESTIONS

1. How do antisuit injunctions lead to escalations of tensions and conflict that may undermine international comity?

2. Hartley argues that while U.S. courts have been aware of the antisuit injunction as a litigation tactic, the approach that U.S. courts have traditionally adopted with respect to antisuit injunction does not fully recognize the extent of the problem. What is the flaw in the approach of U.S. courts?

V. Evidence and Discovery

PROBLEM 8-15

Sisco is an American computer software firm that believes that its products are being copied by Linosoft, an aggressive computer software firm with its headquarters in Brazil that is emerging as a major player in South America. Rather than bring an action in Brazil where Sisco believes that it has little chance of success, Sisco has decided to bring an action in the United States in the jurisdiction where Linosoft has a permanent U.S. office. Sisco is convinced that T.K. Suarez, the CEO of Linosoft, has been engaged in a systematic and widespread effort to copy Sisco's most valuable new products. As T.K. Suarez lives in Rio de Janeiro and there is no basis for jurisdiction over him, Sisco cannot require him to appear in the United States. However, Sisco's in-house lawyers believe that Suarez has information that is crucial to their case and they must obtain this information from him or they will have no chance of prevailing in the U.S. litigation. An in-house lawyer at Sisco has drafted the following document request, "Produce all documents relating to Sisco in your possession or in the possession of anyone in your company." The Brazilian Supreme Court has also recently issued a decree stating, "No documents relating to the computer industry shall be sent abroad in connection with any overseas litigation." The in-house lawyer calls your law firm and wishes to consult with you on the next steps that need to be taken to get these documents. The company lawyer is also concerned about the new decree and asks you what its intended purpose is and what, if anything, can be done to overcome it. What is your advice on how to proceed? Brazil is a party to the Hague Evidence Convention discussed in the *Tulip* case below. *See also* §442 of the Restatement (Third) of Foreign Relations Law.

Tulip Computers International B.V. v. Dell Computer
United States District Court, Delaware, 2003
254 F. Supp. 2d 469

JORDAN, District Judge.

I. INTRODUCTION

Presently before the Court are two motions by defendant Dell Computer Corporation ("Dell"). One of the motions requests international judicial assistance to take evidence from Mr. Gerardus Franciscus Duynisveld and the other motion requests international judicial assistance to take evidence from Mr. Frans Dietz. Both Mr. Duynisveld and Mr. Dietz are citizens of the Netherlands. Dell has filed these motions pursuant to Federal Rule of Civil Procedure 28(b)(2), and the Hague Convention on the Taking of Evidence Abroad in Civil or Commercial Matters ("Hague Evidence Convention" or "Convention"). Plaintiff Tulip Computers International B.V. ("Tulip") opposes the motions.

II. BACKGROUND

Tulip, a Dutch corporation with its principal place of business in the Netherlands, initiated this patent infringement lawsuit on November 24, 2000, asserting that Dell, a Delaware corporation with its principal place of business in Texas, is infringing its U.S. Patent No. 5,594,621 (issued Jan. 14, 1997) ("the '621 patent"). Dell answered Tulip's allegations of infringement on June 19, 2001, denying Tulip's claims of infringement and asserting the invalidity and unenforceability of the '621 patent. Discovery in the case closed on May 10, 2002. The parties completed briefing their pre-trial summary judgment motions by November 1, 2002. On December 9, 2002, the local magistrate judge issued a Report and Recommendation construing the contested '621 patent claim language. The magistrate judge has also issued Reports and Recommendations in this case addressing some of the parties' pre-trial summary judgment motions. The motions presently before the Court stem from a discovery dispute pre-dating the issue date of each of the magistrate judge's Reports and Recommendations.

III. DISCUSSION

A. THE HAGUE EVIDENCE CONVENTION

The Hague Evidence Convention serves as an alternative or "permissive" route to the Federal Rules of Civil Procedure for the taking of evidence abroad from litigants and third parties alike. The Convention allows judicial authorities in one signatory country to obtain evidence located in another signatory country "for use in judicial proceedings, commenced or contemplated." Hague Evidence Convention, Art. 1. The United States and the Netherlands are contracting states under the Hague Evidence Convention.

There are three available methods of taking evidence pursuant to the Convention:

(1) by a Letter of Request or "letter rogatory" from a U.S. judicial authority to the competent authority in the foreign state, (2) by an American or foreign diplomatic or consular officer or agent after permission is obtained from the foreign state, and (3) by a private commissioner duly appointed by the foreign state.

Dell has opted to employ the first mechanism listed, *supra*, Letters of Requests. Pursuant to the Convention, a Letter of Request must provide the contracting state with specific information regarding the lawsuit and the information sought. The signatory state, upon receipt and consideration, "shall [then] apply the appropriate measure of compulsion" as is customary "for the execution of orders issued by the authorities of its own country." Hague Evidence Convention, Art. 10. Signatory states may refuse to execute a Letter of Request if the request "does not fall within the function of the judiciary" or if the "sovereignty or security" of the contracting state would be prejudiced but, execution "may not be refused solely on the ground that under its internal law the State of execution claims exclusive jurisdiction over the subject-matter of the action or that its internal law would not admit a right of action on it." Hague Evidence Convention, Art. 12.

The person to whom the discovery requests in a Letter of Request are directed has the right to "refuse to give evidence" to the extent that the person has a privilege under the law of the State of execution or the State of origin. Hague Evidence Convention, Art. 11. However, the Netherlands has stated that "[o]nly the court which is responsible for executing the Letter of Request shall be competent to decide whether any person concerned by the execution has a privilege or duty to refuse to give evidence under the law of a State other than the State of origin; no such privilege or duty exists under Dutch law." Hague Evidence Convention, Netherlands 2i, Art. 11.

The Netherlands has also adopted reservations to the Hague Evidence Convention pursuant to Article 23 of the Convention, which provides that "[a] Contracting State may at the time of signature, ratification or accession, declare that it will not execute Letters of Request issued for the purpose of obtaining pre-trial discovery of documents as known in Common Law countries." Hague Evidence Convention, Netherlands 2i. Thus, as implemented by the Netherlands, Letters of Request may not be acted upon if "issued for the purpose of obtaining pre-trial discovery of documents as known in Common Law countries." Hague Evidence Convention, Netherlands 2i, Art. 23.

B. THE PARTIES' ARGUMENTS

1. Dell's Position

Dell asserts that "[w]hile in the employment of Tulip, Mr. Duynisveld had knowledge of and participated in R & D activities that may be directly relevant to Dell's defenses in this case." (D.I. 458 at 2.) Similarly, Dell maintains that "[w]hile engaged by Tulip, Mr. Frans Dietz had knowledge of and participated in patent procurement activities that may be directly relevant to Dell's defenses in this case." (D.I. 459 at 2.) In particular, Dell contends that Mr. Duynisveld [and Mr. Dietz] may be able to provide information relating to "the validity of the '621 patent; the enforceability of the '621 patent; and the alleged infringement by Dell of the '621 patent." (D.I. 458 at 2-3; D.I. 459 at 2-3.) Dell contends, therefore, that since Mr. Duynisveld and Mr. Dietz are foreign nationals residing in the Netherlands and are not parties to the present litigation, discovery pursuant to the Hague Evidence Convention is proper.

Dell further asserts that the taking of evidence from these individuals compels proceeding under the Convention since all alternative efforts to obtain the evidence have failed. Dell contends that the Netherlands' reservations pursuant to Article 23 of the Convention do not weigh against its requests. In addition, notes Dell, the parties have, during the course of this case, proceeded pursuant to the Convention to obtain evidence from other individuals. Moreover, argues Dell, Tulip's opposition is not well founded since the Dutch authorities will weigh the breadth of the evidence sought to assure compliance with the Convention and Netherlands judicial procedure. Dell contends that the documents and testimony sought are not privileged as Tulip maintains and, even if the evidence were privileged, it would first be returned to this Court, thus placing the Court in a position "to determine whether any applicable privilege prohibits the production of certain documents to Dell."

2. Tulip's Position

Tulip contends that the Court must apply a much higher standard than is applied in this country when ordering discovery, if the Court authorizes Dell's request to proceed pursuant to the Hague Evidence Convention, since use of the Convention raises issues of territoriality and comity. In particular, Tulip argues that Article 23 of the Convention prohibits the broad document inquiry sought by Dell because Dell's requests do not conform to the Netherlands' reservations with regard to Article 23, which may be characterized as prohibiting American-style discovery "fishing expeditions." (D.I. 468 at 5-7; D.I. 469 at 5-7.) In addition, asserts Tulip, the Court should deny Dell's requests because much of the evidence Dell seeks is privileged information. Moreover, maintains Tulip, the evidence sought is either irrelevant to the proceedings or constitutes inadmissible hearsay.

C. ANALYSIS

"A party which seeks the application of the Hague [Evidence] Convention procedures rather than the Federal Rules [of Civil Procedure] bears the burden of persuading the trial court [ ]" of the necessity of proceeding pursuant to the Hague Evidence Convention. *Valois of Am., Inc. v. Risdon Corp.*, 183 F.R.D. 344, 346 (D. Conn. 1997). That burden is not great, however, since the "Convention procedures are available whenever they will facilitate the gathering of evidence by the means authorized in the Convention." *Aerospatiale*, 482 U.S. at 541, 107 S. Ct. 2542. Factors relevant to the Court's decision include "considerations of comity, the relative interests of the parties including the interest in avoiding abusive discovery, and the ease and efficiency of alternative formats for discovery." *Madanes v. Madanes*, 199 F.R.D. 135, 141 (S.D.N.Y. 2001).

Resort to the Hague Evidence Convention in this instance is appropriate since both Mr. Duynisveld and Mr. Dietz are not parties to the lawsuit, have not voluntarily subjected themselves to discovery, are citizens of the Netherlands, and are not otherwise subject to the jurisdiction of the Court.

Tulip's arguments go more particularly to the scope of the discovery Dell seeks pursuant to the Hague Evidence Convention. The arguments do not justify wholly precluding Dell's efforts to acquire the evidence it seeks. Tulip's primary argument is that the evidence sought is privileged and Mr. Duynisveld and Mr. Dietz, therefore, should not be placed in a position to determine for themselves what information is or is not privileged in the case. Tulip contends, therefore, that in order to prevent an abuse of privilege the Court should deny Dell's requests *in toto*. The Court disagrees. Mr. Duynisveld and Mr. Dietz may avail themselves of the privilege provided in this country and in the executing country under Article 11 of the Convention. Presumably, they may also obtain counsel, if they wish, and Tulip will be free to express its own views on privilege and, if necessary, to seek this Court's opinion with respect to those views.

The Court is also not persuaded by Tulip's assertions with regard to the Netherlands reservations pursuant to Article 23 of the Convention as applied to Dell's proposed document requests. If Dell's document requests are overly broad under the law of the Netherlands, as Tulip maintains, then the requests will presumably be narrowed by the appropriate judicial authorities in the Netherlands before any documents are produced. The Court is content that such officials will make the appropriate determination under their own law.

Accordingly, it is hereby ordered.

That Dell's motions (D.I. 458; D.I. 459) to approve requests for international judicial assistance, pursuant to the Hague Evidence Convention of 18 March 1970 on the taking of evidence in civil or commercial matters, to take evidence from Mr. Duynisveld and Mr. Dietz are granted.

NOTES AND QUESTIONS

1. There is continuing conflict and controversy over carrying out American-style discovery in foreign countries. In *Societé Nationale Industrielle Aerospatiale v. United States District Court*, 482 U.S. 522 (1987), the Supreme Court held that the Hague Evidence Convention is neither the exclusive nor the required first option for discovery outside the United States. The Hague Convention is simply "one method of seeking evidence that a court may elect to employ" 482 U.S. at 540. The Supreme Court further stated that "American courts, in supervising pretrial proceedings, should exercise special vigilance to protect foreign litigants from unnecessary or unduly burdensome discovery. Objections to 'abusive' discovery that foreign litigants advance should therefore receive the most careful consideration." *Id*. at 547. Did the court in *Tulip Computers* comply with this standard?

2. Many countries have passed "blocking statutes" under which government officials can prevent the production of documents or taking of evidence in certain cases. What is the impact of these blocking statutes? Consider the Restatement (Third) of Foreign Relations Law of the United States (1987):

§442. Requests for Disclosure: Law of the United States

(1) (a) A court or agency in the United States, when authorized by statute or rule of court, may order a person subject to its jurisdiction to produce documents, objects, or other information relevant to an action or investigation, even if the information or the person in possession of the information is outside the United States.

(b) Failure to comply with an order to produce information may subject the person to whom the order is directed to sanctions, including dismissal of a claim or defense, or default judgment, or may lead to a determination that the facts to which the order was addressed are as asserted by the opposing party.

(2) If disclosure of information located outside the United States is prohibited by a law, regulation, or order of a court or other authority of the state in which the information or prospective witness is located, or of the state which a prospective witness is a national,

(a) a court or agency in the United States may require the person to whom the order is directed to make a good faith effort to secure permission from the foreign authorities to make the information available;

(b) a court or agency should not ordinarily impose sanctions of contempt, dismissal, or default on a party that has failed to comply with the order for production, except in cases of deliberate concealment or removal of information or of failure to make a good faith effort in accordance with paragraph (a);

(c) a court or agency may, in appropriate cases, make findings of fact adverse to a party that has failed to comply with the order for production, even if that party has made a good faith effort to secure permission from the foreign authorities to make the information available and that effort has been unsuccessful.

3. A United States district court has the authority to grant foreign litigants, without any requirement of reciprocity, special assistance in obtaining evidence in the United States. *See* 28 U.S.C. §1782(a).

VI. Recognition and Foreign Enforcement of Foreign Judgments

PROBLEM 8-16

A group of MNEs with major commercial piracy problems in China has been persuaded by a U.S. law firm to sue the China Small Commodities City Group, Ltd. (CSCG, which is discussed in Chapter 7; see pp. 617-621 *supra*), a major supplier of counterfeit products in China and around the world, in U.S. court. The MNEs have long been frustrated and angry about the lack of effective enforcement through the Chinese legal system and so the U.S. law firm has convinced them that an alternative is to sue the CSCG in a U.S. court. The U.S. law firm argues that as the Chinese legal system is weak, is still developing, is prone to local protectionism, and is notorious for damage awards that are ridiculously low by U.S. standards, a lawsuit in a U.S. court will be a better strategy and will allow the MNEs to assert their claims fully and prove the full measure of damages. Following this advice, the MNEs file suit in Texas against the CSCG, asserting jurisdiction on the basis that the CSCG has a relationship with an independent distributor in Texas. The U.S. law firm conducts extensive discovery, files a large number of motions, and assigns a large number of lawyers to conduct the trial (and, of course, receives very hefty legal fees from the MNEs). As a result, the MNEs recover a judgment against the CSCG for $50 million in damages and are ecstatic. However, as CSCG's property in the U.S. amounts to no more $50,000, the MNEs are now wondering what to do with their judgment and have the following questions.

(1)   Can this judgment be enforced against the CSCG in China? If so, what procedures must the judgment holders follow in China, which follows the general procedures in the international enforcement of judgments described in *Somportex* below?

(2)   What standards or analysis will an international court use in determining whether to enforce a judgment? Assume that China will follow the general approach in *Somportex*.

(3)   Can the CSCG argue that the U.S. judgment is not entitled to recognition in China because the judgment is not valid? How would you make this argument? Will it succeed? Assume that China would follow the same approach on validity and jurisdiction as set forth in *Nippon Emo-Trans Co.* following *Somportex*.

(4)   What are the chances of collecting on the $50 million judgment against CSCG in China?

(5)   Is the strategy of suing the CSCG in the United States a good one?

Somportex Limited v. Philadelphia Chewing Gum Corp.

United States Court of Appeals, Third Circuit, 1971
453 F.2d 435, cert. denied, 405 U.S. 1017 (1972)

ALDISERT, Circuit Judge.

Several interesting questions are presented in this appeal from the district court's order granting summary judgment to enforce a default judgment entered by an English court. To resolve them, a complete recitation of the procedural history of this case is necessary.

This case has its genesis in a transaction between appellant, Philadelphia Chewing Gum Corporation, and Somportex Limited, a British corporation, which was to merchandise appellant's wares in Great Britain under the trade name "Tarzan Bubble Gum." According to the facts as alleged by appellant, there was a proposal which involved the participation of Brewster Leeds and Co., Inc., and M.S. International, Inc., third-party defendants in the court below. Brewster made certain arrangements with Somportex to furnish gum manufactured by Philadelphia; M.S. International, as agent for the licensor of the trade name "Tarzan," was to furnish the African name to the American gum to be sold in England. For reasons not relevant to our limited inquiry, the transaction never reached fruition.

Somportex filed an action against Philadelphia for breach of contract in the Queen's Bench Division of the High Court of England. Notice of the issuance of a Writ of Summons was served, in accordance with the rules and with the leave of the High Court, upon Philadelphia at its registered address in Havertown, Pennsylvania, on May 15, 1967. The extraterritorial service was based on the English version of long-arm statutes utilized by many American states. Philadelphia then consulted a firm of English solicitors, who, by letter of July 14, 1967, advised its Pennsylvania lawyers:

I have arranged with the Solicitors for Somportex Limited that they will let me have a copy of their Affidavit and exhibits to that Affidavit which supported their application to serve out of the Jurisdiction. Subject to the contents of the Affidavit, and any further information that can be provided by Philadelphia Chewing Gum Corporation after we have had the opportunity of seeing the Affidavit, it may be possible to make an application to the Court for an Order setting the Writ aside. But for such an application to be successful we will have to show that on the facts the matter does not fall within the provision of (f) and (g) [of the English long-arm statute].

In the meantime we will enter a conditional Appearance to the Writ in behalf of Philadelphia Chewing Gum Corporation in order to preserve the status quo.

On August 9, 1967, the English solicitors entered a "conditional appearance to the Writ" and filed a motion to set aside the Writ of Summons. At a hearing before a Master on November 13, 1967, the solicitors appeared and disclosed that Philadelphia had elected not to proceed with the summons or to contest the jurisdiction of the English Court, but instead intended to obtain leave of court to withdraw appearance of counsel. The Master then dismissed Philadelphia's summons to set aside plaintiff's Writ of Summons. Four days later, the solicitors sought to withdraw their appearance as counsel for Philadelphia, contending that it was a conditional appearance only. On November 27, 1967, after a Master granted the motion, Somportex appealed. The appeal was denied after hearing before a single judge, but the Court of Appeal, reversing the decision of the Master, held that the appearance was unconditional and that the submission to the jurisdiction by Philadelphia was, therefore, effective. But the court let stand "the original order which was made by the master on Nov. 13 dismissing the application to set aside. The writ therefore will stand. On the other hand, if the American company would wish to appeal from the order of Nov. 13, I see no reason why the time should not be extended and they can argue that matter out at a later stage if they should-so wish."

Thereafter, Philadelphia made a calculated decision: it decided to do nothing. It neither asked for an extension of time nor attempted in any way to proceed with an appeal from the Master's order dismissing its application to set aside the Writ. Instead, it directed its English solicitors to withdraw from the case. There being no appeal, the Master's order became final.

Somportex then filed a Statement of Claim which was duly served in accordance with English Court rules. In addition, by separate letter, it informed Philadelphia of the significance and effect of the pleading, the procedural posture of the case, and its intended course of action.

Philadelphia persisted in its course of inaction; it failed to file a defense. Somportex obtained a default judgment against it in the Queen's Bench Division of the High Court of Justice in England for the sum of 39,562.10.10 (approximately $94,000.00). The award reflected some $45,000.00 for loss of profit; $46,000.00 for loss of good will and $2,500.00 for costs, including attorneys' fees.

Thereafter, Somportex filed a diversity action in the court below, seeking to enforce the foreign judgment, and attached to the complaint a certified transcript of the English proceeding. The district court granted plaintiff's motion for summary judgment.

Appellant presents a cluster of contentions supporting its major thesis that we should not extend hospitality to the English judgment. First, it contends, and we agree, that because our jurisdiction is based solely on diversity, "the law to be applied . . . is the law of the state," in this case, Pennsylvania law. *Erie R. Co. v. Tompkins*.

Pennsylvania distinguishes between judgments obtained in the courts of her sister states, which are entitled to full faith and credit, and those of foreign courts, which are subject to principles of comity. *In re Christoffs Estate*, 411 Pa. 419, 192 A.2d 737, *cert. denied*, 375 U.S. 965 (1964).

Comity is a recognition which one nation extends within its own territory to the legislative, executive, or judicial acts of another. It is not a rule of law, but one of practice, convenience, and expediency. Although more than mere courtesy and accommodation, comity does not achieve the force of an imperative or obligation. Rather, it is a nation's expression of understanding which demonstrates due regard both to international duty and convenience and to the rights of persons protected by its own laws. Comity should be withheld only when its acceptance would be contrary or prejudicial to the interest of the nation called upon to give it effect.

Thus, the court in *Christoff, supra*, 192 A.2d at 739, acknowledged the governing standard enunciated in *Hilton v. Guyot*:

> When an action is brought in a court of this country by a citizen of a foreign country against one of our own citizens . . . and the foreign judgment appears to have been rendered by a competent court, having jurisdiction of the cause and of the parties and upon due allegations and proofs, and opportunity to defend against them, and its proceedings are according to the course of a civilized jurisprudence, and are stated in a clear and formal record, the judgment is prima facie evidence, at least, of the truth of the matter adjudged; and it should be held conclusive upon the merits tried in the foreign court, unless some special ground is shown for impeaching the judgment, as by showing that it was affected by fraud or prejudice, or that by the principles of international law, and by the comity of our own country, it should not be given full credit and effect.

It is by this standard, therefore, that appellant's arguments must be measured.

Appellant's contention that the district court failed to make an independent examination of the factual and legal basis of the jurisdiction of the English Court at once argues too much and says too little. The reality is that the court did examine the legal basis of asserted jurisdiction and decided the issue adversely to appellant.

Indeed, we do not believe it was necessary for the court below to reach the question of whether the factual complex of the contractual dispute permitted extraterritorial service under the English long arm statute. In its opinion denying leave of defense counsel to withdraw, the Court of Appeal specifically gave Philadelphia the opportunity to have the factual issue tested before the courts; moreover, Philadelphia was allocated additional time to do just that. Three months went by with no activity forthcoming and then, as described by the district court, "[d]uring this three month period, defendant changed its strategy and, not wishing to do anything which might result in its submitting to the English Court's jurisdiction, decided to withdraw its appearance altogether." Under these circumstances, we hold that defendant cannot choose its forum to test the factual basis of jurisdiction. It was given, and it waived, the opportunity of making the adequate presentation in the English Court.

Additionally, appellant attacks the English practice wherein a conditional appearance attacking jurisdiction may, by court decision, be converted into an unconditional one. It cannot effectively argue that this practice constitutes "some special ground . . . for impeaching the judgment," as to render the English judgment unwelcome in Pennsylvania under principles of international law and comity because it was obtained by procedures contrary or prejudicial to the host state. The English practice in this respect is identical to that set forth in both the Federal and Pennsylvania rules of civil procedure. F.R.C.P. 12(b)(2) provides the vehicle for attacking jurisdiction over the person, and, in *Orange Theatre Corp. v. Rayherstz Amusement Corp.*, 139 F.2d 871, 874 (3d Cir. 1944), we said that Rule 12 "has abolished for the federal courts the age-old distinction between general and special appearances." Similarly, a conditional or *"de bene esse"* appearance no longer exists in Pennsylvania. A challenge to jurisdiction must be asserted there by a preliminary objection raising a question of jurisdiction. Pa. R.C.P. 1017(b)(l).

English law permits recovery, as compensatory damages in breach of contract, of items reflecting loss of good will and costs, including attorneys' fees. These two items formed substantial portions of the English judgment. Because they are not recoverable under Pennsylvania law, appellant would have the foreign judgment declared unenforceable because it constitutes an ". . . action on the foreign claim [which] could not have been maintained because contrary to the public policy of the forum," citing Restatement, Conflict of Laws, §445. We are satisfied with the district court's disposition of this argument:

> The Court finds that . . . while Pennsylvania may not agree that these elements should be included in damages for breach of contract, the variance with Pennsylvania law is not such that the enforcement "tends clearly to injure the public health, the public morals, the public confidence in the purity of the administration of the law, or to undermine that sense of security for individual rights, whether of personal liberty or of private property, which any citizen ought to feel, is against public policy." *Goodyear v. Brown*, 155 Pa. 514, 518, 26 A. 665, 666 (1893).

Finally, appellant contends that since "it maintains no office or employee in England and transacts no business within the country" there were not sufficient contacts there to meet the due process tests of *International Shoe Co. v. Washington*. It argues that, at best, "the only contact Philadelphia had with England was the negotiations allegedly conducted by an independent New York exporter by letter, telephone and telegram to sell Philadelphia's products in England." In *Hanson v. Denckla*, 357 U.S. 235, 253 (1958), Chief Justice Warren said: "The application of [the requirement of contact] rule will vary with the quality and nature of the defendant's activity, but it is essential in each case that there be some act by which the defendant purposely avails itself of the privilege of conducting business within the forum State, thus invoking the benefits and protection of its laws." We have concluded that whether the New York exporter was an independent contractor or Philadelphia's agent was a matter to be resolved by the English Court.

For the purpose of the constitutional argument, we must assume the proper agency relationship. So construed, we find his activity would constitute the "quality and nature of the defendant's activity" similar to that of the defendant in *McGee v. International Life Ins. Co.*, 355 U.S. 220 (1957), there held to satisfy due process requirements.

In sum, we find that the English proceedings met all the tests enunciated in *Christoff, supra*. We are not persuaded that appellant met its burden of showing that the British "decree is so palpably tainted by fraud or prejudice as to outrage our sense of justice, or [that] the process of the foreign tribunal was invoked to achieve a result contrary to our laws or public policy or to circumvent our laws or public policy." *Christoff, supra*, 192 A.2d at 739.

The judgment of the district court will be affirmed.

Nippon Emo-Trans Co., Ltd. v. Emo-Trans, Inc.
United States District Court, Eastern District of New York, 1990
744 F. Supp. 1215

DEARIE, District Judge.

[Plaintiff Nippon Emo-Trans Co., Ltd. (NET), a Japanese corporation, and defendant Emo-Trans, Inc. (ETI), a New York corporation, are freight forwarders. Their business consists of assembling goods from various sources for shipment, arranging for shipment, and arranging for the shipments to be broken down and delivered to the ultimate recipient. From August 1982 to February 1986, NET and ETI had a contractual relationship in which each agreed to serve as the receiving end for shipments made by the other. A dispute arose between them on the allocation of profits in connection with freight charges collected from consignees. In June 1986, NET sued ETI in the Tokyo district court and obtained a judgment against ETI in the amount of $354,000. ETI thereafter appealed the judgment to the Tokyo High Court and that appeal was still pending when NET brought the present action to attach any property of ETI found in New York up to $400,000. The federal district court, sitting in diversity jurisdiction, applied New York state law under *Klaxon Co. v. Stentor Electric Manufacturing Co.*, 313 U.S. 487 (1941) and granted the attachment. However, under New York state law, NET had to make a motion to confirm the attachment within 5 days after the levy was first made. NET timely moved to confirm the order of attachment after levy on ETI's property in various banks.

NET's motion to confirm was now before the federal district court. Under applicable New York law, the confirmation of the attachment turned on two issues. First, as the attachment was based on a foreign court judgment, the attachment could be confirmed only if the foreign judgment was entitled to recognition by New York courts under New York law. Whether the judgment was entitled to recognition depended on whether the judgment was valid and the validity of the judgment in turn depended on whether the Tokyo district court had *in personam* jurisdiction over ETI. Second, the attachment could be confirmed only if there was a need to continue the attachment.

As to the first issue of jurisdiction, the federal district court first found that ETI waived any jurisdictional objections when it made an appearance in the Tokyo district court and contested the claim on the merits. Although ETI initially made an appearance to contest the court's jurisdiction, ETI's assertion of an additional defense on the merits constituted a waiver and, under New York law, a defendant, once having waived jurisdiction, is precluded from challenging jurisdiction again in a subsequent action. The federal district court, however, went on to conclude that even if ETI were permitted to relitigate the issue of jurisdiction of the Tokyo court, New York law would allow its courts to recognize a foreign country judgment if the foreign court judgment was based on a jurisdictional basis that would be recognized under New York law. In other words, if the Tokyo court could have exercised in personam jurisdiction over ETI in accordance with New York's long-arm statute, then the federal district court is entitled to recognize the Tokyo court judgment. The court then turned to the issue of whether exercise of jurisdiction by the Tokyo court under New York's approach to jurisdiction was proper.]

JURISDICTION UNDER NEW YORK LAW

New York's general jurisdictional statute, Section 301 of the Civil Practice Law & Rules, incorporates all bases of jurisdiction recognized at common law. Of cardinal importance at common law and under Section 301 is jurisdiction based on a finding that a foreign corporation is doing business within the state; so long as a corporation does business "not occasionally or casually, but with a fair measure of permanence and continuity," *Tauza Susquehanna Coal Co.*, 220 N.Y. 259, 267, 115 N.E. 915 (1917), then it is deemed to be "present" within the state, and subject to suit on any cause of action, not merely those arising out of business transacted in the state. *Id.* One of the traditional indicia of "doing business" is "substantial, regular and continuous sales or shipment of goods in the state." 1 J. Weinstein, H. Korn & A. Miller, *New York Civil Practice* ¶301.16 at 3-34 (1989). In *Tauza* itself, the Court relied both on defendant's having an office in the state and in having "obtain[ed] orders which result in continuous shipments . . . to New York"; 220 N.Y. at 265, 115 N.E. at 917; there is reason to believe, however, that substantial and continuous shipments alone would have been a sufficient basis for jurisdiction.

A foreign corporation may also be found to be doing business in the state by virtue of the actions of an in-state agent taken on the defendant's behalf. It is clear from the caselaw that in this context, the term "agent" may at times include a person who, under common law, would more readily have been considered an "independent contractor" than an "agent." *See, e.g., Gelfand v. Tanner Motor Tours, Ltd.*, 385 F.2d 116 (2d Cir. 1967), *cert. denied*, 390 U.S. 996, 88 S. Ct. 1198, 20 L. Ed. 2d 95 (1968). In general, it appears that New York courts will find an agency relationship for purposes of Section 301 if the services performed "are sufficiently important to the foreign corporation that if it did not have a representative to perform them, the corporation's own officials would undertake to perform substantially similar services," *Gelfand*, 385 F.2d at 121, and if the representative is genuinely acting on behalf of the foreign corporation, and not for its own account. In some instances, common ownership may give rise to an inference of agency, although it is neither necessary nor sufficient. In connection with actions on behalf of the foreign corporation, it has been said that the agent must have the power to bind the foreign corporation. While such a test may have particular significance in the context of sales of services such as use of hotel rooms or the sale of tour tickets, it would appear appropriate to look to the nature of the enterprise to determine those actions which can most reliably indicate whether an entity is acting on behalf of the defendant or on its own account.

ETI's business, by its nature, involves the performance and brokering of transportation services. Insofar as the Court understands the business, the freight forwarder typically will enter into a contract with a customer for the delivery of a quantity of goods to a separate country; the forwarder will then assemble goods into quantities suitable for shipment, arrange to have the goods transported by carrier, and engage another party on the other end to receive the shipment, break it down, and deliver (or arrange for delivery of) the goods to the ultimate recipient.

Since 1986, ETI has maintained a relationship with [a Japanese affiliate, Emo-Japan, Ltd. (EJL)] whereby EJL would act as break bulk agent for shipments originated by ETI to Japan; ETI derives approximately 1% of its gross revenues—about $600,000 per year—from its shipments to Japan. Between 1982 and 1986, ETI had had a similar arrangement with NET; the president of ETI had been a director of NET, and he had traveled to Japan to help solicit business for both NET and ETI. Whether ETI's president engages in such activities with EJL is not revealed in the record.

There can be no question but that the value of shipments sent by ETI to Japan is "substantial." ETI argues that the amount in question constitutes an insignificant portion of its gross revenues. While that may be so, this cannot be the only appropriate measure of substantiality; if ETI's argument were accepted, then the larger the foreign corporation, the less likely would it be to be amenable to suit in New York. In this context, the "substantiality" requirement is satisfied by the gross value of business transacted by ETI in Japan, in excess of half a million dollars annually. Further, ETI has engaged in "continuous" activity directed at Japan, as evidenced by its maintaining relationships first with NET and then with EJL, over a period of eight years. Thus, even apart from considerations of ETI's relationship with EJL, it could be said that ETI had directed its activity at Japan with a "fair measure of permanence and continuity."

In addition, it can hardly be argued that EJL is not ETI's "agent," performing actions on ETI's behalf in Japan. The Court notes that ETI itself characterizes EJL as its "break bulk agent." *See Frigger Declaration,* ¶19. To paraphrase the *Gelfand* Court, it must be conceded that since the nature of ETI's business is getting the goods to their ultimate destination, the services performed for it by EJL "are sufficiently important to [ETI] that if it did not have [EJL or some other representative] to perform them, [ETI's] own officials would undertake to perform substantially similar services." *Gelfand,* 385 F.2d at 121. Further, so far as it appears from the record, no argument can be made that in serving as break bulk agent, EJL is really acting on its own account. There is no indication in the record that EJL enters into a separate contract with the party who initially shipped the goods, or that its profits for shipment are independent of ETI's. In addition, ETI relies *solely* on EJL for break bulk services in Japan; thus, in the words of the New York Court of Appeals, EJL does "all the business which [ETI] could do were it here by its own officials." *Frummer,* 19 N.Y.2d at 537, 227 N.E.2d at 854, 281 N.Y.S.2d at 44. In the presence of facts such as these, it is significant that ETI and EJL are affiliated through common ownership and that ETI acts as EJL's break bulk agent in the United States. While certain of the characteristics of a common law agency relationship may not be present here, that is not the test under Section 301; given the nature of the freight forwarding business and the services performed by EJL, the Court is of the view that EJL is ETI's agent, within the meaning of Section 301, and that actions taken by EJL on ETI's behalf are attributable to ETI for purposes of determining whether ETI is "doing business" in Japan.

In view of the volume and continuity of activity initiated by ETI and directed toward Japan, the Court concludes that, were it necessary to reexamine the facts to determine whether ETI is amenable to suit in Japan, it would find that, judged by the standards of Section 301, a New York court would conclude that ETI was doing business in Japan on a substantial, continuous and permanent basis, and that as a result the Tokyo Court could properly have asserted jurisdiction over it. In consequence, whether [ETI is deemed to have waived the jurisdiction objection] or under common law, NET has demonstrated a probability of success on the question of the Tokyo Court's jurisdiction, and thus on the merits of this action.

THE NEED TO CONTINUE THE ATTACHMENT

It remains to be seen whether NET has demonstrated a need to continue the levy, as required by Sections 6212(a) and 6223(b) of the New York Civil Practice Law & Rules.

The Court is of the view that in cases where jurisdiction is not at issue, the standard under Section 6201(4) requires that the plaintiff make some showing of a need to secure the sought-after judgment, both at the time an attachment is sought *ex parte* and on the motion to confirm.

Thus the question for the Court is not merely whether there exists a foreign judgment, likely to merit recognition, and remaining unsatisfied; rather, it is whether NET has shown that confirmation is necessary to secure payment of the Japanese Judgment. The Court concludes it has not. It must be conceded that if ETI's statements regarding its revenues and assets are credited, ETI would have no difficulty satisfying the Japanese Judgment. NET has not presented the Court with any information which tends to cast doubt on ETI's assertions, although it bears the burden of proof on this issue and has had the opportunity to conduct limited discovery. Similarly, in view of the nature and history of ETI's business, it appears unlikely that it would attempt to "flee" the jurisdiction. As to ETI's program of restructuring its operations in some states in order to give key personnel equity interests in majority-owned subsidiaries, NET claims that this amounts to a transfer of assets to third parties. While this may be true, ETI's explanation of the purpose of its restructuring program is a plausible one, and its effect is limited by operation of law; absent stringent supermajority provisions not normally used for such subsidiaries, ETI, as the majority shareholder, would have effective control over the funds and other assets of its subsidiaries.

The Court concludes that NET has not met its burden of proof regarding the need to continue the attachment; as a result, the motion to confirm is DENIED, and the order of this Court dated February 2, 1990, granting such attachment, is vacated subject to the conditions described in the following section.

STAY PENDING APPEAL IN JAPAN

[Although NET was not entitled to the confirmation of the order of attachment, the court realized that NET could next make a motion before the court for recognition of the Tokyo judgment itself and then seek to enforce that judgment immediately against ETI. However, as ETI's appeal of the Tokyo district court judgment before the Tokyo High Court was still pending and would take a year or more to decide, the court realized that recognition of the Tokyo district court judgment at this point was problematic as it might still be reversed on appeal.]

In view of these competing considerations, the Court views it appropriate to order a stay of these proceedings, subject to the following conditions:

> FIRST, the stay shall take effect only upon ETI's posting a bond for the full amount of the Japanese Judgment, plus a reasonable reserve to cover interest for an eighteen-month period; ETI may, in its discretion, post such bond in this Court or in the appropriate court in Japan; and
>
> SECOND, in order to avoid creating any incentive for "strategic behavior" on ETI's part, the effective time of the vacatur of this Court's order of attachment shall be postponed until such time as ETI posts the bond described above.

Subject to the conditions described herein, (i) the motion for an order confirming the attachment is DENIED, and (ii) the proceedings in this action are hereby STAYED pending the outcome of ETI's appeal of the Japanese Judgment. So ordered.

Thieffry and Associés

Enforcement of U.S. Judgments in France (2002)

[As] French courts used at the time to review foreign judgments on the merits before granting enforcement, the U.S. Supreme Court decided in 1895 to refuse to enforce French judgments in the United States on the basis of reciprocity.[32] Times have changed. French courts are now as open to foreign judgments as the courts of most of the other occidental countries.

A. Legal Mechanism by Which U.S. Judgments Are Enforced

With regard to the enforcement of foreign judgments, French law distinguishes between countries which have signed a bilateral treaty with France or are a party to a multilateral convention also ratified by France and those which have not entered into such agreements.

Although France is a part to the Brussels Convention on Jurisdiction and the Enforcement of Judgments in Civil and Commercial Matters[33] (hereinafter, the "Brussels Convention"), and to bilateral treaties[34] with various countries of different legal systems relating to the enforcement of foreign judgments, none of them have been entered into with the United States.

Surprisingly for a civil law country, the enforcement of the foreign judgments made in those countries which, like the United States, have not entered into any convention or bilateral treaty with France is not regulated by any specific statute. Such judgments are enforced according to the general rules elaborated and implemented by case law through the decisions of the French Supreme Court, the Cour de Cassation.

B. Substantive Standards

1. IN GENERAL

The leading case from the French Cour de Cassation is *Munzer vs. Munzer*.[35] According to the main ruling of the *Munzer* decision:

"[T]he French judge must ensure that five conditions are satisfied, namely (1) the jurisdiction of the foreign court which rendered the decision; (2) the regularity of the

---

32. *See Hilton v. Guyot*, 159 U.S. 113 (1895).

33. Convention on Jurisdiction and Enforcement of Judgments in Civil and Commercial Matters, 21 O.J. Eur. Com. (No. L. 304) 77 (1978); 8 I.L.M. 229.

34. More than 40 bilateral treaties have been signed between France and various countries, including countries of Eastern Europe.

35. Judgment of Jan. 7, 1964, Cass. Civ., Fr., Journal de Droit International 302 (1964), casenote Goldmani *Revue Critique de Droit International Prive*, [R.C.D.I.P.]. 344 (1964).

procedure before that court; (3) the application of the law applicable according to French rules of conflict of laws; (4) the compliance with international public policy; and (5) the absence of fraud under law."

2. FINALITY OF THE FOREIGN JUDGMENT

According to the rules developed by the Cour de Cassation, the enforcement of a foreign judgment may be granted as soon as it is enforceable in the country where it was made and even though the foreign judgment is subject to appeal or recourse before the Supreme Court in such country. However, it should be noted that some bilateral treaties are less favorable in that they require that the foreign judgment be final.

3. THE REVIEW ON THE MERITS OF THE U.S. JUDGMENT

The former practice of reviewing the foreign judgment on the merits has been abandoned once and for all, by the French Cour de Cassation in *Munzer*. This decision, which lists limitative grounds for non-recognition, states that:

"[T]his examination which suffices to ensure the protection of the French legal order and interests, the very purpose of the enforcement procedure, *constitutes in all matters both the expression and the limit of the power of review rendering the foreign judgment enforceable in France without the judge carving out any review of the decision on the merits*." (emphasis added)

4. THE JURISDICTIONAL TEST

French courts will examine jurisdiction over the subject matter or venue under the rules provided for by the law of the country where the judgment was made.

However, the question is much more complicated with regard to the "international jurisdiction" of the foreign court, a distinction being based upon whether or not the French courts had "exclusive jurisdiction" over the dispute. If the French courts had, pursuant to a French rule of jurisdiction, exclusive jurisdiction, the foreign court shall be deemed to have lacked jurisdiction over the dispute and enforcement shall be refused. Most commonly, a French judgment debtor may argue that the French courts had exclusive jurisdiction pursuant to article 15 of the Code Civil unless the judgment debtor waived his right to benefit from this provision. However, in this respect, a contractual choice of court in a provision on settlement of disputes is, of course, deemed such a waiver. French courts also have exclusive jurisdiction over all disputes relating to estates located in France, French patents, trademarks, etc.

Failing the exclusive jurisdiction of the French courts, the international jurisdiction of the foreign court shall be examined neither according to the French rules, nor according to the foreign rules on jurisdiction but according to the rule specifically fashioned by the Cour de Cassation in *Simitch* which specifies that:

"[E]very time that the French rule . . . does not grant exclusive jurisdiction to the French courts, the foreign court must be deemed to have had jurisdiction if the dispute is connected in a characterized manner to the country where the decision was made and if the choice of the court was not fraudulent."

5. THE SERVICE OF PROCESS

As a preliminary remark, it should be noted that, under French law, an adequate service of process shall not confer jurisdiction to the French Courts and, for the purpose of enforcement, is required solely for the purpose of ensuring that the judgment debtor had a fair opportunity to appear and to present his defense. Therefore, the adequacy of the service of process shall be examined with regard to its conformity with the public policy requirement independently of the rules of procedure applicable in the country where the judgment was made.

In practice, service is often not effected pursuant to the Hague Convention on the Service Abroad of Judicial and Extrajudicial Documents but under the French rules.

6. THE MEASURE OF DAMAGES OR COMPENSATION

Any review of the measure of damages or compensation determined in the United States would be considered as a review de novo or a modification of the foreign decision prohibited under French law. Several decisions have held that the court where the enforcement is sought cannot modify or increase the measure of damages decided by the foreign courts.

As discussed below, the quantum of damages could be put into question as not conforming to public policy. In fact, penalties imposed in private, civil or commercial matters will usually be enforceable, although it is conceivable that in extreme circumstances they could be found excessive.

7. THE DATE AND RATE OF CURRENCY EXCHANGE

Since the judge is not allowed to modify in any respect the terms of the foreign judgment subject to enforcement, the conversion of the amounts expressed in the foreign judgment in foreign currency into French Francs is not necessary and can be made at the official rate published in the "Journal Official" on the date of payment.

8. JUDGMENTS IN TAX MATTERS, JUDGMENTS AWARDING TREBLE DAMAGES OR PUNITIVE DAMAGES

Judgments rendered in tax matters are not usually enforceable except to the extent provided by treaty, if any.

Punitive damages or treble damages are characterized under French law as private penalties. As such, they may contravene Article 1149 of the French Civil Code which provides for the exact compensation of the injury. However, the rule is not absolute and Articles 1150 through 1155 of the Civil Code provide for some exceptions.

9. THE PROCEDURE IN THE U.S. COURT

As a general rule the procedural standards of fairness will be examined under the public policy requirement and the enforcement shall be refused if the judgment contravenes public policy. It should be noted, however, that the caselaw has developed the concept of international public policy and that looser standards of fairness apply. Under the international public policy requirement, French courts will refuse enforcement of the foreign judgment if the defendant did not receive adequate or proper notice or has not been properly represented or able to present his case.

Therefore, enforcement shall not be granted if the defendant has not been properly served or served in time in order to allow him to appear and prepare his defense or if the foreign judgment is based on the sole ground of the default of the defendant.

With regard to the methods of gathering evidence which are under French law fundamentally different from those provided under American law, some difficulties may arise. A party's testimony under oath has been ruled contrary to public policy.[36]

Thus, a foreign decision based on some discovery-generated evidence might, in particular cases, be presented as non-conforming to public policy and therefore unenforceable.[37]

10. RECIPROCITY

Under the general rule as developed by the Cour de Cassation, the reciprocity requirement does not apply and has never been applied by French courts. The reason most commonly presented is that the relationship between private parties and the resolution of their disputes must not depend on public interest and political considerations.

C. PROCEDURE OF ENFORCEMENT

The enforcement of a U.S. judgment in France is obtained from the Tribunal de Grande Instance, the court having general subject matter jurisdiction at the first degree in France. The particular Tribunal de Grande Instance before which the action in exequatur is to be brought is the court of the judgment debtor's residence or, if the judgment debtor has no residence in France, the court of the place where enforcement is to occur. The action in exequatur is to be introduced like any other action before the courts by means of an assignation (complaint) to be served upon the defendant.

Appeal may be taken from the order refusing to grant exequatur to the foreign judgment before the Court of Appeals within one month of service of the order.

---

36. Judgment of Jan. 22, 1951, Cass. Civ., Fr., R.C.D.I.P. 167 (1951); casenote Francescakis.

37. The French blocking statute makes clear that the refusal to concur to discovery is a matter of public policy. French Law No. 80-538, dated July 16, 1980, Journal Officiel de la Republique Francaise (July 17, 1980).

In case of refusal of exequatur, the judgment creditor may prefer to introduce an action on the merits since the refusal of exequatur does not have *res judicata* effect.

NOTES AND QUESTIONS

1. What is the basis for recognition and enforcement of foreign judgments in the United States? Is this matter governed by state law? Selected provisions of the Uniform Foreign Money-Judgments Recognition Act, 13 U.L.A. 43 (2002), which has been adopted in many states, reads as follows in relevant part:

Section 4:

(a) A foreign judgment is not conclusive if
(1) the judgment was rendered under a system which does not provide impartial tribunals or procedures compatible with the requirements of due process of law;
(2) the foreign court did not have personal jurisdiction over the defendant; or
(3) the foreign court did not have jurisdiction over the subject matter.

Section 5:

(a) The foreign judgment shall not be refused recognition for lack of personal jurisdiction if
(1) the defendant was served personally in the foreign state;
(2) the defendant voluntarily appeared in the proceedings, other than for the purpose of protecting property seized or threatened with seizure in the proceedings or of contesting the jurisdiction of the court over him;
(3) the defendant prior to the commencement of the proceedings had agreed to submit to the jurisdiction of the foreign court with respect to the subject matter involved;
(4) the defendant was domiciled in the foreign state when the proceedings were instituted or, being a body corporate had its principal place of business, was incorporated, or had otherwise acquired corporate status, in the foreign state;
(5) the defendant had a business office in the foreign state and the proceedings in the foreign court involved a [cause of action] arising out of business done by the defendant through that office in the foreign state; or
(b) The courts of this state may recognize other bases of jurisdiction.

2. Certain nations have concluded international treaties to governing mutual recognition of their judgments. The most important is the European Convention on Jurisdiction and the Enforcement of Judgments (1968 as amended) (the Brussels Convention). The Brussels Convention system was enlarged with the accession of new member states to the European Community/Union as well as a "parallel convention" known as the Lugano Convention (1988). In December 2000, the Council of the European Union adopted a new regulation which replaces the Brussels Convention for all EU members except Denmark. *See* Council Regulation 44/2001 on Jurisdiction and Recognition and Enforcement of Judgments in Civil and Commercial Matters, 2001 O.J. (L 12) 1. The Brussels Convention and the Regulation make it relatively easy to enforce a judgment within Europe.

3. Would it be desirable if the United States entered into a multilateral treaty for mutual recognition and enforcement of judgments? Negotiations for such a treaty are ongoing at the Hague Conference on Private International Law. At this writing, these negotiations are deeply stalled.

9 _Corporate Social Responsibility_

I. Introduction

The growth and importance of international business operations raises many issues concerning the social responsibility of business to civil society. Corporate social responsibility (CSR) and business ethics are especially important in the international arena because of the rise of MNEs and the perception that they wield extraordinary power and influence. In fact, in terms of economic power, many MNEs have more annual turnover than the GDP of the majority of states of the world. MNEs usually operate through individual, linked companies so that they consist of a corporate group organized around a holding company and various subsidiary corporations. MNEs, of course, are subject to the national regulatory laws and policies of the countries in which they operate, but, because they are international, they may be able to organize their operations to avoid significant social responsibility within nations, and their economic and political power may allow them to pressure states into complying with their wishes. The recent revelations of international corporate scandals involving MNEs such as Enron have inflamed the belief by many that powerful corporations are controlled by unscrupulous individuals driven purely by greed and profit, view themselves as above the law, and evade their responsibilities to their shareholders and the public. Developing countries in particular may be subject to their influence and control.

This is the perception of many, but is this borne out by the facts? Undoubtedly, there are abuses, but how widespread are they? Is avoidance of CSR the norm or the exceptional case? Furthermore, is it advisable for an MNE to shirk its CSR even if it has the opportunity? Are there reasons besides legal compulsion for an MNE to operate in a socially responsible way? Finally, what standards, guidelines, and procedures should an international company use to be socially responsible? Should it simply comply with the individual national requirements in each country in which it does business or should it adopt uniform minimum standards for all its operations? Although these issues may seem to be theoretical questions for an ivory tower far removed from the corporate board-room, some recent developments provide clear indications that MNEs cannot ignore concerns arising from CSR. The materials below set forth the major developments in this area.

In this chapter, we consider the international law norms that apply to international business as well as voluntary codes of conduct and other incentives and reasons why international business must today be very concerned with CSR.

We introduce these CSR concerns in a practical context in the problems below. To address these problems, consider the following articles by Professors Charney and Paust and the accompanying notes.

PROBLEM 9-1

Dresser, Inc., is a Texas company engaged in the highly competitive and labor-intensive athletic shoe and apparel industry. The CEO of Dresser comes to your law firm and says, "To survive in our business, we need to move our operations overseas and we need to find rock-bottom labor costs. I want a survey done of the world's labor laws and I want you to identify the country with the lowest level of protection and the fewest rights for workers so I can pay the lowest wages and earn the highest profits. Now I want to emphasize that this is 'no race to the bottom' as we do not want to do anything illegal. My strategy is to scrupulously follow the written laws of the country in which we are operating. My position is that so long as we are following local law to the letter and treat employees the same way they are being treated by their local employers, our conduct is lawful and we are protected. In fact, we should be commended for bringing jobs to the local economy." Is this a good strategy?

PROBLEM 9-2

NED Industries, Inc., is a major industrial corporation incorporated in Delaware and with world headquarters in Chicago. NED is a world-class manufacturer of chemicals used in a variety of household and industrial applications. NED has subsidiary companies in Europe and Japan and is now considering selling its products as well as establishing manufacturing facilities in other areas.

NED's expansion plans target developing countries in Africa and South America. NED has a twofold strategy of developing new export markets by an aggressive marketing campaign in these nations. When sales reach a certain volume, NED plans to establish subsidiary companies that will carry out manufacturing operations in several countries. Some of these operations may involve dangerous toxic chemicals. NED's founder and CEO, Ned Burner, is a colorful and idealistic personality who wants to be successful, but is conscious of his company's social responsibility to the countries in which he does business. He also does not want adverse publicity because it could cause NED economic harm. Burner comes to you, his general counsel, with the following questions:

(1) "I know that multinational companies like ours are subject to regulation by domestic legislation but are MNEs also subject to international legal norms that govern corporate behavior? If so, what types of norms might be applicable to our plans in Africa and South America?"

(2) "Explain whether you think we are better off or worse off if our company is subject to public international law norms rather than just subject to domestic regulation."

Jonathan I. Charney, Transnational Corporations and Developing Public International Law
1983 Duke Law Journal 748, 762-769

I. INTRODUCTION

Currently, one of the most significant developments in public international law is the apparent creation of law applicable to transnational corporations

(TNCs). Although public international law has addressed international economic issues for some time, recently, in light of expanded TNC activity and increased third world leverage in international affairs, greater attention has been focused on the establishment of rules to govern TNC behavior. These developments are partly explained as an effort by the third world to increase its international power vis-a-vis the power of both the TNCs and the western developed world, with whom the TNCs are generally aligned, but there are also additional factors encouraging them. First, because one country usually cannot unilaterally regulate TNC power and behavior, even the western, developed countries have an interest in these developments. Second, TNCs themselves recognize the benefits of a uniform regulatory scheme that would avoid many of the difficulties produced by varying national requirements. Although these new rules will be aimed at TNCs, international practice has largely precluded TNCs from directly participating in this rule-making process.

[handwritten margin note: Reasons to make laws for TNC's]

There is evidence that TNCs have had international legal personality and have participated in the international legal system for some time. Examples of such participation include application of public international law to contracts with state entities and participation in dispute settlement forums established either by treaty or intergovernmental organizations. Some principles of public international law have become so widely accepted that they have been viewed as binding on the TNCs' international activities. Finally, TNCs advise international organizations when their interests are at stake and it is clear that they play a direct role in influencing national behavior on relevant international matters.

Some maintain that TNC activities are actually just a new form of western colonialism while others view the TNC as a more benign force that is ultimately subject to state control even without major new international initiatives. Regardless of which view is correct, the international community is moving toward greater international regulation of international business without allowing direct business participation.

There are strong arguments for expanding the role of TNCs in the international legal system. Nation-states aside, TNCs are the most powerful actors in the world today and to not recognize that power would be unrealistic. The international economy depends heavily on the services they provide and they have far greater influence and economic power than unorganized human beings or most other nongovernmental organizations. In fact, even the influence of intergovernmental organizations, which depends on the continued financial and political support of nation-state sponsors, cannot be compared to the power of many TNCs. This argument for increased TNC participation is further supported by the conclusion that the continued viability of the international legal system depends upon the close conformity of public international law to international realities.

Jordan J. Paust, Human Rights Responsibilities of Private Corporations

35 Vanderbilt Journal of Transnational Law 801, 802-815 (2002)

Does human rights law reach private multinational corporations? Despite the lack of widespread early attention to private corporate liability for human rights deprivations, preferences of a few textwriters, and remarkable confusion, human rights law can reach private corporations. More generally, a private corporation as such is simply a juridic person and has no immunity under U.S. domestic or international law. In each nation-state, private corporations, like private individuals, are bound by domestic laws. Similarly, private corporations and entities are bound by international laws applicable to individuals. For example, in the United States and elsewhere, companies and other non-state associations and organizations have been found to have civil and criminal responsibility for various violations of international law, including human rights and related international proscriptions. In the United States, private companies have rights to sue under the Alien Tort Claims Act (ATCA) [28 U.S.C. §1350] and it is only logical and policy-serving that they can also be defendants under the ATCA. In fact, there have been express recognitions to that effect in U.S. cases. For example, in 1997, in *Doe v. Unocal Corp.*,[1] the Central District of California recognized that several human rights and other international law claims made by farmers from Burma against a private corporation and others were viable under the ATCA. These claims included claims of slave or "forced" labor, torture, violence against women, and other human rights violations and crimes against humanity that also occurred in complicity with Burmese military, intelligence groups, and police. Addressing universal jurisdiction through the ATCA and nonimmunity of corporate actors for cruel, inhumane treatment and slave or forced labor, the district court in *Iwanowa v. Ford Motor Co.* added: "No logical reason exists for allowing private individuals and corporations to escape liability for universally condemned violations of international law merely because they were not acting under color of law."[2] In 1907, an Opinion of the U.S. Attorney General recognized that a private U.S. company violated a treaty by diverting the Rio Grande through dredging activities.[3] The Attorney General noted that an International Water Boundary Commission "found . . . [t]hat the . . . Company . . . violated the stipulations of that treaty," and recognized that injuries included "damage to property," including injury to "riparian rights," and "[a]s to indemnity for injuries which may have been caused to citizens of Mexico, I am of the opinion that existing statutes provide a right of action and a forum . . . the statutes [including the ATCA] thus provide a forum and a right of action."[4]

In *Burger-Fischer v. DeGussa AG. & DeGussa Corp.*, claims were made concerning the seizure of property and slave labor.[5] In *Bodner v. Banque Paribas*, the court found that claims against banks for looting, conversion, and withholding of assets of victims of the Nazi Holocaust in violation of human rights and other international law were actionable under the ATCA.[6] Alleged corporate involvement with prison labor also led to suits in *Ge v. Peng*[7] and *Doe v. The Gap, Inc.*[8] *Ge* was later dismissed, however, because, "[u]nlike *Kadic* and its progeny, . . . [the] case involves the use of forced prison labor in the production of soccer balls . . . [and] forced prison labor [according to the court] is not . . . proscribed by international

---

1. *Doe v. Unocal Corp.*, 963 F. Supp. 880 (C.D. Cal. 1997).
2. *Iwanowa v. Ford Motor Co.*, 67 F. Supp. 2d 424, 445 (D.N.J. 1999).
3. 26 Gp. Att'y Gen. 250, 251-54 (1907).
4. *Id.* at 251-53.
5. *Burger-Fischer v. DeGussa Ag. & DeGussa Corp.*, 65 F. Supp. 2d 248, 272-73 (D.N.J. 1999).
6. *Bodner v. Banque Paribas*, 114 F. Supp. 2d 117 (E.D.N.Y. 2000).
7. *Ge v. Peng*, 1999 U.S. Dist. LEXIS 10834, at *6-7, *dismissed*, 2000 U.S. Dist. LEXIS 12711 (Aug. 28, 2000).
8. *Doe v. Gap, Inc.*, No. CV99-77 (D. Haw. 1999).

law."[9] In *Jama v. U.S. I.N.S.*, the court found that violations of human rights prohibitions of cruel, inhuman, or degrading treatment by a private correctional corporation and its officers and employees acting under contract with the Immigration and Naturalization Services—which made the corporate officers "state actors"—were actionable under the ATCA.[10] In *Eastman Kodak Co. v. Kavlin*, the district court found that claims of arbitrary detention involving a Brazilian company and an individual owner thereof who allegedly conspired with local Brazilian officials were actionable under the ATCA.[11]

2. TRENDS IN DECISIONS OUTSIDE THE UNITED STATES

Judicial decisions outside the United States have recognized human rights responsibilities of private persons, companies, and corporations. Japanese and German cases have recognized such forms of private responsibility, and there has been similar recognition by the European Court of Human Rights. More recently, the British House of Lords recognized that a private corporation's responsibilities under domestic employment law are "[s]ubject to observance of fundamental human rights. . . ."[12] In 1998, the Supreme Court of Canada recognized that it is possible "for a non-state actor to perpetuate human rights violations on a scale amounting to persecution" within the reach of the Refugee Convention and, more generally, that private actors can engage in human rights violations.[13]

Most human rights instruments speak generally of particular rights of each person or everyone without any mention of or limitation concerning which person or entities owe a corresponding duty. Thus, most duties are generally not limited to state actors and do reach private persons or entities. Moreover, violations of human rights recognized in particular treaties and customary international law often reach private perpetrators expressly or by implication. For example, the preamble to the Universal Declaration of Human Rights recognizes that the human rights proclaimed therein are "a common standard of achievement for all peoples . . . [including] every individual and every organ of society." Article 29, paragraph 1, affirms that "Everyone has duties to the community . . ."; Article 30 recognizes that no right of "any . . . group or person . . . [exists] to engage in any activity or to perform any act aimed at the destruction of any of the rights and freedoms set forth" in the Universal Declaration. Thus, there are correlative duties of groups and persons not to engage in acts aimed at the destruction of human rights set forth in the Declaration. Indeed, Article 30—like provisions in most major human rights instruments—contains an interpretive command that "[n]othing . . . be interpreted as implying for any State, group or person any right to engage in any activity or to perform any act aimed at the destruction of any of the rights and freedoms set forth herein." Because numerous human rights are set forth in the Declaration without any mention of "state" actors or any limitation to state actor duties or "color," the express and unavoidable

---

9. *Ge v. Peng*, 2000 U.S. Dist. LEXIS 12711, at 18 (Aug. 28, 2000).

10. *Jama v. U.S. I.N.S.*, 22 F. Supp. 2d 353, 362-63 (D.N.J. 1998).

11. *Eastman Kodak Co. v. Kavlin*, 978 F. Supp. 1078, 1090-95 (S.D. Fla. 1997).

12. *Johnson v. Unisys, Ltd.*, UKHL/13, ¶37 (22 March 2001) (Lord Hoffmann).

13. *Pushpanathan v. Canada*, [1998] 160 D.L.R. (4th) 193, 231, 1998 D.L.R. Lexis 512 (Can. 1998), also noting a related practice of Australia.

interpretive command in Article 30 prohibits adding words or implying limitations that the drafters did not choose. Article 30 also should not be read so as to interpret particular human rights articles as if groups or persons can engage in any activity or perform any act aimed at the destruction of such rights, but state actors or those acting under "color"—and only such actors—cannot do so. The correlative reach of Article 30 is to "any" group or person.

The preamble to the International Covenant on Civil and Political Rights (ICCPR)[14] expressly affirms "that the individual, *having duties* to other individuals and to the community to which he belongs, *is under a responsibility* to strive for the promotion and observance of the rights recognized in the present Covenant."[15] Thus, at a minimum, individuals have duties to not violate human rights. Article 5, like Article 30 of the Universal Declaration, also affirms the lack of a right of "any . . . group or person . . . to engage in any activity or to perform any act aimed at the destruction of any of the rights and freedoms set forth" in the Covenant "or at their limitation to a greater extent than is provided,"[16] and thus impliedly affirms the duty of any group or person to not destroy or limit human rights.

Private duties are also expressly recognized in the preamble to and Articles 27 through 29 of the African Charter on Human and Peoples' Rights.[17] Article 17 of the European Convention for the Protection of Human Rights and Fundamental Freedoms contains a "group or person" provision similar to those in the Universal Declaration and the International Covenant.[18] It affirms the lack of a right of "any . . . group or person . . . to engage in any activity or perform any act aimed at the destruction of any of the rights or freedoms set forth . . . [in the European Convention] or at their limitation to a greater extent than is provided for in the Convention."[19] Thus, an implied correlative duty of any group or person exists to not destroy or limit such rights. Indeed, the authoritative European Court of Human Rights has expressly recognized that private "terrorist activities . . . of individuals or groups . . . are in clear disregard of human rights,"[20] therefore affirming that duties of private individuals and groups exist under human rights law.

The preamble to the American Declaration of the Rights and Duties of Man[21] acknowledges that "the fulfillment of duty by each individual is a prerequisite to the rights of all. Rights and duties are interrelated. . . ."[22] Articles XXIX through XXXVIII set forth several express duties of private actors. Indeed, the very title of

---

14. International Covenant on Civil and Political Rights, Dec. 19, 1966, 999 U.N.T.S. 171 (entered into force Mar. 23, 1976).

15. *Id.* pmbl. (emphasis added).

16. *Id.* art. 5, ¶1.

17. O.A.U. Doc. CAB/LEG/67/3 Rev. 5 (1981).

18. Convention for the Protection of Human Rights and Fundamental Freedoms, 213 U.N.T.S. 222, art. 17 (1950).

19. *Id.*

20. *Ireland v. United Kingdom*, 25 Eur. Ct. H.R. (ser. A) at 149 (1977).

21. O.A.S. Res. XX (1948), O.A.S. Off. Rec. OEA/Ser. L/V/I.4 Rev. (1965). The United States, and all states in the Americas, are bound by the American Declaration of the Rights and Duties of Man, which is now a legally authoritative indicia of human rights protected through Article 3(k) of the O.A.S. Charter, Apr. 30, 1948, 119 U.N.T.S. 3, 2 U.S.T. 2394, T.I.A.S. No. 2631, *amended by* the Protocol of Buenos Aires, Feb. 27, 1967, 21 U.S.T. 607, T.I.A.S. No. 6847.

22. O.A.S. Res. XX (1948), pmbl., O.A.S. Off. Rec. OEA/Ser. L./I.4 Rev. (1965).

the American Declaration is an express affirmation of private human rights duties. The American Convention on Human Rights[23] also contains express recognition that "[e]very person has responsibilities to . . . his community, and mankind,"[24] and Article 29(a) commands that the treaty not be interpreted to allow "any . . . group, or person to suppress the enjoyment or exercise of the rights and freedoms recognized . . . or to restrict them to a greater extent than is provided for" in the Convention.[25] Thus, an implied duty of groups and persons exists to not suppress or restrict human rights. The American Convention also contains express references to responsibilities of private companies.[26]

The authoritative Human Rights Committee created under the International Covenant on Civil and Political Rights has also recognized that states should report "the provisions of their criminal law which penalize torture and cruel, inhuman and degrading treatment or punishment, . . . *whether committed* by public officials or other persons acting on behalf of the State, or *by private persons.* Those who violate article 7, whether by encouraging, ordering, tolerating or perpetuating prohibited acts, must be held responsible."[27] The Human Rights Committee added that states have a duty to afford protection against such acts "*whether inflicted by people acting* in their official capacity, outside their official capacity or *in a private capacity*"[28] and "States must not deprive individuals of the right to an effective remedy."[29]

NOTES AND QUESTIONS

1. Professor Charney raises the important question of whether international companies are subject to international law norms. What are his answers? Does he believe that they should be?

2. Professor Paust argues that international companies are increasingly subject to human rights norms in a variety of contexts and forums.

3. There is probably no reason why MNEs could not be considered subjects of international law, but at the present time individuals, including MNEs, are directly affected only exceptionally by international law norms. This is because states are still the primary international law subjects, and in most cases, international obligations are only derivative for individuals and companies. One important area in

---

23. American Convention on Human Rights, opened for signature Nov. 22, 1969, 144 U.N.T.S. 123 (1970) [hereinafter American Convention]. Although the United States signed but has not ratified the American Convention on Human Rights, the United States is obligated to take no action inconsistent with the major purposes of the Convention. *See* Vienna Convention on the Law of Treaties, May 23, 1969, art. 18(a), 1155 U.N.T.S. 331.

24. American Convention, *supra*, art. 32(1).

25. *Id.* art. 29(a).

26. *Id.* arts. 6(3)(a) ("shall not be placed at the disposal of any private party, company, or juridical person") and 14(3) ("company"). See also id. art. 29(a) ("group, or person") and art. 29(d) (incorporating the American Declaration—with its express recognition of private duties—by reference, as does the preamble to the Convention).

27. General Comment No. 20 [concerning violations of Article 7 of the Covenant on Civil and Political Rights] (1992), ¶13, *in* International Human Rights Instruments at 29-32, U.N. Doc. HRI/GEN/1 (1992) (emphasis added).

28. *Id.* ¶2 (emphasis added).

29. *Id.* ¶15 (emphasis added).

which derivative liability can attach to MNEs or other individuals is when MNEs or other individuals act under the "color" of state law. In such cases, individuals may then be subject to public international law norms that by their terms apply only to states and not individuals.

In certain areas, however, individuals, including business entities, are full international participants:

- Individuals can be subject to international criminal liability for international crimes such as genocide and crimes against humanity.
- Certain customary law and treaty-based human rights norms give rise to obligations enforceable against individuals.
- Certain treaty regimes, notably the Convention on Civil Liability for Oil Pollution Damage (1969 and Protocols 1992 and 2000), the Convention on Civil Liability for Damage Resulting from Activities Dangerous to the Environment (1993), and the Convention on Nuclear Safety (1994), provide for direct international liability of responsible individuals.
- Individuals are granted rights against states under certain international investment treaties (see Chapter 6).

4. The question of the social responsibility of international business is addressed comprehensively in a number of international forums. The United Nations has a draft Code of Conduct of Transnational Corporations, but it has not been formally adopted. There is a difference of opinion on whether such an international business code should have universally applicable principles or standards tailored to regional areas or both. A number of voluntary codes and standards of conduct have been promulgated by various organizations. We consider the codes in the following section.

PROBLEM 9-3

Based on the readings so far, consider the following:

Zenos Industries, an Ohio company in the oil and gas business, has been offered a series of lucrative foreign investment projects with governments of countries in Southeast Asia. These governments are known as being repressive and are on watch lists of various nongovernmental organizations concerned with human rights abuses and environmental degradation and are subject to frequent criticism by international law experts that they do not comply with public international legal norms that apply to nation-states. Zenos' general counsel has the following concern: "We are aware that our partners are being criticized for not complying with public law norms that apply to nation-states in the areas of human rights and the environment, but we are a private company and, of course, our activities and actions do not involve state action. However, do we, as a private company, incur liability under norms of public international law applicable to nation-states only just by doing business with a repressive government? Does the nature of a foreign government become part of the business case in deciding whether to make a foreign investment in the country?"

II. Codes and Standards of Conduct

There have been several efforts to develop generally applicable policies and standards to govern the activities of multinational enterprises. Perhaps the most prominent example of a voluntary code is the Organization for Economic Cooperation and Development Guidelines for Multinational Enterprises set forth below. The OECD guidelines advise "due consideration" of the protection of the environment and many other social obligations by multinational enterprises. The following two problems explore some issues associated with the OECD guidelines.

PROBLEM 9-4

The aggressive CEO of an MNE has just learned about the OECD Guidelines for Multinational Enterprises set forth below. The CEO is puzzled, though, because the guidelines are by their terms voluntary, and he has the following questions for your law firm: "I can understand why MNEs need to follow laws and other binding legal norms that create social obligations when they do business overseas. But why would I want to voluntarily adhere to a set of guidelines that seem to create an extensive list of social obligations that might impact on my bottom line? Can you make a business case (i.e., why it might actually help my bottom line) for why MNEs will want to adopt the OECD guidelines or any other of the voluntary codes that are being considered?"

PROBLEM 9-5

Hyde Industries is considering a very large foreign direct investment in an impoverished Southeast Asian nation. During a meeting between Hyde executives and officials of the host country, the Minister of Foreign Trade says, "Look, we know that you are considering a number of countries for your investment but we are on the brink of social disaster and very badly in need of foreign capital. So I talked it over with the President and the other ministers and even though the laws do not provide for such exemptions, we would like to offer you several attractive incentives: (1) A ten-year exemption from all pollution and environmental standards. We need industrialization very badly and we know that you can help us industrialize faster if we do not insist on strict environmental controls. We will also offer you (2) a five-year exemption from all local labor laws regarding your employees and in addition we will offer you five years of 'free labor' from a group of young workers whom we will provide to you at our own expense. We'll take care of their health needs as well so you won't need to worry about that expense. And we will offer you (3) a five-year holiday from all local taxes."

When the Hyde officials return to the United States, the CEO calls you, the general counsel, and asks, "Should we accept these conditions? We didn't ask for them but they look pretty good to me." Assume that Hyde Industries is part of an industry group that has declared its intention to adhere to the OECD guidelines set forth below. Do these conditions violate any of these guidelines?

Organization for Economic Cooperation and Development: The OECD Guidelines for Multinational Enterprises
40 I.L.M. 237 (2000)

I. CONCEPTS AND PRINCIPLES

The Guidelines are recommendations jointly addressed by governments to multinational enterprises. They provide principles and standards of good practice consistent with applicable laws. Observance of the Guidelines by enterprises is voluntary and not legally enforceable.

II. GENERAL POLICIES

Enterprises should take fully into account established policies in the countries in which they operate, and consider the views of other stakeholders. In this regard, enterprises should:

1. Contribute to economic, social and environmental progress with a view to achieving sustainable development.
2. Respect the human rights of those affected by their activities consistent with the host government's international obligations and commitments.
3. Encourage local capacity building through close co-operation with the local community, including business interests, as well as developing the enterprise's activities in domestic and foreign markets, consistent with the need for sound commercial practice.
4. Encourage human capital formation, in particular by creating employment opportunities and facilitating training opportunities for employees.
5. Refrain from seeking or accepting exemptions not contemplated in the statutory or regulatory framework related to environmental, health, safety, labour, taxation, financial incentives, or other issues.
6. Support and uphold good corporate governance principles and develop and apply good corporate governance practices.
7. Develop and apply effective self-regulatory practices and management systems that foster a relationship of confidence and mutual trust between enterprises and the societies in which they operate.
8. Promote employee awareness of, and compliance with, company policies through appropriate dissemination of these policies, including through training programs.
9. Refrain from discriminatory or disciplinary action against employees who make bona fide reports to management or, as appropriate, to the competent public authorities, on practices that contravene the law, the Guidelines or the enterprise's policies.
10. Encourage, where practicable, business partners, including suppliers and sub-contractors, to apply principles of corporate conduct compatible with the Guidelines.
11. Abstain from any improper involvement in local political activities.

III. DISCLOSURE

Enterprises should ensure that timely, regular, reliable and relevant information is disclosed regarding their activities, structure, financial situation and performance.

IV. EMPLOYMENT AND INDUSTRIAL RELATIONS

Enterprises should, within the framework of applicable law, regulations and prevailing labour relations and employment practices:

1. a) Respect the right of their employees to be represented by trade unions and other bona fide representatives of employees, and engage in constructive negotiations, either individually or through employers' associations, with such representatives with a view to reaching agreements or employment conditions;
   b) Contribute to the effective abolition of child labour;
   c) Contribute to the elimination of all forms of forced or compulsory labour;
   d) Not discriminate against their employees with respect to employment or occupation on such grounds as race, colour, sex, religion, political opinion, national extraction or social origin, unless selectivity concerning employee characteristics furthers established governmental policies which specifically promote greater equality of employment opportunity or relates to the inherent requirements of a job period.

2. a) Provide facilities to employee representatives as may be necessary to assist in the development of effective collective agreements;
   b) Provide information to employee representatives which is needed for meaningful negotiations on conditions of employment;
   c) Promote consultation and co-operation between employers and employees and their representatives on matters of mutual concern.

3. Provide information to employees and their representatives which enables them to obtain a true and fair view of the performance of the entity or, where appropriate, the enterprise as a whole.

4. a) Observe standards of employment and industrial relations not less favorable than those observed by comparable employers in the host country;
   b) Take adequate steps to ensure occupational health and safety in their operations.

5. In their operations, to the greatest extent practicable, employ local personnel and provide training with a view to improving skill levels, in co-operation with employee representatives and, where appropriate, relevant governmental authorities.

6. In considering changes in their operations which would have major effects upon the livelihood of their employees, in particular in the case of the closure of an entity involving collective lay-offs or dismissals, provide

reasonable notice of such changes to representatives of their employees, and, where appropriate, to the relevant governmental authorities, and co-operate with the employee representatives and appropriate governmental authorities so as to mitigate to the maximum extent practicable adverse effects.

7. In the context of bona fide negotiations with representatives of employees on conditions of employment, or while employees are exercising a right to organize, not threaten to transfer the whole or part of an operating unit from the country concerned nor transfer employees from the enterprises' component entities in other countries in order to influence unfairly those negotiations or to hinder the exercise of a right to organize.

8. Enable authorized representatives of their employees to negotiate on collective bargaining or labour management relations issues and allow the parties to consult on matters of mutual concern with representatives of management. . . .

V. Environment

Enterprises should, within the framework of laws, regulations and administrative practices in the countries in which they operate, and in consideration of relevant international agreements, principles, objectives, and standards, take due account of the need to protect the environment, public health and safety, and generally to conduct their activities in a manner contributing to the wider goal of sustainable development. In particular, enterprises should:

1. Establish and maintain a system of environmental management appropriate to the enterprise, including:
    *   Collection and evaluation of adequate and timely information regarding the environmental, health, and safety impacts of their activities;
    *   Establishment of measurable objectives and, where appropriate, targets for improved environmental performance, including periodically reviewing the continuing relevance of these objectives; and
    *   Regular monitoring and verification of progress toward environmental, health, and safety objectives or targets.

2. Taking into account concerns about cost, business confidentiality, and the protection of intellectual property rights:
    *   Provide the public and employees with adequate and timely information on the potential environment, health and safety impacts of the activities of the enterprise, which could include reporting on progress in improving environmental performance; and
    *   Engage in adequate and timely communication and consultation with the communities directly affected by the environmental, health and safety policies of the enterprise and by their implementation.

3. Assess, and address in decision-making, the foreseeable environmental, health, and safety-related impacts associated with the processes, goods and services of the enterprise over their full life cycle.

4. Consistent with the scientific and technical understanding of the risks, where there are threats of serious damage to the environment, taking

also into account human health and safety, not use the lack of full scientific certainty as a reason for postponing cost-effective measures to prevent or minimize such damage.

5. Maintain contingency plans for preventing, mitigating, and controlling serious environmental and health damage from their operations, including accidents and emergencies; and mechanisms for immediate reporting to the competent authorities.

6. Continually seek to improve corporate environmental performance, by encouraging, where appropriate, such activities as:

   • Adoption of technologies and operating procedures in all parts of the enterprise that reflect standards concerning environmental performance in the best performing part of the enterprise;

   • Development and provision of products or services that have no undue environmental impacts; are safe in their intended use; are efficient in their consumption of energy and natural resources; can be reused, recycled, or disposed of safely;

   • Promoting higher levels of awareness among customers of the environmental implications of using the products and services of the enterprise; and

   • Research on ways of improving the environmental performance of the enterprise over the longer term.

7. Provide adequate education and training to employees in environmental health and safety matters, including the handling of hazardous materials and the prevention of environmental accidents.

8. Contribute to the development of environmentally meaningful and economically efficient public policy, for example, by means of partnerships or initiatives that will enhance environmental awareness and protection.

VI. Combating Bribery

Enterprises should not, directly or indirectly, offer, promise, give, or demand a bribe or other undue advantage to obtain or retain business or other improper advantage. Nor should enterprises be solicited or expected to render a bribe or other undue advantage.

VII. Consumer Interests

When dealing with consumers, enterprises should act in accordance with fair business, marketing and advertising practices and should take all reasonable steps to ensure the safety and quality of the goods or services they provide.

VIII. Science and Technology

Enterprises should:

1. Endeavor to ensure that their activities are compatible with the science and technology (S&T) policies and plans of the countries in which they

operate and as appropriate contribute to the development of local and national innovative capacity.

2.   Adopt, where practicable in the course of their business activities, practices that permit the transfer and rapid diffusion of technologies and know-how, with due regard to the protection of intellectual property rights.

3.   When appropriate, perform science and technology development work in host countries to address local market needs, as well as employ host country personnel in an S&T capacity and encourage their training, taking into account commercial needs.

4.   When granting licenses for the use of intellectual property rights or when otherwise transferring technology, do so on reasonable terms and conditions and in a manner that contributes to the long term development prospects of the host country.

5.   Where relevant to commercial objectives, develop ties with local universities, public research institutions, and participate in co-operative research projects with local industry or industry associations.

IX. Competition

Enterprises should, within the framework of applicable laws and regulations, conduct their activities in a competitive manner. In particular, enterprises should:

1.   Refrain from entering into or carrying out anti-competitive agreements among competitors:
     a.   To fix prices;
     b.   To make rigged bids (collusive tenders);
     c.   To establish output restrictions or quotas; or
     d.   To share or divide markets by allocating customers, suppliers, territories or lines of commerce.

2.   Conduct all of their activities in a manner consistent with all applicable competition laws, taking into account the applicability of the competition laws of jurisdictions whose economies would be likely to be harmed by anti-competitive activity on their part.

3.   Co-operate with the competition authorities of such jurisdictions by, among other things and subject to applicable law and appropriate safeguards, providing as prompt and complete responses as practicable to requests for information.

4.   Promote employee awareness of the importance of compliance with all applicable competition laws and policies.

X. Taxation

It is important that enterprises contribute to the public finances of host countries by making timely payment of their tax liabilities.

Agenda 21, United Nations Conference on Environment and Development
June 1991, A CONF. ISI/4 (Part III)

CHAPTER 30
STRENGTHENING THE ROLE OF BUSINESS AND INDUSTRY

INTRODUCTION . . .

30.1. Business and industry, including transnational corporations, play a crucial role in the social and economic development of a country. Business and industry, including transnational corporations, and their representative organizations should be full participants in the implementation and evaluation of activities related to Agenda 21. . . .

30.3. Business and industry, including transnational corporations, should recognize environmental management as among the highest corporate priorities and as a key determinant to sustainable development. Some enlightened leaders of enterprises are already implementing "responsible care" and product stewardship policies and programs, fostering openness and dialogue with employees and the public and carrying out environmental audits and assessments of compliance. A positive contribution of business and industry, including transnational corporations, to sustainable development can increasingly be achieved by using economic instruments such as free market mechanisms in which the prices of goods and services should increasingly reflect the environmental costs of their input, production, use, recycling and disposal subject to country-specific conditions.

NOTE ON THE UN CODE OF CONDUCT FOR MNES

The United Nations Commission and Centre on Transnational Corporations has worked on the promulgation of a Code of Conduct for Transnational Corporations. The difficulty of coming to agreement on the norms of international law to be established under such a Code is typified by the following excerpt from the 1985 Report of the Centre on Transnational Corporations on Work on the Formulation of the United Nations Code of Conduct on Transnational Corporations at pp. 12-13:

> There are at least two different schools of thought on this matter. The first maintains that the code should allow for the applicability of customary international legal principles in relevant areas to amplify or qualify the broad standards enunciated in the code. The applicability of international law to the relations between States and transnational corporations is not limited to international obligations expressly founded on conventions, treaties or other international agreements. In addition, customary international law is seen as prescribing principles and rules with respect to such matters as jurisdiction over transnational corporations, permanent sovereignty of States over their natural wealth and resources, renegotiation of State contracts, nationalization and compensation, non-discriminatory treatment of transnational corporations, diplomatic protection of aliens and alien property, and procedures for the settlement of disputes between Governments and transnational

corporations. It follows that the provisions of the code would not derogate from the application of those customary principles of international law, subject of course to the express undertakings of the States concerned under conventions, treaties and other international agreements concluded by such States.

The second school of thought questions the existence of universally recognized principles of customary international law governing the treatment of transnational corporations or foreign investors. Adherents to that school maintain that this area falls primarily within the purview of national law, subject to international legal norms and specific undertakings and obligations expressly stipulated in international instruments, such as codes of conduct and conventions, treaties and other international agreements, to which the States concerned have freely subscribed.

Anita Margrethe Halvorssen, Book Review: Changing Course: A Global Business Perspective on Development and the Environment by Stephen Schmidheiny with the Business Council for Sustainable Development
4 Colorado Journal of International Environmental Law & Policy 241, 243-248 (1993)

The BCSD [Business Council for Sustainable Development] sets the stage for the new action program by describing how a business relies on assessing its opportunities, risks, and trends. In the same way, the report assesses the global environment and patterns of development. Environmental degradation is described as a process in which "the human species is living more off the planet's capital and less off its interest." Population growth and poverty in the developing countries are emphasized as disturbing trends in development patterns, often occurring in the same regions as the deterioration of natural resources. The conclusion is that environment and development are inextricably interwoven: environmental degradation is sure to follow economic decline and vice versa, as is the case in many developing countries today.

The BCSD stresses that the key to sustainable development is a system of open, competitive markets in which prices include the cost of environmental resources. Competition, the BCSD states, is the driving force for new technology, which is needed to enable more efficient use of natural resources and pollution reduction. Giving the right market signals, steering businesses toward sustainable development, is only possible if environmental costs of producing and distributing goods are integrated into economic decision-making.

The BCSD endorses the use of the "polluter pays principle," which requires the polluter to pay for all damage caused in the production process, as the starting point for internalizing environmental costs.

Three well-known mechanisms for internalizing environmental costs are analyzed in the report: government regulations (command and control), self-regulation, and economic instruments. The BCSD states that regulations are needed to create a basic regulatory framework in all countries. However, it feels that most countries rely too heavily on the command and control mechanism. Self-regulation could prove less costly than the other mechanisms but could also lead to the creation of cartels and protectionism. The third mechanism, economic instruments, receives the most favorable reviews. The BCSD characterizes economic instruments as those that involve government intervention in the form of taxes and charges, to create incentives or disincentives, for the purpose of changing behavior. In addition to being more cost efficient than government regulations, they provide the incentive for polluters to change to cleaner technologies rather than requiring the use of a specific technology, which, the report states, is often the case of command approaches.

CHANGING COURSE argues convincingly that all three mechanisms should be used in order to achieve sustainable development. It recommends several factors that should be considered when seeking the optimal combination of mechanisms. Among them are: efficiency for society as a whole, flexibility of response, and a level playing field in the international marketplace.

The report argues that organizational commitment within all companies is necessary in order to integrate environmental aspects into all of their activities. The roles and responsibilities of the boards of directors, top management, and middle management are changing. Some companies, the BCSD notes, have established a high-level position covering all environmental activities in the firm. The report states that a commitment to a vision of sustainable development must in turn produce new strategies and action plans.

CHANGING COURSE emphasizes the need for objective evaluation of a company's performance in the area of sustainable development A novel mechanism, called "sustainable development reporting," would go beyond environmental audits to include performance in both the environment and the economy in terms of present and future quality of life. According to the BCSD, companies have not yet reached this goal.

The BCSD claims that "within the context of sustainable development, environmental concerns become not just a cost of doing business, but a potent source of competitive advantage." The report explains how increased environmental regulations, forcing polluters to pay for damage caused by pollution, will make cleaner technologies the norm. Companies, the BCSD says, are recognizing that environmental management now requires minimizing risks and impacts throughout a product's life cycle, from "cradle to grave." They are realizing that pollution is a sign of inefficiency and that waste reflects raw materials not sold in final products. Efforts to improve efficiencies, the BCSD states, have the corollary effect of reducing pollution while decreasing costs and increasing competitiveness.

PROBLEM 9-6

As part of an effort to take international environmental obligations seriously, Webb Industries, a publicly traded plastics manufacturer incorporated in Delaware with operations around the world, is considering various management changes. One plan under consideration is the appointment of a senior vice president in charge of global environmental responsibility to be located at the company's headquarters in Chicago. The new senior vice president would be in charge of setting company rules and policies and would oversee their implementation in all of Webb's subsidiaries and affiliates in the United States and abroad. Each subsidiary or affiliate would appoint a director of environmental compliance who would report directly to the vice president.

Webb's contemplated changes were prompted in part by recent problems within the company's global operations. The company has recently discovered that its wholly owned subsidiary in Myanmar (formerly Burma) has been involved in an industrial accident that has caused serious damage to the local rainforests. As Webb has a strong relationship with the military government of Myanmar, the government has told Webb that it is willing to control any news coverage of the damage if Webb is willing to repair the damage, estimated to be about $300 million. Webb's CEO wants to do "the right thing" by paying to fix the damage but also wants to prevent any reporting of the event and the adverse publicity that will result.

Webb wants your views on whether its environmental management plan is a good idea and whether it can prevent disclosure of the industrial accident. Consult the readings by Israel and Lyons below.

Brian D. Israel, Environmental and Safety Management in Large Companies: Avoiding Pitfalls
American Bar Association Trends, 4-5 (2004)

Over the last several years, a growing number of companies have recognized the need to adopt comprehensive management systems to ensure environmental and safety compliance. For example, as of the end of 2002, nearly 50,000 organizations worldwide had obtained the ISO [International Standards Organization] 14001 environmental management system (EMS) certification, with more than 2,600 certificates in the United States alone. While it is widely reported that ISO 14001 and other management systems result in improved regulatory compliance and overall performance, there are also important legal and practical pitfalls that can arise in large, complex firms. In some cases, safety or environmental management systems could actually increase environmental and safety problems. Fortunately, there are ways to design an EMS or safety management system to address those risks.

ENVIRONMENT, HEALTH AND SAFETY MANAGEMENT SYSTEMS

An environmental or safety management system is a continuing organizational structure to assist companies in setting and achieving particular goals. An effective system will include policy setting; implementation and control; auditing, inspecting and corrective actions; and management review.

Most observers agree that an effective system requires high-level corporate involvement and policy-setting. High-level corporate involvement in management systems refers not only to corporate officers and directors, but also to parent companies, affiliated companies and corporate shareholders. For example, recent empirical data confirm that parent organizations are a principal driving force behind a facility's adoption of environmental management systems.

PITFALLS OF MANAGEMENT SYSTEMS IN COMPLEX FIRMS

While high-level corporate involvement in management systems is often desirable, such involvement becomes increasingly problematic as the size and complexity of a company increases.

First, a parent company that is deeply involved in environmental or safety management at [its] subsidiary's plant may be exposed for liabilities should something go wrong. A number of recent cases have reiterated this point.

The same can be true in the environmental context. While the Supreme Court held in *United States v. Bestfoods*, 524 U.S. 51 (1998), that normal shareholder monitoring will not trigger CERCLA [Comprehensive Environmental Response, Compensation, and Liability Act of 1980, 42 U.S.C. §9601 *et seq.*] liability, one might infer that the in-depth involvement envisioned by many EMS structures could, in some circumstances, constitute "operation" of the facility. At the very least, significant parent company involvement in environmental audits, inspections and corrective action might allow a litigant to overcome summary judgment.

Second — and for many companies, more important — in-depth involvement by parent or sibling companies will not necessarily lead to better results and could lead to worse results. For instance, in order to achieve workplace safety and environmental compliance, specific individuals must clearly be accountable. If a parent or sibling corporation takes occasional responsibility for environmental or safety management, this involvement could generate ambiguity at the subsidiary as to who is ultimately responsible and accountable for ensuring performance.

Finally, plant employees are often more familiar with the specific manufacturing operations and technology — and sometimes, the applicable regulations — than the staff of the corporate shareholder. To the extent that this is true, any effort of the parent or sibling company to assume responsibility for safety or environmental performance could result in less safety and less environmental benefit, not more.

TIPS FOR STRUCTURING A SYSTEM

Notwithstanding the risks identified above, there are clear benefits to high-level corporate involvement in environmental and safety management systems. Most important, such involvement ensures that all levels of the organization understand the seriousness and depth of the company's commitment to environmental performance and workplace safety. Furthermore, in many firms, corporate staff members possess expertise and experience that will aid in the achievement of environmental and safety goals.

The challenge then becomes to design a management system in a manner that obtains the benefits of high-level involvement while not simultaneously assuming unnecessary liability or inadvertently making performance worse than better. Fortunately, there are several methods that can assist with this effort.

DISTINGUISHING POLICY FROM IMPLEMENTATION

The Supreme Court clearly stated that corporate shareholders are entitled to articulate firm-wide policies. *Bestfoods*, 524 U.S. at 72. That is, parent companies are entitled to set forth generic corporate goals and policies without creating liability for themselves. Accordingly, a parent company should be able to require subsidiaries to maintain environmental or safety management systems and may, in some cases, be able to assist drafting these systems.

However, it is critical to avoiding the legal and practical pitfalls described above that the responsibility for *implementation* of these policies rests with the subsidiary, not the shareholders. Moreover, it is important that there be no ambiguity or confusion in this regard. Subsidiaries and plant personnel must know that they possess ultimate responsibility for ensuring the achievement of environmental and safety benchmarks. This division of responsibility should be stated explicitly and often, in management system documents.

DISTINGUISHING GENERAL MONITORING FROM AUDITS AND INSPECTIONS

Of course, parent companies will want to monitor the results of the management systems and compliance efforts of their subsidiaries. That is normal shareholder behavior and an essential element of any management system. The critical distinction, however, is between monitoring benchmarks (emissions, injuries, near-misses, notices of violation, audit results, etc.) and actually conducting inspections and audits of plant operations. The case law indicates that the mere monitoring of benchmarks will not create parent company liability. *See, e.g., Hinkle v. Dealvan Industries Inc.*, 24 F. Supp. 2d 819 (W.D. Tenn. 1998) (monitoring safety statistics does not constitute assumption of duty).

On the other hand, as discussed above, if a parent of affiliate company itself conducts inspections or detailed audits, there exists the potential of creating unnecessary liability exposure. In addition, there is the pragmatic problem of removing responsibility from the day-to-day operators who know the facility best. Audits and inspections can often be conducted by the plant staff, thereby avoiding the problem. To the extent that an independent audit is deemed necessary, it can be commissioned by the subsidiary, once again avoiding the risks associated with parental involvement.

DISTINGUISHING RECOMMENDATIONS FROM REQUIREMENTS

Environmental and safety management systems are designed to address regular operating procedures as well as response protocols to upset conditions. In many large companies, a shareholder or affiliate possesses technological expertise and/or procedures useful for both. In such cases, the parent company or affiliate may not intend to "take over" responsibility for environmental operations or safety, but only intend to share their knowledge and experience in an effort to assist the related company.

It is important for the companies to consider which entity is responsible and make sure that all documentation reflects that allocation. Parent or affiliate companies wishing only to provide assistance or advice should ensure that all parties understand that their technological expertise or operations procedures are offered as advice or recommendations, not requirements.

DISTINGUISHING SPECIFIC FROM OVERALL RESPONSIBILITY

In some instances, it makes sense for the affiliated or parent company to assume responsibility for a certain environmental or safety function at the related company. For instance, the parent company may possess unique technological expertise thereby justifying detailed involvement and it is not possible to structure that involvement as advice or recommendations.

Also, a parent company may determine that the overall risk to the firm is reduced by allowing the parent or affiliated company to assume certain operational responsibilities at the subsidiary. In such circumstance, there should be clearly articulated documentation describing—and, if appropriate, limiting—the area of involvement. In this way, a company's efforts to audit and correct one aspect of their subsidiary's operations cannot later be used to infer responsibility for other areas.

In summary, comprehensive management systems may indeed improve performance for both environmental and safety benchmarks. Nonetheless, there are natural problems that arise as the size and complexity of a company increases. These problems, if not addressed, could lead to more liability for the company overall and could result in less performance. A well-designed management system can overcome many of these problems.

Francis X. Lyons, Sarbanes-Oxley and the Changing Face of Environmental Liability Disclosure Obligations
American Bar Association Trends, 10-11 (2004)

Disclosure obligations related to environmental liabilities are nothing new to public companies. Yet the Sarbanes-Oxley Act of 2002 (the Act), the recently adopted Securities and Exchange Commission (SEC) implementing regulations, and heightened public interest in corporate governance and disclosure concerns suggest that the time has never been better for public companies to assess the adequacy of their environmental disclosure procedures.

This article highlights potential changes in how public companies should view environmental disclosure obligations in light of the Act and the new SEC regulations.

NEW DISCLOSURE CERTIFICATION REQUIREMENTS

The United States has recently witnessed the financial implosion of a number of large public companies such as Enron, Global Crossing and others. A firestorm of public outrage followed, as investors saw portfolios evaporate and company employees lost their jobs. Congress felt the heat and pledged to enact new laws designed to establish tighter controls over public companies and their senior corporate executives.

To this end, Congress amended the SEC Act of 1934 by adding numerous requirements related to corporate finances, disclosures, audits, conflicts of interest, governance and ethics, and others. The Act and the new SEC implementing regulations require a company's chief executive officer and chief financial officer to certify that for each required financial SEC filing, disclosure controls and procedures are in place to ensure that material information—including environmental information—is brought to the attention of appropriate corporate officers within time to make informed disclosure decisions.

Like most laws, the Act comes equipped with built-in compliance incentive provisions, consisting of severe sanctions, to ensure that corporate officers treat these certifications with their intended importance.

The Section 906 criminal certification requires the CEO and CFO to certify that the periodic report containing the financial statements fully complies with the requirements of the SEC Act of 1934 and that it fairly presents, in all material respects, the financial condition and results of operations of the company.

The Section 302 provisions require, among other things, that the CEO and CFO certify that the report is accurate and materially complete and attest that the company has internal controls over financial reporting that are effective as of the end of the reporting period.

These certification requirements undercut the credibility of a potential "I didn't know" defense from a senior corporate officer in the event of materially deficient disclosures. In essence, the new requirements make it the senior officer's job to know.

HISTORICAL DISCLOSURE REQUIREMENTS

Specific SEC disclosure requirements related to environmental costs and liabilities are summarized below:

- SEC Regulation S-K, Item 101 — Description of Business (17 CFR 229.101). Requires registrant to disclose, among other things, material effects of complying or failing to comply with environmental requirements on capital expenditures, earnings and competitive position of the registrant or its subsidiaries. *Id.*
- SEC Regulation S-K, Item 103 — Legal Proceedings (17 CFR 229.103). Requires registrant to disclose "any material pending legal proceedings, other than ordinary routine litigation incidental to the business, to which the registrant or any of its subsidiaries is a party . . ." as well as any matter, irrespective of materiality, involving a claim that exceeds 10 percent of the registrant's assets or to which a governmental authority is a party to a proceeding that may involve a monetary sanction, unless the registrant reasonably believes that such proceeding will not result in a monetary sanction in excess of $100,000. *Id.*
- SEC Regulation S-K, Item 303 — Management's Discussion and Analysis of Financial Condition and Results of Operations (17 CFR 229.303). Requires registrant to disclose, among other things, environmental contingencies such as any known trends or demands, commitments, events or uncertainties that may reasonably have a material effect on net sales, revenue or income from continuing operations. *Id.* This disclosure requirement would include potential costs associated with environmental compliance.

While these disclosure requirements themselves are not new, the requirement under the Act and the SEC's implementing regulations that corporate officers certify that adequate controls and procedures are in place to accurately disclose material changes in a company's financial condition or results of operations represents a significant change.

These new standards were passed with the intent of holding senior company executives personally accountable for the veracity of representations made in substantive SEC filings, in the belief that this is the best way to ensure the completeness and accuracy of information.

The new requirements provide a good opportunity for companies to assess their own internal systems to ensure that timely and accurate information related to potential environmental costs and liabilities is not only available to the CEO and

CFO but is presented in a manner sufficient to allow full comprehension of the relevant importance of the information. This will ensure that the CEO and CFO can make the necessary certifications with confidence.

To Disclose or Not to Disclose

The threshold question of when potential environmental liabilities are material or otherwise subject to disclosure is critical. Unfortunately, there is no bright-line test that answers this question with certainty in every situation. Rather, responsible corporate officers and their counsel must ensure that adequate systems are in place to determine what disclosures are appropriate with each substantive SEC filing under the totality of the circumstances.

The careful and deliberate analysis of when disclosure is appropriate should not be made in a vacuum. Information related to potential environmental liabilities is readily available through a variety of sources outside the company. The U.S. Environmental Protection Agency (EPA) Web site (www.epa.gov) is one source of information regarding potential environmental liabilities of companies.

Specifically, the EPA Enforcement and Compliance History Online (ECHO) Web site (www.epa.gov/echo/about_site.html) provides compliance and enforcement information for approximately 800,000 regulated facilities nationwide. The site contains information related to inspections, violations, enforcement actions and penalties for the past two years. Similarly, EPA regional Web sites contain additional data regarding past and present enforcement actions, as do comparable sites maintained by state environmental agencies or other units of local government and by nongovernmental organizations.

Companies will put themselves at great risk if they do not have adequate internal systems in place to make an appropriate determination of potential environmental costs and liabilities and the need for disclosure of this information. The specific nature of the internal control procedures will naturally depend on the size of the company and the nature of its operations. But all appropriate internal control procedures will have some common elements if they are to satisfy the new accountability regime established by Sarbanes-Oxley. They will ensure that specific personnel are identified as having specific responsibility for identifying potential environmental costs and liabilities.

This will necessarily include reviewing pending or threatened litigation, current regulatory obligations, emerging trends and potentially new environmental regulations. They will also ensure that senior corporate managers are involved in the evaluation of all information required to assess these costs and liabilities and that these managers are competent to understand the significance of this information. These elements can only be satisfied through the cooperation and regular communication of senior business and environmental managers, outside environmental consultants and legal counsel.

NOTES AND QUESTIONS

1. *United Nations Global Compact.* In 2000, the Office of the Secretary General of the United Nations launched a new initiative to promote human rights, workers' rights, and protection of the environment by multinational corporations. The United Nations Global Compact consists of nine principles drawn from the UN

Universal Declaration of Human Rights, the International Labour Organization's Declaration of Fundamental Principles and Rights at Work, and the Rio
Declaration on the Environment and Development. Companies can join the UN
Global Compact by addressing a letter from the chief executive officer to the
Office of the UN Secretary General. The UN Global Compact is not regulatory
in scope. A participating company agrees voluntarily to implement the nine principles and to publish an annual report on its achievements.

The nine principles are as follows:

Human Rights
Principle 1: Businesses should support and respect the protection of inter-
    nationally proclaimed human rights within their sphere of influence, and
Principle 2: Make sure that they are not complicit in human rights abuses.
Labour Standards
Principle 3: Businesses should uphold the freedom of association and the
    effective recognition of the right to collective bargaining;
Principle 4: Eliminate all forms of forced and compulsory labour;
Principle 5: Eliminate child labour; and
Principle 6: Eliminate discrimination in respect of employment and occupation.
Environment
Principle 7: Businesses should support a precautionary approach to environ-
    mental challenges;
Principle 8: Undertake initiatives to promote greater environmental respon-
    sibility; and
Principle 9: Encourage the development and diffusion of environmentally-
    friendly technologies.

2. *Environmental Management Systems (EMS).* A number of systems exist to
create incentives for voluntary business implementation of environmental protection measures. One of the most prominent is that created by the Geneva-based
International Standards Organization (ISO). ISO 14000, as it is called, has two
components: (1) an environmental management system and (2) environmental
auditing. The ISO system is described in the following excerpt.

Charles M. Denton, Scope of ISO 14001
International Environmental Reporter (BNA), p. 715
(August 7, 1996)

ISO 14001 specifies five core elements necessary for a satisfactory EMS:
(1) *Environmental Policy*: ISO 14001 requires that a company's top management devise an environmental policy that includes a commitment to all applicable
environmental laws and "continual improvement." ISO 14001 defines "continual
improvement" as the process of enhancing the EMS, with the purpose of achieving improvements in overall environmental performance. The policy must be
relevant to the nature, scale, and environmental impacts of the company for
which it is drafted. Moreover, the policy must be documented, communicated
to all employees, and made available to the public. It is important to note that
the environmental policy is the only facet of the ISO 14000 standards that is
required to be made available to the public.

(2) *Planning*: After institution of an environmental policy, ISO 14001 requires that the company implement "environmental planning." The planning stage includes establishment and maintenance of the following procedures: a procedure to identify the environmental impacts of the company's processes, services, and activities; a procedure to identify all statutory and regulatory requirements applicable to the company's range of activities; documented objectives and targets, defined as the overall environmental goals that the organization itself sets to achieve; and an environmental management program for achieving these objectives and targets.

Such a management program is broadly described to include designation of responsibility for achieving these targets at each relevant level within the "company and the means and timeframe by which they are to be achieved." The environmental management program also should contain a review procedure for assessment of all environmental impacts associated with the planning, design, production, marketing, and disposal stages of the company's activities.

(3) *Implementation and Operation*: Implementation and operation (I/O) of the environmental plan is the third step for those companies seeking compliance with ISO 14001. This step mandates that a company devote adequate human, technological, and financial resources to ensure I/O of the EMS. A specific management representative(s) must be appointed who, irrespective of other duties, will be responsible for ensuring the continual I/O of the EMS. This phase also requires training of all employees whose work may impact the environment; internal and external communication procedures; and environmental documentation and document control.

I/O requires that a company identify all activities that result in significant environmental impact so that operational controls may be devised for those activities. Operational controls are established to guide performance so that environmental objectives and targets may be reached. Lastly, a company must define and maintain procedures for responding to emergency situations and for mitigating the environmental impacts associated with such accidents.

(4) *Checking and Corrective Action*: ISO 14001 requires that a firm institute "checking and corrective action" procedures. These procedures include the monitoring of the company's processes that may have a significant impact on the environment so that the company can track performance and demonstrate compliance with the organization's objectives and targets.

In the event of non-conformance with the company's targets and objectives, the company is to establish and maintain procedures for initiating corrective and preventive action. Furthermore, the company must establish a system of periodic EMS audits in order to determine if the EMS conforms to the requirements of ISO 14001 and has been properly implemented and maintained. Such audits may be conducted either internally or externally; ISO 14001 makes no mention of a requirement of external verification of the results ascertained by internal EMS audits (privilege/confidentiality may therefore be maintained). A comprehensive system of environmental records that document the I/O of the EMS and the progress made toward the company's objectives and targets must be kept.

(5) *Management Review*: Lastly, ISO 14001 requires of those firms seeking compliance the documented review of EMSs by management at periodic intervals. This review is designed to address the possible need for changes to the firm's environmental policy, targets and objectives, and procedures, particularly in

light of the EMS audit results, changing legal requirements, and the commitment to continual improvement

NOTES AND QUESTIONS

1. Would you recommend that an international business set up an environmental management system covering its foreign operations? What are the possible disadvantages?

2. Should an international business set up similar systems to monitor and comply with other social concerns?

3. Environmental reporting and "eco-audits" on a voluntary basis are quickly becoming the norm among transnational corporations. There are many national and industry-based voluntary codes of conduct. The European Union has adopted Council Regulation 1836/93, 1993 O.J. (L 168) 1, which provides for voluntary eco-audits by participating companies that are willing to report on corporate environmental performance. Are these codes of conduct useful? What are their advantages and disadvantages? Should they be compulsory?

4. Many developing countries seek to involve transnational corporations in the protection of the environment in developing nations. In 1989, a draft resolution, "Transnational Corporations and Environmental Protection in Developing Countries," was introduced by Tai Kat Meng of Malaysia on behalf of the G77 countries, a group of developing countries. Specifically, it asks the Secretary General of the United Nations to:

- Conduct a study — in consultation with experts, transnational corporations, and international organizations — analyzing the "main sectors of activity" that harm the environment and "the factors that determine the allocation of these activities between developed and developing countries";
- Elaborate a set of criteria and operational principles to strengthen participation of transnational corporations in environmental preservation and protection, "in view of the specific responsibilities of large industrial enterprises in this field";
- Gather existing and emerging data on "environmentally hazardous" technologies and "the availability of alternative technologies," and recommend ways to better transfer the alternative technologies to developing countries;
- Identify ways that developing countries might benefit from the experience of other countries "in their efforts to protect the environment in relation to the activities of industry, including transnational corporations"; and
- Examine — in consultation with governments and "other interested parties" — the feasibility of a fund, to be financed by voluntary contributions from transnational corporations, to support environmental protection efforts by developing countries, "in particular for strengthening the transnational corporations' role" in overall efforts to protect the environment.

Should transnational corporations be compelled to accommodate host country environmental concerns?

PROBLEM 9-7

Global Solutions, Inc. (GSI), a business consulting firm, is a strong proponent of responsible corporate behavior and believes that there has been too much criticism of MNEs in the media. Recently, GSI has been hired to work on media and public relations for a group of chemical companies that have been accused of taking advantage of developing countries by setting up dangerous enterprises that would not be allowed at home. A spokesperson for GSI says, "First of all, the vast majority of companies in our industry just don't behave this way. There may be one or two rogue companies, but basically this is just corporate bashing. Second, while MNEs are often criticized for shirking their environmental responsibilities, some developing countries are actually contributing to this problem." Do you agree with GSI's statements? How might developing countries contribute to irresponsible behavior by MNEs? Consult the articles by Leonard and Bent below. If you were advising developing countries on how to deal with MNEs, what would you suggest?

H. Jeffrey Leonard, Confronting Industrial Pollution in Rapidly Industrializing Countries: Myths, Pitfalls, and Opportunities
12 Ecology Law Quarterly 779, 784-786, 800-801, 811 (1985)

Although there are many clear instances of American multinational corporations and their subsidiaries causing serious pollution problems in developing countries, most of the documented cases have involved discrete and declining types of industries. The most egregious examples of pollution by multinational corporations in the developing world have involved aging industries, industries that are difficult to re-equip, low technology operations such as mineral processing, and industries in which both production and demand are declining in the advanced countries.

In contrast, most high-technology multinational corporations building large integrated production plants today routinely use pollution control measures everywhere they locate. Most of these companies possess the technology and the knowledge to alleviate serious potential pollution problems and to operate modern efficient plants. As a result, some developing countries are beginning to require that incoming industries construct pollution-minimizing facilities that will not substantially exacerbate pollution problems.

Another reason why industrializing nations have some degree of latitude to drive hard bargains on pollution control is that most pollution control standards for industries in developing nations are set on a case-by-case basis. Thus, the stringency of environmental regulations for particular facilities varies according to the preferences of local or national officials, the amount of public pressure, and some rough calculation of the assimilative capacity of the local environment. Because of the ad hoc nature of this process, and the lack of national standards uniformly applied to foreign and domestic industries, most countries require multinational corporations to abide by stricter standards than those applied to locally owned industries.

Countries soliciting multinational corporations to build and operate production facilities can set technology and process constraints to which the multinational corporations must adhere if they wish to locate in the country. The costs to corporations of meeting these constraints and specific pollution control guidelines are often partly subsidized by various government grants and tax breaks. The remaining costs can be included in the companies' overall capital expenditure budgets for their projects. Only rarely will a company's investment decision turn on these incremental costs. If the country seems hospitable, and the long-range potential appears profitable, multinational firms may be quite willing to absorb the extra-capital costs of pollution control as the price of locating in the country.

In contrast, those countries that forbid multinational corporations from owning or operating plants on their soil for ideological or economic reasons, usually experience problems related to their own lack of expertise in pollution matters. Such countries still must often purchase foreign technology for their domestic plants. Technology importing nations have less room to bargain with foreign companies about pollution control than do countries that tolerate or encourage foreign investors.

Industrializing countries seeking to attract international capital must not only assess the immediate pollution problems that incoming industries might cause, but must also try to project the long-term environmental impacts of welcoming such industries. Such projections are difficult because there is seldom adequate information for informed judgment and because some industries at first appear much more environmentally benign than they eventually prove to be. Industrializing countries accepting new industries are therefore playing a sort of Russian roulette both because of their lack of advanced research capabilities, particularly with respect to environmental carcinogens, and because of deficiencies in information transfer from the more technically advanced nations.

Industrializing countries need not accept gross environmental damage by foreign firms as the price of economic development. Most multinational companies — whether American, European, or Japanese — are willing, when required, to take precautions to protect both workers' safety and the surrounding environment. A government that clearly and forthrightly outlines its minimum pollution control standards for foreign investors is likely to encounter few multinational firms that will withdraw from negotiations on this basis alone.

Maureen A. Bent, Exporting Hazardous Industries: Should American Standards Apply?
20 N.Y.U. Journal of International Law & Politics 777, 778-781 (1987)

Multinational corporations play a decisive role in the industrialization of developing countries. They design, construct and operate industrial facilities, and serve as a major conduit of technology transfers. Generally, technology exports to developing countries occur either as a result of intra-firm transfers or participation by multinational corporations and host countries in joint ventures. Where technology transfers occur in a joint venture setting, the host country often shares in the ownership and management of the enterprise. When the technology involved is relatively new, however, MNCs are usually reluctant to relinquish full control. In such cases, MNCs typically establish wholly- or majority-owned subsidiaries.

Since they wish to accelerate industrial development and attract high technology industry, developing countries frequently fail to challenge MNCs' demands to retain control over the technology that they seek to import. In fact, developing countries accord priority and grant preferential treatment to MNCs with more sophisticated technology. MNCs often benefit from liberal investment incentives, and host countries frequently relieve them of more stringent environmental and worker safety regulation. The nature of the parent-subsidiary and joint-venture relationship, as well as the developing countries' desire to attract sophisticated technology, provide MNCs with practically unfettered ability to "export" highly technical, and often hazardous, industries to lesser developed countries.

The United States is one of the leading source countries for foreign investment in the manufacturing industry in developing countries. A significant share of its investment was earmarked for the chemical industry, which accounted for 25.2 percent of the U.S. total foreign investments in 1980. Compared with the lower regulatory standards of developing countries, tougher U.S. environmental regulations may account for the significant presence of chemical industries in those countries. Although some industries seriously consider environmental regulations when determining plant location abroad, such regulations are only one of many factors weighed by U.S. manufacturing industries when determining plant location. Perhaps the driving force behind investments in manufacturing abroad is the ability of MNCs to obtain greater profits than they may otherwise make at home. MNCs maximize profits by taking advantage of limited, and often weakly enforced, environmental regulations in developing countries, as well as minimal requirements for investment in safety equipment to control potential hazards to workers and the general public, low employee wages and benefits, and weak taxation structures.

Whatever the reasons for the significant presence of MNCs in developing countries, one fact is clear: U.S. MNCs adhere to a double standard when operating abroad. The lack of stringent environmental regulations and worker safety standards abroad and the relaxed enforcement of such laws in industries using hazardous processes provide little incentive for MNCs to protect the safety of workers, to obtain liability insurance to guard against the hazard of product defects or toxic tort exposure, or to take precautions to minimize pollution of the environment. This double standard has caused catastrophic damage to the environment and to human lives.

If U.S. MNCs insist on exporting hazardous industries, measures should be taken to prevent or at least reduce the damage from accidents such as the Bhopal disaster. The most effective and expeditious means of achieving these ends would be to impose upon U.S. MNCs operating abroad the environmental and worker protection standards to which they are subjected when operating in the U.S.

QUESTION

Why might some developing countries or some officials within developing countries be willing to waive environmental law requirements even though they realize that this is likely to result in serious and long-term harm to the environment?

III. Exporting Hazardous Wastes: Legal and Ethical Considerations

An international business concern that deals in potentially hazardous waste products must be concerned with the international regimes that regulate the transnational movement of such wastes. The business concern also needs to consider legal regimes that may impose liability as well. We include materials in this section that discuss the relevant international treaties and obligations as well as the *Bhopal* case that deals with liability issues arising from environmental disasters.

Eric Neumeyer, Greening Trade and Investment, 164-166 (2001)

THE BASEL CONVENTION

[R]estrictions on trade are at the heart of the Basel Convention on the Control of Transboundary Movements of Hazardous Wastes and Their Disposal. It aims to "ensure that the management of hazardous wastes and other wastes including their transboundary movement and disposal is consistent with the protection of human health and the environment whatever the place of disposal" (preamble). At the time of this writing, the Convention has been ratified by 136 countries, but not by the United States, which has signed but not ratified the Convention. Some 28 countries were WTO members but not parties to the Convention.

The major trade provisions of the Basel Convention are as follows. Trade in hazardous waste is subjected to a comprehensive control system which is based on the principle of prior informed consent. This means that a country can only export these materials to another country if it has gained the prior written consent from the importing country and all transit countries (Article 6). Trade in these materials with non-parties is prohibited (Article 4:5) unless agreements with these non-parties have been concluded which "do not derogate from the environmentally sound management of hazardous wastes and other wastes as required by this Convention" (Article 11:1). A party has the right to ban the entry or disposal of foreign hazardous waste in its territory (Article 4:1). Furthermore, an amendment to the Convention generally bans trade in these materials between so-called Annex VII (OECD countries) and non-Annex VII countries. However, at the time of this writing, this amendment had been ratified by only 20 countries and it is unclear whether it will reach the necessary ratifications to enter into force.

[T]he Basel Convention does not contain any substantial provisions for financial assistance to developing countries to assist them in implementing their obligations. This has been regarded as one of the major reasons for the poor implementation of hazardous waste trade-control systems in these countries and the consequent substantial illegal trading, which will become exacerbated once the amendment to the Convention banning trade between OECD and non-OECD countries comes into force.

THE ROTTERDAM CONVENTION

The Convention on the Prior Informed Consent Procedure for Certain Hazardous Chemicals and Pesticides in International Trade (Rotterdam Convention) was adopted and opened for signature in Rotterdam in September 1998. Its objective is "to promote shared responsibility and cooperative efforts among Parties in the international trade of certain hazardous chemicals in order to protect human health and the environment from potential harm and to contribute to their environmentally sound use" (Article 1). It needs to be ratified by 50 countries and is not in force yet.

Annex III of the Convention specifies the chemicals that are subject to the Prior Informed Consent (PIC) procedure (initially, Annex III encompasses 30 chemicals). This means that a country may only export one of these chemicals to another country if it has sought and received the PIC of the importing country. Furthermore, the exporting country has the duty to provide for "labeling requirements that ensure adequate availability of information with regard to risks and/or hazards to human health or the environment, taking into account relevant international standards" (Article 13:2). This applies to all chemicals listed in Annex III, all chemicals banned or severely restricted in the exporting country's territory (Article 13:2) as well as to all chemicals subject to environmental or health labeling requirements (Article 13:3). Exports of chemicals, the use of which are banned or severely restricted in the exporting country's territory, are subject to laborious information requirements for export notification as laid down in Annex V of the Convention.

Countries need not give their consent to import Annex III chemicals. According to Article 10 of the Convention, each party has the right not to consent to import or merely consent to import, subject to specified conditions, any of the chemicals contained in Annex III. However, if a country decides to ban imports or consent to import only under specified conditions, then according to Article 10:9 it has to "simultaneously prohibit or make subject to the same conditions" the import of the chemical from any other country and the domestic production of the chemical for domestic use. In other words, a country cannot ban or severely restrict imports of a chemical from one country, but not another, or to ban or severely restrict imports of a chemical, but not domestic production.

THE AGREEMENT ON PERSISTENT ORGANIC POLLUTANTS

In December 2000, in Johannesburg, 122 countries concluded negotiations on a multilateral Agreement on Persistent Organic Pollutants (POPs Agreement). It is supposed to be signed formally at a meeting in Stockholm in May 2001 and will enter into force once it has been ratified by at least 50 countries. The objective of the agreement is the eventual elimination of eight POPs: aldrin; chlordane; dieldrin; endrin; heptachlor; hexachlorobenzene; mirex; and toxaphene. The use of another four POPs becomes severely restricted: dichlorodiphenyltrichloroethane (DDT) for use against malaria; dioxins; furans; and polychlorinated biphenyls (PCBs).

POPs are considered of special danger to human health and the environment as they are persistent and can accumulate in the environment, and therefore can be passed on from one generation to the next. Article D of the agreement allows the importation of the relevant POPs only for the purpose of environmentally-sound disposal or for a specified use permitted explicitly by the agreement. Exportation is only allowed for the same purposes and only to either parties to the agreement or to non-parties that can document that they comply with the provisions of the agreement.

Organization for Economic Cooperation and Development: Council Recommendation on the Application of the Polluter-Pays Principle to Accidental Pollution
July 7, 1989
28 I.L.M. 1320 (1989)

APPENDIX
GUIDING PRINCIPLES RELATING TO ACCIDENTAL POLLUTION

THE POLLUTER-PAYS PRINCIPLE...

3. According to the Recommendation of the Council of 26th May 1972 on the Guiding Principles Concerning International Economic Aspects of Environmental Policies, the "principle to be used for allocating the costs of pollution prevention and control is the so called Polluter-Pays Principle." The implementation of this principle will "encourage rational use of scarce environmental resources." According to the Recommendation of the Council of 14th November 1974 on the Implementation of the Polluter-Pays Principle, "the Polluter-Pays Principle . . . means that the polluter should bear the expenses of carrying out the pollution prevention and control measures introduced by public authorities in Member countries, to ensure that the environment is in an acceptable state. In other words, the cost of these measures should be reflected in the cost of goods and services which cause pollution in production and/or consumption." In the same Recommendation, the Council recommended that "as a general rule, Member countries should not assist the polluters in bearing the costs of pollution control whether by means of subsidies, tax advantages or other measures."

APPLICATION OF THE POLLUTER-PAYS PRINCIPLE

4. In matters of accidental pollution risks, the Polluter-Pays Principle implies that the operator of a hazardous installation should bear the cost of reasonable measures to prevent and control accidental pollution from that installation which are introduced by public authorities in Member countries in conformity with domestic law prior to the occurrence of an accident in order to protect human health or the environment.

5. Domestic law which provides that the cost of reasonable measures to control accidental pollution after an accident should be collected as expeditiously as possible from the legal or natural person who is at the origin of the accident, is consistent with the Polluter-Pays Principle.

6. In most instances and notwithstanding issues concerning the origin of the accident, the cost of such reasonable measures taken by the authorities is initially borne by the operator for administrative convenience or for other reasons. When a third party is liable for the accident, that party reimburses to the operator the cost of reasonable measures to control accidental pollution taken after an accident.

7. If the accidental pollution is caused solely by an event for which the operator clearly cannot be considered liable under national law, such as a serious natural disaster that the operator cannot reasonably have foreseen, it is consistent with the

Polluter-Pays Principle that public authorities do not charge the cost of control measures to the operator. . . .

9. Public authorities of Member countries that "have responsibilities in the implementation of policies for prevention of, and response to, accidents involving hazardous substances" may take specific measures to prevent accidents occurring at hazardous installations and to control accidental pollution. Although the cost entailed is as a general rule met by the general budget, public authorities may with a view to achieving a more economically efficient resource allocation, introduce specific fees or taxes payable by certain installations on account of their hazardous nature (e.g., licensing fees), the proceeds of which are to be allocated to accidental pollution prevention and control.

10. One specific application of the Polluter-Pays Principle consists in adjusting these fees or taxes, in conformity with domestic law, to cover more fully the cost of certain exceptional measures to prevent and control accidental pollution in specific hazardous installations which are taken by public authorities to protect human health and the environment (e.g., special licensing procedures, execution of detailed inspections, drawing up of installation-specific emergency plans or building-up special means of response for the public authorities to be used in connection with a hazardous installation), provided such measures are reasonable and directly connected with accident prevention or with the control of accidental pollution released by the hazardous installation. Lack of laws or regulations on relevant fees or taxes should not, however, prevent public authorities from meeting their responsibilities in connection with accidents involving hazardous substances.

11. A further specific application of the Polluter-Pays Principle consists in charging, in conformity with domestic law, the cost of reasonable pollution control measures decided by the authorities following an accident to the operator of the hazardous installation from which pollution is released. Such measures taken without undue delay by the operator or, in case of need, by the authorities would aim at promptly avoiding the spreading of environmental damage and would concern limiting the release of hazardous substances (e.g., by ceasing emissions at the plant, by erecting floating barriers on a river), the pollution as such (e.g., by cleaning or decontamination), or its ecological effects (e.g., by rehabilitating the polluted environment).

Michael P. Walls, Disclosure Responsibilities
for Exporters
4 Natural Resources & Environment 10 (1990)

A United States–based chemical company receives an order for a hazardous chemical substance or pesticide to be delivered outside the United States. At first glance, it is the start of a typical export transaction. The parties will usually negotiate some type of contract, covering such details as the terms and currency of payment, delivery, risk of loss, and quality control. The exporter must comply with the record keeping and licensing requirements of the Export Administration Act or related statutes, obtain any necessary import license, confirm a letter of credit, and prepare the shipping documents before the chemical can be shipped to its foreign destination. Exports require extensive documentation to support each transaction.

Since the early 1980s, U.S. exporters have been subject to an additional requirement for shipments of hazardous chemicals, pesticides, and hazardous wastes. The Toxic Substances Control Act (TSCA) and the Federal Insecticide, Fungicide, and Rodenticide Act (FIFRA) require that the government of the importing consignee be notified of the impending shipment. The Resource Conservation and Recovery Act (RCRA), in contrast, requires the express consent of importing countries to shipments of hazardous wastes. At least five other U.S. laws require some form of notice to importing countries when hazardous materials are to be exported. *See, e.g.,* Federal Hazardous Substances Act, 15 U.S.C. §1273(d) (1982). Failure to comply with the U.S. notification and/or consent requirements may subject an exporter to penalties, including seizure of the shipment. The distinction between notifications to governments and requiring their consent has no practical effect on an importing government's ability to control imports.

The export notification requirements in U.S. law are generally intended to provide foreign governments with information on the regulatory controls imposed on a particular chemical in the United States. The programs are not intended to function as an import monitoring system.

International criticism has been leveled at developed countries for the lack of effective controls on exports of hazardous chemicals, pesticides, and hazardous wastes. Indeed, the perception has been that the developed world uses developing countries as a dumping ground for dangerous products and wastes. Proposals for more effective control of such exports have included complete export bans, enforced by exporting countries; more complete information exchange programs; and prior informed consent (PIC), by which importing governments would expressly consent to receipt of regulated chemical products. The unmistakable domestic and international trend is toward required disclosures of ever more health and environmental information on export shipments of regulated products.

PROBLEM 9-8

Waste Solutions, Inc. (WSI), is a Texas company in the waste management field. For several years, it has been shipping garbage to landfills in South Carolina, but it has encountered increasing resistance from the local population. In looking for an alternative site, WSI has found that there is also strong resistance from surrounding states as well. Because of the mounting resistance, WSI has begun negotiations with Z, a small impoverished developing country. WSI has now entered into a long-term contract to ship garbage to Z in exchange for generous payments to the government of Z. The Z government then simply dumps the untreated garbage in crudely made open-air dump sites near some large natural lakes. WSI's top management is very pleased with this solution as it relieves them of the headache of finding a suitable dump site in the United States, and Z government officials are happy because they are receiving payments from WSI. (Whether WSI needs to be concerned about where the payments are going is another issue; see Chapter 6, §IV.) The CEO at WSI refers to this arrangement as "the classic win-win situation."

(1) Do any international laws prohibit the "sale" of garbage by WSI to Z? What norms, if any, apply?

(2) In response to a request from the Z government, WSI sets up a wholly foreign-owned subsidiary in Z to help the government treat the garbage before disposal. Later, it is discovered that the treatment of the garbage by the subsidiary leaves some toxic materials in the waste that seep into the nearby lakes and so contaminate the waters that they can no longer be used for drinking unless the water undergoes expensive waste treatment. WSI's sharp in-house counsel has been scrupulously following corporate formalities in dealing with the subsidiary and has the paperwork and electronic records to prove it and all of the technicians in the subsidiary were expertly trained at WSI's corporate headquarters. Does WSI have any liability? In addition to the readings so far, see the article below, the *Union Carbide* case, and the Divan and Rosencranz article discussing the Bhopal litigation.

Stephen C. McCaffrey, Accidents Do Happen: Hazardous Technology and International Tort Litigation
1 The Transnational Lawyer 41 (1988)

[In this article, Professor McCaffrey, taking the facts of the disaster at Bhopal, India, where 2,000 people were killed and 200,000 injured in an industrial disaster in 1984, examines the question of jurisdiction over the subsidiary and parent corporation in that case.]

Assertion of judicial jurisdiction over the subsidiary by local (in the Bhopal case, Indian) courts would present no problem in countries following either the civil or the common law system. However, the target defendant will probably be the parent company or foreign exporter of the hazardous technology, not only because the parent may have controlled the subsidiary, and may be responsible for, e.g., the defective design, process, or method of operation that led to the accident, but also — and perhaps chiefly — because the parent will have the deeper pocket. Further, as in the Bhopal litigation, plaintiffs may wish to sue the parent in order to obtain the most attractive forum. Finally, it may be that no local subsidiary was involved, in which case the foreign manufacturer or exporter may be the only available defendant.

If suit is brought against a foreign entity having no direct presence in the forum state, the question of jurisdiction over that entity is almost certain to be challenged, costing victims time and money. Even in the United States, which has shown perhaps the greatest readiness to "pierce the corporate veil," mere ownership of a majority or even all of the subsidiary's stock would probably not be enough by itself to allow the state in which the subsidiary is incorporated to assert jurisdiction over the parent. On the other hand, earlier reluctance of U.S. courts to reach a foreign parent through a local subsidiary has given way to a recognition that assertion of jurisdiction over the foreign parent is permissible where the parent so controls the subsidiary as to disregard its separate corporate existence. Obviously, however, this theory would not be available where it is claimed that plaintiff's injuries resulted from the foreign corporation's *failure* to exercise adequate supervision and control over a local subsidiary. Still, plaintiff in such a case could seek to hold the foreign corporation directly responsible if its failure to supervise were negligent (i.e., where it had breached a duty of supervision).

In re Union Carbide Corp. Gas Plant Disaster at Bhopal, India in December 1984
United States Court of Appeals, Second Circuit, 1987
809 F.2d 195

MANSFIELD, Circuit Judge.

This appeal raises the question of whether thousands of claims by citizens of India and the Government of India arising out of the most devastating industrial disaster in history — the deaths of over 2,000 persons and injuries of over 200,000 caused by lethal gas known as methyl isocyanate which was released from a chemical plant operated by Union Carbide India Limited (UCIL) in Bhopal, India — should be tried in the United States or in India. The Southern District of New York, John F. Keenan, Judge, granted the motion of Union Carbide Corporation (UCC), a defendant in some 145 actions commenced in federal courts in the United States, to dismiss these actions on grounds of *forum non conveniens* so that the claims may be tried in India, subject to certain conditions. The individual plaintiffs appeal from the order and the court's denial of their motion for a fairness hearing on a proposed settlement. UCC and the Union of India (UOI), a plaintiff, cross-appeal. We eliminate two of the conditions imposed by the district court and in all other respects affirm that court's orders.

The accident occurred on the night of December 2-3, 1984, when winds blew the deadly gas from the plant operated by UCIL into densely occupied parts of the city of Bhopal. UCIL is incorporated under the laws of India. Fifty and nine-tenths percent of its stock is owned by UCC, 22% is owned or controlled by the government of India, and the balance is held by approximately 23,500 Indian citizens. The stock is publicly traded on the Bombay Stock Exchange. The company is engaged in the manufacture of a variety of products, including chemicals, plastics, fertilizers and insecticides, at 14 plants in India and employs over 9,000 Indian citizens. It is managed and operated entirely by Indians in India.

Four days after the Bhopal accident, on December 7, 1984, the first of some 145 purported class actions in federal district courts in the United States was commenced on behalf of victims of the disaster. On January 2, 1985, the Judicial Panel on Multidistrict Litigation assigned the actions to the Southern District of New York where they became the subject of a consolidated complaint filed on June 28, 1985.

In the meantime, on March 29, 1985, India enacted the Bhopal Gas Leak Disaster (Processing of Claims) Act, granting to its government, the UOI, the exclusive right to represent the victims in India or elsewhere. Thereupon the UOI, purporting to act in the capacity of *parens patriae*, and with retainers executed by many of the victims, on April 8, 1985, filed a complaint in the Southern District of New York on behalf of all victims of the Bhopal disaster, similar to the purported class action complaints already filed by individuals in the United States. The UOI's decision to bring suit in the United States was attributed to the fact that, although numerous lawsuits (by now, some 6,500) had been instituted by victims in India against UCIL, the Indian courts did not have jurisdiction over UCC, the parent company, which is a defendant in the United States actions. The actions in India asserted claims not only against UCIL but also against the UOI, the State of Madhya Pradesh, and the Municipality of Bhopal, and were consolidated in the District Court of Bhopal.

By order dated April 25, 1985, Judge Keenan appointed a three-person Executive Committee to represent all plaintiffs in the pre-trial proceedings. It consisted of two lawyers representing the individual plaintiffs and one representing the UOI. On July 31, 1985, UCC moved to dismiss the complaints on grounds of *forum non conveniens*, the plaintiffs' lack of standing to bring the actions in the United States, and their purported attorneys' lack of authority to represent them. After several months of discovery related to *forum non conveniens*, the individual plaintiffs and the UOI opposed UCC's motion. After hearing argument on January 3, 1986, the district court, on May 12, 1986, 634 F. Supp. 842, in a thoroughly reasoned 63-page opinion granted the motion, dismissing the lawsuits before it on condition that UCC:

(1) consent to the jurisdiction of the courts of India and continue to waive defenses based on the statute of limitations,

(2) agree to satisfy any judgment rendered by an Indian court against it and upheld on appeal, provided the judgment and affirmance "comport with the minimal requirements of due process," and

(3) be subject to discovery under the Federal Rules of Civil Procedure of the United States.

On June 12, 1986, UCC accepted these conditions subject to its right to appeal them; and on June 24, 1986, the district court entered its order of dismissal. In September 1986 the UOI, acting pursuant to its authority under the Bhopal Act, brought suit on behalf of all claimants against UCC and UCIL in the District Court of Bhopal, where many individual suits by victims of the disaster were then pending.

In its opinion dismissing the actions the district court analyzed the *forum non conveniens* issues, applying the standards and weighing the factors suggested by the Supreme Court in *Piper Aircraft Co. v. Reyno*, 454 U.S. 235, 102 S. Ct. 252, 70 L. Ed. 2d 419 (1981). At the outset Judge Keenan concluded, in accordance with the Court's expressed views in *Piper* that, since the plaintiffs were not residents of the United States but of a foreign country, their choice of the United States as a forum would not be given the deference to which it would be entitled if this country were their home. Following *Piper*, the district court declined to compare the advantages and disadvantages to the respective parties of American versus Indian Laws or to determine the impact upon plaintiffs' claims of the laws of India, where UCC had acknowledged that it would make itself amenable to process, except to ascertain whether India provided an adequate alternative forum, as distinguished from no remedy at all. Judge Keenan reviewed thoroughly the affidavits of experts on India's law and legal system, which described in detail its procedural and substantive aspects, and concluded that, despite some of the Indian system's disadvantages, it afforded an adequate alternative forum for the enforcement of plaintiffs' claims.

As the district court found, the record shows that the private interests of the respective parties weigh heavily in favor of dismissal on grounds of *forum non conveniens*. The many witnesses and sources of proof are almost entirely located in India, where the accident occurred, and could not be compelled to appear for trial in the United States. The Bhopal plant at the time of the accident was operated by some 193 Indian nationals, including the managers of seven operating units employed by the Agricultural Products Division of UCIL, who reported to Indian Works Managers in Bhopal. The plant was maintained by seven functional departments employing over 200 more Indian nationals.

In short, the plant has been constructed and managed by Indians in India. No Americans were employed at the plant at the time of the accident. In the five years from 1980 to 1984, although more than 1,000 Indians were employed at the plant, only one American was employed there and he left in 1982. No Americans visited the plant for more than one year prior to the accident, and during the 5-year period before the accident the communications between the plant and the United States were almost non-existent.

We are concerned, however, that as it is written the district court's requirement that UCC consent to the enforcement of a final Indian judgment, which was imposed on the erroneous assumption that such a judgment might not otherwise be enforceable in the United States, may create misunderstandings and problems of construction. Although the order's provision that the judgment "comport with the *minimal* requirements of due process" (emphasis supplied) probably is intended to refer to "due process" as used in the New York Foreign Country Money Judgments Law and others like it, there is the risk that it may also be interpreted as providing for a lesser standard than we would otherwise require. Since the court's condition with respect to enforceability of any final Indian judgment is predicated on an erroneous legal assumption and its "due process" language is ambiguous, and since the district court's purpose is fully served by New York's statute providing for recognition of foreign-country money judgments, it was error to impose this condition upon the parties.

We also believe that the district court erred in requiring UCC to consent (which UCC did under protest and subject to its right of appeal) to broad discovery of it by the plaintiffs under the Federal Rules of Civil Procedure when UCC is confined to the more limited discovery authorized under Indian law.

Basic justice dictates that both sides be treated equally, with each having equal access to the evidence in the possession or under the control of the other. Application of this fundamental principle in the present case is especially appropriate since the UOI, as the sovereign government of India, is expected to be a party to the Indian litigation, possibly on both sides.

For these reasons we direct that the condition with respect to the discovery of UCC under the Federal Rules of Civil Procedure be deleted without prejudice to the right of the parties to have reciprocal discovery of each other on equal terms under the Federal Rules, subject to such approval as may be required of the Indian court in which the case will be pending.

As so modified the district court's order is affirmed.

Shyam Divan & Armin Rosencranz, The Bhopal Settlement

1989 Environmental Policy & Law 166

A. INTRODUCTION

On February 14, 1989, the Indian Supreme Court cut the Gordian knot that the Bhopal case had come to resemble. That afternoon, the Court induced the Indian Government and the Union Carbide Corporation (Carbide) to accept its suggestion for an overall settlement of the claims arising from the Bhopal disaster. More than four years earlier, during the early hours of December 3, 1984, forty tons of highly toxic methylisocyanate (MIC) escaped into the atmosphere from

Carbide's pesticide plant in Bhopal and killed over 2,500 people. Another 200,000 people, caught in the path of the dispersing gas, suffered injuries. While hardly a generous amount in terms of Carbide's total worth, the Court-induced settlement does appear to achieve the mixed private and public goals of compensation, corrective justice and deterrence.

B. Summary of the Settlement

The settlement is elaborated in four documents: (1) the Supreme Court's Principal Order dated February 14, 1989; (2) a supplemental order of the Court issued on February 15; and (3) a consequential memorandum of the terms of settlement signed by Carbide's and the Indian Government's attorneys and tendered to the Court on February 15; and (4) an "order" of May 4, 1989, setting forth the Supreme Court's reasons for urging the settlement. This last document seems to have been provoked by the storm of criticism from environmentalists, lawyers and jurists that greeted the Court's February 14 and 15 orders.

Under the settlement, Carbide agreed to pay US$470 million[30] to the Indian Government on behalf of all the Bhopal victims in full and final settlement of all past, present and future claims arising from the Bhopal disaster. The entire amount had to be and was paid by March 31, 1989. In addition, to facilitate the settlement, the Supreme Court exercised its extraordinary jurisdiction and terminated all the civil, criminal and contempt of court proceedings that had arisen out of the Bhopal disaster and were pending in subordinate Indian courts.

C. India's Weak Institutional Framework

Almost any country's regulatory and redressive machinery would have been severely tested by a disaster of Bhopal's magnitude. In India, the challenge was particularly formidable. It quickly became apparent that the institutional framework both for immediate and long term support to the Bhopal victims was remarkably weak. None of the government agencies knew how to contain the damage inflicted by the lethal gas. None had detailed information about the toxicological properties of MIC or the appropriate post-exposure treatment for the victims. Characteristic of an oblivious-to-safety culture, there was no disaster management plan at any level of government. As a result, the medical response to the disaster was entirely voluntary, unplanned and haphazard.

The dim prospect of early compensation under India's judicial system compounded the victims' immediate difficulties. Moreover, Indian lawyers are courtroom advocates, unaccustomed to the searching investigation and fact development that a case like Bhopal demanded. India has an undeveloped tort law. In the decade between 1975-84, there were only 56 non-motor vehicle cases reported in the All India Reporter. These cases, despite their straightforward nature, took an average of 12 years and 9 months from filing to decision. Significantly, average

---

30. In 1985, Carbide had paid US$5 million to the International Red Cross for the relief and rehabilitation of the Bhopal victims.

recoveries among the successful plaintiffs were very low — the Rupee equivalent of US$950.

These weaknesses, together with the risks attending all complex litigation, made the Bhopal lawsuits eminently suitable for settlement. As the Supreme Court itself observed, "The tremendous suffering of thousands of persons compelled us to move into the direction of immediate relief which, we thought, should not be subordinated to the uncertain promises of the law."[31] Indeed, given the formidable obstacles in securing redress, few lawyers would have predicted that the victims would secure US$475 million from Carbide in just four years.

D. THE BHOPAL ACT

To ensure that claims arising out of the disaster were dealt with speedily, effectively and equitably, the Indian Parliament, in March, 1985, enacted the Bhopal Gas Leak Disaster (Processing of Claims) Act of 1985 (the Bhopal Act). The Bhopal Act conferred an exclusive right on the Indian Government to represent all claimants both within and outside India, and directed the Government to organize a plan for the registration and processing of the victims' claims.

Aggrieved at being excluded from the litigation process, some victims challenged the constitutionality of the Government's assumption of an exclusive power to sue. In the wake of the February 1989 settlement, the outcome of this challenge (which is still pending before the Supreme Court) has assumed critical significance. The settlement presumes the constitutionality of the Bhopal Act. If the Act is struck down, the settlement, too, will fall.

The chances of the Act's invalidation, however, are slim. The Supreme Court has put its prestige on the line to bring about the settlement. An invalidation that jeopardizes relief to the victims is likely to invite public reproach. Moreover, the magnitude of the Bhopal tragedy and the weak bargaining power of most of the victims against Carbide — a powerful multinational — provide the Court with an ample rationale for upholding the Bhopal Act.

E. HOW THE BHOPAL CASE REACHED THE INDIAN SUPREME COURT

In April 1985, shortly after the enactment of the Bhopal Act, the Indian Government sued Carbide in the United States. The Government's preference for an American court stemmed from a lack of confidence in its own judicial system, the lure of large damages that an American jury might award, and its uncertainty about whether Carbide would submit to the jurisdiction of an Indian court. The American court, however, declined to try the Bhopal lawsuit, declaring that India was the more appropriate forum. Consequently, in September 1986, nearly two years after the tragedy, the Indian Government sued Carbide in the Court of the District Judge, Bhopal, for U.S.$3 billion in damages.

---

31. Supreme Court of India, Order dated May 4, 1989 (setting out the reasons that persuaded the Court to make the February 14, 1989 Order for settlement in the Bhopal case), p. 24.

The Bhopal case reached the Indian Supreme Court through the separate appeals of Carbide and the Indian Government from the judgment of Justice Seth of the Madhya Pradesh High Court. In April, 1988, Justice Seth awarded interim damages of US$192 million on the basis of "more than a *prima facie* case having been made out" against the defendants. Carbide's lawyers claimed that the judgment was unsustainable because it amounted to a verdict without trial. The Indian Government appealed because Justice Seth reduced by 30% District Judge Deo's earlier interim payment award of US$270 million.

Surveying the Bhopal litigation in December 1988, the five judge Supreme Court Bench must have been dismayed at the lack of progress in the principal lawsuit. The ineffectiveness of the Indian Government's maneuvers, combined with Carbide's apparent disregard for the victims, had dimmed the victims' hopes for early compensation. Proceedings in the original lawsuit before the Bhopal District Judge had stalled. Pre-trial matters such as "discovery" had yet to be addressed. Four years after the tragedy, the Government had still to finalize its list of authentic claimants.

Rather than proceeding rapidly with the trial of the original lawsuit and establishing a legal claim on Carbide's American assets with a determinative final judgment, the Government had preferred to pursue a risky short-cut. Encouraged by an early suggestion of Bhopal District Judge Deo, regarding an "interim" award,"[32] the Attorney General of India's main litigation strategy was the pursuit of such a pre-trial award. More than a year had been consumed in appeals from that award. In separate proceedings, additional efforts had been expended in a contempt of court action against Carbide, its Chairman and its lawyers. Indeed, there was little in the Government's handling of the Bhopal case that might have impressed the Supreme Court Judges with the Government's capacity to devise legal strategies and introduce reformed trial procedures that could bring the Bhopal lawsuit to a swift conclusion.

F. Options Before the Supreme Court

Eager to help the victims, the Supreme Court faced difficult choices. One option before the Court was to uphold the High Court's pre-trial judgment of US$192 million. But American courts (which the Indian government would have had to enlist to enforce any interim award) have no experience with interim payments, and they would almost certainly have dismissed an Indian pretrial judgment as a denial of due process. So certain were Carbide's lawyers of the unenforceability of the Seth Judgment that they did not bother to obtain a stay of the US$192 million award, pending the outcome of their appeal.

Alternatively, the Supreme Court could have struck down the interim award and urged the Government to pay some interim compensation until it secured a final judgment against Carbide. This course, although legally sound, seemed politically unfeasible. Temporarily relieving the multinational of its liability to compensate the victims would have marred the reputation of the Court in the

---

32. Judge Deo relied on Section 151 of the Indian Civil Procedure Code providing for the "inherent power of the Court to make such orders as may be necessary for the ends of justice."

eyes of the Indian public. Besides, it is unlikely that the Indian Government, in an election year, would have consented to pay interim compensation. Such payment could have been criticized as an interest-free loan and sell-out to the insensitive multinational.

Faced with these no-win options from the perspective of the Bhopal victims, the Supreme Court pressured the parties into settling the dispute. In the Court's own words, "[T]he basic consideration motivating the conclusion of the settlement was the compelling need for urgent relief." In the situation facing it, the Court did the best it could.

G. THE SETTLEMENT: AN EVALUATION

The basic analytical question is whether the settlement efficiently achieves the traditional tort goals of compensation, corrective justice and deterrence. The norm of efficiency dictates that the goals of tort law be achieved at a minimum cost to society in terms of expense and time. The goal of compensation requires that an innocent victim be reimbursed for his or her injuries. Corrective justice or fairness means that the tortfeasor is held liable for his or her misdeeds and does not benefit from the action. Imposing liability for injuries also deters the tortfeasor and other potential tortfeasors from repeating the wrong.

The Bhopal settlement is welcome because it obtains compensation efficiently: Future litigation costs have been avoided and compensation has been secured within five years of the disaster—a short time by Indian standards. Frequently, the compensation secured in mass tort cases is dwarfed by the transaction costs of litigation. Attorneys' fees may eat into more than one third of the total award. For example, one study of the asbestos trials in the United States concludes that litigation expenses consumed 63% of the recovery, leaving only 37% for victim relief.[33] The Bhopal settlement both contains transaction costs and cuts long years of expensive litigation. At the sluggish pace at which the Indian Government was proceeding in the case, it might have been 15 more years before the victims saw the colour of their money. By that time, the compensation—so urgently required by the impoverished and displaced victims—would have been meaningless. With the settlement, the victims should begin receiving compensation in a few month's time.

[1] COMPENSATION

The basis for the amount of US$470 million suggested by the Supreme Court and accepted by the Indian Government and Carbide was disclosed by the Court in its post-settlement Order on May 4, 1989. During settlement negotiations, Carbide's best offer had been US$426 million, while the Government's lowest demand was US$500 million. The Court arrived at a middle figure of US$470 million after estimating the amount of appropriate compensation due to the claimants for varying degrees of injury.

---

33. J. Kakalik, P. Ebener, W. Felstiner, G. Haggstrom & M. Shanly, Variations in Asbestos Litigation Compensation and Expenses at XII-XIX (Rand Corp. 1984).

The settlement provides US$44 million for the 3000 dead, US$160 million for the 30,000 permanently disabled, US$60 million for the 20,000 temporarily disabled and an additional US$50 million for 2000 victims who suffered other serious injuries. The Court also set aside US$16 million for specialized medical treatment, after-care and rehabilitation of the victims. The remaining US$140 million was allocated to meet the claims of those with less serious injuries, such as those who lost personal belongings and livestock.

Under the Settlement, compensation for the deceased will average US$14,600. This amount is nearly three times higher than what has been awarded in motor vehicles accident claims under Indian tort law. Moreover, the Supreme Court's May 4, 1989 order implies that the entire US$470 million will go to the victims and that neither the Federal nor the Madhya Pradesh state government will be entitled to draw reimbursements from that amount, for litigation and rehabilitation expenditures incurred by them.

The US$470 million settlement, with its immediate payment condition, compares favorably with Carbide's previous offer in March 1986, to pay US$350 million over 5 to 7 years. Moreover, the March 1986 Carbide offer was made during proceedings before a U.S. District Court. The Bhopal victims were then represented by several American lawyers, who would have skimmed off as much as 40 percent of the $350 million in contingency fees. By contrast, the entire US$470 million will now go to aid the victims.

Could a better settlement have been secured? From Carbide's standpoint, there was no imminent threat to its American assets—Justice Seth's pre-trial award was little more than a paper decree—and apparently there was no urgent need to settle. Apart from the Supreme Court's inducements, the only real pressures working on Carbide were the mounting legal costs and the continuing stain on its reputation. Carbide's officers do not seem to have been much moved by their company's bad publicity and they seem to have held fast to a sum that was relatively modest in terms of Carbide's total assets. Given the negligible progress in the original suit, it seems unlikely that the Indian Government could have secured more favorable terms that it did from the multinational.

[2] CORRECTIVE JUSTICE

Although the Supreme Court's orders do not ascribe liability to Carbide, the settlement implicitly establishes the multinational's accountability. Retributive or corrective justice requires that the tortfeasor not benefit from his or her action or negligence but instead be forced to compensate the victim. The settlement clearly achieves this end. Indeed, the Bhopal settlement is the first in a mass tort case where a multinational has paid for the actions of its local subsidiary. The settlement, therefore, is likely to strengthen the emergent norm of international law that transnational corporations are strictly liable for mishaps from hazardous activities conducted by their subsidiaries around the globe.

[3] DETERRENCE

The US$470 million paid by Carbide to the Supreme Court in February, 1989, pursuant to the settlement, was more than double the corporation's US$200 million insurance coverage. This amount seems large enough to deter foreign and domestic entrepreneurs from recklessly investing in hazardous technologies in India or, indeed, in developing countries generally. At the same time, by consenting to a settlement that will not severely deplete Carbide's assets, the Indian Government has signaled its willingness to permit new investments in hazardous industries, provided that the investors are willing to internalize the social costs resulting from their activities.

H. Conclusion

In the final analysis, the Supreme Court's statesmanship has secured more for the Bhopal victims than the Indian Government could have otherwise obtained, at least for the short term.

As for the future, the Supreme Court must constitute an oversight machinery to ensure that the money actually reaches the victims. It must also issue directions for the speedy distribution of compensation. The Supreme Court's members are undoubtedly equal to these administrative challenges, and will be spurred on by their own keen awareness of the victims' great need.

NOTES AND QUESTIONS

1. As in the case of many lawsuits, one event had a decisive impact on the outcome of the entire litigation. In this case, the decisive event was the dismissal of the U.S. case on the grounds of *forum non conveniens*. Why?

2. Why did the Indian government seek a pretrial award of damages in the Bhopal District Court? What procedures would the Indian government have to follow in enforcing the judgment against UCC? Was UCC concerned about the damages award?

3. As between the Indian government and UCC, which party was under greater pressure to resolve the case? Why?

4. Review the award of damages, particularly the award for wrongful death. Do you find the amount of this award to be fair and adequate? What about in the United States?

Michael J. Bowman, The Convention on Civil Liability for Damage Resulting from Activities Dangerous to the Environment
2 Environmental Liability 11(1994)

On June 21, 1993, the Council of Europe's long-awaited Convention on Civil Liability for Damage Resulting from Activities Dangerous to the Environment was finally concluded at Lugano. According to Article 1, the Convention "aims at ensuring adequate compensation for damage resulting from activities dangerous to the environment and also provides for means of prevention and reinstatement."

Chapter I, entitled "General Provisions," comprises four articles, the first of which sets out the object and purpose of the treaty as indicated above, while the second articulates a lengthy series of definitions of key terms employed in the text. Of particular interest in that regard is the concept of "damage," which is defined to include not only loss of life, personal injury and loss of or damage to property, but also loss or damage by impairment of the environment itself, although compensation here, other than for loss of profit from such impairment, is to be limited to the costs of measures of reinstatement actually or to be undertaken. The costs of preventive measures and loss or damage occasioned by them are also included. Article 3 then provides that the Convention is to apply when the incident occurs within the territory of a party, regardless of where the damage is suffered, or alternatively where the incident occurs elsewhere, but where the law in force for such territory becomes applicable by virtue of conflict of laws rules.

The key provisions of the Convention, which relate to the issue of liability, are to be found in Chapter II. Article 6 establishes principles governing liability for damage arising out of certain dangerous activities undertaken professionally, including the operation of sites or installations for the incineration, treatment, handling or recycling of waste and the production, storage, use or release of dangerous substances or hazardous micro-organisms or genetically-modified organisms. Essentially, the operator (that is, the person who exercises control of the activity) is to be liable for any damage resulting from incidents occurring during his period of Control. Provision is made for the joint and several liability of successive operators if the incident consists of a continuous occurrence or a series of occurrences having the same origin. In either case, however, any operator who can prove that only part of the damage can be attributed to occurrences during his period of control will be liable for that part alone. If the damage only becomes known after all dangerous activity on the site has ceased, the last operator is liable unless it is proved that all or part of the damage resulted from an incident occurring before he became the operator.

Chapter V comprises a single article, Article 25, which lays down that nothing in the Convention limits or derogates from the rights of victims of environmental damage, or any measures concerning environmental protection or reinstatement, under the laws of any party or any other treaty by which it is bound, while at the same time providing that, as between European Community members, Community rules prevail. The Convention itself will therefore apply only to the extent that no relevant Community rule exists.

In conclusion, Chapter VIII enunciates in more or less standard form the final clause of the Convention governing such matters as participation, withdrawal and depositary functions. The most striking features of this chapter are to be found in Articles 32 and 35. The latter provides that parties may reserve the right to allow a "state of the art" defense to operators in certain contexts, to apply the Convention in respect of damage suffered in the territory of non-party states only on the basis of reciprocity, and to exclude the operation of Article 18 in its entirety. Finally, Article 32(3) provides that only three acceptances will be needed in order to bring the Convention into force, though at least two must be by Council of Europe member states. It is to be hoped that this low threshold can be speedily crossed, as the Convention has the potential significantly to advance the interests of victims of pollution incidents.

QUESTIONS

1. What is the nature of the obligations that are created by national and international rules that now apply to the export of chemicals and hazardous materials?

2. What are the concerns of an investor who wants to locate a manufacturing plant in a foreign country? Does incorporation as a foreign subsidiary company under the laws of the foreign country protect the parent or holding company against liability?

IV. The U.S. Alien Tort Statute

The Alien Tort Statute (ATS), codified at 28 U.S.C. §1350, is a legislative product of the very first Congress in 1789. Its current version reads as follows: "The District Courts shall have original jurisdiction of any civil action by an alien for a tort only, committed in violation of the law of nations." Although it may seem unlikely that U.S. corporations need to be concerned about such an ancient and obscure statute in their conduct of international business, recent decisions by U.S. courts indicate that issues concerning the ATS can be an important consideration in IBTs.

Interpreting the ATS has been something of a puzzle because no one is quite sure how or why it was enacted. Furthermore, it provided jurisdiction in only one case during the first 170 years of its existence. For this reason, the distinguished judge of the Second Circuit Court of Appeals, Henry Friendly, called the ATS a "legal Lohengrin,"[34] a reference to the Richard Wagner opera, *Lohengrin*, and its main character, a knight bearing this name, who appears suddenly coming down a river in a boat drawn by a swan.

While in the opera, Lohengrin turns out to be a Knight of the Holy Grail, this may not be the case with the ATS. In the landmark ATS case of *Sosa v. Alvarez-Machain*, 124 S. Ct. 2739 (2004), the U.S. Supreme Court took a "no-nonsense" approach to the interpretation of the act, whose implications will now be worked out by the lower courts.

Reading the opinion of the Court by Justice Souter, one can only come away impressed. The Court did extensive analysis based on original historical research. Justice Souter did an excellent job of uncovering the origin and meaning of the ATS, and the *Sosa* opinion appears to be definitive.

The *Sosa* case determined that the ATS "was intended as jurisdictional in the sense of addressing the power of the courts to entertain cases concerned with a certain subject."[35] Thus the Court (three justices dissenting) concluded that Congress intended to create a private cause of action by passing the ATS; it was not intended to be "placed on the shelf" to await future legislative action.

But what is the contour of the cause of action created? Here the Court concluded that the ATS furnishes "jurisdiction for a relatively modest set of actions alleging violations of the law of nations."[36] This may seem to be a truism, but the Court went on to state that this means a narrow set of common law actions "based on the present-day law of nations to rest on a norm of international character accepted by the civilized world and defined with specificity comparable to the features of the 18th century paradigms we have recognized."[37] The reference to "18th century paradigms" was threefold: Violation of safe conduct, infringement

---

34. *ITT v. Vencap, Ltd.*, 519 F.2d 1001, 1015 (2d Cir. 1975).
35. 124 S. Ct. at 2755.
36. Id. at 2759.
37. Id. at 2761-2762.

of the rights of ambassadors, and piracy. The Court seemed to approve, or at least did not disapprove, the landmark 1980 case involving torture, *Filartiga v. Pena-Irala*, 630 F.2d 876 (2d Cir. 1980). In the *Sosa* case itself, which involved a claim by the plaintiff Alvarez based on wrongful arrest and abduction from Mexico in order that he could stand trial in the United States, the Court held there was no ATS cause of action since the norm advanced "expresses an aspiration that exceeds any binding customary law rule having the specificity that we require."[38] It might be added that this was an easy determination since the Supreme Court in 1992, in *United States v. Alvarez-Machain*, 504 U.S. 655 (1992), had upheld the legality of this very seizure and abduction.

What is the future of the ATS after *Sosa*? The court left the door open for international law claims, but how wide is hard to say. Despite the call for judicial caution in ATS matters, the *Sosa* Court reaffirms that the United States, including the judiciary, is bound by international law norms including customary international law, and that this is one of the narrow areas where federal common law continues to exist.[39]

In the materials that follow, we consider the ATS in the context of international business. After *Sosa*, how will the ATS be used? Even if an ATS complaint is ultimately unsuccessful, what is the implication of the *threat* of such actions?

Beanal v. Freeport-McMoran, Inc.
United States Court of Appeals, Fifth Circuit, 1999
197 F.3d 161

STEWART, Circuit Judge.

[Plaintiff Tom Beanal, a resident of the Republic of Indonesia and leader of a local tribal group, brought an action in the federal district court in Louisiana against Freeport-McMoran, Inc., and Freeport-McMoran Copper & Gold, Inc. (Freeport), Delaware corporations with headquarters in Louisiana. Freeport operated a copper, gold, and silver mine in Indonesia. Beanal argued that Freeport violated the Alien Tort Statute, 28 U.S.C. §1350, and the Torture Victim Protection Act of 1991. In his first complaint, Beanal alleged that Freeport engaged in environmental abuses, human rights violations, and cultural genocide. The district court dismissed the complaint without prejudice, instructing Beanal to amend the complaint to state more specifically his claims of genocide and individual humans violations. After Beanal filed his second amended complaint, the district court again instructed Beanal to plead facts sufficient to support his claims of genocide and human rights violations. In March 1998, the district court granted Freeport's motion to dismiss his third amended complaint and dismissed the complaint, this time with prejudice. Beanal appealed the dismissal to the court of appeals.]

Beanal claims that Freeport engaged in conduct that violated the Alien Tort Statute (the "ATS" or "§1350"). Under §1350:

The district courts shall have original jurisdiction of any civil action by an alien for a tort only, committed in violation of the law of nations or a treaty of the United States.

---

38. Id. at 2769.
39. Id. at 2764.

Rule Section 1350 confers subject matter jurisdiction when the following conditions are met: (1) an alien sues, (2) for a tort, (3) that was committed in violation of the "law of nations" or a treaty of the United States. Beanal does not claim that Freeport violated a United States treaty. Thus, the issue before us is whether Beanal states claims upon which relief can be granted for violations under the "law of nations," i.e., international law. *Issue*

Beanal's allegations under the ATS can be divided into three categories: (1) individual human rights violations; (2) environmental torts; and (3) genocide and cultural genocide. We address each in turn.

1. INDIVIDUAL HUMAN RIGHTS VIOLATIONS

First, Beanal claims that his pleadings sufficiently state claims for individual human rights violations. Essentially, Beanal complains that Freeport engaged in the following conduct: (1) surveillance; (2) mental torture; (3) death threats; and (4) house arrest. *See* Third Amended Complaint ¶25. However, Freeport argues that Beanal's allegations fail to give adequate notice under the federal pleading requirements.

After reviewing Beanal's pleadings de novo, we agree with the district court's ruling. Beanal's complaint merely makes conclusory allegations. Beanal's claims are devoid of names, dates, locations, times or any facts that would put Freeport on notice as to what conduct supports the nature of his claims. Although Beanal argues that the district court inappropriately subjected his complaint to a heightened pleading standard, nonetheless, the notice requirements under Rule 8 require more than "bare bone allegations that a wrong has occurred." *See South Cent. Bell Tel. Co.*, 904 F.2d, at 277.

2. ENVIRONMENTAL TORTS AND ABUSES

Next, Beanal argues that Freeport through its mining activities engaged in environmental abuses which violated international law. In his Third Amended Complaint, Beanal alleges the following:

> FREEPORT, in connection with its Grasberg operations, deposits approximately 100,000 tons of tailings per day in the Aghwagaon, Otomona and Akjwa Rivers. Said tailings have diverted the natural flow of the rivers and have rendered the natural waterways of the plaintiff unusable for traditional uses including bathing and drinking. Furthermore, upon information and belief, the heavy metal content of the tailings have and/or will affect the body tissue of the aquatic life in said rivers. Additionally, tailings have blocked the main flow of the Ajkwa River causing overflow of the tailings into lowland rain forest vegetation destroying the same.
>
> FREEPORT, in connection with its Grasberg operations, has diverted the aforesaid rivers greatly increasing the likelihood of future flooding in Timika, the home of the plaintiff, TOM BEANAL.
>
> FREEPORT, in connection with its Grasberg mining operations, has caused or will cause through the course of its operations 3 billion tons of "overburden" to be dumped into the upper Wanagon and Carstensz creating the likely risk of massive landslides directly injurious to the plaintiff. Furthermore, said "overburden" creates

acid rock damage which has created acid streams and rendering the Lake Wanagon an "acid lake" extremely high in copper concentrations.

However, Freeport argues that Beanal's allegations of environmental torts are not cognizable under the "law of nations" because Beanal fails to show that Freeport's mining activities violate any universally accepted environmental standards or norms. The district court conducted a thorough survey of various international law principles, treaties, and declarations and concluded that Beanal failed to articulate environmental torts that were cognizable under international law.

Beanal and the *amici* refer the court to several sources of international environmental law to show that the alleged environmental abuses caused by Freeport's mining activities are cognizable under international law. Chiefly among these are the *Principles of International Environmental Law I: Frameworks, Standards and Implementation* 183-18 (Phillip Sands ed., 1995) . . . and the Rio Declaration on Environment and Development, June 13, 1992, U.N. Doc. A/CONF. 15 1/5 rev. 1 (1992) (the "Rio Declaration").

Nevertheless, "[i]t is only where the nations of the world have demonstrated that the wrong is of mutual and not merely several, concern, by means of express international accords, that a wrong generally recognized becomes an international law violation in the meaning of the [ATS]." *Filartiga*, 630 F.2d at 888. Thus, the ATS "applies only to shockingly egregious violations of universally recognized principles of international law." *See Zapata v. Quinn*, 707 F.2d 691, 692 (2d Cir. 1983) (per curiam). Beanal fails to show that these treaties and agreements enjoy universal acceptance in the international community. The sources of international law cited by Beanal and the *amici* merely refer to a general sense of environmental responsibility and state abstract rights and liberties devoid of articulable or discernable standards and regulations to identify practices that constitute international environmental abuses or torts. Therefore, the district court did not err when it concluded that Beanal failed to show in his pleadings that Freeport's mining activities constitute environmental torts or abuses under international law.

3. GENOCIDE AND CULTURAL GENOCIDE

Beanal claims that Freeport engaged in acts of genocide and cultural genocide. In his First Amended Complaint, Beanal alleged that Freeport's mining operations caused the Amungme to be displaced and relocate to other areas of the country. He also alleged that Freeport's mining activities destroyed the Amungme's habitat. As such, Beanal asserted that Freeport purposely engaged in activity to destroy the Amungme's cultural and social framework. However, Freeport attacked Beanal's allegations claiming that cultural genocide is not recognized as a discrete violation of international law. The district court relying chiefly on the express language of Article II of the Convention on the Prevention and Punishment of the Crime of Genocide, 78 U.N.T.S. 277 (the "Convention on Genocide"), concluded that cultural genocide was not recognized in the international community as a violation of international law. The district court then instructed Beanal to amend his complaint to allege genocide. Specifically, the court instructed Beanal to allege facts that would demonstrate that "he [was] the victim of acts committed with the intent to destroy the people of the Amungme tribe. . . ." Consequently, the district court found that Beanal's Third Amended Complaint failed to comply with its express instructions.

A review of Beanal's Third Amended Complaint reveals that his claim of genocide suffers from the same pleading defects that plagued his other claims of individual human rights violations. Beanal's complaint is saturated with conclusory allegations devoid of any underlying facts to support his claim of genocide. Although the pleading requirements under Rule 8 are to be liberally construed in favor of the plaintiff, nevertheless, the rule requires more than "bare bone allegations." *See Walker* 904 F.2d at 277.

Notwithstanding Beanal's failure to allege facts to support sufficiently his claim of genocide, Beanal and the *amici* in their respective briefs urge this court to recognize cultural genocide as a discrete violation of international law. Again, they refer the court to several international conventions, agreements, and declarations. Nevertheless, a review of these documents reveals that the documents make pronouncements and proclamations of an amorphous right to "enjoy culture," or a right to "freely pursue" culture, or a right to cultural development. They nonetheless fail to proscribe or identify conduct that would constitute an act of cultural genocide. Furthermore, Beanal has not demonstrated that cultural genocide has achieved universal acceptance as a discrete violation of international law. Accordingly, we find that Beanal's claims of genocide and cultural genocide are facially insufficient to withstand a motion to dismiss under Rule 12(b).

B. TORTURE VICTIM PROTECTION ACT ["TVPA"]

Beanal claims that his allegations of individual human rights violations are also actionable under the TVPA. The TVPA provides an explicit cause of action for torture and extrajudicial killings. *See* 28 U.S.C. §1350, note, §2. In pertinent part, the statute declares that any individual who, under actual or apparent authority, or color of law, of any foreign nation subjects an individual to torture or extrajudicial killing shall, in a civil action, be liable for damages. *Id.* §2(a)(1), and (2).

Beanal's allegations of individual human rights violations under the TVPA are essentially predicated on the same claims of individual human rights violations under the ATS. Because we find that Beanal fails to state with the requisite specificity and definiteness his claims of individual human rights violations under the ATS, we find that his allegations under the TVPA also suffer from the same pleading defects.

Aguinda v. Texaco, Inc.
United States Court of Appeals, Second Circuit, 2002
303 F.3d 470

LEVAL, Circuit Judge.

[In 1964, Texaco Petroleum Company (TexPet), a subsidiary of Texaco, began oil exploration in Ecuador. In 1965, TexPet and Gulf Oil Corporation began operating an oil concession for a Consortium owned in equal shares by TexPet and Gulf. In 1974, the government of Ecuador, through its state-owned oil agency, PetroEcuador, obtained a 25 percent share in the Consortium. PetroEcuador then acquired Gulf's share and gradually began acquiring the remaining interests in the Consortium owned by TexPet. By 1992, TexPet relinquished all of its interests in the Consortium, leaving it wholly owned by the Ecuadorian government. In November 1993, a class action was brought on behalf of Ecuadorian plaintiffs against Texaco in the federal district court for the Southern District of New York. (Texaco's headquarters were in New York at the time.) A second class action against Texaco was brought in December 1994 by plaintiffs from Peru. Both complaints asserted numerous claims against Texaco, the parent company, for directing the oil operations in Ecuador that caused pollution of forests and rivers based on theories of negligence, public and private nuisance, strict liability, medical monitoring, trespass, civil conspiracy, and violations of the Alien Torts Statute, 28 U.S.C. §1350. The trial court dismissed both cases based on grounds of *forum non conveniens* and international comity. On the first appeal, the Second Circuit vacated and remanded the dismissal for reconsideration on the ground that dismissal on *forum non conveniens* grounds was inappropriate absent at least a commitment from Texaco to submit to the jurisdiction of the Ecuadorian courts. On remand, Texaco agreed to submit to jurisdiction in Peru and Ecuador. The district court found that the courts of Ecuador provided an adequate alternative forum for plaintiffs' action. The court also found that the balance of public and private interested favored dismissal. As a result, the district court granted Texaco's motion to dismiss both cases and plaintiffs appealed.]

We modify the judgments in one respect explained below, but otherwise affirm the dismissal of the actions by reason of *forum non conveniens*.

DISCUSSION

Plaintiffs contend that the district court abused its discretion in determining that Ecuador was an adequate alternative forum and that the balance of private and public interest factors tilted in favor of dismissal. Finding no abuse of discretion, we affirm with modification.

After determining the degree of deference owed to a plaintiff's choice of forum, a district court engages in a two-step inquiry. First, the court must consider whether an adequate alternative forum exists. If so, it must "then balance a series of factors involving the private interests of the parties in maintaining the litigation in the competing fora and any public interests at stake." *Wiwa*, 226 F.3d at 100. The defendant seeking dismissal bears the burden as to both questions. After assuming a strong presumption of validity for plaintiffs' choice of forum, the district court found that the presumption was overcome by the balance of public and private interest factors.

A. DOES AN ADEQUATE ALTERNATIVE FORUM EXIST?

Ordinarily, the requirement of an adequate alternative forum "will be satisfied when the defendant is 'amenable to process' in the other jurisdiction. In rare circumstances, however, where the remedy offered by the other forum is clearly unsatisfactory, the other forum may not be an adequate alternative. . . ." *Piper Aircraft Co. v. Reyno*, 454 U.S. 235, 255 n. 22, 102 S. Ct. 252, 70 L. Ed. 2d 419 (1981). Plaintiffs raise several objections to the availability and adequacy of an Ecuadorian forum.

Plaintiffs contend first that Ecuador does not offer an alternative forum because Law 55 precludes them from proceeding in Ecuadorian courts. Law 55 provides, "[S]hould the lawsuit be filed outside Ecuadorian territory, this will definitely terminate national competency as well as any jurisdiction of Ecuadorian judges over the matter." Plaintiffs argue that Law 55 deprives Ecuadorian courts of competency to assert jurisdiction because both suits were first filed in the United States. They contend that dismissal for *forum non conveniens* would leave them without a forum in which to proceed. We agree with the district court's skepticism as to the law's retroactivity, as well as its application to cases dismissed for *forum non conveniens*. We note furthermore that following oral argument the parties submitted to us an April 30, 2002 decision of the Ecuadorian Constitutional Court declaring Law 55 unconstitutional. We need not determine the scope of Law 55, as the district court qualified its dismissal specifying that, in the event the cases were dismissed in Ecuador under Law 55 and this result were affirmed by Ecuador's highest court, it would be open to reconsider the question.

We find no merit in plaintiffs' further argument that Ecuadorian courts are unreceptive to tort claims. The record shows that several plaintiffs have recovered judgments against TexPet and PetroEcuador for claims arising out of the very facts here alleged. In addition, Texaco has offered unrebutted evidence of other types of successful tort claims brought in Ecuadorian courts, including personal injury claims by Ecuadorian oilfield workers against TexPet.

Plaintiffs' contention is predicated on the absence of tort actions on the docket of Ecuador's Supreme Court. Given Texaco's showing that tort judgments are awarded by Ecuador's courts, their absence from the docket of the Supreme Court of Ecuador appears to be of little significance.

Plaintiffs' third objection is that Ecuadorian courts do not recognize class actions. On the other hand, Ecuador permits litigants with similar causes of action arising out of the same facts to join together in a single lawsuit. While the need for thousands of individual plaintiffs to authorize the action in their names is more burdensome than having them represented by a representative in a class action, it is not so burdensome as to deprive the plaintiffs of an effective alternative forum. Plaintiffs point further to several respects in which Ecuadorian procedure is less efficient than U.S. procedure. While Ecuador's judicial procedures may be less streamlined than ours, that does not make Ecuador's procedures ineffective or render Ecuador inadequate as an alternative forum.

Plaintiffs contend that Ecuadorian courts are subject to corrupt influences and are incapable of acting impartially. After ordering supplemental briefing on this question, Judge Rakoff made detailed findings. He found: 1) no evidence of impropriety by Texaco or any past member of the Consortium in any prior judicial proceeding in Ecuador; 2) there are presently pending in Ecuador's courts numerous cases against multinational corporations without any evidence of corruption; 3) Ecuador has recently taken significant steps to further the independence of its judiciary; 4) the State Department's general description of Ecuador's judiciary as politicized applies primarily to cases of confrontations between the police and political protestors; 5) numerous U.S. courts have found Ecuador adequate for the resolution of civil disputes involving U.S. companies; and 6) because these cases will be the subject of close public and political scrutiny, as confirmed by the Republic's involvement in the litigation, there is little chance of undue influence being applied. We cannot say that these findings were an abuse of discretion.

⑤ Finally, plaintiffs challenge the district court's allowance of only 60 days for the assertion of plaintiffs' claims in Ecuador exempt from claims of preclusion. We agree with this objection. In the district court, timely claims were brought on behalf of nearly 55,000 plaintiffs. In Ecuador, because class action procedures are not recognized, signed authorizations would need to be obtained for each individual plaintiff. This presents a formidable administrative task for which we believe 60 days is inadequate time. We therefore direct the district court to modify its ruling to make dismissal conditioned on Texaco's agreeing to waive any defense based on a statute of limitations for limitation periods expiring between the date of filing these United States actions and one year (rather than 60 days) following the dismissal of these actions.

B. BALANCING PRIVATE AND PUBLIC INTEREST FACTORS

Having demonstrated the availability of an adequate alternative forum, Texaco must next establish that the balance of private and public interest factors "tilt[s] strongly in favor of trial in the foreign forum." *Wiwa*, 226 F.3d at 100.

1. Private Interest Factors

Private interests include "the relative ease of access to sources of proof; availability of compulsory process for attendance of unwilling, and the cost of obtaining attendance of willing, witnesses; possibility of view of the premises, if view would be appropriate to the action; and all other practical problems that make trial of a case easy, expeditious and inexpensive." *Gulf Oil Corp. v. Gilbert*, 330 U.S. 501, 508, 67 S. Ct. 839, 91 L. Ed. 1055 (1947). We find no abuse of discretion in the district court's conclusion that these interests "weigh heavily" in favor of an Ecuadorian forum. The relative ease of access to sources of proof favors proceeding in Ecuador. All plaintiffs, as well as members of their putative classes, live in Ecuador or Peru. Plaintiffs sustained their injuries in Ecuador and Peru, and their relevant medical and property records are located there. Also located in Ecuador are the records of decisions taken by the Consortium, along with evidence of Texaco's defenses implicating the roles of PetroEcuador and the Republic. By contrast, plaintiffs have failed to establish that the parent Texaco made decisions regarding oil operations in Ecuador or that evidence of any such decisions is located in the U.S.

If these cases proceeded to trial, it would be onerous for a New York court to manage the translation difficulties arising from cases with 55,000 putative class members of different indigenous groups speaking various dialects. In addition, it would be far more feasible for an Ecuadorian court to view the polluted areas in question than for a New York court to do so. We also find significant that the Republic and PetroEcuador, neither of which are parties to the current suits, could be joined if the cases were resumed in Ecuador. We agree with the district court's observation that in the absence of the Ecuadorian Republic as a party, a U.S. court would be incapable of effectively ordering several aspects of the equitable relief sought in the complaints.

To the extent that evidence exists within the U.S., plaintiffs' concerns are partially addressed by Texaco's stipulation to allow use of the discovery already obtained. Furthermore, Texaco's counsel agreed at oral argument that Texaco would not oppose further discovery in Ecuador that would otherwise be available in the U.S.

2. Public Interest Factors

Public interest considerations include administrative difficulties associated with court congestion; the unfairness of imposing jury duty on a community with no relation to the litigation; the interest in having localized controversies decided at home; and avoiding difficult problems in conflict of laws and the application of foreign law. The district court was within its discretion in concluding that the public interest factors tilt in favor of dismissal.

We conclude that the district court was within its discretion in dismissing the actions on the basis of *forum non conveniens*.

U.S. Oil Firm Leaves Toxic Legacy in Ecuador
The Japan Times, p. 14 (January 30, 2004)

Oil activities conducted by ChevronTexaco in the northeast Amazon region in Ecuador have caused significant environmental damage and serious health consequences for the indigenous population. ChevronTexaco spilled more than 70 billion liters of toxic waste into 600 unlined pits in an area of more than 5,180 square kilometers. This toxic dumping has affected an indigenous community of 30,000 and has led to the loss of 1 million hectares of rain forest.

The health damage incurred by the indigenous population has been documented in the village of San Carlos, which contains more than 30 oil wells constructed by ChevronTexaco. One of the first studies on the effects of oil pollution on people's health in that village was carried out by two medical doctors in collaboration with the University of London's Department of Tropical Medicine and Hygiene. The study found that cancer rates in San Carlos exceed the average by up to 30 times. For several years the residents of San Carlos had been exposed to more than 3.8 million liters of oil and toxic waste-water dumped by ChevronTexaco. Exposure occurred through several routes, including absorption through the skin, ingestion of contaminated food and water, and inhalation of oil and related gases. The water used by local residents for drinking, bathing and laundering contains nearly 150 times the amounts considered safe for substances such as hydrocarbons. The study also found the risk of cancer of the stomach, liver, bile duct and skin for those living in San Carlos was more than double the average. ChevronTexaco claims that these results were only preliminary and not worth analyzing.

In November of 1993, a class-action lawsuit on behalf of residents of the rain forest area known as Oriente was launched in a U.S. District Court in New York. Although the plaintiffs wanted the case to be tried in New York, a federal appeals court in New York ruled that it should be conducted in Ecuador.

NOTES AND QUESTIONS

1. In *Beanal*, the court of appeals used different grounds for dismissing the claims of (1) environmental damage, (2) cultural genocide, and (3) human rights

violations and genocide. What were the grounds for dismissing each of these three sets of claims?   *Pleading issue*

2. Discuss what type of allegations and proof would be sufficient to satisfy the *Beanal* court's requirements on the human rights violations. What obstacles or issues might there be with satisfying these requirements?

3. In *Aguinda*, why were the plaintiffs anxious to file an action against Texaco in the United States as opposed to suing Texaco or its subsidiary in Ecuador or Peru? Why were the defendants so anxious to prevent the case from proceeding in the United States? After the Second Circuit upheld the dismissal of the case by the federal district court, the case went forward to trial in Ecuador in 2003. Is a damage award rendered in Ecuador enforceable in the United States? Do these considerations suggest that U.S. courts have a special role in enforcing corporate responsibility?

PROBLEM 9-9

Executives from Petro-Tech, a gas and oil company located in Texas, have received a very attractive offer from a Southeast Asian country run by a military government to set up an oil exploration venture. The project will involve setting up camps in different parts of the country for several weeks at a time in order to clear local rainforests and to build oil wells and run pipes through large areas of open forest grounds. Petro-Tech will send a small team of engineers to supervise the construction of the wells and the pipes. As the project involves a heavy investment of capital, the local government has offered to provide security for the project. A local general has stated that security is necessary as many local inhabitants live in the forests who might become scavengers.

Petro-Tech's business consultants have raised certain concerns about the country's egregious track record of human rights abuses. After a risk assessment and the input of various consultants, the Petro-Tech executives have decided to proceed with the project but with some modifications. Petro-Tech executives decided that the involvement of the military in providing security was risky and proposed the following alternatives:

(1)   Petro-Tech and the local government and its military will sign an agreement detailing the type of conduct by the military that will be permitted as well as conduct that will be strictly prohibited during the course of completing the project. The military will gives its assurances that it will fully abide by the agreement; or

(2)   The local military would not be involved in providing security at all. Petro-Tech would hire at its own expense a private security firm in the United States that will provide private paramilitary security services for the project. This alternative would save the military the costs of providing security.

Comment on whether Petro-Tech's proposal to deal with the issue of security is a sound one. Would you proceed with the project? What risks might Petro-Tech be exposed to if it decides to go ahead? Consult *Doe v. Unocal* below.

Doe v. Unocal Corp.
United States Court of Appeals, Ninth Circuit, 2002
2002 U.S. App. Lexis 19263

PREGERSON, Circuit Judge.

[In 1992, defendant Unocal Corporation acquired a 28 percent interest in Total Myanmar Exploration and Production (Total Myanmar), a venture for the production, transport, and sale of natural gas established in Myanmar (formerly Burma) by Total S.A. (Total), a French company, under authority from the Myanmar government. As operator of the venture to produce, transport, and sell oil (the Project), Total Myanmar was responsible for hiring employees, determining the hours of work, and compensating employees. Plaintiffs are villagers in Myanmar who allege that Unocal directly or indirectly subjected them to forced labor, murder, rape, and torture when defendants constructed a gas pipeline through their region. Plaintiffs sued Unocal in federal district court in California, alleging violations of the Alien Tort Statute (also known as the Alien Torts Claim Act) and other federal and state laws. Also named as defendants were the Myanmar military government (Myanmar Military) and Myanmar Oil, the government entity that leased the oil and gas rights to Total Myanmar. The district court entered summary judgment in favor of the defendants on all of the plaintiffs' claims. The plaintiffs now appeal to the Ninth Circuit Court of Appeals, which reversed in part and affirmed in part the district court's rulings.]

B. UNOCAL'S KNOWLEDGE THAT THE MYANMAR MILITARY WAS PROVIDING
SECURITY AND OTHER SERVICES FOR THE PROJECT

It is undisputed that the Myanmar Military provided security and other services for the Project, and that Unocal knew about this. The pipeline was to run through Myanmar's rural Tenasserim region. The Myanmar Military increased its presence in the pipeline region to provide security and other services for the Project. A Unocal memorandum documenting Unocal's meetings with Total on March 1 and 2, 1995 reflects Unocal's understanding that "four battalions of 600 men each will protect the [pipeline] corridor" and "fifty soldiers will be assigned to guard each survey team." A former soldier in one of these battalions testified at his deposition that his battalion had been formed in 1996 specifically for this purpose. In addition, the Military built helipads and cleared roads along the proposed pipeline route for the benefit of the Project.

There is also evidence sufficient to raise a genuine issue of material fact whether the Project *hired* the Myanmar Military, through Myanmar Oil, to provide these services, and whether Unocal knew about this. A Production Sharing Contract, entered into by Total Myanmar and Myanmar Oil before Unocal acquired an interest in the Project, provided that "[Myanmar Oil] shall . . . supply [ ] or make available . . . security protection . . . as may be requested by [Total Myanmar and its assigns]," such as Unocal. Unocal was aware of this agreement. Thus, a May 10, 1995 Unocal "briefing document" states that "according to *our contract*, the government of Myanmar is responsible for protecting the pipeline." (Emphasis added.) Similarly, in May 1995, a cable from the U.S. Embassy in Rangoon, Myanmar, reported that Unocal On-Site Representative Joel Robinson ("Unocal Representative Robinson" or "Robinson") "stated forthrightly *that the companies have hired* the Burmese military to provide security for the project." (Emphasis added.)

Unocal disputes that the Project hired the Myanmar Military or, at the least, that Unocal knew about this. For example, Unocal points out that the Production Sharing Contract quoted in the previous paragraph covered only the off-shore Gas Production Joint Venture but not the Gas Transportation Company and the construction of the pipeline which gave rise to the alleged human rights violations. Moreover, Unocal President John Imle ("Unocal President Imle" or "Imle") stated at his deposition that he knew of "no . . . contractual obligation" requiring the Myanmar Military to provide security for the pipeline construction. Likewise, Unocal CEO Roger Beach ("Unocal CEO Beach" or "Beach") stated at his deposition that he also did not know "whether or not Myanmar had a contractual obligation to provide . . . security." Beach further stated that he was not aware of "any support whatsoever of the military[,] . . . either physical or monetary." These assertions by Unocal President Imle and Unocal CEO Beach are called into question by a briefing book which Total prepared for them on the occasion of their April 1996 visit to the Project. The briefing book lists the "numbers of villagers" working as "local helpers hired by battalions," the monthly "amount paid in Kyats" (the currency of Myanmar) to "Project Helpers," and the "amount in Kyats" expended by the Project on "food rations (Army + Villages)."

Furthermore, there is evidence sufficient to raise a genuine issue of material fact whether the Project directed the Myanmar Military in these activities, at least to a degree, and whether Unocal was involved in this. In May 1995, a cable from the U.S. Embassy in Rangoon reported:

> [Unocal Representative] Robinson indicated . . . Total/Unocal uses [aerial photos, precision surveys, and topography maps] to show the [Myanmar] military where they need helipads built and facilities secured. . . . Total's security officials meet with military counterparts to inform them of the next day's activities so that soldiers can ensure the area is secure and guard the work perimeter while the survey team goes about its business.

A November 8, 1995 document apparently authored by Total Myanmar stated that "each working group has a security officer . . . to control the army positions." A January 1996 meeting document lists "daily security coordination with the army" as a "working procedure." Similarly, the briefing book that Total prepared for Unocal President Imle and Unocal CEO Beach on the occasion of their April 1996 visit to the Project mentions that "daily meeting[s]" were "held with the tactical commander" of the army. Moreover, on or about August 29, 1996, Unocal (Singapore) Director of Information Carol Scott ("Unocal Director of Information Scott" or "Scott") discussed with Unocal Media Contact and Spokesperson David Garcia ("Unocal Spokesperson Garcia" or "Garcia") via e-mail how Unocal should publicly address the issue of the alleged movement of villages by the Myanmar Military in connection with the pipeline. Scott cautioned Garcia that "by saying *we* influenced the army not to move a village, you introduce the concept that they would do such a thing; whereas, by saying that no villages have been moved, you skirt the issue of whether it could happen or not." (Emphasis added.) This e-mail is some evidence that Unocal could influence the army not to commit human rights violations, that the army might otherwise commit such violations, and that Unocal knew this.

C. UNOCAL'S KNOWLEDGE THAT THE MYANMAR MILITARY WAS ALLEGEDLY COMMITTING HUMAN RIGHTS VIOLATIONS IN CONNECTION WITH THE PROJECT

Plaintiffs are villagers from Myanmar's Tenasserim region, the rural area through which the Project built the pipeline. Plaintiffs allege that the Myanmar Military forced them, under threat of violence, to work on and serve as porters for the Project. For instance, John Doe IX testified that he was forced to build a helipad near the pipeline site in 1994 that was then used by Unocal and Total officials who visited the pipeline during its planning stages. John Doe VII and John Roe X, described the construction of helipads at Eindayaza and Po Pah Pta, both of which were near the pipeline site, were used to ferry Total/Unocal executives and materials to the construction site, and were constructed using the forced labor of local villagers, including Plaintiffs. John Roes VIII and IX, as well as John Does I, VIII and IX, testified that they were forced to work on building roads leading to the pipeline construction area. Finally, John Does V and IX testified that they were required to serve as "pipeline porters" — workers who performed menial tasks such as hauling materials and cleaning the army camps for the soldiers guarding the pipeline construction.

Plaintiffs also allege in furtherance of the forced labor program just described, the Myanmar Military subjected them to acts of murder, rape, and torture. For instance, Jane Doe I testified that after her husband, John Doe I, attempted to escape the forced labor program, he was shot at by soldiers, and in retaliation for his attempted escape, that she and her baby were thrown into a fire, resulting in injuries to her and the death of the child. Other witnesses described the summary execution of villagers who refused to participate in the forced labor program, or who grew too weak to work effectively. Several Plaintiffs testified that rapes occurred as part of the forced labor program. For instance, both Jane Does II and III testified that while conscripted to work on pipeline-related construction projects, they were raped at knife-point by Myanmar soldiers who were members of a battalion that was supervising the work. Plaintiffs finally allege that Unocal's conduct gives rise to liability for these abuses.

 Before Unocal acquired an interest in the Project, it hired a consulting company, Control Risk Group, to assess the risks involved in the investment. In May 1992, Control Risk Group informed Unocal that "throughout Burma the government habitually makes use of forced labour to construct roads." Control Risk Group concluded that "in such circumstances UNOCAL and its partners will have little freedom of manoeuvre." Unocal's awareness of the risk at that time is also reflected in the deposition testimony of Unocal Vice President of International Affairs Stephen Lipman ("Unocal Vice President Lipman"):

> In our discussions between Unocal and Total [preceding Unocal's acquisition of an interest in the Project], we said that the option of having the [Myanmar] Military provide protection for the pipeline construction and operation of it would be that they might proceed in the manner that would be out of our control and not be in a manner that we would like to see them proceed, I mean, going to excess.

On January 4, 1995, approximately three years after Unocal acquired an interest in the Project, Unocal President Imle met with human rights organizations at Unocal's headquarters in Los Angeles and acknowledged to them that the Myanmar Military might be using forced labor in connection with the Project.

At that meeting, Imle said that "people are threatening physical damage to the pipeline," that "if you threaten the pipeline there's gonna be more military," and that "*if forced labor goes hand and glove with the military yes there will be more forced labor*." (Emphasis added.)

Two months later, on March 16, 1995, Unocal Representative Robinson confirmed to Unocal President Imle that the Myanmar Military might be committing human rights violations in connection with the Project. Thus, Robinson wrote to Imle that he had received publications from human rights organizations "which depicted in more detail than I have seen before the increased encroachment of [the Myanmar Military's] activities into the villages of the pipeline area." Robinson concluded on the basis of these publications that "our assertion that [the Myanmar Military] has not expanded and amplified its usual methods around the pipeline on our behalf may not withstand much scrutiny."

Shortly thereafter, on May 10, 1995, Unocal Representative Robinson wrote to Total's Herve Madeo:

> From Unocal's standpoint, probably the most sensitive issue is "what is forced labor" and "how can you identify it." I am sure that you will be thinking about the demarcation between work done by the project and work done "on behalf of" the project. Where the responsibility of the project ends is *very important*.

In June 1995, Amnesty International informed Unocal that comments from a Myanmar Department of Industry official "could mean that the government plans to use 'voluntary' labor in conjunction with the pipeline." Amnesty International went on to explain that "what they call 'voluntary' labor is called forced labor in other parts of the world."

[O]n December 11, 1995, Unocal Consultant John Haseman ("Unocal Consultant Haseman" or "Haseman"), a former military attache at the U.S. Embassy in Rangoon, reported to Unocal that the Myanmar Military was, in fact, using forced labor and committing other human rights violations in connection with the Project. Haseman told Unocal that "Unocal was particularly discredited when a corporate spokesman was quoted as saying that Unocal was satisfied with . . . assurances [by the Myanmar Military] that no human rights abuses were occurring in the area of pipeline construction." Haseman went on to say:

> [E]gregious human rights violations have occurred, and are occurring now, in southern Burma. The most common are forced relocation without compensation of families from land near/along the pipeline route; forced labor to work on infrastructure projects supporting the pipeline . . . ; and imprisonment and/or execution by the army of those opposing such actions. . . . Unocal, by seeming to have accepted [the Myanmar Military]'s version of events, appears at best naive and at worst a willing partner in the situation.

On February 1, 1996, Total's Herve Chagnoux wrote to Unocal and explained his answers to questions by the press as follows:

> By stating that I could not *guarantee* that the army is not using forced labour, I certainly imply that they might, (and they might) but I am saying that we do not have to monitor the army's behavior: we have our responsibilities; they have their responsibilities; and we refuse to be pushed into assuming more than what we can really guarantee. About

forced labour used by the troops assigned to provide security on our pipeline project, let us admit between Unocal and Total that we might be in a grey zone.

And on September 17, 1996, Total reported to Unocal about a meeting with a European Union civil servant in charge of an investigation of forced labor in Myanmar: "We were told that even if Total is not using forced labor directly, the troops assigned to the protection of our operations use forced labour to build their camps and to carry their equipments." In reply, Total acknowledged that forced labor did indeed occur in connection with the pipeline: "We had to mention that when we had knowledge of such occurrences, the workers have been compensated." Unocal President Imle testified at his deposition that in Unocal's discussions with Total, "surrounding the question of porters for the military and their payment was the issue of whether they were conscripted or volunteer workers." Imle further testified that "the consensus was that it was mixed," i.e., "some porters were conscripted, and some were volunteer." On March 4, 1997, Unocal nevertheless submitted a statement to the City Counsel of New York, in response to a proposed New York City select purchasing law imposed on firms that do business in Myanmar, in which Unocal stated that "no [human rights] violations have taken place" in the vicinity of the pipeline route.

II. ANALYSIS

A. LIABILITY UNDER THE ALIEN TORT CLAIMS ACT

1. Introduction

The District Court granted Unocal's motion for summary judgment on Plaintiffs' ATCA claims. We review a grant of summary judgment *de novo*.

One threshold question in *any* ATCA case is whether the alleged tort is a violation of the law of nations. We have recognized that torture, murder, and slavery are *jus cogens* violations and, thus, violations of the law of nations. *See United States v. Matta-Ballesteros*, 71 F.3d 754, 764 n. 5 (9th Cir. 1995). Rape can be a form of torture. *See Farmer v. Brennan*, 511 U.S. 825, 852, 854, 114 S. Ct. 1970, 128 L. Ed. 2d 811 (1994) (Blackmun, J., concurring) (describing brutal prison rape as "the equivalent of" and "nothing less than torture"); *Kadic v. Karadzic*, 70 F.3d 232, 242 (2d Cir. 1995) (describing allegations of "murder, rape, forced impregnation, and *other forms of torture*" (emphasis added)); *In re Extradition of Suarez-Mason*, 894 F. Supp. 676, 682 (N.D. Cal. 1988) (stating that "shock sessions were interspersed with rapes and *other forms of torture*" (emphasis added)). Moreover, forced labor is so widely condemned that it has achieved the status of a *jus cogens* violation. Accordingly, all torts alleged in the present case are *jus cogens* violations and, thereby, violations of the law of nations.

Another threshold question in any ATCA case *against a private party*, such as Unocal, is whether the alleged tort requires the private party to engage in state action for ATCA liability to attach, and if so, whether the private party in fact engaged in state action. In his concurrence in *Tel-Oren v. Libyan Arab Republic*, 726 F.2d 774 (D.C. Cir. 1984), Judge Edwards observed that while most crimes require state action for ATCA liability to attach, there are a "handful of crimes," including slave trading, "to which the law of nations attributes *individual liability*," such that state action is not required. *Id.* at 794-95. More recently, the Second

Circuit adopted and extended this approach in *Kadic*. The Second Circuit first noted that genocide and war crimes — like slave trading — do not require state action for ATCA liability to attach. *See* 70 F.3d at 242-43. The Second Circuit went on to state that although "acts of rape, torture, and summary execution," like most crimes, "are proscribed by international law only when committed by state officials or under color of law" to the extent that they were committed *in isolation*, these crimes "are actionable under the Alien Tort [Claims] Act, without regard to state action, to the extent that they were committed *in pursuit of genocide or war crimes*." *Id.* at 243-44. Thus, under *Kadic*, even crimes like rape, torture, and summary execution, which by themselves require state action for ATCA liability to attach, do not require state action when committed in furtherance of other crimes like slave trading, genocide or war crimes, which by themselves do *not* require state action for ATCA liability to attach. We agree with this view and apply it below to Plaintiffs' various ATCA claims.

2. Forced Labor

a. Forced labor is a modern variant of slavery to which the law of nations attributes individual liability such that state action is not required.

Our case law strongly supports the conclusion that forced labor is a modern variant of slavery. Accordingly, forced labor, like traditional variants of slave trading, is among the "handful of crimes . . . to which the law of nations attributes *individual liability*," such that state action is not required. *Id.* at 794-95 (Edwards, J., concurring).

b. Unocal may be liable under the ATCA for aiding and abetting the Myanmar Military in subjecting Plaintiffs to forced labor.

[In determining whether the district court erroneously entered summary judgment in favor of defendants on Plaintiffs' claim that Unocal aided and abetted the Myanmar Military in subjecting them to forced labor, the court held that this issue was governed by international law and adopted the standard for aiding and abetting liability under international criminal law, which can be summarized as knowing practical assistance, encouragement, or moral support which has a substantial effect on the perpetration of the crime.]

First, a reasonable factfinder could conclude that Unocal's alleged conduct met the *actus reus* requirement of aiding and abetting as we define it today. Unocal's weak protestations notwithstanding, there is little doubt that the record contains substantial evidence creating a material question of fact as to whether forced labor was used in connection with the construction of the pipeline. Numerous witnesses, including a number of Plaintiffs, testified that they were forced to clear the right of way for the pipeline and to build helipads for the project before construction of the pipeline began.

The evidence also supports the conclusion that Unocal gave practical assistance to the Myanmar Military in subjecting Plaintiffs to forced labor. The practical assistance took the form of hiring the Myanmar Military to provide security and build infrastructure along the pipeline route in exchange for money or food. The practical assistance also took the form of using photos, surveys, and maps in daily meetings to show the Myanmar Military where to provide security and build infrastructure.

This assistance, moreover, had a "substantial effect" on the perpetration of forced labor, which "most probably would not have occurred in the same way" without someone hiring the Myanmar Military to provide security, and without someone showing them where to do it.

Second, a reasonable factfinder could also conclude that Unocal's conduct met the *mens rea* requirement of aiding and abetting as we define it today, namely, actual or constructive (*i.e.*, reasonable) knowledge that the accomplice's actions will assist the perpetrator in the commission of the crime. The District Court found that "the evidence does suggest that Unocal knew that forced labor was being utilized and that the Joint Venturers benefited from the practice." *Doe/Roe II*, 110 F. Supp. 2d at 1310. Moreover, Unocal knew or should reasonably have known that its conduct—including the payments and the instructions where to provide security and build infrastructure—would assist or encourage the Myanmar Military to subject Plaintiffs to forced labor.

Viewing the evidence in the light most favorable to Plaintiffs, we conclude that there are genuine issues of material fact whether Unocal's conduct met the *actus reus* and *mens rea* requirements for liability under the ATCA for aiding and abetting forced labor. Accordingly, we reverse the District Court's grant of Unocal's motion for summary judgment on Plaintiffs' forced labor claims under the ATCA.

3. Murder, Rape, and Torture

a. Because Plaintiffs testified that the alleged acts of murder, rape, and torture occurred in furtherance of forced labor, state action is not required to give rise to liability under the ATCA.

Plaintiffs further allege that the Myanmar Military murdered, raped or tortured a number of the plaintiffs. In section II.A.1, we adopted the Second Circuit's conclusion that "acts of rape, torture, and summary execution," like most crimes, "are proscribed by international law only when committed by state officials or under color of law" to the extent that they were committed *in isolation*. *Kadic*, 70 F.3d at 243-44. We, however, also adopted the Second Circuit's conclusion that these crimes "are actionable under the Alien Tort [Claims] Act, without regard to state action, to the extent that they were committed *in pursuit of genocide or war crimes*," *id.* at 244 (emphasis added), i.e., in pursuit of crimes, such as slavery, which never require state action for ATCA liability to attach. According to Plaintiffs' deposition testimony, all of the acts of murder, rape, and torture alleged by Plaintiffs occurred in furtherance of the forced labor program. As discussed above in section II.A.2.a, forced labor is a modern variant of slavery and does therefore never require state action to give rise to liability under the ATCA. Thus, under *Kadic*, state action is also not required for the acts of murder, rape, and torture which allegedly occurred in furtherance of the forced labor program.

b. Unocal may be liable under the ATCA for aiding and abetting the Myanmar Military in subjecting Plaintiffs to murder and rape, but Unocal is not similarly liable for torture.

The same reasons that convinced us earlier that Unocal may be liable for aiding and abetting the Myanmar Military in subjecting Plaintiffs to forced labor also convince us now that Unocal may likewise be liable under this standard for aiding and abetting the Myanmar Military in subjecting Plaintiffs to murder and rape. We conclude, however, that as a matter of law, Unocal is not similarly liable for torture in this case.

Initially we observe that the evidence in the record creates a genuine question of material fact as to whether Myanmar soldiers engaged in acts of murder and rape involving Plaintiffs. The record does not, however, contain sufficient evidence to establish a claim of torture (other than by means of rape) involving Plaintiffs. Although a number of witnesses described acts of extreme physical abuse that might give rise to a claim of torture, the allegations all involved victims other than Plaintiffs. As this is not a class action, such allegations cannot serve to establish the Plaintiffs' claims of torture here.

Next, a reasonable factfinder could conclude that Unocal's alleged conduct met the *actus reus* requirement of aiding and abetting as we define it today, i.e., practical assistance or encouragement which has a substantial effect on the perpetration of the crimes of murder and rape. As just discussed, the evidence supports the conclusion that the Myanmar Military subjected Plaintiffs to acts of murder and rape while providing security and building infrastructure for the Project. The evidence also supports the conclusion that Unocal gave "practical assistance" to the Myanmar Military in subjecting Plaintiffs to these acts of murder and rape. This assistance, moreover, had a "substantial effect" on the perpetration of murder and rape, which "most probably would not have occurred in the same way" without someone hiring the Myanmar Military to provide security, and without someone showing them where to do it.

Finally, a reasonable factfinder could also conclude that Unocal's conduct met the mens rea requirement of aiding and abetting as we define it today, *i.e.*, actual or constructive (i.e., reasonable) knowledge that the accomplice's actions will assist the perpetrator in the commission of the crime. The District Court found that "Plaintiffs present[ed] evidence demonstrating . . . that the military, while forcing villagers to work . . ., committed numerous acts of violence; and that Unocal knew or should have known that the military did commit, was committing, and would continue to commit these tortious acts." *Doe/Roe II*, 110 F. Supp. 2d at 1306. Moreover, Unocal knew or should reasonably have known that its conduct — including the payments and the instructions where to provide security and build infrastructure — would assist or encourage the Myanmar Military to subject Plaintiffs to these acts of violence. Thus, because Unocal knew that acts of violence would probably be committed, it became liable as an aider and abettor when such acts of violence — specifically, murder and rape — were in fact committed.

[The court of appeals concluded that there were genuine issues of material fact as to whether Unocal was liable for aiding and abetting murder and rape, but not as to torture. Accordingly, the court of appeals reversed the district court's grant of summary judgment on the murder and rape claims but affirmed the lower court's grant of summary judgment on the torture claims.

The court went on to hold that the Myanmar Military and Myanmar Oil were entitled to immunity under the Foreign Sovereign Immunities Act, that the plaintiffs' claims against Unocal were not barred by the act of state doctrine, and that the district court lacked extraterritorial subject matter jurisdiction over the plaintiffs' RICO claim against Unocal and remanded the case to the district court for further proceedings consistent with its opinion.]

NOTES AND QUESTIONS

1. After the decision in *Doe v. Unocal* above, the Ninth Circuit granted a rehearing en banc in February 2003. *See Doe v. Unocal*, 2003 U.S. App. Lexis 2716. As of this writing, no decision has been made in the rehearing.

2. In *Aguinda v. Texaco*, the defendants prevailed on a motion to dismiss on the grounds of *forum non conveniens*. Although the defendants lost on appeal in *Unocal* on the motion for summary judgment, they can now move to dismiss on *forum non conveniens*. What are their chances of success?

3. Is it possible for a private corporation to be liable for violating the law of nations or does the corporation have to be acting under "color" of state action of some type?

4. Before purchasing a part of Total's interests in the oil and gas project, Unocal executives hired a consulting company to conduct a risk assessment, which concluded that the Myanmar Military had a history of using forced labor. Do you think that the executives at Unocal made a decision to go ahead with the oil and gas project knowing that the Myanmar Military would engage in heinous crimes and egregious human rights abuses? Why did the Unocal executives go ahead with the project?

5. During the operation of the project, it appears that numerous incidents of human rights abuses were brought to Unocal's attention. Why did Unocal ignore this information?

6. What lessons does *Doe v. Unocal* provide about corporate responsibility and social obligations? If you were counsel to a large corporation such as Unocal what advice would you give Unocal about its business plans for the future?

PROBLEM 9-10

For the past five years, Z-Mart Department Stores in Columbus, Ohio, has bought and imported large quantities of clothing and apparel from the Juno Textile Trading Company, an export trading company with no manufacturing capability in a developing country in Southeast Asia controlled by an authoritarian government. The factory buys the clothes from a state-run prison in a nearby province that houses political prisoners under harsh conditions and is the prison's only customer. The proceeds from the sale of the clothes have allowed the prison to build a new electric fence and to hire several tough new prison guards. Is Z-Mart in violation of the Alien Tort Statute?

Table of Cases

Principal cases are indicated by italics.

Index